CANADA

Bear's Paw
Mountain

Cow Creek
Canyon

Missouri River

Fort
Benton

Highwood
Mts.

MONTANA
TERRITORY

Snow Mts.

Fort Keogh

Yellowstone River

Canyon
Creek

Bozeman

Fort
Ellis

Big Horn River

Tongue River

Heart
Mountain

Shoshone River

Yellowstone
Lake

YELLOWSTONE
PARK

WYOMING
TERRITORY

Scale in miles

0   100

EYEWITNESSES TO THE INDIAN WARS, 1865–1890

EYEWITNESSES TO THE INDIAN WARS, 1865–1890

The Wars for the Pacific Northwest

EDITED BY PETER COZZENS

STACKPOLE
BOOKS

Published by
STACKPOLE BOOKS
5067 Ritter Road
Mechanicsburg PA 17055
www.stackpolebooks.com

Printed in the United States of America

10 9 8 7 6 5 4 3 2 1

FIRST EDITION

Library of Congress Cataloging-in-Publication Data

Eyewitnesses to the Indian Wars, 1865–1890 / edited by Peter Cozzens.—1st ed.
    p. cm.
    Includes index.
    Contents: v. 2. Wars for the Pacific Northwest
    ISBN: 0-8117-0573-0
    I. Cozzens, Peter, 1957–
E99.A6 E94 2002
973.8—dc21
                                                                    00-52270

For Pam, Tom, Brittany, and Brian

CONTENTS

PART ONE:
The Snake-Paiute War and After, 1866–72

PART TWO:
The Modoc War, 1872–73

PART THREE:
The Nez Perce Campaign, 1877

PART FOUR:
The Bannock War, 1878

PART FIVE:
The Sheepeater Campaign, 1879

ILLUSTRATIONS

PREFACE

Eyewitnesses to the Indian Wars, 1865–1890: The Wars for the Pacific North-west is the second volume of a five-volume series that seeks to tell the saga of the military struggle for the American West in the words of the soldiers, non-combatants, and Native Americans who shaped it. Volume Three will be devoted to the military conquest of the Southern Plains and will also contain a chapter on the Ute War in the Rocky Mountains. Volume Four will be devoted to the dramatic and costly conflicts on the Northern Plains. A fifth volume will feature accounts that transcend a particular region or conflict. Categories will include eyewitness biographical sketches of key military and Native American figures; narratives of army wives and enlisted men; accounts of garrison and reservation life; writings and speeches of army officers on Indian policy and reservation management; narratives of army scouts; and discussions of Indian-fighting doctrine and tactics.

It is the purpose of the present volume to offer as representative a selection of original accounts pertaining to the Indian wars and campaigns of the Pacific Coast as may be assembled under one cover. As in *The Struggle for Apacheria*, most of the accounts presented here are taken from contemporaneous newspapers and magazines, or from unpublished manuscripts.

Several considerations guide the choice of material for inclusion in the *Eyewitnesses to the Indian Wars* series. The events described must have occurred between the end of the Civil War and the tragedy at Wounded Knee. With but few exceptions, the articles featured were published during the authors' lifetimes. Articles published within the last fifty years have been excluded, as they are for the most part readily available.

Because the events described in this volume take the form of discrete wars or campaigns, each of which may be understood individually, I opted against a historical introduction as redundant. Reading the selections in the order in which they are presented should give the reader as clear an appreciation of the causes, events, and consequences of each conflict as I could hope to provide.

I followed generally the same editorial practices in this volume as in *The Struggle for Apacheria*. My goal has been to present accurate and annotated texts of the articles, letters, and manuscripts included in this work. I have added notes to correct errors of fact, clarify obscure references, provide historical context where needed, offer capsule biographies of contributors, and identify more fully persons mentioned in the text.

Editing of the text has been light. Most nineteenth-century writers had a penchant for commas, for commas and hyphens in combination, and for semicolons. I have eliminated them where their overuse clouded the meaning or impeded the rhythm of a sentence. I have regularized capitalization, punctuation, and the spelling of names and places. My only departure from the practices I followed in Volume One has been to replace references to an officer's brevet, or Civil War volunteer, rank with their actual rank at the time of the events described. Thus, Bvt. Maj. Gen. George Crook becomes Lt. Col. George Crook during the Snake-Paiute War, Brig. Gen. Jefferson C. Davis becomes Col. C. Jefferson Davis during the Modoc War, and so forth.

ACKNOWLEDGMENTS

Continued service abroad on diplomatic assignment with the Department of State has posed unique challenges to my gathering the articles and other primary accounts found in *Eyewitnesses to the Indian Wars, 1865–1890: The Wars for the Pacific Northwest.* Without the help of those persons mentioned below, it would have been impossible.

My deepest thanks go to my mother for her many trips to the Wheaton (Illinois) Public Library, submitting OCLC requests and retrieving articles, and to the staff of the periodicals department of the Wheaton Public Library for their kindness and diligence in filling these requests.

Jerome A. Greene of the National Park Service provided helpful suggestions and guidance in the selection of sources pertaining to the Nez Perce War. I heartily recommend his *Nez Perce Summer, 1877: The U.S. Army and the Nee-Me-Poo Crisis* (Helena: Montana Historical Society, 2000), to anyone wishing to learn more about that fascinating and tragic conflict; it is, in my opinion, one of the very best studies of a frontier military campaign ever written.

My friend Scott Forsythe of the National Archives guided me to a number of sources and put me in contact with historians such as Jerry Greene.

Much of the material presented here I obtained during several visits to the Newberry Library in Chicago. The reference staff of that institution was most helpful on every occasion.

I also thank the following individuals for providing me with manuscripts from their collections and, where necessary, for permission to publish this material: Terry Abraham, head of special collections at the University of Idaho, Moscow; John A. Doerner, chief historian at the Little Big Horn National Monument, Crow Agency, Montana; David M. Hays, archivist and instructor at the University of Colorado, Boulder; Robert N. Matuozzi, manuscripts librarian at Washington State University, Pullman; Susan E. Snyder of the Bancroft Library, University of California, Berkeley; Robert G. Trujillo, head of special collections at Stanford University; and Brent Wagner, manuscripts librarian at the Denver Public Library.

My thanks go also to my copyeditor at Stackpole, Joyce Bond, for the excpetional work she did on the long and complex manuscript.

Finally, I thank my editor at Stackpole, Leigh Ann Berry, for her enthusiastic support of this project.

PART ONE

The Snake-Paiute War and After, 1866–72

Fighting in the Sierras

ALBERT G. BRACKETT[1]

United Service, n.s., 6, no. 5 (October 1891): 321–28

An Indian War is always a serious matter, as it generally breaks out suddenly and there is no telling how far reaching it may be in its effects. The
sparse settlements are overrun and many individuals killed before any relief
can be afforded.

The troubles in the states of Nevada and California in 1866 and 1867 have
never been properly appreciated. Bold and fearless bands of savages roamed at
will over large extents of country, murdering unsuspecting and helpless people
and using the torch freely in the infant communities of the states mentioned.
Taking advantage of the disturbed condition of the Union during the Civil War,
the red men thought it the proper time to avenge their fancied wrongs and at
the same time to add to their own wealth. For years they had watched the
immigrants as they slowly toiled across the continent on their way to the new
lands bordering on the Pacific Ocean and, having possessed themselves of
good arms and a plentiful supply of ammunition, sought to arrest their
progress, or at least to take from them what they had. Being in no way scrupu-
lous about the means adopted to bring about this state of affairs, they swarmed
on the thoroughfares and occupied the dark defiles.

The California and Nevada volunteers had rendered good service in keeping back the insolent foemen, and Lieutenant Colonel McDermit[2] of the 2nd
Regiment of California Cavalry Volunteers was killed by them in the summer
of 1865 while out scouting and guarding the roads. Colonel McDermit was a
brave and cautious man, but while leading his horse down a mountainside was
waylaid by one of his wily foemen and shot dead at once.[3] This act greatly
incensed the California Volunteers, who were a superior body of men, utterly
fearless and untiring. From that time forth they put forward their utmost efforts
and spared no pains to find the savages, who mainly belonged to the Paiute and
Snake tribes.

Upon the death of McDermit, Lt. Col. [Ambrose E.] Hooker, who was
promoted to his place in the 2nd Regiment of California Cavalry Volunteers,
took command of the District of Nevada, which he retained until mustered out

2

of the service and until the arrival of regular troops after the close of the Civil War. He was a man of a good deal of energy of character and had his head-quarters at Fort Churchill, some twenty-seven miles from Virginia City, near the banks of Carson River, a well-built post in the midst of a desolate region.[4] The mountains of Nevada furnished ample hiding places, while the warm valleys were safe retreats during the cold winter season for the savages and their animals, as nearly all of them were mounted.

The care of the women and children is always a matter of great moment to the Indians while engaged on the warpath and gives them the greatest anxiety. An effective blow can always be administered to them by capturing their wives and little ones. There is no better place to conceal considerable bodies of people than the rocky gorges of the mountains, many caves of considerable dimensions being found among the great lava fields to be met in all directions. It must be borne in mind that these people had occupied this region for an indefinite period and were well acquainted with all of its secret recesses and handsome valleys. Food supplies of pine nuts, acorns, grass, seeds, and tule could be found easily, and tame cattle and horses made up the wealth of the red men. They had a fair supply of clothing, but from infancy Indians are not well clad and can endure a great degree of cold without much apparent suffering. They wear clothing as much for ornament as for actual use and upon going into battle like to strip off everything. Their tactics in war do not differ from those of their kindred farther to the eastward, they deeming it the height of folly to expose themselves openly to the bullets of their enemies. Every inequality of the ground is taken advantage of, as well as every root, tree, bush, rock, and shrub. They can conceal themselves behind the smallest objects.

The first action of any moment was fought by Capt. George D. Conrad with twenty-five men of Company B and twenty-five of Company I under Lieutenant Duncan—all of the 2nd California Cavalry, who attacked the hostiles on the west side of Quinn's River, near Fish Creek, on January 11, 1866.[5] The savages fought well, but the determination of the volunteers soon caused them to ground, though not until thirty-five of their number had been killed and nine captured. Corporal Biswell and Privates Duffield, Riley, and Shultz were wounded and several of the horses were killed and wounded.[6] This was quite a severe check upon the red men and showed them that the time had arrived when the whites were determined to avenge the wrongs done them on so many occasions.

Their loss caused them deep grief, and there was wailing through the mountain region. For the first time they began to realize the danger they were in, although none of them yet thought of coming in and giving themselves up and suing for peace. They possessed great resolution, and having retained the advantage in numerous small encounters with the settlers, thought this was but a temporary disadvantage and that in the next affair they would retrieve their fallen fortunes and times would continue as they had been before. In this they were mistaken and were obliged to receive still greater chastisement.

On February 15, 1866, Maj. Samuel P. Smith of the 2nd California Cavalry, with a body of troops made up of volunteer citizens, numbering in all eighty-one, encountered the savages near Rock Canyon in Nevada. A severe fight ensued in which 115 Indians were killed and nineteen captured.[7] Private Austin of Company D was killed. Major Smith and Privates Resler, Grimshaw, Balta, and Rhuman of Company D, and Privates Mills and Smith of Company F were wounded. Maj. Henry B. J. Mellen, Captain Starr, and Lieutenant Robinson of the 2nd California Cavalry were with the detachment. Sixty horses which had been stolen from the settlers were recovered, and a large amount of Indian property was destroyed.

On account of the good conduct of Majors Smith and Mellen, they were subsequently appointed officers in the Regular Army, the former a captain in the 8th, and the latter a lieutenant in the 6th Cavalry.[8] This was a very important affair and reflected great credit upon the troops engaged. At one time it was feared that the whole detachment would be cut off, but a vigorous onslaught led by Major Smith in person gave the whites possession of the strong grounds occupied by the enemy, who were soon put to flight with the losses above mentioned. The foemen were considerably disheartened by this defeat, which was a severe one.

Sgt. James T. Edwards, while out with eight men of the 2nd California Cavalry, had an encounter with a war party in Paradise Valley on March 7, 1866, in which six Indians were killed.[9] The skirmish was conducted with great energy and skill, showing that the sergeant understood his profession well and was prepared to make the best of the occasion.

By this time the Indians had been taught some lessons of prudence, and their headmen no longer thought they could overthrow the whites so easily. Their arms were of an excellent quality, having been purchased for them by unscrupulous white men who lived, in some instances, on terms of perfect equality with them. At that day there was an abundance of money in Nevada, the silver mines turning out large quantities of bullion, and each of the Indians as chose to labor earned good wages. The Washo Indians especially were industrious and careful and consequently had more of the comforts of life than they had ever before known. These Indians were by no means friendly to the Paiutes and were glad to see them overthrown by the soldiers. There was a good deal of bitterness of feeling, as the Washo had been overpowered once by their enemies, when the best-looking women were taken away from them and they were allowed to keep only a few horses. Their taskmasters had been very hard on them and oppressed them in various ways until they became little better than slaves of their conquerors, and it was at this time that they learned to work.[10]

In April 1866 Bvt. Col. A. G. Brackett, major, 1st Cavalry, took command of Fort Churchill, being in charge of the first regular cavalry sent to the Pacific Coast after the close of the Civil War. On May 18 one hundred twenty Indian prisoners were brought in and delivered to him. He placed them in camp on the banks of Carson River, where they constructed shades and shelters for themselves, being supplied with rations from the Subsistence Department.

On June 1 Colonel Brackett assumed command of the District of Nevada. Shortly afterwards Major General Halleck, commanding the Military Division of the Pacific,[11] visited the fort, on which occasion there was a brave array of friendly Paiute Indians under Young Winnemucca from the Truckee and Walker River reservations.[12] These savages wished to do honor to the general and were indeed a grim collection, all wishing to shake hands with him. After this ceremony was finished the general expressed a desire to see some of their warlike exercises. They retired a short distance and, having mounted their horses, commenced moving off in front of him, Winnemucca with his war drum being in front, mounted on a fine pony without a saddle and only a rope bridle; he was bareheaded, his long hair sweeping in the breeze. Indians followed in wild, irregular order, chanting their songs and keeping time to the dull thumping of the war drums. Many of them were well dressed, a decided partiality for tall white hats and red shirts being perceptible among them. Still, their costumes varied from the buckskin shirt and moccasins of the wild tribes to the common clothing of the white men, but all of them were profusely ornamented with beads, feathers, and bright-colored blankets. It is doubtful whether there has ever been a finer display of savage life within the limits of the state of Nevada.

After continuing this for some time, and having shown themselves to the best advantage, they suddenly halted in front of the general and commenced making speeches through their interpreter, an Indian who had been educated in the eastern states. Winnemucca's speech was of considerable length and gave great satisfaction to all concerned. When he had finished, Big George, the peace chief, spoke, and then the general left them. The Indians were very much pleased with their visit, and when General Halleck departed, he directed a supply of rations to be issued to them, which gladdened their hearts.

A few days afterwards Winnemucca's Indians started for the Truckee reservation, taking with them all of the Indian prisoners which had been brought in, the little ones being carried along in army wagons, much to their delight. All went along pleasantly, except one surly and insolent fellow, who was put in the guardhouse for his bad behavior. His squaw sat down on the ground, utterly disconsolate, and had to be put in one of the wagons and was trundled off with the rest. They reached the reservation in safety and there found peace and quietness.

A dreadful slaughter of a large party of Chinese occurred in the spring of 1866 near the line between Nevada and Idaho. The party started from Virginia City, intending to go to the silver mines of Idaho. They had with them a four-horse wagon and an American driver, the men walking along the road as innocent and incapable of defense as so many school children. They carried sluice forks, umbrellas, and bamboo poles and seemed utterly unconscious that there was any kind of danger. A few of the men had pistols, but even these they may not have known how to use. However this might have been, they journeyed along until they came near a deep ravine leading into the Owyhee River, when they were suddenly assailed by a large band of Indians who shot down those in front, who made no effort to defend themselves; in fact, those having pistols surrendered them to the savages, thinking in this way to conciliate them, but the slaughter went on until the whole of them, some fifty in number, were killed. Never was there a more inhuman massacre. The Chinese were willing to give up all they had on earth, but this would not satisfy the devilish spirit of the red men, who thirsted for blood. The bodies of these poor creatures were left on the ground as food for the wolves and ravens swarming in that region.[13]

After mustering out the volunteers, the troops in the district consisted of portions of the 1st United States Cavalry and 9th United States Infantry. On June 1 an Indian named Captain George was killed near Camp McDermit by a soldier of Company I, 1st Cavalry, and on the sixteenth of the same month an Indian murderer was killed near Fort Churchill while endeavoring to escape by Pvt. John Gould of Company F, 9th Infantry.

In August the headquarters of the district were moved from Churchill to Camp McGarry, near Summit Lake, on the road leading to Idaho. The Indians had been quite bold on this road,[14] attacking a train from Susanville, California, severely wounding one of the teamsters, who, returning the fire, left one savage dead on the ground.

The autumn passed away in comparative quiet, the Indians having concealed themselves in the mountains. A small number spent the winter near Camp McGarry, coming into the post occasionally at night and robbing the blacksmith's shop; though [a] strict search was made, nothing of them could be found. A long torch, made of the inner fibers of the sagebrush, by which fire could be preserved and carried for a long time, was discovered. With snow covering the country for many miles around, it was a mystery how these people eked out a living.

About January 1, 1867, Mr. Westover, the mail carrier between Camp McGarry and Trout Creek, was captured and killed by the Indians. Upon it being reported to the commanding officer, he sent out a detachment of twenty men of the 1st Cavalry under Lt. George F. Foote of the 9th Infantry. This detachment was attacked by the savages on the night of February 7 above the Vicksburg mines, near a cave which was evidently their home and stronghold. The Indians were driven off and followed until their trail was lost. Upon their return, the soldiers burnt the huts of the savages. Pvt. William Hill was very severely wounded by the enemy, and Pvt. Samuel Hollister was dangerously wounded by accident.

The following autumn the district commander [Brackett] was sent to Camp Bidwell with his headquarters and had been there but a short time when he was ordered to Camp McDermit in Nevada.

On November 25, 1867, Capt. James N. McElroy, who was out scouting with a part of his company of the 8th Cavalry, a portion of which had been sent to the district upon its organization, discovered a party of Indians near the base of some hills, who retreated to the banks of Quinn's River, which they attempted to cross. In so doing the soldiers attacked them, and two warriors were left dead on the field. Lt. Aaron B. Jerome accompanied Capt. McElroy on this scout and in personal conflict killed an Indian who was pressing him too closely.[15]

Nearly all of the troops were sent out from Camp McDermit for the purpose of engaging the Indians. Col. John P. Baker of the 1st Cavalry succeeded in capturing quite a number, at the same time leaving three dead on the field.[16] In another scout, Lt. John Lafferty of the 8th Cavalry killed two warriors with his own hands.[17]

While the troops were absent, Colonel Brackett learned there was a large party in the vicinity of Eight-Mile Creek and, sending out Lt. Frank K. Upham, who was his acting assistant adjutant general, with a party of soldiers, received the surrender of the whole band. This was on November 20, 1867. The savages had become disheartened by their several defeats and were only too glad to lay down their arms.

In addition to the officers named, Captains Charles O. Wood and Frederick Mears of the 9th Infantry, and Capt. James A. Hall of the 1st Cavalry had rendered excellent service in bringing about this desirable state of affairs.

About guarding the roads leading to Idaho, the editor of a Susanville, California, paper said,

> As many of our citizens are engaged in freighting goods to Idaho and are constantly passing and repassing over this dangerous road, we have frequent opportunities of hearing their views with regard to the manner in which the route is protected. All with whom we have conversed on the subject are unanimous in the opinion that no officer could have done more, and few as much, as Col. Brackett has done with the limited force at his disposal to make the route safe. All speak in the highest terms of the promptitude with which assistance has been rendered when needed and are loud in their praise of the kindness and courtesy extended to them by Col. Brackett and the officers and men under his command.

So far as Nevada was concerned, the war was ended, but certain bands in California continued to give some trouble. A small remnant of the Nevada Indians went north and was met by a force under command of Capt. Samuel Munson of the 9th Infantry in Warner Valley, Oregon, on May 1, 1868. In this fight, the guide, Mr. Daniel Hoag, was killed and Lt. Hayden De Lany[18] was wounded, the latter receiving a brevet for gallant and meritorious service on that occasion.[19] In the affair the Indians evinced unwonted bravery, and being well fortified behind rocks, a good deal of work was necessary to dislodge them, but the soldiers accomplished it.

Thus ended a serious Indian outbreak in Nevada, and peace was restored to the miners and settlers. Old Winnemucca, who was the leading man among the Paiute Indians, had during most of these disturbances been near Steen's Mountain, in Oregon, not caring to take part in the war. He was a man of great power and possessed of a far-reaching mind. No one could concentrate the strength of the savages as he could, as was well shown at the battle of Pyramid Lake in the month of July 1860.[20] Young Winnemucca was not related to the old chief in any way, though he had the same name.[21] He too was a man of strong mind, who sought to elevate his people as much as was in his power. Though a war chief, he believed in peace and thought cultivated farms and the means of cultivation excellent things, and things to be worked for. He wished to strengthen his band and was much pleased when the whole of the prisoners were turned over to him, as with their assistance he could open new farms and till more ground. He was thoroughly reliable and trustworthy and not addicted to gambling like many of his race. He loved power but did not wish to obtain it by questionable ways. While all this was true with regard to this man, the same could not be said of many other members of his tribe, as it contained some skillful sharpers, who thought deception and dishonesty extremely praiseworthy.

The peace following the events here recorded was lasting and of the utmost benefit to the white people. Never since has there been any serious outbreak. The Indians have remained quietly on their reservations, or when off have been assisting the white men in their labors. They work in nearly every department of labor, making efforts to secure good homes for themselves. Quite a number are fair workmen as carpenters, blacksmiths, horseshoers, ditchers, and gardeners. Half the men can talk enough English to make themselves understood about ordinary work. They have done a great deal of farm labor and are constantly adding to their stock of knowledge, so that they will soon be a desirable class of laborers. Besides farming, their fisheries are valuable, the trout from the Truckee and Walker Rivers finding ready sale. Their old feuds and misunderstandings have pretty much passed out of their minds, and all things have improved so far as they are concerned. Having no incentive to go to war, they are rapidly learning the arts of peace, forming thrifty communities and adding to the wealth and material prosperity of the states in which they dwell, forming a striking contrast to their condition twenty-five years ago.

During the disturbances in Nevada, there was a peddler passing through the northern portion of the state who had a two-horse wagonload of groceries, especially fine preserves. He was waylaid in a lonely portion of the road and killed. The Indians then killed the horses and prepared for a great feast. They encamped near the road and, breaking open the cans and jars of preserves, poured the contents on the ground. What they could not use they were determined to destroy. They remained until they ate up the two horses, having a notable feast, and all around they poured the preserves in great circles out of mere wantonness. They seemed to have a great partiality for horsemeat and fairly gorged themselves.

Operations against Hostile Indians with General Crook, 1867–1868

WILLIAM R. PARNELL[1]

United Service, n.s., 1, nos. 5 and 6 (May and June 1889): 482–98, 628–35.

In the spring of 1867 I was relieved from duty with the 8th U.S. Cavalry, then being organized, and ordered to report for duty with my own company and regiment at Camp C. F. Smith, Oregon. I was at the time stationed at Benicia Barracks, California, and proceeded by boat to Sacramento, thence marching across the Sierra Nevada, over the old stage road, through Carson, Fort Churchill, and McDermit, Nevada, to my own station in southern Oregon.

Twenty-one years ago the Indian tribes were not concentrated as they are today, but were scattered over an immense territory, broken up into small bands of from twenty to fifty roaming at will, destroying or stealing stock, and murdering small parties of prospectors or other travelers whenever found unprepared. Small military posts were located at isolated places near stage roads or mining camps, but they were usually composed of but one small company of cavalry or infantry, rendering effective scouting almost impossible, for to send out a sufficient number of men to meet any emergency would be to reduce the strength of the garrison to such a degree as to leave it entirely defenseless in case of attack. All this is now changed, and military garrisons are large enough to send out a strong command and retain enough men not only to protect life and property at the post, but also to afford support to those in the field should it be necessary.

From Lemhi, in Idaho, to Klamath, in Oregon, an almost uninterrupted tract of country abounding in game, fish, and bunchgrass feed for animals lay at the mercy and control of those itinerant bands of Paiute, Snake, Klamath, Modoc, and Pit River Indians; their weapons consisted chiefly of bows and arrows and old shotguns; occasionally rifles of various patterns would be found among them, taken no doubt from some of their victims, either teamsters or miners waylaid in their long and solitary journey to the goldfields in the mountains.

It was no easy task that Colonel Crook[2] had before him. Were it possible for him to concentrate those scattered bands and with his troops give them battle, the problem would soon be solved, but for hundreds of miles the country

William R. Parnell as a retired colonel.
CYRUS T. BRADY. *NORTHWESTERN FIGHTS AND FIGHTERS.*

had to be thoroughly scouted to find—after perhaps weeks of hard and tedious marching—but a small band of warriors, who would scatter to the four winds at the approach of troops. It was only when they had every advantage in position and numbers that they would show any disposition to fight, or when cornered, and then they would fight to the death. Every shot and every arrow was sent to kill, their firearms usually being loaded with slugs and their steel or flint-headed arrows poisoned, the process of poisoning being done by taking a deer's or other animal's liver and holding it on the end of a long stick to a frenzied rattlesnake to bite and thus impregnate it with poison, or else leave it in the sun to become putrid, then rub the arrowhead in it and leave it to dry. A wound from one of those would usually prove fatal, but if the arrow became exposed to moisture, the poison would evaporate and become ineffective, and for this reason the Indians always carried their arrows in quivers made from the skin of fur animals, with the fur inside.[3]

Colonel Crook's long experience and study of the Indian character in Oregon prior to the War of the Rebellion placed him par excellence the man to successfully cope with the settlement of the Indian question in this portion of the Pacific states and territories, and the confidence of the authorities in Washington and of the people of the Pacific Coast was fully justified by the results. The soldiers under his command had just passed through a four years' war and were young, hardy fellows, full of fight and capable of enduring any amount of fatigue and hardship; indeed, had it not been so, the successful termination of this particular war in 1868 could not have been accomplished, leaving as it did thousands of acres of fertile land to be taken advantage of by the thrifty settler and enterprising stock raiser. Railroads, towns, villages, and productive farms now occupy the sites of Indian wickiups and battlegrounds in this beautiful garden of the Pacific Coast.

The troops composing the expedition in preparation for the campaign against these Indians consisted of Companies F, H, M, 1st Cavalry, and a detachment of Company D, 23rd Infantry, mounted.

On July 22 the command left Camp C. F. Smith for Camp Warner,[4] distant about 100 miles due west. On this march we crossed Steen's Mountain[5] and passed many peculiar formations of rock and earth. Skull Creek Canyon, a narrow pass in the mountains, is lined on either side with basalt rock resembling church spires and the long, narrow, arched windows of European cathedrals, many of them being almost as perfect as if done by the skillful hand of the architect. Thirty miles west, in the vicinity of Beaty's Butte,[6] we passed a perfect amphitheatre of earth covering a space of about two acres, the angles being surmounted by earth towers of fifty to sixty feet in height, the surrounding walls being ten to twelve feet thick and partially (and apparently) in ruins; to stand about half a mile from it the effect and delusion were perfect. Yet it was evidently but work of volcanic action.

We remained at Camp Warner a few days waiting the arrival of a company of Warm Springs Indians from the Dalles, who were to act as scouts and trailers during the expedition. So daring were the hostile Indians that a few days before we reached Warner, a party of them had killed a soldier of the 23rd Infantry and wounded another not more than 200 yards from the post. The garrison consisted of two companies of the 23rd Infantry.

Public animals and cattle had to be strongly guarded by armed men and then only within sight of the post; even with all this precaution, the Indians would sometimes attack the herd and succeed in stampeding some of them. On one or two occasions they crawled up to the stockade corral at night and killed some of the animals with arrows; at another time they stampeded the herd half a mile from camp and got away with thirteen government mules. There was no cavalry at the post to follow them, and they got off with their plunder. After the arrival of our Indian allies, we took up the line of march for the Goose Lake[7] country, which today is dotted with towns and productive farms, but at that time was the home of the hostile Indians.

Passing through Goose Lake Valley, we again got into the mountains, making occasional halts for one or two days to graze our animals and to give our Indians an opportunity of scouting the country ahead of us for Indian signs. Some days our march would take us up the rugged mountainside away above the snow line, giving us an excellent view of the surrounding country many miles in every direction. Our guide, on one of those occasions, remarked that "a fellow couldn't very well get lost in such a country, there were so many permanent peaks about," meaning, of course, prominent points. The country was rich in its numbers of warm, sheltered valleys, with grass in abundance, game plentiful, and clear mountain streams abounding in trout—the regular, orthodox, speckled, solid-fleshed, gamy fellows that make the angler's heart rejoice.

Scarcely a day passed that did not see Colonel Crook's mess well supplied in this line. There is no better fly fisher in the country than Colonel Crook, and with his rifle he is equally expert, as I can attest from witnessing his unerring aim at deer and antelope, as well as Indians. We continued our search for "Lo; the poor Indian," up and down mountain ranges, steep and rugged as nature could have made them, with now and again a few miles completely blocked by fallen timber in every conceivable direction. Slowly we would make our way over and through such obstructions leading our horses. Until September 13 we had not so far encountered any hostiles, yet the colonel was certain that several small bands were concentrated somewhere in some secluded spot in the mountains—fishing, hunting, and gambling, as was their usual custom at this season of the year. The colonel therefore concluded to divide the command and send one party north and take the other with him in a southerly direction. So Companies F and M, and a party of scouts, all under command of Captain D. Perry,[8] were ordered north, and Companies H (mine) and D, 23rd Infantry, with Archie McIntosh's[9] Warm Springs scouts, remained with the general for work southward.

We had constant rains and snow for several days after our party divided, but we continued our work looking for our lost Indians. We cross the boundary line into California on the twenty-second, and Indian signs began to get plentiful and interesting. While in camp that night we noticed two or three fires west of us, and three parties of scouts were sent out to locate them, their instructions being to get as near as possible unobserved, get an approximate idea of their numbers and situation, then return cautiously and report, the general's plan being to make a night march on them and attack at daybreak.

Our guide—Wilson[10]—went with one party of our Indians and McIntosh with another. Wilson came upon a large party early the next morning, situated beneath a small bluff overlooking a large, open plain—a magnificent place for an attack; but in direct disobedience to his orders, he fired on the Indians and then ran for his life instead of getting away unobserved and returning to camp to report, when the whole command would have been fresh for a general attack. This piece of stupidity of Wilson's gave the Indians the alarm at once, and signal fires were visible in every direction, the whole country was ablaze, and our other scouts reported Indian runners everywhere. They waylaid and killed two or three of them. The colonel was terribly annoyed and disgusted with the guide, whom he immediately discharged, and some of the men of my company were so incensed at his perfidy that they actually got a lariat and had him under a tree ready to swing until Lieutenant Eskridge, 23rd Infantry (the quartermaster),[11] discovered them in time to save the fellow's life. I think sometimes it would have been but meted justice to have let the rope serve its work then, for a few days afterwards many valuable lives were lost by his disobedience and insubordination. The next two or three days was anticipation and excitement; Indian signs were plentiful. Now and then one or two bucks would be seen on the side of some mountain and then disappear in the timber;

they were evidently watching our movements and did not propose to be caught napping.

On the morning of September 26 we moved down the mountainside into the Pit River Valley and had just reached the flat country when our chief of scouts (McIntosh) rode up and reported a large band of warriors entrenched in rocks and caves above us and wanting to fight. I was ordered to dismount my company and move up from the south side, while Lieutenant Madigan,[12] my second lieutenant, who was in command of the mounted infantry, was directed to ascend from the north; the east side was the valley, with our lead horses and pack train; and the west was protected by a perpendicular bluff about 500 feet high. We commenced climbing up the steep mountainside, over rocks and huge boulders, down through a deep ravine, and up again through rocks and juniper trees, when the Indians opened a heavy fire upon us. We made quick work up that steep ascent, driving the Indians before us, until we reached a rocky plateau about 600 feet above the valley and there found the Indians in force. They were in a natural fortification, strengthened by artificial means, with loopholes and embrasures. There was a main fort, of a basin-like formation, with a balcony nearly all round it, and above this a wall of rock about eight or nine feet in height, with a rocky gulch, about twenty-five feet, being the only space distant between us and the Indians; but they were behind their stone wall, while we were more or less exposed.[13]

Our men, however, sought shelter behind rocks and boulders. The firing was lively from both sides. Several other strong forts were near the main one, with caves connecting them, so that the Indians could pass from one to the other in perfect security. Some of the Indians posted themselves at the entrance to these subterranean passages, and lying flat on their stomachs, they would pick off our men, while we could not discern where the shots came from owing to the dark background and the Indians being about the same color as the rocks surrounding them. Before our men had sought shelter behind rocks, 1st Sgt. Albert Brachett[14] and Pvt. [James] Lyons were killed, and Lieutenant Madigan and half a dozen men were wounded. The afternoon was consumed in forming our line so as to completely surround the position held by the Indians, movements being made by the men on all fours, or crawling to the position desired, for at twenty paces a man exposing himself was bound to be hit. The bodies of the two men who were killed could not be removed until after dark, as they lay in a position fully exposed to the Indian fire.

Soon after sundown one-half of the command were sent down to the camp in the valley to get something to eat. We had not had a mouthful since 5:00 A.M., and our attack on the Indians commenced about noon. After all had supper and our wounded were attended to and the dead removed, we again took up our position around the forts. The night was clear and cold. All night long the Indian medicine man kept up a monotonous and loud talk, evidently giving counsel and courage to his people. An occasional shot would relieve the monotony of this doleful cry. Just about sundown I climbed up on a high rock near me to try and get a view of the Indian fort. I was seen, and in an instant arrows flew thick and fast around me from both flanks and front, but none hit. About midnight Lieutenant Eskridge came to me to go round to where Lieutenant Madigan was and cheer him up. He said he had just left him, very despondent. I went around and gave him a drink of whiskey, as his whole frame was shaking and shivering. I did and said all I could to cheer him up, but he evidently had a premonition of death, and nothing I could say or do had any effect whatever. The poor fellow was killed in the attack next morning. A brilliant officer and a brave man was Lt. John Madigan.

About an hour before daylight next morning, Colonel Crook directed me to draw in my line, form my men, and storm the works. This (the concentration) was done with the loss of two or three wounded. So near had they closed in on the Indians during the night that when they wanted to get back, they had to pass over an exposed position and thus became a target for the ever-watchful Indian.

Everything being ready, the men were directed to take off their overcoats, as hard climbing was before us. Lieutenant Madigan neglected to do this. I took the right, with twenty-two men, with Lieutenant Madigan and eighteen men on my left. The rest of our available men were either attending the wounded of the day before or were guarding our pack train, which had been attacked in the valley during the night by Indians on the outside. At the command "forward," we went with a rush down into the gulch surrounding the main fort. We were met by a perfect hailstorm of arrows as we rose in full view of the Indians, but not a man was touched. We were down at the bottom of the gulch in an instant, where we were secure, as a shot, to be effective, must be fired from a perpendicular height above, and to do this the Indians would have had to come outside of their works and be exposed to our fire.

Our forty or fifty feet of climbing now commenced. The boulders were large, too large for a man to climb unaided, so that two or three men would be pushed up and they, in turn, would drag up their comrades. Up, up we went this way until we reached the balcony mentioned, when we were on the same level with the Indians, with a wall of loose rock eight or nine feet high above us. "Make a breach" was the order given, and "Let no man stand still for a moment but keep moving."

While these orders were being given, Sgt. Michael Meara, looking through one of the loopholes, shouted, "Here they are boys!" and in an instant he was shot through the head. The gun could not have been more than six or seven inches from him at the time, as his face was badly burned with powder. A few moments after Meara's death, Pvt. [Willoughby] Sawyer was killed in a similar manner, his head and face being badly powder burned. Private Shay, another old soldier and an excellent fighter, received a shot in the wrist, his carbine stock was broken, and the shock hurled him down that steep, rocky wall forty feet below. It was not long before he was back with his comrades, swearing like [the] trooper that he was. In the meantime, a breach was made in the wall of rocks, and our men swarmed into the fort, using revolvers and clubbed carbines on the skedaddling Indians. Some got down through their underground passage; others jumped over the wall on the opposite side to us, while others remained in the fort, past the power of doing any more deviltry.

It was while Chief Si-e-ta was jumping over the wall like a jackrabbit that Colonel Crook, with his unerring Spencer, hit him square in the spine, and Mr. Indian fell headlong down the gulch and his body buried itself between two large boulders. In the meantime, Lieutenant Madigan's men moved forward when the order was given and, on reaching the edge of the gulch, found the banks too steep and ran round to our position and followed us. Lieutenant Madigan, with his overcoat on, stood still for a few moments to give some directions, or to examine the position, when he became a target for the Indians and was shot through the head, the wound and the place where he was standing being identical with that of Private Lyons, who was killed the day before. After we gained possession of the fort, heavy firing from the smaller forts and from caves and holes continued for several hours, our men returning the fire when an opportunity presented itself.

About 9:00 A.M. one of the infantrymen was on my left, watching through a small opening in the rocks. A small sprig or weed somewhat obstructed his view, and he was about to remove it when one of the men cautioned him not to do it, but he replied that "it wouldn't make any difference," and he broke it off. An instant after, a ball passed clean through his head above his ear. The shot came through that hole, for there was no other place that it could possibly have come. Strange to say, this man lived unconscious for two or three weeks. He was carried to Camp Warner on a double travois across a range of mountains, a distance of 150 miles.

About 11:00 A.M. a small detachment was left in charge of the fort and skirmish line, and the remainder were ordered down to camp for breakfast. We had not been down but a few minutes when a messenger came down and reported that the Indians had attacked the fort and recaptured it. I hurried back and found that they had attacked the fort and had driven our men out, but that other men on the line rallied to their support and had in turn again driven the Indians back, but a short time after the Indians moved by both flanks through the underground passages and, taking position at the entrances to those caves, had command of the approaches to the fort, while our men had command of the fort itself. Our dead lay where they had fallen. We therefore had to keep men in such a position as to command their bodies, so as to prevent the approach of Indians for scalping or mutilating villainy.

All the afternoon of the twenty-seventh a desultory firing was indulged in on both sides. We could not reach the Indians in their retreat in the caves, as two or three men could successfully resist any number, as but one man could approach any of the numerous entrances at a time. Their retreat was a perfect honeycomb, and they would not come out to fight. After supper the line was again formed, as we supposed, completely around the position held by the

Indians. The medicine man's talk was not heard this second night; he had been killed in the attack in the morning.

From 8:00 to 10:00 P.M. the arrows flew thick and fast around us, but doing no injury. Then there was a lull for an hour. We were expecting a night attack from the redskins, with a view of breaking through our lines and escaping. Our herd and pack train were being annoyed by straggling Indians in the valley, hoping that we would reduce our force on the hill to protect our train; but we had armed all our packers with the arms of the dead and wounded and made them stand guard that night. I went round the line and cautioned every man to be alert in case Indians should try and escape. About midnight another volley of arrows came from the Indians. They fired them in the air, hoping they would drop down on us, as we were quite close to them; but the angle of elevation was not enough, and the arrows buried themselves in the ground thirty or forty feet in rear of us. After about half an hour of this sort of amusement, everything was quiet again, and again we looked for an effort by the Indians to escape. But day-light came and we breathed easier. Shortly after, we discovered that the Indians had actually escaped during the night; but how? We did not know until McIntosh and some of his scouts discovered their trail and some broken guns near a cave about seventy-five yards in rear of our line. They had passed through the subterranean passages under our feet and emerged to the open air in rear of our position soon after midnight and softly stole away in the dark.

A sergeant in charge of a squad captured a wounded squaw who, when questioned by our chief of scouts, told so many lies that finally a rope was put around her neck and threats to hang her made if she did not speak the truth. Finally she stated that there were 100 warriors in the fight, sixteen of whom were killed and nine wounded, the rest escaping during the night. Some women and children and wounded men were yet in the various underground passageways, where they could not be got at, nor would they come out.[15] Some of the men undertook to examine and explore some of the caves. Dead Indians were found in several of them. Pvt. [Bryan] Carey of Company H had been down into one of those places and had actually taken some of their scalps. He was about to enter another large cave when he was shot dead by a wounded Indian inside. His body fell to the bottom of the cave, and it took about two hours to recover it.

I sent down to camp and directed the blacksmith to get a long pole and work a horseshoe into a drag hook, attach it to pole, and send it up. We then got a lariat and tied it to the end of the pole. One man got as near the entrance of the cave as safety would permit, so as to handle the pole and work the hook into Carey's waist belt, the men on the rocks above holding on to the lariat, ready to haul up the body when secured by the hook, and thus we got poor Carey's body out of the hole for decent burial.[16]

An examination of the position held by the Indians proved it to be much more formidable than we anticipated. There were four immensely strong natural forts of a circular formation like extinct craters, further strengthened by piling up large rocks all around, and all communicating with each other, in addition to which were a number of smaller detached forts capable of holding half a dozen men; besides these were the underground passages, the entrances to which were all protected by rocks. I quote from my diary of September 28, 1867:

> Around the large fort, north and west, was a continuation of the deep gulch, where it was impossible to climb; on the south of it were several smaller forts and breastworks. These were nearly on the same level where the troops were formed for the attack on the morning of the twenty-seventh and where Lieutenant Madigan was killed and seven men of Company D, Twenty-third Infantry wounded. But to get to this ground several ravines and chasms had to be crossed—dangerous to jump, even when not confronted by the enemy.

Such is a brief idea or outline of the character of the Infernal Caverns, Pit River, California, the official title by which it is recognized by the War Department.

On the afternoon of the twenty-eighth we buried our dead, obliterating all traces of the graves, so that the Indians could not find the bodies to mutilate them. Lieutenant Madigan's body was carried one day's march and was buried at midnight near the forks of Pit River, his grave also being so obliterated as to avoid detection.

We prepared double and single travois for our wounded before marching on our return to our military station. The double travois was made by getting two long poles or saplings and strapping them to the aparejos on two pack mules, tandem fashion, with a space between the mules for the man, then canvas and blankets were made fast to the poles, and it at once became a stretcher on mules, where a wounded man could lie quite comfortably and much easier than in an ambulance. The single travois had but one mule, the ends of the poles being on the ground. On two or three mules we had rigged easy chairs by lashing short poles on each side of the aparejos, slanting backward, and then padding up with grass and blankets the top and sides of the aparejos until quite a comfortable seat was made. In this way we got all our wounded along without any unnecessary suffering, although it took seven days' fair marching with wounded men to return across the mountains to Camp Warner. Two of our wounded died some time after, one of them being a packer who was wounded in the thigh, and whom the doctor said really died more from fretting than from the character of the wound, which he did not consider dangerous.

This particular expedition was now finished and preparations were immediately made for another in the Steen's Mountain country, which occurred during the winter months.

A packer and pack mule. NELSON A. MILES. *PERSONAL RECOLLECTIONS AND OBSERVATIONS.*

THE WINTER CAMPAIGN

After the return of the troops from the campaign against the hostile Indians in the Goose Lake country and the three days' fight at the Infernal Caverns, active preparations were commenced to carry on a winter campaign against bands of the Paiute, whose winter haunts lay in secluded and sheltered valleys of the Steen's Mountain country, distant from our post about 100 miles northeast. It was here where Indians would cache their winter supply of dried fish, venison, and camas, the various small bands uniting as soon as snow commenced to fall, and pass the winter months in gambling, etc., unless disturbed by some of Uncle Sam's soldier boys.

During the days of the volunteer troops, 1861–66, very little winter campaigning was indulged in, in this particular section of country, and the Indians did not anticipate any variation from this time-honored custom—they did not know anything about the status of the troops then occupying the various military posts on the frontier. Volunteers or regulars were alike to them—they were their deadly enemies in either case, and the presence of a blue coat meant fight.

Colonel Crook understood the situation thoroughly; his purpose was to attack them in their winter homes, kill the bucks, capture their women, and destroy their supply of provisions, and thus so cripple them that they would be glad to surrender and beg for peace. But much had to be done before a winter campaign could be undertaken. Our cavalry horses and pack mules were sadly run down after the severity of the four months' campaign finished. The blacksmith was kept busy from early morning until sundown. We had lost many horses from sickness and exhaustion in the fall months. Others had to be supplied and drilled to replace them, and recruits recently joined had to be drilled ready for field service. Our supply of forage was very limited. We had enough grain on hand to feed three or four pounds a day to the animals and moldy hay enough to last two or three months, so that the recuperation of the animals was very slow. The men fared but little better. Old Camp Warner was abandoned, and the troops occupying it moved to and established the new post, about forty-five miles west of the old one and situated at the base of Mount Crook, altitude about 5,000 feet above sea level.[17]

The subsistence department was not in those days as well equipped as it is now. A little tea, white sugar, and Java coffee would sometimes be on hand for sale to officers. The other supplies were made up of the ordinary rations of flour, pork, Rio coffee, sugar, salt, etc.; canned goods were in the prospective only. But even the ordinary ration allowance was down to the lowest ebb, and many times it was but repeating the old story of the war days when cavalry were ordered out—i.e., three days' rations to last five—except that in the latter case we could always make up for the other two by foraging, while in the former there was nothing to forage, the nearest habitation being probably two or three hundred miles distant. We had a few tough old steers, called by courtesy beef cattle, with their ribs and hip bones prominently sticking out, their hides laying close down to their skeleton carcass. To kill them would be an act of humanity; to eat them meant a funeral at the post. Several attempts were made to secure assistance from the supplies at Camps McGarry, Nevada, Bidwell, California, and Harney, Oregon, with some trifling success. On one or two occasions, the party sent out to Bidwell or McGarry had to return on account of deep snow, some of the men being badly frozen on the trip, the snow on the parade ground at Warner being quite three feet deep, and the thermometer on several occasions registering eighteen to twenty degrees below zero. When it is understood that there was not a building at the post, some conception may be had of what military life on the frontier meant in those days. Officers and men alike were under canvas, officers' and soldiers' wives and children having to suffer with the rest, not only in the matter of shelter, but also of food. Even the luxury of a little milk for young children was not obtainable at any price— there was no place where it could be purchased, and no animals at the post to supply it. Yet I heard no complaints. It was an illustration of heroism on the part of women unsurpassed since the days of the Revolution. On the part of the troops, it was patient endurance and discipline worthy of any age.

The troops composing the garrison consisted of Company H, 1st Cavalry, and Companies B, D, and I, 23rd Infantry, Colonel Crook and staff with headquarters, 23rd U.S. Infantry, and the headquarters, District of the Lakes.

Several scouts were made to Warner and Alert Lakes in November and December without any results. Our Warm Springs Indians, who were enlisted for four moons in the fall campaign, had been discharged and sent home. It was therefore necessary to secure friendly Indians from some source for trailing and scouting during the winter months. The colonel decided to send to Fort Boise, Idaho, and try and secure twenty-five or thirty from the reservation there.

On December 17, 1867, Lt. O. W. Pollock, 23rd U.S. Infantry, and myself, with a small escort, started from Warner for Fort Boise, via Camp Harney, with letters to the governor of Idaho Territory and others, soliciting their assistance in securing the services of reservation Indians for four or five months (the Indians enlisted for lunar months only; they would bargain for so many "moons"). We had plenty of snow during the trip, but so far it was soft in the valleys and did not impede our travel very much. We reached Boise on December 30 and immediately commenced negotiating for Indian volunteers. They were very reluctant to leave their warm and comfortable dwellings for hard work and exposure in the mountains; but the prospect of a little money in the end overcame their objections, and we secured twenty-three for four moons and commenced our return journey on January 7, 1868.

During our week's delay at Boise, much snow had fallen in the mountains, and the weather was exceedingly cold. When we arrived at the ferry on the Snake River, forty-five miles from Boise, we found the boat tied up and frozen in solid. The ice was about sixteen inches thick on the river, which at the crossing is about 300 yards wide, and for 100 yards from the banks on either side it was solid, the rapidly running water in the center being full of floating ice, some of the immense cakes being seventy-five or eighty feet across. Sometimes several large cakes, piled one on top of another, would pass swiftly along, crushing and destroying anything that obstructed their course. It was a problem difficult to solve, how we were to get to the other side. At one time we concluded to return to Boise and await the spring opening; yet such a course would be, we thought, cowardly and would frustrate all of Colonel Crook's plans and prolong the Indian war another year. We quickly abandoned that idea and then thought of trying the road by way of Silver City and Camp C. F. Smith; but to reach Silver City would entail encountering as much snow as we would have to pass through on the direct road we were on, if we could only cross the river, as Silver City is seven thousand feet above sea level. We made several excursions up and down the river, hoping to find some place where the ice was jammed and frozen solid from bank to bank, so that we could cross on the ice, but at no point was it completely frozen over—a gap of several yards would exist where we thought we had found solid ice. If we had [had] no animals to cross, we could ourselves have crossed in a small boat, but we had thirty-one horses and thirty pack mules in the outfit.

We tried every possible way to get the ferryman to cut the boat out from the ice and make the effort to cross, but to no purpose. He declared that the immense cakes of floating ice in midstream would cross the boat, snap the cable, and send everybody to eternity. Finally we decided to take control of the ferry business ourselves as a military necessity. The old man would not aid us in any way, either by advice or otherwise, but his hired man Smith, under promise of good compensation, agreed to lend a hand. So, after three days' delay, we made a beginning on the fourth day. We procured a long ice saw and commenced to cut a channel from the water's edge to where the boat was tied.

We got the channel cut by dark on the first day, but half of the next day was consumed in cutting away the fresh ice formed during the night and scraping the mush ice from around the bottom of the boat. In the afternoon we put a few horses and mules on board, with eight or ten Indians and some provisions, and started our load through the channel. All went well until we got into the stream, and then the danger confronted us. We had armed half a dozen Indians with long poles to push aside floating cakes of ice as they would come along at a seven miles an hour speed. Every eye was on the wire cable that held the boat to her place. Every exertion was made by the Indians to keep off the ice, but the great cakes came thick and fast, and when one would strike us, the boat would curve downstream, the wire and rope lines giving with every blow, and then a sudden jerk back to their places, to be again put to the test by another blow. With the frost in the wire and every rope connecting the boat with the cable covered with ice, it was wonderful that one or the other did not snap. Had such an accident occurred, the boat would have instantly capsized and men and horses would have perished. But we finally reached the solid ice on the other side and made fast to stakes driven in the ice. We disembarked our load and camped on the bank of the river.

The next morning we had again to get rid of the ice that accumulated around the boat during the night, and with our poles working at the bow we re-crossed to the edge of the ice on the other side, as our canal was again frozen over. We got one small load over in the forenoon and one in the afternoon, watching carefully the floating ice. The loads had necessarily to be small, as a crash with an ordinary load on would have been too much for the cable. The day following we made two more trips—one in the forenoon and one in the afternoon—completing the job. We were very much elated at our success after our seven days' delay at the ferry. Not the slightest accident occurred to man, horse, or provisions, and we camped that night with light hearts, little dreaming of the snow banks ahead of us. Next morning we started bright and early toward the Blue Mountains,[18] where we expected to find plenty of snow.

The second day out from the river we commenced to ascend the mountain ranges and found the snow five feet deep by actual measurement. Of course, we had to lead our animals, or more correctly speaking, the men would take the lead single file and break trail for horses and pack train, the man leading battling with the virgin snow for a few yards, when he would drop out and take the rear, and the next man take it up. By this means the passage of thirty men over the snow would make a fair trail for the horses and the pack train in the rear of all. Sometimes we would make a march of seven or eight miles and at other times not more than four, it depended entirely on whether our route took us over the backbone of a ridge, where the snow was blown off, or whether we were marching in the timber, where no drifts occurred. We camped each night in the timber, so as to get shelter as well as firewood. Our animals suffered severely, as we had but little grain—about three pounds per day—and of course no hay or grass. The trees would be completely stripped of bark and small branches every morning wherever our horses were tied. Two or three times we lost our way in a blinding snowstorm and had to camp each time. Our animals had nothing but snow in place of water for several days, and we had to melt it down in our camp kettles to get water to drink or to make coffee. On one of our marches, we did not make more than a quarter of a mile; at night, where we went into camp, one could almost throw a stone to the place where we left in the morning. Soon after leaving camp, we undertook to cross a ravine which we thought was not deep, as the snow was on a level with us, but we found twenty or twenty-five feet of snow there, and it took us nearly all day to break a trail and get our animals across.

We reached Camp Harney on January 24, [1868,] in a violent snowstorm. Our friends at the post had about given us up, some thinking that we could not get out of the Boise Valley, while others thought we had perished in the mountains.

The distance from Boise to Camp Harney by the route traveled was about 210 miles, and we had yet 140 miles of heavy snow between us and our destination, Camp Warner. We therefore laid over at Harney for a couple of days to rest ourselves and our animals and then bid adieu to our hospitable friends at Harney. We reached Warner on the evening of February 1, where we were joyfully received by the entire garrison, but more especially by the members of our own family. They also had about abandoned any hopes of seeing us, supposing that we had perished in the mountains. However, everything reached camp all right, not an animal lost or the occurrence of any accident worth mentioning, although for forty-eight hours before reaching Harney, we had neither provisions nor forage. We were notified that a week's rest would be granted, and then be ready to start on a scout toward Steen's Mountain.

When we reached the Malheur River, forty-five or fifty miles from Harney, we came across a train of wagons that had been caught in the snow and had to remain in camp there until the following June, when the roads became passable. Some of the teamsters had tried to reach the post on horseback, but one of their number had his feet badly frozen in the attempt, and they were compelled to return. We found the man who had been frozen in a bad plight: one of his feet had swelled to an enormous size and then burst. The flesh appeared to be dropping off in flakes as large as an egg. The poor fellow had nothing but a little coal oil to dress it with and a lot of old rags supplied by his comrades. We had him fixed up as well as possible and took him with us to the post, where he was sent to the hospital for treatment. He remained in the hospital about four months, receiving every attention from the surgeon, who saved both his feet, and then the ungrateful fellow left camp during the night without even a word of thanks and stole a pair of blankets from the hospital as well, which the doctor had to make good to the government. And yet it was known that the miserable specimen of manhood had two or three thousand dollars in his possession at the time.

We come across meanness in our fellow man occasionally, but seldom is it found among frontiersmen, whether they be teamsters, cowboys, miners, or army men. As a rule, they are generous and brave and appreciate any act of kindness done them, especially in sickness. They will fight on slight provocation and are reckless, daredevil kind of fellows; but do them an act of kindness at any time, and they are your friend and champion ever after. If a scabby sheep happens to get in among them, they soon find him out and run him out of camp.

On February 11 Company H, 1st Cavalry (mine), thirty men of Company D, 23rd Infantry, Lt. F. L. Dodge, and fourteen Indian scouts, all under command of Colonel Crook, left Warner for an expedition to Steen's Mountain, hoping to get on to a band of Indians in their winter home. Our direction for two or three days was north. When we reached Warner Lakes,[19] fifteen miles from the post, the entire command, pack train and all, crossed the lake on the ice—I suppose a distance of five or six miles—and then we had the shelter of high bluffs all along the east shore and not more than a foot of snow on the ground. On this trip our transportation was very limited, so that the luxury of a tent was not admissible. We therefore would lay our rubber blankets or heavy canvas on the snow, then our blankets, and then turn in for the night with a piece of canvas or rubber coat on top, and our soft, comfortable snow bed would be down in the morning a foot or more, caused by the heat of our bodies. We generally rested very comfortable, especially after the snow had settled under us, so as to let us down below the surface of the snow level, where the cold wind could not reach us.

After we left the Warner Valley we got up on to the high tableland and deep snow, where progress was slow; the men had to break trail, the horses and pack train following. We reached the head of Dunder and Blitzen Valley[20] in Steen's Mountain on the fifth day out and halted until about 9:00 P.M., when we again started for the valley, hoping to surprise an Indian camp before daylight, as our scouts, who had started several hours ahead of us in the morning, had reported a camp about eight or ten miles down the valley, with Chief We-ah-we-ah in command.[21]

We found the snow in the valley about eighteen inches deep, with a hard crust on top, making it very hard work for both men and horses to get along. We proceeded cautiously down the valley. The night was clear and exceedingly cold. Soon after midnight our advance ran on to a small party of Indians camped in the willows along the banks of the Dunder and Blitzen Creek. The Indians made for the thick underbrush, and firing on both sides was quite lively for nearly an hour. We could not see the Indians, of course; neither could they see us, the direction of fire being obtained only when the flash of a gun revealed the location of the shooter. We remained about an hour trying to get them out, but the brush was so thick and spread over such a large surface of ground that it was useless to waste time, as we hoped to get larger game at daylight. We therefore continued our march until about 3:00 A.M. The scouts intimated that we were not far from the large camp and it would be well to remain in a secluded position until it was light enough to see what we were doing. We therefore dismounted and stood to horse for four long hours. Daybreak did not come until about 7:00 A.M., so there we stood in single file in the snow trail, stamping our feet and hands to keep up circulation, our poor horses humped up like an enraged cat, their bodies a mass of frost, and mane and tail almost a solid mass of icicles. Perfect quiet was enjoined on the command, as we did not know just how near we might be to our prospective and unsuspecting Indian camp. Even the lighting of a match to get a smoke had to be done under the shelter of the capes of our overcoats and then extinguished before throwing it away. It was a weary watching, those long four hours before dawn, with the thermometer not less than ten or twelve degrees below zero.

With the first streak of day, we mounted and pushed on, in the meantime getting ammunition ready and convenient for handling if we should happen to jump a camp of hostiles. But on and on we went, and no Indians. We marched until 11:00 A.M. and not a sign of an Indian, and as all hands were very much in need of breakfast, the colonel put us into camp where we could get water from a stream instead of waiting for a couple of hours to get enough snow melted down to make coffee, as we had been doing for several days previous. Our horses also got water instead of snow, and then nibbled the tops off the sagebrush and ryegrass that appeared above the snow. If any camp had been seen by our scouts, the midnight attack must have given the alarm, and the entire band moved to a more secure place. But no trail or other indication of their presence was anywhere visible. We remained in camp the balance of the day, hoping that our scouts, who were out, might possibly run on to a rancheria; but nothing of the kind occurred, and having but a few more days' rations on hand, we were ordered back to Warner for more rations and a sufficient number of pack mules to carry a month's supply. We had but a few pack animals on the trip, as the train proper was in the Surprise Valley, south of Camp Bidwell,[22] after grain and flour. We reached the post on February 23 and immediately commenced putting things in order for a longer scout early in March.

━━━ ❈ ━━━

Our experience during the month of February while crossing the great plains in the southern and eastern portions of the state of Oregon—which were covered with snow, without a vestige of shrub or tree to relieve the eye as the blazing midday sun shone like a mirror on its level surface—cautioned us to make special precautions against snow blindness.

On the last expedition a few of the men became snow-blind and suffered intense pain; the eyes became very much inflamed, some being so much swelled up as to be entirely closed, and the men's horses had to be led on the march. As many as could procured goggles. All had campaign hats issued to them, and instructions were given for every man to keep his face blackened with burnt cork, which will relieve the eyes from the terrible glare of the sun and snow.

The troops consisted of Company H, 1st Cavalry, fifty-two men; with twelve men of Company I, 23rd Infantry, attached and mounted; twenty-seven men of Company D, 23rd Infantry, mounted (Lieutenant Eschenburg);[23] and fourteen Indian scouts—all under the command of Colonel Crook; Lt. A. H. Nickerson,[24] acting assistant adjutant general, and Acting Assistant Surgeon Dickson as medical officer. Lt. Duncan Sherman[25] was my second lieutenant and acted as aide-de-camp to the colonel. We started from Warner on March 9, 1868, with a month's rations and a limited quantity of grain, taking the trail for Steen's Mountain again.

The men presented a very comical appearance as they formed line preparatory to moving out: all had heavy black marks around their eyes, just as if they had been in the prize ring for half a dozen rounds. Some had gone in for artistic work and smeared their faces all over, while others had blue or green goggles, but while they made good use of the burnt cork, they need have no fear of snow blindness. At the head of Warner Lakes we were joined by Company C, 8th Cavalry, from Fort Harney, Captain Kelly commanding.[26] We struck our old trail leading toward Steen's Mountain and reached the bluffs overlooking Dunder and Blitzen Valley on the thirteenth. Our scouts had been out two days in advance and returned to our camp at the bluffs, reporting fires in the valley.

Next morning we moved down and about 10:00 A.M. came across a band of Indians camped in a rocky canyon near the Dunder and Blitzen Creek. After the first few shots from our carbines, a portion of the command made an effort to charge with revolvers on the stampeded Indians, but the canyon was narrow and the sides very steep and rocky. We therefore deployed the men dismounted and advanced up the canyon, the line extending from one bluff to the other; those on the slopes finding it very difficult to get along, owing not only to the steepness of the sides, but also to large boulders and loose, sliding rock.

We soon came upon some of the Indians hiding behind the rocks, but they kept so close that it was almost an impossibility to get a shot at any of them. Very soon, however, the arrows began to fly thick and fast, and as the location of the shooters was thus established, the troops who were on the side hill near the top advanced quickly and maneuvered so as to get above the Indians and shoot down on them. Two or three men got within fifteen or twenty yards of the redskins before they could see them plainly enough to shoot with any accuracy; their clothes were literally riddled with arrows. One man received a steel-headed poisoned arrow through the left arm, the arrow passing half its length through the arm. Several other men were wounded more or less severely. One arrow struck me in the hip, penetrating a couple of inches, but did not prove serious.

When the arrows discontinued we found but one dead Indian—a great big, savage-looking fellow, who was riddled with bullets before he was killed; both legs and both his arms were broken, and he had half a dozen or more shots through his body, one or two in the face, and one that sent him to the happy hunting ground through the right eye. Farther on, more "good" Indians were found who had succumbed to the fire of our men.[27]

The skirmish lasted about three or four hours. We scoured the country thoroughly and then made camp on the creek in the valley, where we could obtain water and dry willows for firewood. It was not very pleasant camping; the winter was breaking up and the snow in the valleys was melting, so that we had to pack sagebrush on the ground to lay our blankets on in order to keep out of the mud and slush. The next few days we continued our march through the spurs and ranges above the valley in a northeasterly direction, sometimes struggling through miles of snowdrifts, and at other times wading through mud and slush up to our saddle girths, with frequent blizzards of snow, sleet, or rain beating in our faces.

In the low, flat country and on the side hills where the snow had melted off, the horses' feet would sink down into the soggy mire, and in their struggles to drag their feet up again, the sharp, jagged rocks that covered the ground would tear and lacerate their legs until the blood would come; then the poor animals would have to stand all night exposed to frost and snow in a small space controlled by the length of their lariat. Many a man deprived himself of his shirt-sleeves to make bandages to protect his horse's legs; the poor dumb animals would indicate their appreciation of the kindness shown them by their riders by every sign known and readily recognized by the true cavalryman.

Among cavalrymen generally there is everywhere a peculiar bond of affection that is not understood by the ordinary mortal. When a cavalryman loses his horse, he loses his best friend, and his usefulness is gone for the time being. More especially is this the case with United States cavalry on a scout, with perhaps two or three hundred miles between them and the nearest military station or settlement of any kind, with the intervening country beset with roving bands of hostile Indians; it therefore behooves a man to even sacrifice his own comforts to benefit his horse under such conditions as surrounded us on this occasion, even if the man's own nature did not prompt him to it. Many a time have I seen men of my company take their own blankets to cover their horses on those cold, clear, frosty nights in the Steen's Mountain country during that unusually cold winter of 1867–68. I have seen them, too, take their hardtack and share it with their horses when ordinary grazing, or even white sage, was covered with snow. As for grain, we had none after being out a week or so. When it is remembered that the allowance of hard bread (hardtack) is one pound per day per man, it will be seen that the man and horse had not very much to make a square meal on. The horses would eat the hard biscuit with much relish, but salt pork or bacon they respectfully declined.

On March 17 we camped about 1:00 P.M. on a knoll in a valley overlooking the Malheur country; the entire valley was almost a lake, caused by the melting snow. We found bunch grass for our animals about a mile distant on a side hill, which was the first grazing of any account since we left our garrison. Late that afternoon we discovered a long column of mounted men passing across the valley about five miles off; our first thought was Indians, but very soon after our field glasses brought into view a pack train in rear of the column, and we knew that it was some organized command, and our chief of scouts rode out to obtain particulars. The command was Company F, 1st Cavalry (Captain Perry), return-ing to Camp Harney after a month's scouting through the country we were heading for; he had not seen any Indian signs during the month's expedition. It was therefore useless for us to proceed farther, and the colonel decided to return to Warner. We were not more than two days' march from Harney, so Captain Kelly's company of the 8th Cavalry was ordered to return to its proper station, and one or two of our own badly wounded men were sent there, rather than have them suffer several days' hard marching back to Warner.

Next day we commenced our return march. The whole country was one mass of water, except on the ridges, of course; the warm noonday sun sent the melting snow down into the flat country in great streams, and men were soak-ing wet to their waists, for horses could not travel with men on their backs. Every man had to dismount and lead his horse, sometimes for several miles across the flats. Early in the morning a sheet of ice would cover the ground, through which men and horses would break, making our progress still more difficult and exceedingly uncomfortable.

On the night of the twentieth we camped at the mouth of the canyon where we had the fight on the fourteenth; before daylight next morning Mr. Corliss, our chief packer, came to me and said, "There are some Indian signs here." I jumped from my blankets (I was already dressed, having slept in my clothes all night) and found Mr. Corliss holding his favorite saddle mule, with three arrows buried in the poor animal's body. It was still dark, but I ordered the herd in at once. Our horses had been hobbled and lariated on a plateau above our camp about two or three hundred yards and sufficiently far apart to avoid getting tangled up, as well as to give them a chance to graze. We had nine men and a non-commissioned officer guarding them. When the herd came in, we found several animals wounded with arrows and seven horses and four-teen mules missing, Colonel Crook's horse, "Old Buckskin," being among the number. The night was very dark and rain fell heavily nearly all night; the Indi-ans had taken advantage of this and had crawled in through the sagebrush between the lines of sentinels, and had cut the leather hobbles and lariats and then quietly worked the animals out of the herd, the darkness preventing the men on guard from seeing what was going on. But three men were on post at the time, and the large herd being so scattered necessarily involved the dis-tance between the men being unusually great.

Lieutenant Sherman and seventeen men were immediately sent out to fol-low the trail; they returned in a short time and reported having come on to the missing animals about two and a half miles from camp, on the bank of the Dunder and Blitzen Creek all dead. The Indians had driven them as far as the condition of the swampy valley would allow and then killed them, hoping to get enough meat off of them to last a long time, but we took means to upset their fondest hopes.

After breakfast we dismounted our spare aparejos, as our pack train was light, mounted our dismounted men on mules, moved back four miles, and camped. In the afternoon the colonel gave me permission to take half a dozen men to where the dead animals were, as I was certain the Indians would be busy cutting them up, preparatory to manufacturing jerked beef. So, with Dr. Dickson, Donald McKay, chief of scouts,[28] and six men, we started for our horseflesh.

After passing our old camp of the morning, and within about a mile of the dead animals, we rounded a point and came in view of five or six Indians busy enough cutting up our war horses; so far they had not seen us. We dropped back well out of sight and dismounted. Leaving one man in charge of the horses, we commenced a cautious advance on the would-be butchers; the melting snow left about a foot of water all over the low, flat country, and the creek itself was above its banks. So, wading through the water and stooping low, we were able to keep ourselves concealed through the tall ryegrass until we got to within about 300 yards of them; here was a stretch of rising ground that must be passed over to reach them.

Cautiously we crept along, hoping to get near enough to make no mistake about our shooting; we got over seventy-five or eighty yards in this fashion when one of the Indians, tired from stooping evidently, raised up and stretched his arms above his head and then took a survey all round. Just as he did so, I knew we were seen and gave the order to fire. This fellow and another dropped, and all hands ran for the others, but they ran too; they swam the swollen creek and got into the tule on the other side. We soon reached the bank, and one of the men dropped down to a kneeling position and took a shot at an Indian, apparently wounded, struggling along through the tule. He dropped but was up again in a minute; the Spencer pill was again sent on its mission of death, and again he fell; again he got up and moved a few steps, and again another shot, which terminated his career of deviltry. Of the number engaged in preparing the fresh beef for the "Indian market," but one escaped, and he was seen soon after off on the side hill making for the mountains. Determined that none of the tribe should profit by their plunder and our misfortune, we sprinkled every carcass liberally with flour; in this condition the Indians would not dare to touch it, supposing it to be poison. We then returned to camp very well satisfied with the result of our trip.

We started next morning for Warner. When we reached the head of Warner Lakes again, the ice was breaking up; during the night, when the heavy frost commenced to act on the great field of ice (the lake is about sixty miles long and ten wide), the noise resembled heavy peals of thunder or distant cannonading; the contraction would cause great fissures in the nearly two feet thick ice, and it would separate for miles, down or across, with loud explosions.

On March 26 we reached the post and found a great scarcity of provisions and no forage. The greatest deprivation we had to endure was want of vegetables. We had to resort to sending out details into the side hills and sagebrush flats for wild onions and a weed commonly known as lamb's quarters, which, when cooked, was very palatable and helped keep off scorbutic attacks.

Peace rested on our isolated garrison for a few weeks; the cavalry horses were all sent down into the valley to pick up a little flesh—grazing was now fair down along the lake shore and side hills—and it was while our horses were away from the post a small band of Indians attacked the herd of the quartermaster's animals and succeeded in running off a dozen mules. The cavalry horses were ordered back from their grazing ground, about twenty-six miles down the valley, and a strong detachment sent after the renegades. The country over which the Indians had driven the stock was a mass of loose slate rock, over which it was impossible to follow a trail for the simple reason no trail or footprints were made, but a general direction was followed for several days without any result. The Indians had forty-eight hours' good start and drove the animals day and night, as they always do with stolen stock as long as the animals stand it. We never learned in what direction they had driven the stolen mules, but it was supposed that they had driven them down into northern California by way of Goose Lake Valley and the Madeline Plains.

On April 29 a detachment of Company D, 23rd Infantry, came across a small band of hostiles under Chief Oitz-oi-ou.[29] Lieutenant Eschenburg was in command of the detachment, thoroughly conversant with Indian warfare, but Lt. A H. Nickerson, being his senior and acting assistant adjutant general of the district, arrogated to himself the honor of making the attack and the disposition of the troops for this purpose. So completely ignorant of the presence of soldiers were the Indians that during the night, the men got so close to them in the thick sagebrush and ryegrass that they could distinctly hear the Indians gambling and enjoying the discomfort of the losers, and yet at daylight, when the camp should have been completely surrounded, every one of them escaped. The troops lost one man mortally wounded.

In the meantime, our neighbors at Harney were not idle. Captain Perry, with his own company, and Captain Kelly, with Company C, 8th Cavalry, had been scouting in the Malheur country and early in April attacked a large band of Indians commanded by We-ah-we-ah, Eh-gau,[30] and Oytez and almost annihilated the entire outfit.[31] The constant harassing, winter and summer, day and night, by the regular troops since their arrival from scenes of war in the East had so demoralized the Indians, by destroying their provisions and lodges, capturing their women and children, and killing many of their chiefs and braves, that nothing was left them but to surrender and beg for clemency.[32] They were completely subdued and very near starvation's gate. Sometime in the latter part of June, a courier arrived from Harney, notifying Colonel Crook that the whole tribe of Paiute Indians were either at Harney or en route there, ready to surrender, unconditionally. Runners had been sent out by the Indian chiefs all through the Blue Mountain and Steen's Mountain country to notify scattered bands to come in and surrender according to the decree of their council. One band of about twenty-five or thirty came in to Warner and surrendered.

On June 26 Colonel Crook started for Harney to make final arrangements with the Indians, Lieutenant Nickerson and myself, with a small escort, accompanying him. We reached the post on the evening of the twenty-ninth. As we entered the canyon where the post was established, the creek bank for a mile or more was lined with Indian wickiups, called by some tribes tepees; they were simply long poles set up in tripod fashion and covered with robes, matting, old blankets, or anything else they could get. Each family had its own lodge, or where a buck had two wives, then there was a lodge for each wife, just as in Mormondom, where each wife has a separate house or an addition to one.

The next day a grand council was held at the garrison; the United States government was represented by Colonel Crook and the Indians by We-ah-we-ah, E. E. Gantt, Big Head, and a lot of small fry. The chiefs made long speeches, expressing sorrow at having done so much deviltry; that now they felt assured that they could depend on the soldiers as their friends, and they had buried the rope (not the hatchet) and would not steal horses any more, nor do any bad act, etc. One of them made quite a graphic speech, gesticulating with both hands and marking on the ground with a stick. Among other things, he said, "Your great white people are like the grass; the more you cut it down the more it grows and the more numerous its blades. We kill your white soldiers, and ten more come for every one that is killed; but when you kill one of our warriors, or one of our people, no more come to replace them. We are very weak and can not recuperate."

The colonel informed them that the soldiers were there to fight when it was necessary; they did not ask the Indians to make peace; the soldiers would follow them day and night, winter and summer, until the last one of them was killed as long as they (the Indians) remained hostile and continued to kill people and to rob and steal, but if they were sincere in their pledges and continued to be good Indians, the soldiers and the government would be their friends.

The powwow lasted about three or four hours; immediately after its conclusion the colonel called upon the chief We-ah-we-ah for ten of his men to go with him as scouts on an expedition into the Goose Lake country after the Pit River Indians. In an instant ten fine, strapping young bucks stepped out as volunteers, only too anxious to get a chance at another tribe, or even some of their own, for that matter, so long as it was the excitement of war. I think nothing could have more fully illustrated the character and ambition of the Indian. Just from the field of defeat and subjection by their historic foe, the white man, they were ready in a moment to join with him in any enterprise of a warlike nature that would give them an opportunity to heal their wounded spirit by wreaking vengeance on a weaker foe, backed up as they were by the soldiers whom they had so recently been fighting. Wild by nature, nurtured and fed on the traditions of their race, they heard nothing in their nomadic homes but stories and legends of their warlike ancestors and the prowess of the young warriors of their people. No wonder, then, that they were ready again to take the field with the troops whom they had good reason to know were a brave and generous foe. It took but a short time to clothe them in Uncle Sam's uniform and arm and equip them as soldiers; they were then prepared for a business in which they took a delight.

Next morning we were on our way back to Camp Warner with our volunteer Indian detachment. A few days after our arrival at Warner, an expedition started for the Pit River country. The command consisted of Companies A, H, and I, 1st Cavalry, and Company G, 8th Cavalry, from Camp Bidwell; Company A, of the 1st, coming from Klamath; and Company I from Camp Watson. On August 6 our Indian scouts came across a party of twenty-five hostiles and had a short brush with them, but they came in and surrendered and were sent under escort to the reservation. We continued our scout as far as the Madeline Plains but found no sign of Indians anywhere; the roving bands had followed the example of those at Harney and had sought shelter and protection on some of the reservations either at Harney, Klamath, or Pyramid Lake, Nevada. Thus was concluded one of the most determined and successful campaigns ever organized against the bands of hostile Indians that kept northern California, Oregon, Washington Territory, Idaho, and Nevada in perpetual commotion, retarding the prosperity of the country, and a constant menace to life and property.

Colonel Crook's Campaign

JOSEPH WASSON[1]

Owyhee Avalanche, July 27, 1867[2]

CAMP C. F. SMITH, BAKER COUNTY, OREGON,
SATURDAY, JULY 20, 1867

Left the Owyhee ferry Thursday last at 4:00 P.M. Arrived at the head of Crooked Creek at 9:30 P.M. same evening—twenty-four miles. Sagebrush scenery and road rough and smooth by turns, but generally a good road. Three soldiers stop at the old station as a sort of relief and convenience for the government express. Left Crooked Creek to the rear at 6:30 A.M. yesterday and arrived at this place at 1:00 P.M.—an individual as nearly used up as one could be.[3] Have been endeavoring to recruit ever since to be ready for another advance, which will be at 6:00 P.M.—leaving me but a little time to scribble, but will save your readers a lengthy infliction of trash thereby. I should be glad to torment them all that is possible. The road from Crook Creek pretty much the same as beyond, if anything rockier and is ten miles longer.

Camp Smith[4] is the liveliest place I've seen in the upper country since the early days of the Boise basin. O. R. Johnson, Alf Mix, and others arrived here a day or two ago from Chico, bringing five or six hundred horses and mules, which added to those already here, make a camp of upwards of a thousand, and there are over a hundred head of cattle grazing on the valley round about. White Horse Creek is a series of creeks at this point, get together soon and sink. The valley is several miles long and two or three wide, covered with rye grass. There are one or two ranches in successful cultivation.

The inspection of the new supply of horseflesh constituted several days' rare amusement, closing this morning. No serious accidents that I have heard of occurred. The stock looks pretty well on the average. There is a lack of saddles, aparejos,[5] and supplies of that character. There are about two hundred men round the post now, besides near a hundred Indians, the latter mostly equipped as scouts. Captain Darragh,[6] in command of about fifty Wasco and Warm Springs Indians, arrived here yesterday afternoon from the Dalles country via the John Day and Malheur [Rivers]. They had a little fight somewhere on the way, killing four and getting one killed.[7] They made a display of scalps

An army mule team. OUTING MAGAZINE, 1887.

and parade on their advent here. Their war songs may be music to them. Together with the Boise Indians here, they made camp howl last night. I didn't go to bed as early myself last night as my fatigued condition demanded. I blame the officers of this post for that; they said it was customary evenings before a long campaign. The expedition leaving here tonight will consist of about one hundred fifty soldiers and one hundred Indian scouts. They will go round the Pueblo [Mountain] into the Goose Lake country and bring up at Camp Warner the last of the month, where an addition of over one hundred men will be ready to join the command. It was the intention of the commanding officer [Crook] to go up the Malheur, but the opinion of Captain Darragh that the Indians are south changed the program. Information from the chief We-ah-we-ah, commanding the enemy out there, goes to show that they are in constant communication with the Truckee country;[8] in fact, they say they like the whites down there better than those residing up this way—they can get all sorts of materials for war. Which is a good joke on the whites up this way. We-ah-we-ah is represented as bearing a charmed life; has white hair so long that he can sit on it—very handy, I should think, for a cushion or for scalping.

Camp Smith is rather pleasantly located on a plateau overlooking White Horse Valley, but occasionally the wind blows tremendously and then things are not so pleasant—as today, for instance, when the demand for paper-sand in no wise equals the supply sifted through a two-foot wall. Camp Smith is to be continued as a military post, and considerable building will be done ere winter comes again. They need more shelter here, and Captain Walker[9] is making arrangements accordingly. Captain Coppinger[10] is here for a share of horses for Camp Winthrop, from which place he will make a campaign up the Owyhee soon. Some of the stock goes to Fort Boise and Camp Lyon.[11] I infer that Camp Warner will be the place to operate from by next fall. Colonel Crook wants to get as near the Indians as possible and is satisfied that a good cleaning out where he is going will put a damper on their raiding out in the settlements and along the highways. A surprise accompanying a defeat of Indians is said to sicken them more than double the amount of destruction in a pitched battle. They don't like to be beat at their own game of stealth. The expedition going out tonight will travel altogether in the nighttime and endeavor to camp during the day in places as unobservable as possible. It will go hard, this turning night into day and vice versa, but I know some who have been practicing it lately and may be specially adapted to the service forthcoming. If there is nothing to prevent, you may hear from me at Camp Warner. The expedition takes two months' rations, and I am likely to stay as long as the rations last and as close to them as I can conveniently.

I am not much on the ceremony business, but all the officers I have met here have treated me better than I could have expected, and if the trip is not agreeable to the end, the fault will not be theirs. Speaking of officers, I am reliably informed that Col. Jeff C. Davis[12] will soon be in chief command of this district. I don't suppose the program will be interfered with in the least, as he has the reputation of being a practical sort of man.

—•— ≊◆≊ —•—

Owyhee Avalanche, August 3, 1867

CAMP NUMBER ONE, JULY 21, 1867

This place is doubtless in Baker County, Oregon, on what is known as Trout Creek, and about eighteen miles south of Camp C. F. Smith, which post the commanding officer left at 6:30 P.M. last evening and pitched the temporary wickiups[13] at 12:30 A.M. The road traveled was the Chico, up to within a few miles, where we left it to the right and took a cut-off supposed to save five miles. From Camp Smith the road leaves Steen's Mountain to the right about twenty-five miles. Steen's Mountain is of the butte character, standing out on the level plain; but in another sense it is but a higher portion of a long, low chain extending into Nevada. It supplies the South Fork of the Malheur and is yet spotted with snow; its timber is scrubby. Camp Smith overlooks the valley of White Horse to the west and south, and along which the road takes its way some distance; but four miles from Smith brings us to Willow Creek. Thence to Trout Creek, along which we traveled several miles previous to camping.

As everything was in such a jumble at the post the little while I was there, and everybody so busy, I failed to connect with any great amount of information, and that was not very correct. I've been taking an inventory of the outfit today and find it composed about as follows: Captain Perry, commanding Company F, First Cavalry, forty-five men; Captain Harris,[14] Company M, First Cavalry, thirty-seven men; Captain Darragh, thirty-seven Warm Springs Indians and eleven employees—forty-nine; Captain McKay,[15] thirty five same Indians, eleven employees—forty-six; Archie McIntosh, twenty-five Snake Indians—making about two hundred men mounted. Add to the column two

George Crook in his preferred campaign attire.
JOHN G. BOURKE. *ON THE BORDER WITH CROOK.*

hundred pack animals, and it strings along single file to a respectable length; as it moved off from the post about sundown presented a unique appearance—motley rather, with the Indians in as much or little dress as suits their taste, boys in blue, and the usual variety of employees. I may add that Colonel Crook[16] commands the expedition; Dr. Wagner[17] is chief surgeon, and Dr. Tompkins, assistant surgeon. It may be of the utmost importance to add that the undersigned is in charge of Company I—I being the only one in the company at this time. Having one of the biggest and the toughest horses in the command, I may make an imposing appearance, but am satisfied I am regularly imposing on the good nature of all hands and the cook—especially the latter. Such trips as this fetches one to his appetite, but frequently takes one to where there isn't anything else. However, we are going where there is [an] abundance of game—and maybe where "game" will be required and found wanting. Speaking of game, this creek is aptly named, and all hands and all colors of hands are feasting on or fishing for trout—the regular brook species. A nice stream and an accommodating one, bubbling up to the lips of the way-worn traveler, accompanying him through the desert as far as it can, and then sinks as if tired of the barren prospects above and, as it were, goes in quest of Wild Horse and Willow Creeks gone before. To appreciate the beauties of nature where the bounties are limited, the traveler needs to experience a good sagebrush thirst and then come down on a pure, cool stream when least expecting it.

Lieutenants Madigan and Bacon leave Camp Smith today for Camp Warner, taking all at Smith except the old garrison of about fifty men under Major Walker, who will run the concern satisfactorily if given but half a chance. The officers aforesaid—also, Lieutenant Eskridge,[18] a bully boy and doing considerable business in the A.Q.M. Department—will immediately outfit more men to join the expedition at Warner and swell its number to upwards of four hundred effectives. But more of this again, perhaps.

CAMP NUMBER TWO, JULY 22—This place of rest is undoubtedly in Humboldt County, Nevada, but Oregon may claim it by a mile or two until the surveyors settle it;[19] but I am not caring a cent one way or the other—nor carrying a cent, either, which is the old thing, you know. Came down Trout Creek from 6:00 P.M. last evening until we struck the old stage-road station. Passed through some rough canyons, high, black walls on either side, resembling columns jostled over to an angle of forty-five degrees and then left to shift for themselves; at intervals reminding one of the front of a paint shop where green and yellow is daubed regardless of expense. However, nature furnishes the original for every production of art, and we should not find fault with her profusion of colors even if we half suspect the birds contributed a share by way of variety. As my friend Madigan might say, "Nothing in this menagerie, ladies and gentlemen, to shock the modesty of the most fastidious."

Leaving Trout Creek, the command continued south on the Chico road, which winds along the foot of the east side of the Pueblo range—rather an extension of Steen's Mountain. The camp today is eighteen miles from that of yesterday, in a canyon about a quarter of a mile west of, and at the mouth of which is, a deserted village known as Pueblo City. Another interesting illustration of the naming of towns, as I am told that "pueblo" means city in the original. However, as it is in ruins and ruined no one but its founders, we should be satisfied. What a pity some other cities of magnificent distances—in the distance—started on imaginary wealth and maintained on promises of equal sensibility, had not been similarly loved by the gods and died young? I have no doubt it was money in the pockets of the proprietors of Pueblo that they were fools enough to commence life at the mouth of a canyon where one Indian could come down and clean out ten to one any time; they were thus enabled to get acquainted early in business and have something to start elsewhere. This view embraces all of Pueblo Valley—several miles in width and perhaps twenty long, surrounded by low mountains; to better describe it, it looks like a billiard table stripped of its green—the bed is mostly alkali, but in these mountains there is plenty of slate mixed with quartz, the latter being hard and white, the former lead color and soapstonish. Having seen some specimens that indicate silver, considerable antimony and colored by copper. The Vicksburg mines are farther south and on the opposite side of the valley; a few men are at work there and a little machinery pointing that way.

The command thus far has marched leisurely and has had some trouble with wild pack mules, but is now getting in shape to come to time. Archie McIntosh was ordered to the front this morning, and from this on, the expedition may expect forced marches occasionally, be the result something or nothing. McIntosh is no throw off, as many are in the profession he is acting. He was brought up by the Hudson Bay Company, who meant business all the time. The McKay family (pronounce it McKye) is represented quite numerously in the district. Donald is with Coppinger as scout and I understand is trustworthy; besides the captain there is another brother here. The captain—known also as "Doctor" and "Billy"—is an educated man and one who has traveled. He is a gentlemanly fellow and sociable, and I like him much. His family name is Scotch, but his complexion corresponds more aptly to the celebrated snuff of that name.

McKay and Darragh's commands are regularly enlisted in the U.S. service for one year or "the war," which may mean more or less. McIntosh's Snakes are a temporary command so far, but one most likely to continue right along; their leader will so long as Colonel Crook runs the machine and can get him. There is a young buck who was captured last winter at the fight on Teara's Plain. He is bright as an antelope, and it's interesting to see some old one put him through a dance and singing operation—a mixture of juba and coyote. But what I was going to say, the little devil during the fight observed the soldiers making rather rough but necessary examinations for the purpose of distinguishing the sexes of the enemy, so that the feminine might not be put to the sword—especially at that time. When captured, he expected instant death, but with his hands he managed the fig-leaf dance so successfully that his life was spared—more out of admiration for his sagacity than love for him as the poor Indian. By the way, Captain McKay is satisfied of the death of old Paulina[20] and that the Snakes over towards John Day are without a leader and have gone south to join We-ah-we-ah or are badly scattered. Paulina was killed about thirty miles south of the Warm Springs reservation.

I have been reading the reports of Colonel Curry and his under-officers, who traveled over this country two and three years ago as Oregon volunteers.[21] Find considerable to interest just now, as the colonel deals in the descriptive occasionally. At the Owyhee ferry, where I found use for such words as played out, gone in, etc., he employed weird, antiquated, fanciful, and other terms, and positively asserts that those curiously wrought hills and shores were caused by the winds alone. A close examination thereabouts will disprove his theory and more firmly establish that those strange curiosities in nature were produced by the action of waves instead of the wind, and that all the Great Basin was once the sea. I think, however, that between wind and water the colonel and I will strike it somewhere; and as he inclines to wind in other respects in his report, I'll let him have his way. Out here, from necessity, I incline to water frequently—for drinking purposes, of course.

From this camp on, I hope to find something to interest you more than a draw on the fancy. It interests me, however, and I don't care so much for your welfare as to worry about it under such circumstances. I find some droll old characters among the soldiers, most of whom have seen service of some kind or other. One old steed I met at the ferry was a remarkable man, as he told it. I traced his life and adventures through his own conversation—down through all the wars since the battle of the Byone to the last fight at Steen's Mountain, and a rough estimate would require forty cords of wood and other materials to replace his sacrifices of limbs, head, etc. Science tells us that a human being undergoes an entire change of material once every seven years in the ordinary course of life; just think of my hero, then! I gave him a glass of whiskey, showed him the side of a bale of hay, and started for Camp Smith, but on the way, at a certain place on the road, I experienced a dose of rough living that set me to thinking of home. The living was better than the sleeping. I come out on this trip to get revived up, and expected and preferred something active. The adobe abode was about the size of an old fashioned bake oven and looked so much like one that if I could have gone to sleep, there would have been no trouble about dreaming of the "days of my boyhood," etc.; however, as to the matter of health, I was not in bed over two seconds by the watch—I was on the night watch, and by moonlight I could see anything, no matter how large— until I could feel new life (new to me) coming upon me from every point of the compass,[22] and it occurred to me that if this expedition should all get killed but one, and that one was me, it would come back with a million more lives than it started with. But I am happy since getting to Camp Smith, all right.

I get a chance to send this in tomorrow, which pleases me mightily, as I don't like any more of the memoranda business than can be got along with conveniently. O. R. Johnson started back to Chico today and will return to Camp Warner as soon as possible, and perhaps stay out that way some time; all of which is in the program.

8:30 P.M.—Two Indians have just arrived from McIntosh, in which he states that he struck the trail of four Indians early this morning, followed them nearly all day, caught, and killed them. The messengers brought in a bow and quiver of arrows and seemed highly elated. The affair took place west of this place about twelve miles and is important from the fact of their not getting away with any information.

Owyhee Avalanche, August 10, 1867

CAMP NUMBER 3, TUESDAY, JULY 23

Left Number Two at Pueblo City at 6:30 A.M. McIntosh's success, of which I wrote last night, believed to have cleared the way so that one march could be made in daylight. I treated the Pueblo prospects cavalierly, but I could see nothing there to encourage immigration when there are so many more favorably located districts; there is no timber nearer than fifty or one hundred miles of Pueblo but sage.

Our route today is south along the Chico road, at the side of which, about two miles from camp, we saw the remains of the little mill which was taken to Silver [City] two years ago; at the ruins were several tons of quartz, which looked as if much of it would assay well in silver; the ore is tinged with copper. About eight miles south of camp a road leads to the mountains, which, I was told, was the one to the copper mines; but copper will have to be found almost pure in this far-off place to be of particular value. I believe a few colors of gold were panned out at camp, but the mountains do not indicate an abundance of the article in any shape. There is a promontory extending north from the Vicksburg range into the Pueblo Valley, which gives it a forked appearance looking south. Opposite the northern extremity of this point, on the west side of the valley, is a scalding hot spring, several feet in diameter and deep. It rises in a marsh and scatters round and sinks within a quarter of a mile.

At this point is an old Chico stage station—adobe, containing its quota of portholes, a characteristic of every habitation from Jordan Valley down. The remark that the steam from the spring smelled like scalded feathers suggested the idea that maybe here is where the devil "cooks his goose"—geese, rather. But a mile or two farther on brings us to a large, yellow-colored lake of alkaline proclivities, and being so near hot water, the supposition is that the devil's laundry may be hereabouts, and that he had used the mountainsides for a washboard—the west shore being volcanic, steep, high, and marked along its sides with those curious lines so common in these lava formations, giving the walls the appearance of having a series of mining ditches located one above another and of various ages. At the south end of the aforesaid lake, the command left the road and took up a canyon, cutting off several hours' necessary travel, had it followed round the south end of the Pueblo range.

It is a curious range, extending almost from the Owyhee River nearly to Summer Lake, and very narrow, fronting abruptly on the Chico road and along it for at least one hundred miles (including Steen's Mountain, of course); it forms a splendid screen for Indians to overlook the operations of whites with impunity and then fall back into the canyons and sage in the rear with perfect safety. The Vicksburg range—trending east and west, mostly—is high enough to retain snow at this season of the year; as to anything further of its character, I know nothing.

As we approach the low lands west of the Pueblo range, off to the south-west about ten miles the tules surrounding a boiling hot lake of half a mile in length are seen. The lake was discovered by Colonel Crook and soldiers last winter. It is a permanent body of water, apparently, and quite deep. It is a curiosity I should like to have seen on the trip. The route traveled so far today has been about southwest. Could a pass have been discovered, about ten miles of the day's march could have been saved; but as it enabled me to see several miles further into Humboldt, don't mind the heat, sage, and exercise. Knowing so many persons who saw their way into Humboldt and couldn't see it out, I am content to let Humboldt rip with Camp Number Four, 3:00 P.M., July 23.

This is nearly west of Number Three, on a creek that has ceased to run water this year; good water for stock in places and plenty for drinking pur-poses obtained by sinking a foot or two beneath the sod. Good grass and quite a valley covered with a thick matting of rye and other swamp grass. Nothing particular occurred—reading, sleeping, etc.—until 5:00 P.M. on the twenty-fifth, when we started for Camp Number Five, Isaac's Springs, July 25. Arrived here at 12:30 A.M. This is an excellent camp after traveling about twenty miles north of west over rough lava and sage; this is on the old Drew trail, which we struck back seven or eight miles. It was the result of a trip from California several years ago by Colonel Drew—who drew on the imagination as a general thing, but didn't draw on government subsequently to pay for it, as is too often the case.[23] A few wagons have passed over it, as the crushed sage indicates in places. Some of McKay's scouts came in during the night with six papooses and a grown scalp, which showed that the wearer was on the decline of life—and the decline greatly hastened. Got them about twelve miles to the southwest; several bucks evidently escaped, but McIntosh is now on the track. It was his thunder, and there is considerable rivalry existing between the dif-ferent bands of Indian scouts. There are at least two detachments out all the time, and the country scoured pretty thoroughly for ten miles ahead of the command. Leave here at 5:00 P.M., twenty-sixth, for Camp Number Six, Satur-day, July 27.

Traveled northwest over a very rough road—just as we found and made it—until 2:00 A.M., when it became evident that we were slightly lost. The command stopped, built fires, and worried it out till daylight, when we struck off west over several miles of excessively rocky country and brought up in a dry canyon—plenty of grass, water having departed several weeks. Made a dry camp from 7:00 A.M. till 10:30 A.M., when we started for Camp Warner, Baker County, Oregon, July 27, where we arrived about 3:00 P.M. Had some little profitable excitement today, of which I will attempt to give some idea. When about coming out on the Warner and Camp Smith road, seven or eight miles back from here, a fresh moccasin and pony track were discovered crossing our trail to the south. A detachment of Darragh's Indians were ordered to follow the trail, which led over a lava bed a mile or two and overlooking a grassy flat extending back from the road two or three miles. Captains McKay and Darragh followed the Indian scouts, who, when at the edge of the marsh, discovered quite a rancheria[24] of natives at the upper end and motioned to the command to go out. All hands started across lots, but when about halfway across the lava, the colonel thought the alarm to have been founded on the discovery of the "lone horseman," etc., and that the scouts would be sufficient, and halted the cavalry.

McKay and Darragh kept going and were "on the ranch" nearly as soon as their scouts; the undersigned, having a fast horse, also got up in time to get two shots at the nest with a Henry rifle. The rancheria was evidently not expecting an attack and had but little time to take to the rocks, which, on the west, were bounded by the flat, and east they (the runaways) were liable to be met by the rear end of the command—the packers. After skirmishing round for half an hour or so, and everything seemed to be quieted and the chase abandoned, I started after the command. When I left the place, as nearly as I could ascertain, there were four dead warriors, six or eight squaws and papooses, and six horses captured. In the wickiups were much Indian provisions, nets, etc., indicating a permanent residence. The Columbia Indians went through the spoils for everything they could find, and it appeared to me were more inclined to look after the spoils than follow up, but it seems some of them got on the track of three or four runaway bucks, who hid in the rocks, and between Indian scouts and packers, were all smoked out and killed. Tom McKay and Frank Cunningham, among the packers, each shot an Indian, I am informed. Captain McKay thinks that one buck got away alive, but McIntosh is still out, and it will go hard with any he gets the scent of; also, some of Darragh's men are in the same direction.

One or two of the savages had guns, the remainder bows and arrows. I suppose it will be safe to say there are fifteen Indians less from today's encounter[25] and twenty-five for the week ending tonight, having left Camp Smith just one week ago. The only casualties so far were two of McKay's horses wounded by arrows today. The captured animals bore the "U.S." brand, and the colonel, I think, is favorably impressed with the results thus far. Since June 15 some fifty Indians have been killed or captured in his district, and such hauls will soon tell severely on the savages. It will be several days before the next and summer campaign will commence, but will write again from this place.

—+— ⊫◆⊨ —+—

Owyhee Avalanche, August 17, 1868

CAMP WARNER, BAKER COUNTY, OREGON
SUNDAY, JULY 28, 1867

Last evening I wrote and this morning sent you some account of our trip and doings after leaving Pueblo on the twenty-third up to arriving at this place yesterday P.M. Of the summing up of the fight [we] had back ten miles yesterday at noon, I gave the number of killed and captured at fifteen. The showing made here this morning is larger by seven—twenty-two in all; eleven scalps of warriors, the remainder squaws and papooses. I was inclined to believe that the first estimate was too high, but am pleased to know the error was on the other side of the ledger. Darragh and McKay allowed their Indians to go in after their own style, and the scene was scattered over half a mile of sage and rocks, and besides the little shooting necessary, jargon was the only sound I heard. Little shooting, I said; I notice that Darragh, McKay, the subscriber, and another savage had two shots apiece at a buck in the sage about two hundred yards distant before killing him; but the army statistics say it requires 272 pounds of metal to kill a man, and so I should be satisfied, it being a new experience to me.

Now, since leaving Camp Smith one week last evening, the campaign figures up thirty-five Indians killed and captured, all ages and sexes; just about one-half were warriors. McIntosh is still out, and the chances are in his favor that he will have increased the loss to the natives. The Snakes are the superior Indian every way in this outfit for "fighting the devil with fire"—three fires, I may say, for there are three tribes against the Snakes aside from the soldiers. The fight yesterday terminated with fire surely, for three Indians had to be literally burned out of the rocks, one being cooked almost white; they would not yield on more tolerable terms. One of the besieged Snakes made a defiant speech from his position in the rocks.

McKay and Darragh have tolerably good command over their Columbia River tribes, who are armed with Maynard carbines. General Steele[26] did a good thing when he organized these two companies, but he would have conferred additional advantages on the service had he sent up improved arms; but then, he perhaps did the best he could at the time.

The captured Indians, I am told, are to be taken care of by the enlisted Indians, experience proving that they do better with their own kind, and besides, the government has to foot the bills whatever the situation. Among the seven captured Wednesday last are one or two papooses whose complexion suggests a mixed origin, and it may be that when they are washed out of their savage tints, the physiognomies of some of the members of the past legislatures of Nevada and Idaho may be developed, as during such assemblies, when the capital cities are overdone, members frequently become very hard up in more ways than one. This is merely an allusion to the natural results of the straits of society—especially when it includes wickiups and reservations. These papooses could doubtless find homes in white families and be very acceptable where the matrimonial relations have failed to correspond to the requirements of the Scriptural injunction "multiply and replenish," but the better plan all around, I suppose, is to keep the Indians by themselves as much as possible, and then the case will be bad enough and soon enough. Some of the little imps take the matter of capture as a matter of course, while others frown like young hyenas for about a week, and their appetites increase in the same ratio, but after the first clean-up (a mining phrase, you will recollect) and the intestines get filled, the animal organs continue operation with not so much dispatch as cheapness for the commissary. When first captured, [they] have a commissary of their own where they can put their fingers upon it; the living afforded thereby cannot be said to be fast, as they seem to catch it whenever they want it. Like the Chinaman's, the variety is confined to "lice." The Indian soldiers immediately put the squaws to work round camp or, in accordance with orders from the colonel, take them out to assist the scouts in finding the haunts of others. His idea is, as I infer, to keep about three bands of scouts ahead and on either flank at a distance of ten to twenty miles from the main command, and either band large enough to take in any ordinary wickiup of natives; also, to find favorable camping places for the main command, which will do its traveling in the night, and thus, should any of the Indians escape the scouts, they can only inform to that extent. In case a large number of Indians are seen together, then the whole outfit makes a forced march in the night and surrounds them. Nine time out of ten, when the combatants are equal, the fight results in a fruitless footrace—the soldiers being able to attack the Indians only upon one side or point.

The success of the command so far, and upon success alone is everything judged in this practical world, implies that Colonel Crook's plan is as good as any, and I believe he has the Indian character a little nearer down to a scratch than any man in the regular service. By having sufficient men to surround and whip any band liable to be met, and good scouts with change of horses, he can sweep a wide belt of country and keep it up continually.

The best information locates the bulk of the hostile Indians in the country marked in outline by Camps Bidwell, Warner, Watson, and Fort Klamath; a band of about sixty is supposed to be operating above the forks of the Owyhee, and Captain Coppinger at Winthrop is amply able to clean them out if he has the luck to corral them. He has a detachment of Snake scouts and a good man at their head, and orders, I believe, to go on the campaign within a very short time. The delay of supplies has caused a delay generally in the campaign. This evening Captain Perry, with his company, and McKay, with a detachment of his Indians, go with several days' rations on a scout to the southeast. Now, a word for Camp Warner, which is about one hundred miles west of Camp Smith and located at the eastern base of Warner Mountain,[27] the eastern shores of Warner Lakes—all of which take their name in honor of Captain Warner, of engineers, killed in a canyon near here by Indians as early as '49. In the summer season and until snow falls, Warner is a nice camp, and the country all round for miles—especially north and south—is a beautiful contrast to anything I've seen since leaving upper Jordan Valley. Right at the present camp there has been a thick grove of pine, but the wants of the camp have thinned it out to a few trees for ornament. The quarters are low log structures; altogether the arrangements are comfortable and of very cheap getup. At present there are two companies of the 23d Infantry stationed here—Captain Collins, Company D, and Captain

Hinton,[28] Company B; Lieutenant Jack of the latter is quartermaster of the post.[29] The commandants aforesaid—Hinton and Collins—keep things neat round here. A very hospitable people they are, even to a vagabond like myself. Lieutenant Eskridge, district quartermaster, and Lieutenants Madigan and Parnell have just arrived from Camp Smith with all the materials for fitting out Company H, 1st Cavalry, for the coming campaign and otherwise strengthening things necessary. George H. Bailey is sutler at this post. Notwithstanding Camp Warner is the finest located post in the district from a summer and fall view of the case, it is entirely out of all favor with Colonel Crook, who came near losing his own life and endangered his men in getting to and from it last winter, and he is determined to change it every way just as fast as it can be done after selecting a new site. This is a terrible place for snow in winter, and so swampy for several months afterwards that its removal on that score is imperative.

MONDAY, JULY 29, 1867—In camp on Darragh Creek—stream putting into Warner Lakes from the west and perhaps fifteen miles northwest of Camp Warner. Darragh, with a detachment of Indians, left Warner last night to scout the way to the new post, and this morning Colonel Crook, with Captain Harris and company, followed. Darragh got lost in the rocks west of the lakes and encamped here just in advance of the balance of the command—11:00 A.M. To get here, we followed southerly along the base of Warner Mountains several miles, thence down an immense hill and a rocky one to the lakes; thence north a mile or two to a narrow place, over which Captain Hinton had made a very substantial stone crossing; thence northwest along the margin of the lake, or marsh rather, to the debouch of this stream.

The lakes are a series of marshes—at times miles of clear, uninterrupted water—extending north and south upwards of forty miles and in places fifteen wide; the mountains making a high, steep, and rocky shore on the east, and on the west the lakes are bordered by the usual variety of sage scenery and formations, varied with low rye alkali flats on a level with the tules, which is the principal vegetable and nearest thing to timber I've seen on the lakes; am told, however, that sagebrush islands abound farther north where the lakes widen. Ducks, geese, and gulls innumerable in sight.

The Warner Mountains contain considerable timber of mahogany and juniper species, but I have heard of no mineralogical prospects. Substituting sagebrush plains for these lakes, and Warner Mountains are in a manner very similar to Steen's. Snow in places yet. Indians can have a good view of matters east from the mountains, and a retreat into the lakes and sage west. By the way, I should not forget that there is a very perceptible current in the lakes setting north, and the question arises whether they are not the outcropping of a large subterranean river; besides, I am told that the water rose in them one foot during one day last spring, which would require a hundred times more water than the natural watershed of the surrounding country can produce. Here, then, may be something of a solution of the problem of what becomes of the waters that sink in Nevada. To continue the subject a little farther, these lakes are on a level with the Harney, Malheur, etc., and the latter, I believe, have no outlet above ground, and the presumption is that all are connected, though Harney Lake tastes salty while Warner Lakes are fresh and clear—and cool. As I may learn more of the subject during the summer, I will only add that on the east side of Warner are many large, detached boulders presenting smooth sides, whereupon are traced in outline pictures of mountain sheep, deer, etc., with a species of indelible ink, but by whom is not known. Persons who are conversant with [John C.] Fremont's journals of explorations say the location and hieroglyphics correspond to those mentioned therein many years ago.

TUESDAY, JULY 30—Camped today on same creek, ten or more miles above yesterday's camp, where we remained till noon today. Found Darragh, who has several scouts out north and south. Creek heads in the mountains about four miles farther up—mountains, a nicely timbered range, trending north and south; snow patches frequently along the summit. Going up this stream, the view ahead is a perfect picture in the way of mountain scenery.

WEDNESDAY, JULY 31—The colonel, with a part of the command, goes in quest of a suitable place for establishing a new post. Continue up same creek a couple of miles, then strike north out of the mountain basin just discovered and travel several miles through an open-timbered country, a bench of the mountains, which, in the absence of any other known title, it is proposed to call Crook's Mountain.[30] It is the only thing in the country unnamed fit to receive any particular appellation, and this is certainly a cheering landscape, and the aroma of pitch and pure, cool air in connection affords a welcome relief from the nauseating mixture of sage, alkali, sand, and heat so monotonous and omnipresent in the "golden land of dross and stones."

This mountain looks placer-like from the foothills, but I have no authority for saying, as yet, that a color has been found. It is a section of U.S. domain scarcely scratched by the toenails of white men. The sign of game is abundant. Four miles' travel, and the outfit halted on the skirts of the timber and in a depression of mountain and plain, in which is found several small streams of excellent water. Here Colonel Crook selected a site for the new post, which it is intended shall be known as Camp Woods—a double signification: in honor of Governor Woods of Oregon, but should that fail to connect in any ways soon, the post can fall back on its own resources and safely continue its name for the next century.[31]

The belt of timber continues northwest from the new post as far as the eye can [see] and till the mountains seem to cease in the plain; straight, clean pines and so thick as to hide the ground. The new location is about on the line of longitude which forms the eastern boundary of California, and perhaps thirty miles in Oregon, and the latter may feel proud that there are some redeeming features in the southeastern section of the state. The supplies at present must come via Chico.

There is [in] much of this country natural grazing land, and here and there good yields of hay are obtained; but that article will have to be carried several

Placer mining. NELSON A. MILES. *PERSONAL RECOLLECTIONS AND OBSERVATIONS.*

miles to supply Camp Woods. Colonel Crook has in view the comfort of his men, and the new site will have the advantages over that of any post now occupied in the district—wood and a shelter against the wind. Trees are a nice size for building. The altitude is evidently five hundred feet lower than Camp Warner—a point, again, in the matter of temperature. Captain Hinton is along getting the lay of the land and instructions regarding the erection of the necessary buildings, which he will commence in a few days and occupy when finished.

Back to camp about 1:00 P.M. Darragh Creek is almost one continual camping place from mouth to source—large willows, grassy bottoms, a healthy stream of cold water, and currants and gooseberries in profusion. No permanent Indian sign along the east side of Crook's Mountain, but several very distinct trails trending south. Scouts discovered where two horses had been slaughtered at intervals on one trail about two weeks ago. Followed trails south about fifteen miles, where they became numerous and pretty fresh.

They say a small river puts into Warner Lakes from the southwest and that the country is favorable to immediate communication to Camp Bidwell, barring a range of mountains running across the north end of Surprise Valley, and on which snow is visible from present standpoint. Up to this time the weather has been so uniform that I failed to notice it, but as we traveled mostly in the night, the heat and dust were in a manner avoided, and otherwise, this country is not blessed with much variety in the summer season. This evening, however, we had a nice little shower of rain, accompanied with thunder and lightning. I must say a good word for the mosquitoes, a chief source of annoyance in camp life. So far I have found them few, and those badly disciplined, whatever others may say. The amount of rations on this trip not justifying much of a raid after Indians, it is resolved to return to Camp Warner, August 1, by the nearest cutoff to the crossing before mentioned. Say ten miles over tableland of lava, etc., to the shores of the lakes, to which we got down to through a dry, rocky canyon and thickly lined with large juniper trees, among which the evidences of Indian life a month or so back are abundant. Got to the big hill at noon, and with the sun reflecting in full power on the black wall, the prospect heavenward suggested feelings decidedly opposite, and before I reached the summit—on a level too with this place—I recalled "John Phoenix's" experience at Fort Yuma, Arizona. I believe he stated that a soldier, having died there from sunstroke, went to purgatory and immediately returned to Fort Yuma for his blankets!

Find things at Warner running pretty level. Captain Perry returned without the color of an Indian, and Archie McIntosh, who had not got in from the first week's scout, in camp here with eleven more natives to add to the list—forty-six at least. He got into a good-sized wickiup, off some distance southwest, killed two bucks; others, squaws, etc., captured. Most of the bucks got into the rocks before he could cut them off and gave him and his few Snakes a determined fight. The love of plunder—imbibed, I suppose, from the whites along the Columbia—rendered the other Indians useless on the occasion, and after it became apparent to McIntosh that he must lose all of his men (only four in number) in more desperate attempts to dislodge the enemy, he concluded to come in to Warner. He is considerably disgruntled, and for one who works very hard, he is entitled to some relief. I infer there will be some pretty sharp talk to the Siwash[32] supports before another campaign, which may not commence for ten days yet; besides, a brief cessation of raids may throw the hostile fellows off their guard and into the belief that everything is permanently quiet on the part of the military.

Colonel Crook, with a small command, is going on a skirmish trip to Silvies River—running south into Malheur Lake from the west, east, and north of this place about a hundred miles—for the purpose of selecting a site for another military post. There is a company temporarily stationed at Camp Wright,[33] which will come to the new post. Since arriving here at 3:00 P.M. the place has been visited by a thunderstorm and small shower of rain.

AUGUST 2—The colonel starts for Silvies River tomorrow morning, the express to Camp Smith on the fifth, and returns about the tenth, when I may send you some more stuff. Indians are reported very numerous round Goose Lake, where I presume the next expedition will go first. Captain Collins has his company of infantry mounted now—an addition to the outfit in the way of cavalry. Lieutenant Stanton,[34] with a portion of Captain Perry's company, and McIntosh, with fifteen of his "boys," as he calls them, go on the Silvies River trip. Archie thinks some of taking a few wickiups northeast of here and feels glad to get out alone with his Snakes. The command will take fifteen days' rations.

Owyhee Avalanche, September 14, 1867

CAMP WARNER, GRANT COUNTY, OREGON,
AUGUST 16, 1867

Following is something of an account of a jaunt from Camp Warner north to Camp Wright, thence via Camp Curry back to this place. The object, to locate and start a new military post and scout the country for information or anything pertaining to Indians. Colonel Crook, with twenty-five men of Captain Perry's company, Lieutenant Stanton commanding, and McIntosh, with fifteen Indians, aside from the packers, etc., composed the expedition. Stanton is an Ohio boy who has tramped over considerable of my old ground but has no recollection of my career and has no advantage of me on that score. However, I don't believe he would insist on exposing things at this late day.

The outfit left Camp Warner on the morning of August 3, kept along the eastern base of Warner Mountains and a creek which runs the entire distance, twenty-five miles, where Camp Number One was made. From Warner to head of that creek, over the divide and down this several miles, the land is rolling prairie and, for as many miles in width, excellent grazing range. Three soldiers hunting stock were chased some distance for Indian spies; eighteen antelope, about 10:00 A.M., afforded some of us another chase, no more profitable than the first. Chickens, rabbits, etc., abundant and readily taken in. Road from that hour into camp very rocky. The creek at this point turns to the right, zigzags a few miles to its sink in the plains.

Camp Number Two, west side of Harney Lake. To get here today made doubly the hardest march yet. Forty to forty-five miles without water and very hot. Road, however, very rocky. Cayuse measurement calculates miles by fives—all marches, you see, must conclude with some certain number of fives. I expect we really came forty-five miles, as it was a steady go from sunup till 9:00 P.M. Since learned that water could have been obtained fifteen miles back at springs in a canyon, which but aggravates the case. Men and animals suffered much—increased, perhaps, by indulging some about noon in a puddle of warm alkali, equally as palatable as secondhand soapsuds. I never experienced the want of drink more keenly but once—coming from the Owyhee ferry to Camp Smith. The express man had two kegs of lager beer in charge, the mule carrying it running just ahead, and the last thirty-five miles without water. Whiskey all gone the first day. I supposed the Irish soldier in the company would not hesitate to forage a little where a unanimous feeling seemed evident, the express man being a German. But when I proposed to the former, he objected on the grounds that the kegs did not contain whiskey, and the latter pled that much of the article would be lost in the sagebrush were we to attempt such a rough and impromptu opening, and he never could get over sacrificing a drop of lager were he to die with thirst. Confound such discriminating discipline!

Now a word or two as to the route today. A mile or so brought us to the northern extremity of Warner Mountain, when a descent was made to the level of the lake, when a ten-mile stretch of alkali flat and greasewood introduced us to the balance of the trip—sage, sand, and an occasional rocky outcrop on the windup before coming out on this valley. The route is plainly outlined as if following between the barren banks of a sunken river quite as large as the Snake, connecting apparently by some subterranean arrangement the Warner, Harney, and Malheur Lakes, the two last named being several hundred feet lower than the former, as indicated by the surrounding sandstone strata. Having twice alluded to the probable effects of an inland sea, I again recur to the matter of an underground river now in active operation and draining the sinking streams of Nevada and southern Oregon into the Columbia, or to some place lower down and where the demand for water may be much greater. Warner Lakes, at the narrowest point, near a quarter of a mile wide, with a strong current setting north, are suggestive of more than a passing notice, but the evidence afforded today is almost conclusive in favor of the theory; besides, the road is dry enough to have several large streams decidedly beneath it. Pilot's Peak, a fine conical landmark, was visible today for many miles and is located on the southwest side of the valley; we came close to the eastern base of it and five miles to this camp—[the] side of a marsh of shallow water.

Camp Number Three, north side of Harney Lake and fifteen miles west of south of old Camp Wright. Two miles farther last night would have brought the command to a large spring, but the first taste of water seemed to better satisfy than the Indians' knowledge of things ahead. August and September are the worst months of the year for water, and many places of anticipated moisture are found utterly dry. October, it is said, though there may be no rain or other visible causes, brings much more of the desired element again to the surface. Today's march was about east—first, alkali flats with hedge fences of greasewood; then sagebrush, sand, and a belt of it very rocky, promising in the morning to be a worse day than yesterday for water; plenty of big flies to develop the horses' tactics of traveling stiff-legged and swinging and stumbling about, rendering riding about as pleasant as trying to run a race over a mixture of hedge and picket fence.

The mirage occasionally brought almost within reach visions of willow-shaded streams, only to vanish into sagebrush and alkali prospects barren as brickyards—the most cruelly deceptive thing one can imagine. A broad, dreary landscape apparently without end, with an occasional glimpse of Harney Lake on the right. On reaching the lake, it was concluded to make a tolerable camp and rest over at the end of fifteen or twenty miles. Water tastes of the land around, but by sinking holes to get it cooler and building a tule pontoon, men and animals were enabled to enjoy it, compared to the experience of yesterday. Geese, ducks, cranes, etc., flying and floating about in great numbers, but for want of a boat, few of them were brought in out of the wet.

Camp Number Four, August 6, on a branch of Silvies River (Sylvester's River, McIntosh says, was the original title),[35] near Camp Wright, temporarily occupied by Lieutenant Goodale,[36] with Company K, 23d Infantry; I rather like Goodale. Fifteen miles from timber larger than fish poles, and adobe ruins scattered around. Curry's subordinates' and Crook's ideas of locating posts differ like that of some folks regarding a residence—one had rather exist in the dust and noise of the city than live among the comforts afforded in the suburbs or country surrounding. An old flatboat found nearby enabled the lieutenant to improvise a flagstaff for his tent camp, and during the summer, wood is not the most imperative necessity of camp life. The water here is sickly sluggish.

Camp Wright is at the extreme southeastern point of a triangular plateau, extending down through the plain from the northwest eight or ten miles, making a rather singular and very noticeable landmark; at this point, at least one hundred feet high.

As to that flatboat: Some of Colonel Curry's subordinates were seized with the brilliant idea of fighting the enemy by water, using a mountain howitzer, among other things. It was intended to float down the river into the lakes and then just rake things right and left. Aside from the fact (I think I am correctly informed) that the stream does not reach the lake above ground by several miles, it was frequently and impassably damned by the beavers and consequently were the prospects of what may otherwise terminated the most brilliant naval exploit of modern times.

Lieutenant Goodale conducted a party of us over east two miles to the main stream about 5:00 P.M., where there is a rookery of wild waterfowl, the broad margin of willows along the eastern bank being literally black and white with several varieties of cranes and cormorants, and the water alive with them and ducks, geese, etc., as far up and downstream as one could see with the naked eye. In numbers the birds seemed as incalculable as the pigeons in old-fashioned roosts of Ohio and Indiana; in variety of species, sufficient to puzzle a naturalist—altogether a scene indescribable and one I would not have missed for a consideration. Those cormorants (next thing to a black wild goose) are known to the sportsmen of northern California as shags. However, I got three of them and one goose in as many minutes and shots, and it wasn't a good day, either, I was told, and I know I was the poorest shot in the crowd, but at that stage of the sport, Henry cartridges began to look bigger in value than the birds, and further operations were postponed.

But I came near forgetting the main question—Indians, of which Captain Baker killed and captured twenty about two weeks ago while out on a scout from Camp Watson, via Camp Curry, across to Steen's Mountain, round by the Middle Malheur Mountains, and back via this place. Killed four bucks in the Malheur country and captured a squaw or two; the remainder west of Camp Curry, squaws and children, captured.[37] The latter had no information more than that they belonged to no particular band. Archie McIntosh and his boys are down at Camp Wright today pumping the Malheur squaws for anything they may know, or rather, are willing to tell. They say there are but few Indians in that country, but that We-ah-we-ah is there. I am beginning to believe there is no such animal and that I am being imposed upon. However, there is a company of cavalry at the mouth of the Malheur, and they may see to the case of We-ah-we-ah this summer—granting that he is anybody and is over that way. As I have acquired the habit of trying to be particular as to pronunciation and orthography, just broadly accent We-ah-we-ah on the second syllable and sound the whole thing as if you were attempting to swallow a hot potato by mistake; and if you should dislocate your windpipe or get the diphtheria by the operation, charge it to me or forever hold your tongue.

Camp Number Five, August 7; fifteen miles north of Camp Wright, in a wide, grassy canyon containing a fine rivulet of water—all located in the foothills of the southern extremity of the Blue Mountains. This place is known to some as Rattlesnake Camp. Hills covered with juniper and but three or four miles back into the spurs covered with pine. Trout or other fish abundant in all the streams.

Lieutenant Goodale and command will commence here immediately to build quarters for a new post to be known as Camp Steele.[38] It will be about sixty miles west of south from Canyon City. The new post will be an important one, pretty well sheltered and very accessible from the west, south, and east. This location don't suit Colonel Crook, but it is perhaps the best that the limited time enabled him to select. The canyon is most[ly] too narrow and faces to the south—better shelter from wind being obtained in this country on the east or north side of the mountains; then, the timber is not within arm's length of the point needed. This must be in Grant County, Oregon, and hence Warner must be instead of in Baker as before written. Any quantity of hay can be had in the valley south, and grazing is good everywhere. A few miles back today, we had another chase after forty antelope. I think, though, that an animal that can run so fast can't be fat enough for good eating, and hereafter I, for one, will make no effort to get a shot at the brutes. I don't want any antelope anyhow.

August 8, still at Rattlesnake Camp, fishing and tramping through the hills, viewing and contemplating the landscape. In these broad plains, mountain ranges, and many streams, the breadth of observation and line of travel occupied by a person on horseback is about as important in comparison as a spider's thread stretched across an Illinois farm, yet men will ride through such a country on schedule time and have the impudence to tell about it "to the marines" or people on the Atlantic Coast.

I expect to be pretty well satisfied in my own mind regarding the geography of this section by the close of the campaign, but as to imparting any knowledge of it correctly is another thing. This Harney and Malheur Lake country is a great, high, level plain—perhaps a hundred miles long and on the average half as wide; Malheur, somewhat circular, and twenty-six in diameter. A very few streams emptying into either above ground. On the southeast, Dunder and Blitzen (named by Curry's men during a thunderstorm) puts into the latter lake from the west of Steen's Mountain. (I am told by good authority that said mountain was named after Major Enoch Steen.) The continuation of Steen's Mountain north is very broken, is the source of the South Fork of the Malheur River, and east of here, joining the Blue Range, heads the Middle Fork, side by side with Silvies River (running in opposite direction) in a high mountain flat; farther along is the Blue Range, the North Fork, etc.—the whole forming a semicircular wall round the south, east, and north sides of the great valley. Neither lake has any outlet above ground, but both are connected by a sloughy strait. There must be much land in the valley that would grow barley, potatoes, etc., and it would seem that a market for such produce is about to be afforded. But with a market for the products of grazing, this must be a most valuable section of Oregon. These military posts should be ample protection at once for extensive settlements. Is well watered by branches and bayous of Silvies River.

Camp Number Six, August 9, fifteen miles west of Camp Wright and thirty miles round the foothills from Camp Steele. This morning, overhanging Camp Wright, was a beautiful specimen of the mirage—a large lake, inverted sagebrush through the middle representing a line of weeping willows, and beyond, along the horizon, a border of trees made by elevated sage—all "in the eye." The route today was very agreeable, till we struck the flat foothills in the rear of the triangular promontory before alluded to, and an improvement in soil, grass, etc. This camp is on a little creek and alongside of what is evidently an old emigrant road to the Willamette Valley. The same emigrants, perhaps, who originated the legend of the Bluebucket Diggings, to find which several large parties have vainly searched and came within one of "kicking the bucket" en masse; all set afoot by Indians.[39] Pick it up by chunks! What damn nonsense! Yet of such stuff are prospectors made, and all their lives spent in fatigue and famine and rounded off by their last holes constituting their graves. In Arizona the Indians have furnished the golden bullet stories, yet are ever ready to supply the adventurous miner with leaden ones in the usual way.

But I must tell you of the last thing in that line. (I can't give names, as I am confidentially enjoined, you know, for a share of the immensely imaginary profit!) Indians should have exhibited golden arrowheads last spring in Susanville as having coming from the section north and where the coming campaign is to be made. I know of several men of good sense and judgment (in other things) that are going for the source of those charming missiles, and were there no mixture of metals, it might be some consolation to be in the secret; besides, I am in as good condition to be shot that way a few times as anyone I know of. Perhaps the savages may have exhibited an arrow or two tipped out with the contents of some poor devil's vest or trouser pocket after scalping him. I never could be the unfortunate in such circumstances, but then I have known folks to have a twenty or other valuable jewelry ahead.

Camp Number Seven, August 10, on Silver Creek, seven miles below old Camp Curry. Twenty-five miles today—first half, low juniper hills; second, up

Silver Valley, the latter thirty miles in length and average width, of fine, red-top grass, wild pea vine (excellent forage, green or dry), and clover—if anything, a better section, so far as it goes, than Silvies River. The creek sinks before reaching Harney Lake.

Sunday, August 11—Layover at this point; fishing good and large creek. Some of the command went up to prospect the old post—now in charred ruins—and fished out of the creek much iron, steel, and rusted horseshoes.

Camp Number Eight, August 12, twenty miles southwest of Silver Creek at Wagontire Springs; excellent water and grazing at eastern base of a small range of mountains.[40] Passed over considerable country today that resembles the Black Hills east of the Rocky range; black, rocky, and covered with scrub juniper. Also passed to the west of a butte that may be Pilot's Peak, or Pleasanton's Butte, or vice versa, as the maps can't tell and I find opinions differ. Both prominent teats on the bosom of mother earth, but in a section not flowing with milk, and if there is any honey discovered I'll make a note of it.

Camp Number Nine, August 13, at a big spring at the north end of Mount Juniper—a huge bump on the tableland and covered with the timber suggested by the title; it is about west of the north end of Warner Lakes and close to the eastern bluff of Lake Abert.[41] Deposits of alkali, etc. Thirty miles today—first ten over more black hill country, leaving a small range of dingy mountains, a black peak in the middle, to the east; balance of the route high tableland and very rocky.

Camp Number Ten, August 14, in a canyon putting east to Warner Lakes; a little water in places and sufficient grass. Left Mount Juniper to the left this morning, and then continued all day till 3:00 P.M. over still higher plains and rockier than before—twenty-five miles. Nothing but a fight between two packers to remember this camp by, except that Archie turned up in the night after several days' scout. No sign on this expedition but pony tracks many weeks old and a cache of provisions near Lake Abert.

Camp Number Eleven, August 15, on Warner Lakes, near Hinton's riprap causeway, before alluded to as the crossing of the lakes. Out of the canyon this morning and over a rocky range of high hills extending east and west; then over a rocky plain to Darragh's Creek, running east into the lakes from Crook's Mountain; from creek to this camp along the lakes eight miles—twenty-five miles today.

Since leaving Wagontire Camp, excepting the last eight miles, the entire route has been not nearly so much over a bed of roses as rises of bedrock—a high, bleak, barren waste. I don't wonder that there is no Indian sign, as there are but few places on which they could make an impression with a cold chisel. The direction from Camp Curry to this place—first day southwest, then south till today, which has tended east, the route coming back being about parallel with the one going out but averaging at least thirty miles west. From Camp Woods to Camp Steele, a comparatively smooth road for wagons can be had after getting from Crook's Mountain out to Warner Lakes and following the trail of this expedition north. No mountains to cross on the whole route and but a few miles of stony country west of Warner Lakes to Camp Woods.

These posts will be on a line with Camp Bidwell and must soon establish a road from Camp Steele to Susanville to Harney Lake Valley, at which place barley, oats, vegetables, etc., can be had for about one cent per pound. From what I saw and could learn, a better wagon road from the mouth of the Malheur to the headwaters of the Willamette can be readily obtained, and the distance no greater than that from the Malheur to the Columbia at Umatilla. With the new posts so near the center of the hostile ground and consequent successful campaign, southern Oregon east of the Cascade range must, by next summer, be made pretty safe for citizens in any civil pursuit. Of course, the military may be hindered in diverse ways by citizens who talk loudest for protection but pray in secret for an eternal hold on the government teat; who would chuckle over the scalping of every honest adventurer, so long as the soldier could be kept at posts within easy supply and at exorbitant rates.

The little expedition arrived at Camp Warner this (Friday) morning, August 17, where nothing particular has transpired since the third. Some of the Chico supplies have arrived and are forwarded to Camp Woods, to which Captain Hinton is transferring Camp Warner. In the meantime, Lieutenants Parnell, Madigan, Eskridge, and others have been getting ready for the coming campaign, which will be detained a few days again on account of non-arrival of supplies from Boise. The colonel found more transportation provided for Lieutenant Goodale's detachment of infantry than could up to this time be obtained for this entire command. If I were in the packing business, I'd prefer to hire the mules to government at $1.75 per day in coin, and "U.S." furnish the employees besides.

I suppose the next move will be south of Goose Lake and round to the west and north, as everything points there as the present rendezvous of the "lost tribes." The country will be effactually scouted for fifty to seventy-five miles wide, and the campaign may well result in gobbling up a goodly number in detail, but any large take-in can hardly be expected this time of year. However, everything will be ready for a big fight or little, and it must result at least in getting a good knowledge of their whereabouts. A better management of McKay's, Darragh's, and McIntosh's Indians will be had—several causes of the jealousy and consequent detriment to the campaign (hinted at before) being ascertained and removed. An Indian is a singular beast, and to get the most good service out of him in the business requires careful handling. With the best of civilization, he frequently becomes as low in the scale of humanity as a white man.

Owyhee Avalanche, September 21, 1867

SOUTH FORK, DARRAGH CREEK, OREGON
AUGUST 25, 1867

Having nothing to do and nothing to write you, I have a mind to scribble about two columns of stuff and thus pass the Sunday. My experience has been that whether it is nonsense or news set before the public, the one finds as many readers as the other. Have the exchanges stopped coming, or has the *Avalanche* ceased to slide and all the proprietors vamoosed the ranch? Haven't had a thing from the outside world for weeks.

The colonel has ordered the packing of one month's additional rations, extending the campaign till October 20, and as I have heard of no order commanding me to leave the camp, I expect to make the round trip. I expect to get out of this adventure alive, if I can keep the officers from seeing what I have said about them till I can get away. The only orders he [Crook] ever gave me were at the table and always were to "help myself," or words to that effect; and I'll bet something that in all his extensive and varied soldier life, he never saw a more willing subordinate than your humble servant.

I am foraging on Captain Perry now, and so long as Captain Harris don't shut his tent against me at night, I shall not try to desert. There is nothing to keep me out late—have no guard duty to perform, unless a sort of blackguard duty, which is rather a pleasure. To be sure, there may be good Dalles female society down among the Indians, but I did not come out here to engage in the root-digging business.

Madigan is back at Warner and will bring out the balance of the menagerie, consisting of Captain Collins's Company D, mounted infantry, as soon as the colonel comes to start the machine again; a week, perhaps. Collins has gone to Fort Goodwin, Arizona, only one step this side of purgatory, and I am sorry for Collins; orders must be obeyed.

Lieutenant Jack is packing the effects of Camp Warner over to Woods, and Captain Hinton (that good-natured soul) remains at Warner a few days to receive an addition to his infantry; Dr. Wagner is yet there. I have not fell out with Captain Darragh yet, and Captain McKay has not beat me to death for that curious notice I gave him sometime since. By the way, in my letter from Camp Smith, I made a bad mistake in regard to him. It was he and scouts that had the fight coming over from the Dalles, and not Darragh—where he killed five, captured several, and lost one of his men. This is a matter of importance to them, and I wish to set the matter right. The only thing I am never mistaken in is my appetite on this trip. Altogether, my chances to stay awhile yet are better than average.

Lieutenant Stanton, my Ohio neighbor, is not out with me, though he is out on a little scout south of Warner now. There is a great variety of human nature in this outfit, and representatives of all parts of the world and every battlefield celebrated during the last twenty years—nearly. Here is my good

Trials of a mounted infantryman. CENTURY MAGAZINE, 1891.

neighbor, Lieutenant Parnell, one of the "Six Hundred" at Balaclava (I believe that is the place); [he] is married and doing well, and nearly all the officers and men of this outfit were through all the ups and downs along the Potomac and James Rivers. I get many interesting things from these veterans of the war that never saw type and many that knocks the gloss off incidents in print and accepted as history. I find a goodly number of old Regular army men here— men who can tell of nearly every expedition on this coast. It is a noticeable feature that the cavalry is composed of Americans, while the infantry, on the other hand, is mostly made up of foreigners, Germans and Irish predominating.

The bulk of the expedition (Captain Perry in command) left Camp Warner last Thursday [August 22] for this place (west of the lakes), and McIntosh, with eighteen of his Indians, started south for the Goose Lake section on a scout preparatory to a general move ahead again. This morning Archie and command came in to this place; as he says, "whipped back." He captured two squaws while out, who told him of a band of ten warriors in the mountains east of Goose Lake, about twenty miles from Fort Bidwell. He endeavored to surprise them yesterday morning at daylight and take them in, but the steep, rocky, swampy, and bushy character of the mountainside[42] delayed his ascent, and the thing was reversed—they jumped him in more than equal numbers. He sent Boise George and a squaw into the wickiup headquarters with peace propositions, which were rejected very indignantly, accompanied with threats that they intended to kill everybody that came to molest them. Evidences of this determination were soon manifest, as George came back with a shot through his arm.

Then the fight commenced, and the scouts all chose a rock or bush and got behind them Indian fashion except a tall, rash cuss whom Archie called "Coppinger," who got on top of a rock and sauced back, telling those on the inside that they couldn't shoot much anyhow; but the sequel was they put a bullet through him while there—and he is there yet. He was one of Archie's best men.

The hostiles came out once, so that Archie's men killed three of them at one round and perhaps wounded some others, but by this time Archie saw about twenty making across the country to head him off in a canyon through which he must go to get out of the affair with the horses, and he retreated accordingly, during which a running fight took place most of the distance. He counted at one time over twenty after him, mostly armed with guns; killed one more of the pursuers that he knows of and lost one of his horses, shot. He could hear them whoop occasionally last night in his rear, but he took a round-about way to get back and eluded them. He says they are mostly the same crowd that repulsed him last winter south of Warner, telling him to go home, that they were doing well on horse meat;[43] also, the same that repulsed Captain Hinton and detachment—killing one of his sergeants—near the same place last April;[44] the same that fought back Archie and several of his men and a number of the Warm Springs—the latter not coming to the scratch, as alluded to before—on the late trip out from Camp Smith to Warner. So this makes the fourth success, and they think they have a dead thing and take occasion to say so. I have heard Colonel Crook hint several times that some of that horse meat belonged to him, or words to that effect, and when he heard of this last talk, I imagine things will soon be finished up at Warner and this outfit started for Goose Lake and kept going lively for about six weeks to come.

Archie says the Indian that does all this defiant talking is known as Chee-oh—the Warner Lakes chief.[45] Now, I never heard of him before this affair and am loath to believe in his corporeal existence. No sooner had I got rid of We-ah-we-ah than here comes Chee-oh. Oh, damn Chee-oh! In sounding his name abroad, you must accent the chee part with a good sneeze—the remaining part will naturally follow. Archie don't say that Chee-oh was killed in the last fight and that he saw his friends carry him off before he had time to scalp him, as many "Indian fighters" would. I wish Chee-oh and We-ah-we-ah were dead and that Winnemucca would stay on the reservation—without any mental reservation—instead of coming back with powder, lead, guns, etc. I'm tired of writing about something I don't see and am eternally hearing of. If Archie's scouts could exchange their weapons for some others not bearing the brand of "Harpers Ferry, 1845," and get revolvers swung to them also, their confidence would be enhanced and better accounts rendered in these skirmishes.

P.S.—Wednesday, August 28—Several of the Boise wagons arrived here last night, and among other things, brought Spencer carbines for Lieutenant Parnell's company, and today Archie's men get the best of his Sharp's guns. He has done the most of the rough work so far with the poorest tools, and it is time that his outfit be improved. It is my belief the boys will all see much rough travel the next six weeks, and that with the new posts and policy established and carried out, few of them will see the line of the Owyhee and Boise the coming winter. All the reliable indications point to the country south and west of this as the general rendezvous of the hostiles, and I think time will develop the wisdom of going for them where they live in lieu of keeping the troops in useless suspense along the line aforesaid. September and October, to be sure, is the time the Indians are most scattered, but this expedition will scout the country fifty miles wide at least and must result in waking them up to judgment in numerous instances. The party of twenty-two gobbled near Camp Warner several weeks ago were en route from Steen's Mountain to the Goose Lake section and were most terribly surprised at the advent of the command from the direction of Pueblo; having marched in the night, Mr. Indian did not see the joke until he struck the floor heavy.

Thursday, August 29—Colonel Crook, Lieutenant Eskridge, and M. W. Hawley[46] came out from Warner last evening; also, Lieutenant Madigan with Collins's mounted infantry, which about deserts Warner. They brought out a little mail matter too, which interested me very much—that obituary notice in the *Avalanche,* letting me out of the institution.[47] As a specimen of fine writing, that pleases me better than anything I've seen in that sheet for some time. If it was not entirely satisfactory, I'd ask the author to do it some more. The menagerie suits me pretty well, and better, it will leave tomorrow at early candlelight to slow music.

▬◄◆►▬

Owyhee Avalanche, September 28, 1867

EDITORS, *AVALANCHE:* Although I have no viable interest in the concern, I entertain thoughts of its welfare, and this expedition partaking of a local character in Owyhee, a continuation of my account of its movement may be read. One thing in regard to my scribbling for a newspaper, I never discover the little difference between it and a running, random conversation with some of the boys until I see the blasted stuff in print, and then am astonished to see what an amount of human cussedness and conceit a single individual under no restraint can produce. I will faithfully promise to be more concise and choice in my use of words from this out.

Camp Number One, South Fork, Darragh's Creek, Friday, August 30—This rendezvous is about twenty-five miles west of Camp Warner and eight south of Camp Woods. One of Darragh's Indians committed suicide this morning. He had been sick for some time, and the news that the squaw prisoners were to be left at Camp Woods today may have caused him to shoot himself. The joke of the day is on two blacksmiths who went down to the mouth of the creek yesterday morning on business; they had about twelve miles to go over tableland alone. One, a big, blustering American, was armed; the other, an Irishman, was not. Coming back last night, it was quite dark, and when about halfway they got stampeded and ran back to camp at a breakneck gait—the latter says he went over his mule's head twice and rolled one time fifty feet; the other won't admit anything but swears there were at least fifteen mounted

Indians crossing the road ahead of them and that he called out to them, but got no answer. He was simply frightened at a row of juniper trees. Since Archie's late repulse, Indians are seen everywhere by packers and others.

The command broke camp at 4:00 P.M.—280 soldiers (officers and men, white and Indian); 360 men, including packers. A pretty large expedition for this country, but it is such that several detachments thirty to fifty strong can be on the scout in different directions at one time and all the time on comparatively fresh horses. Route along the eastern base of Crook's Mountain to the south; grassy tableland four or five miles, then breaks up into ravines and rides very rocky; small creeks at intervals.

Eight miles brought the column to a swampy creek. By the time the packers got up, it was very dark, and the animals got all mixed and filed in together and stuck in the mud. Such a scene I never saw. Oaths and imprecations rent the air in English, Spanish, French, Dutch, Irish, and Indian; straight, then again a mixture of all—a literal packer's pandemonium. One tall cuss from Pike was particularly distinguishable, and I asked him in regard to his bringing up. Said he never was farther away from home than in hearing of the geese until he was eighteen, and supposed that what made him so tall was that his father was six feet six, his mother five feet ten, and that he was their only child and never left the maternal dairy until seven years old, and then weaned himself out of shame. He's a specimen.

About 10:00 P.M., the bulk of the column having got through to a large creek two miles ahead, Camp Number Two was made, where the command remained during Saturday, thirty-first. A fine camp (when things get straightened out) on One Mule Creek, heading in south end of Crook's Mountain and running into Warner Lakes on Drew's trail to Klamath. Wide grass bottom and pitch pine timber thick on all the mountains and foothills roundabout. Some of the Indians brought in a deer this morning. The chief manager of the menagerie arranges the program for another performance—advance agents sent ahead to post the hills.

McKay and McIntosh, with twenty each of their respective Indians, swung into a circle for instructions. Papooses in arms—including the arms—and all horses captured to be turned over to government invariably, and only warriors in arms, etc., to be disposed of after their own style. The two bands started about 10:00 A.M. with three days' rations for the scene of Archie's last fight—southwest. About noon another band of scouts were sent in a northwesterly direction, with old "Dad" Wilson in command. He is an old stager that Captain Perry picked up somewhere last summer and has since employed as a guide, etc., but till today has had no particular service to perform during this summer's campaign. Has superstitiously adhered to an oldfashioned rifle and not indulged in none of the innovations in firearms beyond a six-shooter, being very much prejudiced in favor of the old weapon. But today notes an important epoch (to him) in his career—he has bought a Henry rifle; in consequence, he says, of a wild Cayuse having bucked the hindsight off the old gun. He is a subject for remark today, and the boys indulge it to his great discomfort. "Now Dad, you must stick some feathers in your horse's tail or you won't have any luck!" Dad intimates that if they furnish the feathers, they can go beyond that with them, if they like. "I say, Dad, your cinch is under your horse's belly." "Don't I know it is?" says Dad; and with that he started.

Camp Number Three, Sunday, September 1—From Number Two, the balance of the command traveled south a short distance to the South Fork of One Mule Creek, up that seven or eight miles west, through a grassy, level avenue into Camas Prairie,[48] on the west side of which this camp is made. The scenery today is very similar to that of the Willamette Valley—low mountains set in thick timber but bare on top. A stiff frost this morning notes the approach of fall. This prairie is about four miles long, half as wide, and properly named.

About noon some of Darragh's Indians came in from hunting in the mountains just west and overlooking Goose Lake Valley, and reported "hi-yu Snakes." As that unqualified adjective may mean five or fifty, an expedition is at once organized to go in pursuit. In the meantime, the remainder of McKay's scouts started on their own hook without orders and soon were far ahead of Darragh, with the balance of his, and Captain Perry, with thirty men. They passed through to the valley northwest, where they discovered many pony tracks going round the north end of the lake, but evidently several days old; also, about dark, saw a couple of Indians off in the high, bald mountain north of this basin or prairie, but by 9:00 P.M. nearly all hands are back in camp; result—nothing as yet.

This evening the camas question came up, and the colonel proposed that he'd give some of us a lesson in Oregon, or aboriginal, agriculture. After a brisk use of a spade and sheath knives, with poor results, the district quartermaster made a calculation of how long it would be (at that rate) before he would starve to death were camas the only base of supplies. But the colonel said the natives had a knack of telling from a surface standpoint where to go for the biggest roots and most of them. Knowing that it is the universal custom for squaws to do this work (and also that the colonel is an old coaster), I ventured to ask him if it was not a natural weakness on the part of female humanity to always go for the biggest, etc.? The good man intimated that about one more such break as that and he'd order me out of camp and see that I went. Since then there has been nothing said in this menagerie. This is undoubtedly a rich country for Indians and a fine one to look at generally.

Monday, [September] 2—Still at the prairie. The balance of Darragh's party of yesterday report this morning that they saw nearly twenty Indians—big and little of either sex—after he returned last night, but they were on the lookout and unget-at-able. Several had guns, but all were afoot. The thoughtless haste of McKay's Indians undoubtedly prevented their surprise, as they were heading across the valley at first. No use to fret now.

Wilson and crowd returned this afternoon, having seen nothing but a few tracks. McKay and McIntosh returned to main command about sundown, having been over the ground where Archie got repulsed. The hostile occupants had evidently left it soon after the affair, going round the north end of Goose Lake to the west side. Lookout Mountain (as they call the place) is doubtless on the California line and, according to McKay, must be the most impregnable of all Indian haunts. He says he was over three hours in getting down from the summit to the Goose Lake level, yet up there the hostile cusses lived in "elegant leisure," and so secure that this whole command would have had all the work it wanted to have successfully stormed the place. It was an unfortunate move generally for Archie to attempt it. The enemy had a chain of rough breastworks added to the natural strength of the place, thus connecting the various steps or benches of the rocky rise for several hundred yards. A heavy bank of snow on the northeast side of the summit furnishes the place a perpetual stream of water. Down next to the lake, the sign of cattle is abundant, doubtless hundreds of them have been sacrificed to appease the Indian's god—the stomach. McKay thinks this the best country for Indians he ever saw—all kinds of roots, seeds, berries, fish, flesh, and fowl in profusion. As I expect to see round the lake myself, I will postpone further account of it.

Thursday, [September] 3—same place. Darragh and all his Indians (thirty-four) started today with six to ten days' rations on a scout north through the country west of Crook's Mountain, hoping to head off the party of twenty before alluded to. Darragh is entirely reliable himself and has some excellent Indians for the business. McKay and McIntosh have got a change of horses, four or more days' rations, and start tonight on the trail of the large party west of the lake. They counted seventeen campfires where only a portion of the retreating party first halted—ample evidence of a healthy old band.

I should like to take a hand in these scouts, but it is the rule that none but those properly belonging to the bands shall accompany them. Besides, some of these officers say that I couldn't be got within shooting distance of a hostile Indian anyhow. Confound them! Moreover, one of them makes it a standing bet of $4.50 that I can't shoot a hole through an army tent twenty steps offhand. Not having a cent, I have to endure this, but the worst feature of it is, no one will risk anything on it in my behalf. It looks bad. I think there is a combination to ruin my reputation, but never having had any in particular, they can't make a point of me there. You might start a collection for my benefit—that people have frequently contributed much to less important matters—if possible. I see where I could use a few dollars legitimately. My stock of ready-made clothing will soon be reduced to a short breechclout, and were the rags at hand converted into paper, it wouldn't make a one-cent postage stamp. A mess of camas for dinner tonight was entirely satisfactory, however, and should it come to the worst, I will be every way prepared to make both ends meet. I don't think there is as much danger of being burnt at the stake among the hostiles running at large as among those captured, as shown on the medical records of this campaign.

Camp Warner, Oregon, in 1873. NATIONAL ARCHIVES.

Dr. Wagner and small escort came in from Camp Warner via Camp Woods this evening, and as communication towards Idaho will be accidental from this on, I will tear off a slice of this most interesting journal and start it for Owyhee tomorrow morning. It may be a month before another opportunity will occur. I have an idea that the command will go across to the west side of Goose Lake Valley one of these nights soon, but after that it will move according to circumstances. The enemy is to the right, left, and front in various places, and as to the rear, you may know more than you want by this time. The maneuvers for the next six weeks will be to corral them, if possible, and I am satisfied everything to that end is being done. I like this Goose Lake country better than any I've seen east of the Cascade range, and if some mishap don't cook my goose, I hope to give you a good account of it, if not of myself. So, yours truly, decidedly ragged, undoubtedly getting fat, and altogether things are lovely and working.

◆—◆ ≡◆≡ ◆—◆

Owyhee Avalanche, November 2, 1867

EDITORS, *OWYHEE AVALANCHE:* On September 3 I sent you a batch of matter for swearing at from Camp Number Three of the Goose Lake campaign—said camp in Camas Prairie, on the Drew road east of the north end of the lake. All the scouts were employed in determining the destination of the abundant sign; that is, Darragh and scouts had been sent north to the Lake Abert country, McIntosh and McKay's to the mountains west of Goose Lake. During the night of the fourth, the main command left the prairie, came out through a canyon to the northwest seven miles to Goose Lake Valley, crossed over to the mountains west, and camped in the timbered valley of Kelly's Creek.[49] Twenty miles altogether of this night's march. The fifth, sixth, seventh, and eighth were passed by the command at this camp. On the morning of the sixth, Archie and McKay came in with four scalps and reported the probable whereabouts of others,[50] and on the eighth started for the place and a two days' scout. Went along but saw nothing except fine mountain scenery and considerable game. On the ninth the command moved up the creek fifteen miles, where we found it and encamped and Darragh returned. He had trailed a party of Indians into the tules round the Abert lakes, and after figuring round two or three days had to abandon the hunt. He found two respectably sized lakes in addition to what are noted on the maps. On the tenth the entire command marched together northwest through the mountains, passing through a beautiful valley six miles in length, with as fine a stream of water running through it into Lake Abert as I ever saw; swarming with brook trout.[51]

McKay Valley[52] may be known by two rocky buttes in the center. Camped on a branch of said stream after fifteen miles today. On the eleventh a short march (six miles) north—Indian sign, and fresh in the vicinity. Seemed to tend to the southeast. A part of Darragh's Indians sent that way with several days' rations. The balance of the command (on the twelfth) started off to the southwest through the mountains twelve miles, and camped high up on the nice stream aforesaid. The colonel had become satisfied by this time that the Indians he had "lost" had gone south, but concluded to split the command and go in opposite directions.

On the morning of the twelfth, Captain Perry with Company F, First Cavalry, Captain Harris with Company M, same regiment, and Captains Darragh and McKay with their respective companies of scouts were sent north—Perry commanding—with orders to scout the country across from Summer and Silver Lakes to the head of Deschutes River, via Crooked River, and bring up at Camp Harney, sixty miles south of Canyon City. Colonel Crook, with the smaller part of the expedition, consisting of Company H, First Cavalry, and Company D, 23d Infantry (mounted)—the former commanded by Lt. W. R. Parnell, the latter temporarily by Lt. John Madigan—and Archie McIntosh with his Snakes, started south. Lieutenant Eskridge (district quartermaster) accompanied the colonel. Dr. Wagner went north, Dr. Tompkins south. The colonel remarked that if his venture on this southern tour failed to in any way meet public expectations, the blame should fall upon him alone. He put little faith in a summer campaign but believed this one a necessity. Ten miles' march south through the mountains, and camped on a branch of Sprague River, which helps make the Klamath Lakes.

Equinoctial influence made marching very disagreeable, and the fourteenth was passed here. On the fifteenth continued south across the valley (the infernal regions must be full of such valleys, else this would be included) and camped on the South Fork. It was a long twelve miles—a blinding storm of rain, hail, and snow, and altogether the rockiest of the trip—but not entirely devoid of interest. During a halt among the juniper, three grizzly bears (an old she one and two half-grown cubs) crossed just in rear of the column. The word "bear" soon got to the front, when the colonel, Eskridge, and others broke for the rear—Eskridge almost running on to the old one as she stood up to inspect the troops, he mistaking her for his chief packmaster. This part of the menagerie soon disappeared in the brush, the colonel shooting at a cub by way of revoking the order about firing, which confused the men, who had such good opportunities to have taken in the whole patch perhaps. To see grizzlies running round loose was more of a sight than I ever expected to see, besides having a good joke on the quartermaster, hence I was pretty well satisfied.

On the sixteenth marched southwest through the mountains; re-crossed the divide, from which a good view of the Modoc Mountains to the west was had; and camped southwest of Drew Valley, through which West End Creek runs into the north end of Goose Lake. Fifteen miles today. The seventeenth, marched southeast twelve miles through nice mountain country, passing a beautifully located lake on which wild fowl were abundant. A big buck antelope stopped in front this morning long enough for the colonel to revoke the order on him. It is told of some gruff old officer that when Sergeant So-and-So shot and hit the game, he exclaimed, "All right, send me up a quarter"; when he missed, "Arrest him" was the word.

From a high point of mountain above camp, an extensive view of country was obtained: east, the entire Warner (Sierra Nevada) range; the mountains south of Pit River; and west were Mount Shasta, Wright Lake, etc. This camp supposed to be about on the California line.

On the eighteenth marched southeast through high, level timberland fifteen miles; camp in a canyon next to Goose Lake, opposite the Lassen Pass in the Warner Range. Came by the ground this morning on which old Dad Wilson said he "fit" [fought] a grizzly last evening; all we had to do was to go out and find the animal in a certain willow patch and finish him at leisure. With the aid of two Indians, it was ascertained that "Dad shot a bear"—but you know the balance of the rhyme; the antagonists had gone in opposite directions as fast as man and beast ever did. Saw dozens of deer and antelope today, and the Indians manage to keep their commissary full of that sort of ration despite the orders. Command remained in camp here during the nineteenth and twentieth for the purpose of recruiting the stock a little.

A paragraph in regard to the country passed over. All the maps yet in vogue are nothing like correct respecting that part of Oregon west of the Owyhee to the Klamath and Deschutes country, and north of the Warner and Goose Lakes. There is fifteen miles square of good bunch grass prairie between the north end of Goose Lake and the mountains north and west, which are high, sharp, thickly timbered ridges interspersed with small lakes, camas prairies, patches of pea vine, [and] broad, grassy ravines. Pitch, sugar, and white pine, white and red fir, cedar, juniper, and cottonwood constitute the variety of timber. On the foothills and in the canyons north of the lakes, wild plums are abundant, elderberries abound, and nearly every stream in the aforesaid mountains is prolific in brook trout. No indications of the precious metals.

If one wishes to indulge in a tramp through the mountains west of Goose and the Abert lakes, old Wilson says they can be easily known by the "many permanent peaks."

On September 21 command marched through the juniper and lava about eight miles to a canyon near the south end of the lake [Abert]. The lake is about forty miles in length and will average say ten miles in width; it is almost an uninterrupted sheet of water, and along the west shore rocky or gravelly, with the waves lashing thereupon, it seems more like a lake than anything in the District of the Lakes. The water has a sort of milky color that I have not heard explained.[53]

On the twenty-second marched fifteen miles south over the plain to springs. Here the trouble commenced. Archie, with some of his Indians, was sent ahead in the evening to look for sign, and Wilson was entrusted with six Indians to go in a southwest direction for the same purpose and to join Archie in the night. This was the second time only during the summer that Wilson was allowed to go on a responsible errand—the colonel don't want any stock in a person who is always talking of how many "year" he has "fit" Indians and of taking scalps as if it were as easily done as said. Good horseflesh was above par at this time, and for the reason that Wilson possessed a couple of good animals, he was deemed a necessary evil on this part of the expedition.

About 9:00 P.M. the old fellow discovered all his knowledge of scouting and put the natives on the lookout by building a large fire on an exposed point in view of the camp of the soldiers—said fire being answered soon after on the Warner Range twenty-five miles east.

If this affair caused uneasiness at headquarters, it were nothing to what followed the next day, the twenty-third, when the command marched south several miles and camped on Pit River. At the crossing of the Forts Crook and Bidwell road, two Indian boys were captured and brought along. About noon old Wilson came puffing and sweating into headquarters with the story that early that morning he "fit" a camp of at least "fifty warrior" (ten miles west) and that his Indian scouts had run. By this time seven or eight big signal fires were in active operation ten miles down the river. When the colonel asked Wilson why he had not reported (as strictly enjoined) instead of alarming the camp discovered in the morning, the poor old fool stammered out something about wanting to find Archie and went off with his head down like a sheep.

After marching the command for two weeks over the most infernal ground for the purpose of keeping under cover, and it had been quietly landed within one night's march of its destination, and now that the whole campaign seemed to be rendered a complete failure, the disgust exhibited round headquarters was the most expressive I had ever seen. The scouts that should have run away came in toward evening as leisurely as if nothing had happened; the fact is, they don't demoralize so easily as white men, being much better judges in such cases of when danger is real or imaginary. The old man, it was plain, had fired a few shots promiscuously and broke like a quarter horse for the main command.

Archie and party came in soon after with the scalp and gun of a buck whom they caught near the signal fires down the valley.

Pit River (which name originated in the fact that the Indians used to trap deer by means of deep pits) is a stream the color of Goose Lake, is about fifty feet wide and three in depth at this time, and runs through a wide rye grass, sagebrush, alkali valley; north of the valley and west of the lake (in California, which claims two-thirds of it) is a high, rocky plain thickly timbered with juniper and extending off as far as the eye can reach towards Mount Shasta and the Klamath country.

On the twentieth-fourth, considering that the hostile natives were well alarmed, the colonel marched the command down the wagon road in daylight about twenty miles and within that distance of Fort Crook, as if he were en route to the Sacramento, and where the mountains came up to the river on the south side, crossed over and camped in a timbered canyon. Here, he having become satisfied that the two captives belonged at Fort Crook and had been following a detachment of soldiers up the road toward Bidwell on a begging tour, they were started on their way downstream rejoicing.

On the twenty-fifth started southeast along the foot of a timbered spur of mountain. While going up one side of a rough canyon, a wickiup of Indians were jumped up on the opposite—the several bucks scattered and hid; the squaws and papooses were not molested, the state of the country already being such that their capture would make little difference one way or the other. Struck a much-used Indian trail which tended towards the head of the South Fork of Pit River—fresh sign, both horse and moccasin tracks, thick and thickening. Camped in a timbered canyon; a hard fifteen miles' march; good bunch grazing everywhere since crossing the river and fine creeks. If I had seen huge disgust and chagrin round headquarters of the District of the Lakes three days ago, the cup of indignation was more than full tonight, and to add to the gloom, the clouds were black and raining. The colonel was off by himself under a big pine tree roasting the pods, trying to whittle and whistle, and had a face on longer than this report with two veto messages added. I never wanted to make a suggestion so bad in my life—that I should go out and dig some roots, and with the pine tops we'd have a warm supper—but I was afraid to indulge. He considered the campaign "all up." Archie's horses were about on their last legs for scouting; all this stock weary and much of it sick; the country alive with hostile Indians on the alert; and whether scattered or concentrated or both, as yet undetermined.

On Thursday, September 26, the command moved eastward along the Indian trail aforesaid several miles over high tableland; fresh horse tracks, as if there had been much galloping back and forth during the night, and moccasin tracks as usual. Arrived at a small lake; the sign seemed to scatter but the general direction northeast. Archie and several of his boys traced the indications ahead, and the command marched southeast to the lava bluffs overlooking the South Fork of Pit River; two miles down a canyon—twelve in all from the last camp—and the valley was reached. Turned north along foot of bluffs, and when about five miles north of the place Williamson's map calls Camp S. F. Meadows,[54] Archie came galloping down off the high bluffs with the word that he had tracked Indians into the rocks but could only guess at the number.

The command was within half a mile of the south line of the occupied rocks. The colonel ordered Parnell to dismount half his men and take them up and form a line across the side, Madigan to move farther along and act on the same order with regard to the north side—under the circumstances, the Indians would hardly try to escape to the pine below. Archie had got the remainder of his boys and returned to the high bluffs. I went along with him, satisfied that a good view of the performance could be obtained up there.

We got up through a canyon on the south side and round to the brink of the bluffs about 1:00 P.M., and just as Madigan's men got in line; not understanding the disposition of troops as yet, his men gave us a volley of Springfield rifle balls—no one hurt. Some blasphemous remarks (in the American language) in return fixed that matter. The boys got into position Indian style, and as I was taking an opera-glass view of the menagerie beneath, a couple of slugs from the inside sounded as though a similar position would be acceptable.

I got a place that seemed tolerably comfortable, and a bird's-eye view of the enemy's works appeared in outline as follows: a perpendicular lava wall three hundred feet high and a third of a mile in length from the west side; on the north, running down toward the valley, is a ridge of great lava boulders; on the south a canyon. From the valley, it is a gradual rise (coming west) till within about four hundred yards of the high wall, where it forms a low, sharp ridge with loose boulders along the crest—this forming the eastern side and giving the whole a basin-like appearance. Running into this basin from the southeast side are two promontories of rock one hundred fifty feet in length, fifty wide, and thirty high, and walls perpendicular; the two points are parallel with each other and thirty feet apart, thus marking an impassable gorge between. On the north end of the eastern point is a circular, artificial fort twenty feet in diameter, breast-high with portholes; on the western point are two of the aforesaid forts on a larger scale. Between the forts and the bluff, the canyon on the south and ridge on the north, it is a mass of shapeless lava boulders from the size of an A-tent up. The Indians well knew the value of position, for the only practicable approach is from the eastern slope, and they seemed to make the fort next to it their headquarters at this time—3:00 P.M.

When Parnell approached the canyon from the south, he got a volley from fifteen to twenty Indians, who then fell back into the forts, making defiant gestures and exclamations. Parnell's men were then enabled to get a position within fifty yards of the forts under the rocky crest, but in attempting to reconnoiter in advance of this, a volley from the fort mortally wounded Sergeant Barchet,[55] killed Private Lyons, and wounded Privates Clancy and Fisher. This repulse, which we could plainly see from above, was noticed by Eskridge, in charge of the stock, herders, etc., on the plain below, who went into camp.

A regular siege was inevitable. All hands round the circle, from the time they got into position and a lay of the land, poured a constant stream of bullets into and round the forts, and with the sound of the firing, mashing, and glancing of balls, and the yelling from both sides, the occasion was interesting, to say the least. One old chief, or medicine man, from a safe standpoint, kept up an almost ceaseless talk in a loud voice, the burden of which no one on the outside could or cared to interpret—it was but too evident that a large number of the faction had centered here and were waiting for the soldiers to tread on the tails of their coats, which the latter at once proceeded to do.

The colonel was busy reconnoitering the enemy's works—getting a close call occasionally—until about 5:00 P.M. and had sent a squad of Parnell's men up to join Archie, and after being persuaded that it was improper to shoot us from the rear, they helped throw lead down at the forts. One Indian made his escape by way of the ridge and bluffs to our left. Thinking it one of Madigan's men crawling up through the juniper trees and rocks, the slippery cuss got too much the start; as he gained the level, he made some saucy gestures, gave a whoop, and ran for a lava canyon north. Archie made him a good chase, however. Madigan, while attempting a close inspection of the forts, got a slight wound in the right arm.

From the bluff line down to the forts, the range was about fifty yards, at an angle of about forty-five degrees, yet the east fort would make it warm for a person venturing but a momentary exposure of head and shoulders. Hundreds of shots from the bluff must have struck inside the forts during the afternoon, while below from three sides there was a volley in readiness for every Indian that showed himself. All the bucks that were seen up to this time were in a very simple dress—naked to the waist, a short shirt, and head stuck full of feathers. About a dozen bucks were hidden in a gorge between the rocky promontories. Two good animals were allowed to come out through the lines.

The colonel came up above for a final observation, ordered Archie's command to supper and the soldiers to watch the bluffs till further notice. Parnell (executive officer) was ordered to see that the soldiers got their regular rations and a strong picket kept up. About dark, all the available men were ordered to crawl as near the forts as possible and prevent any escape—Archie's men to occupy the ridge below between the soldiers, the latter to connect their lines west of the forts but under the high wall. For good reasons (this time), I chanced it with the scouts during the night. But nothing ever looked so damned ridiculous as their war dance after supper—as much as to say the show couldn't go on at all without some of that sort of thing.

The loose boulders along the crest of the ridge made good breastworks for the boys, and they crawled up to within one hundred feet of the east fort and about on a level with the same. Soon as darkness set in, the besieged devils turned loose with their Paiute toothpicks (arrows), and what with those and throwing stones we had no occasion to go asleep. The bodies of Barchet and Lyons were recovered from the rocks early in the night, and one of Madigan's men—Carl Bross[56]—killed accidentally; he had crawled too far ahead, and the soldiers couldn't distinguish in the dark so well as Archie's boys, perhaps. Some more of the horses attempted to come out, when their proprietors called them back with arrows. In and round the forts, there was a constant sound of the rolling down or piling up of rocks, as if they were building additional breastworks, and every time the pickets would fire a volley, that interesting talk was heard, sounding at times as if it proceeded from a cavern.

Till midnight thunder and lightning added a peculiar interest to the scene; vivid flashes of the latter lending an infernal coloring to the black basin and wall to the west. The clouds that lowered upon our house were ominous, but I had got an inkling at suppertime of what was yet to come. In the first place, the colonel said the siege should be continued from day to day until the red devils were all killed or starved to death, provided it could be done with the means at hand; secondly, considering that it had become a chronic thing for soldiers to follow Indians into rocks and leave them, the moral effect of such an affair would be worth several ordinary victories; and lastly, the taking of all those artificial forts by storm would heighten the effect and shorten the siege, besides saving the men, as the latter would then have additional advantages with less exposure.

He was up from camp about daylight, and after hearing the reports, ordered Parnell and Madigan to bring all their available men from picket duty and form under the crest facing the east fort. They had each about twenty men. Archie and boys were ordered to go round and get positions on the opposite side in the rocks of the ridge. The storming parties (Madigan on the left) were ordered to crawl up the slope as far as possible without discovering themselves and halt. One Lawrence Traynor (citizen) took Lyons's carbine, and he and I volunteered to go in with the boys in blue—it was our funeral, and we joined Madigan's right. The colonel talked to the men like a father—told them that at the word "Forward," they should rise up quick, go with a yell and keep yelling, and never think of stopping until they had crossed the ditch, scaled the wall, and broke through the breastworks—and the faster, the better.

About sunup of the twenty-seventh, word was given. We had gone about twenty feet when a volley of all sorts of slugs and arrows knocked eight of Madigan's men out of line, killing the lieutenant himself; badly wounding Corporals [Patrick] McCann, [Thomas] Fogerty, and [Edward] Furman; wounding Privates [Frank] McGuire, [Joseph T.] Etabler,[57] and [William] Barbes—the latter two with arrows; and badly wounding Traynor. The remainder of the boys kept going, a canyon or natural ditch wide and deep to cross notwithstanding. There were but two points along the wall that seemed like practicable ascents, and the men immediately commenced to climb—on the left, Sergeant Bassler of Company D; on the right, Sergeant Meara and Private Sawyer of Company H; these men leading at the different places. About twenty-five feet deep, the wall receded into a natural parapet six feet wide and continuing round the east and north sides of the artificial fort.

Meara jumped across and looked over into the fort and exclaimed, "Come on boys, we've got 'em," but instantly fell on the parapet dead, his head, with a bullet hole through it, striking about a foot to the left of me. At the same moment, on the left, Bassler got his gun through a porthole, fired, and looking over, said, "Get out of that, you sons of bitches!" I went round the parapet to the north side of the fort to get a shot as they came out, but they dropped their empty guns and slid over the west side and disappeared in the gorge in an instant like so many lizards.[58] I found Sawyer, who had preceded me but a moment, stretched on the parapet, the brain oozing out his left temple. Saw James Shea[59] of Company H down under the wall to the right waiting for them to come out, and could see no other live human being round about or in the gorge beneath except, through a porthole, I could see the soldiers getting into the fort.

But an instant afterwards, a volley of arrows and bullets came across from the west forts and apparently from the natural rocks below—one striking the guard iron of Shea's carbine, splitting the breech wide open, and others wounding him (not seriously) in three places. The prospects for continuing in that good state of health of which I had been boasting were not now very bright, and I went back to the southeast end of the parapet, by which time Parnell had all the soldiers up and the fort full of them.

Inside and on the west side lay a buck with two dead shots through him—some of the men on the left had caught him, or the colonel himself, who, from the ridge where Madigan fell, shot twice at the retreating devils over the men's heads. He makes few mistakes with that long Spencer of his.

While a number of us were lounging round outside the fort on the south side taking loose observations, another of those mysterious volleys came from the west, most of it ranging up and over us, only cutting clothes and scratching a few men, but strongly indicative that in taking the fort we had got hold of something we couldn't let go. But things remained quiet for some time, when the colonel ordered a detachment of men to remain in the fort and hold it, the picket line kept up, the men their rations as usual; if he had a huge fighting mad on at first, the morning's operations only seemed to increase it, and all hands prayed for nitroglycerine or Greek fire but felt as though those Indians were ours anyhow. William Enser (Company H), on picket duty several yards to the left of where the charge was made, got a deep wound in the right shoulder at that time—to some extent significant of the enemy's strength and watchfulness. Eskridge thought he had been where bullets and things were thick, but the volley that killed Madigan seemed to him the most stinging, face-slapping affair yet encountered. He and Dr. Tompkins had been kept pretty busy in consequence. The fluttering noise of those toothpicks mingled with the whistle of lead and pewter slugs produced at a range of less than fifty yards did constitute queer music, perhaps, to a man up a tree.

The effect of the storming and running over the artificial forts upon the superstitious minds of the besieged was more than could have been expected, considering the nature of their retreat. After the lull of the morning, only scattering shots were fired up till noon, and the men exposed themselves all round and over them. One of the men—[James] Kingston of Company D—in the east fort received a dangerous wound in the right temple. The shot came from the west fort and through a porthole at which the man was stationed. He had got hold of that fatal carbine of Lyons. It was significant of the preference for breechloaders to see the infantrymen exchange their guns as fast as the Spencers became idle.

The picket guard and firing were kept up stronger than ever, if possible, during the afternoon and night of the twenty-seventh, after the manner of a free fight—whenever you see a head, hit it. The curious quiet of the afternoon on the part of the enemy was rendered the more singular by the squalling of papooses during the night, which was very dark, in front and rear of the men.

The morning of the twenty-eighth developed the tactics adopted by the savages soon after the storming and successfully acted upon during the night. About 8:00 A.M. a young squaw was allowed to come out through the lines, and her story was that all the bucks had escaped during the night, leaving nothing but squaws and papooses. Archie's men searched round the circle and found that the story was but too true. Running from the fortified promontories to the southwest and the canyon is a deep strata of lava threaded with fissures and subterranean passages, and the pickets having crawled in close to the forts, the slippery devils wormed out under the feet of the men many rods to the rear, into the canyon and over the bluffs. Beyond the canyon, in their flight, guns, bows and arrows, ammunition, etc., were dropped, showing a state of demoralization never anticipated by the saucy fiends two days before. After the fact of their escape being fully established, all hands went into an examination of the premises—every man venturing according to the extent of his fearless curiosity.

Thus far I have only attempted a description of what appeared on the surface. To begin with, those promontories and surroundings constitute a most remarkable fortress of natural engineering, and the sagacity of the Indians in selecting it is only equaled by their ingenuity in completing its defensive character in the building of those bird-nest bastions and guarding every approach and parapet with breastworks of suitable dimensions. There are natural shelves, fissures, and caverns in ten acres inclusive and surrounding that, thoroughly known, ten thousand men could be stowed out of sight in fifteen minutes, and five hundred men unacquainted with the place could never capture five well posted, armed, and supplied to stand a siege within. Regular hatchway holes run down through from the artificial forts, many of which are worn smooth from the climbing up and down to and from the subterranean resorts. In scaling the walls and overrunning the rocky promontories, the fissures facing and underfoot are every few steps and of such depth that a man can be shot within three feet of him and never know what did it. That the place is an old (but lately active) volcano is probable. To thoroughly explore those caverns containing wounded and armed savages who knew all the exits and entrances and possessed the advantages of light and darkness was too much to demand of the officers and men who had acted so well from the first, and the colonel permitted everyone to use his own discretion in the matter. Lieutenant Parnell acted very earnestly and bravely from first to last.

In the ditch, or gorge, is an entrance to a cave under the east fort. About 11:00 A.M. James Carey[60] of Company H started down into the dark den, head foremost and six-shooter in hand; he reached a shelf with a bullet through his heart. In recovering the body, one of the men said he got sight of a cave in which "you could camp the command." The bulk of the volleys came from in and round this gorge, the artificial forts being used, as it were, for sharpshoot-ers, about a dozen of whom occupied the east fort and seemed to be reserving of their fire, as evinced in their waiting till we got up to their portholes, then emptying and leaving their guns. It was not ascertained whether any natural supply of drinking water existed in the caves. The only indication of an eco-nomical use of ammunition was discovered in the east fort; they had sacked up the battered balls thrown in from the bluffs the first day and sent some of them back at us the next morning. Plenty of powder and caps, bows and arrows were found in and round the fort—some of the former in sacks; considerable in almost brand-new cans and boxes. The guns were mostly of the American half-stocked pattern, showing a particular source of supply. The great number and depth of the caves rendered the idea of burning and smoking the occupants futile; if anything were lacking to complete their demoralization, hand grenades or shells to roll down the openings would have done the work, and what a pleasure it would have been to those on the outside. The hammering of all the artillery extant could not have dislodged the occupants, had they decided to remain. But they had no idea of the soldiers staying with them right along, and the cause of their sudden change of tactics was now apparent. Whether they will ever make another stand in such a place—not knowing what to expect next, and they won't if Crook goes down there again on "business"— remains to be seen.

I heard no man complain of the charge, but rather that the whole siege was conducted and finished on the cheapest plan, and there was a universal feeling of regret that the savages knew all about the rocks and we didn't. The largest estimate of their dead claimed by the men was but fifteen, and yet the wonder was that even that number were killed.[61] Five dead bucks were found in one hole, the bodies partly covered with rocks. The number of dead (if any) in the unexplored caves, not ascertained. The east fort was a very bloody affair, and the wall down to the gorge in the rear was streaked with the article. An old, one-eyed, crop-haired squaw, whom the command gave bread back at the aforesaid wickiup, was found dead in the rocks and added to the list of slain. About noon, while Archie and boys were crawling round the forts, he fired at what seemed a moving shadow in a deep shelf of rock and killed a squaw. This was the last casualty on either side in the three days' fight at this Indian Gibral-tar. The scouts remained round the place till dark, but nothing new developed except that Boise Jimmy found the corpse of a chief that was at the head of stealing H Company's horses last winter. The boys have got the fur cap tasseled off with the queues of massacred Chinamen and the scalp it covered. There were only eight horses saved—several fine ones, the others much jaded.

That young squaw told some palpable lies at first, when Archie and crowd took her to a tree [and] threatened her in a way which an Indian could quickly understand. She then told the following story, which agreed with circumstances taken place. The chief band in the fight was Si-e-ta's, numbering about seventy-five Paiute warriors and thirty Pit Rivers, besides some of the Modocs. The bulk of the Chee-oh party had gone from North End Mountain to Eagle Lakes, saying that "by and by, before snow," they would go "up north" (Idaho?) on a raid. They took H Company's horses west from Dunder and Blitzen Creek to Lake Abert and so on down; and that during six months they captured over one thousand horses and had killed and eaten or traded them off about Pyramid Lake and [the] Truckee reservation for whatever they wanted. The Pit Rivers, she says, furnished a large proportion of the firearms. In Archie's fight on North End Mountain, he killed two and wounded seven— three mortally; that one of the former was a medicine man (the one with whom Archie had the "peace conference") and that the fur capped fellow then joined Si-e-ta's band. There has been a big trade between Pyramid Lake and Virginia [City], white men doing a good business trading ammunition, etc., for fish. Now, before the expedition left Camp Smith, parties arrived overland via Goose Lake and stated that large bands of mounted Indians were going north for the purpose, they said, of hunting. Billy McKay and Darragh made some captures on their way to Camp Smith, from whom information was obtained that Si-e-ta came north but, on getting a glimpse of those large bands of scouts at once retraced his steps. The Chee-oh party made several fights between Pueblo and Goose Lake. The Indians killed in that clearing up just east of old Camp Warner were all from the Pyramid Lake country[62] and en route north. Scores of artificial forts are found to correspond with their line of travel up along Goose and Abert Lakes and east to Steen's Mountain and the Malheur. The squaw frequently alluded to a convention of chiefs that was soon to be held to consider the best course for future deviltry. If it should be true (as she says) that Si-e-ta was killed, the convention will not be very well represented from two particularly strong precincts.

When Colonel Crook came to Idaho last winter, he set about whipping the Indians and learning their haunts with an energy unparalleled, meeting with much success and some vexatious loss. He soon became satisfied that from the impudent nature of the depredations on the Humboldt Road and the Owyhee settlements, that the perpetrators had some far-off place of retreat and where they lived in apparent innocence. From much experience, he concludes that Indians seldom go less than one hundred miles to commit deviltry, and oftener two or three; that they are never peaceable from principle and their best policy is to have a portion of the tribe "peaceable" and the remainder hostile; that the overwhelming Washo settlements overawed the Paiutes, when they turned their attention north to Humboldt and Owyhee, and have had the Goose and Eagle Lake and Pit River country all to themselves for a quiet shelter—a warm climate and rich in their kind of vegetables, which they must have, and it is folly to say that they live round on cold rocks and horsemeat alone; that it is the Paiutes instead of the Snakes that are doing the bulk of the deviltry—and it is well known that the Paiute "grounds" originally extended to the Owyhee. Of course, there is more or less intercourse between all the tribes or remnants mentioned, and the colonel is satisfied, from the information gathered this summer, that there is a fine trade going on between the Nez Perce and Indians on the Malheur and Burnt Rivers, but that the greater portion of the Snakes were crowded east by the big emigration to Boise and were well settled through the influence of General Connor.[63] That there is something of a general misunderstanding is indicated from another source—by some of Archie's Paiute captives from the Truckee reservation, who occasionally forget themselves and talk as good Chinook jargon[64] as the more highly educated citizens of Oregon.

Colonel Crook was determined to make the aforesaid campaign this summer, cost would it would, and demonstrate to the authorities and public interested certain disputed facts. He took a broad view of the matter, and this campaign should satisfy the most incredulous of the correctness thereof. And if there were no large bands of well-armed and mounted savages carousing along the Owyhee this summer, as of old, it is evidence of the good disposition of the troops. The colonel will take a pleasure in fighting those devils this winter if he can get the reasonable means he asks for at Camp Warner.

Regarding the history of the men killed, this was learned—of Company H, 1st Cavalry: Charles Barchet, German, through the war with 7th Vermont Volunteers, has relatives in Texas; James Lyons, father and brother living in Place Dale, Rhode Island; Michael Meara, born in Galway, Ireland, has been in the U.S. Army eighteen years, relatives in Boston; Willoughby Sawyer, a native of Canada west; James Carey, for a long time a resident of New Orleans. Of Company D, 23rd Infantry, Carl Bross, German, family in Newark, New Jersey.

These men were buried on the river flat north of where the fight occurred about one mile. Buried in separate graves side by side, the earth tramped in, the surplus dirt removed, and the whole burned over after the manner of a log heap. Bad enough to be killed by savages, but there is additional horror attendant in knowing that one has to be left hundreds of miles in the wilderness without so much as a little lumber to designate the line of demarcation between human and Mother Earth; but on the other hand, the greatest respect that can be afforded is to have every trace obliterated. The well-known practices of the human hyenas that inhabit the country render this sort of ceremony a necessity.

The unfortunate officer, Madigan, it was resolved to take along one day's march from the battlefield. The wounded unable to ride horseback were placed on two-mule litters, and on the twenty-ninth the command marched north along the west bank of the South Fork; curious stream—clear as crystal, solid bottom, but the tule shore makes it impassable. Get in at one side and you can't get out at the other. Fifteen miles to the main stream, which is bad enough, and a crossing was effected. The South Fork Valley is at least fifteen miles wide by thirty long—or much longer, for anything I know. There is doubtless much rich land available on either side—on the west along the bluffs; on the east the Warner Range, numerous creeks and rivulets. The South Fork is a great resort for fishing by the Indians. About twenty rods north of the main stream and thirty below the junction of the South Fork, Lieutenant John Madigan of Company H, 1st U.S. Cavalry, was buried with extra ceremony, of the kind. He was born and brought up in Jersey City, New Jersey, served through the war with the Army of the Potomac, and for gallantry therein received a commission in the regular service. His friendship was of the genuine sort, and possessing a droll originality and humor, his presence at the campfire had become almost indispensable with Crook's officers, and no one could more regret his taking off in the prime of life than the colonel himself. Alas, poor Madigan! Where are your oddities now? Hushed amid the yells of fiends, and no sound but the bugle call of Judgment can awake you to glory again. Madigan was shot through the left temple, tearing a hole through his head an inch in diameter, and of course never knew what hurt him. He fell about where Lyons was killed the first day, also shot through the head.

On the thirtieth the command marched up the west bank of Pit River several miles, crossed to the east bank, where is a most singular collection of soft sand cones not unlike inverted hornets' nests and about the same color. They are from five to forty feet high and stand round over several acres in pairs and threes—an old one with one or two young ones, as it were; if that isn't a graphic description, I don't want a cent. A few miles north and camped. Only ten miles today. Scouts kept in the rear for the purpose of getting in a back-handed lick on some of the lurking natives, but such satisfaction was barely probable. The mineralogical corps found a fair prospect of gold in the creek here, and Warner Range east round Saddle Mountain looks like a gold country.

On October 1 north fifteen miles and camped below Lassen Pass. Passed where large signal fires had been made in answer to those down the river and followed by others near the rocks, showing a perfect system of telegraphy, of the kind. The source of Pit River [having] been a source of dispute with many so long, the colonel concluded to make a detour from the command and follow the stream up towards Goose Lake. It was found to run out of said lake, and for ten miles next to the lake was a stream apparently larger than below the forks. Great numbers of ducks, but why such a nice lake should have such a goose of a name did not appear. Found bunches of plump, ripe wheat and oats at the wagon road crossing several miles below the lake; think there is much land down there that will pay for surveying. The temperature is favorably shown up by the freshness of the bunch grass and other vegetation. On the second marched fifteen miles along the west base of the Warner Range to near the

Oregon line. Next day same distance to north end of lake. Passed near North End Mountain, on which Archie "fit" with Chee-oh and company. It is a high and rocky makeup surely and is one of the fortified stations on the Paiute route to Idaho. The wild plums were found to be ripe, and to say they were worth going for and we went is no name for it. Counting the prairie north of the lake, there is a range of most superior bunch-grass grazing land along the Warner Range and in extent at least fifteen miles wide by one hundred in length. The Warner Range is very high, broad, bald, and rugged; timbered ravines with fine creeks every few miles, fish and game abundant. Altogether a superior section of interior public domain. That fair-paying mines will be found and the reclaiming of the country follow, and soon, is a reasonable conclusion. From the Drew road, the command continued north over a low divide to the valley of Lake Abert, fifteen miles. [On] the fourth, six or eight miles up over high bluffs to the east, and Camp Woods (new Camp Warner) was reached again.

The soldiers were truly glad to see a chance to rest, especially the wounded, who seemed to get along finely. Lieutenant Powell, regular surgeon,[65] had arrived and is there assigned. Among the letters awaiting Madigan was a promotion. Lieutenant Small's reported success killing and capturing thirty Indians in the tules of Lake Abert agrees in time and circumstances so well that I think Captain Darragh helped him to that "bowl of blood."[66] The news came up via Bidwell that the two Winnemuccas had lately come into Susanville with passes from the Truckee reservation to go hunting in the Eagle Lake section—good sign—and that, in a muddle wherein the citizens were going to kill them, got away. On the seventh Thomas Dean and party came in to Warner from Fort Crook. He had two pulls at it, being driven back once by the Indians. He was attacked on the morning the fight commenced, but near where the command first struck Pit River. Nothing like having the natives show their hand where they live.

On the seventh [also] the colonel started to Camp Harney, and from which point I expect to furnish you a few items. Incidents of interest occurred every day of the campaign that must go by the board. I have endeavored to give you a plain statement of one month's operations developed from day to day.

Had a bully time and have no excuses to make.

Owyhee Avalanche, November 9, 1867

EDITORS, *OWYHEE AVALANCHE:* Arriving at Camp Woods—now Camp Warner—on October 5, Colonel Crook concluded to remain over one day and then proceed north to the other post in course of construction—Camp Harney—and complete arrangements for a winter campaign. There were no buildings completed at Camp Warner. George B. Cosby (sutler) was to have a turbine sawmill running in a few weeks, and the officers were waiting for lumber. Several new officers had arrived there—Lieutenants Eschenburg, Sherman, and

Fisher[67]—and twenty recruits for Captain Perry's company. Three of Captain Hinton's company had deserted, got nearly to the Humboldt road, were attacked by Indians, and Private Myers killed, when the other two concluded to give it up as a bad job and return to Warner, which is their story of it. Captain Hinton had also been recruiting for his infantry about this wise: Born—to the wife of Captain Hinton, September 17, a daughter. There will soon be quite a number of married ladies at Warner, no other arrangements to the contrary—Mrs. Crook, Hinton, Parnell, Eschenberg, Jack, Lewis, and Cosby. The general found an order here from department headquarters removing Companies F (Perry) and H (Parnell), 1st Cavalry, out of his district, which, if not revoked, will leave him little to operate with this winter.[68]

Camp Warner is located most favorably for making a winter campaign round the Warner, Abert, and Goose Lakes—within one day's easy march of either, and all are infested more or less with the gentle savages; and south of the latter it is literally lousy with them. Fort Bidwell is still more favorably located for operating against the Paiutes but has no troops, it is said. If that post were added to the District of the Lakes, it would be no detriment to the service. Camp Warner is a peculiarly central point and should be well supplied with the materials for Indian war, and there is little fear that they will not be judiciously and effectively sent right along.

On the seventh the colonel, Lieutenant Eskridge, with Perry's recruits and Archie's Indians, started north, the advance getting into Harney on the eleventh; owing to the condition of the stock, the recruits and scouts had a rough trip of it, one of the former lost, and Archie was taken down with rheumatism. The Indian prisoners taken during the summer were brought over to Harney, from where they will go to reservations.

Captain Perry's part of the expedition had got into Harney on the fifth; Darragh's scouts a few days previously. From Separation Camp, west of Lake Abert, Perry went north, touching Summer and Silver Lakes, thence through open timbered country, sandy soil, to the Deschutes River; traveled down that three days, thence one day east to Crooked River—branch of the former—up said river southeast and into Harney. From Silver Lake, Darragh struck east and had some long stretches without water. There is an immense amount of high, sage desert country north from the latitude of Silver, Summer, Abert, and Warner Lakes to Crook River, about which the Warm Springs and Wasco Indians have many superstitious notions and legends of immense suffering, but Darragh is of [the] opinion, now that he has been over most of that dreaded landscape, that water can be found at convenient distances any direction if such discovery is deemed essential to a continuation of earthly affairs. The opinion is a reasonable one with regard to such matters anywhere, as travelers may pass within a few rods of secluded springs and rivulets and yet die of thirst. As to the object of the campaign, no part of Perry's command struck any of the hostiles and but little sign of any, and all hands are now convinced that "Crook was right after all" regarding their whereabouts.

A friendly scout. CENTURY MAGAZINE, 1891.

Lieutenant Dodge,[69] in going through from Auburn[70] to Harney with some recruits and property, had several mules driven off somewhere on the headwaters of the Middle Malheur—supposed to have been done by Indians. On the evening of the twelfth, Captain Kelly, with fifty men of Company C, 8th Cavalry, and Capt. Billy McKay, with ten of his boys, started with fifteen days' rations for the purpose of looking into that matter and to otherwise scout the Malheur haunts.[71]

On October 13 Lieutenant Eskridge started to Portland (department headquarters) with important papers from Colonel Crook pertaining to carrying out the war in the District of the Lakes. He asks that Companies F and H be retained, else the former goes to Boise and the latter to Camp Smith, leaving the colonel but two companies of cavalry (Captain Kelly's at Harney and Captain Bassford's,[72] not arrived, at Warner), at posts with one hundred fifty miles of desert between, with which to conduct a winter campaign. He is anxious to continue the thankless task of settling the savages' hash, now that he has got a thorough knowledge of their manner and scene of operations, and were it well for the good of all honestly interested in the country that his most reasonable wants be in some way supplied. But the fact is, he anticipates more trouble from that "power behind the throne,"[73] which boasts that it "can buy department headquarters for a horse," than from the Paiutes. To ask for tough mustang stock and receive an indifferent makeup of unacclimated, gangling horses that one day's march will play out is not very flattering to men willing to risk and wear out their lives in a service which, nine times in ten, the pay and promotion will increase as rapidly sitting in comfortable quarters issuing orders. And to know that large and small contracts for supplies are so let or tampered with, no moneyed man of integrity or honest laborer ever getting a hearing, and all this species of robbery boasted of by a set of chronic thieves, is a pleasant state of affairs to contend with.

Everything was peculiarly lovely at Camp Steele, now Camp Harney. The hay contract—old doormats would be luscious nutriment in comparison—was considered filled at about $40 coin per ton; was being hauled two miles and undergoing the process of stacking by soldiers at $16 per month greenbacks. All there was lacking was Eskridge's name to the papers, which at last accounts was not there. These large citizen mule teams suddenly commenced hauling two loads of logs instead of one per day; some nine or ten fancy carpenters got an eternal leave of absence, and one practical old man substituted in their stead, and who, in charge of the hay stackers (infantry), did more in four days toward building the quarters at Camp Harney than had been accomplished for four weeks previous. The wood contract, $14 coin, I am told can be filled at one-half the figure with good margin. Pack trains, hired at $1.75 per head per day coin, realized to their citizen owners, through detention or manipulation of instructions, many thousands of dollars before the quartermaster could take them on his papers as purchased at a set price. Mr. Robles, a few miles north of camp, would have a good sawmill in operation in ten days; he intends to furnish lumber to government at $30 per thousand and depend on the quantity taken to make anything by the venture. He anticipates considerable custom from new settlements that are expected to spring up in the country. He certainly deserves success.

This post will be the most important of all for operating across the headquarters of the Malheur to the Owyhee, west of Steen's Mountain, etc., the Harney Valley furnishing a short and easy road to any of the aforesaid points and in the rear of all. There are two companies of cavalry needed at Harney for that purpose, and it would seem that Company F could see more of the "lost tribes" from that standpoint than from the little more genial clime of Boise. However, Captain Kelly's company may expect to rot next winter. He is the ranking officer stationed at Harney; should Captain Perry remain there, he will command the post. I hope Perry will have to "suffer." He swore on the point— of taking something with the officer of the day—that I came under the special ban of the following order from the post commander of date October 16 and exposed in several conspicuous places:

> In pursuance of instructions from Headquarters, District Lakes for the purpose of protecting all honest and industrious citizens who may visit the post and the public property, horse thieves and other disreputable persons being known to be in the vicinity, all citizens now on the military reservation not in the employ of the government, or who have been employed, and all persons having no visible occupation, will leave the reservation at once.
>
> The officer of the day is charged with the execution of this order and will see that its provisions are strictly carried out and obeyed.

Now, the only horse I ever contemplated stealing died a natural death near where the late unpleasantness occurred between Colonel Crook and the Paiutes. "Old Buster" was about the last of the Oregon cavalry—had webbed feet and only lacked wings to make him a complete swamp angel. He carried me about twelve hundred miles, but got the "California fever" and died like a hero. He could keep fat on greasewood with the bits in his mouth, but loved a square meal, and now that he is unencumbered by any mortal picket rope, he is doubtless reveling in pastures ever green. He could snuff the battle far off—farther than I could—and at the sound of a rifle would say "hay, hay," which sometimes annoyed the district quartermaster—and that suited crooks much. The fact is the contractors and their bummers had left nothing to steal, and I didn't come out with so much as a shoddy overcoat—couldn't have had a wooden overcoat if I'd happened to stayed with Old Buster. Peace to his manes.

It was a sight, though, to see the scattering caused by the foregoing bull. Pack trains returning below had back loads in passengers, and many adventurers left camp with blankets on their backs. The "Oregon War" school of thieves had disseminated the idea [of robbing] the government of more than went to feed or fight the Indians, and after years of uninterrupted practice, it will go hard to meet with a check.

Now that Colonel Crook has got a thorough knowledge of the hostile country, it would be a great drawback to have a promising winter's campaign go by the board, as it surely looks. With two companies of cavalry at Harney and Archie's scouts increased and well mounted, the colonel intended to scour the Malheur and Owyhee during the first of the winter, and then with two companies of cavalry at Warner again start for the Paiute headquarters. From information obtained last winter, he believes there is a band of about sixty above the forks of the Owyhee, and from indications discovered the past summer, the scattering sneaks in the Malheur and Burnt Rivers sometimes get supplied through the Nez Perce traffic, and that one more winter can be made to settle their hash and close out their business. He believes in applying to the race the principle so desirable in civilized warfare—make one-half of the enemy oppose the other, and is bound to use the Boise and Brunean Snakes to that end. They can be made to do it, and as is the case with Archie's—they soon come to like hunting the Paiutes.

Archie's band possesses much independence of character, mind their own business, are fat, jolly, and contented (because they are treated justly), and the soldiers rather like to see them round. It would seem that if there were a company of them enlisted and mounted for the District of the Owyhee and put in charge of some suitable person—Donald McKay, perhaps—the business of keeping the peace would be greatly aided and the saving to the government immense. These Snake scouts are invaluable as guides and herders, their keen power of perception infallible. A mere pittance of coin will satisfy them as to pay, and any one of them for scouting purposes is worth all the government guides, bilks, and bummers.

Captain Gilliss,[74] wife, and Mrs. Crook were expected to arrive at Harney about the twentieth, and Lieutenant Eskridge with the result of his errand about the twenty-fifth. Should the latter signify that the Indians shall be fought from the carpet "down below," the colonel may make Warner his headquarters, himself comfortable, and go to issuing orders. But more likely Captain Perry and Archie will scout the country across to Boise, the Indians see their folks and then return to Harney, when Crook will start the marching again with whatever means there is. Darragh's and McKay's Indians were to start home about the thirtieth—whether to return to the field again, I can't say. If I have talked pretty plain and apparently familiar about many things seen and learned while "swinging round the circle" the last four months, there has been nothing said on that score which the public should not (for once) know through the papers and nothing that need offend except in the right places.

On the twentieth Captain Harris and company started for Camp Lyon. The undersigned, "having no visible occupation," was allowed to come out of the District of the Lakes the first opportunity. It is about five easy marches from Harney to Lyon—125 miles—but owing to the "guides," it took seven. Twenty miles from Harney, and there is a gap through the eastern rim of the Harney Valley basin, and about as low as the lakes, to the South Malheur, heading in Steen's Mountain. It is not the worst road, considering the meanness of the country across the Malheur, Owyhee, etc., to Lyon. Two fresh barefooted horse tracks had passed up the Malheur about the twenty-third, and the sign of several signal fires on the bottom indicated that Billy McKay and Captain Kelley may have been stirring up the natives; and it is hoped the expedition has been successful. McKay is a good scout and has been lucky.[75] Company M's horses needed rest and forage very much, and the captain and men felt glad when

Camp Lyon again appeared in sight. With recruits and other additions, the post will soon be able to turn out near a full company of cavalry with the best of arms.

I shall always fell indebted to Captain Harris, Captain Perry, Lieutenants Eskridge, Parnell, and Stanton for favors tending to make the campaign a pleasant affair from first to last; also to Captain Hinton and Lieutenant Jack at Warner, and Lieutenants Goodale, Rice, and others at Harney, for kindnesses. If I have not said enough already to make the colonel wish the devil had me, I'd say he was one of God's own men in the right place—thoroughly in earnest; regardless of fear or favor from any source.

The Battle of the Infernal Caverns

RICHARD I. ESKRIDGE[1]

Austin A. Parker to William C. Brown, November 20, 1928,
William Carey Brown Papers, Box 21, Folder 41,
University of Colorado Library, Boulder[2]

Following a plain trail on September 26,[3] [1867,] our advance encountered about thirty Indians, who opened fire from a ravine coming down from a high bluff on the west side of the South Fork Valley. The troops, fighting on foot, drove the Indians to a plain lava rock about 500 by 300 yards in area, bounded on the west side by a wall of rock 150 feet high,[4] and on the east side by a ridge about thirty feet higher than the plain, covered with grass, brush, and large boulders, and sloping away to the valley.

About midway of this plain, up against the ridge which we occupied, are two promontories of rock, which rise about fifteen feet above the plain, about eight feet apart, on a line perpendicular to the ridge, each about twenty feet across the top and having a chamber eight or ten feet square inside, with an opening of two or three on top and a similar one into the space within, besides an exit into the caverns and continuous subterranean passages with which the plain is honeycombed. In these two chambers were provisions and water. The tops were fortified with breastworks of stone three feet high, with loopholes. The Indians numbered ninety bucks.

From the top of the ridge, the ground slopes at an angle of forty-five degrees down to the base of the nearest promontory, the sides of which are so steep as to necessitate the use of hands in climbing up.

Having posted ten men on the high bluff in rear, the colonel [Crook] formed the two companies, about thirty men strong each, at the first gray of dawn on September 27 under cover of the ridge, where they had bivouacked the night before. Parnell was ordered to attack on the right or north side and Madigan on the left or south side. I was ordered to superintend operations on left. Madigan's company, advancing down the steep descent to the base of the promontory, received a withering volley from the breastworks, caves, and crevices at thirty or forty feet range. Lieutenant Madigan was killed and about ten of his men killed or wounded, but the men stood the shock with wonderful coolness and advanced steadily to the base, then climbed up as best they could.

Parnell swept around on the right and, with great gallantry and energy, reached the breastworks. His men, elated at getting their first objective, attempted to rush in over the works, when they received a volley which fairly paralyzed them and sent a dozen tumbling to the bottom. Meantime, Sergeant Russler of Company D, who with great gallantry and alacrity in the face of such fire was the first to reach the breastworks on our side, thrust his piece into one of the loopholes and fired, killing and wounding several of the fifteen or twenty Indians inside and stampeding the rest. In retiring, they were exposed to the keen eye of the colonel, who stood on top of the ridge directing the movements of both companies; two sharp reports of his deadly rifle were heard over our heads, two bodies fell with a dull thud to the rocks at our feet, both companies rushed in with a yell, and the place was ours.

The Indians were under us but not confined, as caves led off in every direction. The ten men on the bluff in rear, which commanded the situation generally, held them in check, while twenty men were left to hold the fort. The remainder retired to camp in the valley, taking the wounded, to care for them and get something to eat.

One of the Indians killed by the colonel was the medicine man,[5] a large buck covered with hideous paint and wearing a large war bonnet, profusely decorated with feathers and silver ornaments, who had kept up a constant harangue in a loud voice throughout the previous day and night. His voice was forever silenced, which struck terror to the souls of the savages, for not another sound was heard from them except the report of a rifle whenever one of our party attempted to enter the caverns or inadvertently exposed himself to their rifle fire from some unseen crevice.

When night came on, the Indians who were able to travel took a hurried departure, leaving wounded, squaws, and children. Our scouts were on the alert and shot several of them as they came up out of the caverns of the lava bed during the night. The wounded left in the caverns made it certain death for anyone of our party to attempt to enter. Their skeletons were found there several years later.

Race with the Indians

GEORGE CROOK

The Daily Oregonian (Portland), July 29, 1868

The following letter, though evidently not written for publication, is handed to us by Governor Ballard with a view to giving the widest publicity to the fact the Indian war in Idaho has, for the present at least, come to an end:

CAMP HARNEY, Oregon, July 1, 1868

Governor Ballard,
Dear Sir:

I made a treaty yesterday with the concentrated rascality of the Paiute tribe. They have been suing for peace for the last month, and I met them here yesterday and told them that I was not anxious for peace, for they had lied to me before, and I did not know but that they would do so now; that I had plenty of soldiers here and more coming; and if I killed them all off, they would not lie to me again. I have no doubt but this desire for peace on their part is sincere from the fact that about half of their number have been killed, and those that are left don't know what day their turn might come. Ten of them have volunteered to help us fight the Pitt Rivers and other hostile Indians, and leave today for Camp Warner for that purpose.

The only thing I fear now is that white men will commit outrages on the Indians in retaliation. If this thing can be controlled, I feel satisfied that the bloody scenes of the last four years are at end, and we will have a permanent peace with the Indians.

It occurs to me that you can do more towards preventing a renewal of hostilities than any other person I know of in the country. Get the newspapers in your territory to interest themselves in the matter, and enjoin upon all good citizens the necessity of refraining from retaliation. Give the Indians a chance to show their hand on the peace side of the question, and I feel satisfied that our troubles with them are over.

Yours sincerely,
Crook

Indian Affairs on the Pacific Coast

JOSEPH W. KARGE AND SAMUEL MUNSON

Army and Navy Journal 5, no. 45 (June 27, 1868): 711–12

The following interesting reports contain accounts of two affairs with the Indians on the Pacific Coast which took place this spring:

CAMP WINFIELD SCOTT, NEVADA, MAY 1, 1868
Col. John P. Sherburne, Assistant Adjutant General, Department of California.

COLONEL: I have the honor to report that on the twenty-ninth ultimo, a citizen residing in the vicinity of this post reported at 7:00 A.M. that a horse, tied within 100 yards of his dwelling, had been cut loose the night previous and led off by Indians. I ordered Lieutenant Hunter[1] to take three men and an Indian guide and go in pursuit, believing, however, at the time that the horse had either strayed or been taken by some white men. I cautioned Lieutenant Hunter, in case he struck an Indian trail, to be careful and not allow himself to be drawn into a snare. The owner of the horse accompanied the detachment.

At 11:00 A.M. another report reached camp that three yoke of cattle were also missing from within a mile and a half of the locality where the horses were stolen. No longer doubting Indians were the perpetrators, I immediately ordered Lt. [John] Lafferty, who was temporarily attached to this post, to proceed with six men and one day's rations in the direction taken by Lieutenant Hunter and, having struck his trail, to follow up and afford him such assistance as circumstances might require.

No tidings were received from either party until 6:00 P.M, when a citizen came in and reported that the detachment under Lieutenant Hunter had been surprised by Indians in a canyon eight miles from camp, all their horses shot dead, and that the men, badly wounded, were in a cave keeping the Indians at bay. As Lieutenant Lafferty had not yet returned, I requested Maj. [Frederick] Mears, United

States paymaster, who happened to be at the post, to take charge of the camp. Leaving him thirteen men, with the remainder, ten in number, I left camp within five minutes from the receipt of the news.

Some 600 yards from camp I met Lieutenant Lafferty on his return. He reported that he had failed to strike Lieutenant Hunter's trail, and having learned that the cattle reported lost had turned up safe, he doubted the reports in regard to Indians; under this impression he returned to camp, expecting to meet Lieutenant Hunter on his arrival.

I therefore left Lieutenant Lafferty in charge of the camp and proceeded at a gallop under the guidance of the Indian guide and the citizens who had made their escape from the place of action on foot. I reached the mouth of a canyon eight miles from camp at sundown and, after a march of four miles more through intricate defiles, reached the reported beleaguered party at dusk.

An oblong cave some 100 feet in circumference, surrounded on all sides by high and perpendicular rocks, with a solitary entrance not more than six feet wide, had fortunately afforded a temporary refuge to the retreating detachment, who were hotly pursued by their bloodthirsty foes. Owing, however, to the coolness and intrepidity of Lieutenant Hunter, who, although badly wounded and more rolling than walking, covered the retreat of his wounded men with his Spencer carbine, the cowardly savages, seventeen in number and apparently well armed with repeating rifles, as the nature of the wounds attest, dared not attack the four men under shelter. I found but one man, Private Reid, capable of defense, and he was pacing his beat at the mouth of the cave. Lieutenant Hunter, Sergeant Kelly, and Private Ward were stretched at full length on the rocks—the former with his carbine in his hands; the latter two groaning under excruciating pain. Lieutenant Hunter, who withal seemed cheerful and composed, had received a gunshot wound in the right hip, the ball, of small caliber, ranging inwardly toward the bladder, where it still remains. Another ball struck him across the chest, perforating all his clothing save the undershirt, and inflicting a slight wound on his right wrist. His right ankle was badly strained, causing him more inconvenience and pain than the more serious wound. Sergeant Kelly was struck by a large, conical bullet, injuring his collarbone and the first rib. Private Ward was shot through the lung with a conical bullet. He has since died.

I did my utmost to make the wounded as comfortable as possible under the existing circumstances, the night being cold and the snow several feet deep in the cave. Lieutenant Hunter, although suffering severely from his wounds, mounted a horse and, with an escort of five men, rode to a ranch in the valley, six miles distant. Before start-

On the lookout. OUTING MAGAZINE 1887.

ing from the camp, I ordered Acting Assistant Surgeon Hays to accompany my detachment on horseback with instruments, etc., and also to bring an ambulance as far as the nature of the ground would permit, which was to the mouth of the canyon. I am pained to say that the surgeon failed to appear when his services were most needed, although I had taken due precaution to have him piloted to the ground in case he lost his way in the darkness.

The only cover I was in possession of to keep the wounded from freezing was a pair of my own blankets and six saddle blankets; the emergency of the case and our great haste made us forget to bring overcoats and blankets, as well as canteens. Water was brought to the wounded from a distance of half a mile in boots, and shirts and drawers were used as bandages and compresses to stop the flow of blood. The night was passed in anxiety and suffering by both sick and well.

On the morning of the thirtieth, I took five men and a citizen who had joined the detachment, and went on foot to examine the ground on which the affray had taken place and to recover, if possible, some of the horse equipment. Leaving two men in charge of the wounded, I followed the tracks which had been made by Lieutenant Hunter's retreating party over deep and frozen snow about two miles, across ground strewn with rocks and offering at every step natural fortifications in projecting ledges of rocks. A deep but gradually sloping gulch intervenes between two mountains, affording from either of its acclivities an extensive view of the surrounding country. The mountain on which the action took place has a gradual slope of some 2,000 feet. Irregular cones of black rock project horizontally along the slope some 500 feet from its summit, forming an excellent breastwork for defense.

On this last elevation, I found three dead horses, all shot through the head, despoiled of their equipment and the best part of the flesh. Examining further, I found that the foe had not been more than twenty feet from the approaching soldiers when the fatal volley was fired; that the party escaped immediate death is miraculous. The other three horses reported by their riders as also killed could not be found and had probably been led off by the enemy.

After a three hours' search, I returned to the cave at 7:30 A.M., where I found five men who had been sent the previous night to the camp for stretchers and to hunt up the missing surgeon, whom they had at last unearthed somewhere in the sagebrush.

The wounded men were placed on stretchers and carried four miles to the mouth of the canyon, whence the ambulance took them to camp. Lieutenant Hunter was also sent for, and judging from appearances, he is doing well. In conclusion, I cannot forebear to make special mention of the heroic behavior of Pvt. James C. Reid, who, being the only sound man in the party, stood nobly to his work in defending the lives of his disabled comrades.

I have the honor to remain, very respectfully, your obedient servant,

JOSEPH W. KARGE,[2]
First Lieutenant, 8th U.S. Cavalry, Commanding

HEADQUARTERS CAMP BIDWELL, CA.,
SURPRISE VALLEY, CA., MAY 15, 1868
Col. John P. Sherburne, A.A.G., Headquarters Department of California.
SIR: I have the honor to report that I left camp on April 28 with Lt. [Hayden] De Lany and thirty-one enlisted men of Company C, 9th Infantry, nineteen enlisted men of Company G, 8th Cavalry, post surgeon, and guide.

On May 7 we discovered a party of thirty or forty Indians on the side of a mountain about thirty-five miles northeast of this camp.[3] We attacked them at once and drove them slowly toward the top (some three miles). On arriving at the summit, they attempted to hold it, but we pressed forward, and they scattered and fled in different directions.

The fight lasted four hours, with a loss on our side of the post guide killed, Lieutenant De Lany wounded (shot through the arm), and Pvt. Charles Amstedt, Company G, 8th U.S. Infantry, shot in the leg.

Several of the Indians were killed, but I am unable to report the exact number, as it was almost dark when we reached the summit, and the extent and nature of the ground and the exhaustion of the men prevented any search for their dead.[4]

The band was a new one in this part of the country. Nearly all had rifles and were dressed in citizens' clothing, and five of their horses that we shot on the trail at the commencement of the fight were shod and had not been long in their possession.

Mr. Daniel Hoag, the guide who was killed, had been under my command in three different skirmishes and in many long and successful marches, and had so well and cheerfully performed his duty that he was beloved by all in the command.[5]

I would respectfully call the attention of the general commanding the department to the good conduct of Lieutenant De Lany, who showed great promptness, energy, and bravery.

Very respectfully, your obedient servant,

S. MUNSON,[6] Captain, 8th U. S. Cavalry, Commanding

A Scout to Steen's Mountain

ALBERT G. FORSE[1]

Army and Navy Journal 11, no. 4 (September 6, 1873): 52–53

L t. A. G. Forse of the U.S. Army, a resident of Brooklyn when at home, writes to his uncle, Mayor Powell of that city, a letter, from which the following extracts are made in the *Brooklyn Eagle:*

CAMP McDERMIT, NEVADA,
AUGUST 23, 1873

On Thursday I returned from [a] scout to Steen's Mountain, Oregon, where I was seven days with fifteen men, fully armed and equipped, and an acting assistant surgeon as medical officer. We have orders to make a scout once a month to look after the Indians in that quarter, as they are the most to be feared and largest tribe on the coast, with the exception, probably, of the Apaches.

The Indians are the Paiutes and number about 8,000,[2] and should they break out and get into Steen's Mountain, as they certainly would do, it would take more men to get them out than in the Lava Beds, for it is a worse place. The mountain top is never free from snow, giving them plenty of water, which the Modocs did not have in the Lava Beds. Besides, there is but one point that I saw where troops could get to the top, and there a few Indians could keep back an army by rolling rocks above, as it is almost perpendicular. Should the troops gain the summit, they would find it twenty miles across and cut up more than the Lava Beds, having chasms and fissures hundreds of feet deep. Worse than all, the mortars and howitzers could not be brought into play upon them, as the mountain is too high.

I had an interview with Pah-a-coy, chief of the Steen's Mountain band of Paiutes. He was willing to go on a reservation, and started for the one at Camp Harney the same night I saw him, but the head chief of all the tribes of the Paiutes, whose name is Winnemucca, I could not find, nor would the Indians tell me his whereabouts. I think he is in the mountains, hiding to keep from going on a reservation.

As long as he keeps his Indians from stealing cattle, the government will not disturb him, but I fear he cannot do that very well, as they will steal. They steal very expertly, however, so that the settlers cannot catch them very easily. Some of the settlers told me that the Indians stole their cattle more or less all the time, but that they could not catch them in the act, and when they did they would kill the thieves. An Indian never steals alone, and they are not slow to kill a white man, if by doing so they can cover their tracks.

The difficulties between the settlers and Indians increase every year. It must soon be settled one way or another as to what the Paiutes will do. Winnemucca and his tribe will have to go on a reservation or fight, as the cattlemen will force a fight on him if he does not go. Winnemucca says that he has been driven out of all his hunting places by the cattlemen and that he is determined to hold Barren Valley. He did burn out one or two cattlemen who went there. One of the principal cattlemen told me that he intended to put one or two thousand head of cattle in that valley next spring and settle the point. The government, unfortunately for Winnemucca, does not acknowledge his right to the land, and it holds out inducements for him to go on a reservation. The cattlemen can go to the valley and take their chances, if they see fit, knowing well that if they do stir up a war, the troops will be sent to their protection.[3]

The chief, Pah-a-coy, whom I saw, is a fine-looking Indian and very friendly. We shook hands and sat down together. I gave him some smoking tobacco, and he handed it to one of his bucks, who made him a cigarette, first lighting it and smoking it awhile before giving it to the chief, who then took about a dozen puffs, inhaling the smoke in his lungs, and then passed the cigarette back to the buck. They never take but a few whiffs at a time. I was amused at the surgeon I had with me. He is a young man and not accustomed to riding. With us on the march we have but two gaits, the walk and the trot, as the gallop injures the horses and knocks off their shoes. The first day after riding, and when we had encamped, he said, "I cannot see how your men can laugh and talk after a march; I should think they would be so stiff and sore they would not feel like being lively." He evidently did not know, poor fellow, that all the others were used to it and rather enjoyed it than otherwise. I don't think that he fancies cavalry life, for he says it is too hard work. I always had him up in the morning to breakfast, never later than 3:00 A.M. nor earlier than 1:00 A.M., and then only gave him bacon, coffee, and bread. I had to get up early for breakfast to make an early start and get into camp before noon, so as to give my horses time to graze before night came on, as I then had them tied up and a guard placed over them during the night for fear of Indians.

The trooper and his mount. RUFUS F. ZOGBAUM. *HORSE, FOOT, AND DRAGOON.*

This is a great country for grazing. There are about fifty thousand cattle and sheep in Quinn River Valley, which is about a mile from here. The cattlemen locate themselves, build a hovel, and claim the land for so many miles, which means all the grass land in the neighborhood. Their claims are not valid, but as they urge them with a double-barreled shotgun or revolver, they generally hold good. Their ranches are on an average from twenty to thirty miles apart.

In addition to my going out as officer of the day every other day, when I have to get up at reveille, 4:30 A.M., see that the horses are groomed twice a day, drill one hour and a half mounted and one hour dismounted, attend all general roll calls, and visit the guards between 12:00 P.M. and 4:30 P.M., I have to issue every day provisions to the troops and officers, and every other day to the Indians for two days at a time, receive fresh beef every day, have it weighed and issued. These belong to my duties as commissary.

As quartermaster, I issue all grain for the government animals, of which there are 112, receive hay and straw, see that it is weighed and in good condition, also have all government supplies hauled from Winnemucca, distant eighty miles. I have been hauling for nearly two months and still have one hundred fifty thousand pounds there. When the stores arrive, I have to count every article and see that it is in good order and condition, for I have to receipt for everything and become responsible for it in the future. Those are some of my duties as quartermaster.

I have all the post adjutant's duties to do—mount the guards, etc. As post treasurer, I have to see that the baker furnishes the command with good bread, that he is kept in flour, potatoes, hops, etc., for baking. As signal officer, once a week I have to take all the noncommissioned officers out and drill them in signaling, in sending and receiving messages. As instructor of target practice, once a week I have to take out the command and instruct them in firing. Besides the above mentioned duties, I have to see that the post is kept in repair, mules shod, wagons in order, and do numerous other things. The reason of my having so much to do is that there are but two officers to the command now, and I, not being commanding officer, have to do the work. In a large command there are plenty of officers, and five, if not six, would do the work I am doing.

PART TWO

The Modoc War, 1872–73

The Modoc War—Its Origin, Incidents, and Peculiarities

JAMES JACKSON[1]

United Service, n.s., 8, no. 1 (July 1892): 1–122[2]

During the winter of 1872–73 in southern Oregon and northern California occurred an Indian outbreak remarkable in many respects. Remarkable for the loss of life on the part of troops in proportion to the number of Indians they were endeavoring to subdue; remarkable for the tenacity with which a comparatively small number of Indian warriors held out against the arms, solicitations, and promises of a government so powerful and a people so numerous as ours, and with whose power and numbers they were quite familiar; remarkable for the peculiar and almost indescribable country in which they had taken refuge and which enabled them to hold out as they did against the forces endeavoring to bring to them to terms; remarkable for the vengeful treachery which closed the labors of the "peace commission," by which one of our most capable commanders, Brig. Gen. E. S. Canby,[3] lost his life, ending a career of great usefulness, quiet benevolence, unselfish patriotism, and soldierly devotion to duty, by the bullet of a treacherous savage; remarkable, finally, for the complete stamping out of this causeless Indian rebellion and the well-merited, prompt, and exemplary punishment of its leading spirits, something unusual in the history of Indian wars.

The home of these Modoc Indians was in a district of country just east of the Cascade Mountains and lying on both sides of the boundary line between Oregon and California, a rocky, broken, sagebrush region containing a number of alkaline lakes, some fertile valleys, and a few mountain streams, but covered by the most part by volcanic scoria. Their principal habitat was the valley of Lost River and the basin of Tule Lake, into which the valley opens.[4]

The rivers and lakes abounded in fish and were the resort of vast numbers of waterfowl; game was plentiful in the adjacent mountains, the bunch grass was luxuriant, the climate mild; snow seldom fell and never remained long in the valleys. Taken altogether, it was a paradise for nomadic Indians.

At the eastern extremity of the Tule Lake basin was a district of country known as the Lava Beds, which at the outbreak of hostilities was, to the white man, a *terra incognita*, being for miles each way a confused jumble of lava

James Jackson as a lieutenant colonel.
CYRUS T. BRADY. *NORTHWESTERN FIGHTS AND FIGHTERS.*

which had in some prehistoric period rolled down the slopes of the volcanic peaks on its eastern border and, lashed into furious foam and toppling waves by the obstructions in the lake valley, had—apparently while at the height of the disturbance—solidified into a hard, blackish rock, honeycombed by bursting air bubbles caught in the lava flow, leaving a surface over which no white man ventured of his own accord and whose intricate passages and cavernous retreats were known only to this tribe of Indians and the mountain lion as he stalked them in search of prey. The ocean breakers as they dash on a rocky coast, suddenly petrified in all the wildness of their fury, would give some idea of the character of a portion of this lava surface and induce a realizing sense of the difficulty of carrying on military operations in such a country.

Along a mile or more of the lakefront, the molten lava had poured over the abrupt and irregular bluffs, forming as it cooled a rock wall whose almost vertical face was impossible of direct ascent. On the crest of this wall the lava, in cooling, had broken away from the horizontal flow, forming a deep crevice which in an irregular line followed the indentations of the lakeshore and, curiously enough, made almost as perfect a defensive work as a military engineer could have laid out. There was no part of this abrupt rocky glacis that was not covered by a line of fire from the natural rifle trench, while at the angles masses of rock had fallen forward, forming lunettes, covering the receding lines, affording loopholes or windows through which all approaches could be observed, and serving as admirable picket or lookout stations for a defending foe. When the line of crevices had been broken through, or failed to give sufficient defense, the Indians supplemented it with a double wall of broken lava, carried to and around the caves used for sleeping purposes, affording a continuous channel of unexposed communication from one flank to the other, completing and making impregnable against a small force this Modoc stronghold.

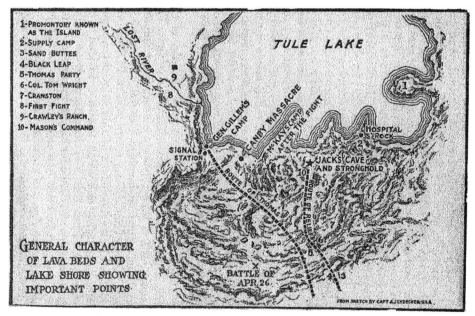

1- PROMONTORY KNOWN AS THE ISLAND
2- SUPPLY CAMP
3- SAND BUTTES
4- BLACK LEAP
5- THOMAS PARTY
6- COL. TOM WRIGHT
7- CRANSTON
8- FIRST FIGHT
9- CRAWLEY'S RANCH.
10- MASON'S COMMAND

TULE LAKE

GENERAL CHARACTER OF LAVA BEDS AND LAKE SHORE SHOWING IMPORTANT POINTS

The Lava Beds. CYRUS T. BRADY. *NORTHWESTERN FIGHTS AND FIGHTERS.*

The Modoc Indians belong generally to the races known as "Digger Indians,"[5] from living largely upon esculent [edible] roots which the squaws dig, dry, and cache for winter subsistence, but they are much superior to the average Digger Indians and are more nearly allied in character and by intermarriage to the Rogue Rivers, a warlike tribe[6] now about extinct, inhabiting at one time the western slope of the Cascade Mountains in Oregon, and with whom portions of the old army under Captains C. C. Augur, A. J. Smith, Benjamin Alvord, and others whom the stars have since fallen upon had frequent warfare, and whose last war chief, Old John, while being transported as a prisoner in a sailing vessel to San Francisco, attempted singly and alone to capture the vessel and crew and came very near succeeding.

The Modocs were treacherous and bloodthirsty. In the "Days of '49" and subsequent years, they proved very troublesome to emigrants, frequently waylaying their trains and sparing neither men, women, nor children. "Bloody Point," a rocky projection on the north shore of Tule Lake, received its baptism from one of these periodic massacres.[7]

Their combative disposition prevented them from living in harmony even in their own tribe, which split into three parts or families, known to the whites as Hot Springs Modocs,[8] located in northern California; Rock Modocs, living in the vicinity of the Lava Beds; and the Lost River Modocs, whose country was principally Oregon. This last was the principal division and contained the chief or governing family, the Schonchins.

A Schonchin was chief of the tribe when the treaty was made with the Klamaths, Modocs, and Yainaskin Snakes, by which these tribes, for the consideration offered by the Indian Bureau, agreed to live upon the Klamath reservation, then just established.[9]

The Indian title to the Lost River and Tule Lake country was thus extinguished, and the land thrown open to settlement. The Klamath reserve proving to have a much colder climate than the Modocs were accustomed to, and the Klamath Indians, their ancient foes,[10] taunting them with living on "their" land, catching "their" fish, and killing "their" game, the Modocs became discontented. The governing chief, Old Schonchin,[11] with a large part of the tribe, got as far away from the Klamaths as he could and lived up to the terms of the treaty, but the restless and desperate spirits of the tribe under the leadership of the Indian afterwards widely known as Captain Jack[12] and John Schonchin, a brother of the hereditary chief, left the reservation and returned to the Tule Lake basin, declaring that they would live in their old home and nowhere else.

It is with this band of desperados that history has to deal when treating of the Modoc War, though subsequent to the breaking out of hostilities, they were joined by the Hot Spring and Rock Modocs. Many of these Indians were what would be called "half civilized." A number of them had been born and raised near the outlying California settlements and had worked for white men on their ranches and cattle ranges. They dressed like the frontier white men, talked some English, and were familiar with the ways of white people, including all their vices. They were well armed with breech loading and other rifles, which by constant practice at game and waterfowl they had learned to handle with skill and precision.

The settlers in the country thrown open to settlement by the treaty soon began to complain of Captain Jack's band of desperados, charging them with killing cattle and abusing the settlers' families when their men were absent. The Indian agent of the Klamath reserve made repeated efforts to induce them to return to the reservation, but every effort was met with contemptuous refusal and the declaration that they would fight rather than leave their present location.

In June 1871 the Indian agent Mr. John Meacham requested the commanding officer at Fort Klamath, Capt. James Jackson, 1st Cavalry, to have Captain Jack arrested by a military force; he had rendered himself liable to criminal action by killing an Indian doctor—shooting him through the head while asleep in his tepee—for failing to cure one of Jack's children of some malignant disease—a facetious way of settling his doctor's bill, but one quite in accordance with Indian custom.[13]

To avoid jeopardizing the lives of settlers by provoking hostilities with Jack's people, who, it was known, would resist his arrest, it was decided to capture him under the aegis of civil law at Yreka, California, whither he generally repaired with his band and their families on the Fourth of July and other festive occasions to pick up money for the purchase of arms and ammunition.

A detachment of cavalry was sent to Yreka to effect the arrest, but Jack, warned by the squaw men[14] who infested that section of country of the movement of the troops, took to the woods and hid in the mountains for some time.

In the fall of 1872 the settlers in southern Oregon procured an order from the Interior Department for the removal of Jack's band to the Klamath reservation, "peaceably if possible, forcibly if necessary." The superintendent of Indian Affairs for Oregon, Mr. [Thomas B.] Odeneal, visited their village and tried to induce them to comply with the orders he had received, but failed in his attempt,[15] and while negotiations were still pending, but with no uncertainty as to the result, turned the matter over to the military authorities, sending his agent, Mr. Ivan Applegate,[16] to Fort Klamath to request the commanding officer there, at that time Major John Green, 1st Cavalry,[17] to send a force to the Modoc Camp to compel their compliance with the orders from the Department of the Interior, and insisting upon it that only a show of force (about twelve or fifteen men mentioned) was necessary to accomplish the object.

Major Green directed Captain Jackson to take all available men of his troop (B, 1st Cavalry) and proceed by forced march to the Modoc camp and induce them to comply with the orders given by Superintendent Odeneal or, failing in this, to arrest the Indians. Captain Jackson, with thirty men, accompanied by Lt. F. A. Boutelle and the post surgeon, Dr. [Henry] McElderry, who had volunteered to go with the command, was soon on the march.[18]

Mr. Ivan Applegate, in the capacity of interpreter, and a few citizens joined the column while en route. Those citizens were detached at the ford on Lost River to take post at Crawley's ranch[19] to protect the family there and prevent an attack on the rear of the troops, the ranch being situated between the two Modoc villages or camps, which were about a half mile apart on opposite sides of Lost River, a deep, sluggish stream with abrupt banks that could be crossed only by boat.

Marching continuously day and night, the troops arrived at the Modoc village about daylight[20] and formed line among the tepees,[21] taking the Indians completely by surprise. Had they been undoubtedly hostile, there would have been no Modoc War. The chiefs and leaders were called for, particularly Captain Jack, but he did not put in an appearance and, so far as is known, took no part in the subsequent fight. Some of the subchiefs gathered around, and the orders of the Indian superintendent were explained by the commander of the troops to such Indians as could understand English and to all of them by Mr. Applegate, who visited both villages to carry out his instructions.

The time given to parleying was used by the Indians to recover from their surprise and get ready for the resistance which they had previously determined upon. While some talked to gain time, the boldest spirits disappeared in their tepees and soon came out painted, stripped to the buff, and carrying from one to three rifles. The interpreter, after using every effort to persuade the tribe of the folly of resisting United States authority, gave it up and, convinced that no compliance with the orders of the Indian superintendent could be obtained, so informed Captain Jackson.

Battle of Lost River. CYRUS T. BRADY. *NORTHWESTERN FIGHTS AND FIGHTERS.*

It was then determined to carry out the second part of the instructions before alluded to and arrest the leaders. A squad of the best known warriors having taken position near some tepees about thirty yards in front of the line of dismounted cavalrymen—seventeen men in skirmish order—Lieutenant Boutelle was directed to advance some men from the left and secure these Indians. At the order to move forward, all of the Indians aimed their rifles at the line, and one of them fired, apparently at Lieutenant Boutelle. The troops instantly returned the fire, pouring volley after volley in and through the tepees, behind which the Indians had taken cover and from which they were rapidly firing at the soldiers.

This firing beginning to weaken the line, a charge was ordered which drove the Indians from cover of the tepees into the surrounding brush and left in the village only a few squaws bemoaning their dead and wounded. The Indians continued the fire from distant cover, a line of pickets was thrown around the captured camp in such shelter as could be found or improvised, while the wounded were being cared for by the surgeon and then transported across the river by canoe to Crawley's ranch.[22] This done, an advance was ordered, when the owner of the ranch came galloping up on the other side of the river, imploring assistance to protect his family and the wounded men at his house from a threatened attack on that side of the river, the citizens stationed there having left to notify the settlements of the breaking out of hostilities. He was told to hold the place at all hazards, and the troop, carrying its dead, moved quickly up the river to the ford, Lieutenant Boutelle with a small skirmish line protecting the rear and keeping the Indians at a respectful distance. The command arrived at the ranch in time to prevent any catastrophe there.

The Indians lingered around until sundown, burned a few haystacks, and then retired to the "rock fort," which they had told the settlers was to be their refuge and stronghold. What this rock fort was, no one knew, further than that it was a place in the Lava Beds which Jack had boasted he could hold against any number of white men and where he had cached the possessions of the tribe and a sufficiency of dried roots and jerked beef to last his people a year. Thus commenced the Modoc War.

The Indians, in retreating to their stronghold, had murdered a number of citizens and threatened to raid the settlements.[23]

More troops were dispatched to the scene of action, and Lieutenant Colonel Wheaton, the district commander,[24] came from Camp Warner to take command of the forces in the field. The assembling of troops was necessarily tedious; they came from distant posts, and marching was the only means of transportation.[25]

In January [1873], the troops having assembled and being joined by a contingent force of California [and Oregon] volunteers and Klamath Indians,[26] Colonel Wheaton organized an attack on both sides of the Indian position, expecting certainly to crush them out between the two forces.

Captain Bernard, 1st Cavalry,[27] with two cavalry companies and the Klamath Indian allies, was directed to move upon the Modocs from the north, while Colonel Wheaton, with a battalion of the 21st Infantry, two cavalry companies, and the California [and Oregon] volunteers, attacked from the south; the lake on which the Stronghold faced being respectively the right and left of the assaulting lines.[28]

The Lava Beds being impracticable for horses, the cavalry companies were dismounted and operated on foot. As the troops marched into position the day before that appointed for the combined assault, a fog settled down over the whole lake basin so dense that objects a few yards distant could hardly be distinguished.

The troops from the south had comparatively easy traveling until they arrived at the edge of the lava fields, a mile or more from the Stronghold, but Bernard's battalion had ten miles of scrambling over lava before they could reach the point from which the attack was to be made on the following morning, and in getting there ran on the Indian outposts and had a lively skirmish with them, capturing the largest part of their pony herd and demonstrating the unreliability of some of the Indian auxiliaries.[29]

The next morning [January 17] the fog was, if possible, denser than the day before, but the lines formed in skirmish order at daylight and advanced to the attack, expecting soon to meet and greet each other over a victory won. Lines of battle have seldom or never before crossed such a difficult country; every step had to be watched or the men came to grief. Through fissures and chasms, over jagged heights, around masses of vertical rock, across wave crests of inky lava—in file, in bunches, in open order, as best they could make some headway, the troops moved forward until the crack of Indian rifles told that their outposts had been reached. Then, with a cheer, the lines charged—if scrambling over rocks where a misstep would prove as deadly as an Indian bullet can be called charging—and moved rapidly on, seeing nothing of the Indians but the flash of their rifles from behind rocky points, until men were shot down from almost underfoot and the character of the terrain became simply impassable for any military organization.

The troops had run up against the Stronghold, and human feet could go no farther and retain any governable formation. Colonel Wheaton's line had struck the lava wall on the southwest, too long to flank and too abrupt to scale. Bernard, finding he could make no headway in such a country, and unable even to see it, halted at one of the rocky wave crests near the Stronghold. The men, quickly taking such advantageous positions as could be found, sought in vain through the blinding mist to discover the Indian warriors, though the crack of their rifles showed them to be not many yards distant.

Stripped to the buff and of the same color as the rocks, they glided stealthily from cover to cover through the intricate rocky passages and could not be seen. Efforts were made to discover some way to flank the position of the Indians, but the fog and exceedingly difficult nature of the country baffled all efforts.

Hospitals were improvised for the wounded, and the troops waited in the hope that the fog would lift and enable some communication between the two forces to be had, so that acting in concert they could gradually surround the Indians. After some hours the fog did lift a little, and the signal flags on each side of the bay fronting the Stronghold commenced to work, but before a message could be sent or received, the mist settled down thicker and darker than before. Then came a rapid fusillade from the south, answered by volleys from Bernard's line and another effort to penetrate the inaccessible conglomeration of jagged lava in front of the troops.

Major John Green, from Colonel Wheaton's command, endeavoring to get in rear of the Indians, struck the rocky glacis that faced the Stronghold and, following its trend, passed with his command under the guns of the savages in the natural rifle trench along the lakefront, forcing his way over the broken rocks until he joined Bernard's right, resting on the lake, losing heavily in killed and wounded.[30] That his men were not annihilated was due principally to the density of the fog.

The attack from both sides had failed, more on account of natural obstacles than the resistance of the Indians, the two days' rations taken along were exhausted, ammunition was getting short, and the wounded had to be cared for, so it was decided to draw out that night, dispose of the wounded, and with the knowledge of the country obtained by this reconnaissance in force and better weather, renew the attack under more favorable auspices.[31]

On arriving in camp[32] the following morning, Colonel Wheaton received a dispatch from Washington forbidding an attack on the Modoc Indians.[33] It had come too late for those who lost their lives, and it prevented any further effort to force these Indians into submission until a peace commission had duly labored with their untutored minds, wasted their time, and sacrificed their lives to persuade them to become good citizens.

Humanly speaking, there is but little doubt that had the day been clear so that the country could have been observed and taken advantage of, there would have been no need of a peace commission. The Modocs would have been surrounded in their stronghold, and their surrender only a question of days. The order to suspend operations was unexpected and, in the end, unfortunate. Another attack with the additional forces then en route and a tolerably accurate knowledge of the terrain would have closed the campaign and left the Modocs prisoners in the hands of the troops.

Retiring to their camps, and scouting the country to prevent the Indians leaving their chosen places of refuge to raid the settlements, the troops sat down to await the advent and labors of a peace commission composed of General Canby, the department commander, Colonel Gillem,[34] the recently selected commander of the troops in the field, Dr. Thomas,[35] a Methodist divine from San Francisco, Mr. A. B. Meacham,[36] ex-superintendent of Indian Affairs for Oregon, and Mr. Dyar,[37] then agent of the Klamath Indians.[38]

After assembling, the peace commission with considerable difficulty opened negotiations with the Indians and "dragged its slow length along" through the winter, renewing after each failure the futile effort to make terms with or procure the surrender of the Modocs.[39] Officers, agents of the commissioners, and representatives of the press, taking their lives in their hands, visited these savages in their rocky crevices to talk with them, ascertain what terms of peace would be acceptable, and represent the solicitude of the government for their best welfare. The Indians would listen to nothing but a withdrawal of the troops and a return to the ante-war status. Once it seemed that they were about to accept the amnesty and generous terms offered by the commissioners and agreed to come if wagons were sent to a certain point on the lake to haul their families and effects. Wagons were sent, tents pitched for them to live in, first built to keep them warm, and every arrangement made for the comfort of these misguided brethren, but, alas! The weary eyes of the commissioners were strained until dark looking for the dusky forms and saw returning only empty wagons.[40]

General Canby, now weary of this trifling, moved the troops closer to the Indians, stationing Maj. E. C. Mason[41] with a battalion of the 21st Infantry and 1st Cavalry on the north and Col. A. C. Gillem with battalions of the 4th Artillery, 12th Infantry, and 1st Cavalry on the south, about two miles from the Indian stronghold.[42]

The peace commissioners, camped with Colonel Gillem's command, reopened negotiations and unfortunately yielded to the solicitations of the Indians to have the conference, or "peace," tent placed a half mile from the camps of the troops, in a rocky depression not visible from the picket stations. To impress them with the power of the white man's government and the numerical strength of the troops assembled to enforce, if necessary, the requirements of the commissioners, the Indians were invited to come unarmed to Colonel Gillem's camp and did so, frequently trading at the extemporized store for tobacco and other luxuries.

Dr. Thomas, a kindly man and devoted Christian, fed some of them at his own table and made them many presents to evince the good feeling and friendly intentions of the commissioners. He was particularly kind and generous to Boston Charley,[43] subsequently Dr. Thomas's murderer; he heaped favors upon him, but when, after being mortally wounded by this fiendish savage, the doctor pled with him for the remaining hours of his life, the only answer was a shot through the head.

After placing the peace tent, a few unimportant councils were held, always under the agreement that each party should come unarmed. The Modocs, intending treachery and desiring to lull the commissioners into security, put off from time to time the final decision, waiting for spring and a good opportunity to carry out their devilish purpose.

A Modoc squaw—Mrs. Riddle, a white man's wife[44]—who acted as interpreter for the commission, had frequently warned them that while the Modocs talked of accepting terms, she thought they did not mean it and that in her opinion they would eventually commit some act of bad faith; she did not know exactly what. This warning was repeated on the morning of April 13, when the last and decisive council was to take place.[45]

A message was signaled to Major Mason that a council would be held, and it was reported that treachery was intended. The commissioners evidently did not believe it and repaired to the tent in the usual manner, making no arrangement for relief in case of an attack.

About the time for the conference to take place, two Indians with a white flag appeared on a rocky ridge in front of Major Mason's camp and indicated a desire to talk. Major Mason directed the officer of the day, Lieutenant Sherwood, 21st Infantry,[46] to ascertain what was wanted. Sherwood, in starting out, was joined by Lieutenant Boyle,[47] who, having been an Indian agent, was quite familiar with the Chinook jargon spoken by all the Pacific Coast Indians. Passing the pickets, they picked their way slowly through the rough lava towards the Indian with the white flag, who, as they approached, fell back slowly towards the Stronghold. Nearing a chasm in the rocks, the officers halted and evidently refused to be tolled any farther away from camp. After a few moments' conversation with the Indian, the officers faced about to return. As they did so, the Indian fired at Sherwood with a pistol. At this, these officers commenced running toward the pickets, their pace accelerated by the crack of several rifles from Indians concealed in the chasm. Sherwood fell, and Boyle came under the protection of the pickets, who immediately opened fire and drove the Indians to cover.

An officer of the signal station, watching these proceedings and remembering that it was near the hour for General Canby to be in council with the

Indians at the peace tent on the other side of the Stronghold, and knowing that treachery to these officers meant death to him, seized the signal flag and, calling for the operator, directed that a message be sent instantly to Colonel Gillem's camp, that the commissioners might be rescued if possible. The message was sent, the troops were warned, and the companies sprang into line in their streets and awaited orders. Before they were given, firing in front told of the tragedy that had occurred.

The Indians had timed their actions well. The pistol fired at Sherwood was the signal for attack upon the commissioners nearly two miles away, and ere assistance could be sent them from the unprepared camp, resting in the security of Indian faith, General Canby and Dr. Thomas had been killed, Meacham wounded and left for dead, while Agent Dyar, who had failed to comply with the agreement in regard to carrying arms, pointed his hitherto concealed pistol at the Indian detailed to kill him and so astonished his would-be assassin that he missed his mark, and before he could reload, the long legs of the agent had carried him out of danger. Colonel Gillem, on account of sickness, did not attend the council.

The massacre of the commissioners was followed in a short time by an attack upon the Modoc stronghold.[48] The lakefront was captured, cutting off their unlimited supply of water. The troops pushed forward by degrees, covering each advance with rifle pits of rock to prevent an unnecessary loss of life. A mountain-howitzer battery was carried to the crest of the rock formation and, opening upon the rear of the defenses, shelled the Indians from cover and forced the evacuation of the Stronghold. They retreated through a channel or chasm in the rocks and took up a position in the black lava near the volcanic peaks, rather more inaccessible than that from which they had been driven and where the only water to be had for miles was in caves held by the Indians.

Then came the gallant but unfortunate reconnaissance of Captain Thomas of the 4th Artillery[49] to the vicinity of this black lava, which ended so disastrously to the officers and men engaged, and which demonstrated how little chance regular troops, as usually handled and fought, have against these wily warriors with all the advantages of terrain in their favor.[50]

Following this effort to locate the Indians, the cavalry and Warm Springs allies scouted the borders of the lava fields to place them and prevent their escape. On the morning of May 10, the bivouac of the cavalry and Indian allies at Dry Lake,[51] on the northeastern edge of the Lava Beds, was savagely attacked just about daybreak by all the hostile Modocs, a number of whom had crept inside the pickets through crevices in the lava and, posting themselves in the rocks about sixty yards from the bivouac, opened at dawn of day a rapid fire upon the sleeping soldiers. Jumping the men from their blankets, the Indians were charged in front by the cavalry, and the Warm Springs were moved out on the flank to cut off their retreat. The Modocs were quickly driven back from the camp and, seeing the Warm Springs making for their flank, broke into such rapid retreat through the lava that the troops could not keep up with them.[52]

Hasbrouck and Jackson now closed on them from the north and east, Mason from the west, and Perry from the south.[53] Their situation was getting desperate. Quarreling among themselves as to what should be done, they came to blows and, separating on the old lines, crept out of the lava at night—the Hot Spring to the south, the Lost River under Jack to the north, seeking safety in flight to the mountains.[54]

Striking the trail of the Hot Spring Modocs, the cavalry pursued rapidly and brought them to bay in the mountains of northern California and compelled their surrender to Col. Jefferson C. Davis,[55] who had succeeded Canby in command of the department and of the troops in the field.

The party with Captain Jack so thoroughly covered their tracks that it was some time before they could be located. Their hiding place was eventually revealed by some of the bucks who had surrendered to Colonel Davis and who, to save their own necks, agreed to guide the cavalry to Jack's retreat.[56]

They were found in a deep gorge in the mountains north of Clear Lake, driven from it, followed closely, overtaken, surrounded in a rocky canyon near the head of Lost River Valley,[57] and seeing the "game was up," surrendered to Major John Green, commanding the cavalry battalions.[58]

Captain Jack, with two or three bucks, escaped during the night but was trailed to Willow Spring Canyon and captured by Captain Perry's command of the 1st Cavalry.[59] The Modoc War was ended. Colonel Davis intended to hang the leaders immediately and erected gallows for that purpose, but a telegram from Washington caused him to change his mind.[60]

The Modocs, with no one missing but the dead, were taken as prisoners of war to Fort Klamath, Oregon, whence a handful of men had marched just six months before to put them upon their reservation.

The leaders were tried by a military commission; six of the participants in the massacre were condemned to be hung; the sentences of two of these were commuted to imprisonment for life; the remainder of the band was banished to the Indian Territory. Captain Jack made a strong plea to have a cousin of his wife, Scarfaced Charley, hung in his stead, but the white man's justice could not accept the vicarious sacrifice.

On an October morning in 1873,[61] in the presence of the troops who had captured them—the Klamath Indians in their gayest attire and the nonhostile reservation Modocs under Old Schonchin—Captain Jack, John Schonchin, Black Jim, and Boston Charley expiated the killing of the peace commissioners and numerous other crimes.

The Initial Shot of the Modoc War

IVAN D. APPLEGATE[1]

Klamath Falls *Express,* January 10, 1895

Perhaps few places on earth of like area have cost so much in blood and treasure as Klamath land, and yet it may be worth the price, dear as it was, for it is one of nature's brightest gems. The native possessor held it with a tenacity which compels us to admire his patriotism, his reverence for the land of his ancestors, while we deprecate the methods of his warfare. As he would put it: "Here is the dust of my fathers. Better for me to die here than to be removed to any other country. If I die here I go down to dust with my father and my people. If I die in some other land I shall be lost forever."

The Modocs stood as bloody sentinels along the line of the Emigrant Road. As far back as 1852, they began the work of ambush and slaughter, and Modoc land was for a quarter of a century the scene not only of savage treachery and cruelty, but of heroic deeds and tragic incident. Weary immigrants toiling onward toward the setting sun—no record tells how many—were here sacrificed almost on the very threshold of their land of promise.

Later, when the enterprising white man, having seen and appreciated this land of green meadows, silvery lakes, and crystal streams, determined to possess it, brave settlers, representing that hardy race of men and women who have led the hosts of civilization across the continent, planted settlements here; but a band of about 300 renegade Modocs under the leadership of Captain Jack, renouncing the authority of brave Old Schonchin, the rightful chief, inaugurated a reign of terror throughout the lake country.

During the summer of 1872, many petitions were forwarded through the Indian Department, asking the authorities at Washington to order the removal of Captain Jack's band from the vicinity of Tule Lake, their ancient home, to the Klamath reservation, and to keep them there. Orders were finally received by the superintendent of Indian affairs in Oregon, Hon. Thomas B. Odeneal, to secure their removal, peaceably if possible, but by force if necessary.

On his arrival from Salem, Mr. Odeneal, having by messenger called upon the Modocs to return to the reservation without avail, determined to place the matter in the hands of Capt. James Jackson of the United States Army, an offi-

110

Captain Jack. NELSON A. MILES. *PERSONAL RECOLLECTIONS AND OBSERVATIONS.*

cer of well-known discretion and courage. At noon on November 28, 1872, Captain Jackson, with thirty-five men of Company B, 1st U.S. Cavalry, left Fort Klamath and arrived at the pioneer town of Linkville at a little after dark. Here he met Superintendent Odeneal and received instructions as follows:

> When you arrive at the camp of the Modocs, request an interview with the head men and say to them that you did not come to fight or to harm them, but to have them go peaceably to Camp Yainax on Klamath reservation, where ample provision has been made for their comfort and subsistence, and where, by treaty, they agreed to live. Talk kindly but firmly to them, and whatever else you may do, I desire to urge that if there is any fighting, let the Indians be the aggressors. Fire no gun except in self-defense, after they have first fired upon you. I. D. Applegate will accompany you as my representative; will also act as guide and interpreter.

During that dark, rainy night, we made our way from Linkville down the Klamath Valley toward the stone bridge on Lost River, where Captain Jack was encamped on the west side of the river. About a third of his forces, under Hooker Jim and Curly Headed Doctor and some other of his trusty lieutenants, were encamped on the east side of the river near the Dennis Crawley cabin.

We found it very difficult in the darkness to make our way through the heavy sagebrush, for we had to leave the road in order to avoid being discovered by the wily Indians, who doubtless were observing as closely as possible every movement. We followed along the foot of the chain of hills west from Lost River, and at daylight we were about one mile west of the Modoc camp, which was at that point on the riverbank where Dan Colwell's residence now stands.

The company was formed into two platoons, and we rode directly through the village and halted upon the riverbank, facing the encampment. As we came near the river, Scarfaced Charley, who had crossed just before we came up, fired at us from the other side of the river, shouting at the same time to arouse the sleeping Indians. In a moment, there was great excitement and commotion. As soon as the men were dismounted and advanced in line, standing at order arms in front of the horses, I was directed to enter the camp to see Captain Jack and inform him of our friendly mission and assure him that no harm was intended, but that he would be required to remove with his people to the reservation. Going from camp to camp, I was not able to find Captain Jack.

As I came out of one of the huts, I saw Scarfaced coming up the riverbank. As he passed Captain Jackson, who was still mounted, the captain ordered him to halt, at the same time drawing his revolver. To this Scarfaced paid no attention, but came on into the village, all the time haranguing his people and demanding that they fight to the death; telling them that if they would be quick enough, they could kill every soldier without the loss of a man. With an oath, he rushed past me and went into Bogus Charley's tent, and in a moment both Scarfaced and Bogus appeared with their guns drawn and called to the women and children to throw themselves flat on the ground. Then I knew they were going to fire upon us. I immediately started toward our men, saying, "[Captain], they are going to fire!"

At this, the captain ordered Lieutenant Boutelle, who stood in advance of the line, to take four men and arrest the two Indians who had guns in their hands. As Boutelle stepped forward with the four men, the two Indians fired. The warriors in the camps and in the heavy sagebrush in the rear of the village fired almost simultaneously. Then all was din and commotion; men were falling in the line, the riderless horses were dashing here and there. The attack was so sudden and desperate, the Modocs rushing onto us with demonlike yells, that the men were forced back a step or two, and it seemed for a moment that the thinned line would yield and break. But immediately came the order "Forward!" and it was like an inspiration. The men sprang forward, under the leadership of the brave Boutelle, delivering a deadly fire, and the Indians were forced back.

Scarfaced's first shot struck Boutelle's revolver, disabling it, and cutting through the sleeve of his blouse, passed through the clothing on his right shoulder. Scarfaced was knocked down by a bullet which cut through the handkerchief he had tied around his head, and Watchman, Captain Jack's most daring lieutenant, fell, riddled with bullets, almost at our feet. Boutelle's calmness saved us. Speaking to the men coolly and confidently, he led the charge into and through the village, driving the Indians out, advancing his skirmish line far beyond into the heavy sagebrush.

O. C. Applegate, who was to take charge of Captain Jack's band in case they came onto the reservation, rode from his station at Yainax on November 28th, reaching Linkville (Klamath Falls) late in the evening. Superintendent

Odeneal informed him of the movement on foot and requested him to be present to assist in securing, if possible, a peaceable removal of the Modocs. With the Klamath scout, Dave Hill, and five trusty citizens, he forded Lost River near the Lone Pine that night and reached the Crawley cabin, near Hooker Jim's camp, about daylight on the morning of the twenty-ninth, finding there Messenger Brown of the Indian Department, Dennis Crawley, Dan Colwell, and a few other citizens. When daylight revealed the presence of the cavalry in Captain Jack's camp, Hooker's men made a rush for their canoes, evidently to reinforce Captain Jack, but were prevented by the citizens. The object of the authorities was explained to the Indians, and a few of them were in the act of giving up their arms when the firing began at Captain Jack's camp.

Instantly the Modocs fired on the citizens, and a fierce fight at close range took place, so that, looking across the river during the fight with Captain Jack, we could see another battle going on almost opposite to us. Two citizens, Jack Thurber and William Nus, were killed, and Joe Penning was maimed for life, and the Indians, securing their own horses, which were near at hand, escaped to the long, rocky ridge east of where the Frank Adams farm is now located, while the citizens rallied at the Crawley cabin.

Captain Jack, with most of his best and most desperate men, had made good his escape, though at the time, both he and Scarfaced were reported among the killed, even by the prisoners. We had lost Sergeant Harris, killed, and as nearly as I can remember, six men were mortally wounded, and several others painfully though not dangerously hurt. Among the Indians killed were Watchman and We-sing-ko-pos, leading warriors; Black Jim, Long Jim, and Miller's Charley were among the wounded. The loss on our side amounted to fully a third of the military force then in the field and was quite sufficient to disable Captain Jackson's small force for the time being.

After the fight, Captain Jackson sent his wounded across the river in a canoe, Dave Hill being the oarsman; Surgeon McElderry and a few more as a guard were also taken over, and the men were conveyed to the Crawley cabin. The remaining troopers mounted their jaded horses and, as there was no ford in the vicinity, hastily rode up toward the Stukel Ford seven miles distant. Before arriving at the ford, word reached them that Jack and his infuriated men had renewed the fight. Looking toward Tule Lake, great volumes of smoke could be seen arising from burning buildings. Dashing through the rapid ford, the poor horses seemed to realize the awful situation as they put forth renewed effort down the river with utmost speed on the east side, and soon the cavalry rode onto the ground where the citizens and Hooker's men had so lately fought, but the wily savage was already wreaking vengeance on the inoffensive settlers beyond the ridge on the plains at the head of Tule Lake.

The butchering and devastation on Tule Lake had already begun, and eighteen settlers were added that day to the long list of Modoc victims.

On that fateful day, a few miles below the scene of the fight, a mule team was seen coming toward the Boddy residence, but no driver held the reins.

Mrs. Boddy secured, unhitched, and stabled the team. Very uneasy, she called to her married daughter, Mrs. Schira, and hastily the two women started toward the woods where the men had gone that morning to their accustomed work. They had not gone far when they saw the Indians not far away and heard the awful war whoop. Soon they came upon the stripped and mutilated body of Mr. Schira, and soon after those of Mr. Boddy and his older son.

The younger boy, who had been on the plain below herding sheep, could not be seen, and the sheep were wandering at will among the sage. The heroic but horror-stricken women knew that all were killed; that nothing remained for them but to seek their own safety in flight, to hide themselves among the juniper and mahogany in the almost trackless and, to them, unknown woods. Struggling onward, they knew not whither, only that they felt that they were going away from a sad and awful scene, soon night settled upon them among the mountain solitudes. As they shivered amid the snow and strove to look down through tears of burning anguish toward the mutilated forms of dear ones and upon desolated homes, what tongue could tell, what pen depict the poignancy of their grief?

The Modoc War

MAURICE FITZGERALD[1]

Americana 21, no. 4 (October 1927): 498–521[2]

The stubborn and spectacular fight waged against overwhelming odds by Captain Jack and his band of Modocs to retain possession of the ancient hunting ground of their tribe stands distinct in the annals of Indian warfare, if not without parallel. In every other instance where the aborigines achieved temporary successes over white troops, the former invariably had the superiority of numbers. But a mere handful of Modocs, not to exceed one hundred, capable of bearing arms and with inferior weapons, held in check and on more than one occasion actually defeated greater numbers of regular soldiers of the United States Army, sometimes reinforced and assisted by Oregon volunteers, and maintained their ground against such odds for more than six months. It was a remarkable achievement, even though they possessed a great advantage in the nature and character of the ground occupied—the famous Lava Beds.

In the latter part of November 1872, Maj. John Green, commanding officer at Fort Klamath, Oregon, received orders from the Honorable Thomas B. Odeneal, commissioner of Indian affairs for Oregon, to round up the Indians known as Captain Jack's band of Modocs, then inhabiting the Tule Lake region, and have them removed to a place selected for them on the Klamath reservation, where they must remain in the future. Major Green ordered Capt. James Jackson of Troop B, 1st Cavalry, to take his troops and compel compliance of the order by the Indians, even to the extent of using force.

Captain Jackson and Lieutenant F. A. Boutelle, with about forty troopers, set out from Fort Klamath and rode through a pelting rain down to a point on Lost River not far from where it empties into Tule Lake. Reaching there just before daylight on November 29, they found the Indians encamped on both sides of the river, the larger number on the west side under Captain Jack, while Hooker Jim had a band of some fifteen to twenty on the east side. They were aware that the government meant to remove them from the lake, but not expecting such quick action, were completely surprised at dawn to find the soldiers lined up in front of their tepees.

The purpose was immediately made known to them by Ivan Applegate, representative of the commissioner of Indian affairs for Oregon, but the Indians were sullen and disinclined to obey. One of their chiefs, Scarfaced Charley, swore, with a rifle in his hands, that they would never go on a reservation. Captain Jackson then ordered Lieutenant Boutelle to have him disarmed.

As quick as a move was made for that purpose, the Indians began firing from their lodges, whereupon the troopers returned the fire, and a sharp skirmish ensued. The Modocs were compelled to leave their dwellings, and from positions in the heavy growth of sagebrush close by, they kept up an intermittent fire for some time, gradually moving away towards Tule Lake, where they embarked in canoes for the Lava Beds.

Captain Jackson's losses were too great to permit of pursuit. Fully one-third of his command was killed or wounded in the short encounter; so he returned with his wounded to Fort Klamath and reported what had happened.[3] Because less exposed, the Indians also suffered some losses in the fray, although not as great as the white troops.

Arriving at Fort Klamath with news of the disastrous ending of the expedition, a messenger was dispatched across the mountains to the nearest telegraph station, Ashland, Oregon, one hundred miles away, to notify General Canby by wire of what had transpired. The news was flashed all over the country that the Modocs were on the warpath.

About this time, a number of settlers, mostly small stockmen, had established themselves upon the north and east margins of Tule Lake. Some of these had fairly good homes and other improvements, while others were living in shacks. The primary reason for requiring the Modocs to be removed and placed on a reservation was to obviate causes of friction between them and the incoming settlers, sure to arise were the Indians allowed to continue roaming at large.

At the time of the skirmish with Captain Jack's band on the west side of Lost River, Hooker Jim's band on the east side had a small encounter with some citizens who had come down from Linkville to see if the Indians would obey the orders for their removal and, if not, to render any assistance within their power to Captain Jackson. The Indians, from all accounts, had a slight advantage in the scrimmage and compelled the citizens to retire.

Hooker Jim and his bloodthirsty band then started to raid the Lake Tule settlement. The settlers, in complete ignorance of the serious happenings on Lost River, had no reason to anticipate any trouble and were taken by surprise. Hooker and his red devils butchered every isolated settler that could be found, sparing neither age nor sex.[4] They burned the dwellings, slaughtered the livestock, and in every way upheld the traditional cruelty of their race when engaged in warfare.

When their bloody purpose had been accomplished with brand and rifle, and desolation reigned where only the day before had been a prosperous and happy settlement, the Indians betook themselves to the fastnesses of the extensive Lava Beds contiguous to the southern shore of Tule Lake. There they joined with Captain Jack and established their headquarters in the famous Stronghold, where for months they defied the military arm of the government to bring them to submission. While these events were transpiring around Tule Lake, the writer was a private in Troop K, 1st U.S. Cavalry then stationed at Camp Halleck, Nevada. With a dozen or more young fellows from the eastern states, he had but lately joined as a recruit; in fact, only three months before, he landed in New York from the shores of a little island on the other side of the Atlantic famous in story and song.

The new arrivals were not attracted by the prospect of spending any great portion of their military terms in the dull routine duties of a frontier post. When enlisting, they had been told of many opportunities for active service "out west," which appealed to them. They longed for adventure and excitement and fervently wished that some *casus belli* might speedily arise to give them an opportunity to show of what kind of stuff they were made.

In those years the western Indians were becoming more and more alarmed at the encroachments of the whites. The ever-increasing stream of land seekers forewarned them that the end of their long dominion was approaching. Unless something (they knew not what) intervened, their hunting grounds would soon be overrun by palefaces and their sequestered valleys and grassy meads disturbed. These conditions and this spirit were manifest throughout the West; recourse to arms was the only alternative open to them to avert the impending peril.

When the news came that the Modocs were murdering settlers and destroying property in southern Oregon and northern California, and it was whispered around that unless the uprising was speedily suppressed, very likely Troop K would be called upon to go to the front, a majority of the men hoped that the trouble might not end until their troop could have a hand in bringing it to a successful termination. Such is the thoughtless way in which young and immature minds view matters of the most serious import; with them, consequences count for nothing.

For six long weeks or thereabouts, no order came. Occasionally we received scraps of news that things were not progressing favorably and that great difficulty was being experienced in bringing on troops and supplies. Transportation facilities in that region were then of the most primitive kind. Two companies of volunteers were being organized in Oregon—one by Capt. Harrison Kelley in Jacksonville, the other by Capt. O. C. Applegate[5] in Linkville and vicinity—to aid in punishing the Indians, but it took quite a while to equip them and get them to the front.

One cold morning in January 1873,[6] the long-anticipated hour at last arrived, and Troop K received the order to proceed to the scene of hostilities. Eagerly and hurriedly, everything was made ready; the second day after receiving the summons, the troops entrained at Halleck Station on the Central Pacific for Reno, about 250 miles distant.

Here we detrained and, mounting our horses, set out for Fort Bidwell, Surprise Valley, California, 150 miles north. Traveling through Nevada in midwinter is anything but a picnic, particularly when one must camp out in all kinds of weather with very light covering and subsist on the meager allowance of food issued to a U.S. soldier on the march. So the enthusiasm felt at starting out soon vanished, and the journey resolved itself into a very prosaic affair.

Arriving at Fort Bidwell about the last of the month, we learned from some wounded soldiers invalided home from the Lava Beds to barracks that a desperate fight had taken place near the Stronghold on the seventeenth. Colonel Wheaton, commanding some 300 regulars, reinforced by two companies of Oregon volunteers under Captains Kelley and Applegate, entered the Lava Beds at daylight and continued till nightfall; but though the soldiers had a great superiority in numbers, all their efforts to dislodge the Indians were unavailing.

As the shadows of night descended upon the jaded combatants, the retreat was sounded, and the chagrined and hungry troopers straggled back through the rocks to their camp, leaving the victorious Modocs in possession of the field. Many men were killed and wounded in this encounter; even Captain Perry, second in command, received a severe wound in his arm and side.[7]

After so futile an effort to subdue the Indians, even with a considerable force, it was determined to await the arrival of reinforcements before undertaking any further aggressive movement. Our commander, Maj. James Biddle,[8] saw the necessity of hurrying our movement to the front. So, leaving Fort Bidwell, we traveled as fast as possible through snow and ice, and after six days arrived at the southeast corner of Tule Lake and almost on the edge of the Lava Beds.[9] Our camping place was known as the Louis Land ranch, but the owner had fled from the wrath of the redskins to some safer locality.

The problem of obtaining fodder for our horses and pack mules was now becoming serious; no hay could be had, and what little grass there might be was snowed under. In view of this condition, we were directed to proceed to what was known as the Applegate ranch[10] on Clear Lake, about eight miles east of Tule Lake. There we were able to get hay and grain, and as the weather was very severe, we remained ten days.

At the end of that time, we were ordered by Col. Alvan C. Gillem of the 1st Cavalry to proceed forthwith to the temporary headquarters of the command, which had been established at Van Bremer's ranch, a few miles west of the Lava Beds. A guide was furnished to conduct us by a little-used Indian trail which passed through the lava rocks about five miles south of the Stronghold.[11] Strict injunctions were given not to fire upon or molest any Indians that we might encounter on the journey, unless they took the aggressive.

Since the beginning of hostilities, an influential element in the eastern states had become active in an endeavor to have a radical change made in the methods heretofore followed by the government in its dealing with the "wards of the nation," especially in adjusting disputes. It was alleged that the military authorities were too prone to resort to force, even in matters of trivial import; that methods up to that time had been cruel and inhuman, contrary to the dictates of humanity and the teachings of Christianity; and that it would be possible, in most cases, to prevent disturbances by kindness and conciliation rather than by "big stick" tactics.

Never was this influence stronger, or more in the nature of an intrigue, than during the second administration of President Grant. When it was learned that the Modocs were fighting to retain possession of their ancient heritage against the alleged encroachments of a turbulent and lawless class of whites, great pressure was brought to bear upon the president to call a halt to the military preparations for the punishment of the Indians.

He finally agreed to the appointment of a peace commission to go upon the ground, examine into and report upon all the facts relevant to the matter at issue. Until such commission had had time to investigate and report, military operations were to be at a standstill.

The personnel of the commission was Brig. Gen. E. R. S. Canby, commanding the Department of the Columbia, A. B. Meacham, ex-commissioner of Indian affairs for Oregon, and Reverend Eleazar Thomas of California. Though its purpose was well intentioned and praiseworthy, the commission was destined for a deplorable ending, as will subsequently appear.

Our journey from Clear Lake to Van Bremer's ranch was made partly over a trail that I venture to say had never been traveled before by United States soldiers, and probably not since. We crossed the famous Lava Beds, which cover an area of probably about ten by twelve miles, along a dim path, invisible to ordinary eyes, winding through endless defiles, or narrow passages, between immense quantities of basaltic rock, scattered in great confusion over the extensive area. As we passed by Sugar Loaf Peak,[12] one of the few distinctive features of the lava bed region, we caught sight of two Indians nearby, but they quickly scampered out of sight as soon as they observed us.

It was difficult to restrain some of the boys from pursuing them, but our orders not to fire or attack unless fired upon were imperative. We next came upon a considerable number of mountain sheep, and it was really wonderful to see how these peculiar animals ran with the greatest fleetness over the tract of crags and rocks, across yawning chasms and piles of boulders.

After spending almost an entire day in crossing this unique and freakish expanse of broken and jagged rock, interspersed here and there with scoria, we at length emerged upon a reasonably good tract and reached our destination about sundown.[13]

We found a considerable number of troops at Van Bremer's under the command of Colonel Gillem. General Canby was also there but had not assumed active command. Two days after our arrival, a reconnoitering expedition of three troops, of which ours was one, was organized to proceed to the vicinity of the Lava Beds and observe, if possible, what the Indians were doing.[14] Both General Canby and Colonel Gillem went along.

Col. Alvan C. Gillem. ILLUSTRATED LONDON NEWS, 1873.

Proceeding easterly, skirting for some miles the southern margin of Lower Klamath Lake and then ascending a stretch of tableland, we found ourselves upon the top of a bluff, or volcanic escarpment, some five hundred feet above the surface of Tule Lake and the adjoining Lava Beds, at the southeast corner of the lake[15] and about two and one half miles from Captain Jack's Stronghold.

We halted on the edge of the bluff and dismounted. From that vantage point, the eye could range over the placid expanse of Tule Lake, stretching away many miles northward and eastward, while to the east and south lay the seemingly level expanse of the Lava Beds, the western edge of which began almost at the foot of the bluff on which we were halted.

While leisurely gazing over the imposing landscape, we suddenly heard a shout from the rocks near the foot of the bluff and then observed an Indian waving his cap and yelling that he wanted to talk with the "hyas tyee [chiefs]." General Canby and Colonel Gillem consulted for a time over the advisability of complying with the request and finally agreed that by taking their six-shooters along and being within range of the carbines of the soldiers, the risk was negligible.[16]

By this time the Modocs had become aware that a commission had been appointed to investigate their grievances and that in the meantime the soldiers were not to molest them. The officers went down afoot to the spot where the Indian was awaiting them, had a friendly handshake with the Modoc spokesman, and "powwowed" with him for about twenty minutes.[17]

Meanwhile, those in the dismounted command on the top of the bluff were interested spectators of this peculiar conference but could only conjecture as to what was being said. After bidding the Indian goodbye, the officers climbed the hill in safety, and we then retraced our steps to Van Bremer's.

During the short time we were there, the U.S. Army paymaster visited the camp and paid the men their bimonthly wages. Several hundred soldiers, at least two hundred civilians—teamsters, packers, scouts, stockmen, and settlers, and even a few squaw men were there. It was a motley crowd, and all had money.

A saturnalia of gambling naturally followed. It would have done the heart of a forty-niner good to behold the layouts for the accommodation of those sportingly inclined and brought back to his mind "the days of old and the days of gold." Monte seemed to be the favorite game, while chuck-a-luck, Honest John, and twenty-one had their votaries.

The games were dealt under the canopy of heaven upon blankets spread upon the bosom of Mother Earth. No limit was placed upon the amount you chose to hazard, provided you didn't exceed your bankroll; "your money and your conscience" was the motto. With supreme recklessness, soldier and civilian alike risked his last dollar upon the turn of a card. By the end of the second day, the bulk of the money had gone into the hands of a few men, and the gambling fever subsided for the time being.

The peace commissioners being anxious to make progress with the important task assigned them by the president, it was decided to break camp at Van Bremer's and move the command of Colonel Gillem closer to the Stronghold. This was presumably to impress the Indians, should they be obdurate in their demands, that they might expect to be summarily dealt with by the armed forces of Uncle Sam. About the last of March we moved to a point selected at the southwest corner of Tule Lake, and by the foot of the bluff where General Canby and Colonel Gillem held the powwow with the representative of Captain Jack a few days before.[18] At the same time, another camp, of which Major Mason was the commander, with between three and four hundred soldiers, was established near the southeast corner of the lake and about three miles on the other side of the Stronghold.[19]

Every few days an Indian emissary would come in from Captain Jack to talk with the peace commissioners regarding the time and place for holding the council. Even Captain Jack once approached within a half a mile of the camp and had a talk with General Canby and Mr. Meacham. It was finally mutually agreed that a council tent should be pitched at a point half a mile east of our camp and nearby the trail leading to the Stronghold. April 11 was the date set for the big powwow, and it was agreed that not more than five were to represent either side at the conference.[20] All those participating were to come unarmed. On the evening of the tenth, all arrangements were completed for the fateful meeting on the morrow.

Boston Charley, one of the Indian leaders, came into camp that evening for the purpose of conducting General Canby and his colleagues to the rendezvous in the morning. I recollect him well; his appearance and actions made quite an impression upon me at the time, for I scrutinized him closely, and that impression has never been effaced. He was a stocky little Indian of the California

Boston Charley. NATIONAL ARCHIVES.

"Digger" type, not much over five feet in height; his dress was that worn by the ordinary civilian of the working class—brown coat, calico shirt, dark pants and cap, all a little the worse for wear. The expression on his face showed a dogged determination, and his eye was of the keenest, but his glance was rather sly and furtive. His appearance did not in the least resemble the redskin warriors of popular fiction, or the Plains Indian of a later day. He spoke English fairly well, went through the camp and among the soldiers with the utmost nonchalance, talked freely about the trouble between his people and the government, and expressed the opinion there would be no more fighting.

A few months later this same Charley mounted the scaffold at Fort Klamath with firm step and seemingly the most stoical indifference; his only request was for a "chaw" of tobacco—in expiation of his treacherous conduct on this occasion—such was the judgment of the military court. But can it be said impartially that the sentence was a just one, or that it was right to condemn him according to our standards? However, he died like a brave man and upheld the traditions of his race.

On the morning of the eleventh, all were astir bright and early. Our camp was situated at the base of the bluff already mentioned, and about halfway up the bluff, a signal station from which messages were exchanged with Major Mason's command on the other side of the Stronghold had been established. After breakfast all the men of the camp, except those engaged in special duties, gathered in the vicinity of the signal station, a point of vantage from which all the preliminary movements of those about to participate in the peace conference could be seen.

From that point, and in the clear atmosphere prevailing in that region, the council tent seemed not more than a quarter of a mile distant, although actually a little more than half a mile. The day was ideal; the April sun shone brightly from a cloudless sky. Not a ripple disturbed the surface of the lake, and the air was redolent with the perfume of myriads of delicate wildflowers that grow in the springtime among the rocks and boulders of that semiarid region.

About 8:00 A.M. or 9:00 A.M. we saw General Canby, Mr. Meacham, and Rev. Thomas leave headquarters and, accompanied by Boston Charley, set out on foot (Meacham was mounted) towards the council tent. Shortly afterwards, Mr. L. S. Dyar, Indian agent of the Klamath reservation, who had recently been appointed a member of the peace commission, started out afoot[21] for the same destination, accompanied by Riddle the interpreter and his squaw, Toby, the latter mounted on a pony. All members of the party arrived about the same time upon the level piece of ground where the council tent was pitched. They stood and talked a little while, evidently awaiting the arrival of the Modoc contingent, which they soon saw approaching around the head of the lake. In a few moments we also caught sight of Captain Jack and his fellows advancing towards the group of white men. When they met, there was a general handshake, and from the manner and movements of all concerned, we surmised that the greetings were cordial.

After a brief time spent in this manner, all moved towards the council tent, which to us they seemed to enter; but they actually stopped on the east side of the tent. Then all sat down upon some large stones that had been placed there by the Indians and began their deliberations. We observers on the bluff expressed our opinions as to what the result of the conference would be. Some thought an amicable arrangement would be reached by a compromise, whereby a part of the Tule Lake country would be given to Captain Jack as a reservation for his people. This would have obviated the necessity of placing them on the Klamath reservation, to which they had a great repugnance. Others reasoned that as the Tule Lake country was already well settled by whites, the government, after allowing them to take up the land, could not now consistently eject them, but no one considered it possible that the peace conference would end in bloodshed.

As we sat there whiling away the time for probably an hour or so, awaiting the conference to disperse, suddenly the sergeant in charge of the signal station shouted, "They're firing on the peace tent." Just as he spoke, we saw the white men run from behind the tent and scatter in different directions; at the same time, puffs of smoke arose from near the tent, followed by the rapid report of several shots. Instantly every man sprang to his feet and darted down the hillside to the line of tents below, where our arms were stacked.

We knew then that the proverbial treachery of the Indian was again exemplified. Each man grabbed his gun and started at top speed towards the council tent; but before we had gone many steps, the command "fall in" rang out clear and strong, and the military instinct of obedience prevailed over our individual or human impulses. We quickly formed in line and were given the command "Forward, march; double time, march," and started off at a good stiff gait.

It didn't take long to reach the peace tent. On the way, we met long-legged Dyar running towards camp, almost out of breath and greatly excited; a short distance behind him came Toby, the squaw. Both had been shot at by the Modocs several times as they ran and dodged but had escaped without a scratch.[22] Luckily for them, the Indians had larger game to absorb their attention. Riddle, the interpreter, had taken a different route to reach headquarters.

When we reached the tent, a gruesome sight was presented to our view. About twenty feet to the south lay General Canby on his back; his body was pierced by three bullets,[23] and all of his clothing had been removed by the Indians. A little farther off to the south and west lay the dead body of Reverend Thomas, also stark naked, and a short distance from the tent on the north and west, we found Mr. Meacham, lying on his side and stripped of all his clothing save a pair of red flannel drawers.

He had been partly scalped; in their hurry, they left the job incomplete. Dr. Cabaniss, a physician of Yreka, California, who accompanied the troops,[24] found by examination that life was not extinct, so he poured a little whiskey from his flask down the throat of Mr. Meacham, who soon began to show signs of returning consciousness. His wounds did not prove fatal; by careful nursing and medical skill, he soon regained his former strength and vigor, and enjoyed life for several years thereafter at his famous homestead in the Blue Mountains of Oregon. Meacham was an ardent prohibitionist, and during his long life never indulged in alcoholic beverages. It is said that when afterwards informed of it, he greatly resented the action of Dr. Cabaniss in using whiskey to resuscitate him!

General Canby, a man of unblemished character with an excellent record in the Civil War, was sixty-eight years old.[25] He was of a most kindly disposition and unassuming character, and enjoyed in a marked degree the esteem and respect of those who served under him. Of the unfortunate divine who perished with General Canby in the praiseworthy effort to stop bloodshed and harmonize difficulties, I know nothing but presume he must have been worthy of selection by President Grant as a member of so important a commission.

All who gazed upon that scene of perfidious and cowardly murder, where the folly of confiding in the promises of the wily and ferocious Indian was again demonstrated, were inflamed by a desire for speedy vengeance. The first impulse of the hotheaded young men was to press forward towards the Stronghold and inflict summary punishment upon the whole brood of accursed redskins. But fortunately wiser counsels prevailed. Had we then, in our unpreparedness, advanced into the Lava Beds, there would have been few if any left to tell the tale of the disastrous adventure. At the command of our superior officers, we slowly and reluctantly retraced our steps to camp.

Almost at the same instant that the firing on the council tent was announced, a signal message from Major Mason's command was received to the effect that some Modocs had approached within a short distance of the camp and, raising a white flag, asked that the big tyees come out for a powwow. Major Mason thereupon delegated Lieutenants W. H. Boyle and Walter Sherwood to go and see what was wanted.

When the two had got within a short distance of the Modoc contingent, the latter opened fire upon them, killing Lieutenant Sherwood but missing Lieutenant Boyle, who ran back to camp uninjured. If further proof were needed that the Indians deliberately planned the killing of the peace commissioners, this incident furnished it. In their illogical minds, the idea found lodgment that if the commanders were killed, the soldiers would go home and leave the Indians in possession of their hunting grounds. They soon learned that their treacherous conduct had the opposite effect.

Preparations were now begun for a purpose which everyone knew, though little or nothing was said about it; the Indians had to be punished, and no time was to be lost. The temporizing and peace-talking policy had a sanguinary, sudden ending and was discredited. Militarism was again in the ascendant, and the strong arm of Uncle Sam was invoked for the purpose of inflicting upon those savages such chastisement for their misdeeds as would not be forgotten in a generation.

The signal corps was kept busy sending and receiving messages between our camp and that of Major Mason. A concerted attack was to be made upon the Indians by the troops of both camps, so that danger of failure would be reduced to a minimum. By the evening of the fourteenth, three days after the murder of General Canby, everything was in readiness for starting the punitive expedition.

Soon after midnight the troops in our camp moved silently out; we had somewhat over 300 men, two-thirds cavalry, but dismounted on this occasion, for the nature of the ground would not admit of movements on horseback.[26] Major Mason, with about the same number,[27] moved at the same time with the purpose of cooperating with us. We advanced in single file, each with carbine and sixty rounds of ammunition; in his haversack each carried fifteen hardtack and a small piece of bacon to sustain the inner man while the fight might last.

It was a beautiful and balmy night; not a breath of air was stirring, nor could the slightest sound to break the prevailing stillness be heard from any direction. Everything was so ominously silent as to seem really uncanny. There was no moonlight, but a star-bespangled sky afforded enough light to enable us to pick our footsteps over the jagged rocks without stumbling. We were cautioned not to make the slightest noise, lest the Indians become aware of our movement and thus very likely prevent our forming a junction with the forces of Major Mason.

At this time, we were under the command of Maj. John Green, a capable and efficient officer. Moving noiselessly along the southern margin of the lake, past the spot where the tragedy of the peace tent was enacted, every breast was filled with a desire to avenge the treachery. Our progress was unavoidably slow, but everything went well until just after we had passed the corner of the lake at the southwest angle of the triangular shaped lava peninsula that jutted for more than a mile into Tule Lake. Upon that peninsula, near its apex, the Stronghold was situated.[28]

The intention was for both forces to approach from opposite directions and form a junction somewhere near the center of the base of the triangle, then close in on the Stronghold, compelling the Modocs to surrender or be driven into the lake. Something unexpected quite upset this well-laid plan. The infantry contingent of our force was in the lead, groping its way over heaps of broken rock and around cavernous pits that impeded its progress, when one of the men stumbled and accidentally discharged his gun.[29]

The sudden report of the rifle caused every man to halt in his tracks and hold his breath; but before the sound died away, another more ominous, and seemingly not a hundred yards away, broke upon our ears. It was the warning cry of an Indian picket, "wow-ow-ow," made by rapidly tapping the half-opened mouth with the palm of the hand and emitting a "wow" sound at the same time.

We were in the midst of a vast stretch of lava beds, extending for miles on every side but one, and on that the waters of the lake; in the darkness of the night, without accurate knowledge of our location, and in close proximity of our lurking foe, who was familiar with every boulder and crevice. Is it any wonder that when we heard that weird and awesome signal, making known our location to his bloodthirsty fellows, for the moment our hats seemed lifted by some unusual action, the blood left our cheeks, and great beads of perspiration stood out upon our foreheads?

While in dreadful expectancy, and much quicker than I can tell it, there burst forth from every crag, fissure, and cavern that same blood-curdling war signal, as if the rocky peninsula were alive with ten thousand fiendish redskins ready to bear down upon and annihilate us. The mouth of every Modoc sent forth that terrifying cry, every gloomy recess and cavern took it up, and from the bowels of the earth and the bosom of the placid lake, the echo kept reverberating until only a whisper of it came back to us from the naked bluffs beyond.

Not until dawn began to break and our eyes could discern the landmarks around us did that spell of dread stupefaction seem to depart. As the darkness vanished and objects became visible, firing began on our front. The Indians seemed to have anticipated the intention of uniting our forces against them and set out with all their power and cunning to prevent it.

I belonged to a detachment of cavalry that halted on a rocky eminence, from which we could observe what was transpiring on our right. There, the infantry, instead of pressing forward to form a junction with Major Mason's command, whose men—judging from the frequent rattle of firearms in the distance—were already engaged with the enemy, were compelled to turn and face the Indians, who were annoying them by persistent sniping on the flank.

We could plainly see how the fighting progressed. The soldiers, about five paces apart, were deployed as skirmishers, and after advancing at a run where the ground would admit for a short distance, would then fall flat on the ground behind some cover, observe the spot where smoke of the Indians' rifle came from, fire at that spot, then jump up and advance again. We would frequently get a glimpse of a Modoc dodging cautiously behind the jutting rocks.

When they caught sight of a bluecoat, we would see the puff of smoke and hear the soft ping of the Henry rifle in contrast to the sharp bang of the soldier's gun. The Indians didn't waste any ammunition, for they knew the difficulty of replenishing their stock. A great part of the day was spent in this kind of desultory fighting, the Modocs gradually retiring toward their Stronghold.

Under such circumstances, time certainly flies. As we sat on the mound of rocks watching the "doughboys" and the redskins playing the game of hide and seek and snipe, and occasionally munching a hardtack, we suddenly received orders to move to the front. Only then did we realize that we had been there for hours, and noticed that the sun was rapidly sinking towards the west.[30]

During the day, a pack mule carrying a small Coehorn mortar, not more than thirty inches in length, was led along a kind of trail by the edge of the lake where the action of the water had made the surface of the lava rocks reasonably smooth. This baby mortar, intended for throwing shells into the Stronghold just before an assault was to be made, arrived safely at our command.

After having been onlookers up to that time, our troops were ordered to advance up the peninsula, keeping close to the lake until we were slightly in advance of the engaged infantry. Then we were deployed as skirmishers, facing the outer works of the Modoc citadel.

When the natural formation did not meet all the requirements of their fortification, the Indians had constructed artificial barriers of stone about four feet in height as breastworks with loopholes to shoot through. We were now facing several of these defenses, from behind which the Indians took frequent shots at us. To make our attack more certain of success, the little mortar was now brought up and placed in position for shelling the breastworks.

The position taken was immediately behind Troop K, and we were to lie prone while it was being fired. It was loaded, sighted, and touched off; but through some oversight or defect, the shell, instead of being hurled behind the breastworks, fell about fifteen feet in front of our line and spun around, hissing and sputtering like a thing of life. Some of the men jumped up and started to run; others seemed too dazed to move and looked upon the antics of the shell as if they were charmed by it.

An officer, who took in the situation and the imminent danger to which the men were exposed, shouted, "Everyone lie close to the ground." He was instantly obeyed, and then the thing exploded, scattering fragments through the air in every direction; no one was hit, but everyone was badly scared. The next shot was more successful and fell behind the works, and was followed by others equally well directed.

The shots from a mortar in their trajectory describe a curve, or arc of a circle, and are visible in their course to the eye; this caused the Indians to waste some good ammunition trying to hit the fiery projectile as it descended in their proximity. We were now ordered to charge at double time, which we did with a will, firing, running, stumbling, and clambering over rocks, the Indians pegging away at us in the meantime until we reached the breastworks. Most of these we found abandoned, the Indians not seeming to relish hand-to-hand fighting. But behind a barrier which three or four of us reached at the same moment, a Modoc had the temerity to remain, until one of our party named [Pvt. Charles] Johnson looked over it and received a bullet through the head, killing him instantly. The Indian disappeared like a flash through the crevices in the rocks. In this charge a few were killed and wounded, though I never learned the exact number. As it was now getting dusk, we were ordered to bivouac on the line just taken.

Supper that night consisted of a few hardtack and a piece of fat bacon. Our longing for a cup of coffee as a bracer was in vain. We sat, lay, or crouched among the lava rocks throughout the night, tightly gripping our carbines, and found very little rest.

In the morning[31] we had orders to again make every possible effort to unite our line with that engaged on the other side of the peninsula.[32] With that object, our command all moved to the right, keeping up at the same time an intermittent exchange of shots with the Indians hovering on our left, equally intent upon keeping the two commands apart.

As we moved eastward, the character of the ground became rougher, and the persistence of the redskins in attacking us on the flank more annoying. We could make little if any headway, and judging from the distant report of firearms in that direction, the other command was not having any better success in its efforts to reach us.

It was determined, therefore, to retrace our steps, take a position as close as possible to the Stronghold, and attempt to storm it the next morning. In conformity with the change of plans, we straggled back tired and hungry through the rocks, harassed all the time by a galling fire, to very near the place we occupied the night before, though a little closer to the Stronghold.

It was now the evening of the second day, and our stomachs and haversacks were empty. Though the prospect of another sleepless night among the rocks was not a pleasant outlook, not a murmur was heard; everyone felt that the Modoc fortress must be taken at any cost and the foul murder of General Canby avenged. As the evening advanced, the Indians became much more active than on the previous night; they moved out from the Stronghold and in the darkness approached very near to our line. At times they would call us in very plain, if not classical, English names unfit to print. Then our men would pour a regular volley at the point whence the voices came; but this was ineffective, as the Modocs kept a screen of rocks between themselves and danger. They continued these tricks through the greater part of the night, moving along the line from one place to another and shouting frequent volleys of profanity at the soldiers. The boys in blue were not above returning the compliment in just

The entrance to Captain Jack's cave. ILLUSTRATED LONDON NEWS, 1873.

as choice billingsgate. We afterwards found out that they were feeling for a weak place to pass through our line.

As our eyes turned toward the Stronghold early the next morning, it was evident that no change had taken place during the night. If a soldier's hat was raised upon a gun barrel, it quickly became a target for the watchful foe. Gradually, however, it dawned upon us that the Indians had played us a foxy trick. When it was good daylight, the command was given for the whole line to advance. As we raised from our recumbent positions, we became aware that there were hostiles behind us, for bullets began whizzing from that direction as well as from the front. We pressed forward, however, heedless of what might be behind, fully determined to enter the Stronghold or perish in the attempt. The task was much easier than we had anticipated, for we found only a few crippled and wounded Modocs holding the place; all the others had decamped during the night and were now somewhere in our rear. A few wounded, left as a sort of decoy, kept fighting to the last; they expected no quarter, and none was given. After a long and arduous effort, we had attained the coveted goal, but the quarry had escaped us.

The famous Stronghold that we had heard so much about, and which had taken so many fantastic shapes in our imagination, was nothing more than a deep, dish-shaped hole, or cavernous depression, perhaps an old crater, about a hundred yards in diameter. It was encircled by reefs of basaltic rock, and the surrounding ground gradually sloped away from the edge; manned by cool headed and determined men, with plenty of arms and ammunition, it would have been a very difficult place to take by assault.

When we entered the foul-smelling and nauseous hole, heaps of bones, rags, and filth of every kind were seen all over the place, and here and there the body of a dead Indian, some mutilated. I remember distinctly seeing the head of a Modoc severed from the trunk, perhaps by some soldier, that was as black as the darkest native of the Congo. Passing troopers generally saluted it with a vicious kick.

One incident connected with the taking of this Indian fortress has never been mentioned in print, and but little orally. When Company K, 1st Cavalry, to which I belonged, at the time under the command of a lieutenant, a West Point graduate whose name I will refrain from mentioning, and while others were doing what they could for the few wounded though still fighting Indians, we found a squaw, probably eighty or ninety years old, squatted on her haunches among the rocks on the edge of the Stronghold. Her gray hair was hanging in disorder over her wizened and wrinkled countenance; her long and emaciated arms were bare; and her skinny hands, with fingernails like the talons of some bird of prey, rested on either knee.

As we were passing by this wretched specimen of superannuated human- ity, abandoned to her fate by her own people as too old and feeble to be taken along, we stopped to gaze upon her, but with no thought of inflicting punish- ment upon such a helpless being. Probably she knew that no prisoners were being taken, or had a presentiment of impending danger; so while we looked at her, she piteously whined in plain enough language, "Me hurt no one; me very old woman; me no fight."

Turning his cold blue eye upon her, Lieutenant [George R. Bacon] said, "Is there anyone here who will put that old hag out of the way?" A Pennsylva- nia Dutchman stepped from the ranks and said, "I'll fix her, Lieutenant." He then deliberately placed his carbine to her head and blew out her brains. We then moved forward; not a word was said, but some strong expressions in the minds and on the lips of the men dared not find utterance. I do not believe that there was another man in the company, save the perpetrator of the deed and the epauletted officer, who didn't feel shocked at such inhumanity.

Many years ago this lieutenant retired from the army and became a wealthy manufacturer in a large industrial city of Illinois.[33] Less than a decade ago I received a copy of a newspaper published there, containing an account of his death and three columns of fulsome eulogy of this "splendid citizen and Christian gentleman." Reading it, I wondered if any memory of the poor old Modoc squaw, whom he caused to be wantonly murdered years ago in the Lava Beds, ever came before his vision as he lay awaiting the summons to appear before his Creator!

This incident goes to show that humanity is about the same the world over and not to any great extent affected by religion, language, or national bound- aries. In some men of every clime and color, the barbaric instinct only slum- bers and is easily aroused to action when passions are aroused and nations or individuals are engaged in deadly strife. That only the other fellow is capable of doing acts of that kind is a theory disproved.

While the Stronghold was in our hands, the main body of the hostiles was still at large. Our next move was to return to camp and make preparations to

·head off the Indians in case they should evacuate the Lava Beds, and our steps were turned in that direction.

It was only about two and one-half miles of rough trail, but before we had trudged any considerable part of the distance, all began to feel the cumulative effects of sleepless nights, strenuous days, and empty stomachs; by the time we reached camp, we were "all in." Never have I been so completely exhausted as after that walk to camp at the end of the memorable three days' fight.[34]

On our return journey, about half a mile from the Stronghold, we found the mutilated body of a packer[35] who had left camp early in the morning with a pack mule, carrying supplies for the men on the firing line. He had no idea of meeting any Indians, as he thought we had hemmed them in. Some who had broken through met him, killed both man and mule, and flattened the packer's head between two rocks to almost the thickness of one's hand.

After our arrival in camp, a mess of well-cooked beans and coffee had a wonderful effect in restoring our impaired vitality. Dinner over, we saddled our horses and, accompanied by Donald McKay and his twenty-five Warm Springs Indian scouts, started to encircle the Lava Beds with the object of locating the escaped Modocs. Towards sundown,[36] when near the southeast corner of the Lava Beds and in the vicinity of Sorass Lake, the scouts came upon two Modocs, whom they killed and scalped. We camped close by where this happened, and that night the Warm Springs Indians held a scalp dance in celebration of their victory over the two Modocs. They howled and danced all night long with hands joined in a circle, while one brave held a pole in the center from which both scalps dangled. So strenuous was the barbaric performance that the participants worked themselves nearly into a frenzy of excitement, while the perspiration streamed from their almost naked bodies. These Warm Springs Indians, hereditary enemies of the Modocs, entertained a wholesome dread of them begotten of many encounters in bygone days and would not think of fighting them man for man.

McKay and his dusky scouts returned to camp next day, and our command spent a few days looking around for some traces of the Indians. Finding none, we concluded that they must still be somewhere in the Lava Beds. Then we also returned to camp, which was all flurry and excitement; more than two score of dead and wounded were there, and we soon learned what the Modocs had been doing in our absence.

In the early evening, a few days after our departure, a fire was noted somewhere near the center of the Lava Beds, and it was rightly conjectured that Captain Jack and his band were still there. To determine the correctness of this view, a detachment of sixty-odd artillerymen under Capt. Evan Thomas was ordered to make a reconnaissance the next morning.[37] McKay and his Indian scouts were also instructed to move in the same direction through the Lava Beds and keep somewhere near Captain Thomas's command.

The detachment started about 7:00 A.M., intending to be back by sundown. About noon, after traveling some four miles through the rocks without seeing anything to indicate the presence of hostiles, it was planned to take a little rest and eat the lunch that had been taken along, and a small, sandy knoll among the lava rocks was selected for that purpose. While seated and enjoying their slight repast, they were fired upon suddenly from apparently all directions by the Modocs, who had them surrounded. Every officer, including Captain Thomas, Lieutenants Albion Howe, Arthur Cranston, G. M. Harris, and T. F. Wright, were killed. Assistant Surgeon B. G. Semig, who accompanied the command, was badly wounded and afterwards had to undergo amputation of the leg.

News of the disaster was first learned when a few of the detachment who escaped through the rocks arrived at headquarters in the evening and told how the greater part of their comrades had been killed by the Modocs. Their statement at first was considered an exaggeration or received with incredulity; officers and men thought it hardly possible that upwards of sixty trained and well-equipped soldiers could be annihilated by a small band of discouraged Indians. But soon a few more straggled into camp, exhausted and bleeding from many wounds, and the full truth became apparent.

One splendid specimen of physical manhood made his way to camp over that awful trail (a truly wonderful feat) with more than twenty bullet wounds in his body and lived about thirty-six hours thereafter. It might truly be said that he was "shot to pieces." Just as soon as the news was verified, relief parties were organized and started for the scene of the disaster. One of them was in charge of Lt. F. A. Boutelle, who had taken such a prominent part in the first encounter on Lost River. He spent two nights and a day without rest in a most heroic effort to relieve the suffering of the wounded and have them moved to camp, where they could receive proper treatment. The task of carrying badly wounded and dying men over such an execrable stretch of jagged and broken rock is almost beyond the power of description. By untiring effort, and with only the crude appliances at hand, Lieutenant Boutelle accomplished this in the most creditable and satisfactory manner and received unstinted praise from officers and men.

I had never seen this splendid type of U.S. Army officer from that time until a few years ago, when I called at his office in Seattle, Washington, and spent a very pleasant hour or so talking over the thrilling events of bygone days. He died a little more than three years ago, having passed his eighty-third milestone; yet almost up to the last, his mind was as clear, his step as light, and his carriage as erect as it was more than half a century ago in the Lava Beds. As he was occasionally seen walking down the principal streets in his military uniform (for he was a retired colonel), people stopped and turned to admire his very impressive and distinguished bearing.

I said to him one day before his demise, "How is it, Colonel, that you and I hold our age so well and keep in such good health, when most of those with whom we were associated in those troublous times have long since gone the way of all flesh?" "Fitzgerald, because we didn't spend most of our time trying to drink up all the whiskey made in Kentucky." Perhaps he was right.

Though McKay and his twenty-five Warm Springs Indians scouts were only a few hundred yards away, they attempted no resistance, but later gave for an excuse that they had to construct a temporary barricade in the rocks or they would have been annihilated.[38] Their abject fear of the Modocs unnerved them and rendered them practically useless in such emergencies.

This was the last trump played by Captain Jack and his band. Shortly afterwards, through the difficulty of obtaining water, and probably also from scarcity of ammunition, they left both the Lava Beds and their fighting spirit behind them. Divided into small bands, they wandered around the adjacent country, apparently having no aim except to keep out of the way of the soldiers. But in this they could only meet with disappointment, for the purpose of the government was to pursue them relentlessly until all were captured and then to deal with them summarily for their misdeeds.

By following the various trails, detachments of troops soon ran down these scattered bands and forced them to surrender. Once or twice when overtaken, a few of them put up a spirited fight for a short time, but usually when closely pressed, they would find some elevated point, raise a dirty white rag on a piece of stick, and then await the signal to come down. When surrendering, they had a dejected and crestfallen appearance and would say little or nothing.

Toward evening one day in the latter part of May or early June 1873,[39] our troop received the submission of Scarfaced Charley, a prominent chief, and six others. It is said that Charley was not a Modoc, but a Rogue River Indian.[40] About the same time, Captain Perry of Troop F and Captain Trimble[41] of Troop H, 1st Cavalry, after a long and tiresome chase, ran down Captain Jack and John Schonchin in a deep and narrow canyon not far from the southern edge of Langell Valley. The remainder now quickly gave themselves up.

Thus ended the famous Modoc War, which, except the Custer massacre of June 25, 1876, created more widespread interest and involved more casualties than any Indian trouble of recent times. Taking everything into consideration, it must be admitted that the government dealt harshly with this little band of brave, if treacherous, savages. They were fighting for what they deemed an inalienable right to retain possession of a locality that had belonged to them and their ancestors from time immemorial, and from which it was sought to forcibly eject them for no good cause, as they could see it. No punishment can be greater for an Indian than death or banishment.

Those known to have participated in the atrocious murder of General Canby and Reverend Thomas, and the attempted murder of Mr. Meacham, were taken to Fort Klamath, tried by a military court, and sentenced to pay the extreme penalty upon the scaffold. Later in the season Captain Jack, John Schonchin, Boston Charley, and Black Jim were hanged at that place. The remainder of the unfortunate band was removed temporarily to Fort D. A. Russell, near Cheyenne, Wyoming. Later they were placed on a small reservation set apart for them in what was then the Indian Territory, where many succumbed to the enforced exile and unfavorable climatic conditions, though I have been informed that a small remnant still exists. A few of the Modocs are said to have found their way back across two-thirds of the continent to their native heath and are dwelling quietly and peaceably among the ever-increasing white population of that region, where once their forefathers held undisputed sway.[42]

The Modocs Laugh at the Soldiers

ANONYMOUS

New York *Herald,* February 16, 1873[1]

A correspondent of the Oregon *Herald,* writing under date of January 22 from the camp of the Oregon militia operating in the Modoc country, tells the story of the battle of the seventeenth ultimo as follows:

Captain Bernard's forces, together with that portion of Fairchild's party and the soldiers that made the junction with Bernard during the battle, arrived at this camp lasts night, a footsore, shattered, and demoralized troop. A portion of these men were compelled to lie behind rocks and in crevices, sheltered from the deadly fire of an unseen enemy, until darkness gave them a chance to escape.

Their retreat began at midnight and continued until daylight without a halt. The sufferings of the wounded during that terrible night must have been extreme. One of these rode on horseback through the night, over the worst imaginable trail, with his thigh bone broken in splinters—said, in this instance, to be a mortal wound.

The forces upon the east side were in a position equally critical but were more fortunate in their retreat. I despair of making it clear how so formidable and carefully prepared an expedition could have accomplished such disastrous results. Everybody affected contempt for the enemy, and it is but fair to say that the enemy affected the greatest contempt for us.

When Captain Bernard opened his fire on the east, although the engagement had already begun on the west, a shout of derisive laughter arose upon the Indian right and ran along and around their line, through rocky canyons, a distance of nearly two miles. In close quarters the Indians showed themselves proficient in the use of slang English. Their remarks were more exasperating than edifying. This profanity and obscenity was enough to provoke the envy of the most accomplished American gentleman. One of them, hearing Major Green's name mentioned, said, "Is that you Green? Well, go along, you infernal old [bastard], we won't hurt you."

Oregon volunteers. RUFUS F. ZOGBAUM. *HORSE, FOOT, AND DRAGOON.*

The Fairchild party formed themselves with a part of the infantry battalion in a rocky gorge, when a voice, recognized as that of Steamboat Frank, shouted across to another voice—Scarfaced Charley's—on the opposite side: "Hello, Charley, here is some Yreka boys; don't you see them?"

"Yes."

"Boys, what do you want? What makes you come here to fight us?" And the same voice continued, "Charley, there is old Dorris. Dorris, what do you want here? Say Dorris, how long are you going to fight us?"

All this talk was accompanied by a lively shower of bullets. Only an occasional glimpse of an Indian was seen. Four of the little party had already been shot. The men were lying flat behind rocks and sagebrushes. Any exposure or movement, however slight, invited a shot. No answer was made to this Indian talk. Steamboat Frank persisted in trying to draw Dorris out.

"What's the matter with you, Dorris? Can't you hear? Ain't you got ears? Can't you talk? Ain't you got a mouth?"

But Dorris knew his man and laid low, occasionally blazing away at the rock from which these questions seemed to proceed, and conscious that his rock was being peppered in turn. A soldier nearby peered over his cover in the direction of the voice a moment—a shot, and he sank back with a bullet hole in his forehead, mortally wounded. Near this spot, Captain Perry, an officer of great gallantry, was shot through the arm and breast. He involuntarily moaned, "Oh, I'm shot!"

A shrill voice, that of a squaw, likely, mocking him, said, "You come here to fight Indians and you make noise like that; you no man, you squaw."

The number of narrow escapes, where bullets were stopped or turned aside by cartridge belts, pistol handles, etc., was large. An awkward German, unaccustomed to the use of arms, carried his pistol at full cock on his abdomen. A Springfield rifle bullet struck in that vicinity, and that pistol remains at half cock yet. His pistol is ruined, yet the man lives and is happy. Donald McKay's horse was shot dead under him. Donald is a nephew of the celebrated Dr. McKay.

To sum up, we were eager to get in and glad to get out, anxious in the morning that the Indians should not escape, and at evening anxious that we should. The nature and impregnable character of the Modoc position, and the number of the enemy, were not understood. Better information was not attainable except only by a reconnaissance in force and at the sacrifice of life. All that was known in these respects was obtained by observations made at a distance of five miles, except what Fairchild learned in his visit to Captain Jack, and that was limited.[2]

It is impossible to imagine the character of that terrible place, or even to approach it. It stretches away in expansive awfulness. As you approach the Modoc position, its ruggedness increases, and it breaks into an endless succession of canyons, chasms, gorges, extinct volcano craters, and mountains of rock, jagged, splintered, and toppling. From the extreme and commanding points occupied by our skirmish lines, the scene has a sort of infernal grandeur in it. From the lake to the east, south, and southeast, the rugged plain reaches to the mountains with a gradually increasing elevation. Although within a few feet of the main camp (we passed over several deserted ones), we saw nothing of the celebrated cave. It is, however, universally believed in here.

Personal Observations on the Conduct of the Modoc War

WILLIAM H. BOYLE[1]

Bancroft Collection, University of California Library, Berkeley[2]

My brother officers said to me, "Lieutenant, you are in for it, and I am very glad that 'Bobby' (the pet name the officers called Colonel Granger)[3] appointed you post quartermaster, for I will not have to take that trip to Jacksonville and back through the mud without accomplishing anything; for do you know, that as soon as Maj. John Green goes after those Indians, he will clean them out sooner than a man can say 'Jack Robinson.' Didn't he whenever he went after the Apaches? Did he not jump them and make a good killing? He will soon clean out the Modocs. I can tell you that, but let us go and see the little colonel, and see what he has to say."

So we went and were informed that we could pack our blankets and get ready to leave at once on the steamboat for Portland, en route to the Modoc country. At 7:00 P.M. that evening, the battalion, 21st Infantry, composed of Companies B and C,[4] commanded by Major E. C. Mason, with the following named officers: Captains George H. Burton and V. M. C. Silva; Lieutenants W. H. Boyle and H. De Witt Moore, left Vancouver, Washington Territory, December 3, 1872, to take part in the Modoc muddle that ended in the loss of five officers and sixty men, and a total of 130 killed and wounded.

On our arrival at Portland, we were met by General Canby and staff, who greeted us with a good, hearty welcome and adieu, and sent us on our way rejoicing. Little did we think, as we shook hands with that good old officer, that his life was to be offered up [as] a sacrifice in the attempt to pacify a lot of miserable scalawag Indians, with their hands dripping with [the blood] of citizens and brave soldiers that they had so recently murdered.

Well, to my text. On the following morning we arrived at Roseburg, Oregon, without any mishap, and our quartermaster, Lieutenant Boyle, was all day getting the transportation ready to transport the baggage up the valley to Jacksonville. Many were the growls of the old soldiers as they remained in the rain waiting for the battalion to move. One laughable circumstance occurred at that camp. A deserter from the 23rd Infantry delivered himself up to the guard, and the sergeant reported to Captain Burton, officer of the day, as is customary, and

Brig. Gen. Edward R. S. Canby.

he reported the fact to the colonel commanding, who informed him it was impossible to take him with the battalion on the march, and to inform the deserter he must report to the battalion upon its return from the Modoc country. The captain informed the sergeant, an old soldier, who called the deserter to him and informed him in this language, "Look here, we can't take you now, but when we return, you may report; do you hear, sir?" "Yes," said the deserter, "I did not care much whether I went or not." So the poor fellow is no doubt waiting for the return of the battalion, as we did not return that way, but marched through by the way of Camp Kearny and Walla Walla.

The next morning the battalion started on its march up the Umpqua Valley through the mud. The transportation was all day, from early in the morning until late at night, making two miles, when the battalion marched past the wagons. The last I saw of our quartermaster was in the mud up to his middle trying to get the wagons out of the mud that contained the provisions, so the officers need not go supperless to bed. We dined that evening by the light of the moon; after seven days' hard marching, we arrived at Jacksonville, where we changed transportation and began our march at once for Linkville.

There we began to experience the hardships of the trip. The rains began to pour down, and the roads became so soft that it was impossible to draw an empty wagon up the mountainside, and we had to double the teams on the wagons and get the men to assist, to enable the teams to keep pace with the men. The men were footsore, and for the first time since our leaving Vancouver, I began to see dissatisfaction on the faces of the men. Still, they were cheerful and did their duty.

On the evening of the thirteenth, we encamped on the side of the Cascades at a place called Green Camp, and the snow fell that night to the depth of about one foot. All the next, through the driving snow, the troops marched on, elated with the news we had obtained from a courier that evening that the attack would not be made until the arrival of the battalion. There was some chance of a fight with the Indians, and the trip would not be a fruitless one, as we had expected at the commencement of the march. The command rested on the summit of the mountains and encamped over Sunday, as [it] was the custom of our company never to march on the Sabbath.

One of our officers, Lieutenant Silva, became so sick that he requested to be sent back to Vancouver for medical treatment. The request was granted, and we lost the service of one officer. But his place was ably filled, as will be seen, by Lieutenant Moore, a young officer of merit, who acted as signal officer and participated in all the engagements during the campaign.

In two days' hard marches, anxious to get to the Modoc country and close out the war, we arrived at Linkville, where we were met by Colonel Wheaton and his assistant adjutant general, Lieutenant Adams;[5] also General Ross, the volunteer commander who had come to confer with the colonel as to the mode of attack, his command being at the ferry on the Klamath River.

After a long consultation, the colonel decided to send to Vancouver and procure two howitzers to use in the Lava Beds to demoralize the Indians. This caused a delay and a great deal of discontent among the troops, who had just come from Arizona, where we only had to find the Indians, and then go in and whip them; the idea of sending for howitzers to fight the Modocs was absurd. But the sequel will show that Colonel Wheaton was right, and if the "powers that be" had only listened more to his advice, and not relieved him after his reconnaissance, the war would have ended without the horrid massacre of Thomas's command, and the Indians would never have left the Lava Beds.

After a rest of two days, the battalion resumed their march and encamped at Crawley's ranch[6] on Lost River, with the cavalry command under Maj. John Green, 1st Cavalry, and anxiously awaited the arrival of the howitzers.

During this time, Capt. R .F. Bernard, 1st Cavalry, was stationed at Land's ranch, Tule Lake, about twenty-five miles from Lost River. On about December [21, 1872,] a wagon belonging to his command, in charge of a corporal and two men[7] from Camp Bidwell, California, loaded with commissary stores and ammunition for his company, when about two miles from his camp, was attacked by the Modocs, and two men and one mule [were] killed. But by the bravery of the commanding officer in charge, the wagon was saved. Captain Bernard, as soon as the news reached him, went to their assistance,[8] and the presence of the troops drove the Indians again into their Stronghold, without any fighting.

Upon the news being brought to headquarters, Captain Jackson was dispatched with his Troop B, 1st Cavalry, to the assistance of Captain Bernard, but his service was not required, as the Indians had retired on the appearance of the command of Captain Bernard.

Captain Jackson was attached to that command, and they were ordered to watch the enemy and see that they did not escape from the Lava Beds or make raids on the citizens in the vicinity of Langell Valley. No great change was

Jack's cave. CYRUS T. BRADY. *NORTHWESTERN FIGHTS AND FIGHTERS.*

made in the movement of the troops but to send the volunteers to Van Bremer's ranch; also, Captain Perry's troops, where they could watch the enemy from that side and be used in case of an attack. The colonel, finding that the volunteers were dissatisfied owing to the short rations issued by the state, and the time being about to expire, ordered the troops under Majors Green and Mason to Van Bremer's ranch; also, the depot of supplies in charge of Lieutenant Boyle, head quartermaster.

On January 1, 1873, they crossed Lost River and proceeded to their destination, where they remained until the fight of January 17. During the time, it was found necessary to issue rations to the volunteers and forage their horses to keep them in the field. The howitzers arrived on the fifteenth.

The morning of the sixteenth dawned smoky and foggy, so much so that it was almost impossible to discern an object ten paces from you. The officers were pleased, as they were of the opinion that they could the more easily come upon the enemy without their seeing them. But what seemed a godsend for our troops was also to the advantage of the enemy.

Our troops arrived at the Lava Beds on the evening of the sixteenth, and a skirmish occurred between the advance of our line in front to alarm the enemy, and the troops went into camp behind the bluffs that overlooked the Lava Beds. There was no trouble to supply the troops with water, as the lake ran by the foot of the bluff, and the position was in the hands of our troops. All the troops were in good spirits, expecting the fight to be very short the next morning, and [that] we would walk over the Lava Beds without any amount of trouble, but we found this could not so easily be done, and to our cost.

It was the intention of Colonel Wheaton to make the attack on the morning of the seventeenth by a bold maneuver unknown to the Indians, but by a blunder of Captain Bernard, who came on the east side of the lake, the enemy had learned our positions. Bernard, who had relied more on his own judgment than upon the man employed as guide, marched into the center of the Lava Beds, or rather, into the caves occupied by Captain Jack, and a sharp engagement ensued, causing the troops to fall back two or three hundred yards and take up a strong position behind a ledge of rocks, where they remained all night. In this affair Captain Bernard lost four killed and wounded. It was very unfortunate, as he gained nothing by the movement and only discouraged the troops, who were all night engaged in attending to the wounded, when they should have been getting into a good position for the coming attack. It was indeed a sad blunder, for had the troops taken their positions at night and without the knowledge of the Indians, how different might have been the result of the next day's fight.

The morning of the seventeenth opened with the same gloomy fog as the day previous, and as the troops looked down upon the Lava Beds, it looked like one grand sea. Nothing could be discerned but a vast fog bed, as far as the eye could reach.

Colonel Wheaton was up early, and the troops, both volunteers and regulars, and their officers were anxious for the fray by the time it was light. Major Mason, in charge of the battalion, was placed on the left of the line, resting on the lake; the company of California volunteers, Captain Fairchild's, acting as flankers; Captain Perry's Troop H, 1st Cavalry, in the center; and the volunteers under Gen. John Ross on the right; Maj. John Green commanding the whole. Maj. Gen. John F. Miller, Oregon volunteers, had been ordered by the governor to the field, and although present during the fight, he did not take part in the affair.

In this formation the troops advanced to the Lava Beds. At about 7:00 A.M. the skirmishing began, and Colonel Wheaton ordered up the howitzers, in charge of Lieutenant Miller, 1st Cavalry.[9] He only fired three shots; as the fog was so very dense, he was afraid he would do more harm to our troops than to the enemy. It was a very unfortunate circumstance for the howitzers that we had waited so long, as the troops had to depend on their rifles. Hardly had the troops entered the rocks when the Indians began firing on them, and owing to the rough and rocky country we had to pass over, the Indians could fire and retreat before the troops without loss to them, but a great loss to the troops, [who] were being shot down by an unseen foe. Yet the troops advanced steadily until they came to a great chasm, which divided the regulars from the volunteers. Major Green, who by his cool bearing and his bravery before the enemy had gained the confidence of the officers and men, had driven the Indians across the chasm, placed his troops between the Indians and the lake, and determined to connect with Captain Bernard's right. It was a very daring operation, and the only way to succeed in driving the enemy and joining all the commands; but in order to do so, he had to fight his way over the worst position of the Lava Beds, across large chasms and over rocks, under the muzzles of the Indians' rifles.

About this time, the Oregon volunteers had learned that the Indians would fight and would not run at the approach of the soldiers. They were not so anxious to shoot Indians as they were in the morning, and by some unaccountable circumstance failed to keep up the connection with the right of Perry's troops, and in fact were discouraged as regarded advancing farther over the Stronghold. So when the command was given by Major Green to move by the left and join Captain Bernard's right, they were left behind. The battalion, 21st Infantry, 1st Cavalry, and Fairchild's company, California volunteers, consisting in all of about 200 men, now left to make the final movement to connect with Bernard and to cut the Indians from water; never did soldiers show more cool courage than did the small handful of men about to make this movement. When the order was given for them to advance, with one accord they moved to the front through the most deadly fire of musketry. As their comrades fell alongside of the chasm, they knew that killed or wounded they would fall into the hands of the Indians, and they fought like crazed tigers. Many a brave soldier fell as they crossed that chasm. Soon the connection was made, but with fearful loss. At that point, Captain Perry and Lieutenant Kyle, 1st Cavalry, were wounded, and about thirty percent of the men killed and wounded.

Now the connection was made, and night began to settle upon the scene. The troops had done all that was required of them. They had found the enemy in a strong position, and it had required time to get them out. This Colonel Wheaton would have done, had he been allowed time, but he was superseded; with what a cost, the sequel will show. But to my text.

As soon as the volunteers found that the regulars had passed beyond the chasm and formed a connection with Bernard's troops, they fell back to the bluff by the cover of darkness, when a conference was held [by] Wheaton,

Miller, and Ross, and they decided to withdraw the troops from the Lava Beds and encamp on the bluff, also to signal Major Green to withdraw his command. But darkness came upon them, and they could only get part of the message to Green. But this brave soldier, knowing that the troops had done all they could, or that was required of them, gathered up the wounded and dead, and that night fell back to Land's ranch.

Captain Bernard's command, although they could not advance, kept up a continual fire upon the Indians during the day and assisted to keep the Indians engaged while the movement to the left was being made.

Colonel Wheaton, after he had determined to withdraw the troops, found he had only the volunteers and a small detachment of regulars, amounting in all to about seventy-five men. The enemy following on their trail, and some chance of their being surrounded, [Wheaton] gave orders to fall back to the bluffs. After some very hard scrambling, he succeeded in getting all the command safely up the steep hill.

An incident occurred that I must relate in connection with General Ross. That evening I asked him who commanded the volunteers that day. He replied that the only order he gave was to "get up the bluff, " and he seized hold of the tail of his mule, took a double hitch on his arm, and went up the hill.

All that night the troops under Colonel Wheaton remained on the bluff. The weather was cold, and they suffered from cold and want of food, as they had lost or thrown away most of their rations on going into the fight that morning. At early dawn the troops began their march back to Van Bremer's ranch, where they arrived at 2:00 P.M., footsore and not so anxious to kill Modocs as when they left the day previous, the volunteers very anxious to get home, or to place the Cascade Range of mountains between them and the Modocs. In all due regard for some of the brave men that were among the volunteers—such as Captain [Harrison] Kelley, Lieutenant Rhein, and others—their service did not remunerate the government for the rations consumed by them and the large amount of forage furnished their horses.

But to return to Major Green and his little band, still before the enemy. Finding his men tired and footsore, having worn out their shoes scrambling among the rocks during the two days since they left their camp; with two of their officers—Captain Perry and Lieutenant Kyle—wounded, and a heavy percentage of the men without the means of transporting their wounded from the Lava Beds; and with a relentless foe hanging about them, ready to take any advantage they could to massacre the small party that was left, after a consultation Major Green decided to withdraw to Land's ranch, where the march commenced over the rocky path that only a chamois could make its way on such a dark morning. The wounded were carried in blankets and on the backs of the Indian ponies captured that day. To hear the groans of the poor fellows as they were jostled against the rocks was quite horrible. One circumstance was particularly so. Crook, one of the California Volunteers, who was wounded in the leg, breaking the bone, could not be carried in a blanket and preferred to ride on the back of a pony; but his leg hung loose and would strike against the sharp rocks and sagebrush as he moved along, so some of his command tied a rope to his leg, so as to lift it up when he came to an obstacle. It was sickening to see the expression of his face; the pain he must have endured was excruciating. I give this as only one of the many horrible incidents that occurred on that retreat to Land's ranch.

The men and officers were so thoroughly worn out by the two days' marching and fighting that as soon as the order [to] halt was given, they at once fell asleep. I saw many riding and walking in their sleep that morning. It was a great relief to all to arrive at Land's ranch in safety; for had the Indians attacked the small party, fagged out as they were, they would have fallen an easy prey to the two-legged wolves that hung on their trail.

I should have mentioned that we had some Klamath Indians as allies, but they did so little, and it has since been proven by the Modoc Indians that they were an assistance to them and furnished them with ball and powder, and kept them informed of all that was transpiring among the troops. On the day of the fight, they only fired their rifles in the air and did some tall shooting, but did no service, as I have been able to ascertain.

On the following day the troops under Major Green were marched to Lost River, and on the following day[10] to Van Bremer's ranch. When all had camped, with the exception of Captain Bernard's company, the volunteers, thinking they had done all that was required of them and wishing to return to their homes, were marched back to Jacksonville by General Ross, and the Indians discharged and sent to Klamath.

Colonel Wheaton called the officers together and informed them that he had determined to withdraw the troops to Lost River Ford, some thirty miles from Van Bremer's ranch, where he intended to remain until he was reinforced by troops that he had asked for and had been sent to report to him. The camp, he stated, would be the base of his operations, and he intended to build two mortar boats, and should attack from the lake side as well as from the land, so the Indians could not get away—first to surround them, and then batter down their Stronghold. Had his plans been carried out, we would not have to record the massacre of Captain Thomas and party, and the others that were sacrificed for want of a competent commanding officer.

On the following day, January 21, 1873, the troops took up their march from Van Bremer's ranch to Lost River and arrived that evening, making in all about thirty miles. We went into camp and remained until Colonel Wheaton was relieved and Colonel Gillem took command.

COMMENTS ON THE BATTLE OF JANUARY 17, 1873

I am positive that no more could have been done under the circumstances we had to contend with, and the only mistakes that occurred that could have been avoided were these: Had the volunteers maintained their line during the day and not have fallen back, and the Indian allies under Captain Applegate been of any assistance, we might have succeeded in killing some Modocs, but as the troops had only three days' rations and no way of cooking, it was impossible for them to hold their position in the Lava Beds.

Captain Bernard did not obey the orders of Major Green when ordered to advance his left, so as to draw the fire of the Indians and to allow Major Mason and Captain Kelley's command to get around the point and across the chasm when fired upon by the Modocs. But never did men fight better than did the regular troops during that day's fight, and without exception, the officers did all that could be expected of them.

MASSACRE OF THE PEACE COMMISSIONERS

The battle of [January] 17 having been fought, and it finally understood that the Indians before us were not the kind that the troops had been used to fight, as most of the troops had been in Arizona and had fought the Apaches. Whenever they did find them, they had only to go for them, and the Indians would fire a few shots and then run. But not so the Modocs. They were ready to exchange shot for shot, were in a strong position, and could hold their own. Colonel Wheaton had found out that strategy had to be used to dislodge them from these positions, and being a humane man and experienced soldier, he at once set about a campaign [in which] we could capture or make them surrender with but very little loss of life. Requisitions were at once forwarded to Portland and San Francisco headquarters for the proper material to build two mortar boats and for the supplies to carry on a campaign. A depot was established at Lost River Ford, and the supplies were to be brought there.

The troops were awaiting the arrival of the troops, mortars, and supplies that Colonel Wheaton had sent for, when the news came that Colonel Alvan Gillem, 1st Cavalry, had superseded Colonel Wheaton. Never since General McClellan had been relieved from the Army of the Potomac did I see such consternation rest on the faces of officers and men.[11] All the knowledge that Colonel Wheaton had gained by dearly bought experience was to be lost by the change of commanders, and it is so proven, as will be seen. On the top of this news came the news that a peace commission had been appointed to treat with the Indians, and no further active operation would be made against them.

Soon after, Colonel Gillem made his appearance at Lost River camp and relieved Colonel Wheaton from command. He never asked any information or allowed Wheaton to give him any, but blustered around the camp for a few days, bragging what he would do and how he would capture and kill the Modocs, had he the opportunity. When Colonel Wheaton was about to leave, he said in his lofty way, "Frank, should a fight occur, I will send for you, and you can have half the 'chicken pie.'" Wheaton asked what he meant by that. He replied, "Should a fight arise, you can come on the one side, and I on the other." "I am much obliged to you for the proposition, and will be glad to assist you, should a fight occur," said Wheaton. But when the fight did come off, Gillem did not keep his promise, and as he had no plan, he consequently failed.

The whole winter [was] passed, while we were in camp on Lost River, in drilling the troops every good day. Two companies of the 4th Artillery and two of the 12th Infantry arrived from San Francisco and went into camp at Van Bremer's ranch, where Colonel Gillem made his headquarters. Our company of the 1st Cavalry was stationed at Dorris's ranch,[12] and a few were at Fairchild's, all waiting for the arrival of the peace commissioners.

I had almost forgotten an affair that occurred about the time the troops arrived at Lost River, I think on January 22.[13] Captain Bernard, Co. F, 1st Cavalry, had been ordered to withdraw his troops from Land's ranch to Applegate's on Clear Creek and had removed all the property but 6,000 lbs. of grain. He sent two wagons in charge of [the] first sergeant and twenty men, ample to protect the wagons against all the Modocs in an open fight. They had been to the ranch, loaded their wagons, and returned on the road about two miles, when a party of Modocs lying in ambush surprised the party, drove them away from their wagons, and undertook to drive the wagons off. A messenger was sent to Captain Bernard at Applegate's, and he with the troops soon arrived on the ground. A sharp fight ensued. The wagons were recaptured, although partly burnt, and one Modoc killed and one wounded. The troops followed the Indians to the rocks and brought the wagons into camp. This was the first victory over the Modocs, if it might have been called so, but very little fighting was done, and it is believed that had the sergeant and his men shown fight, they could have driven them off at first.

The commission, as you are aware, was composed of Gen. E. B. Canby, Hon. A. B. Meacham, and Rev. [Eleazar] Thomas. The officers who knew the Indians had but very [little] faith in the commission, but I will not say anything about that, as it is always the way, "I told you so." But you know how it ended, and I will now skip to the day before the massacre, when the troops were in position to fight. After the many times that Jack had said tomorrow I will talk, and when it came the time to do so did not appear, the military had come to the conclusion he must fight and [was] preparing for war.

Colonel Gillem had moved his camp, consisting of three companies of the 4th Artillery, two of the 12th Infantry, and three companies of cavalry, making eight in all, to the bluff on the southeast border of Tule Lake and about one mile or one and a half miles from Jack's Stronghold. Major Mason, who was commanding on the other side of the lake, had moved his troops to Hospital Rock, less than one mile from Jack's camp and about five miles from [the] supply camp. The stores had been removed from Lost River when it was found impossible to make a treaty with Jack and a fight was almost a sure thing. Now everything was a tumult in camp. Some said Jack will come in, and others said not. Dispatches were frequent, and the troops were anxious to fight.

The writer visited Colonel Gillem's camp on the evening before the massacre of Canby and Thomas, and talked [with] both. He found them confident

Maj. John W. Green. CYRUS T. BRADY. *NORTHWESTERN FIGHTS AND FIGHTERS.*

that the Modocs would treat and suspicious that Riddle and his wife had not given the proper interpretation of the proposition offered to them. But as Bogus Charley, a Modoc Indian, had agreed to interpret to them the following day, they thought that Jack would be there and that they could come to some terms. Meacham was not so confident and often told me that he was afraid that there would be trouble and that we would have to fight it over again.

Well, about 9:00 P.M. that evening[14] Bogus Charley and his squaw came into camp, and he then told Riddle and his squaw that the Modocs meant to massacre the peace commissioners. He [Riddle] at once told Meacham, but everyone laughed at him and intimated to him that he was a coward.

The next morning Boston Charley came riding into camp and told them that Jack would meet them that day. Every one of the military thought that the Indians would treat that day, and I left that camp that morning for Hospital Rock to join the command there, expecting no more trouble from the Indians. But upon my arrival I found that a telegram had been received to the effect that the authorities were informed that Jack meant treachery.

About this time, a white flag was discovered advancing from Jack's camp. Lieutenant Sherwood, 21st Infantry, officer of the day, went to meet them. He soon returned and reported that it was three Modocs who wished to talk with the big *tyee,* or chief. Major Mason ordered him to return and inform the Indians that they would have to come in to the picket post to see him. Lt. W. H. Boyle, 21st Infantry, who was present and understood the Chinook jargon, asked permission to accompany him.

The two left to meet the flag of truce, passed the picket post, and proceeded about one-half mile farther in the direction of the Lava Beds, where they were met by an Indian in advance of the flag, who said his name was [Curly] Haired Jack [and] that Steamboat Frank and Comstock Dave were with the flag and wanted to talk with the tyee. He then asked Sherwood if Boyle was the tyee and was informed he was not. He then urged the officers to go up where Steamboat Frank was, and they would talk. But the officers began to see that they meant treachery. As they were without arms of any kind, they declined to go farther, but told the Indians to come where they were and they would talk with them, and that the commanding officer had directed them to come in to the picket post. He would there meet them and hear what they had to say. This the Indians refused to do. The officers saw at once that they were in for it, and being some half mile from the pickets and a good mile from camp, and in the power of three well-armed Indians, men chosen for the purpose, that their chance was very poor for getting back. So after some more parleying with the Indians to show that they [did] not fear them, they bid them good day and started for camp.

As soon as their backs were turned on the Indians, they began firing at the officers, and the officers began dodging behind the rocks. Boyle told Sherwood they best separate, one going to the right and the other to the left, which they did. But poor Sherwood had not gone over thirty paces when he was shot in the arm and leg and, as it proved, mortally wounded. When he fell, the Indians concentrated the fire upon Boyle and were following him up, but a soldier on post at the outer picket began firing on the Indians, who in turn, turned and fled towards the Lava Beds.

The troops were at once under arms and came to the rescue of Boyle. They met him sitting on a rock outside of the pickets, very much excited by scrambling among the rocks to keep out of the range of the Indians' rifles.

Sherwood was found where he fell and brought in to camp, where he died on the third day after. A better or more gentlemanly officer never wore the uniform of the U.S. Army, and all regretted his loss. An officer he was that few could fill his place in talent, gentlemanly conduct, etc. He had just returned from a trip to Europe, having visited London, Paris, Vienna, and all the large cities of note on the eastern continent. Young and energetic, with a long life before him, it was too hard to lose his life by such treachery.

While this act was transpiring, the Indians under Jack were doing their bloody work that has been so often told—the massacre of Canby and Thomas.

Colonel Gillem ordered all the troops to return to camp that evening. Two days passed, and all were anxious to close out the war, but he awaited orders from division headquarters. The troops in the meantime were preparing for the bloody encounter that followed. I only promised to give you my version of the battle. You can gain all the rest from others, but the fight I will give you the whole plan of, if a plan it could be called.

<hr />

SECOND BATTLE

Everything was now in readiness, and the day had been determined, April 15, 1873, to make the attack on Captain Jack's Stronghold. A consultation was held at headquarters. Colonel Gillem had decided to make the attack at

7:00 A.M., but Major Mason, who had been with Wheaton in the previous fight, asked to be allowed to take his command (consisting of three companies, 21st Infantry; two companies, 1st Cavalry; and the Warm Springs Indians, who had arrived the same day and were commanded by Captain Donald McKay, a half-breed Indian) that very same evening so he could take up a position without loss of any of his men. He was allowed to do so.

The command left camp at midnight, succeeded in getting into position, and would have almost advanced to the Stronghold, had it not been for some of the Indians being fishing on the lake that night. They went into position in the following order: the battalion, 21st Infantry, on the right, resting on the lake; the two companies of cavalry (dismounted) on the left of them; the Indians on the extreme left; and a battery of two howitzers in charge of Lieutenant Chapin, 4th Artillery, with their left in the air.

Colonel Gillem, who remained in camp, although in command, sent the troops on his side, in charge of Major Green, at 8:00 A.M. to take their position. They were met by the Indians some distance from the Lava Beds, and held the troops in check. This shows they should have taken their position at night and not waited until daylight to make their advance. Major Green's command consisted of Companies E, K, and M, 4th Artillery; Companies E and G, 12th Infantry. Thomas's Battalion A, 4th Artillery, remained in camp with the mortars, ready mounted for use. Captain Perry with Co. F, 1st Cavalry [took] up a position during the night without loss of any men.

At about 9:00 A.M. the battle became general along the whole line. Mason's command, being under cover, suffered no loss, with the exception of one Warm Springs Indian wounded. On Major Green's side of the Lava Beds, the loss was one officer, Lieutenant Eagan, wounded in the leg, three enlisted men killed, and nine wounded. Major Green made one or two unsuccessful attempts to carry the enemy positions, and as the darkness came on, the troops remained in the position they had taken that day, Colonel Gillem and staff [in] their camp, and the remainder of the officers remaining at their post with the troops. Cooked rations and hot coffee were furnished the troops. They passed the night building breastworks to cover them and taking up a more advanced position. Occasional firing occurred along the line during the night, but no general engagement ensued.

April 16, 1873. The day broke fair. As soon as it was light, the Indians discovered that the troops had advanced during the night. They commenced firing on the pickets, but without doing any damage. At about 10:00 A.M. a general advance was made, but with little success and with a loss on our side of two killed and four wounded, these being in Major Green's command. A general fusillade was kept up all day, and at evening the firing ceased on both sides. Our troops were rationed during the night, which they passed much in the same manner as the last. The soldiers were instructed to build stone breastworks sufficient to hold five or six men, and at no time to allow themselves to be surprised. They managed to allow two or three to sleep while the others watched. You could see the soldiers sleeping as soundly, with their heads pillowed on a rock, as if they had been in their camp.

Lieutenant Chapin took advantage of the darkness to advance his howitzers during the night on[to] a small hill that overlooked the Stronghold of Jack. In the morning he was prepared to throw his shell into the very mouth of the cave. Captain Thomas succeeded in getting his mortars in a good position to land his shell on the heads of the Modocs.

Everything was in splendid condition to do execution in the morning. The troops were in fine condition to fight and in good spirits. As the Modocs had been cut off from water the previous evening, they thought they had them sure. But while this preparation was going on outside of the caves, Jack and his warriors were also at work removing all of their property and women and children from the caves, about two miles to a safe retreat. When the army rested the previous evening, there was a gap left open between the right of Miller's[15] command and the left of the Warm Springs Indians, through which the Modocs carried their property, women and children, and old men. The Warm Springs Indians reported hearing children crying during the night, but did not report the fact to the commanding officer. So the Modocs were permitted to escape and take with them all their property, leaving sufficient men to make an appearance of their being still in position.

April 17, 1873. This day was as fine as could be expected. As soon as it was light, the firing began on our side, seemingly with little attention from the Modocs, until about 11:00 A.M., when the few that were left in the caves were reinforced by a few more of the party that had assisted the women and children to escape. A general engagement ensued. All the troops were brought into the field and advanced over the Lava Beds, but the Modocs had made good their escape and were again perched on top of the rocks about two miles distant.[16]

How they escaped was a miracle to the soldiers. But when they came to examine the cave, they found a fissure in the rocks, thrown up by nature, leading from the caves to the distant hills, making an avenue protected on both sides by rocks. This pass the Modocs had carefully guarded and marked by sticks and stones piled on top of one another, so that they could pass out as well by night as day.

The troops marched over the dreaded caves searching for the Modocs. In one fissure they found two squaws, more dead than alive, and soon after an old man, who had been left behind. The dead bodies of three Indians were also found. Some of the rags and plunder of the Indians, too worthless to carry, were left behind. Thus ended the three-day fight under Colonel Gillem, with the only success of having driven the Indians from their caves to a better position in the rocky hills.

The cavalry under Captains Bernard and Perry were in the afternoon ordered back to camp, with instructions to pursue the Indians that the colonel imagined had escaped from the Lava Beds. Bernard was to take the trail by the peninsula, and Perry was to make a circuit of the Lava Beds. The next morning they started. Indeed, they did make a good circuit, for the Indians were only some two miles from their former stronghold, and the cavalry made a march of about fifty miles and returned without doing any good but to disable their horses for future service.

Mason's command was ordered to hold the Lava Beds, or the cave Jack had formerly occupied. Some of the troops were ordered to Colonel Gillem's camp to protect it. All the property belonging to the infantry command was taken to the caves, and the cavalry to the peninsular camp formerly established by Major Mason. All were surprised to see the strong position held by Captain Jack. It was a natural strong position without being fortified. But the Indians had not been idle during the peace talk, but had built themselves a strong fort, all having avenues running one to another so that [they] could reinforce either portion of their work without exposing themselves. It was no longer a wonder that so small a party could hold out against so large a number of good troops, armed with the improved arms of the present day, for one good man in the position held by Jack would be equal to at least ten men on the outside.

April 18, 1873. During the day there was occasionally a shot fired by the Modoc Indians, who were in plain sight. They had a fire built and seemed to be burning their dead. Mason's command had fortified the caves, and the how-itzers and mortars were in position to protect them against an attack. Every-thing seemed to be inactive. Colonel Gillem, during the day, crossed over to Hospital Rock and ordered the property to be taken back to the peninsula, and the place to be abandoned. That evening everything that belonged to the infantry was moved to the caves, and the property of the cavalry and [friendly] Indians was in readiness to move back to their former camp.

Early the next morning, before it was light, the pack train was loaded and the Indian horses corralled. As soon as it was light, the whole train, in charge of Lieutenant Boyle, the quartermaster, started over the trail for camp. Had the Modoc Indians made an attack on the train, they could have with ease taken and destroyed the train and property in charge, as it was only guarded by a few sick men and superannuated Indians left by the Warm Springs to guard their dead. The train was stretched out over the trail for at least one mile and at the mercy of the Modocs. But fortunately they arrived in safety at their destina-tion. This closed the three days' fight, and the troops held the Stronghold of Jack. Our loss during this time amounted to one officer wounded, six enlisted men killed, and thirteen wounded.[17]

The cavalry arrived at the camp on the following day, and after stopping overnight, left their horses and again reported to Major Green for duty, dis-mounted. The following day Captain Perry arrived at the peninsula and reported that no Modocs were out of the Lava Beds, he having made a complete circuit of the Lava Beds, [with] stops at Van Bremer's, Ball's, and Dry Lake.

The Warm Springs Indians who had been sent by Colonel Gillem to the south of the Lava Beds also returned and reported no signs of the Indians hav-ing left the Lava Beds. The same day[18] a party of the Modocs were seen to go from the position they occupied to the lake for water. In plain sight of Colonel Gillem's camp, they procured water, and some of them had the audacity to bathe themselves in the lake, and only a feeble attempt was made to get them or attack them.

April 21, 1873. Colonel Gillem at this time sends the following telegram:

Lava Beds, April 21, 1873

To Maj. Gen. J. M. Schofield,
San Francisco, Ca.

The Indians have been found in the southern part of the Lava Beds, about four miles south of their old stronghold. It may seem incredible that they could have remained so near us three days undiscovered, but an examination of the lava fields, with their innumerable caves, crevices, and chasms, would explain how difficult it is to find a man who is endeavoring to conceal himself. They are about three miles from water; it was the want of water that forced them from their hiding place. So soon as Mendenhall[19] and Hasbrouck arrive, if not before, I shall again endeavor to surround the Indians.

Yesterday they fired from the rocks on an escort of fifty men, killing one and wounding one man.[20] I have requested Mendenhall to move as rapidly as possible. The Indians are here.

(Signed) Gillem,
Colonel 1st Cavalry

Now there was not a day during the three days passed that the Indians had not shown themselves, and Colonel Gillem had himself heard them firing. The first day after he had sent out the cavalry, he was at the camp at Hospital Rock, and the Indians fired on the Warm Springs Indians while they were bringing their dead. The next day they attacked four Indians sent by Lieutenant Boyle to carry a dispatch to Colonel Gillem, announcing the arrival of the cavalry and that they report no Indians have been seen outside of the Lava Beds. These Indians were attacked by the Modocs at the old camp, Hospital Rock, and one of the Warm Springs lost a horse, but they succeeded in driving off the small party of Modocs and arrived safely at Mason's camp in the Lava Beds. The Modocs had been down to the deserted camp, no doubt searching for cartridges that had been dropped by the soldiers.

On the third day the Modocs attacked a mule train inside of the pickets of Major Green taking rations to the soldiers, and killed one citizen, Mr. Hovey,[21] a young man from Yreka, California, and wounded a soldier. The Warm Springs Indians were then ordered to take post at the head of the bay, to keep the Indians from coming to that point for water; also, to keep the Modocs from coming into Gillem's camp to carry rumors.

Everything was now quiet, the soldiers and officers anxious to do something, but Colonel Gillem disposed to await the arrival of the two companies of artillery under Captain Mendenhall, now en route from San Francisco. And with the enemy in plain sight, [the] army rested.

Delays are dangerous, and it was so in this case, for failing to follow up the attack after driving the Indians from their stronghold gave them (the Indians) time to recuperate, and bred discontent among the officers and men of the command, who were anxious to close out this disgusting war. No one could tell what Colonel Gillem was waiting for, as Mendenhall's two companies were not required to surround the Indians. They had to be assailed in their strong position and either killed or captured. It was impossible to surround them.

Major Green was anxious to attack at once, and so was Major Mason, but an apathy had settled on Colonel Gillem and, like a nightmare, seemed to follow him about. His own personal safety was all he seemed to think of. As many of the troops as possible were brought to his camp, and to have viewed the affair, one would have thought that the Modocs were expected to attack him at most any moment.

About this time, news was received that Colonel Davis was to take command, and those who knew him, and all [who] had heard of his good fighting abilities, were glad to hear of his appointment, for all had lost confidence in their present commander.

The cavalry having returned without finding the Modocs (who had never been out of sight), Colonel Gillem sent Donald McKay, the chief of the scouts, with some of his men to find the exact position of the Modocs and a trail, so as to bring the howitzers and mortars up to the position the enemy occupied, to again begin an attack.

McKay explored the route [and] found the enemy in a strong position. A good trail led to their stronghold, he so reported to Colonel Gillem, but Colonel Gillem not being satisfied with the report of McKay, conferred with Major Green, and they determined to send Captain Thomas, 4th Artillery, with Cos. A and K, 4th Artillery; E, 12th Infantry; and a party of Warm Springs scouts. About eighty-five men in all left the camp of Colonel Gillem on the morning of April 26 to make a reconnaissance over the same trail that Donald McKay had been and [had] reported to Colonel Gillem as practicable to pass the guns and troops over. This party met with no opposition and had reached the point designated for them to go—a sand butte near the position where the Modocs had taken up their position. From that point, Colonel Gillem had determined to plant his mortars and howitzers. They moved about 12:00 P.M., and seeing no signs of the enemy, the party halted to rest themselves and to take a lunch, without proper provision in sending out flankers and pickets to ascertain if any of the enemy were in order.

While clustered together in a friendly group, they were fired upon by the enemy, who, seeing the disadvantage the troops were under, at once demoralized and disorganized the whole command. All the officers fell wounded and killed in the first fire,[22] trying to rally the men. Some of the men deserted the officers, but most all remained and were killed, as reported by Colonel Davis in his report. All the brave men remained and were killed, and the cowards ran away and were saved. Of the whole party that left camp on that morning, not one of the officers were left. Captain Thomas of the 4th Artillery was killed almost at the first fire, trying to rally his men. Lieutenants Wright, Howe, and Cranston followed soon after. Thirteen enlisted men were killed and sixteen wounded.[23] Most of the wounded have died since from their wounds and exposure, during the time they were wounded and the time they were brought to the camp for medical treatment—some twenty-four hours.

The firing commenced about 12:00 P.M. and could be heard very plainly at Gillem's and Mason's camp and at the quartermaster's depot at Scorpion Point. Stragglers began coming to Gillem's camp at 1:30 P.M. and reported that the troops were being worsted. All the troops were at this time ready and anxious to go to their support. But Colonel Gillem, as usual, lost all control of himself and would not act, nor let others.

Before the troops left camp under Major Green, darkness had settled, and the weather that had been unusually pleasant now turned blustery, stormy, and disagreeable. The troops were about six hours making the distance of four miles, and when they did arrive, what a sight met their gaze. In a small space, less than 100 feet square, lay the dead, dying, and wounded men and officers. It was almost impossible to find the wounded, as they were afraid to answer when called to, thinking it was some device of the Modocs to get them out and massacre them. When the troops arrived, they at once gathered together the wounded and the dead. Officers, Captain Thomas, Lieutenants Wright, Howe, Harris, and Dr. Semig—the last two wounded, the other three dead. Lieutenant Cranston's body could not be found. The officers had all died fighting. The body of Lieutenant Wright was pierced with a number of balls, and he lay dead, still grasping his rifle in the act of firing, with the dead body of a sergeant lying across his body, who had no doubt died defending him. It was so in almost every case, and [with] all that fell that day, when the bravest of the brave died.

Had they been commanded by some experienced Indian fighter, the surprise could not have happened. The officers who commanded were as brave [as] any men could be, but being just from the East and never having seen any frontier duty, it was an oversight to place him [Thomas] in command of troops that were to meet a subtle foe like the Modocs. He was not to blame, but those who sent him to perform that duty. Had he sent out flankers and made the proper disposition of his troops when he came to halt, the Indians could not have taken him at a disadvantage. When attacked he should have at once charged the enemy and drove them from their position. He would have lost some men, but he would not have suffered as he did by falling back to an open country and allowing the enemy to shoot down his men without retaliating, or even doing any harm to the enemy.

The troops, having succeeded in finding most of the wounded and dead, placed the wounded on the pack mules, buried the dead soldiers in a row, covered them with sagebrush, and then started for camp.

The elements seemed at that time to be trying to cover this awful scene by one of the most fearful storms I ever beheld. All the fore part of the evening it had been raining; now it turned to snow and hail, and never did men suffer as did the officers and soldiers on that night, hearing the wails of the dying and the fearful spectacle of dead men packed on the backs of mules, and the war of the elements. It was a picture too fearful to contemplate or describe. The suffering of that night's march made many a young man old, spent as it was among their dead and dying comrades. And what the wounded suffered before the troops came to their succor cannot be described, lying helpless, hearing the powwow of the Indians, and expecting to be killed and scalped by those bloodhounds, who were lying in wait for them to come from their hiding places.

The troops arrived at Gillem's camp at daybreak the next morning, being out all night. This ended the Thomas affair.

The Modoc Muddle

EDWARD FOX[1]

New York *Herald,* February 21, 1873[2]

HERALD HEADQUARTERS,
FAIRCHILD'S RANCH, SISKIYOU COUNTY,
UPPER CALIFORNIA, February 5, 1873

I have at last arrived in the neighborhood of the famous Lava Beds, a spot which will be celebrated for years to come as the scene of one of the most decided victories the Indians ever achieved in this state. After arriving in San Francisco, I was shown a dispatch from the neighborhood of Yreka stating that they had experienced a very heavy fall of snow, rendering the roads nearly impassable, and consequently obstructing the portage of ammunition and rations to the front. I, however, decided to leave immediately and started last Saturday morning by rail to Redding, via Sacramento. The journey by rail to Redding took seventeen hours, bringing me to the latter spot at 11:00 P.M. the same day. I resumed my journey on the following day by stage, leaving at 6:00 A.M. After a tedious journey, lasting about six hours, over a very bad road, and part of the journey through eighteen inches of snow, I arrived at Yreka last Monday at noon.

Yreka is a small mining town of about 1,500 inhabitants and situated in Siskiyou County, some 400 miles due north of San Francisco and about sixty or seventy miles south of the borderline between Oregon and California. There was considerable excitement in this little community about the Indian troubles, and on the whole the business portion of the residents were rather jubilant, as trade was good. In consequence of the demand for grain to supply the troops, the price of the latter article had risen from two cents to four cents, but at the latter figure there was plenty to be had. Colonel Hague, who was stationed at Yreka forwarding up supplies, stated that the troops were now well furnished with rations, forage, and ammunition. Finding the news at Yreka relative to the war was of the most opposite nature, I deemed it prudent to visit the scene of action before sending my first letter. In fact, it was hard to find two people with the same story, and having no inclination to be "steamboated," as they call it, I paid a visit to a livery stable and contracted with the proprietor for passage to the army headquarters, some seventy miles distant in an easterly direction. Having learned that there were no accommodations at the front and, in fact, no tents for the men, I supplied myself with a rubber sheet and plenty of blankets, in order to be prepared for camping out.

I left Yreka early Tuesday morning, in company with a correspondent of a Sacramento newspaper,[3] and after a pleasant drive of about eighteen miles across Little Shasta Valley, we began the ascent of Goose Nest Mountain. This proved to be a rather tedious undertaking, as the incline was steep and the road heavy. The country through which we passed gave evidence of a volcanic origin, as some very abrupt strata of rock were visible in all directions, giving the appearance of a mass of rock suddenly uplifted by some violent action and hurled in every direction. After about twelve miles of ascent, we arrived at the top of the range and continued along its summit for a short distance, passing through a considerable depth of snow. The mountain was well timbered with immense sugar, yellow, and bastard pines, spruce, fir, redwood, and mountain maple. During the ascent, we passed several empty wagons returning from the front, and also two United States cavalrymen.

These gentlemen told us they were going down to escort some grain wagons, but I have since learned they were deserting. The descent on the northern side of the mountain was tolerably easy, as the road was well graded; but in some places it was very soft, and our wagon sank in on several occasions up the axletrees. Descending the mountain, we obtained a view of Butte Creek Valley, with Mount Shasta in the distance away to the eastward. Mount Shasta is the highest mountain in the neighborhood, being over 14,000 feet above the level of the sea, and was originally a volcano, a fact which probably accounts for the nature of the surrounding country. The hundreds of cattle and horses that dotted Butte Creek Valley showed plainly the calling pursued by the residents of that locality, and we presently had the pleasure of making the acquaintance of one of the occupants of the valley, at whose ranch we passed the night. We arrived at Ball's ranch about 5:00 P.M. and camped there for the night, having made the journey from Yreka, thirty-eight miles, in about nine hours. It may appear rather slow traveling to those accustomed to the civilized regions of the East, but I was most agreeably pleased at not being swamped and left on the mountain at night. Mr. Ball and his brother received us with the accustomed hospitality of the frontier settler, and after doing ample justice to a bountiful supper, I unrolled my blankets and, stretching out on the floor, enjoyed a good sleep before a log fire. Before lying down, however, I made some inquiries as to the locality of Colonel Gillem's headquarters, and was informed that he had just pitched his camp at Van Bremer's station, some twenty-five miles distant.

We started next morning and crossed Butte Creek Flat, but missed the road to Van Bremer's, and finally struck Dorris's[4] ranch. There we learned that Colonel Gillem's was expected shortly from Fairchild's ranch, and so we started out and met the colonel about two miles from Dorris's, riding in an open wagon, and I delivered him some dispatches that had been entrusted to my charge at Yreka. The colonel informed me that he was going to stop the night at Dorris's and proceed in the morning to Lost River. As the colonel stated I could get a horse at Fairchild's, we resumed our journey and arrived at the last-named place at 4:00 P.M. this afternoon.

I will now give a brief sketch of the Modoc troubles and their origin, as far as I have been able to learn from the settlers who have resided here for the past eighteen years. The Modoc tribe have for the last forty years resided on Lost River and this section of the country and, in fact, claim it as their own. Since the whites first located this section of the country, on the borders of Oregon and California, they have occasionally had trouble with the Modocs, but in nearly all cases it was between the Oregon settlers and the Indians. About eighteen years ago Ben Wright, an old Indian fighter, invited a number of this tribe to a peace feast, and when he got them all together, his men fired into the crowd and killed some forty or fifty.[5] This naturally created considerable distrust between the whites and Indians, and after this country was tolerably well settled, in about the year 1857 there was some movement to get the tribe on a reservation. In the year 1864 the Modoc tribe, or what was left of them, were residing on Lost River, near Tule Lake, under the leadership of a chief named Schonchin, and an effort was then made by the resident Indian commissioner[6] to get them to move to Yainax reservation, on Martin River. After considerable talk, Schonchin and about thirty warriors, with their wives and papooses, left for the reservation, but the remainder of the tribe decided to remain where they were and recognized Captain Jack as their chief.[7]

This, however, did not satisfy the Oregon settlers, and persistent efforts were made to get Captain Jack and the rest of the tribe to move in the same direction. They, however, had paid occasional visits to the reservation, and finding that game was scarce, preferred the plentiful supply of fish from Lost River to taking the chances of living at the government expense. The troubles, however, still continued, and in the fall of 1867 Mr. Lindsey Applegate induced Captain Jack to accept the hospitality of Uncle Sam, and they consequently moved up to Yainax reservation. They remained there during the months of September, October, November, December, and January, and then returned to their old quarters on Lost River.

Captain Jack stated his reasons for returning were because they had nothing to eat on the reservation, and they actually had to kill and eat some of their horses in order to prevent starvation. They have now resided on Lost River since February 1868 and have obtained a living by fishing, hunting, and trapping. The California settlers do not appear to have had much trouble with them since their return; but they were perpetually quarrelling with the settlers on the Oregon side of the line, on whom, it appears, they were in the habit of levying a mild kind of blackmail in the shape of axes, knives, rope, etc. There was, however, no open outbreak, and last summer the Modoc tribe were camped on Lost River in two bands, one on each side of the river. Captain Jack had about fourteen warriors in his camp on the west side of the river, and there were about twelve on the other side under the command of an Indian known as Curly Headed Doctor. There were also some few scattered about around Tule Lake, making in all about thirty-one or thirty-two warriors. Another band of the same tribe were camped near Fairchild's and Dorris's ranches.

The two latter gentlemen and some of the other settlers made treaties with these Modocs for the privilege of living and grazing their stock on Butte Creek Flat. The first treaty was made with Ike, an Indian who claimed the right over that section of the country. A second treaty was made with Big Jack, and finally a third with Captain Jack, [John] Schonchin, and others. A consideration was paid the Indians on each occasion. This party of Indians, residing near Fairchild's and Dorris's ranches, mustered about thirteen braves and were considered to belong to Captain Jack's band, though they denied his authority and rather looked up to an Indian blessed with the romantic name Shacknasty Jim. I allude especially to this band, as I shall have occasion to give them prominent mention further on.

Towards the fall of last year, Mr. Odeneal, the president Indian commissioner, annoyed by the perpetual complaints of Oregon settlers, determined to remove the Modoc Indians to Yainax reservation. A combined movement was made on Thanksgiving Day last November. A party of soldiers from Fort Klamath, under the command of Captain Jackson and accompanied by Mr. Ivan Applegate, the son of the late Indian commissioner, visited Captain Jack's party; simultaneously, a party of Oregon settlers, well armed and under the command of Mr. Oliver Applegate, went to the camp of the party under the leadership of Curly Headed Doctor.

A discussion ensued between the troops and Captain Jack's band, as the latter refused to leave their present quarters, which ended in a fight, and both parties claim that the other fired first. In this fight, two Indians were killed and several soldiers killed and wounded. In the meantime, the settlers had nearly prevailed on Curly Headed Doctor's band to go to the reservation, as they stated that Captain Jack's band had surrendered; but hearing the firing on the other side of the river, they refused to go, and presently both sides began firing. The citizens finally retreated, leaving one of their party on the field, and the Indians state the whites killed a squaw and two papooses in the fight. This party then broke loose over the country and murdered some twelve or thirteen white settlers, and then, going round the northern end of Tule or Rhett Lake, joined Captain Jack in the Lava Beds.

Captain Jack and his party had retreated there immediately after the fight with the soldiers, but kept on the California side of the river and went into the Lava Beds from the southern side. They did not murder any citizens on their retreat and, in fact, told a settler named Samuel Watson to go home, as they only wanted to fight with soldiers, not settlers. The first intelligence of the

Thanksgiving fight that was brought to the Butte Creek Flat settlers came by Samuel Watson, the man who had been sent back by Captain Jack unharmed.

Messrs. Fairchild, Dorris, Ball, and others then paid a visit to Shacknasty Jim's party, who were residing near Fairchild's ranch, and found them very much excited, as they heard the Oregon settlers were coming over to clean them out. Fairchild, Dorris, and party told them to keep quiet, and they would see they were not harmed. These Indians had considerable confidence in the above named men, as they had lived close to them for years without trouble. Fairchild then wrote to Captain Jackson, stating that he wished to take this party of Indians to the reservation. His letter was forwarded by Captain Jackson to Major Green at Fort Klamath, and the latter immediately wrote to Fairchild, telling him to bring them on, and also stating on what terms he would receive the surrender of Captain Jack and his party.

A consultation was then held between the Battle Creek Flat settlers, and it was arranged that Fairchild, Dorris, Ball, and Beawick should accompany the Shacknasty party to the reservation. They accordingly started, and reached Klamath River the same evening and stopped at the ferry run by Bob Whittle. When they were there, some man called out from the other side that a party of Oregon settlers had crossed the river further down and intended coming up to massacre the Indians. Fairchild and the other whites then went down to meet this party and had a talk with them. They stated they did not intend to hurt the Indians, but had come over to protect a settler of the name of Small,[8] who they heard was in danger. Fairchild and party then returned to the ferry, and about midnight Mr. Dyar, the subagent, came over and said the Indians must be got through that night, as the settlers in Linkville were very excited and, if they saw the Indians, might massacre them.

There was some trouble then about getting their horses, and it was 2:30 A.M. before they were ready to start. They then came to the conclusion that they could not get through Linkville before light, and the Indians, getting scared, started back for the mountains. They were, however, induced to return to their settlement at Fairchild's, and while the latter was arranging to get troops to protect them to the reservation, they all started off one night and joined Captain Jack in the Lava Beds, reinforcing his command with fourteen of the best warriors in the tribe. Some days before this party finally left, Messrs. Fairchild, Dorris, Beawick, and Murray went to Captain Jack's camp, accompanied by three of the Indians, and had a big talk. When there Fairchild read Major Green's letter to them, which stated that the only terms that could be offered was an unconditional surrender of the murderers and the immediate departure of the rest of the band for the reservation. Captain Jack did not make any direct reply to this communication, but decline to go to the reservation, as the country was too cold and he wanted something to eat. The mission consequently resulted in nothing.[9]

New York *Herald,* February 24, 1873[10]

HERALD HEADQUARTERS,
LOST RIVER CAMP, Oregon, February 8, 1873

The battle of the Lava Beds has attracted so much general attention, both from the fact of the United States troops receiving such a severe check and from the varied descriptions of the scene of the contest, that I have prepared a pretty full report of that memorable engagement, feeling convinced that the details will be read with interest by the public in general.

After Captain Jack was driven from his camp on Lost River and took refuge in the Lava Beds, it was thought at first that he would come to terms and the war would be ended without further bloodshed. The addition, however, of fourteen warriors[11] to his forces that were really driven to the Lava Beds by the threats of Linkville citizens, heated by Linkville whiskey, resulted in Captain Jack wishing to make his own terms.

But Lt. Col. Frank Wheaton, who, as the commanding officer of the lakes, had come down in person to attend to this affair, soon arrived at the conclusion that if fighting was to be done, the sooner this lava bed was inspected the better. Arrangements were then made for an attack, and as soon as the available troops had arrived in the neighborhood, Colonel Wheaton had several councils with Major Green, Major Mason, and others as to the best means of getting at Jack in his lair. The Lava Beds were inspected and all the old settlers interrogated as to the geography, with reference to the moving of troops in that direction.

There appeared to be a good many opinions as to the nature of the ground, and although all agreed in saying it was a very rough country, no one was competent to describe the extraordinary volcanic formations that were afterwards discovered by the troops when they made the assault.

After mature consideration of the various plans of attack that were suggested, Colonel Wheaton decided to make a movement in force which, should it not prove successful, would at least enable him to obtain a satisfactory reconnaissance of the ground upon which to base his plans for any future aggressive movement. Everything being arranged, the following orders were issued to the officers in command:

THE ORDERS FOR THE ATTACK
HEADQUARTERS, DISTRICT OF THE LAKES,
AND OF THE TROOPS OPERATING IN THE MODOC COUNTRY
CAMP NEAR VAN BREMER'S RANCH, Cal.,

Jan. 12, 1873
GENERAL FIELD ORDERS NO. 3

1. The troops will move from their present camp east and west of the Lava Beds on Thursday, January 16, and take positions for the attack on the Modoc camp at sunrise on the following morning.

2. At 4:00 A.M. on Thursday next, Maj. John Green will detach Capt. D. Perry's Troop F, 1st Cavalry, and order it to clear the bluff southwest of Tule of Indian pickets and scouts, and cover the movement of the main force to a camp some three miles west of the Modoc position.

3. Maj. E. C. Mason's battalion 21st Infantry, two companies— C, Capt. G. H. Burton,[12] and B, commanded by 2d Lt. H. D. W. Moore—and a detachment of twenty men of F Company, 21st Infantry, under 1st Sgt. John McNamara; Gen. J. E. Ross, Oregon volunteer militia, two companies—A, Capt. Hugh Kelley, and B, Capt. O. E. Applegate; and Lt. W. H. Miller's battery—a section of mountain howitzers—will march from Van Bremer's ranch to camp on bluff west of Tule Lake in time to reach the designated camp not later than 3:00 P.M. on the sixteenth instant. The camp will be so located and arranged as to be secure from observation by the Modocs, and every precaution taken to prevent the Indians from discovering our numbers and precise location.

4. District headquarters will accompany the troops.

5. Early on January 17 the troops above named will move into the Lava Beds to attack the Modoc camp, and in the following order: Maj. E. C. Mason's battalion, 21st Infantry, leading, followed by Gen. J. E. Ross's Oregon volunteer militia, and the section of mountain howitzers packed. Capt. D. Perry, Troop F, 1st Cavalry, will follow the howitzer battery.

6. When the troops have reached a position near the Modoc camp, the main force will be deployed on the right of the infantry battalion in close skirmish order, and a left half-wheel of the whole line will be executed in order to enclose the southern side of the Modoc position and connect the right of the main force with the left of Captain Bernard's troop, who are simultaneously to attack on the east.

7. Also, the troops operating against the Modocs are to move from the camp with three days' cooked rations in haversacks, two blankets, 100 rounds of ammunition on the person, and fifty rounds in close reserve. Canteens will be filled at Little Klamath Lake by the troops moving from Van Bremer's ranch, and care taken to water every horse and pack mule at that point, as there is no water on the bluff where the main force will encamp on the night of the sixteenth inst.

8. Maj. John Green, 1st Cavalry, is charged with the execution of these movements and the details of the attack.

9. Lt. W. H. Miller, 1st Cavalry, commanding the howitzer battery, will report to Major Green for orders and instructions as to when and where to prepare his guns for action in the proposed attack.

10. The troops on the east side of the Lava Beds at Land's ranch, Troops G, Capt. R. F. Bernard, and B, Capt. James Jackson, 1st Cavalry, and the Klamath Indian scouts under Dave Hill will move from camp on the sixteenth inst. to a point not more than two miles from the Modoc position. At sunrise on the seventeenth, this force will attack the Modoc camp, with their right resting on or near Tule Lake, and when sufficiently near to render the movement advisable, a right half-wheel will be executed, in order to connect the left of this force with the troops attacking from the west. In his advance Captain Bernard, 1st Cavalry, will take steps to capture any canoes the Modocs may have near their camp, or at least use every effort to prevent Indians escaping by water. Capt. R. F. Bernard, 1st Cavalry, will execute these movements under such detailed instructions as he may receive from Maj. John Green, 1st Cavalry.

11. After the first three shots have been fired by the howitzer battery as the signal for the troops attacking on the east side of the Modoc camp, firing will cease for fifteen minutes, and an Indian scout directed to notify the nearest Modocs that ten minutes' time will be allowed them to permit their women and children to come into our lines. Any proposition by the Modocs to surrender will be referred at once to the district commander, who will be present.

12. Lt. W. H. Boyle, 21st Infantry, acting field quartermaster and commissary of subsistence and a guard of ten men will remain at this camp in charge of the temporary field depot until further orders.

13. Lt. John Adams, 1st Cavalry, acting assistant adjutant general, District of the Lakes, and commanding detachment, H Troop, 1st Cavalry, will furnish from his command such details as may be required for the howitzer battery and accompany this district commander. Lieutenant Adams will be prepared to communicate by signals with the signal sergeant, who has been detailed for duty with the troops on the east side of the Modoc position.

14. Assistant Surgeon Henry McElderry, United States Army, will give the necessary directions and instructions to the medical officers with the different commands and detachments in the field.

By order of Bvt. Maj. Gen. Frank Wheaton, 21st Infantry,
Commanding District of the Lakes.
John Q. Adams, first lieutenant, 21st Cavalry,
Acting Assistant Adjutant General.

In pursuance of the above, and according to instructions, the troops moved from their quarters on the sixteenth inst. and camped in the respective locations to which they were assigned. Captain Bernard, with two troops of the 1st Cavalry, had a little skirmish on the evening of the sixteenth, as in the fog, which is very prevalent in that section of the country, he advanced rather nearer to Jack's Stronghold than he intended, and when he found out his mistake and made a move to retire, the Indians opened fire from a position they had taken in the rocks. They were finally driven from their shelter and forced to retreat to their stronghold, but not before they had wounded three of the cavalry.

On the following morning the troops had all arrived at their assigned positions, and at daybreak Lieutenant Adams reported to Colonel Wheaton the following force in the field:

Corps	Commanding Officer	Muster
1st Cavalry	Captain Perry, F Troop	46
1st Cavalry	Captain Jackson, B Troop	42
1st Cavalry	Captain Bernard, G Troop	47
1st Cavalry	Lieutenant Adams, H Troop	16
21st Infantry	Lieutenant Ross, B Company	38
21st Infantry	Captain Burton, C Company	57
Oregon Field Officers		7
Oregon Volunteers	Capt. O. Applegate, A Company	56
Oregon Volunteers	Captain Kelley, B Company	46
California Volunteers	Captain Fairchild	25
Indian scouts	Dave Hill	20
	Total	400

There was also a section of mountain howitzers under the charge of Lieutenant Miller of the 1st Cavalry. The troops on the west side moved down the precipitous bluff from their campground in the direction of the Lava Beds, Major Mason's battalion of the 21st Infantry leading, followed by Captain Fairchild's California riflemen, General Ross's two companies of Oregon volunteers, the howitzer section packed on mules, under the command of Lt. W. H. Miller of the 1st Cavalry, and Capt. D. Perry's troop of the 1st Cavalry bringing up the rear.

The morning was damp and cold, and the Lava Beds were nearly obscured from sight by a dense fog, which, however, only hung over that section and did not rise to the bluff which the troops had just left. The troops on the east side, commanded by Capt. R. B. Bernard of the 1st Cavalry, comprising his Troop G and Capt. James Jackson's Troop B, 1st Cavalry, with twenty Klamath scouts commanded by Dave Hill, simultaneously advanced from the position they had taken the previous evening, two miles from Captain Jack's Stronghold. On account of the deep chasm and gorge in his front, Captain Bernard was unable to advance farther than the position he had reached by severe skirmishing on the evening of the sixteenth.

The advance, attack, and management of the troops were conducted by Maj. John Green, 1st Cavalry, and the district commander, Lt. Col. Frank Wheaton of the 21st Infantry, accompanied the troops operating on the west side. This force had moved forward from the base of the bluffs, with Captain Burton's company of the 21st Infantry ahead, in skirmishing order. Upon the arrival of the troops at the lake, a rush was made for water, as the men were naturally thirsty, having passed the night at a dry camp. The advance was then resumed across this rugged country, and it was with the greatest difficulty the men were kept in line, as the unnatural irregularities of the volcanic rock formed nearly insurmountable obstacles to their progress. The line was now being deployed to the right, stretching into the heart of this fastness about a mile and a half, while Captain Burton moved with his company on the extreme left, supported by Lieutenant Moore and his command on his right. The Oregon and California volunteers spread out the line between the extreme points and kept a steady advance, although the nature of the ground kept an irregularity in the face of the line.

The plan of attack was to keep deploying in a half wheel to the right until Captain Perry should connect with Captain Bernard, who was adopting similar tactics but moving from the left. The fog still hung low and shrouded the mysteries of this craggy fastness from these daring explorers, though the frequent crack of a rifle, followed by an unearthly war whoop, denoted some fresh victim to the unerring marksmanship of these dusky warriors. It was impossible for men to do more than both the soldiers and the volunteers did on this occasion, and although every now and then there would be a vacancy in the muster roll, and some gallant soul would fall by the bullet of an unseen foe, another brave heart would fill up the gap and press on with the steadiness of a disciplined soldier. In vain the troops looked high and low for some Indian sign, and although the fog would rise every now and then, not an Indian showed as much as the top of his head feathers.

About noon Captain Perry, on the extreme right, arrived at an impassable chasm;[13] at least, it was impassable without a fearful sacrifice of life. Captain Perry sent back to the district commander that it would be impossible for him to connect with Captain Bernard by the right except by an immense loss of life, and added that if necessary he would carry the chasm, but he did not expect to take ten men across. Colonel Wheaton then came to the conclusion that if the proposed connection could not be made, they might as well retire and wait for a few days, and consequently issued orders to that effect, but gave Major Green a discretionary power to push forward and connect by the left if he deemed it feasible.

Major Green then ordered a flank movement by the left, and skirting along the lake under the shadow of some craggy strata of volcanic rock in the possession of the enemy, they finally made the desired connection, but not before the galling fire to which they had been subjected had thinned their ranks considerably. It would fill columns to detail the incidents of this fight, which proved such a trial to the officers, soldiers, and volunteers that formed the attacking party. Colonel Wheaton told me the other day that he had been through all the principal battles during the Rebellion, and he had never seen officers and men appear so indifferent to danger or so cool and steady under such a harassing fire.

The Indians did not waste much powder and shot, as they were excellent marksmen and, having the advantage of a rest for the rifle and perfect safety

Gillem's camp and Tule Lake. NATIONAL ARCHIVES.

from a return fire, were unerring in their aim. Often a man would fall badly wounded and, looking eagerly around for his enemy, would only see the smoke of a rifle curling up from a small hole on some inaccessible crag overhanging his position. On one occasion a man was shot dead at a certain spot, and another man was sent with a stretcher to carry away his body. The second met the fate of the first, and a third, who went on the same errand, fell badly wounded. These men all fell without knowing the position of the Indians who had shot them. Every little, narrow passage between the rocks that was likely to be of importance was guarded by two or three rifles, peeping out from loopholes that the Indians had formed for that purpose.

On the move along the lake to the left, the men had to move with the greatest caution, as the Indians had lined the overhanging bluffs with their men, and to show yourself in full view was nearly certain death. They crawled on their hands and feet, making a dart every now and then from one rock to another, but still pushing forward in the direction of Captain Bernard. Captain Perry, who was with his troops on the left, while stretched behind a rock accidentally turned on his side and exposed a portion of his shoulder and arm, receiving a severe flesh wound, which compelled him to retire. Major Green and Major Mason were perpetually in the hottest of the fire and appear to have charmed lives as, although their uniforms were in many instances cut by a passing ball, neither received a scratch during the fight. There was not an officer that went into the Lava Beds that did not come out with some portion of his clothing marked or torn by a bullet. When the troops on the west side finally connected with Captain Bernard, they found him stopped from further advance by an immense chasm that appeared impassable, and which was strongly defended by Indians.

Shortly before dark the fog lifted slightly and showed the Oregon volunteers, a portion of Captain Perry's troop, and the infantry reserve still on the west side, and at a signal from the district commander, Major Green fell back to

Land's ranch to camp for the night with Bernard's command and the infantry battalion. The Oregon and California Volunteers retired by the west side and fell back to Van Bremer's ranch.

I cannot conclude without saying something of the difficulties experienced in the retreat to Land's ranch, and of the bravery and heroism exhibited by the officers and men on that occasion. They had been up since 4:00 A.M. and fighting since 6:30 A.M. up to dark. The retreat commenced at 10:30 P.M. and continued all night and up to 1:00 P.M. next day. Thirty-three hours without rest or food are enough to try the patience and endurance of most men, but these gallant fellows never uttered a word and were always ready to relieve one another at the end of a blanket, carrying the sick and wounded. Surgeon McElderry worked unceasingly and, through the day, was exposed on several occasions to a dangerous fire, but never flinched from his duty, and rushed from place to place to the assistance of the wounded.[14]

━━ ≡◆≡ ━━

New York *Herald,* February 27, 1873

HERALD HEADQUARTERS,
LOST RIVER CAMP, February 12, 1873

Affairs here are progressing rather slowly, and until the peace commission arrive and get through their talk, there will be no aggressive move against Captain Jack and his forces. That redoubtable warrior is still ensconced in his lava stronghold and, as he is well posted about everything going on outside, will remain there until he hears what proposals the peace commissioners have to make. There is very little doubt Jack is willing to make terms, but he is powerless to a certain extent, as Curly Headed Doctor, who leads the party of Indians that committed all the murders, is strongly in favor of fighting, on the principle that they might as well die in arms as give themselves up and be hanged for murder. Scarfaced Charley, the Indian that is credited with firing the first shot of the campaign, is also said to be a strong peace man and a firm supporter of Captain Jack. They have about ten others with them, which leaves nearly thirty-five in favor of fight. It is estimated by the settlers, who have known these Indians for years, that there are about forty-four or forty-five warriors in the Lava Beds, but they are assisted by some forty to forty-five old men, squaws, and children. The latter portion are of considerable use in such a natural fortification as they occupy at present, as anyone that can hold a rifle and pull a trigger is equal to ten men on the attack.

I had a talk the other day with a squaw[15] of the Modoc tribe who had been in to see Captain Jack. She said that Captain Jack, Scarfaced Charley, and about ten others are in favor of peace, but the rest of the tribe are decidedly against it. It is very amusing to listen to the opinions of different people around this section of the country as to the origins of the disturbance, as they are of the most opposite nature and vary according to the exact locale of the informant.

When I arrived first at Yreka, I received various accounts from persons, but on the whole they appeared of the opinion that the Indians had been treated badly, and that Davis and Fairchild were the prime workers in the entire movement, and rather encouraged war in order to get a good bill out of Uncle Sam. The nearer I approached the region of the Lava Beds, on the California side, the stronger became the feeling that the Indians were badly used, but the blame was thrown on the Indian agent and the Applegate family. A member of the latter family, Mr. Jesse Applegate, has been appointed peace commissioner. He is a large real estate proprietor in Oregon and has considerable interests in some land lately taken up in this neighborhood under the Swamp or Over-flowed Land Act. Here in Oregon the settlers are rather bitter against the Indians, and many of them coolly assert that Captain Jack was advised to hold his position at all hazards by Mr. Elijah Steele, a man of high standing in this section, but a resident of Yreka and a friend of the Indians as far as right and wrong are concerned.

There is, however, little doubt that the Indians have been badly treated, and if the whites had kept faith with them, there would have been no disturbance at all. The late Indian agent, Mr. Meacham, thoroughly understood this Modoc tribe and took some interest in their case, so far as to forward their claim to this Lost River slip of land to Washington. From all accounts, Captain Jack appears to be a "very square" Indian, and he has on several occasions returned property to the settlers that some of his tribe had stolen. The present Indian agent, Mr. Odeneal, was evidently misinformed as to the class of Indians he had to deal with when he sent Mr. Ivan Applegate to Major Green for twelve or fifteen men to assist him in forcing Captain Jack and his warriors onto the Yainax reservation. Major Green, however, was a little better posted and sent Captain Jackson, of the 1st Cavalry, with his troop.

The action of the troops on one side of Lost River and the gallant Oregon citizens on the other has already been fully described, and it is generally thought that some warning should have been given to the settlers before making an aggressive movement against these Indians. The residents of Linkville, or the bad whiskey sold in that region, are also responsible for the reinforcement of fourteen picked warriors that Captain Jack received shortly after his arrival in the Lava Beds. If they had not threatened to kill those Indians on sight and frightened Mr. Dyar, the subagent, out of his wits, Captain Jack would be minus the assistance of Shacknasty Jim, Big Jack, Frank, and some eleven others that are said to be the bravest warriors in the tribe.

Colonel Gillem of the 1st Cavalry, commanding the troops in this section; Lieutenant Rockwell of the 1st Cavalry, acting adjutant general; and the *Herald* correspondent left Dorris's ranch on the seventh and arrived here the same day, eleven hours in the saddle. As the colonel was anxious to have an interview with a Modoc woman living at the Klamath River ferry, with a view to obtaining her services as interpreter in case of a talk with Captain Jack, we went round that way, giving us about sixteen miles longer to ride. The nearest route by Van Bremer's ranch to this point is about twenty-two miles, but by the trail we took round Little Klamath Lake, the distance is said to be forty miles. We were ferried across Klamath River, and also Link River, a large stream connecting Klamath Lake with Little Klamath Lake, and arrive at the camp at about 8:00 P.M.

Lost River Camp is at present the headquarters of the army, and yesterday Lt. Col. Frank Wheaton, who has been in charge up to the present, turned over his command to Colonel Gillem, who now assumes control of operations in this section of the country. It is the intention of Colonel Gillem to remove headquarters to Dorris's ranch or some place in that neighborhood, but as definite news arrived yesterday that the peace commissioners are to meet on the fifteenth, no movement of importance will be made until they have transacted their business.

It is the general feeling among the army officers that there will not be another shot fired, which is rather a disappointment to them, as they would like to have had another turn at Jack, in order to get even for the disaster of January 17. If there is a continuation of hostilities, Jack will find it rather a hot place in the Lava Beds, as shells will be in order, and a plentiful supply sent into his stronghold at Uncle Sam's expense. The attack will probably be made from the lake upon a plan suggested by Major Mason, bringing some floating batteries into service. The land forces will be divided into two battalions, one commanded by Colonel Gillem and the other by Colonel Wheaton, and as fast as the shells begin to operate upon the Indian stronghold, the troops will advance and carry the position by storm.

It is pleasant to find that for once the settlers are satisfied with the work of the regular troops, and it is safe to say that there is not one of the volunteers that took part in the fight of the seventeenth that will not speak enthusiastically as to the cool bravery exhibited by the military. Lt. Col. Frank Wheaton, although obliged to retire on that occasion through force of circumstances, cannot be blamed for the result, as the elements were against him in a perfectly strange country. No man had any idea of what lava beds were until that morning, and there are few that were there then that want to go in again. Of course, as soldiers, they will do their duty, and do it gallantly, but they all agreed it was one of the hottest places they had ever struck. The impression that Colonel Wheaton was relieved of his command on account of incapacity is simply ridiculous, as in truth Colonel Gillem was sent up by General Canby, commanding the Department of the Pacific, because the latter deemed the disturbance of sufficient importance to render necessary the presence of the senior officer on the coast.

Now that the peace commissioners are to meet on Saturday, there is considerable anxiety as to what measures they will take and what will be the results of their talk. They have a rather difficult task before them in order to satisfy both Indians and whites. Justice demands the death of those Indians that murdered the fourteen settlers, but perhaps prudence and the interests of the

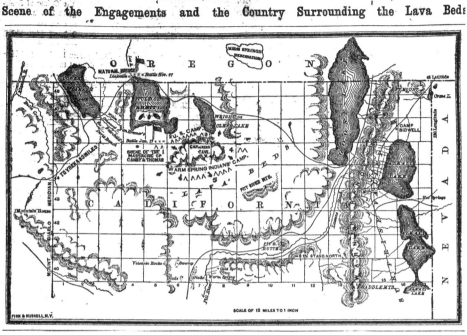

The Lava Beds battleground. NEW YORK HERALD, 1877.

country may disarm the terrible majesty of the law and preserve those outlaws from the fate they have so richly earned. It is highly improbable that the Indians will make any treaty whatsoever unless assured of a pardon for these aforesaid murderers; even should Captain Jack agree to give them up, he would be powerless to do so. It is generally believed that the administration are in favor of granting their claims to the strip of land along Lost River, but is sincerely hoped that the commissioners will be firm enough to insist on the giving up of the murderers at all hazards as, should they be pardoned and allowed to reside on this Lost River land, there could never be any security to settlers living in that section of the country. Men that will commit such offenses against the laws of human nature on one occasion are liable to repeat the offense again and again.

Colonel Wheaton left here yesterday en route for Camp Warner, via Fort Klamath and Yainax reservation, but will return in case of a renewal of hostilities. General Canby is expected to arrive in this vicinity before long, via

Jacksonville. The roads are all in a very bad state, and we have eight inches of snow on the ground today.

The troops are beginning to get rather impatient here and want to have the affairs settled up one way or the other so that they can get back to their stations, instead of being forced to endure the discomforts and expenses of camp life. It is rather hard on officers and men to serve in California [and] to be always paid in greenbacks, making a considerable loss in their receipts, besides having the discomfort and bother of getting their paper exchanged for specie. This camp will probably not be broken up for another month, as the negotiations with Captain Jack and his party will take at least a fortnight to consider the propositions of the peace commissioners.

—◦—▰◦▰—◦—

New York *Herald,* February 17, 1873

LINKVILLE, Oregon, Via ASHLAND, February 15, 1873
Colonel Gillem and staff and the *Herald* commissioner[16] left Lost River Camp at noon today and rode over here, where they found General Canby, commander of the District of the Pacific, and staff, who had just arrived from California via Jacksonville. By appointment of the secretary of the interior, the commission to arrange peace with the Modoc Indians, comprising Messrs. Meacham, Jesse Applegate, and Samuel Case, were to meet at Linkville on February 15.

The commission met at 4:00 P.M. Present: Jesse Applegate and Samuel Case, Mr. Jesse Applegate in the chair. On motion of Mr. Samuel Case, Mr. O. P. Applegate was appointed clerk of the commission.

The following communication was then received from the secretary of the governor of Oregon and read by Mr. Jesse Applegate:

STATE OF OREGON, EXECUTIVE OFFICE,
SALEM, February 10, 1873
TO THE COMMISSIONERS APPOINTED TO CONCLUDE PEACE
WITH THE MODOC INDIANS:
GENTLEMEN: As the state of Oregon is deeply interested in the results of the pending Indian special commission, I desire to express to you a few suggestions bearing upon the subject about to engage your attention. From official reports made to me, and from other reliable information, it appeared conclusively to establish that the massacre of eighteen citizens of Oregon, on November 29 last, was committed without provocation and without notice—cutting and shooting men down in cold blood at their houses and in their fields one by one as they were found—by Indians who had not been attacked by the soldiery nor otherwise molested, and who could not speak our language, and were personally acquainted with the vic-

tims. The homes and farms of the slaughtered settlers were upon lands to which the Indian title had long since been extinguished by treaty. These acts I hold to be deliberate and willful murder. Over such offenses I conceive the civil authorities of this state constitute the only competent and final tribunal.

I desire, therefore, to protest, on behalf of the state of Oregon, against any action of the commission which shall purport to condone the crimes of the Modocs or compound their offenses. The people of Oregon desire that the murderers shall be given up and delivered to the civil authorities for trial and punishment. As to the lands on Lost River, which some have suggested should be surrendered to the Modocs as a peace offering, allow me to say that these lands lie wholly within the state of Oregon, and within the jurisdiction of the superintendent of Indian affairs for Oregon; that the Indian title to these lands was extinguished by treaty, fairly made through the Oregon superintendency, between the Modocs and the general government, on October 14, 1864. They have been surveyed under the direction of the surveyor general of Oregon, and the surveys were long since approved by the General Land Office. These lands have been extensively taken, and are now occupied by bona fide settlers under the homestead and preemption laws of the United States. The commission will, therefore, have no more power to declare a reservation on Lost River under these settlements to make the same basis of peace with those Indians than they have to provide for their establishment on any other settled portion of the state. For the interests of southern Oregon and for the future peace of our southern frontier, I will express the hope and confidence that the project of a reservation on Lost River will not be entertained by the commission, and that the Modocs will either consent to return to their own reservation or be assigned to bounds beyond the settlements. With great respect, I am your obedient servant,

L. F. GROVER, governor of Oregon

On motion, the letter was laid on the table. Owing to the absence of Mr. A. B. Meacham, the commission adjourned to meet at Van Bremer's ranch on Monday, February 17.

There is a very strong feeling in Oregon against peace, and especially against locating these Indians on the Lost River strip of land, as the settlers declare the country will not be safe with the Modocs in the neighborhood.

General Canby, Colonel Gillem, the officers attached to their staffs, Messrs. Jesse Applegate and Samuel Case of the peace commission, and the *Herald* correspondent leave tomorrow morning for Van Bremer's, forty miles distant.

A party of four or five Modocs, out on a scout, burnt Dennis Crawley's log hut on Friday evening. Colonel Gillem saw the smoke from the Lost River Camp and sent out a detachment of cavalry to investigate the matter. They found the house in ruins and the tracks of Indians, but it was too dark to follow them up. In the morning another party of cavalry were sent out, but the Indians had taken refuge in their stronghold in the Lava Beds.

━·━ ≕◆≕ ━·━

New York *Herald,* March 1, 1873

HERALD HEADQUARTERS,
DORRIS'S RANCH, February 17, 1873

Awaiting the arrival of the peace commission appointed by the secretary of the interior to arrange the troubles with the Modoc Indians, the troops are in a state of inactivity, encamped at Lost River, Clear Lake, Van Bremer's, and Dorris's ranch. It has been definitely announced that Messrs. Jesse Applegate, A. B. Meacham, and Samuel Case are the three gentlemen who have been entrusted with the diplomatic arrangements about to be entered into with Captain Jack and his tribe.

Mr. Jesse Applegate is one of the oldest settlers and explorers of Oregon and, in the pursuance of his profession as surveyor, has traveled over the greater part of the state and is personally acquainted with the Modoc Indians. He is said to be on good terms with Captain Jack and some of the party, but there are some of the men who do not entertain the most kindly feelings towards him and are reported to have expressed an extreme interest as to the length of his hair, with a view to adorning their wigwam with those revered gray hairs. I have talked with Mr. Applegate on the likelihood of peace, and he evidently appreciates the difficulties that are before him in the attempt to make a treaty with the Modocs that will prove satisfactory to the government and the settlers. The latter portion of the community, especially those residing in Oregon, are decidedly warlike in their aspirations, thirst for the blood of the Lava Bed Indians, and are evidently opposed to all movements in favor of peace.

Mr. A. B. Meacham was formerly superintendent of Indian affairs in the state of Oregon and was succeeded in that office by Mr. Odeneal, the present superintendent. Mr. Meacham was in office at the time that Jack and his tribe went to the Yainax reservation and, after stopping there a couple of months, left in disgust, stating that they were starved and had to kill their horses and eat them in order to keep body and soul together. This statement is, however, contradicted by the friends of Mr. Meacham, who state that the Modoc Indians were well treated on the reservation, and that Captain Jack only made the above statement in order to make an excuse for returning to Lost River.

There are others, however, who place implicit confidence in Captain Jack's story and state positively that it was only actual starvation [that] drove

Jack's party from the reservation back to their hunting and fishing grounds on Lost River.

Mr. Meacham certainly, while in office, took a lively interest in the case of those Modoc Indians and forwarded their claims to this Lost River land to Washington, with a recommendation that it should be granted. It is also stated that in consequence of the lively interest Mr. Meacham assumed in behalf of these Indians, interest was brought to bear in Washington which caused his removal and the nomination of Mr. Odeneal to the office. It is therefore assumed, as Mr. Meacham is appointed one of the peace commission, that the government have come to the conclusion that his policy was right.

Mr. Samuel Case, the third commissioner, is the Indian agent on the Alsen reservation.[17] This reservation is situated on the coast, about 130 miles south of the Columbia River. He has been connected and engaged in the management of Indians for the past ten years but has never had any business whatever with the Modoc Indians. It appears, therefore, that Mr. Case has been selected with a view to being a kind of umpire between the two other commissioners, who are thoroughly well acquainted with the Modocs and their grievances.

Life at Lost River Camp has been very monotonous, and with the exception of an occasional crack at a prairie hen or a jackrabbit, there was literally nothing to do. On last Thursday evening[18] a little excitement was effected by the discovery of some smoke in the distance, and as it appeared to rise from the neighborhood of Dennis Crawley's log hut, Colonel Gillem sent out a detachment of cavalry under the charge of Lieutenant Rockwell to investigate the matter. The cavalry returned in about three hours' time, and Lieutenant Rockwell reported that Crawley's hut was burned to the ground; but he was unable to ascertain the cause, it being too dark to see any tracks. In the morning Major Green, several officers, and a troop of cavalry rode out to the same spot and discovered the tracks of three or four Indian ponies, and also the tracks of two men who had crossed the river in a canoe, gone up to the hut, and afterwards beat a hasty retreat. From this it was surmised that a party of Indians, numbering probably four or five, had been out on a scout and on their way home had sent two men across the river to burn Crawley's hut by way of bravado, as they knew the smoke would be seen at the Lost River Camp.

On Saturday morning Colonel Gillem, Lieutenant Rockwell, Mr. Jesse Applegate, Surgeon McElderry, and the *Herald* correspondent left Lost River camp and rode over to Linkville in order to be present at the meeting of the peace commission. Linkville is about fifteen miles due west of Lost River Camp and is situated on Link River, about halfway between the two Klamath Lakes. It consists of a store, a hotel, a barroom, a land office, and a blacksmith's shop and has also been rendered famous in this war as the headquarters of those settlers whose bloodthirsty threats were the means of adding fourteen warriors to Captain Jack's band in the Lava Beds.

When we arrived, we found General Canby and his aide-de-camp, Lieutenant Anderson,[19] in possession of the hotel. General Canby is the officer in command of the Department of the Columbia but, in the absence of General Schofield, is commanding the Division of the Pacific. Mr. Samuel Case had also arrived, but Mr. A. B. Meacham, the other commissioner, had not been heard from. Colonel Gillem joined forces with General Canby and put up at the hotel, and the balance of the party were billeted elsewhere.

⊷ ⊯⬥⊨ ⊶

New York *Herald,* March 6, 1873

HERALD HEADQUARTERS,
FAIRCHILD'S RANCH, February 20, 1873

My last letter, dated from Dorris's ranch, was dispatched in rather a hurry, as the courier was sent earlier than usual with some important government dispatches, and I was therefore forced to break off in the middle of my description of the first meeting of the peace commissioners.

We did not arrive at Linkville until late in the afternoon of Saturday, February 15, and at about 4:00 P.M. the peace commission met in a small room under the land office. Messrs. Jesse Applegate and Samuel Case were present. The former took the chair, and Mr. Case immediately moved the appointment of Mr. Oliver Applegate, Indian agent at Yainax, as clerk of the commission. Mr. Jesse Applegate seconded the motion, and Mr. Oliver Applegate was declared duly elected. The private secretary of the governor of Oregon then came forward and handed an official document to the commissioners. Both gentlemen eyed it in rather a suspicious manner,[20] but it was finally opened and read by Mr. Jesse Applegate—the substance of which, I see from a dispatch, has already been reported in the *Herald.* Both gentlemen appeared rather "flabbergasted" at the letter, and some remarks were made respecting the sanity of the aforesaid governor; but final "Uncle Jesse," as he is best known in this section of the country, took the bull by the horns, and the objectionable document was laid on the table. The commissioners, on motion of Mr. Case, then adjourned, to meet at Van Bremer's ranch on Monday, February 17.

Saturday night was passed at Linkville, and at about 9:00 A.M. on Sunday a start was effected for Dorris's ranch. The mounted party consisted of Colonel Gillem, Acting Adjutant General Rockwell, Lieutenant Anderson, Capt. Oliver Applegate, and Mr. Samuel Case. The three ambulances were occupied by General Canby, Uncle Jesse Applegate, and your correspondent. In a weak moment, I lent my horse to Lieutenant Anderson, thinking that a drive would be a pleasant change, and I must confess that up to that time I had not formed a correct opinion of the roads in that vicinity. During the first two miles the sidlings were so bad and the ruts to port so deep that General Canby got out and walked, while I hung out on the starboard side, holding fast to the weather rigging. As ballast, I proved a success, and probably saved the ship capsizing on two or three occasions.

We arrived at Klamath ferry about 2:00 P.M., and General Canby had a talk with Mrs. Whittle, an intelligent Klamath squaw, the wife of the ferryman,[21] which resulted in her promising to take a message into the Lava Beds if required. The remainder of the road was pretty good, with the exception of one hill which appeared to be covered by loose rocks of considerable size, and over which we drove regardless of consequences. Dorris's ranch came in sight just before dark, and at 7:00 P.M. all hands were sitting down to supper, a meal which was eaten with relish by the travelers. There was rather a pinch that evening for accommodations, and the floor of the storeroom was pretty closely packed, making it all the warmer during these cold, frosty nights.

Monday morning[22] was passed very quietly at Dorris's, and in the afternoon General Canby, his staff officers, and the peace commission moved up to Fairchild's ranch, where they now have their headquarters. I waited until Tuesday, and then rode up and joined them. In the afternoon Mr. A. B. Meacham arrived, and the same evening the peace commissioners and General Canby sat in secret session in a small outhouse. That habitation had been furnished with two short benches and a three-legged stool in honor of the occasion. Their deliberations resulted in the dispatch of a messenger for Mrs. Whittle and Modoc Sally, a squaw on the Klamath reservation. Mr. Meacham was elected chairman of the commission, and after the meeting was over, he kindly posted the *Herald* correspondent as to the business transacted. Mr. Meacham said as soon as one of the squaws arrives she will be sent into Captain Jack's camp to see if he is willing to talk. If she should return and report favorably, another messenger will be sent in to arrange for a meeting between Captain Jack and the commissioners.

On Wednesday[23] I rode over to Van Bremer's ranch and passed the day with Lieutenant Miller, Captain Throckmorton, and the other officers at the camp. We talked over the prospects of peace, and it appeared to be the general opinion that the instructions from Washington were of such a peaceful nature as to make the business of the peace commissioners an affair easy to arrange. When I returned to Fairchild's, I found that Mrs. Whittle had arrived, and in the evening Mr. Meacham had a talk with her and gave his instructions, which were simply to explain how peacefully inclined President Grant was and the desire of the peace commissioners to talk over the question with Captain Jack. Mrs. Whittle and a squaw called Artinie [Choakus] left early this morning for Captain Jack's camp.

It is the general opinion in this neighborhood that the peace commission will fizzle out, as the right men are not on it. It is, in fact, more plainly expressed in a remark made to me yesterday: "They can't be elected, as the wrong men are on the ticket." It certainly does appear strange that some names were not put on the peace commission of men known to the Indians and in whom they could trust and have reliance. Again, there are many complaints that California has no representatives on the council. The war is in California and the Indians are in California, yet three Oregon men have been selected to decide what is to be done with them. The settlers in this neighborhood say that nothing can be done by the present commission, as the Indians will not talk with them. Mr. Meacham was the superintendent of Indian affairs when Captain Jack went on the Klamath reservation.

Jack states that he left the reservation because he was starved and only half blankets were served out to him and his people. The squaws in this neighborhood all reiterate the same complaint. Again, in justice to Mr. Meacham, he denies the complaint in toto, says that he furnished the blankets to the Indians with his own hands, and that the Indians were well fed while on the reservation. Several Indian agents attached to adjoining reservations also support Mr. Meacham's statement.

Capt. Oliver Applegate, the agent at Yainax, states that he never heard Jack make such a complaint, he having always stated that he left Klamath reservation on account of the Klamath Indians, and also because he had been advised to remain at Lost River, as that land belonged to him and the white people could not turn him out.

It is very hard to say what instructions the peace commission have received from the president, but it is generally understood they are of a peaceful nature. They will have to be very liberal to make peace, as it is hardly probable the Indians will come out of the Lava Beds unless they are all pardoned. At present, Curly Headed Doctor's party, or the murderers' party, are in the ascendant, numbering about twenty-five to Captain Jack's ten or twelve. Now even if it is true that Captain Jack is anxious for peace, he would not have the power to give up the murderers to the civil authorities, and even should he wish to come out himself, the others would probably not allow him to move. It would certainly be highly impolitic to give the Lost River land to these Modoc Indians under existing circumstances, as it will simply depopulate the surrounding country of white people. Should these Indians be placed on the Lost River land, they would become so saucy and independent that it would be impossible for them and whites to occupy the same section of country.

It is reported that the Indians are to be removed to a distant reservation on the seacoast, and if the peace commission can get them out of the Lava Beds, the murderers given up, and the rest located on the seacoast, they will confer a benefit on this community that should reap for them the thanks of the people of the United States.

—+— ≡◆≡ —+—

New York *Herald,* March 8, 1873

HERALD HEADQUARTERS,
FAIRCHILD'S RANCH, February 22, 1873

The weather has moderated slightly during the past few days, and a warm sun has cleared the low lands of their white and fleecy covering, substituting the most unromantic slush. The peace commission are busy in the discharge of their duties and hold mysterious talks together, which result in more work for the clerk, Capt. Oliver E. Applegate, who left his reservation at Yainax in order to devote his services to the cause of peace. The settlers in this neighborhood have not much confidence in the peace commission and openly assert that the Indians will not talk with either Meacham or Applegate, as both those men have broken faith with them before. In justice to Meacham, however, I believe he states that he is not responsible for their being starved on the reservation as, though he was superintendent of Indian affairs, the agent on the reservation was Captain Knapp,[24] and he had charge of them.

Some time was lost here arranging to send in a messenger, but at last a Klamath squaw, Matilda, the wife of Bob Whittle, and the Modoc squaw, Artinie, were sent off last Thursday evening with the following message:

> That the president of the United States, General Grant, had heard about the war and was very sorry his children were fighting. He looked upon all the people of every color as his children, and he did not want them to spill each other's blood. He thought this might have been a misunderstanding between the whites and the Indians, and he wanted to see about it. That he was trying to have a new kind of law made that would do away with war, and that's why he said "stop until we talk awhile." Then he sent a man, A. B. Meacham, all the way from Washington, and another man, Samuel Case, that was a friend to Indians and acquainted with their character, to have a talk. They must not mistake the reason why he "done" it and think he was weak or a coward, or think that he was whipped, because he was not. The soldiers were beyond the Indians' power in numbers; if he had to fight and had not enough here, he could send enough; he never failed to win in war; that he would rather settle it without blood.

Matilda was instructed to deliver the above message and to talk with the Indians, ascertain their feelings, and see if they were willing to have a talk. They both started about 11:00 A.M., Artinie in her war paint, with a white handkerchief tied round her head, and Matilda in a neat-fitting red dress, with a white cloth tied round her chest. Matilda was evidently a little nervous as to the result of her mission, as she was afraid she would find the Indians rather wild, and although she is related to some of them, her brother was fighting against them in the last battle. She, however, was gifted with the indomitable Indian pluck and started off to make good her promise, but first left all her jewels and trinkets with her husband, in case she should not come out again. As soon as these emissaries of peace had fairly started, the ravens around the campfire began to croak as to the danger they would encounter and spun yarns about the visit of One-eyed Dixie—how they licked her when she went in, although she was closely related to many of the leading bucks and sister of the charming Mrs. Shacknasty Jim.

This ranch is now filled with attaches of the Indian Department, as we have Capt. Ferree,[25] one of the contractors supplying the Yainax agency; Capt. Oliver C. Applegate, Indian agent and commissary at Yainax; Capt. Ivan Applegate, late interpreter and messenger; Mr. Samuel Case, peace commissioner and Indian agent at Alsen reservation; Mr. A. B. Meacham, peace commissioner and ex-superintendent of Indian affairs in Oregon; and some others. Mr. Jesse Applegate, the other peace commissioner, is also here, and General Canby and aide-de-camp Lieutenant Anderson have their quarters in the same building. The rest of our party consists of a newspaper correspondent, settlers, and the vaqueros attached to the ranch.

Accommodations are rather limited, as about fourteen occupy the floor of one room fifteen feet square; seven sleep in an adjoining apartment, nine by fifteen, and General Canby and staff have an adjoining shed about eight feet square. We have two meals per diem, one at 8:00 A.M. and the other at 4:00 P.M. These meals are decidedly simple in their nature and are served with a fair allowance of dirt, which has accumulated by its constant service during the past few years without being introduced to water. Although the proprietor of this ranch, Captain Fairchild—a very good fellow, by the way—is the happy possessor of over 3,000 head of cattle, the lacteal produce of the bovine race has never been used in the ranch, and even the butter that graces the hospitable board is brought all the way from Yreka. The staple article of food at both meals is beef, fried in grease in the morning and boiled in fat in the afternoon. Flour made up to the style of hot biscuits is also used at each meal, as vegetables have not yet made their appearance here. The fluid in use is called coffee and has a brown appearance resembling a liquid we have seen before bearing the same name; but perhaps, on the whole, a man might make a campaign under worse auspices.

On [Thursday] I rode with Lieutenant Anderson to Van Bremer's Camp and stopped there for the night. It is very neatly laid out at the foot of Van Bremer's hill, which overlooks the Lava Beds. The little shelter tents are all laid out in streets, and everything around the camp is kept clean and orderly. Captain Miller of the 4th Artillery is in command. He arrived about a week ago and relieved Captain Throckmorton, who was in command at that time. I returned on Friday morning[26] and passed a rather dismal afternoon awaiting the return of the two squaws, Matilda and Artinie. As the afternoon passed away, and anxious gazers discerned no sign of approaching horsewomen on the distant knoll over which the trail mounted and fell, the ravens began to croak again with redoubled energy and uttered fearful prophecies as to their fate. Shortly after 5:00 P.M. a solitary horsewoman was seen riding over the crest of the hill, followed immediately afterwards by another, and the quick eye of a looker-on discerned the expected messengers.

Uncle Jesse Applegate walked down to the corner of the fence to meet them and, for fear that unhallowed ears should first receive the message from the famous Captain Jack, ordered the squaws to ride straight to the ranch and speak to no one before they saw the peace commissioners. After they had partaken of the standard ranch meals, they were escorted by the commissioners and General Canby to an outlying hut, where the session was to take place. As I was rather anxious to hear the squaws tell their story in their own language, I asked Mr. Meacham for permission to be present. He said he had no objection and would ask his colleagues. Mr. Meacham finally returned and said his colleagues objected. Mr. Case said bluntly and honestly he objected, but finally agreed to admit me if Mr. Meacham did not object. As all three by this time had decided not to admit me, they finally concluded to throw the onus of the refusal on General Canby, and having extracted a mild negative to my request from that gentleman, I was politely informed that the interview would be strictly private.

The star chamber was thereupon convened, and the grand inquisitor, Mr. Meacham, put the squaws through a most interesting "course of sprouts." After about two hours' talk the session was closed, and they all came up to the ranch. Mr. Meacham then came forward and said that the peace commissioners were willing to give the press the following information:

> The Klamath squaw made the following statement to them: When she arrived in the camp the Modocs received her kindly. Said they were glad she had come. Were tired of waiting. Out of clothes, out of provisions. They wanted no more war and were ready to wash their hands of blood. Captain Jack, John Schonchin, brother of the old chief, and another old buck were the only speakers. Captain Jack commenced by complaining that the Indians were pitched into when asleep. They did not intend to trouble the citizens. Wanted to fight soldiers. Citizens should not have troubled them. They went to the rocks for safety, and soldiers came and hunted them as if they were coyotes. Did not want to live like that; wanted the blockade raised. They were tired of seeing women come to them; women did not understand; often lied; he was a chief still; Squire Steele had made him a chief; he did not want to talk to little tyees or people who had been in the fight; wanted to see them come in there; they would not be hurt. I am ready to talk, and I want to talk to these men that come from a long way off.
>
> John Schonchin, the brother of the old chief Schonchin, and one of the surviving Modocs that took part in the war of 1852, then spoke and said he was very tired waiting for someone to come and talk because he could not go out and talk. He remembered the Ben Wright treachery. These boys (pointing to the other Indians) have all grown up since then. He wanted to wash everybody's hands of blood—all the past buried. He was the eldest there, would control the boys and bring peace. He was glad men had come to talk with them. Wanted to see Mr. Case because he had come from a distance; wanted to see Mr.

Meacham because he had come from a distance. A man of his name, or like it, had talked to him before and made his heart strong. Since then very much bloodshed, and he did not want any more. He had given up all his country but a very little place at Lost River. Soldiers pitched into him there. Always tried to be friendly with the citizens. Boys got wild when soldiers pitched in; could not control boys then, but could now. His heart had been wild; getting better now; thought the wild got out of the boys the same way. He liked the talk sent by the woman from the president. "All the people were his children; he did not want them to fight." He felt like being a peacemaker among his own children; breaking the trouble as he would a string in the middle. These men were coming to do that. When troubles came among his people, he tried to separate them and prevent blood. He had a red skin but a white heart.

His heart was wild while fight, but good news sent out wild spirit. He was ready to see and talk at any time; did not want any more women; they did not understand things well. When next messenger came, they would arrange to meet the men from afar off, where there were grass and water. They were to come out and not be afraid. I can control my people, but I am afraid you cannot control your people. My men will do what they agree; we are afraid your people will not. I am not afraid myself, and these men need not be afraid; they will not be hurt; nobody will kill them. Went on the reservation, promised place by Lost River. No let stop there, only little while. Captain Knapp move me to Williamson River, and then again between the Klamaths; had to live on mud (meaning roots, etc.); could not see happy home and rest, and came away. Did not want any time lost about council; clothes worn out, sent men and women to our caches for roots on Lost River; got scared and turned back. Send this woman Matilda back with the next messenger, and they will come out of roots and talk. We like all the words that have been sent to us; they did not send very many—we have replied all we want to send; when send more talk, we send more back.

The other old Modoc that talked did not say much, but the drift of his observations was in favor of peace, but he was afraid of treachery like Ben Wright's. All the Modocs were very attentive to the speakers and grunted their approval at the words that had been sent to them. There were no dissenting voices to the speeches, and the Indians seemed all to be in accord, except a little jealousy on the part of Captain Jack lest he should not be recognized as chief. The squaw Matilda was of the opinion he had lost his influence, and that John Schonchin was the acknowledged leader by the majority of the bucks. She did not think that the jealousy would result in a conflict, as Schonchin had a large majority on his side. She has the utmost confidence in their pretensions for peace. The Indians sent no propositions.

I afterward learnt from Mr. Whittle, who had a talk with his wife, that Captain Jack appeared more anxious to talk with Elijah Steele or Judge Ros-borough,[27] and that he also spoke very bitterly about being attacked by the soldiers in the dark. He also said the citizens on the other side of the river fired the first shot and killed a squaw and two papooses, which so maddened the young men that five of them started on the raid and killed white men, but spared the women. He also complained about the broken treaty and how they were frozen out and starved on the reservation. The other squaw, Artinie, also said that Captain Jack would not make peace unless he was given a portion of land on Lost River.

The result of this first mission to Captain Jack formed the subject of discussion that evening, and all the settlers appeared surprised at finding the Indians so anxious for peace. There were many opinions as to what terms the Indians wanted, but the majority were impressed with the belief that nothing except a general amnesty would effect peace. This morning Bob Whittle and his squaw started off to meet the Modocs and arrange for a meeting with the commissioners. The meeting will probably take place next Tuesday somewhere between Van Bremer's and the Lava Beds.

FAIRCHILD'S RANCH,
February 23, 1873

Yesterday Capt. O. Applegate and Captain Ferree left for the Yainax reservation in order to attend to the delivery of some supplies to their Indians. Lalake, a Klamath chief, John Parker, Klamath Indian, and Modoc Sally arrived from the reservation per order of the peace commissioners. They will be used in the negotiations with Captain Jack's Indians, as Modoc Sally speaks tolerably good English. At 11:00 P.M. Bob Whittle and his squaw returned from Captain Jack's camp, bringing with them a Modoc named Dave,[28] who had been sent by Captain Jack to hear what the commissioners had to say. Bob Whittle says that the Indians appear willing to talk and that he thinks Captain Jack is still in power. They asked him how many citizens had been whipped in the fight, meaning how many were killed. Whittle told them, and then asked how many Indians had been whipped. Captain Jack said none. He thought white man no try to kill Indian; lay on back and fire in air. Whittle said he counted between forty-two and forty-three bucks present at the talk, which will verify their statement, as that is about the number the settlers thought were in the fight.

A telegraphic dispatch was received yesterday from Secretary Delano stating that Judge Rosborough of Yreka had been appointed on the commission. There are fears, however, entertained here that as the judge is now on circuit, he will be unable to come. His presence would certainly be of material benefit, as the Indians have confidence in him and would believe any promise he made. At present there is no man on the commission in whom they have confidence.

The peace commission met this morning and heard Whittle's report. The squaws Matilda and Artinie and the Modoc Indian Dave were present. Mr.

Whittle stated that when he got within a mile and a half, he saw some mounted Indians riding along the crest of a hill. I then saw about twenty Indians on foot, who stopped when 100 yards distant. I got off my horse, and Long Jim and Steamboat Frank came up, and I shook hands with them. They then laid down their guns, and the rest of the Indians on foot then came up and I shook hands with them. Captain Jack then rode up with his party, dismounted, and shook hands. They all sat down, Captain Jack in the center, John Schonchin on the left, and Curly Headed Doctor on the right. I told them what Mr. Meacham had said about his trying to get them that land on Lost River, and also that he was away when they were put on the reservation and not responsible for their treatment when there.

Captain Jack remembered his meeting with Jesse Applegate and Judge Rosborough and their talk about the Lost River land. I then told them about the other commissioners, and they said they were glad they had come, as they wanted to talk. They said they were willing to meet on the Platte, about twenty-one miles distant from Van Bremer's, and have a talk on Tuesday at noon. They would all come, as they all wanted to hear what the commissioners had to say. They wanted to talk to their friends, Fairchild, Steele, and Rosborough; did not know these commissioners, whether their hearts were good. Wanted especially to see Fairchild.

The squaw Matilda then pointed out to the Indian Dave who the commissioners were, and he went back today, bearing the instructions that Fairchild, Whittle, and the two squaws would come to see them tomorrow and have a talk, and make arrangements for the grand meeting.

Mr. Meacham and the commissioners appear to be throwing every obstruction in the way of a public investigation of this matter, and ordered Whittle and Fairchild on no account to allow any reporters to go with them. This is not the first attempt that has been made to prevent the press from obtaining direct information, as we were excluded from the examination of the squaw Matilda after her return from the first visit to the Lava Beds.

⤙ ⛊ ⤚

New York *Herald,* February 28, 1873

HEADQUARTERS CAPTAIN JACK'S CAMP,
LAVA BEDS, February 25, 1873,
Via YREKA, February 26, 1873

I write this dispatch in Captain Jack's cave in the Lava Beds, having at last reached this spot, though not without considerable difficulty. In my last dispatch I stated that John Fairchild, Bob Whittle, and the two squaws, Matilda and Artinie, were to leave on the morning of the twenty-fourth for Captain Jack's camp, with instructions to arrange a meeting between the Modocs and the peace commissioners. I also stated that I had applied for permission to Mr. Meacham to accompany these men into the Lava Beds, in order to give the public, through the *Herald,* some idea of this band of warriors and the stronghold which they defend so bravely.

As you already know, my request was peremptorily denied, and Whittle had given the most decided orders not to permit any member of the press to accompany his expedition. I finally concluded that Mr. Meacham had no authority to govern my going and coming in this section of the country and therefore determined to make an attempt to go on my own responsibility. Knowing that my movements at Fairchild's ranch would be rather closely scrutinized, I left there on the afternoon of Sunday, the twenty-third, saying that I intended riding over to Van Bremer's ranch and stopping through the night with the officers of the 4th Artillery. This movement was not suspected, and before leaving I casually asked Fairchild at what time they intended to start next morning, and he replied, "7:00 A.M."

I felt considerably relieved when I got clear of the headquarters of the peace commissioners, as Mr. Meacham might have asked General Canby to give orders that I was not to leave the neighborhood, which would naturally have left me in rather an awkward position.

After a good night's sleep at Van Bremer's, I got up at reveille and made a start at 7:30 A.M., riding down the road towards Fairchild's in order to meet the party. It had been snowing some two or three hours, and the ground was covered with a white, fleecy coating. When I arrived at the bridge over Willow Creek, I found, as there were no tracks, that the party had not come up, so I rode on to meet them. They finally came in sight, Fairchild and Artinie leading and Whittle and Matilda bringing up the rear. I immediately rode up to Fairchild and told him I wanted to accompany him. He replied that personally he had no objection, but as the party was under the charge of Bob Whittle, I must get his permission. I then rode back to Whittle, and my request was very firmly but politely refused. He said, "If you had spoken to me before I was engaged by the peace commission, I would have been happy to have gone with you, but now I am in the government employ, and you know yourself what my instructions were."

I talked to him for about five minutes, until at last he said, "I am very sorry, but either you or I must go back."

I thought at first of going in alone, but after mature consideration I concluded to turn back, as to hunt for a place twenty miles distant without any further idea as to the locality to be found would probably result in failure. I then said, "Good-bye," and started back, and after trotting along for about half a mile, my eye fell on the freshly imprinted horse tracks that were so clearly seen in the newly fallen snow.

I immediately wheeled around, as in an instant I saw my guide to the Lava Beds. Those tracks would take me there. I rode slowly at first and was always cautious going uphill to peep over the top before I exposed myself and my horse to the plain that lay before me.

On picket duty in the Lava Beds. NATIONAL ARCHIVES.

After a ride of about two hours along the southwestern shore of Klamath Lake, the tracks turned sharply to the right, up a hill, and led through a mass of loose rocks, which proved rather an obstacle to fast traveling. At the top of the hill, seeing nobody on the flat before me, I quickened my pace, as I thought the Modoc country could not be very far off. My judgment was not in error, as from the next eminence I saw the party about a mile and a half ahead, with the squaw Artinie in advance.

I then concluded that they were in Indian country and so rode on pretty fast, and presently Fairchild and Whittle caught sight of me. They immediately pulled up and waited until I came up. Whittle appeared rather annoyed at first but finally said, "Well, well, now you have come; you had better keep up close, as we have been seen by the Modocs before now." He added, "If I had seen you a couple of minutes further back I would have turned back, but as we have been seen, it would be unwise to return now." We all rode on quietly and in about three-quarters of an hour arrived at the bluffs overlooking the Lava Beds without having seen an Indian. As Whittle expected to meet the Indians on that spot, he gathered some brush together and lit a fire in order to let them know we had arrived. In about twenty minutes' time we saw a couple of horsemen and a man on foot coming across the plain below in the direction of the foot of the bluff. They finally came up the hill towards us, and I had the pleasure of an introduction to Hooker Jim,[29] Modoc Dave, and Steamboat Frank. These three men were armed to the teeth. Two of them had Springfield rifles, and the other, Frank, had a cavalry Spencer carbine with equipment. Each of them had a revolver and large sheath knife.

After a little talk and smoke round the fire, Frank said that Captain Jack wanted to see Mr. Fairchild in camp. We then walked down the bluff, leading

Hooker (Hooka) Jim. NATIONAL ARCHIVES.

our horses, and on arriving at its base, I discovered what I had taken to be a flat plain was a rolling surface, covered with sharp-edged rocks and interspersed with large and deep holes, half filled with broken scoria. The trail was very rough, and we walked slowly along, our horses feeling the traveling rather bad. We came presently on one of Captain Jack's scouting parties and found half a dozen warriors warming themselves around a fire, while their horses were nibbling at the bunch grass in the vicinity. We got off, and I was again introduced and went through some more handshaking and more smoking. My smoking qualities were evidently much admired by the Modocs, and they also expressed themselves favorably of the quality of my tobacco.

This party were also well armed and all painted. They were all painted pretty much alike—that is, the entire lower part of the face was smeared with a brownish or black composition of a greasy nature. It gave them a very hideous appearance, and coming upon this group standing round the blazing fire, each with a musket in his hand and revolver and knife in the belt, they were not calculated to reassure the visitors of the pacific nature of the inhabitants of the Lava Bed. We did not make a very long stay, however, and moved along, our party being now reinforced by these half dozen scouts. About a half mile farther on, we came upon another camp of about fifty men, women, and children. They were nearly all lying in a rocky spur, around a blazing fire, but as we approached, they rose and came down to meet us. Their costume was of a very heterogeneous nature, showing that their clothing was collected at different epochs of time. Most of them, however, had soldiers' overcoats, and the squaws appeared very partial to red petticoats.

Here I was introduced to John Schonchin, the brother of Schonchin, the old chief of the tribe, and several other notabilities. After a delay of about five minutes, we started again, accompanied by our new acquaintances, which consequently swelled our train considerably.

The road became worse and worse, and the country more hillish-looking every minute. It defies description, and now I can perfectly understand how forty or fifty men so demoralized the 300 regulars and volunteers that [attacked] them on January 17. The Modocs appeared to skip nimbly over the rocks, but our horses were completely nonplussed, and my quadruped required considerable persuasion in order to induce him to move forward.

We were presently met by Bogus Charley, who was evidently glad to see Fairchild, and a few minutes afterward a most diabolical-looking Indian, called Charley Miller,[30] came riding down toward us, motioning us back with his hand. A lively discussion then ensued in the Modoc tongue, a language with which I have not yet become acquainted; but the Modoc squaw, Matilda, acting as interpreter, told me that Captain Jack had sent orders for us to camp where we were and not advance any farther. Bogus Charley, Frank, and Dave appeared considerably exercised over this order, as Charley stated that Fairchild should come and sleep at his house. Dave added that Whittle and the *Herald* correspondent should stop at his.

I cannot say that at the moment I was very grateful to Mr. Dave for this exercise of hospitality, as I concluded that should these gentlemen come to blows over this little question of etiquette, the guest would probably fare the worst of all. At this juncture, however, Scarfaced Charley came up and immediately settled the matter by saying we all could come into camp. Fairchild and Artinie here left us, taking the left-hand trail to Captain Jack's house, and we went to the right, led by Mr. Dave, who was quite happy at having captured his guests. I now dismounted, as the trail became nearly impassable, and after passing through a wild-looking gorge with walls of craggy rock about twenty-five feet in height, we climbed up some rocks, and then, suddenly descending a nearly perpendicular wall of broken scoria, landed in a chasm surrounded by walls about thirty feet in height, formed of broken rock apparently piled indiscriminately one on top of the other. There were three or four Indian rancherias located in this wild-looking spot. As our guide entered one of these primitive habitations, we dismounted and, taking off our saddles, made our horses fast to some of the large rocks that had evidently been scattered around with a liberal hand.

We then entered the rancheria and squatted down in Indian fashion round the fire, which was built in a cavity formed by two rocks that nature had placed in a position similar to the apex of an equilateral triangle. This rancheria, or "wickiup," was only built up to the rocks, so that the fire was really in the open air, and I afterwards found, when the fire was out, the keen frosty air was rather biting and sharp when it attacked the pedal extremities. After sitting for about half an hour round the fire, which time was passed in distributing tobacco and making the acquaintance of several other painted savages, I was told by Matilda that there was a difference of opinion as to whether the *Herald* correspondent was to be admitted to the council. To the credit of the Modoc nation, I am happy to say that the friends of literature predominated, and a messenger presently arrived with orders to convey our party to the council cave, accompanied by Bob Whittle and his squaw.

I followed our guide, and after clambering up the rough walls of the chasm, we walked, or rather crawled, about 100 yards over some broken rocks, when the guide suddenly disappeared down a dark hole. The *Herald* correspondent followed but, not being acquainted with the nature of the country, went down faster than necessary and found himself in a large cave, lit up by the blaze of a fire, which was burning in the center and gave sufficient light to enable me to see some fifty or sixty Modocs seated round in circles four or five deep. Edging my way through this motley throng, I came to a vacant spot in the front circle but, before sitting down, shook hands with Captain Jack and Scarfaced Charley, on whose left, with considerable courtesy, I was placed. I took my seat there like the rest.

It was a strange scene and a fit subject for some figure artist, for certainly no troop of Italian bandits could have made a wilder or more picturesque picture. As soon as I had recovered from the first flutter, which the presence of so many celebrities had excited, I ventured to take a quiet look around and found that I was the object of general attention, and judging from the favorable glances received, it appeared the party was inclined to tolerate my presence. Mr. Fairchild explained that I was a paper man and that I had come from far off, from the big city by the sea, and that I was anxious to hear the Indians' own story of their troubles, and that I had followed their trail in the snow. This speech was translated by Bogus Charley and was received with general approbation, expressed by a chorus of grunts sounding like a guttural pronunciation of the letter "A."

Captain Jack looked very sick and was sitting with a blanket around his limbs and supporting himself by resting his hands on the handle of one of their root diggers, which was stuck in the ground before him. Bogus Charley sat on his right and officiated as interpreter, and Schonchin was to the right of Charley. Shacknasty Jim sat to the left of Captain Jack, the *Herald* correspondent and Bob Whittle in the order named here. The rest of the Modocs were seated around in circles, and I noticed that many had washed off their paint and come to the council without their arms.

Shortly after my introduction, Mr. Fairchild produced his instructions from the peace commissioners and read them by sentences in English, and Bogus Charley translated them. They simply informed Captain Jack who comprised the peace commissioners that the president had sent and how they were willing to delay the grand council until the arrival of Judge Rosborough and their friend Elijah Steele. It also alluded to Ben Wright's treachery and said that Ben Wright was a bad man. This allusion was, however, rather an unhappy one as, when it was translated, the noble savage evinced the most decided disgust at the introduction of such reminiscence.

After Fairchild had got through and stated he had come to make arrangements for the meeting, John Schonchin spoke. He talked for about two hours, and in this dispatch I will only give the pith of his remarks. Bogus Charley, assisted by Steamboat Frank, officiated as interpreter. Schonchin said,

[I] knew Mr. Meacham. He says he big chief. I seen him long time ago. He talked well; told me straight. He told me I was a big chief. Come with me; make you good home. Showed me good home. Said, "You like that?" Took me to live at Fort Klamath; then he tell Captain Knapp treat him good, this Modoc Indian. Captain Knapp no like me. Go Meacham; told him watch them good. Captain Knapp bad man. He come my door; I say, "Don't come to my house, no like you." Saw Mr. Meacham long ago put the axe in the ground; no want to take it out. I know Mr. Meacham; tell him talk straight. I want to live in good place at Klamath, where I live first. Meacham go away. Agent make it bad; hang Indian, that Captain Knapp.

Mr. Schonchin made a diversion in my favor to give an account of the first fight on Lost River. He spoke about the fight when the citizens attacked the Indians. He said,

White chief tell your people white men shoot first. I tell no lie. I give away all. My country keep little piece on Lost River, yet they shoot me. I don't know what for, I thought. I gave them all my land, water, grass, everything. I don't charge nothing for my country; give all away, yet they shoot me. Want little piece on Lost River. I don't like to fight; I told them so. They shoot squaws, children, little girl. My friend there, white man, shoot him. I got up early in the morning, went out to shoot geese, come back, see so many men both sides of river. What the matter? Bad place. Now Applegate's son tell me lie; children scared; nobody in house.

Bogus Charley now talked and said,

Applegate's son and One-Armed Brown[31] one day talk good; next day all lie on the other side. Captain Jackson don't know what the matter with him. Come before day, plenty soldiers with him, pistol in hand, like to see Captain Jack. I said, "Stop!" He say, "Like to see Captain Jack in bed." They tell me plenty of men coming. I asleep house. Come out, see soldiers. Say, "Stop, boys! I don't want you come near." Go camp. Children scared. Still they come closer to house. All carry gun and ask for Captain Jack. Captain Jack no clothes on, no gun loaded, no pistol loaded. Old squaw give Jack shirt. He go out, have no gun. I go down to see Captain Jackson. I say, "Why you come, what you come for?"

Scarfaced Charley come down side of river from Dennis Crawley's; so soldiers now fall down; gun go off 400 yards away. Soldiers hear shoot. One man shoots me in side, fifty yards away. All soldier shoot. Two Indians dead. Few Indians shoot; only two or three guns. Then on other side, bad men took guns from Indians. George Fiocke shoot first and Dennis Crawley. Both shoot. Shot woman.

Ivan Applegate come down with Brown before. Says I, "Come back, three men, and talk till Big Tee he come back with soldiers." Captain Jackson so quick shoot quick. Scarfaced Charley asked him what chief he come from? He say he come from the mountain, as Captain Jack was very sick.

The council was then adjourned until morning, and I returned to my house and got some supper. I then gave an audience and received John Schonchin, Scarfaced Charley, Bogus Charley, and several others, and heard more about the way the Indians were treated on the reservation. They were moved three times from place to place; were only given half a blanket, and the squaws none at all. It was the winter season. They were given no food and had to dig in the hard, frosty ground for some camas roots and kill their horses for meat. I only give the facts now, as my report in detail will be forwarded by mail. Before lying down, I went back to Captain Jack, who presently commenced to talk. He said,

I see Mr. Meacham a long time ago at Fort Klamath. I don't know what may become now. Got plenty of soldiers. I afraid I don't know him. Maybe he don't feel good. I got one heart. Maybe Meacham got two hearts. My thoughts straight. I don't want Meacham to be scared. All come; don't be afraid. I tell my one heart; other chiefs sometimes lie. I don't know what I have done bad. I tell truth. I am a Yreka man. I conceal nothing. I know good many men treat me well want to fight. I don't so. I am not ashamed to talk to white people. I did not steal their horses. I got up in the morning. Soldiers distrust me. I done nothing. I told them. Yreka man give me letter. Letter make blood. He tell you a lie. I don't want no move before day. Look something to eat, not blood. No shoot, no more want at all. Good then. Indians done shooting. No tell lie. I want things done quick. I told to quit, all quit. I got good sense; boys use my sense not. Party quit, all quit.

Mr. Meacham, maybe, got two tongues. I talk with one tongue. Mr. Meacham got too many friends. Maybe half white good, half white bad. All boys here one mind. Want whites all one mind. I tell him truth. I want tell him gas before fight, same as white man after fight. Indian, I want no Indian law. Want same law for white and Indian. Want Indian same as white man. When Meacham done talking, if he tell no lies, be same as white man. Meacham's side only half minded. This side all one mind. I go Yreka. I go as white man, money in pockets. Go to store, buy what I want. I make more friends with whites. Mr. Meacham must not think treachery from any boys. They all act all right. Wash all the blood from these boys, make them same as women. I only got new men. Sorry white man afraid to travel this way. Like people travel every way.

Captain Jack then went over the story of the fight on Lost River and directly denied that the Indians shot first, and then said, "Tell Meacham I want him to come too, no gassing. Tell him not be scared, this man from paper afar off. He come to hear me talk. He hear no lie. He hear no more hard stories about me. Did not make first fight. I want every good. I am not ashamed of first fight. Glad to see white come to talk."

Mr. Fairchild then put a series of questions in order to find out where they wished to meet, how many they were going to bring, and whether they objected to the commissioners bringing soldiers, and Captain Jack answered, saying, "All [my] boys wanted to hear talk. White men might come, but no soldiers. Soldiers make [my] boys feel bad. Twelve or fifteen white men come; want paper man to come. No want Lalake, Jim Parker, or Modoc Sally. No like them. Keep soldiers where they are. Come tomorrow; come first day ready. Come soon; tired waiting. Want to talk."

Schonchin then spoke for a little, chiefly against Meacham and the commission bringing soldiers: "Indians bury the hatchet. No want to see soldiers, make him feel bad. Meacham not be scared. Boys waste all the blood. Mean good. Talk truth. Meacham mean peace; soldiers no good for peace. Afraid somebody your side wants to make blood again. Don't like it. Perhaps tell lies. I want to make all good; tell no lies. Soldiers like dogs—they come, want blood. White men come all right."

VAN BREMER'S RANCH, February 25—10:00 P.M.

As soon as Schonchin had finished, we started for our horses, and I arrived here about 7:00 P.M. Although the route is only twenty miles, it is over a very rough country. From what I have seen of the Indians in the Lava Beds, and from what I have learned of their history, I think they have been badly treated and that the origin of the war can easily be traced to a few Oregonians. The California settlers have never had any trouble with these Indians. They are now in a stronghold that is nearly impregnable, and as they have many men and good marksmen, it will require a force of a thousand men to clean them out, and it cannot be done without a fearful sacrifice of life.

They hold themselves innocent of any crime, as after the white men attacked they do not consider it any wrong to kill white men, and when they made their raid they spared women and children. If the peace commissioners expect them to give up the Indians that killed the settlers, they need not for one moment flatter themselves of obtaining such a result, as the Indians will fight to the last man, believing they have done no wrong. They are, however, willing to go on a reservation, and if the whites only keep faith with them and the Indians agents do not rob them of their supplies, for which the government pays, they will remain quiet like the rest of their tribe and give no further trouble. It is very doubtful, however, whether the present peace commission will do any good with these Indians, as I am satisfied from what I have seen in the Lava Beds that they distrust them. I sincerely trust that peace will be made, as more war can only result in much bloodshed and very little honor. I send this by special messenger to Yreka.

—•→ ⟨≓◆≓⟩ ←•—

New York *Herald,* March 17, 1873

HERALD HEADQUARTERS, VAN BREMER'S RANCH,
SISKIYOU COUNTY, March 1, 1873[32]

For nearly half a century, the history of this country has recorded many celebrated Indian fights, in which numbers of brave men have bitten the dust, but during the past ten years, there has not been a battle with the red men of the forest which created a greater sensation throughout the United States than the recent fight with Captain Jack and his band of Modoc Indians.

I shall not attempt to criticize the generalship that was exhibited on this particular occasion, as in a former letter I have endeavored to give a clear and impartial history of the events that transpired on January 17, and therefore every reader of the *Herald* can form his own opinion on the question, bearing in mind, however, that my sketch of the Lava Beds does not approach an adequate description of the natural fortifications against which the regular troops had to contend. I make the above statement as, since writing my account of the Lava Bed fight, I have succeeded in obtaining ocular demonstration as to the impregnable nature of the Indian stronghold, and I hasten to correct any false impression I may have unwittingly made in that respect. Colonel Wheaton had no idea of the nature of the ground on which he fought—at least, his engineers had given him a wrong impression in regard to its strength—and in fact, the only point that appeared to trouble the regular troops was the fear that perhaps, owing to the extent of the country they had to attack, some of the Indians might break through the line and escape.

A survey of the Lava Beds from the bluff above would certainly give no idea of the rough and broken country below, as I remember when I stood on that point and looked down, I made the remark, "Where are the Lava Beds? This country below looks like a flat plain that a mounted man could gallop across without difficulty or impediment." It was not until the troops were in action that the command arrived at a correct estimate of the character of the field of operations.

Their experience, though rather dearly bought at the cost of about fifteen brave men, has given a comprehension of the geography of the Lava Beds that was hitherto unknown. It is to be hoped, however, that no further aggressive movements may be necessary, as from my personal inspection of the position now occupied by the Modoc Indians, a victory will be dearly bought, even should the attacking party be 1,000 strong.

Ever since the arrival of the peace commission, there has been a hope that war was at an end, but since I have made the personal acquaintance of Captain Jack and his forty-two braves, I do not feel so certain about the negotiations terminating peacefully, as from what I can learn, Mr. Meacham is the only member of the peace commission who appears inclined to grant these Indians a general pardon, and without such liberal action there are no hopes of peace, as the Modocs will fight to the last man rather than give up one of their number to suffer for the death of those citizens who, in their belief, were only killed in honorable warfare. Mr. Case and Mr. Applegate, it is understood, are both in favor of, as they say, upholding the dignity of the government they represent and claiming the so-called murderers to be handed over to the civil powers of Oregon, to be tried for their crimes. The action of the Oregon grand jury finding a true bill of murder in the first degree against Hooker Jim, Charley Miller, Curly Headed Doctor, and two others has certainly rather complicated the business in the hands of the peace commission as, supposing they should pardon all these Indians and decide to move them to Klamath or some other reservation within the boundaries of the state of Oregon, the sheriff might put in an appearance and claim the above named men, and thus make a conflict between the military and civil authorities, as the former would certainly protect the Modocs from the hands of the law.

For the past three weeks I have traveled pretty well around the section, with a view to obtaining a correct opinion as to the origin of these troubles, and after a careful estimate of the different stories that I have heard, I feel satisfied that these Indians have been badly treated and forced into a war which they appear perfectly able to sustain. At first I was very much puzzled by the conflicting accounts one heard from the Californians and Oregonians, but the letter of the governor of Oregon, stating that the Lost River land had been located under the Homestead Act, and the reservation being all located in the same state, enabled me to comprehend the motives of the Oregonians in attempting to force these Indians from their homes on coveted land to a government reservation, where Indian agents would have more heads to include in their requisitions, and therefore more government funds at their disposal.

These Indians, however, had an experience of the comforts of a reservation and preferred their little settlement on the banks of Lost River, where fish and game were plenty, to starvation at the expense of the government. For three years they lived in peace and quiet, traveling backwards and forwards without molesting or disturbing any of the settlers, and occasionally visiting Yreka to dispose of furs and feathers, which formed their chief means of subsistence. Some of them, however, were scattered through the country, located on different ranches, where they made themselves generally useful, splitting rails and stock riding. This peaceful state of affairs did not suit the Oregonian settlers, and when they complained to the Indian superintendent and trumped up stories of repeated insults offered their families by the Modocs, the government sent down a company of thirty-five soldiers to move them onto a reservation, peaceably if they could, but forcibly if necessary. The soldiers came before daylight and, as the Indians say themselves, before they were out of their beds.

Captain Jack distinctly denies the story that the Indians fired first, but says that Scarfaced Charley had been out shooting wild geese and, returning, saw the soldiers in the camp, ran up to see what was the matter, and when 300 yards from the soldiers, fell down, and his gun was accidentally discharged, and the report started the firing on the part of the soldiers. In justice, however, to the military, I must state that Captain Jackson, who was in command of the soldiers, distinctly affirms that Scarfaced Charley fired the first shot when close upon the troops. On the other side of the river, John Schonchin states that a man named George Fiocke of Yreka fired the first shot, which was followed by several others on the part of the citizens, which resulted in the killing of a papoose, wounding of a squaw, and scaring all the party in the encampment. The attack was considered by the Indians to be, to all intents and purposes, a declaration of war, and putting on their war paint, they started for the Lava Beds. The party attacked by the citizens made a raid on the settlers and killed twelve men, but spared all women and children with the exception of a boy aged eleven. The latter they evidently considered able to carry arms, as the other day, when in the Lava Beds, I saw an Indian boy, certainly not over twelve years of age, carrying rifle and ammunition.

The subsequent events, and the fight of January 17, have already been fully described and need no further comment. The next move in this campaign of importance was the arrival of the peace commission, and here we commence a history of political trickery which, although it may result in a quiet settlement of the Modoc troubles, will be owing mainly to the influence of Elijah Steele, the instructions of President Grant, and the common sense of General Canby. Ever since Messrs. Meacham, Applegate, and Case have been in session, it was evident that private interests were consulted instead of the public welfare. Mr. Meacham, the late superintendent of Indian affairs in Oregon, although one of the most peacefully disposed of the three, takes every opportunity that his position affords him to cloak the misdeeds enacted in his reign by throwing the onus upon Captain Knapp, the Indian agent at Klamath at that time. He has also evinced great eagerness in ferreting out the causes and troubles leading to this war with, as some people say, the charitable view of establishing the blame upon his successor in office, Mr. Odeneal.

Both Messrs. Meacham and Applegate are Oregonians, who feel it their duty to stand by their state and are steadfast in their opinion that the murderers should be given up to justice. Mr. Meacham, however, does not despair and hopes to convince Judge Rosborough of the expediency, if not the justice, of his views. Should he prove successful, the commission will be divided, and General Canby will have the casting vote. That officer has kept carefully aloof from all the squabbles and bickering of the three first named gentlemen, and will doubtless come forward at the proper moment in a manner that will rather astonish their weak nerves.

The commission have been very careful as to what information they furnished the correspondents of the different newspapers, and what they did give them was furnished as a special favor. One of the commissioners was kind enough to promise me all the current news on the condition that I should submit my correspondence for the approval of the commission before mailing it to its destination. It is needless to say that I was unable to avail myself of this very kind offer, and consequently they retaliated by refusing me permission to be present at the interview with the squaws Matilda and Artinie when they returned from their first visit to the Lava Beds.

I then came to the conclusion that there must be some mystery that these gentlemen were attempting to hide from the public and decided that the only way to arrive at the truth was to see Captain Jack and hear his own story. Bob Whittle went in the next day with his squaw, Matilda, and a Modoc Indian named Dave, and they gave a rather favorable report as to the intentions and disposition of the Modocs in relation to peace. After hearing Whittle's story, the commissioners decided that as Captain Jack was anxious to see Mr. John Fairchild before having any big talk, his wishes should be gratified, and therefore Whittle, Fairchild, and the squaws Matilda and Artinie were given instructions to go to Jack's camp on Monday, February 25, and Modoc Dave returned on Sunday to prepare Captain Jack for their coming.

This appeared to be a favorable chance for visiting the Lava Beds, and I accordingly had a talk with John Fairchild early Sunday morning, and he said that I might accompany them in their trip. Before Dave left, Mr. Meacham called in Whittle, Fairchild, Dave, and the squaws Matilda and Artinie to give them their instructions. He commenced by handing a document to Mr. Fairchild, who was authorized to do the talking, and which proved to be a letter from the commissioners addressed to Captain Jack, John Schonchin, Scarfaced Charley, and other prominent men of the tribe, telling them who the commissioners were that the president had appointed to treat with them. It also told them that Judge Rosborough was a member of the commission, and that their friend Elijah Steele had been sent for; in order to allow them time to get to Fairchild's, it was necessary to delay a few days before holding the big talk. Mr. Fairchild was also instructed to find out on what terms the Modocs proposed to meet, and whether they would agree to allow the peace commissioners to be accompanied by as many soldiers as there were Modocs.

Parleying in the Lava Beds. NELSON A. MILES. *PERSONAL RECOLLECTIONS AND OBSERVATIONS.*

Mr. Meacham then turned to Whittle and told him to tell his squaw to point out to Dave and tell him the persons that were going in on Monday morning. Whittle told the squaw to tell him that their party and perhaps a couple of white men were going; but as he spoke, Mr. Meacham caught the last words and immediately turned to Whittle and told him that he was in the government employ, and he was to take Fairchild and no other man with him, especially newspaper reporters. I did not say anything at the moment, but afterwards I went to Mr. Meacham and asked him to allow me to accompany Whittle, and he most emphatically refused. Being thus thrown entirely on my own resources, I went out and had a talk with John Fairchild, and as he said personally he had no objection to my going, I concluded that I would make the attempt.

During the afternoon there was a good deal of private conversation between the members of the peace commission, and as I saw they appeared a little doubtful as to my intentions, I concluded it would be best to ride over to Van Bremer's and pass the night at that camp. Before going I had a little talk with Artinie, and she pointed out to me the gap in the range, where the road they were to follow left the main road between Fairchild's and Van Bremer's. I then started off, telling everybody I was going up to dine and pass the night with the officers of the 4th Artillery, who were then encamped at Van Bremer's. I had made the same trip on several occasions before anything was suspected, and I rode off without hindrance of any kind. On my way, I prospected the country a little and discovered where the road turned off and led to the bridge over Willow Creek. At Van Bremer's I kept my intentions quiet, as I was afraid I might place the officers in an unpleasant position if I told them what I intended to do contrary to the orders of the commissioners. Before going to bed, I went down to the sutler's, bought a couple of pounds of tobacco, and had my flask filled, in case I should require a little stimulant to help me out.

I awoke early and was up and dressed by 6:00 A.M. and found that it had been snowing during the night. The ground was covered with white, fleecy particles, lying about three inches deep. After swallowing a hasty breakfast, I saddled my horse and started along the road to Fairchild's in order to meet the other party, who I knew were to leave the ranch at 7:00 A.M. Instead of going directly down to the bridge, I made an attempt to ford the creek higher up, which resulted in a difference of opinion between myself and my horse, and as I had neither whip nor spurs, the quadruped succeeded in defeating my intentions. I dismounted and, having secured the services of a club, returned to my former position and renewed the discussion. The horse was, however, deaf to all arguments and insinuations of the club, and I consequently gave up the point and moved down toward the bridge. When I got there, the unbroken snow gave no signs of any horses having passed over that morning, so I rode back towards Fairchild's to meet them. After a few minutes' ride, I saw them coming over a spur, Fairchild and Artinie leading, with Whittle and Matilda about twenty yards behind. As soon as Fairchild and Artinie came up, I turned my horse round and rode alongside of them.

FAIRCHILD—Where are you going?

HERALD CORRESPONDENT—To the Lava Beds, with you.

FAIRCHILD—Well, personally I have not any objection, and in fact I would be glad to have you with us; but as I am only accompanying Whittle, you had better see him.

I said, "All right," and rode back to join Whittle and his squaw. When I joined them, the following conversation ensued:

WHITTLE—Where are you off this morning?

HERALD CORRESPONDENT—I hardly know—just taking a little ride.

WHITTLE—I am sorry the commissioners would not let you go with us.

HERALD CORRESPONDENT—Yes, it was rather mean of them. But I have an idea of going without their permission, as I do not see what authority they have to govern my traveling to any part of the country I deem proper.

WHITTLE—That is so, but then you cannot go with me.

HERALD CORRESPONDENT—But if I choose to ride along after you, there is nobody who can prevent my going into the Lava Beds.

WHITTLE—If you go there, you will have to find the way yourself as, if you follow me, I shall turn back.

HERALD CORRESPONDENT—You need not do that; nobody can blame you if I follow you.

WHITTLE—Yes, they will. If you had asked me before I was engaged by the government, I would have taken you, but as it is, if you go I go back.

HERALD CORRESPONDENT—Is there no way I can fix it?

WHITTLE—None that I know of.

HERALD CORRESPONDENT—Well, if that is the case, I suppose I must defer my visit.

WHITTLE—I am very sorry, but it cannot be helped.

Whittle then rode on after Fairchild and the squaws, and I turned round and rode back in not a very pleasant frame of mind. As the horse walked slowly on, I began to think how I could get into that lava bed without getting Whittle into trouble, and just as I was giving up all hopes, my eyes happened to light upon the fresh tracks made by Fairchild's party in the snow. It suddenly flashed across my mind that those tracks would lead me to the Lava Beds, and the commissioners could then throw no blame on Whittle.

I turned round in my saddle, and seeing that the party had passed over the next hill and were out of sight, I wheeled and followed slowly after them. For some minutes I let the horse walk slowly along, until we came close to the top of the first hill, when I dismounted and peeped cautiously over. Whittle and party were out of sight, so I mounted and trotted leisurely along the trail.

About twenty minutes' ride brought me down to the edge of Little Klamath Lake, a large sheet of water that appeared entirely frozen over. Turning a point of rocks near the border of the lake, I saw my unconscious guides about two miles ahead. I waited behind the rocks until they turned the next point jutting out into the lake, and then resumed my journey, trotting leisurely along.

It was not a very pleasant morning, as the snow was still falling and the air was keen and sharp. The road led along the edge of the lake, and although the frost of the two or three preceding days had hardened it to some extent, there were many soft and miry places. From what I heard, I knew that this must be the old California trail to the Atlantic states, and that I could not be far from a portion of the road that had been the scene of many an emigrant massacre, in which some five and twenty years ago the fathers of these very Modocs whom I desired so much to see had taken a prominent part in butchering hundreds of victims.

This train of thought had rather an unpleasant effect on my peace of mind, and the close proximity of two large ravens that kept slowly hovering over my head did not tend to enliven my spirits. These birds kept right above my head, not five yards distant, and kept slowly fanning the air with their wings, and for two miles they never flew twenty yards away. Several times they came so close to my head that I raised my hand to strike them; but they were not easily frightened and still kept their position, flying faster when my horse trotted and slower when he walked. The road kept along the edge of the lake for about eight miles, and then went straight up a long hill.

I had been riding up this hill about five or ten minutes, when I suddenly perceived that the snow was unbroken and there were no fresh tracks of horses ahead. I immediately turned my horse's head and rode slowly back, looking out for tracks, and when I got down to the edge of the lake, I found a fresh trail leading sharp up to the right of the main road. I dismounted and, finding the tracks of four horses, followed it up a wild ravine, gradually mounting all the time until we reached the top of the spur. As Whittle, Fairchild, and party were not in sight, I trotted along pretty fast, but in many places the ground was so rocky that I was obliged to walk my horse, and mounting again at its base, [I] rode fast to the top of the next spur. As I passed over its crest, I saw Whittle and party on the flat below, and they saw me at the same time. They immediately pulled up, and as Whittle waved his hand to me, I thought it best to ride on fast and soon came up with them.

Whittle waited until I rode up, and then said, "So you were determined to come?" I replied that as the tracks on the snow were a good guide to the Lava Beds, I thought it best to take advantage of the chance and not wait until the sun had effaced all tracks of their ride. Whittle laughed and said, "Well, as the tracks have seen you before this, you had better keep up and go along with us." He added, "If I had seen you before you came over that last hill, I should have turned back, and you would have had to find the road the best way you could." I did not attempt to argue the question but accepted the position and rode up alongside of Fairchild and Artinie.

We now began to look out for Indians, as we were nearing the place where Whittle held his first talk on the Saturday previous. They did not appear to be on the lookout, as we reached the top of the bluff overlooking the Lava Beds without coming across a single scout. The squaws immediately went to work and pulled up some sagebrush and lit a fire, in order to let the Indians know we had arrived. In the meantime, I took a look about and saw the Lava Beds below me and Tule Lake to the left.

The Lava Beds, seen from the bluffs, looked more like a flat plain, dotted over with sagebrush shrubs, than the rocky, broken ground that those present in the fight had such difficulty in getting over. It lay right at the foot of the bluff and about halfway across the flat. The squaw Matilda pointed out a little knoll, thinly covered with patches of juniper, which she said was close to Captain Jack's cave. After waiting about a quarter of an hour, Matilda said she saw a Modoc riding across the flat towards the foot of the bluff. We all looked in that direction, but with the exception of the other squaw, Artinie, nobody could see any sign of the Indians. It was fully ten minutes before we were able to see what the keen eye of the squaw had already discerned, and then the approaching horseman looked like a small, black speck, moving rapidly across the plain. Presently another horseman was seen following after the first, and when about half a mile from the foot of the bluff, we also discovered an Indian on foot, running along with the horses. The ascent of the bluff was very steep, but the mounted Indians rode their horses halfway up, and then, tying them up to a juniper tree, came the remainder of the distance on foot. Before they arrived, I asked Whittle what to do when they came up, and he said shake hands with them, give them a smoke, but do not appear too familiar.

In a few minutes the head of Dave, the Modoc that had been into the ranch on Saturday, appeared over the crest of the hill, followed shortly afterwards by Hooker Jim, one of the most notable ruffians in the tribe. Dave had no paint on and wore a pair of buckskin pants and a soldier's overcoat. He carried on his arm an old Springfield muzzleloader, and the necessary equipments were hung over his shoulder. I immediately stepped forward, shook hands with him, and a few seconds afterward my hand was grasped by Hooker Jim with a kind of sullen grip. There was certainly no friendship evinced in that shake, and a look at the gentleman's countenance did not tend to reassure me of his pacific intentions. He wore a flannel shirt and a pair of gray pants considerably the worse for wear; an old-fashioned muzzle-loading rifle rested on his arm, and a buckhorn powder flask was suspended from his waist.

Hooker Jim was in mourning, and if anything could make him more hideous and ruffianly, this tribute to the memory of the departed, which consisted of a black, greasy paste laid on over the lower part of the face, close up to the eyes, was certainly a success. Hooker Jim I should take to be a man of about thirty years of age, five feet nine inches in height, 175 pounds in weight, and of stout and compact proportions. His name has become celebrated in this late war as one of the leaders of the band that murdered the Oregon settlers on the day of the first fight at Lost River. He has been indicted by the Oregon grand jury for murder in the first degree, but I think the sheriff and his posse will have some trouble in arraigning him before the bar.

Both these Indians stood round the fire talking with the squaws, and in the meantime, Steamboat Frank walked up and joined the party. Frank is not a bad-looking Indian, about twenty-three years of age, five foot eight in stature and weighing about 160 pounds. He had on his war paint, smudged roughly on the cheeks and forehead, and was armed with a Spencer breech-loading carbine and equipment adorned with the letters U.S. This weapon was probably obtained from one of the cavalry killed in the fight of January 17. He had a belt full of cartridges slung over his shoulder and a revolver and knife in his belt. Both the other Indians carried revolvers and sheath knives. Frank belongs to the Hot Creek band of Indians and was one of that party that Fairchild and Dorris would have taken safely to Yainax reservation if they had not been stopped by the drunken Linkville roughs.

For a few minutes the conversation was confined to the squaws and the Indians, and in the meantime, I filled and lit my pipe, and passing it around, they took two or three whiffs. Presently Frank began to talk to Fairchild in English, and we found that Captain Jack was very sick and would not be able to come out and talk, but he wanted Fairchild to come in and see him. Whittle then asked if he and the paper man (the name under which the *Herald* correspondent was introduced to the Indians) were to come along, and Frank responding in the affirmative, we all started, leading our horses down the bluff. The descent was very steep, making nearly an angle of forty-five degrees, and it took us nearly twenty minutes to make the base. Arriving there, we mounted and continued our journey at a walk.

The track led in an easterly direction, along the southerly edge of Tule Lake and across a country that appeared one mass of broken rocks, firmly imbedded in a dark, loamy soil. The rocks were all rough, with jagged edges; on the track, although some were worn down a little, the traveling was very bad.

We walked quietly along in single file, and Mr. Hooker Jim kept close to me and appeared very much taken by an Ulster overcoat I had on. He afterwards evinced such an interest in that article of apparel that he proposed a trade, offering me in exchange an old soldier's overcoat. I certainly felt flattered at the proposal, and under the influence of the persuaders which Mr. Hooker Jim carried in his hand would probably have complied with his request, but I finally concluded that it would not be wise to give way to the avaricious desires of the wily savage and told the squaw to tell him the coat did not belong to me.

After riding slowly along for about half an hour, we came upon half a dozen Modoc scouts standing round a sagebrush fire and talking and laughing among themselves. Fairchild dismounted, and Whittle and I followed his example. Leaving our horses to browse on the bunch grass, we walked up and joined the party by the fire.

They were a wild looking group, nearly all clad in woolen shirts and secondhand soldiers' clothes. They were all armed to the teeth and painted. Some were in mourning, but the majority had their faces daubed with the reddish brown mixture which they use as war paint. Fairchild, after shaking hands with the party, introduced me as the paper man from afar off, from the big town by the sea, Boston Illihee. The Indians in the West call all the white men Bostons, and the word Illihee means country or land. After shaking hands with the entire party, my pipe was again brought into requisition and went the rounds of the group, each man taking a whiff and then passing it to his neighbor. Some of these Modocs were quite young, and I noticed one boy in the group, certainly not more than fifteen years of age, with his face plentifully bedaubed with red paint and armed with an old-fashioned muzzle-loading rifle.

After a short talk, we mounted our horses and rode on, escorted by our new friends. Some of them were riding their little Indian ponies, and the others came along on foot. The trail then led to the border of the lake, and for a short distance we just skirted the water's edge, passing through the tule, or long bulrushes, from which the lake takes its name. After traversing about half a mile of a very rocky country, we saw another Indian camp that at the distance made a picturesque scene. A large party of the Modocs were standing and lying around a fire, built on the summit of a rocky bluff rising about twenty feet above the surrounding country. There were about fifty or sixty bucks, squaws, and papooses in the group, and the squaws, attired in their red petticoats with their papooses on their backs, gave one the picture of what might be taken for a gypsy encampment.

When we got to the base of the rocks, we all dismounted, and after the usual form of introduction, I shook hands with about twenty more Modocs, including John Schonchin, the brother of Schonchin, the old chief of the tribe, now residing on the Yainax reservation. John Schonchin is a fine-looking Indian, about fifty-five years of age, with an intelligent countenance not disfigured with paint. He was unarmed and expressed himself very glad to see the paper man.

I set my pipe going and handed it to Schonchin, who took a smoke and then passed it on to Long Jim, a fine-looking Indian who had his right arm in a sling. He received a bad gunshot wound in the first fight, which shattered his arm pretty badly, but the squaw Matilda told me it would be healed in a few days. Speaking of wounds, I may add that these Indians take a wonderful amount of killing. Shacknasty Jim and Bogus Charley were both shot through the body at the first fight, and four days afterwards they were walking about, apparently in perfect health, with a patch of sticking plaster over the holes made by the bullets.

We only stopped about five minutes at this camp, and then started off for Captain Jack's headquarters, accompanied by the entire party, some riding, but the majority on foot. The trail now became very rocky and rough, and the horses had some trouble in keeping on their legs. The ground was rolling and completely covered with rocks, giving one the idea that the whole country had been suddenly upheaved and left nothing but rocks on the surface. The formation of the rocks is very curious, as there is no similarity between one pile of rocks and the other, as to the right we pass a deep hole filled with loose rocks and on the left there runs a trail leading into a chasm about fifteen or twenty feet deep, with walls so perpendicular that they give me the impression of being the work of man rather than the work of nature.

About a quarter of a mile further on, we were met by rather a nice-looking Indian, who immediately greeted Fairchild in English and shook hands with him in a friendly manner. The newcomer, Mr. Bogus Charley, was rather a nice-looking boy, about twenty years of age, belonging to the Hot Creek party, and he appeared to speak English tolerably well. Our march was presently interrupted by the arrival of Charley Miller, a repulsive-looking Indian who waved us back with his hand as he came. This young man, I have been given to understand, is one of the worst Indians in the tribe, and certainly first appearances did not give a favorable impression. He immediately commenced talking and gesticulating in a violent manner, and Bogus Charley, Steamboat Frank, and Tame answered him back somewhat sharply.

Although the conversation was carried on in the Modoc language, I could easily perceive that rather an animated discussion was being carried on, and that we were in some way or the other the origin of the row. I must say that I did not like the look of things, as the Modocs were evidently getting very hot over their talk, and it did not appear improbable that they would wind up with a fight. Such a conclusion I did not desire, as an Indian with his blood up might not have much respect for a newspaper correspondent, especially one who had hair about ten inches long. I asked Matilda what was the matter, and she said that Charley Miller had come down with a message from Captain Jack that we were to camp where we were, and that Fairchild alone would be received by him. Although the evening was bitterly cold and the prospect not inviting, I displayed unusual alacrity, and immediately jumped off my horse and expressed my readiness to camp anywhere that Captain Jack desired. Matilda told me not to be in a hurry, as Tame, who was living with his cousin Wild Gas, insisted that we should go to his house for the night. Although Mr. Tame certainly displayed the greatest zeal in our behalf, I inwardly cursed his well-meant hospitality, as Charley Miller looked more savage every minute, and [I] felt nervous for fear the Springfield resting on his arm might go off "accidentally in earnest."

The pressure brought to bear by Bogus Charley, Frank, and Tame finally succeeded in squelching Mr. Miller, and we resumed our march without further hindrance. Scarfaced Charley presently rode up and settled all doubts on the matter by telling us to come on. At this juncture, Scarfaced Charley, Bogus Charley, Frank, Fairchild, and Artinie took the trail to the left, and Tame took Whittle, Matilda, and the *Herald* correspondent straight ahead. We were now evidently approaching Captain Jack's headquarters, as we passed through two or three gulches about fifty feet in width and walls of broken rock about twenty feet high. In each of these natural fortifications were one or two Indian rancherias, or wickiups. After climbing up out of one of these rocky canyons, we suddenly descended into the largest of the kind I had yet seen, being about 100 feet square and with walls about forty feet in height. There were four or five rancherias in this place, and at one of these Tame stopped and, lifting up the blanket that served as a door, went inside. We all dismounted and, after tying up our horses to some safe brush stumps that had escaped the fire, took off our saddles and bridles and went into Hotel de Tame.

The accommodation was certainly limited, as the reed matting [hanging] over a few tent poles stuck in the ground in an oval shape did not cover an area of more than ten feet by eight. The fire was built against the rocks in the open air, and under two rocks that had fallen together and formed two sides of an equilateral triangle. Indians do not appear to care for a genial warmth but prefer a system of roasting that requires something of the nature of a salamander to endure. On entering the wickiup, I was introduced to my hostess, Mrs. Wild Gal Tame, who appeared rather better looking than the average run of Modoc squaws. Miss Wild Gal Tame, a pretty little papoose about three or four years of age, sat on her knee playing with a dead mouse.

We all sat down on the matting round the fire, and Whittle then told me that there was a difference of opinion among the Modocs as to whether I should be admitted to the council. Several of the bucks came around and were introduced, and nearly all of them carried their guns, as if suspicious of treachery. I pulled out my pipe and set it going the rounds, and then cut up a plug of tobacco in small pieces and divided it among them. This bribery and corruption, I believe, defeated the opposition, as a few minutes afterwards, Long Jim came up and told us to come along to the council. We then followed our guide across the canyon and, after a scramble up one of its rocky walls, came out upon a table of broken scoria, which we crossed with some difficulty, and then our guide suddenly disappeared down a deep hole. When I came up to the spot where he so mysteriously disappeared, I found a deep hole with foot tracks leading down about twelve feet; I let myself down gently, and then, after about ten paces down an inclined plane, found myself in a large cave filled with Indian bucks and squaws.

The *coup d'oeil* was striking, as the fire shed a glare over the faces of the brown warriors, who were seated round in circles. The light also flashed on their musket barrels, showing that not even in council did they leave their treasured weapons. The cave was lofty, and the walls ran round in circular form about forty feet apart. The fire was in the center, and sitting up with a blanket wrapped round his lower limbs was Captain Jack, the chief of these few Indians that had given such practical evidence of their fighting capacity. He had a white handkerchief round his head and wore a gray flannel shirt. His left hand rested upon the handle of a root digger that was planted in the ground before him, and when I stepped into the circle, he put out his right hand and shook me a cordial welcome.

I then shook hands with Scarfaced Charley, Shacknasty Jim, Black Jim, and some half a dozen others, and took a seat in the front circle to the left of Scarfaced, and with Whittle on my right. On the opposite side of the fire reclined a fine looking Indian who had been shot through both arms and was then under treatment of Curly Headed Doctor. Two long arrows stood in the ground, one at each side of his head, and the doctor's wife sat alongside of him, ministering to his wants. On Jack's right sat Bogus Charley, Steamboat Frank, John Schonchin, and Hooker Jim, in the order named, and on his left were Shacknasty Jim, John Fairchild, Scarfaced Charley, the *Herald* correspondent, Whittle, and the two squaws Matilda and Artinie.

When all were quiet, John Fairchild got up and introduced the *Herald* correspondent by name to the assembled Indians and told how I came from afar off, from Boston Illihee, and wrote for a paper that told all the white people what was doing in all parts of the world. He said I had heard what the white people said about the Modoc troubles, and that I wanted so bad to hear the Modocs' story that though the commissioners had forbidden him to take me in, I had followed their tracks in the snow to the top of the bluffs. Bogus Charley, who officiated as interpreter, then translated this speech to the sachems, and when he concluded, they expressed their approbation in a perfect chorus of "A's," the nearest approach to their approving grunt being a sound resembling the pronunciation of the letter A.

John Fairchild then proceeded to carry out his mission and read the letter of the commission, which was translated, sentence by sentence, by Bogus Charley. The letter simply informed the Indians of the names of the four commissioners and that they were anxious to delay the big talk until Judge Rosborough and Mr. Elijah Steele should arrive. As each sentence was translated, the Indians grunted their approval.

Fairchild then asked to hear them speak, and in the meantime, I sent my pipe on its rounds. John Schonchin finally got up, and in order to give an idea of a Modoc speech, as rendered by the interpreter, I will give it verbatim:

Well, glad to see men; glad to see the paper man from afar off; my heart feels good when men talk; tired of hearing squaw talk; Indian not ashamed to talk when white man come to see him. You tell me a name; I know him; Mr. Meacham; I see him; he says I am big chief; first time see him he say I big chief; I see him long time ago; I knew him, Mr. Meacham, tell me all straight, "I come now big chief; I make you good place." Tell me first time; show me good house; long time ago; that man, I say I know him, Mr. Meacham; he told me out at Fort Klamath; he tell Captain Knapp, "You treat him good this Modoc Indian." Captain Knapp no like me; he scare me, Captain Knapp. Mr. Meacham told him to watch me good; I know Mr. Meacham; he say big talk; tell me straight, tell truth. Captain Knapp bad man; he come to my door; I say I do not want you come to my house, no like you. I knew Mr. Meacham; tell me the truth; give me good say; say want to tell me truth, no want to tell me lie. I knew Mr. Meacham at Fort Klamath; put the axe in the ground; I tell him straight, Fort Klamath; I make no first blood; I want to talk right, tell him, Mr. Meacham, I want to live in good place, where I live first (Fort Klamath).

Man from afar off, hear Indian speak. Hear him speak truth. That agent make it bad, hang Indian; Captain Knapp, he bad man. Four moons ago (first fight), white man make trouble. He shoot me first; white man shoot first. I same as white man; they come attack me. I want the chief to tell me good; no lie. He shoot me; I don't know him. I give you all my country; I keep a little piece of land, yet they shoot me. I do not know what he shoot me for. What makes them shoot me? I keep a little piece of land. I don't like fight; no want fight. He comes; I tell them no fight. You come in, Mr. Fairchild, that's all right. All true when you come. I see you; all right after you come. You like grass in this country; that's all right. White man shoot children, little girl, big girl; my friend, he shoot him. I get up soon in morning; I hunt geese. When I look back see too many men both sides of the river. I look back, both sides of Lost River. What the matter? Bad work. Applegate's son (meaning Lindsay Applegate's son) tell me lie. Applegate's son say he go back tomorrow; he tell me lie; me feel bad. When I go back, he kill my friend. I come home, I call my children; no breakfast, no home. I like to see him. Applegate's son, he bad man. One day he tell me good, with One-Arm Brown. All hic hic. I see him; he said plenty of men; I see them. I don't know what the matter with Jackson. He come early morning; soldier men coming, pistol in hand; like to see Captain Jack; all carry gun.

Bogus Charley here took up the story, saying:

> I say stop; like to see Captain Jack; I say stop boys; Ivan Applegate. I got up early morning; told Charley go get me water; he say, "Plenty of men come." I hardly get up; I sleep in house; he come slow; say, "Boys, soldier come." What he want? I say, "Stop boys, I don't want you come near; make you place there, camp there." All children scared; still they come, close to house. All carry gun; ask for Captain Jack. Captain Jack asleep, no clothes on, no gun loaded, no pistol loaded. Old woman gave Jack shirt. He said, "No hurry, plenty of time." He go out. We have nothing; no gun. I go down to see him, "Major Jackson, how are you?" He said nothing. "Why you come for this morning. What you come hurry?" Sets big shoot, all guns. I never do anything against soldiers. Scarfaced Charley come from other side; been to Dennis McCann's house. He came slow; he see soldiers; he run up; carry gun to kill duck 400 yards away. He fall down; gun go off. Soldier hear shoot; he shoot, kill Indian. One man shoot me. Jackson talk, "Come boys, get off horses, stop all together." I think Ivan Applegate make him bad. Man shoot me, fifty yards away. All soldiers shoot; two Indians dead. Big shoot other side; George Fiocke shoot first. Dove and Crawley both fire shotguns; shot women and papoose, take guns from Indian. Ivan said want run, go to Yainax; soldiers shoot you; I want you go. I say want to stay with my father. Ivan come down two days before, say he come back, two men, have big talk, hi, hi. Come back with soldiers; would not go off; camp and talk. Major Jackson no talk. Scarfaced say, "Jackson, what chief you come from?" He say come from the mountains.

Fairchild then suggested that we should break up the council for the present and go to supper. This proposition appeared to meet with general satisfaction, and the Indians all retired to their respective rancherias and caves, leaving Captain Jack in the charge of Curly Headed Doctor and wife. Fairchild, Whittle, and myself returned to Mr. Tames' rancheria and, pulling out a bag of biscuit and cold meat, set to work at supper, and Mrs. Wild Gal Tame boiled some water and made up some coffee. A number of Indians sat around outside and munched greedily at some pieces of bread that we gave them. After supper Bogus Charley, Scarfaced Charley, John Schonchin, and several others arrived, and Bogus told me that Captain Jack was too sick to talk to me himself and had sent them to tell me all about their wrongs.

They first told me about going on the reservation, where they had nearly frozen to death, as the agent only gave them half a blanket and none to the squaws. He also said they had only been issued provisions for the first two or three days, and afterwards they had to dig camas roots in the depth of winter and kill and eat their horses to keep from starvation. Charley said that he and three or four others had split some two or three thousand rails and had never been paid for their work, and added that starvation finally drove them back to Lost River, after they had been about ten weeks on the reservation. Speaking about the last fight, they told me each two or three men had about two miles of rock to defend. They did not have a high opinion of the Oregon volunteers and said they lay on their backs behind rocks and shot up in the air. They asked me all about the *Herald* and were evidently much amazed and astonished at the magnitude of the establishment connected with that paper. Finally, Scarfaced Charley told me they were going to doctor Captain Jack, and so I went over to see the performance.

A good many Indians were in the cave, and in the center were two other Indians, jumping up and down on the ground and singing some unintelligible words to a meaningless kind of tune. Captain Jack was lying down alongside the fire, and the doctor and his squaw were evidently trying the effect of magnetism on his system. Captain Jack's squaw, a nice-looking woman with a magnificent eye, soft and full of expression, sat at the head of the bed. After a little quiet work upon his patient, the doctor appeared presently to get quite excited, and finally turning Captain Jack on his face, he gave a howl, jumped on his back, laying all over him, and put his teeth in Jack's shoulder blade. He held on there for a couple of minutes, writhing and twisting his body about, and then Dave, a stout-looking Indian weighing about 160 pounds, jumped on top of the doctor, in order to keep him in his position. In the meanwhile, the men kept up their dancing and howling in the middle of the room, being relieved every now and then by fresh recruits. Presently Dave got off, and the doctor rose from the body of his patient and, going up to the entrance of the cave, vomited. All the Indians ran up after him to see what he threw up, as their belief is that he had sucked all the disease out of the sick man, and they wanted to see what it looked like. My curiosity did not lead me to join in the prospecting party, so I sat and watched them bathe Jack in cold water and then continue their rubbing and singing. I finally returned to my wickiup, not at all satisfied with the performance I had just seen, as I was inwardly convinced that Jack would be dead next morning, and as such an event might cause a revolution in this peaceful family, the position of the guests in such a case would be rather unpleasant.

On my way back to the Tame rancheria, I passed a group of bucks dancing round in a circle and singing a peace song. They all appeared in good humor, which is said to be graded in accordance to their exact feelings. I found the house pretty full, and after sitting up for about an hour, my hostess, Mrs. Wild Gal, proceeded to arrange the bed. After shaking out the matting, the blankets were thrown on top, and taking off my boots, I lay down and made an attempt to sleep, but it was so cold I never closed my eyes all night. If animal warmth could have kept my blood in circulation, I would have been all right, as our party consisted of four gentlemen and three ladies, all stretched out on a matting eight feet wide.

A little before daylight the squaw Matilda got up and lit the fire, and I was glad to get a little warmth in my feet. After eating a light breakfast and smoking a pipe, we went over to Captain Jack's cave and found the council already in session, waiting for our arrival. Captain Jack was sitting up, supported by his squaw, who had her arms around his waist, and he looked a little better this morning, as if the treatment he received on the previous evening had really done him good.

As soon as we were all seated, Captain Jack commenced his talk, which was translated as follows:

> I know Mr. Meacham; I see him long time ago at Fort Klamath. I don't know which way he comes from now. He tell me truth. He got plenty of soldiers. I afraid I don't know him; maybe he don't feel good. I got one heart; maybe Meacham got two hearts. My thoughts straight. I don't want to scare Meacham; he come here, don't be afraid. I don't tell nobody hard; I tell truth. I tell my own heart; other chiefs lie. I want you, Mr. Fairchild, tell how you know me long time, hear me speak truth. I don't know what I have done bad. I tell truth. I am Yreka man. I conceal nothing; I tell truth all. I know good many men, treat me well. Want to fight; I don't go. I tell you glad to see paper man from afar off. I know you better; not ashamed to talk to white people. I did not steal your horse.

He then turned to me and said:

> Tell your people I just got up in morning. They disturb me; I done nothing. I told them Yreka men gave me a letter; good words in letter. White men no like. He tell you a lie; you say all right. I don't want to see more before day. You go home, you fellows; want people to look good, no watch anymore. Get up in morning, just look for something to eat, not blood. I tell him [Jackson] not going to steal your horse; not ashamed to speak. No shoot; no more want, it all good. These Indians done shooting; no tell lie. I want things done quick; no wait long, talk quick. I can tell them to quit; I say, "Boys, quit." I got good sense; my boys use my sense. That's all.

FAIRCHILD—Meacham wants to know if when you say quit, that every Modoc quit.

CAPTAIN JACK—My boys think as me; I say quit, they all quit. Mr. Meacham maybe got two tongues; I speak with one tongue. These all my people. I make good sense, give them my sense. Meacham got too many friends. I don't want Meacham talk that way; maybe half white good, maybe half bad. All boys here one mind; want whites all one mind. I tell him truth, I won't tell guess. I laugh and feel good to see Mr. Meacham. Before fight we same as white men; after fight Indian.

I want no Indian law, got no Indian law; want same law for Indian and white man. Indian want to be same as white man. When Mr. Meacham done talking, if he tells no lies, I be same as white man. Meacham's side only half minded, this side all one mind. I go to Yreka, I same as white man, money in pockets. Went to store my things; I make more friends with white; I tell him truth, all straight, shake hands, want no more bad. Mr. Meacham must not think treachery from my boys; they all act right. Wash all the blood from these boys, make them same as women. He must not talk that. I got only few men; I got one house. Sorry white man afraid to travel this road; I like people everywhere.

Well, John Fairchild, you look after your cattle; watch them well. I don't know what chief want to make blood again. Mr. Meacham perhaps not know they were going to make blood; very bad, every Indian agent did. Want Mr. Meacham talk quick, stop making blood. I don't know why send Maj. Jackson; he want to kill me quick, he bad man. I like to see him. He tell me lie, he make me crazy. I want him to talk straight. He came before morning; all dark. Ivan came days before; tell me he come back three men; he tell me lie. When Jackson come, my gun not loaded, no pistol loaded, no clothes on, my friends all asleep. I tell the boys all bad, told all to get up. Scarfaced, coming back into camp, fall down; gun go off. I tell him soldiers shoot. They say want to find Captain Jack; they come pistols in hand, me no clothes on. I told Maj. Jackson to make a camp, come back and talk. He don't want to talk; tell men to get off, keep together. Ivan say, "Clean them all out today, kill these Indians." Boys won't talk, want to kill these tricks. All soldiers get off, pull off his coats. My boys get scared. I don't shoot first. They shoot one of my friends; he fall down dead. Tell you truth; I don't shoot first.

I did not want to fight. He come, kill my friend, my dear friend. I don't care about dead; let them go. I want good for alive. I told Fairchild, when he come first, I quit. They come fight, get all fight; come again, get more fight. I saw Klamath Indians. I tell him I want to quit; no want fight. He tell me all coming to fight tomorrow; soldiers camped very close. I did not go near, did not want to fight; could have fought them before day, did not want to fight. I tell my boys, and we go any place and fight; my boys not afraid. Did not want to fight them. Long time ago Indian get fighting, many of them, big chief could not stop them. Now not so many, stop them. Want Meacham and one, three, or five come talk; no gassing, want them to come. Tell him not to be scared, this man from paper afar off.

This man with good eye, he come to see me; he not afraid. Indian glad to see him, want paper man come again. He hear same story, hear me speak truth. Hear no more hard stories about me when done talking with white men. I did not make first fight. I want everybody good. I hold up my head; I not ashamed of first fight. Glad to see men come to see me; tired of hearing squaw talk. That's all.

FAIRCHILD—What place would you like to hold the meeting?

CAPTAIN JACK—Glad to talk. Little flat by the lake, near foot of the bluff; plenty water and grass. Want to see white men. I don't want soldiers come; want Fairchild, paper man from afar off, he come hear me speak truth. I want to show my boys to Mr. Meacham. We don't want to make gas; meet down on flat by the lake, plenty of water and grass.

FAIRCHILD—How many Indians come? Mr. Meacham says he bring many soldiers as Indians. He don't like to come with few men to meet all Modocs.

CAPTAIN JACK—I don't like to see soldiers, keep the soldiers where they are; don't like their faces, make me feel bad. Want to see Mr. Meacham and white men. If he want peace, what he want soldiers? He come, Meacham and four others; you three come—eight altogether.

FAIRCHILD—Meacham want Lalake, Joe Parker, and Modoc Sally come.

CAPTAIN JACK—I don't like them, no want to see them.

FAIRCHILD—This party come: Meacham, Case, Applegate, Canby, writer, waiter, clerk, Rosborough, Steele.

CAPTAIN JACK—All right, ten altogether. No soldiers. Talk good; tell me truth. You three come.

FAIRCHILD—Other paper men want to come.

CAPTAIN JACK—That's all right; want to see paper men. No soldiers. Soldiers stop where they are, mad with them; make my boys feel bad.

FAIRCHILD—What day shall they come?

CAPTAIN JACK—I am tired; I want you to come tomorrow. Tell him to do right. I am sick, ready any time; come soon.

FAIRCHILD—All right, we come when Steele and Rosborough come. When they come, I come down and tell you.

These matters being all arranged satisfactorily, we were arranging to go when John Schonchin said he wanted to talk, and according to Indian etiquette, we remained where we were and heard the following speech:

When I see Fairchild I not ashamed; I don't gas about anything. You tell me what Mr. Meacham says all good. I like Meacham well; no more bad. I know Meacham; he wants good talk. I don't like to wait long; like Meacham good, like him well. Meacham says he big chief. Little chief wants to talk quick; big chief slow. I want to talk good, wash my hands. Mr. Meacham may be good talk; what he want to bring soldiers? Soldiers no good for peace. I don't like soldiers. I like good roads, all open. People travel right and left; don't scare when you hunt your cattle, you need not watch them—all good. These boys only look for good—no bad. I feel good now as if I stood in high place, saw all peace. See cattle graze, leave them alone. Men get scared, go hunt their cattle; don't like to see that. I am chief of this country; the bricks like to work round the country, chop wood, look for things. If Meacham wants to stop fight, all right; that would be good. I guess someone on your side want to make blood again; don't like it, perhaps tell lies. This side tells all truth. The big soldier chief, he come here, all right. Your side think good; want no soldiers, no gas this side. You know my heart, Mr. Fairchild. You know me, you know whether I am crazy. I make no bad sense. I think you do on your side. I have got no bad heart. I don't think of making it bad again. Maybe you do; that why you want bring soldiers here again. He send good word; want to make no more blood. If Mr. Meacham stood here and talked no more blood, soldiers same as dogs; when they come, look like blood. Don't like Mr. Meacham fetch soldiers. I am telling paper man all about it. Talk with one heart, all truth. Squaw tell me come big chief. Mr. Meacham make my heart good; next time he tell me straight. Don't want to see more soldiers. I tell you truth, white men. Come and see me, all right. That's all.

Schonchin's speech wound up the council, and we all got up and, after a round of handshaking, started for our ranches and saddled our horses. As we left the camp, the Indians crowded on the rocks and, shouting our names, said, "Good-bye, come again." Bogus Charley rode back with us and went on with the party to Fairchild's, and I left them after crossing Willow Creek and rode up to Van Bremer's. During the night, Hooker Jim, Curly Jack, and another Indian rode in and had a talk with Lalake, the Klamath chief, and got their horses and rode back.

On Thursday evening Judge Rosborough and Steele arrived, and I had the pleasure of hearing from Mr. Steele that my visit to the Lava Beds, he was certain, had done more to establish confidence between the Indians and whites than anything that the peace commission had yet accomplished. Mr. Steele, John Fairchild, Frank Riddle and squaw, and three California newspaper correspondents went into the Lava Beds on Friday morning. Mr. Steele was the bearer of the following proposition, which was suggested by General Canby: "For the Indians to surrender as prisoners of war and go on some reservation in California or Oregon."

New York *Herald,* March 3, 1873

FAIRCHILD'S RANCH, VIA YREKA,
March 1, 1873

Messrs. Elijah Steele, John Fairchild, Frank Riddle and squaw, and members of the press[33] arrived at 5:00 P.M. this evening from Captain Jack's camp, accompanied by Shacknasty Jim, Bogus Charley, Curly Headed Jack, Mary (sister of Captain Jack), Hooker Jim, and several other Indians.

The party left Fairchild's on Friday morning and slept last night in the Lava Beds. Mr. Steele was the bearer of the following terms to the Indians: To surrender to the military as prisoners of war and to be removed to a reservation, either in California or Arizona. Captain Jack was very sick but received the party in his cave, and they had a long talk last night and another council this morning.

Mr. Steele explained to them the difficulties there were to contend against in removing them to a reservation in Oregon, on account of the action of the grand jury of that state in indicting five of the tribe for murder. He also explained to them how, if they surrendered as prisoners of war, they would be protected by the military from the civil authorities. They expressed themselves pleased with the proposition and also stated that the visit of the *Herald* correspondent to their camp had given them confidence that the white people meant well, as he was not afraid to trust them. Captain Jack did the most of the talking and said that their boys were willing to go anywhere to a place by themselves. They seemed to think favorably of going south.

The delegation that accompanied Mr. Steele back to Fairchild's are empowered to arrange the details of the treaty. It is now safe to say there will be no more trouble with the Modoc Indians, and General Canby deserves the credit of having suggested the solution to a problem that appeared rather a difficult matter to settle. Captain Jack was too sick to come in himself but said that he would like to go to Washington with two or three of his young men and talk with the big chief and tell him his troubles.

The peace commissioners will have a talk tomorrow with the eight Modocs that came in this evening, and they will return the same day and inform Captain Jack of the details of the treaty. Some of the party that went into the Lava Beds and heard the conversation that took place during the council are not so confident that Captain Jack stated that he was willing to go on a reservation out of Oregon or far away from Lost River.

Last Tuesday morning, when I was in the Lava Beds and talking to John Schonchin, the second chief in power after Captain Jack, he said they would prefer going to the Klamath reservation, where they had been before. Mr. Steele, however, says that Captain Jack told him he and his braves were willing to go wherever he (Mr. Steele) advised them. Steele then asked them if they would go south and each man live on his own little farm. To this question they answered in the affirmative, and in order to be sure of it, he repeated the question, and they said they were willing to go.

The talk over the details and particulars will probably take some time, especially as Captain Jack is too sick to come out and see the commissioners. This sickness will probably entail a number of conferences and some journeys between Fairchild's and the Lava Beds before the matter is finally settled.

New York *Herald,* March 6, 1873

FAIRCHILD'S RANCH, March 4,
VIA YREKA, March 5, 1873

The prospects of peace with the Modoc Indians are not so favorable today, as Mr. Elijah Steele has just returned from the Lava Beds, bringing the intelligence that after a long council, the Indians decided against going away from their own country and are evidently determined to fight it out on that line.

Mr. Steele went yesterday morning into the Lava Beds the bearer of the following terms:

First—To surrender to General Canby and receive full amnesty for the past.

Second—To be removed to Angel Island, where they are to be fed with soldiers' allowance and clothed until a new home can be provided for them and they are able to support themselves in it.

Third—To be furnished by General Canby with transportation for their women and children to the island, and thence to their new home, perhaps in Arizona.

Fourth—General Canby is of the opinion that he can promise that Jack and some of his headmen should go to visit the president, and that the president will permit them to select for themselves a new home in a warmer climate.

They had a long talk over the matter, but from the first they evinced a marked dislike to leaving the home of their forefathers, and finally sent back word by Mr. Steele that they would only live in their own country. This alters the aspect of affairs, and the commissioners have telegraphed Washington for instructions. The first talk was held last evening in Jack's cave, and everything went on smoothly until Mr. Steele read out the terms and they were translated to the Indians.

Only two or three appeared to approve of their tenor, and presently John Schonchin got up and spoke rather wildly, saying that the commissioners were talking with two tongues, and that he wondered Steele had the courage to make such a proposition to them. Schonchin's speech fired up the warriors, and if the envoys had not preserved their presence of mind, they might have fared badly.

Steele counted sixty-nine warriors present, all fully armed, which makes twenty-five more than I saw when I was in the Lava Beds. These last twenty-five are supposed to belong to the Snake tribe, as some of them wore mustaches.

Captain Jack spoke and said he did not understand what Mr. Steele meant when he was in before, but now he knows the nature of the proposition. He felt sorry, because he could not go away from his own country. His heart was good. He did not want to fight, and he would give up all his land in Oregon to live on a little piece of land in California, but he would not go away from this country. Mr. Steele finally concluded that it would be better to defer the talk until the morning, and the council adjourned.

Steele and party did not pass a very pleasant night, as it was evident from the actions of Scarfaced Charley and Captain Jack that they were afraid of treachery. Steele and the clerk who went in with them slept in Jack's cave, with Scarfaced Charley on one side of them and Mary, Jack's sister, on the other. Captain Jack sent away his wives and slept at their feet.

The night, however, passed over without any outbreak, and in the morning they had another talk, but there were only about twenty warriors present. Captain Jack and Schonchin both spoke for some time in an excited and insolent manner.

Steele tried to temporize with them a little and proposed an interview with the commissioners somewhere near the Lava Beds. To this they assented, but only wanted to see Meacham and Applegate and no soldiers.

Mr. Steele finally left and came back with his report to the commissioners, accompanied by several squaws, who are determined not to go back again and say that the bucks are mad and want more blood. It is hard to account for this sudden change in their bearing, and I can only account for it by the appearance of those strange Indians who are supposed to be the Snakes.

When I was in there, Jack said overtures had come from the same source.[34] Mr. Steele has had enough of the Lava Beds, and I do not think he will go back there anymore.

The commissioners are looking very blue, and Meacham said tonight that he wanted a good horse, as he was a peace man, not a soldier, and from the look of things the Modocs appeared to be anxious for a lock of his hair, which he had no intention of giving away if he could prevent it.

A message will be sent in tomorrow by some Indians that the commissioners will only meet them on honorable terms and will not go into the Lava Beds; they also send word that they will guarantee clothing, food, and protection to any that may choose to come out. Things look rather like fighting as, since the Indians have been round the house, a flask of powder and some caps have been stolen.

Two wounded Modocs, Duffy and Long Jim, have surrendered and are being taken care of by the military.

New York *Herald,* March 5, 1873

FAIRCHILD'S RANCH, COTTONWOOD CREEK, CA.,
March 5, 1873

The peaceful aspect of affairs has disappeared, and present indications look very like war, as the Indians do not appear inclined to leave this country and have set a bold front against all overtures of the kind. Mr. Elijah Steele and party returned from their first mission to the Lava Beds, accompanied by seven or eight Modoc bucks and the squaw Mary, sister of Captain Jack. Mr. Steele was evidently pleased with his visit, and reported to the commissioners that the Indians were willing to surrender as prisoners of war and go to some warmer country. This was indeed good news, and we were all calculating upon the prospects of a speedy return home, when Mr. John Fairchild, one of Steele's party, said that he was afraid the Indians had not properly understood Mr. Steele's proposition for them to leave this country, and that they were under the impression they were to remain where they had been on Lost River or to go to Klamath. Mr. Steele, however, would not give up the point and insisted that everything was favorable and that the Indians perfectly understood what he said and replied in the affirmative.

It was finally determined that Mr. Steele should go in again on Monday, and consequently he started, accompanied by Mr. Atwell, Frank Riddle the interpreter and squaw Mary, and six Modoc bucks. Two of the bucks, Long Jim and Duffy, surrendered and remained where they were, under the charge of the military. They arrived at the Lava Beds about dusk and did not receive a very cheering welcome, as the bucks looked sullen and discontented. After taking off their saddles and tying up their horses, they went to Wild Gal's ranch and ate supper. They then waited for a messenger to bid them to council; but finally, getting tired, they went over there themselves.

As they came up to the entrance to the cave, they heard the Indians wrangling among themselves and talking in loud tones of voice, and several of them came out as they were descending the rather precipitous entrance. The cave was very full, and before sitting down, Mr. Steele and Mr. Atwell stepped across the circle and shook hands with Captain Jack and Schonchin, and it was plainly evident from their greeting that trouble was brewing. To anyone conversant with Indian manners and customs, the signs around the cave were of no good portent, as even the woman's cap on Captain Jack's head showed that he thought he had been fooled, and the arrows at the head of the wounded warrior were placed side by side, in the same position as they are placed at the grave. There were more present than Mr. Steele had seen before, and he counted sixty-nine warriors in all, many of whom were strangers to him and wore hair on their upper lips. This is a fashion not familiar to the Modoc tribe, and [it] gave Mr. Steele the impression that they had been reinforced by some Snake Indians. It is certainly probable that they have received an addition to their force, as I only counted forty-four or forty-five warriors present on the occasion of my visit.

After cutting up and presenting the tobacco they had brought with them, Mr. Steele read the terms offered by General Canby and the peace commissioners, which were that they were to surrender to the military and be removed to Angel Island and fed, clothed, and cared for at the government expense. Jack and several of his headmen were to go to Washington, see the president, and arrange about their new home—probably in Arizona. These terms were heard in sullen silence, and Scarfaced Charley and two others were the only ones that grunted an assent. Captain Jack finally spoke and evidently showed that he did not appreciate the proposed terms. He accused Mr. Steele of duplicity; said he had never sold his land and would never leave it, and then spoke in a wild strain, every word of which told on his savage auditors, and their eyes sparkled and told a tale of blood that their fingers itched to shed.

Mr. Steele then spoke again, going over the terms once more, and he was followed by John Schonchin, who made a regular war speech, pitching into everybody all around that had had any hand in the proposed treaty; accused Steele of lying, and finally asked him if he was not afraid to lie down and sleep among them after bringing them such a message. Steele replied that he was not afraid, that he was afraid of no man, and that he was old and to die did not hurt much. He then told them he had deceived no one and explained the terms of the treaty again, and how it was impossible for them to live peaceably in Oregon. Captain Jack and Schonchin then spoke again in rather hot language, and finally they accepted Steele's proposition to have a talk again in the morning, and the warriors dispersed, muttering and talking loudly among themselves.

When Steele and Atwell got up to retire to Wild Gal's ranch, Scarfaced Charley got up and whispered to them, "Make your bed here; I will lay down alongside of you." They concluded to accept his advice and, unfastening their blankets, spread them down on the ground near the rocks. Charley slept alongside of them and Captain Jack at their feet, showing that these two were determined to guard them against treachery. The night passed without any incident occurring to break their rest.

In the morning, after breakfasting in Wild Gal's ranch, they returned to the cave for a talk.

After taking their seats, business commenced with the following speech from John Schonchin:

> I have heard the talk; Captain Jack has heard it; Captain Jack don't know anything about another country—don't want to go there. Captain Jack has talked good about the country; Captain Jack and I have talked much about these things; we have talked enough; I have talked enough. It looks like another heart has entered into the talk now; I want to talk good to you; I want a good country to live in; I will speak the truth; I have talked about it till I am tired; expect you are tired coming out here to talk about it. These boys are tired going to and fro talking. I want to talk good just what comes in my mind; I want to say yes to this thing, but I don't know about it; don't know as I can; I want everything wiped out and to live as we used to; that is the way I want to settle this matter. I would like to know the names of the bad men that want to harm us; I want to know where they live; I want to know why they are mad; I am afraid of them; I want to talk good and straight. I am not afraid of these men; these are my men here; all my

people; they will do just what they agree to do; what I talk now I talk forever; I am not good today and bad tomorrow. This matter has all been talked over. I did not exactly understand then as I do now; the first time you told it to us, you did not tell it to us this way. I have talked to my people some about it; we are all of the same mind; I have told all my men to lay down their arms, and you can see that they have done so. What I understood the last time was that we should lay down our arms, we should have peace, and that was all we had to do.

I understood that the commissioners would come here and talk to us. I expected them this time, instead of which none have come. I am willing they should. You must be tired coming so often to talk good for us. I want them to come to talk; I want these commissioners to come and talk. I want them to come and settle this trouble soon, so that you need not be coming always to talk; I want to talk the truth and have this trouble settled. Why don't these men quit and have peace? Don't trouble them (Oregonians). These are my men; they think like me. I have told the truth as near as I can. What is the reason these men won't make peace, these men over there (Oregonians)? Why don't they quit fighting? We have. I told my friends what to do; if they do not do right, I would make them do right. It scares me; they won't quit fighting and let us alone. I have no horse to go see these commissioners or anywhere else—let them come here. That's all.

Mr. Steele replied as follows:

I have come a long way to talk to you as a friend; the commissioners came to Linkville and did not intend to come any further. I asked them to come to Fairchild's ranch, and they came, only a half day's ride from you. They did this because they are your friends and want to do good and stop this war. Some of the commissioners have ridden for four weeks to meet and talk with you and try to stop this fighting. General Canby, an old man, has ridden 300 miles to talk because his heart is good to you. These young men who went into Fairchild's saw him; they can tell you if they think he tells lies. He is your friend. He wants you to show confidence enough in him to come out and talk with him. He promises you will be safe. The first time I came here, I came here as your friend because I trusted you. I was not afraid of you then; I am not afraid of you now. I am not afraid of any man in the world, but I am afraid to do anything wrong. I don't fear when I talk with a good heart. I told you then that I thought it best for you to go to a warmer climate under the charge of General Canby, because he is a soldier and can protect you.

Our people are many, the Great Chief can't watch over all the bad ones; your people are few. The Oregonians are very mad at your peo-

ple, and if you live here, they will kill some of your men. Then your
young people will act wild and kill some good people. These men say
that your young men have stolen some of their horses, killed their cattle, and murdered their people. They say they will kill you if you stay
here. They are very mad. They are not your friends or mine. They talk
bad of me because I have been your friend. The Great Chief knows
that you are not to blame in the matter, and to keep you from being
harmed by them, he wants you to go with General Canby, who will
take you to a good home where none will hurt you. He thinks this
trouble is from a misunderstanding. It is liable to occur again if you
remain here.

Bad men will drink whiskey and, when drunk, will shoot Modocs,
then war will be again. There are plenty of bad men, and the Great
Chief cannot watch them all. They will live close to your land, your
people will meet them, and there will be trouble all the time, for when
they see each other, each party will get mad. That is why I talk peace
and why I want you to go to a warmer country. If I told you you could
live here in peace when I knew you could not, I would be speaking
lies. If you live here, in two months there will be war again, and then
you will say Squire Steele lied to us, when I could not help it. We
can't move our people, they are too many. Your people are few, we
can move them. When I told you I wanted you to go to this warmer
country, I could not tell you where it was; I had not been told by the
commissioners to do so. I knew that the Great Chief had plenty of
land that he would give to you.

I then went back to the commissioners and General Canby and
told them your hearts were good, and they sent me back to tell you
what they would do for you. He told me to come in and make peace
with you for them, if you would not talk with them. But they want to
shake hands with the headmen, for they came a long way to see you. If
your hearts are good, you can go a little way to meet them. They
don't want this war to stop because they are afraid of you. They have
plenty of soldiers. You might killed a thousand of them, but it would
not stop the war. He can in two months bring more soldiers than he
can stand on these lava beds.

He wants to stop this war to prevent all your people being killed,
because he thinks you are a good people. If you go to that new home,
you will be fed, clothed, and protected till you can take care of yourselves. You can have your own land, raise grass, melons, grain,
horses, cattle, and live like the white men. If you do not agree to this,
you will stay here and be killed. He will send soldiers enough here to
kill all, and I don't want that done. I told the Great Chief that I did not
want him to fight this people, for I had been their friend for many
years. The tyee chief, General Canby, has not much clothing but will

send to get more for you if you make peace, and now he can give you enough to make you comfortable. When you go to that island, you will be where no one can disturb you, while Captain Jack goes to Washington and then looks at his new home. He will send soldiers to guard them from bad men, so that no Oregon men can harm them. I think it is not safe for you to leave the Lava Beds without an escort of soldiers to protect you from these bad men. If you go as I want you to, I promise you that none shall be hurt.

Now I want you to go and talk with General Canby and make a treaty with him; you need not deal with the commissioners if you don't want to, for I heard them say whatever General Canby promises, they would agree to. He gave me this paper to show you what he will do for you if you agree to his terms. Jack and his head-men will go to Washington, while his people remain on Angel Island; then he can go out and find a new home, and then all can go there. There you will find no bad men to bother you. Your children can learn to read and write like the whites. The people there will all shake hands with you in peace.

I do not know the names of these bad men in Linkville. I can't point them out, but I see by the papers that they are all mad. There are men way up in Salem who are mad at you, and it is not safe for you to live here. I know they are mad because they write me. Knowing that I am your friend, I don't fear them, but I fear for you. I am an old man and can't last long anyway, and while I live, I want to do right between Indians and white people. I hope they will take my advice and make this treaty. I have no more to say.

Captain Jack then responded as follows:

The talk that we have made has taken such a turn that I hardly know what to think of it. I did not study the first talk much, and this seems to be somewhat different. I thought of the talk we had a long time ago, and I thought this would be like it. My heart was good then, and I thought it would remain so forever. I would like to know why we can't sleep and live here as we can in any place. What I talked first, talk now. I want these men to come here and fix that thing up right away. I did not understand the last talk as I do now. I see that there is a difference in that and this talk. My heart told me there would be no difference when you came back. What I spoke about I spoke from my heart. I thought that the commission would come this time to talk with us, but now they want us to come to them. I thought everything was to be wiped out, and we were to live as we did before.

I want these men to come and see us, that we won't have to go back and forward so often. I am tired of it. These are all my people; I have no other, and they are like me; we talk with one mouth. I don't know how it is I can't live here as I was when I made peace here before. I expected to make peace that way now. I don't know how it is that one man talks one way and another talks differently. One says it is all right, and now you talk of coming here with soldiers. The talk now is just what it was when it caused the bloodshed. I never talked or thought of going away off, and if one of my men should talk so to you, I would send him away as a bad man. Some bad men have been talking about me; I want it stopped.

Why did Matilda tell us the soldiers were gone? My young men saw plenty of soldiers; I want them all to go away and leave us alone. I did not want Matilda to come here; why did she not tell us about going away off? She did not want to tell us that, and now it is new to me. It is just as I thought—the Oregon men want to fight, and the others do not. It is strange your Great Chief cannot rule your people alike. I am not like the Oregonians; I want everything wiped out; I have been staying around here and am willing to stay here; let them have that side of the lake, and I will keep this side. I don't know of any other country; I don't want any but this and have nothing to say about another country. Why did they not tell me of this at first? Why kill me if I stay? I don't know anything about another country; have no money with which to buy a new country. This is my home; I was born here, always lived here, and I don't want to leave here. I have heard a great deal of talk about moving from here, and I am afraid again. I have done.

Mr. Steele then said:

I told you the first time I talked with you that the Oregon men were so mad that they and the Modocs could not live in peace when they and the Modocs were so close together. It would not last; there would soon be fighting. Your people are few, and I wanted them to move to a warmer country where you would be happy and safe, and I tell you again I want you to go there. Your people will be safe and increase and grow strong. Stay here, fight the soldiers, and you will be killed. If you make this treaty, you can sleep as soundly as I slept last night.

The people of Oregon are under one chief, those of California under another; one wants war, the other wants peace. One says kill all the Modocs unless they give up these men and have these men hanged; the others say, "No," and I say, "No," for I want you to go away from here and make peace. These men want to hang Scarfaced Charley, Hooker Jim, and several others, and they will if you stay here and fight the soldiers, for they are too many for your men. They want this done as the only condition on which they will make peace with you. I know that living on the borders, you cannot keep peace.

The last time we talked, you told me you wanted to leave this place, that it was a bad place to live in, that you did not want to live near the Oregonians. That is different from what you talk now. The talk we had some time ago I wrote to the Big Chief. He said it was good; he was pleased with it. A little while after that, you made another treaty with Huntington—a different man. In that paper you said you wanted to go on the Klamath reservation. The Big Chief then said these people did not like my talk, but had sent another talk, saying they would go on the reservation instead of living here. He then told me I was chief no longer. He put in a man whom they understood better. Since then I have been no chief, only Modocs' friend. I will go back and tell the soldiers' chief about what you say today. My heart is sick about your talk. You want me to trust you all the time, but you trust no one. I will go and tell them what you say, and see what they will do. I don't know what they will do. I don't know what they will say or do about it. That is all.

Schonchin then said:

I would like to live in my own country. I know the Oregonians are mad at me; still, I hate to give up this land. I don't see why they want to take me away. I did not start first, and I want you to think of that. If my men had fired the first shot, I would not say one word about going away. But they did not. I want to know why they want to hang my men. I never told my men to shoot. I know the soldiers shot first. I want you to think that all over.

Mr. Steele then said:

When Schonchin's brother, who is on the reservation, talked with Huntington, he sold him all the land—so the papers say. He stays on the reservation and keeps his promises. Captain Jack's party came away and broke their promises. The tyee sent soldiers to bring them back, and that brought on the fight. The soldiers think the Indians fired first. I don't know, but I do know they killed Miller, Brotherton, and Boddy in cold blood after the fight was over, and their best friends too. This is what makes the Linkville men mad at the Modocs. These men were at Linkville the day before the fight, and the people did not tell them that the soldiers were coming, because they knew these men were your friends and would tell you of it. You then murdered them, and that is why these Linkville people want to hang these Indians. The Oregon chief thinks it right to hang them. I thought at first that some mistake had been made and that all might be washed out. But I know now that to make a sure peace, you must go away, and that is why I advise my friends to make this treaty. If your hearts were as good as mine, you would go this little way to talk with these men and arrange this thing. Your men went with me and came back safe. I promise you to bring you back safe; if you go, you shall be equally safe.

Schonchin replied:

I thought the talk the other day settled everything; buried and wiped all out. What I said then, I say now. I want to quit and live as we did before. I want to know who will come here and kill me when I am asleep. Your talk is so different, I don't understand it. You talk now of the soldiers coming. Are they mad too because I want to live here? I don't want much more talk about it. I want these men to come and fix this trouble right and straight.

Captain Jack then said they would meet the peace commission in the Lava Beds at the foot of the bluff in two days' time. He only wanted to see Meacham and Applegate. John Fairchild might also come, and two or three reporters, but nobody else. The council then broke up, and Mr. Steele and party went and saddled their horses and started off, accompanied by Mary, Wild Gal, Boston Charley, and another squaw. Lucy, another squaw, wanted to come, but the Modocs would not let her. Scarfaced Charley also told Mr. Steele that he would like to come in, but he dare not, as the others would kill him if they saw him making such an attempt.

The party arrived at Fairchild's at dusk last night, and Mr. Steele made his report to the commissioners. The news rather astonished those gentlemen, and they now became satisfied that their mission was near a close, and that matters would now be entrusted to the care of General Canby.

Boston Charley, Mary, Artinie, and two other squaws returned today, bearing the information that the peace commissioners were tired of talking; that they would not go in to see them. They would meet them on honorable terms on neutral ground, with an equal number of men on each side, or they would guarantee the safety of the headmen if they would come to Fairchild's and have a talk. They would wait for their answer until tomorrow evening, and if they did not hear by that time, their mission would cease and General Canby would have to deal with them. General Canby also sent word that any that chose to come in and surrender would be cared for and fed and clothed. The messengers departed in a very bad humor, some of them refusing to shake hands.

I believe this will end my peaceful correspondence.

New York *Herald,* March 26, 1873

VAN BREMER'S RANCH,
March 14, 1873

The Modoc question is still puzzling the Indian Bureau at Washington, and from the present aspect of affairs, they will probably succeed in running up a bill bordered upon a couple of millions before their peace policy is successfully carried out.

We have just had the painful experience of the efficacy of a peace commission acting under the authority of the Indian Bureau, and their labors have formed a fit subject for the laughter of the citizens of California and Oregon. The history of this peace commission may be told in a few words. The Modoc trouble broke out, and Mr. A. B. Meacham, the late superintendent of Indian affairs in Oregon, happened to be in Washington at the time. This gentlemen is a gifted orator; as described by a contemporary, "Words fell from his silvery tongue like peas rolling off a hot platter," and he has for a long time felt deeply aggrieved at his removal from office and the substitution of Mr. Odeneal in his place. This war was a perfect godsend to this Micawber politician, and seizing the opportunity, he went forthwith to Secretary Delano and exploded one of those shells of oratory, sending pellets of peace in every direction.

The secretary forthwith appointed a peace commission to arrange these Modoc troubles, in which Mr. Meacham was to act in conjunction with Mr. Odeneal and the Rev. Mr. Wilbur[35] of Oregon. This, however, did not suit Mr. Meacham, as perhaps in his dreams of the future he had seen a picture in which a war that broke out through the mismanagement of the present superintendent was settled by the late superintendent, a happy termination of affairs which resulted in the reinstating of the late superintendent to full power, adorned by a wreath of laurels. The silvery tongued orator, therefore, went once more to the secretary, and once more his dulcet tones charmed the ear of Mr. Delano, and the names of Odeneal and Wilbur were struck out, and Jesse Applegate and Samuel Case substituted in their place.[36]

Everything satisfactorily arranged, Meacham started for the Modoc country and arrived at Dorris's ranch like a conqueror come to deliver an oppressed people. He had no doubt of the success of his mission, as he could easily manage the rest of the commission. Sam Case was an old friend, he could be relied on; as for Uncle Jesse Applegate, there could be no difficulty there, as Meacham knew Uncle Jesse and his partner (another man by the name of Jesse) had a little interest in certain swamplands in which he might be able to lend assistance.

The peace commission established their headquarters at Fairchild's ranch, and in two days after their first meeting, Meacham's face wore the expression of a much-abused man. It soon leaked out that the commission were at loggerheads, as both Uncle Jesse and old friend Sam expressed different ideas on the Modoc question to those propagated by the oily-tongued Meacham. His eloquence was wasted upon these two Oregonians, who only listened and laughed in their sleeve; in fact, one of them openly stated that the peace commission was "a mere humbug, used simply as a cloak to cover the attack of Meacham against Odeneal."

Under existing circumstances, it may be naturally inferred that the peace commission proved a stupendous humbug, or as more explicitly termed by Applegate, "an expensive blunder." General Canby, however, fortunately arrived, and his suggestions were accepted by the commission and would probably have resulted in the surrender of the Indians if the latter had not been scared by the statement of a man named Blair, a pardoned convict residing in Oregon, who told them he had a warrant to hang nine of them when they came in and gave themselves up. These Indians have cause to be afraid of treachery, as some years back Ben Wright murdered forty-seven of their tribe at a peace feast; therefore, such a statement totally destroyed the negotiations of weeks, and the work will have to begin again.

During the past week, Messrs. Applegate and Case both resigned their positions on the peace commission and returned to their respective avocations. Mr. Meacham, however, determined not to give up so soon and remained a commission of one at Fairchild's.

Before leaving, Mr. Applegate sent the following characteristic letter to Mr. Clum at Washington as a minority report:

HEADQUARTERS PEACE COMMISSION,
FAIRCHILD'S RANCH, CAL., March 1873

Hon. H. B. Clum, Acting Commissioner of Indian Affairs:

SIR—The commission appointed to examine into the causes and bring to a conclusion the Modoc War, having concluded its labors, submit the following as its final report, to wit:

First—The causes leading to war were the dissatisfaction of Captain Jack's band of Modocs with the provisions and execution of the treaty of October 1864 and refusal to abide thereby. To what extent wrongs justified resistance, the commission, having no power judicially to investigate, cannot say.

Second—The immediate cause of hostilities was resistance by the Indians to military coercion.

Third—Unconditional surrender of the Indians, and the trial and punishment of the guilty by the civil authorities, would have been more satisfactory to the whites and a better example to the Indians than more lenient conditions.

Fourth—Terms of surrender were offered the Indians to save the further effusion of blood and secure a permanent peace by the removal of the whole tribe out of the country, a result scarcely to be hoped for by continued hostilities.

Fifth—The terms agreed to by the commission were suggested and must be carried into effect by the military. A commission to negotiate a peace was therefore unnecessary.

Sixth—A commission to inquire into the causes of the war should be composed of men wholly disinterested in the findings of the commission, directly or indirectly, and clothed with full power to investigate.

Seventh—Some of the personnel of this commission being obnoxious to the Indians, it was a hindrance to negotiations. Having no power to administer oaths nor send for persons and papers, and the official acts of the chairman to be revised, its finding must have been imperfect and unsatisfactory in regard to the cause of the war. We therefore consider the commission an expensive blunder.

JESSE APPLEGATE

Before the commission broke up, Judge Rosborough of Yreka had been added to the commission at the suggestion of General Canby, and that gentleman, assisted by Mr. Elijah Steele of Yreka, did good service in the negotiations that followed General Canby's proposition. Mr. Steele made several trips to the Lava Beds and would have succeeded in obtaining the surrender of Captain Jack and his party if the lies of Blair had not upset their calculations. The Indians had gone so far as to agree to come out and surrender. They were to be met by wagons halfway to carry their baggage, but on the appointed day, not an Indian made his appearance. Things since then have been in a state of status quo, and rumors were current that the Indians had deserted the Lava Beds.

General Canby finally ordered Major Biddle of the 1st Cavalry to come from Bernard's Camp at Clear Lake to Van Bremer's with his troop and, on the way, make a scout through the Lava Beds. Major Biddle arrived here last evening and brought in thirty-four Indian ponies with him. Major Biddle reported to General Canby, who arrived here yesterday morning, that when about four miles south of Captain Jack's Stronghold, they came upon a nest of ponies guarded by five Indians—four bucks and a squaw. Not knowing how peace matters were going on, they did not fire at the Indians but simply surrounded the ponies and drove them into camp.

Matters are now on rather a peculiar basis, as a dispatch arrived today from Washington stating that Mr. Odeneal has been added to the commission. This brings matters to a most interesting crisis, as the commission will now compose Meacham, Odeneal, and Judge Rosborough, the other two having resigned. It is very doubtful, however, whether Odeneal will accept and face the music of the silvery-tongued Meacham.

How long this farce will be carried on by the Indian Bureau is hard to say, but it does seem an outrage that they should have the power of running up such an unnecessary debt as they are rapidly accumulating. Grain is now twelve and a half cents a pound, which is cheap compared with the thirty-five cents per pound paid during the first part of the war. On an average, each horse in the government employ costs about $1.75 a day for subsistence, and as there are about 300 horses now in this county for cavalry and fighting purposes, we can easily account for an expenditure of $500 per day on that branch of service alone. The cost of freight on ammunition and rations for 700 or 800 forms also no inconsiderable item of expenditure. There are also hundreds of other things that help to foot the bill to one of gigantic dimensions.

This camp is at present the headquarters of the army, and we have here Batteries B, E, and M of the 4th Artillery; Companies E and G of the 12th Infantry; and Troop K of the 1st Cavalry, making in all about 260 rank and file. Everybody is getting very tired of the inactive state of affairs and hopes for some move that will lead to a conclusion of these troubles.

New York *Herald,* March 20, 1873

VAN BREMER'S RANCH, Cal., March 18,
VIA YREKA, Cal., March 19, 1873

Everything is quiet at the seat of war, and excepting the occasional moving of troops from post to post, there is really nothing going on.

A squaw came from Captain Jack's camp the other day and said that the Indians were mad at losing the ponies which Major Biddle captured.

We have now in camp three batteries of the 4th Artillery, two companies of the 12th Infantry, and one troop of the 1st Cavalry, making in all about 250 rank and file. There are two troops of the 1st Cavalry at Dorris's ranch, four companies of the 21st Infantry at Lost River, and two troops of the 1st Cavalry at Clear Lake—the total number of troops amounting to about 550 or 600.

General Canby is very reticent as to what move he intends to make for fear the Indians would learn his intentions through the agency of some of the squaws and men. From preparations that are being made, I am led to believe that we will move camp before long and completely surround the Lava Beds.

There will be three or four camps—one on the banks of Tule Lake, at the foot of the bluffs, about two miles due west of Jack's cave; another at the foot of the Love Butte, about four miles south of Jack's cave; another at Land's ranch, on the eastern side; and perhaps some on the peninsula, to the northeast of the cave. These movements will probably be made in the course of a few days.

Mr. Odeneal, the new addition to the peace commission, will arrive in about five days.

New York *Herald,* March 22, 1873

VAN BREMER'S RANCH, March 20,
VIA YREKA, Cal., March 21, 1873

There has been considerable activity in camp during the past few days, and although the future movement of the troops is kept very quiet at headquarters, I have just learned that the Lost River Camp will be broken up on Saturday and the troops there moved into camp on the southeastern shore of Tule Lake, about three and a half miles from Captain Jack's cave.

Lieutenant Chapin of the 4th Artillery leaves tomorrow for Lost River to take charge of the howitzers of that camp. Four twenty-four-pound Coehorn mortars arrived here yesterday and have been given in charge of Capt. Evan Thomas of the 4th Artillery, who will be assisted by Lieutenant Cranston of Battery M of the same regiment. The troops from Dorris's and this camp will probably move about Monday or Tuesday[37] and take up a position at the southwest of Tule Lake, close to the bluffs, about two and a half miles distant from Jack's cave.

I am going tomorrow on Colonel Gillem's staff on a reconnaissance with two troops of the 1st Cavalry. We shall probably go to the Lava Beds and return the same evening.

The Indian Bureau have just put a clincher on their peace policy by the appointment of Mr. Dyar, the Indian agent for Oregon, who has been excused. Dyar is the man who scared fifteen of these Modocs out of a year's growth and sent them back to fight when they were on their way to a reservation.

⊷ ≖◊≖ ⊶

New York *Herald,* March 25, 1873

YREKA, Cal., March 24, 1873

The new members of the peace commission, Messrs. Dyar and the Rev. Thomas, are hourly expected at Van Bremer's ranch, and we shall probably have divine services next Sunday in Captain Jack's cave.

Last Friday[38] General Canby and Colonel Gillem, accompanied by Major Biddle and Captain Perry, and Troops M and F of the 1st Cavalry, made a reconnaissance of the Lava Beds. They arrived at the top of the bluffs about noon, and there the cavalry were dismounted and the [officers] surveyed the Lava Beds through their field glasses. Several Indians were seen on a ledge of rocks about a mile distant from the foot of the bluffs, and they shouted for someone to come down and talk. Acting Assistant Surgeon Cabaniss was then halfway down the bluffs, and he immediately asked permission of General Canby to go and see what they wanted.

His request was granted, and he presently returned, saying that Captain Jack wished to talk with General Canby and Colonel Gillem. As he asked for one more to come down, the *Herald* correspondent joined him and returned to the Modocs. Outpost Williams and three other Indians were there in full war paint, and some of them stripped to their waist, so as to be free from all encumbrances while fighting.

We then agreed that General Canby and Colonel Gillem were to meet Captain Jack at a juniper tree situated about halfway between the foot of the bluffs and the Modoc outposts. Assistant Surgeon Cabaniss then went back to inform General Canby of the arrangement, and shortly after he had returned from his mission, Captain Jack arrived.

The latter at first objected to going to the juniper tree; but as Dr. Cabaniss and the *Herald* correspondent offered to remain as hostages for his safety, he finally agreed to the proposition. Jack was accompanied by Scarfaced Charley, Curly Headed Doctor, Curly Jack, and two other Indians.

The talk did not amount to much, as Captain Jack simply signified his wish for peace and to be left where he was or on Lost River. He also informed General Canby that if he had anything to give him, he might send it down to the Lava Beds. He made no answer when General Canby asked him why he did not come out when the wagons were sent to meet him. As soon as the conference was over, Dr. Cabaniss and the *Herald* correspondent left the outpost and returned to the top of the bluffs. Two of the Indians had their shot pouches covered with scalps that were taken in the last fight. The troops returned to camp the same evening, returning about midnight.

The Lost River Camp was broken up yesterday, and the troops from there went into camp on the east side of Tule Lake, about three miles from Captain Jack's cave.

Major Green of the 1st Cavalry arrived at Van Bremer's today and took command of the troops from Dorris's and Van Bremer's, who will go into camp on Tule Lake at the foot of the bluffs in two or three days, as soon as the road is passable.

The Reverend Thomas, the new peace commissioner, will arrive at Van Bremer's tomorrow evening and join Mr. Meacham.

It is now reported that the Indian Bureau intend giving Captain Jack a reservation on Lost River. There is no doubt in my mind that they will not be satisfied with anything else. They will have to place a military post on the reservation to protect the Indians from the Oregonians.

——+ ☰◆☰ +——

New York *Herald,* April 7, 1873

YREKA, Cal., March 26, 1873

The prospects of peace with the Modoc Indians are not very promising, as they appear to grow more independent every day, and consequently more grasping in their demands. Mr. Meacham still represents the peace commission at Van Bremer's, and was joined yesterday by the Reverend Thomas, a newly appointed member sent by the Indian Bureau to practice the theory of moral suasion. Mr. Dyar is expected from Oregon every day. Judge Rosborough will come as soon as he can leave his court at Shasta. Great things are expected from the new peace delegation, but I am an unbeliever and maintain that the Modocs will not leave this section of the country until the military have exercised a little physical suasion. At present the Modocs are firmly imbued with the belief that they can "lick" all the soldiers that can be brought against them, and consequently intend remaining where they are.

As General Canby is evidently getting rather tired of the peace manipulations, the troops will soon be moved into position surrounding the Lava Beds, and then some aggressive movements will be made in order to impress the Modocs with an idea of the number of soldiers that can be brought against them. It is expected that the mortars will have a very salutary effect on their weak nerves, as in the last fight they expressed considerable curiosity about the guns that "shot twice." On that occasion, however, only a few shots were fired from the howitzers, and none of them took effect, only one shell bursting within their neighborhood, and that about 150 feet above their heads.

Last Friday we made a reconnaissance of the Lava Beds in force and did not get back until midnight the same day. The object of the scout was to give General Canby and Colonel Gillem a chance to examine the country, with a view to selecting a camp on Tule Lake somewhere near the foot of the bluffs. General Canby and aide-de-camp, Lieutenant Anderson; Major Mason; Captains Throckmorton and Thomas of the 4th Artillery; Dr. Cabaniss; the *Herald* correspondent; Major Biddle and Lieutenants Cresson and Bacon, with Troop K of the 1st Cavalry, left Van Bremer's ranch at 6:30 A.M. and met Colonel Gillem, Assistant Surgeon McMillan, Captain Trimble, Lieutenant Rockwell, Captain Perry, Mr. McKay, and Troop F of the 1st Cavalry at the bridge over Willow Creek.

The entire force, numbering over 100 rank and file, then followed the trail to the top of the bluff overlooking the Lava Beds and were then dismounted. They arrived at this point about noon, and General Canby and Colonel Gillem got out their field glasses and took a good look at the Lava Beds that lay directly beneath them. The Indians were seen below us, moving about as if in rather an excited state and gathering in about twelve or fifteen horses that were scattered over the plain. Presently three or four of them took up a position on a ledge of rock about a mile from the foot of the bluffs, which appeared to be their first line of fortifications.

They began to shout to us in English, and finally asked one man to come down and talk, saying that he would not be hurt. Dr. Cabaniss was then sitting about halfway down the bluffs, and when he heard their request, he asked permission of General Canby to go and see what they wanted. The general answering in the affirmative, Dr. Cabaniss went down the hill and walked across to where the Indians were sitting behind the rocks. Looking through our glasses, we saw him shake hands with them and sit down for a talk. Presently one of the party got up and, bringing out a white horse from behind the rocks, rode off in the direction of Captain Jack's cave. Dr. Cabaniss then returned to the foot of the bluffs and shouted up that he wanted another man to come down. I then got up and started down the hill, preceded by Lieutenant Moore, who was called back by General Canby and returned to the top of the bluff.

When I got about halfway down, I heard Dr. Cabaniss's message, which was that Captain Jack and Schonchin would talk with General Canby and Colonel Gillem at the juniper tree, halfway between the foot of the bluffs and their present position. I passed the message on to General Canby, who was seated at the top of the bluffs, and after receiving his approval of the proposition, continued on and joined Dr. Cabaniss at the foot of the hill, and we both walked across to where the Indians were awaiting our return. They all shook hands with me when I arrived, and after setting my pipe on its rounds, sat down and had a talk. There were only four Modocs on duty when I came up, and one of them, William, my host on the occasion of my former visit to the Lava Beds, was stripped to the waist and in full war paint.

They occupied a rather ingenious fortification of about thirty feet front. It was originally a wall of rock about twenty feet high, with a projecting ledge about ten feet from the ground. On the edge of this ledge, they had built a breastwork of loose rocks about four feet high, which allowed them a space about three feet deep to work in, with the main rock at their backs. They were all armed, two with Springfield rifles, one with a Spencer carbine, and the other with an old-fashioned Kentucky rifle. We sat some time talking but, as none of those present spoke English well, gained no information of importance.

The messengers sent after Captain Jack returned shortly afterwards and said he was on his way, but wished to meet General Canby and Colonel Gillem nearer to his own camp. We, however, overruled that suggestion, stating that General Canby was a big tyee and an old man, and therefore would not come any farther than the juniper tree, which they had designated for a place of meeting. They finally agreed to stand to the old arrangement, and Dr. Cabaniss started for the bluffs to get General Canby and Colonel Gillem down to the appointed place. I remained with the Modocs, who were presently reinforced by Scarfaced Charley, Boston Charley, Wild Gal, and several others. We presently saw General Canby and Colonel Gillem come down the hill and sit down, awaiting the arrival of Captain Jack. Dr. Cabaniss then returned to where we were and sat down in the circle.

The Indians appeared rather nettled about the loss of their horses and were rather particular in their inquiries who were the soldiers that took them away. I told them they were taken by 100 new soldiers, hoping that the knowledge of such an addition to our forces might have a wholesome effect, but I am grieved to say they did not look very scared. One gentleman, on hearing the news, passed his hand affectionately over a scalp of curly brown hair that covered his shot pouch, as if congratulating himself on the speedy acquisition of more of the same sort. This was too much for my refined and well-educated wool to endure, and it gently raised my hat, as if it desired to remind me of the company I was in. I took the hint, and when I got back to Van Bremer's, had my hair cut off, thinking it might not wear well as a pouch cover.

After waiting about an hour, Captain Jack arrived, accompanied by Curly Headed Doctor, Steamboat Frank, and about a dozen others. After shaking hands with the party, I showed Captain Jack where General Canby and Colonel Gillem were sitting, awaiting his arrival.

He did not show any very great eagerness for an interview and thought General Canby had better come where he was. To this motion, however, I put a most decided veto but, in order to reassure him of his safety, said that Dr. Cabaniss and I would remain where we were as hostages for his safe return. He then appeared more satisfied and started to meet the generals, accompanied by Scarfaced Charley, Steamboat Frank, Curly Headed Doctor, and three others. Just as they were going, I noticed that they had their guns and immediately told them they must leave them behind. To this, however, they objected; but finally, after I had explained that General Canby and Colonel Gillem were unarmed, Scarfaced Charley set the example by laying down his gun, and the others did the same, with the exception of Steamboat Frank, who got sulky and asked me what I was afraid of. I told him I was not afraid, as I had come to see twenty of them, all armed, but General Canby was a big tyee, and when he talked peace, he came without arms and expected to meet Indians without arms.

This satisfied the others, but Steamboat was evidently in a bad humor and sat down, refusing to go. The others started off. Before they had got halfway, I noticed that three of them had not taken off their revolvers. As they were then pretty close to the place of meeting, I thought it better to let them go on, trusting that there would be no contretemps to mar the harmony of the meeting. Our position would not have been very pleasant if one of those revolvers had gone off accidentally, as the soldiers on the bluff would immediately have come tearing down to see what was the matter, and our scalps would probably have suffered before they were halfway down.

The conference, however, concluded peacefully, and as soon as we saw General Canby and Colonel Gillem on their way back, we left our friends and started for the top of the bluffs. On the way, we met Captain Jack and his party returning from the talk, and we stopped for a few minutes to find out the result of the conference. Captain Jack said he had not talked much and did not think that the soldier tyee had much good to offer. He said he wanted peace and wanted to remain where he was. We then shook hands and left them, pushing on up the hill to join the rest of the party. As soon as we got to the top of the hill, we mounted our horses and started to return to Van Bremer's. It was 6:30 P.M. when we left the bluffs, and our party did not get to Van Bremer's until after midnight, after a ride of about forty-four miles. Colonel Gillem and party returned to Dorris' ranch.

On the way back, General Canby told me that he did not think Jack wanted peace unless he could get Lost River. Captain Jack told him as he was going away that if he had anything to give him, he could send it down to the Lava Beds. General Canby asked him why they did not come out and meet the wagons according to their own proposal, and to that question could get no answer. The general is of the opinion that nothing can be done with the Modocs until they have experienced the power of the troops and thoroughly understand their position.

The Lost River troops marched last Sunday from their old camp and are now located on the east side of Tule Lake, about three miles from Captain Jack's cave. The howitzers, under command of Lieutenant Chapin, are with them. Colonel Gillem and the two troops of cavalry at Dorris's are expected at Van Bremer's tomorrow, and in a few days all the troops from the latter place will move into camp at Tule Lake, at the foot of the bluffs, about two and one-half miles this side of Captain Jack's cave. The Modocs will then be between the two camps. Major Mason is in command on the east side, and Major Green will take charge on this side. If the peace commissioners do not succeed with moral suasion, General Canby will probably try the power of the military. The attack will be made in skirmishing order, quietly but firmly, and the troops will take their blankets and hold their position during the night. Under cover of night they will be supplied with rations and fresh water. The mortars will cover the advance of the troops and keep shelling Captain Jack's Stronghold day and night. These tactics will, I am satisfied, have more effect upon Captain Jack and his band than all the moral suasion of the peace commission and the Indian Bureau combined.

I return to Van Bremer's tomorrow morning.

New York *Herald,* April 9, 1873

LAVA BED CAMP, April 7,
VIA YREKA, Cal., April 8, 1873

The peace commission have not as yet accomplished anything. They have had but one talk with the leading Indians since they arrived in the Lava Beds, but unreliable Indians such as Bogus and Boston Charley come in every day and always receive some present from Mr. Meacham.

Battery K, 4th Artillery, arrived here at noon today. Major Mason has moved his command from Sand's ranch to Hospital Rock, about two miles east of Captain Jack. Signal stations have been established at different points and work well.

Two or three boats have been put upon the lake, and communications is now frequent between the different camps.

New York *Herald,* April 11, 1873

LAVA BEDS CAMP, April 8,
VIA YREKA, Cal., April 10, 1873

Yesterday the peace commission sent Frank Riddle's Indian woman to Captain Jack's Stronghold for the purpose of arranging for a talk at some point between Jack's camp and ours. She returned in the evening and reports that while she was there, Captain Bernard's men, camped at Hospital Rock, made a reconnaissance and captured four horses belonging to Jack. This made them (the Indians) very angry, and they abused her roundly and refused to make any arrangement to talk with the commission. Orders have been given by signal to return the captured horses.

I am informed by Mr. Fairchild that the commission begin to feel very despondent. It is the general opinion that if the commission would withdraw, this farce would be ended within three days.

Jack's men were busily engaged this morning in building rock fortifications.

＊—＊　≡♦≡　＊—＊

New York *Herald,* April 13, 1873

LAVA BEDS CAMP, April 11—3:00 P.M.,
VIA YREKA, April 12, 1873

Peace policy and the Indian Bureau have accomplished the bitter end, and offered as martyrs to the cause the lives of Brig. Gen. E. R. S. Canby, commanding the District of the Columbia, and the Reverend Thomas of Petaluma, California, presiding elder of the Presbyterian Church. As my courier leaves instantly, having eighty miles to ride, I can only give a brief details of one of the most treacherous massacres ever perpetrated by the Indians.

For several days past there have been endeavors made by the peace commission and General Canby to obtain an interview with Captain Jack and the leading chiefs of the Modoc band. The prospects of peace seemed to be better, as orders had been sent from Washington to the peace commissioners to give the Indians, if necessary, a reservation in this neighborhood.

Yesterday evening Bogus Charley came in and said that Captain Jack, Schonchin, and three or four others would meet the peace commissioners on a spot near the lake, about three-quarters of a mile from camp. Bogus Charley stopped in our camp all night, and in the morning Boston Charley also came and said that everything was all right, as Captain Jack was coming out to meet the commissioners.

Between 10:00 and 11:00 A.M. the peace commission party—comprising General Canby, Mr. Meacham, Dr. Thomas, Mr. Dyar, Riddle the interpreter and squaw, and Bogus Charley and Boston Charley—went out to the designated spot.

There they met Captain Jack, John Schonchin, Black Jim, Shacknasty Jim, Ellen's Man, and Hooker Jim. They had no guns with them, but each carried a pistol at his belt. This, however, was not much noticed, as in previous interviews they had had their guns with them.

They sat down in a kind of broken circle, and General Canby, Meacham, and Dr. Thomas sat together, faced by Captain Jack and Schonchin. Mr. Dyar stood by Jack, holding his horse, with Hooker Jim and Shacknasty Jim to his left.

Meacham opened the talk, and gave a long history of what they wanted to do for them, after which General Canby and Dr. Thomas both talked for some time. Captain Jack then talked in an apparently good, serious strain, and when he finished, stepped back to the rear where Meacham's horse was hitched. John Schonchin then began to talk, and while he was speaking, my informant, Mr. Dyar, heard a cap misfire, and looking around, saw Captain Jack to his left with his pistol pointed at General Canby. This was the signal for a general massacre, and a dozen shots were fired inside of half a minute.

Mr. Dyar, after hearing the cap misfire, turned and fled, followed closely by Hooker Jim, who fired two shots after him. Dyar, finding Hooker Jim gaining on him, turned and drew his derringer, whereupon Hooker Jim retreated, and Dyar made the best of his way to the camp.

Captain Jack fired again on General Canby, and the noble old gentleman ran off to the left but was speedily shot down and killed instantly. Meacham was shot at by Schonchin and wounded in the head. He tried to draw his derringer, when two Indians ran up and knocked him down. Dr. Thomas was killed almost instantly by two pistol shots in the head. Riddle ran off, and it appears they did not fire at him, but they knocked his squaw down. Dyar, Riddle, and the squaw returned in safety to the camp.

The above story I obtained from Mr. Dyar.

I was lying down in my tent just after lunch, reading a book and rather sulky with the peace commissioners for refusing the press access to the talk, when I heard a shout from the signal station on the side of the bluff, "They are firing on the peace commissioners." I jumped up and, buckling on my revolver, ran out just as the drums and bugles were sounding the call to arms. I then learned from Colonel Gillem that the Indians had attacked Major Mason's camp on the east side of Tule Lake, and he showed me a half-written note which he had hastily penned to send as a warning to General Canby.

I rushed out with Captains Miller and Throckmorton's two batteries that were leading the skirmish line, and after about five minutes' tramp over the broken rocks, we arrived at the scene of the massacre. In the distance I saw three of the perpetrators of the murders running round the edge of the lake on their way back to their rocky fastness. About 100 yards to the west of the place of meeting, we found Mr. Meacham badly wounded with a pistol shot over the left eye. He was immediately attended to and carried back for medical treatment. Fifty yards further on was the body of the Rev. Dr. Thomas, lying on his face and stripped to the waist. Life was extinct from pistol shot wounds in his head. The body of General Canby, the hero of many a fight, was stripped of every vestige of clothing and lay about 100 yards to the southward, with two pistol shot wounds in the head.

Pausing only to cast a glance on the body of the man they both loved and respected, the troops dashed on, and the two leading batteries were within a mile of the murderers when the bugle sounded a halt. Lieutenant Eagan and Lieutenant Wright's companies of the 12th Infantry were behind the artillery, and then came the cavalry.

Colonel Gillem and Major Green and staff were up with the men, but as soon as they found that the Indians had all got back to their stronghold, the troops were ordered to fall back, and active operations will commence tomorrow or the day after.

The attack on Mason's camp, as I learn through Lieutenant Adams, signal officer, commenced by the Indians firing on Lieutenants Boyle and Sherwood, who had wandered some 500 yards outside their picket lines. Lieutenant Sherwood was shot through the arm and leg, but Lieutenant Boyle escaped without injury. Both officers got safely back to their camp.

In justice to Riddle and his squaw, it should be stated that they both warned the peace commissioners and General Canby not to trust implicitly in the Indians, and added, "If they will go, I wash my hands of all blame in the matter."

The murder of General Canby has thrown a gloom over this camp and created a bitter feeling in the hearts of the men that will exact a bitter reckoning from these treacherous savages. I have never known an officer so universally respected and esteemed as General Canby. He was a true Christian and brave soldier, and died in what he believed was the discharge of his duty. For the past few days he had clothed and fed these Indians, giving them blankets, food, and tobacco. I saw him give Boston Charley money out of his pocket to go and buy some things at the sutler's. When the squaws came into camp, they rushed to General Canby, and they went back laden with provisions and calico. Yet the first to fall was their kindest and noblest benefactor.

Dr. Thomas was the most earnest and best member of the peace commission, and never hesitated to go to meet these savages when he deemed his duty called him there.

Mr. Meacham is still in a dangerous condition, suffering from a flesh wound on the right forearm and a pistol shot entering behind his right ear and escaping three inches above. He also has an incised wound on the head, where the Indians tried to scalp him.

New York *Herald,* April 14, 1873

CAMP IN THE LAVA BEDS,
VIA YREKA, Cal., April 12, 1873

The massacre of yesterday was entirely preconcerted, as I find this morning that Lieutenants Boyle and Sherwood were induced to leave Major Mason's camp by the Indians waving a white flag and shouting that they wanted to talk.

Lieutenant Boyle miraculously escaped without a scratch, but Lieutenant Sherwood fell wounded in two places. He was afterwards brought into camp on a stretcher by some of his own regiment, who had been sent out on a skirmish line. The wounds are pronounced severe but not dangerous.

Mr. Meacham is still in a precarious condition, but hopes are entertained of his recovery.

All the troops in camp turned out under arms at 2:00 A.M. this morning, as firing commenced along the picket line; but the enemy finally dwindled down to two horses grazing, and we returned to our beds. In the hurry of getting under arms, Major Green narrowly escaped death, as an accidental pistol shot passed through the front of his forage cap, tearing away the cross saber insignia.

We move tomorrow into camp about 1,200 yards from Captain Jack's cave, and active operations will immediately commence. The Warm Springs Indians under Donald McKay are expected at Major Mason's camp tomorrow.

The remains of General Canby and Dr. Thomas left today under charge of Lieutenant Anderson.

<hr />

New York *Herald,* May 5, 1873

CAMP ON LAVA BEDS, April 14, 1873

Three days have now elapsed since the massacre of General Canby and Dr. Thomas, and tomorrow we go into action. I write this in case any stray shot might prevent my giving a detailed account of this most heartless and treacherous act. In some such instances, the brutal and treacherous nature of the Indian has been passed over, and his deeds of blood laid to the account of ignorance, but here no such palliation can be offered, as the Modoc Indians are far above the average in intelligence, having associated freely for the past ten years with the whites. The knowledge of civilization which they have obtained has, however, only rendered them more dangerous, and I do not scruple to say that they are one of the worst bands of Indians in the United States.

I have followed very closely the negotiations that have passed between the peace commissioners appointed by the government and these Indians, and although at one time I was inclined to believe they were peaceably disposed, I am now assured that the insolent manner in which they carried themselves, the result of their fight on January 17, could only be destroyed by a sound thrashing. They felt like a victorious army and received the friendly offers of the government as a victorious people would treat the solicitations of their vanquished foes. On the occasion of my visits to their stronghold, I always found them talking of the late fight—how one of their men had defended a line of rocks two miles in length; how their little band had whipped 300 soldiers without losing a man, when the soldiers lost some forty killed and wounded. They always said, "If the soldiers go away, we will stop where we are and shoot no man; but if the soldiers want more, we will give them what they want." To tell them that more soldiers were coming only made their eyes glisten, as if the thought flashed across their minds, "All the more to kill."

Thomas at that time was of the opinion that Captain Jack was tired of fighting and would make peace, but I freely acknowledge that the surrounding settlers, such as Fairchild and Dorris, and the squaws of the men Whittle and Riddle, always held the opinion they would fight rather than leave Lost River. In a letter written some time ago, I stated that the fiend incarnate of these Modocs, Boston Charley, who had been acting as a kind of courier and spy for Captain Jack, had arranged on behalf of the Modocs to accept the terms then offered by General Canby to go to Angel Island until a reservation had been selected for them in some distant country. In pursuance of this treaty, he asked for three or four wagons to come and meet them at Klamath Lake on the Monday following at noon. He said General Canby and the members of the peace commission might come, but no soldiers.

On the Sunday evening Toby, Riddle's squaw, came to General Canby's tent and beseeched him not to go, saying it was a plot among the Indians to massacre them all and secure the horses out of the teams. Both General Canby and Colonel Gillem, Mr. Elijah Steele, and numbers of others, including your correspondent, laughed at the idea of such a thing, and both Riddle and his squaw were looked upon as playing a double game. Mr. Steele accompanied the wagons to the appointed place, but no Indians came in sight, probably thinking that by exercising a little patience they would get a better haul. At the time nothing was thought of it, but now I feel assured that the Indians meant treachery.

Again, when I remained with Dr. Cabaniss at one of their picket stations while Captain Jack and five others of the tribe had a talk with General Canby and Colonel Gillem, they objected to leaving their guns before going to talk, and although they finally conceded that point, they managed to smuggle their pistols with them. I believed then they meant treachery but on afterthought concluded it would be better to wait for some of the peace commission.

After we arrived at this camp, there were several meetings between the peace commission and the Indians, and although Messrs. Meacham and Dyar both distrusted the intentions of the Modocs, General Canby and Dr. Thomas felt confident that no treachery was intended. For over a week, not a day passed by without one or more Modocs coming into camp, ostensibly to talk, but in reality to beg and trade with the sutler. They brought in their feathers and sold them to the sutler for clothing, calicoes, soap, matches, and other articles. Food they got in plenty, as General Canby was too kindhearted to refuse any of their demands for food, and they generally returned to their camp each carrying a bag full of provisions. Boston Charley was in nearly every day and was in the habit of making his headquarters in General Canby's tent. His talks with General Canby and Mr. Meacham generally resulted in his getting a couple of blankets from them, ostensibly to cover some sick Indian of their tribe.

The day before the massacre, Boston Charley and Bogus Charley both came into camp and made arrangements for the meeting of the succeeding day. They arranged to meet at a spot about half a mile from our camp, near the edge of the second inlet of the lake. Two meetings had been held on the same spot, and a wall tent was pitched on the ground so as to give shelter in case of rain. This little flat, covered with bunch grass and loose scoria, that has since become notorious as the scene of the massacre, was hid from our camp by some intervening rolling and broken ground but was in full view of the signal station on the bluff at our backs.

Early Friday morning,[39] the day of the massacre, Toby came to Mr. Meacham and beseeched him not to go out, as she was certain the Indians meant to kill them. She said that the last time she had been in their camp on a message, William, Wild Gal's man, ran alongside of her horse as she was leaving and told her that the Modocs were talking bad and meant to kill all the men at the next talk. Mr. Meacham then went to General Canby and the other commissioners and told them this story, but neither General Canby, Colonel Gillem, nor Dr. Thomas would put any credence in the statement. Mr. Dyar felt somewhat like Mr. Meacham and said that he could not see what Toby had to gain by lying on such a subject. General Canby said that he looked at the matter in another light and could not see how the Indians would help their case by murdering them; it would be only precipitating a war which they were anxious to avert. Mr. Meacham then called John Fairchild and asked him to sound Bogus Charley and see if he could find anything out of him.

Fairchild had a long talk with Bogus, getting quietly to the point, but could get no more information. Bogus asked Fairchild if he was going out with the commission, and receiving an answer in the negative, then said everything would be all right: "Captain Jack hurt no one." When Dr. Thomas heard the story, he went to Bogus, an Indian to whom he had taken rather a fancy, and asked him if there was anything in the story, and very naturally Bogus denied it, saying it was a squaw yarn. Dr. Thomas then said he was satisfied that the Indians meant no treachery and that he should go, as he felt certain that the God in whom he trusted would guard over him while he went on such a mission.

After some reluctance, and with evident misgivings as to the result, Messrs. Meacham and Dyar consented to go, and the party was preparing to start when Riddle called them all into Colonel Gillem's tent and said, "Gentlemen, I want you to hold me blameless if any harm comes to you today, as I am confident

The peace commissioners' tent. NATIONAL ARCHIVES.

that the Modocs mean no good. They will not shoot me, because I am married to one of their tribe, but I greatly fear they have treacherous intentions." General Canby and Colonel Gillem rather laughed at his fears, and the party finally started on their mission, from which two never came back alive. Just before leaving, Boston Charley asked Mr. Dyar's permission to tie a bag of provisions on his horse, a favor which was granted. The party consisted of General Canby, Dr. Thomas, Boston and Bogus Charley on foot, and Mr. Meacham, Mr. Dyar, Riddle, and his squaw on horseback. Colonel Gillem did not go, as he was on the sick list, having been in the doctor's hands for the past three days.

They all walked quietly towards the rendezvous and arrived there without any incident of importance occurring, but it was noticed that Boston Charley stopped behind them a little and looked about, as if to see that there were no soldiers about. General Canby and the peace commissioners, when they arrived at the tent, were shortly afterwards joined by Captain Jack, John Schonchin, Shacknasty Jim, Hooker Jim, Ellen's Man, and Black Jim. The party finally sat down in a kind of broken circle. General Canby sat facing the west, with Mr. Meacham on his left. Dr. Thomas sat to the left of Mr. Meacham, a little back, and adjoining him were Riddle and his squaw.

Captain Jack sat nearly opposite General Canby, with Schonchin, Black Jim, and Ellen's Man on his left, and on his right were Mr. Dyar, Shacknasty Jim, Hooker Jim, and Boston Charley. Mr. Dyar was standing alongside of Jack during the conference, holding his horse, and Mr. Meacham's was tied a little in his rear. Bogus Charley was not sitting down, but kept moving about in a restless manner.

Mr. Meacham opened the talk with a long speech, in which he told the Indians how anxious he was to arrange a peace with them, so that the president would be pleased and there would be no more fighting. He told them how difficult it was to get a place where they could live unmolested in this section of the country, and that it would be better for them to decide upon going some distance, where they would be away from the Oregonians, who wished to annoy them. Mr. Meacham spoke for nearly half an hour, after which General Canby talked, telling them not to be afraid of the soldiers; they were their friends and would not hurt them. He also told them how the president wished all his children, Indians and whites, to be at peace and not fighting with one another. Nothing could have been kinder than his speech to these savages, and the kind old gentleman talked to them as if they had been his own children.

Captain Jack and Schonchin then spoke to the effect that they wanted the soldiers sent away, and then they would make peace and take a reservation on Cottonwood, Hot Creek, or Willow Creek, in the country that they knew and where they had lived many years. Dr. Thomas then talked in his kind, quiet way and was telling them how difficult it would be for them to live at peace in this part of the country, and how much better it would be for them to go with their families to some other part of the country where they would be fed and clothed by the government.

While Dr. Thomas was speaking, Captain Jack got up and walked back to where Meacham's horse was tied, and then returning, said aloud, "*Hetuck?*" (Are you ready?), and, pulling his hand out of his pocket, snapped a pistol at General Canby. This was the signal for the murderers, and they immediately commenced their bloody work. There was no hurry or confusion in their manner; each man had selected his victim, and they had only been awaiting the signal. At the first snap of Captain Jack's pistol, General Canby got up and ran in a southerly direction, followed by Captain Jack and Shacknasty Jim, who both fired at him. The poor old gentleman ran about fifty yards, when he threw up his hands and fell. Bogus Charley, Shacknasty Jim, and another Indian then threw themselves upon him and, after stabbing him in the throat, stripped him of everything he had on. They did not leave a vestige of clothing on his body, and the only portion of his apparel found was a small black necktie.[40]

Mr. Meacham rose at the same time as General Canby, to receive a bullet from the pistol of John Schonchin, but he ran off a short distance, about seventy or eighty yards, and then fell, shot in four places. His murderers then stripped him to his underclothing and left him, as they supposed, a ghastly, bleeding corpse.

Poor Dr. Thomas was shot through the head in the first fire by Boston Charley,[41] the treacherous brute who had breakfasted with him the same morning. He staggered a few yards and fell on his knees, at the same time asking Boston Charley to spare his life. The fiend replied by firing another bullet through his head, and at the same time said to him, "Why you no believe squaw?" Boston Charley, after stripping the body of Dr. Thomas to the waist, ran to where Meacham was lying and commenced scalping him, when the squaw Toby shouted, "The soldiers are coming," and the cowardly devil ran off.

Mr. Dyar was standing on Jack's right when the first shot was fired, and he immediately turned and ran for camp, followed by Hooker Jim, who fired two

The murder of the peace commissioners. ILLUSTRATED LONDON NEWS, 1873.

shots after him. Dyar, thinking that Hooker Jim was gaining, drew his derringer and, turning around, snapped it. The pistol did not go off; but the coward no sooner saw the weapon than he wheeled and ran back to where the rest
of his party was finishing their bloody work. The whole scene was enacted in a
very few minutes, and before the troops got on the ground, the murders were
safe in their rocky fastness.

I was lying down in my tent reading, when I heard a shout that came from
above me at the signal station, "They are firing at the peace commissioners!
General Canby is killed!" I rushed out just as the bugle notes were calling the
men to arms. Captain Miller's and Captain Throckmorton's batteries of artillery
were soon skirmishing across the rolling ground between the camp and the
scene of the murder, followed closely by Lieutenant Wright and Lieutenant
Eagan, with two companies of the 12th Infantry. Major Biddle and Captain
Trimble came next, with Troops K and F of the 1st Cavalry.

When the troops came to where the body of their beloved general was
lying cold and dead, disfigured with his wounds, they did not at first recognize
him, but learning the horrid truth, they dashed forward among the rocks, eager
to revenge his murder.

While some were attending to the dead and dying, the troops were moving
rapidly forward, and it was with difficulty that Colonel Gillem kept them back,
to reserve their vengeance for another day. It was a sad march, that walk back to
camp with the dead bodies of General Canby and Dr. Thomas and the almost
hopelessly wounded Meacham. The squaw Toby was in despair, crying inces-
santly and muttering, "Why would they not believe me?"

At first it was thought in camp that the murder had not been premeditated,
and that the Indians had started the shooting when they found the peace commissioners would not give them a reservation in their old country. When we
came back from the scene of the murder, I went into Colonel Gillem's tent, and

as I sat down, he gave me a piece of paper on which was written, "General Canby—The Modocs have attacked Mason's pickets, wounding Lieutenant Boyle." As I read it, he said, "I was just writing a note to General Canby, which Dr. Cabaniss had volunteered to take out, when the warning from the signal station told me it was too late to save the life of one of the best and noblest men in the United States Army." It appears that during the morning, some Indians, including Scarfaced Charley and Steamboat Frank,[42] came out on the rocks on the east side and waved a white flag. Lieutenant Sherwood of the 21st Infantry, who was the officer of the day, went out to see what they wanted, accompanied by Lieutenant Boyle, quartermaster of Major Mason's command.

When they arrived within about sixty yards, Lieutenant Sherwood asked what they wanted, and [Curly Headed Jack] answered [that] they wanted to talk with the "little tyees" and asked them to come upon the rocks where they were. This Lieutenant Sherwood refused to do, and the Indians immediately fired upon them, wounding Lieutenant Sherwood severely in two places. Lieutenant Boyle ran away on hearing the first shot and succeeded in escaping unhurt. On hearing the shots, a company immediately left Major Mason's camp, led by Lieutenant Eagan, who happened to be there at the time, and accompanied by Assistant Surgeon DeWitt. They soon came up to where Lieutenant Sherwood was lying and brought him back to camp. His wounds have proved fatal, and he died two days afterwards. Mr. Meacham has been doing remarkably well and, although shot in four places and half scalped, will probably recover. I trust that by this time tomorrow, the punishment of these treacherous murderers will have begun, and that some will have paid the penalty of their crimes.

* * *

New York *Herald,* April 19, 1873

CAMP ON LAVA BEDS, April 15—10:00 P.M.
The work of retribution has commenced, and the troops are now encircled around Captain Jack's Stronghold, within 250 yards of his cave, awaiting daylight to resume the attack.

The position they attained today was the result of much hard fighting and will probably cost the United States the lives of four or five soldiers and the maiming of seven or eight others.

Yesterday evening Colonel Gillem decided that any further delay in the punishment of the Modocs was unnecessary, as the stores arrived from Van Bremer's and the command was supplied with boots. People may think it odd that shoe leather should form an important item in the necessaries required for an attack on Captain Jack and his treacherous band of assassins; but I take the liberty to assure them from personal experience that a pair of shoes will not last more than one day's tramping in the Lava Beds.

Last night the orders were issued that the infantry and artillery would move from this camp at daybreak, and the cavalry at 3:00 A.M. The latter were instructed to advance until they reached the Modoc pickets, then take the strongest position they could get and hold it until the remainder of the command arrived. Major Mason's command, consisting of Companies B, C, and M of the 21st Infantry; Troops B and G of the 1st Cavalry; and seventy-two Warm Springs Indians, moved into position last night on the east side of the lake.

During the afternoon, a cavalry detachment arrived from Van Bremer's, bringing with them Long Jim, a squaw, and two papooses. Long Jim is a Modoc Indian that was wounded in the last fight, and who since came in and surrendered, as the wounds rendered him useless in a fighting capacity. After the murder of General Canby and Dr. Thomas, Long Jim was put under arrest and on being searched, was found to carry four pounds of powder and some lead in his clothes. About 12:00 A.M. last night the camp was alarmed by several shots, which proved to be a parting salute in honor of Long Jim, who quietly shook the dust off his feet and returned to Captain Jack. He jumped suddenly out of the guardhouse, dashing between the officer of the guard and the sentry, and got clean away, escaping about a dozen shots that were fired after his retreating figure.

At 3:00 A.M. this morning Captain Perry started with the cavalry battalion, consisting of his own Troop F and Troop K, under Lt. Charles C. Cresson. I tried then to snatch an hour's sleep, but at daylight the sounds of musketry soon roused me out of bed, and upon the signal station I found that Major Mason's command were already at work, and looking through the glass saw the howitzers brought into position, and presently a shell burst over Captain Jack's cave, eliciting, as I have since been told, a howling of disapprobation from his band of murderers.

Our camp soon began to present a lively appearance, and shortly after 7:00 A.M. Batteries A, E, K, and M of the 4th Artillery, and Companies E and G of the 12th Infantry, were paraded before Maj. John Green, who commanded the western division. The men carried their overcoats, one blanket, haversack with three days' cooked rations, and 100 rounds of ammunition. Major Green soon gave the order to march, and Capt. Marcus P. Miller led the advance, with K Battery in skirmishing order.[43] The remainder of the troops followed in double file. The march out was undisturbed until shortly after the command had been deployed in skirmishing order. Lieutenant Eagan of the 12th Infantry, with his company, had the extreme left, with Lieutenant Wright, of the same regiment, next, and then Captain Throckmorton, Lieutenant Harris, and Captain Miller, with their respective batteries, in the order named.

I was toting a Springfield and doing duty for the time being with Captain Miller's battery, then on the extreme right, and about 9:00 A.M. we charged up a rise, but no sooner reached the crest than—"tip, tip, tip"—bullets out the sagebrush all around us. We immediately fell back under cover, and a few minutes afterwards charged and took the next bluff, some 150 yards distant. The whole line was now under fire, and the troops behaved splendidly, advancing steadily in good order. We soon passed the position held by the cavalry, who were halted and given a rest.

After crossing several ridges, we came to a flat about 300 or 400 yards in width and broken by a couple of small ridges. Major Green, who was up with the troops, ordered his bugler to sound the advance. The line then moved forward and became exposed to a harassing fire from a fortified position held by the Modocs on a ridge on the other side of the flat. They soon found the fire very hot and halted, every man seeking cover under the sagebrush. Presently Major Green ordered the charge, and the troops, rising, took the position on the run.

It was one of the most dashing charges of the day. The officers led their men and cheered them on under a galling fire. In this charge Lieutenant Eagan received a flesh wound in the thigh after making a brilliant rush with his company. A corporal of his company was killed in the same charge. It would be hardly fair, however, to single out any company for special praise, as both infantry and artillery did splendidly.

Up to this time I had been keeping with the front, skirmishing in the hope of getting a shot at an Indian, but as the only intimation I received of their presence came from oral testimony of sundry bullets, I concluded the amusement and returned to Colonel Gillem's headquarters.

The colonel and staff occupied a bluff some 300 yards in the rear, which they had selected as it afforded a good view of the attack and also served as a signal station. The signal corps, under Lieutenants Adams and Moore, proved of invaluable service to Colonel Gillem, as through their aid, communication was kept up all day with Major Mason's camp.

After taking the bluff on the other side of the flat, the troops were given a rest of about a couple of hours, during which time, however, the infantry and artillery succeeded in improving their position.

Shortly after 2:00 P.M. the mortars arrived from camp, under the command of Captain Thomas and Lieutenants Cranston and Howe. Major Green then ordered Troops F and K of the 1st Cavalry to advance on the left, with the lake as their guiding line.

The two troops formed in skirmishing order and made a dashing charge, capturing the opposite bluffs, but not without the loss of two killed and one wounded. I should say one killed, one mortally wounded, and one severely wounded. One man, Delaney, of Troop K, was shot through the eye and died instantaneously. Searles, the bugler of F Troop, was shot in the head alongside Captain Perry, but he survived his injuries several hours.

After the bluffs on the left had been captured, the mortars were moved forward and a battery opened on the other side of the flat. After a few trial shots they obtained the range and soon began to burst their shells in the vicinity of Captain Jack's Stronghold. While the cavalry were taking those bluffs, the infantry and artillery had not been idle, and Captain Miller, pushing forward on the extreme right, captured a very strong point and dislodged the Modocs.

When night set in, the troops had extended their line to a point about 300 yards from the Stronghold, and I anticipate pretty severe fighting tomorrow.

Assistant Surgeon Henry McElderry and Acting Assistant Surgeon Cabaniss were both indefatigable in their attentions to the wounded and did not hesitate to expose themselves to fire when their presence was required.

The wounded were carried in hand litters to a temporary field hospital in the field, under the charge of Assistant Surgeon McElderry, and they were all conveyed the same evening to the hospital in the camp, where Assistant Surgeon Semig was officiating.

The troops on the eastern division under Major Mason, acting in conjunction with the Warm Springs Indians, took and held a strong position, and have reported no casualties. Assistant Surgeon Calvin De Witt and Acting Assistant Surgeon Jenner were on duty with Major Mason.

The troops all remain tonight in the position occupied by them at sundown, and as I write, the occasional boom of the mortars and cracks from the rifles serve as a reminder that all are not asleep on the Lava Beds.

It is impossible to arrive at a correct estimate of killed and wounded among the Modocs, but as far as I can judge, they have lost two or three in the fight. The following is a list of casualties on our side during the day's fight:

Lieutenant Eagan, G Company, 12th Infantry, gunshot wound in left thigh.

Sgt. H. Gude, G Company, 12th Infantry, gunshot fracture of right tibia; severely wounded.

Cpl. Drew, G Company, 12th Infantry, gunshot wound through head; dead.

Cpl. E. Killebeck, Battery——, 4th Artillery, scalp wound; slight.

Cpl. Dennis Delaney, K Battery, 4th Artillery, gunshot wound through right eye; dead.

Bugler W. F. Searles, F Troop, 1st Cavalry, gunshot wound through head; mortally wounded, may survive a few hours.

Pvt. E. O'Connor, E Battery, 4th Artillery, gunshot flesh wound, left leg.

Pvt. Owen Dooley, K Battery, 4th Artillery, gunshot flesh wound, left leg.

Pvt. T. McManus, E Battery, 4th Artillery, gunshot fracture of left thigh; dangerous.

Pvt. Martin Conner, G Company, 12th Infantry, gunshot flesh wound, right leg.

Pvt. Thomas Bernard, K Troop, 1st Cavalry, gunshot, apex of left shoulder, fracturing clavicle.

I return to the line at daylight.

April 16—4:00 A.M.

The shelling has continued all night at intervals of ten minutes. The general attack will be renewed at 7:00 A.M. this morning.

CAMP ON LAVA BEDS, April 16, 1873

The whang of the mortar and the crack of the muskets are still the only music enjoyed by the Modocs, and Colonel Gillem may be congratulated on the success he has thus far achieved, although the Indians are not yet conquered. The colonel has succeeded today in connecting his line on the left and thus securing the waterfront, which naturally deprives the Modocs of a necessity of life. They have also, I am satisfied, been forced to leave the Stronghold and take up a position farther south in order to escape the hot shelling they received from Captain Thomas's battery of mortars.

Their final destruction is now assured, and although it may take a few days longer than at first anticipated, the result will be obtained with a smaller percentage of killed and wounded. As a last resort they may break out to the southward—a consummation, in my opinion, much to be desired, as it would be impossible to find a worse country to whip them in than that they now hold. They could not go far, as they are without horses, and we have seventy mounted Indians and five troops of cavalry to put on their trail.

I left this camp this morning shortly after 6:00 A.M. and rode out to the front. The troops were in about the same position as I left them on the previous evening. Excepting the play of the mortars, there was very little going on along the line. Looking through the glass, I could discover no sign of Modocs in the neighborhood of Jack's Stronghold, and I then learned that the shelling during the night had been a complete success, eventually driving the enemy from that position. During the night, a shell burst in the vicinity of their campfire, and the domestic circle dispersed, venting their wrath in frantic war whoops.

About 9:00 A.M. firing commenced on the extreme right, and we found that the Modocs had taken up a new position some three-quarters of a mile to the southward and were actively engaged with Captain Miller's battery and our allies, the Warm Springs Indians. During the evening, Captain Miller's command, on the extreme right, and the Warm Springs Indians had some pretty severe fighting with the Modocs. As far as I can learn, it resulted in about an equal loss on both sides.

Captain Miller had advanced pretty far in the face of the ridge towards Jack's Stronghold and was holding a strong point, assisted by about a dozen of his company, when a shell burst near his position and forced him to fall back. In his retreat he lost one man killed and one wounded. The Warm Springs Indians also lost a man, but they claim three Modocs killed.[44]

The troops held their line on the bluffs commanding the left shore, and during the evening I paid a visit to a commanding point held by Captain Perry of the 1st Cavalry. When I arrived, Captain Burton of the 21st Infantry was chatting with [Perry], they having succeeded in gaining the line. They were then sitting on a rocky bluff about 200 yards from Jack's cave, and from what I could ascertain, they intended to remain on the defensive, as the Modocs would probably attack them in their efforts to get at water.

At 3:00 A.M., after my return to camp, I heard heavy firing in the direction of the waterfront, which I surmised must have been occasioned by a visit from the thirsty redskins in search of a drink. They were, however, driven back, as the firing soon ceased, and nothing now disturbed the solitude of the night except the occasional whang of a mortar and crack of a solitary musket shot.

Tomorrow will probably settle the Modoc War, unless they beat a retreat during the night. I rather fancy, however, they will fight it out on this line as, if they take to the country, they will have to travel twenty-five miles before they strike water, which would be rather a long journey to carry their squaws and papooses. I also am satisfied that they fully appreciate the strength of the Lava Beds, and with the proverbial love of an Indian for his old home, they will stick by the rocks to the last. From what I could learn today, I am satisfied they must have lost ten or twelve men killed or wounded.

Our casualties today were Bugler William Smith, Battery M, 4th Artillery, gunshot wound through neck. Private Harmon, Battery E, 4th Artillery, gunshot wound through breast; dead. Private Wiggan, Battery E, 4th Artillery, shot through leg; seriously wounded.

⊷⊷ ☰◊☰ ⊷⊷

New York *Herald,* May 7, 1873

CAMP ON LAVA BEDS, April 20, 1873

The massacre of April 11 effectually solved the peace problem, and Colonel Gillem immediately commenced preparations, with a view to surrounding and meting out the punishment the Modocs so richly deserved. The duties of the peace commission were ended, and the Modocs were handed over to the tender mercies of the military. The troops were impatient to be led to the attack, and although those that had figured in the fight of January 17 would rather have met their foes in a different country, they were impatient to avenge the murder of their general.

On Monday, April 14, Colonel Gillem decided to commence operations on the following day, and orders were issued to the company commanders to that effect. The colonel determined that in order to avoid loss of life, the advance should be made very slowly, keeping the men as much as possible under cover. On Monday afternoon, while walking through the camp, I found the men unusually cheerful, and during the evening singing and laughing were heard in every direction.

It had been first proposed that the troops from both sides were to advance simultaneously at daybreak on Tuesday morning and press forward until the enemy's fire made it prudent to take shelter. The Warm Springs Indians, seventy-two in number, under Donald McKay, a well-known half-breed scout, arrived at Major Mason's camp on Sunday evening, and they received orders to advance with that command. As the operations in the Lava Beds could only be conducted on foot, they were instructed to keep their horses on herd at Hospital

Rock. On Monday afternoon Major Mason requested and obtained permission to move his line at midnight of that day, so that he might be able to obtain a good position under the cover of night and preserve his men as much as possible from the fire of the enemy. Colonel Gillem then decided to move two troops of cavalry from our side with a similar object in view, and also with the hope that they might get under cover unseen by the Modocs, and perhaps be able to flank them if they advanced too far to meet our main line. All the troops in the command were ordered to take with them a blanket, overcoat, canteen full of water, 100 rounds of ammunition, and three days' cooked rations.

At 12:00 A.M. on Monday, April 14, the camp at Hospital Rock was quietly broken up, and Major Mason moved out with his command and succeeded in taking up an excellent position without hearing a shot fired. Major Mason's command comprised Company C, 21st Infantry, Capt. George H. Burton; Company B, 21st Infantry, 1st Lt. John M. Ross; Company I, 1st Lt. E. R. Theller; Troop G, 1st Cavalry, Captain R. F. Bernard,[45] brevet colonel, 2nd Lt. John G. Kyle; Troop B, 1st Cavalry, Capt. James Jackson, brevet major; 1st Lt. Henry Moss, 2nd Lt. F. A. Boutelle, and seventy-two Warm Springs, commanded by Donald McKay. The infantry were on the right, the cavalry in the center, and the Warm Springs Indians on the left.

Shortly before 3:00 A.M. on the morning of Tuesday, April 15, the cavalry moved out of our camp under the command of Captain Perry, brevet colonel. His command comprised Troop J, 1st Cavalry, 1st Lt. Charles C. Cresson, brevet major, 2nd Lt. George R. Bacon; Troop F, 2nd Lt. W. H. Miller. Captain Perry succeeded in obtaining an excellent position within a mile of the Stronghold without firing a shot. They threw up some slight breastworks and lay behind them, awaiting the arrival of the rest of the troops.

The main body of troops left camp about 7:00 A.M. on Tuesday, April 15. The command comprised Battery E, 4th Artillery, Capt. M. P. Miller, brevet colonel, 1st Lt. Peter Leary, Jr.; Battery M, Capt. C. B. Throckmorton, brevet major; Battery K, 4th Artillery, 2nd Lt. George M. Harris; Company E, 12th Infantry, 1st Lt. Thomas F. Wright, colonel of volunteers, and Company G, 12th Infantry, 1st Lt. Charles P. Eagan. The camp was left under the command of Capt. J. G. Trimble, brevet major, with a detachment of B Troop, 1st Cavalry. Capt. C. N. Hoyt, chief quartermaster of the expedition, 1st Lt. A. M. Camp, and 1st Lt. M. E. Guedas, acting quartermaster, remained in camp.

The medical department, under the command of Assistant Surgeon Henry McElderry, was divided up as follows: Assistant Surgeon Calvin DeWitt, in charge of hospital at Hospital Rock; Acting Assistant Surgeons J. O. Skinner and F. S. Stirling,[46] in the field with Major Mason's command; Acting Assistant Surgeon B. Semig in charge of hospital at Captain Trimble's camp, and Assistant Surgeon H. McElderry and Acting Assistant Surgeon F. Cabaniss, in the field with Major Green's command. Battery A, 4th Artillery, Capt. Evan Thomas, brevet major; 1st Lt. Albion F. Howe and 1st Lt. Arthur Cranston, detached from Battery M, were left in camp with four Coehorn mortars, awaiting orders; 2nd Lt. E. S. Chapin, detached from Battery E, 4th Artillery, with a detachment from Battery A, was in command of the two howitzers in a position on Major Mason's line.

The troops moved slowly out of camp, with Captain Miller's battery in skirmishing order as the advance guard. Major Green followed, accompanied by his aide-de-camp, 2nd Lt. S. W. Taylor of the 4th Artillery, and the *Herald* correspondent. For the rear of the command came Colonel Gillem, Major Biddle, 6th Cavalry; 2nd Lt. James Rockwell, 1st Cavalry, acting assistant adjutant general, and 1st Lt. John Quincy Adams, acting signal officer. (2nd Lt. H. De Witt Moore was acting signal officer on Major Mason's side.)

The advance guard, in skirmishing order at five paces' interval, advanced slowly over the rough, rocky ground, passing the spot still red with the life blood of the martyred General Canby and Dr. Thomas and, rounding the little inlet of the lake, closed in by the right and faced in the direction of Captain Jack's Stronghold.

Stumbling over the rocks, the troops advanced by the right, allowing Batteries K and M and Companies G and E to be thrown out as skirmishers in the order named, with Company E on the extreme left. The cavalry were ordered to remain in the position they had taken until further orders. Although we advanced as far as the cavalry line without opposition, the rolls of musketry from the other side, mingled with the occasional sharp crack of the Kentucky rifle, told a tale of war on Mason's line. The howitzers were also at work, and we could see the shells occasionally burst over the enemy's fortifications.

I was on the extreme right, with Captain Miller's battery, and we had the honor of receiving the first Modoc fire. We had shown ourselves on the top of a small bluff, when five or six bullets went zip, zip past our heads. We all fell on our faces and moved back like crabs under the shelter of the bluff, and soon the troops on our left were exposed to fire and laid down for shelter. The Modocs were in a position some 600 yards ahead of us, behind a fortified pile of stones, halfway up a rocky bluff. After a short halt, Major Miller ordered us to advance again; but instead of moving across the high ground, we passed through a hollow to the left and gained the next rise, about 100 yards further on. Here the fire became rather warm, and we hugged the rocks pretty closely, as we were under the fire from ahead and another from two or three Indians on our right. Four or five men were deployed to the right to try and dislodge the above party, and then Major Green came forward and ordered the whole line forward.

The troops behaved very well and advanced as far as the middle of a flat about 500 yards wide, when they became exposed to a crossfire and had to lie down in the sagebrush for shelter. I remained with Major Green on a rising ground a little in the rear and covered by a large rock—a safeguard which the major disdained to make use of, as he stood up watching his troops, regardless of the balls that were whizzing around him. After the men had rested a little, Major Green sent his aide-de-camp, Lieutenant Taylor, to Major Miller, with orders to advance the artillery and infantry and take the position held by the

Indians. Lieutenant Taylor started off with his message, and shortly afterwards I saw a stir along the line, which was followed by a simultaneous dash forward of the whole force. Lieutenant Leary charged in advance of Battery E, leading his men, and Lieutenant Eagan, on the extreme left, rushed forward with Company E of the 12th Infantry. Tom Wright, on the left center—a scarred veteran of many Indian fights—took off his hat and cheered on Company G.

The charge was one of the most brilliant events of the day, and our troops were soon in possession of the place from where a few seconds before the Indians had rattled in such hot fire. Lieutenant Eagan, while rushing on his men, was unfortunately shot through the fleshy part of the upper thigh; but even then he refused to leave his command and was supported by his men to a shelter under the rocks, where his wants were attended to by Acting Assistant Surgeon Cabaniss. I then followed Major Green up to where the line was established and Lieutenant Wright and his men [were] resting under shelter of a dark and craggy bluff of rocks. His company had escaped without a scratch, but Lieutenant Eagan had not been so fortunate, losing one killed and one wounded. Our line having now secured a strong position, I returned with Major Green across the flat to the bluffs where the cavalry were, and there found Colonel Gillem and staff. The signal officer, Lieutenant Adams, was sending a message to Major Mason, which, however, had to be sent first to our camp and then across to Lieutenant Moore on the other side. The message had to take this circuitous route, as we had not yet secured a position from where we could communicate directly with Lieutenant Moore.

An orderly was shortly afterwards sent back to camp with orders to Captain Thomas to bring up the mortars, and in the meanwhile, Colonel Gillem and Major Green decided to put them in position on the left. As this point was, however, still in possession of the Modocs, Captain Perry was ordered to move forward with the cavalry and, forming his left on the lakeshore, push forward and connect his right with Lieutenant Eagan's left. The two troops moved off very quietly in single file, halted in the middle of the flat, and extended in skirmishing order at five paces' interval. F Troop was on the extreme left, with K Troop on the right.

They made a magnificent line and charged in splendid order, led by Captain Perry, Lieutenant Cresson, and Lieutenants Bacon and Miller. Nothing could exceed the cool gallantry displayed by both officers and men in this charge, which drove the Modocs back into their stronghold and connected Lieutenant Eagan's left with the water. This charge, however, cost K Troop one killed and two wounded, and F Troop one killed.

The pack train now moved up, carrying the mortars and ammunition, and Captain Thomas was soon busy arranging his battery on the edge of the flat, in the rear of the cavalry line. The Modocs, however, did not let them alone and kept up a hot fire, which the officers and men of Battery A stood gallantly while they were getting the mortars into position. Assistant Surgeon McElderry was hard at work with the wounded at a temporary hospital which he had established on the other side, but as soon as he had disposed of the wounded infantry and artillery and sent them on hand litters to the boat to be taken to camp, he moved his position to a sheltered spot under a bluff to the left of the mortar battery and gave his attention to the wounded cavalry.

The mortars got to work about 5:00 P.M., and soon the shells began to play the devil with the Modocs. On one occasion we noticed a shell fall in the Stronghold, and immediately after the explosion, some twenty or thirty Indians ran up on top of the rocks, yelling and cursing at a lively rate. One Indian was so mad that he fired his gun off in the air and jumped from rock to rock like a lunatic. We have since learned from a squaw that a shell fell close to the council fire, and that One-Eyed Jack picked it up and ran toward Schonchin and his nephew. All three commenced biting the shell, and while they were taking the edge off their teeth, the shell burst, and the Modoc tribe were minus three warriors.[47]

During the day, we heard a lively fire from Major Mason's command, and when at night I received a dispatch from Assistant Surgeon DeWitt, saying they had no casualties, I was rather astonished. It appears, however, that Major Mason took up his position at night and held it during the day, keeping his men under cover. At about 7:30 P.M. I returned to camp with Colonel Gillem and staff. Dr. McElderry returned with me after he had seen Lieutenant Eagan and the other wounded safely in the boat.

We left camp shortly after daybreak Wednesday morning,[48] and when I arrived at the line, I heard the mortars had been doing considerable execution during the night. On one occasion a shell burst close to one of their fires and made them so mad that one of the party got up and made a speech in tolerably good English, calling the soldiers all the names his limited knowledge of the language commanded. Although they were few, it would be hard to excel them in vulgarity and profanity. Our men answered back, and finally some of the Modocs advanced under cover of the night and opened fire on the mortars, but Howe's men gave them such a hot reception they retired quicker than they came.

During the night, Major Mason advanced his command some distance, and at daylight the troops had closed in pretty near the Modocs. The mortars still kept up an incessant fire, but at about 10:00 A.M. had to let up, awaiting the arrival of some more ammunition. During the morning, the cavalry advanced their lines considerably, and K Troop, led by Lieutenants Cresson and Bacon, made a brilliant dash and captured an important ridge of rocks. Captain Miller kept moving to the right in hope of connecting with the Warm Springs Indians, who were deployed on Major Mason's left, but he could not effect a junction or get beyond an immense ravine that appeared to divide the Lava Beds.

About 1:00 P.M. Captain Miller and eight or nine of his men got cut off from the rest of the line by some Modocs who had got in their rear, but they built up a breastwork of rocks for cover and intended remaining there until dark.

At noon the mortar battery was moved up into a new position on the extreme left, just in rear of Captain Perry's advancing line, and they were soon pitching shells all along the Modoc fortifications. One of these shells went rather far, and almost close to where Maj. Miller was entrenched, forcing him and his nine men to break back and join the line. On their retreat, one man was killed and another wounded. The wounded man was carried back behind our lines, but the dead [man] was not recovered until the next day.

During the afternoon, C Company of the 21st Infantry, under the command of Captain Burton, acting on Major Mason's right, connected with F Troop, 1st Cavalry, under Captain Perry, on our extreme left. This junction gave us the waterfront, and its consummation was hailed by a cheer that passed all along the line.

Donald McKay and about twenty of the Warm Spring Indians, who were trying to connect with our right, were flanked by some Modocs, and one of the Warm Springs, "Bob," was wounded in the fleshy part of the leg. About 3:00 P.M. an order was given by one of Major Green's orderlies to move by the left flank. The men soon began to move along the line, and before Major Green, who immediately saw the mistake, had time to correct it, many of the best positions that had taken some trouble to capture were given up, and the gap to the right made wider than ever. The order as sent by Major Green had been "move by the right flank," and the orderly had carelessly substituted left for right. The men were soon halted and ordered to hold their positions during the night. I returned to camp about 7:00 P.M.

During the night, we heard a very lively fusillade, and it was kept up pretty well all night. The fact was, the Modocs were getting thirsty and made several attempts to get through our lines to the water, but were repulsed on every occasion. At one time during the night, a Modoc came out to a point on the right and made a speech, saying: "Soldiers good men; Warm Springs good; want no more fight." He was saluted, however, with a volley after about each three words, and he finally got mad and cursed the soldiers, saying he could lick any four of them.

I left camp about 7:00 A.M., riding with Dr. McElderry, and some distance ahead were the colonel's orderly, Mr. Tickner, and Mr. Atwell, a correspondent of some San Francisco papers. We rode along quietly round the bend in the lake and presently arrived at the cluster of rocks where Colonel Gillem had taken up his position during the first day's fight. We had then about a thousand yards to ride across a flat to reach the field hospital, situated under a bluff of rocks behind Captain Perry's line. We continued riding quietly along, when I noticed the colonel's orderly, who was some two hundred yards ahead, suddenly dismount and take to the sagebrush, and Tickner and Atwell started running as if they had a mad bull at their heels.

Atwell had a game leg, but on this occasion he would have distanced Dexter on the homestretch. While I was laughing at the gymnastic display of my collaborator, the doctor turned to me and said, "They must be firing this way." He had hardly got the words out of his mouth before four or five bullets came whizzing by our ears. We both dismounted, and the doctor started leading his horse to get behind a ridge to his left. I stood for a minute, but a couple more bullets cured me of hesitation, and letting go my horse, [I] started on a run to get behind the cluster of rocks we had just left. They were about a hundred yards off, and I don't think I could have been more than thirteen seconds making the distance, hampered as I was with cartridge box and Springfield. I had murderous intentions and crept up behind these rocks in order to get a shot at the red devils who had caused all this commotion; but just as I was slipping a cartridge in the breech, two fresh leaden messengers—one so unpleasantly close that it made my left ear tingle—changed my tactics, so that I made a flank movement, left my rear open to the fire of the enemy, and rejoined the doctor after a brilliant dash of some two hundred yards. Some officers who had been watching my evolutions with the aid of a powerful glass afterwards acknowledged that I had made the most brilliant retreat of the day.

With the assistance of the doctor, I recaptured my steed, and we made a detour to the left, under cover of some low bluffs, and succeeded in arriving at the field hospital safe and sound. The boat was just leaving, bound for camp, and in the stern sheets I perceived the burly form of the San Francisco correspondent, who was returning in order to dispatch a special with the full and correct account of the day's fight. After tying up my horse, I sat down alongside of Lieutenant Wright, who was stretched out on a blanket with a badly sprained ankle, and we were talking about the firing and wondering who the Indians were that had got behind our lines, when one of the Warm Springs Indians attached to the pack train came up and told us he had seen eleven Modocs making towards the little inlet of the lake to get some water. We shortly afterwards heard some shots from that direction, and an orderly presently came in and said the same party had just fired upon two citizens and killed one of them. These citizens were bringing out four horses to carry the litters and had just turned the bend of the lake when the Modocs fired upon them, killing Hovey and capturing the horses. The other man, Watson, started off on a run and got safely back to camp.

About 10:00 A.M. I walked up at the back of the lines to the mortar battery and found Colonel Gillem, Major Mason, Major Green, and a number of officers sitting round the mortars discussing the position of affairs. Major Green was of the opinion that the Modocs had deserted the Stronghold and intended taking to the open country. No Modoc was to be seen, and the men were sitting on the rocks along the line, offering some very tempting shots, but there was not a gun fired. About noon word passed from our left that the Warm Springs were advancing, and looking from a position occupied by Captain Perry's men, I saw some Indians on the other side of Jack's Stronghold, creeping quietly along. They moved stealthily but quickly, making a dash from the friendly cover of a rock to the next shelter. Presently Donald McKay, their chief, made his appearance, and although about six feet three inches in height and weighing about two hundred thirty pounds, he skipped from rock to rock like a two-year-old.

Our lines then began to advance under orders from Major Green, and in a few minutes the Stronghold was captured, amid the deafening cheers of our men and the ringing war whoops of the Warm Springs. Lieutenant Cresson of Troop K, 1st Cavalry, an officer who during the Rebellion commanded a regiment in action at the age of eighteen, was foremost in the line, and presently climbed up a pile of rocks and captured the Modoc medicine standard, which consisted of a mink skin tied at the end of a stick; a bundle of feathers and beads were also attached to the end of the skin. The soldiers and Warm Springs were soon scattered all through the rocks, and occasional shots tolled the death knell of some wounded Modocs that were pulled out of holes in the rocks, where they had been left when the main body retreated.

Colonel Gillem advanced with the line that was thrown across the rocks, and after passing over the Stronghold in a southerly fashion, they were suddenly fired upon by a party of ten or twelve Indians some hundred yards ahead. Everybody immediately sought cover, and the colonel dropped down into a hole to his right, followed pell-mell by Nigger Bill (Captain Bernard's servant) and Lieutenant Kyle. Our men soon got under cover and opened fire on the Indians, forcing them back from their position.

Orders were now sent by Colonel Gillem to Captain Perry to return with Troops F and K to camp and get ready for a scout round the western edge of the Lava Beds. Orders were also sent to Captain Bernard and Donald McKay to prepare for a similar movement on the eastern side. Major Mason was left in command of the Lava Beds, with three companies of the 21st Infantry, two companies of the 12th Infantry, and four batteries of the 4th Artillery, with the mortars, as a garrison.

I returned to camp with Colonel Gillem and staff, following in the rear of the cavalry. On the way we passed the body of the citizen Hovey, which presented a horrible picture. His entire scalp had been taken off and his stomach slashed through with a knife, making a fearful gash from which the entrails were protruding.

Shortly after arriving in camp, I paid a visit to the hospital and found the doctors hard at work alleviating the sufferings of the wounded. Their hospital room was rather limited, but they succeeded in obtaining accommodation for all.

Captains Bernard and Jackson, with Troops G and B of the 1st Cavalry and the Warm Springs Indians, left Major Mason's old camp at midnight and in a southerly direction, with three days' rations, in order to find where the Modocs had gone. Captain Perry, Captain Trimble, and Lieutenant Cresson, with Troops F, H, and K, started at 3:00 A.M. on April 16 on the same errand. It is uncertain where the Modocs are, but I feel satisfied they are somewhere in the Lava Beds, and we shall hear of them before long. The Modoc loss is estimated at about sixteen killed, including John Schonchin.[49]

New York *Herald,* April 23, 1873

CAMP ON LAVA BEDS, April 20, 1873

The Modoc War is now reduced to a serious guerrilla warfare, which will prove tedious and harassing to our army. The Modocs appear to have broken up into two or three parties and, judging from their actions, are reduced to desperation and will fight to the last man.

Today they attacked the escort that was coming to meet the pack train running from here to Major Mason's camp and killed Private Welch of Company G, 12th Infantry, and wounded Private Dorsey of the 4th Artillery. Later in the afternoon four Modocs came to a rocky bluff about 800 yards from camp and fired into us, but happily their bullets did not find a billet in anything of a living kind.

Some fourteen or fifteen bucks and squaws are encamped on a back ledge of rock about three miles due southeast of this camp, and we were watching their movements this morning from the signal station.

The pack train carrying rations from this camp to Major Mason's headquarters at Captain Jack's old stronghold is generally escorted by twenty-five men from this camp about half the distance, where they are met by twenty-five men from the other camp and taken the rest of their journey and back to our men, who bring them home.

The train was rather late starting this morning, and in the meantime Lieutenant Leary,[50] with twenty-five men, had advanced as far as the edge of the lake, near where the citizen was killed the other day,[51] when his command was fired upon from an adjoining bluff, and one of his men was killed and another wounded. We could see from the signal station the three Modocs that fired at Lieutenant Leary and watched them fall back as he charged and took the bluff. In the meantime, the pack train left our camp under escort of twenty-five men, under the command of Lieutenant Howe, and passed the dangerous point in safety. Lieutenant Leary then escorted the train to Mason's camp and back, and delivered them to Lieutenant Howe to bring them back to us.

On his [Howe's] return, he was fired upon by four Indians, who followed up his rear guard, firing all the time, but happily without effect. They finally came to a rocky ridge, about 700 or 800 yards off, and fired half a dozen shots into camp, sending the bullets whizzing over our heads. They occupied that position for about a quarter of an hour, during which time twelve bucks came down from their camp to the lake and enjoyed a good drink. The troops were called to arms, but as soon as the Modocs heard our bugle sound, they broke back to the rocks and returned to their camp.

The Warm Springs Indians have been sent for and will probably get here tomorrow. They will then be employed against this party, and a picket will be placed near the lake to pick the Modocs off as they come to water.

We heard some shots this morning from the other side of the Lava Beds, and I have since learned that some Modocs fired upon a few of the Warm Springs Indians who were herding stock.

The cavalry that left on Friday morning[52] on a scout are expected back tomorrow.

Mr. Simpson, special artist of the *London Illustrated News,* arrived here today from San Francisco.[53] He proposes making some sketches of the Lava Beds. He also hopes to get a portrait of Captain Jack, but I am afraid he will be disappointed, as there is such a rush among the boys for the head of that chief [that] by the time the artist arrives on the spot, there will not be much to draw.

A report was brought in tonight that some of the teamsters were fired upon this evening near Klamath Lake. The country is dangerous to travel in without a strong escort, and even then it is far from safe, as the Modocs today laid in ambush for twenty-five soldiers. I have great faith, however, that the cavalry and the Warm Springs Indians will soon clear the "varmints" out.

CAMP ON LAVA BEDS, April 21—7:00 A.M.

The camp was not attacked last night, as we anticipated, but we experienced a light fall of snow, which will be received with thanks by thirsty Modocs in the rocks. The Modocs have been seen this morning in their camp, and directly the Warm Springs Indians arrive, they will be put on their trail.

Mr. Meacham will soon leave for his home in Oregon, and all our wounded are doing well.

New York *Herald,* April 26, 1873

CAMP ON THE LAVA BEDS, April 23, 1873

The cavalry have returned from their scouts and report that they have seen no Modoc signs. This news, however, was already anticipated, as we have seen twelve or fourteen Indians some two miles south of the inlet in the lake.

Colonel Gillem sent over orders to Donald McKay to hunt the Lava Beds and discover where the Indians were. Donald arrived in camp today and reports forty or fifty Modoc bucks and squaws in the black rocks, where we saw them moving the other day. Donald says that if anything, they have a stronger place than they had before.

Colonel Gillem proposes attacking them next Friday.[54] The Modocs are scattered through the country, as one of my couriers was fired on the other day between here and Klamath Lake, and Mr. Tickner saw two Modocs on Monday carrying bundles and traveling in a westerly direction.

Frank Riddle believes that some of the Indians who were not connected with the murders have left the rest of the band and will try to hide themselves among other Indians on some of the reservations. Colonel Gillem purposes a very quiet attack this time and will only advance his lines sufficiently to allow the mortars to operate.

Our cavalry are all dismounted, as the epizooty[55] is raging among the horses.

LAVA BEDS, April 24—11:00 A.M.

The Warm Springs Indians encamped last night near the lake, between us and Major Mason's command. We have not seen an Indian today, although a sharp lookout has been kept from the signal station.

Donald McKay is of the opinion they have left as, finding his party had taken up a position between them and water, they concluded another attack was meditated. The Warm Springs Indians are to hunt them up at night, in order to try and find where they have located. Two squaws captured by Captain Miller's battery were brought into camp yesterday. They state that two Yainax Modocs have deserted from the band. They were probably the two seen by Tickner traveling west, in the direction of the Yainax reservation.

The reinforcements from San Francisco of two batteries of the 4th Artillery will be here in about five days. The Indians are supposed to still have about thirty fighting bucks. Donald McKay is of the opinion they have gone in an easterly direction, towards Goose Lake. The epizooty is very bad, nearly every horse being sick.

—→·——◼◆◼——·←—

New York *Herald,* April 29, 1873

CAMP ON LAVA BEDS, April 26, 1873

Affairs in the Lava Beds are at present in a state of status quo, as we have not had a shot fired during the past three days. There appears to be a difference of opinion as to the location of the Modocs, but Donald McKay, who returned from a scout yesterday, believes they are still secreted in the caves and crevices of the Lava Beds, about four miles southeast of our present camp.

I am tolerably well satisfied that they will not stand together in a body and will have to be exterminated by ones and twos. There is a summer scout in prospective for the cavalry, and there will not be much security for the ranchers. These Modocs are now desperate, and they will rob, plunder, and murder indiscriminately. I understand that Col. Jefferson C. Davis, commanding the Department of the Columbia, Captain Sumner,[56] and Captain Lydecker of the engineers[57] are now on their way to this camp and will arrive about Tuesday next. Colonel Davis will assume command of the forces uniting in the Modoc expedition.

The wounded are doing remarkably well, and many will soon be able to resume duty.

A reconnaissance will be made of the ground where the Modocs are supposed to be hid. The party will comprise Company G, 12th Infantry, and Batteries A and K, 4th Artillery. They will be under the command of Captain Thomas, Battery A, 4th Artillery.[58]

The Modoc Indian War,
by One Who Was There

P. W. HAMONT[1]

Miscellaneous Manuscript 0289, Department of Special Collections, Stanford
University Libraries, Stanford, California[2]

Thirty-seven years is a good while back, but I can shut my eyes, and a panorama of that war, which is so indelibly stamped on my memory, will pass as a moving picture before me. Imagine the molten lava from an active volcano, fifteen miles wide, running down and across the plain into a lake. Then imagine, as the lava cools, an earthquake to tear up the lava and pile it in ridges with heaps fifty feet high in places, with frightful black and yawning figures in every direction, with one place at the lake where the lava was cooled suddenly by the water [and] piled 100 feet high with galleries, caves, and a big hollow cup in the center, which was known as Captain Jack's Stronghold, and you will have a sort of an idea of how the 120 square miles which compose the Lava Beds look.

This delightful spot was sparsely sprinkled with sagebrush and grease-wood, and also produced bears, coyotes, scorpions, innumerable rattlers, and millions of blue bottle flies. Except Tule Lake on the border, and a few small springs liable to go dry at any time, it was waterless.

After the battle of [January 17, 1873], the troops were withdrawn to Van Bremer's ranch, Colonel Wheaton was relieved, and Col. Alvan C. Gillem was assigned to the command. Reinforcements of four companies of the 4th U.S. Artillery were rushed to the front from San Francisco.[3] Active operations ceased, and a series of powwows followed. Our pious philanthropists way back east did not want the soldiers to kill the poor innocent Indians who might torture, burn, scalp, and kill the troops, and it would be all right; so nothing would do but they must have a peace commission, which they got.

Here is a case in point. When the Modocs were driven out of their stronghold, they caught a lot of plunder that they could not take with them, some of which the boys found and opened. In opening a cache just outside of the Stronghold, they uncovered the dead body of a bugler belonging to Troop F, 1st U.S. Cavalry, whom [the Modocs] captured in Wheaton's fight. The body was nude, its legs crossed and tied with a deer thong at the ankles, its hands tied at the wrists. The toes were cut off at the second joint, the scalp was torn from off the head, and finally his brains were dashed out by a jagged rock, making a three-cornered hole [and] raising the skull at least one half an inch, where the blow was struck that ended his torture. It was said that the squaws did this, and the bones were to be made into a necklace for some brave. Our pious friends thought that was all right, as that was what soldiers enlisted for.

On April 1, 1873, the whole command broke camp and moved to Tule Lake in the Lava Beds. Battery A, 4th Artillery, being divided into two sections, the first section under the command of Captain Thomas and Lieutenant Howe, took charge of four brass Coehorn mortars, which four men could carry. They used a twelve-pound shell. The second section, under command of Lieutenant Chapin, had two twelve-pound mountain howitzers, with Sgt. P. W. Hamont, Battalion 4th Artillery, as chief of section. The howitzers joined Major Mason's command on Lost River, [which] marched around Tule Lake and took up a position on the east side of the Lava Beds, on the shore of the lake, as Colonel Gillem and the peace commissioners did on the west side, with six miles of lava beds and Modoc Indians between the two forces.

The day before the council, Riddle, the interpreter, told General Canby that he was convinced the Indians meant treachery. It was a painful dilemma. On the one hand, General Canby still hoped and believed that he might persuade the Indians to go peaceably and felt that he ought to exhaust every hope of reconciliation. On the other hand, he knew that they were never to be trusted where treachery seemed profitable, and he was satisfied that Riddle was no alarmist. So he took a characteristic decision in deciding that it was his duty to go and take all the risks. The venerable preacher, Mr. Thomas, was equally aware of the danger and equally brave, and these soldiers of peace and righteousness went calmly and fearlessly to the hideous death trap.

When the Indian representatives assembled, Canby must have felt instinctively the hopelessness of his mission. No element of treachery and bloodshed was missing. There was cunning Schonchin, the secret and unceasing advocate of war; Boston Charley, who had been deputed to quiet Riddle's suspicions by protesting his love for all white men; Hooker Jim, a dark, scowling ruffian who had led the raid on the settlements and murdered men, women, and children; Shacknasty Jim, looking like an unevolved ape; and Black Jim, another of the murderers who had scalp locks, the hair on some of them being two feet long and silky in texture.

Unfortunately, I have lost the memorandum I made of the proceedings in the council tent just previous to the murder of the commissioners, as given by Meacham, who escaped. As my memory serves me, it was about this way: General Canby opened the council, telling the Indians how the Great Father in Washington loved them and had sent as commissioners the Rev. Mr. Thomas, Mr. Meacham, and himself to treat with them, explaining what a good, and how much better, a reservation was allotted to them than the one they were being expelled from; all of which the Indians did not believe, and wanted to know why the soldiers were on both sides of them. [They asked] a lot of questions, which General Canby answered to the best of his ability, even going so far as to offer them another reservation for them to choose from. The Reverend Thomas followed Canby, talking to the Modocs as only a preacher can who has the love of God in his heart and believes the Indians are like Cooper portrays them in his novels—a noble red man who is cheated, wronged, and defrauded by the white man, and endorsing what General Canby had already told them.

Schonchin then took the floor and delivered an oration portraying his notion [of] the wrongs done them in the past and getting down to the present, actually frothing at the mouth. In the meantime, two bucks had slipped up to the tent with their arms full of loaded rifles. (I believe they got a life sentence on Alcatraz Island in San Francisco Bay for their part in the massacre.)[4] When the bucks arrived at the tent with the rifles, they gave a signal. Captain Jack turned to General Canby, shouting, "It is time," and drawing a pistol from under his clothes, fired point-blank at the general, killing him on the spot. Schonchin is said to have slain the Reverend Thomas.[5] In the melee, Meacham was knocked down and left for dead. Riddle ran for his life, with two Indians after him. At the first sign of treachery, Dyar broke for camp, pursued for a short distance by some of the Indians, who soon returned to the tent to help finish the deviltry there.

The camp was alarmed, and the men pushing to the front as Dyar passed by, shouting, "They are all killed but me." The Modocs tried to get Meacham's scalp but did not have time, as Riddle's squaw, who was outside the tent, shouted, "The soldiers are coming." They ran back to their lines, taking General Canby's uniform coat with its gold epaulets and his field glasses with them. When the troops rushed the council tent, they found Canby and Thomas both dead and Meacham, who had been clubbed with the butt of a rifle, covered with blood and frightfully disfigured.[6] He eventually recovered.

It is probable that Captain Jack and Schonchin, fearing that the peace sentiment might prevail, planned the massacre so as to close all doors to reconciliation. At any rate, the Modoc War was now on in earnest. General Canby's treacherous taking off horrified the country and wakened up the authorities to the fact that they had a serious war on their hands. Every available man in the department was hurried forward; even the light battery at San Francisco was sent, equipped as cavalry.

What was more important than fresh troops were [the Warm Springs] Indians, under their chief, Donald McKay, [who] joined Major Mason's command. They were near neighbors of the Modocs and yet entirely different. The Modocs were foot Indians, only using their ponies to carry their ammunition, traps, and families, never to fight from. The Warm Springs were mounted fighters. Their ponies were models for that country—hardy, quick, and surefooted. The Warm Springs were not as good shots as the Modocs, and not much to fight on foot, but put him astride his pony and he is a born fighter.

Their chief, Donald McKay, was a handsome and intelligent half-breed, his father being a Hudson Bay trader. He wrote and spoke English well. He was captain, first sergeant, company clerk, and everything else, for they were armed, equipped, mustered, and paid like regular soldiers. Their muster rolls were queer looking, with their long names made up of a great many short syllables. The idea of calling such a roll made me shiver, though Donald probably did it.

After General Canby's assassination, the Indians took a position in the lava near Tule Lake. Their chief defense was a precipitous pile of rocks in the edge of the lake, known as Jack's Stronghold. This naturally strong place they had fortified so ingeniously that an army engineer who went over the place after the evacuation declared that it would have been creditable to any engineers on earth. A path barely wide enough for one man would go up the almost perpendicular slope in short and steep zigzags, each one entirely commanded by the one above it. In several places there were natural galleries in the rocks by which the Indians could, after holding the zigzag to the last moment, be at the next one long before the assailants. At the top was a deep, circular pit or small crater, just large enough to hold all their ammunition, stores, and families safe from a direct fire. Imagine men toiling in single file up this steep slope, exposed at every step to the well-aimed fire of men entirely hidden and protected. In fact, 500 men could not have taken it by assault. There was but one thing to do: drive them into it; surround it, which was not hard, for it did not cover much ground, being closed on one side by the lake, and we had by this time between five and six hundred men; then fortifying our lines in the lava, wait patiently, and starve them out.

The attack was directed from two sides, Maj. John Green, 1st Cavalry, commanding the west side, and Major Mason, 21st Infantry, the east side. The two commands on the night of April 14 moved as close to the Modocs as possible under cover of darkness, displayed their men in line of battle north and south, each line with one flank resting on the lake, and the Modocs between them in their stronghold, one mile from Mason's command and two and a half from Green's. The idea [was] to close in the outer flanks as they advanced, and finally to form a complete semicircle around the Stronghold. This, as will be seen, had the inevitable disadvantage of combined movements, which in this instance was aggravated by the want of a competent head. Colonel Gillem's health and mind had so far given way that he seemed incapable of any vigorous or sustained effort.

For three days—April 15, 16, and 17—the battle raged, gaining some ground every day and driving them closer to the Stronghold, but with considerable loss at every charge; as Green's men had more open country, cut up with fissures and ravines, his loss was heaviest. If, in one of their rushes, they ran up against a fissure, they would have to flank the same in order to advance. In so doing, if two men got together, one or both were sure to be hit. Mason's line was closer to the Stronghold, but he had to contend with piles of rock, holes in the lava, and also a bluff some sixty-odd feet high, with Indian sharpshooters under cover on the top, before they could arrive within striking distance of the Stronghold, which was some 800 yards beyond the bluff, with fissures, pits, piles of rocks, and Indian sharpshooters between.

The troops would advance against the nearest ridge, seeing no enemy but keenly conscious that they were there from the shower of bullets that greeted them as they toiled and clambered over the rugged masses, avoiding the deep pits, like miniature craters of endless volcanoes. The Modocs, perfectly safe in their rocky recesses from a fire wild and badly aimed, as all advancing fire must be, would coolly wait until the troops got within fifteen or twenty yards of the crest. Then the fire would cease, and as the soldiers reached the top, they might perhaps catch a glimpse of a lean brown figure running, as men stripped to moccasins and belts, and as active as cats, can run. Of course, it would be a miracle if shots fired by men panting and blowing from such a rush hit such a target. The affair was over—our men had taken a lava ridge at a cost of several lives.

When night came and the firing ceased, our men would advance their lines under cover of darkness as near the enemy as possible, so that at least that ground would not have to be fought over in the morning. As soon as all got quiet, those Modocs who could speak English would get out on some high point and begin blackguarding the soldiers, taunting and defying them, which would be returned by some of the troops in kind—which would have been amusing had we not known that hell would break loose in the morning. The next day would be largely a repetition of the first, gradually driving the Indians to their stronghold and trying to connect the two wings. But [that failed] for some reason, probably the want of a leader able to take in the whole field, Colonel Gillem being back at the main camp with something the matter— opinions differ as to what. He got the credit for driving the Modocs out of their stronghold and, after he sent Captain Thomas and his men to their death, was relieved by Colonel Davis. At any rate, Green was forever trying to close with Mason and never effecting it.[7]

Finally, when the two forces were almost in touch, as Mason had worked his lines up to the foot of the bluff, and after shelling the Modocs from cover, [Mason] rushed and captured it. [That] placed him on the same plateau as Green and about 800 yards from the Stronghold, with all of its approaches fortified with rock walls, which a rifle ball would not faze, but the howitzers sent them flying in every direction.

The two wings were now in plain sight of each other and ought to [have] come together.[8] It appears a stupid blunder of a bugler bringing orders caused Green to close to his left instead of his right, thus widening the gap. Through this gap the Warm Springs, who formed Mason's left wing, let Captain Jack and his whole tribe (Green taking them for Warm Springs) slip out of their stronghold and the trap set for them, making their escape into the Lava Beds. Thus, through someone's blunder, the Modocs were still at large, with a barbarous war in full swing, besides their fear of being surrounded.

Captain Thomas's four little brass Coehorn mortars, which four men could have carried, had helped to drive them out. The circular pit in the Stronghold was no protection against vertical fire, and whenever night came, Captain Thomas got busy and kept the Indians not only awake, but guessing where the next shell would drop.

On the night of the sixteenth, the Coehorns got busy. One of the first shells dropped by chance in the crater, where the Indians were holding a powwow, where it burst and killed and wounded several. [That] had a tendency to make them watch and keep cover. Bogus Charley, after the surrender, gave that as the chief reason for evacuating. During the three days' fighting, the Indians' fire was so rapid, and covered so large a front, that many of the officers engaged were satisfied the original sixty-odd Modocs had been joined by the Klamath and the Pitt River Indians, as many of them were missing from agencies.

For some days after their flight from the Stronghold, the whereabouts of the Indians was uncertain, though it was thought that they were in the neighborhood of a sand butte about 400 feet high, which decidedly overtopped all the surrounding ridges, being about five miles from Colonel Gillem's camp on Tule Lake. Colonel Gillem ordered a reconnaissance to ascertain their position. Of all the mistakes of this unlucky war, this was the worst, as it was to be the most costly. In civilized war, in an ordinary country, a small party can often get valuable information with little risk, for such expeditions are generally mounted, or if infantry is used, they are lightly equipped for rapid marches. But in this labyrinth of lava, it was certain that no Indians would be seen until they wanted to be seen. Anyone who knows the A, B, C of Indian war knows that they never attack unless they think the chances are greatly in their favor.

As over 400 men had been held in check by these same Indians for two days, what insanity to send fifty-nine men and six officers against them when it was certain that every step they took would be watched. If Gillem only wanted information, half a dozen Warm Springs would [have] got it with little trouble or risk. Fifty-nine men of Batteries A and K, 4th Artillery, and Companies E and G, 12th U.S. Infantry,[9] were detailed to this service. At about 8:00 A.M. on April 26, the unlucky expedition marched out. It was commanded by Capt. Evan Thomas, a young officer who had done gallant service during the Civil War but who had never, until this campaign, seen a hostile Indian.

They started with the advance guard, commanded by Lieutenant Cranston,[10] deployed as skirmishers. The expedition was headed for the sand butte, as the Indians were supposed to be somewhere in that vicinity. After marching about four miles, they struck a rift in the lava, which had the appearance of a dry riverbed from five to twenty yards wide in places, covered with sand that had washed down from the butte, on which a lot of sagebrush had grown. The main body of the expedition marched along this rift. In the meantime, the advance guard's front was so small that they did not cover the most elevated ridges on the right and left of the column, and as they groped and stumbled over the rugged masses, and saw and heard nothing but the endless gray-green of the sagebrush and the whirr of an occasional rattler, they became confident and careless. When the column struck the sand rift, the advance guard soon assumed the shape of a horseshoe, with the bow in front and the calks extending down each side of the column in the form of flankers. Huddled together in front, they were making slow progress, moving from ridge to ridge,

Capt. Evan Thomas. ILLUSTRATED LONDON NEWS, 1873.

and it was lonely tramping along with a lava ridge between you and the fellow next to you.

At 11:50 A.M. the column arrived at the foot of the sand butte and halted for dinner; many a poor fellow never finished that meal in this world. The advance guard was pushed to the front a little to the left. Flankers were thrown out on both flanks in the lava ridges, but unfortunately the formation of the ground at that place was commanded by higher ridges on both flanks, and the sand butte dominated over all with a high ridge butting off from the west side. Captain Thomas and Lieutenant Howe[11] started up the sand butte to the right of the advance guard in order to signal the main camp and see if they could locate the Modoc camp. The troops were seated in groups on the ground, partaking the noonday meal, when like a clap of thunder from a clear sky, three rifle shots rang out, fired from the high ridge on the right, and one poor fellow sprang to his feet crying, "Oh, my God," and fell at full length on his back. Pandemonium now broke loose. Showers of bullets came among the troops from every high ridge; discipline was cast to the wind. The troops on the flanks came rushing in on the main body. Captain Thomas and Lieutenant Howe came back on the run and did their best to rally the men. But deadly fear seemed to possess them, some getting down behind sagebrush, as if that would turn a bullet.

Finally the most of the main body fell back about 200 yards, where the rift of sand was about thirty yards wide and thickly covered with sagebrush, which seemed a little better adapted for defense. In the meantime, the Indians were closing in and occupying the ridges vacated by the flankers. The Indian fire was now continuous from every ridge and elevated point, and the excitement became terrible. Men rushed wildly for cover in every direction, but they were in low ground, and the only cover available was the sagebrush.

There was one thing that might have saved them, even after the panic began. If they had made a rush for the top of the sand butte, the chance of being hit would be less than if they had remained behind the sagebrush. With the bayonet which they all carried, ten minutes of work would have thrown up a breastwork of sand, behind which they could stand off the whole Modoc nation.

Lt. Tom Wright, of Company E, with some of his men, attempted to flank the ridge. That was the last seen of him alive. He was afterward found dead, with his men dead around him, in a hollow at the foot of the ridge. Lieutenant Cranston and his men were reported missing. Their bodies were found two weeks later, stripped and mutilated behind the little rock breastworks they had piled up, the Indians crawling up and shooting them from behind.

All direction had now ceased. The survivors took what cover they could get and fought with heart sickening alternations of despair and hope. At times the Indians approached so near that they could hear them talking. Then the firing ceased entirely for a while, which gave the few left time to dig deeper into the sand, which, with the sagebrush, gave considerable protection. At the beginning of the fight, several of the men [became] demoralized [and] struck out for the main camp. Among them were a tall slim soldier and a Dutch bugler of Battery A. I mention those two, as they were the only ones that got to camp safe, and how that soldier could run! He kept straight down the crevice of sand and seemed to strike the ground about every ten feet, with the whiz of Modoc bullets stimulating him to greater efforts, so that he fairly flew. He arrived at camp about 2:30 P.M., slightly wounded, and reported all killed or being killed. This being the first news Colonel Gillem received from the expedition, [he] did not order out a relief column until late that evening.

As for the bugler, the Modocs made it so hot for him that he left the sand and struck the Lava Beds, and finally ran into a party of Warm Springs, who thought to help the troops by making believe help was near, [and] ordered the bugler to sound the assembly. This was about 4:00 P.M. The troops, hearing the bugle, thought they were saved, but could not locate the spot amid the wilderness of lava where the sound came from. The only result was to hasten their fate, as the Modocs resolved to make short work of it and advanced to close quarters, throwing rocks among the sagebrush where the survivors crouched and shooting wherever the bushes stirred, and sometimes shooting into a dead body to make sure, as some of the dead had two or more bullets shot into them.

About this time, Captain Thomas was wounded in an artery and rapidly bled to death, firing his carbine until his strength failed, then drawing his revolver and emptying that in the face of his foes as he passed to the Great Beyond. Thus died a true gentleman and a brave man, sacrificed, he and his men, through incompetence, if nothing worse. And the brave Lieutenant Howe, no one knew when he was killed, but he was found lying on his elbows and knees holding his loaded carbine at a ready shot, paralyzed in that position by a bullet through the head, with his brains lying on the ground. Lieutenant Harris [was] badly wounded and Dr. Semig shot in the shoulder and the leg, which was afterwards amputated. Dark came at last, which saved the remnants, as two hours more of daylight and the Indians would have got the last man. With the darkness, the Indians ceased firing.

During the night, a strong force of cavalry arrived and rescued the few survivors. Out of fifty-nine men and six officers, forty-two men were killed or wounded, and four officers killed and two wounded.[12] That night the dead were buried under sagebrush loaded with rock. The wounded, with the dead officers, were carried to camp in blankets, and the one stretcher the doctor brought out for someone else, he came back in himself. The wounded were not much trouble, as the Modocs shot most of them a second time to make sure of them. Lieutenant Cranston and his men were not found until an expedition was sent out to ascertain their fate and bring in the dead for burial. When the expedition arrived at the battleground, they found the Indians had taken the dead from under the sagebrush, stripped the clothes from their bodies, and mutilated some of them in a most horrible manner.[13] Most of the Indians now had soldiers' clothes, arms, and ammunition, captured first and last from Uncle Sam's troops. They got one box of 1,000 rounds in the Thomas fight that never had been opened.

April 29 brought the last reinforcements, consisting of Hasbrouck's Light Battery B, acting as cavalry, and Mendenhall's Battery M, 4th U.S. Artillery, from San Francisco. Soon after, Colonel Gillem was relieved by Col. Jefferson C. Davis, who combined [the] coolness of an old frontier man with the dash of a cavalry leader. Dry weather was our best ally. We had discovered a trail leading to the lake, by which they packed water every night. This trail was guarded, and their supply cut off. The few small springs in the Lava Beds had dried up, and the want of water drove them out. But for that, they could have kept up this running fight over the 120 square miles of lava until our entire force had been used up.

Suspecting that they would try to escape, Colonel Davis sent Captain Hasbrouck with Light Battery B, 4th Artillery; Troops [B and] G, 1st Cavalry; and the Warm Springs Indians to Dry Lake on the east edge of the Lava Beds to watch that side. Just before daylight on May 10, Captain Jack's whole band, on their way out, came upon the camp of the cavalry. They could easily have avoided the troops, but the apparent helplessness of the sleeping command and the chance of getting horses and plunder was too strong a temptation. They took possession of a line of bluffs about 400 yards from the camp without being seen by the pickets and stampeded the horses, [which] galloped wildly through the camp.

The men were awakened by a shower of bullets. For a few minutes it looked like a repetition of the Thomas disaster. The men seemed reluctant to get up in that deadly fire, but a tall corporal of Battery B sprang to his feet, calling out, "Come on boys, we must charge them."[14] The example was contagious; the men were up, deployed, and commenced advancing. At the first shot, the Warm Springs had leapt to their feet [and] caught their ponies, which they had kept near them instead of herding them with the cavalry horses. As fast as each buck bridled his pony, he threw himself on and pushed at a smart gallop for either flank of the rapidly forming line. Hasbrouck led the center, pistol in hand, Captain Jackson the right, and Lieutenants Kyle and Moss the left. Right up the bluff went the charging and cheering line, the Warm Springs circling on the flanks like whooping vultures.

The position was carried with moderate losses, [and] the Modocs driven back four miles into the Lava Beds. But for the want of food and water, the war would have ended that day. As it was, their spirit was broken, and the fact was established that on any decent ground, these much-dreaded Indians would not stand a chance. Among the killed was the brave corporal who first told his comrades they must charge. The Warm Springs had one man wounded[15] but dragged with a lariat into camp a dead Modoc known as Ellen's Man.[16] Major Mason, in the meantime, had marched the entire infantry and artillery command across the Lava Beds in the direction of Dry Lake, leaving the artillery [pieces] on a peninsula in Tule Lake the night before the two forces united.

The Modocs again managed to slip out, owing to Mason's excess of caution. They were followed until their trail branched, showing that a portion of them were heading for Steen's Mountains, which were even more inaccessible than the Lava Beds. Captain Hasbrouck was sent to head them off.[17]

This was the [Hot Creek] band headed by Hooker Jim, and who had been at the time of the conference inclined to peace and had gone on the warpath reluctantly. They were dissatisfied with Captain Jack, claiming that he made them do the lion's share of the watching and fighting, and saved his own men. Ellen's Man [George] belonged to the [band], and his taking off by the Warm Springs at the fight at the bluff caused a row between the two branches of the Modocs. The [Hot Creeks] pulled off, with Hasbrouck after them, who struck them just outside the Lava Beds, and after a running fight, they sent in two squaws to ask for terms.

About sundown on May 25, the artillery and infantry being on the march, Colonel Davis was seen approaching with several soldiers, two citizens, and four Indians, who wore soldiers' uniforms and each had a breech-loading rifle lying across the pommel of his saddle with cartridge box full of government cartridges, who appeared to be strangers. One soldier said, "They don't look like Warm Springs." Another said, "I believe they are Modocs." One of the survivors of the Thomas massacre shouted, "My God, that is Hooker Jim!" There was no mistake in the savage, scowling face. The next one recognized was Bogus Charley, who looked like a good-natured, bright mulatto. The third was Steamboat Frank, and the fourth, Shacknasty Jim. Every one of them helped murder innocent women and children,[18] some of them helped murder General Canby and Preacher Thomas, and all were at the Thomas massacre. Still, Colonel Davis, without even a pistol, had ridden sixteen miles through a desolate country with five white men, three of them unarmed, with those bloodstained traitors. It looked like utter foolishness but was the result of a cool calculation of chances and thorough knowledge of Indians. Learning through Hasbrouck that some of the worst Indians [Hot Creeks] were dissatisfied and wanted terms, he got them word through the squaws, the invariable flag of truce of Indian war, that he would guarantee the life of any Indian who would assist in Captain Jack's capture.

The men were much excited, and the officers had to exert their authority to restrain them until they could explain how entirely Colonel Davis's plans depended on exciting no alarm or distrust in the minds of the Indians. The soldiers were particularly bitter against Hooker Jim as the murderer of inoffensive settlers, and as a precaution against resistance, Colonel Davis placed him in a tent within six feet of his own. The result vindicated his pluck and judgment. These Indians kept faith with him and hunted their late companions with the vindictiveness of lifetime enemies. They rounded up and helped capture all of Jack's crowd.

The two branches of Captain Jack's Modocs were rounded up into two camps on the peninsula in the lake, with the artillery on the point farthest from the mainland and the infantry next to it. When the irons were put on, at first Jack's immediate family painted half of their faces black and kept up a moaning and groaning all night, keeping the irons hid with their rags, as six months in the Lava Beds had about wore out the shape of clothes. They were a hard-looking crowd, hardly human, as toward the last they could not get water to wash their bodies, and being smoked, squatting around their fires of sagebrush and cow chips, they presented an appearance that could only be indescribable.

I remember the names of only two of the squaws, as they seemed to have charge of the younger. The Indians were kept under close guard. The squaws only were allowed to go to the lake for water, there being a line of sentinels across the peninsula from water to water on both sides of the Indians; also, guards among them to keep them safe, as we already had all the fighting we wanted. The two boss squaws were Princess Mary and One-Eyed Dixie, who saw that the balance cut the wood and did all the work, the bucks doing nothing. One-Eyed Dixie was an old hag, and Princess Mary was a regal looking Indian of about twenty-five or thirty years. Some of the women were dark as Negroes, others like bright mulattoes, with two girls almost white. Along about June 20 the whole band was moved to Fort Klamath. Thus ended the Modoc War.

The Modoc Peace Commission Massacre

OLIVER C. APPLEGATE[1]

Winners of the West 3, no. 2 (January 1926): 7

During the Modoc War of 1872 and 1873, a truce was declared by the authorities at Washington, and a commission was sent to the headquarters of the army in the lava country south of Tule Lake in northern California. After a month or so had been consumed in communications with the hostile Modocs, mainly through Indian messengers, it was arranged for the commissioners to meet the hostile chief and four of his principal men in the Lava Beds, between the military camp and the Indian stronghold among the rocks, distant from the army camp three-fourths of a mile.

The commission then consisted of Mr. A. B. Meacham, formerly superintendent of Indian affairs in Oregon, chairman of the commission; Brig. Gen. E. R. S. Canby, U.S. Army, department commander; Rev. Eleazar Thomas, a Methodist minister of California; and [the] Honorable Leroy S. Dyar, U.S. Indian agent of Klamath agency, Oregon. The interpreters were Toby Riddle (since known as Winema), a Modoc Indian woman, a second cousin to Captain Jack, the hostile chief, and her husband, Frank Riddle, a Kentuckian.

On the part of the Modocs, Captain Jack, chief of the hostile Modocs, a signer of the great treaty of 1864 as Kientpoos; Schonchin John, subchief of that band, brother of Old Schonchin, chief of the friendly Modocs then at Camp Yainax on the Klamath reservation; Black Jim, half-brother of Captain Jack; Boston Charley and Hooker Jim, headmen of the band. It is true that there were other warriors at hand when the attack was made on the commissioners, whose presence was not authorized.

Capt. O. C. Applegate, officer in charge of the Modocs, Paiutes, and Klamaths at Camp Yainax on the Indian reservation, was under detail to assist the commission and, at the request of General Canby, brought to the headquarters of the commission at Colonel Gillem's camp in the Lava Beds the loyal old Chief Schonchin from Yainax to assist the commission in negotiations, or more particularly, to observe while with them the conduct and appearance of the hostiles to determine whether or not they were acting in good faith.

Oliver C. Applegate. CYRUS T. BRADY. *NORTHWESTERN FIGHTS AND FIGHTERS.*

Meetings were held on successive days at the agreed place in the Lava Beds, Schonchin being present with the commission on two occasions. Before the third meeting, word was received from Camp Yainax that some of Captain Jack's emissaries were there, probably for the purpose of influencing the old chief's Modocs to join the hostiles.

The old chief, being greatly disturbed by the news, asked General Canby to return him at once under conduct of Captain Applegate to Yainax to prevent dissatisfaction among his people. This the general agreed to. The evening before departure, with the few Modocs who had accompanied him from Yainax, Captain Applegate conferred with Mr. Meacham and Mr. Dyar of the commission, and they both, being experienced men with Indians, assured Captain Applegate that Captain Jack's party was coming every day to the council armed and in a morose temper, and they felt that they were risking their lives at every meeting at a place so remote from the camp of the army and in a rugged terrain where hostile warriors could be easily concealed. Neither General Canby nor Reverend Thomas seemed fearful of danger and were bent on continued efforts for peace, and Mr. Meacham and Mr. Dyar were determined to take chances with them at any risk.

Captain [Oliver C.] Applegate took from his pocket a little two-barreled derringer and gave it to Mr. Dyar, saying, "Put this in your pocket with these cartridges. In some possible emergency, it may help you." Mr. Meacham already had a little pocket pistol, but neither General Canby nor Reverend Thomas would consent to carry arms, even such innocent weapons as these little pocket pistols.

The next morning, before Captain [Oliver C.] Applegate started to Camp Yainax with his party, he, with the old chief and Little John, his Klamath interpreter, went into the peace commission tent at military headquarters to say good-bye to the commissioners, who were all seated around a table. Mr. Meacham, evidently wishing confirmation of his own views, said to Captain Applegate, "Oliver, can you give us any hope?" The answer was not encouraging. It was that the commissioners were in great danger, dependent as they were upon the caprice of Indians already proven treacherous and having an evident advantage.

The meeting with Captain Jack and his cabinet passed that day without unusual incident, but Winema, who was sent with a message to Captain Jack after he had returned to his stronghold, was secretly intercepted on her return by Faithful Williams, one of Jack's men, an old-time friend of hers, with the statement that the Modocs had already decided to kill the commissioners, and if they should go to the place of the meeting that day, it would certainly be their death. This dread news she immediately communicated to the commissioners, and she and her husband pled with them vehemently not to go.

The morning of that fatal day, April 11, 1873, General Canby and Reverend Thomas being still unconvinced, the entire party went as before, and with them Bogus Charley, one of Jack's men who had remained overnight in the military camp with the soldiers, professing warm friendship.

The council opened peacefully as usual, General Canby distributing cigars among the party and expressing his hopes for peace. As the council proceeded, however, signs of an approaching crisis appeared, and finally Kientpoos, springing up and drawing his pistol, shouted, "Otwe Katuck (Now it ends)," and shot General Canby in the face at a distance of probably not over eight feet. The attack on all the commissioners began at once, each Modoc knowing beforehand who his victim was to be. Other warriors appeared, armed, from the surrounding rocks. General Canby and Dr. Thomas were soon killed and their clothes stripped from them. Mr. Meacham, bleeding from several wounds, was prostrate and unconscious among the rocks.

Mr. Riddle succeeded in escaping to a rugged lava field near the lakeshore, and Mr. Dyar ran towards the military camp through the rocks, pursued by Hooker Jim, who fired at his intended victim as he ran. Mr. Dyar expected momentarily to be killed but marvelously escaped being shot by one of the best marksmen in the hostile band. At a distance of probably a hundred yards from the place of attack, he turned toward his pursuer, menacing his foe with the derringer but not firing, as the books have it, for it would have been impossible with such a weapon to have harmed his foe at a distance of fifty yards. The menace was effectual, and Jim threw himself on the ground to escape a possible shot, while Mr. Dyar gained distance enough to meet the relief party of soldiers from Colonel Gillem's camp, who had been notified from the signal station on the cliffs above the camp of the attack on the commissioners.

Winema remained on the ground where the murderous attack occurred, was once knocked down by an Indian gun, and prevented one Indian from shooting Mr. Meacham through the head and another from scalping him while he was yet unconscious. At last she cried out in the Modoc tongue, "Sojers capcopila (Soldiers are coming)," and the Modocs stopped the bloody work and soon disappeared inside the rugged fastness of the Lava Beds.

The noble Canby, famous as a major general in the War of the Rebellion, and Reverend Thomas, peace loving divine as he was, lay prone and naked among the rocks, and Alfred B. Meacham, enthusiastic and almost fanatical friend of the red man, lay bleeding where he had risked his life rather than desert his companions, who could not realize the danger with him. He slowly recovered from the awful ordeal and lived for several years, and until his death remained a friend to the Indian.

Mr. Dyar's escape was marvelous, for both Black Jim and Hooker Jim had been selected to kill him, but their bullets went wild, and as he claimed the menace with the little pistol had saved his life, Captain Applegate made him a present of it.

After more than fifty years, when Mr. Dyar finally passed away, his daughter, Miss Helen Dyar of Ontario, California, sent the little pistol by mail to Captain Applegate at Klamath Falls, Oregon. It is only a month ago that he received it, and you may be sure that he prizes it as one of his most interesting souvenirs of the tragic drama of the Modoc War.

The Twelfth U.S. Infantry
in the Lava Beds

GEORGE W. KINGSBURY[1]

Army and Navy Journal 10, no. 4 (June 14, 1873): 697

We have received the following letter, dated camp at Fairchild's ranch, California, May 25, 1873:

In your issue of May 10, I have read with pain and surprise an extract from a dispatch in the [New York] *Herald* dated Lava Beds, May 1, 1873, in which the conduct of Company E, 12th U.S. Infantry, is severely criticized for its part in the action of April 26. It says, "The great loss of life on the twenty-sixth is attributed to the giving way of Company E, 12th U.S. Infantry, and some few of the artillery, who were ordered to fall back and hold a bluff in the rear of the troops to cover their retreat." It further says, "If these orders had been executed, there would have been comparatively slight loss, but the men went straight to camp, etc." As the successor of the late lamented Lieutenant Wright, and in justice to the brave men of his command, I pronounce the above to be a most heartless and unjust statement, without a particle of truth to justify the assertion. What are the facts? These: During the advance and at the time of the attack, Company E, under command of Lieutenant Wright, was deployed as skirmishers[2] while the artillery marched in column. Arriving at the sand hill, a halt was ordered, the skirmish line being held intact while the artillery rested, after which an advance was ordered. Almost immediately the Indians opened fire. Lieutenant Wright, seeing and comprehending the situation at a glance, immediately ordered the set of fours on the left of his skirmish line, consisting of three men of Company E and one man of the artillery, to advance, "not to retreat," and hold a bluff on the left and front of the skirmish line, perhaps fifty yards in advance of it.

The three men of Company E immediately proceeded to obey his order, but the man of the artillery failed to obey it. This poor fellow, however, nobly retrieved any dereliction of duty at that time by subsequently surrendering his life on the field of battle. The three men ordered forward had approached the bluff indicated to within about thirty yards, when they were fired upon from the very point they were sent to hold, proving that the Indians held that position from the first. These men, McCann, Cavin, and Waga, returning the fire of

274

The last stand of Captain Thomas and his command.
CYRUS T. BRADY. *NORTHWESTERN FIGHTS AND FIGHTERS.*

the Indians, did not "return to camp," as stated in the dispatch above noted, but retreated to and joined their company and Lieutenant Wright.

It is a notorious fact that the first man in camp was an artilleryman, he having returned without firing a shot; his piece, being inspected, was found to be perfectly clean. Lieutenant Wright was an old Indian fighter—his whole life had been spent on the frontier. A braver officer never lived. His men had the utmost confidence in his ability to command them. This is proved from the promptness with which his men obeyed his every command, retreating in good order to the ridge of rocks in their rear, fighting as only true and brave soldiers can fight, losing a comrade here and there, until they succeeded in reaching the bluff where their idolized commander, who had already received four wounds, was stricken down by a ball passing through the heart.[3]

Here is the official report of the men engaged, with a list of the killed and wounded: Battery A, 4th Artillery, had three officers and eighteen men in the fight; loss, three officers and eight men killed, and five men wounded. Battery K, 4th Artillery, had one officer and eighteen men in the fight; loss, four men and one officer [killed], and five men wounded. Lieutenant Harris[4] of this battery has since died. Company E, 12th U.S. Infantry, had one officer and twenty-three men in the fight; loss, one officer and seven men killed, and six wounded. Do these figures show that the men of Company E, 12th U.S. Infantry, with seven-twelfths of their number either killed or wounded, left the field in disgrace and "went straight to the camp?"

"Gosh Dash It, Let's Charge": A Story of the Modoc War

CHARLES B. HARDIN[1]

Winners of the West 10, no. 6 (May 1933): 4

The Modocs had been driven out of their stronghold on Tule Lake, California, on April 17, 1873, and it was believed that they had established another stronghold somewhere towards the southern end of the Lava Beds. On April 26 Capt. Evan Thomas, 4th Artillery, with his Battery A serving as infantry, Company E, 12th Infantry,[2] and about twenty Warm Springs Indian scouts, had been sent out from Gillem's camp, our field headquarters, to locate this new stronghold and had met with disaster, losing all of the five officers killed or mortally wounded, about half of the sixty-five killed, and most of the remainder of the command wounded before relief could reach them. Still the new stronghold had not been located.

On May 9 a mounted command consisting of Light Battery B, 4th Artillery, serving as cavalry, Troops B and G, 1st Cavalry, and a part of Donald McKay's troop of Warm Springs Indian scouts, all under command of Capt. Henry Hasbrouck, 4th Artillery, was sent out from Boyle's Camp,[3] on the east side of Tule Lake, to scout around the Lava Beds. Just what was expected of this mounted command, I have never known.[4] Certainly we could have done nothing with our horses in the Lava Beds, where the Indians were located.

Upon arriving at Sorass, or Dry, Lake, about twelve miles south of Boyle's camp, Troops B, G, and perhaps ten of the Indian scouts bivouacked for the night. Battery B, under command of its first lieutenant, proceeded about two miles further south, to bivouac in the edge of a pine forest.[5] Captain Hasbrouck remained with us at Sorass Lake.

Our horses and pack mules were turned loose to graze under a herd guard, this herd guard also serving as camp guard for the night. In fact, there was no camp guard, as the herders had to remain with the herd.[6] It appears that all arrangements for the camp were made under the supposition that the Modocs would not come to us, but would wait quietly for us to go to them. There was no order or formation to this camp. Each man made his own selection of the spot where he would make his bed, consisting of his saddle blanket, folded for use as a mattress, one blanket for covering, and a pillow made with saddle and folded

The Herd guard. RUFUS F. ZOGBAUM. *HORSE, FOOT, AND DRAGOON.*

overcoat. We were well scattered. The officers formed a group of their own about sixty yards from their men, and the packers formed another group nearby.

We slept peacefully, without either security or information, until the sounding of first call for reveille. This call, of course, awakened all hands, but did not get them up. The men just remained on the ground, stretching, swearing at that "damned windjammer," and suggesting various methods for his torture. No necessity for getting up until time for assembly. Suddenly a single rifle shot was heard. Some one shouted, "There goes another thumb." This referred to the fact that previously, during the war, two of our men had shot off their thumbs, hoping thereby to escape further violent action with the Modocs. We all thought that this was an accidental shot fired by a member of the herd guard.

But we had little time for speculation before we received a heavy volley, fired from the semicircle of lava hummocks on the north and west sides of our camp and distant about one hundred yards.[7] This volley, accompanied by the unmusical yells of the Modocs, was much more effective than had been the efforts of the trumpeter. We became very much alive and full of action. But this action was poorly directed, as it consisted only of men bobbing about from place to place, vainly seeking better shelter than was afforded by their saddles, with some firing of carbines at nothing. Meanwhile, the Modocs were pouring in a hot fire, sending showers of gravel over us and adding considerably to our celerity of action. The situation was becoming serious. The men were milling like frightened animals. It began to look like the prelude of a stampede. No command had come from our officers, who had been delayed by their having to pull on their boots and cover the distance separating them from us.

Then, suddenly, all was changed. Those nearest to him heard our quartermaster sergeant, Thomas Kelley of Troop G, shout, "Gosh dash it, let's charge."[8] Instantly every man who heard Kelley seemed to realize that this was just what should be done, and those who had not heard were quick at catching on. With loud cheers that would drown the best efforts of any band of Indians, the charge was on, the two troops all mixed up and charging without order. It was a real foot race, with every man going as if he liked it. Men were falling fast: some shot, and others hit with gravel, only thinking that they were shot. Nothing could stop that charge.

The officers caught up with us just as we got well started, and they too seemed to like it. The Modocs, remembering their recent success with the command of Captain Thomas, and seeing that our force was fewer in number than they had handled with Thomas, held on until we were clambering over the lava hummocks, when they gave way, leaving behind them their clothing that they had stripped off for the fight and many small piles of cartridges that they had laid out to have them handy for use. They also left two of their dead, but got away with three others who afterwards died of their wounds.[9]

That was the prettiest fight that I ever saw, and it was the decisive fight of the war. The Modocs never made another attack, though later on the same command bivouacked for several days within gunshot of their new position while waiting for others to come to attack them from another direction. The loss of Ellen's Man, a popular hero of the Modocs, at Sorass Lake, and the leaving of his body with us, together with the complete failure of their attack, caused dissension in their ranks and a division into two bands, both of which were soon run down and captured with little further resistance. Our loss of seventeen men killed and wounded was rather heavy,[10] considering the fact that we had less than sixty men in the fight. But twice that loss would not have stopped the charge. The wonder of it all was seeing a near panic turned into an unbeatable offensive by the magic words, "Gosh dash it, let's charge."

The single shot first heard by us that morning killed one of our Indians, who had gone out to look for his pony and had flushed the enemy lying quietly, waiting for our formation for roll call, which would have given them a fine target. Our Indians probably saved the lives of many of us.

In my opinion, Kelley's action would have graded about [a] Distinguished Service Cross, had this honor been in vogue at that time. But the Distinguished Service Cross had not yet been introduced, so Kelley received no reward. So far as I know, none of the officers who were in that fight ever heard of what Kelley had done that morning. For a few days after the fight, we occasionally heard men shout, "Gosh dash it, let's charge," and laughing over it. Then the subject was dropped. We had all become accustomed to witnessing the bravery of Sergeant Kelley in action. This had only been the usual thing.

As I grow older, I realize more and more the importance of our having Kelley with us at Sorass Lake. Had there been a Kelley with Captain Thomas on April 26, 1873, and had he been permitted to live for only a couple of minutes, that command would not have been scattered, to be shot down in small bunches over a large area. As a member of the relief party sent out to that field, I could plainly see that there had been a wild panic. That this charge was not ordered was probably due to the fact that the officers were picked off first as they sat eating their luncheon, with no pickets out to give warning. At any rate, there was no Kelley to shout, "Gosh dash it, let's charge."

Observations on the Modoc War

JEFFERSON C. DAVIS[1]

Army and Navy Journal 10, no. 45 (June 21, 1873): 714

Colonel Davis, in conversation with the special correspondent of the San Francisco *Bulletin*[2] on June 11, gave the following statement:

When I arrived on the field, I found the troops engaged in a war with a band of Indian outlaws and murderers, wards of the government who had revolted against its authority. They were fighting mercilessly, neither giving nor exacting quarter. I then thought that captives taken in the future should be executed on the spot, as the surest and speediest method of settling the Modoc problem. When captured while fighting against the military forces of the United States, and as a separate nation and tribe, I was disposed to deal with them accordingly. Since their capture, I have ascertained that the authorities of Jackson County, Oregon, have found indictments against certain members of the band. I have not deemed it proper to turn them over to the civil courts, because they were waging war against the government at the time the murders upon which the indictments were based were committed; also for the reason that after the capture, they were prisoners of the government and not directly amenable to the civil laws.

During my command here, I have observed that the citizens, when desiring protection for person and property, or indemnification for loss, invariably appeal to the authority of the United States; but now that the war is over and the marauders captives, both the public and local authorities want to take the punishment of the offenders into their own hands. The threats of the people and the recent bloody act in this neighborhood, when four old, defenseless captives en route from Fairchild's ranch to this camp were murdered by civilians, indicate that a trial by civil law would be a useless farce.[3]

The people have made up their minds that the prisoners are guilty. It is suggested that a military commission be ordered to try the criminals. If the idea is carried out, the officers composing the court should be of high rank, and men who have had no immediate connection with the Modoc difficulty. Such a commission would probably try each case separately. It will require

Jefferson C. Davis as a major general of volunteers during the Civil War.
CYRUS T. BRADY. *NORTHWESTERN FIGHTS AND FIGHTERS.*

about six months to perform the work, to say nothing of the expense involved in such proceedings to the government. Besides, everybody, civil as well as military, knows that the Indians are guilty of murder in the first degree and ought to be hanged. I thought to avoid the unnecessary expense of the farce of a trial by doing the work myself. Owing to the dilatory manner in which the Modocs were treated by those in charge at the beginning of these difficulties, the Indians obtained a fearful advantage over us. They slaughtered so many people that the country was astonished—even shocked—and now fear they will get the advantage in the closing scenes.

This same fear was disturbing the minds of the citizens of the frontier. Justice has already been very tardy, and its coming is approaching from so many directions and in such questionable shape and garb that I doubt her success in meeting the requirements of the case. The Indians do not recognize the jurisdiction of civil or military courts because they are incapable of understanding their working. These Modocs cannot comprehend what is meant by court. They have been interrogated on that subject, and they would regard a court trial, with its technicalities, testimony, etc., as a kind of jugglery, and if convicted and sentenced to death, could not be made to understand that justice figured in the business at all. They believe they have committed deeds that merit death, in fact, are real murderers, and have daily expected to be hanged. They believe the military have the power and right to inflict punishment.

The murders and arrests occurred in Oregon and California, and the case is badly mixed. My proposed course would have settled the question by a single stroke. The Gordian knot was to be cut. The Indians are cooped up in tents—men, women, and children, guilty and innocent alike, fearing a massacre all the time. They must remain in this condition of suspense for months.

I had procured lumber, chains, ropes, and tackle, and all the paraphernalia of execution, and had selected Friday last as doomsday. Thursday forenoon I drew up this declaration of charges and read it to Jack later in the day:

HEADQUARTERS DEPARTMENT OF COLUMBIA,
IN THE FIELD, LAKE TULE, CAL., JUNE 1873

JACK—Since white men first began to travel through or settle in the country occupied by the Modocs, a people of which you claim to be one of the chiefs, the Modocs have been known as a band of merciless robbers and murderers. The history of your tribe is filled with accounts of the murders of the white race. Even among your Indian neighbors you are known as a domineering and tyrannical tribe. Old settlers in the country report as many as three hundred murders committed by your people within the limits of the present generation. Along the shores of this beautiful little lake, in view of which we now stand, are the graves of over sixty victims of Modoc barbarity, all murdered by your immediate ancestors in brutal acts. They were peaceful emigrants—men, women, and children—passing quietly through the country on the public highway.

For these many crimes no adequate punishment has ever been visited upon the guilty—even as a tribe or individually. Upon the contrary, the government has tacitly overlooked them. A few years ago, regardless of these acts of treachery, it gave you a reservation of land for a home where, if you chose, you could remain and enjoy the annual bounties of the government unmolested. But you and your band seem to have preferred the warpath. You left the reservation, you spurned the kindness of the government, and even resisted the soldiers in the execution of their duty while endeavoring to force you back to the reservation. You hastened to fight. Emulating the bloody deeds of your fathers, you again strewed the shores of Tule Lake with the slain victims of your bloody band. All those victims were peaceful and unsuspecting citizens and were slaughtered while at their daily avocations.

You then fled to your stronghold, the Lava Beds, prepared for war, and defied the power of the government. Still, the president at Washington ordered the soldiers to desist until the peace commissioners could have a talk with you and, if possible, avoid shedding more blood. Their efforts were fruitless. After much delay and many attempts at conciliation on their part, you decoyed the commissioners into your hands. Armed or unarmed, these acts have placed you and your band outside of the rules of civilized warfare. In other words, you have made yourselves outlaws, and as such, since my arrival here as the successor of General Canby (whom you murdered with your own hands), I have made unremitting war upon your race and upon you, until at last you have been captured after much expense to the government and the loss of many valuable lives. Now that I have recounted your history and that of your tribe, the recent acts of yourself and band, I will close this interview by informing you that I have this day directed that you and your confederates, members of your band, be executed at sunset tomorrow in the presence of the troops, your people, and the assembled citizens of the country.

While I was preparing a list of those I intended to execute, a courier arrived with the instructions from Washington, "Hold the prisoners until further orders." After the execution, I intended organizing a force for the purpose of starting for Columbia and probably for Lapwai, seeing and talking with as many chiefs as possible while en route. I knew that the prompt execution of Modoc outlaws would facilitate peace talks among the Indians of Oregon and Washington Territory, as well as California, and have a tendency to quiet the Indians all through the country. The Indians all know that we have captured the Modocs, and they will quickly learn the news if the death penalty is inflicted. The chastisement would result in a mutual benefit to both Indians and whites. With the prestige the Modocs have gained, we could do great good by such a campaign.

The Capture of Captain Jack

"VERITAS"

Army and Navy Journal 12, no. 22 (January 23, 1875): 378–79

To the Editor of the *Army and Navy Journal:*

SIR: As the subject, although a little stale, may be interesting to some of your readers, I take the liberty of sending you an extract from the journal of a comrade of mine, who has ere this turned his saber into a hoe, or some other agricultural implement. The extract relates to the capture of the famous, or infamous, Captain Jack of Lava Bed notoriety.

→ ⊠⊹⊠ ←

On May 26, 1873, the cavalry portion of the Modoc expedition left Fairchild's ranch in search of Captain Jack, who had abandoned his position in the Lava Beds a few days previous. The movements were made by squadrons. The squadron in which I have the honor of serving, commanded by Captain Perry and consisting of Troop F (Captain Perry) and a large detachment of Troop H (Captain Trimble), both of the 1st Cavalry, was the last to leave. We arrived at Applegate's ranch on the second day and went into camp. Meanwhile, the other squadrons were engaged in hunting up the Modocs. On the morning of May 31, we were ordered to saddle up, and about noon we were en route. After marching a few miles in the direction of Langell's Valley, we met the rest of the expedition, who were returning for rations. They told us that they had corralled the Modocs and succeeded in capturing several. I forget the precise number, but amongst them was Scarfaced Charley, the "Chevalier Bayard," as Dr. Cabaniss called him, of the Modocs,[1] but Jack and a few immediate followers had eluded them. After gaining some information as to the supposed whereabouts of the fugitives, we commenced our hunt and became amateur pathfinders for the nonce.

Our Warm Springs allies, of which there were a fair sprinkling along, were of great service to us in this emergency, and it was not long before we struck the trail. But night came on, and we went into camp in Willow Creek Canyon. Next morning, June 1, 1873, we were again in the saddle and recommenced the

Scarfaced Charley. ILLUSTRATED LONDON NEWS, 1873.

search, keeping close to the creek most of the time, as the trails we had found led in that direction, and we were pretty certain that our missing friends, the Modocs, were secreted someplace in the canyon. About 11:00 A.M. Captain Trimble was detached from the main body with two noncommissioned officers and about thirteen privates of his own troop and ordered to cross the creek and scout the other side.

As I afterwards learned from one of the detached party, and for whose veracity and intelligence I can vouch, the detachment, after crossing the creek, continued to search parallel to the main body. In the course of half an hour, they came suddenly upon one of Captain Jack's vedettes, who was stationed on a promontory jutting into the canyon, his attention being evidently directed to the movements of the main body on the opposite side; the detachment formed rather an unpleasant surprise party to that gentleman. As soon as he discovered their approach, he attempted to escape, but was surrounded and captured in a trice. He proved to be a hunchback, one of Jack's most attached followers.[2] When he was first captured, he was so badly scared that he could not talk, but he gradually became more composed and even a trifle saucy. He, however, readily answered all the questions put to him in a jargon (a sort of lingua franca devised by the Hudson Bay Company for trade purposes, and which is understood by nearly all the Indians on the coast). He said that Jack was in the canyon below, and that he had only a few boys and squaws and papooses with him. After extracting all the information attainable from him, the soldiers and the Warm Springs advanced a short distance and were ordered to halt and stoop down.

The captured Modoc was then conducted to the edge of the canyon by a couple of Warm Springs and ordered to halloo down to Captain Jack and tell him to come up; that the soldiers would not shoot him, but if he refused, he would be killed on the spot. After some parleying, Jack, preceded by his retinue of boys, squaws, and papooses, emerged from his hiding place. He surrendered himself to Captain Trimble, to whom he gave his gun. Jack's appearance at that moment was not at all distinguished. He had no fancy Indian trappings on his person; neither was he dressed in any of the clothes of General Canby, as was erroneously reported. He appeared to be about five feet eight inches in height, rather slim built, was dressed in a suit of dirty blue overalls and an old white hat, with the leaf turned in all around, except a small portion in front, which formed a sort of visor; to this dress he added, directly after his capture, a striped calico shirt. He was altogether a commonplace specimen of the genus Lo! Immediately after the capture of Jack, Captain Trimble's party commenced cheering, and the cheer was taken up by the main body on the other side, who were witnesses but not participants in the capture, but whose appearance in such close proximity no doubt contributed thereto.

After the detachment and the prisoners joined the main body, the Modocs were turned over to the Warm Springs, and the whole party commenced the return march to the Applegates', which was, I should judge, about seven or eight miles distant. On our arrival in camp, the prisoners were placed under guard, and were a few days thereafter removed to the supply camp on the isthmus. The capture of Jack was the grand finale of the Modoc War, which had proved to be the bloodiest in our annals, considering the small number of hostile Indians engaged.

The Modoc Misery

H. WALLACE ATWELL[1]

New York *Herald,* June 2, 1873

NEW YORK *HERALD* HEADQUARTERS,
MODOC EXPEDITION, May 22, 1873

A short account of what has transpired lately here may not prove uninteresting to the many readers of the *Herald.* Therefore, I will give you, in as few words as possible, the main features of the operations of the last few days, beginning about the first of the month, or rather, I might say, on April 26, the date of the Thomas massacre.

Several dead and missing were left on the battlefield, the troops being unable to find the first or remove the second, and consequently great anxiety was felt regarding the fate of the missing, for one was an officer—gallant Lieutenant Cranston—a better or braver man we rarely see. It was expected that an effort would be made to find his body, at least, for it is well known that if the troops would not be ordered out to search for the body of an officer, the bodies of the privates stood but little chance of being recovered. But for once officer and private fared alike and were left where they fell until the time I am about to write.

On the arrival of Colonel Davis, it became apparent that matters were to be pressed a little, and that the American soldier would be called upon to attempt in all seriousness the task of subduing the gentle Modoc. As a first step, it was determined to recover the bodies and give them Christian burial if possible. To my unmilitary mind, the effort should have been made sooner, if the morale of the troops could be trusted. But we must not criticize the acts of those in power, for we are not supposed to understand the working of some of the mighty minds, whose chief ornaments are shoulder straps and an education won at the expense of the government. As yet, I hardly like to write of this sad affair, but prefer to wait until some of the fawning sycophancy, which has characterized some accounts of this sad affair, shall have worn away and men be able and willing to get the shoulder straps out of their eyes and place the blame of this wholesale murder where it rightfully belongs without fear of mortally offending some of the embryo veterans, whose only knowledge of

Indian warfare before this campaign consisted in sundry encounters they have had with tobacconists' signs in some of their nightly revels. I do not refer to all or any officers who belong to this expedition, for we have some gallant gentlemen here. But this is merely written for the benefit of future young warriors who think their uniforms hide their want of brains or lack of civility.

Before I proceed further, I will relate the attack on the wagon train that took place on the peninsula May 7, I think. It had or has little significance, only to show the troops that the Modocs were on the offensive and had not left the Lava Beds. It was then determined to ascertain whether this was supposition or a fixed fact. Therefore, Capt. John A. Fairchild, by and with the consent of the military, sent out One-Eyed Dixie and Artinie Choakus (Long Legs), half-civilized Modoc squaws, to spy out the land and report thereon. He went with them to within about three miles of the stronghold,[2] camped all night, and sent them in the morning with instructions [that] if the Modocs were there, to light a fire if they could; if not, report to him at his ranch at night.

The squaws hardly could be persuaded to go, for fear of the Warm Springs Indians and soldiers. But still they went, returned at night, and reported [the] Modocs gone, and gone for good, as there was no water left, the natural cistern having been exhausted. They also reported that they had found the body of Lieutenant Cranston and those of the missing men.

This intelligence was given to the colonel [Davis] in the afternoon, and that evening Capt. Donald McKay and his Warm Springs Indians were ordered out to verify the report. When darkness had enveloped the Lava Beds, Donald and his men proceeded to the dreaded place, and in the morning their fires told us that again the squaws had been true to their task, and that the dreaded Modocs had really left their stronghold, and it was decided that the day following a detachment should be sent out to gather and bury the dead. The soldiers, or many of them at least, would not believe the Modocs had fled and said the whole thing was a ruse to get them out to build another graveyard (to be slaughtered).

Well, the expedition, consisting of the infantry and artillery under Lieutenant Field, Battery A, 4th Artillery,[3] started on May 9, just thirteen days after the first ill-starred expedition left camp for the same place, but with altogether a different object. The formation of this detachment gave another evidence that reason had not altogether deserted our camp, for as much care was displayed in this as though they expected to meet the enemy. Had the same prudence been observed in the case of the first expedition, the sad result might have been avoided.

The troops formed three sides of a hollow square, with pack train in the center, and flanked out thirty yards on either wing. The ground was reached, the bodies passed, and the troops took up high ground commanding the position, while a part proceeded to gather the dead.

Cranston and four men were found side by side, probably laid in that position by the Modocs, in a position where they could rake any party who came for them. The other body was but a little way off. Cranston was scalped, hair and whiskers, and two of the other bodies mutilated badly. It was found impossible to remove them, decomposition having rendered them almost putrid masses, and they were buried there, with headboards to mark their lonely resting place. The bodies of the eight soldiers left there were reinterred, the Modocs having burned off the sagebrush with which they were covered, leaving most of them but charred remains. Having accomplished this sad duty, the party returned unmolested to camp.

I will now return to the attack on the wagon train on the peninsula, which was of little moment save to help convince the military mind that it was sometimes unsafe to send out small parties as escorts, and also that at times the Modocs would whip the soldiers evenhanded—the former always having the choice of ground, of course.

This little affair occurred on the seventh and was about like this: A train of five wagons[4]—one six-horse, the others four animals each—left Boyle's supply camp to go down the peninsula to his old camp for some lumber left them. They had an escort of fifteen or twenty men under Sergeant Murphy. At a point where the neck is very narrow, they were attacked by about twenty Modocs, who fortified themselves across this narrow place where they could not be flanked. The first fire wounded three soldiers, who fell back, and a running fight of a few minutes resulted, ending in the capture of four wagons and seventeen animals, the six-horse team being behind and thus escaping.

As soon as the firing was heard, Lieutenant Boutelle, with reinforcements, started for the scene, but although his command rode hard, they did not come up in time to save the train, which was yet burning, and the Modocs, having taken to the rocks, could not be followed. On the following day they returned and finished burning the wagons.

It now becoming evident that the Modocs were really out and hunting the soldiers, it was resolved to start a scout after them, and to this end a force under command of Captain Hasbrouck, consisting of the mounted men of Major Mason's camp and Captain Jackson's and Lieutenant Kyle's troops of cavalry, with the Warm Springs under McKay, started on the ninth for a scout around the head of Sorass Lake, where it was rightly supposed the enemy had fled.

The cavalry camped the first night on the head of Sorass Lake, while the light battery tethered their horses and camped in a juniper grove some three miles distant. The troops dug for water but found none, the lake being little else now but a dry marsh, as it is every dry season. About two hours after the cavalry had encamped, McKay and his Indians came up and camped with them, apparently unknown to the Modocs, who were in the rocks a few miles away. It was rather an open country where the cavalry were encamped—one in which horses could be used to some advantage. In the gray of the following morning, the Modocs came down from their rocky fastness, stripped for the fight, and with their terrible war whoop opened fire on the sleeping soldiers.

The first fire killed one outright and wounded eight others, two of whom have since died. The most of the horses were stampeded, but were afterwards recovered by those who kept their stock. The Warm Springs sprung to their ponies and in a few seconds were on the flanks of the Modocs, who evidently did not expect them. With the aid of the dismounted cavalry, they drove them about five miles, when, reaching that portion of the Lava Beds that is almost impossible to move in, the troops returned to their camp about 10:00 A.M., where they remained until night, when they returned to Scorpion Point, bringing their dead and wounded with them. The Warm Springs lost one warrior killed, two wounded, one of whom has since died, and the other probably will not recover.

The fruits of this victory were one Modoc killed, four ponies, one mule, and about 100 rounds of ammunition captured. Still, it was a victory, and though an insignificant one, it possessed great advantages in one point of view, for it taught the soldiers that if they stand their ground, they could whip the Modocs, when they could not do it by running.

Reinforcements were sent out the next morning, hoping to surround the Modocs from this side, and two or three days were spent in "feeling" their position, when it was discovered that the Modocs had fled and were making for the timbered range leading around to the head of Butte Valley, which lies between them and Goose Nest Mountain, from which they could easily reach Bogus Creek.

The cavalry and Warm Springs[5] were soon after them, going as far west as Boyce's ranch, nearby Beal's. They struck the trail on Sunday last,[6] and finding it was leading back to Fairchild's ranch, they spurred on for about eight miles, when they caught sight of the Modocs on foot in a sagebrush plain which skirts Sheep Mountain on the east and immediately gave chase. There horses being jaded, they did not get very close to the Modocs before they gained the hills about three miles south of Fairchild's ranch, where the horses could not follow them. In this running fight, the Modocs lost one man and two squaws killed, and ten or a dozen women and children captured, while we had no killed or wounded to report.[7]

On Monday evening Captain Fairchild went to the Warm Springs camp and, by the aid of One-Eyed Dixie and Artinie, interviewed the captured squaws. From them he learned that the band was on its way to Fairchild with a view of surrendering themselves when attacked. This he communicated to Captain Hasbrouck, who took the responsibility of delaying the chase for two or three days, in order to give them time to surrender.

One-Eyed Dixie and Artinie were sent out with one of the captured squaws to find the party and tell them to come in. They left on Tuesday [and] returned on Wednesday,[8] reporting that they were anxious to surrender if they had someone they knew and had confidence in to come and bring them in. They were sent back this morning, assured by Fairchild that he would meet them when they neared camp and talk with them.

The squaws found them over by Indian Springs, an almost impregnable position some fifteen miles northwest of this place and about seven miles west of the Hole in the Ground. They found there Bogus Charley, just returned from Bogus Creek, and by his aid and that of Steamboat Frank and Shacknasty Jim, the party consented to return and meet Fairchild, which they did, about four miles from his house. A long talk ensued, when finally they agreed to come in and surrender unconditionally; at 6:00 P.M. the poor, misguided fellows came in and laid down their arms to Colonel Davis.

It was a sorry sight, this squalid, weary, half-starved band, comprising about seventy souls all told, sixteen of whom were able to bear arms, though several were only boys of twelve and fourteen years, who seemed hardly able to bear the Springfield muskets with which they were armed. The names of some of the most famous among them are Curly Headed Doctor, the main cause of the war;[9] Steamboat Frank, a daring warrior, one of the best of Captain Jack's men; Hooker Jim, who shot at Dyar, peace commissioner at the time of the massacre; Shacknasty Jim, Bogus Charley, and William, the last two, it is said, being the ones who stood guard at the mouth of the cave the night Steele and Atwell were there, and when but for Scarfaced Charley and Captain Jack, assisted by these two, they would undoubtedly have been murdered.

This is a sad blow to Captain Jack, for it takes away the best of his fighting men, leaving him an easy prey when he is found. This band of Hot Creek Modocs have been considered the bravest and most cunning warriors of the tribe, and their defection will be sorely felt.

They are now under guard, and what will be done with them I cannot yet determine, but certain it is that Bogus Charley, Hooker Jim, and Curly Headed Doctor will be tried for their lives. Bogus Charley, it will be remembered, was with Boston Charley when the peace commission was treacherously attacked. Bogus Charley says that their party and Captain Jack's had a quarrel when they learned of their intention of surrendering, and that Captain Jack and William had a fight because the former wished to disarm the band. He says they have been wandering around, trying to get in.

When they laid down their guns, the stoutest could hardly withhold their tears. I never saw Indians exhibit so much emotion before. Great credit is due Captain Fairchild for the success of this undertaking, by which half the band has become prisoners. We get fifteen guns and about 100 rounds of ammunition. Bogus Charley says Boston Charley must be dead, as he has been missing since the fight of Sunday. He asked Colonel Davis today that one of his men might go out with some soldiers tomorrow to hunt for his body. He says Captain Jack has gone to Pit River or Goose Lake, and that before he left he robbed them of all their best guns and their horses and left them with only the arms they now have.

I am inclined to believe the robbery, just to please the Modocs, though I think they have their guns cached nearby, and that Captain Jack is lurking around in this neighborhood, waiting to see how those who have surrendered will be treated. He may be at this moment on Bogus Creek or some other equally strong place, for I do not think he will leave this section of the country. He is politic and wants to live, and could he be assured his life would be spared, I believe he would surrender in less than a week.

◆═◆═ ◆

New York *Herald,* June 16, 1873

HEADQUARTERS MODOC ARMY,
BOYLE'S CAMP, June 6, 1873

The close of this tragedy of war appears to degenerate into a farce, so rapidly has the little Modoc force disappeared, when once pressed to the wall. First came the surrender of the Hot Creek Indians (sixteen in number), and this broke the back of the rebellion. Captain Fairchild proposed taking four of those who had surrendered—Bogus Charley, Hooker Jim, Shacknasty Jim, and Steamboat Frank—and by their aid to discover the hiding place of the Modocs. Colonel Davis at once acted on this suggestion, and on the twenty-sixth he, Captain Fairchild, three soldiers, your correspondent, and the four Modocs started from Fairchild's, riding around the lake and reaching our present camp on the day following. On the twenty-seventh the Modocs were sent out, returning on the twenty-eighth, reporting the camp of Captain Jack to be on Willow Creek, twenty miles east of this place.

The commands of Captains Hasbrouck and Jackson left camp on the twenty-ninth, your correspondent accompanying them. Arriving near the supposed camp, the command divided, one wing going down on the right hand bank, the other on the left. Owing to miscalculating the distance, Captain Jackson's command reached the place first, surprising the Modocs, who all fled across the creek about half a mile in advance of Hasbrouck's command. Boston, who murdered Dr. Thomas, surrendered. Seven squaws—including Mary, Jack's sister—were captured, with several horses and mules. The troops went into camp, and Boston went out and attempted to find his fleeing people, but without success.

On the following morning the trail was taken up and followed all day. First it led to the west, then north, then south, making three sides of a square, over high, rocky ridges covered with steep pines, where an animal could not step without treading on a rock; and still the four Modocs and Warm Springs Indians followed the trail as unerringly as hounds after game. After riding about twenty-five miles, just as we reached the head of Langell Valley on Lost River, a few were seen in the bluffs. The command was halted, and an effort was made to have a talk with the Modocs, but they fled.

A charge was made, and the command swept down around the bluffs into the valley, reaching a slope where they could ascend to the bluffs and head the fugitives off. The sun was just going down, and the Indians, seeing they were about to be corralled, threw up the sponge at once. Scarfaced Charley came into our lines, gave up his gun, and said he would fight no more. He wanted to see John Fairchild, but that person was scouting some miles away. Major Green, who commanded the expedition, told Charley to go back and bring in his family and all that wanted to surrender at once, or he should charge them at once. As Charley returned, Dr. Cabaniss, who was with the little party which had started to head the Modocs off, but was then at a halt, went along with Charley and talked with Captain Jack and the others. Of course, the troops could not move against the Modocs with him in their midst, and as darkness was coming on, the troops filed down onto Lost River and went into camp for the night.

After a while, Dr. Cabaniss returned with Mose and the message that the Modocs would come in in the morning. On the following morning Scarfaced Charley and nine others came in, making eleven Modocs we had taken. Several squaws came along also. Charley expected that Captain Jack and his companions had run away. The day was spent in an effort to find them, and the day following, the commands scattered around searching for the fugitives.

The scene of the capture was about fifteen miles from where we started them up the day previous. On June 1 Captain Perry's command, which had joined the expedition, was on the trail, his Warm Springs Indians following it back near to the camp on Willow Creek. A Warm Springs discovered one of Jack's scouts, stole upon him, and disarmed him. He promised to show where Jack was, and the Warm Springs soon had that doughty warrior in their hands. Warm Springs George had command of the detachment of Warm Springs, but Bowlegged Charley, We-na-shet, and Car-pi-o-in were the ones who were "in at the death."

We now had Captain Jack, Schonchin Jim, and Boston Charley—the murderers of the peace commissioners—and Scarfaced Charley, their engineer and general. Still, twelve men were out, and the soldiers continued the scout. On June 2 four more were taken by the Oregon volunteers. The remainder are expected daily and will probably be found at Yainax. Bogus Charley and Jim have been sent to hunt them up, and when found, the last of this desperate band will be in captivity. From this rapid review, your readers can see the situation of affairs and the end of the Modoc War.

The prisoners are all here, Captain Jack, Schonchin, Boston, and others being shackled. What will be done with them I know not, but think they will be hung. The Warm Springs will go home in a few days, their time being out on the tenth. They will not reenlist, even in the event of hostilities with other tribes. They have been treated rather badly. They say they have been on many scouts, but never have received such bad treatment before. They were promised grain for their horses and also the shoeing of them, but like many other promises, they were not kept. Donald says the Wascan-pins[10]—about one-third of his command—can enlist again if they want to, but the Warm Springs would not.

To these people really belongs the credit of closing the war, for without their skill it would have been impossible to have hunted the Modocs down.

There is one man who deserves especial credit—Captain John Fairchild. By the stroke of policy which brought into use the captured Modocs, by his untiring energy in the pursuit of the wily foe, and through his knowledge of the country and the Indians, his services have been invaluable. Cool and brave, possessing the confidence of the Indians, he could succeed in persuading them to surrender when all others would have failed. Still, few army men would feel inclined to give him the credit he deserves; though the civilians know and appreciate his worth.

◄—◆ ☰◆☰ ◆—►

New York *Herald,* June 23, 1873

BOYLE'S CAMP, June 9, 1873

I am physically unfit[11] to write much of a letter but will endeavor to give you a resume of what has passed since my last letter. First, I will give you an item substantiating my account as to who really captured Captain Jack, the Modoc chief. I telegraphed that he was captured by Warm Springs George's detachment of Warm Springs, under Captain Perry's command. Owing to a morbid jealousy, some of the military rather doubt the assertion, or affect to, claiming that Captain Trimble took him. While I am willing to give the captain all the credit he deserves, I will not permit him or anyone but the real captors to have the credit of this capture. Car-pi-o-in and We-na-shet, two Indians of Warm Springs George's division, captain of McKay's command, captured the redoubtable chief, and to them he surrendered.[12] They then reported the capture to Captain Trimble and turned over their prisoner. He had no gun when he first surrendered, all accounts to the contrary not withstanding. He might have taken his gun when going to Captain Trimble, as he was permitted time to change his clothes.

In proof of this, I give my authority, Charles Putnam, grandson of Jesse Applegate, who was with the two Warm Springs and [was] the only white man with them when the capture was made, and I think his veracity is beyond question. It amuses a civilian to see the jealousy manifested by some of the officers regarding the distribution of the little honor won in this farcical campaign, though all profess to not care a rush as to what the papers say of them.

A cold-blooded massacre was perpetrated on Saturday evening, June 7, by some Oregon volunteers, it is supposed, in which four Modoc males (prisoners) were killed and one squaw wounded. It happened in this way. Captain Fairchild and J. C. Burgess had been sent out by Colonel Davis to get some stragglers who were on Shovel Creek, a tributary of Bogus Creek. They had secured four bucks, with their families, [and] brought them to Fairchild's ranch, from whence they started for this camp to turn over their prisoners to the military. "Uncle Jimmy," brother to Captain Fairchild, drove the team of four mules. The others, mounted, rode on ahead with Shacknasty Jim and Bogus Charley, who went with them after the Modocs and came into camp safe. "Uncle Jimmy," with his prisoners, had reached a point about eight miles from camp, when two men rode around a bluff, gained his front, and sitting by the roadside, awaited his approach. As he came up, one put a gun to his head [and] halted him, while the other cut the mules loose from the wagon. They commenced an indiscriminate massacre of the unarmed Indians in the wagon, in which the party of males were murdered.[13] No doubt the cowardly wretches would have butchered the women and children had not a detachment of ten soldiers under Sergeant Murphy hove in sight, when the miscreants fled.

There is no doubt but what the party—there were three or four more seen—intended to catch Captain Fairchild with the two Modocs, Bogus Charley and Shacknasty Jim, and murder the whole party. They would rather kill Fairchild than Captain Jack, but if he and Burgess had been with the prisoners, the cowardly ruffians would not have dared to attack them. This is on a stripe of all the cowardly acts which have heretofore provoked Indian wars. Cowardly, brutal acts have marked the frontier history, and Oregon has her full share of these stains on a people's honor. We boil with indignation because these Modocs slew settlers after having been attacked by them, and because they slew General Canby; but I question if either case equals in atrocity and cold-blooded cowardice the massacre of these defenseless prisoners, two of whom were old, feeble men and wounded, and neither of the band had been implicated in anything but fighting. Two of the party had fought in the Lava Beds, and two had never been with Captain Jack at all. This is a glorious record for the Oregon volunteers, and may God give them joy of it. But if this band, or the ruffianly portion of it, is not disbanded, it will provoke a general war along the border. There is far more danger in their disturbing existing peace than that the Indians will rebel. And peaceful citizens had better take their chances with hostile Indians than with such allies.

Of such a spirit was the attempt of Mrs. Boddy[14] to kill Hooker Jim. Though she has suffered much and is in a measure excusable for her passionate act, the principle is about the same and not to be commended. Her husband and the husband of his daughter were among those slain on the lakeshore after the attack by Oregon citizens on the Modoc camp at Lost River. These ladies[15] were here to give evidence and identify the murderers. Hooker Jim and Shacknasty Jim were sent to the tent where the ladies were by Colonel Davis, that they might be identified. The women recognized Hooker Jim at once and accused him of the murder. The elder went to her valise for a pistol. A gentleman informed Colonel Davis of his suspicions,[16] and the colonel entered the tent just in time to wrest the pistol from her hand. She had another, which was taken from her also. Her daughter had a pistol and a knife; in fact, they have had arms enough with which to stock a small arsenal.

I am not sorry that their amiable intentions were frustrated, for had they killed Hooker Jim, it would have placed Colonel Davis in a bad position. I doubt not he deserves death at the hangman's hand, but murder by anyone while a prisoner of war is to be reprobated; besides, we want no more murders committed by the whites. If Indians are to be hung for murdering whites, we call on Colonel Davis to hunt down the white murderers of Indian prisoners and hang them also.[17] The rule has been too long in Oregon that law is for the Indians alone; the whites are not bound to respect it where an Indian is concerned. I refer only to these border men, who have nothing at stake, everything to gain, and nothing to lose in the event of a continuance of the war or the outbreak of other tribes. But I am glad to know that the citizens, the respectable portion of them, condemn such proceedings. Governor Grover has already been petitioned to strike Lieutenant Hyzer and his company from the muster rolls, and in so doing remove as far as possible the foul stain cast on the good name of the state. The editor of the Salem *Mercury* is doing all in his power to have the murderers punished and their crime atoned for. Had this crime been committed by those who had lost relatives to the Modocs, there would have been some palliation for it. But such was not the case. Evidence now gathered points to the fact that Lieutenant Hyzer's company contains the villains, and probably an investigation will disclose the facts to be as now suspisioned.

We are having a court martial here today for the trial of six deserters, brought here in irons yesterday. It will probably go hard with them, for they deserted in the face of the foe.[18] At one time I feared the larger half of the army would desert, so badly were the troops demoralized. This has been denied, but it is nevertheless true. If it was not so, why did the bodies of those slain at Thomas's massacre lie thirteen days on the field before the men were sent to recover them? Simply because the officers feared that some of the commands would not stand if attacked. Why were the Warm Springs Indians and the reserve ordered to fire into those suspected men if they ran in case of an attack, if they did not fear their action? All this and much more remains to be told, and it will be told in good time, too, when this war shall have been written up without prejudice to any party.

I will mention the capture by Hyzer's volunteers of Black Jim and three other of his men a few days since.[19] These men struck their trails and followed it for two days, coming up with them at first about 3:00 P.M., finding one who was wounded up a juniper tree near the camp where the squaws and children were. He was taken, and they learned from him, through Hooker Jim and Steamboat Frank, that they were in the rocks some two miles away. They followed them up, when two came out and surrendered, but Black Jim showed fight when the lieutenant covered him with his rifle, and he threw down his gun and gave himself up. After he was taken, some of the volunteers wanted to kill the prisoners, but the lieutenant would not permit it, and eventually they were brought into camp, guarded by the company, and turned over to the commanding officer. For this they deserve credit, and shall have it, and I wish I could give credit to them at all times.

I expected to chronicle the movement of the army through to the north but cannot, for I learn it will not take place, orders to that effect having reached here today. It was the intention of Colonel Davis to take all but the light

Captain Jack's family. NATIONAL ARCHIVES.

artillery, who would be left here to guard the prisoners, and make a tour of the Indian agencies, via Warner, Harney, Nez Perce, and Walla Walla country. It was certainly a very desirable move and would have had a very beneficial effect on the disaffected tribes in showing them the resources of the nation, but it seems this is not to be.

Again, we expected to see just a little wholesome hanging. Of the murderers of General Canby and the settlers on the lakeshore, it was understood that they were to swing on the sixth, but an order was received which put the matter by for a while. I learned that an order was received today by Colonel Davis permitting him to settle the matter right here. We have every confidence in his wisdom and doubt not that he will settle it satisfactorily to all. These murderers must be hung. Nothing less will satisfy the demands of justice—nothing else will. No puling, mawkish sentiment of pity for the "poor Indian" must intervene and defeat the ends of justice. The refractory tribes must be taught a lesson, and a severe one. They must know that treachery cannot be overlooked, that brutal murders will be surely punished by the death of the murderers. One such lesson will be worth to them more than the extermination of a tribe by actual fighting. An Indian does not fear death by the bullet or knife, but he fears death by the rope, for it rules them out of the happy hunting grounds of the spirit land.

Another little episode occurred, a capture of Modocs by the Pits, which occurred three days since. Chief Chip of the Hot Spring Pits notified Preston

Hays, temporary agent there, that Modocs had been seen near his camp. Hays told them to get them in his camp and disarm them. He acted on this advice and sent Dick out, who decoyed them in, when they were disarmed. Messrs. Hays and Hess were notified and came and took them in charge. After this, some eight citizens gathered and wanted to kill them, but were prevented by Hays, Hess, Chief Chip, and his men. These two gentlemen, Chief Chip and his half brother, Captain John; Tom Dickson, another brother of the chief, and several other Pits brought them through and turned them over to the authorities yesterday, three men, eight women and children being in the party. When the Modocs were disarmed, one Kelley, who had come to assist in securing them, became very much excited and liked to have spoiled all by his recklessness. Had all been as excited as Kelley, the Modocs would have been murdered there, and another dark stain added to the history of this singularly conducted campaign against the Modocs.

PART THREE

The Nez Perce Campaign, 1877

Chief Joseph's Own Story[1]

HEINMOT TOOYALAKEKT (CHIEF JOSEPH)[2]

North American Review 128 (April 1879): 412–33

My friends, I have been asked to show you my heart. I am glad to have a chance to do so. I want the white people to understand my people. Some of you think an Indian is like a wild animal. This is a great mistake. I will tell you all about our people, and then you can judge whether an Indian is a man or not. I believe much trouble and blood would be saved if we opened our hearts more. I will tell you in my way how the Indian sees things. The white man has more words to tell you how they look at him, but it does not require many words to speak the truth. What I have to say will come from my heart, and I will speak with a straight tongue. Ah-cumkin-i-ma-me-hut (the Great Spirit) is looking at me, and will hear me.

My name is Heinmot Tooyalakekt [or In-mut-too-yah-lat-lat] (Thunder Traveling Over The Mountains). I am chief of the Wal-lam-watkin[3] band of Chute-pa-lu, or Nez Perce (nose-pierced Indians).[4] I was born in eastern Oregon thirty-eight winters ago. My father was chief before me.[5] When a young man he was called Joseph by Mr. Spalding, a missionary.[6] He died a few years ago. There was no stain on his hands of the blood of a white man. He left a good name on the earth. He advised me well for my people.

Our fathers gave us many laws, which they had learned from their fathers. These laws were good. They told us to treat all men as they treated us; that we should never be the first to break a bargain; that it was a disgrace to tell a lie; that we should speak only the truth; that it was a shame for one man to take from another his wife, or his property, without paying for it. We were taught to believe that the Great Spirit sees and hears everything, and that He never forgets; that hereafter He will give every man a spirit home according to his deserts; if he has been a good man, he will have a good home; if he has been a bad man, he will have a bad home. This I believe, and all my people believe the same.

We did not know there were other people besides the Indian until about one hundred winters ago, when some men with white faces came to our country. They brought many things with them to trade for furs and skins. They brought

Chief Joseph. NATIONAL ANTHROPOLOGICAL MUSEUM, SMITHSONIAN INSTITUTION.

tobacco, which was new to us. They brought guns with flint stones on them, which frightened our women and children. Our people could not talk with these white-faced men, but they used signs which all people understood. These men were Frenchmen, and they called our people "Nez Perces," because they wore rings in their noses for ornaments. Although very few of our people wear them now, we are still called by the same name. These French trappers said a great many things to our fathers, which have been planted in our hearts. Some were good for us, but some were bad. Our people were divided in opinion about these men. Some thought they taught more bad than good. An Indian respects a brave man, but he despises a coward. He loves a straight tongue, but he hates a forked tongue. The French trappers told us some truths and some lies.

The first white men of your people who came to our country were named Lewis and Clark. They also brought many things that our people had never seen. They talked straight, and our people gave them a great feast as a proof that their hearts were friendly. These men were very kind. They made presents to our chiefs, and our people made presents to them. We had a great many horses, of which we gave them what they needed, and they gave us guns and tobacco in return. All the Nez Perces made friends with Lewis and Clark and agreed to let them pass through their country and never to make war on white men. This promise the Nez Perces have never broken. No white man can accuse them of bad faith, and speak with a straight tongue. It has always been the pride of the Nez Perces that they were the friends of the white men.

When my father was a young man there came to our country a white man (Rev. Mr. Spalding) who talked spirit law. He won the affections of our people because he spoke good things to them. At first he did not say anything about white men wanting to settle on our lands. Nothing was said about that until about twenty winters ago, when a number of white people came into our country and built houses and made farms. At first our people made no complaint. They thought there was room enough for all to live in peace, and they were learning many things from the white men that seemed to be good. But we soon found that the white men were growing rich very fast, and were greedy to possess everything the Indian had.

My father was the first to see through the schemes of the white men, and he warned his tribe to be careful about trading with them. He had a suspicion of men who seemed so anxious to make money. I was a boy then, but I remember well my father's caution. He had sharper eyes than the rest of our people.

Next there came a white officer (Governor Stevens), who invited all the Nez Perces to a treaty council.[7] After the council was opened, he made known his heart. He said there were a great many white people in the country, and many more would come; that he wanted the land marked out so that the Indians and white men could be separated. If they were to live in peace, it was necessary, he said, that the Indians should have a country set apart for them, and in that country they must stay. My father, who represented his band, refused to have anything to do with the council, because he wished to be a free man. He claimed that no man owned any part of the earth, and a man could not sell what was not his own.

Mr. Spalding took hold of my father's arm and said, "Come and sign the treaty." My father pushed him away and said, "Why do you ask me to sign away my country? It is your business to talk to us about spirit matters, and not to talk to us about parting with our land." Governor Stevens urged my father to sign his treaty, but he refused. "I will not sign your paper," he said. "You go where you please, so do I. You are not a child, I am no child; I can think for myself. No man can think for me. I have no other home than this. I will not give it up to any man. My people would have no home. Take away your paper. I will not touch it with my hand."

My father left the council. Some of the chiefs of the other bands of the Nez Perces signed the treaty, and then Governor Stevens gave them presents of blankets. My father cautioned his people to take no presents, for after a while, he said, "they will claim that you accepted pay for your country." Since that time four bands of the Nez Perces have received annuities from the United States. My father was invited to many councils, and they tried hard to make him sign the treaty, but he was firm as the rock and would not sign away his home. His refusal caused a difference among the Nez Perces.

Eight years later (1863) was the next treaty council. A chief called Lawyer,[8] because he was a great talker, took the lead in this council and sold nearly all of the Nez Perces' country. My father was not there. He said to me, "When you go into council with the white man, always remember your country.

Do not give it away. The white man will cheat you out of your home. I have taken no pay from the United States. I have never sold our land."

In this treaty, Lawyer acted without authority from our band. He had no right to sell the Wallowa (Winding River) country. That had always belonged to my father's own people, and the other bands had never disputed our right to it. No other Indians ever claimed Wallowa.

In order to have all people understand how much land we owned, my father planted poles around it and said, "Inside is the home of my people—the white man may take the land outside. Inside this boundary, all our people were born. It circles around the graves of our fathers, and we will never give up these graves to any man."

The United States claimed they had bought all the Nez Perces' country outside the Lapwai reservation from Lawyer and other chiefs, but we continued to live on this land in peace until eight years ago, when white men began to come inside the bounds my father had set. We warned them against this great wrong, but they would not leave our land, and some bad blood was raised. The white man represented that we were going upon the warpath. They reported many things that were false.

The United States government again asked for a treaty council. My father had become blind and feeble. He could no longer speak for his people. It was then I took my father's place as chief. In this council, I made my first speech to white men. I said to the agent who held the council:

I did not want to come to this council, but I came hoping that we could save blood. The white man has no right to come here and take our country. We have never accepted presents from the government. Neither Lawyer nor any other chief had authority to sell this land. It has always belonged to my people. It came unclouded to them from our fathers, and we will defend this land as long as a drop of Indian blood warms the hearts of our men.

The agent said he had orders from the Great White Chief at Washington for us to go upon the Lapwai reservation, and that if we obeyed he would help us in many ways. "You *must* move to the agency," he said.

I answered him:

I will not. I do not need your help; we have plenty, and we are contented and happy if the white man will let us alone. The reservation is too small for so many people with all their stock. You can keep your presents; we can go to your towns and pay for all we need; we have plenty of horses and cattle to sell, and we won't have any help from you; we are free now; we can go where we please. Our fathers were born here. Here they lived, here they died, here are their graves. We will never leave them.

The agent went away, and we had peace for a while. Soon after this, my father sent for me. I saw he was dying. I took his hand in mine. He said:

My son, my body is returning to my mother earth, and my spirit is going very soon to see the Great Spirit Chief. When I am gone, think of your country. You are the chief of these people. They look to you to guide them. Always remember that your father never sold his country. You must stop your ears whenever you are asked to sign a treaty selling your home. A few years more, and white men will be all around you. They have their eyes on this land. My son, never forget my dying words. This country holds your father's body. Never sell the bones of your father and your mother.

I pressed my father's hand and told him that I would protect his grave with my life. My father smiled and passed away to the spirit land. I buried him in that beautiful valley of winding waters. I love that land more than all the rest of the world. A man who would not love his father's grave is worse than a wild animal.

For a short time we lived quietly. But this could not last. White men had found gold in the mountains around the land of the winding water. They stole a great many horses from us, and we could not get them back because we were Indians. The white men told lies for each other. They drove off a great many of our cattle. Some white men branded our young cattle so they could claim them. We had no friend who would plead our cause before the law councils. It seemed to me that some of the white men in Wallowa were doing these things on purpose to get up a war. They knew that we were not strong enough to fight them.

I labored hard to avoid trouble and bloodshed. We gave up some of our country to the white men, thinking that then we could have peace. We were mistaken. The white man would not let us alone. We could have avenged our wrongs many times, but we did not. Whenever the government has asked us to help them against other Indians, we have never refused. When the white men were few and we were strong, we could have killed them off, but the Nez Perces wished to live at peace.

If we have not done so, we have not been to blame. I believe that the old treaty has never been correctly reported. If we ever owned the land, we own it still, for we never sold it. In the treaty councils, the commissioners have claimed that our country had been sold to the government. Suppose a white man should come to me and say, "Joseph, I like your horses, and I want to buy them." I say to him, "No, my horses suit me, I will not sell them." Then he goes to my neighbor, and says to him, "Joseph has some good horses. I want to buy them, but he refuses to sell." My neighbor answers, "Pay me the money, and I will sell you Joseph's horses." The white man returns to me and says, "Joseph, I have bought your horses, and you must let me have them." If we sold our lands to the government, this is the way they were bought.

On account of the treaty made by the other bands of Nez Perces, the white men claimed my lands. We were troubled greatly by white men crowding over the line. Some of these were good men, and we lived on peaceful terms with them, but they were not all good.

Nearly every year the agent came over from Lapwai and ordered us onto the reservation. We always replied that we were satisfied to live in Wallowa. We were careful to refuse the presents or annuities which he offered.

Through all the years since the white man came to Wallowa, we have been threatened and taunted by them and the treaty Nez Perces. They have given us no rest. We have had a few good friends among white men, and they have always advised my people to bear these taunts without fighting. Our young men were quick tempered, and I have had great trouble in keeping them from doing rash things. I have carried a heavy load on my back ever since I was a boy. I learned then that we were but few, while the white men were many, and that we could not hold our own with them. We were like deer. They were like grizzly bears. We had a small country. Their country was large. We were contented to let things remain as the Great Spirit Chief made them. They were not, and would change the rivers and mountains if they did not suit them.

Year after year we have been threatened, but no war was made upon my people until General Howard[9] came to our country two years ago and told us that he was the white war chief of all that country. He said, "I have a great many soldiers at my back. I am going to bring them up here, and then I will talk to you again. I will not let white men laugh at me the next time I come. The country belongs to the government, and I intend to make you go upon the reservation."

I remonstrated with him against bringing more soldiers to the Nez Perces' country. He had one house full of troops all the time at Fort Lapwai.

The next spring the agent at Umatilla agency sent an Indian runner to tell me to meet General Howard at Walla Walla. I could not go myself, but I sent my brother and five other headmen to meet him, and they had a long talk.

General Howard said, "You have talked straight, and it is all right. You can stay at Wallowa." He insisted that my brother and his company should go with him to Fort Lapwai. When the party arrived there, General Howard sent out runners and called all the Indians to a grand council. I was in that council. I said to General Howard, "We are ready to listen." He answered that he would not talk then, but would hold a council next day, when he would talk plainly. I said to General Howard:

> I am ready to talk today. I have been in a great many councils, but I am no wiser. We are all sprung from a woman, although we are unlike in many things. We cannot be made over again. You are as you were made, and as you were made you can remain. We are just as we were made by the Great Spirit, and you cannot change us; then why should children of one mother and one father quarrel—why should

one try to cheat the other? I do not believe that the Great Spirit Chief gave one kind of men the right to tell another kind of men what they must do.

General Howard replied, "You deny my authority, do you? You want to dictate to me, do you?"

Then one of my chiefs, Toohoolhoolzote,[10] rose in the council and said to General Howard, "The Great Spirit Chief made the world as it is, and as He wanted it, and He made a part of it for us to live upon. I do not see where you get authority to say that we shall not live where He placed us."

General Howard lost his temper and said, "Shut up! I don't want to hear any more of such talk. The law says you shall go upon the reservation to live, and I want you to do so, but you persist in disobeying the law (meaning the treaty). If you do not move, I will take the matter into my own hand, and make you suffer for your disobedience."

Toohoolhoolzote answered, "Who are you, that you ask us to talk, and then tell me I shan't talk? Are you the Great Spirit? Did you make the world? Did you make the sun? Did you make the rivers to run for us to drink? Did you make the grass to grow? Did you make all these things, that you talk to us as though we were boys? If you did, then you have the right to talk as you do."

General Howard replied, "You are an impudent fellow, and I will put you in the guardhouse," and then ordered a soldier to arrest him.

Toohoolhoolzote made no resistance. He asked General Howard, "Is this your order? I don't care. I have expressed my heart to you. I have nothing to take back. I have spoken for my country. You can arrest me, but you cannot change me or make me take back what I have said."

The soldiers came forward and seized my friend and took him to the guardhouse. My men whispered among themselves whether they would let this thing be done. I counseled them to submit. I knew if we resisted, that all the white men present, including General Howard, would be killed in a moment, and we would be blamed. If I had said nothing, General Howard would never have given an unjust order against my men. I saw the danger and while they dragged Toohoolhoolzote to prison, I arose and said, "I am going to talk now. I don't care whether you arrest me or not." I turned to my people and said, "The arrest of Toohoolhoolzote was wrong, but we will not resent the insult. We were invited to this council to express our hearts, and we have done so." Toohoolhoolzote was prisoner for five days before he was released.

The council broke up that day. On the next morning, General Howard came to my lodge, and invited me to go with him and White Bird[11] and Looking Glass[12] to look for land for my people. As we rode along, we came to some good land that was already occupied by Indians and white people. General Howard, pointing to this land, said, "If you will come on to the reservation, I will give you these lands and move these people off."

I replied, "No. It would be wrong to disturb these people. I have no right to take their homes. I have never taken what did not belong to me. I will not now."

We rode all day upon the reservation and found no good land unoccupied. I have been informed by men who do not lie that General Howard sent a letter that night telling the soldiers at Walla Walla to go to Wallowa Valley and drive us out upon our return home.

In the council next day, General Howard informed us in a haughty spirit that he would give my people thirty days to go back home, collect all their stock, and move onto the reservation, saying, "If you are not here in that time, I shall consider that you want to fight, and will send my soldiers to drive you on."

I said, "War can be avoided, and it ought to be avoided. I want no war. My people have always been the friends of the white man. Why are you in such a hurry? I cannot get ready to move in thirty days. Our stock is scattered, and Snake River is very high. Let us wait until fall, then the river will be low. We want time to hunt our stock and gather our supplies for the winter."

General Howard replied, "If you let the time run over one day, the soldiers will be there to drive you onto the reservation, and all your cattle and horses outside of the reservation at that time will fall into the hands of the white men."

I knew I had never sold my country and that I had no land in Lapwai, but I did not want bloodshed. I did not want my people killed. I did not want anybody killed. Some of my people had been murdered by white men, and the white murderers were never punished for it. I told General Howard about this, and again said I wanted no war. I wanted the people who live upon the lands I was to occupy at Lapwai to have time to gather their harvest.

I said in my heart that rather than have war, I would give up my country. I would rather give up my father's grave. I would give up everything rather than have the blood of white men upon the hands of my people.

General Howard refused to allow me more than thirty days to move my people and their stock. I am sure that he began to prepare for war at once.

When I returned to Wallowa, I found my people very much excited upon discovering that the soldiers were already in the Wallowa Valley. We held a council and decided to move immediately to avoid bloodshed.

Toohoolhoolzote, who felt outraged by his imprisonment, talked for war and made many of my young men willing to fight rather than be driven like dogs from the land where they were born. He declared that blood alone would wash out the disgrace General Howard had put upon him. It required a strong heart to stand up against such talk, but I urged my people to be quiet and not to begin a war.

We gathered all the stock we could find and made an attempt to move. We left many of our horses and cattle in Wallowa, and we lost several hundred in crossing the river. All my people succeeded in getting across in safety. Many of the Nez Perces came together in Rocky Canyon to hold a grand council. I went with all my people. This council lasted ten days. There was a great deal of war talk and a great deal of excitement. There was one young brave present whose father had been killed by a white man five years before. This man's blood was bad against white men, and he left the council calling for revenge.

Again I counseled peace, and I thought the danger was past. We had not complied with General Howard's order because we could not, but we intended to do so as soon as possible. I was leaving the council to kill beef for my family, when news came that the young man whose father had been killed had gone out with several hot-blooded young braves and killed four white men. He rode up to the council and shouted, "Why do you sit here like women? The war has begun already."

I was deeply grieved. All the lodges were moved except my brother's and my own. I saw clearly that the war was upon us when I learned that my young men had been secretly buying ammunition. I heard then that Toohoolhoolzote, who had been imprisoned by General Howard, had succeeded in organizing a war party. I knew that their acts would involve all my people. I saw that the war could not then be prevented. The time had passed. I counseled peace from the beginning. I knew that we were too weak to fight the United States. We had many grievances, but I knew that war would bring more. We had good white friends who advised us against taking the warpath. My friend and brother, Mr. Chapman,[13] who has been with us since the surrender, told us just how the war would end. Mr. Chapman took sides against us and helped General Howard. I do not blame him for doing so. He tried hard to prevent bloodshed. We hoped the white settlers would not join the soldiers. Before the war commenced, we had discussed this matter all over, and many of my people were in favor of warning them that if they took no part against us they should not be molested in the event of war being begun by General Howard. This plan was voted down in the war council.

There were bad men among my people who had quarreled with white men, and they talked of their wrongs until they roused all the bad hearts in the council. Still, I could not believe that they would begin the war. I know that my young men did a great wrong, but I ask who was first to blame? They had been insulted a thousand times; their fathers and brothers had been killed; their mothers and wives had been disgraced; they had been driven to madness by the whiskey sold to them by the white men; they had been told by General Howard that all their horses and cattle which they had been unable to drive out of Wallowa were to fall into the hands of white men; and added to all this, they were homeless and desperate.

I would have given my own life if I could have undone the killing of white men by my people. I blame my young men and I blame the white men. I blame General Howard for not giving my people time to get their stock away from Wallowa. I do not acknowledge that he had the right to order me to leave Wallowa at any time. I deny that either my father or myself ever sold that land. It is still our land. It may never again be our home, but my father sleeps there, and I love it as I love my mother. I left there hoping to avoid bloodshed.

If General Howard had given me plenty of time to gather up my stock, and treated Toohoolhoolzote as a man should be treated, there would have been no war. My friends among white men have blamed me for the war. I am not to blame. When my young men began the killing, my heart was hurt. Although I did not justify them, I remembered all the insults I had endured, and my blood was on fire. Still, I would have taken my people to the buffalo country without fighting if possible.

I could see no other way to avoid a war. We moved over to White Bird Creek, sixteen miles away, and there encamped, intending to collect our stock before leaving; but the soldiers attacked us, and the first battle was fought. We numbered in that battle sixty men, and the soldiers a hundred. The fight lasted but a few minutes, when the soldiers retreated before us for twelve miles. They lost thirty-three killed and had seven wounded. When an Indian fights, he only shoots to kill, but soldiers shoot at random. None of the soldiers were scalped. We do not believe in scalping, or in killing wounded men. Soldiers do not kill many Indians unless they are wounded and left upon the battlefield. Then they kill Indians.

Seven days after the first battle, General Howard arrived in the Nez Perces' country, bringing 700 more soldiers. It was now war in earnest. We crossed over Salmon River, hoping General Howard would follow. We were not disappointed. He did follow us, and we got between him and his supplies, and cut him off for three days. He sent out two companies to open the way. We attacked them, killing one officer, two guides, and ten men.

We withdrew, hoping the soldiers would follow, but they had got fighting enough for that day. They entrenched themselves, and next day we attacked again. The battle lasted all day, and was renewed next morning. We killed four and wounded seven or eight.

About this time, General Howard found out that we were in his rear. Five days later he attacked us with 350 soldiers and settlers. We had 250 warriors. The fight lasted twenty-seven hours. We lost four killed and several wounded. General Howard's loss was twenty-nine men killed and sixty wounded.

The following day the soldiers charged upon us, and we retreated with our families and stock a few miles, leaving eighty lodges to fall into General Howard's hands.

Finding that we were outnumbered, we retreated to Bitterroot Valley. Here another body of soldiers came upon us and demanded our surrender. We refused. They said, "You cannot get by us." We answered, "We are going by you without fighting if you will let us, but we are going by you anyhow." We then made a treaty with these soldiers. We agreed not to molest anyone, and they agreed that we might pass through the Bitterroot country in peace. We bought provisions and traded stock with white men there.

We understood that there was to be no war. We intended to go peaceably to the buffalo country, and leave the question of returning to our country to be settled afterward.

With this understanding, we traveled on for four days, and thinking that the trouble was all over, we stopped and prepared tent poles to take with us. We started again, and at the end of two days, we saw three white men passing our camp. Thinking that peace had been made, we did not molest them. We could have killed or taken them prisoners, but we did not suspect them of being spies, which they were.

That night the soldiers surrounded our camp. About daybreak one of my men went out to look after his horses. The soldiers saw him and shot him down like a coyote. I have since learned that these soldiers were not those we had left behind. They had come upon us from another direction. The new white war chief's name was Gibbon.[14] He charged upon us while some of my people were still asleep. We had a hard fight. Some of my men crept around and attacked the soldiers from the rear. In this battle we lost nearly all our lodges, but we finally drove Colonel Gibbon back.

Finding that he was not able to capture us, he sent to his camp a few miles away for his big guns (cannons), but my men had captured them and all the ammunition. We damaged the big guns all we could and carried away the powder and lead. In the fight with Colonel Gibbon, we lost fifty women and children and thirty fighting men. We remained long enough to bury our dead. The Nez Perces never make war on women and children; we could have killed a great many women and children while the war lasted, but we would feel ashamed to do so cowardly an act.

We never scalp our enemies, but when General Howard came up and joined Colonel Gibbon, their Indian scouts dug up our dead and scalped them. I have been told that General Howard did not order this great shame to be done.

We retreated as rapidly as we could toward the buffalo country. After six days General Howard came close to us, and we went out and attacked him, and captured nearly all his horses and mules (about 250 head). We then marched on to the Yellowstone Basin.

On the way we captured one white man and two white women. We released them at the end of three days. They were treated kindly. The women were not insulted. Can the white soldiers tell me of one time when Indian women were taken prisoners and held three days, and then released without being insulted? Were the Nez Perce women who fell into the hands of General Howard's soldiers treated with as much respect? I deny that a Nez Perce was ever guilty of such a crime.

A few days later we captured two more white men. One of them stole a horse and escaped. We gave the other a poor horse and told him that he was free.

Nine days' march brought us to the mouth of Clark's Fork of the Yellowstone. We did not know what had become of General Howard, but we supposed that he had sent for more horses and mules. He did not come up, but another new war chief (Colonel Sturgis)[15] attacked us. We held him in check while we moved all our women and children and stock out of danger, leaving a few men to cover our retreat.

Several days passed, and we heard nothing of General Howard, Colonel Gibbon, or Colonel Sturgis. We had repulsed each in turn and began to feel secure when another army, under Colonel Miles,[16] struck us. This was the fourth army, each of which outnumbered our fighting force, that we had encountered within sixty days.

We had no knowledge of Colonel Miles's army until a short time before he made a charge upon us, cutting our camp in two and capturing nearly all of our horses. About seventy men, myself among them, were cut off. My little daughter, twelve years of age, was with me. I gave her a rope and told her to catch a horse and join the others who were cut off from the camp. I have not seen her since, but I have learned that she is alive and well.

I thought of my wife and children, who were now surrounded by soldiers, and I resolved to go to them or die. With a prayer in my mouth to the Great Spirit Chief who rules above, I dashed unarmed through the line of soldiers. It seemed to me that there were guns on every side, before and behind me. My clothes were cut to pieces and my horse was wounded, but I was not hurt. As I reached the door of my lodge, my wife handed me my rifle, saying, "Here's your gun. Fight!"

The soldiers kept up a continuous fire. Six of my men were killed in one spot near me. Ten or twelve soldiers charged into our camp and got possession of two lodges, killing three Nez Perces and losing three of their men, who fell inside our lines. I called my men to drive them back. We fought at close range, not more than twenty steps apart, and drove the soldiers back upon their main line, leaving their dead in our hands. We secured their arms and ammunition. We lost, the first day and night, eighteen men and three women. Colonel Miles lost twenty-six killed and forty wounded. The following day Colonel Miles sent a messenger into my camp under protection of a white flag. I sent my friend Yellow Bull[17] to meet him.

Yellow Bull understood the messenger to say that Colonel Miles wished me to consider the situation; that he did not want to kill my people unnecessarily. Yellow Bull understood this to be a demand for me to surrender and save blood. Upon reporting this message to me, Yellow Bull said he wondered whether Colonel Miles was in earnest. I sent him back with my answer, that I had not made up my mind but would think about it and send word soon. A little later he sent some Cheyenne scouts with another message. I went out to meet them. They said they believed that Colonel Miles was sincere and really wanted peace. I walked on to Colonel Miles's tent. He met me and we shook hands. He said, "Come, let us sit down by the fire and talk this matter over." I remained with him all night; next morning, Yellow Bull came over to see if I was alive, and why I did not return. Colonel Miles would not let me leave the tent to see my friend alone.

Yellow Bull said to me, "They have got you in their power, and I am afraid they will never let you go again. I have an officer in our camp, and I will hold him until they let you go free."

I said, "I do not know what they mean to do with me, but if they kill me, you must not kill the officer. It will do no good to avenge my death by killing him."

Yellow Bull returned to my camp. I did not make any agreement that day with Colonel Miles. The battle was renewed while I was with him. I was very anxious about my people. I knew that we were near Sitting Bull's camp in King George's land, and I thought maybe the Nez Perces who had escaped would return with assistance. No great damage was done to either party during the night.

On the following morning I returned to my camp by agreement, meeting the officer who had been held a prisoner in my camp at the flag of truce. My people were divided about surrendering. We could have escaped from Bear's Paw Mountain if we had left our wounded, old women, and children behind. We were unwilling to do this. We had never heard of a wounded Indian recovering while in the hands of white men.

On the evening of the fourth day, General Howard came in with a small escort, together with my friend Chapman. We could now talk understandingly. Colonel Miles said to me in plain words, "If you will come out and give up your arms, I will spare your lives and send you back to the reservation." I do not know what passed between Colonel Miles and General Howard.

I could not bear to see my wounded men and women suffer any longer; we had lost enough already. Colonel Miles had promised that we might return to our country with what stock we had left. I thought we could start again. I believed Colonel Miles, *or I never would have surrendered.* I have heard that he has been censured for making the promise to return us to Lapwai. He could not have made any other terms with me at that time. I would have held him in check until my friends came to my assistance, and then neither of the generals nor their soldiers would have ever left Bear's Paw Mountains alive.

On the fifth day I went to Colonel Miles and gave up my gun, and said, "From where the sun now stands, I will fight no more." My people needed rest—we wanted peace.

I was told we could go with Colonel Miles to Tongue River and stay there until spring, when we would be sent back to our country. Finally, it was decided that we were to be taken to Tongue River. We had nothing to say about it. After our arrival at Tongue River, Colonel Miles received orders to take us to Bismarck. The reason given was that subsistence would be cheaper there.

Colonel Miles was opposed to this order. He said, "You must not blame me. I have endeavored to keep my word, but the chief who is over me has given the order, and I must obey it or resign. That would do you no good. Some other officer would carry out the order."

I believe Colonel Miles would have kept his word if he could have done so. I do not blame him for what we have suffered since the surrender. I do not know who is to blame. We gave up all our horses—over 1,100—and all our saddles—over 100—and we have not heard from them since. Somebody has got our horses.

Colonel Miles turned my people over to another soldier, and we were taken to Bismarck. Captain Johnson, who now had charge of us, received an order to take us to Fort Leavenworth. At Leavenworth we were placed on a low river bottom, with no water except river water to drink and cook with. We had always lived in a healthy country, where the mountains were high and the water was cold and clear. Many of our people sickened and died, and we buried them in this strange land. I cannot tell how much my heart suffered for my people while at Leavenworth. The Great Spirit Chief who rules above seemed to be looking some other way and did not see what was being done to my people.

During the hot days (July 1878), we received notice that we were to be moved farther away from our own country. We were not asked if we were willing to go. We were ordered to get into the railroad cars. Three of my people died on the way to Baxter Springs. It was worse to die there than to die fighting in the mountains.

We were moved from Baxter Springs (Kansas) to the Indian Territory and set down without our lodges. We had but little medicine, and we were nearly all sick. Seventy of my people have died since we moved there.

We have had a great many visitors who have talked many ways. Some of the chiefs from Washington came to see us and selected land for us to live upon. We have not moved to that land, for it is not a good place to live.

The commissioner chief (E. A. Hayt)[18] came to see us. I told him, as I told everyone, that I expected Colonel Miles's word would be carried out. He said it could not be done; that white men now lived in my country, and all the land was taken up; that if I returned to Wallowa, I could not live in peace; that law papers were out against my young men who began the war, and that the government could not protect my people. This talk fell like a heavy stone upon my heart. I saw that I could not gain anything by talking to him. Other law chiefs (congressional committee) came to see us and said they would help me to get a healthy country. I did not know whom to believe. The white people have too many chiefs. They do not understand each other. They do not talk alike.

The commissioner chief invited me to go with him and hunt for a better home than we have now. I like the land we found (west of the Osage reservation) better than any place I have seen in that country; but it is not a healthy land. There are no mountains and rivers. The water is warm. It is not a good country for stock. I do not believe my people can live there. I am afraid they will all die. The Indians who occupy that country are dying off. I promised Chief Hayt to go there and do the best I could until the government got ready to make good Colonel Miles's word. I was not satisfied, but I could not help myself. Then the inspector chief (McNeill)[19] came to my camp, and we had a long talk. He said I ought to have a home in the mountain country north, and that he would write a letter to the Great Chief in Washington. Again, the hope of seeing the mountains of Idaho and Oregon grew up in my heart.

At last I was granted permission to come to Washington and bring my friend Yellow Bull and our interpreter with me. I am glad we came. I have shaken hands with a great many friends, but there are some things I want to know which no one seems able to explain. I cannot understand how the government sends a man out to fight us, as it did Colonel Miles, and then breaks his word. Such a government has something wrong about it. I cannot understand why so many chiefs are allowed to talk so many different ways, and promise so many different things. I have seen the Great Father Chief (the president); the next great chief (secretary of the interior); the commissioner chief; the law chief (General Butler),[20] and many other law chiefs (congressmen), and they all say they are my friends, and that I shall have justice, but while their mouths all talk right, I do not understand why nothing is done for my people. I have heard talk and talk, but nothing is done. Good words do not last long until they amount to something. Words do not pay for my dead people. They do not pay for my country, now overrun by white men. They do not protect my father's grave. They do not pay for my horses and cattle. Good words will not give me back my children. Good words will not make good the promise of your War Chief, Colonel Miles. Good words will not give my people good health and stop them from dying. Good words will not get my people a home where they can live in peace and take care of themselves.

I am tired of talk that comes to nothing. It makes my heart sick when I remember all the good words and all the broken promises. There has been too much talking by men who had no right to talk. Too many misrepresentations have been made, too many misunderstandings have come up between the white men about the Indians. If the white man wants to live in peace with the Indian, he can live in peace. There need be no trouble. Treat all men alike. Give them all the same law. Give them all an even chance to live and grow. All men were made by the same Great Spirit Chief. They are all brothers. The earth is the mother of all people, and all people should have equal rights upon it. You might as well expect the rivers to run backward as that any man who was born a free man should be contented penned up and denied liberty to go where he pleases. If you tie a horse to a stake, do you expect he will grow fat? If you pen an Indian up on a small spot of earth and compel him to stay there, he will not be contented, nor will he grow and prosper. I have asked some of the great white chiefs where they get their authority to say to the Indian that he shall stay in one place, while he sees white men going where they please. They cannot tell me.

I only ask of the government to be treated as all other men are treated. If I cannot go to my own home, let me have a home in some country where my people will not die so fast. I would like to go to Bitterroot Valley. There my

Chief Joseph's winter tepee at the Nespelem agency.
NEZ PERCE NATIONAL HISTORIC PARK.

people would be healthy; where they are now, they are dying. Three have died since I left my camp to come to Washington. When I think of our condition, my heart is heavy. I see men of my race treated as outlaws and driven from country to country, or shot down like animals.

I know that my race must change. We cannot hold our own with the white men as we are. We only ask an even chance to live as other men live. We ask to be recognized as men. We ask that the same law shall work alike on all men. If the Indian breaks the law, punish him by the law. If the white man breaks the law, punish him also.

Let me be a free man—free to travel, free to stop, free to work, free to trade, where I choose, free to choose my own teachers, free to follow the religion of my fathers, free to think and talk and act for myself, and I will obey every law, or submit to the penalty.

Whenever the white man treats the Indian as they treat each other, then we shall have no more wars. We shall be all alike—brothers of one father and one mother, with one sky above us and one country around us, and one government for all. Then the Great Spirit Chief who rules above will smile upon this land, and send rain to wash out the bloody spots made by brothers' hands upon the face of the earth. For this time the Indian race are waiting and praying. I hope that no more groans of wounded men and women will ever go to the ear of the Great Spirit Chief above, and that all people may be one people.

In-mut-too-yah-lat-lat has spoken for his people.

The True Story of the Wallowa Campaign

OLIVER O. HOWARD[1]

North American Review 128 (July 1879): 53–64[2]

O n reading in the *North American Review* for April the article entitled "An Indian's View of Indian Affairs," I was so pleased with Joseph's statement, necessarily ex parte though it was, and naturally inspired by resentment toward me as a supposed enemy, that at first I had no purpose of making a rejoinder. But when I saw in the *Army and Navy Journal* long passages quoted from Joseph's tale, which appeared to reflect unfavorably upon my official conduct, to lay upon me the blame of the atrocious murders committed by the Indians, and to convict me of glaring faults where I had deemed myself worthy only of commendation, I addressed to the editor of that journal a communication (which has been published) correcting misstatements and briefly setting forth the facts of the case.

Now I find eastern newspapers insisting that if Joseph's statements are borne out by the facts of history, General Howard should be removed from his department.

May I say that I am profoundly concerned about this subject of the management of Indian affairs, and if I am an obstacle in the way of order, justice, obedience to law, and the advancement of civilization among the Indians, I deserve to be deprived of command. But is it not a strange idea that the army commander who is subject to the requisition of the Indian Department, of which he forms no part; who on that requisition is ordered to use the force under his command to stop citizens and Indians in armed array against each other from fighting; to put bands of roaming and nomadic Indians on reservations set apart for them; and finally, to restore the peace where fiendish murders have already begun—is it not a strange idea that he should be held accountable for all the mischief that has been brewing; for the depredations of the nomads; for the quarrels between the citizens and Indians; for the dispositions of the Indian Department; and for the horrid murders that inaugurate the war? This is a very unfair distribution of power and accountability. If I had had the power and the management entirely in my hands, I believe I could have healed that old

Brigadier General Oliver O. Howard. NATIONAL ARCHIVES.

sore and established peace and amity with Joseph's Indians. It could only have been done, first by a retrocession of Wallowa (already belonging to Oregon) to the United States, and then setting that country apart forever for the Indians without the retention of any government authority whatever; and second, by the removal therefrom of every white settler, making to each a proper remuneration for his land and improvements. But this power I did not have, and the Indian management did not belong to my department.

There were two ways in which I was brought into this matter as department commander: first, by the yearly appeal of the scattered white people for protection against the depredations, misconduct, and threats of the Indians; these appeals, coming from an alarmed population and taking official form, had to be met. Second, the requisition of the Indian Department through its several channels, resulting in positive military orders. Now permit me to present a few simple facts which will show whether, in manner or matter, I have failed to meet the requirements of the situation. These facts I wrote and published when the whole subject was fresh in memory, and will endeavor before long to place again at the disposal of the public, in book form, with a more complete account of this notable Indian war.

Governor Stevens and Joel Palmer[3] in 1855 made a treaty with the Nez Perce, including all the different bands. Joseph's band were parties to the treaty, and Joseph's father signed it. This ceded and relinquished to the United States all land that the Nez Perce claimed outside of the limits then fixed and agreed upon.

This treaty, be it remembered, included Wallowa and Imnaha Valleys. In 1863 the United States, by their commissioners, made another treaty with the

Nez Perce, fifty-one chiefs participating. This treaty reduced the limits so as to constitute the reservation in Lapwai as it now is and ceded all the land outside to the United States. Wallowa and Imnaha were left out.

Joseph's band and a few other bands, now known as the Salmon River or White Bird's band, lived east of the reservation, and the Palouse or Hush-hush-cute's band, west of the same. These, with a few more on and off the reserve, constitute what are called "nontreaties." The vast majority who made the treaty have kept good faith and are called "treaty Indians." James Lawyer, the present head chief, is an excellent man; dresses as a white man and has a good house and farm. Now, notice the difference: Joseph says, "Governor Stevens urged my father to sign the treaty (1855), but he refused." Then he goes on to give us a graphic account of this refusal and its consequences. He "cautioned his people to take no presents." He "was invited to many councils, and they tried hard to make him sign the treaty, but he was firm as the rock and would not sign away his home," etc. Now all this is very fine; yet his father did sign the treaty. His name is the third on the list, and there are eleven white witnesses, besides the makers of the instrument.

Governor Grover says in his message, "The reservation named became the common property of the whole tribe." Joseph and his band acknowledged these conclusions also by accepting the benefit of the treaty of 1855.

Such is the record of history, in precise contradiction to Young Joseph's traditional statement. But he states truly the *claim* (based on the treaty of 1863) of the United States to Wallowa, and Joseph's constant *demurrer* thereto. The underlying cause of all the troubles, finally resulting in the war, is Joseph's assumption that as subchief he is not bound by this last treaty, inasmuch as he has ever refused to sign it. This disputed territory was finally surveyed and is within the limits of Oregon. Stockmen began to pasture portions of it, and enterprising frontiersmen settled in and near one of the valleys. They took up land and gained their titles to homesteads in the usual way. Again and again the government tried to convince the Indians that they all had common right inside of the Lapwai reserve, but that "the Indian title was extinguished" for those Oregon lands.

Nothing but restlessness and dissatisfaction resulted for a while—no serious outbreak, though the quarrels with settlers, especially in the Salmon River country, were perpetual, several times resulting in loss of life.

Again, the account of Joseph concerning his father's death and his home is beautiful and quite affecting. I dislike to mar the effect of it, yet it is a known fact that when the United States agents sought to make some definite arrangement, proposing to give this land to the tribe as a *home,* the offer was refused. The governor of Oregon writes in 1873: "This small band wish the possession of this large section of Oregon simply to gratify a wild, roaming disposition, and *not for a home.*" And even up to the last peace council, the objection was not that "you take from us our *home*" (for they intended to live part of the year with the remainder of the tribe), but "you take away our liberty; fix bounds to our habitation, and give law to us. The land is ours, and not yours."

Joseph's pictures of frontier troubles between whites and Indians are graphic and true. The killing of a member of his tribe by a white man he refers to. This came near causing an outbreak. The troops intervened between the settlers and the Indians, and the latter quieted down.[4] But the slow process of the civil law, and the prejudice against Indians in all frontier courts, almost invariably prevent the punishment of crimes against Indians. I did what I could to further the ends of justice, in bringing the guilty to trial; but my efforts in this case resulted in nothing. The Indian has a complaint against us (army and agents), because we can and do punish *him,* but do not and cannot punish *white men* who steal the Indian's property and take life.

"But no war was made on my people until General Howard came to our country two years ago," etc. This has all the summary brevity of Shakespeare's history but is not more accurate. The facts are that I had been in command of the department since the fall of 1874 and had many dealings with Joseph and his people.

The "nontreaties" became suspiciously restless during the Modoc troubles. This was quieted by my worthy predecessor by sending a considerable force among them just after the Modoc War. Colonel Davis, speaking of a large gathering of Indians that boded difficulty at the Wee-ipe, says: "The troops did not interfere with the council (twelve hundred Indians), but their presence there for about ten days had the effect to disperse it. General dissatisfaction, however, seemed to prevail among the 'non-treaty Nez Perce.' This was particularly the case with Joseph's band, the claimants of Wallowa Valley."

Again, the *same year* (1874), these Indians were so restless and threatening that Maj. John Green, 1st Cavalry, was sent to Wallowa Valley with two companies and remained till the Indians left for their winter quarters.

The next year (1875) I say in my report: "The troubles at Lapwai and Wallowa Valley have not thus far resulted in bloodshed, but it has been prevented by great carefulness and provision on the part of the government agents."

The year following (1876), my report goes into the trouble again at length, mentioning the grave fact that "an Indian was killed by a white man in a dispute concerning some stock"[5] and winds up with these words: "And renew my recommendation of a commission to hear and settle the whole matter, before war is even thought of." The commission was at last ordered, but not until after blood had been shed—not till after the Indians had stood up in battle array against armed citizens in Wallowa, and a conflict was averted only by the intervention of regular troops. The commission came, held its memorable sessions at Lapwai in November of 1876, and labored hard and long to get the consent of the disaffected nontreaty Indians to some measures of adjustment.

Here are a few of the facts developed by this commission:

The Dreamers, among other pernicious doctrines, teach that the earth, being created by God complete, should not be disturbed by man; and that any cultivation of the soil or other improvements to interfere with its natural productions; any voluntary submission to the control of the government; any improvement in the way of schools, churches, etc., are crimes from which they shrink. This fanaticism is kept alive by the superstition of these Dreamers, who industriously teach that if they continue steadfast in their present belief, a leader will be raised up (in the East), who will restore all the dead Indians to life, who will unite with them in expelling the whites from their country, when they will again enter upon and repossess the lands of their ancestors.[6]

Influenced by such belief, Joseph and his band firmly declined to enter into any negotiations, or make any arrangements that looked to a final settlement of the question pending between him and the government yet, in view of the fact that these Indians do not claim simply this (rights of occupancy), but set up an absolute title to the lands, an absolute and independent sovereignty, and refuse even to be limited in their claim and control, necessity, humanity, and good sense constrain the government to set metes and bounds and give regulations to these nontreaty Indians. And if the principle usually applied by the government, of holding that the Indians with whom they have treaties are bound by majorities, is here applied, Joseph should be required to live within the limits of the present reservation.

The commission, though firm and strong in the expression of its opinion, was very patient with and kind to the Indians. I was a member of this commission and earnestly desired peace. I took Joseph's brother by himself and showed him how much it would be for the Indians' advantage to come to some settlement and spent a long time in giving him and his brother, in the kindest manner, the benefit of my counsel. They appeared at one time almost on the point of yielding, but bad advice intervened to renew the Dreamer sophistry. The commission promised that they should annually visit Wallowa, and so recommended. But here are a few closing words: "If these Indians overrun land belonging to the whites and commit depredations on their property, disturb the peace by threats or otherwise, or commit other overt acts of hostility, we recommend the employment of sufficient force to bring them into subjection, and to place them upon the Nez Perce reservation. The Indian agent at Lapwai should be fully instructed to carry into execution these suggestions, relying at all times upon the department commander for aid when necessary."

Now, there was nothing like precipitancy in all this; so that the wonderfully abrupt advent of General Howard, with a fear of the laughter of the white man in his heart and a threat of violence on his tongue, is all fiction. Doubtless Joseph was told that the commission had recommended "that Wallowa should be held by military occupation" to *prevent* and not to make war, and that I should have the work to do.

This commissioner's report was approved at Washington. The Indian agent, Mr. [John B.] Monteith, did all that lay in his power to carry out the recommendations at first without military aid.

The Indians called me to an interview first at Walla Walla, afterward at Lapwai. At Walla Walla the talk with Joseph's brother Ollokot was exceedingly pleasant. I write of it,

> The old medicine man looks happy, and Ollokot believes we shall have no trouble. I made the appointment for Lapwai in twelve days, but I went to Lewiston immediately to meet the officers of Fort Lapwai, and Indian agent Monteith, to read to them carefully the full instructions from the hon. secretary of war, [from] General Sherman, and [from] the commanding general of the military division, in relation especially to the agency the military was to have in placing the Indians upon the reservation.

I made a visit to Wallula, and then returned by stage to meet the nontreaties at Lapwai May 3, 1877. This is the council to which Joseph invited me, and not I him, as he alleges.

Before giving points in this interview in answer to Joseph's statements, I must state that Mr. Monteith had been instructed by his chief at Washington to bring the nontreaty Nez Perce upon their reservation. He had made his official demand upon me. I had been positively ordered to give the essential aid. There was now nothing left to parley about, yet to please the Indians, I had promised to meet them again, and I did.

These picturesque people came in sight, after keeping us waiting long enough for effect. They drew near the hollow square of the post and in sight of us, the small company to be interviewed. They struck up their song. They were not armed except with a few tomahawk pipes that could be smoked with the peaceful tobacco or penetrate the skull bone of an enemy, at the will of the holder; yet somehow, this wild song produces a strange effect. Our ladies, thinking it a war song, ask with some show of trepidation, "Do you think Joseph means to fight?" The Indians sweep around the fence and make the entire circuit, still keeping up the song as they ride, the buildings breaking the refrain into irregular bubblings of sound till the ceremony was completed.

After all had finally gathered at the tent and Father Cataldo had opened by a prayer in the Nez Perce language, I turned to Joseph and said through Mr. Whitman (the interpreter), "I heard from your brother Ollokot, twelve days ago at Walla Walla, that you wished to see me. I am now here to listen to what you have to say."

Joseph then told me of other Indians coming and said, "You must not be in a hurry to go until all get in to have a talk." I replied, "Mr. Monteith and I have our instructions from Washington. They send us to your people. If you decide at once to comply with the wishes of the government, you can have the first pick of vacant land. We will wait for White Bird if you desire it. Instructions to him are the same as to you. He can have his turn." And [to] an old Dreamer intimating that they wished a long talk, the answer is, "Mr. Monteith and I wished to hear what you have to say, whatever time it may take; but you may as well know at the outset that in any event, the Indians must obey the orders of the government of the United States."

Mr. Monteith then read his instructions from the Indian Bureau to the Indians and had them carefully interpreted to them, and also explained how he had already informed them of the orders to come on the reservation through Reuben (then head chief at Lapwai)[7] and that they had scorned his message. "Now, you *must* come, and there is no getting out of it. Your Indians and White Bird's can pick up your horses and cattle and come on the reservation. General Howard will stay till matters are settled."

Ollokot replied at length, objecting to considering matters settled.

I rejoined, "Joseph, the agent Mr. Monteith and myself are under the same government. What it commands us to do, that we must do. The Indians are to come on the reservation first; *then* they may have privileges, as the agent has shown, to hunt and to fish in the Imnaha Valley. If the Indians hesitate to come to the reservation, the government directs that soldiers be used to bring them hither. Joseph and Ollokot know that we are friends to them, and that if they comply, there will be no trouble."

Everybody at this council was in good humor except two old Dreamers, who tried to make a disturbance. I told them pointedly to give good advice. My manner I will not judge of. It is my usual manner, proceeding from the kindest of feelings and from an endeavor to behave as a gentleman to the weakest or most ignorant human being. The Indians, excepting the two I have named, made no angry remarks. We shook hands and separated, to wait as Joseph had requested.

Joseph has turned this right about in the article published in the *Review,* where it is stated that he said, "I am ready to talk today," and that General Howard would not. His account runs two days' interviews into one. Joseph never made that interesting speech ending with "I do not believe that the Great Spirit Chief gave one kind of men the right to tell another kind of men what they must do." And I did never reply, "You want to dictate to me, do you?" We always treated each other with the most marked courtesy.

On May 4 Joseph made a brief speech: "This is White Bird; I spoke to you of him; this is the first time he has seen you and you him. I want him and his Indians to understand what has been said to us."

White Bird was a demure-looking Indian, about five feet eight inches in height. His face assumed the condition of impassability while in council; he kept his ceremonial hat on and placed a large eagle's wing in front of his eyes and nose.

The subchief and Dreamer, Toohoolhoolzote, was broad-shouldered, deep-chested, five feet ten in height, had a deep guttural voice, and betrayed in every word a strong and settled hatred of all Caucasians. This man the Indians now put forward to speak for them—not that they had already decided to endorse his sentiments, but because he always counseled war; they evidently desired to see what effect his public utterance would produce upon us.

Now, instead of the mild and respectful speech attributed to this surly Indian by Joseph, a speech that was followed by my causeless loss of temper, Mr. Monteith and I heard him patiently, for quite a length of time, asserting his independence and uttering rebellious speeches against the Washington authority. We replied firmly and kindly as before, explaining everything and showing the imperative nature of our instructions.

The White Bird Indians were very tired that day, and Joseph again asked for delay. The record reads, "Let the Indians take time; let them wait till Monday morning and meanwhile talk among themselves. So, with pleasant faces and cordial handshaking, the second interview broke up."

How different this is from Joseph's account of the affair, in which he condenses the whole narrative into the arrest of Toohoolhoolzote upon his first appearance, and without provocation.

Now (Monday, May 7) we came together again. The nontreaties had received large accessions. The display (previous to seating themselves) gave them great boldness. Our garrison was but a handful, and the manner of the Indians was now defiant. Mr. Monteith began in the kindest manner to show the Indians that their religion would not be interfered with, nor their ceremonies, unless the peace was disturbed by excessive drumming.

Then Toohoolhoolzote began in the most offensive style. We listened to the oftrepeated Dreamer nonsense with no impatience, till finally he accused us of speaking untruthfully about the chieftainship of the earth.

I thought the time had come to check his tirade. I was not in the least angry, if I recall my mood with accuracy; I did not lose my temper, but I did assume a severity of tone sufficient to show that I understood the drift of the council, and that we were not to be intimidated. My first words were, "I do not want to interfere with your religion, but you must talk about practicable things. Twenty times over I hear that the earth is your mother, and about the chieftainship of the earth; I want to hear it no more, but to come to business at once."

He then talked against the treaty Indians and said they had no law, or their law was born of today; then against us white people for attempting to divide the earth, and defiantly asking, "What do you mean?"

Mr. Monteith explained, "The law is, you must come to the reservation. The law is made in Washington; we don't make it." Then, again, the Dreamer goes over the same ground and becomes fiercer and fiercer. The crowd of Indians are becoming excited, and I saw that I must act, and that very promptly. The record is, "The rough old fellow, in his most provoking tone, says something in a short sentence, looking fiercely at me. The interpreter quickly says, 'He demands what person pretends to divide the land and put me on it?' In the most decided voice, I said, 'I am the man; I stand here for the president, and there is no spirit, good or bad, that will hinder me. My orders are plain and will be executed. I hoped that the Indians had good sense enough to make me their friend and not their enemy.'"

From various unmistakable signs (I am no novice with Indians), I saw that immediate trouble was at hand. Joseph, White Bird, and Looking Glass endorsed and encouraged this malcontent. I must somehow put a wedge between them; so I turned to this Dreamer and said, "Then you do not propose to comply with the orders of the government?"

After considerable more growling and impudence of manner, he answered with additional fierceness, "The Indians may do what they like, but I am not going on the reservation." After telling the Indians that this bad advice would be their ruin, I asked the chiefs to go with me to look at their land. "The old man shall not go. I will leave him with Captain Perry." He says, "Do you want to scare me with reference to my body?" I said, "I will leave your body with Captain Perry." I then arose and led him out of the council, and gave him in charge of Captain Perry.[8]

The whole tone of the Indians now changed, and they readily agreed to go with me to look at their new homes. They may have thought of killing me then and there, but a bold, quick, unexpected action will often save you in extreme peril. Joseph's manner was never defiant. He rode with me to look at what Mr. Monteith had intended for him. A few Indians and some white sojourners would have to remove to other lands, to put Joseph's people together. We lunched together at Mr. Colwell's, and then returned to the fort. White Bird and Looking Glass appeared to be happy and contented. They pleaded for the release of Toohoolhoolzote, but I told them to wait until I had shown them their land, which Mr. Monteith would designate. The next day we rode to Kamiah (sixty-five miles), and the next went to the lands intended. White Bird picked his near Looking Glass's farms, and then we returned to Kamiah, and the next day following to Lapwai.

Toohoolhoolzote was released on the pledge of Looking Glass and White Bird, and on his earnest promise to behave better and give good advice.

Now we must have our final interview, May 14. Joseph concluded to go, too, near Kamiah with the rest. The promises were put in writing. No objection was made to thirty days, except by Hush-hush-cute. I gave him thirty-five days because he had not had so early notice of removal.

I withheld the protection papers from Hush-hush-cute because of something he said which indicated that he was attempting to conceal his intentions. So I left his papers with the agent. There was general joy among the treaty Indians, nontreaty Indians, and whites at the peaceful outcome of the councils, and I returned to Portland.

This idea that General Howard caused the war is an afterthought.

That story that Joseph asked me for more time is not true. That I sent orders to the soldiers to drive them out on their return to Wallowa is, of course, untrue; that would have disconcerted everything. On the contrary, the officers and soldiers were simply to occupy Wallowa in the interest of peace and not use constraint unless forced to do so.

The statements with reference to our losses and those of the Indians are all wrong, and Joseph does not tell how his own Indians, White Bird and his followers, who treacherously escaped after the terms of the surrender had been agreed upon between us at Colonel Miles's battlefield, being permitted by himself, did in fact utterly break and make void the said terms of surrender.

These Indians were to return to Idaho, not because of any promise, but because of General McDowell's orders requiring all the Nez Perce prisoners to be kept in my department. This order was changed by General Sherman or at Washington.

Should the Indians return to the scene of their horrid outrages, they could have no peace. There is not an Indian there now. The Bitterroot country puts them at the throat of our eastern connections and makes another war very probable.

Let them settle down and keep quiet in the Indian Territory, as the Modocs have done, and they will thrive as they do.

Origin of the Difficulties with the Nez Perces

MELVILLE C. WILKINSON[1]

Army and Navy Journal 15, no. 1 (August 18, 1877): 22

The Elmira (NY) *Advertiser* prints a letter from Lt. M. C. Wilkinson of General Howard's staff, giving some interesting particulars of the campaign against the Nez Perce Indians. The letter is dated at Camp M. T. Miller, Kamiah, [Idaho] Territory, July 17, and says:

Just thirty days ago, the exact time specified and the time agreed upon between General Howard and Mr. Monteith, their agent, did these nontreaty Nez Perce Indians commence murdering men, women, and children. Few in the East can understand the cause of this Nez Perce war. Years ago, at the time this tribe was given a reservation, Joseph held that he was not bound to go upon it, submitting to the United States authorities, because he did not sign the treaty. No majority rule for him.

Three years went by, and he gathered to himself a sort of miscellaneous lot, and finally, within the past two years, growing stronger, it was thought best, prudent, and all that, to seek to mollify this savage chieftain by holding councils, talks, and the like with him. His ambition was the Wallowa Valley, a rich and fertile one in this northern Idaho, letting into another, the Imnaha, both abounding in game, and whose streams have abundant fish. Why not? Who wouldn't have so much, if he could only get it? So Joseph stuck and hung, till last fall a commission was sent from Washington, and after much labor, this commission finally consented to give a part of this coveted land to Joseph and his people. Gaining the inch, he went for the mile, and must have all or nothing, and so we have the war. This is about the long and short of this whole business. Joseph was offered a good house (I wish I had as good a one), with barns [and] an orchard in the valley of the Lapwai, on the reservation. This would not do. He had promised his flock of malcontents to stick for Wallowa and Imnaha.

Fort Lapwai in 1877. HARPER'S WEEKLY, 1877.

In May last the final council began, and at Fort Lapwai. On the eleventh Joseph and his people, about seventy-five warriors with their families, came. The Interior Department, through its agent, read to Joseph his instructions, viz.: that unless he came on the reservation peaceably, he must call on the military to put him on by force. Then General Howard read his instructions from the War Department, viz.: that when the agent called upon the military, he must act. Well, Joseph, he sat for a while and then said White Bird was coming, was in the mountains just above us, and he wanted to wait for him. So the council adjourned until tomorrow at 9:00 A.M.

Nine o'clock A.M. tomorrow came. No Indians. At about 10:00 A.M. there is a big dust in the direction of Joseph's camp, and soon the head of the column appears, this time about 150 strong. In platoons, singing their unearthly songs, in war paint and feathers, do these savages march twice around our little garrison, and then dismount and gather about our council tent. White Bird shields the most of his fine specimen of an Indian's face behind an eagle's wing. Joseph sits, as he always does, with a noncommittal air. Again are the instructions read, and again is time asked in order that they may talk it all over together in their Indian council. This time the general gives two days, for he is pushing troops from Walla Walla to the Wallowa and bringing them to our rear (Lewiston).

The two days are up, again the same pomp and circumstance, and we are seated in council. Now Looking Glass is present, giving us all the nontreaty chiefs of any account, viz.: Joseph, Looking Glass, and White Bird, with followers about 175. A Quaker meeting is the sendoff. Finally the general asks Joseph to talk, which he don't do. White Bird ditto and Looking Glass the same. But an oldish and very savage-looking medicine man, six feet and over of badness, takes a seat in front of the general and the agent and tells his tumtum (heart).

Speaking of medicine men on this Northwest Coast, they beat the average one. They are spiritualists, with the theory that by and by the Indians are to have a general resurrection, and then good bye whites. So this old fraud, by name Toohoolhoolzote, gives forth the predetermined voice of all these Indians. Says he, "I will say a few words. The earth is my mother. Who is it that takes away my mother? Who did I tell in Washington to give my land away? The earth will take care of me. I am not coming on the reservation."

General Howard—Do you speak for yourself?

Toohoolhoolzote—Yes.

Joseph, White Bird, and Looking Glass are each asked if he speaks for them, and each answers yes. This old rascal is then taken out of the council by force and put in charge of an officer. Then the chiefs are informed that tomorrow they must be prepared to select each a place on the reserve and will be given thirty days to come in. Next day Joseph is shown the fine place to which reference has been made, and he tacitly consents to take it. The next day we are traveling across the great Nez Perce plains to this very place where I sit writing this, with White Bird and Looking Glass as companions. The next day we are up this Clearwater River, eighteen miles above this point, and where the hard battle of the eleventh was fought. Yes. White Bird and Looking Glass would come in, in thirty days. They were our brothers. They were each other's brothers—in short, the most brotherly pair of everybody's brother one can imagine.

But the story entire is too long. This whole country to a man and woman, the worst Indian hater in all of it, firmly believed these three chiefs meant every word they said. Hence the unpreparedness of the murdered settlers. So much had been done by the commission, the work of the Interior Department. But the thirty days are up. On a little stream called John Day, running into the Salmon River, two of Joseph's men—without the knowledge, it is said, of Joseph—strike, killing three men. With stolen horses, and one with a stolen Henry rifle, they ride early into Joseph's camp, saying, "What are you women doing? See this gun, look at these horses. What are you sitting here for?"

It is said that these murderers really decided the undecided ones. They must give up the murderers and go on the reservation; this or

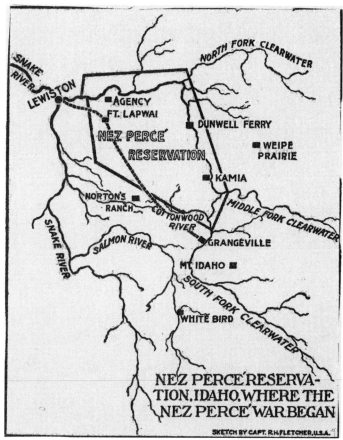

The Nez Perce reservation, where the Nez Perce war began.
CYRUS T. BRADY. *NORTHWESTERN FIGHTS AND FIGHTERS.*

war. The war party was too strong, and there right and left about Mount Idaho, State Creek, [and] White Bird Creek, in these widely separated settlements, seventeen men, women, and children were murdered, and worse than murdered were some of the women who are yet alive whom I saw at Mount Idaho. Scarcely alive were two of them whom these fiends so cruelly outraged that it were not decent or right to print it. Even death did not stop them in the case of one woman, and that in the presence of her aged father, whom they did not notice enough to kill. With streaming eyes, broken heart, and choked voice, this poor old man told me of the cruel death of his precious child.

We had been busy in getting on certain renegade Indians along the Columbia River and had worked back by canoe and steamer to Fort Lapwai just as the thirty days were up. Friday, June 15, a corporal and three men having been sent out to Camas Prairie to ascertain the position of the Indians, they are met by two Indians escaping from Joseph's camp, who turn them back to us with the first news of the murders on the John Day. Then Perry is sent that evening to head them off from their work of destruction, and an officer is sent to the nearest telegraph station at Walla Walla, to ride without rest with orders for the concentration of all the troops in the department. Already you have heard of Perry's battle, almost a second Custer's. Troops are marched with almost incredible speed, Indians cross and recross these rivers, which are torrents, swift, deep, and dangerous, until last Wednesday, July 11, we have so pressed them that we are now on them.

We are upon a plateau. A bluff near reveals part of the Indians in their camp in the valley of the north fork of the Clearwater, near the mouth of the Cottonwood. We must go back about one mile and a half to secure the head of the ravine up which they are pouring. A howitzer is sent with all speed thither, supported by a company of cavalry and a Gatling gun, and a company of infantry put under double-time, and none too soon, for the enemy appear in great force and madly seek to outflank this little band.

Other troops are ordered up, prolonging our right, and in less than thirty minutes the battle is opened along the line, which now has been extended on the left by the cavalry, so that we have a front of nearly two and a half miles, against which 300 and over of the enemy, in every way known to savage warfare, seek to break our lines. They ride up behind little elevations, throw themselves from their ponies, fire, and are off like rockets. Lines of them creep and crawl and twist themselves through the grass until within range, and with pieces as good as ours, tell with deadly aim that they are marksmen. They tie grass upon their heads so that it is hard to tell which bunch of grass does not conceal an Indian with a globe-sighted rifle. They climb trees and shoot from them, and for seven hours we put our boys in where they are greatly needed, and also bring many back to our surgeons, already too busy. Captain Bancroft,[2] leading his Company A, 4th Artillery, is shot through the lungs. Seeing him soon after, he said, "I saw the black snakes crawling up and believe I fixed some of them." A brave man, a patient sufferer. We are glad to know his wound is not necessarily fatal. Lieutenant Williams[3] is soon brought back from the mouth of the gulch, shot through the wrist and thigh.

The fight commenced at about 1:00 P.M. At 3:30 P.M. General Howard ordered a charge on the left, and away under Captain Miller, 4th Battalion, go our brave men, leaving, as I have been told, eight Indians closely laid out together.

Darkness alone closes this day's work. The night finds us busy throwing up entrenchments, caring for the wounded (twenty-four), bringing in the dead, of which seven are found, and setting at work packers and all who can bake bread, for our hard bread is gone and we are nearly out of rations. We are nearly 375 strong and have this long line to defend. Our pack animals are corralled in the center, while our cavalry horses, unsaddled, remain at most convenient points for the opening of the morning's work. The bright stars looked down on our little army, exhausted and not discouraged. Our torn and bleeding comrades give us cheer by their brave words spoken and silent suffering.

This is all that can be written now and is the first opportunity when it has been possible to put aside pressing work at every halt, to do what I have wanted to do, viz.: give you, and through you, your readers, some account of this fight.

Chief Joseph as a Commander

ALBERT G. FORSE

Winners of the West 13, no. 12 (November 1936): 1, 3–5

Heinmot Tooyalakekt (Thunder Rolling in the Mountains), or Joseph, chief of the Nez Perce, as he is known to the whites, is without doubt the greatest Indian as a leader of which we have any record; not only brave and fearless in battle, but possessing that rare gift—military genius—which is of far greater importance to a commander than mere personal valor, and which I hope to be able to prove to my readers he possessed to a remarkable degree.

The first time I ever met Joseph was in September 1876, the day upon which he had told the settlers in the Wallowa Valley, in northeastern Oregon, and volunteers from Indian and Grande Ronde Valleys that he would meet them and decide the question then in dispute, the right to the Wallowa Valley.[1] Fortunately I succeeded, by making a forced march of eighty-eight miles in a little over twenty-five hours, in arriving in time to prevent hostilities; feeling satisfied that if I could get an interview with Joseph he would give up his hostile intentions, I secured a guide and found him seven miles distant, where he had informed the volunteers he would meet them.

His command was posted upon quite a high bluff, the approaches to which, although pretty steep, were free from brush, trees, and everything that would obstruct his fire or shelter an enemy, being a natural glacis. His men were mounted in line, in war paint and with but few exceptions stripped to the breechclout, although it was in September in a high altitude and, moreover, a very cold day.

As Joseph rode out and dismounted, I thought he was the finest looking Indian I had ever seen, not only physically, but intelligently. He was about six feet in height, powerfully built, and strength of character [was] written on every feature.

After a parley of two hours, we came to terms, and during my stay with him of nearly three weeks, in which time we had several councils, I became more and more impressed with his worth.

Returning to his position taken up on the day above referred to, I found later, upon visiting his camp a mile in the rear, where his women and children were, that it was ably chosen. An enemy could not approach him without being under his fire for the distance of more than half a mile. At the same time, it perfectly protected his camp, which was in an angle formed on the right by Wallowa Lake and on the left by a very high, rugged, and steep mountain, which could not be descended on his side if climbed, and which could not be turned. The only way by which his camp could be approached was by the right and front, in which case the enemy would have had to cross the Wallowa River, which was perfectly commanded from his position. His right, in the position on which I saw it, would have only had to refuse its flank.

Had the volunteers attacked him there, I do not believe one would have escaped. Joseph could easily have fallen upon the settlers in detail, killing them and destroying their property. They had called outsiders to their assistance and said they were going to kill him (Joseph) and his Indians, but he was willing to give them an opportunity to do so in a fair fight, even sending word to his enemies where he could be found, something unheard of in Indian warfare.

I saw he had complete control over his warriors during our parley of two hours. Although his men were naked and shivering with cold, not one moved out of ranks except the subchiefs and an interpreter.

I will not dwell upon the cause of the outbreak the next year, 1877, into which Joseph was reluctantly drawn, nor upon Perry's defeat at White Bird Canyon, in which two troops and a few volunteers were badly whipped, losing nearly half their numbers, but will pass on to July 1877, when General Howard, with his command and with the aid of all the boats which he could collect on the Salmon River, crossed over in pursuit of Joseph, who led him in a chase of two or three days over the adjoining mountains, then gave him the slip, recrossed the Salmon—which was deep, broad, and very swift—some distance below where he had crossed, swimming his horses, and crossing his women and children in rawhide boats hastily constructed. And this, one might also say, within sight of a command composed of cavalry, artillery, and infantry.

With the assistance of the boats, it took the command about two days to recross. Joseph went over Craig Mountain, passing around two troops sent by General Howard (as Captain S. G. Whipple[2] says in his report) to hold in check Joseph. This was at Cottonwood, where Lt. S. M. Rains,[3] ten soldiers, and two scouts were killed.[4]

Joseph did his best to take the place, but the men had had time to throw up rocks and earth, so he gave up, passing around our flank and crossing Camas Prairie to the Clearwater River, where it was not until later that General Howard found him.

About 11:00 A.M. of July 11 the Indians were discovered in the river bottom some distance up. The command was on bluffs 2,000 feet in height above them. The howitzers were brought into requisition and shelling began, but at each explosion the Indians would shout in derision. Captain W. H. Winters[5] was finally sent, with his troop supported by a company of infantry, to a projecting bluff higher up the river, from which it was thought the howitzers

Nez Perces on the lookout. NELSON A. MILES. *PERSONAL RECOLLECTIONS AND OBSERVATIONS.*

would be effective. But before reaching the point indicated a citizen fortunately rode up and asked if there were any troops in that canyon to our front. A
negative reply was given, when he said, "Well, then, it is filled with Indians."
By this time a few scattering Indians had been seen on the bluffs to our front.

The troop was deployed, halted, and dismounted until supports came up.
The Indians were now seen in great numbers at the head of the small canyon
above mentioned and a larger one farther on. Both canyons led from the high
bluffs to the river bottom where Joseph's camp was, and besides were connected by a natural depression, through which the Indians could pass from one
to the other and be secure from our fire.

The position chosen by Joseph was well selected. The ground at the head
of the larger canyon was higher than that occupied by the troops and commanded all the mesa, or tableland, from the bluffs to heavy timber beyond our
left. This ground had been chosen in advance, and General Howard forced to
fight on it. This was proven by the breastworks of logs which were thrown up at
the river to protect his retreat in case of defeat and found by the troops during
the final charge of the second day's fight.[6]

The battle of the eleventh was quite severe, three charges having been
made before the smaller canyon was reached. It was from this one that most of
the damage was done, the center and left being enfiladed from it; the Indians
being well protected by large trees and bushes with which the heads of the
canyons were filled.

Quite a number of casualties would have been prevented had the third
charge been carried a little farther, but it was stopped just as the troops reached
the head and the sides of the canyon, the Indians taking cover behind trees and
bushes. By concentrating our fire wherever the smoke of a rifle could be seen,
and by some of the bravest men taking the run and throwing themselves into

the bushes and behind trees, they finally cleared it. But the Indians were not whipped.

In the charges referred to, the Indians fought desperately and held their ground until we were almost upon them, some of the troops falling dead upon the logs behind which the Indians were protected.

The skirmish line was occupied all night, but not until 12:00 A.M. did the right succeed in throwing up some rocks for protection for the next day's fight. In the early part of the night it was attempted, but the troops, being on higher ground, could be seen against the sky, and whenever a man showed himself, he was fired at from the canyon, which the Indians had taken possession of after the men occupying it had been withdrawn at dark.

The next day the fight recommenced very early, and firing continued until nearly noon, when the right was ordered to extend intervals so as to have some companies on the left withdrawn, preparatory to a charge of the enemy in echelon. When the first company moved out, the Indians tried to get on their left flank, then another company was sent forward, and so on, the Indians all the while trying to get on the extreme flank, but going so far to the left was the cause of their defeat. By the time they succeeded in getting on the left of the last company, the right, or first, company was almost to the canyon, the occupation of which would cut them off from their camp of women and children.

To save them was now their only thought, giving way and rushing their horses down the canyon, and some even riding down the bluffs, where it was almost impossible for a man to go down on foot and which took up two hours' hard work after the charge. Seeing the troops getting in between them and their camp demoralized them, and as Joseph said afterwards, it was impossible to hold them, and said further that he was sanguine of success and would have had 400 more warriors in a few days.

Twice on the first day the Indians massed under shelter, leaving their war horses in the timber, and charged the line savagely, which had to be met by a countercharge as savage, the men almost meeting when the Indians sought cover.

After this fight Joseph was called the "war chief." He was everywhere along the line, running from point to point. He directed the flanking movements and charges. It was his long, fierce calls which sometimes were heard loudly in front of us, and sometimes resounding from the distant rocks.

Had Joseph been able to hold his men, there would have been a different ending to that two days' fight. They were on our flanks and rear and being mounted, could have charged through the camp without much opposition, the cavalry being deployed and very much extended in order to protect the large trains and a spring, our only source of water.

If the Indians had once gotten possession, we could not have done much to prevent a stampede of the stock, and the troops to the front would have been powerless, for to reach the Indians, they would have had to fire through the camp, where the hospital and headquarters were. But granting that they had been repulsed in their attack on our left, they could have taken position in the heavy timber, and we would have been driven from our position.

This was the first and only time they were ever demoralized. They were afterwards surprised, but quickly recovered themselves. In this fight the troops were about 500 strong; the Indians not over 350, if as many. The former had, in addition to numbers, the advantages of howitzers and gatling guns, and were commanded by many officers who had seen service during the late war. Moreover, this was the first time the Nez Perces had really had an opportunity to pit themselves against the whites, the fight in the White Bird Canyon being from all reports and accounts nothing more than a stampede.

Our loss at Clearwater was forty-three killed and wounded. Joseph claims to have lost more.[7]

Captain Perry was ordered to pursue with the cavalry, consisting of B, F, H, and L Troops—E not being available, as it was at the river, having joined in the charge dismounted with the artillery and infantry, leaving the horses on the bluff. He went to the river and there halted, and was censured by General Howard for not continuing the pursuit, but proved before his court of inquiry that such were his orders. Had he pursued, a great many captives would have been the result, principally women and children.

The pursuit did not commence until the next day. In the meantime, Joseph had collected his warriors, women, and children and was leisurely making his way down to Kamiah, where he crossed over the Clearwater. The last had just gotten over when the cavalry hove in sight. A few shots were exchanged, but it was too late to accomplish anything.

The next day was occupied in watching each other across the river. On the fifteenth General Howard took four troops and started down the Clearwater for Dunwell's Ferry, hiding his movements as much as possible from Joseph. His object [was] to cross over and get in Joseph's rear, cutting off his retreat over the Lolo Trail to Montana. Joseph discovered the movement and divined the object of it at once. When Howard was only eight miles from Kamiah, his starting point, he was informed by courier that Joseph had sent in a flag of truce. He returned at once with part of the cavalry. The rest proceeded to the ferry but were recalled the next day.

Joseph, owing to the almost impassable condition of the Lolo Trail, required time to get his noncombatants well over before he commenced the retreat. This he did under a flag of truce. Having gained his object and outwitted his adversary, he as much as told him no treaty could be made and started for Montana.

Joseph, when hostilities commenced, was for peace and did not want to go on the warpath, and by many was accused of cowardice. When at Kamiah, he was opposed to going over the mountains and said, "What are we fighting for but our lands and homes; why leave them and go we know not where? Let us hide our women and children in the forests and remain and fight. You accused me of cowardice; now who are the cowards?"

They were all against him, so he had to yield and made his plans accordingly. When over the mountains, he found the Lolo Trail occupied by troops and citizens. How to get by them was the next difficulty. He could easily have whipped them, as the command consisted of only two small infantry companies and a few citizens.

A rectangular work of logs about breast high had been thrown up in the center of the valley but was in easy range of the high ground or mountainsides on each side of the valley, and from which it could have been enfiladed and the occupants driven out in a few moments. But Joseph did not want to antagonize the citizens whose country he was going to pass, and upon whom he had to depend for fresh horses, supplies, ammunitions, and arms, all of which he obtained a little later. So he began parleying with them and told them that if they would go home and not take part in the conflict, he would see that they and their property were respected. Finding they had nothing to fight for and everything to gain by trading, they left for home.

It appears negotiations lasted for two days, at the end of which time it failed. Joseph then notified Capt. C. C. Rawn[8] that he would go into the valley the next day in spite of all opposition.

Accordingly, at daylight[9] light firing was heard on the skirmish line, and it was supposed that the Indians would at once assault the main line. Stray shots continued for some time, and as all the attention of officers and men were concentrated on the front, a man called the attention of Lt. C. A. Coolidge[10] to the fact that he had seen the heads of a few Indians moving down one of the gulches in the rear of the extreme right. This proved to be the rear guard of Joseph's outfit. The wily savage had again outwitted the troops. He left a few men to skirmish with Rawn's pickets, and while the command was expecting an attack in front, he had filed down through the gulches past the works and escaped.

Rawn deployed and started in pursuit, but did not overtake them until they had reached the Bitterroot Valley and turned up it. Three miles from its mouth, he found them strongly posted on a ridge in some timber. They defied him to fight, but having been deserted by the volunteers and not feeling strong enough for an attack, he withdrew to Missoula.

Joseph moved slowly up the Bitterroot Valley, and when near the headwaters crossed over the high divide to the Big Hole River and went into camp. This was on August 8. Rawn had left them on July 28. They crossed over to the south bank and camped in a bend of the river which was partially surrounded by dense thickets of willows.

It was here that Col. John Gibbon completely surprised Joseph at daylight on August 9 with his command, consisting of five companies of the 7th Infantry and thirty-six volunteers. Colonel Gibbon had been telegraphed by General Howard that Joseph had gone to Montana by the Lolo Trail. He immediately collected what companies he could: one from his own post, Shaw; one from Camp Baker; one from Fort Benton; one from Fort Ellis; and one from Missoula.[11]

Colonel Gibbon deserves great credit for the manner in which he succeeded in getting his command around the hostile camp without being discovered. The men had to wade through the river with the water almost to their armpits to get into position. This was a little before daylight. They then deployed and, when approaching the camp, were discovered by an Indian who was going out to round up the herd. He was immediately shot down.[12] The first shot having been agreed upon as the signal to charge, the whole line moved forward, charging, and captured the camp. Had Colonel Gibbon pursued the Indians beyond their camp, destroyed their tepees, provisions, and camp equipage, and then put his command in a position to secure the advantage he had gained, his victory would have been complete.

Although Joseph neglected a precaution he had always taken before and afterwards, to keep his men well out to watch the approach of an enemy, he neglected it this time for the reason [that] he knew of no other troops in the vicinity than those of Missoula, and those he had seen return to their post. General Howard was too far in the rear to give him any uneasiness.

It was his first campaign, and he had to learn by experience. He was surprised, but not whipped. Colonel Gibbon had a different Indian to contend against than the Sioux.

While his men were wandering around the captured camp, pillaging and off their guard, Joseph saw his opportunity and succeeded in completely surrounding Colonel Gibbon's command, and from the dense willows where they were concealed, poured into the troops a murderous fire. Colonel Gibbon deserves credit for the manner in which he surrounded the Indian camp, as I have said, but Joseph deserves much more for surrounding Gibbon, who knew that Joseph was in the vicinity, whereas Joseph had not known of Gibbon's nearness.[13]

The troops were compelled to retreat and took refuge in the mouth of a gulch in some timber, but the Indians got upon higher ground and, by taking advantage of the riverbanks below, completely surrounded them. It was then every man for himself to get under cover as quickly as possible, which they did by digging rifle pits with their trowel bayonets and by piling up rocks.

They were kept in this condition about two days, and had it not been for General Howard's command, which was hurrying forward, but few would have escaped. No man could expose any part of his body without being shot at, and from the close range the Indians were at, nearly every shot was effective.

When the Indians withdrew, the troops had been reduced to eating horseflesh, and some of that tainted. The wounded had been without attention, as there was no surgeon with the command.

The Indians, under cover of their sharpshooters, took down some of the tepees. Joseph, the first night of the fight, sent his women and children under escort to the Lemhi country, making peace with the settlers, where he joined them upon General Howard's approach.

An attack on an Indian village. RUFUS F. ZOGBAUM. *HORSE, FOOT, AND DRAGOON.*

Colonel Gibbon reported twenty-nine officers and men killed, and forty officers and men wounded. Of the enemy, eighty-nine were found dead on the field, but several officers who were in the fight, and with whom I camped a short time afterwards, told me that they estimated the number of women and children killed at about seventy, which would leave but about nineteen warriors killed. I do not wish to criticize Colonel Gibbon's report, but it certainly gave the public a wrong impression.

The killing of the women and children could not be avoided, as the tepees fired into contained many more women and children in proportion to the warriors, thus they naturally suffered the most; besides, not being able to seek shelter so quickly, they were longer under fire. It was here Joseph's wife was killed, leaving her infant who was born during Perry's fight and a girl of ten.

Joseph only withdrew at the approach of superior numbers but, when he did so, had command of the field and had converted a surprise, and what would have been to many commanders a defeat, into victory.

Joseph, after joining his people at Lemhi, started northeastward toward the national park of Yellowstone, and his rear guard had crossed the Corinne stage road a few hours before General Howard's command reached the same point.

The next night, just before dawn, General Howard's camp was startled by the firing of rifles. Joseph had sent about forty of his young men to stampede the herd.[14] They succeeded in getting the mules, but the horses, having been picketed, fared better. It was these Joseph wanted, and he said after his surrender that the above number of warriors, forty, had made all the noise and firing of the attack.

At dawn the mule herd was discovered in the distance. The cavalry went in hot pursuit and soon captured them, but it was only for a moment. Joseph had so planned that at this point, our troops ran into an ambuscade of the whole Indian force and had to neglect the herd, which the Indians mostly secured.

Joseph was tired of having Howard always on his trail and wanted to put him afoot. He said, "You did not picket your horses other nights, and I did not expect it this night." Joseph partly accomplished his object. Howard, for want of mules, was forced to stay where he was three days.

Col. S. D. Sturgis and the 7th Cavalry, fresh in the field, were ahead of Joseph, and General Howard confidently expected to hold him in the mountains, from which there was but one pass in the direction Joseph was going, and [the] other toward the Stinking Water [River]. But every attempt to communicate with Sturgis was unsuccessful. The bodies were found of every courier sent out.

Joseph made a feint toward the Stinking Water Pass and, having gotten Colonel Sturgis moving in that direction, slipped out under cover of the hills by way of Clark Fork and crossed the Yellowstone toward the Musselshell Basin. He had led his people much over 1,000 miles, through the ruggedest wilderness of the continent, and again paused to rest at Canyon Creek. But Sturgis, reinforced by Howard's fresh cavalry, overtook him there, and he again started the women, old men, and children under escort, while he and the warriors held their position and protected the retreat.[15]

Thus he made a running fight of two days, extending 150 miles to the lakes near the Musselshell. Here he distanced all pursuit and was never again overtaken until he had crossed the Missouri, nearly completing a retreat of almost 2,000 miles, and was within thirty or forty miles of the British line, and not much farther from the hostile camp of Sitting Bull.

On September 12 General Howard sent word to Colonel Miles that Joseph had foiled all attempts to stop him and requested him to make every effort to intercept the Indians. This dispatch was received by Colonel Miles September 17, and the next day he began the march which resulted in Joseph's capture.

Joseph's camp lay in the sheltering hollows of a bare, rolling country which was covered with a light fall of snow and therefore, for fighting purposes, the worst situation. Joseph said he thought he had taken every precaution against surprise, having his scouts for forty miles in every direction except to the north, from which he anticipated no trouble; but Miles came in from that direction under cover of a blinding snowstorm September 30 and was not discovered until almost upon them.[16] Instantly, on discovering the advance, the Indians seized the crests of the knolls immediately surrounding the camp, and the cavalry charge was successfully repulsed. To show their contempt for the charge, when Capt. Owen Hale[17] gave the order to charge, an Indian yelled out in good English, "Oh hell! You are not charging the Sioux." In this charge every officer or noncommissioned officer who wore a badge of rank was killed or wounded, save one.[18]

Joseph and his elder daughter were on the other side of the creek among the horse herd when the first charge was made. Calling to the girl to follow, he dashed across and joined his men, taking command. But his daughter and many others were cut off by the cavalry charge, which captured and drove off the herd. Joseph's daughter was restored to him six months afterwards.

The troops held most of the higher crests commanding the camp. The Indians, with great labor, honeycombed a portion of the site of their camp [with] transverse gulches, with subterranean dwelling places [and] communicating galleries. Their dead horses were used as fortifications and as food.

Here they held their own, refusing all offers of surrender and saying, in effect, if you want us, come and take us. Joseph visited Colonel Miles under a flag of truce but at that time would not surrender. His people held Lt. L. H. Jerome[19] until Joseph was returned to them.

On October 4 General Howard, with two aides [and] two friendly Nez Perces, both of whom had daughters in the hostile camp, arrived at Colonel Miles's camp. These two Nez Perces, George and Captain John, rode into Joseph's camp the next day and begged Joseph to surrender. He said he would if allowed to go back to Idaho. The following is the message they brought back from Joseph:

Tell General Howard I know his heart. I am tired of fighting. Our chiefs are killed. Looking Glass is dead. Toohoolhoolzote is dead. The old men are all dead. It is now the young men who say yes or no. He who led the young men (Joseph's brother, Ollokot) is dead. It is cold and we have no blankets. The little children are freezing to death. My people, some of them, have run away to the hills and have no blankets, no food. No one knows where they are; perhaps they are freezing to death. I want to have time to look for my children and see how many of them I can find. Maybe I shall find them among the dead. Hear me, my chiefs. My heart is sick and sad. From where the sun now stands, I will fight no more forever.

About sunset Joseph rode in to deliver himself up. Had he not lost his herd, it is more than probable Joseph would have made another of his successful fights in retreat.

When he surrendered, he wore a gray woolen shawl, through which were four or five bullet holes from the last fight; his forehead and wrist were also scratched by bullets. The blanket was given to Colonel Miles by request. An officer present told me of all the rifles surrendered, he did not see one worth having. It is probable White Bird and the few who escaped with him took all that were serviceable. Joseph surrendered 79 warriors, 178 women, and 174 children; in other words, nearly five times more noncombatants than combatants.

It was to rest his women and children that he went into camp near Bear's Paw Mountain, where he was captured; had it not been for them, there would have been a different ending to the campaign.

Joseph had Howard in pursuit; Gibbon, Sturgis, C. C. Gilbert,[20] and Miles trying to head him off—everyone, with possibly one exception, had more fighting men than he, but notwithstanding, he was only brought to bay after a retreat of nearly 2,000 miles and by superior numbers.

Colonel Miles promised to send Joseph back to Idaho, but the government sent him to Fort Leavenworth; put them into camp about two miles above the fort on the Missouri River bottom, between a lagoon and the river, which was filled with malaria, and which the prisoners in their reduced state soon contracted. By the time they reached the Indian Territory, twenty-one had already died. Shortly after their arrival, out of 410 remaining, 260 were sick at one time. Within a few months, they lost more than one-fourth of their number.

This is the way that one of the bravest and most magnanimous warriors we have ever known was treated. By magnanimous, I mean as related to our North American Indians. It is true that he killed all males who bore arms against him when they fell into his power, but he did not allow them to be scalped or their bodies mutilated.[21]

When he finally decided to take up arms against the whites, he sent Ollokot to White Bird to tell him that during the campaign, he did not want to hear of any of White Bird's band injuring a woman or child; that if they did, they would hear from him.

When White Bird's band commenced the war by killing settlers on the Salmon River, White Bird Canyon, and Camas Prairie, they committed all kinds of excesses. Women and children were shot, and the former, when spared, suffered a worse fate. But afterwards not an instance is known where a woman or child was molested. Even after the loss of women and children at the battle of the Big Hole, he never harbored revenge, going so far as to conduct to a place of safety the women captured in the national park.

In White Bird Canyon, when Emanuel's ranch was attacked and he wounded by White Bird's men, he succeeded in getting in the brush along the creek, as did one of his little girls and a young Irishman. He stood her pleadings for two or three days. When he could stand it no longer, he picked her up in his arms and carried her into Joseph's camp, and told Joseph he wanted him to send the child up to Camas Prairie among friends, but with me you can do as you please.

Joseph looked at him a moment or two, and then said, "I do not want to kill you; you can take the child up yourself." But when he was about starting, Joseph called him back and told him to stay, saying, "Some of my young men are out and under the influence of drink, and you may run across them. They, not knowing that I have sent you, may kill you. Wait awhile, and I will send you up under an escort," which he did. What civilized man would have done as much for an Indian?

Joseph's men were accused of scalping the dead at White Bird, but such was not the case. The dead had been lying for about twelve days before General Howard's command came to bury them. By that time, through the effects of heat, sun, and rain, they were in such a state that when a body was lifted up or rolled over into his grave, his hair and whiskers would adhere to the ground, tearing off the scalp and skin, which gave to the uninitiated the appearance of their being scalped and caused the circulation of the rumor. I did not see all the dead, but from inquiries made at the time, I failed to find anyone who had seen a body that had been scalped or mutilated in any way.

An officer of the 7th Infantry reported that upon visiting the battlefield of the Big Hole, he found some of the bodies dug up by the coyotes and Indians, and that some of the dead had been scalped; this after six weeks of burial and exposure. The Indians had long since gone. They were not scalped when buried, and it is not likely, as he suggests, that it was done by Indians who were left behind wounded. An Indian so badly wounded would have something else to think of than digging up dead bodies and scalping them.

Joseph, after the remnant of his tribe which had been taken to the Indian Territory had lost more than half its number, was in 1885, or eight years after his surrender, sent back—not to Idaho, but to the Colville reservation in northeastern Washington with Chief Mose.

The Nez Perce War, 1877:
Battle of White Bird Canyon

WILLIAM R. PARNELL

United Service, n.s., 2 (October 1889): 364–74

The Wallowa Valley is fifteen or twenty miles east of the Grande Ronde Valley in eastern Oregon and had long been a bone of contention between the whites and a band of nontreaty Nez Perce Indians under Chief Joseph.. The whites claimed the right of settlement under the United States land acts, and while no determined effort on their part was made to take up homestead, pre-emption, or other claims, yet they kept it as a grazing ground for their cattle while the Indians denied them the right to such privileges, claiming to themselves the entire control of the valley and surrounding hills for hunting and fishing, a right ceded to them by the government in 1855. But by subsequent authority from Washington, the land was thrown open for settlement, and still later on again withdrawn. Those conflicting rulings the Indians did not clearly understand and evidently did not propose to be trifled with like a child with a toy, to be taken away from and given again at pleasure. Quarrels were continually arising between the two parties, an occasional steer would be missing from the white man's herd, and ponies would be, in turn, missing from the Indian herd. Fort Walla Walla was the nearest military station, and the troops were constantly moving to and from the Grande Ronde and Wallowa Valleys, settling differences and preserving the peace, from the date of regarrisoning it in 1873 until hostilities commenced in 1877.

During the summer months, two troops of cavalry were kept in camp in the Wallowa Valley, returning to Walla Walla for the winter; but even the severity of winter did not appear to cool the hot blood of either the white man or the Indian, for on New Year's Day 1876, two troops of the 1st Cavalry had to forgo their New Year's calls, eggnog, and other attractions and start out on an expedition across the Blue Mountains to Grande Ronde Valley, with the thermometer at twelve degrees below zero, to quell an anticipated outbreak of the Indians for some grievance against the whites.

It would seem an anomaly to the military mind to read the regular annual presidential message to Congress that "the country was at peace," etc., when war within our own borders was never ceasing; a few years ago not a month in the year passed that war did not exist in one section or another within the boundaries of the United States; if not in Washington Territory, Oregon, Nevada, or California, we had it in Montana and Dakota, or down in Arizona, New Mexico, or Texas. So far as the cavalry arm of the army was concerned, cessation from hostilities did not exist, and even today, with all the advantages of railroads and constantly increasing population on our frontier, cavalry are continually on the alert; the ever-watchful eye of an army are either in the saddle or virtually standing to horse.

Such was the condition of affairs closely following the terrible Custer massacre, when General Howard, commanding the Department of the Columbia, was instructed from Washington to proceed to Fort Lapwai, Idaho, and hold council with Chief Joseph and his tribe regarding the disputed territory, and to formulate a plan by which the nontreaty Indians should come in on the Nez Perce Indian reservation at Lapwai.

There were stationed at Fort Lapwai in May 1877 Troop F, 1st U.S. Cavalry, and a small company of the 21st U.S. Infantry, the post being under command of Capt. David Perry, 1st Cavalry. General Howard ordered Troop H, 1st Cavalry, from Walla Walla to Lewiston, Idaho, a small town at the junction of the Snake and Clearwater Rivers. This troop was to remain in camp on the west bank of the Snake, so as to be ready to move up the Snake River, or to move into the Wallowa Valley and reinforce Troops E and L, 1st Cavalry, should occasion require it, as it was well known that the Indians were ugly and strongly opposed to going on a reservation or surrendering their alleged rights to the Wallowa.

The Nez Perce Indian Reservation covers an immense tract of perhaps the most fertile soil in Idaho, abundantly supplied with water and timberland. The agency is beautifully situated on the Clearwater about three miles from the military post, Fort Lapwai. It has a subagency at Kamiah, sixty miles higher up on the Clearwater, and it is here where the celebrated Lolo Trail across the Bitterroot Mountains into Montana commences.

It was with much difficulty that the Indians could be induced to come in and hold council; several preliminary talks had occurred with one or another of the subchiefs. On May 15 the grand council was held in a large tent pitched on the parade ground of the posts. The attitude of the Indians indicated anything but friendly feelings; they wore a sullen, dogged, and defiant demeanor; treachery on their part was at least anticipated. Although the stipulations were that each party should appear unarmed, it was afterwards discovered that every Indian present at the council, besides many on the outside, were armed with revolvers, hid away under their blankets. To provide against such an emergency, the general gave orders to have all the troops remain in quarters, and under arms. The Indians were represented by Chiefs Joseph, Ollokot, White Bird, Looking Glass, and Husis Kute, chief of the Palouse Indians, strong allies through intermarriage of the Nez Perces.

The council lasted from about 10:00 A.M. until late in the afternoon. Many times during the day, hot and defiant words fell from the lips of the Indians, more particularly those of White Bird, who was the worst devil of the lot. Towards the close of the council, the excitement grew intense. Every moment General Howard and the officers present anticipated an attack by the Indians, whose every motion indicated that they were armed, though none were shown. So arrogant and defiant were they that few white men could have restrained themselves; indeed, at one time General Howard was on the point of committing one of them to the guardhouse in irons, but his cooler judgment and proverbial desire for peace restrained him, and the storm subsided for the time being. The most trivial spark of indiscretion on the part of any officer present would have caused the massacre of the entire party. Chief Joseph and Looking Glass favored the proposition of going on the reservation, and the termination of the council was with that understanding. Thirty days were allowed for this purpose; June 14 was to see the entire band of nontreaty Indians on the Nez Perce reservation, among their own people.

During the conference, Chief Joseph's brother, Ollokot, sometimes called Young Joseph, exhibited a map of the disputed territory of the Wallowa which was, to say the least, unique. It was a novel specimen of draughtsmanship. If I remember correctly, it was on a peculiar piece of paper or parchment of a muddy yellow tinge, about sixteen or eighteen inches square, the ink lines being of a pea green color. The geography of the country was delineated by natural history; for instance, the Wallowa Lake was represented by a single ink line showing the boundary line and a crude drawing of a fish in the center. The mountains were represented by the figures of deer, the Wallowa River by a zigzag line, with trees here and there along its length. The wagon road was probably the most peculiar and interesting part of it: a double column of very small circles running the entire length of the valley was the impression one received at first glance, the circles not larger than a pin's head, but upon closer inspection, the circles were incomplete; they were minute representations of horseshoes, indicating the impress of the shoe on the soft earth. A tragedy that occurred a short time before, in which an Indian was killed by a white man, occasioned by a dispute about the removal of a rail fence to allow horses to pass through, was shown on the map as near the vicinity as guesswork could make it by figures representing a white man and two or three Indians struggling for a gun; the figures of men and animals were a good deal after the style of Egyptian figures—straight lines and angles. An effort was made by General Howard and Lieutenant Fletcher[1] of the 21st Infantry to make an exact copy of the map, but under no consideration would the Indians allow them to retain it long enough for that purpose.

General Howard returned to Portland next day to await the termination of the allotted month, and the Indians returned to their camp on the Salmon River.

As the June 14 drew near, speculation was rife as to the probabilities of the Indians abiding by the decision of the council or not. Nothing had been heard from them, nor had any of them as yet come in.

The morning of June 14 arrived, and with it brought General Howard from department headquarters. The day wore along, clear, warm, and peaceful; troops were to return to their stations if all went well; but all didn't go well, for about 6:00 P.M. a messenger arrived with a letter from Mount Idaho to General Howard, stating that Joseph's band were giving the settlers much trouble and annoyance, causing fears of an outbreak.

Early next morning four cavalrymen and the interpreter from the agency started for Mount Idaho to learn particulars. Much uneasiness was manifest throughout the garrison. We knew that the Indians should now be within the boundary of the reservation, and they were not. We were satisfied in our own minds that they did not intend to obey the mandate of the council, and from their demeanor during the deliberations of the council, we could see no other prospect than war. They were a brave type of the Indian, strong, tall, and well formed, armed with weapons equal if not superior to ours, for theirs were Winchesters, sixteen shooters; ours were the Springfield single breechloaders. They had a large herd of good, strong ponies, giving them almost unlimited relays for their mount, either for pursuit or retreat. We therefore began our preparations for business on the return of the messengers.

Scarcely three hours had elapsed ere the party came galloping into camp, very much excited. They had been fired on and driven back by some of the Indians, who were about ten miles from Lapwai in the timber, watching the road to Mount Idaho. Our dream of a peaceful settlement of the question was now at an end; hostilities had commenced, and another protracted Indian war confronted us.

The Indians had failed to comply with the action of their council; the young bloods had defied the action of the older and wiser heads of their tribe and demanded recognition from their people for the cold-blooded murder of innocent and unsuspecting white settlers along the Salmon River.

On June 14, the day they should have been on the reservation, three of their young men went to a store and post office, six miles above Slate Creek on the Salmon River, kept by a Mr. Elfers[2], whom they shot and killed while plowing. His unfortunate wife witnessed the murder of her husband, and then fled from the house and sought shelter in the thick underbrush along the creek. The Indians thoroughly ransacked the house, procured one or two rifles and shotguns, a quantity of ammunition, and a large supply of provisions. A party fleeing from Cottonwood to Mount Idaho, eighteen miles distant, was also attacked. One man was killed, one wounded, and one woman was badly wounded.[3] A settler at the mouth of White Bird Creek on the Salmon River was also killed, his wife made prisoner, and his house burned. Those were acts which demanded recognition and approval at the hands of the tribe, or at least the condoning of them. We learned afterwards that a grand council was held by the leading men of the tribe, and after a lengthy debate, it was determined to give their support to the murderers and defy the United States authorities; in other words, they determined to go to war rather than surrender the offenders against law or to go on the reservation.

Troops F and H, 1st Cavalry, therefore left Fort Lapwai for Mount Idaho at 8:00 P.M. on June 15. The command mustered about eighty men, Captain Perry, Company F, in command. After marching until about 1:00 A.M. on the sixteenth, skirmishers and flankers were thrown out. We were in the mountains, and heavy timber, deep ravines, and a wild, broken country confronted us. The night was dark, and at any moment we might be saluted with a volley from the usually unerring rifles of the Indians; but the men were vigilant and careful, and we reached Cottonwood—eighteen miles from Mount Idaho—unmolested. Here we remained long enough to get breakfast, and then proceeded across Camas Prairie to Mount Idaho, which was reached about sundown. We found the citizens all armed and very much excited. In the course of the evening, a delegation waited on Captain Perry, urging him to move on down to the Salmon River where the Indians were camped and attack and punish them for the murders committed by them. Captain Perry called the officers of the command together (Captain Trimble and Lieutenant Parnell, Company H, and Lieutenant Theller, 21st Infantry, attached to Company F), and after a long conversation with the citizens, who professed to know the situation and strength of the Indians, claiming an easy victory, it was decided to make the attempt. We fed our men and horses, and started at 10 o'clock P.M. for the Salmon River, distant about twenty-five miles. About half a dozen citizens accompanied us to act as guides and assist in the prospective fight also, their leader being George Shearer, an ex-Confederate major, a brave man, and a genial good fellow.

We plodded along in the dark until about 1:00 A.M., when we reached the head of White Bird Canyon; here we made a halt until dawn of day. Captain Perry ordered perfect quiet, and under no circumstances was a light of any kind to be made; yet one of the men of his own company lit a match. Almost immediately the cry of a coyote was heard on the hills above us—a long, howling cry, winding up, however, in a very peculiar way not characteristic of the coyote. Little heed was paid to it at the time, yet it was a fatal cry to the command: It was made by an Indian picket on the watch for the soldiers, whom they knew were already on the march. This signal was carried by others to the camp, so that they were thoroughly prepared for our coming.

As dawn approached, we continued our march down the ravine into the White Bird Canyon; a trail led us down the narrow defile, now and again crossing a dry creek bed, with here and there heavy growths of willows and underbrush. Now we would be skirting along the steep side hill, and again following the creek bed. High bluffs and mountains lined each side of the canyon, while the trail led over rolling country, up and down little knolls or rises, but still descending. About 3:00 A.M. that fatal morning, as we passed in single file along the crest of the hill, a sad and pitiable sight presented itself to us. An unfortunate woman,[4] whose husband was killed, was in the gulch below us

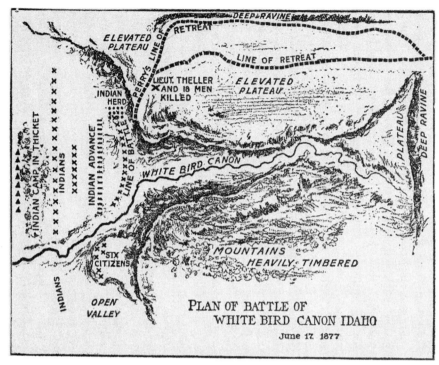

Plan of battle of White Bird Canyon.

CYRUS T. BRADY. *NORTHWESTERN FIGHTS AND FIGHTERS.*

with a little four-year-old girl in her arms. The little one's arm was broken, yet bearing it with fortitude, the poor mother and child [were] shivering with cold and thanking God for their timely deliverance. They had been hiding in the brush from the Indians since the fourteenth, and it was now the morning of June 17.

I have never seen a sight that called for sympathy, compassion, and action like it; it was a terrible illustration of Indian deviltry and Indian warfare. The contents of haversacks were freely given to the unfortunates, and we passed on to the work before us. In a short time we found the canyon widening out, and as we descended, the bluffs on either side appeared to grow higher and higher. Bearing round to the left, we found ourselves in a valley about four or five hundred yards wide. We had not gone more than a hundred yards, when I noticed Captain Perry's troop moving into line at a trot. It was now fairly daylight; the Indians were seen advancing, and fighting commenced at once. Troop H moved up at a trot and formed line on the right of F; the citizens were on the extreme left and in good position on a knoll, which virtually commanded all approaches from the left.

The ground to the right of the line was a steady rise of an angle of about twenty degrees for a distance of perhaps 200 yards; then quite a steep ascent for some distance to the plateau above. The ground to the left of Troop H, and occupied by F, gradually swayed downward and upward again to the position occupied by the citizens. It was bad judgment, and certainly not tactical, to put the entire command on the line, leaving no reserves whatever in either troop. To increase the dangers of such a fatal error, the men were in the saddle in an exposed position, while the Indians were seeking cover in the grass and behind rocks. Very soon the men dismounted of their own accord; some were shot off their horses, and while the firing became hotter, many loose horses were galloping away in rear of the line.

About half an hour had elapsed, and several men had been either killed or wounded, when Perry's men began moving by the right flank to the higher ground on our right. It appears that an attack had been made on the position held by the citizens, two of whom were wounded and the rest driven from their position. This left it an easy matter for the Indians to pass round Perry's left under cover of the knoll and get position in his rear, which compelled him to change his position. In the meantime, the Indians had driven a band of some 500 ponies through the line, and scattered in among the ponies were some sixty or seventy of their men, which so thoroughly demoralized the troops, many of whom were recruits, that it became utterly impossible to control them. As Perry passed on to the right, I supposed he would halt the line when in position on the right of Troop H; but not so, he kept on gaining ground to the right and rear, until I saw him finally ascend the steep rise to the bluffs above. He afterwards explained this officially, "that the men were beyond control." Captain Trimble, it appears, went with Perry until the plateau was reached, and then was seen no more until Perry and myself, with a handful of men, reached our camp near Mount Idaho, where we learned he had preceded us with undue haste by nearly three hours. Lieutenant Theller[5] also endeavored to follow Perry. I had, a short time previous, secured a horse for him, he having lost his. He made an effort to reach the bluffs at a very steep place and was overtaken by the Indians and killed, as were a small party of men with him.

With what men I could collect together, I now commenced falling back by the way we came; that is, up the White Bird Canyon. I saw it would be suicidal to attempt to reach the bluffs on our right, so we slowly retreated up the ravine, holding the Indians in check from knoll to knoll. I saw that a halt must be made very soon to tighten up our saddle girths; so, posting a few men on a little rise to hold the Indians, I dismounted and readjusted my saddle, directing the men to do the same; we then took position on the next knoll and held it until the other men tightened up; and so on, little by little, we moved back, the few brave fellows with me obeying every command with alacrity. I think there were thirteen or fourteen men altogether.

The Indians followed us, not daring, however, to approach too near, but yet near enough for my last and only pistol shot to hit one of them in the thigh. We had several miles of this kind of work up through the canyon, with Indians in front and flanks, but the men had now fully recovered themselves and were cool and determined. At last we emerged from our contracted space to the plateau and fortunately made a junction with Captain Perry, who had with him fifteen or twenty men.

There was mutual rejoicing at our providential meeting. I had not seen him since he reached the bluffs two hours before, and neither of us knew anything of the whereabouts or fate of the other. Our uniting no doubt saved the massacre of either or both parties, for we had yet about eighteen miles to fight our way back ere we could hope for succor. Immediately in our rear was a deep ravine to be crossed. Perry requested me to hold the ridge we were on while he crossed, and he would then cover my passage from a commanding position on the other side. I watched his crossing so as to be ready to move when he had his men in position, but again his men failed him; they had not yet recovered from their unfortunate stampeded condition. I crossed the ravine at a gallop, and then halted on the other side to welcome the Indians, who appeared to swarm on every hill. They halted abruptly on receiving a salute from our carbines. We then moved quietly down to Johnston's ranch, a mile in our rear, where Perry had his men dismounted in good position in the rocks. I dismounted my roan, had the horses tied to a rail fence, and took position in the rocks; the house and barn was to our left a short distance, and a small creek between us and the house.

Presently shots came flying over our heads from the front and right flank. The Indians had taken position among clumps of rocks in our front and flank, which was on higher ground and therefore commanded our position. At the same time, I noticed some of them coming down on our left flank under cover of a fence that ran from the house up the hill perpendicular to our front. I mentioned this to Captain Perry. Our ammunition was getting very short, as we had but forty rounds starting out. After a short consultation under a very hot fire, we determined to abandon our position, mount our horses, and continue a retreating fight back to Mount Idaho.

Perry moved his men down and mounted. I then ordered my small detachment to move down and mount, waiting to see that every man was away. I followed, and to my consternation found my horse gone; he had either broken loose or had been untied by mistake, and had followed the command, which was now more than 100 yards from me, although it was the understanding that they were to have waited until every man was out of the rocks and in the saddle. I hallooed out to "hold on until I got my horse," but evidently nobody heard me, as the command continued to move on. The Indians were now gaining on me, and shots kept whizzing past me from every direction in rear. I looked round for a hiding place, but nothing presented itself that would secure me from observation. I finally made up my mind that I would not be taken prisoner and determined to use my hunting knife or a small derringer pistol I always carried in my vest pocket. These thoughts and final determination flashed through my mind in a few seconds, as I kept moving on, trying to overhaul the command. Finally some of my own men missed me and, looking

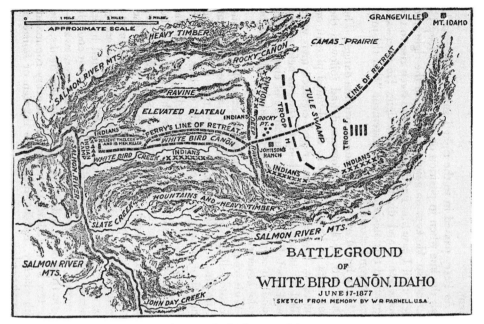

Battleground of White Bird Canyon.

CYRUS T. BRADY. *NORTHWESTERN FIGHTS AND FIGHTERS.*

back, saw me and reported it to Captain Perry. The troops were halted, and my horse caught and led back to me.

I then joined the command and got the men into column of fours. A few minutes after, Perry halted the command and requested me to organize it. I called the men of Troop F to the front, mounted fours, and then closed in the men of H. I asked Captain Perry to support me with his men, while I would form a skirmish line with mine. Wheeling the men to the front, I threw them out as skirmishers with unusually great intervals so as to cover as much front as possible, and then, after a few words of caution and instruction, we waited the coming of the Indians, who at a distance had been closely watching us. We did not have long to wait, for they came upon us with a yell. Not a shot was fired by the men until the red devils rode up to within 100 yards of us, when I gave the order to commence firing. Several redskins and half a dozen horses went down from our fire.[6] We then moved to the rear at a walk and again halted, the Indians making for us again. Once more our fire sent some to grass, and we quietly fell back seventy-five or one hundred yards more. Thus we continued retreating for several miles. A bold attempt was made by White Bird with about seventy-five warriors to drive us off to the right into Rocky Canyon, which, if they had succeeded in doing, would have sounded our death knell, but Captain Perry moved his men so as to protect our left, and with a few well-directed volleys drove them back.

In passing over a marsh, my attention was called to a man struggling through the swampy ground and long tule grass, about halfway between us and the Indians; his head could just be seen above the grass. In few minutes more the Indians would have been upon him. I advanced the line firing, driving the Indians back, and rescued a man of Troop F, whose horse had been shot. The poor fellow was almost played out; he was taken up behind another man, and we continued our retreat.

When we got to within a few miles of Mount Idaho, a party of citizens came out to help us. While we fully appreciated their action, it was too late for them to be of any service, as the Indians had disappeared just as they came in view over the hill. Men and horses were completely exhausted. We had been on the move ever since Friday, without sleep for two nights, and under too much excitement to hope for sleep even now when we reached comparative safety.

Our loss was severe. Troop F lost Lieutenant Theller and twenty men killed; Troop H, thirteen men killed. One man in each troop was wounded. The first sergeant of Troop H was supposed to be killed, but he turned up on Tuesday, having been two days hiding away in the mountains. He was captured and turned over to some squaws for safekeeping, but escaped from them and got up into the thick underbrush until night, when he moved out and marched towards camp until daylight on Monday, hiding again until dark, and reached us about 10:00 A.M. the next day.

A correspondent of the New York *Herald,* in giving an account of the Nez Perce Indian campaign, says of the battle of White Bird Canyon,

> The hostiles commenced operations by murdering all the white settlers they could find, of whom there were many; burning their houses, driving off their stock, and taking all the valuables they wanted. The terrible massacre of thirty-three of these soldiers under command of Captain Perry on June 17 first attracts our attention. Captain Perry attacked the Indians in White Bird Canyon, situated on a creek of the same name, at a point about three miles from where the stream empties into the Salmon River.
>
> This canyon is very deep and extensive, and the trail leading down to it is very steep and in places extremely narrow, necessitating for part of the way a march by file. It is seven miles from the point of descent to the creek, the first three miles being almost perpendicular. The canyon gradually widens as you approach the creek, sloping down to the water's edge. The width of the canyon contiguous to the stream is about five miles. It here presents the appearance of a rolling prairie, being dotted here and there with wave-like swells.

The correspondent is somewhat in error about the width of the canyon, as in no part of it is it anywhere near half that distance. There is also some slight discrepancies in his account of the orders given and the conduct of the engagement. He says, "Captain Perry led his command down the narrow trail at daylight on the morning of June 17 after marching all night, with men and horses hungry and weary. The Indians permitted him to advance to within seventy-five yards without resistance or even showing themselves to the troops. When the redskins were visible, the command was given, "Left front into line; forward, charge!'"

The correspondent then goes on to explain the action, in which are many errors. He, however, says truly enough that "Captain Perry did attempt to rally his men, but he could not get one-twentieth of them together, scattered as they were, especially as he could not find either of his trumpeters." True enough, for one of his trumpeters was killed, and the other was demoralized and had got out of range of the Indians' rifles as soon as the retreat commenced.

He says again, "However, with the few men under his immediate eye, he occupied a semicircle of knolls, with himself and a few citizens inside the curve thus defended, until an opportunity occurred to retreat still farther in a similar manner, and his party reached the top of the canyon, whither all who had horses ran as if for their lives."

Captain Perry did not retreat up the canyon. He did just as stated by me—he ascended to the plateau above the canyon and retreated along that until our parties united. Neither did all those who had horses "run as if for their lives." That some did I have a lively recollection; yet when either commissioned or noncommissioned officers show an example of such unmilitary conduct, young or timid soldiers are very likely to follow.

The correspondent generously speaks in very flattering terms of my humble—although happily—successful attempts to hold the Indians in check with the few gallant fellows who fought up the canyon. He says, "There is no doubt but the Indians would have pursued and massacred every one of the command were it not for the bravery and determined pluck of Lieutenant Parnell of the 1st Cavalry. This officer, gathering a few men around him, occupied knolls here and there after gaining the high ground, and so vigorous and effective was the fire poured into the victorious Indians that they [the Indians] did not deem it prudent to come within range, but instead circled to the right and left, when Lieutenant Parnell would so change his position as to again check them."

It might seem a pity to spoil a good story, especially where one is so particularly interested as the *Herald* correspondent indicates, but he is in error when he says that "they [the Indians] did not deem it prudent to come within range." The jubilant devils did come within range, and pretty close range too, on more occasions than one; but the men were now steady, and gave them a withering fire every time. White Bird Canyon was a terrible defeat to the troops engaged in it; it put the Indians in "high feather," largely increased their warriors from the reservation Indians, and from those along the Palouse and Snake Rivers, resulting as it did in the massacre of the brave young Lieutenant Rains and his party of ten men at Cottonwood; the battle of Clearwater, July 11 and 12; the pursuit across the Lolo Trail into Montana; the severe fighting by troops under Colonel Miles; and the combined action of troops under Howard and Miles, which finally terminated in the surrender of Chief Joseph and his warriors, with the exception of White Bird and about sixty of his followers, who escaped into Canada.

The White Bird Fight

JOHN P. SCHORR[1]

Winners of the West 6, no. 3 (February 1929): 4

The following statement is my recollection of the White Bird Fight; that is, the outbreak of the Nez Perces. A powwow was held at Fort Lapwai, Idaho, in June 1877, with the Indians mentioned by Gen. O. O. Howard and his staff.

As far as we enlisted men learned, everything was clear, and the Nez Perces were to be on the reservation by June 15. I was on guard duty the night of the fourteenth, and the Indians were going back and forth all night and were apparently making their preparations to return to the reservation. But that was only a move to deceive us, for on the fifteenth we received the information "Indians on the warpath."

About a week previous to this, Medicine Chief Toohoolhoolzote, who seemed to be the most stubborn, refused any and all propositions put up to the Indians by General Howard. He finally had said chief placed under arrest and confined in the guardhouse. Trumpeter Jones of my troop was also in confinement, and he and the chief became quite friendly and "chummy." I recall hearing the trumpeter make the statement that if the Indians did break out, they would not molest him (Jones). Unfortunately, he was the first to be picked off,[2] and his horse was also killed.

On that day, June 15, 1877, Corporal Lytle and myself were on detached duty to see why the Indians did not come in, and at this time there was a detachment cutting timber about twelve miles from Fort Lapwai, when an Indian courier came and notified us that the Indians had "gone out," and we returned to the post. The courier reached the post about 6:00 P.M. with the message "Indians on the warpath." About ten minutes later, "Boots and Saddles" was sounded, and an hour later we were in the saddle with five days' rations. Capt. David Perry was in command of the outfit, [with] Captain Trimble of H Troop; Lieutenant Parnell, H Troop; and Lieutenant Theller of Company G, 21st Infantry, attached to Troop F, 1st Cavalry.

We marched from Fort Lapwai about 7:00 P.M.[3] and made a forced march, riding about forty miles all night. About 5:00 or 6:00 A.M. the following day,

356

Scene of Perry's battle on White Bird Creek . June 27th 1877.

Scene of Perry's battle on White Bird Creek. STEPHEN P. JOCELYN. *MOSTLY ALKALI.*

we made a rest long enough to get a snack and forage for the animals. We then took up the march again, headed for Grangeville. On this day, the sixteenth, we saw many depredations committed by the Indians, such as killing horses and plundering prairie schooners; evidently the Indians were very much loaded with "fire water," for in the plunder left behind, we found an empty whiskey barrel with one of the heads knocked out.

From this point we threw out our advance guard, and at noon that day we reached Cottonwood, or Norton's ranch. Here we found more of the Indians' dirty work, as household goods were strewn about the place, and by some miracle the ranch escaped being burned down. One of the reds set fire to an open trunk containing papers and clothing, but through some unknown process, the lid closed and smothered the fire. Norton was killed.

After another snack and a short rest, we were off again for Grangeville. We reached this point about 10:00 P.M., and about 2:00 A.M. the next morning (June 17), we were again mounted and off for the White Bird Canyon, eighteen miles away, so as to make a daylight attack.[4] But let me remark that we received the surprise of our lives, for as soon as we started the march, there was the signal of a coyote, evidently a fake by one of the Indian spies, imitating a coyote. The Indians were prepared for us and anticipated our arrival, for as we got into the canyon, they had us flanked on all sides. We were completely routed, and it seemed to be a case of "God for us all, and the devil get the hindmost."

In going into the canyon, we met a Mrs. Benedict with her two children, hiding in the brushes, nearly starved and in rags—the father and husband was killed and their home in ashes, as well as several other ranches in the locality. Mrs. Benedict advised our commander and pleaded with him not to proceed any farther, for we would run into an ambush and all be killed. She and the children were suffering with hunger, so we emptied our saddle bags to relieve their suffering, but without heeding her advice advanced, and in three-quarters of an hour were routed, retreating in disorder. Captain Perry was called before a court of inquiry, as we understood that he went beyond his orders, being sent merely to protect the citizens of Grangeville. In this engagement Troops F and H, 1st Cavalry, participated. We lost thirty-three men in a very short time. Most of their horses got away but were captured by the Indians; they also got the soldiers' equipment, guns, etc., but little ammunition, if any, as the men fought hard and left only empty shells.

In this engagement thirty-three men were killed, but only one wounded.[5] Pvt. [Thomas] McLaughlin was wounded in his [right] arm. We had no chance to bury our comrades until a week later, and it was a painful duty to perform. We did not at the time bury them, but simply covered the bodies with rocks to keep the coyotes from mutilating the bodies.

Coming out of the canyon on the morning of the seventeenth, we rallied at Grangeville, excepting Cpl. [Charles W.] Fuller of F Troop, who rode direct to Fort Lapwai, bringing the information to the post. On June 18 General Howard, with his aide, reinforced us with two troops of the 1st Cavalry. I have forgotten the names of the troops.[6] The remainder of F Troop was ordered to Fort Lapwai for supplies, and on returning July 3, we got word that twelve men had been killed, among them Lt. Rains.

Our next skirmish was on July 4 and 5 at Cottonwood. We had a lively time of it. Fortunately we lost none of our men, but as far as we could determine, our men did effective work and sent some of the Indians to their happy hunting grounds.[7] Here is where we were reinforced by Troop E, 1st Cavalry, who used a Gatling gun and soon routed the Indians.

Our next move was to trail the Indians to White Bird Canyon and make camp, but only for a day, as the Indians were crossing the Salmon River. During this time we were reinforced by more artillery, cavalry, and infantry, and our force now numbered about 450. During this time, the Indians also gained strength and were estimated somewhere between 1,600 to 2,000.[8]

We struck them at the Clearwater on the eleventh, and here is where we had some hard fighting, taking two days to drive them out of their stronghold. We had forty men killed and wounded, and it is, and always has been, a mystery to me why they did not pick off General Howard, who was always on the front line giving orders, at the same time gave the command to sacrifice as few lives as possible. An Indian sniper in a tree picked off some of our men; every time he fired, one of our men was killed or wounded. We had a mountain howitzer with Civil War ammunition, but none of us could handle it. Finally an infantryman volunteered, and, after getting the range did a lot of damage to the Indians. He had served some time in the artillery. The Indians then began packing and to retreat, and were driven over into Montana. We found and destroyed caches and a large number of cooking utensils.

We followed up the advantage gained, until we drove them across the Clearwater, swimming our horses across, and followed them as far as the Lolo Pass. Troop F was then relieved, as men and animals were giving out. We returned to the post and kept up the usual camp routine.

Narratives of the Nez Perce War

LUTHER P. WILMOT[1]

Luther P. Wilmot Papers, Special Collections, University of Idaho Library, Moscow

THE BATTLE OF COTTONWOOD

July 4, 1877, was an anxious day for the settlers on Camas Prairie, Idaho. The Indians were reported to be in many places. In the evening Captain Randall[2] came to me and said, "Lew, will you take ten men and go across the prairie tomorrow and see if you can locate the Indians?"

My reply was yes. I had lived on the prairie over ten years. I knew all the trails leading from the Salmon River to the Clearwater. I began to select the boys I wanted to accompany me. I told them to get up early and have their horses ready so we could get an early start, and for each one to bring a lunch.[3] The trip would be an all-day one. With these instructions, we separated, the boys to rest and I to the bed of a sick wife and to help care for a four-day-old baby.

It seemed but a few minutes before it was time to turn out and feed and saddle our horses. By the time that was done, the cook in the hotel had our breakfast ready. The ten of us was soon on our way. We had not gone half a mile when we met Dan Crooks.[4] Dan asked me where we was going. I told him we had heard so many rumors as to where the Indians were [that] Captain Randall had asked me to take the boys and see if we could locate them. Dan said the Indians are camped near Cottonwood Butte, and yesterday they killed Lieutenant Rains, ten soldiers, and Blewett and Billy Foster, scouts,[5] and had told the soldiers at the Cottonwood House they—the Indians—intended to kill them tomorrow. And the commander had sent him to tell Captain Randall to come to their assistance.

We turned and went back to Mount Idaho and reported to Captain Randall. Dan told Captain Randall what he had told us. When Dan got through, Captain Randall called for twenty-five volunteers to go to the assistance of the soldiers at Cottonwood. Seventeen was all that could go. I shall never forget. Ben Evans came to me and said, "Lew, I would like to, but I have not got a horse."

"If you want to go, I will let you have my horse." Johnny Rice had told me that whenever I wanted to go out, I could have his horse "Frank." I went and got Frank.

We got ready as soon as we could, and by 8:00 A.M.[6] we started. There was Capt. D. B. Randall, J. C. Cearley,[7] 1st Lt. W. P. Wilmot, 2nd Lt. Frank A. Fenn, Orderly Sgt. H. C. Johnson,[8] C. M. Day, D. Howser, Ben Evans, Al Leland, A. D. Bartley, George Riggins, Frank Vansise, Charley Case, Jim Buchanan, W. B. Beamer, and Eph Bunker. There was seven men in that bunch that had no business in such an expedition. While they were good and brave men, they had never been under fire and were not good marksmen.

Once we got under way, we rode as fast as our horses could stand it. We were not long in passing the carcasses of the two horses that was killed when the Indians jumped the Ben Norton party and killed Ben Norton, mortally wounded Joe Moore, and wounded Mrs. Norton. The next wreck we came to was where the Indians chased Peter H. Ready[9] and me away from our freight wagons.

We did not go far when we could see large droves of stock coming off from the mountains. There was a great difference in opinion as to what they were. Some thought it was a big drove of stock being drove by soldiers. Some of the boys had a small pair of binoculars. It was Henry Johnson, and someone stopped and took a look while the rest of the boys kept on. I could tell they were Indians. I begged and coaxed Captain Randall to retreat. This he declined to do. I used all the persuasive power I had. I told him the Indians outnumbered us at least ten to one and so far had not met with defeat; then, if they whipped us, what was to become of our families?

Captain Randall said, "If you are afraid, you can go back. I have started to the relief of the soldiers, and I am going to go." Finally he said, "You can get behind me."

I said, "Captain Randall, the situation is too serious to be made a joke of. I can stand it if you can."

All Indian tribes have a way of signaling when they want all to come as quick as they can. They ride around in a circle, and all the warriors who can see that hurry to them as fast as they can go. When the Indians began circling on the mountains, [they] done the same thing. A lot of Indians had attracted the soldiers at Cottonwood, the Cottonwood buildings being on the creek. Captain Perry had moved his command up onto some small hills and had thrown up an embankment and had two Gatling guns mounted. They called the embankment Fort Perry.[10]

During the attack, before Captain Randall came in sight, an Indian rode out onto a hill and cut a lot of didoes. The soldiers turned one of them Gatling guns onto him but could not silence his battery.

The boys who stopped to use the glass reported Indians. The warriors had answered them signals and had come together. They took up a position across the road about a mile from Shebang Creek and there awaited our approach. I said to Captain Randall, "What are your orders, and what are you going to do?" He said, "We will charge them. And if anyone's horse gets killed, the nearest one to him must stop and pick him up."[11]

We was not long in getting in range of the Indians. As soon as we got near enough to the line, H. C. Johnson got down from his horse and fired. This seemed to awaken the Indians, who then began to fire. As soon as Henry fired, he got on his horse and started on. He had not gone very far when he came to Frank Vansise, whose horse had been shot. Frank did not know what to do. Henry stopped and told him to get on behind him, which Frank did. I had stopped to take a shot, and as soon as I did, I started on.

By this time we had got through the Indians' line. They broke and run to get out from our way, and as soon as we passed they took in behind us. Soon I came to where Captain Randall was standing by his horse, which had been killed. I passed within about fifty yards from him. He said, "Lew, don't run; let's fight 'em." Captain Randall was in a swale, which was lower than the prairie. I kept on for over 100 yards to a piece of higher ground. I wanted to be where I could see all around.

As soon as I got off from my horse, I began shooting. The Indians began to run for cover. I was down but a few minutes when Henry Johnson, W. B. Beamer, C. M. Day, and Charley Case joined me.[12] Eph Bunker and Jim Buchanan wanted to go on to the Cottonwood House for help. I said all right. I told Frank Vansise and George Riggins to go over to the fence and care for D. H. Howser, who was wounded but could still ride. Cash Day I told had better go a little to our left to protect our flank. Jim Cearley, Charley Johnson, Al Leland, Ben Evans, and Randall were caught in the swale, and I never seen any of them until the fight was over, and do not think that any one of them fired a shot after the charge through the Indian line, and Charley Case never fired a shot after he got down by me.

During the fight, Henry Johnson, who was not very far from me, hollered, "Look out, Lew, that Indian near that horse is getting your range." During the fight an Indian had chased us until we took the stand. Then, when he started to run, he stopped in a swale about 300 or 350 yards from us. The swale was deep enough for the Indian to crawl along. He would raise his head, which could hardly be seen through the grass. He would shoot, then shift his position.

I had been shooting at a group over 1,000 yards [away] when Henry called my attention to the Indian by the horse. I watched for him to come up. I had not long to wait when I could see a dark object raise up in the grass. I drew down and fired. At the crack of the rifle, I saw the dirt fly. Beyond the swale, I had overshot probably one foot. I had been shooting [and] had not got my rear sight low enough. I put in another cartridge, and waited and watched. Soon I seen the dark object coming up down the swale below the horse. I took all the pains I knew how and fired. I did not see any dirt or anything fly. I did not see anything more of the dark spot. I hollered to Cash Day to shoot the horse. Cash took a shot at the horse with his needle .50-caliber rifle, and when the bullet hit that cayuse down he went. It sounded like hitting an object with a board.

We then steadied down to a siege. We would shoot at any Indians that would show up. Along about 3:00 P.M. [or] 4:00 P.M., Captain Winters come

2nd Lt. Sevier M. Rains. SPECIAL COLLECTIONS, UNITED STATES MILITARY ACADEMY LIBRARY.

down to within 200 yards of us.[13] He sent his orderly down. George Shearer came down just ahead of the orderly. He rode up near me. I told him to get down; that the Indians might hit him. He made light of the idea. Just then I seen a puff of smoke from an Indian's rifle, and soon a .45-70 bullet hit George's horse through the top of his withers. George got down. That was the last shot being fired. I hollered to Captain Randall for him and the boys to come up and we would go to the Cottonwood House with the soldiers. Jim Cearley answered and said Randall was wounded, Ben Evans was killed, and Al Leland and Charley Johnson were wounded.

I ran down to where Captain Randall lay. I said to him, "Are you badly hurt?" He said, "I am mortally wounded."

He pulled up his shirt, and then I seen where the bullet had hit him. It was about four inches below the heart. He complained of being hot. I hollered for the soldier to bring his canteen. I sat down, took his hat, and fanned until the soldier got there with the water. I gave him a drink, which he threw up. He straightened out and died in my arms.

Captain Winters was getting very anxious to return to the Cottonwood House. The Indians were all together about one mile from us. Captain Winters thought there was going to be a charge. He said, "We can carry the wounded on our horses. The Indians cannot hurt the dead." I said, "We are not going to leave any of our men."

A civilian named Peter H. Ready had come down with the soldiers. He is the man whom, with me, the Indians had attacked June 16. I said to him, "Ready, you take my horse and go to the Cottonwood House, and with yours bring the wagon. We will wait." It being one mile and an eighth, it did not take him very long to make the trip.

It was 4:30 P.M. when we reached Cottonwood. We did not receive from the commanding officer, Captain Perry, a hearty welcome. It was different with the subordinates and the soldiers.

Just as dark set in, the camp was thrown into quite a commotion. The sentry who was on the beat out toward the Indians come in and reported a big body of horsemen approaching from where we seen the Indians at sundown. The situation was soon relieved by two men riding into camp. It was Captain Hunter[14] and an orderly, who said it was their men. They felt very much grieved to hear of the death of our men, and the death of the Rains men and Billy Foster and Blewett. There were seventy-four men in Hunter's company.

That night it was agreed that Captain Hunter and his men should accompany us to Mount Idaho the next day.[15]

The next morning early, we put our dead and wounded in the wagon, and I drove home. In some respects, rumors had reached Mount Idaho that all of the seventeen had been killed. That threw the whole community into consternation and sorrow. While it was a terrible shock to the family and friends of Captain Randall and Ben Evans, they were glad it was no worse. The wounded were cared for. The dead was buried with military honors, and thus ended the Cottonwood fight as seen by Luther P. Wilmot.

━◄◆►━

THE STORY OF THE RAINS MASSACRE[16]

Although the hostile Indians numbered over 400 and kept with them several thousand horses for several days during the first [part] of July, their whereabouts was unknown to either the settlers or the soldiers. Rumor reached Captain Whipple, who had been left in command of the troops at Cottonwood House during the absence of Captain Perry, who had taken a pack train and gone to Fort Lapwai for supplies. Captain Perry had twenty soldiers for an escort. Some squaw man had reported that the Indians had crossed the Salmon River at the mouth of Maloney Creek, and to verify that report, Captain Whipple sent a half-breed Indian named Billy Foster and a young white man named Blewett out to make a reconnoiter.[17]

It was early in the day[18] when they left. They followed the stage road to where it crossed Boardhouse Creek. Here the trail for Salmon River bore off to the left and went up over quite a hill. The scouts took this trail.

When they reached the top of the hill where the trail starts down toward Lawyer's Canyon, the scouts met about 100 warriors who were coming up the hill. The Indians were close enough for Billy Foster to recognize several of them. Among those he knew was James Reuben. When the scouts saw the Indians, they wheeled their horses around and started to run. As they turned, Blewett's horse began to buck and threw him. Billy hollered to Blewett to run for the brush, which was only a short distance. Billy was riding a very fast horse, and although the Indians fired many shots at him, none took effect. Billy kept in the road and soon was back to the command at the Cottonwood House and reported.

Lieutenant Rains called for ten men to go to the relief of Blewett. Billy went also. The Indians killed Blewett near the place where his horse threw him. The Indians followed Billy to the top of the mountain overlooking the prairie and halted.

They had not long to wait when they saw the relief party coming. The Indians divided. Some went down a draw to the right of the road; some went down to the left, in order to get between the Rains party and Cottonwood; and some of the Indians stayed on top of the mountain. The soldiers, being greatly outnumbered, ran, and the Indians ran after them. When the soldiers reached the foot of the mountain, they were attacked by the Indians who had gone down the draw. Billy and his horse were killed, together with four soldiers. Lieutenant Rains got nearly one-half mile farther down the road toward the Cottonwood House. About 100 yards from the road, nature had built a fort. Here some ledges of rocks were thrown up, some of them six feet high, with spaces between where a man could crawl.

Six soldiers took refuge in this fort. The Indians ran for cover and besieged the soldiers. One Indian had taken a position behind a pine stump that was five feet high and not 100 yards from the rocks. The soldiers, in shooting at the Indian, had hit the stump several times. Finally a bullet hit the stump so near the top that it glanced and hit the Indian through the head. That was the only Indian that was killed.[19]

Soon after the Rains party left the Cottonwood House, Captain Whipple ordered all hands to saddle up and follow the Rains party. They were not long in getting under way and had gone a little over one mile when the command came to the top of the first hill out from the Cottonwood House. Here they could see the Indians who were besieging the six soldiers. The troops could not see the soldiers, but they could see the smoke from their rifles and plainly hear the reports from the rifles. When the Indians saw the command come up to the top of the hill, most of them formed in a line reaching across the road not far from the six men. The command could not see any of the Rains party. All they could see was the smoke from the soldiers' rifles and hear the reports. Here the command stopped for over six hours. Finally the command returned to the Cottonwood House, believing the Rains party had all been killed, and they did not know anything definite until afternoon the next day.

Captain Perry, who had gone to Fort Lapwai for supplies, came through the next day and found Billy Foster, Lieutenant Rains, and all but the six boys at the rocks, who had held the Indians off until their ammunition gave out. Then the Indians had come and shot all of them in the head. The Indians moved camp the day Captain Perry came through, from where they were camped over near Grave Creek. The Indians moving camp that day was all that saved Captain Perry's command from the fate of Lieutenant Rains.[20]

—+— ⊠⬦⊠ —+—

MISERY HILL

July 7, 1877, was a busy day in and around Mount Idaho. The hostile Indians had recrossed the Salmon River and joined with Koolkool Snehee and Looking Glass on the Clearwater.

After the burial of Captain Randall and Ben Evans, Colonel Hunter with the Dayton volunteers done some scouting in the vicinity. There was some bad blood brewing between Eugene Wilson[21] and Hunter. It was claimed that Colonel Hunter had obtained some whiskey and was under the influence. In returning from a scouting, they got into a heated argument. Eugene thought the colonel was going to shoot him. Eugene jerked out his revolver and fired at the colonel. The bullet took effect in the colonel's shoulder. The boys come on to Mount Idaho, where the colonel was put in the hospital and Eugene was arrested by civil authorities and put in jail.

I had been very busy making cartridges in Oliver's blacksmith shop. It was along in the afternoon when I had got through. I came out from the shop, which was just across the street from the jail. My attention was attracted by the Dayton volunteers riding around the jail, swearing vengeance on Eugene. I asked someone what all the trouble was about. I was told. I went to the hotel, which was the headquarters of our company. We talked the matter over, and it was decided that the best way to quiet the boys down would be to take them from town. I was selected to take them on a scouting trip, if they would go.

I got my rifle, got on my horse, rode up to the front of the jail, and called the boys to attention. I said, "You boys have come up here to help us protect our homes, and we all feel very grateful to all of you. We are very sorry this has happened. Since Eugene has been legally arrested and is now in the hands of the civil authorities, you boys cannot take him out. And now all of you boys that would rather go and hunt Indians than to try to take Eugene out follow me, and I will show you all the Indians you will want to see." The boys gave a big whoop and said, "Light out."

We rode up to the hotel, packed a horse, and made arrangements to meet them somewhere on the trail near Kamiah. We left Mount Idaho and went northwest.[22] I knew the Indians had followed the main trails from Salmon River to the Clearwater. Quite a while before we reached the main trails, we could see where the ground was cut up by large bands of stock. We followed on the main trails until we had reached the last range of hills on the south of the Clearwater. Here we stopped in order to determine what we should do. I told the boys we were then less than a mile and a half of Looking Glass's camp, and I was certain that was where Joseph would go.

There was quite a number of the Mount Idaho volunteers along, so we were about seventy-five all told. It was decided we would camp where we were. It was a very well sheltered place. Good water and feed for our horses. We were not very long in getting our supper. Then Colonel McConville, who was in command of the expedition, put out his guards for the night. Colonel

McConville, Capt. Jim Cearley, and several of the boys came to where I had made my bed and we discussed. It was agreed that Captain Cearley and myself should get up in the morning as soon as we could see and go down on to the mountain and see where the Indians were camped.

Just before the boys bid me goodnight, the sound of the tom-tom and the war whoop come in. And it sounded like the Indians were very near. It was the first sound of Indians most of the boys had ever heard. They grabbed their rifles and got ready to fight. Of course, all of the boys were gathered around Captain Cearley and I. We knew the country thoroughly. We told them there was a draw come up from the Clearwater through to the divide near where we were camped and the sound come in, and it seemed to be so near, quite a number asked to go on guard. I lay down and was soon asleep. Captain Cearley made his bed near mine.

In the morning, as soon as we could see, Captain Cearley and I got up. We rode down near the top of the mountain and tied our horses in some brush. We walked down to the bluff. That brought us in less than one-half mile of the Indian camp. We counted 72 big tepees. We counted over 150 horses tied at different places around the tepees. We was satisfied the whole band [of] the Indians were in this camp. We watched until the sun come up and begin to shine on the tepees. Soon life began to show. First squaws began to come out. Fires began to start, and once in a while men began to move around. Boys began to start out on the hills on to the opposite side of the river. Finally we went back to our camp and reported.

All hands had a say as to what was best to do. Some was for going back (only a few). When it come my time to speak my little piece, I told them as there was at least 300 warriors in the Indian camp and but 75 of us, and not a dozen who had ever been under fire, it was too great odds against us to attack the Indians, and as all the women and children was in camp, the bucks would put up a big fight. I thought the best thing for us to do would be to secret ourselves and horses and stay where we were; that John McPherson and Dave Baldwin would be along with a couple of pack horses loaded with grub. Then when it come night, we could send [to] General Howard (who was camped at Wall's, about twelve miles from where we were), telling where the Indians were camped and for him to attack them from where we were camped. The main fork of the Clearwater was high. The Indians could not cross it in a hurry. We would have them in a trap.

But the best laid plans of mice and men oft gang agley. We cached our horses and kept a guard out to watch the trail. Everything was going fine until about 10:00 A.M. Johnny Atkinson, while monkeying with a .50-caliber Springfield, let it go off accidentally. Never did I hear, or think I had heard, a rifle make such a report.

We did not have very long to wait until we saw a couple of Indians come out onto a piece of high ground, from where they could see our horses and some of us.

They went back in a hurry. Our camp was thrown into quite a commotion. About one-half mile from where we were, there was quite a high hill. It was flat on top and one of [the] finest places anyone could wish to make a stand. We filled kettles and canteens with water and moved up to the top of what was afterwards known as "Misery Hill."

We had not long to wait after we got moved before we had callers. First nineteen Indians come up onto a mountain overlooking us. They stayed for quite a while and dared us to come over and fight. It was not long before more than 100 come up. We did not try to shoot any; they were over one-half mile from our position.

A little while after noon, quite a number left the group and started south. That was the direction in which John McPherson and Dave Baldwin would come. One of our boys seen dust arise on the trail. My attention was called to it. I took in the situation in an instant. I run to Colonel McConville and said, "Mac, that is our boys coming and the Indians are going to try to cut them off in that gap in the hills. Send some of your men quick. See the Indians making for that hill by the gap?" He said, "You take ten men and go." I said, "Let some of the Dayton boys go."

Colonel McConville called for ten men to go. Not one would go. I said, "If no one will go, I will, rather than see our boys cut off." I jumped onto my horse and started. I had to go down quite a hill before I struck level prairie. When I got to the foot of the hill, I looked back to see how many boys were coming. There was but one. It was M. S. Martin. I run my horse as fast as he could go until I come to the top of a rise. I jumped down, raised my peep sight for 1,000 yards, and fired. When Colonel McConville seen I was going to shoot, he turned his glass onto the Indians, and at the crack of the rifle, he said he saw one Indian fall from his horse. By the time I got back onto my horse, a lot of the boys come. No sooner than I was mounted, the Indians opened fire on me. I was riding a fast horse and soon passed the boys. As I passed one he said, "Lew, I am shot." I said, "Are you badly hurt?" He said, "No, I have the bullet in my hand." I said, "Stick it in your pocket and come on." We gained the hill before the Indians and saved our two friends and our grub.[23] The young fellow who was hit was riding to my right when I got down and shot. The Indians overshot me, and the bullet passed through his shirtsleeve and drew blood on his forearm, then hit the receiver of his rifle, and after denting the barrel of the rifle, the bullet fell into his hand.

When we all got back to the hill, McConville gave his boys quite a lecture for not going out to the assistance of our friends. Our friends not only brought us grub, but also the news that General Howard was camped at Wall's and expected to move on down the Clearwater the next day. After we had our dinner, we held a council of war. It was decided the best thing to be done was to hold the hill, send a couple of men over and tell General Howard where the Indians were camped, and ask him to attack them in the morning, and McConville could attack with our boys.

Ben Penny and I was selected to carry the dispatch. When we got there, we was to build a big bon fire when [Howard] started to go to the attack. We had a lot of very deep canyons to cross and the Clearwater, which was swimming at most of the fords. I knew one where we could cross without getting wet. We went there. The road, or I mean the country, was so rough our progress was slow. It was daylight when we reached the soldiers' camp. I was taken with a very sick spell and could not ride any farther. I sent Ben on with the dispatch. Ben told General Howard I had become sick and had to lie down. The general sent a couple of soldiers back with Ben, and I went into camp. The boys gave me some strong coffee, which revived me, and I went to the general's tent.

When I got to the tent, I found the general surrounded by a lot of officers. Among them was the captain who would not go to the assistance of Captain Randall. The general said, "Lieutenant Wilmot, this is Captain Perry, the officer whom you volunteers accused of cowardice." I said, "How?" Captain Perry said, "You told General Howard I did not send anyone to your assistance, and you told the general you were not a mile and a half from where I was stationed, when it was nearer Cottonwood. We measured it afterwards, and it was exactly one mile and three-eighths."

After he got through, I told him the facts, and I called him all the dirty names I had in my vocabulary. Captain Babbitt[24] spoke up and said, "Captain Perry, if I were you, I would kick him (meaning me) out from camp." I said, "Suppose you try it in Captain Perry's place."

When I got through cussing Perry, General Howard ordered me arrested. I jumped onto my horse and was going to bolt, when an orderly caught my horse by the bridle. I got down [and] gave up my rifle and revolver. Then I told Howard what I thought of him and used language more forcible than elegant. Among the things I told the general was "When I was at your camp on Salmon River, you told me to make out charges against Captain Perry, and you would have him court-martialed. You know that he and I could not settle this. We made out the charges and sent them to you." The general said it made his blood boil to hear an officer blasphemed. I said, "General, it does not make your blood boil half as much as it does mine to hear a dirty coward stand up and lie."

General Howard ordered me released. They gave me my rifle and revolver. I said I wanted my cartridges, which they gave up. Then the general said, "I am very sorry this has occurred." I said, "I'm not, for it was no fault of mine." General Howard said they should not move against the Indians, as it was the Sabbath, and he said, "Will you go and show us the way to the Indian camp?" I said, "No, I will not." "Then what are you going to do?" I said, "I am going back home to Mount Idaho, then to Misery Hill." The general said, "You cannot get through the Indian lines." I said, "I would much rather take my chances with the Indians than with your officers." I got on my horse and rode away. I soon struck off into the timber, and by keeping out from open ground I crossed Clearwater about ten miles above where Ben and I crossed. Ben stayed and went with General Howard.

Our people were greatly surprised when I put in an appearance about 4:00 P.M. I did not tarry long. I got a man to go with me, and we went back to Misery Hill, which we reached about 11:00 P.M. You cannot imagine our surprise when we reached the top. By the aid of matches, we found several rifle [pits], a lot of empty shells, and several dead horses. All we had to do was to retrace our steps. We could surmise all we wanted to. We could not find out anything until we got communication with some of the boys I had left on Misery Hill.

We got back to Mount Idaho before noon. There we found most of our boys, who told us of the fight. Not long after dark, the Indians crawled up the brink of the hill and opened fire, and set up such an unearthly yell the horses nearly all stampeded. A few was killed. They kept up the attack for an hour or so, then withdrew. The next morning[25] the boys packed the horses—the few they had left with their saddles—and started back to Mount Idaho, and when they got opposite Jim Cearley's ranch, they went there and camped. That was how we missed them when we visited Misery Hill. They said they waited quite a while and watched for the bonfire Ben and I was to start, so they give it up and were going back home disgusted. After we left, Hunter got better. Him and Eugene settled their difficulty. Eugene nursed the colonel until he was able to travel, when he went back to Dayton. Thus ends the Misery Hill fight as seen by Luther P. Wilmot.

━━◆◧◆━━

THE BATTLE OF THE CLEARWATER

It was Wednesday[26] morning, July 11. The general started to move to attract the Indians who were camped at the forks of the Clearwater. The Indians moved up and recrossed the south fork of the Clearwater and moved up to where the Cottonwood Creek puts into that stream. General Howard's Indian scouts kept Joseph's band informed of every move the general made.[27]

The general, with his command, moved down the main trails and went a little over halfway to where the Indians were at. The command had passed Little's ranch and come out onto an open ridge. The Indians attacked the general. First they cut off Louie Booket and another packer who had several mules loaded with medical supplies. These the Indians got. The ridge on which the general was attacked was destitute of water. The weather was very hot in the afternoon. The Indians had an ideal place to fight. The soldiers were out on the open prairie. The Indians had the bluffs of the Clearwater and in some places lumber to protect them.

Down near the bluff stood a lone pine tree over two feet in diameter. This tree was about 600 yards from the general's headquarters. An Indian had made a fort out of a couple of pieces of burnt pine snags, one of which he leaned up against the tree. The soldiers could see the tree perfectly and had tried to dislodge the Indian. I was at the tree the day after the fight, and on examining the

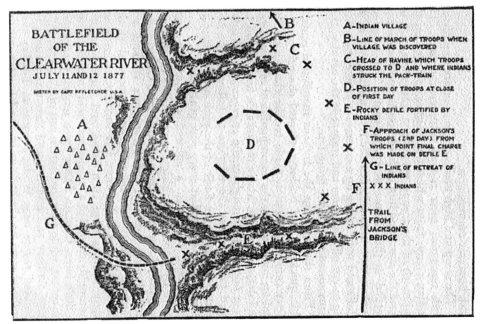

Battlefield of the Clearwater River. CYRUS T. BRADY. *NORTHWESTERN FIGHTS AND FIGHTERS.*

tree, I found many bullet marks on the tree. Only one struck the tree less than four feet from the ground. This bullet struck the tree in the center. Many bullets hit the tree above. I picked up more than fifty empty .45-70 government shells. The fight was kept up all day, and when night came, some of the soldiers and civilians made their way to a spring and got some water.

The next morning[28] the fight was renewed by the Indians and continued until 2:00 P.M., when Captain Miller hove in sight with eight companies of infantry[29] and Captain Jackson's company of cavalry. When the Indians saw this big cavalcade coming, they broke and ran. Their camp was not one mile from the battlefield. The Indians packed up and moved down the Clearwater to Kamiah and crossed the main Clearwater the next day. General Howard moved his command down to Kamiah and camped on Lawyer's Canyon. At first the general halted the troops in the flat not far from the river. The Indians opened fire on the troops and wounded two soldiers.[30] Then the general moved back into Lawyer's Canyon. The general lost fourteen soldiers and two civilians killed, and two wounded. The Indians lost one warrior—the top of his head was blown off by a shell from a mountain howitzer.[31]

Colonel McConville, with the boys I had left at Misery Hill, had been attacked about an hour after Ben Penny and I had left. Although the Indians stampeded a lot of the horses and kept up the fight for several hours, no one was hurt. The boys lost forty-eight horses. They having failed to see any of the signals we were supposed to give, the command moved toward Grangeville the next day and camped at Cearley's ranch, six miles north of Mount Idaho. Here they heard that the soldiers and Indians fought [Wednesday] and were still fighting. The boys started to go down, but before they got there, the Indians ran. [Thursday] night I caught up with the boys and camped with them, and the next day we went down to General Howard's camp. Here we were camped on the south of the Clearwater, and all the Indians were camped in plain sight on the north.

That evening General Howard sent for Colonel McConville and wanted to know if he would take his men and go with Captain Jackson's cavalry down and cross the Clearwater at Greer's Ferry,[32] and go in on to the Lolo Trail to head Joseph off from the old Nez Perce trails that lead to Bitterroot and the buffalo country. Mac told him he would. We were supposed to move at daylight.

Instead of moving at daylight, the sun was way up, and it made a beautiful sight as we climbed the mountain. We could see over into the Indian camp. All was a bustle over there. Tents were being struck [and] horses were being driven in from every quarter. The Indians could see us as we marched out. Captain Jackson asked Colonel McConville if he had a couple of men who were acquainted with the country [whom] he could send ahead and keep not over a mile ahead of the command. Colonel Mac sent Jim Cearley and I. All went well for about an hour, when we received orders to halt. We were quite fortunate in being near a small pine tree. Here we waited for orders. When the Indians saw us marching out, they knew what it meant. They sent a flag of truce. That was the reason we were ordered to halt.

Here we were kept until after 3:00 P.M., when we received orders to move on. When we got to Wilson Creek, about three miles from Greer's Ferry, we were ordered to halt. When Captain Jackson came up, we told him how far it was to the ferry. He ordered us to camp, and he wanted two of us to go with his orderly and see if the ferry boat was there. Jim, the orderly, and I went down. The ferry boat had been turned loose but had lodged against a sandbar on the opposite side of the river. We returned and reported. The colonel wanted to know if we could get the boat. We told him we could cross on a raft, which we could make in a short time. We got our suppers and a good night's rest.

In the morning Captain Jackson received a message from General Howard to return to Kamiah. Joseph had left a lot of his real old people and had pulled out for the Lolo Trail, and of course it would take the general a few days to reorganize his command. Quite a number of the young men from our company joined the general as miners and sappers. There would be a lot of work to be done in following the Indians through the Bitterroot Mountains.

I told McConville I had enough, so I, with about twenty others, pulled out for Mount Idaho. I worked around Mount Idaho and went on a few scouting parties and escorted a stageload of women. It was September before we moved back home, yet such is the life of the early settler.

Howard's Campaign against the Nez Perce Indians, 1877

THOMAS A. SUTHERLAND[1]

Portland, Oregon: A. G. Walling, 1878[2]

BEGINNING THE PURSUIT OF THE NEZ PERCE

Feeling rather inadequate to the task of doing all, or anything like all, that was announced flatteringly in the *Standard,* as my intention, respecting a brief sketch of the campaign against the hostile Nez Perces, I nevertheless plunge *in medias res.* I joined General Howard's command at the end of June, where it was encamped on the Salmon River, near the mouth of White Bird Creek. The Indians were on the west side of the river and, flushed with their victory over Perry, flaunted their blankets in defiance at our troops from the bare hillsides. Passing along a bald mountain in single file, yelling derisively, they marched off in the direction of Snake River. General Howard was now determined to make them fight, if possible, and began immediately rigging a ferry across this most turbulent and rapid stream—exceedingly difficult to cross. Being unable to procure a good pulley, the rope crossing had to be abandoned, and some men sent up the river to get a couple of rowboats, and with which slender means the entire command, about 400 strong, was landed safely on the other side. These unavoidable delays of course gave the Indians considerable start; and as they were familiar with the country and we unable to get a man who knew ten miles of it, they scampered away from us very readily. The only white man we met living on the west side of the Salmon was a farmer named Brown, but so ignorant of the surrounding country that he had never ascended any of the mountains that almost encircled his little home. Left entirely on our own resources, we were compelled to travel slowly and cautiously. Having marched for five days in a crescent shape to where we again struck Salmon River at Craig's Ferry, we discovered from some friendly Indians that Joseph had crossed about a day's journey up the stream from where we were and was heading towards Camas Prairie. Ineffectually, General Howard endeavored to cross, making a raft out of the only house at the ferry, which was lost in launching by the violence of the stream. Just about that time, James Reuben and Captain John, friendly Nez Perces, brought the news that the principal portion of Joseph's people had passed Norton's (where Perry was located) towards the Clearwater, this making the journey back, the way we had come, as short as any other.

We thereupon broke camp immediately[3] and hurried for the mouth of the White Bird. On arriving at a point nearly opposite Rocky Canyon, we for the first time heard of Lieutenant Rains's death and the skirmishes between Perry of the 1st Cavalry and the hostiles. McConville and Hunter's volunteers were dispatched here and sent directly to Norton's. Prior to leaving our camp on the east side of Salmon River, Captain Whipple had been sent to capture Looking Glass and his band, who were reported to be killing cattle in extraordinarily large numbers, drying the beef, and showing other signs of preparing for war. Whipple being forced to rest the worn horses of his command on reaching Mount Idaho, Looking Glass got wind of the movement, and on Whipple's arrival at his camp, the wily Indian and his followers took to their horses and ran away, joining Joseph on Camas Prairie. The camp however, and about 700 wild cayuse ponies fell into the hands of the troops. After this movement and skirmish, Captain Whipple was sent to Norton's as an observing force to see what direction the Indians might take, protect supplies coming under Perry from Lewiston, and keep General Howard informed. Bendire's[4] company of cavalry, having previously come to Indian Valley from Harney, prevented Joseph from going in that direction and necessarily from joining forces with the Weiser or Malheur Indians. The result of General Howard's demonstration on the west side of Salmon River had several beneficial effects. He drove the Indians from mountain fastnesses and kept them from reaching the naturally fortified country of the Wallowa, which Joseph at all times considered his last resort, or "ditch," as it was called in the Civil War. They were forced out on the open prairie near Mount Idaho, where General Howard had located troops and where, had all the volunteers of the neighborhood been united, the Indians could have been annihilated or driven back upon the force of the commanding general. Minor advantages resulting from Howard's crossing the Salmon River were the discovery of many rich caches filled with tobacco, clothing, Indian food, several hundred sacks of flour, dried beef, etc. Several large bands of cayuse ponies belonging to Black Tail and White Bird were captured, and large numbers of fat cattle. This movement cannot otherwise than be called wise and successful. General Howard could not stand tamely by and see the Indians march into the rugged Wallowa or entrench themselves among their cattle in the precipitous mountains of the Salmon River country. They had to be driven out, and they were. So much for the wisdom of the maneuver—the advantages have already been cited.

* * *

BATTLES AT COTTONWOOD CREEK AND CLEARWATER RIVER

General Howard recrossed the Salmon River early in the second week of July (after great difficulty, losing several horses by drowning), finding Captain Haughey[5] and his company fortified in our old camp, ready to resist any

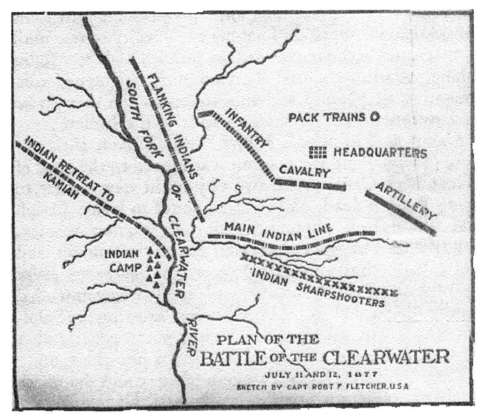

Plan of Battle of the Clearwater. CYRUS T. BRADY. *NORTHWESTERN FIGHTS AND FIGHTERS.*

demonstration of the hostiles in that quarter. Taking him with us, we moved towards Grangeville, where we were joined by Perry and his cavalry command.

Hearing that Joseph, with over 300 warriors[6] and about as many squaws and boys able to bear arms, was encamped on the South Fork of the Clearwater, General Howard's intention was to get beyond them, so as to keep the enemy between him and a force of about 90 volunteers, fortified on a hill almost over-looking the Clearwater, sent thither about two days before from Mount Idaho to reconnoiter and report. So he crossed the river several miles above the Indian camp on what was left of Jackson's bridge (for the Indians had almost succeeded in burning it) and got well to the rear of Joseph, when Ad Chapman discovered the camp on the other side of the river (the Indians having crossed the stream near the mouth of Cottonwood Creek).

The celerity of General Howard's movements in this instance is deserving of more than a passing notice. His little force was spread over a great deal of country, necessitated by the uncertainty of the Indians' movements and the desire to hold all advantageous positions. As if by magic, all the various commands from the different directions came marching into Grangeville, and not a moment was lost by waiting for dilatory officers—for there were none. In order to expedite matters, the foot troops—artillery and infantry—were put into farm wagons and trundled over the roads as rapidly as the anxious soldiers could make the horses go. We came upon Joseph on July 11, about ten days from the time we last saw him on the west side of the Salmon River.

On the night of the tenth, the Indians attacked the volunteers on their fortified hill and succeeded in killing and stampeding about fifty of their horses. This seemed to demoralize the citizens, and they moved to Three-Mile Creek, about six miles from Mount Idaho, to protect the settlements, leaving General Howard to do the fighting himself. Before Chapman had discovered the camp (for it was hidden in a narrow defile between two mountains), the column had marched down the river and beyond it. The Indians were taken completely by surprise and, had it not been for their inaccessible position, would have fallen as easy a prey as the British at Ticonderoga. While I do not intend to go into the details, I will give a few general outlines of the battle to show its general conduct and importance. In the first place, General Howard completely surprised the Indians, as was shown by their consternation and scattering; their loud cries for assembly; their driving off their stock to a place of safety; and their disinclination at this time to fight back. Another evidence was the absence of all fortifications facing toward our side of the river, as they all pointed in the direction of the volunteers' camp, as if their expectation was for us to join the citizens and fall upon the Indians from the Camas Prairie side of the river. Another proof that Howard's attack was unexpected is that the Indians had made a trail up a very steep declivity on our side of the river, so that they might have a means of escape, should they be defeated. There were also some valuable caches discovered here, tending to prove that should Joseph be driven from his camp hurriedly, something would be waiting for him on the other side. There are other evidences of the surprise, such as the story told by a captured squaw; but we think the point has already been made sufficiently clear without more argument.

The question naturally arises, if the Indians were surprised, why were they not captured? Simply on account of their inaccessible position. A navy might surprise Gibraltar—that is, get near it without those in the fort knowing it—yet be powerless to make it capitulate. Where we first placed our big guns, we could not reach the Indians at all, and instead of killing any of them, we unfortunately gave them warning of our presence, owing to the depth of the canyon made by the junction of the Cottonwood Creek and Clearwater River. On hurrying to another point, from which we could drop shells into the hostile camp, we found Indians already behind breastworks on our side of the river, ready to receive us. The distance in a direct line from where we discovered the enemy to the new position was not more than half a mile, but by the detour we had to make to our left, around a deep and impassable ravine, the distance was fully a mile and a half. Firing here commenced on both sides, and Howard's whole command was brought up and placed in a circular form, with the provisions, horses, etc., in the center. The Indians fired from all conceivable places, trying every now and then to flank us or break our line by joining together and firing upon one part of our defense, but they were invariably unsuccessful.

On the second day of the fight, the troops charged the Indians in their rifle pits and drove them down the steep path before alluded to, into and across the river and up the precipitous hills on the other side—where the volunteers, unfortunately, were not waiting. As the Indians were all mounted, it was impossible for foot troops to pursue them further. Captain Perry of the cavalry was then ordered to continue the chase, but in the transmission of the order, it was not delivered to him. Independent of this, Captain Perry found his cavalry scattered and fighting as infantry, away from their horses; a portion of Jackson's was obstructed by the mountain descent in its front and after trial had to turn back and go another way, consuming time; and all the horses but his had been two days shut off from food—under fire—and absolutely without water, so that the condition of the cavalry was not such as to induce Perry to use it before a few hours given for recuperation. On Perry's reaching the other side of the Clearwater, he simply waited the arrival of the foot troops, which he ferried over.

The tangible and moral effects of this battle were without equal in the entire campaign. In the first place, there were eight or ten Umatilla and as many Spokane and Coeur d'Alene Indians in this fight, and should Joseph have been successful (as Joseph himself told me), the Indians from the Weiser to the Spokane country would have joined him, and the remnant of soldiers been annihilated. Joseph also told me, while conversing with him on the Upper Missouri, that the two days' fight on the Clearwater was the only one during the campaign where his ambition was victory; his highest aim ever after being simply to escape. This is the only time he fought when he was not compelled to, and Joseph says he afterwards considered he carried the day when he got off with fewer men killed than the attacking party. The battle taught the Indians that no matter how courageously they might fight, how well armed they might be, or how well fortified, the United States troops, when well generaled, are vastly their superiors.[7] This disheartened the young bucks of the different tribes who had joined Joseph merely for the excitement and plunder, and they all scattered and went to their different reservations and homes. Some twenty odd of the renegade Nez Perces themselves felt their inferiority and surrendered, and Joseph says that he too wanted to come in but was overpowered in the council by White Bird, Looking Glass, and other chiefs. Another discouraging effect the Clearwater fight had upon the hostiles (to say nothing of the impression that the killed and wounded made upon them), was the loss of their entire camp, as they got off with nothing more than their guns and horses. Hundreds of buffalo robes, skins of all kinds in abundance, camas and coos roots dried and in flour, quantities of dried beef with their different utensils—in fact, their entire camp equipage was captured. For people who intended to make the long march to the buffalo country, to be thus stripped at the very outset was a most severe blow, and we can but coicide with Joseph that "the Clearwater fight broke his heart and his command's back."

⊶ ⋐◊⋑ ⊷

NEAR SURRENDER OF JOSEPH AND HIS RETREAT OVER THE LOLO PASS

The night after the defeat of Joseph and his warriors at Clearwater, General Howard and his command pitched their tents in the old Indian camp. The next morning most of the troops were engaged in destroying the caches and burning the tepees. About 7:00 A.M. James Reuben, a friendly Nez Perce, rode into camp and informed General Howard that the hostiles were crossing the river at the ford near Kamiah and were intent upon either destroying the homes of the James Lawyer Indians or making for the buffalo country via Lolo Trail. No time was to be lost, and with all the speed that could be spurred from our over-worked men and horses, General Howard hurried ahead with the cavalry, the foot troops hastening closely behind.

When we reached the highlands overlooking the beautiful Kamiah Valley, by the aid of field glasses we could see the hostiles crossing the river about a mile below the village, their stock, squaws, and children being already on the other side.

With all possible speed, we hastened down the almost vertical mountains. Arriving in the valley, General Howard divided his cavalry into two bodies, sending Whipple around by the river, while he himself accompanied Jackson along the base of the mountains, both commands to form a junction at the ford where the Indians had crossed. Among other news brought by James Reuben to General Howard on the morning of this day was a challenge from Chief Joseph to fight at Kamiah, or rather an announcement that he would fight Howard there should he put in an appearance. Having only the cavalry and a Gatling gun at this time, General Howard's movements one would suppose would be slow and cautious, but he had no sooner given his orders than the whole force was put to a brisk run to the river crossing.

General Howard with Captain Jackson was the first to reach the destination, as the road taken by Whipple was more circuitous. The Gatling gun was hurried into position, and under command of Captain Wilkinson did good work in driving the Indian sharpshooters from their different breastworks on the mountains opposite. The river road taken by Whipple wound around in one place very close to the bank on the Indian side, and as he arrived at this point, he was met with a very brisk fire (say fifty shots in two minutes) from some hostiles in ambuscade. The men jumped from their horses and took to the grain fields on their left, and joined us on foot at the ford. The Gatling gun was now used to dislodge the Indians who had fired upon Whipple, and some of our best shots were stationed in good positions to pick off every Indian who might show himself. The firing was kept up until dark on both sides, although of a very desultory character. General Howard then drew off and went into camp on a plain near the wire ferry over the Clearwater. As the smoke from the hostile camp could be plainly seen just over the first mountains on the Lolo Trail, it was not so sure that Joseph intended going to the buffalo country and that he did not intend to make good his boast of giving Howard a fight. Captain Jackson and Colonel McConville of the volunteers, who joined us this day, were ordered by a roundabout route down the river to Dunwell's Ferry to learn if the bridge there was destroyed—from which point it was thought Joseph might be attacked unawares, in the rear—and with a view of proceeding by that ferry to the junction of its trail with the Lolo Pass, the general hoping to get his troops to that point before the hostiles.

The next day General Howard left camp with the cavalry, apparently going toward Lewiston, but with the real purpose of carrying out the object referred to. He had not proceeded far when a messenger arrived, stating that Joseph was anxious to surrender, whereupon General Howard sent his cavalry on to Dunwell's Ferry but returned himself to Kamiah. On reaching Kamiah, General Howard proceeded immediately to the river, where he was met by Kulkulsuithim—a messenger from Joseph—and during the talk, he was fired upon by a hostile in ambush on the other side of the river. This, of course, closed all negotiations; General Howard, however, told Joseph's envoy that if his chief and warriors would come in, they would be tried by a military court and get justice. This did not seem to satisfy the chief of Wallowa, for he sent no other messengers and struck camp the next morning, starting across the almost impenetrable Lolo Trail, evidently discovering our movement toward Dunwell's Ferry.

Here I will take occasion to throw a little light on the course pursued by General Howard, which has been criticized so generally by people ignorant of surrounding circumstances. These stay-at-home heroes look upon Joseph's offer for surrender as a ruse only to gain time, and that Howard must have been easily gulled to have placed any confidence in it. Now the truth is, Joseph did want to surrender, and General Howard lost not a moment of time by conferring with him, nor did he place any too much confidence in his peace protestations. It is absurd to talk of Joseph's "ruse to gain time," for did he not wait at Kamiah for more than a day, when he need not have waited five minutes? And did he not hover about the place after Howard had gone a good day's march towards Lewiston? He showed an utter disregard for time, and it is not likely he would have resorted to a *ruse de guerre* which was at once unnecessary and not intended to be taken advantage of. In substantiation of my assertion that Joseph wished to surrender, I will briefly state that the Indians spent over a day near Kamiah in council; over twenty warriors deserted and surrendered;[8] and Joseph himself says that his voice was for peace, but he was overpowered by the other chiefs, and when he talked of surrendering at all events, he was threatened with death. Furthermore, General Howard lost no time in consulting with Joseph's peace messenger, as he could not move until everything was in readiness for the long tramp, and he might as well be negotiating for the surrender of Joseph as "sitting like patience on a monument." He lost no time coming back from his cavalry when en route to Dunwell's Ferry, for he sent the command on, they not halting an instant on account of Joseph's so-called ruse. Another little item that we wish to call our readers' attention to is General Howard's answer to Joseph when he proposed to surrender:

> Clearwater, July, 15
>
> Joseph may make a complete surrender to-morrow morning. My troops will meet him at the Ferry. He and his people will be treated with justice. Their conduct to be completely investigated by a court composed of none of my army, selected by myself. Captain Miller is designated to receive Joseph and his arms.
>
> (Signed,)   O. O. Howard,
>   Brigadier General U.S.A.

When we reached Colonel Sturgis's command some time afterward, that officer informed me that he had received instructions from the War Department to promise Joseph his life should he surrender. Had latitude of this kind been given General Howard, who is supposed by those who know nothing of the Nez Perce campaign to be a most peaceful foe, I venture to say that the hostiles would never have crossed the Lolo Trail and many a dollar and life would have been saved. General Howard took a bold stand and would listen to nothing but unconditional surrender. So much for the general who has been slandered about his desire to let all the Indians go free if they would but surrender to him.

⊷ ⩳⧆⧆ ⊶

BATTLE ON THE LOLO TRAIL

As soon as it was positively discovered that the Indians had begun to cross Lolo Trail towards the mountains, General Howard crossed the Clearwater with his command as speedily as possible, it taking a day, as considerable time was lost in repairing the wire ferry. Before daybreak the next morning (July 17), Major Mason, with the entire cavalry force and some Indian scouts— under orders from General Howard to make a two days' march beyond the intersection of Lolo and Oro Fino Trails to find the direction taken by the Indians—started from camp.

By hard marching, Major Mason succeeded in carrying out General Howard's order in one day, making all the necessary discovering concerning the direction taken by the Indians. He came upon them in a narrow and densely wooded defile in the Lolo Trail near the Camas Weippe, where the Indians had taken a position in the timber. The Kamiah Indian scouts fell into the trap (as they were riding ahead), two of them being wounded and one killed, two others being disarmed and allowed to escape, as they were recognized by the hostiles as acquaintances.

Major Mason immediately ordered his men to dismount and form skirmish lines. He proceeded cautiously into the thick forest, driving the Indians slowly until they took a position in a place not unlike the pass of Thermopylae, shaping themselves like an inverted arrowhead. Knowing it would be suicide—cavalry as they were, in a wooded country—to force his small command on to the fortified hostiles, and having carried out General Howard's orders to the letter, Major Mason returned to Kamiah. One hostile was killed[9] and two mules laden with provisions captured by the men under Lieutenant Hoyle.[10] On this day General Howard telegraphed Captain Sladen[11] to inform General Sherman and posts east of the Bitterroot Mountains of Joseph's start across the Lolo Trail for Montana.

Thinking he could kill two birds with one stone, General Howard determined to refit his command at Lewiston and go through the Spokane country, establish the needed reservations, and be at the Missoula end of the Lolo Trail in time to meet Joseph on his exit. Captain Throckmorton was left at Kamiah with a company of artillery, a company of infantry, and a company of cavalry to resist any attempt on the part of the hostiles to return, and with the assurance that a large cavalry reinforcement from Boise City under Major Green would join him. Howard thereupon recrossed the Clearwater and had marched his command thirty-five miles to Cold Spring in one day, when news arrived from Captain Throckmorton,[12] Colonel Watkins,[13] and Mr. Monteith, that forty renegades had secretly returned to Kamiah and had driven off about four hundred ponies. This news, with the earnest entreaties of influential men like L. P. Brown of Mount Idaho, Mr. Croasdaile of Camas Prairie,[14] and delegate to Congress from Idaho S.S. Fenn, that the troops remain awhile to assure the people against a return of the murderous redskins, settled General Howard in his purpose to pursue the Indians in a direct line across the Lolo Trail as soon as Major Green and his cavalry should arrive.

Howard's command had now been a month in the field, and the Boise column had not yet heard the whistle of a hostile bullet. The time taken by this cavalry very much interfered with the general's plans, as all his old cavalry—Jackson's troop excepted—under Captain Perry was ordered to accompany the Spokane column under Colonel Wheaton, as this cavalry was not in as good condition as Sanford's. It not being wise for us to leave the vicinity of Camas Prairie while the peaceful Indians and white settlers were in such an excited state and without cavalry, we had to cast about the country like a steamer off the Columbia bar awaiting our opportunity to go ahead. From Cold Spring we went to Lawyer's Canyon, where we were joined by two companies of the 4th Artillery under Captains Cushing and Field,[15] a company of the 12th Infantry under Captain Viven,[16] and one of the 8th Infantry under Captain Wells.[17] From this camp—named after Surgeon C. T. Alexander[18]—we moved on to Camas Prairie near Croasdaile's farm, at the intersection of six trails, for the double purpose of establishing a debouche and protecting the farmers in gathering their crops and herds. General Howard sent Jack Carlton, a lumberman, to Lewiston to engage fifty men to precede us on the Lolo Trail, to cut away the fallen timber and improve the path in dangerous and impassable places. From this place Captain Wilkinson was ordered to the Dalles to secure, if possible, some Warm Springs Indians as scouts, then to report to Colonel Wheaton and accompany him on the Spokane expedition.

Hearing that the cavalry column would soon reach Kamiah, General Howard proceeded to that place, and on July 28, the date of Sanford's arrival, had crossed all his command. Sanford increased Howard's command [to] 150 cavalrymen and 20 Bannock scouts.[19] Again, on the twenty-eighth, General Howard telegraphed Captain Sladen in Portland: "Ask to have the troops at Missoula detained until we can strike his (Joseph's) rear." This made two dispatches, one under the date of the July 17 and the other dated the twenty-eighth (to say nothing of warning dispatches sent even earlier than July 17), that General Howard had sent to apprise the officers at the Montana end of the Lolo Trail that the Indians were coming that way, and to be prepared for them. On the night of July 30, Sanford's command, less a company under Captain Sumner[20]—left behind to protect the settlers and await Major Green's arrival— crossed the Clearwater and joined Howard's command, in readiness to begin the march across the mountainous Lolo Trail.

Joseph, starting on July 16, had just two weeks the start of Howard. Before breaking camp on Camas Prairie, General Howard issued the following order, which explains itself, and which it is necessary that my readers thoroughly comprehend if they wish to keep the thread of these brief articles constantly in hand:

HEADQUARTERS DEPARTMENT OF THE COLUMBIA,
In the Field, Camp Sully (Idaho), July 13
The following field order No. 2 has been promulgated by General Howard:

The hostile Indians, according to the latest information, have retreated by the Lolo Trail towards Montana, leaving but a few families, who are possibly concealed in the rocky fastness of the Snake and Salmon River country. It is directed that the two columns and a reserve shall operate as follows:

A, the right column, personally commanded by the department commander, consisting of the battalion of artillery under command of Capt. Marcus P. Miller, the battalion of infantry commanded by Capt. Evan Miles, and a battalion of four companies of cavalry under command of Maj. George B. Sanford, will immediately, upon the arrival of Major Green's force from Boise City, enter upon a direct pursuit of the Indians over the Lolo Trail, the objective point being Missoula City, Montana Territory.

B, the left column, commanded by Col. Frank Wheaton of the 2nd Infantry, consisting of his force of infantry, increased by a battalion of cavalry, to be commanded by Colonel Grover[21] of the 1st Cavalry, and composed as follows, viz.: Companies F (Perry's) and H (Trimble's), 1st Cavalry and two companies, 200 each, of Washington Territory mounted volunteers, will proceed northward by way of Hangman's Creek and the Coeur d'Alene Mission, the objective point being Missoula City, Montana Territory. The design of this column will be first, a cooperation with the right column, a frequent communication to be kept up by means of reliable sources, via the reserve column at Mount Idaho; second, by overawing malcontent Indians or occupying their attention, to prevent any reinforcement of the hostile Indians, and should the latter attempt to return through the Coeur d'Alene country, to engage them; third, to quiet the fears and apprehensions of the settlers, that they may return to their peaceful pursuits; fourth, a cordial cooperation with the officials of the Interior Department in their endeavor to settle disputes and controversies between the so-called friendly Indians and the settlers.

Colonel Wheaton will, as soon as practicable, furnish the commanding officer of Fort Lapwai, Idaho Territory, with a small detachment of ten or fifteen men and will leave a guard at Lewiston sufficient to protect the main depot. Finally, the recent indication of a reconcentration of fugitive hostile Indians on the Lolo Trail having altered the department commander's original intention of pursuing this northern route in person, he desires that the commander of the left column exercise the greatest caution in the anticipation and prevention of complications tending to cause an increase of allies, either direct or indirect, to those Indians now actually at war.

C, the reserve column, will be commanded by Maj. John Green of the 1st Cavalry and will consist of the troops from Boise City, excepting the cavalry designated to accompany the night column, increased by Company C (Whipple's) and Company E (Winter's) of the 1st Cavalry, and a body of Warm Springs Indian scouts. Major Green will allocate his main force at or near Croasdaile's farm on Cottonwood Creek, protecting with at least one company and two pieces of artillery the subdepot at Kamiah and maintaining a small outpost at Mount Idaho as a nucleus for the Mount Idaho and Grangeville volunteers. He will closely watch, by means of scouting parties and patrols, the crossings of the south fork of the Clearwater River and Salmon River—that is, the forks of Kamiah, Dunwell's Ferry, etc., on the former, and White Bird Creek, Rocky Canyon, etc., on the latter.

The country between the Salmon and Snake Rivers and beyond the forks of the south fork of the Clearwater River will be thoroughly and constantly scoured by scouting parties, and its most hidden recesses probed by the Warm Springs Indians, and any scouts, little parties, or hiding families left by the hostile Indians will be captured and brought in.

Major Green will forward promptly all communications between the operating columns.

Second—The right column will move across the south fork of the Clearwater River, so as to be ready to make its departure from the Weiser on Monday the thirtieth instant. Colonel Wheaton will endeavor to make the movement of the left column northward as nearly simultaneous with the movements of the right as possible. It is desirable that any necessary delay in the left column take place as far northward near the Coeur d'Alene country as possible.

Each column will be supplied with twenty days' small rations and will take with it a herd of as many steers as necessary. As a general rule, forage will not be camped, but will be obtained en route.

Third—The Lewiston depot is designated as the main depot for the army in the field. The general staff will keep it well furnished with at least three months' supplies in advance.

Brig. Gen. O. O. Howard, commanding

[On] July 30 General Howard, with his command (about 700 strong), began the march across the Lolo Trail.

As was announced before our first article on the Nez Perce campaign, I will deal only with the salient facts bearing directly on the military conduct of the war and, for that reason, will confine my remarks about the hardships of the Lolo Trail to the following brief clipping, written by me for another paper. The trip through Lolo Trail was made in excellent time, and to General Howard is due the full credit, as he alone appeared to be the man anxious to hurry ahead at all hazards to life or limb, and at all times.

On leaving Kamiah, we were accompanied by a severe rain which kept us company for the entire day, making the march, which was single file on account of the narrowness of the path, [by] far the most slippery, sticky, muddy, and filthy of the trip. The first night we camped at the Weippe (Nez Perce for a marshy place in the mountains), where camas was so plentiful that the path taken by our men was in many places actually white with that favorite Indian bulb. I should like to carry you with me through the different camps, but as there, was a great sameness in these I shall confine myself to presenting a few outlines.

About twelve years ago several thousand dollars were appropriated by Congress to have the Lolo Trail surveyed, and judging from the great distances between the mile posts, the engineers were in league with someone who wanted to get a further appropriation for a wagon road. In connection with the extraordinary length of these miles, they are nearly all straight up and down mountains, which in height—and in the language of the Oregon trapper Joe Meek—make ordinary picnic mountains, as for instance, the Adirondacks, "appear as holes in the ground." For about three days and a half of our experience on this trail, our horses are entirely without grass, the only semblance of it being a tough species of wire growth which mules and horses refuse to eat. The rapid marches, lack of food, and camping on the sides of the mountains, which deprive the poor brutes of rest at night, made our last tramps before reaching the east end of the Lolo very laborious, not to say of the order in which a man "works his passage."

On the very day that we began our march towards Montana, Joseph and his warriors issued from the other end of the trail, having made the trip in fifteen days—a journey that Howard made in nine days. While Howard was behind pursuing the Indians there was no possibility of their returning, and as he had telegraphed thirteen days before the Indians reached the east end of the trail that they were going in that direction, he had every confidence that they were being driven to their destruction. The following is the last dispatch he sent to Montana:

Camp Alfred Sully, July 25,1877

Commanding Officer, Post of Missoula, Montana:

Sir:—All reports seem to indicate that what are left of the hostile Indians, with their stock and plunder, have escaped by the Lolo Trail and may reach you before this dispatch. I shall start with my right column from Kamiah, in direct pursuit next Monday, the thirtieth inst. My guides say that if you could move your force this way as far as (the canyon of) the Lolo Fork, which runs into the Bitterroot River, you could prevent their escape. They have a thousand horses at least, and much stuff of one kind and another, and will not go fast after they escape from the mountains (probably will stop to graze animals). If you simply bother them and keep them back until I can close in, their destruction or surrender will be sure. I shall make the march as rapidly as it can be done over a rough trail. Colonel Wheaton's column will have the same objective point, viz.: Missoula, Montana, moving via Coeur d'Alene Mission and Sohon Pass. Please notify all neighboring commanders, both regular and volunteers, of my movement. We must not let these hostile Indians escape.

Very respectfully,

O. O. HOWARD, Brigadier General, U.S.A.

When very near the end of the trail, a courier came from Colonel Gibbon announcing that the Indians had passed around Captain Rawn, and that he himself wanted reinforcements from Howard. Howard immediately started ahead with his entire cavalry command, about 250 strong, to join Gibbon in his proposed attack on the Indians. As a description of the way in which the Indians passed Rawn would take up too much space in this chapter, and as it is too important to be hurried over, I have concluded to close this article here and devote the next to Captain Rawn and the escape of the hostiles from the Lolo Trail into the Bitterroot Valley.

—•— ≍◈≍ —•—

ESCAPE OF JOSEPH AT THE EAST END OF THE LOLO TRAIL

In the entire campaign against the hostile Nez Perces, no one transaction is more open to criticism than the escape of Joseph and his followers from the east end of the Lolo Trail. As has already been shown, the troops in Montana had been warned thirteen days in advance that the hostiles were in the Lolo Trail heading towards Missoula and could easily be checked and held there for months. The fact that Howard was behind them with about 600 fighting men utterly excluded all hope on the part of the Indians of returning. Howard was steadily driving them upon hostile bayonets, and whether he was actually on their heels or nine days behind them, the efficacy of the movement was the same—they could not countermarch and must either stand between two fires or assault the fortifications. Howard's plan made it compulsory that the Indians take either of these horns of the dilemma.

The trail was exceedingly narrow and so precipitous that even Rocky Mountain sheep could not scale the granite walls, making it impossible for the hostiles to escape by any side march; they must either keep straight ahead and storm the breastworks at the east end of the trail or return to meet the victorious Howard, with overpowering numbers.

This was the plan—and now we will consider its execution. All available troops in Montana had received notification from Howard in ample time to have barricaded the narrow trail, but for some inexplicable reason, only twenty-five soldiers could be raised in two weeks to oppose the Indians' progress—or rather to consummate the plan that was sure to end in their destruction. On whom should the blame fall? On Howard, who had given ample time to the different commanders to be prepared and who had impressed upon them the necessity of speed? Surely not. Should we condemn Captain Rawn, who was the only man at the post and in command of only a handful of men? We see no just reason to find fault with him for at least making an effort to carry out Howard's instructions—the only man in that vicinity who appeared to be untainted by jealousy or indifference. The detachment from Fort Hall moved so slowly as almost to appear either anxious to avoid perfecting Howard's plan or keep from fighting the Indians, while Governor Potts became disgusted at the refusal of the War Department to authorize him to raise volunteers and took no part. While I do not imagine for an instant that I am capable of judging correctly at all times of the efficacy or folly of military maneuvers, I feel no hesitation in criticizing Captain Rawn, insofar as he fortified himself too near the mouth of the trail, where canyons running at right angles with the main pass were staring the Indians in the face like so many invitations to escape. Had Rawn moved his command further into the trail, he would have left these passes in his rear and the escape of the hostiles [would have] been, then impossible.

Rawn had with him volunteers enough to make his force 216 men, while the Indians (unfortified) were but 200 strong. Finding themselves in a trap with no apparent means of escape, the wily rascals began to parley, with the object of gaining time to examine the country for a means of exit to the Bitterroot Valley. Having consumed four days in pretended negotiations, the hostiles became thoroughly familiar with the different canyons and so, at the end of that time, in full view of the entrenched troops and citizens, moved up a canyon on the right and over the mountains unobstructed.

In justice to Captain Rawn, we are compelled to say that he undoubtedly would have struck Joseph with his superior force had he any command over it. Looking Glass promised the volunteers that if they would let his followers pass unmolested, he would see to it that the Indians should shed no blood in the Bitterroot Valley. This disgraceful proposition was accepted by the volunteers, and Rawn, with his insignificant regular force, was compelled to abide by their decision. This is the whole story of the Indians' escape from the Lolo Trail. Howard had planned their capture here, and had his instructions been carried out and his solicitation for cooperation properly heeded, the Indians would never have got away to commit new robberies and murders. This unfortunate escape of Joseph I look upon as the most disgraceful feature in the entire Nez Perce War. The Indians were fagged out, their cayuses scarcely able to walk, and their cartridge belts almost empty. To let them go by was equivalent to giving them new horses, plenty of ammunition, and ample provisions—it was, in a word, breathing new life into a corpse. Here was the golden opportunity of the war, which for indifference on one side, cowardice or selfishness on another, and impecuniosity of the government on the other, irretrievably lost. The official proofs of Howard's forewarning the commands east of the Lolo Trail in ample time for service, and of the little advantage taken of it by the different officers, are extant and would be gladly published by me had I not determined upon excluding everything of that kind from these articles. Somebody was criminally negligent in allowing the hostiles to escape from Lolo Trail, and who it was I will leave to my readers, with the naked statement of facts, to decide.

—•—⊫♦⊨—•—

PASSAGE THROUGH THE BITTERROOT VALLEY AND THE BIG HOLE BATTLEFIELD

With the assurance from the settlers that they would not be interfered with in their passage through the Bitterroot Valley, the Indians moved very slowly from the time they issued from Lolo Trail until overtaken by Gibbon, as they were anxious to trade with the whites and recruit their jaded horses. At a little place

Making camp in the Bitterroot country. CENTURY MAGAZINE, 1889.

called Stevensville, the whites behaved most despicably. They sold the hostiles not only provisions, horses, and cartridges, but followed them up with wagons trying to sell them goods while on the march. Some half-breed Indians engaged in horse raising traded fresh horses to the Nez Perces for their worn-out cayuses, which gave them a great advantage over their pursuers. It was in this valley that Joseph was reinforced by eighteen lodges of Nez Perces who lived off the regular reservation, chief of whom was the deceased Poker Joe.[22]

Knowing that Howard was considerably behind them, the hostiles moved very leisurely for, as Joseph told me afterwards, he had been guaranteed against attack in Bitterroot Valley in consideration of his spilling no white blood there.

Believing what he had been told, he had no rear scouts and traveled about ten to fifteen miles a day for the purpose of recuperating. Arriving at Ruby Creek,[23] in the Big Hole, the hostiles went into camp for the purpose of making preparations for the treeless plains of the buffalo country. They were all employed in cutting and barking lodge poles, with the intention of spending four or five days at it, when Gibbon overtook them. While Gibbon was pursuing Joseph, Howard dispatched Sergeant Sutherland, Co. B, 1st Cavalry, with the request that the Indians be delayed as much as possible by Gibbon until he could catch up—he then being a little more than two days behind.

At this time, General Howard, with thirty-seven men,[24] left Skal-ka-hoe (Sleeping Child) with the purpose of forming a junction at all hazards with Gibbon, supposed to be seventy-five miles distant. That day General Howard and his handful of men made fifty-three miles. When in the midst of a dense forest beyond Ross' Hole, they were met by six citizens coming from Gibbon, who were the first to give information that a fight had taken place. As these men were sadly demoralized, they told very exaggerated stories of Gibbon's defeat, saying that he had lost 100 men killed, had been 48 hours without food or water, that he was completely surrounded, and the country was swarming with victorious Indians.

Discouraging as was this news to such a little band, General Howard determined to push on, and he arrived at the scene of the battle early next morning, the Indians having a short time previously broken camp. When General Howard received the news of the Ruby Creek battle and the precarious situation of the soldiers, he dispatched Mr. G. H. Bonny, chief clerk at headquarters, back to the command with instructions to Major Mason to bring up all the troops as rapidly as possible and send ahead some surgeons immediately. This ride was made at night and was carried out in most gallant style, Mr. Bonny having delivered the message and returned to General Howard within 37 hours, having made 151 miles in that time and slept but four hours. Surgeon Alexander and Dr. Fitzgerald, under a cavalry escort, set out instantly and, by traveling all night in a rapid way, arrived considerably ahead of the main command at the battlefield, where they rendered efficient service in caring for the wounded.

Colonel Gibbon, apparently not believing that the Indians would remain long in their Ruby Creek camp, and not heeding Howard's dispatch to delay the Indians until a junction could be formed, struck them early on the morning of August 9.

The scene of the fight was on a narrow plain between slightly wooded hills on one side and bare tablelands on the other, through which Ruby Creek flowed, the banks of which were covered with stunted willows, very dense and tangled. On the tableland side of the creek, in an opening along the willows, the Indians had pitched their camp. Gibbon, the night previous to the fight, was three or four miles off and breaking camp at 1:00 A.M.[25] with his entire force, moved along the creek just opposite the Indians, taking up a position in front of the hostiles' stock at the base of the wooded hill until it was light enough to distinguish objects.

The troops were then ordered to cross, but before they got over, the Indian herders discovered them and fired two or more shots, and then ran. The troops and citizens then charged the camp, most of the bucks escaping in two bands, one taking to the brush and the other to the tableland. The whites began firing into the tepees, killing some bucks and several squaws and children. Stopping to pillage, the Indians in the undergrowth opened crossfire on our men, who immediately charged the party in the willows. In the meantime, the bucks who had gone to the tableland rallied and began a galling fire on Gibbon's men. The Indians who had run to the tableland were mounted, and dividing into two parties, crossed the river and began attacking the troops on the flanks. One of these parties discovering a corporal and some men bringing a howitzer and a mule loaded with cartridges, they cut them off, capturing the ammunition and destroying the gun. Gibbon and men then fell back and recrossed the river and, as I understand the situation, finding he was surrounded, began fortifying on a little wooded knoll. Here was a most difficult undertaking, and the hidden Indian sharpshooters picked off many men, being able to shoot down immediately into the barricade. In order to get Gibbon's men out, the Indians set fire to the grass on the bare part of the hill, a quarter of a mile from the fort, with the idea of burning the entrenchments, but fortunately the wind was not sufficiently strong, and the fire went out about 300 yards from the trees in which the whites were barricaded.

The Indians remained here the next day, firing every time a soldier showed himself, and left with the utmost leisure on the eleventh, apparently indifferent to pursuit. The number of Indians killed was about fourteen bucks and from forty to fifty squaws and children,[26] and in addition, our men burned several tepees [and] captured some tent poles and a few Indian trinkets. The hostiles got the guns from most of the white dead, say twenty-five in number, captured 2,000 rounds of cartridges and a howitzer, [and] leaving out the women and children shot by the soldiers, killed more men than Gibbon did.

Looking at this fight impartially, Colonel Gibbon got worsted. He was compelled to fortify, was cut off from water and provisions, and actually lost more than the Indians. The blow he struck, however, severely crippled the hostiles, and the attack was one of the best-planned schemes in the entire war. The only trouble with it was that from evidence abundant, such as preparing tent poles for the buffalo country and other signs, the Indians intended to stay here several days, and Gibbon was rather too hasty in his attack, when he knew Howard and his full cavalry force were not two days' travel off. His precipitancy robbed him of a splendid victory.

Among Gibbon's killed were Captain Logan,[27] Lieutenant Bradley,[28] and several soldiers outright, and Lieutenant English,[29] who died shortly after of wounds received. There were seventeen citizens killed. Colonel Gibbon, Captain Williams, Lieutenants Coolidge and Woodruff,[30] and thirty-six men[31] and four citizens were wounded.

The morning after Howard's arrival at the scene of the Big Hole battle, Major Mason came up with the cavalry command and, after burying the Indians, preparations were made to start the next day in pursuit of the hostiles, said to have gone into Lemhi Valley.

SUCCESSFUL RETREAT OF JOSEPH THROUGH CAMAS MEADOWS

We had marched about two days from the Big Hole battleground when a messenger rode into camp with the news that the Indians had killed several settlers in Lemhi Valley and robbed nearly all the ranchmen of Horse Prairie of their stock. The detour made by the Indians into the Lemhi country, and the assurance from the fortified settlers at the mouth of Stephenson's Canyon that they would oppose the passage of the Indians by that trail, gave General Howard every confidence that by hurrying along the Salt Lake and Montana stage road, he would be able to head off the hostiles at a crossing, usually made by the Indians en route for the buffalo country. We passed in sight of Bannock City, the entire town turning out in holiday attire to welcome General Howard and his brave soldiers, whom they looked upon as their deliverers.

In this march we were accompanied by two companies of infantry, kindly spared us for a short time (too short, however, to be of any service) by Colonel Gibbon. A company of the 4th Artillery, under Lieutenant Humphrey,[32] and one of the 8th Infantry commanded by Captain Wells, by forced marches succeeded in overtaking us just before the companies belonging to Gibbon's command had returned to Deer Lodge.

About August 16, when at a little stage station called Junction, Major Sanford reported to General Howard that his horses were in such worn-out condition it would be impossible for him to continue the pursuit without at least a day's rest. Prior to arriving at this place, sixty volunteers under Messrs. Stuart and Clark from Deer Lodge joined us, but apparently not wishing to fight the Indians if they had to chase them for it, they returned home after traveling about five miles in the direction of the hostiles. At Junction [Station] we were joined by about forty more volunteers from Virginia City, commanded by Captain [James E.] Callaway, a large proportion of whom followed the example of the Deer Lodge citizens and went home before we had made a day's march towards the stage road crossing; a small portion of them, however, continued on to Camas Prairie.[33] With the assurance that the settlers who had fortified at the end of Stephenson's Canyon would hold the Indians until the arrival of the troops near Camas Meadows, General Howard left Sanford's cavalry command at Junction to recuperate for a few hours (with the exception of an important detachment under Lieutenant Bacon,[34] which will be spoken of hereafter) and went ahead, followed by a company of the 2nd Cavalry under Captain Norwood—who had just joined us[35]—to learn the exact whereabouts of the Indians.

The general had not been gone long when a dispatch was received at Junction [that] the Indians were crossing the stage road and heading towards Henry's Lake, an order coming at the same time to Sanford, commanding him to saddle immediately and make all haste for the place where the Indians had crossed. Before setting out, a picked command of forty cavalrymen under Lieutenants Bacon and Hoyle of the 1st Cavalry, and some Indian scouts had been sent out at midnight to go to Henry's Lake by a shortcut to report the doings of the Indians and harass their progress. Of course, it was a great surprise to General Howard to hear that the Indians had eluded him, as he had relied upon the citizens of Stephenson's Canyon to be as good as their word and at least resist the Indians' passage.

Like their brethren of the Bitterroot Valley, however, these fortified men, holding a position like that of the Lolo Trail, which the Indians could not possibly have stormed, disgracefully allowed the hostiles—the same who had but a couple of days before murdered perhaps their own brothers in Lemhi Valley—to pass, on condition they would do no harm to them or theirs. Facts are truly stubborn things, we have not one word to say in extenuation of the abject cowardice on the part of the settlers—a class of men whom we had been taught in early life to regard as courageous as lions.

On arriving late at night at the stage station[36] near where the hostiles had crossed the road going towards Henry's Lake, General Howard was informed by his scouts that Joseph was encamped about sixteen miles from there, on a grassy plain called Camas Meadows. The general immediately consulted his different officers on the feasibility of keeping on through the night but, on the assurance of the cavalry commander and other officers that the horses and men could not possibly withstand the hardship, reluctantly abandoned the project until morning.

At early dawn the command was already on the way towards the Indian camp, with the infantry and artillery hurrying after us, in country wagons, about a day behind. Reaching Camas Meadows, we found "the birds had flown," but as the place was well watered and rich grass was in abundance, and the men and horses were fatigued and the foot troops but a short distance behind, General Howard moved across two parallel creeks in that neighborhood and encamped on a rocky knoll, with a view of holding a strong position and feeding his animals in the bottom. The few volunteers of Callaway's company took up their position between the two creeks[37] about 200 yards from the main camp.

THE NEZ PERCE SURPRISE NIGHT ATTACK

The camp on Camas Meadows was named in honor of Captain Callaway of the Virginia City volunteers.

As was shown in the last article, General Howard encamped on a rocky eminence as a defense against their running off with our horses, as the bell mares were hobbled on this night, a thing that had not been done before in the campaign—probably because they had to graze outside the main lines. Major Mason was more particular than ever in the placing of pickets, our little camp being completely surrounded by them, out beyond the grazing herd.

This night the entire command went to sleep with a confidence that everything was safe, it being the first time that many of us had taken off all our clothes on retiring since the Clearwater battle. At the first streaking of dawn,

"Our guns were almost useless." CENTURY MAGAZINE, 1891.

or rather, just after the intense darkness that precedes the daylight had passed away,[38] our camp was awakened by sharp firing and the diabolical yelling of Indians, about 200 yards from the headquarter tents. We all ran out as quickly as possible, but as it was dark, and as the volunteers had camped across the creek from the main command in the immediate vicinity of the firing and war whoops, our guns were almost useless. Immediately the command was given to saddle, and as quickly as the confusion would permit, the men were standing at their horses' heads, waiting for daylight to mount and chase the Indians. Sweeping around our camp could be distinguished a herd of stampeded horses and mules, galloping at their highest possible speed, with a considerable band of Indians behind them goading them on with loud cries and discharge of rifles.

As soon as the sun had thrown rays enough over the valley to permit our men to see before them, Major Sanford started with three companies of cavalry to attempt to overtake the hostiles and recover the stolen stock. The different companies were commanded by Captains Carr[39] and Jackson of the 1st Cavalry, and Captain Norwood of the 2nd Cavalry, with Lieutenant Benson of the 7th Infantry acting as lieutenant. After riding several miles as rapidly as the exhausted animals could go, sight was caught of the stampeded herd. Captain Carr was ordered to charge the hostiles, which he did most gallantly, cutting off some thirty-six horses and mules. A messenger then came into camp from the front and informed General Howard that the hostiles were in force in some lava beds about eight miles to the southeast. General Howard took all the available men from the little body defending the camp and started to join Sanford. On reaching the fighting ground, it was found that Major Sanford, not wishing to precipitate an engagement with his inferior force, had given orders to fall back. This command was obeyed by all except Captain Norwood, who, being surrounded by Indians and dismounted, sent back word that it would be impossible for him to leave his position without creating a panic among his men, and so he gallantly held his own until the Indians drew off and left his exit clear. Although nothing very serious happened in this little skirmish beyond the killing of a bugler and the wounding of six men and one officer, Lieutenant Benson,[40] it cannot be denied that whatever glory is attached to it belongs to Joseph, to say nothing of his stampeding our pack train and thus robbing us of nearly $10,000 worth of animals.

It seems strange that at a time when unusual precautions were taken against a surprise, that at that very moment the Indians should make an attack and get away successfully. As an evidence of the unusual care taken this night, all the cavalry horses and wagon mules were tied up on the rocky mound where we were encamped, and fortunately it was so, as these were the animals the Indians had hoped to run off.

The hostiles who took part in this attack rode up to our picket line in columns of fours like cavalry, coming apparently from the direction from which we expected the return of Lieutenant Bacon from Henry's Lake with his detachment of horses. This misled our guards, and they did not fire until the Indians had got within easy speaking distance. As the glen where our pack animals were grazing was cut up by two parallel creeks, the banks of which were covered with a dense scrub willow thicket, it was not very difficult for Indians to conceal themselves in it and creep into our camp in the darkness. As quickly as the first picket fired on the hostiles, those who had stolen into the meadows among our pack animals cut the hobbles from the bell mares and, with the yelling and firing of their rifles, succeeded in frightening the whole herd into a stampede, which the main body, being in readiness of, took immediate advantage of and drove them as rapidly as possible towards the Indian breastworks in the lava beds. It cannot be denied that the Indians behaved courageously and that they successfully carried into effect their well-laid plans, or that they also are entitled to all the glory of the skirmish; but on the other hand, it is equally certain that every precaution was taken to prevent a surprise, and blame can be attached to no one.

⊷ ⊱◆⊰ ⊶

THE TROOPS REST AT HENRY'S LAKE

At about sunset the day of the Camas Meadows skirmish, by dint of forced marches, the artillery and infantry under Captains Miller and Miles, respectively, caught up with General Howard and the cavalry command.

Early the next morning the entire force was en route for Henry's Lake, at which place it was hoped that the Indians would either camp or be held at bay by the cavalry force under Lieutenant Bacon. Unfortunately, neither was the case. As we were so close upon the hostiles, they only stopped at the lake long enough to cook breakfast, and were off again in the direction of Yellowstone Park. Lieutenant Bacon, having reached Henry's Lake considerably ahead of the Indians, and seeing no signs of them up to the time they were expected, took it for granted they had gone in some other direction. He thereupon broke camp and, striking the stage road in our rear, rejoined us in the stern chase. On the way to Henry's Lake, we were joined by fifty Bannock Indians under a very daring scout from Fort Hall named Fisher.[41]

On reaching the lake, it was found impossible to proceed farther without refitting and rest. Surgeon Alexander reported about thirty men as completely worn out and many more in a condition imperatively demanding rest. Our horses were nearly exhausted, and the men and officers alike needed shoes, blankets, and clothing. General Howard inquired how many days would be needed to bring the necessary clothing to the camp from Virginia City and was informed that it could not be done in less than five. The general was positive it could be done in less time and, without more ado, started for Virginia City, traveling night and day, until he returned with all the stock of blankets, shoes, etc., in the town.[42] Besides communicating with Generals Sherman and McDowell through the telegraph office while at Virginia City, Howard also directed further clothing supplies, [which] he had previously requested through Colonel Gibbon by telegraphing to Fort Ellis. These followed and overtook us at Mud Springs. A herd of cayuse horses was also brought to serve as pack animals.

Before leaving for Virginia City, General Howard had sent those of the Bannock Indians who had not returned to Fort Hall, on account of the cold, ahead under Fisher to steal the hostiles' horses, harass them at every opportunity, and keep them constantly in view to inform us of their different movements. As it was very evident from the direction taken by the Indians that they intended to move toward the Crow agency, Captains Cushing and Field of the 4th Artillery, and Norwood of the 2nd Cavalry, were detached and sent by a shortcut in that direction via Fort Ellis, with instructions to take up any available force en route.

On reaching Henry's Lake, it was generally believed that orders would be received informing us that inasmuch as General Howard had driven the Indians considerably beyond the limits of his department and was in too exhausted a state to continue driving them without great suffering, through territory commanded by other officers, we must retrace our footsteps to Lewiston. Instead of this, however, a dispatch announcing that we must keep on to the bitter end was received—and right loyally was it obeyed. The few days' rest at Henry's Lake had a very good effect upon our men and horses, nearly all of them gaining strength and spirits, as the rapidity of our subsequent movements clearly demonstrated. It is true that our worn-out men, having been of the opinion that their forced marches would end at Henry's Lake, were a little disappointed to learn that they must continue through the winter, as they feared, in the same old way, with little rest, often insufficient food, and frequently without water for twelve hours at a time; but they never once complained, and a more willing command to keep on, under all circumstances, can scarcely be imagined.

⊷ ⚔ ⊶

CONFUSION ON THE YELLOWSTONE RIVER

General Howard broke camp at Henry's Lake on August 22 and continued on the trail of the hostiles towards the Yellowstone River and national park. Before leaving Camp Ebstein, a man came into camp who told us of a party from Radersburg that had been robbed and attacked by the hostiles in the Geyser Basin. As this is an episode not properly connected with the military conduct of the campaign, we pass it over with the remark that Joseph behaved honorably towards the captives, and we hope it may be remembered in his favor when brought to trial.

Passing through that wonderful laboratory of nature, the geysers of the national park, we reached the Yellowstone River about September 1. Our marches at this time averaged about fifteen miles a day, the object in making such small distances being to enable certain supplies from Virginia City to overtake us. The command had to make a road from Henry's Lake to the geysers, and the wagons that followed us were the first, we believe, that ever succeeded in making that trip. The tree choppers and graders were kept very busy, and much credit is due Captain Spurgin,[43] 21st Infantry, who commanded this corps of pioneers, for the successful result of his labors.

While encamped on the Yellowstone River, a discharged soldier named Irwin, who had been captured in the Lower Basin by the hostiles, escaped and reported to General Howard. He informed us that the Indians were about forty miles ahead of us, wandering about in a seemingly aimless way among the dense pine forests. They told a miner named Shively,[44] whom they had captured, that they were lost and wanted to get out of the entanglement of woods and mountains to the buffalo plains. He agreed to pilot them through, knowing he could thus prolong his life, and told Irwin they would go through Clark Fork.

About this time, Fisher, the Fort Hall scout, sent a messenger to camp informing us of the hostiles' whereabouts and probable future movements. General Howard learning from Irwin that a shortcut could be made by way of Baronett's Bridge and Soda Butte Canyon to the point of outlet from the mountains to the plains near Heart Mountain, he resolved upon that course and, without more delay, hurried with all speed in that direction.

On arriving at Baronett's Bridge, we found that a small raiding party had been there and had made an unsuccessful attempt to burn the bridge. We were delayed here several hours in repairing the damage, and then learned for the first time of the attack made by the small scouting force of hostiles at Mammoth Springs and Henderson's ranch. Lieutenant Colonel Gilbert arrived with Norwood's company of the 2nd Cavalry a day after this attack, but for some unaccountable reason, instead of keeping on, he swung far around to our rear, where he kept during the entire campaign.

On arriving at the entrance of Soda Butte Canyon, a party of scouts was put upon the Indian trail, which was discovered here (running almost at right angles with the route we pursued), and sent by that way to keep us informed of any backward movement on the part of the hostiles, while the main command took the path through the canyon, expecting to either head off the hostiles at Clark Fork Canyon or be so close upon them as to make their capture an easy undertaking. Passing through these canyons and Lodge Pole Trail, we struck Crandall Creek the day after the hostiles had left. The Bannock scouts found a wounded Nez Perce there and inhumanly killed him. Near Crandall Creek, we were met by some scouts from Colonel Sturgis, who informed us that that officer, with Custer's old 7th Cavalry, was only two days' travel off, near Heart Mountain on the other side of the mountains, at the entrance to the buffalo country. General Howard immediately sent two of these men back to their commander with instructions concerning our proximity and the certainty of our driving the Indians upon him. There was but one outlet, and the Indians were as much entrapped as at Lolo Trail. General Howard was behind them with a superior force, Sturgis was at the other end of the narrow trail with six companies of cavalry, and the Indians between us with no opportunity to escape on the side—the one narrow trail being the only outlet in this rugged country to the plains. How our trap worked will be the subject of the next article.

<hr />

THE NEZ PERCE AGAIN ESCAPE

On or about September 10 we discovered, as was related in the previous article, that the hostiles were between us and Sturgis, and our hopes of their speedy capture were of the most buoyant kind. Leading from us to the supposed whereabouts of the 7th Cavalry was a trail over a very high mountain, which trail degenerated into a narrow gully on the other side between the high walls of rock that, almost meeting at the top in places, made it appear as if we were passing through an incline tunnel. It was through this natural screening pass that Joseph and his warriors escaped to the buffalo plains. Colonel Sturgis did not receive any of the late dispatches sent him by Howard to watch for the exit of the Indians near Heart Mountain, and supposing that the common impression was correct, that the hostiles intended to move toward Stinking Water, he started off with his cavalry force in that direction. On that very day,[45] Joseph and his followers—men, women and children, horses and pack animals—came swarming down the mountainside, through the tunnel trail, and escaped out on the long sought buffalo plains.

Here was a repetition of the misfortune that met the troops on arriving at the east end of the Lolo Trail. The game was almost in hand, but apparently disdained. Colonel Sturgis explains his course by saying that he had no scouts

The Battle of Canyon Creek.
HARPER'S WEEKLY, 1877.

acquainted with the country, with the exception of a Canadian of doubtful honesty, and was informed that there was no possible way by which the Indians could get from the west side of the mountains to the buffalo country, unless by the direction of the Stinking Water. Having made up his mind to head them off at this place, Sturgis listened to the Canadian's counsel and left his true position, and thus gave the Indians free exit.

General Howard had no sooner arrived on the lowlands near Heart Mountains than about eight bodies of Scandinavian miners were discovered, pierced with bullets and pockets rifled. Discovering that the Indian trail led towards Canyon Creek and the Yellowstone River, General Howard dispatched a messenger to bring back Sturgis from his wild goose chase, and continued on himself to Clark Fork.

Being overtaken here by the 7th Cavalry, General Howard held a council with Sturgis and assumed formal command; resolving that as the latter's horses were comparatively fresh, to send them on with their utmost speed to overtake the hostiles, detaching from his own command Captain Bendire's company, as having the strongest appearing animals, Lieutenant Otis[46] with the battery, and Lieutenant Fletcher with the white and Indian scouts—all under Major Sanford of the 1st Cavalry. It will be seen that the force thus constituted was now part and parcel of General Howard's own command.

On September 13 the hostiles were overtaken by this advance pursuing force in a little valley surrounded by a series of hills, the melting snow running from the sides of which had made deep canyons, affording an excellent battleground for the Indian style of warfare. Near the center of the valley was a dry creek at the bottom of a deep and crooked ravine, between high perpendicular banks, into which the hostiles drove all their stock, leaving it in charge of the squaws and boys. There were scarcely five trees in the entire valley, and only in the vicinity of the creek was anything like a sheltering shrub, sagebrush being very luxuriant there. The warriors took possession of the different heights almost immediately and, by their courage and good shooting, baffled all the attempts of our men to get to the other end of the canyon, through which the stock was being driven. When the ponies had all gone safely through the pass and were well on their way to the Buffalo (or Round) Lakes, the Indians' opposition to the troops gradually decreased, and by sunset all firing had stopped. In this skirmish, although at long range, three soldiers were killed and nine wounded. Six Nez Perce bodies were found,[47] and about 100 of their horses were driven off, principally by the Crows.

At 6:00 A.M. next morning[48] Sturgis continued the pursuit, and a running fire was kept up nearly all day between our advance and the hostile rear guard—several Indians being killed and about 600 horses captured.[49] Howard, with a small escort, hearing of Sturgis's engagement, rode all night toward the Dry [Canyon] Creek battleground, where he arrived the next morning about four hours after the departure of the advance column. Taking into consideration the worn-out condition of his men and animals, which precluded anything like a rapid pursuit, Howard determined to keep the comparatively fresh Sturgis on the heels of the Indians, while he, with the main command, would go around by the Yellowstone near [Pompey's Pillar] for supplies, on to the Musselshell, and then try to head off Joseph in his attempt to join the hostile Sioux.

Colonel Sturgis deserves much credit for the vigorous blow he struck the Indians and the speed and steadfastness of his pursuit. He traveled so fast in his chase that he got two days ahead of his supplies and was compelled to live on mule meat. In his dispatch to General Howard, Sturgis pluckily said he would keep after the hostiles until either his or their horses should give out; and he did it, too, but unfortunately his horses were the first to succumb. General Howard then returned from Sturgis's battlefield to the Yellowstone River, took command of the main column, and started for the Musselshell, where he and Sturgis afterwards effected a junction.

❀

THE FINAL BATTLE NORTH OF BEAR'S PAW MOUNTAIN
After Howard's and Sturgis's commands had come together at the Musselshell River, the chase was kept up through the alkali plains and Judith Basin at comparatively slow marches, the reason being that General Howard had sent couriers ahead to Colonel Miles to look out for the Indians making towards the Upper Missouri. Miles sent back word that if eight days could be given him, he would succeed in getting beyond the hostiles and would strike them. To bring

about so favorable a result, our marches were slowed so that the Indians, not finding us within a dangerous proximity, would slacken their pace too.

After we had passed through the Judith Basin, and our supplies from the Bighorn post had reached us, General Howard resolved upon sending back the 1st Cavalry and the mule pack train. Winter was threatening around us, and as the cavalry horses of the 1st Regiment were nearly all worn out, it would be impossible to keep them alive in a country covered with snow. As for the pack animals, they were hired by the month at Lewiston, and as we were now in a country where wagons could be used, it was deemed best not to risk any longer their being snowed in for the winter at a heavy expense to the government, so they were sent home, took via the Mullan road. The very day that the 1st Cavalry and the pack train left us, news was brought that the Indians had crossed the Missouri River at Cow Island—a day's march from where we then were—had killed one or two men there in a skirmish, and robbed and burned the store.[50]

As soon as Miles was apprised of this, he started from the mouth of the Musselshell with his cavalry and mounted infantry by a circuitous route and forced marches to intercept the Indians before they could reach Sitting Bull across the border, knowing that it was useless to join Howard in a stern chase and that the Indians were ignorant of his whereabouts.

Howard's first dispatch to Miles concerning the direction taken by the Indians was dated September 12, and on the thirtieth of that month Miles succeeded in striking the Indians on the right flank, a little to the front, on Snake Creek just north of Bear's Paw Mountains. The country there is barren and broken, with steep, precipitous ravines running in every direction. At first sight of the camp, Miles gave the order to charge it—the mounted 5th Infantry in the center, flanked by companies of the 2nd and 7th Cavalry, carried out the command. At the very first onset, the 2nd Cavalry succeeded in cutting off about half the warriors and horses from the camp; the latter they captured. The charge made by the 7th Cavalry on the rifle pits was not quite so fortunate, Captain Hale and Lieutenant Biddle being killed almost immediately, besides several men. All the while the 5th Infantry was marching slowly and surely upon the Indian fortifications, and being joined on the wings by the cavalry companies, the little camp was completely surrounded.

Desultory firing was kept up for three days by 300 United States troops on one side and 75 Indians on the other, when a flag sign was made in the Indian camp and Joseph announced that he wanted to make peace. On guarantee from Miles of good treatment, Joseph came in and held a council. Lieutenant Jerome, who ventured too near the enemy's line, was about this time taken prisoner and held as hostage for Joseph's safe return. The result of the conference was that Joseph was promised his life and safe return to Idaho unchained if he would surrender. Joseph wanted to retain his arms, but finding Miles determined against it, he waived the demand and left with the apparent intention of surrendering with his entire force. It turns out, however, that Joseph was unsuccessful in his peace mission, his warriors stoutly refusing to give up. Firing was recommenced, and kept up when General Howard with a small bodyguard arrived on the scene. Immediately negotiations for the surrender of Joseph were again entered into, and our two Nez Perce herders, Captain John and [Old] George, were sent into the hostile camp to reopen the question. After a great deal of message sending to and fro, and diplomatic *finesse,* it was finally arranged that the Indians would surrender on substantially the same terms offered by Miles in the first place.

At sunset Joseph rode into camp, surrounded by a few warriors on foot, and going up to General Howard, as commander of the expedition, proffered him his rifle. The general instantly stepped back and told Joseph that he must surrender his gun to Miles, who, although successful under his instructions, was in reality the conqueror. This courtesy on the part of General Howard was not lost on Colonel Miles, who took occasion to show the general several times how keenly he appreciated his services in the victory. Joseph had scarcely turned over his gun to Miles, when the Indians were seen in every direction coming in to follow his example, the wily White Bird among the rest. This latter individual, regretting the step he had taken almost as quickly as made, stole away from camp that night and joined the warriors—those who had been cut off by the 2nd Cavalry—in their march to Cypress Mountains, the camping place of Sitting Bull.

About 375 Indians surrendered at this Snake Creek battle, only 75 of whom, however, were actual fighters. It was promised Joseph that he would be taken to Tongue River and kept there till spring, and then be returned to Idaho. General Sheridan, ignoring the promises made on the battlefield, ostensibly on account of the difficulty of getting supplies there from Fort Buford, ordered the hostiles to Leavenworth, where they now are, which doubtless they deserve; but different treatment was promised them when they held rifles in their hands, and we think it should have been adhered to. Howard's command then took steamboat from Carroll [City] to Omaha, and via Pacific Railroad home, thus ending the first campaign against the hostile Nez Perce Indians.

—+— ≡✦≡ —+—

CHARACTER OF THE COUNTRY

A brief sketch of the general character of the country passed through by Howard's command in its chase after the hostile Nez Perces properly belongs to this series.

Coming over Craig's Mountain from Lewiston, we entered upon the rich, undulating Camas Prairie; a country almost destitute of trees, though fringed with pine forests along the mountain boundaries and so rich in grass that the earth could only be distinguished in the paths. The valley is well watered and admirably adapted for grazing and dairying purposes. The land between Camas Prairie and the Salmon River is hilly, rich in grass, and bare of trees, the descent from the summit to Salmon River being seven miles. The character of country on the west side of the Salmon River, for a few miles inland, is about the same as on the east side but differs beyond, as you are met with a densely wooded section a short distance in and confronted by so steep and lofty mountains that it took part of our command over a day to make the ascent of one of them, and several mules were lost by tumbling over the grade. To climb this mountain, it was absolutely necessary to cling to the rocks with fingers and nails to keep from sharing the same fate as the unfortunate pack animals. On reaching the summit, a beautiful tableland was spread out before us, luxuriant in herbage, well wooded and watered, and actually cold in temperature in the middle of July. The country from the heavily timbered Clearwater to Kamiah was "up and down" and not unlike the hilly neighborhood of the Salmon River, except that little groves of trees dotted the different canyons here and there, in a way to break the monotony.

The country dividing Kamiah, Idaho, from Missoula, Montana, is mountainous, rugged, and wild. The trail led over steep heights, winding about abysses, sloughing through marshes, and groping through fallen timber and dense and tangled undergrowth. At times we were encamped on the summit of bald, rocky mountains, at others on the sides of steep declivities, and at others in rank swamps. At one part of this Lolo Trail there is no grass for upwards of 120 miles, and it was with the greatest difficulty that we kept our horses alive through the march. The east end of this route is a great improvement, however, on the center and west end, there being frequent little oval-shaped openings rich in grass and water, and the timber is not so dense nor the mountains so precipitous.

On issuing from the Lolo Trail, we entered the beautiful Bitterroot Valley—as level as a college campus and "as green as the shamrock at Blarney Castle." From here we passed through a series of semimarshy places, run together like a string of zeroes, called "holes," the connecting, or rather separating, bonds being rocky ridges covered with pines. We then recrossed the Rocky Mountains from the east side to the west, entering Pleasant Valley. The country from here to Henry's Lake was filled with beautiful little trout streams and elegant grazing lands, abundant with game and rich in all kinds of timber. The country around Henry's Lake, though diversified, is well supplied with nutritious grasses and an abundance of water.

From Henry's Lake to the Yellowstone River, the face of the land is very much broken, and so thickly covered with forests that our axe men were kept very busy cutting places even wide enough for horsemen at single file to ride, to say nothing of the exertions that were made to cut paths wide enough for our wagons. The scenery around Yellowstone River—the national park—is at once picturesque and grand. The spouting streams of hot water; the boiling vats of different colored mud; the wild, weird appearance of this entire sulphurous country; the mighty Yellowstone Canyon, with its walls tinted with gold, pink, russet, and scarlet, bounded at one end by the beautiful falls of the Yellowstone

River; the river itself; the silvery Yellowstone Lake, all tend to make up one of the most enchanting pictures in all nature.

The trip from Yellowstone Canyon to the plains was over a very rough section; rugged mountains, snow capped, surrounding us on every side. On this march we passed through Soda Butte Canyon, one of the sublimest spots in the world, renamed by General Howard Jocelyn Canyon, after Captain Jocelyn[51] of the 21st Infantry. Immense mountains on both sides, as ragged as the Needles of Interlaken and as solemn as old Mount Blank himself, stand like giant sentinels along the trail. Mighty as is the Yellowstone Canyon, it is as insignificant compared with this home of thunderstorms as the so-called *Mauvais-pas* of Switzerland, and I seriously doubt if there is a place in all nature so mighty and magnificent.

Struggling through the forests along Clark Fork, and up and down the vertical and jaggy mountains, we reach the plains—the buffalo country—at Heart Mountain. Between the Yellowstone River and this mountain we are given a taste of what we are to get in the future, water fortunately being plentiful, but timber scarce. Between the Yellowstone and the Musselshell Rivers, land is almost entirely without trees and water is exceedingly scarce, only to be had in alkali holes, which are made doubly distasteful by buffaloes having wallowed in them. The landscape is very uneven, grass being scarce—the whole appearing like a tempestuous sea of sagebrush and greasewood. We here saw our first buffaloes, which with antelope and deer were very plentiful. The general aspect of the country was pretty much the same from the Musselshell to Judith Basin as that between Musselshell and Yellowstone Rivers—bare of trees, grass poor, and water bad and difficult to find.

The Judith Basin is a large prairie surrounded by timbered hills and crossed by numerous little crystal streams. Vegetation grows luxuriously, and the general appearance of the place is not unlike Camas Prairie, only more level, better watered, and decidedly more windy.

From Judith Basin to Carroll [City] on the Missouri River, and across the Missouri to the Bear's Paw Mountains, the command passed through the much-dreaded badlands. Even sagebrush and greasewood can scarcely exist there. The surface of this section is very rough and hilly, and composed of a black, sticky earth that when moistened by rain sticks to the feet of pedestrians and horses in great lumps, seriously impeding progress. Taking it altogether, General Howard's command had to pass through some of the very worst country in the United States. The first half of the campaign was over steep mountains—we crossed the Rockies three times—through dense forests; the other half was over a vast waste of sterile land, dreary and tiresome, without water, fuel, or grass, monotonously level at times, and others a succession of ascents and descents every few hundred yards that even wearied our sturdy foot troops. When it is considered that the artillery and infantry went through this terrible region, tiring out the cavalry twice over, making an average of over seventeen miles a day, the fact is undeniable that they performed a feat never before equaled, whether we compare it with Sherman's March to the Sea, or Xenophon's celebrated retreat of the ten thousand. With this "hurry graph" of the country passed through I close this article, to prepare for a chapter on the American private soldier.

DESCRIPTION OF THE TROOPS

The following concerning "the boys in blue" was written editorially, but as it is my intention to close this pamphlet with a few remarks on the citizen employees under Howard, I hope I may be pardoned for publishing it here, as none are more deserving than the brave private soldiers.

There has been a disposition among newspapermen, ignorant of "war and its wild alarms" (if we except the occasional infuriated citizen who hunts the editor with a cowhide), to jeer at our private soldiers, speaking of them as a hodge-podge of scum of the world, being men only one step, perhaps, above thieves on the social ladder. This is a base slander, and the more quickly the heroes, "invincible in peace and invisible in war," awaken to the fact, the earlier they will make amends for a rank injustice.

Among the soldiers may be found mechanics of every description, and often a man who had held high office among his citizen brothers. As a class they are intelligent men, as many being exceptionally intelligent and exceptionally ignorant. Every company has among its members a carpenter, a shoe-maker, a tailor, a barber, some five or six able to fill first-class clerkships, and men, in fact, of almost every condition of life; besides, almost every post has its reading room and library. Why such men join the army is beyond our province. Each man has his own sad story. Some have lost everything in business and in desperation have carried a musket; others have seen, perhaps, the adored one of their bosoms play them false, and have tried to bury themselves and their heart wounds under a blue coat; whilst others, perhaps having gone on a spree, and on sobering, keenly feeling, and nervously magnifying, their disgrace, have resolved to go off into some distant country and hide themselves in a rifle-pit grave.

We call to mind a gallant little sergeant[52] who had applied for leave from his post to join his company in the field, and with whom we became acquainted on the road from Portland to General Howard's command on the Salmon River. He was a very intelligent young man, being one of the best Shakespearean scholars and readiest quoters from standard English poets we have ever met. We never have seen a man so anxious to get where the Indians were supposed to be, nor happier while traveling rapidly or sadder when resting.

At the battle of the Clearwater, this young man started up once of his own accord to charge the Indians and was pulled back, but jumping up again, he rushed forth firing, but almost instantly fell flat on his face, pierced by Nez Perce bullets on every side. Perhaps this was foolhardy, but how do we know what load the lead in this poor fellow's body took from his mind? Which of us could blame the man, weighed down with troubles and bitter recollections, with no light in the future, for dying as he did? At the same battle a private came into where the doctors had put a hospital tent, badly wounded in the arm and face. No sooner were his wounds dressed than off he started. The doctor who had bandaged him called out, "Go over there with the wounded." "Never mind about me, doctor," the brave fellow answered, "I'm as good as two dead Indians yet," and off he went for a picket line, where it was almost suicide to show the top of one's head. It is possible there are some who scoff at the private soldier who would have done the same and not taken the doctor's permission to keep out of danger, but we hope we may be pardoned for doubting it.

These, however, are but samples of many cases called to our attention. Through the entire chase after Joseph (unparalleled in warfare), the foot-sore soldiers never once flagged, and no officer in the entire command was more anxious than they to reach the Indians. On one occasion, after they had tramped thirty miles over a barren waste and had just thrown themselves on the ground in sheer exhaustion, the news came that the Indians were only twenty-five miles ahead. Soon after, the different battalion commanders came to General Howard and said their men—God bless their brave hearts!—were anxious to keep on marching through the night. This is the stuff our American soldiers are made of. And when they were in actual combat, *not a man flinched,* and when they were told to charge, a yell of delight went up, and not a living soul held back. This is the American soldier as we found him by actual contact.

THE CITIZENS WITH GENERAL HOWARD
The citizens under General Howard were the packers in charge of the mule trains, guides, interpreters, couriers, scouts, and volunteers. The scouts were also used in the passage through the dense forests of Lolo Trail as woodchoppers and graders. The packers were a splendid class of men physically, and better accustomed to the hardships of the camp than even the soldiers or volunteers. Most of them were Americans, with a small sprinkling of Mexicans— just enough to give the proper pronunciation of *aparejos* and swear in a musical tone. In the long tramps, they were always the happiest, and in camp their fires were the first made, their suppers first ready and better provided and cooked than any others. In time of fighting, they were never known to falter, and at the two days' Clearwater battle, when at one time the Indians were thought to have broken our lines, they all took guns and ran to the breach. The report that General Howard was delayed in the Lolo Trail by a strike among the packers is false, for they were willing at all times to keep going, and never once hesitated. The guides were men picked up in the different regions we passed through and dropped usually at the end of their usefulness.

Through Idaho to Montana, Ad Chapman was the guide, and was at once one of the most intelligent and bravest men in the command. He is generally acknowledged to be the best horseman in northern Idaho, and the way he would tear down a steep mountain, jumping rocks and fallen timber with his horse at full speed, would make even the Indian herders hold their breath. At the Clearwater fight, several companies on the picket line were out of ammunition, with no way to get back after more. Who would volunteer to carry it out? Ad Chapman jumped on his spirited horse, and with a heavy box of cartridges on back hip, started at full run amid a shower of balls for the front, where he safely landed his precious burden. Chapman was also our chief interpreter, being the only white man in the command who could speak the Nez Perce language perfectly.

Our chief guide through Montana was George Huston, a modest man, one of the oldest hunters in the country and as brave as a Nez Perce chief. We found him in the heart of the Rocky Mountains, and the services rendered by him were of the most important kind. From the time the Indians struck the plains at Heart Mountain, he kept on their track and was one of the few who was "in at the death." We met with a great many so-called guides, of the long hair, buckskin-suit, overly armed order, with high sounding titles, but invariably found them to be the guides of fiction and of no practical use, being in fact almost as great cowards as they were boasters.

On reaching the Crow country, our interpreter was a Canadian, dressed in a variegated blanket overcoat and answering to the sobriquet of "Frenchy." He was a rollicking fellow and bore the reputation of not caring very much whose horse he took in a pinch, being what they call in the Upper Missouri region a "J.S." man. [The] J.S. man is one who steals government horses and changes the U.S. brand by lengthening the right line of the U, making it look like a big J.

The couriers were men well acquainted with the country and excellent and enduring horsemen. They were sent often hundreds of miles at a time with letters, and in but few instances failed to reach their destination in good season. Our best courier was "Pike" Davenport of Idaho; he having made the trip all the way from Lewiston to the Upper Missouri with letters from the rear for General Howard, alone, and in remarkably short time. Tom Chapman in Idaho, and "Baptiste" (a Canadian half-breed) from Fort Hall in Montana, Blake from the Pataha, and the brave Nez Perce James Reuben from Kamiah all rendered valuable services in this calling.

In Idaho our volunteers were from the vicinity of Walla Walla, Lewiston, and Mount Idaho. They were a fine looking set of fellows, excellent horsemen, accustomed to endurance, and with their wide hats, rifles across their pommels, cartridge belts, and Bowie knives, presented a very threatening appearance. Seventeen of them on one occasion did some very brave fighting at Camas Prairie, actually shooting their way through surrounding Indians. The volunteers deserving the most praise were those from Lewiston under Colonel McConville, a brave and honorable young man. Those from the Pataha appeared to pay more attention to gathering Indian ponies than in actual fighting, while the Montana volunteers mostly were failures. We had companies from almost every town we passed near, which would come out in a cloud of dust, thirsting for gore, and on finding that they could not usurp General Howard's command of the expedition, and that they were getting unpleasantly near the Indians, would suddenly recollect business at home and leave us. A few of the Virginia City delegation, I believe, stuck to us till we caught up with the Indians at Camas Meadows, but performed no great deeds of heroism.

Our principal scouts were Fisher from Fort Hall (the only man we met in the entire campaign who wore buckskin and amounted to anything), who actually camped on the Nez Perces' trail; Lieutenant Jack Carlton of Lewiston, a power in this vocation; Frank J. Parker, of Boise City; the well-known correspondent J. L. Penseroso; W. D. Curry of Portland, Oregon; Capt. [Orlando] Robbins of Boise City; and a young Bannock chief named Buffalo Horn. All made enviable reputations for themselves. It was on these men that we depended chiefly for our information as to the whereabouts of the Indians, and for game. A braver set of men never put spurs to horse, nor a more cheerful set, under hardships, ever gathered around a sagebrush fire.

Here ends the last tramp. Our destination is reached, and in taking leave of my old comrades in arms, while as yet but few of us have gone to our final camping ground, I wish to say that if this little book has helped in any way to keep green the memories of our mutual pleasures and hardships, or aided in cementing the friendships formed during the campaign, I shall feel more than compensated for my labors, and glad indeed that the work has been done.

An Infantryman in the Nez Perce War of 1877

HARRY L. BAILEY[1]

Lucullus McWhorter Papers, Washington State University Libraries, Pullman[2]

I was born in Ohio, October 4, 1854; graduated with honors from the Lima, Ohio, high schools June 14, 1872; and from the United States Military Academy same day, 1876.

I started to join my Company, B of the 21st Infantry, at Fort Wrangle, Alaska, but met my department commander, Brig. Gen. O. O. Howard, "the great Christian soldier," in Portland, Oregon, in October 1876, and after being most agreeably entertained by him at a luncheon at his residence, was informed by him that he had what was called the worst company of my regiment[3] stationed at Fort Klamath, Oregon, and he wished me to go and take command of it for reforms, as its captain had been absent on "sick leave" for five years, and he found me active in church affairs. Thus I had a memorable experience with a cavalry and infantry command in a remote military post through the first winter, and then was ordered to join my own company, on its way from Alaska to Fort Walla Walla, Washington Territory, in March 1877, Capt. S. P. Jocelyn, commanding.

The post then had only cavalry troops, and the officers tried all kinds of jokes, as usual, on the new "doughboy" of the infantry, and though I succeeded in dodging their tricks so far as being caught, the tricks were so good that I gave them away.

I wish space permitted telling the tricks. At that time, after the Civil War, nearly all the officers above lieutenants were veterans of that great struggle and deemed their experience sufficient to meet the needs of military study, and often left the main part of the drills and court-martial recording to us novices, a good experience for us. Moreover, a fact little known to the average citizens, those old veterans in many cases had had during the Civil War the most strenuous struggles with our frontier Indians but, in the fearful and exciting events of the war, received scant notice or credit for their work and sacrifices, and even in my own time, it was usual to see a fine print with one's name misspelled in the corner of the press after some serious Indian battles.

While I was at lonely Fort Klamath, I took advantage of an offer of Rev. Mr. Stubbs to ask him explanations about difficult questions in the Holy Scriptures, being very earnest in my boyhood Presbyterian Church, and the kindly gentleman took my questions to the "great Christian soldier," my commander, but without telling my name. When I returned to Portland, the general read me my own letter, or described it to me, and I was faced with either silence as a kind of hypocrite or supposed disfavor with my commander, so I told him that I was the "critic of the Gospel." The general acted very disturbed, and there were times in my subsequent service under him that I seemed selected for discrimination, but each case gave me hard but valuable experience, so that I believe I was the gainer in the end.

The general was graduated from West Point in the year I was born, 1854, and his life is one of the greatest of our country's history. I have seen him under a shower of bullets in battle and was inspired by his example to stop dodging bullets, and hence can testify to his wonderful courage, as well as to his wonderful qualities as a soldier who would not send anyone into dangers and hardships he would not share. And yet he was ambitious and very sensitive to the press.

He was so honest himself that others could lead him into trouble by careless tales about facts of Indian conditions and roads and trails, as we might illustrate in a more detailed account than this can become. As an example, in one situation the citizens had caused the general to change his mind or plans often, so that his temporary staff officer was exasperated into saying he was "acting like a chicken with its head cut off." The remark got to his ears, and the staff officer was quickly placed under arrest, and we friends of the officer were worried. The general, however, finally forgave the offense, and the officer was one of our most useful men in the campaign.

During the general's immense work and worry over the Indian situation, he was carrying a load of worry about his Freedmen's Bureau troubles, and he told me one day, while walking the floor in great restlessness, that he had just sent his lawyers the last of $3,000 (I think it was), which he had saved and also earned by lecture tours, on account of those problems. That he was poorly educated in politics and publicity is shown by the fact, if my memory is correct, that one whole volume of his two [volume] memoirs is taken up with explanations of that trouble.[4]

I thought it an example of his sensitiveness to the press when I overheard him explain to a Walla Walla newspaper editor one of the failures to catch a trick of Joseph in misleading us, but after my years of experience, I will say that I may have misunderstood the situation.

West Point, with few exceptions, and a few apparent exceptions, is the most democratic body in the world, and I served with my own captain[5] for two or three years before I became corrected of an impression that he was a graduate of West Point. He had been a private, lieutenant, etc., in the Civil War, and when he came to retirement, his Civil War service gave him a grade in promotion, as in all such cases. He was very efficient and left to me most of the duties except the care of the little company fund. He had a long, excellent service, filling high places with honor. He once took a year's leave in Europe, giving me the command of the company, an excellent experience. After my promotion, my next captain's absence on duty at West Point gave me command of his company for six years, thus making much easier the long service, due to slow promotion following the Civil War, of twenty-one years as a first and second lieutenant.

It required many years to heal the spiritual wounds of the Confederate after the Civil War, and one or two churches are still "North" and "South," and the superior education of this age is already bringing understanding between Germany and her late antagonists, but even today, after 100 years, we have some citizens who see in the American Indians only savages who are "good" only when "dead." And yet a review of General Howard's book about Nez Perce Joseph, and the general's series of articles in the *Chicago Advance* of about 1878,[6] will show how we can see two sides to the Indian question, though this case is the fairest, perhaps, for both sides in our "civilization" pushing the Indians into deserts, of any in the long list of violated treaties. And another chapter we should remember is that of the 3,000 friendly Indians of the same Nez Perces who not only remained neutral, but even helped us in the war against their own kind, under their Christian training by missionaries.

For some three years we had had a few troops each summer in the fine Wallowa Valley to prevent friction between the Indians and increasing settlers, and I should like space to relate amusing events when the last cavalry force left Fort Walla Walla for that valley, due to new officers and men, and new or untrained horses.

On May 18, 1877, three days after my return from a very interesting trip as escort to Fort Colville, my classmate, Lt. Sevier M. Rains, 1st Cavalry, came back with sad news of the drowning of our esteemed comrade, Dr. Going, veterinary surgeon, 1st Cavalry, in attempting a crossing by swimming his horse along with the lieutenant, the current of the Grande Ronde River being too turbulent for such risks, but the bearing of important dispatches made duty first to such soldiers. That was perhaps one of the first sacrifices of the Nez Perce War of 1877. Lieutenant Rains, of a fine, historical family of Georgia, was one of the finest and bravest men I have known, and we all loved him, and he had on this trip a very narrow escape but was reserved for "the great sacrifice" later in the war.

On June 16, 1877, Lieutenant Wilkinson, 3rd Infantry, General Howard's aide, arrived about noon in Walla Walla full of excitement and rushed everywhere to send dispatches [and] order supplies and troops, under his chief's directions, and made an alarming advance agent indeed. He brought news of commencing hostilities by Joseph and Chief White Bird's bands and said all available cavalry was ordered to Fort Lapwai, Idaho, the starting point of our troops, and soon we had news of our regimental comrades being ordered to

Ft. Walla Walla—Capt. Evan Miles of Vancouver Barracks, Capt. George Burton of Ft. Townsend, Washington Territory, and Capt. Marcus P. Miller, 4th Artillery, of Ft. Stevens, Oregon. Lt. Joseph W. Duncan, 21st Infantry, was ordered to go at once to Fort Lapwai with the cavalry detachments left here by the troops in the Wallowa Valley.

On June 19, 1877, sudden orders came for our Fort Walla Walla infantry companies to proceed to the base at Fort Lapwai at all speed, and my captain gave me details of preparing the company for the rush, so that I had no time to prepare my personal self. At 4:00 P.M. we took the thirty-mile railway for Wallula and the expected river boats, and I found myself wearing a white shirt with stiff collar and gold studs and collar buttons, and a couple of blankets and my .45 Colt, purchased after leaving West Point, and I did not have a chance to get into field garb until we were lucky enough to find a few issue clothes and boots and shoes at Fort Lapwai's quartermaster department.

In the absence of its own officers, I was given command of Company H of my regiment, but Captain Haughey relieved me en route on the river steamer, and I rejoined my own company.

Arriving at Fort Lapwai, Idaho Territory, we were soon rushing such preparations as could be made at a small two-company post for the hurry into the stricken region of Indian murders and outrages, while reports and rumors and calls for help came every hour.

It was here that I bought a bottle of whiskey (for five dollars), though I did not at that time know the ordinary size of a drink. After carrying that bottle untouched through the toils, fatigue, and shivering of mountain nights, with only my saddle blanket for the rocky and stubble "beds" of the march, it was stolen during the night of my first battle by a citizen. But when I looked for sympathy, my old comrades said that anybody would steal whiskey under such conditions.

While trying to fit a gunnysack on the Indian pony given me of those brought in by the friendly Nez Perces, Lieutenant Theller's grieving but brave widow sent me her late husband's little English racing saddle by the post blacksmith, and though it could not afford any hold for even a tin cup of my baggage, it was vastly superior to none at all, and served many times to relieve footsore soldiers whom I saw along the mountain trails as we toiled after the enemy.

Men were paying as much as sixty dollars in gold for old saddles, but few were to be had at any price. Not being able to sleep at nights most of the march, I many times found myself sound asleep on my saddle during the day, when awakened for a five-minute halt and rest. And during the short rest, I would fall asleep immediately upon touching the ground. To the younger officers, the rushing march and the wilderness were entirely new experiences and required some days before we could be adapted and comfortable.

One of our bravest and best young officers was of the nervous type, and it adds to his credit for bravery that he saw and felt dangers far beyond the normal, and one of his worries, affording us much amusement later, ever a song of doggerel for the campfires, was the howling of coyotes, because the settlers had told us that the Nez Perce war cry was the coyote howl. And I must say that we had some almost unbelievable cases of such war cries, as though we were actually surrounded by a thousand warriors. Once, for instance, when I was away out from the main command at an outpost, with half a dozen men, and it was surely expected that the camp would be attacked at any moment, there was a single coyote cry on one side of men, then after a minute an answering cry on the opposite side, the same on the other two sides, and then a deep silence for a half hour, when all hell broke loose on every side of the command [except] my outpost. Then, suddenly, a deep silence again for some minutes. After I had arranged my little outpost along a big log for defense, came a single shot in the midst of the main command. Then a few lights moving about in the main camp, but no other sign of life there. My young mind imagined every kind of disaster, such as a sudden, silent rush upon the tired soldiers and every throat cut.

No other sounds until morning, and then I took my guard, as previously ordered, out to meet the head of the column for commencing the day's march. All the way, until I met one of my silent comrades, Lieutenant Duncan,[7] did I fathom the strange silence of that usually lively morning marching body of brave soldiers. Then my chum, Lieutenant Duncan, told me that one of our comrades of the artillery had shot one of the soldiers who was going out for a necessary purpose, and that the poor soldier lingered in pain but brave resignation until morning, when he died, forgiving the wretched lieutenant, saying he knew it was an unavoidable accident. I had to be with that lieutenant for days afterward in another post and may say that so far as I know he was never the same man again. Such are the side sorrows of war.

I was fortunate, after all, in the footwear matter, for I had to take a pair of coarse issue shoes, a size too large, but happened to have a few pair of those thick woolen socks, knitted by my paternal grandmother, and they cushioned my feet so that I never had foot trouble, and even two little corns acquired at West Point disappeared during the hundreds of miles of that long chase.

When we neared Camas Prairie we heard much about the camas root, which was a large part of the Indians' food supply, and someone showed me a few of the roots, as he supposed, and I tried a very small bite, only to find that my informant was a long way wrong, for I had eaten a piece of a kind of "flag," which the medicine books say is a bitter purge, and for two or three days and nights I was nearly purged to death. The camas root itself is a fine and pleasant fruit or vegetable.

It was here we came upon the ransacked ranches,[8] every pillow and mattress being torn to pieces in the hunt for gold and currency (crimes wrongfully charged to Indians), and some damage looking rather civilized, for we know that war gives excuse for additional damage. About this time also, we saw the poor wounded citizens crawling out for food and protection after days of terrible suffering.

And then, on June 27, 1877, we marched down into that White Bird Canyon of awful death, my company being the advance skirmish line, until we saw the Indians across the wide and torrential Salmon River beyond rifle reach, though they sent a few shots toward us and made demonstrations of force to hide the fact that their main body was marching around to our late rear.

My own company buried eighteen of the thirty-three bodies which had lain ten days exposed to the elements [and] the hot sun, until they were swollen and changed into awful shapes too dreadful for eyes and our olfactory nerves, so that we had to run a distance every little while during the making of shallow graves in the rocky soil with entrenching bayonets, and trying to find enough of our scarce blankets into which to pull the bodies for the semblance of a decent interment. I think all but one of the bodies I saw were stripped of all outer clothing, boots, and shoes. I did not see the body of the brave and unfortunate Lieutenant Theller, though it was eventually found and is now buried at San Francisco.

Of course, we were ever on the lookout for sudden attack, and one body of a cavalry soldier gave us some anxious moments, for it was thrust so hard into a shallow thorn tree in the full and lifelike position of firing that we did not approach without guns cocked until near enough to see that the poor fellow was also dead and swollen beyond recognition. He must have worried his foes very greatly for some time, for his body was torn and torn with bullets. It was very difficult to remove that body.

We heard the stories of mutilation and scalping, as did the general public, but in the light of later information and experience, I am sure there was no mutilation, and that the appearance of scalping was due to the falling off of the decayed hair.

Of course, not a sign of any ammunition nor other property was left on the field. While intent, with every nerve stretched, in the search and burial of the dead heroes, the sky became dark with a great cloud, and suddenly two or three sheets of flame, like a series of rifle volleys, burst from the edge of the middle butte in the valley of the canyon, and I was shocked involuntarily to my knees and prepared for an attack, only to find a moment later that it was lightning.

It is a story in itself how we were welcomed by the suffering citizens, wives, and children of Mount Idaho and vicinity, and how some of them who had not been robbed tried to give the soldiers food and coffee, even in some cases baking fresh loaves of fine bread. I tried to give some of them my little savings in appreciation. On the other hand, let it be said in sorrow that certain citizens tried to "graft" on the awful situation, as happens in wars.

The White Bird massacre has been told in several accounts, and I had at first hand stories about it while in the field and later, and have the usual opinions of the participants as sifted from many views, with sorrow for some failures of men's souls, and with sadness that the real heroes do not always receive proper credit. There are times when suicide seems justifiable, and so we must recognize that a time comes when even an old soldier of great past bravery has a "failing case." So it seemed in the White Bird Canyon battle.

We had no doubts about the wonderful Lieutenant Parnell, and I still believe he saved the remnant of brave soldiers who escaped. (Of course, with those marvelous sergeants, corporals, and other soldiers we do have so frequently in our American army.) The failures of some volunteer citizens was natural, and some of us even felt sorry that any of them were present in such a trying case of surprise and overwhelming numbers of the enemy. I sometimes remember that we had the usual idea about savage torture becoming our fate in case of capture, and one should give those soldiers and volunteers credit for the nerve to go in a great wilderness against so brave a lot of foes as those Nez Perces had proven. I actually had in mind myself to save the last cartridge for myself in case of capture, as often advised by old officers.

June 29, 1877, we were encamped on the Salmon River at the foot of White Bird Canyon, and all wondering what direction the Nez Perces would take next, being terribly anxious for the safety of the settlers both ahead and behind us, and having for an "information service" little more than the vague guesses and rumors of the good citizens and some good scouts, who were in some cases very fine, and in others quite unreliable, as in one instance where I discovered the scout made a practice of charging wildly out of camp until he arrived at a safe place not far away, and then hid and smoked until what seemed a proper time to rush in and tell wild stories of his guesses.

I suggested to some of the officers of my regiment that I would like to sneak down the river, to a quiet place below the Indians across the river and swim over to find out whether they were all opposite us or had kept merely a small body of warriors to run around and around the small hills, as it appeared, while the main body had gone somewhere else, but my old friends said my plan was foolish, and for me to remember that all "volunteers" met disaster, as in poor Lieutenant Theller's case and so many others. Hence I subsided. We were trying also to do some signaling, but few officers and other soldiers were adept, and the signaling outfits were scarce, as were most supplies.

By the wonderful good luck of Uncle Sam, other events caused the commanding general to send a few troops back to Craig's Mountain, and although it was the cause of a sorrowful loss, the death of Lieutenant Rains and his eleven brave men, it got us on the trail of the Indians before they could do much more killing of citizens.

All the signs showed that the lieutenant and his men had made a very brave, though hopeless, fight against the whole of Joseph's forces. The bodies were stripped to the underwear, but for some reason the lieutenant's riding gloves were still on his hands, and his West Point class ring was still on his finger and eventually was sent to his sister, with whom I afterward saw it.

On June 30, 1877, we crossed the Salmon[9] with much unavoidable delay, on account of having to send far for boats and ropes, and that crossing was in itself a story of bravery and great risks to life, especially of our fine pack mules and our horses. I have never been sure that we did not lose a number of animals, for I saw several whirled over and over in the awful current as they were swept down, but some of the packers told me all got across safely, though in some cases it took long to bring them back to working form.

We were led over terrible but cunningly made false trails to another even worse crossing, where we tried making a raft and were finally compelled to give up and return on our route—back to Camas Prairie, and then on the rush to catch the cunning foe.

What a blind man's bluff it was for ten days, until at last, seemingly by accident, we were forced to fight the battle of Clearwater, July 11 and 12, 1877, on ground which may have been chosen by Joseph himself, although I do not now think so. I do know that the citizen scouts and so-called guides[10] took us far around and onto the wrong side of the Clearwater River, and almost gave us a defeat.

I had heard citizens tell of brave riding over hill and dale until they, they said, found the Indians across the river, talked to them, and dared them to come over and fight, and my boyish heart was filled with great admiration for our wonderful volunteers. By accident, I found that the good citizens had made a wonderful stone fort on the same side of the river, at a place about nine miles from it, and that fort was far from any supply of water. I do not blame those volunteers, but I have felt sorry that they spoiled my wonderful opinion of them.

We were marching along, hoping for anything if only we might some day finish the hard, hard forced marching on two meals a day, when along the edge of the bluffs of the river, some of our officers saw some Indians on the other side—just the side we had left "on information"—and at first it was a question whether we might not have come upon a camp of the friendly Indians. But after hurrying along for two or three miles, the artillery of one mountain howitzer[11] and two Gatling guns was taken to the edge of the bluff and some shots fired at a very long distance, while the rest of us hurried on, wondering how and where we might get into the attack, and were brought up by an attack, at first scattering, [then] more and more severe, as the Indians succeeded in crossing the river and climbing the very high and steep bluffs. I do not doubt that they were as much surprised by our attack as we were to find them in their very comfortable old home ground by the gurgling stream, all evidence after the two days' battle showing that the camp had long been occupied and had wonderful stores of supplies.

Intelligent Indians like Nez Perce Joseph would never have chosen to expose [their] families and such tons of excellent supplies to an uncertain battle. It seems apparent by this time that the many false directions and tales were the very lucky cause of our striking the enemy in his worst position, where he had so much at stake and only a chance selection, if any, of a battlefield.

But our choice of a battlefield was mere accident, for we had no water, nor any protection except one or two small trees and bare, broken, rocky upland, so that even entrenching was difficult.

The bluffs proved a protection on our river flank, until after considerable time, when some Indians seemed to have succeeded in climbing them to our level, but not many, and some troops were ordered to rout them, which seemed effective to a considerable extent. The general and his staff soon made a kind of headquarters with the aid of the pack saddles piled in a circular manner, though the protection was very slight, except that that position was not so near the hottest fire.

My Company, B, 21st Infantry, under Captain Jocelyn, was on the flank nearest the river, and along the edge of the largest ravine on the most dangerous front—for we were really surrounded in a short time, so that all sides were fronts.

When the attack commenced along the bluff, and along the edge of the small ravine, the general ordered Capt. Marcus B. Miller into that position, and soon he was busy on all sides like the rest of us, when some of his men and some of ours commenced to take each other for the enemy, making one of those terrible errors which occur in so many battles but are generally kept out of the reports. I saw Private Winters of my company wounded, and he kept saying that some of our own men had shot him.[12]

Then I saw the truth, that the artillery and my company, and some of the others, were jumping up and shooting at each other at a range of one or two hundred yards. Although the bullets were flying in a shower, I rushed out between the artillery company[13] and mine, yelling, "Cease firing! You are firing into your own men!"

The time seemed long, but was a few minutes, when order was again restored. I noticed Captain Miller at that time, and he was walking about with his short pipe in his mouth as though the day were not filled with many deaths, and it is no surprise to learn that his is a record of many battles and honors through many years, including the great Civil War. He was a big help in stopping that demoralizing, self-destructive firing.

Capt. Robert Pollock[14] of my regiment was not far from my left, commanding his company like an old veteran, which he certainly was, and to see him bareheaded and in red flannel shirtsleeves going from place to place as his men needed was a fine example, and I was imitating him when for the third time, my captain told me that I must lie down; that he would "not tell me again," one of the sensible things in a rain of bullets. However, I had checked several of my men who were crawling back, though there was no protection anywhere. One old private said, when I scolded him, "I tell you, Lieutenant, this is a ticklish business." I told him it would be more ticklish if he did not keep his place. At that moment a rattlesnake reared up at his elbow, and he forgot the bullets for a second.

There was one small tree not far back of my position, and Lieutenant Hoyle of the 1st Cavalry was standing beside it with Musician Keller, Company B, and by a sudden mysterious impulse, Lieutenant Hoyle suddenly grabbed the musician by the arm and jerked him down, when a bullet struck the tree just behind the position where the musician's head had been.

In about the same location was a hole of slimy, muddy water. Although we cautioned everyone within hearing not to drink of it, some were so famished for water that they used it, and especially my chum Lieutenant Duncan. As he told me afterward at Fort Lapwai when invalided home, he suffered almost death and was certainly sorry he had not observed our caution. Meanwhile, the want of water became so pressing that the general sent details to a spring which someone had discovered in the small ravine, and by the loss of a few lives, we finally got a little relief from it.

We saw an Indian in one of the large trees in the big ravine in our front, and after many hundreds of shots, he was tumbled down in death. I believe he had caused several of our casualties.

At this era of our army, we had had almost no target practice, and we were like the Indians themselves, with whom poverty and their way of hunting made it the custom to shoot only at short distances, and so not only they but ourselves sent most of our shots too high, as was evident by the showers going overhead until the Indians succeeded in getting within about 100 yards of us—some 30—when we suffered our many casualties and narrow escapes. I found the worst complaint to be that we could seldom see any Indians, notwithstanding the rain of bullets, for they certainly had the modern rule of hiding and creeping down to a science.

A number of us saw a poor old horse, probably wounded, standing for some hours out in my front, and I suppose several hundred bullets were fired at him without apparent effect. That was one of the lessons I had about our shooting, when we had in our army but three shots per man per month for target practice. Think of it!

As it grew dusk, I heard the piling of cobblestones some thirty yards in my front and the sound of voices, probably the talking of squaws, and I asked my captain to get the howitzer to my right rear to fire some shots at the point. But about the time I thought, different orders had been given. I was amazed to see the flash of a discharge close behind me, and then came the shell, so near over my head that I could have touched it by reaching up. To my joy, the shell exploded right in the place I had indicated, and the voices and stone piling ceased. Finding myself alone, where I had had several men by me, I asked permission to withdraw to join the company. As I arose to go back, a shot at close range blew off my hat. I dropped, suddenly turned, fired my rifle, and then drew my revolver, but no more sounds came from that place. After some minutes, I slowly withdrew to the company.

During the forenoon, I had one of those mysterious experiences which do affect even a man free from superstition, for as I was shooting at every excuse for a shot, having laid down by order, I noticed that some hidden Indian was hitting the ground closer and closer to my body, as I was fully exposed to the enemy's view, when suddenly I seemed to hear a voice say, "Move over." I said to myself, this is the beginning of fear; I'll pay no attention to it. But again came the voice, and I repeated my resolve to pay no attention to it, when it seemed that a force, very gentle but very firm, simply moved me over, when two bullets struck the ground where my body had just been lying. You may believe there was a reassurance in it.

As usual in Indian fighting, the firing became less—and even ceased—as the darkness increased, and we were able to make shallow trenches in the rocky soil, while some of the packers, having tools, made real holes, as I saw when next morning I had to go all along our part of the line to make arrangements for the disposition of the troops to make a general charge later.

The firing was much lighter as I went from company to company, and I was much assisted by Lt. Charles F. Humphrey, 4th Artillery, who was as cool as every day all through the battle. He insisted on my going back to the headquarters, where the pack saddle barricade was, to get some coffee, as we had had nothing since commencing the fight, but I asked him to go. At last he solved the problem by having us draw straws. I won and went back to find about all the officers there. No one, however, was ready to go out and help in arranging the troops for the charge, and so Humphrey and I did it alone. When approaching the trench of Captain Haughey and Lieutenant Eltonhead,[15] they yelled at me to lie down, as I was drawing fire, but I was inconsiderate until a bullet struck the top of their little trench a few inches from the captain's head and my ankles. They had stuck to their trench all through and certainly looked very sweaty and dirty.

Were this not a very hasty article, I should like to tell of individual experiences, as when my dear chum Lt. Charles A. Williams was struck, and then, as I saw, was hit again as he was being carried back to the headquarters.[16] He was taken back to civilization with others soon after, and it was long before we met again, as days go in campaigns. He was one of the bravest, and so cheery.

On June 12 came the general charge, which swept the foe down that ravine which had brought most of them up on our bare field. The rout was rapid and very complete, and I saw one chief lose his fine head feathers as they caught in the branch of a tree in the ravine.

The current of the river was too dangerous for foot troops, and so we were ordered to wait for the cavalry to ferry us over, when we scattered up the hills beyond the Indian camp after the wonderfully rapid and fleeing foe. Being recalled after a time, there came the examination and destruction of the Indian camp, and it appeared to have been their home for a long, long time.[17]

The orders were to burn everything, and the packers and citizens (for it was marvelous how many citizens seemed to arrive) showed us how to find the Indian caches, or storage places, in the ground by sticking ramrods into the earth. It was a wonder to see the tons and tons of food and fine Indian goods, jewelry, etc., some of which I judged came from early Hudson's Bay days, which we brought to sight. The packers helped themselves, and the citizens the same, while I tried to get a few things as souvenirs. But as fast as I got a little

Filling canteens during the Battle of the Clearwater. OUTING MAGAZINE, 1888.

bundle, someone took it while I was looking after the troops. At last I saved a few, and was so fortunate as to have them taken to Fort Lapwai by a pack train going in for supplies under escort.

An echo of this plunder came when our pack trains were attempting some of the false Indian trails on steep mountainsides. In one such place I saw six of the overloaded mules slip and go wheeling down several hundred feet, with a spurt of flour at every turn, no doubt breaking the packers' hearts, for our regular fare was only two meals a day of the Civil War kind of hardtack, unwrapped bacon, and black "issue" coffee. (But how good those field rations were with appetites made by unexampled mountain marches!)

After plans and subterfuges, and marching and countermarching, we at last took the Lolo Trail on July 30, 1877, in real chase of the fleeing foe. Although we made marvelous time for such awful trails, and the delays due to misinformation or ignorance of the location and direction of the enemy, we certainly were tricked into additional delays by the Indians, where we took apparently good, broad trails, only to find ourselves in terrible tangles of rock, brush, and steep cliff sides.

One of my pleasant memoirs is of a rest I had when I came, as commander of the rear guard, to that beautiful valley with meadows on one side, a grand cliff on the other, and a natural temple at the head, with a few great springs of crystal water in circular basins at its side—some of steaming hot water, and some of delightfully cold water.

At last came the march into civilization again, when we arrived at St. Mary's River and had news of Gibbon's Big Hole fight. It was on August 10 that the general decided to send a courier to stop the further march of his left column under Col. Frank Wheaton, 2nd Infantry, and have him return to look after the upper Columbia Indians, if necessary.

The older officers not desiring the detail, it was given to me, with directions to leave my Indian pony (which had become like a pet) and select three pack mules and one of the packers, and proceed at once via Missoula to carry important orders to Colonel Wheaton, who would be, by the time I reached him, at the "Summit" on the old Mullan road.[18]

My guide proved to be a half-breed Canadian French, Antoine Perez, who had packed over some of the proposed route, and an excellent guide he proved to be. I have given him much credit, but am sorry I never made an official report of my trip so as to make a government record of his good services. He selected fine mules, and although we had marched eight or ten miles that day, we set out about 3:00 P.M. at a steady trot and, with but one brief halt of a minute, made the thirty-three miles into Missoula, Montana, by 11:00 or 12:00 P.M. that night. [We] camped at the site of the proposed new military post of Fort Missoula, four miles from the city, [and] using an empty wall tent already there, with a hardboard floor and with saddle blankets for a bed, soon slept the sleep of the very tired. I had never ridden a mule more than a few miles, and so that unaccustomed jolt of the pack mule's trot, along with the hard floor and cool night, found me so stiff in every muscle by sunrise that it seemed I should break at every motion.

But duty ignores mere comfort, to say nothing of youthful pride, and we rode into the city, after a visit to my classmate, Lt. William M. Medcalfe, 4th Artillery, in a neighboring tent, who was on his way back to his post at San Francisco with his battery and, when I awoke him, was startled by the impression he was ordered back to field duty. He was one of our high West Point graduates and a very dear friend. That was perhaps the last time I ever saw him, for duty separated us, and after transferring to the Ordnance Department, he was killed by the accidental explosion of a shell [on] October 21, 1886.

I went into the bank in Missoula and asked for an army pay voucher blank, which was handed to me, duly filled for a month's pay four months back, and paid without a word. I joined my guide and went about buying food for the days necessary to reach the Summit. The bacon, sugar, etc., were wrapped in strong paper, which caused us disaster after a few miles of the jolting pack mule, so that for several days we had only salty sugar and some crumbs of hardtack, the bacon having been lost.

Fortunately we were able to get a little game, though our rate of travel made hunting almost impossible. My first game was a Montana "fool hen," which sat on a near limb and let me shoot off one of its legs, with only some blinking while it stood on its one leg, when my guide said in his deliberate way, "If the Lieutenant will wait a moment, I'll get him for you." He dropped off his mule and knocked the fool hen down with a bit of tree branch.

We made twenty-seven miles from Missoula that afternoon and camped in a place made smooth by the act of a bear having eaten a deer in the brush under a tree, the remnants being scattered around. The next day we made forty-eight miles. In fact, we traveled from sunrise till dark every day, but after reaching the end of civilization, the distances were very uncertain because of lost trails or having to wade the mountain streams for many yards hunting for the trail traces, and all that, to say nothing of the poor pack mule becoming lame and requiring much care.

In Missoula some friend gave the guide a bottle of what he called "Forty Rod," or some kind of whiskey, and as we were trotting over the hot, open, gravelly plain out of the city, every bone in my body aching from the first day's jog-trotting, he asked me if I would like a drink. I took one swallow, only to find my dry throat strangled so shut that I could not get a breath. Looking ahead, I saw the water of an irrigating ditch. [I] dashed my mule up to it and dropped off by throwing my body to the edge of the ditch, getting a swallow of water just in time to save my life. I never took another drop of that whiskey. (And I do not know whether the guide did, for that matter.)

I had my Springfield rifle and .45 Colt, and sometimes felt that such arms were merely a temptation to any chance enemies, but I was young and, after my many escapes from death in battles, felt no worries.

A number of hostiles passed us, especially at night, but we did not know they were enemies until afterwards from chance citizens and friendly Indians who were generally friends of my guide, or knew of him. After the defeat of Nez Perce Joseph at Clearwater and Big Hole, there was not much danger of further manifestation.

On the evening before we had to cross the ferry of the Missoula, or Clark Fork, we were camped near a ranch of white men, enjoying [an] exchange of news about the Indian situation, when in the night came a cavalcade of six or seven men on horseback terribly excited, with horses covered in sweat and the news that the ferryman had been attacked by some notorious renegade at his ferry house and shot through the woolen shirt, as he showed us by running his fingers through the two holes in front. The men said they were going to get more men and go after the scoundrel in the morning. I told them that I was the bearer of important government dispatches and must cross that ferry, but at first they said it might be impossible to wait for me and my mules. I simply told them it would be high treason to hinder a public messenger on government business, and they said they would consider it. At any rate, they said, I would have to be ready to start during the night, as they were going after the renegade as soon as their horses could stand the trip.

The next morning at my usual time, about sunrise, my guide and mules were setting out to resume our journey when the ranchers came from somewhere on the road at a rapid run. I called to them to remember that I must be ferried over the river. Then they left us, and we continued on as though nothing unusual had happened. Arriving a few hundred yards from the ferry, the men came from the woods, and one of them told me to wait, hiding in the trees; they would steal around up and down the river to see whether that renegade was still holding the ferryman's house. The ferryman's house was in plain sight across the river, and the ferryboat was on our side, just as it had no doubt been left last night by the ferryman. It was of the kind run by a cable, with a large sideboard to take advantage of the strong current, and a big wheel for regulating the angle of the sideboard.

I judged from rumors we had heard, and from the general situation, that the renegade had been as anxious to get away as the frontiersmen were to catch him, and called my guide to come along, and we started down to the boat. After a minute the ferryman and his friends slowly followed us. When we got to the boat the ferryman, trembling with excitement, took his wheel, and we started across, all the time watching the ferry house for any movement, but no sign of life. As soon as we were landed, I went straight up to the house and threw open the door, to find upon search that no one was there.

Then the frontiersmen started along the trail toward the west, saying they would find that son-of-a-gun or die in the attempt, and left my party to travel along as usual. After a half hour or so, we found the man hunters halted. They said they had to go back and attend to their stock, but if I should come across the renegade, to capture him. And thus we parted good friends.

Incidentally, I paid the ferryman three dollars, a dollar each for the U.S. mules, out of my own pocket. When I submitted my claim for the money, [I] was told I must have a receipt in a certain form because Congress had made no appropriation that summer, so I went back and got the receipt, only to find that another change had been made under later laws. So it went until I started to tear up the paper, and I have that paper in my baggage to this day, unpaid. (Red tape.)

We were pretty low in hardtack crumbs when we came to the Coeur d'Alene mission and the fine father, Alexander Diomedi, who gave us a wonderful welcome and fed us like Thanksgiving Day. [We had] a long chat about the Indians, the father's twenty-five years at the mission, and his 3,000 lbs. of Indian bacon curing, which he hoped to sell to the 2nd Infantry on its march. He had packed for us a big, new pillowcase of roast chicken, loaves of fresh bread, and other good food, so that the memory is a marvel to this day. His Indians seemed to have a very civilized country all about, just as good as in the surrounding civilized sections.

Leaving him with many expressions of gratitude, we soon came to a great marsh, two or three miles across and apparently dry enough to accommodate our mules. As the only other way was some nine miles, we chose the risk of the shortcut.

It would take a long story to describe our dangers and toils of that crossing: how we had to unload, load, and unload our pack mule many times to dig him out of quicksand, and how we were nearly caught ourselves, so that by night we were just able to drop on the first solid ground, and drop sound asleep, to awaken in an hour so swollen by mosquito bites that existence was almost unendurable. But we had food, and our journey was nearing its end, for we were coming to the lake and the Spokane River, and the friends [in] the 2nd Infantry.

The Battle of the Big Hole

CHARLES A. WOODRUFF[1]

Contributions to the Historical Society of Montana 7 (1910): 97–116[2]

Of all the Indians I have ever met, I consider the Nez Perces second to none of our wild Indians. They were polygamists, but when we consider that the squaws did all the work, you realize that polygamy was a blessing to the women, in that it divided the drudgery and didn't diminish the affection bestowed upon them. They would steal horses occasionally, but that was a weakness inherited for so many generations that it had become a manly excellence, but they had more virtues and less vices than generally belong to wild Indians.

Of them General Howard said, "The Nez Perces have never been, up to the present time, hostile to our people."

Colonel Miles said, "The Nez Perces are the boldest men and best marksmen of any Indians I have ever encountered."

Nine months before the events I am about to describe, some of these same Indians gave a sham battle at Colonel Gibbon's post, and with rifle and fire rehearsed the very tactics that were enacted in this real tragedy.

The Nez Perces had been inoculated with the Catholic, the Methodist, and the Presbyterian religions. It had "taken" in each instance; no case was a severe one, but it generally prevented them from engaging in the awful barbarities that usually characterize Indian hostilities.

In 1863 a treaty was made by the United States with three chiefs of the Nez Perce tribe, by which they agreed to relinquish certain lands, including the Wallowa Valley, Oregon. Chief Joseph repudiated this treaty and refused to be bound by it. In time he was joined by White Bird, Looking Glass, and Toohoolhoolzote and several hundred warriors. These were called the "non-treaty" Nez Perce Indians.

In 1875, by executive order, Wallowa Valley was opened to settlement, and the trouble began. Wrongs were perpetrated on both sides, and it was decided to force the Indians upon the reservation. In this case, as usual, when the Indians were ready, a number of defenseless white men and women were

Charles Woodruff in later life. CONTRIBUTIONS TO THE MONTANA HISTORICAL SOCIETY, 1896.

killed, and a small body of troops was sent to the scene of hostilities. At White Bird Canyon they were attacked by overwhelming numbers and defeated, with a loss of one officer and thirty-three enlisted men killed.

General Howard took the field in June 1877 with a strong force; after several skirmishes and two lively fights, resulting in severe losses to both whites and Indians, the latter scattered and thus evaded the troops. They afterwards concentrated, to the number of about 400 warriors, 150 women, and as many children, and started for Montana by way of the Lolo Trail. It had been the custom each year for large bands of these Indians to cross the mountains to Montana for the purpose of hunting buffalo (I have hunted with them myself), so that while they were forced by the presence of troops into unusual routes, the country generally was familiar to them.

As soon as Colonel Gibbon,[3] who commanded the District of Montana, learned that the Indians were heading his way, he made preparations to meet them. Gathering three companies of his scattered regiment, Comba's[4] battalion, he took the field at their head and, starting from Fort Shaw, crossed the Rocky Mountains at Cadotte Pass on foot, with pack mules for transportation. The transportation was so limited that only one blanket was allowed to each individual; no separate mess for officers, but all lived on bacon, hard bread, and coffee. By forced marches he reached Fort Missoula August 3, covering the distance (150 miles over the roughest kind of mountain trail) in seven days.

Here he was joined by three more companies, one of which had come 259 miles with wagons. Leaving Fort Missoula August 4, with 17 officers and 146 men with wagon transportation, he pushed on in rapid pursuit of the hostiles, whose trail coming out of the Lolo Pass was struck, four days old, six miles beyond Fort Missoula, going up the Bitterroot River.

While in this valley, Joseph was joined by eighteen lodges under Chief "Poker Joe." His stock of ammunition had been nearly exhausted in his fights with Howard and, strange as it may appear, along the Bitterroot he found white men who sold him all the arms and ammunition he wanted, taking in payment gold [that was] red with the blood of men, women, and children in Idaho.

The Indians seemed in no great haste. White Bird is said to have scented danger and urged a more rapid movement. One of their medicine men had cautioned the chiefs that death was on their trail. "What are we doing here?" he asked. "While I slept, my medicine told me to move on, that death was approaching. If you take my advice you can avoid death, and that advice is to speed on through this country. If we do not, there will be tears in your eyes." But Looking Glass replied, "We are in no hurry; the little bunch of walking soldiers at Missoula are not fools enough to attack us."

Gibbon pushed on, covering thirty to thirty-five miles per day. He ascertained by personal examination of their campground about how many Indians there were, and that he was covering two of their daily marches with one of his. He was joined by thirty-four citizens[5] who did not sympathize with those who had supplied the wants of the hostiles.

When the command reached the foot of the Rocky Mountains at Ross's Hole, the head of the Bitterroot, and found the Indians had crossed the mountains, many of the citizens became discouraged; they were out of provisions, and their affairs at home demanded their attention. But the colonel assured them that he meant business and should strike the Indians a terrible blow, once he should overtake them. He told these volunteers that they should have all the fighting they wanted (they got it). Also that they might have all the horses that could be captured, save enough to mount the command, and that his men would divide their last rations with the citizen comrades. The latter decided to follow their gallant leader, and they did it with honor to themselves and credit to American manhood. Most of these volunteers were veterans of the Civil War, and during the next few days they all showed the heroic spirit of '61.

On the night of August 7, Lieutenants Bradley and Jacobs,[6] with most of the mounted men—soldiers and volunteers (about fifty in number)[7]—pushed on over the mountains to locate the village and try to stampede the stock, the Indians having about 2,000 head of horses. But daylight found them still on the trail, and they concealed themselves in a secluded ravine. Lieutenants Bradley and Jacobs now did a piece of reconnoitering for which they deserve great credit. Leaving the camp in charge of Captain Catlin of the volunteers and Sergeant Wilson, Bradley and Jacobs, keeping under cover as much as possible, went forward until they could hear the sounds of axes in the woods where they were. Then, crawling along until they could distinguish the voices of the squaws, who were cutting lodge poles, they climbed a tall tree and a few hundred yards from them saw the Indian camp. Knowing that Howard was far in the rear, and fearing no other foe, the Indians were resting and preparing a supply of lodge poles to replace those thrown aside in Idaho.

At 5:00 A.M. on August 8, the command started up the main divide of the Rocky Mountains. Three miles of hard climbing were before them—three miles of steep mountain trail, filled with rocks and fallen trees. Teams were doubled and dragropes manned, and at 11:00 A.M., after six hours of hard, unremitting toil, the summit was reached. Just before the last wagon was up, a dispatch from Bradley was received stating that the trail was hot; that the Indians were moving and that if discovered, he would be in great danger.

The colonel read the dispatch and simply said, "Keep the column closed," and pushed down the mountain. From time to time, played-out mules were left along the trail, but the men never flinched. At bad crossings, axes, shovels, and picks were plied with desperate energy; their comrades in front were in danger. It seems as if the men were doing all that nerve and muscle could do, but when later in the day a second courier met us with the news that the village was located, renewed life was thrown into the step, and at sundown the column filed into Bradley's bivouac. After a scanty supper of hard bread and raw bacon, the tired men lay down to rest. The genial campfire, stimulating coffee, and soothing pipe were forbidden. After making his dispositions for the proposed attack, Colonel Gibbon ordered his adjutant [Woodruff] to call him at 11:00 P.M. and, lying down under the spreading branches of a pine tree, slept as peacefully as a child.

The train was carefully parked near the creek[8] so that, if attacked, there might be no trouble in getting water. In the corral thus formed, all the animals save two horses (for the colonel and his adjutant) were secured and left in charge of a small guard. Overcoats and canteens were discarded; nothing but arms and 100 rounds of ammunition per man was taken.

In silence the column was formed, and at 11:00 P.M. the little band, 182 all told, filed down the trail through dark groves of pine and fir; now through tangled underbrush, soon wading the cold mountain brook and struggling through deep marsh. The only light [was] a few stars amid the bank of clouds. Pointing to one of these, Gibbon whispered to his adjutant, "Old Mars is smiling upon us tonight; that's a favorable omen."

Five miles were stealthily covered, when the narrow valley of Trail Creek opened into what is known as Big Hole Basin. A mile ahead, the soldiers saw the smoldering campfires of the enemy, heard the baying of his dogs responding to the howls of prowling coyotes, and saw the flickering lights, the smoky lodges of the warriors. The trail now led along the bluffs that bound the left bank of the river, passing through a grove of second growth pine (with which we shall become better acquainted later on), and emerged upon a steep side hill covered with grass, upon which an immense herd of ponies was grazing. Slowly, for fear of disturbing them, the column moved through the herd. It was thought that they were in charge of a guard who must be sleeping nearby, and for fear of alarming the Indians, no attempt was made to capture the herd at this time.

It was about 2:00 A.M.[9] when the command arrived opposite the village, which was in the valley about 150 yards from and 50 feet below the trail. There were eighty-nine lodges pitched in the form of a "V," with the angle upstream, which was between the bluff and the village, the intervening valley being traversed by a slough and covered with bunches of large willows; beyond the village was a long stretch of open, rolling prairie.

Comba and Sanno's[10] companies were quietly placed in skirmish line at the foot of the bluff, covering about half the front—the upper half of the village. Bradley, with the volunteers and about fifteen soldiers, was on the extreme left as we faced and somewhat detached so as to be able to strike the lower end of the village. Rawn, Browning,[11] and Williams's[12] companies [were] in line behind Comba and Sanno; Logan[13] in line ready to strike the extreme right flank. The plan [was] to force the Indians out of the village onto the open plain, away from their animals, where, with our long range rifles and superior discipline they would be at our mercy, but unfortunately we didn't have men enough to cover the whole front of the village. Save the barking of the dogs, the occasional cry of a wakeful child, and the gentle crooning of its mother as she hushed it to sleep, all was quiet.

The thoughts of that little band were serious. They knew that day would bring with it a reveille of blood; still there was no flinching, but the suspense was trying. They longed for fight, for action.

Unless you have experienced it, one can hardly realize the nervous strain attendant upon the waiting for a battle to commence. Few men go rejoicing to a bloody conflict, but anything is preferable to the suspense when you realize that it must come; once in, there is little romance in the actual hero, amidst the melee of a hard fight, face seamed with the lines of brutal passion and grimed with dust, perspiration, and smoke. Half human, half brute. These men had a human hatred of bloodshed, yet they knew that the hard but single road to full duty demanded it.

At last the eastern sky begins to take on the rosy hue of the coming day; one by one the tops of the lodges come into view above the blackness of the valley. The hour had come. Quickly the whispered order is given for the two skirmish lines to "forward, guide center." The men tighten the grasp on their rifles as they give a trial glance along the sights. While they are silently moving forward, a solitary Indian going out to look at the herd approached the volunteers. He leans forward on his horse to try make out in the dim light what is before him. Two rifle shots ring out; the Indian falls dead.[14] The battle is on: "Charge!"

The remaining companies are ordered in on the run. The adjutant bounds on his horse and gallops to Bradley (who runs to meet him, so eager is he for the fray), shouts the order, "Go in and strike them hard," and followed by a shower of bullets, returns on the run to his chief, who is coolly watching the movements, unconscious that his position on the hill renders him a conspicuous target. But the adjutant is troubled by no such imperceptibility and advises an instantaneous advance to the valley, and they are soon with the line.

The troops plunge through the river, in places waist deep, and strike the village. A lovely, peaceful valley is in a moment changed to an inferno. The Indians, aroused by the first shots, rush from their lodges half clad but fully armed and, fortunately for us, a little dazed and nervous from the shock of surprise. Men, white and red, women, and boys all take part in the fight, which is actually hand to hand; a regular melee, rifles and revolvers in full play. Men are powder burned, so close are they to death dealing guns. The dingy lodges are lighted up by the constant discharge; the ground is covered with the dead and dying; the morning air laden with smoke and rent by cheers, savage yells, shrieks, curses, [and] groans. No one asks or expects mercy—our only commands are "Give it to 'em, push 'em, push 'em."

In a few minutes the upper end of the village is ours, and we sweep down the stream, expecting every moment to see Bradley's column at the lower end of the village—but this was not to be. After receiving his order, he had scarcely gone twenty yards before he was shot dead, and his men, without a recognized leader, naturally drifted upstream and joined the main command.

Soon from the willows in the rear, we receive a fire; the Indians from the lower end of the village have taken the brush and passed around our left flank. Lines are quickly formed and we sweep the willows; it is literally bushwhacking. They are driven back to the hills, and we return to destroy the village. But soon from all directions is heard the sharp crack of rifles—the enemy is invisible. The Indians have recovered from the shock of surprise. They now know how small is the attacking force and are fighting for everything that man, civilized or savage, holds dear. The village has become the hottest place in the vicinity, and the colonel reluctantly gives orders to retire to the wooded point before mentioned, about 1,000 yards up the river. Taking the wounded with us, the movement is deliberately executed. The colonel is severely wounded and his horse killed. It isn't a very healthy place for a dismounted man; the adjutant recognizes this fact and urges him to accept his horse, the only one left, and wounded at that. This generous offer is kindly but firmly declined.

When the command reaches the point of timber, it is found in possession of the hostiles, but a determined charge changes its ownership. We wanted that timber, and we wanted it badly. A barricade of logs and an active use of the trowel bayonet soon makes the command feel secure. In a short time the Indians returned to the village and hurriedly packed up, stimulated by an occasional shot, and started east. We thought that they were willing to call it quits, but we were mistaken; they wanted revenge, and the warriors returned to get it. They tried sharp shooting awhile but soon got discouraged at that, for the revenge account kept on increasing. Soon great clouds of smoke came rolling over, and fine ashes dropped down among us. They had fired the grass, hoping to have it run into the timber, and do what they can, cannot drive us out. Matters begin to look serious.

Nez Perce warriors trying to burn out Gibbon's command.
NELSON A. MILES. *PERSONAL RECOLLECTIONS AND OBSERVATIONS.*

But the colonel is not discouraged. He said, "If the fire reaches us, we will charge through it to the river, taking our wounded with us, and then from the cover of the banks send the redskins to a hotter place than they have prepared for us." Fortunately the wind shifted, and we were saved from that danger; but while it lasted, the situation was very trying. More than one wounded man examined his weapon to see how to work it, when the muzzle was pointed his way, to be ready in case the worst should come.

Scattering shots are constantly falling inside the barricade, and every little while a dull thud tells of mangled flesh or shattered limb; but they are having no picnic themselves, for our best shots are giving them as good as they send us. Night closes down upon the scene, but the fight continues. The Indians try a few feeble charges, but individual courage unsupported by discipline isn't suited to that kind of work.

About 11:00 P.M. most of them withdraw to follow the fast-moving camp. It seemed as if daylight would never come. The nights are cold in the mountains, even in summer. The men have no covering; their clothes have been soaked in crossing and recrossing the river. More than one-third of the command are killed and wounded; they have no medical attendance, and some of the wounded suffer intensely, and their groans are very trying. In addition to all this, the yelling and shooting of the Indians during the first part of the night didn't add to the comfort of the survivors. Bill Edwards, one of our citizen comrades, volunteered to carry dispatches to Deer Lodge; it was a brave deed, and gallantly performed. He left us at 11:00 P.M. Thursday, crawled through the encircling line of Indians, walked forty miles to French's Gulch, obtained a horse, and rode forty more, [and] at 10:00 A.M. was in the telegraph office at Deer Lodge.

After daylight[15] fires were lighted, and the adjutant's horse, killed by the hostiles within the barricade, furnished a much needed breakfast—the first mouthful of food since our cold supper thirty-six hours before, after which the men buried their own and the enemy's dead. During the day, a detachment returned for the wagons, which were brought up, and then with plenty [of] bedding and an abundance of food, we were as comfortable as could be expected.

At the risk of trespassing upon your generosity, I will relate two incidents of a personal nature.

I was passing along the skirmish line just before the attack was made and saw an officer (a colonel during the Civil War, with a gallant record) rubbing black mud over his trousers, which were of white corduroy. Being asked what he was doing, he answered, "You see, Woodruff my boy, as we are about to attack, it has occurred to me that these trousers will be a trifle conspicuous in this light, and I am trying to tone them down a bit."

I had somehow gotten a reputation of knowing about wounds, and in the midst of the fight in the village, one of the men[16] came up to me and, exposing his breast, showed me where a bullet had entered and said, "Do you think I will live, Lieutenant?" Knowing from the bubbles of air in the flowing blood that the shot had entered the lungs, I told him to let me see his back, where I found the ball had come out. I described the nature of the wound and said, "Alberts, you have a severe wound, but there is no need of your dying if you have got the nerve to keep up your courage." Two years later Alberts, a hotel runner, was the first man I met in getting off a train in St. Paul. He rushed up to me, grasped my hand and luggage, and said, "You see, I had the nerve, Lieutenant."

The second day after the fight, at 10:00 A.M.,[17] General Howard arrived with a detachment of twenty-seven soldiers[18] and seventeen Indian scouts. His movement was a heroic one, even though the results proved it was unnecessary. Hearing that Colonel Gibbon was surrounded and cut off from water, he took his little command and pushed on to the rescue, ordering the men to fill their canteens and on no account to use any of the water, as it would be needed by Gibbon's beleaguered troops. He said, "I was intensely anxious for Gibbon's command till I came in sight of it. His wagons were then near his fortified camp; his men were bathing and washing their clothes at the creek, and the horses quietly grazing in the bottom. There was no sign of an enemy in the vicinity. On reaching his position, which was on a wooded point just above the willow bottom, we found Colonel Gibbon's command covered by small barricades, within which were many wounded, including Colonel Gibbon himself, but all were cheerful and confident as troops were wont to be who have remained in position and slept on the field of battle."

Of the seventeen officers, fourteen bullets found their billets in their bodies. Three were killed or died of wounds, and four were severely wounded.[19] The entire command lost thirty-one killed or mortally wounded and thirty-eight wounded (all but five severely), but Gibbon had not blundered. It was magnificent, but it was war.

The Indians left 89 dead unburied on the field, and Joseph admitted a loss of 208 killed or mortally wounded; 26 more than Gibbon took into the fight.[20] Someone was commenting upon the fact that every officer killed and wounded was a married man, when a bystander remarked, "Well, it would take a sharp-shooter to find a bachelor in the 7th Infantry."

Owing to the rapidity of the movements for concentration, the command was unable to secure the services of a surgeon and received no professional attendance until the arrival of Howard's medical officers three days after the fight.[21] On Monday,[22] four days after the battle, we started home via Deer Lodge, the wounded in army wagons.

The army wagon is not a luxurious vehicle, but as an exercising machine for invalids, it has few equals and no superiors. As there were no roads, and the route lay across a bunchgrass country, you can imagine that the wounded did not enjoy the excursion. Their bodies were full of aches, and their hearts of delight, when we met a party of citizens from Butte, Deer Lodge, and Helena, accompanied by doctors and supplies of every conceivable kind. We had forty miles to go before reaching a house or road. After that, our journey was almost a triumphal procession, the people vying with each other in their efforts to cheer and comfort the wounded. As an illustration, a wagon containing three wounded officers halted at a ranch kept by a kind old lady who prepared a din-ner that would have done credit to a "quarterly meeting." Two of the officers were helpless as to locomotion, the other, who was badly wounded in the head and severely in the side, though he could manage to get around, asked for the bill. She replied, "Nothing for those poor wounded fellows, but seventy-five cents for you."

Twelve days after the fight, at the end of a 240-mile ride, we reached our post and home.[23]

From Fort Fizzle to the Big Hole

CHARLES N. LOYNES[1]

Winners of the West 2, no. 4 (March 1925): 7–8

Those were eventful days from 1875–1880 in the then territory of Montana. Col. John Gibbon, at that moment [was] commanding the regiment, with headquarters and six companies stationed at Fort Shaw. Other companies were at Fort Benton, Fort Ellis, and Camp Baker. On March 17, 1876, with drums and bugles playing "St. Patrick's Day in the Morning," we left Fort Shaw, the snow knee deep, and did not return until October.

The 7th [Infantry] was to be part of the force ordered to meet Colonel Terry for the Yellowstone expedition and attack the Sioux under Sitting Bull. In the month of June, two days after the Custer massacre, we were in the vicinity of the Little Bighorn country when Lieutenant Bradley, who had charge of the mounted detachment and who was in advance, sent back word to the main column that Custer and his command had been massacred. Of course, officers and men could not credit such a report, but soon found it to be true. The regiment immediately advanced and rescued Major Reno, who with the remaining companies of the 7th Cavalry had made such a gallant stand against the savages by using their dead horses and hardtack boxes for breastworks. During that summer the 7th Infantry marched over 2,100 miles.

After the expedition to the Yellowstone, the companies returned to their respective forts for the winter and not until the following year, 1877, did they move again. At that period, the government intended to establish a post west of the Rocky Mountains, in the Bitterroot Valley near a small settlement called Missoula.[2] For that purpose two companies of the 7th—Companies I and A, commanded respectively by Captains Rawn and Logan—were ordered there. On a beautiful June day, we entered the then struggling village of Missoula, composed at that time of a gristmill, about twenty log houses, and a camp of two or three hundred friendly Indians under an old chief about eighty years of age by the name of Big Canoe. We soon crossed the Blackfoot and Hell Gate rivers, which meet at that point, and after passing over a level stretch of prairie four miles across, we found ourselves under the shadow of the Bitterroot Mountains, and near the river of the same name.

Many will remember that at that time, Brig Gen. O. O. Howard, with cavalry, infantry, and a section of the 4th Artillery, started his long trip from Oregon to the Missouri River in pursuit of the Nez Perce Indians under the great Chief Joseph. Being advised of the approach of the Indians in our direction, we at once commenced to fortify our camp as best we could by throwing up rifle pits, cutting away the brush that would shelter the Indians, and piling up sacks of grain in such a position as to give protection to the wives and children of officers and the laundresses of the companies.

About seven miles to the south of our camp was what is known as the Lolo Pass, through which we expected the Nez Perces to come. A detachment from both companies was accompanied by a few friendly Indians and thirty or forty citizens, all under command of Capt. Charles C. Rawn, and a better officer never lived. His entire force numbered about one hundred, while that of the Indians was about five hundred, and they were mostly armed with Winchester repeating rifles, while we had the Springfield single loader, caliber .45. We soon arrived at the entrance to the pass, or canyon, and with our skirmish lines thrown out in front and on flank, we advanced to meet the Indians.[3]

Going forward about three miles, we were suddenly accosted by a number of shots coming in our direction from brush in front, evidently fired by the outposts of the hostiles. Our answer was a yell, and the friendly Indians with us giving their war whoops, we pushed forward, the few Indians in front retreating back to their main body.

The canyon at this point was becoming less broad; on our sides were high stone precipices, some underbrush and scattering Norway pines, and a small stream of water called the Lolo. Here we met the main body, and the firing from both sides became more rapid. We were ordered then to check their further advance, and for that purpose men and axes were soon felling trees across the canyon in our rear. A tree would be dropped, then another, called a head log, would be placed upon it, with a small limb in between giving the required space to get the rifles through. In the meantime, the shadows of evening were coming on, a drizzling rain had set in, and the citizens who accompanied us— principally for the ponies they might capture—perceiving the large body of Indians we had to contend with, had already deserted, with the exception of about a dozen.

Among those who remained was a man by the name of Andrews, as we remember him, who ran the gristmill at Missoula, and a daring, brave man he was too. During the early evening, his attention was attracted to a slight noise in front, where he and some soldiers were posted; so getting over the works, they advanced cautiously forward and soon covered four Indians with their rifles, and brought them in as prisoners. They were conducted to the rear, their feet and hands tied, and a guard placed over them. Among the prisoners was one by the name of John Hill,[4] who had a good English education; another was what is termed a squaw Indian, who had during the trip from Oregon killed a ranchman's wife [and] was consequently, when captured, enjoying the privileges of a brave. He afterwards escaped from the guard tent one dark, rainy night while guarded by a drummer boy.

Chief Joseph must get by us, for he knew General Howard's command was coming up in his rear. In this he might be successful, but only at a great loss to himself. During the night, we made preparations to receive him, believing he would try to force his way through on the following morning. Before the first streak of daylight,[5] every man was on the alert, with rifles ready, to meet the expected attack. At last daylight came, and with it an occasional shot—just enough to keep our attention. We were beginning to get somewhat impatient, and were preparing to throw out a skirmish line to feel them, when on a high, rocky point to our right were seen six or eight Indians working their Winchesters right into us. Volunteers were called for, and fourteen sprang forward,[6] led by Lieutenant Coolidge, and started up the steep mountainside to drive them off. We had gotten quite well up, when they vanished out of sight.

We soon discovered that during the night, Joseph had moved his whole camp up the steep mountainside, had passed around us, and was then making rapid time to get to the Bitterroot Valley, and at the same time had left a number of his warriors to keep our attention and delay us as long as possible.[7] When he arrived at the mouth of the Lolo Pass, he turned to the right and went up the Bitterroot Valley, going in the direction of Corvallis and Phillipsburg toward the Big Hole basin, where, a week later, on August 9, we attacked him.

Not having at the time [a] force large enough to follow, we at once returned to camp near Missoula.

On August 3 Colonel Gibbon arrived at Missoula from Fort Shaw with Companies D, F, G, and K, and men from other companies attached. The day following, the above named companies, including A and I, left Missoula in pursuit of the Nez Perces. In addition to our command were a number of citizen volunteers, making the entire force about 182 men, including a [twelve-pounder mountain] howitzer. We followed the Indians for five days, passing over the roughest country imaginable. In places the trail was so steep that the mules were detached from the army wagons and, with ropes, were drawn up the steep sides. The scattered settlers were congregated in a square-built adobe fort for protection, and the men informed us that, if necessary, the women could use firearms as well as they. One night[8] we encamped on a high point of the mountain with no water or food. The next morning we descended to the valley below, where we got water for men and animals, who by this time were nearly famished. Here the Indians had camped four or five days previous, many wickiups being in evidence. They are made by bending over the young willows, forming a circular arch, upon which are thrown buffalo hides or blankets for protection of the occupants.

About the third night[9] Lieutenant Bradley, with the mounted detachment and accompanied by Lieutenant Jacobs, started ahead to locate the Indians. Two days following their departure,[10] we had entered what is called the Big Hole Basin, when Lieutenant Bradley sent word back that the Indians were encamped about seven miles in our front. We then marched to within three miles of their camp, halted, and made preparations to attack. Here we left our wagon train in charge of Kirkendall and Sergeant Frederick, also our howitzer in charge of Sergeant Watson[11] and Corporal Sale,[12] both former artillerymen [who] lost their lives the next morning, although Watson's wound caused his death some days later in Deer Lodge. They had orders not to advance until they heard us attack the camp. After eating hardtack with water, and being issued 100 rounds of ammunition per man, we waited until about 11:00 P.M., when we received orders to fall in, in single file, all orders being given in whispers. At this time we were in a deep valley thickly covered with underbrush and scattered Norway pines. Taking the side of the hill on our left, we advanced quietly toward the Indian camp. It was quite dark where there was brush; now and then a soldier would stumble or fall in some manner, but absolute quiet was demanded.

About 1:00 A.M.[13] we found ourselves on the side of a hill facing the Indian village, their herd of ponies on the crest of the hill in our rear. It was part of the plan to capture that herd. With the exception of the restlessness of the Indian ponies, it was very quiet just at that time, but it was the quiet that precedes the tornado, before death and destruction follow. How unsuspicious they were of the approaching danger. Now and then a tepee would flash up with light, as perhaps someone in it would throw a stick on the fire, for the nights were chilly there. Fallon[14] of Company I could not resist an inclination to smoke, so he lighted a match for that purpose but soon discovered that he had made a mistake. Thirty or forty yards below us flowed the Big Hole River, into which we must soon plunge, for the camp was on the other side. The river was fringed on either side by alder bush.

Chief Joseph intended to move his camp that day, so at the first signs of the coming morn, three Indian herders were seen coming in our direction on their way to their herd. Concealment now was no longer possible. We had previously received orders to give three volleys through the camp and then charge, so that as the Indians stepped up the bank on our side of the stream, they instantly fell. As we gave three volleys into the camp, we rushed to the water's edge, everyone seeming to want to get to the opposite side first. So into the water we leaped, not knowing its depth in the dim light of the moon. Through it and into the camp of the Indians, we followed with a yell that would do credit to the Indians themselves.

We will never forget that day, how we fought with those savages—kill or be killed, no time to load our rifles. With the butts and muzzles of our guns, we struck right and left. The shouts of soldiers, the war whoops of the Indians, the screeching of the squaws, who with Winchesters in their hands were as much to be feared as the bucks. Our attack was a complete surprise, and we gradually forced them back to the opposite side of their camp, where the river makes a complete bend. Into the water they jumped, some of them who had a blanket first throwing it in and getting underneath, trying thus to escape. But they had to have air, so as soon as we discovered this trick, we only had to notice where the blanket or buffalo hide was slightly raised, and a bullet at that spot would be sufficient for the body to float down the stream. Although at this time the sun had not yet risen, it was quite light.

Most of the Indians had taken to the brush on the east side of the camp, where they soon discovered how few in number we were compared to them. Soldiers were constantly falling, and we soon discovered they were being hit by shots coming from the tepees occupied by Indians who had not time to get away or had retreated into them at the first attack. It was necessary to get them out at once. To do so, three or four soldiers would throw a lariat over the top of the tepee, and with others on the opposite side lying on the ground with rifles ready, the tepee would be pulled over, exposing an Indian who of course, with his last shot at so close a distance, would kill or wound a soldier. Those detailed to run off the Indian ponies had failed in their mission; many of the Indians at the first firing had gone to save their ponies and succeeded.

When we rushed them in early morning, many Indians had gone in the direction of our field piece, which was hurrying to our relief, and we met it quite near the camp. Above the din of firing, we heard one or two shots. They killed or wounded those in charge. Corporal Sales's body was afterward found stripped, and one of the horse collars about his neck. Privates Gould and Scott were never heard of again.[15] John Bennett, a veteran of the Civil and Mexican Wars who rode the horse attached to the fieldpiece, merely escaped with his life.

We supposed at this time we were masters of the camp. It was not so, however. It was the old story of the government in those days sending a handful of soldiers against a host of Indians better armed than ourselves. They rallied from all directions, and soon every bush and tree covered an Indian.

Something must be done quickly. At this point, Colonel Gibbon, while washing a wound he had received in the foot or ankle, directed Captain Rawn of Company I, then the senior captain in the regiment, to form and deploy his company toward the bush some eighty yards distant, now full of Indians. Then the discipline of the regular soldier showed itself, for the company formed under fire and advanced toward the Indians. On they went, over dead and wounded soldiers and Indians. The move was simply to cover the retreat of the main body, who were to fall back, cross the creek, and fortify as best they could on the side of the hill, where today stands a monument erected by Congress to commemorate one of the most stubborn conflicts in frontier history. The main body had now left the camp. Captain Rawn must now retreat with the remnant of his company. With faces toward the exultant savages, we gradually fell back. As we did so, our wounded would clutch at our legs and beg not to be left behind.

Poor Broetz, whose knee had been shattered by a ball, reached up and grasped Sergeant Murphy's rifle and would not let go.[16] The sergeant quickly found another. Fighting thus every step of our way, we slowly retreated.

But what a sight met our view in that short time. There was Bostwick, our scout and guide, sitting with his back against a clump of alders, a bullet having pierced his chest, the blood streaming from his mouth, and his hands tearing at his shirt in agony; he realized his situation when the Indians would find him. There lay the gallant Captain Logan, for he was a soldier who won his shoulder straps through bravery in the Civil War, his iron gray hair mingled with the green grass. Here lay Lieutenant Bradley, and no regiment ever had a more fearless or better officer; First Sergeant Stortz,[17] with the glaze of death coming in his light blue eyes; First Sergeant Edgeworth,[18] who left two sisters in England whom he was never to see, Sergeant Hogan, with a mother in Dayton, Ohio; Sergeants Martin and Clark;[19] Corporals McCaffery, O'Connor, Payne, and Eisenhut;[20] and the many privates, making a total of over sixty killed and wounded. Lieutenant English, with other wounded, was carried to Deer Lodge, where he afterwards died. Sgt. Edward Page of Troop L, 2nd Cavalry, [was] also killed.

One incident made an impression upon our minds which is not easily forgotten. A squaw was found lying on her back dead, with wide open eyes staring heavenward, an infant upon her bare breast, alive and crying as it painfully waved its little arm, which had been shattered by a bullet. It was probably hit when we sent three volleys into the camp before charging, and perhaps the shot that killed the mother wounded the little one.

Among the last to leave the camp was Captain Rawn and the few members of his company. Recrossing the creek [and] going in a westerly direction for about 250 yards, they met the main body trying to entrench by throwing up the dirt, using the Rice trowel bayonet for that purpose. One man would scrape up the dirt, while every second man would continue to fire. We were now completely surrounded by the savages, some of whom would climb the trees on the upper side of us, but our best marksmen soon dislodged them. We now lay in a square, probably forty feet each way, the Indians on every side, and not a man expecting to leave alive.

That was a long day to us. The sun seemed to stand still. We wanted the night to come that we might get water, for the cries of our wounded for water were most distressing. On the lower side of us flowed the Big Hole River, only distant about thirty yards. Oh, for the darkness of night, for by this time we had no water or food—nothing since the day before. But as there must be an end to all things, so there was to that day. As the shades of night came on, so the Indians kept closing in, particularly upon that side where the water was. When it was dark, a few volunteered to get water, and loaded with canteens, they crawled out into the darkness. But soon we saw the flash and heard the reports of rifle shots, and [Myron] Lockwood, a citizen, and one soldier had lost their lives in the attempt.

Among the head war chiefs of Joseph were Looking Glass and White Bird, the latter a brave warrior and great chief whose strong voice could be heard all through the night, first on one side of us, and then on the other, urging the braves to get ready to charge us in the morning, for he told them we had killed their braves and squaws. Every word he uttered was interpreted to us in a low voice by a half-breed by the name of Pete Matte, whom we had met on our way up the Bitterroot. The officers were a little suspicious of Pete, so a sergeant and two privates rode beside him, with orders to shoot him on sight if he proved treacherous. He was a horse thief with $500 on his head, offered by the ranchmen in Idaho. He was afterward captured and hung.

During the time we lay there, digging and fighting for our lives, we could hear the last cries of our helpless wounded in the camp below as the Indians closed in and finished them. Pitiful and awful as they were, they rang in our ears for days afterwards.

The first night, there was not much we could do to strengthen our position, for what few limbs of trees [that] were scattered about we had already used. To the north, or upper side, were a few saplings, so Corporal Loynes and Helder were ordered to leave their guns behind, crawl out, and with the Rice trowel bayonet, which is sharp on one side, try to cut down a few. The former, followed by Helder, was soon chopping them down, but the noise quickly attracted the Indians, and their dark forms were seen creeping in that direction by the men who were stationed on that side to watch. The cry "Come back quick" soon brought them back, amidst a volley from both sides.

Colonel Gibbon's horse, a large, dark sorrel, had been with us up to the time when we were first surrounded, but he was soon hit, and with pain he commenced to rave and pitch, greatly to the danger of Lieutenant Woodruff, who was wounded through the hips and, with a revolver in each hand, was doing his best to repel the Indians while sitting with his back to the tree to which the horse was tied. "Better finish him, Woodruff," an officer cried out, "for we may need him." During the following night, some crawled to where the bloated dead horse lay. They cut off some of the flank but, being without salt or a fire, preferred to remain hungry.

The night passed with a shot now and then, mingled with groans of the wounded and their cries for water, some of whom at times became delirious, when the name of mother or some loved one could be heard. When the first signs of day were seen, most of us were posted on the west side, for at that point we expected they would charge us, because twenty yards away was a narrow ravine, the opposite side being covered with a dense underbrush. We had not long to wait, for soon a heavy column of smoke began to arise. We saw their intention was to either smoke us out or probably to charge under its cover.[21] We crouched down behind our slight earthwork, with rifles loaded and cocked, prepared for what we believed to be our last struggle. But the smoke did not take the direction the Indians hoped for. It rose steadily, going in a direction to the right of us, and our hearts beat more hopefully for that.

As it became lighter, the firing increased. We were cautioned now to use our ammunition sparingly, for it was getting low. The sun was getting higher, and as its hot rays beat down upon us, our throats became parched, and the deep, sunken eyes and powder-stained faces of our comrades told of the strain which was upon them. We realized our situation was a desperate one, but there was fight left in that band of 7th Infantrymen, as there always is in the American soldier. General Howard and Colonel Miles, and a few remaining officers and men who at that time met the Nez Perces, will testify to the fighting qualities of the Indians while under the leadership of the great Chief Joseph, many of the Indians at Big Hole showing courage to a marked degree. One great warrior was particularly noticeable. He crept through the light brush to within thirty yards of us in daylight, wearing a blue shirt upon the front of which was a red star, and as the red glistened a second, it made a shining mark, and he fell dead.

Thus the fighting went on, but we had one hope. We knew that grand soldier, Brig. Gen. O. O. Howard, was some three days back on the trail of Chief Joseph, and if we could hold them off a while longer, we would be saved. It was during the third day that the shots from the enemy became less and less, and finally ceased entirely. Evidently their outposts had discovered the approach of General Howard. Suddenly there appeared in our midst one of the advance scouts of General Howard, who soon informed us that the general was only a few miles back and would soon be here. Needless to say, it was a happy moment to us when we saw him approach with the 1st Cavalry and a detachment of the 8th and 21st Infantry, also a band of friendly Bannock Indians as scouts, uniformed in blue trousers, buck tails hanging from their black campaign hats. Very soon his surgeons were at work on our wounded. General Howard and Colonel Gibbon had a conference. Soon the cavalry bugles sounded, and they dashed away to the south of us after the fleeing Indians. The Bannocks soon found the dead Indians who were too near us to be taken away and commenced to scalp them. They took the entire scalp from the head and, after carefully washing it, had what they most highly prized. But to us it was not a pleasant sight, considering the state of our empty stomachs, the air laden with the stench of dead bodies and ponies from the camp below, mingled with burning sagebrush and the ether the surgeons were using. A detail under Captain Browning was soon deployed down into the abandoned Indian camp, where we found our dead comrades stripped of all their clothing, their bodies swollen to twice their normal size from the heat of the sun, very few being mutilated. They were buried as best we could at that time, but some few weeks after, a burial detail was sent to more properly perform that duty. Some of the bodies were found torn up by bears and wolves that inhabited that wild region. In the meantime, we went back and were surprised to find the wagon train safe. We at once made preparation to move our wounded to Deer Lodge, probably sixty miles distant. They could not be carried in the army wagons, for the jolting would be too rough, so we took tepee poles, and then, skinning the dead ponies lying around, we cut the hides into strips, and braiding them over the poles, improvised what is termed a travois, upon which we laid our wounded, the other ends dragging on the ground, where a soldier walked for the purpose of lifting it while crossing streams or when the ground was too rough.

We finally arrived at Deer Lodge,[22] where we left our most dangerously wounded, some of whom died there. First Lieutenant English, who had been married only a few months previously in the states, and whose wife was among those who came to greet us as we entered the town, was one of the number.

Deer Lodge at that time was only a small place of log houses, but the people did everything for our wounded they could, and they felt only too grateful that the Indians turned in another direction, for Deer Lodge was in the path of the hostiles. Two white girls were held captive by the Indians at the time of our attack on the camp but were liberated when the surrender of the tribe took place to Colonel Miles. We are informed that they are now married and having families living in Montana.

Most of the officers of our regiment were men who had served and won promotion in the Civil War. Its colonel was Maj. Gen. John Gibbon, a division and corps commander in the Civil War and captain of artillery in the Mexican War; also General C. C. Gilbert, our lieutenant colonel. His major was Gildo Ilges.[23] The captains were Rawn, Benham, Freeman, Clifford, Kirtland, and Logan. Most of the officers and men of the 7th Infantry of that day have all reported for roll call to the Great Commander of the army on the other side.

The Battle of the Big Hole

JOHN B. CATLIN

Society of Montana Pioneers, *Forty-fourth Annual Convention, Missoula, Montana, August 4, 5, and 6, 1927, Historians Annual Report,* Missoula, n.p., 1927: 9–15

The battle of the Big Hole occurred August 9, 1877. The story of this memorable battle, following upon the Custer massacre, has been written and every detail of the action discussed, and yet I am not satisfied with the accounts given. Being a part of the affair, I will give my version as I saw it.

In the summer of 1877 word was brought the settlers of Missoula, in the Bitterroot Valley, that Chief Joseph of the Nez Perces and several hundred of his tribe were coming eastward through Idaho by way of the Lolo Pass. The statement was made that they were killing all white persons whom they encountered and burning the property of the settlers on every side. The report was exaggerated but had a definite basis, for the savages had killed settlers in the Sweetwater Valley, burned the ranch buildings, and driven off the stock. Steps were taken to organize local companies at once for protection of settlers living in sections of the country through which the Indians would pass.

Several companies organized—one at Corvallis and one at Skalkaho, where I was residing on a ranch with my family. I took an active part in organizing the Skalkaho company and was elected captain of the company. I received arms and ammunition from Governor Potts, Helena. Our guns were the old army Springfields, made over into breechloaders, and were serviceable weapons. The governor also sent me one thousand rounds of ammunition. The fort was being built at Missoula at the time. Captain Rawn was in command, with three companies of regular soldiers. The citizens of the city of Stevensville repaired to Fort Owen. Corvallis built a sod fort; Skalkaho built a stockade of logs, and then built a house inside large enough to accommodate the women and children. By the time all these preparations were made, Joseph put in an appearance.

When Joseph met the command of Captain Rawn and a party of citizens on the Lolo, there was a parley for a couple of days, and then Joseph pushed out past the troops and traveled up the valley.

They took their time going through, traded with the settlers en route, paying for all they secured. When it was found that they intended to do no harm, I was perfectly willing to let them go. But a few days later, Colonel Gibbon with a small force had joined Captain Rawn at Missoula, and they at once started in pursuit of the Indians. When they passed our place, a great many of the boys wanted to join the soldiers and wipe out the whole outfit. I opposed this and refused to until the boys insisted, as I had organized a company and, having had some experience with Indian fighting, should go and command them.

I finally told them I would be on hand at sunrise on the following day, and if we had enough men to make a showing, we would try and overtake the soldiers. We overtook the soldiers the first day out, and there we were informed the colonel did not care to be encumbered with citizens, but we stuck. Just before night the colonel sent for me and wanted to know if I had any men in my company that knew the country ahead of us. I told him that we to a man knew every inch of it. I was asked to take ten men and cross the hills and see if the Indians had gone over the mountains or were still on our side of the range. Our detail proceeded to go far enough to see that the Indians had crossed the divide. Nearly the entire day following was taken up with the troops reaching our camp. They arrived at our camp in the afternoon, and Colonel Gibbon immediately commenced preparations for sending out a party to locate the Indians.

Notwithstanding Gibbon had no use for the citizens, we were invited to join Lieutenant Bradley, who had come from Fort Shaw with twenty-five or thirty mounted men. When we started from home, we had not less than seventy-five men, but a great many of them had become discouraged and thought we would never locate the Indians and had gone home. Lieutenant Bradley with his thirty or thereabouts men, and my command consisting of thirty-four men all told, crossed the divide with Lieutenant Bradley, in command to locate the Indians. This was about 5:00 P.M.[1] It soon got dark on us and the trail was obstructed with lodge pole pine [so] that in places it was almost impossible to lead our horses through, and owing to delay, we did not get down until daylight.

We located the Indians, all right, and after we had found them, the only thing for us to do was not to let them find us until we could join forces with Colonel Gibbon, who finally reached us at night, after we had remained hidden the entire day. The colonel did not have any use for civilians, but for all that, he sent his adjutant to see if I could take two men and picket a trail until 11:00 P.M., at which time he prepared to move on the camp. When the time arrived for the command to move, we were called in, and a detail was made to take care of our horses. Lieutenant Bradley, with his men, was in the advance, and Catlin's men next. Then came Captains Rawn and Logan. The entire command moved opposite the Indians about 2:00 A.M.[2] and waited for daylight. I was asked to detail ten men for picket duty. I refused to make a detail but told the adjutant[3] I would furnish the required number.

I then called for volunteers, and the entire command volunteered. I then counted off the required number of men, and by that time the adjutant was back to know if I would take charge of the picket line. I saw the situation and fully realized that we were in for a fight of no mean proportions. I told the

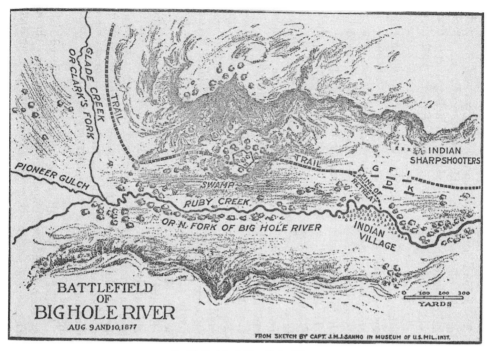

Battlefield of Big Hole River.

adjutant I would go with them, as I would not ask men to go where I would not go myself.

Our skirmishers were advanced a short distance, where we remained for the signs of coming daylight, when a solitary Indian came out from the lodges, riding directly towards us, evidently going to their herd of horses. They had between two or three thousand horses, and we had come in between the camp and their stock. In order for the Indian to reach their horses, he would have to come through our line, and we could not remain long without being discovered. My men had been instructed, and the poor devil paid the penalty. Some four or five of the boys helped him on his way. Of course, this opened the fight, and from that time on it was a severe one. When I say that, I speak from experience gained during three years of army service in the Civil War.

The Indians were taken entirely by surprise, and without waiting for arms or clothing, they fled to the willows, and the squaws in several instances were seen running after them with gun and belt. We waded the creek through water waist deep, and then we lost a lot of valuable time trying to burn the lodges. While we were thus engaged, the Indians recovered from their surprise, and we soon found that we had more important work on hand than burning lodges.

Colonel Gibbon's horse was shot and the colonel wounded. The fight became so fierce that Colonel Gibbon ordered us to fall back into a better position, and when the Indians saw that, they seemed to think that we were about to give up and get out.

Colonel Gibbon had a talk with some of his officers a short time before the battle and was planning to send fifty men up the mountains to capture the Indians' horses. Mr. [H. S.] Bostwick, Colonel Gibbon's scout, remarked to the colonel, "Colonel, you had better keep your command together, you are not going to fight Sioux now." There were but a few sent up the mountain. Lieutenant English[4] came down the line and asked Captain Catlin to make a small detail out of his men to go out on the skirmish line. The captain remarked, "My men are here for business, and they are ready for anything."

At this stage of the game, our forces, take them all told, were badly whipped. Colonel Gibbon rode up the right bank of the creek and ordered a retreat. Our forces then fell back one-half mile up the creek, to a point of the mountain that extends to the creek bottom. Here Colonel Gibbon called a halt and told his men that we would make this place our final stand. Our men were mad and desperate. When I came up and took in the situation very quickly, [I] asked, "Who in hell called a halt here?" When told that Colonel Gibbon had ordered it, I replied, "I don't give a damn, it's a hell of a place to camp!" This so amused Colonel Gibbon that he did not call me to account for my disrespect.

Here we began to throw up an entrenchment. The Indians had by this time surrounded our quarters. They were firing from every side, while we were digging and firing, doing the best we could. We lay there a day in the hot sun with not drop of water nor a mouthful of food, with the exception of Lieutenant Woodruff's dead horse, [and] with the Indians pelting us from about every side until 11:00 P.M. During the night, we had thrown up a strong breastwork and were able to stand quite a long siege.

After dark on the evening of the ninth, Colonel Gibbon called for volunteers to take dispatches to Deer Lodge, the nearest telegraph station, and to get teams and physicians to take care of the wounded. Billy Edwards of Catlin's company told the colonel that he would go. A number of others volunteered their services, but Edwards preferred to go alone. The colonel gave Edwards a few dollars and told him that he did not have a mouthful of provisions to give him. He also gave him a horse to ride. Edwards said, "I will risk my life to save you and your men." With a "God bless you" from the colonel, Billy Edwards passed the outer guard, perhaps to see the face of a white man no more; with a distance of sixty miles to travel, without a mouthful of food and the country infested with merciless savages, Edwards made the trip and fulfilled his duty.

On the morning of the tenth, the Indians had nearly disappeared; about fifteen of their best warriors still hung around our breastworks, firing an occasional volley among us. On the evening of the tenth, Hugh Kirkendall, who had charge of the transportation for Colonel Gibbon, came down with teams and provisions. This was the first mouthful of food we had had since Wednesday night when we left camp for the battle. The colonel gave Captain Catlin a box of hardtack, and from Kirkendall we got coffee and bacon. This food was eaten with a relish. On Saturday we were ordered out on the battlefield to bury the dead. In our company there were five killed and four wounded. The killed were Lynde Elliott, Campbell Mitchell, Dave Morrow, John Armstrong, and Al Lockwood. The wounded were Myron Lockwood, severe; Jacob Backer, slight; Fred Heldt, slight; [and] Otto Leifer, severe. (Leifer was wounded by an accidental shot from a soldier.)

The artillery that was ordered to come down at daylight on the morning of the battle fired only two shots, and then was captured by the Indians. The gunner was killed, and the other two men escaped into the mountains and finally made their way back to Fort Ellis.

Of Colonel Gibbon's command, I can only refer you to the colonel's report to the War Department as to the killed and wounded.

After the fight was over and we were making preparations to return to our Bitterroot homes, Colonel Gibbon sent for me, and in the talk he made at that time, he extolled the citizens to the skies and virtually admitted that had it not been for the citizens, it might have been another Custer affair.

I have always regretted that he did not give due credit in his report. For my part, I do not care, but when men fight as my men did, and under the eyes of the colonel, I think it shabby not to recognize us. I sized it up this way: We were whipped in the Big Hole, and there was not glory enough to go around, so the citizens were left out.

Colonel Gibbon had a brilliant war record, but I shall always believe there was mismanagement on his part. In the first place, it was bad management on his part to lose valuable time trying to burn lodges that were covered with frost and would not burn. If we whipped the Indians, the lodges could be burned when we had more time for that kind of work. Another mistake, and a most serious one, was when we retreated from the fields to occupy a new position. I have long since learned to not show my head twice in the same place when an Indian was watching to get a shot at me, and another thing, never back up, but always go ahead, or an Indian will think you are whipped and thus renew his courage.

I am not bragging when I say that my men were worth three to one of the large portion of the soldiers, who were recruits and had never heard the yell of all Indian.

I want to say the little handful of men in my command were heroes, every one of them, and if it had not been for them, Colonel Gibbon's command would have been wiped out. All of my men killed were young men, except one, and three of them single. I must have had a charmed life to escape as I did, as Lieutenant Bradley was killed at my side early in the engagement, and David Morrow, one of my men, a few minutes later. Every man fought on his own hook, and the one thing that was impressed on my men was to take advantage of shelter where available and to make every shot tell.

My recollection is that Colonel Gibbon reported his loss as follows: two officers, six citizens, and twenty-one enlisted men killed; five officers, five citizens, and thirty-one men wounded. Chief Joseph admitted the loss of 208 warriors killed in the battle, so there were a larger number of Indians killed than of white men engaged.[5]

In due time the physicians, men, and teams, with an abundance of provisions, came from Deer Lodge and Butte and cared for the wounded and took them to the Deer Lodge hospital. On Saturday General Howard's scouts under Captain Robbins came into our camp and assured us that Howard was still on the trail. Strange to say, when the Nez Perces buried their dead, they would not touch their medicine man. He was left on the field unburied. When Howard's scouts were taken to him they got off their horses, and each gave him a kick, saying, "No good Medicine Man."

You may ask why did we kill the women and children. We answer that when we came up on the second charge, we found that the women were using the Winchesters with as much skill and as bravely as did the bucks. As to the children, though many were killed, we do not think that a citizen or soldier killed a child on purpose. They were there with their fathers and mothers, and their fathers and mothers were violating the laws of our land, and we as soldiers were ordered to fire, and we did.

You ask what right had the citizens to go into the fight when the Nez Perces passed through our valleys peaceably; we answer, "To avenge the wrongs they had committed on the early settlers at Mount Idaho." We know too that had not Charlot, chief of the Flathead Indians here, taken part with the whites, that we might not have had a whole building left in the whole Bitterroot Valley. It was through fear that they passed through quietly.

In conclusion, I will say that though we were whipped, we broke the backbone of the Nez Perce nation. They never rallied again, so to speak. Looking Glass was killed somewhere on the Yellowstone; Chief Joseph surrendered to Colonel Miles, near the British line; White Bird never surrendered and is still somewhere in the British possessions.

As to Colonel Gibbon, we have nothing but kind words, save that when he made his report to the War Department, he failed to give my men their just praise that duly belonged to them, and they will ever look upon the matter with regret. It was my men who fired the first shot that brought down the great medicine man, in whom the Nez Perce tribe had full confidence that he could not be killed. It was one of my men, who in the dead hour of night, without food or blanket, carried the dispatches to Deer Lodge afoot and alone, through a country infested with merciless savages. It was my men who fought for three days side by side with the soldiers and shared hunger alike, and yet Colonel Gibbon failed to make special mention of them in his report that went out to the world.

To Colonel Gibbon's officers and men, we extend our thanks for your kindness, for you too were true to your cause and brought honor to your country, and to our old friend, Hugh Kirkendall, we give thanks for the coffee and bacon that helped to make out a meal when we had nothing but hardtack.

An Incident of the Nez Perce Campaign

HARRY J. DAVIS[1]

Journal of the Military Service Institution of the United States 36 (May–June 1905): 560–64

During the memorable campaign against the Nez Perce Indians in the year 1877, there were many stirring incidents that have never been given to the public, and notably among these is the Camas Meadow fight of Capt. Randolph Norwood's[2] Company L of the 2nd Cavalry. In the early part of the summer, we had assisted the 5th Infantry under Col. Nelson A. Miles in rounding up and capturing the remnant band of Cheyenne Sioux under Lame Deer and bringing them into the cantonment at the mouth of Tongue River. Shortly after arriving there, Maj. Gen. W. T. Sherman and staff, and the general's son Thomas, came up the Yellowstone on a tour of inspection, and we were ordered to escort them to Fort Ellis, which was our home station. Arriving there, a portion of the company was detailed to accompany our distinguished visitors on a trip of sightseeing to the Yellowstone Park. They had scarcely departed when dispatches arrived telling of a disastrous engagement of Col. John Gibbon's troops with the Nez Perces at Big Hole Pass, something like 160 miles away; saying he was in desperate circumstances and in danger of annihilation and ordering us to hasten with all speed to his relief.

Our company was depleted by various details to about fifty men, and with this force we started within the hour, which was already late in the day. Virginia City, sixty miles, was made on the night of the following day; the next ninety miles were made without halt except for coffee for the men and short rests for the horses. It was a tedious ride; all day, all night, and all day again, the steady plod, plod of the horses broken at night by the occasional smothered exclamation or oath of some trooper who had dropped asleep and nearly fallen from his horse.

On the second night out from Virginia City, we went into camp late, moved early the following morning, and had not been on the road long before we met a wagon and travois train bringing wounded from the battlefield. They told us that they had been soundly whipped, with great loss, and that the Indians, unable to dislodge them, had after a three days' siege departed, taking a southeasterly course and following the main range of the Rocky Mountains.

They would, without question, have killed or captured every man of Gibbon's force had they not been apprised of a large force of soldiers coming from the West. This was General Howard's command, consisting of two companies of the 1st U.S. Cavalry, two or three batteries of the 4th U. S. Artillery, and the 21st U.S. Infantry. The artillery was equipped as infantry. This force we joined,[3] and then began a stern chase which proved to be the traditional long chase.

Our course was the same as the Indians had taken. But with our heavier impedimenta, the best we could do was to keep from fifteen to twenty miles behind them. We crossed to the south side of the main range, and for seven nights we slept booted and spurred. We were following the trail, which, after crossing the mountains, led through a good grazing country, and from the numerous carcasses of cattle which lined the trail, we knew that the Indians were well sustained. An interesting fact, to those not acquainted with Indian ways, is that these dead steers were disemboweled and the bulk of the internal arrangements had disappeared, while the loins, rump, and in fact, all choice parts from a white man's point of view had not been disturbed.

The trail was easily followed, as it was from 50 to 150 feet wide, and the vegetation was almost entirely obliterated by the tramping of their several hundred ponies and the dragging of scores of travois poles. At their halting places, we found many freshly made graves, showing that their wounded list was rapidly growing smaller. We also noticed at such resting spots numbers of conical piles of pony droppings, evidently built by hand, which our scouts told us were constructed by the young bucks to show their contempt for us.

When we struck Camas Creek,[4] General Howard decided to give the men and horses a chance to rest, as our march had been arduous and the Indians seemed about to strike for the headwaters of Snake River, and from there enter the then almost wholly unexplored Yellowstone Park. We camped on the east bank of Camas Creek, on open ground. Opposite and above the camp, the creek was fringed with cottonwoods and alders, and below, the banks were clear and the stream flowed over a natural meadow to "the Sink" a few miles below, where it disappeared. The creek was literally alive with trout from twelve to twenty inches long and offered the finest sport I have ever seen. With only a small portion of the men fishing, enough were taken to feed the entire command. In the immediate vicinity of that campground,[5] there is now a company, with a capital of $200,000, engaged in raising trout for market, and they supply Ogden, Salt Lake City, and even San Francisco; the waters are ideal for the purpose. At night guards were posted, and a picket post was established some 500 yards upstream, near the creek and on a rocky knoll, and two at other points. The mule herd was turned loose to graze in the space between the camp and the principal picket post mentioned above.

Some of the men slept under the wagons and others pitched shelter tents; I chose the latter method, and with Private Monaghan for a "bunky" was soon in a state of "innocuous desuetude." Either our pickets fell asleep or the Indians were very astute, for during the dark half hour that generally precedes daylight, we were awakened by a disconcerting concert of demoniacal yells and a cracking of rifles, while the whizzing of bullets could be heard well overhead.[6] Everyone was out in a minute, and all we could see was a magnified imitation of a swarm of fireflies flittering in the alders as the rifles spoke; while the tramping of hundreds of hoofs added to the din,

We had no sooner sent them "a Roland for their Oliver" than the fireflies ceased winking, and except the noise we were making ourselves, nothing could be heard but receding hoofbeats and faint yells, as the enemy returned from whence they came, taking with them as a souvenir about 150 mules—our pack train. Our company horses had pulled one picket pin and had them milled round and round, and twisted themselves into a grotesque puzzle.

Orders came quickly for the three companies of cavalry to saddle, pursue, and try to recapture the pack train.[7] One company of the 1st Cavalry was to make a detour to the right and the other to the left, and our company was to follow the trail. The morning air was extremely chilly and crisp, and the horses rank, so that what was an orderly gallop at first soon developed into a race. After half an hour of this, we approached a ridge, which was the first roll of the foothills. The first ones to make the summit of the ridge suddenly stopped and then quickly returned to the foot; as the rest of us came up, we soon learned that the Indians had made a stand just over the ridge.

We dismounted, and the number fours,[8] each holding four horses, being unable to fight, left about thirty-five of us to meet the Indians. Crawling to the top, we saw a line of dismounted skirmishers standing behind their ponies on open ground and about 1,000 yards away. We deployed along the ridge and for twenty minutes or so exchanged shots with them, with but little damage on either side, as the range was long for our Springfields and longer for their Winchesters.

Lieutenant Benson[9] of the 7th Infantry, who was attached to our company for the day, standing up for an instant just at my side, received a bullet which entered at the hip-pocket and went out at the other, having passed entirely through both buttocks;[10] this, while we were facing the enemy, caused us to realize that we had no ordinary Indians to deal with, for while we had been frolicking with the skirmishers in front, Chief Joseph had engineered as neat a double flank movement as could be imagined, and we were exposed to a raking fire coming from right and left.

The horses had been withdrawn more than 500 yards to a clump of cottonwoods; and when we turned around, there was no sight nor sign of them. For a brief period there was a panic, and then we heard the notes of a bugle blowing "recall" from the cottonwood thicket. The race to that thicket was something never to be forgotten, for a cavalryman is not trained for a 500-yard sprint.[11] Luck was with us, however, and no man was hit in that mad race for safety. I had a horse's nosebag slung over my shoulder containing extra cartridges, and a bullet cut the strap and let it fall to the ground. A hero would have stopped, gone back, and recovered that bag, but not I.

We all reached the horses and found the place an admirable one for defense; it was a sort of basin, an acre or so in extent, with a rim high enough to protect our horses, and filled with young cottonwoods in full leaf.[12] It was oval in shape, and we deployed in all directions around the rim.

For two hours it was a sniping game, and our casualties were eight. The Indians crawled very close, one shooting Harry Trevor in the back at about fifteen feet, as we knew by the moccasin tracks and empty shells found behind a rock after the engagement. Poor Trevor's wound was mortal, as was that of Sam Glass, who was shot through the bladder; a bullet hit Corporal Garland's cartridge belt and drove two cartridges from it clear through his body; his wound never healed, and he blew out his brains a few years later. Will Clark had his shoulder partly torn away by an explosive ball; Sergeant Wilkins, a head wound, and [William H.] Jones, a busted knee; a citizen attache, a bullet through the foot, and the lieutenant, wounded as told above.[13] This was the amount of damage done to us, and what we did to the Indians we never knew, as they retreated in good order, taking their dead or injured with them after they found they could not dislodge us. Three dead ponies and some pools of blood were all the records we found of their casualties.[14]

The real hero of the occasion was Sgt. Hugh McCafferty, who climbed a cottonwood tree and, in short range of every Indian and only concealed by the foliage, kept us posted on their movements by passing the word to a man stationed under the tree. For this act he was given a certificate of merit and a medal by Congress. It should have been mentioned that we recovered twenty mules that were dropped by the Indians about midway between the camp and battleground. The others were never retaken, but were worn out or died before the final surrender of the few survivors to Colonel Miles.

We took up the trail the next day, after our wounded had been started for the post under escort. I could never understand how those two companies of the 1st Cavalry could have missed the Indians and gotten entirely out of touch with us, when we started together, and we were fighting within half an hour and kept it up for nearly three hours. More could be told of our chase through forest and canyon, over mountains and across gorges, where wagons had to be let down almost perpendicular walls by hand, for two hundred feet. But that is another story.

The Nez Perce War of 1877—
The Inside History from
Indian Sources

DUNCAN MCDONALD[1]

Deer Lodge *New North-West,* July 26, 1878–March 28, 1879[2]

It will be remembered that in the year 1847, Dr. Whitman and wife were murdered by a Cayuse Indian named Ta-ma-has, who was supposed to have been influenced to commit this by a Mexican named Jo. This murder resulted in a conflict between the U.S. government and the above named tribe. After the Indians were defeated, the government demanded the murderers, and Ta-ma-has and several others were hanged in Willamette Valley, Oregon. At the time the Cayuses were engaged in this war, a young man of the Nez Perce nation named Yellow Bull abandoned his parents and tribe. Ta-ma-has had a young and beautiful daughter, loved and respected by all who knew her. Yellow Bull, by his coolness and personal bravery, had won her affections and the confidence of her father, and it was soon agreed upon that the two should wed each other.

After Ta-ma-has was hanged, the young couple came back to the Nez Perce country, and shortly after, the girl gave birth to a son. Little worthy of note transpired regarding this couple until the boy reached the age of manhood. One day, whilst conversing with his mother, he asked her if he ever had a grandfather, and if so, he would like very much to pay him a visit. Hesitating for a few moments, the woman told him that he had a grandfather, and that his grandfather was dead, having been hanged by the Americans a long time ago. This same young man was one of the three who committed the depredations in Idaho last summer.

Later on, in the year 1854, the Nez Perces, then under Chiefs Lawyer and We-we-tzin-mae, concluded a treaty with the United States government. Shortly after this treaty was formed, several Indians and their women were murdered by the whites, probably without just cause, as we shall endeavor to show.

We refer to one instance in particular, when three Indians started out to the mountains in search of game. Arriving where game was plentiful, they had little or no difficulty in procuring a reasonable supply. After caching it, they returned to their homes, making an agreement to return at a certain time and take the game home. This being agreed upon, the three separated, and upon their return, two met at the cache about the same time. Feeling somewhat

Nez Perce Caches. CENTURY MAGAZINE, 1889.

fatigued by their trip, they dismounted to take a short rest, when two white men approached them in a rude manner, disarmed them, and asked one of the Indians whether or not he was the man who interpreted for Chief Joseph.[3]

The man answered him to the contrary. Thompson, the white man, called him a liar, at the same time knocking the Indian down and abusing him in a brutal manner. The Indian's companion made no resistance or attempt to save him, but the third one of the party referred to, named Willatiah, arrived while the scuffle was going on and made inquiries as to the cause of it. On being informed that the Indian had been thus treated without any cause or provocation whatever, Willatiah at once interfered in hopes to stop the white man from offering any further abuse, when suddenly the white man sprang upon him. But Willatiah, being a man of considerable nerve and strength, soon had the white man upon the ground, when the latter called to his companion to "shoot the bastard." The companion obeyed this command—Willatiah fell, a corpse.

The white man who committed this rash act was one of the squatters of Wallowa Valley, and it was supposed a little difficulty he had had with Chief Joseph a short time before was what prompted him to do the deed. It seems Chief Joseph had ordered him to quit Wallowa, as he himself claimed that section of country, and requested him to ask Lawyer to give him land, as that he, Lawyer, had sold his country for molasses sugar to the government. As soon as Willatiah expired, the remaining two Nez Perces started off quite panic stricken. A short time afterward, another Indian reached the scene of the late conflict and found his dead friend and companion, and immediately set out to ascertain the cause. Satisfying himself, he informed Chief Joseph, who at once summoned his warriors and started to interview Agent Monteith, demanding at the same time the murderers. This request the agent refused to comply with, only trying to satisfy them by telling them that they ought to kill the white men.

—•— ⚎⬦⚎ —•—

Wahlitits was the man who fired the first shot in the late Nez Perce war. He was the son of a well-to-do farmer named Tip-piala-natzit-kan, who is a brother of the once favorite Eagle of the Light,[4] and who was murdered by a white man four years ago. Tip-piala-natzit-kan was well known throughout the tribe, and his duty it was to call the councils together. As was mentioned before, the father of Wahlitits was a farmer and, in good circumstances, peaceably inclined toward all, accommodating, and he undoubtedly desired the settlement of the country in which he lived. About a year prior to the murder of Tip-piala-natzit-kan, a white man came to his house and stated that he would like to take up a piece of land. The man requested Tip-piala-natzit-kan to show him a piece of land unclaimed by anyone, promising him (the Indian) to be a good neighbor. Tip-piala-natzit-kan, liking the appearance of the man, at once granted his request and proceeded to show him the unclaimed land. No difficulty arose between the white man and the Indian until about a year afterward, when the white man wanted to fence a piece of land that the Indian claimed. It seems that early one morning, the man was engaged in hauling some rails a short distance from the Indian's house, when the wife of the Indian roused him up and told him that his white friend was putting some rails upon their land. Tip-piala-natzit-kan at once aroused the other Indians who were living in his house and asked them to accompany him, as he wished to talk with the white man and find out what were his intentions, and said that he was afraid to visit him alone. But it seems that no one wanted to accompany him, and accordingly he went alone. Upon reaching the designated place, he asked the white man if he had forgotten the promise he made to him during their first interview, and asked him in a friendly manner not to put any rails on his land, but put them on the land that he was owner of. The white man at once became wrathy, took his rifle from the pile of rails, and shot the Indian, wounding him mortally. The Indian at once started for home, suffering great pain and much exhausted from the loss of blood. His son Wahlitits was then in the Cayuse country. The wounded man addressed his people in the following words,

> I know that my days are short upon this earth, and it is my desire that you do not get excited at this event. Send this message to my son Wahlitits: Tell him for my sake, and for the sake of his brothers and sisters, and in fact, for the whole of the Nez Perce nation, to hold his temper and let not his heart get the best of him. We are as a nation poor in circumstances, in fact we have nothing. The white man has plenty of things that we have not. We can manufacture neither arms nor ammunition. We love our country and above all, our families. Do not go to war. You will lose your country by it, and above all the loss

of life will be great. Tell my son I should like to see and shake hands with him before I die, but I am afraid I cannot. When I am dead, tell him all I have said, and lastly of all not to wage war upon the whites.

Saying this, he expired a few moments afterward.

A few days later his son came home, and naturally enough his relatives delivered to him the message left by his dying parent. Wahlitits hung his head as the message was related to him and, with tears running down his cheeks, said that he was very sorry to hear of his father being killed in that way, and that he felt proud of his last remarks warning himself and people to keep at peace and hold in abhorrence war. Chief Joseph and others demanded the murderer of Tip-piala-natzit-kan, but the authorities refused to take any steps to either arrest or punish him. Joseph then warned the whites that if they did not punish the murderer, there would be trouble. Wahlitits, Tap-sis-ill-pilp,[5] and a young boy whose name is not known, are the three who commenced the depredations in Idaho last summer. Both Wahlitits and Tap-sis-ill-pilp were killed in the battle of Big Hole.

As further evidence in proof that the attack of the Nez Perces on the white race was not the result of inborn deviltry on the part of the red man, but rather a continuous abuse and violence exercised by the former on their so-called savage neighbors, I will now give you the history of the murder of a native in the vicinity of Slate Creek, Idaho. Ta-wai-a-wai-we, or Bear Thinker, one of the chiefs of that region, with the accustomed friendliness shown by his people ten years ago toward the whites, received into his family as son-in-law and endowed with a portion of his worldly goods an American whose love of ease overleapt his ambition. Unfortunately also for Bear Thinker, the mind of his son-in-law was as stagnant as his body and seemed to have belonged to the Dark Ages when the superstitions of his race were more remarkable than those of the Indians today. Among other beliefs indulged in by him was one that his father-in-law, being a chief and a medicine man, or wizard, was proof against death otherwise than by old age. This conviction being conveyed to a white acquaintance and backed by a bet, the pair tested the matter by administering to the chief a dose of strychnine, which, it is hardly necessary to add, quickly conveyed him to the happy hunting grounds. Granting that this act originated in an almost incredible ignorance, it appears that a devilish recklessness went hand in hand therewith, as the Indians state that the poisoners enjoyed a hearty laugh while the old man was "kicking his last" and remained wholly unpunished for their crime.

About nine years ago a Nez Perce woman was murdered near Kamiah, but I have not been able to gather any particulars. I have also been informed of the killing of Ta-akill-see-waits, son of a chief of the same name. Of his death, nothing is known except that he started on a short trip with a white friend from which he did not return. Sometime after, however, some Indians engaged in hunting discovered traces of blood which, being followed, led them to the bank of a small creek, where they found the remains of their friend covered with earth and brush. Their applications for the arrest of those involved and other of their assailants and murderers were of no avail, meeting always with the response that the punishment of a white man would instigate a war, and as yet they were not sufficiently desperate to accept such an issue.

＊→ ≡◆≡ ←＊

On their annual trip to the plains, about the year 1864, the Nez Perces, having dug what camas they required at Big Hole, proceeded down the Missouri and camped at the junction of a stream which heads in the Rocky Mountains southeast of Deer Lodge. While at that place, it seems that a party of Flatheads under Stalassna, which had been on an unsuccessful horse-stealing expedition to the Snake country, arrived within a short distance of the camp. Upon discovering it, however, instead of making themselves known, they cached themselves till night, when they stole four fine horses and also stole themselves away. On the following day, while the Nez Perces were moving camp, they were overtaken by four well-armed white men who accused them of stealing horses from the vicinity of Virginia City. Their denial was, of course, received with utter disbelief because the whites had tracked their horses almost into the camp—in fact, to the stopping place of the Flatheads, who were the true thieves. Although the Nez Perces declared that there must be some mistake and they themselves had had horses stolen, their assertions still met with no credence. The white men accordingly followed the camp until it reached the neighborhood of Bozeman, when, emboldened by the proximity of the settlements, they shot two Indians, named respectively Ta-wis-wy and Hym-py-ya-se-ni, who had gone there to trade. The former was killed at once, but the latter escaped and recovered, although a bullet entered at the base of the nose and made its exit at the back of his neck. At the same period also, the whites, determined on a supposed revenge, caught and killed another Indian who was hunting about eight miles from Bozeman. These acts were more than Indian nature could be expected to submit to, and accordingly, the Indians determined on an assault on the settlements. Such an unfortunate occurrence was, however, at that time avoided by the intervention of a Delaware named John Hill, who, acting as interpreter between the races, procured the holding of a common council in which the Nez Perces were promised that the murderers should be arrested, taken to Virginia City, and made to undergo a lawful punishment for their acts. Of course, the promises were a dead letter. Equally, of course, no one who has followed the published accounts of the Nez Perce War will argue that the then peaceful result of the conference was due to cowardice on the part of the Indians.

Reckless as the actions of the above-mentioned whites really were, there are yet many men in the West who would sympathize therewith, and with some show of reason, as the former certainly had strong cause for belief that the Nez Perces had stolen their horses; but who can excuse the killing of U-mas-na-cow and Key-la-tzie-augh (Hand Otter), two of the tribe murdered in the vicinity of Lewiston in 1868 or 1869, simply because they attempted to prevent two white men who had brought whiskey into their lodge from debauching their women? The next murder of my list seems to have been committed merely on account of the belief (shared and stated, according to a late report, by General Sheridan) that only a dead Indian can be a good one. The circumstances connected therewith being as follows: In 1871 my informant had his lodge pitched on the present site of the Missoula post, when two Nez Perces arrived there on the way from the main camp, then on the Gallatin, to their homes in Idaho. During the night of their stay with him, another Nez Perce en route from Idaho also made his appearance, and in giving the home news, told one of the others that his wife was anxiously awaiting his return. This much pleased the Indian addressed, for in some manner he had been led to believe that during his winter's hunt on the plains, the woman had allowed proximity to have the stronger charms and replaced him with another husband. Such a story having been circulated in the camp, the forsaken husband, being a man of mark, had been offered as second wife a young girl, one of the most eligible of the tribe. Being, however, of a constant disposition, before stating his acceptance he determined to more accurately inquire as to his wife's faithlessness. For this reason he had started for home ahead of the camp, leaving therewith his baggage and extra animals. Upon hearing the news as above stated, he concluded to return to the camp for his belongings so as not to arrive at home empty handed. He therefore left the Bitterroot and was on the road wthin twenty or twenty-five miles of Bozeman, when a man stepped out of a roadside house and, without speech of any description, shot him through the body. By catching the saddle, he managed to remain on his horse until he was carried some distance from the scene of the attack. He then fell to the ground and crawled sufficiently to be out of sight of white passers. Thus he remained for two days and nights, without food or water, when at last some Indians came along, and they bore him to their camp a few miles on the other side of Bozeman. Soon after his arrival there, some soldiers appeared with an order for the camp to move, the order having originated on account of some depredations committed in the vicinity by other Indians— Sioux or Crows. All the Nez Perces then—with the exception of Eagle of the Light, who had a dying brother in his lodge and preferred to take the responsibility of staying to either leaving his brother or killing him by travel—left for the Yellowstone, and on their way the wounded man died. An Indian more or less is truly no great matter, but surely a great country which can afford to free her Negroes may also exhibit a slight feeling of humanity for the family ties of a poor red man.

Many more cases of outrage committed against the Nez Perces as individuals could be added to the foregoing, but a surfeit, perhaps, having already been given, it is now appropriate to call attention to the great cause of dissatisfaction on the part of that tribe. The Stevens' Treaty of 1855, under which the government claims the control of those Indians, was obtained by a ruse which, if understood, could hardly receive the commendation of a great nation. Not being able to gain to his aim the consent of any of the real chiefs, Governor Stevens, a man of much ability and few scruples, cut the Gordian knot for the government by providing a chief freshly manufactured for the occasion. Lawyer, recognized by the Indians as a tobacco cutter (a sort of undersecretary) for the chiefs Looking Glass, Eagle of the Light,[6] Joseph, and Red Owl, was the chosen man. In other words, for certain considerations he was prevailed upon to sign away the rights of his brethren—rights over which he had not the slightest authority—and although he was a man of no influence with his tribe, the government, as if duty bound on account of his great services, conferred upon him the title and granted him the emoluments of head chief of the Nez Perces.[7] The feelings of the Indians were at that time aroused to such a pitch of indignation that they at first determined to hang their new superior, but as so often has been the case with them, milder counsels prevailed, and indifference and contempt took the place of revenge. However the government chose to look upon the result, the true chiefs and body of the people regarded the treaty as void. Thus the case stood—gradual encroachments being made on one side and protests being made by the other—until last year, when the old story of a love affair produced the grand denouement.

Before, however, proceeding with a description of attendant circumstances thereof, I will, to prevent misconception, give a short resume regarding the chiefs connected with the council held during the formation of the aforesaid treaty. As previously hinted, there were at that time four noted chiefs, and these were: First Eagle of the Light, chief of the Took-peh-mas and Lum-ta-mas, first among his peers as to eloquence, and chosen by them as main spokesman at the council. Partly on account of old age, and partly due to a conviction arrived at through an intelligent intercourse with white men that his people had no chance of redressing their wrongs by fighting, he declined to take part in the later war and has, since its commencement, chiefly resided in Montana.

Second: Flint Color, or as better known by Americans, Looking Glass, a chief of the Took-peh-mas and perhaps the most influential man of the nation. He was father of the late Looking Glass, known to the Flatheads as Big Hawk, who was killed in the battle with Colonel Miles north of Fort Benton.

Third: Joseph, chief of the Ca-moo-ey-nahs, father of the present well-known leader. Before death, he cautioned his son against giving white men any opportunity to claim his land. "The Wallowa Valley," said he, "is yours. It is a fine country and belonged to your fathers, who are buried here. It will yield a subsistence for you and yours. Let the white man travel through it, and while doing so, eat your fish and partake of your meat, but receive from him no goods or other presents, or he will assert that he has purchased your country."

And fourth, Red Owl, another chief of the Took-peh-mas, an eloquent, sagacious Indian, noted as an Apollo among belles of the tribe. He was wounded during the attack made by Miles, but whether fatally or not, I have been unable to learn.

It may be here added that at the period now spoken of, White Bird, latterly of so much notoriety, was young and of no particular prominence. Since then, however, he gradually rose in the estimation of his associates and, on the resignation of Eagle of the Light, became first chief of the Lum-ta-mas.

⋆⋅—⋅ 〓✦〓 ⋅—⋅⋆

It seems the Nez Perces and the Crows were [the] greatest of friends once. They used to camp together and kill buffalo every winter for many years. The "Women Nation," the Crows, is what the Nez Perces have called them since the Nez Perce campaign against the United States government in 1877. The Crows are named women and sometimes traitors. It will be explained how they were named. It seems the Nez Perces were influenced by the Crows and urged in a good many respects. The main blame lies on the shoulders of the Crow nation. It is true a man has no right to murder when he is told to do so by another party, but ignorance commits the crime sometimes. Ignorance makes the Indian think all white men are thieves and nothing else, and sometimes they think they can whip the United States government and they really think that there are no good, honest white men. We know that many an Indian has been made chief not for his shrewdness, but for his bravery. Any brave Indian can be made a chief. If he were really an idiot, as long as he is brave, his valor covers a multitude of sins. But it is not often the case with wise Indians. It is a hard matter for a wise Indian to become a chief, but any stupid brave can be one with but very little opposition.

No doubt the well-known Crow chief named The Eagle That Shakes Himself was a brave man, but he was not a man of knowledge. Many a day and night, the Crow chiefs and Nez Perces spent their time counciling in their lodges about the pale-faced white men. We remember about it. For three years before the war broke out in 1877 between the United States government and the Nez Perces, it was told around our campfires what the Crow tribe were trying to do to make an agreement between the two mentioned tribes. We will state an incident that took place about two years ago between the Nez Perce and Crow nations.

We know it to be a fact that The Eagle That Shakes Himself once spoke and told Looking Glass and White Bird about the time when the two Nez Perces were murdered by white men, one of them near Bozeman and the other near the Missouri River. Exclaimed this chief,

> I understand. You are chiefs. Listen to me. I want to let you know how my heart feels towards the white man. Do you see my eyes are open? As long as I live these eyes are open. Never will I allow a white man to take or kill any of my people. You are cowards. You have not the heart that I have. You are a lot of cowards and like to eat the white man's sugar and molasses. You allow them to take your people's lives. You allow them to spill your own blood on your own soil

because they don't tell the truth to the red man. I say, fight them. Take their murderers and kill them. What are they good for, only to murder the Indians and take our country away? You will get all the help from me. Let us go to war against the white man. You go back to your country and start in, and as soon as I get the news I shall do the same thing. At the same time move this way, and I will go to Sitting Bull and make peace with him, and we will all give the white man a game.

Unfortunately, this chief was made a game of by Sitting Bull's warriors. He was killed by the Sioux Indians in a fight between the Sioux tribe and the Crows.

This kind of advice from the Crows had quite an effect on the Nez Perce tribe, especially among the young braves. It was repeated over and over. But Looking Glass never was made a fool of, never was fool enough to take such advice from any of his Indian friends. Looking Glass, after the Crow chief had made his speech, raised his head and, resting his eyes on The Eagle That Shakes Himself as though they would pierce him, said to the Crow chief,

You say you have eyes. You say you can see. You can flatter a fool, but not me. Those eyes of yours and your heart do not see far. You are like a child; you can see, but cannot see far ahead. You are the men who are fond of sugar and molasses. You are the men who suckle the white man. You are the men that can be bought and sold for a plug of tobacco. I, Looking Glass, Eagle of the Light, and Joseph's father were the ones who wanted to hang Lawyer for signing treaties with Governor Stevens. What right had he, or authority, to sign treaties? He does not belong to the blood. He is the offspring of a foreigner. We blame him in signing the treaty. But he was not half as bad as Stevens. What right has Stevens to put Lawyer at the head of a nation that really does not belong to him? Is it right for any Indian to go to whoever the head man of the United States may be and put him out of his office and have anyone he pleases succeed him? Will the people of the United States like it? No. The Indian that would put the president out of his office would be killed at once. This is what Governor Stevens did with our Indians. We don't want any treaties. Whoever made this world never told the red man to sell his country. For this reason, we want to live in peace. If we sign treaties and then turn and fight the government, it would be breaking up treaties. We do not want to fight as long as we have justice. That is all we want. If the white man punishes his murderers, we shall do the same. But he does not. He does not even ask us to help him. The first thing he calls on is his weapon to kill the Indians. I want peace with the white man. My hand is open to the white man. I do not know what they mean. Whenever one of my Indians gets killed, they do not even arrest the perpetrators. By the looks of things, we will be compelled to go to war.

These Indians, on reaching Idaho from the buffalo stamping ground, learned that Willatiah was innocently murdered in the mountains by two white men. This Indian's life was really a cause of many a poor innocent settler losing his life in Idaho. Willatiah was the last man murdered before the war broke out in 1877. I give below a list of Nez Perce Indians killed by whites before the war of 1877.

Chief Bear Thinker was poisoned; Juliah was killed near Bozeman without cause; Taivisyact was shot while passing a house on horseback near the Missouri River on the road to Bozeman; Took-kay-lay-yoot, Lapwai, by a soldier on account of liquor; Yalmay-whotzoot, Lapwai, was killed while looking for horses; Him-paugh was killed on account of buying a pistol; Tip-iala-huana-chino-mouch at Elk City, cause unknown; Koyotes was killed on a spree with supposed friends at Slate Creek; Maltze-qui was killed because he was falsely accused of stealing a bottle of whiskey; Eya-makoot, a woman, was killed with a pick on account of her dog whipping a white man's dog; Cass-say-u was accidentally killed by the son of their own minister, Spalding, who shot at another Indian while gambling and killed the wrong man; Took-ooghp-ya-mool on Salmon River; Usay-kay-act was taken away by a white friend and never seen again; T-nan-na-say, a councilman, was shot by a soldier in a council south of Yakima; Tipia-la-natzi-kan because his field was taken from him; Willatiah in the mountains near Wallowa.

As I have stated before, none of the murderers of these people were ever arrested or punished. At the time of this last occurrence, Joseph and his band were so excited at seeing the murderer of Willatiah go at large that they threatened the settlers of Idaho. The settlers, frightened by these threats, sent a dispatch to the soldiers at Walla Walla. When the soldiers arrived, the officer in command[8] asked Joseph if he wished to fight the whites. Joseph answered, "If I am compelled, I will have to fight. The man we wanted to fight for is dead and gone. It is better to be at peace once more. But I warn the whites to not kill any more of my Indians. I would not mind if you were killing Indians who are trying to do something wrong, but it seems you want to kill my best men, and for this cause I will not stand any more murder. I did not ask you to come and settle in my country. If you do not like us, keep away."

It was then the Nez Perces first heard there was a big chief of the soldiers coming to see the Nez Perce nation.

They were told this by the soldiers, and the big chief coming was Howard. This was in 1876. It should be remembered that there are two brothers, each named Joseph. Joseph Senior (Chief Joseph) is the one now a prisoner at Leavenworth. On hearing of this appointed council, Wa-lame-moot-key, a Cayuse chief and a relative of the Josephs, sent for all the Nez Perce chiefs, saying he wished to have a council with them near Walla Walla. But the chiefs were not disposed to have a council and remained at home.

But Joseph Junior (Ollokot), who had heard from other sources that Howard was at Walla Walla, took four or five other Indians and went there to see him.

Howard met him and said, "Joseph, I am glad to see you. But you have come alone; I would like to see the other chiefs also, and tomorrow I will see you." Howard told them to find lodgings in some of the houses of the town and ordered that they should have something to eat. Ollokot declined to be quartered off on the town or to accept government board and did not remain in town.

Next morning they were called to the military post by Howard and entered the room where he was. Before taking their seats, General Howard said to Ollokot, "The Sioux chief Spotted Tail has concluded to move to a new reservation."

Ollokot merely replied, "And so Spotted Tail finally concluded to remove."

While Ollokot was being seated, Howard drew some papers from his pocket and said to him, "These papers are my instructions from the Great Father to move all Indians to the reservation. I want to move the Indians to three different reserves. These Indians must go either across the Columbia, to Lapwai, or Kamiah reserves." Ollokot made no reply. Howard drew out more papers and said, "Do you understand? All Nez Perce Indians must move to their reserve. Have you anything to say?"

Ollokot replied, "Yes, I have. Howard, you are a chief and I am a chief. You know what is good for your white friends and I know what is good for my people. I think it is better to leave all the Indians alone and to leave all the whites alone. I always feel happy in seeing both living in peace. Both peoples are getting civilized and making progress in this part of the country. Both are growing wealthy. When the whites first came here, they were poor and we helped them by trading. We gave them everything they wanted. All these things I tell you come from the root of my heart. It is impossible to order all white men to leave; I think it is impossible for all Indians to leave. As I said before, the white man helps the Indian to become civilized and the Indian helps the white man to get rich."

Howard answered, "Yes, Joseph, but you must move."

Ollokot again said, "Howard, you had better leave the Indians alone. You are well paid to move Indians from their homes. These Indians are rich and well fixed. I like to see both nations progress. Let the white man raise his children and harvests. The Indian will do the same. We are nontreaty Indians. Therefore, we wish to live among the white men and live in peace. It makes me happy when I travel through this fertile country and see that it will support both the Indian and the white man. I have good reason for not wishing to remove to the reserve. It is too small to sustain half my stock. How could we keep our stock on a reserve that is only half large enough to feed it?"

Howard replied, "You must go to the reserve."

Ollokot said, "Well, you will have to talk with the other chiefs. You are made a chief by your people. You have now a good part of the country. It is better to leave the Indians alone on their own farms. You are working for the white man and I am doing the same for the red man. We are self-supporting Indians. We ask nothing from the government but protection in our rights."

Howard answered, "Your argument is very good, but I am sorry to say you must go to the reserve." At the same time, he told Ollokot that he would telegraph to Washington.

Ollokot rose and said, "I am telling you how the Indians feel about this country. You say these Indians must go to three different reserves—Lapwai, Kamiah, and across the Columbia River. If I must go to a reserve, I want to go to the Cayuse reserve, and if the Cayuse Indians want to go to Lapwai, they can. My Indians can do as they please, but I know they will not go. I do not want a white man to select a place for them. Let the Indians select a place for themselves as white men do. I do not wish the Nez Perces to go to three different reserves. If the Cayuses go to Lapwai, I want the whites to leave that part of the country, because it is too small for the Indians alone. We are rich and have many horses and cattle."

Howard replied, "There are too many settlers in the country to be removed on account of the Indians' wishes."

Ollokot said, "There is the trouble. You say your people are too well settled to be disturbed, and I say the Indians are too well settled to be disturbed. So it is better to leave the Indians alone. Why are you so determined to remove them? This is where we were born and raised. It is our native country. It is impossible for us to leave. We have never sold our country. Here we have all we possess, and here we wish to remain."

Howard merely said, "It is impossible. I wish to have a big talk with all the Indians at Lapwai in ten days' notice."

Ollokot then drew out a paper on which were written the words of his father a few moments before he expired. It was as follows: "My sons, this country is ours. My sons, do not give up this part of the country to the white man." The paper was handed to Howard who, after reading it, said, "Joseph, you and all the other chiefs come to Lapwai in ten days." It was so agreed.

In fulfillment of the wish expressed by Howard to Ollokot, the Nez Perce chiefs congregated at the Lapwai agency at the time specified. Ollokot, on reaching home, had related to the Nez Perces what Howard had said about removal, and they were much alarmed. Ollokot said to his people that he had done his best to prevent their being removed and asked them to keep quiet, and so they went to Lapwai. After arriving there, Monteith, the Indian agent, told a member of the tribe named Reuben, "You go and see Joseph and tell him to come to the reservation at once. Why are they humbugging and holding councils?" Reuben reported to the Indians what Monteith had said, and it seems [he] had said still more that the Indians "must move."

Much anger was created among the Indians at this message. On seeing Howard afterward, Reuben told him, "If you are determined to move these peaceful Indians to a place where they cannot graze half their stock, you will have to do it with soldiers. We will always tell you the place is too small."

Nez Perce warriors. CYRUS T. BRADY. *NORTHWESTERN FIGHTS AND FIGHTERS.*

Howard did get soldiers, and when the Indians saw them reach Lapwai, they became more angry than ever. The next question was who the Indians would have for a speaker at the council. They held a council among themselves to select an Indian who was a good talker. The Nez Perce chiefs were all present except Looking Glass and Red Owl, who were in the mountains hunting, and neither they nor their people had any intimation of what Howard proposed to do with them. The result of the council was the election for speaker of an Indian named Toohoolhoolzote, who was supposed to be a smart, intelligent Indian. Ollokot was barred out, the council deciding that he was not smart nor bold enough to represent them in a council with Howard.

When the day for the great council arrived, all the Indians were present except the two chiefs mentioned and their people. Ollokot, feeling aggrieved at the action of his people in electing another instead of himself as speaker, withdrew from active participation, and the reader will not often see his name mentioned during the campaign.

When the council assembled, General Howard and the Indians took their seats. The general then arose and said, "I want all these Indians to go to their reserve at once. If you do not go voluntarily, I will compel you to do so with my soldiers. I have instructions from Washington to move all Indians to their reserves, and according to my instruction, I must make you move. If you will not move for my words, you shall go to the reserve by the points of my soldiers' bayonets."

The elected chief, or speaker, Toohoolhoolzote, rose and said, "Howard, I understand you to say you have instructions from Washington to move all the Nez Perce nation to the reserve. You are always talking about Washington. I would like to know who Washington is. Is he a chief, or a common man, or a house, or a place? Every time you have a council, you speak of Washington. Leave Mr. Washington, that is, if he is a man, alone. He has no sense. He does not know anything about our country. He never was here. And you are always talking about your soldiers. What do we care about your fighting qualities? You are chief, Howard, and I am elected by the Nez Perces to speak for them and do the best I can for my people. Let us settle the matter between you and me."

Howard replied, "I have instructions from Washington to move all Indians to the reserves and put them under charge of Agent Monteith."

Toohoolhoolzote said, "Howard, are you trying to scare me? Are you going to tell me the day on which I shall die? I know I must die some day."

Howard then turned to White Bird and said, "Have you anything to say?"

White Bird answered, "We have elected Toohoolhoolzote to speak for all the Nez Perces. Whatever he says or does is law with us."

Toohoolhoolzote was at once arrested and put in the guardhouse, where he remained about a week. If I have been rightly informed, Howard in the council came near being a victim at the hands of the Nez Perce warriors.

＊-＊　≡◆≡　＊-＊

When Howard saw the Indians abandoning him on account of their elected speaker going to jail, he sent for White Bird. When the chief arrived, Howard said to him, "I want you and Joseph and all the rest of the Nez Perces to go to the reservation."

Little Bald Head (also known as The Preacher), said to Howard, "I would like to select a place for my people. The place where I want to live is opposite Lapwai."

"I don't want any Indian to select a place outside of the reserve," said Howard. "I want Joseph, White Bird, and all Nez Perces to go where I want them to go. If not, as I said before, I shall move the Indians with bullets or bayonets. I only give you ten days to move to the reserve. If you do not do what I have said, I shall send my soldiers and drive all your stock to the reserve, and also the Indians, and disarm them."

White Bird replied, "We like our country; we are wealthy Indians and self-supporting; we do not wish the government to spend a dollar toward the Nez Perces. My white neighbors are my friends."

Then and there Joseph said to Howard, "You give us ten days to move our livestock and property. You must be joking. I notice when you want to move, it takes a long time to do it, especially when there are rivers to cross. I notice whenever you go after Indians in time of war, it takes you months to cross a river. I want you to understand that we have more horses than the soldiers ever had in the Indian wars. We want time. Ten days is not time for us. When the generals have a handful of soldiers and a few animals to cross a river, it takes them weeks and months to cross. We have plenty of children, women, horses, and cattle, and the rivers are high." This is the only speech Joseph ever made during the year of 1877.

Howard said again, "I don't want any humbugging. Do as I tell you to do—move immediately to the reserve."

Joseph said, "We like hunting; why should we stop on the reserve all the time for the balance of our days?"

Howard said, "If you want to hunt, you have to get a permit from the United States Indian agent. Whenever you want to hunt, do not take many horses; take as few as possible, then you will not bother the settlers. Those settlers are the ones who sent a petition to Washington to get all Indians removed."

All this time Wahlitits, Tap-sis-ill-pilp, and U-em-till-lilp-cown were listening to what Howard and their chiefs had said. Howard told the chiefs, "You can have any houses on the reserve belonging to the whites, and white men will leave their homes and go to some other places. Those houses are on the reserve. If you wish to occupy those houses, all right, and those white men can take your places outside of the reserve—a kind of an exchange."

On these conditions, Joseph, White Bird, and Little Baldhead, or The Preacher, started out with the general to select homes for themselves. While riding around the country, Howard had a few soldiers and an interpreter along with him. Howard said to White Bird, "What made you a chief? I am a chief because I lost my arm while fighting in big battles and fought bravely." Joseph and White Bird were surprised at these remarks and said amongst themselves, "Howard is anxious for war."

All this time there was news amongst the Indians that the soldiers were increasing at Lapwai or some place near.

The Indians were advised by their white friends they would be compelled to move, that Howard was determined to move all Indians. Ollokot, on hearing that there were plenty of soldiers arriving near them, exclaimed, "I see that Howard is determined to move Indians and stock. If Howard tries to move my stock or troubles me, I shall fight him at once."

When the Indians saw Howard's actions, they thought they were bound to fight. Then the Indians concentrated at Camas Prairie to have councils and decide how they should act and what was the best thing for them to do. While camped at Camas Prairie [in] council, the three murderers made up their minds what to do.

At this time, Looking Glass and Red Owl were camped in another place near Clearwater by themselves. Again and again the Indians were told by their

white friends, "You must go; if not, you will be compelled to fight Howard."
At the same time, the three murderers were told, "The settlers at Camas Prairie
were the ones who sent a petition to Washington to get the Indians removed."
Looking Glass, on hearing that the soldiers and Indians were at the point of
war, sent his brother, Took-alex-see-ma, who is now with Sitting Bull, to tell
Joseph and White Bird not to fight. Took-alex-see-ma went from Looking
Glass's camp three different times. He was sent by his brother to do the best he
could to keep the Indians in peace. He was an influential man.

The murderers, on learning the parties that were trying to get the Indians
removed, said, "Well, there is nothing dearer than our country and our lives. I,
Wahlitits, was insulted on account of a girl I took for a wife. Now, my friends,
let us go and buy arms from the settlers. Some of our friends tell us to buy
arms and be prepared for Howard. We might as well start in. Let us kill the
parties around Camas Prairie, because they are the ones that sent the petition to
Washington. We must make them leave our dear soil before we do. It was bad
enough to kill our fathers and they get no punishment, and now they, not satisfied by getting the greatest part of our country and arresting our speaker, must
send a petition to Washington to get soldiers to take our country that is dear to
us. Let us all die and let somebody else get our country."

While having councils at Camas Prairie, Joseph was preparing to go to the
buffalo country. The two brothers Joseph started from Camas back towards
Wallowa Valley to kill some cattle and dry some meat. Took-alex-see-ma was
running around, detailed by his brother Looking Glass to keep the Indians
quiet. As Took-alex-see-ma told us once in his tent, "When I reached White
Bird's camp the third time my brother sent me, we were in a large lodge and
eating dinner, and while I was delivering the message that my brothers sent to
the other chiefs, I heard an Indian making a speech on horseback. I recognized
him as Big of the Light, mounted on a black horse and with a gun in his hand,
saying, What are you counciling about? War is commenced. This black horse
I am riding is a white man's horse. This gun is a white man's gun. Wahlitits,
Tap-sis-ill-pilp, U-em-till-lilp-cown just got back. They murdered four white
men and they brought this horse, gun, saddle, etc.'" At the same time, neither
Joseph nor Looking Glass was in camp. White Bird was the only chief there.

The insult of Wahlitits by other Indians and Howard arresting their
speaker were their reasons for starting out to murder. Besides, Howard's
actions toward them were rather mean, telling them he would move them with
bullets or bayonets.

━┅━ ᚌ◆ᚎ ━┅━

When the tidings that the three Indians mentioned had murdered four
white men the night previous reached White Bird's camp, that chief said,
"Now, my people, we must do the best we can. It is a great crime to murder
white men, especially innocent ones. In time of peace you have no right to kill
people, either by night or day. If we are forced to go to war, then you can do as

you please, except that you must not kill women. Neither I nor Joseph told you to kill these men."

As stated before, both the Josephs were absent at the time of the murder of these four men. It seems, however, a messenger went speedily across the Salmon River and towards Wallowa Valley searching for the Josephs to tell them the news of the murders committed on Camas Prairie. The two brothers were met by the messenger and were told of the crimes committed by Wahli-tits, Tap-sis-ill-pilp and U-em-till-lilp-cown. As soon as the brothers Joseph learned the news, they dismounted, cut the ropes by which the loaded meat was lashed to their pack animals, and proceeded with all speed to White Bird's camp. On reaching it, Joseph and White Bird ordered camp to be moved towards the camp of Looking Glass and Red Owl, but before reaching it these latter chiefs had heard from Took-aliz-see-na [also Took-alex-see-ma], a brother of Looking Glass, of the crimes committed by White Bird's band. Before reaching the camp of Looking Glass, the three murderers again started out in the dead of night and murdered five or six more men.

Anger is an insufficient expression to convey the feeling of Looking Glass when he saw White Bird's camp moving toward him. He said to Joseph and White Bird, "My hands are clean of white men's blood, and I want you to know they shall so remain. You have acted like fools in murdering white men. I will have no part in these things and have nothing to do with such men. If you are determined to fight, go and fight yourselves, and do not attempt to embroil me or my people. Go back to your warriors; I do not want any of your band in my camp. I wish to live in peace."

On hearing these words, Joseph and White Bird made camp a few miles from Looking Glass. They made up their minds not to trouble him, because he did not wish to go to war. The next day they moved towards Salmon River in nearly the same direction from which they had come and camped at a place called Camas Prairie. Early in the morning the camp was alarmed by one of the Indians. This Indian had been out nearly all night, and about dawn of day he saw some soldiers approaching the camp. (Before the fight with these soldiers, they attacked some freight teams on the road and killed two or three men.)[9] White Bird had only seventy-five warriors in the camp,[10] but they rallied and started out to meet the soldiers and ascertain what they wanted. But before White Bird had a chance to speak, the soldiers opened fire on the Nez Perces. Then the fight opened, and there they fought I know not how many hours, but in a short time they surrounded the troops, and the Indians charged upon them. White Bird urged his warriors on, saying, "Now is your time to fight. We are attacked. You have been looking for a fight with the white men, and now you have got it. Fight now to the last. I want my warriors shot in the breast, not in the back."

They defeated the troops in a short time and killed thirty-five of them. Of the Indians, not one was killed and only four wounded. It is said by some that Joseph was away at the time of this fight. The Nez Perces did not move camp that day. This was the first battle of the campaign and occurred near Salmon River.

(The above presumably refers to Colonel Perry's fight with the Nez Perces at the fork of White Bird Canyon about June 15. General Howard reported that Perry had twenty-seven men, including Captain Theller, killed and wounded in the engagement. The troops numbered 150, with some citizens and twenty friendly Indians. The fight lasted three hours, and the soldiers were driven sixteen miles. The Indian strength was estimated at one hundred twenty-five. Editor, *New North-West.*)

❧ ═◆═ ❧

White Bird did not move camp the day succeeding the defeat of the soldiers, but the next he moved and crossed the Salmon River the same day. Here he went into camp and remained about four days. Their next move was in a southwesterly direction through Joseph's country—that is, Wallowa Valley—and they camped in the mountains. Joseph and White Bird ordered camp to move at daybreak the next morning, and they moved back to and across the Salmon River again. The following day they moved again and reached a large plain where there are some pine trees. Here they camped again.

All this time they were counciling to determine what was best to do—whether they should leave the region which they were in and move toward the Snake country, or go to the Buffalo Plains and join Sitting Bull in the British possessions. Some wanted to surrender to Howard, but they feared they would be shot or hanged.

All this time, Red Owl and Looking Glass were camped on a tributary of Clearwater. Looking Glass believed he was safe from assault, believing he had done that which would commend him to the whites by rejecting the proposals of Joseph and White Bird to go to war and sending them peremptorily away from his camp.

Looking Glass even saved the life of a white man who was captured and who happened to be a friend of theirs. He told his warriors not to molest the man, as he did not wish to see any war between the whites and Indians. At this time, he knew a force of soldiers was moving toward his camp. He said to the white man, "Go and tell the whites that I, Looking Glass, am not with the hostiles. I do not wish to fight and will not unless I am compelled to in self-defense. I saved your life because I am a friend of the whites. I do not wish to be regarded or treated as a hostile. I even quarreled with my relatives who were coming to my camp because they were hostiles. Now, my friend, go and meet the soldiers. Tell them I am camped at this place and wish very much to see the officer in command. I do not want any trouble."

The man started with the message, but instead of meeting it he avoided the command and returned to the camp. He told the chief the soldiers were coming and not far off, and he believed they would attack the camp. Looking Glass ordered some of his men to go and see how far away the soldiers were. This was early in the morning. Two or three of the Indians started in the direction the soldiers were coming, but just as the soldiers reached the bank of the creek, the soldiers charged on the camp.

When the chief saw the soldiers coming, he started toward them with the white man he had tried to send as a messenger.[11] Looking Glass made signs to the soldiers to halt, that he wished to speak to them, but his signs had no effect. Almost immediately the bullets were flying thick. The white man got away from the chief and ran to the soldiers. Looking Glass returned to his camp and told his men to do the best they could. He then had about eleven lodges. The Nez Perces fled in all directions. One woman who tried to swim across the stream with her child in her arms had gotten about halfway across when she was shot and drowned. The soldiers captured about 1,200 head of horses. Most of these animals belonged to the two chiefs. The soldiers burnt everything Looking Glass had in his camp.

Talk about savages being bloodthirsty fiends! If these soldiers were not bloodthirsty fiends, then there is no savage in this world. Even had it been Joseph or White Bird who endeavored to have a talk with the commanding officer of the opposing force, they were entitled to it. There is no law of civilized war that gives a right to shoot a man when he is trying to surrender. Neither Joseph nor White Bird knew of the fight. The soldiers killed no one but the woman who was trying to cross the stream with her child. Is it possible that if a soldier cannot kill a buck Indian that he has a right to shoot at a woman?

Before continuing the narrative succeeding the attack on Looking Glass's camp, I will relate an incident preceding. It seems that at the earliest commencement of the Nez Perce War, there were two white women murdered. One of them was murdered by an Indian who was drunk. The other white woman was burned in a house with her child. When her husband and others were murdered by the Nez Perces, she went upstairs. The Indians say they did not see her at the time of killing the men. When the Indians got possession of the house, Ollokot was present. He was sitting at one side of the place smoking his pipe. He was asked by the warriors what should be done—whether they should set fire to the house or leave without destroying it. All this time the woman and child were upstairs, but the Indians say they did not know it. Ollokot answered, "You have done worse deeds than burning a house. You never asked our chiefs what was best to be done. You have murdered many men and not asked advice of your chiefs. You can do as you please about the house."

Some of the young men lit a match and set fire to the building. They then went back a little and sat down to watch it burn. They were suddenly startled by the piercing screams of a woman in the second story of the house. Ollokot ordered them to put out the fire. The young Indians ran down to the water, filled their hats, threw it on the flames, and tried every way they knew to extinguish the fire and to save the woman. But it was too late. She and her child perished.

The same young warriors who were with Ollokot at the time told me that when he left the place, Ollokot held down his head for a long time, and at last looking up, he said they had done very wrong in burning the woman, that he was very sorry, that he had believed the house empty.

The burning of this poor, harmless woman looks very bad for the Indian side. Still, there is some blame should attach to the white man. The white man does wrong in allowing the Indian to have whiskey. It is easy to reply that the Indians take the whiskey away from them by force, but there are many whites who are ready to sell whiskey to them in time of Indian wars.

⊷ ⊯◊⊨ ⊶

While the Nez Perces were camped in the pine grove, the chiefs sent two spies toward Cottonwood to see if any soldiers were advancing from that direction. While these spies were concealing themselves on their trip to Cottonwood, they discovered and killed two soldiers.[12] The same day, the whole Nez Perce camp mounted, but the camp did not move except the horsemen who approached Cottonwood. They knew there were soldiers there and they wanted to attack them. Before reaching Cottonwood, they ascended a high ridge on the road from the Lapwai reservation. Here they stopped and were looking through their field glasses to see the soldiers at Cottonwood.

Suddenly they noticed eleven mounted soldiers at some distance, and in another direction saw some Indians. Joseph immediately dispatched two Indians mounted on their swiftest ponies to ascertain what tribe the Indians belonged to. On reaching them, they met Looking Glass and Red Owl with their little band of men, women, and children, nearly all on foot. It will be remembered that Looking Glass drove Joseph and White Bird from his camp and refused to join them in hostilities. After this he had been attacked by the soldiers, his camp destroyed, his stock taken, and one woman killed. When the two envoys from the hostiles now reached him, he pressed on and reached Joseph and White Bird, who were preparing to charge on the soldiers and citizens at Cottonwood. Looking Glass approached the chiefs and said,

My relations and friends. I had no idea of fighting the white man. My father had traveled many a mile in time of war. My father's warriors fought many battles as allies of the United States soldiers west of the Rocky Mountains. We had friends and relations killed in fighting along with the United States troops. The Indians the troops fought were more our relations than the white man. Why is it that the Nez Perces, having sided with the soldiers in fighting the Cayuses, Yakimas, Umatillas, Spokanes, and others, that today I am compelled to raise my hand against the white man? Two days ago my camp was attacked by the soldiers. I tried to surrender in every way I could. My horses, lodges, and everything I had was taken away from me by the soldiers we had done so much for. Now, my people, as long as I live, I will never make peace with the treacherous Americans. I did everything I knew to preserve their friendship and be friends with the

Americans. What more could I have done? It was because I was too good a friend of theirs that I was attacked. The officer may say it was a mistake. It is a lie. He is a dog, and I have been treated worse than a dog by him. He lies if he says he did not know it was my camp. I am ready for war. Come on and let us attack the soldiers at Cottonwood. Many a man dies for his dear native land, and we might as well die in battle as any other way.

During this speech, the mounted soldiers who were carrying dispatches were approaching on the Lapwai. Looking Glass, after joining the hostiles, took command, and an attack was made on the approaching soldiers.[13] The Indians cut them off from Cottonwood as the soldiers veered off in another direction instead of endeavoring to return to that place, apparently determined to take chances on their horses. Before reaching a high ridge, four of the soldiers dismounted and fought bravely. The four who dismounted were all killed by one Indian, a noted warrior named Wat-zam-yas. The other seven were overtaken on the ridge, the principal murderers being in the advance. The soldiers lasted but a few minutes. I did not ascertain how far this was from Cottonwood. In this fight, no Indians were killed or wounded. One horse was shot under Wahlitits, the warrior who fired the first shot in the war. Another horse was shot under Smoker. White Bird says the soldiers at Cottonwood could have saved this party if they had been brave enough, but they did not even start out from their camp.

That evening the warriors all returned to their camp. The next day Looking Glass ordered camp to move and be made again in a ravine three or four miles distant from Cottonwood, where there are a few pine trees. As soon as camp was pitched, Looking Glass gave orders to the warriors to catch their horses and they would attack the soldiers. Joseph took his Indians and attacked the soldiers, while the rest of the Indians charged on the corral and endeavored to capture the horses. But the corral was well guarded and defended, and they only got twenty-four horses. The soldiers held their position. No Indian was killed in this fight, only one horse shot under Way-uch-ti-mamy. On the third day[14] the Indians raised camp. While packing up, Joseph said to the other chiefs it would be a good plan to pass with their whole camp near Cottonwood but not to attack the soldiers, and thus entice them out of the breastworks and get them to attack the Indians when the Indians could easily whip them. But unfortunately for the success of this plan, some young warriors, without informing the chiefs, had concealed themselves near Cottonwood to attack it.

All this time the Nez Perces believed there was a strong force of soldiers at Cottonwood, and besides, they believed Howard was there. They would rather have him than a hundred soldiers. They wanted Howard badly. The three murderers well knew that whenever the Nez Perces surrendered to Howard, they would be the first Indians hanged, and what they wanted was to see "the Indian Herder," as they call Howard, and kill him. In fact, the great cry in the

Nez Perce camp was to kill Howard at first sight. He was the one who got the Indians dissatisfied.

The camp moved as suggested by Joseph, but while traveling along and expecting momentarily the Cottonwood garrison to come out and attack them, word was brought that the young warriors who had concealed themselves were already fighting the soldiers. This vexed the chiefs very much, and they did not go in that fight. One Indian was killed and two wounded.

The same evening, a noted warrior, the same one who killed the four soldiers, took thirty picked warriors, attacked the soldiers in the night, and captured forty-five head of horses from them without the loss of a man. Thus ended the Cottonwood battles, only one Indian having been killed and two wounded.

It is a well-known fact that when Joseph, White Bird, and Looking Glass joined forces, they had, all told, just 220 warriors, twenty-five percent of whom were armed with only bows and arrows, which are poor weapons against needle guns except in close quarters.

The Nez Perces started from Idaho with seventy-seven lodges. They got twelve more lodges in Bitterroot Valley, taking them by force, making eighty-nine lodges in all.

⊷ ⩤◈⩥ ⊶

After the fighting in the vicinity of Cottonwood, the Nez Perces moved and made camp near Red Owl's farm.[15] Early in the morning the chiefs were told by one of the peaceable Indians that Howard was approaching them with a strong force of soldiers. But they were prepared all this time for Howard's "traps." The camp was in a little ravine. They put up some breastworks on a ridge between their camp and the approaching soldiers. Howard did the same thing. His breastworks were also on a ridge, and there was a ravine between the two bodies of fighting men. Howard, with all his military ability, did nothing better than to fire across the ravine to where the Indians were lying behind their defenses. He could have taken the whole camp by storm. The Indians think he well knew it was their determination to have his life, even if they had to charge into the midst of his troops and sacrifice themselves to accomplish their purpose. He knew what would be the result if he exposed himself. I have no wish to say offensive things of General Howard, but these are the words White Bird said to me sitting by our campfires in the Sioux camp last summer, "If Howard had been as bold as Colonel Gibbon, we might have been all taken, although we intended to fight to the last."

During the first day's fighting, four Indians [were] killed and four wounded.[16] They fought through the night until daybreak. No Indians were killed in the night fighting. The second day the battle continued the same as the first, but no Indians were killed or wounded. The firing was all at long range. I do not know how many men Howard had in these great battles, but as near as I can ascertain, he must have had two or three men to each Indian.

About the middle of the afternoon of the second day's fighting, Looking Glass ordered camp to be moved, and the entire camp was accordingly moved before Howard's eyes. It seems, therefore, that Looking Glass was a better general than Howard, as he withdrew his camp from the front of the enemy and moved away without the loss of either women, children, horses, or lodges.

At this time, Looking Glass had sole control of the camp, although Joseph ranked as high, or perhaps higher, as chief. Joseph's reason for not leading the camp was that there was more or less discontent and growling among the warriors, and Joseph thought he had best have nothing to do with the camp except to follow the movements ordered by Looking Glass.

After moving camp, they reached a creek near Kamiah, where they passed another night, expecting to be attacked by Howard at any moment. But no soldiers appeared. The third day they crossed the Clearwater. The river was high. Only about half the camp was across the river when they saw Howard's troops approaching. There was quick work done then. It only took a few minutes to cross the balance of the camp. Shortly after they got across, the troops reached the river and tried to cross. But Looking Glass was on the alert and, rallying his warriors, opened fire on the soldiers and compelled them to fall back. This ended the great battles of Idaho. Howard could not cross the Clearwater, and Looking Glass left the field. It is a well-established fact among the Nez Perces that Howard only killed four Nez Perce Indians during his operations in Idaho, and one other killed at Cottonwood foots up the grand total of men killed at five.

━━━◄◆►━━━

After the Idaho battles had ended, the Nez Perce camp moved from near Clearwater to a place called Wyap-p [Weippe]. The second day they made camp at a placed called Sah-wis-nin-mah. The next day Looking Glass took a portion of the warriors back to harass Howard, and the camp moved but a few miles. Looking Glass did not, however, attack or discover himself to Howard, but made a night raid to capture the horses of the "friendly" Indians who were in Howard's service. They captured and drove away sixty-five head. After reaching camp with them, a number of Nez Perce scouts were sent back to look for Howard. They had a very good plan laid to destroy Howard's command, but he did not have [the] nerve to push the Indians. Although they did everything they could to entice him, he was rather shy and took good care not to follow too closely on the Nez Perces after they got on the Lolo Trail, always sending his Nez Perce scouts a few days' march ahead of his command.

While Looking Glass's rear guard scouts were watching the trail one day,[17] they discovered three Indians following it. These three Indians were scouts for Howard. Unfortunately for them, they were surrounded before they knew what to do. Looking Glass's scouts were under command of Watz-am-yas, a brave warrior whom I have before mentioned, an honest, good man as ever lived, and who, like Looking Glass, had used every endeavor to preserve peace. When Howard's scouts were captured, Watz-am-yas addressed the prisoners as follows, "We are your relations. Your skins, your hair, your bodies, everything you are or have about you are the same as ours. Your supposed friends, that is, the Americans, have marked our native country with the blood of your relations. The white man has been drawing Nez Perce blood for many years. Our chiefs have put all their nerves between their teeth to keep peace with the white man. And yet you are not satisfied with the way in which we have been treated, but are assisting in working against us. We have captured you before and let you go. We knew you had taken up arms against us, but for relations sake we let you go. You promised us before that you would remain at your homes and not help Howard destroy us. We have kept our promises to you, while your promises have been lies. We have spared your lives many times. We will do so again if you promise me one thing, that when we let you go, you will return to your homes and never make another move or step to fight your relations now under Looking Glass."

The prisoners replied, "Yes. We are so glad to be allowed to go unharmed we will never make another attempt to pursue you. You have spared our lives during the battles in our own country and have acted manly with us."

Watz-am-yas said again, "I want you to understand that the next Nez Perce scouts we capture acting under Howard we will kill at once." Watz-am-yas then took all the cartridges they had and two horses, and told them to go home and never make their appearance again during the war.

After the prisoners had been set at liberty, Watz-am-yas moved his band a short distance, and they concealed themselves to await the approach of the soldiers. Suddenly they discovered some more Indians moving on their trail. These were more of Howard's scouts. Watz-am-yas quickly formed his men in a horseshoe-shaped line in the brush and encompassing the trail. When Howard's scouts had fairly entered the ambush, Captain John, the well-known scout of the general's, exclaimed, "Here are some fresh tracks. Let us go back. There is danger around here."

They turned to retreat, but just as they did so Watz-am-yas opened fire. The brush was so dense, however, that all the army scouts, except one that was dangerously wounded, got away. When Watz-am-yas reached the wounded man the latter said, "Spare my life; I am badly wounded and have news to tell you."

"Yes," replied Watz-am-yas, "we have spared your lives too often. You can tell your news in the happy hunting grounds." With that, he put a bullet through the scout's head.

The Nez Perces were nine days in coming from Clearwater to Lolo.

When the Nez Perce camp reached the Hot Springs on the Lolo Trail, not far from Bitterroot Valley, three Indians met them in their camp. One of these Indians was a Nez Perce, but his home was in the Bitterroot Valley. He told Looking Glass there were some soldiers on the trail watching for them to come.

Looking Glass said he did not want any troubles on this side of the Lolo Range, that he did not want to fight either soldiers or citizens east of the Lolo because they were not the ones who had fought them in Idaho. The idea among the Indians, uneducated as they were, was that the people of Montana had no identity with the people of Idaho, and that they were entirely separate and distinct, having nothing to do with each other. If they had to fight, they believed it was Idaho people they should fight and not Montanans. Looking Glass therefore gave orders to his warriors that in case they should see any white men, either citizens or soldiers, on the Lolo, not to molest them unless, as they had compelled him in Idaho, these citizens or soldiers should compel them to fight in self-defense. He said, "We are going to buffalo country. We want to go through the settlements quietly. We do not wish to harm anyone if we can help it."

The chief then sent an Indian called John Hill and two others in advance of his camp while coming down the Lolo. These three came to a post of four or five white men. This was Captain Kinney's camp, and this was the night John Hill was arrested and taken to camp. Hill told Kinney the chiefs had sent him ahead to ascertain if the Nez Perce camp could pass through peaceably. Hill was sent back to invite the chiefs to come to the white man's camp, saying that these white men wished to see the chiefs. This was on Wednesday. Looking Glass immediately started down with a band of warriors to meet Captain Kinney of the volunteers. When Looking Glass reached Kinney's camp, the chief reiterated to him that he did not wish to harm the whites east of the Lolo Mountains, that it was true he had fought the soldiers in Idaho when he was compelled to, that he did not want to fight anymore, and that he only wanted permission to go through to buffalo country. At this time, the Nez Perces believed that Sitting Bull still retained possession of the Yellowstone country, and that if the soldiers still pursued them, they could join Sitting Bull. Kinney replied that he had no authority to treat with them but appointed a council for the next day in the afternoon.

By this time, Captain Rawn was preparing in the Lolo a splendid trap for Looking Glass and his band. Looking Glass knew nothing about this trap. He only thought the soldiers were camped in the customary manner and had no idea of entrenchments being prepared to obstruct the passage of himself and his warriors. Readers, I do not wish my motives misconstrued in giving Looking Glass the leading position in these movements and councils. I am not censuring Joseph when I do not give him preference, nor am I influenced by kinship with Looking Glass. My statements are simply the truth of history. I know it was understood, and probably is yet, by nearly all that Joseph was the commanding chief of the Nez Perce force during the war, and that he really is the man who should have credit for the good work in restraining his warriors from excesses in their passage into and through Bitterroot. It is an error. Joseph was a good man, but he had nothing to do with the camp after Looking Glass joined it near Cottonwood, only by following it to shelter himself from the retributive hands of the white man. It was Looking Glass who saved many a white man's life during the campaign; he was the commander. As he ordered, camp was moved or remained stationary, and what military credit is due for the conduct of the campaign is due to him. Knowing Looking Glass to be well known to many whites, and that he was entitled to his reputation as a really good, kindhearted red man, I submit these facts, incidentally, to correct a popular error. White Bird was a fighting cock, but with the exception of an instance on Salmon River, he awaited orders from his superior chiefs.

Captain Rawn's camp, where he had erected rifle pits in the canyon, was about sixteen miles from Missoula and about four miles above the mouth of Lolo. The mountains on the south side of Lolo are precipitous and densely covered with standing timber, so that escape on that side was impossible. On the north side, grassy ridges stretched away from the stream, allowing a passage in almost any direction.

On Thursday[18] Looking Glass and White Bird met Captain Rawn and a few armed men and shook hands with Rawn. Of course, the latter wanted the feather in his hat and told Looking Glass he must give up his arms. Captain Rawn and Looking Glass then appointed another day to have a talk.

Looking Glass returned to his camp and told his warriors the conditions demanded of them. By this time they well knew about the "corral," as Looking Glass termed Rawn's fortifications. The Indians thought it was ridiculous to give up their arms to their foes. White Bird made a speech and said, "We remember a big war that took place once on the Columbia River. The United States troops fought against the Yakimas, Cayuses, Umatillas, Spokanes, and Coeur d'Alene. Colonel Wright was the big chief of the soldiers. After many battles, the Indians were defeated. Colonel Wright told the Indians that if they would surrender, he would treat them well and hurt no one but the murderers. On these conditions, the Indians surrendered. Then Col. Wright hanged many innocent Indians. Some of them deserved hanging, but many others' hands were clear of white men's blood. These soldiers camped below us are of the same kind. How do we know but that Joseph, Looking Glass, and others will be hanged immediately after we surrender? The officer tells us he does not know who will be hanged, that the government has to decide on that question." There were manifestations of approval when White Bird had spoken.

Looking Glass said, "Yes. We do not want to fight. I tried to surrender in Idaho, but my offer was rejected. The soldiers came upon my camp, and the first thing I knew the bullets were flying around my head. The soldiers lie, so that I have no more confidence in them. They have had their way for a long time; now we must have ours. We *must* go to buffalo country. If we are not allowed to go peaceably, we shall do the best we can. If the officer wishes to build corrals for the Nez Perces, he may, but they will not hold us back. We are not horses. The country is large. I think we are as smart as he is and know the roads and mountains as well."

The Nez Perces, however, concluded to have another council and try to make peace without giving up their arms—the Indian way of making treaties. On Friday Captain Rawn made his appearance about a half mile below the Indian village with about 100 men and halted. An Indian by the name of Pierre, a Flathead, was sent forward by the officer. When Looking Glass saw so many men near his camp, he thought they had certainly come to fight. Looking Glass returned word by Pierre that he would meet Captain Rawn, unarmed, halfway between the forces. The council was held, and Looking Glass proposed to surrender all the ammunition of the camp as a guarantee that the Indians intended to go through the country peaceably. When told that nothing but an unconditional surrender would be accepted, he asked for another meeting next day to give him time to consult with the other chiefs. Captain Rawn told him that any further communication he had to make must be made under a flag of truce at the fortified camp.

On considering the matter further, the Indians decided not to trust themselves under the condition demanded. They thought perhaps the white man was anxious to make peace, but still they feared treachery: I remember hearing Delaware Jim, the acting interpreter, relate that when Rawn met Looking Glass and demanded the surrender of the Indian guns, Looking Glass replied through the interpreter, "If you want my arms so bad you can start in taking them. I made up my mind before leaving Idaho that we would talk with the white man only through our guns. When I promise, I fulfill and do not lie as the white man does. When a Chinaman travels, he carries no arms. Do you think I am a Chinaman? It is foolish to think of a whole camp going to the buffalo country and not carrying a single gun."

While the Nez Perces were camped on the Lolo and it was supposed they could not get past the corral without surrendering, Joseph said to Looking Glass, "Let us go on. If not allowed to pass, we will fight our way through Lolo and next fight our way through Montana. We want peace, but the whites want us to be kept in the Lolo Canyon. Let us go through the best way we can, whether it is by peace or war."

Looking Glass answered, "Did you or did you not, with other chiefs, elect me for leader through this country because I knew it and the people, and did you not promise that I should have the whole command and do as I please? You and the other chiefs told me these words. Now, Joseph, I wish to know if you are going to break your promise. If you are anxious to fight, I will withdraw my people, and you can fight as pleases you. I fight when I cannot avoid it, but not otherwise. Still, I can fight my battles as well as anybody. At the fortifications in our way, there are some Flatheads aiding the whites. If we fight the whites, we must fight the Flatheads. Some of them are our relations. Now you can make your choice."

Joseph replied, "You are right, Looking Glass. We did elect you head man of the camp. Go ahead and do the best." So Looking Glass remained in supreme command.

On Saturday Looking Glass ordered camp to be raised and directed the women to travel on the north side of Lolo until they passed the "Nez Perce Corral," then cross the Lolo and turn in a southerly direction up Bitterroot Valley. The warriors were to cover the movement. The camp moved. The soldiers and volunteers got into position in the earthworks, and while they were uselessly standing to arms, the Indians passed deliberately by without any fight whatever.

While the camp was moving in this manner, the Indians captured Henry McFarland, Jack Walsh, and another man. These men were volunteers. Looking Glass told them they could go home and attend to their own business. During the day, several white men fell into the hands of the Nez Perces, and to all of them Looking Glass repeated the remark, "Go home and mind your own business; we will harm no man."

It has been discussed whether Rawn acted cowardly or not in permitting the Nez Perces to pass. The Nez Perces gave him credit for wisdom in not opening fire on them. The bravest of their warriors would have done the same. Had he attacked them, he would have been severely whipped. It is a well-known fact that the biggest "Indian eaters" at Lolo were less courageous than those who professed less.

That evening the Nez Perces made camp on McLain's place, about eight miles above the mouth of Lolo, in Bitterroot Valley.

The same evening, W. J. Stephens and about fifty or sixty volunteers reached the camp of Looking Glass. The old chief himself was the first one to meet and speak to them. Some of these volunteers were on their way back to their homes in the Bitterroot Valley and had run into the Nez Perce camp unintentionally. Doubtless some of them thought their lives not very valuable when they found themselves encompassed by the Nez Perces. Looking Glass well knew the facts. He said to them, "You are volunteers; you come over to fight us. I could kill you if I wanted to, but I do not. We have many women and children. I do not care for my own life, but I have pity for them. You can go to your homes. I give you my word of honor that I will harm nobody." After this talk, the volunteers dispersed in all directions for their homes.

About this same time, three Nez Perces arrived at the Flathead agency. They came direct from the Yellowstone country via Missoula. Eagle of the Light was at that time camped at Flathead agency, and they came here to see him and exchange news. These three Indians had been acting as scouts for Colonel Miles, looking after Sitting Bull's Sioux on the Yellowstone, but while on a scout in that valley, they were told by some white men that the Nez Perces had broken out in Idaho, and they deserted Miles to go to their homes in Idaho. The name of the headman of these three was Grizzly Bear Youth. He acted like a grizzly bear in the Big Hole battle. This man had many engagements with the Sioux and always got away with the white feather. When he learned the hostile Nez Perces were on the Lolo Trail, he remained at the agency waiting for them to pass Missoula County. He was at the agency about one week. The news reached Missoula that these three Indians were at the agency obtaining cartridges from the trader Duncan McDonald, and it caused quite a disturbance of public feeling. But it was an error. These three men had a pack mule, but it was for blankets and cooking utensils, and not to pack cartridges. Duncan McDonald knows better than to let hostile Indians have cartridges. During his stay here, Grizzly Bear Youth found how near this point is to the national boundary line, and he thought he would go over to Lolo and see Looking Glass and tell him. Grizzly Bear Youth was, however, one of Lawyer's Nez Perces, was rich in horses, and desired to get back to the reserve in Idaho. Even before this, he tried to go through by the other route, but after reaching Horse Plains, forty-five miles from the agency, he turned back, thinking it was not safe to attempt to get through that way. Duncan McDonald told him he had better go by Lolo Trail and surrender to Howard.

Accordingly, the three Nez Perces started from the agency on Sunday afternoon for the Lolo Trail. Before leaving, Grizzly Bear Youth said here that if he should see Looking Glass, he would try to influence the Nez Perces to go through the Flathead reservation to Tobacco Plains and not through the settlements of the [Idaho] Territory. When he reached Lolo, he found that the Nez Perce camp was only a few miles above, and he concluded he might go over and see his relations, although he did not propose to join the camp. Before dismounting from his horse, he told the chiefs they were a band of fools, that it was folly for a handful of Indians to think of fighting the United States government. After dismounting, he went to Looking Glass and White Bird and told them what he thought it best for them to do—that was to turn back and go by the Flathead reservation and Flathead Lake to the British possessions.

Looking Glass then called a council and told Joseph and the others what Grizzly Bear Youth had said. White Bird and Red Owl agreed; they wanted to go by the reserve. Joseph did not say a word. Looking Glass wanted to go by Big Hole and down the Yellowstone and join the Crows, according to agreement, because the Crows had promised them that whenever the Nez Perces fought the whites, they would join them. There was a disagreement, but after quarreling among themselves, they concluded it was best to let Looking Glass have his way. This council was held about a mile or a mile and a half above McLain's ranch on the Bitterroot.

When the Indians were marching past the fortifications and down Lolo, the voice of Looking Glass could be distinctly heard addressing his warriors, "Don't shoot, don't shoot. Let the white men shoot first." This he repeated over and over. All this time, the soldiers and volunteers kept their positions in the breastworks. When the volunteers saw that Captain Rawn would not fire on the Indians, some of them started down the stream to head the Indians off. Looking Glass was on the alert for a movement of this kind and placed his best warriors between the volunteers and his women, children, and pack horses—in fact, as they passed down, the women and children were advanced ahead and the warriors held back to act as a rear guard. As they were moving down Lolo, they saw these volunteers dashing down Lolo with the evident purpose of cutting off the women and children. At the sight of this, the warriors believed certainly that they were going to have a fight and started with a yell in the direction of the volunteers. Captain Rawn, seeing the demonstrations of the volunteers and believing a collision was likely to occur between them and the Nez Perces, dispatched a half-breed named Pete Matte and a few Flatheads to ascertain whether a fight occurred and to report to him immediately. While Matte and his Flatheads were proceeding down Lolo, they met John Scott riding rapidly back toward Rawn's camp. He had his hat in his hand, using it as a whip, and his war horse was putting in his best licks. On meeting Matte, he told him an engagement was going on—that the volunteers were fighting. He wanted Matte to turn back lest he should be killed. But Matte kept on as he was ordered by Rawn, who desired to reinforce the volunteers if they engaged the Nez Perces. Matte came in sight of the volunteers just as the Nez Perce warriors started for them. The Indian fighters thought sure they had seen their last day and stampeded up Lolo toward Rawn's camp. A few halted when they had gone a little distance or when they had reached Matte and the Flatheads. Looking Glass and his warriors had swift horses and could have intercepted them in their line of retreat, and in case of a fight would have cut them off from Rawn and had the two parties at their mercy. The builders of the Lolo fortifications may have thought they were [in] a shelter, but they were mistaken. The rifle pits were exposed on one side, and on that side there was a steep mountain, covered with trees, fallen timber, and rocks, affording excellent cover for the Indian sharpshooters, from which they could have picked off those in the rifle pits at their leisure. It is true that there were a few splendid shots in the force, but two-thirds of them were not, and all the Indians were hunters, experienced fighters, and good marksmen.

I remember White Bird said that if war had opened on Lolo, the whole country would have been fired, and many a farmer would have lost his crops and home and perhaps his scalp. It is probable that the Nez Perces would then have moved north through the Flathead reservation. Whatever the chiefs of the reserve and Bitterroot Valley may have said about the peaceable disposition of their Indians, and that there was no danger of their joining the Nez Perces, such was a mistake. There were Indians on the Bitterroot and Flathead reserve who had their guns ready for use if a battle occurred at Lolo. Indians had been whispering at these places long before the hostiles reached Lolo. The writer of these papers stated in Missoula before ever Wahlitits, Tap-sis-ill-pilp, and U-em-till-lip-cown raised their hands in Idaho that a Nez Perce war would soon break out in that territory. My prediction was laughed at. Who would believe that the Nez Perces would take to the warpath? The situation was but little less threatening with some of the Flatheads and Pend'Oreilles in Missoula County.

After raising camp at McLain's, there was still some discussion as to the route to be taken—whether to the British possessions through the Flathead reservation, or to the Yellowstone via the Big Hole. If forced to fight, they proposed to join the Sioux or Crows in the Yellowstone country; if not, they designed to return to Idaho the next spring after getting their dried meat. Finally Looking Glass urged that he wanted to go by Big Hole because he knew the country better, and although this was only a pretext, as they could have found their way just as well northward, his wishes were respected, and they started up the Bitterroot Valley.

On reaching the place of Charlot, the Flathead chief, Looking Glass summoned a number of his warriors to accompany him to visit Charlot and inquire of him where the best place to camp was to find good grass. On approaching Charlot's house, Looking Glass thought it would be honorable to extend his hand to Charlot before making his inquiry. But Charlot refused to accept the extended hand, saying, "Why should I shake hands with men whose hands are bloody? My hands are clean of blood." Looking Glass replied, "Your hands are as red with the blood of your enemies as mine are. Why should my hands be clean when I have been forced to fight the white man? Your hands are as bloody as ours. I did not come to talk about blood. I came to ask you the best place to camp." Charlot answered, "Above my house is the best spot to camp," and there they accordingly pitched their tents.

Looking Glass kept close watch of his warriors while camped near Stevensville, in which town they did considerable trading. He sent several to camp for being disorderly. It was very fine for the officers sitting in camp and indulging in strong drink to condemn the people of Stevensville for selling these Indians goods and provisions, and allege that they were aiding the Nez Perces to recruit for their march, and that they should be punished therefore. This talk was something like Howard's. Their words have more force than their deeds. These Nez Perces would never stand before a little town like Stevensville and perish of starvation when plenty could be had there. The Nez Perces under Looking Glass offered to buy from the first, but if they had been refused and obliged to resort to that measure, they would have plundered. Had as many soldiers as there were men been stationed in Stevensville and a band of starving Nez Perces like these been refused food, the soldiers with all the laws of the United States on their side would have lasted but a short time. It was fortunate for Stevensville that citizens and not soldiers had possession of it. Under the circumstances, the citizens of Stevensville did right.

An incident happened during the time of the encampment near Stevensville that illustrates the indisposition of the Nez Perces to have any conflict with the people of Montana. A citizen wished to visit the Indian camp. He mounted his best riding horse and, accompanied by a half-breed who had presented Looking Glass with fifty pounds of flour, rode thereto. It should be remembered that Looking Glass had no lodge nor even cooking utensils. He camped in the open air and received his meals from his warriors. He was so glad to receive as a visitor the half-breed who had presented him with the sack of flour that he invited him to have a smoke. He noticed the actions of the citizen and told him there was a certain portion of the camp which it would be best for him not to visit— that some of their relations had been killed in Idaho, and it was not best for him to go near them. The citizen, however, wanted to trade off his horse for a fortune and went charging around the camp promiscuously, making his steed prance and caper, and asking the Nez Perces three of their good horses for his one. He had many good offers to trade but always refused. In any other camp than the Nez Perces, he would have been packed off, and that would have been the last of him and his funny horse. In one of his circuits, he went to that part of the camp which he had been advised by Looking Glass to avoid. A wounded Nez Perce, some of whose relations had been killed in Idaho, was standing by a log and resting on his gun. On seeing the white man cavorting around in an impudent way, the Indian said in English, "Me give you three horses; my horses very good ones." The white man refused. It seemed that he only wanted to put on style. This made the warrior angry and he exclaimed, "You go home, you damn white man; you [bastard]." It was a wonder he was not killed. But he left hastily, and if that funny horse of his had a 1:40 gait in him, it was brought out as the citizen lit out for Stevensville.

Not being acquainted with the country above Stevensville, I am unable to designate the other camping places. An incident, however, occurred near the head of Bitterroot Valley, at Lockwood's ranch I believe, which I wish to relate. A certain band of the Nez Perces were under command of Toohoolhoolzote, the same Indian who was made prisoner by Howard in Idaho when he was elected speaker of the tribe at the council. This was the worst band in the whole camp and a very unruly lot. While passing Lockwood's ranch, some of this band went into the cabin and helped themselves to about two hundred pounds of flour, thirty or forty pounds of coffee, one file, two or three shirts, and some other small articles. On reaching camp, they went to Looking Glass and told him what they had done. Looking Glass was very angry and told Toohoolhoolzote that unless they obeyed his orders, they should be put out of the camp. He said he would not permit plundering and demanded seven head of horses from those Indians as payment for the articles they had stolen. The thieves consented to give up seven head of horses and leave them at the ranch, but Looking Glass would not be satisfied until they branded the horses with Lockwood's brand and left them at his ranch. I understand that Lockwood, not satisfied with the seven horses left him, went on the warpath, joined Gibbon's command, got shot at the Big Hole battle and lost his brother at the same place.

While traveling slowly toward Big Hole, dragging their lodge poles, White Bird went to Looking Glass and said, "Why do you allow the camp to drag lodge poles? By the way you are acting, you seem to anticipate no danger. How do we know but that some of these days or nights we shall be attacked by the whites. We should be prepared for trouble. Let your lodge poles be destroyed and move as rapidly as possible without them to the buffalo plains."

Looking Glass answered, "That is all nonsense and bosh. Who is going to trouble us? What wrong did we do in passing through the Bitterroot settlements? I think that we did very well in going through the country peaceably with a band of hostiles like we have got. We are in no hurry. The little bunch of soldiers from Missoula are not fools enough to attack us. We had best take the world as easily as possible. We are not fighting with the people of this country."

White Bird replied, "Well, it is no harm to be prepared. We know the whites want us to surrender our arms to them. We were told while in the Bitterroot Valley there were soldiers and volunteers all over the country, in front and rear, looking for us. If they want us to surrender our arms to them, they will have to fight for them."

Looking Glass said, "Oh, there is no danger."

Another Indian, well known among themselves as a medicine man, said to the chiefs a day before the battle of Big Hole, "What are we doing here?" After singing his song, he continued, "While I slept, my medicine told me to move on, that death is approaching us. Chief, I only tell you this because it may be of some good to this camp. If you take my advice, we can avoid death, and that advice is to speed through this country. If not, there will be tears in our eyes in a short time."

Now, reader, let me explain about Indian "medicine." The Indians' belief may seem ridiculous to civilized people, but the Indians believe in their medicine as implicitly as Ignatius, Loyola, or the Jesuits believed or believe in Christ, or a Chinaman believes in Confucius. The Indian medicine man goes to the mountains and starves himself for several days to obtain his medicines. So long as his stomach contains any food whatever he can obtain no medicine. His system must be purified from all edible matter, his body must be made clean by ablutions, and he must have faith that his desires for medicine will be granted. These medicines are chiefly beast, fowls, insects, and fishes of all kinds, which come to him and tell him what is going to happen. It seems the Spiritualists have somewhat similar beliefs.

I am not speaking of the semicivilized tribes, but of the native Indians in their wildest state. Their superstition on this point has cost many a life. The writer of these papers has had many difficulties because he does not choose to believe in what the medicine men say. It is not strange. A man in the south of Ireland who abused a priest might be killed by some devout believer. The Indians are as fixed in their belief in the medicine man. I do not ask readers to believe as they do; I am, however, explaining a matter that has a great deal to do with the actions of Indians.

When the medicine man had advised the chiefs of what to do, Looking Glass, although he protested his inability to see where danger was to come from, ordered camp to be moved forward, and they camped that night on the Big Hole battleground. The Nez Perces say they had seen white men moving down the distant hills. These were some of Bradley's scouts, who have believed they were not discovered by the Indians. The Indians gave the matter little attention. They thought they were merely scouts watching their movements, a surveillance to which they had become accustomed, and they knew that the little band of soldiers that had tried to bar their passage of the Lolo was following them. They did not know this little band had been reinforced by

Gibbon's command from Fort Shaw. They had no idea they would be attacked by the Lolo soldiers.

On the night they camped at the battleground, most of the warriors were up until a late hour engaged in their war dance. This caused a deep sleep to fall on them after they went to their lodges. Some of them slept so soundly they never awakened. The camp, not apprehending danger, was sleeping soundly, when suddenly the rifles of the soldiers belched forth their deadly fire. The camp was awakened to find their enemies plunging through it, dealing death and destruction in every direction. Colonel Gibbon had all the advantage of a complete surprise.

With the soldiers in the midst of their camp before they were even awakened, those who could fled to the brush along a brook. Here it was that White Bird and Looking Glass displayed the valor of true chieftains, rallied their warriors from a rout, and plucked a victory from the very jaws of defeat. White Bird was the first to rally his warriors to a charge upon the soldiers. "Why are we retreating?" he shouted in Nez Perce. "Since the world was made, brave men fight for their women and children. Are we going to run to the mountains and let the whites kill our women and children before our eyes? It is better we should be killed fighting. Now is our time; fight! These soldiers cannot fight harder than the ones we defeated on Salmon River and in White Bird Canyon. Fight! Shoot them down. We can shoot as well as any of these soldiers." At these words, the warriors wheeled around and started back to fight the soldiers in their camp.

Looking Glass was at the other end of the camp. His voice was heard calling out, "Wahlitits! Tap-sis-ill-pilp! U-em-till-lip-cown! This is a battle! These men are not asleep as were those you murdered in Idaho! These soldiers mean battle. You tried to break my promise at Lolo. You wanted to fire at the fortified place. Now is the time to show your courage and fight. You can kill right and left. I would rather see you killed than the rest of the warriors, for you commenced the war. Now go ahead and fight."

The warriors addressed were so angered and aroused they did not care for their lives, and rallied to the charge with those led by White Bird. Some of them said they had heard the white man was a good fighter, but he seemed to fight best when his enemy was asleep.

Many women and children were killed before getting out of their beds. In one lodge there were five children. One soldier went into it and killed every one of them. When the warriors rallied and opened fire, they poured their shot into the soldiers so rapidly and effectively that the soldiers suffered considerable loss and soon retreated to a point of timber near the trail. In the midst of the hottest of the fight, Tap-sis-ill-pilp was killed. Wahlitits, on being told his companion was dead, ran right into the soldiers and was shot down dead in his tracks.[19] Thus did two of the three murderers who brought on the war expiate their offense, and it is due to them to say that they died as brave as the bravest.

Before these two men were killed, an episode of interest occurred at the lodges. In a fight between an officer and a warrior, the warrior was shot down dead. The warrior's sister was standing by him when he fell, and as he lay there, his six-shooter lay by his side. The woman, seeing her brother dying and the blood running from his mouth, seized the six-shooter, leveled it at the officer, fired, shot him through the head, and killed him. From all the information I can obtain, I believe the officer was Captain Logan.

While the soldiers were retreating across to the timber, Grizzly Bear Youth followed them and was doing rapid work with his Henry rifle. If I remember correctly the description, there was a crossing or slough the soldiers had to go over that impeded them. While the soldiers were at this place, a volunteer turned around and commenced damning the Indians lustily. He is described as a tall, ugly looking man, and I will describe the incident following as it was related to me by Grizzly Bear Youth last summer at the Sioux camp near Fort Walsh.

"When I was following the soldiers, trying to kill as many of them as possible, a big, ugly volunteer turned around swearing and made for me. I suppose he had no time to load his needle gun, so he swung it over his head by the barrel and rushed at me to strike me over the head with the butt end. I did the same thing. We both struck, and each received a blow on the head. The volunteer's gun put a brand on my forehead that will be seen as long as I live. My blow on his head made him fall on his back. I jumped on him and tried to hold him down. The volunteer was a powerful man. He turned me over and got on top. He got his hand on my throat and commenced choking me. I was almost gone and had just strength left to make signs to a warrior who was coming up to shoot him. This was Red Owl's son, who ran up, put his needle gun to the volunteer's side, and fired. The ball passed through him and killed him. But I had my arm around the waist of the man when the shot was fired, and the ball, after going through the volunteer, broke my arm."

This was the second scuffle Grizzly Bear Youth had in the Big Hole battle. The other man was a soldier, but he did not last long.

I dissent from the plea that the women had to be shot because they fought as well as the men. It was shameful the way women and children were shot down in that fight. The five children I mentioned were sleeping when they were killed. It was reported Sergeant Wilson killed nine Indians. Yes, nine women and children. I understand he received a medal from the government for his bravery at Big Hole. Instead of receiving a medal, he should have been court-martialed. It is a well-known fact that the command wasted more powder and lead on the women and children than on the warriors. There were seventy-eight Indians, all told, killed in the Big Hole battle. Of these, only thirty were warriors. The others were women and children. About forty women and children were piled up in one little ravine where they had run for shelter. Many women, with from one to three children in their arms, were found dead in that ravine. Some of the children had their mother's breasts in their mouths when both were found there dead. What reason could the soldiers have had to kill them? Had the warriors been with them, we might have believed the soldiers could not help it. A daughter of Looking Glass, now north of the line, had hundreds of bullets whiz past her while crawling with a child in her arms to find shelter. The gallant 7th Infantry! It should be called the Cursed 7th! They were not satisfied in killing Indians whom they found asleep. They must kill women and children, too. Why, if they wanted to kill women, did they not kill the woman who killed Captain Logan? It is said she was killed on the spot. It is a lie. I do not even blame her. Any woman would have done the same. There was her brother dying at her feet, his loaded revolver lying by his side. What sister would not have seized it and avenged her brother's death?

While the fight was going on in the morning, some of the Nez Perces noticed the howitzer approaching the battleground. They charged upon the squad with it, killing, I believe, the man in command. After capturing the howitzer, they damaged it so that, as they believed, it could not be used. A few minutes later an Indian reached the gun and expressed great regrets that it was rendered useless. He said, "It is a great pity. I know how to use this kind of gun. I learned when I was with Colonel Wright fighting Cayuses and Yakimas."

According to White Bird's statement, Gibbon's command retreated to a high point and entrenched itself. It was thereby saved temporarily, but White Bird did not deem the place impregnable. It was another circumstance that saved Gibbon—the Indians were informed Howard's command was close up on their trail and that volunteers were coming from the eastern part of the territory. They continued to harass Gibbon and would have stayed with him till they wore him out, had they not been apprehensive of his receiving reinforcements. They got their news in this way. About the time the main fight was over and the warriors were examining their dead, they discovered a white man, a citizen, breathing, with his eyes closed and pretending to be dead, although he was not even wounded. When they found he was playing possum, they took hold of his arms and raised him up. Finding the Indians were too smart to let him get away, he jumped to his feet. Looking Glass ordered the warriors not to kill him, saying that he was a citizen and they might obtain information from him concerning Howard. They then questioned him, and in reply, he said Howard would be there in a short time, and that plenty of volunteers were coming from Virginia [City] to head them off. While he was telling the news, a woman who had lost her brother and some of her children in the fight came up. She was crying at the time and, on seeing the citizen, slapped him in the face. He instantly gave her a vigorous kick with his boot. He had not more than kicked her when some of the warriors killed him. He would not have been killed had he refrained from kicking her. His statement decided them to raise camp and move on to a more secure place.

White Bird says the volunteers fought better than the regular soldiers, but it was a shame for the Bitterroot volunteers, after the Nez Perces had treated them so well, to join Gibbon and fight them. A white man must have no respect for himself. It makes no difference how well he is treated by the Indians, he will take the advantage. The Nez Perces felt that they behaved themselves while passing through the Bitterroot, and now feel sorer toward the people of that valley than they do toward the soldiers. The officer remembered as having acted most manly in the Big Hole fight is Captain Browning. He stopped his soldiers from killing two women in front of him.

The Nez Perces were crippled more in the Big Hole battle by Colonel Gibbon than in any battle before or after. It was in this fight they lost their best warriors.

And here I wish to make a correction. In my article last week I stated that the woman who shot Captain Logan escaped unharmed. In this I was mistaken. She was killed on the spot by a soldier.

The particulars of the killing of the murderers of the Hayden party and the ranchmen at Horse Prairie and Birch Creek[20] are not generally known to the Nez Perces After numerous inquiries, I find there were two men killed at one place. One of them was murdered in his cabin, and the other while endeavoring to escape from the cabin. It must be remembered the Nez Perces were actuated at this time to commit murders by a spirit of revenge. They had just met with a considerable loss in the battle of the Big Hole and felt that every white man in their path was their enemy, and by taking his life they could thereby avenge the death of their comrades. After the battle with Gibbon's command, the march was resumed. The Indians first came in contact with a party in which there were several white men and two Chinamen. The exact number of whites is not known, but it is thought the number did not exceed six. The party had wagons and a lot of mules, and the Indians came upon them while they were in camp; the Indian camp was made near the train. The whites had in their possession some whiskey, which they proposed trading to the Indians for articles of which they stood in need. While the trade was in progress, it began to grow dark. This suited the young and reckless Indians, and as soon as it was dark, they proceeded to help themselves. Under the influence and stimulated by copious draughts of the intoxicant, their hatred for the white race was intensified, and they fired their guns into the train. As soon as the firing was begun, the whites and Chinamen beat a retreat. I say they beat a retreat. The Indians did not make an examination to find whether or not they had killed any of the party, but after the volley, they approached and rifled the train, taking all the articles in the wagons and camp. They also took the animals. This ended the fight at this place.

The place at which this occurred is not known to either the Indians or the writer. As has been stated, the route was new and unknown to the Indians. Following is the language of my informant: "We did not ask the whites under whose command they were. The fact that they were under command of Hayden was of no interest to us. All we wanted was the whiskey in their possession. Once that was obtained, the appropriation of the rest of the possessions was merely a question of time. An Indian under the influence of whiskey has no more sense than a white man when drunk and is not any more responsible for his actions. When an Indian is drunk, he will commit crimes he would not think of when sober. As an evidence of the truth of this statement only to say that while under the influence of the whiskey captured from the train, one of the bravest and best warriors in the Nez Perce band was killed and another narrowly escaped death at the hands of their comrades."

While the Nez Perce camp was moving beyond Camas Meadow, two days ahead of Howard's command, Grizzly Bear Youth lay in his tent suffering from the wounds received in the Big Hole fight. Here a great bird, that never alights on the earth or trees but rests only in the clouds, appeared to the sufferer in his lodge. In regard to this bird, it is claimed by the Nez Perces to live in their country, that it is never seen except by those wishing it for their medicine. They also say it is much larger and far superior to the eagle and will pick up game of any kind and fly with it. This bird was the medicine of Grizzly Bear Youth, who was awakened from a troubled sleep into which he had fallen by the voice of the bird, which said, "I see you have tears in your eyes, caused by grieving over the loss of your relatives, your country, and your arm. Why do you cry? Look behind about two days' travel and you will see two creeks. These creeks are at Camas Meadow. The big chief of the Idaho soldiers, 'Cut Arm,'[21] and his force are camped there. It is rather a strong force, but fear them not. The Nez Perces will kill some of his men and get possession of his animals. There are two kinds of animals in the camp. I can tell you the name of only one kind. This kind is horses. The other differ from the horse in many ways. Now I must leave you. You may rely on what I have told you. Good luck to you." The bird then disappeared.

It is customary for Indians, when they have received news from their medicine, to summon all their brethren and inform them of what they have been told. Grizzly Bear Youth sent for the warriors, who came to his lodge. After singing his medicine song, he told the Indians of the news he had received from his medicine, the Air Bird. He told them that next night Cut Arm's animals would be in their possession. One-half of the animals were horses; the other half he could not describe. He further said, "I want all the warriors to go back to Camas Meadow tomorrow evening."

When the talk at Grizzly Bear Youth's lodge was over, the warriors retired and the camp was soon quiet. While they slept, two scouts who had been sent to look for Howard's command returned to the camp. They immediately went to Looking Glass and told him that Howard would camp next day at Camas Meadow and that he had with him a large pack train. Looking Glass at once summoned the Nez Perces and told them that he wanted the warriors, with the exception of twenty-five who were to remain under charge of White Bird to guard the camp, to get ready to go and attack Howard. Accordingly, about two hundred and twenty-five warriors, under command of Looking Glass and Joseph, left the camp next morning. They sent scouts all over the country and, traveling slowly, reached Howard's camp about midnight. The Indians were told not to approach the camp until so ordered by Looking Glass, who first sent spies to examine the location. The report made to the camp showed that there were two creeks about three hundred yards apart. Howard's command crossed both creeks and went into camp. The Virginia [City] volunteers made their camp before crossing the second creek. The night was so dark the spies had not discovered the volunteer camp, and they were under the impression that their enemies were all with Howard. It was very lucky indeed for the volunteers that their presence was not known.

On learning the situation, Looking Glass thought it best to have no fight. He told the warriors he only wanted to capture the stock, and that they were to make no move until so ordered by him. A short time before daybreak, he gave the order to approach the camp. In obeying, a deathlike stillness was observed. The Indians made their way on their hands and knees. Howard's pickets could be heard conversing in a low tone of voice. The Indians afterward said they could have captured all the cavalry horses if they had only known where they were, but the night was so dark that they feared the reports of the spies might be incorrect, and they were consequently in doubt as to the real position of the soldiers. After getting close to the camp, Looking Glass ordered his men to prepare for a charge, and told them if they could capture the animals without fighting, it would be the better way, as he only wanted the animals. He also said, "We know American horses are afraid of Indians; make all the noise you possibly can, as by so doing we may be able to stampede the whole herd at once."

The order to charge was given, and the work of stampeding the stock commenced. Ever and anon the voice of Looking Glass could be heard, calling on the Indians to pay no heed to the soldiers but secure the horses. His men obeyed his commands and rent the air with the most hideous yells. They succeeded in capturing over two hundred head of animals—one-half of which were mules. (These latter were the ones which the medicine bird could not describe.) While driving the herd a short distance from the scene of attack, some soldiers were discovered in pursuit. The first thought was that Howard's command was after them, but it subsequently proved to be only a small body of cavalry. These were the troops which were subjected to the whitewashing process in the newspapers—Captain Norwood's command, I believe. Looking Glass ordered the stolen animals to be left in charge of three warriors and the rest of his force to conceal themselves. He said, "Let the fool in command of the soldiers come up to us. Does he think he can take these animals from us with the force he has? Make haste and hide yourselves."

The Indian force was divided and two lines formed, the warriors concealing themselves behind trees, rocks, etc. Looking Glass wanted Norwood to advance between the lines formed, but the officer was too wary to be drawn

Nez Perce driving ponies at Camas Meadow. HARPER'S WEEKLY, 1877.

into the trap. He stationed his men some distance away and commenced firing. Looking Glass ordered his men not to fire; he thought the soldiers had not yet seen them and were only firing by guesswork. The troops failing to advance, orders were given to the Indians to fire, and the fight commenced. The Indians endeavored to get the soldiers between the lines formed, and had they succeeded, there would have been a massacre similar to that when Custer's command were killed by Sitting Bull and his warriors. The Indians finally made a charge, and the troops retreated to a point of timber. While here the Nez Perces became uneasy lest Howard's command should have heard the firing and reinforce the troops under Norwood. Joseph and Looking Glass held a consultation, and as they had suffered no loss whatever, they started back to their camp.

This ended the great battle of Camas Meadow. About noon the Indians halted, and Looking Glass divided the stolen animals among his warriors.

━━ ≍◊≍ ━━

When the Nez Perces were camped at Bear's Paw Mountains, Poker Joe grew dissatisfied with the other chiefs for not making their way into the British possessions. Poker Joe had a good deal of influence over the Indians, but after a discussion with the chiefs, and they not agreeing to his plans, he declined having anything further to do with their future movements. Howard's whereabouts were known to the Indians. They knew his animals were worn out, while their own were in splendid condition. As a consequence, they were in no hurry to move their camp and spent their time in making merry, as they then had no doubt but they would effect their escape without difficulty. They had no intimation of the approach of the troops under Colonel Miles.

While resting in fancied security on the morning of the attack, the scouts being all in camp, an alarm was suddenly given. The cry was "Prepare for a fight; there is a large body of soldiers close on us." White Bird ordered his warriors to prepare for a defense and said, "What a pity we did not have scouts out. Had we known this half an hour ago, how differently might we now have been situated. Had I known then of the approach of the soldiers, we would not have to fight. Our horses are fresh and we could have made our escape. But it is too late now. Escape is impossible—fight we must."

About the battle of Bear's Paw, I have not much to write, as the Indian version is but a repetition of the published accounts. The Indians got worsted in the engagement, as is well known, and the white man's version was the true one. I propose relating, however, the conversation between Looking Glass and White Bird, some facts in relation to the officer who was taken prisoner, and the promises made Joseph by the commanding officer in charge of the soldiers in case the Indians would surrender.

Colonel Miles, like many others, supposed Joseph to be the leader of the hostiles and wanted his surrender in place of the real leader—Looking Glass. This suited the Indians exactly, and they allowed Joseph to go to the camp of the soldiers. That night he remained in the tent of Colonel Miles. During the truce, the Indians were engaged in fortifying their position, and some soldiers under command of Lieutenant [Jerome] who ventured into the Indian camp were taken prisoners and held as hostages for the return of Joseph. The fight was renewed at this time. In the afternoon of the second day, an exchange was effected, the soldiers returning to their command and Joseph to the Indian camp. Before the exchange, while the fight was in progress, one of the warriors was in need of some needle-gun cartridges. He went to the officer who was yet a prisoner and told him what he wanted. He asked for two cartridges and was given five by the officer, whose name I was told was Lieutenant [Jerome]. A few such men as him in the Indian camp would have made more trouble for the soldiers.

While the fight was in progress, many of the Indian women and a few children made their escape. A large part of the camp believed that Sitting Bull was near at hand and that he would come to their rescue. One of the women had escaped at the first appearance of the soldiers, and it was thought she had gone to the Sioux camp. But such was not the case, as the woman went but a short distance and remained until the fight was over.

On the evening of the fourth day, a flag of truce was raised for the third time. Colonel Miles told the Indians that if they surrendered, he would treat them well, that he would take them to Tongue River that winter, and in the spring would send them back to Idaho. He furthermore said that any promises he might make to them would be fulfilled. Joseph wanted to surrender, but the other chiefs kept him from doing so. They feared that in case they were to surrender to Colonel Miles, they would be treated similarly to the Indians who surrendered to Colonel Wright on the Columbia in 1858. After surrendering, the principals were all hanged by command of the officer to whom they surrendered. Joseph endeavored to persuade the chiefs that the best thing they could do was to accede to the demands made by Colonel Miles. Looking Glass and White Bird then said, "Joseph, you do not know the Americans as well as we do. Never in the world will they fulfill the promises made the Indians. The commanding officer speaks sweet, but it is doubtful whether he will send the Indians back to their country." Next morning Joseph told Looking Glass he had concluded to surrender to Colonel Miles. The latter chief then went to White Bird, told him the conclusion arrived at by Joseph, and said, "We will leave here tonight. I know we will never see our country again."

Near the Indian camp was a ridge on which some of the warriors lay watching the movements of the soldiers. Looking Glass, his brother, and the other chiefs were in the camp talking over the proposed flight in the evening. Looking Glass requested his brother to get him his pipe, saying he wanted a smoke. While his brother had gone for the pipe, Looking Glass had his attention attracted by the movements of the warriors on the ridge. He started towards them. He was asked to remain where he was, but the chief replied that he would return shortly, that he wanted to see what the warriors on the ridge were doing. He reached the place where the warriors were. It was some five or six hundred yards from the soldiers' position. He raised himself up to view the surroundings. As he did so, a volley from the guns of the soldiers was directed towards him, and one of the bullets entered his forehead, throwing him some distance down the hill and killing him instantly. Poker Joe, the friend of the lady prisoners taken in the national park, was also killed in the Bear's Paw fight.

White Bird and his warriors escaped that night. In the escaping party were one hundred three warriors, sixty women, eight children, and about two hundred head of horses. One remarkable feature of the party was that there were no dogs with them. An Indian procession is usually considered incomplete unless there are in it a number of these latter animals. In a residence of thirty years in the Indian country, I have not heard of a parallel case.

Joseph could have escaped as well as White Bird, but the conditions promised him by Colonel Miles influenced him to surrender. If he had endeavored to escape, he would have had on his hands his wounded warriors and helpless women and children. He thought it the better plan to rely on the word of the officer to whom he surrendered—the representative of a nation of forty million people.

→+ ⚔ +←

After White Bird made his escape from the U.S. troops at Bear's Paw and before he reached Sitting Bull's camp, he lost seven warriors by the Assiniboine and Gros Ventres. One of the killed was U-em-till-lilp-cown, the third and last of the Nez Perces who committed the murders in Idaho which brought on the war.

White Bird did not know whether or not it would be safe for him to go to Sitting Bull's camp, but after a consultation with his followers, they came to the conclusion they might as well be killed by Indian enemies as by the whites.

Coming to a half-breed camp near Milk River, they hired one of the party to guide them to Sitting Bull. As they were proceeding toward the Sioux camp, they came upon an Indian skinning a buffalo. The hunter appeared rather shy but, after considerable parley, told White Bird that he was a Sioux and that he had come from Sitting Bull's camp. White Bird told him to go to Sitting Bull and tell him the Nez Perces were anxious to see him, that they were refugees, fleeing for protection from the U.S. troops. The buffalo hunter started on his mission, and the Nez Perce camp moved slowly in the direction he had gone. After marching a few miles, they discovered a large body of mounted Indians coming toward them. They numbered nearly three thousand warriors and were coming at full speed. A short distance in advance of the main body rode an Indian warrior on a magnificent war horse. When within hailing distance of the Nez Perces, the command halted. The warrior in advance asked White Bird, by signs, to what tribe he belonged. White Bird made answer, saying he was a Nez Perce. The other then said, "I am Sitting Bull, and these," pointing to his followers, "are my warriors." Sitting Bull then came up and shook hands with White Bird and his warriors. After bidding them welcome, he said, "I am sorry indeed that your skin is like mine, that your hair is like mine, and that every one around you is a pure red man like myself. We, too, have lost our country by falsehood and theft."

Although the Indians were now north of the line, they expected to be followed and attacked by U.S. soldiers. The Sioux had not thus far been attacked, but they did not know but now that so many soldiers were near them they would follow the Indians and give them battle. Sitting Bull, after hearing of the Bear's Paw fight, said, "If I had known you were surrounded by soldiers at Bear's Paw Mountains, I certainly would have helped you. What a pity that I was not there with my warriors. But now you are here, and as long as you are with me, I will not allow the Americans to take even a child from you without fighting for it." Sitting Bull received a present of seven horses from White Bird. The Nez Perces were welcomed in the Sioux camp and received from Sitting Bull and his followers nothing but the kindest of treatment.

Yellow Bull's Story

CHUSLUM MOXMOX (YELLOW BULL)[1]

Walter M. Camp Papers, Folder 59, Little Bighorn National Monument, Crow Agency, Montana

When the Nez Perces left Kamiah, they had no intention of going to Canada, but had planned to cut a circle and come back to the Salmon River. After the battle of Big Hole River they crossed the mountains and went back into Idaho, but later changed their minds and started for Canada.

Just after they crossed the Yellowstone on the way to Canada, they had a fight with the soldiers at Canyon Creek and lost a large part of their herd of horses. After this there was continual dissension and quarreling among the Nez Perces. Looking Glass insisted on short marches, and his advice prevailed. Joseph was chief only of his own band and had no authority over the Nez Perces as a whole. The planning of the fighting was in the hands of a committee of chiefs and warriors, and Pile of Clouds was at the head of this committee.[2]

We got to the place where the battle of Bear's Paw Mountain was fought the day before the fight. Nearly everyone wanted to go on, as we knew that we had not reached Canada yet, but Looking Glass again had his own way, and so we stopped and began to dry buffalo skins and meat. The night before the fight, two of our scouts came in and reported that they had seen signs which seemed to indicate the approach of soldiers a long way off. The matter was discussed. It was thought that soldiers could not be so near us, and that the scouts must be mistaken. We did not believe that the one-arm general and his soldiers could follow us so closely, and we did not know that other soldiers were in that part of the country.

The next morning about 8:00 A.M.[3] there was a sudden alarm of the approach of soldiers, and the soldiers charged right up to our village. We stood our ground, and the soldiers fell back. Ollokot and some others pursued them, and Ollokot was shot through the head and killed. The fighting stopped about noon. Most of the killed on both sides were killed during the fighting of this forenoon.

That night we dug rifle pits with knives and hatchets. We had a council, at which I was present, and White Bird told Joseph that he would remain and help fight it out. He broke his word, however, for he soon skipped out without

Yellow Bull. NATIONAL ANTHROPOLOGICAL MUSEUM, SMITHSONIAN INSTITUTION.

saying anything, taking 103 people with him.[4] The next morning we had dirt and rocks piled up and were ready to fight the soldiers.

About thirty of our men mounted up and started to make a sally to deceive the soldiers. This movement was unknown to Looking Glass, and as he raised his head to see what the whooping and yelling was about, he was shot and killed. Toohoolhoolzote and five more were killed in one of the pits. Husis Kute[5] was not killed, but died in Idaho afterward. White Bird never came back to Idaho. He was killed in Canada by one of his own people during a quarrel.[6]

The Story of the Nez Perce Campaign during the Summer of 1877

HENRY BUCK[1]

Great Falls (Montana) *Tribune,* December 24, 1944–February 11, 1945[2]

The summer of 1877 was the most eventful and exciting time in all history as pertains to the Bitterroot Valley and many parts of Montana. Indian troubles were always considered hair-raising events, and people generally on the frontier were suspicious that something awful might happen when there was a raising of bad blood amongst the natives.

In this special summer our government was having trouble with the Nez Perce Indians just over the range of Bitterroot Mountains, at Lapwai and Mount Idaho, in Idaho, in regard to the tribe's removal to the reservation set apart for their new home. A portion of the Nez Perce tribe had signed the treaty, accepted their allotments, and had removed. But a certain portion were refractory and had refused to go, although many parleys had been held and persuasion used to induce them all to abide by the provisions that Uncle Sam thought best for their well-being. All efforts seemed to have failed, hence Brig. Gen. O. O. Howard was sent into their midst with troops to carry out, with force if necessary, their removal.

Up to this time the Nez Perce Indians were considered a peaceable, energetic, and active tribe of more than ordinary intelligence. They often boasted that they had never shed the blood of a white man, but upon the appearance of troops, it seemed to fire them to wrath, and they openly avowed that they would fight if the soldiers attempted to interfere. Up to this time the chiefs—Joseph, Looking Glass, and White Bird—of the refractory portion of the Nez Perces were not resolved to make the stand and fight; but on the other hand, were almost persuaded to accept the wishes of the government and remove in peace to their new home on the Lapwai reservation.

TROUBLE BEGINS

This trouble, which had been brewing for some time, finally culminated on June 14, when a party of marauding Nez Perces belonging to the refractory band murdered some three or four white men at Slate Creek, about forty miles from Mount Idaho.[3] The torch of war was thus ignited, and immediately the

Indians brought a heavy pressure to bear on their chiefs to go at once on the warpath—fight, murder, and plunder—holding that they were in their homes, the country was theirs, and they would hold it at all hazards.

The chiefs and headmen of the tribe, therefore, held a council and were unable to resist the pressure brought upon them by the tribesmen, hence war was declared in earnest.

Realizing the despotism of the Indians, the following dispatch was sent on the fifteenth by L. P. Brown, one of the leading citizens of Mount Idaho, to the commanding officer[4] at Fort Lapwai:

> Last night we started a messenger[5] to you who reached Cottonwood House, where he was wounded and driven back by the Indians. The people of Cottonwood undertook to come here during the night [and] were intercepted—all wounded or killed.[6] Parties this morning found some of them on the prairie. The wounded will be here shortly, and we will get full particulars. The whites—about forty of them—are engaged in getting the wounded. One thing is certain, we are in the midst of an Indian war. Every family is here, and we will take all precautions we can but are poorly armed. We want arms and ammunition and help at once. Don't delay a moment. We have report that some whites were killed yesterday on the Salmon River; no later word from them. Fear that the people were all killed as a party of Indians was seen going that way last night. Send to Lewistown and hasten up. You can't imagine people in a worse position than they are here. Mr. West has volunteered to go to Lapwai. Rely on his statements.

In answer to this message two companies of cavalry were dispatched to their relief at 5:00 P.M. the same day and arrived at Mount Idaho (sixty-two miles) the following day. From this time on until their final expulsion from Idaho, killing, destroying property, plundering, insulting women, and fighting were their [the Indians'] determinations.

General Howard immediately began getting his forces together to combat the enemy—all the time hoping that the Indians would eventually realize their hopeless condition, surrender, and accept the terms of the government. But bad led to worse, fighting ensued, and General Howard spent a whole month chasing this refractory band of Indians from place to place, indulging in small skirmishes here and there. Being naturally very tenderhearted and also religiously inclined, he avoided a clash as much as possible rather than strike a decisive blow that would bring these fugitives to justice and end the conflict then and there.

RESULTS OF THE CAMPAIGN IN IDAHO

In pursuing the chase, the Indians were kept out of the settlements as much as possible. At one time on the Clearwater, I was subsequently informed by some

of General Howard's soldiers that he had them corralled and could have conquered them, but was afraid he might hurt some of the Indians if he should
strike too hard, so eased up and let the whole band get away over the Lolo Trail.

About this juncture, the Idaho press said many uncomplimentary things
about General Howard's maneuvers, and judging from my own experience
while with the army under General Howard's command, I have often thought
that his soldiers had good reason for censuring the general for lack of initiative
in prosecuting the capture. He was constantly criticized for being too slow;
that he had sadly missed his calling, for he would have made a far better Sunday school teacher than an Indian fighter.

Summing up results thus far, we find that General Howard succeeded in
driving the Indians out of the settlements, while on the other hand the Indians
had defeated two companies of soldiers in a pitched battle; eluded their pursuers; crossed the Salmon River and cut off Howard's communications; kept
the cavalry on the defensive; defeated a company of soldiers; concentrated and
fought the army for two days; then, on July 18, stole away silently over the
Lolo Trail in search of a new home. Although the tribe had been victorious
thus far, they decided it would be better to settle in a new territory where they
could remain at peace rather than maintain their supremacy in Idaho under
constant strife, and so set out for Canada to establish their future abode.

GENERAL HOWARD PREPARES TO FOLLOW THE INDIANS

Our people in the Bitterroot, and in Montana generally, felt very sore at General Howard and severely censured him for chasing the Indians out of Idaho
and onto us while in peaceful pursuit of our daily avocations. This practically
ended the campaign so far as General Howard was concerned, as the Nez
Perces were out of his jurisdiction. The department at Washington, however,
did not feel satisfied to let General Howard cease the chase, so ordered him to
take up the trail and follow whither it might lead; strike the fugitives to defeat,
if possible, and bring them to justice.

Preparations were then made for the long march to the Bitterroot River in
Montana. It was necessary for Howard to concentrate his troops, gather supplies for the trip, organize a company of civilians for special duties, and work
out all details before a move could be made toward following the Indians
across that vast, unpopulated wilderness, leading over the high range of mountains that lay between them and the Bitterroot Valley.

It took until July 29, or eleven days, to get all in readiness. This day being
Sunday, a head chief of the treaty portion of the Nez Perces by the name of
James Lawyer called a prayer meeting, to which he invited Howard's Bannock
Indian scouts, together with the general and many of his officers, to participate.
A temporary stay was called for the day to attend in prayer. According the
General Howard's own report, an earnest meeting was indulged in. He deemed
it wise and proper to ask God's blessing before going forth to battle on the trail
of merciless Indians, not knowing the fate that might befall them at the hands of
these savages.

STRENGTH OF THE ARMIES

At this time, Howard's strength consisted of about 300 infantry, 200 cavalry, 50 Bannock scouts, and 50 civilians.[7] The latter were mounted on horseback and provided with axes, picks, shovels, saws, and all necessary tools for the construction of roads, trails, bridges, and in clearing the way for the train. They were also armed with rifles so that they might reinforce the cavalry in case of a conflict. The artillery consisted of two mountain howitzers and one Gatling gun, which Howard carried along on pack mules.[8]

Joseph was considered the head chief of this refractory band of Nez Perces,[9] hence we will, in referring to them, call the fugitives "Joseph's band." His strength at this time was considered something over 300 warriors, besides all their squaws and families, which made a total of about 1,000; and by way of passing, it is well to add that his strength was not limited to the 300 warriors, for the squaws and older children were just as handy with a gun as were any of the bucks.

These Indians had plenty of ammunition and were all armed with Henry rifles, said to have been obtained sometime prior to the outbreak through one of the government officials at the Nez Perce agency on the pretext of hunting wild game. They spent a great deal of their time hunting and were always given credit for being crack shots with a rifle.

PEOPLE OF THE BITTERROOT VALLEY BECOME ALARMED

On the morning of July 30, General Howard made the start over the Lolo Trail in pursuit of Joseph's band, which was now twelve days in the lead. Meantime, the people of the Bitterroot Valley were eagerly watching proceedings over the range with a suspicious eye. Reports came slowly, as our manner of communication was limited. Our mail service was triweekly. It was sometimes carried on horseback and sometimes in a light, two-horse wagon through the Bitterroot Valley, while a Concord coach carried the mail daily from Deer Lodge to Missoula. Deer Lodge was our nearest telegraph station, and Corinne, Utah, our nearest railroad point. From the meager news that we were able to get, we deemed it wise to fortify ourselves as well as possible for the protection of our families. Three forts were therefore built—one at Stevensville, one about a mile north of Corvallis, and one just south of where Hamilton now stands. The one at Stevensville, located about a half mile north of the town, was a reconstruction of old Fort Owen. At that time, the fort was quite well intact, only the front had crumbled down, so we cut green sods and built the walls up again, making it quite a formidable affair.

DESCRIPTION AND OWNERSHIP OF FORT OWEN

Major John Owen, a sutler in the United States Army and stationed on Snake River for the winter of 1849–50, resigned his position in the spring and resolved to go further north to establish a trading post, where he would trade with the Indians. He, in company with his wife, Nancy Owen, a Snake Indian, came to the bountiful Bitterroot Valley and was favorably impressed with the outlay for the present, as well as prospects to build up a future. The major found in the heart of this beautiful country a Catholic mission, previously established by Father De Smet sometime in the early forties and known as St. Mary's Mission.

During these years, it was customary for the Blackfeet Indians to come down from the north into the Bitterroot Valley, make war on the Flatheads, or Salish tribe, as they were then known, and drive off their ponies. This menace became so prevalent, and the mission [so] many times threatened, that the priests and their attendants, being so thoroughly harassed, determined to abandon their mission. Upon the appearance of Major Owen in their midst, they bantered him for a trade, and in short, the deal was consummated and transfer made, Owen becoming sole owner of all their improvements and belongings. Whereupon the fathers departed for the west.

This country was then a part of Oregon, and as the land laws ran a married man could file on and hold a full section of land, hence the major proceeded to stake out his claim and make the necessary improvements. Owen at first built a stockade and established a trading post, and subsequently, in the year 1856, laid the foundation for his permanent fort, built especially as a protection against these marauding bands of Blackfeet Indians, who continued their yearly visits for war and plunder. The Salish tribe was always friendly to the whites for helping them ward off their common foe.

The old historic fort was made of adobe, or sun-dried bricks, and covered an area 250 feet north and south by 125 feet east and west; the walls were 15 feet high and two feet thick. On the south end were two square bastions built and raised to two stories high, one on each corner. Long, narrow, perpendicular portholes were constructed on either side to serve as lookouts and for rifle shooting in case of an attack. Prior to the Nez Perce War, there had been four of these bastions, one on each of the four corners of the enclosure, but by 1877 only the two at the south end were standing. The end walls were carried to two large, square gateposts, from which were hung two massive plank gates that swung together in the center and locked. The gateposts were spanned together by an archway, nicely constructed out of lumber. The north end, and main entrance, to the fort was similarly constructed, only in addition, a very large pair of elk horns surmounted the archway as an ornament. The roof of each bastion was carried up on the four sides to a point in the middle, supporting a flagpole, from whence floated the American flag. Along both sides of walls, for the full length of the enclosure, were built rooms sixteen feet deep, which were used for living rooms, store rooms, office rooms, etc. These walls were also made of adobe and carried high enough to give sufficient slope to the roof that lay on top of the main walls of the fort. Large poles were then placed upon these walls for the support of an adobe roof that answered a good purpose for protection against inclement weather. A little south of the center of the main court, a well was dug for a supply of sufficient good water at all times within the enclosure. A nice well house was built over it, having an iron wheel swung to the roof, over which a rope passed with a water bucket attached to either end of it.

Washington J. McCormick had possession of the fort at this particular time, having obtained it through foreclosure of a mortgage given by John Owen to a Dr. Nichols, a dentist of Stevensville, for a trifling sum of money. Said mortgage was then transferred to Mr. McCormick, who seized the opportunity of really getting something for a mere nothing and possession of which, even to this day, rests with Mr. McCormick and his widow. Mrs. Nancy Owen passed away without issue, and John Owen became insane.

In the winter of 1876–77 the territorial legislature appropriated funds to carry Owen to his people in Philadelphia, Pennsylvania. Mr. W. E. Bass of Stevensville was named as the one to accompany him to join his relatives in his far-off home. This was done in March 1877.

Think of us people of Stevensville and vicinity falling heir to the use of such valuable property when in dire need for protection. The fort at this time was in good repair, except a portion of the front, or north end, which had crumbled down. We cut green sods and built it up again, and then said to ourselves, "Come on Joseph; if you want us, come and get us." Each fort was honored with a name after the war clouds had rolled by. Ours at Stevensville was "Fort Brave," presumably because we felt quite secure within its walls.

THE FORT AT CORVALLIS

The fort at Corvallis was built of green sod for a surrounding wall. Inside were living rooms partitioned off with lumber, also tents and wagon sheets were used, and the families made as comfortable as could be under existing circumstances. This section of the valley was peopled largely by Missourians, who during the Civil War received warnings often to "Get up and go" to a safer place or refuge. We had at that time no word in the English language that would exactly fit their case, hence the new coined word "skedaddle" came into vogue, and the stockade was thereupon christened "Fort Skedaddle."

THE FORT AT SKALKAHO

The fort at Skalkaho was very similarly built out of green sod and fixed up quite comfortable inside. To this fort, the little word of "run" was applied, for the reason that when finished, the occupants lost no time in getting within its gates. So it was thereafter known and talked of as "Fort Run."

Thus equipped with forts to house our women and children, we felt quite confident that we would be able to stand off a considerable force of Indians in the event of a fight.

POPULATION OF THE BITTERROOT AND MILITARY STRENGTH

Governor Potts, then governor of the territory of Montana, was earnestly petitioned for guns and ammunition. After considerable delay, a few muskets were sent us. Most of the white people at that time had some sort of shooting iron of their own, either for hunting or kept for self-defense, so taking it all in all, we were fairly well armed.

The white people in the valley at that time were few; the lands had just recently been surveyed and opened for settlement, but owing to the lack of industries, markets, and transportation, the influx of home seekers came very slowly.

Our neighbors, the Flathead Indians, who proved in the crisis to be our best friends, and who are deserving of far more credit than ever accorded them, numbered somewhere around 550. I note from reading the Montana history that the census of 1880 gave the valley's Indian population as 350. I remember very distinctly the time the government surveyed ranches for them that sixty-two places were laid out, and a good many more refused to accept land as allotments. Taking this as a basis, together with my experiences in trading and mingling with them, I am satisfied that 550 is not far from being correct at the time of the Nez Perce outbreak.

Generally speaking, the Flatheads were poorly armed and not considered nearly as good marksmen as the Nez Perces. Their guns, being all styles and makes, had been acquired by trading here and there with the white settlers of the valley and were used mostly for hunting rather than for self-protection. It was always customary for the Flatheads to make a pilgrimage once a year to the Yellowstone country in quest of buffalo that abounded there for their supply of meat and hides.

CONDITIONS IN BITTERROOT
In this particular summer, crops had been planted in the spring as usual, and everything looked promising up to the time of the Indian outbreak in Idaho; but from that time on throughout most of the summer, work on ranches was necessarily suspended, crops neglected, rail fences were blown down, stock entered the fields and wrought destruction, and in short, when the harvest time came and a summary of our year's labors made, we found our assets dwindled to a mere pittance. "None are so poor as those who have nothing to sell." This was our condition of affairs, and with winter staring us in the face, the prospect was anything but encouraging.

— ⋉◆⋈ —

BOYS CAPTURED BY THE INDIANS AT LOLO SPRINGS
While we were eagerly awaiting news of developments from over the range in Idaho, Joseph's band had pressed forward across the mountains and camped at Lolo Hot Springs, arriving there on July 21. Meantime, two Stevensville lads, not knowing or realizing the danger, had gone to the springs for a summer's outing and were there when the Indians arrived. The two were William Silverthorne, a brother of John Silverthorne, who resided on the west side of the Bitterroot River on a ranch adjoining that of Charlo, the chief of the Flathead nation; and Pete Matte, a son of Louis Matte, one of our blacksmiths at Stevensville.

The Indians, wishing to remain at the springs a few days to recuperate, but fearing that the boys would spread the alarm, took them prisoners. Under cover of the night, when all was quiet, the boys crept out of camp and made their escape. They each stole a good saddle horse from the Indian herd—Matte's horse especially being a fine, large, showy sorrel—and succeeded in reaching Stevensville about noon the next day to give us the first definite news of the location of the Indians. Thereupon, couriers were sent immediately out for help to all the towns and mining camps within reach, and our calls were readily responded to.

CAPTAIN RAWN ESTABLISHING A FORT ON THE LOLO

Fort Missoula had been previously established, and a few soldiers were stationed there under command of Captains Rawn and Logan, Rawn being the senior officer. In answer to the call, Captain Rawn hurriedly began preparations to take a hand in our defense, and on the twenty-fifth made his departure for Lolo Canyon, taking with him all the force that could be spared from the fort, which consisted of five commissioned officers and thirty enlisted men. As he proceeded up the creek, his force kept constantly growing by the addition of volunteers who gathered in from all directions, until the army finally numbered somewhere around four hundred.

Some eight miles up the Lolo, at a rather narrow canyon, where the hills on either side are steep and quite high, Captain Rawn called a halt and commenced digging trenches and throwing up breastworks of logs, thus making quite a formidable defense against the enemy. With this task completed, he felt quite sure he had the Indians where he could run them into his bag, pretty much after the style we kids used to go "sniping."

FAMILIES GATHER IN FORTS AND COMPANIES ORGANIZED

We at Stevensville and other places gathered our families all in the respective forts, while the men who could be spared from guard duty hurriedly organized themselves into companies and went to the front. Some of the captains, as I recall them, were John Landram, R. W. Martin, Alexander Matt, J. B. Catlin, and Jeffrey Niles.

My brothers, Fred and Amos, were supposed to belong to Landram's company (not mentioned in Colonel Gibbon's list), while I, with fourteen others, was detailed to remain as guard at Fort Owen under Dick Buker as captain. Many of the men who belonged to these companies were never enrolled, as no regular system of enlistment or keeping account of personnel was carried out. The only object was to get there, and to get there quickly, regardless of who their captains were or who made up the list of volunteers. We were fighting for our families and our homes, not for the paltry sum of "one dollar a day," as our governor saw fit later to pay some of the men who so willingly volunteered their services in these trying times. I may also mention the fact in passing that one John Gibbons was sent to Helena and other places in Montana in 1881 by the government to gather an official list of the names and addresses of all persons who participated in the campaign.

Yes, he proceeded to Helena (not elsewhere), gathered the names of those that were easily obtained, leaving out many that spent their time and money throughout all the campaign—even some who helped to fight the battle of the Big Hole—and reported his findings as including "all." The unfortunate part of it is that his list, being so incomplete, is considered in the records as "official and final," which wrought a great injustice to many who took an active part in the campaign. Later on it developed that Congress passed a pension bill for the benefit of those few whom Mr. Gibbons reported, leaving out all those whose names failed to appear on his roll. The bill does not provide further that a participant who had rendered service could prove his claim by living witnesses.

JOSEPH MOVES DOWN THE LOLO

On the twenty-sixth, Chief Joseph moved his force down from the springs and camped on a little prairie about two miles above Captain Rawn's fortifications. This prairie, now known as the Woodman Flats,[11] is located near the mouth of the south fork of Lolo Creek.

That evening Captain Rawn, accompanied by William Baker, Amos Buck, and Cole B. Sanders, proceeded up to the flat with a flag of truce, fashioned by tying a white handkerchief to a gun barrel, asking an interview with Chief Joseph. The Indians, being very reluctant to get into trouble with our people, recognized the flag and gladly granted the interview. During the parley, Captain Rawn demanded of Joseph the unconditional surrender of the entire tribe with all their belongings. This, of course, was refused, but a meeting was appointed for the next day, wherein the three chiefs—Joseph, Looking Glass, and White Bird—were to participate.

THE FLATHEADS PLEDGE ALLEGIANCE TO THE WHITES

The Nez Perces and Flathead Indians had always been on the best of terms, having for years hunted the buffalo together along the Yellowstone, and in many instances had intermarried, hence the Nez Perces, as well as ourselves, were for a time perplexed to know how matters would stand between us and the Flatheads when it came to a test.

The Flathead Indians at that time claimed the Bitterroot Valley as their home under the leadership of Chief Charlot,[12] who was seriously considering the policy they should follow in the crisis. At dawn on July 27, the old chief, in company with twenty of his best warriors, presented himself to Captain Rawn, stating that they had resolved to stand on the side of the white man, claiming their interests were in common with ours, and accordingly took their places in the new fort, all ready for battle if necessary. White handkerchiefs were tied around their heads for identification so, in case of a fight, no mistakes might be made as to their identity.

CAPTAIN RAWN DEMANDS JOSEPH'S SURRENDER

At the appointed hour, about 2:00 P.M., Captains Rawn and Logan, in company with William Baker, Amos Buck, C. B. Sanders, Chief Charlot, and about three other Flathead Indians, together with Delaware Jim as interpreter—Jim was a representative of the old Delaware nation but had allied himself with the Flatheads—met the representatives of Chief Joseph in council about halfway between forces. Joseph's representatives were himself, Chiefs Looking Glass and White Bird, and some two or three other Indians.

At this interview Captain Rawn, as on the previous day, demanded an unconditional surrender of all arms and ammunition, together with camp equipment, horses, and in fact, all their belongings. This Chief Joseph again flatly refused. Nothing was accomplished any more than to arrange for a third parley to be held the following day.

CHIEFS CHARLOT AND JOSEPH MAKE A TREATY

The representatives of the two tribes of Indians, Nez Perces and Flatheads, then entered into council among themselves, in which Chief Joseph repre- sented to Chief Charlot that he was on his way to Canada to look for a new home for himself and his followers and did not wish to fight anymore; that the Flathead Indians were his friends; and he had no enmity toward the white peo- ple of the Bitterroot, but only asked permission to pass through the country peaceably, promising not to disturb any persons or property of the Flathead Indians or whites.

To this request, Chief Charlot's reply was in substance, "Joseph, you and your people are our friends; the white people of the Bitterroot Valley are our friends, and I will grant your request. But remember, Joseph, if you kill any of my people or the white people, or disturb any of the property belonging to my people or the white people in my country, I will fight you."

This was the understanding had at this interview between the two tribes, to which the citizens present gave their consent, knowing that their forces were far inadequate to cope with such a large band as the Nez Perces without the aid of Chief Charlot and his warriors.

JOSEPH REFUSES TO SURRENDER: WAR DECLARED

By this time, some 400 citizens had assembled in the fort to confront the Nez Perce band. On the following day (July 28) Captain Rawn, in company with his picked men, as agreed, met Chief Joseph and his representatives in council. At this interview Captain Rawn, knowing of the treaty entered into between the two tribes of Indians, modified his conditions of surrender by demanding that they at least give up their ammunition.

To this Joseph replied, "If we have to give up our ammunition, it will be through the muzzles of our guns."

Joseph frankly gave Captain Rawn to understand in unmistakable terms that he would parley no more with him, but on the morrow he would move.

Captains Rawn and Logan, now realizing that Joseph meant business, settled back behind their breastworks, feeling that war had been declared and fully determined in their own minds to bag the whole army of Nez Perces in the morning when they advanced.

A vigil watch was kept all through the night, that no surprises might be sprung before the appointed zero hour. As the evening emerged into darkness, the suspense grew more and more intense, which mustered all the courage on the part of the command. Under such circumstances, it seemed only fitting and proper, in order to stimulate their nerves up to the occasion, to interview the "little brown jug," which is always supposed to lend comfort and relief under such trying conditions. Consequently, the officers indulged that night in the motto "Take the spirits down to keep the spirits up," until they were all intoxicated. Luckily for them, the Indians remained peaceable through the night.

THE BATTLE OF "FORT FIZZLE"

On the next morning (July 29) Joseph, true to his word, broke camp and started moving down the Lolo. All was excitement within the little fort. The band advanced to within a half mile of Rawn's impenetrable breastworks, then, to their surprise, turned up a ridge on the left side of the canyon, which they followed to the top, thereby passing entirely around the fortifications and leaving Captain Rawn sitting quietly, "holding the bag."

The Indians fired a few shots from the hilltops while passing, and one shot was fired from the fort by a white man by the name of Gird, whom Captain Rawn severely criticized for so doing. Nobody was hurt, but the truth was, some of our citizens were pretty badly scared.

As soon as Joseph's band had passed the trap, they descended down another ridge, striking the Lolo Trail again, and thence on down the creek to the Bitterroot Valley.

This strong fort of Captain Rawn's, appropriate to the occasion, was then dubbed "Fort Fizzle" and is known by that name to this day by the older citizens of Montana.

Upon the realization of the fact that the "big game" had passed and no fight called, our citizens commenced scampering home down the trail in the rear of Joseph. He and his tribe took the lead up the Bitterroot Valley to a small flat on Carlton Creek, where a halt was called and camp made for the night. Our people were soon given to understand that the Nez Perces would do us no harm, and in fact told the volunteers to pass through their camp—that they did not want to fight them. "Go home and take care of your women and children" were the words passed to our citizens by the supposedly hostile band.

ANXIETY IN FORT OWEN

A great deal of anxiety was felt in old Fort Owen as to what our fate in this hour of trial might be. A census was taken, which showed we had 258 women and children, including fifteen guardsmen, within our gates. I was on guard duty this day. My station was on the main thoroughfare of the valley, where the road crosses Burnt Fork Creek, some 200 yards northeast of the fort.

About noontime I spied an Indian coming up the road on horseback toward me as fast as his pony could run. His long, black hair streaming behind in the swiftness of his flight presented a picture I shall never forget, while at the same time I realized, from his actions, that whoever he was and wherever he was going, his message was a grave one. Upon his approach, I recognized him as being "Fransway," one of our staunch Flathead Indians, who lived on a ranch located near the river, about two miles north of the fort. I halted him and inquired, "What is the news?" He answered, "My friend, I am afraid that all our people will be killed; they are fighting now at Lolo." His hurry was to inform his people to be ready for the worst. I told him to pass on and hurriedly sent the word to our captain, Dick Buker, in the fort.

The next man who came was a man by the name of N. B. Liter, on horseback. Liter's residence was on Sweathouse Creek, near where Victor now stands. He told of the fighting, and he had a hole shot through his coat but had miraculously gotten away. He was very fearful of our boys on the Lolo being all cut to pieces and advised getting plenty of bandages ready to tie up their wounds.

About this time, excitement ran wild in our fort. Moments seemed hours, awaiting the horrible news that we thought sure to come. As time went on and man after man came in, we eventually learned to our joy that no fighting had taken place and nobody hurt; that these first men coming in had left [Fort] Fizzle in advance of the Indians and, upon hearing the few shots fired from the top of the ridge, took it for granted that the fight was on. Being too badly scared for fear of losing their own scalps, [they] never even stopped long enough to look back, lest they should lose a moment in the race for dear life to get under cover of old Fort Owen.

CITIZENS AT FORT FIZZLE DISBAND
The volunteers belonging in Missoula and beyond coursed homeward from the mouth of Lolo Creek as soon as Joseph and his band turned up the Bitterroot Valley, our citizens passing through the supposedly hostile camp at Carlton Creek unharmed.

All, by nightfall, who belonged here were safely lodged in our fort, while those from Corvallis and Skalkaho sped on that night to join their families in their respective forts. We all now felt quite at ease, knowing that the Flathead Indians, who at that time were quite a formidable force, were with us, and of the agreement of the Nez Perces to keep peace on their journey southward.

NEZ PERCES MOVE TO SILVERTHORNE
That night, Captain Dick Buker resigned his office as commander of Fort Owen in favor of my brother Fred Buck, who, having served as a captain in the

Civil War, was considered more efficient to fill the office. All passed quietly for the night, but the next morning, July 30, we all watched uneasily for the coming of the Nez Perce band. About 10:00 A.M. the advance hove in sight on the west side of the river, following the old Indian trail up the valley.

At this time, there was no bridge across the Bitterroot River, hence it was always necessary to ford. I sat on top of the fort, where I had a plain view of the caravan and watched their passing. As was always customary with Indians traveling on horseback, they jogged their ponies along on a little dog trot. Being curious enough to gain some idea of their number, [I] took out my watch and timed their passing to a given point. It took just one hour and a quarter for all to move by, and there were no gaps in the continuous train. There was no unusual confusion or disorder, and none came over on our side of the river. Developments afterward showed that their herd of horses numbered more than three thousand, many of them being of very fine stock.

The band moved on up the valley to a small prairie near the mouth of Silverthorne Creek and in close proximity to Chief Charlot's home, where a halt was called and camp made for the night, and in fact two nights were spent there. We now felt sure that all danger had passed, yet no move was made to return to our respective homes that day.

NEZ PERCE SQUAWS VISIT STEVENSVILLE

Buck brothers (Fred, Amos, and myself) were at that time conducting a general store business in Stevensville about one-half mile south of Fort Owen. We had, during these trying times, moved all our goods to the fort for safety, but that morning, July 31, decided to move back into the store again. We had one wagonload brought in and were busy arranging the goods on the shelves when, lo and behold, a band of squaws from the Nez Perce camp, accompanied by a few armed warriors, appeared. They soon made known their wants to us, saying they needed supplies and had money to pay for them, but if we refused to sell, would take them anyway. Our stock comprised but a handful of such articles as they wanted. However, we held a consultation over the matter and decided that "prudence was the better part of valor," so decided to trade with them. Flour was their main desire, and we had none; but near Fort Owen was located the flourmill, to where they repaired for a supply. Philip Gripp was the miller and E. T. Buker of Stevensville was working for him in the mill.

All passed quietly that day, but not trusting too much to the honor of an Indian, especially when on the warpath, we again returned to the fort for the night.

Peace and quiet reigned supreme, and when morning came, August 1, we felt sure that no more would be seen of the intruders, yet with a grain of caution concluded not to remove the balance of our stock of merchandise to the store for a day or two, but rather take our time in watching maneuvers.

NEZ PERCE WARRIORS VISIT STEVENSVILLE

Brothers Fred, Amos, and myself went uptown to the store that morning, August 1, and about 10:00 A.M. were surprised by the appearance of 115 warriors, well armed with Henry rifles, riding into our little village under the leadership of Looking Glass.[13] We were lost to know what this day would bring forth. Never shall I forget their formidable appearance, their stern looks, their aggressiveness, and their actions, which in themselves placed us immediately on the defensive. This added another stimulus to our present fear, which made a lifelong impression.

They were all well dressed, with apparently new showy blankets, well armed, and rode the finest of horses. Many of these horses, I well remember, were branded "B" and said to have been taken from a man by the name of Baker,[14] who lived near their old home in Idaho. The Nez Perces were by far the finest looking tribe of Indians I have ever seen and so much superior to the Flatheads in intelligence, physique, manner of dress, equipment, and arms that they were hardly to be compared. We had always considered the Nez Perces as a wealthy tribe, and on this visit they seemed to have plenty of money, all in gold coin, but they did not come to trade this day, nor did they buy anything, to my knowledge, except some whiskey sold them by unscrupulous individuals who had no care of the well-being of our community.

During their stay in town, many of them came into the store, some of whom I knew personally. They told me that they held no animosity against the white people of the Bitterroot, as they had always treated them kindly. They also told me of their troubles at home, causes leading up to the outbreak, depredations they had committed, and in short were free to talk to me—speaking good English—of their oppression in Idaho; how the white settlers wished to crowd them onto a reservation and the resulting conflict which crystallized their determination to seek a new home rather than submit to the will of their oppressors.

As a safeguard and caution against trouble, Chief Looking Glass took his stand about across the street from our store, where he sat on his horse all the time the Indians were in town and talked to them constantly in the Nez Perce tongue.

A goodly number of friendly Flathead Indians, armed with rifles such as they had, gathered in to protect us, seeing there were but a handful of us white people to defend ourselves.

NEZ PERCES GET DRUNK

Finally it was noticed that some of the Nez Perces were getting drunk, and on investigation, [we] found that a white man by the name of Dave Spooner, who tended bar in the Reeves saloon, was selling the whiskey. The liquor was seized by a party of us and transported on a wagon to the fort. Strong talk of lynching the dispenser of the firewater was indulged in, yet at the same time we were afraid that if we enforced the vigilante act, it would incite the Indians to violence. The next move was to enter the general store of Jerry Fahy, the only other place in town where liquor was sold.

I might explain that in those days it was customary for storekeepers to have a barrel of whiskey, not especially for sale, but to treat customers, thereby retaining their trade and goodwill; but Fahy, like Spooner in his eagerness for the almighty dollar, forgot the graveness of the situation, and it developed upon a party of our citizens to demand that his barrel be given up. Fahy at first resented and wished to know by what authority we had for making such a demand. One man amongst our number—a Southern Methodist minister by the name of Reverend T. W. Flowers—stepped forward with his pistol in hand, leveled it, and said, "By this authority." Jerry, realizing the situation, remarked, "That's pretty good authority all right; there is the barrel, take it." The whiskey was then loaded onto a wagon and also taken to the fort.

I had a Henry rifle and plenty of ammunition lying on a shelf under a closed counter and took special care to keep close to it all the time that the Nez Perces were in town, as well I knew, from maneuvers and the number of drunken Indians in sight, that it only wanted one shot to be fired, and all would be off and the crisis at hand. I thoroughly determined to sell my life as dearly as possible. I had no thought of ever going through the day alive, yet I was as cool and deliberate as one could be under such circumstances.

The older people of the Nez Perce tribe were well disposed and tried in every way to keep the peace and deal squarely with us; but the younger warriors knew no bounds and were hard to control, especially while under the influence of liquor. I talked with Poker Joe, a subchief whom I knew quite well, he being in the valley a good portion of his time. He used to make his home with either Perish or George Red Crow, two Nez Perce families that lived on ranches about two miles south of Corvallis. He told me about their troubles in Idaho and subsequently their murders and fights with Howard, and [that they] now were on their way to Canada to look for a new country in which they could build up a new home unmolested.[15]

While in town, the tribe as a rule meant peace, but the drunken Indians sought trouble. An Indian, when he gets loaded up with firewater, is by nature right on the peck. One of them, going to the home of our village blacksmith, Jacob Herman, who lived in the building adjoining his shop on Main Street, was boisterous and insulting. He drew up his gun to shoot Mrs. Herman, when a Flathead Indian standing nearby grabbed the firearm and thus saved her life, which really meant saving the lives of us all.

I saw Mr. Herman some six years ago, who at that time reiterated the story and told me that through all these years, he had kept that Flathead Indian in provisions as a token of appreciation for his kindly act in saving the life of his beloved wife.

About 2:00 P.M. a little squad of half a dozen Nez Perces sat on the ground directly across the street in front of our store, in company with three Flathead

Indians who were on guard. One of the Nez Perces drew up his gun, saying, "See me kill that man in the store." But by a quick move of one of the Flatheads, his gun was wrenched from him before he could pull the trigger. At this juncture Looking Glass, sitting on his horse some fifty feet away and seeing the fracas, alighted from his pony and sprang at the Indian, gave him a whipping with his quirt, and then sent him and his little band up the road to camp.

From this time on, the Nez Perces followed in little squads, until about 3:00 P.M., when all had left town.

At that time, the country south of town was open sagebrush, flat and not fenced. The Indians forded the river about a half mile above the mission and went diagonally straight ahead through the woods to Silverthorne—their camp.

As soon as the Indians had gone and the town was quiet again, I turned the key on the store door and made good my getaway to Fort Owen. Upon arriving, my nerves gave way to the awful strain, and I collapsed, trembling like a leaf when I looked back over the scene which we had just passed through, and realizing how near we came to the close of our earthly careers.

CHIEF CHARLOT, A TRUE FRIEND
Now, after all these years of reflection and viewing the situation from every angle, I can truthfully and earnestly say that we, the people of the Bitterroot Valley, owe our lives and well-being to Chief Charlot and his warriors of the Flathead nation. The old saying "A friend in need is a friend indeed" is here applicable, yet neither General Howard, Captain Rawn, nor General Gibbon ever made mention of Chief Charlot and the kindly office he served in saving the lives and property of the people of the valley.

WHITE GIRL WITH THE NEZ PERCES
During the Nez Perce Indian stay at the Silverthorne flat, it was currently reported that they had a young white girl of sixteen summers with them, but nobody ventured to say who she was, where she came from, or why she was in company with this hostile band. This girl was afterward shot in the battle of the Big Hole.

CITIZENS MOVE BACK HOME
On August 2, the next day after the Nez Perces had visited Stevensville and gotten drunk, they broke camp at Silverthorne and moved up the valley.

Believing now that the danger was over, the families housed in the fort began, that day, moving to their homes, and we started transferring our stock of goods back to the store. At the time the call to arms was sounded, my brother Fred was coming down Hellgate Canyon with a load of goods from Helena. He left his whole outfit, except one horse to ride, and hurried on to take part in the battle at Fort Fizzle; so he now returned to gather up his outfit and bring the new supplies on to Stevensville.

COLONEL GIBBON ORDERED TO PURSUE

Colonel Gibbon, stationed at Fort Shaw on the Sun River, had been ordered to take all available troops and proceed to Missoula to intercept the Indians. Going via Cadotte Pass, thence down the Blackfoot River, he arrived at Fort Missoula August 3. The next day he left the fort in hot pursuit of Joseph, taking with him all available troops from there, making in the aggregate nearly 150 men. One cannon was taken along that Major John Owen had brought to Montana and left at Stevensville, but which was subsequently taken to Fort Missoula when that post was established.

Colonel Gibbon, at Missoula, engaged Hugh Kirkendall's wagon train to transport his supplies. This army moved up the Bitterroot Valley as fast as possible, reaching Stevensville in the edge of the evening, three days behind the Indians, and made camp on the bank of the river about a mile and a half south of town, on what is known as the Jim Stuart ranch, north of Pine Hollow, on the east side of the river. Much excitement prevailed throughout the valley, and many citizens joined Gibbon to take part in the chase.

VOLUNTEERS ORGANIZE

Captain John B. Catlin organized a small company of volunteers, consisting of thirty-four persons, to join Colonel Gibbon, and among those enlisted were my brother Amos and my wife's brother Lynde Elliott. In view of the fact that Joseph had promised to pass through the valley in peace, there was a dissenting opinion as to the right of our citizens to take up arms in pursuit, and consequently only a few were persuaded to join Catlin's command. The only argument in their defense for such actions was that their mission was to revenge the wrongs perpetrated upon the whites of Idaho.

GENERAL HOWARD ON THE LOLO

Returning again to General Howard's movements, we next find him in camp at Lolo Hot Springs after making the trip over the trail from Clearwater in eight days. This inviting camp spot, with its hot sulphur water [and] plenty of wood and grass, held its charm for Howard. While enjoying this little spot, a courier by the name of Joe Pardee, who lived on a ranch at Gird's Creek, rode in bearing a dispatch from Colonel Gibbon to General Howard, asking him for 100 cavalry to be sent immediately on a forced march to join his forces and strike the enemy. The reply read, "I am sending you 200 cavalry on a forced march with instructions to continue until your forces are met."

HOWARD SENDS REINFORCEMENTS TO GIBBON

On the morning of August 7, General Howard broke camp and started with 200 cavalry, leaving orders for the infantry to follow as fast as they could. Twenty-two miles were covered the first day out on this forced march.[16] Next morning, August 8, they started out early on a good trail and soon came to

Captain Rawn's temporary fort, located between steep hills, and where Joseph had stopped to parley with the whites. [Here] they halted for inspection.

Viewing the high hills on either side and the excellent barricade of logs appearing in their front, these questions naturally arose and were asked among themselves. How could the Indians get by? Why did not Captain Rawn and his volunteers stop them here? Was Looking Glass always considered a good Indian in the Bitterroot country? The silent answer comes: Joseph was too smart for them.

The cavalry then pressed on to the mouth of the Lolo, where a halt was called for two hours to rest themselves and graze their animals. [They] then resumed their march up the Bitterroot Valley and, after having covered some thirty-four miles for the day, camped for the night south of the town of Stevensville on the same site that Gibbon had occupied the night of August 4.

On the morning of the ninth, that most terrible and historic day for Colonel Gibbon in the Big Hole, and Howard's cavalry 100 miles behind, they left camp quite early, traveling along the excellent road up the valley until they reached the mouth of Rye Creek, where they camped for the night, making some forty miles for the third day's forced march.

Next morning, August 10, General Howard picked out twenty of his best men and horses [and], together with seventeen Indian scouts, struck out in advance of the rest of the cavalry in hopes of overtaking Colonel Gibbon. He took the trail, or rude wagon road, that led up the hill on the south side of Rye Creek and over the mountain down into Ross's Hole. This was, in fact, the only road or trail that led southward at this time.

Passing through Ross's Hole, he came to the foot of the main divide of the Rocky Mountains, where a halt of one hour was called for rest and refreshment, and then resumed the march up the steep mountain, over a crudely constructed road for seven miles to the summit. From there, they had a good trail down Trail Creek on a very easy grade, where they made camp for the night, making about forty miles for the fourth day's march.

HOWARD HEARS OF THE BIG HOLE BATTLE

Here in camp, [Orlando] Robbins, who had charge of Howard's Bannock Indian scouts, came in with a few men on foot, who gave the first information of Gibbon's fight with Chief Joseph's band. This report was to the effect that Colonel Gibbon had struck the enemy on the morning of the ninth and has lost half his men, and that the fight was going hard with the colonel. Developments showed that these few men whom Howard mentions were those who had charge of the cannon when the Nez Perces captured the gun and, being cut off from the main command, were forced to make their getaway as best they could.

General Howard took their story with considerable credence, yet at the same time was enough frightened over it to construct breastworks out of logs for protection during the night and build numerous campfires around his quarters to make believe that he had a large force with him. He at once dispatched a courier to inform the main force of his cavalry, which had camped for the night on the west side of the divide, of the news received and ordered a hurried advance.

Next morning, August 11, General Howard, with his few men, broke camp early and moved down Trail Creek over a good mountain road, reaching Colonel Gibbon's command about 10:00 A.M., where he met the colonel and learned the particulars of the fight. The battle had commenced early on the morning of the ninth, the day Howard left Stevensville, and ran in substance as follows:

BATTLE OF THE BIG HOLE[17]

Colonel Gibbon's scouts had located the Nez Perce camp about one mile below where Ruby Creek and Trail Creek come together to form the headwaters of the west fork of the Big Hole River, a small stream some twenty feet across and waist deep. The level creek bottom, which is about one-quarter of a mile wide where the battle took place, is an open meadow on the east side of the stream, while the west side was covered with thickets of willows, interspersed with small clearings. To the eastward, a high, rolling bench forms the floor of the Big Hole Basin, while the mountain range terminated rather abruptly on the westward of the meadow.

In this meadow, Joseph had pitched his tents and was seemingly at ease, knowing that General Howard was far in the distance and not aware of Colonel Gibbon being on his trail.

Colonel Gibbon, being advised by his scouts of Joseph's location, moved his train down to near the mouth of Trail Creek on the evening of the eighth and made camp for a few hours to rest. Shortly after midnight, he and his men took the trail and followed [it] down to a point on the hillside opposite where the Indians were encamped, leaving his train and supplies in the rear in the hands of a dozen men. The cannon he had brought with him was placed in the hands of a few men to follow up at daybreak. Gibbon and his soldiers took their stand along the trail on the west side of the creek, some twenty feet in elevation above the creek bottom, and sat quietly waiting for dawn to appear. The Indian herd of ponies was feeding on the mountainside just above them.

When the first streaks of dawn were gleaming in the east, orders were given to leave the trail, go in the direction of the Indian village, and shoot the first Indian seen. At the crack of the first gun, a volley was to be fired and a charge made into the camp. The citizens, in the advance, occupied the extreme left. When about halfway to the creek, an Indian, who afterward proved to be their great medicine man,[18] came riding up in front of the citizens, mounted on a large gray horse. Four shots were fired simultaneously by Amos Buck, Oscar Clark, Alexander Mitchell, and John B. Catlin. The Indian fell, and the fight was on.

Such a complete surprise was made that the Indians were at first frustrated, and Colonel Gibbon, thinking he had them well in hand, ordered his men to burn the camps, thereby forcing them to surrender. While this was being done, the Indians crossed the creek and, under cover of the brush, commenced pouring forth a deadly fire. Vincent Burch, one of our citizens, noticed it first and shouted, "Look out boys. They have gone to the brush and are cross-firing us." Colonel Gibbon immediately ordered a charge across the creek and through the brush, quartering upstream and continuing a half mile until a small wooded bench was reached on the west side of the creek. Here he called a halt. Captain Catlin of the volunteers asked, "Who in hell called a halt here?" When informed that it was Colonel Gibbon, he remarked, "Well, I don't care, this is a hell of a place to camp."

Gibbon then ordered his men to dig rifle pits for their protection, which they did with the bayonets of their guns. The Indians soon had them surrounded in the little thicket of small pines, where they poured in a deadly fire all the rest of the day and night, and the next day and evening. If it had not been for Howard's cavalry pressing on to reinforce Gibbon, the scene would have undoubtedly ended in another Custer massacre, but the Indians, realizing Howard's proximity, fired a farewell volley at 11:00 P.M. the second day of the battle, and then took their departure.[19]

All this time the men were without food or water, save a little slough water obtained after dark by someone who dared to crawl down the hill to the slough and bring up a canteen full.[20] Realizing that the command was whipped to a frazzle, all they hoped to do was to hold the Indians at bay until help could come up.

RESULTS OF THE BATTLE

Summing up results of the fight, we find Colonel Gibbon reported two officers and twenty-one enlisted men killed; five officers, including himself, and thirty-one enlisted men were wounded.[21] In addition to this, six of our citizens were killed; namely, Lynde C. Elliott (my wife's brother), John Armstrong, David Morrow, Alvin Lockwood, Campbell Mitchell, and Henry S. Bostwick. The following four were wounded: Myron Lockwood, Otto Leifer, Jacob Baker, and William Ryan.

Of Joseph's band, eighty-nine dead were counted,[22] and of course a large number were wounded, of which no accounting could be made.

The Nez Perces moved up the Big Hole River after scantily burying their dead. It was learned afterwards that a hospital camp had been established some fifteen miles up Ruby Creek, where their wounded were cared for.

COLONEL GIBBON'S REPORT

When Colonel Gibbon's report was made, we were utterly surprised and chagrined to note that he severely criticized the people of the Bitterroot Valley for giving aid to Joseph's band by selling them supplies. It is said that a man is not accountable for what he does not know, hence if Colonel Gibbon had been correctly informed of the dire situation, his report would have read quite differently. The unkindest cut of all, however, was his neglect to even make mention of the thirty-four citizens who so gallantly fought by his side to save the day from entire destruction; undoubtedly, without their assistance in the hour of need, history would have recorded another Custer massacre, this time on the banks of the Big Hole River.

HOWARD'S INFANTRY
On August 10 General Howard's infantry, which he had left at Lolo Hot Springs to bring up the rear, passed through Stevensville on their way up the valley and camped that night on the same ground above town that his cavalry had occupied the night before. The next day they moved on up the valley some twenty-five miles and camped at Sleeping Child Creek, at which place I was drafted into service and continued with the command through the Yellowstone Park.

NEWS OF THE BATTLE REACHES STEVENSVILLE
About 9:00 A.M. on the eleventh, a courier came into Stevensville bearing the news of Colonel Gibbon's battle with the Nez Perces and enumerating the citizens killed. This of course created great excitement. Knowing that brother Amos was in the fight, and we were unable to get any word from him, I told my brother Fred that I was going to hitch up our freight team and go in search of him, and his answer was "Go."

I gathered up the four horses, got them freshly shod, and fixed up my camp outfit with provisions enough to last me a week. Although it was late in the day when I got all in readiness for the start, I had no time to lose, so pulled out that evening, bound to overtake Howard's infantry sometime during the night.

⛓⬦☰⬦⛓

I JOINED HOWARD'S COMMAND
I drove quite hard until about 1:00 A.M., when I found the infantry in camp at Sleeping Child Creek. I halted, unhitched my horses and turned them out in the commons as usual to graze, and then made down my bed in the wagon for the balance of the night.

Early in the morning a young lieutenant came over to my wagon and asked me to haul a load of flour for the command. When I told him my mission, he promised to let me go as soon as I could find my brother.

MY FREIGHT OUTFIT
My freight outfit consisted of four horses. The leaders, Prince and Grant, were sorrels, six years old, weighing 1,300 lbs. each, quick in action but easy to manage; the wheel team, Dick and Jack, were dark bays, eight years old, weighing 1,500 lbs. each, steady and true. My wagon was a new Schuttler with

double box, having an excellent spring seat in front and a fine footrest outside of the box. Under the footrest was a box for carrying wrenches, hammers, rough locks, etc., and attached to the rear end of the wagon was a large, commodious box for carrying camp equipment and grub. Bows were fixed over the wagon, with a good sheet stretched across the bows to keep everything dry in rainy weather.

Thus equipped, my outfit was considered first class, and its superior appearance no doubt had a great deal to do with the lieutenant pressing me into service and my subsequent trip through the Yellowstone Park with the command.

FROM RYE CREEK TO THE BATTLEGROUND

The lieutenant loaded me up pretty heavily, and we pulled out early in the morning. All went well until we came to the mouth of Rye Creek, where the trail, or rude wagon road, led up over the mountain, following a ridge on the south side of the creek. This was steep and I was heavily loaded, so was forced to make haste slowly. I gained the summit just at dark. The rest of the command was in advance of me. I could not see to drive further, so halted, unhitched my horses, tied them to the wagon, and made a dry camp for the night.

This, I think, was the most miserable night I ever spent in all my life. The day had been hot, and there was no water from the time I started to climb, and none on the summit. I slept but little, and when I did doze off for a few moments, it was in a dream for water. In the morning, the thirteenth, as soon as it showed light enough to see to travel, I hooked up and was on my way again—this time on a downhill pull. I reached the command just as they were leaving a fine camp at a large spring of ice cold water at the foot of the mountain as you enter Ross's Hole.

Here, myself and horses sure did justice in quenching our fiery thirst. To my surprise and joy, I met my brother Amos there making his way homeward. He was well and had survived the fight, although his clothes bore the scars of battle, having one bullet hole shot through the rim of his hat and another through his coat under the arm.

I asked relief from my little lieutenant, but he informed me that I would have to continue with the command until evening, then he would let me go, so I persuaded my brother to accompany me back with the understanding that we would return home together.

That evening we camped in a fine meadow by the side of a clear, rippling brook at the foot of the main chain of the Rockies, which divides the waters of the Atlantic and Pacific Oceans. Shortly after supper, the lieutenant came to my camp to inform me that I could now be relieved and return home.

Next morning, August 14, he came again with a different story and told me that I would have to continue with them to the battleground, as he could not get over the mountain without my help. Of course, I was in for it, as the command had orders to live on the country and conscript anybody or anything needed, so I again persuaded my brother to accompany me to the battleground, where I was promised relief.

We got quite an early start that morning and made the seven-mile uphill pull to the summit of the mountains over a very rudely constructed wagon road without serious trouble, and camped in a beautiful, little meadow on Trail Creek for the noonday meal; thence pulled down Trail Creek in the afternoon on a nice, even grade to the battleground, some twenty miles further. Nearing our objective camp, Amos pointed out the spot where the Indians captured the cannon and then rolled the big gun down off the trail into the creek. It is said that the cannon was fired three times prior to its capture.

REVIEWING THE BATTLEGROUND

Upon our arrival at the battleground an hour before sundown, we unhooked our horses and turned them out to graze while Amos and I took a stroll over the grounds, where he pointed out to me the many things that had happened on that memorable August 9. In our stroll we came to the grave of our dear friend Dave Morrow. His hat was lying on the ground, having a bullet hole through the crown, plainly telling the cause of death.

Howard's scouts (Bannock Indians) were in the advance of us and, being curious to know what Indians were killed, had taken poles and pried up many bodies of the dead, hence the battleground presented a very gruesome picture. While wandering about we came to a very large squaw sitting up in her grave, half covered. I recognized her as one who used to come to our store in Stevensville to trade, and I also recognized the calico dress that she wore as being made from cloth that I had sold her only a few days before. She was the largest Indian woman that I ever saw and would have weighed fully 300 lbs.

Another place of particular mention was in the bend of a creek, where a good many bodies of Indians were thrown on a sandbar formed by the eddying waters, then the bank had been caved in onto them for a partial covering.

We tried to cross the creek and get onto the ground where Colonel Gibbon made his stand and held the Indians at bay, awaiting help from General Howard, but could find no crossing. As it was now getting dusk, we made our way back to the wagon with the infantry command, where we built a fire and made a cup of coffee in connection with other edibles for the evening meal.

That evening, while sitting by the campfire, my little lieutenant came over for a short visit. He then told me that I could go and wished me a safe journey home. This was on the fourteenth—five days after the battle.

All passed quietly for the night. In the morning I had gathered up my horses and was hitching up preparatory to my departure for home, when my little lieutenant came up and informed me that I would have to go with the command, as they did not have transportation enough without me to move their supplies, although they had numbers of wagons in the train from Bitter-root, Missoula, and Frenchtown Valleys. I have often thought that the reason for retaining me was that I had a first-class transportation outfit and they were loath to give me up.

Numbers of Bitterroot people and others from elsewhere were on the battleground at this time, and among the rest was Dr. R. A. Wells of Stevensville. My brother got a chance to return home with him, so I bade Amos good bye, and our command moved out over a stretch of benchlands about eight miles distant, where we struck the main Big Hole River, which we followed upstream and made camp for the night—twenty-five miles from the battleground.

HOWARD'S CAVALRY FOLLOWS JOSEPH

The balance of Howard's cavalry (some 180) soon overtook the advance detachment at the battleground, where they rested for two days, then left on the morning of the thirteenth, two days in our advance, following the trail of the Nez Perces up the Big Hole River to Poplar Creek, thence across a low divide to Horse Prairie Creek. At this latter place, the Indians murdered eight men (settlers), the news of which reached our command on the fifteenth.[23]

Somewhere along the upper Horse Prairie Valley, the Indians turned southward and crossed over the main range of the Rockies into Idaho, then traveled in a southwesterly course until they struck Dry Creek, which is some ten or fifteen miles below the present town of Spencer. By taking this course, they hoped to foil the cavalry into the belief that they were going to turn down the Salmon River and go back to their old home, but Howard's Indian scouts insisted that the Nez Perces were headed for the buffalo country along the Yellowstone. The cavalry thereupon did not try to follow over the rough mountain, but continued down Horse Prairie Creek to its mouth, then up Red Rock, with a view of intercepting the Indians somewhere along the stage road leading to Salt Lake.

HOWARD'S TRANSPORTATION TRAIN

Howard's transportation train now consisted of numerous two-horse wagons from Frenchtown and Missoula Valleys, also from the Bitterroot, together with three four-horse outfits, two of which belonged to W. E. Bass of Stevensville— one driven by himself and the other by Neil Brooks, a young lad Mr. Bass had taken to raise; the third was my own and driven by myself. The cavalry had pack animals for their transportation.

GIBBON'S ARMY DISBANDED

The few available soldiers that Colonel Gibbon had left were now placed under General Howard's command and became part of his army.[24] Colonel Gibbon and his wounded and disabled men were taken to Deer Lodge for treatment, while the citizens were allowed to return to their homes in the Bitterroot, except Myron Lockwood, who was severely wounded [and] taken to Deer Lodge with Colonel Gibbon. No discharges of any kind were given to the citizens further than verbally told that they could return home.

INFANTRY MOVES ON TO BANNACK

On leaving the battleground, my little lieutenant took his seat with me on the wagon, and it was then that I really formed his acquaintance. His name was F. E. Eltonhead[25] of the 21st Infantry, and he proved to be a very congenial companion for the trip. He was about my age, and we took very kindly to each other. He rode with me all the way to Henry's Lake. I was directly under his command. My duty mostly was to pick up and haul footsore and worn-out soldiers as we traveled along. I usually started out empty, but by camp time—say twelve or one o'clock—I would have all the men that could get into the wagon.

On the sixteenth we traveled another twenty-five miles and made camp somewhere at or near Grasshopper Divide. Nothing of material interest transpired for the day, so we quietly settled down for the night, turning our horses out to graze as usual on the luscious grasses that were everywhere abundant. Some of the soldiers were always detailed to look out for the herd.

Here my stock of provisions ran out, hence I commenced drawing on the commissary for daily food. I soon got used to soldier's fare and really enjoyed my rations of hardtack, bacon, beans, and coffee.

HOWARD'S INFANTRY AT BANNACK

On the morning of August 17, we broke camp, crossed the Grasshopper Divide, and drove into Bannack quite early in the day, where we halted for two hours to get supplies. Mr. Bass and myself, finding ourselves sore in need of some few things, as both of us came away from home without being prepared for an extended journey and had no money, walked down the street to see if we could find someone we knew. There seemed to be no one in the mining town either of us recognized, so we decided to walk boldly into a store to ask for credit. The man we interviewed was a storekeeper by the name of Graves (his son now keeps store at the same little log building). We told him where we came from, our mission there, our sad financial plight, and asked for credit in the amount of $25.00, promising to send him the money as soon as we returned home. He did not know us, but sized us up pretty thoroughly and concluded that we were rather likely looking chaps, so consented to extend the credit. It would be useless to say that we fulfilled our pledge some eight weeks later, on our arrival home.

Major W. F. Spurgin[26] of the 21st U.S. Infantry had charge under Howard of the axe men (road and bridge builders), which were called "skilled workmen," and for short, we dubbed them "skillets." Also, he had charge of the transportation teams. By this time, Mr. Bass and myself had formed his personal acquaintance. Somehow or other, the major took a liking to us and invited us to join in mess with him. We lost no time in accepting such a proposition as that, so the major detailed a Dutchman we called "Hans" for cook. Turning in our rations, it indeed made it very fine for us not to have any cooking to do. Our mess now consisted of Major Spurgin, Hans, Bass, Neil Brooks, and myself.

The major was very fond of a little nip occasionally, so in Bannack, one of the items of our bill of purchase was for one little brown jug and one gallon of old Scotch for the major. We were then ready to resume our march [and] pulled out over a low divide into a spacious valley called Horse Prairie, where, on the banks of the creek, we made camp for the night.

The nights were now getting cold, and none of us had any too much bedding, so young Brooks and I spliced blankets and prepared to sleep together in my wagon for the remainder of the trip.

A JOKE ON "DOC" WOODMANCY

At this camp, a little incident happened that amused me very much, and I think worth relating. While sitting by the campfire telling stories, one of our neighbors, who lived on Sweathouse Creek near Stevensville, by the name of "Doc" Van R. Woodmancy, came over to join our party. Now Doc was considerable of a storyteller and loved to get a joke off the other fellow whenever opportunity presented itself, and Van liked his bitters at all times, more especially on a trip like this, when it was scarce and not easily obtained. During the evening, while enjoying the bright light of a good fire that Hans had made for us, the major retired to his tent for a moment, brought out his jug, sat down by the side of Woodmancy, turned the jug up, and took a dram. A moment later he turned to Doc and said, "See here, Doc, how would you like to have a smell of this," holding the jug toward him. "Well," said Doc, "Major, at this time, nothing could please me better." [He] reached out his hand to receive the jug, but the major did not [let the] jar loose. "Oh no, you don't," said the major, "all you get is a smell." The jug was returned to the tent, and the laugh was on Doc.

WE LEARN THE WHEREABOUTS OF THE CAVALRY AND INDIANS

At the bugle call on the eighteenth, the command had prepared to get an early start in order to cover as many miles as possible, thereby to catch up with the cavalry, then some distance ahead. We were all on the move by 7:00 A.M., traveling down Horse Prairie Creek and across country to Red Rock, where we struck the stage road that led to Salt Lake. We followed this road toward Pleasant Valley. During the day, we learned that General Howard's cavalry was at Pleasant Valley and the Indians were at Dry Creek in Idaho, some ten or fifteen miles below the present town of Spencer, where the stage road crossed the creek. They were busily engaged in intercepting travelers, cutting telegraph wires, and doing such damage as lay in their power. We made a good day's march and camped by the roadside for the night.

On the nineteenth General Howard, with his cavalry, left Pleasant Valley, going down the stage road through Beaver Canyon until emerging into the Snake River Valley at the base of the mountain, some eighteen miles to Camas Meadows, where they found the Indians' trail. Here they went into camp early on a rocky spot in the meadow, tied up their pack mules and horses, and apparently felt safe from an attack.

INDIANS STEAL ANIMALS, FIGHT ENSUES

About daybreak on the morning of August 20,[27] numerous Nez Perce warriors returned, surprised the camp, stampeded the animals that broke loose from their fastenings, capturing 150 horses and mules [and] driving them forward across country to the base of the mountains, thence following the mountains toward Henry's Lake, among the most tangling mess of lava that one could imagine.[28] This route was chosen undoubtedly in order to handicap Howard's progress, as it proved to be extremely difficult to follow. A few shots were fired, but no damage was done.

As soon as it was light enough to see, Howard gathered up his remaining horses and started in pursuit with two companies of cavalry.[29] They overtook the Indians some twelve or fifteen miles out in a fringe of timber, and a fight ensued in which one soldier was killed and several wounded. No results were reported as to Indians killed or hurt.[30] Howard succeeded in recapturing about half of the stolen animals. Among the missing ones was a pack train of twenty mules that belonged to Alfred Cave of Missoula, and a bell mare that was the property of Hill Cave, his stepson. These animals, I think, constituted the finest pack train that I ever saw; they were entrusted to the care of Dick Johnson, a packer who handled the train for Mr. Cave. These animals were never recovered but were subsequently paid for by our government.

INFANTRY ORDERED ON A FORCED MARCH

All this time we, with the infantry, were plodding along the stage road, making as good time as we deemed advisable under the heavy weight of our command. We never for once entertained any fears for our safety, as we were always at a safe distance behind the Indians.

The day of the nineteenth was spent traveling southward along the stage road, and we camped that night within about ten miles of Pleasant Valley. This uneventful day added no new thrills to our campaign.

On the morning of August 20, however, we were fired into action when a courier from Howard confronted us on the road, bringing word of [the] raid the Indians had made on the cavalry, and ordered a hurry up of the troops. On receipt of this order, we piled all the men we could into all the wagons, and then, quickening our pace, marched as rapidly as possible, changing off footmen for riders and vice versa. We passed through Pleasant Valley and on down the stage road to Snake River Valley, then, taking the cavalry trail to the left at the base of the mountains, arrived at [Camas] Meadows at sundown, making forty-six miles for our day's travel. This we prided ourselves as "going some," even on a forced march.

Upon coming into camp, we were apprised of what had happened. The soldier that was killed in the battle[31] was buried at this rocky point in the meadows with military honors just as we arrived. The camp, now safe from the excitement that had just passed over, quieted down to near normal.

━◄━ ⚔ ━►━

HOWARD'S FORCES ALL TOGETHER

Here, for the first time while I was with the command, General Howard's forces were all together. We now felt sure that we had enough men to whip Joseph in case of an attack, but nevertheless, every precaution was taken so that no marauding parties could again run off our horses, thereby leaving us afoot.

The night passed quietly without a shot being fired or an alarm sounded. In the morning the sweet sound of the bugle's call awakened us from our slumber; soon the camp was astir again, each man going to his respective duties of getting ready for another day's march.

THE INDIANS MOVE TO HENRY'S LAKE

From this campsite on the meadows where Joseph stole Howard's animals,[32] the Indians departed from the well-beaten trail and traveled due north about twelve miles across the broad valley, then entered the mountains again; thence in a northeasterly direction, striking the North Fork of the Snake River about ten miles below Henry's Lake, thus making nearly a direct course from the meadows to the lake.

This route was doubtless chosen for two reasons: first, to shorten their travel onward; secondly, to lead Howard's train through the entanglements which might well be said to be impossible to travel with wagons, thereby throwing a handicap across Howard's progress to enable them to gain another good lead.

HOWARD PURSUES IN MILITARY STYLE

This morning [August 21] we were late in getting started, but when ready, we sure did move in military style. The wagon train and pack animals were placed in the center; ahead of us was a company of cavalry to lead the way, while another company of cavalry brought up the rear. The infantry marched on either side of the wagons about 100 feet distant, while on the outside of these, the balance of the cavalry took their places in the grand parade across the prairie following Joseph's trail.

As far as appearances were concerned, one might expect to jump the whole Indian band at any moment, but Joseph did not want it that way, so hurried on to avoid a collision. This was on the twenty-first. Many places it seemed almost impossible to get a wagon over the huge rocks formed by lava deposits at some remote day in the past. We made only eighteen miles for the day's march and were tired and worn out at that, and camped on a little creek[33] that came tumbling down from the nearby mountain. Only two Indians were reported as seen during the day.

That night we had some reasons to fear an attack, being in the lava beds, where an Indian could skulk around and do his best fighting. Extra precautions were taken, all hands being on the alert should an alarm be sounded. None came, and we slept in peace until daybreak.

At this point my shoes utterly gave out, and I found myself practically barefoot. My little lieutenant companion, F. E. Eltonhead, came gladly to my assistance; drew from the commissary a pair of shoes for himself, then passed them over to me as a present. Oh, how glad I was; I sure appreciated his kindness.

After the usual routine of getting breakfast over and all in readiness, we moved onward over the Indian trail. The country now became smoother and travel easier, and hence we made better time.

THE INDIANS ARE GETTING HUNGRY
Soon after leaving camp, we came to a meadow where the Indians had made camp—presumably at the time when the marauding party stampeded and captured Howard's animals. Here grew a plant having a wide leaf and a yellow blossom, which none of us could name. The Indians had dug over acres of this land for the roots of these plants; also, on the outskirts of the meadow grew quantities of small pine trees. [From] these trees they stripped off the outer bark, then ate the inner bark for food. These maneuvers led us to believe that their provisions were running low.

We pushed on as rapidly as possible, making a long march, and camped on the North, or Henry's, Fork of the Snake River that night. No Indians were reported as seen that day.

FOUND MY HORSE STOLEN BY INDIANS AT STEVENSVILLE
While quietly lying in camp after sundown, some parties came in with a large band of horses of every description. While looking over them, I recognized a roan horse of mine that disappeared from home about the time the Nez Perces passed Stevensville. This horse, called by name "Caribou," we sometimes used in our freight team as a leader, and a good one he was, too. My first thought was that if I could recover him, he would come [in] handy in case one of my team horses should become disabled in any way, to make up the loss, so I immediately repaired to General Howard's headquarters to obtain an order for the animal. I met the general in person and made known my wants. He immediately ordered the necessary papers filled out and signed. This red tape, of course, took a little time, and when I came to look for the lost horse, the herd had been driven away, and I never saw the animal again.

INDIAN WAR DANCE
When dusk had hovered around us and the bright lights of our campfire were burning, our scouts (Bannock Indians) conceived a little entertainment for us

in the way of a war dance. General Howard was interviewed in the matter, and consent asked for them to be allowed to indulge in their old-time customs when out on the warpath. The general's answer was that he could see no harm in it, and he gave his sanction. Soon the tom-tom was sounded, and the dance was on. We all enjoyed it very much. The dance was permitted to continue until 12:00 A.M., when orders came to cease these hilarious performances for the balance of the night.

HOWARD'S FORCE MOVES TO HENRY'S LAKE

Next morning, the twenty-third, we made a start up the river, bound for Henry's Lake. We were compelled to ford the river several times on our way. On so doing, the infantry had to cross in our wagons, taking a load of soldiers over, then driving back after another load, and so on until all were transported. At one of these fords, the riverbed was filled with large boulders and consequently a very bad crossing. One of our Frenchtown teamsters, after making several trips, balked on the job and refused to go back after another load. Major Spurgin immediately called up a soldier and commanded him to take charge of this man, and then another to jump into the wagon and drive the team. After all were safely crossed over, Major Spurgin called for this man to be brought in his presence. He then gave him a sharp reprimand, and the calling down that man got would make one feel like a two-cent piece. He then gave him possession of his team and warned him never to have a recurrence of such actions again.

Traveling on upstream, we arrived at Henry's Lake about midday and struck camp at the cabin of an old trapper by the name of Sawtell. We had a fine camp on the margin of the lake, which was teeming with trout. Lots of ducks and swans were swimming about; not realizing the terrors of men, [they] were loath to get out of our reach. Young Brooks was noted for being an expert fisherman, and he kept our table well supplied with trout and grayling.

Our orders from Washington were to live on the country, hence certain men were detailed as butchers, whose business it was to keep the command well supplied with beef. Cattle seemed plentiful everywhere. The butchers kept tab on the army's wants, selected animals suitable to fill them, and slaughtered daily, care being taken to note the brands and probable worth, so that the owners would sooner or later by paid by our government for the animals.

Hans was a good cook and sure knew how to serve a good beefsteak. At mealtime he would often ask, "Well, boys, will you have your steak fried on a stick today?" This, of course, calls for an explanation. He would slice the meat quite thick, salt and pepper it, then spread both sides with butter; now, with a stick sharpened especially for the occasion, [he] would hold the meat before the fire and broil it until done. Served hot, it can be relished by the most fastidious men. Now if you don't think meat is good cooked in this way, then I say just try it.

During our stay at the lake, one of the boys killed a swan, and Hans fell heir to a portion. He boiled it for a long, long time, until tender and thoroughly done, making a very palatable meal.

MYSELF AND ALL TEAMS DISCHARGED AT HENRY'S LAKE

On our arrival at the lake in the afternoon of the twenty-third, we were informed that Joseph was two days' march ahead of us. At this news, General Howard became disheartened and sought to be relieved from following any longer. The teams, I think, were all discharged—I know I was, and also the Frenchtown and Missoula teams were.

It seemed that a man by the name of Thomas Williams of Missoula had a contract from the government to furnish a given number of teams for the transportation of General Howard's supplies at a given price. Williams was sent for to meet the command at the lake and make settlement. The morning after our arrival, Williams was on hand and settled up with his men. These teamsters planned to return home by way of Virginia City, and I intended to go with them, but after a second thought, I concluded best to tarry until the command moved, thereby resting up my horses.

During the day, Williams came to my wagon and asked me to report to the quartermaster, my team being in his contract, and that as soon as we arrived in Missoula, he would pay me for my time at $10 per day. This was the first intimation that I had had in regard to pay from any source. I told him that I knew nothing about it but would let him know later. In about a half hour, our quartermaster, Lieutenant Ebstein,[34] came to my camp and asked me if I was included in Williams's contract. I answered that I did not know, and then explained to him how I came to be with the command. His answer was "You are one of our teams and Williams has nothing to do with you," and turned and walked away.

HOWARD GOES TO VIRGINIA CITY TO ASK RELIEF

Shortly after this, the Frenchtown and Missoula teams pulled out over the hill for home. General Howard, with two teams, early in the morning left for Virginia City, where he could confer with the officials at Washington, as a telegraph station was then connected with the outside world.

A dispatch was sent to General Sherman, setting forth a pitiful story that the army was tired and worn out, footsore, and wholly unfit to go further; also, that the animals were so jaded that it was almost impossible to club them along, and asked that he might be relieved from further chase, to return with his army to the land from whence they came. The answer read in these words: "Where Indians can subsist, the army can live. The country and the government expect you to do your duty. No troops are near enough to take your place. Continue the pursuit. If you are tired, General, put in a younger man and return to Oregon, but the troops must go on."

General Howard then gathered up such supplies as he could get in this little mining town of Virginia City and returned to camp.

LOCATION OF THE INDIANS

The day we arrived at Henry's Lake, the Indians were in Firehole [Basin], and the following day moved on over the divide from the headwaters of the Madison to the Yellowstone River, and camped at the crossing of the river and Mud Geysers.[35] Here they remained all the day of the twenty-fifth, knowing Howard's whereabouts and caring only to keep far enough in advance to be out of his way.

On August 26 the main camp of the Nez Perces crossed the Yellowstone at this point, then ascended along the river to Yellowstone Lake, where they took the Pelican Creek Trail that leads to the Lamar River Valley in the northeast corner of the park, where my story leaves them.

A party of marauders, however, went down the river on the left side, passed the Yellowstone Falls and Mount Washburn, thence on down to Baronett's Bridge, where they crossed over near the mouth of the Lamar River, thence followed this stream up to join their main camp again. In their route they committed some murders, destroyed property, fired timber in numerous places, and attempted to burn the Baronett Bridge after crossing it, but the fire went out when it was only partially destroyed.

HOWARD PREPARES TO RESUME THE CHASE

General Howard, on his return from Virginia City at noon on the twenty-seventh, began making preparations to renew the chase, gathering up transportation in such teams as were available in connection with his pack train. Our quartermaster, Lieutenant Ebstein, came to my camp and asked me to go with them through the park and whither the Indians might lead us. My answer was, "Yes, I'll go and do my bit toward the capture of the Indians."

Our wagon train as now made up consisted of W. E. Bass, with two four-horse wagons; myself, with one four-horse wagon; J. A. J. Chapman, with one two-horse wagon; Jacob Goff, with one two-horse wagon; Dr. Van R. Woodmancy, with one two-horse light spring-wagon, all from the Bitterroot Valley; together with some four or five other two-horse wagons that came, I think, into camp with supplies for us.

HOWARD FOLLOWS INTO YELLOWSTONE PARK

After having had a four days' rest, we packed up at 7:00 A.M. on the morning of August 28 and, with considerable reluctance, left our lovely camp by the lake, which we had christened "Camp Ebstein" in honor of our worthy quartermaster. Joseph's trail led us over the main range of the Rockies, through a very low pass called Tachers Pass, and thence down a gradual descent, over bunchgrass lands and through thickets of lodgepole pines, to the Madison River, where we camped for the night, quietly and peacefully, knowing that Joseph was fully a week's march in our advance.

The next morning, the twenty-ninth, we rolled out as usual in hot pursuit. We were now near the west boundary of Yellowstone Park, following the Madison River upstream and into the canyon. We were obliged to ford the stream a number of times, cut out timber and brush, and build roads, all of which took much time, rendering our progress slow.

That night we camped in the Madison Canyon, within the boundary of Yellowstone Park. Nothing of note transpired, so we slept soundly until awakened by the bugle call. In the morning, the thirtieth, we again rolled along up the canyon, making roads and fording the river as we had done the day before; crossed a small river coming in from our left, now called Gibbon River. The river on up now changes to Firehole River. The two coming together form the Madison. Following the Firehole but a short distance, we came to a bend in the river where there was an inviting little meadow and called a halt for the noonday meal, in the P.M. of the thirtieth.

FOUND MR. OLDHAM SHOT BY THE INDIANS

Soon after leaving camp, and while working our way up Firehole Canyon, we picked up a poor, unfortunate young man by the name of Al Oldham.[36] He had been shot through both cheeks and was all covered with blood, and withal was a sad-looking spectacle. I took him in my wagon, and he gave me a graphic account of what had happened, which, as I now remember, was about as follows:

I came from Helena to Radersburg; from thence I came in company with the Carpenter party, sightseeing through the "Wonderland" of America. The party consisted of Mr. Cowan and wife, she being a Carpenter girl; a sister, Miss Carpenter, about sixteen years of age; a brother about twenty-one; myself; [and] two other men.[37] We had seen the park and were just about ready to leave for home. Our outfit consisted of two light spring-wagons—one to ride in, and the other to haul our camp equipment [and] provisions; also, we had several extra horses for riding. We were unaware of any hostile Indians being in the country.

Suddenly, early in the morning of the twenty-fourth, we were confronted by a considerable number of red men, not knowing at the time who they were. Some of our party had arisen and were preparing breakfast. At the approach of the Indians, all sprang to our feet and dressed quickly. On inquiring who they were and what they wanted, was told that this was Looking Glass's band of Nez Perces. They advised us to get ready quickly and go with them, as Joseph's band was coming, and if we waited here, he would kill the last one of us. At this news, we all became alarmed, and Cowan, who was at the head of our party, ordered the teams hooked up at once to move. Some rode in the spring-wagon, and some on horseback. Our camp was about one-half mile west of Fountain Geyser, in a fringe of small pines. Soon after the start was made, we came to a sudden stop.

Directly in front of us was a line of mounted warriors, well armed with rifles hanging by their sides. The Indians, after a short parley, ordered our party to move on up the trail, which led up a small valley toward Mary Lake. Going but a short distance, we came to thick timber, where our wagons could go no further. We were now ordered to mount our horses and proceed on horseback, leaving our wagons under some small pine trees. The Indians now confiscated all our provisions, then the march was resumed, reaching the foot of Mary Mountain at noon. A halt was called and camp struck for refreshments. Our party was ordered to dismount. An Indian called Poker Joe, who could speak good English—a notable character in the Nez Perce tribe, being a subchief among them—acted as spokesman.

The chiefs and headmen of the party held a meeting on one side of the camp, while the squaws were busily preparing the noonday meal. This meeting, of course, meant the decision of our fate, and we were wholly at their mercy. Poker Joe asked us a good many questions as to where we came from, whither we wished to go, and what we were doing here. All questions were answered, seemingly to their satisfaction.

After a short deliberation, we were told that we could now go, but before leaving, our guns and ammunition were taken from us, while our horses were exchanged, giving us old, jaded, and worn-out ponies to travel with. We immediately took the back track, thankful even at this to get away with our lives.

After descending the creek for about one mile, we looked back, only to observe something like 75 or 100 renegade warriors following our trail at full speed. We were halted for a while, then ordered forward on the trail again. [We] passed our noonday camp about one-fourth mile on the side of the mountain, when presently a shot was fired, and I saw Cowan fall dead from his horse. Our party then scattered for the nearby timber. Many shots were then fired at us, one striking me, as you see here. It so stunned me that I knew nothing for some time. I had fallen alongside of a tree that had blown over, and presume the Indian making the shot found the blood oozing out of my head, took it for granted that I had received a fatal wound, and left me for dead. When I came to, I did not move, for I could hear Indians talking. One passing near me stopped for a moment, gave me a kick, and, as I did not move, took it for granted I was dead and passed on.

I lay there quietly until after dark, then, as I could hear no sound, took chances that the Indians had gone. I raised up and cautiously crawled away. I found some water, took a drink, and bathed my face, which relieved my suffering considerably. From that time on, I wandered about, seeing nobody until picked up by your command today. I think all of our party was killed, for if not, I should have found some one of them.

This being August 30, making six days without a mouthful of food—long and dreary ones, too—we gave him something to eat, then slowly worked our way up Firehole Canyon to Nez Perce Creek, finally reaching a fine, level piece of land, partly covered with pines and partly meadow, nearly a mile above its mouth.

Here we made camp for the night. Mr. Bass and I took it upon ourselves to look after Mr. Oldham. I had an extra shirt in the boot of my wagon, and Mr. Bass had an extra pair of pants. With these we fixed him up a change of outer garments. The command gave him surgical attention, and in all we made him quite comfortable, and he also looked very respectable.

WE FOUND MR. COWAN ALIVE

Word soon reached us, when settled in camp, that Mr. Cowan had been found about one-fourth mile in advance of us and was still alive; surgical and medical attention was given him, and he was made as comfortable as possible. George F. Cowan was a young attorney who lived in Helena and was a member of the Carpenter party.

His story of the day's happenings was about the same as told me by Mr. Oldham, only adding thereto his own experiences, which were, to say the least, most horrible. "When the property was being confiscated and worn-out ponies were given to us," Mr. Cowan said, "I watched to see what Indian fell heir to my noble steed. The noted Poker Joe, always on the alert, rode him away."

After being shot from his horse, the ball entering his right hip, he rolled down the hillside, lodging against a fallen tree. His wife leaped from her horse and ran to him to administer what aid she could. Several Indians came up and tried to shoot him again, as the wound he had received was not necessarily a fatal one. She threw her arms around his neck and tried to shield him as best she could. An Indian they called "Charley" was the one who sought his life. After tussling for a little while with Mrs. Cowan, trying to pull her away so that he could shoot him with his revolver, he finally succeeded in doing so, then called upon another Indian to shoot; holding his pistol very near Cowan's head [the other Nez Perce] fired. The ball, striking a glancing blow, only stunned him. This was the last he knew for a long time.

Late in the day, Mr. Cowan came to and sought to raise himself up to take a look at the surroundings. He took hold of a small sapling that was growing by his side and pulled himself up in a standing position. Looking back on the trail, he spied an Indian pulling up his gun to shoot. In an instant, the crack of the gun was heard, the bullet striking him in the back. He fell over again, expecting this time the Indian to come up and dispatch him, but for some reason he never came. He lay in this condition until late at night, when he made the attempt to crawl away very cautiously. Looking up the trail in the bright moonlight, he saw an Indian raise up and look all around him, and then settle down again. Mr. Cowan made a wide detour around him, crawling as best he could. Finally, near morning, he reached the creek and got some much-needed water.

He continued his crawling down the trail until finally reaching his abandoned wagons, but found nobody there nor anything to eat. He concluded it would be best for him to continue on down the creek, where his chances were better of being picked up by friendly hands sooner or later, than to remain on the trail of the Indians.

He saw no human being until the afternoon of the twenty-ninth, when two men came riding by. He hailed them and learned that they were General Howard's scouts. They gave him something to eat and made him a fire, and told him that on the morrow the command would be along and would give him proper attention.

On the next day, Howard's advanced troops picked him up just as they were going into camp nearby, about 2:30 P.M. They gave him surgical and medical treatment and the best of care. This camp General Howard christened "Camp Cowan," in honor of this heroic victim.

THE CARPENTER PARTY STILL ALIVE

At this camp, we also received tidings through a scout arriving in our midst that the Carpenter people were still alive. After Mr. Cowan was shot and left for dead, the Indians took Mrs. Cowan, Ida Carpenter, and Frank Carpenter prisoners and kept them for a few days unharmed, then turned them over to Lieutenant Schofield, who had a small command of troops at Mount Washburn.[38]

COMMAND MOVES UP NEZ PERCE CREEK

Before starting the next morning, August 31, a comfortable bed was made with plenty of blankets in the bottom of Doc Van R. Woodmancy's light spring-wagon, thus forming a sort of ambulance for Mr. Cowan, as he was not able to sit up.

We moved out quite early, following the Indian trail up the creek, which we called Nez Perce Creek; the bottom being full of timber and brush made our progress slow. Soon after leaving Camp Cowan, our trail, after crossing the creek, led up alongside the Lower Geyser Basin, which lay just over a low hill from us. On seeing so much steam arising, our curiosity was excited to know its cause, so we called a halt of the team for an investigation. On ascending the hill and looking down over the field, lo and behold, the sight of our lives presented itself to our view. For a distance of some length, the surface of the earth

Castle Geyser, Yellowstone National Park.
NELSON A. MILES. *PERSONAL RECOLLECTIONS AND OBSERVATIONS.*

seemed to be covered with a white limey crust, caused by the hot boiling springs, pools, and geysers [that] seemed everywhere present.

We wandered about for a while around this curious and interesting region, coming to a conclusion that it stood us well in hand to watch carefully our footsteps, lest we walk right into one of these boiling cauldrons, and that would be our finish. They forcibly reminded me of air holes through the ice where I used to skate in Michigan. The lime crust extending to the margin of the water [became] thinner and thinner, even down to a featheredge.

CARPENTER'S WAGON FOUND
Reluctantly we repaired our wagons again and moved on over a stretch of land full of boiling pools. A short distance above—say one mile—we came to one of the spring-wagons that belonged to the Radersburg party. The wagon stood about fifty feet to the right of the trail. I stopped my team and went over to it. In the wagon I found a box containing many pretty specimens. I took a number of them, fixed them up as best I could, and brought them home with me, and I still have them among my collection of specimens and curios.

QUEER TEAMING EXPERIENCES
Resuming our journey up Nez Perce Creek, we camped on a little warm spring creek for our noonday meal. I always kept a close watch over my horses. After lunch I looked for them and could see but three. Naturally wondering what had become of the fourth one—as they always fed together—I began investigating and found he had attempted to cross the small, warm spring creek, which had a

quagmire in it not over twenty feet across. There was my horse, all buried in soft mud save his neck, head, and back, which were sticking out.

I hurriedly procured a rope, throwing a sling noose over his head, and our party dragged him out to terra firma again. He was a sad looking spectacle. I got a pail of water and a piece of cloth, sponged off the black mud, and then hooked up again for the afternoon drive.

After traveling a short distance, I met with the most singular coincidence with a team of horses that I ever had or ever heard of. The trail crossed a small creek, and on going out on the other side, the yellow clay banks were very slippery from recent rains. On going up the bank, my near wheel horse lost his footing and fell across the tongue, over to the side of the off horse; this tripped the off wheeler, and he fell clear over the near horse, and there they both lay on their backs with all legs up in the air. I spoke to them gently, and they lay there quietly until our help unhitched and unharnessed them. Then, taking them by the legs, we turned them over and away from the tongue, when both horses sprang to their feet. Neither one was hurt, nor was there any harm done to the harness. We then hooked up again and were soon off, following Joseph's trail up Nez Perce Creek.

CAMPED TO BUILD ROAD TO TOP OF MARY MOUNTAIN

Upon coming to the foot of Mary Mountain, the trail led over the very steep mountainside. As we stood gazing upon the situation, we could not help comparing it to the old Indian tree, "so straight up that it leaned a little." Here we camped for the night, with a pretty tough job staring us in the face. Next morning, September 1, our skilled workmen had a chance to show some of their cunning. A route was laid out, not continuing on the old Indian trail, but following up ridges and gullies, also along some very steep side hills to pass from one ridge to another, where it would be necessary to use guy ropes fastened to the top of the wagon box and [to have] men walk alongside of the wagon holding fast, thus preventing its capsizing. The last stretch of about one-half mile of heavy grade followed a sort of canyon or washout that was wide enough for the passage of our wagons. The bottom was filled with huge rocks, many of which it was necessary to roll aside before we could proceed.

Our camp was on a nice, little prairie at the foot of Mary Mountain, thence it was a dense forest to the summit, an estimated distance of three miles. There had been a fire that had swept through the pines,[39] and trees lay crisscross over each other on the way; much chopping had to be done, and also some pick and shovel work. It took until the middle of the afternoon of the second before we could make a start with the train.

INDIAN SCOUTS DESERT AND STEAL OUR HORSES

On the morning of September 1, our herders failed to bring in all the horses—some forty head missing, mostly belonging to the road makers. Howard's command had moved forward in our advance and was in camp just beyond Mary

Lake. A courier was dispatched to General Howard, informing him of the situation. He at once sent an officer with a few cavalrymen to our assistance in the search for the missing animals.

It was noticed that the Bannock Indian scouts were deserting General Howard and were acting quite strangely. Among the rest were eight men that we suspicioned knew where the horses were. Howard's officer[40] arrested them, took their horses and arms away, and then informed them that they would be held as hostages until the missing herd was returned. One of the Indians, acting as chief, pled for their release, but nothing doing. The officer told him that Indians were good in following tracks, and as soon as the missing animals were brought in, these men could go.

The old Indian, with a shrug of the shoulders, went galloping off. Early in the afternoon, he came into our camp, with the help of a few Bannocks, bringing about one-half of the missing herd, and again pled for the release of the eight men prisoners. He was again told by the officer that every horse must be brought in before his request could be granted, as it was now plain that they had them cached somewhere. These Indians again departed, and about dusk they came in with the balance of the remaining horses. The men then under arrest were released and their ponies and arms were given back to them, save one who seemed to be the leader, [who] was retained and sent to Fort Ellis.

BROOKS AND I REACH MARY LAKE

Our "skillets" worked like beavers all this time preparing the road for us to travel. In the afternoon of the second day, word came "'tis finished," then came the climb. My wagon was in the lead; we hooked eight horses to it and made the start; other teams were doubled up in like manner, and our train was on the move. Only a few feet were made at a hitch, consequently [we] did not gain the top very quickly.

When about halfway up, one of the men exclaimed, "Oh, look there," pointing over the following country to the south. At an estimated distance of eight miles, an immense geyser was spouting volumes of water and steam to a great height. We all stopped to admire this strange spectacle for twenty minutes or more, all wishing that we could be over there, as it would have been a wonderful sight to have seen at close range. Further developments showed that this big geyser that we witnessed on display at long range was the noted Excelsior, now extinct, but at that time the largest in the known world.

Resuming our arduous task again, we pulled on up over our newly made road, my wagon being the only one to reach the top that night. It was dusk when we drew up to the shore of that beautiful sheet of water called Mary Lake. My camp equipment and a little grub were in my wagon, so Neil Brooks and I held down this camp alone for the night. The rest of the men, taking the horses with them, returned to the camp at the foot of the mountain for the night.

BEAUTIFUL SULPHUR FORMATIONS

Next morning, September 3, Brooks and I went down to the camp below to assist in getting up the rest of the wagons. Success crowned our efforts, and by noon we were all in camp at Mary Lake for lunch. Hooking up again, we made the start for Yellowstone Lake; going along the side of the mountain, travel was quite good. We christened this "Sulphur Mountain," there being loads of pure sulphur on the surface of the ground. Steam in many places was issuing from between rocks. In some places the noise was sufficient to be heard a mile, sounding like a steam engine blowing off. There was lots of hot water present everywhere.

We stopped our teams for a few moments to take a look at the many wonders that nature here had on display. In some places stalactites and stalagmites of pure sulphur were observed, which steam had deposited among the rocks. They were the most beautiful things that one might wish to see, but with a touch of the fingers would crumble into dust. At one place I looked down a crevice in the rocks some four feet across and perhaps twenty feet long, at the bottom of which, say twenty-five feet deep, ran swiftly a very large stream of boiling water.

FROM MARY LAKE TO YELLOWSTONE FALLS

Traveling on down, we struck Alum Creek, which we followed for a short distance. Here again were mud springs, where the mud was boiling and bubbling after the fashion of mush in a kettle that mother was cooking for supper. About this time, a courier came from General Howard directing us to turn to the left and make our way to Yellowstone Falls. Obeying orders, we passed over a high plateau of easy going. At one place on our route, we could plainly see Yellowstone Lake. Suddenly we came up to a full stop on a timbered ridge that extended toward the river. Medium sized pine trees grew here. We took a survey of the whole situation and came to the conclusion that the only way to get down was to take a jump of some 500 feet. Someone suggested to prepare a slide and go downhill like a beaver. The pines were not thick, and the ground was smooth, although about as steep as the roof of an ordinary house. We picked out a place that looked most suitable for our descent and commenced clearing a roadway. The job was soon finished, and "now comes the tug," as the boy said when he slid off the roof of the house and came to the eaves.

DESCENDING THE "BEAVER SLIDE"

We had with us a very large rope—100 feet long—for emergency cases and were now all ready to go. The crowd called out, "Here, Buck, you take the lead, and if you can't make it, we will try it." One end of the rope was fastened to the hind axle of my wagon, then two turns were made around a substantial tree, with several men holding on to the end of the rope so that the wagon could not get away; they played it out as fast as the descent was made. Nothing daunted,

Yellowstone Falls, Yellowstone National Park.

NELSON A. MILES. *PERSONAL RECOLLECTIONS AND OBSERVATIONS.*

I climbed up into my spring seat and gathered up the lines—not even taking off my leaders.

I made the start downward and nearly stood up straight on the footrest of the wagon, it was so steep. Slowly and carefully we went the length of the rope, when a halt was called, and with the aid of a short rope made fast to the hind axle and securely tied to another tree, we then loosened the long rope and came down and made another two turns around a nearby tree, and was then ready for a second drive, thence a third, and so on, until the bottom was reached in safety.

The rope was then carried up the hill, and another teamster took courage to try his luck, and his wagon too was landed at the bottom of the hill. This routine was continued until all the wagons in our train were safely landed on the little flat together. It was now about dusk, and a drive to the nearest water was to be made for camp, which was the Yellowstone River itself, about a mile away and about two miles above the Upper Falls.

CAVALRY AND INFANTRY MOVE TO YELLOWSTONE FALLS

Howard's cavalry and infantry, in the meantime, on September 3 broke camp at the ford of the Yellowstone near Mud Springs and advanced down the river, going into camp on a little flat just above and nearly abreast of the Lower Falls.

Next morning, the fourth, we made quite an early start. Everything went along just fairly well, having some deep-cut creeks to cross and some bridges to build, until we came squarely up against a deep-cut canyon. This we called Cascade Creek, presumably because the water went in leaps and bounds, until it finally took a jump off into the Yellowstone River below. From here we could see our soldiers' camp on the high plateau across the canyon, about on the same ground where the Canyon Hotel now stands. A roadway was selected and cleared through the timber and brush, and a pole bridge built across the stream. The rope act was here repeated to get our wagons down, and teams again doubled up for the long climb to camp on the flat where the command was waiting for us. It was noon when we struck camp, in company with the soldiers whom we had learned to love so well.

We found this country extremely difficult for wagon travel, being full of deep-cut creeks and canyons. General Howard got discouraged in trying to pull his wagon train any farther, it being utterly impossible to keep up with the command, so he gave Major Spurgin orders to take the wagon train and citizens and work his way out of this wilderness as best he could, take the outfit to Fort Ellis, and give all an honorable discharge.

HOWARD ABANDONS WAGON TRAIN

General Howard then took all supplies on pack animals from this camp at the Lower Yellowstone Falls on the morning of September 5 and moved on down the river. We bade them good-bye, as we were never to see them again. The command, consisting of all the cavalry and infantry, followed the trail down the river on the left side until they reached the Baronett Bridge, where they crossed the Yellowstone River near the mouth of the Lamar River, which stream they followed up until striking Joseph's trail, again ascending Soda Butte Creek.

Here our story leaves General Howard and his command to continue the pursuit of Joseph and fight their own battles as best they could, while Major Spurgin in command of the citizens and wagon train pressed forward to work their way out to civilization and Fort Ellis, thence to return home to the lands from whence we came.[41]

Although I was forced in the beginning to go with General Howard's command, the trip was most interesting; the lure of the wild had its charms for me, and although our pathway was beset with many a trial, I thoroughly enjoyed it; so full of beautiful and strange scenes, with many and varied experiences, through a vast wilderness with a military force of arms. Our line of march was filled with thrills that enlivened our pace onward, and now, after a lapse of forty-five years, I can look backward and say, in spite of the hardships, that it proved to be the pleasure trip of my life.

Where Is Chief Joseph?

CHARLES KING[1]

Milwaukee *Sentinel,* April 21, 1889

S herman's March to the Sea was the dramatic and picturesque episode of our great war. The admirably organized and disciplined army, complete in its commissariat and transportation and unencumbered with deadwood of any kind, cut loose from Atlanta and tramped through the heart of the Confederacy to Savannah, meeting hardly any opposition that its advance guard could not easily brush away. In proportion to numbers engaged and obstacles to be surmounted, an Indian chief, Joseph by name, simply triple-discounted this brilliant exploit of our brave and brilliant general, and despite pursuing forces, despite incessant effort to head him off, despite five times his number in fighting foemen, despite the fact that he was burdened with all the women and children of his tribe, this coolheaded yet daring Indian general, this modern Moses, led his people through the wilderness from the eastern border of Washington Territory, through the camas prairies of Idaho, up the valley of the Salmon River, across the Bitterroot Mountains, through Montana to the Yellowstone Park, down Clark Fork, across the Yellowstone, then straightaway northward for the British possessions, and not until within a day's march of the Big Missouri—not until two days more would have landed him safely across the line—was he finally hemmed in and captured, by which time just about half the cavalry and one-fourth of the infantry of the United States Army were in the field engaged in the chase.

Sherman's storied March to the Sea was completed in two hundred fifty miles with little to hinder. Chief Joseph's rush across the continent carried him some seven hundred fifty miles by the way he had to go, and it was fight or dodge every inch of the route. Behind him, close at his heels, was Sherman's wing commander Howard with a strong array of cavalry and infantry—stronger far than Joseph's fighting force.

Every now and then they overhauled and made the Indians turn and fight—every time with disastrous results. Lieutenant Theller, 21st Infantry, was killed in consequence at White Bird Creek on June 17. Lieutenant Rains,

1st Cavalry, was killed in another tussle July 3 at Craig's Mountain, Idaho. Col. John Gibbon packed what men he had in wagons and made a dash from Fort Shaw to head them off at Big Hole Pass as they crossed the Bitterroot Range. He hardly had one hundred fifty effective soldiers when, like the born fighter that he is, he flew at the throat of his foe at dawn on August 9. He had not half that number at noon when forced to drop his hold and let the fierce Nez Perce go. Captain Logan and Lieutenants Bradley and English, 7th Infantry, with over a score of soldiers, were wounded. Chief Joseph went on his way and Howard came up just too late. Sturgis, with the 7th Cavalry, threw himself across his path at Clark Fork, and Joseph tricked him into a wild goose chase down around Cedar Mountain, leaving the way clear. After a long stern chase, with worn-out horses, the 7th Cavalry flew at his heels again just after he had crossed the Yellowstone, but it was an unavailing fight. At last, on September 30, three months from the time of his start, the worn and weary chieftain was halted at Battle Eagle Creek among the Bear's Paw Mountains. Snake Creek is the name of the main stream. Colonel Miles, with his hard regiment, the 5th Infantry, mounted on Indian ponies, and with detachments of the 2nd and 7th Cavalry, had made one of his quick dashes—250 miles cross-country—and barred the way. Even when they rode in to the charge, Capt. Owen Hale and Lt. J. Williams Biddle of the 7th Cavalry met their soldier deaths, but Joseph could go no farther. He and his little remnant of his band surrendered, and the Nez Perce War of 1877 was at an end. Over three months had he withstood the power of the government. Over seven hundred miles had he fought his way to freedom, as it looked to him, and his exploit stands, to my thnking, without a parallel in modern warfare.

If ever an Indian deserved success it was this fellow Joseph. He and his people had their grievances at the old reservation on the western border of Idaho. The Nez Perces were not a savage tribe. Many of them spoke English fairly well; many of them had embraced the Roman Catholic religion. Misunderstandings arose between them and the settlers, in which the chances are ten to one the settlers were as much at fault as the aborigines. The matter was not judiciously handled by the Indian Bureau, and threats of punishment only put the Indians on their mettle. When it had played its last trump and lost the game, the bureau demanded troops to enforce its orders, and the soldiers who had long been stationed among these Nez Perces, and knew and liked them, were compelled to take the field against them. We have no choice in such matters. Had such a man as General Crook been sent thither at the first appearances of a cloud on the horizon, a few words from him would have put a stop to all the trouble, but he, whom they trusted and respected from old association, was far away on duty in another department. Almost before we knew anything about the matter, the news was flashed in by telegraph that General Howard, with all his available troops, was moving on Joseph's camps, and that Joseph had sworn that he and his people should never be taken.

At the outbreak of the war, we of the 5th Cavalry were stationed on the Union Pacific Railway, headquarters and six troops (companies) at Fort D. A. Russell, just west of Cheyenne, the others at Fort McPherson down in the Platte Valley and at Sidney Barracks midway. Early in the season General Crook had sent five of the six troops from Fort Russell to establish a camp of observation way up along the northeastern foothills of the Bighorn range, where he fought the Sioux the previous summer, and we had only the band and Captain Payne's Troop F to "hold the fort" at Russell. Similarly, all the troops from McPherson and Sidney, except a mere post guard, were in the field scouting toward the Sioux reservations when the great railway riot of 1877 burst upon the land. Pittsburgh was in flames, the militia overpowered. Chicago was in the hands of the mob, and the police exhausted.

Then came the order for the regulars, and all the 5th Cavalry within reaching distance of the railway were hurried in. The McPherson battalion rode like mad for the nearest station; left their horses with the quartermaster and a small guard, and were whirled through to Lake Michigan by special train. The 9th Infantry started first from Omaha, but the strikers sidetracked them somewhere, and the first command to reach Chicago was this tough looking battalion of troopers from the plains[2]—bearded, bronzed, dusty, destitute of anything like glitter or gold lace; dressed in their roughest scouting rig, flannel shirts, buckskin or canvas reinforced breeches, and old slouch hats, but Chicago gave them a welcome they have never forgotten. "These fellers ain't got no bouquets in their muskets" was the remark of a newsboy that made the troopers grin.

While the regulars in Nebraska were hurried to Chicago, those along the railway in Wyoming and Utah were similarly hurried to Omaha, and our colonel, Wesley Merritt, was assigned the command at this latter point. Here we guarded the big bridge across the Missouri and kept order from July 26 until August 9, when we were sent back to our stations, the troubles being over. Meantime, General Crook had got in from a scout through the extreme northwestern section of his department, and the very day we started for home, Gibbon, with his little command, was having his death grapple with the Indians at Big Hole Pass.

The next thing we heard was that Chief Joseph was across the mountains, coming east. Still the War Department hesitated. Still it was believed that despite his ill luck so far, Howard with his big force must overhaul the wily Nez Perce. But day after day crept by; every dispatch showed the Indian still ahead, and at last it became suddenly apparent to the powers at Washington that he was almost at the Yellowstone Park and meant to cross the Shoshone Mountains. Once over, there were just three ways for him to escape: northeastward by way of Clark Fork, eastward by the Stinking River to the Bighorn, or southeastward through the Wind River Valley.

The 7th Cavalry, already out along the Yellowstone, was ordered to block the first gap. Hart's[3] battalion of the 5th Cavalry, already up on the Bighorn range at the headwater of Tongue River, was ordered to march via the Custer battlefield of the previous year, where some Sioux and Cheyenne scouts would join them, then up Pryor's Fork and the Stinking River Valley until they reached its head, and so stop the second hole, while Colonel Merritt at Russell received telegraphic orders to go at once to Camp Brown (now Fort Washakie), in the Wind River Valley, and organize a force to meet Chief Joseph should he come that way. All the 3rd and 5th Cavalry near the railway were hustled aboard the cars and shipped to Green River Station, whither the general and his adjutant, hastened by first train, reached there the morning of August 30, jumped on a buckboard, drove northward all that day, that night, and the next day, reaching Camp Brown at 4:30 P.M. The cavalry followed by forced marches.

General Crook soon arrived, and on September 9, with seven fine troops of veteran cavalry and thirty-five picked Shoshone scouts, away we went, still northward, under orders to reach the headwater of the Stinking River and tackle Joseph if we could possibly find him. It was not certain he was coming southeast, and General Crook, who had not been consulted apparently in the orders coming from his superior, shook his head over the plan. "You won't be apt to find him," he said. "He will be over and away long before you can get there, and he is making for the British possessions, or I'm mistaken."

Never have I seen anything in wild beauty to match the magnificent mountain country through which we marched day after day. We climbed and crossed the Owl Creek Mountains on September 12—a wonderful experience. Then came range after range, valley after valley—the Meeyero, the Beaver, the Gray Bull, the Meeteetse; all clear-running streams from the towering Shoshone peaks on our left. We lugged our wagons along until the fourteenth, but they hampered us so that Merritt could stand it no longer, and we left them.

We ran into a blinding snowstorm on the fifteenth, and I, as usual out on the flanks, lost all sight or trail of the regiment until, catching a view of some four-footed objects a few yards ahead, I trotted unhesitatingly among them, never discovering until my horse almost turned a back somersault in his fright that we had darted into the midst of a herd of buffalo. Then it cleared as suddenly as it stormed, leaving the face of nature six inches deep in powdery white, with our column crawling like a blacksnake over the divide to the next valley. Finally, after a rapid twenty-five-mile march on the morning of September 17 through an atmosphere as clear as a bell and a sweep of scenery simply superb, we reached the forks of the Stinking River and struck a recent and heavy cavalry trail.

Sturgis or Hart? Seventh or Fifth? That was the question. At 3:00 P.M. the colonel had his command bivouacked between the beautiful streams, the north and south branches of the river with the infelicitous name. Cedar Mountain loomed right to the east of us. Pure as snow, clear as crystal, the waters plunge into and under it on the western side and reissue on the other, slimy, yellow, and thick, and smelling like Sheol.[4]

And now came the longest ride of my life.

It was necessary that the colonel should know at once whether the Indians had passed or were coming this way. It was necessary that he should know at once whether Sturgis or Hart had made these trails and whither the makers had gone. "Take any lieutenant in the regiment you choose and what scouts you need, and find out," were his brief orders to me. After a cup of steaming coffee and a hearty lunch, mounting my spare horse, which had been led along during our twenty-five-mile jog of the morning, at 4:30 P.M. I rode out northward with seven companions—six Shoshone Indians on their wiry ponies and my "statesman," Lieutenant Bishop.[5] I had chosen him because he was all muscle and sinew—a man who never tired, and who could stand all night's work if need be and be just as ready for a chase on the morrow.

We rode light burdened, with nothing but our arms and ammunition, and at sunset we were loping—up, up, up—following a winding trail leading to the summit of the lofty crest, beyond which lay the valley of Clark Fork. It was the old Bannock trail, said one of our Shoshones. To our right was the long, narrow range that at its southeastern end is called Cedar Mountain. To our left, the main divide between us and Yellowstone Lake—the backbone of the continent. Ahead of us the bold range connecting the two.

We had ridden miles along that twisting, tortuous trail and still could not say whether it was made by the 7th or the 5th. That they had gone in eager haste was evident. We passed horseshoes, we picked up abandoned lariats, a saddle blanket, two canteens, but oddly enough there was no distinguishing mark. At last, under the rays of the full moon, I found the evidence I wanted. Generally, the trail was that of a double file of horses following in each other's track. Here and there were places, though, where in crossing the brook, or ascending or descending steep places, each troop leader (company commander) had chosen a separate path for his men. We had passed several where four and five separate trails were made, but Hart had five troops, and that proved nothing. Far up in the narrowing gorge, we came upon a grassy ridge they had clambered across and here were seven distinct trails of troops in columns of twos. It was the 7th Cavalry, and they had unquestionably crossed the range to Clark Fork.

So, much was settled. Back down the Bannock trail we cantered—the full moon high in the heavens now—and turning westward when we reached the broad, beautiful valley of the North Fork, we rode in wide, dispersed order, scouting it for miles toward Yellowstone Lake, finding game trails innumerable but not a trace of lodge pole, pony hoof, or Indian property. At last, at 11:00 P.M., I gave the word to rein about and made for camp—a glorious gallop over springing turf, through silvery moonlight that made the valley bright as day. At midnight we were challenged by our sentries after our forty-five-mile jaunt.

At daybreak, changing horses once more, Bishop and I, with five of our six Shoshones, were off again. Twenty miles we trotted around Cedar Mountain to the fords of the Stinking River, fifteen miles further up the highlands to the north we went back on the Sturgis trail, nearly running over a magnificent elk as we rounded a sudden turn, and then my field glasses detect a dust cloud miles away down in the valley. Thither we gallop, and in an hour, waving our hats, we ride full tilt into the halted column of Hart's battalion. Twenty-five miles we led them back around the mountain to Merritt's camp, reaching there at 6:00 P.M., in time for supper, having been in saddle twenty-nine hours out of thirty-six and ridden nearly one hundred forty miles. Where was Joseph? Oh! He had dodged past Sturgis ten days before we got there and was far beyond the Yellowstone.

A Pleasure Ride in Montana

THEODORE W. GOLDIN[1]

Ours, a Military Magazine 2, no. 5 (November 1887): 87–88

As many of the readers of *Ours* will no doubt remember, in 1877, following closely on the merciless slaughter of Custer and his gallant command, occurred the campaign against the Nez Perces, in which campaign the old "Seventh" were called to take a leading part. It is to an incident of that campaign that our mind now turns.

The first engagement in which the 7th took part was at Canyon Creek, and owing to the fact that the Indians were supposed to be a long distance in our front, and the suddenness with which we were called on to attack them, gave them the advantage we sought to wrest from them, and they were enabled to temporarily elude the troops by gaining access to the Musselshell Valley and then crossing the Missouri by passing through the canyon which gave name to the battleground.

The morning following[2] our hard-fought engagement there, Colonel Sturgis, seeing that in the present exhausted condition of his command it would be impossible for him to overtake the fleeing foe, decided to acquaint Colonel Miles at Tongue River with the situation and invoke his aid in capturing the hostiles ere they could reach British territory, for which they were evidently aiming.

Shortly after the reveille had sounded and the men had eaten their frugal breakfast, three men might have been seen leaving the camp in different directions. These men who had taken their lives in their hands were couriers with the dispatches to Colonel Miles. Each bore the same news, but it was deemed best that three should go, each taking a different course, so that at least one of the number must be sure to reach the destination.

One of them we have met before—let us follow him[3] as he gallops away in the early morning light. A sharp ride of two or three miles, and he pulls up his horse, springs from the saddle, taking from the saddle pocket his compass, with which he gets his bearings. He replaces the instrument in its place, stops for a moment for a hasty caress of his horse, and he is again in the saddle and, shaping his course nearly due [south[4]], is off. Steadily he rides all day long and far into the night; not a human being has he seen since leaving the camp in the morning, but there is no appearance of timidness or alarm; yet, were we near enough, we should see that his keen eyes were searching every foot of the country over which he passed; nothing escaped him.

It is now almost midnight; he has at last struck a wagon trail and is urging his tired horse to renewed efforts; half a mile further, and he rides up to the door of a rude frontier shack and kicks loudly at the door with his riding boot. "Who's thar?" comes gruffly from within." "A friend, and in a devil of a hurry," is the not over-polite response. A moment's silence, and the upper part of the door swings open, disclosing a burly bearded rancher, rifle at an advance, while just behind him stands his "pardner," shading as best he can the flickering flame of a candle. "Well, what in thunder de ye want?" is the curt question. The courier's errand is hastily made known, and the now thoroughly awakened rancher disappears in the direction of the corral, leaving the tired and hungry horseman to the tender mercies of him of the candle, thanks to whose aid he is soon discussing the merits of a boiled shoulder of antelope and a huge loaf of soft bread.

In a few moments the rancher is back, leading a raw-boned bronco. The saddle is speedily transferred from the worn-out cavalry horse to the new mount; a cheery "all ready stranger," and the courier dashes out of the house. A hurried handshake, a word of thanks, a gruff good-bye, and he is in the saddle, and a moment later the regular hoofbeats of the horse can be heard far down the valley. The tired cavalry steed is led away to the corral, there to rest in peace until he is exchanged for the one ridden away.

Just before daybreak, the thoroughly exhausted rider seeks the shelter of an inviting grove, waters and pickets his horse, and throws himself down for a brief rest. Two hours pass and he is awake; again watering his horse, he swings into the saddle and pushes forward, rested and refreshed by even this brief halt. As he gets nearer his destination, he begins to meet an occasional prospector and once in a while a train of wagons bound for some of the settlements up the river.

But exhausted nature can stand no more; he at last pulls up—weak for want of food and exhausted for want of rest—at the door of a friendly ranch, states his mission, and asks for food for himself and horse and a chance for a few hours' rest. His requests are cheerfully granted, and within half an hour he is snoring contentedly on a pile of robes in the corner.

By sunset he is awake and ready for another start; his generous hosts will accept nothing for their kindness, so with a hearty good-bye he is off, well knowing that he has lost valuable time, but realizing that the few hours' rest can easily be made up by the increase in speed gained thereby. Cantering gaily away, he is soon out of sight. Darkness soon settles over the land, but there is no halt; every rod of the country is familiar to him, and just as the sound of the morning gun at the Tongue River cantonment is echoing and re-echoing among the hills, tired and weary he draws reins in front of the colonel's headquarters and, after a short wait at the door, is admitted, the first of the three to arrive.

The companies just assembling on the parade ground for the morning roll call are no doubt surprised to see their usually dignified commander dashing full speed toward the adjutant's office, followed closely by a dust-covered cavalryman leading a sorry-looking bronco.

Roll call over, the adjutant puts in an appearance. Officers' call is sounded, and in an hour it is known that the four troops of the 7th, the battalion of the 2nd, and all the infantry but one company are to take the trail at once. All day long the notes of preparation resound through the garrison, and by 7:00 A.M. the last man and horses are on the other side of the river and en route to the front, while the poor, worn-out courier is seated at the trader's store, going over in detail the fight at Canyon Creek, interspersing his tale with an occasional invigorator from the trader's "wet grocery" counter.

Military Expedition and Campaign and Battle of Bear's Paw Mountain, Montana Territory, September 30, 1877

PETER ALLEN

Packet FF 12, Walter M. Camp Papers, Western Historical Department, Denver Public Library[1]

I enlisted in the United States Army at Indianapolis, Ind., September 4, 1876, as one of Custer's avengers. We remained at Indianapolis three days after I enlisted, and were then transferred to St. Louis, Mo., where we remained in the barracks for three weeks, having our first experience in being drilled and study of the U.S. military tactics. We were then transferred from St. Louis, via Chicago and St. Paul, Minn., to Bismarck, Dakota Territory, and thence across the Missouri River to Fort A. Lincoln, Dakota Territory, where we were assigned to the 7th U.S. Cavalry, I being assigned to Troop K. I was on a short expedition down the Missouri River during the fall of 1876, where we apprehended and disarmed Cheyenne Indians, and returned to Fort A. Lincoln to winter quarters.

On May 1, 1877, the 7th U.S. Cavalry left Fort A. Lincoln under command of Colonel Sturgis, going north up the Missouri River, pitching camp occasionally to rest and graze our horses.[2] Our first camp for ten days was at Fort Buford, where the Yellowstone empties into the Missouri River. From there we continued the expedition up the Yellowstone until we arrived at Fort Keogh, now Fort Custer. Colonel Sturgis proceeded up the Yellowstone, leaving a small detachment of the 7th Cavalry at Fort Keogh, Troop K being one that remained.[3]

Colonel Sturgis and his command had an engagement with the hostile Nez Perces soon after leaving Keogh,[4] then a hurried dispatch came from Colonel Sturgis to Col. Nelson A. Miles, who was commanding the 5th U.S. Infantry, to take the detachment of the 7th Cavalry remaining at Keogh and proceed on a forced march northeast to cut off the hostiles before reaching Canada. Colonel Miles made good and intercepted Chief Joseph, who was in command of the hostile Nez Perces, who was camped on Snake Creek in Bear's Paw Mountains, Montana Territory.

During our hurried trip from Keogh, we were in camp on the night of September 29, 1877, within three or four miles of the Indian village. Leaving camp on the morning of the thirtieth, we only marched a short distance, passing

Lo! The wide Missouri. RUFUS F. ZOGBAUM. *HORSE, FOOT, AND DRAGOON.*

over a high elevation on the plains, from the top of which we could see the Indian village.[5]

On reaching the plain below, the command "trot" was given, then "gallop." Deploying into line of battle, the command "charge" came, with revolvers in hand, ready for the fray. Before arriving close up to the Indian camp, to our surprise, the hostiles had formed a line of battle out from their breastworks toward our command, and as we came near, they arose with a war whoop and fired a volley at us, and hastily retreated to their breastworks.

On they went, with our command in hot pursuit, using our revolvers and side arms to good advantage. When the Indians that remained alive were in their pits, our command was within less than one hundred yards of the enemy. Dismounting,[6] the battle lasted for about an hour before retreat was ordered. During this short period of time, several comrades were killed and wounded, Lieutenant Biddle of Troop K being killed close on my right side.

While we were on our retreat, I was wounded, one bullet crushing my left arm from elbow to wrist; another passed through my belt and clothing, grazing the skin on my right side; and a third bullet passing through my hat, plowing a furrow through my hair across the top of my head, which rendered me unconscious for a short time. After I realized my condition and the position I was in, being about midway between the two lines of battle under cross firing, I gave the comrade in front of me a signal to cease firing while I crawled over in rear of our line of battle, my overcoat having nine bullet holes in it.[7]

Capt. Owen Hale, who was commanding Troop K, directed me and comrade Fleck,[8] who was wounded in both arms, to go to the hospital. Captain Hale was killed in the battle later.

Arriving at the hospital tent, several wounded were already there, all calling for the doctor and begging for water; some cursing, some praying, some crying, some laughing. This scene impressed me so deeply I never will forget. Soon after we arrived, Dr. Tilton,[9] who was our regimental surgeon, came to where I was sitting on a cracker box, leaning upon an ambulance wheel, and remarked, "Young man, I'll wait on you now. I notice you haven't been calling for the doctor." Until the doctor came to me, I had been sitting there taking in the entire situation.

After my wound was dressed, there came a soldier by the name of "Toba"[10] who had been wounded in the head, and blood was all over his face and breast. The hospital steward[11] became excited because his friend Taube was wounded. He went up and got his gun. The doctor remarked to him, "Stay here, I need your help." His reply was "I am going to kill the damned Indian that shot Toba." He went up to the line of battle, where a small piece of artillery[12] was pouring hot shots down upon the Indians, and he received a gunshot wound in the ankle and fell to the ground calling, "Oh! Doctor, doctor, doctor."

The battle began on September 30, 1877, about 8:00 A.M. Once during the battle, all firing ceased, an exchange being made, Chief Joseph coming up to confer with Colonel Miles and an officer from the 5th Infantry taking his place with the Indians during the negotiations for peace.[13] The conference, however, was of no effect, and after some delay, the exchange of the officer and Joseph was returned, they meeting about midway between the two lines of battle, greeting each other with a handshake, and after they were back in their lines of battle, the firing reopened and continued until the third day, when Chief Joseph and warriors surrendered.[14]

On October 5, 1877, Dr. Tilton amputated my left arm above the elbow. One other soldier[15] lost his arm, and one lost a leg amputated below the knee. Still another lost a thumb.[16]

About the time [of], or just after, the surrender, Brig. Gen. O. O. Howard, who had only one arm, with his command came to our relief.[17]

In a few days after all the amputations were performed, and the wounded men were able to march or be carried in ambulances, we left the battleground on Snake Creek in Bear's Paw Mountains and was about a week crossing over the plains to the government relief boat on the Missouri River.[18] I was placed on the boat and carried down to Fort A. Lincoln, and there remained in the general hospital until February 1878, being discharged February 18, and came back to East Tennessee.[19]

After The Nez Perces

HENRY R. TILTON[1]

Forest and Stream and Rod and Gun 9 (December 1877): 403–4

CANTONMENT AT TONGUE RIVER, M.T.,
November 25, 1877

Joseph and his band, after marching through Idaho and western Montana, and having various conflicts with the military—regular and volunteer—came sufficiently near to invite the attention of Colonel Miles at Tongue River, M.T.

Orders were issued. We crossed the swift Yellowstone on September 18, passed up a ravine where two of Custer's men were killed by the Indians in 1873,[2] over a high plateau which gives commanding views in very direction, cast one long, lingering look at the fair forms and waving handkerchiefs on the other side of the river, and our march began.

We soon reached the valley of Sunday Creek and passed through a camp of Cheyenne and Sioux, our enemies of last year but now firm friends. They surrendered last March, and the only secret of their conversion, after fighting them, is summed up in one word—"Justice." Their main camp is near the post. They are treated fairly, have sufficient food, and from time to time small parties, with an escort of soldiers, have been permitted to go out hunting buffalo. In this way they have provided themselves with new skin lodges and are better off in every respect than before their surrender. This camp has just started out for a hunt and greet us with hearty "Hows" as we march by them. A ride of seventeen miles through the dust, and our first camp was made.

Sunday Creek varies from a roaring torrent after heavy rains to an insignificant thread of alkali water, which is the usual condition. As progress is made toward the head of the creek, water is found in pools, and these at long intervals. Our second day's march is again over a dusty trail, through barren, fantastic badlands alternating with patches of luxuriant grass.

After making camp, several men go out hunting. The pickets report buffalo in sight. Result of the hunt, one black-tailed deer. A few jackrabbits were seen during the day, but there is so much cactus that dogs have no show.

The next morning ushered in a bright, lovely day. I bagged a splendid black antelope, whose horns would have been a fine trophy, but some teamster

Dr. Henry R. Tilton. NATIONAL LIBRARY OF MEDICINE, BETHESDA, MD.

who had no appreciation in his soul threw them out of a wagon after a few days' march. One young officer, who had never seen a buffalo in his native haunts, killed two, and it would require a Nast to do pictorial justice to the scene. All sportsmen can appreciate the feelings of an ardent hunter as he bags his first specimen.

The command had a hard day's march and camped on a branch of the Big Dry Fork of the Missouri River.[3] Just at dark we heard the war song of thirty Cheyenne and Sioux as they came riding into camp. They are our allies on this occasion.

Each warrior has one or two extra ponies, which are not ridden until in the immediate vicinity of an enemy. The loose ponies trot along in front, nipping the grass now and then. They don't present to the eye any indication of the fire within, but when the time arrives for action, sooner than I can tell it the warrior strips for fight, catches up his favorite war pony, and what a change comes over rider and horse. The small, snaky eyes of the former no longer look sleepy; they are flashing fire, while his pony pricks up his ears, dilates his nostrils, and darts off with the speed of the wind.

Our next day's march is over a rolling, picturesque country. We see recent signs, but no buffalo. Antelope are around us in great numbers. I knocked one over at the first fire; my orderly killed another. A great many were secured, and everybody had antelope for his supper.

We have rain in the night. Our beef cattle herd ran off, but on we march, leaving a cavalry company with the herders to bring up the strays when found.

We see plenty of buffalo, but orders have been issued to prevent firing. The lumbering fellows act as if they had received a copy of the order. They cross our trail, running between the advance guard and the next battalion. To accustom my horse to buffalo, I gave chase to one and ran by his side for two hundred yards; but we have a long journey before us, and it behooves us to take good care of the beast that is to carry him in a chase after Indians.

If we can't do any shooting, we have the pleasure of seeing the Cheyenne kill a buffalo. Orders have no effect on our red allies. An Indian is as much excited over a buffalo as he is over an enemy.

We passed over a godforsaken country today.[4] For miles there was not enough grass to sustain a donkey. We camp in the valley of Squaw Creek and discuss the prospect of finding Joseph. Again we have rain. As we travel down Squaw Creek, we see fresh buffalo trails; some of them are worn two feet deep. The hills bordering the valley are covered with cedar and pine—fine places for blacktail and mountain sheep—but for the present we are intent on other business. A steamer transfers us to the north side of the Missouri River. We learn that Joseph has crossed the Big Muddy two days before us. Ferrying a command over the Missouri River means hard work for the men. It is a tedious job. While this is going on, our camp is in a beautiful cottonwood grove on the left bank of the river.

It is evening. Our battalion marches out of the valley, over the hills, the men singing as they go. With the campfires, the scattered animals, the rumble of the moving train, the crack of the drivers' whips, the occasional scream of the steamer's whistle, and the song of the cavalrymen as they march off, the scene is intensely interesting, and it is difficult to realize that we are in the wilderness.

Next morning[5] the balance of the command toils up the hills and follows the trail. The Cheyenne Indians wound an antelope and chase it down. We have a windy, disagreeable day. Next day we see plenty of buffalo. We make a noon halt to allow the wagon train to close up. Buffalo come among the mules and ponies and quietly feed, looking up occasionally to see what their strange neighbors are doing. We march in the afternoon with the pack train, leaving the wagon train to follow more leisurely.

The Little Judith Mountains are to the southwest, while the Little Rockies are to the west and in front of us. Buffalo are on either side; one herd ran across the trail just in front of the column. Next day we have clouds and rain. We cross a branch of Milk River. Buffalo are all around us, and occasionally a herd dashes across our trail. In the forenoon we reach a gap in the Little Rockies. A swift-running stream bordered by willows and filled with beaver dams tumbles and dashes by, singing as it goes. Not far away there is a large pond, upon which countless numbers of ducks plume their feathers, while others circle about in the air at the sight of their intruders. Some are lighting and dashing the spray, others are moving gracefully or taking wing. They need have no fear; we are not hunting ducks today. As we travel up the valley of the mountain stream,[6] buffalo look in wonderment and dash across the trail or leisurely walk over the hills.

The scenery is very picturesque—rolling, grassy slopes, ending in pine-covered hills on either side; pretty green valleys hemmed in by precipitous, white limestone walls, crowned by mountain pine; amphitheatres, terraces, ravines, swift clear streams with beautiful little cascades made by the beaver dams—these greet and charm the eye and overcome all sense of fatigue.

There is evidently more rainfall here than on the prairie; the luxuriant, bright green grass and abundance of water indicates it. The cactus and sagebrush, our constant companions on the prairie, disappear. This would be a hunter's paradise. The water is palatable and wholesome, a very important matter. The majority of the waterholes and prairie streams are strongly impregnated with alkali. Besides the buffalo, elk, black-tailed deer, bear, and antelope abound.

Next morning[7] we had rain, but march as early as we can see to move, and go to the Bear's Paw Mountains, over a country which is much less interesting than the Little Rockies, although antelope and buffalo are seen. Much of the grass has been closely cropped by the vast numbers of buffalo recently here. As we approach the Bear's Paw there is an improvement. We camp in a valley near a pond filled with ducks. Two great hills tower above us.[8] It soon begins to rain in the valley, while snow falls in the mountains. Our scouts report the Indian trail not far away.

September 30—Reveille at 2:00 A.M. The moon and stars shine in a clear sky; the air is chilly. We march as early as we can see to move. A wolf serenades us at our first halt by the side of a stream. We soon come upon the broad Indian trail. Our Cheyenne and Sioux undergo a sudden transformation; they are painted, stripped for fight, on their favorite chargers and are a study for an artist. The picture lasts but a moment; they are bounding over the plain on either side of the column, which is now in rapid motion. To be astride of a good horse on the open prairie, rifle in hand, has an exhilarating effect on the majority of men. To be one of four hundred horsemen, galloping on a hot trail, sends a thrill through the body which is but seldom experienced.

It is not long before the sharp crack of the rifle greets the ear; volley after volley from Springfields are answered by Sharps, Remingtons, and Winchesters. A Hotchkiss mountain gun, throwing a percussion shell, adds its roar to the general din. The bullets hum all the notes of the gamut, fit music for the dance of death. Zip, zip, zip, thud, thud; the dirt is thrown up here and there, while others go singing overhead. Riderless horses are galloping over the hills; others are stretched lifeless on the field. Men are being struck on every side, and some so full of life a few moments before have no need of the surgeon's aid.

The explosive balls are not all on our side. One officer[9] as he rides down the line is struck by a bullet which explodes, shatters the bone, tears a fearful hole in his arm, and carries off a good portion of his ear. Our gallant commander,[10] on a splendid steed, is here, there, everywhere. When the first horse is blown, a fresh one is mounted, and off again. Three horses are ridden down during the day; their rider appears never to tire.

The Indian herd, seven hundred head, has been captured, their village surrounded, and we can take our time. In the afternoon a charge is ordered and gallantly made. It develops the fact that more warriors are opposed to us than we supposed. A regular siege follows. At the first attempt to talk with them, the reply is "Come and take our hair." A dreary night succeeds an exciting day.

October 1—A cheerless morning, with clouds and wind and mist, succeeded by rain and finally snow. Early in the day we discovered in our rear two long lines of cavalry marching toward us on either flank. Were these Colonel Sturgis's troops, or the warriors of Sitting Bull? Many anxious moments were spent before we determined that they were buffalo marching in single file, with all the regularity and precision of soldiers.

The Indians were again hailed. They come out with a flag of truce, and we see Joseph face to face. He is a man of splendid physique, dignified bearing, and handsome features. His usual expression was serious, but occasionally a smile would light up his face, which impressed us very favorably. Several chiefs had been killed the day before, Looking Glass and Joseph's brother among them. Joseph appeared very sad; he was inclined to surrender but did not have control of the entire camp. Joseph remained with us that night, while Jerome,[11] 2nd Cavalry, remained in the Indian village. One wagon train arrived in the afternoon, bringing a twelve-pounder brass piece, which was of great service to us, as the Indians had been industriously digging rifle pits and holes for protection, which sheltered them from small arms very effectually.

When the firing began that evening, there was great anxiety in regard to the fate of Jerome, but we learned next morning that the Indians had put him in a safe place and said no harm should come to him if Joseph was returned safely to them. On the morning of October 2, Joseph was exchanged for Jerome, who reports that there are at least 100 warriors in camp, and about three hundred fifty people altogether.

October 3—The camp is moved to a better position. Firing begins with both field pieces and small arms. We are in a snowstorm.

October 4—A disagreeable, raw, chilly, cloudy day; firing all day long. Gen. Howard, with two aides and a small escort, arrives in the evening.

October 5 ushers in a beautiful morning. Firing was kept up all last night.

Joseph and several followers visit us again today. They are getting very tired of the siege; they don't like the big guns. The runners they had sent to the Assiniboine had been killed. The soldiers fired at them, the citizens fired at them, Indians fired at them; they were ready to surrender and soon afterwards gave up their arms.

We begin our return march October 7 with 405 Nez Perces, from the octogenarian to the papoose born during the siege. The country is rolling and picturesque, with snow and pine-covered mountains in the background. Sunshine and cloud shadows add to the beauty of the scene. The Indians, clad in lively colors and strung out in a long line; the pack train, the pony herd, the mounted troops, the wagons, the wounded on travois, all combine to make an unusual and striking picture.

Soon after camping, dark clouds roll up, and lightning, thunder, wind, and rain threaten to cause a stampede, but the storm soon passes over. Next morning dull clouds and rain, which finally pours down in a torrent, keep us in camp all day.

It is interesting to watch the Indian boys at a game of mimic warfare. They take sides, select their ground, and each party mixes up a lot of mud. A piece the size of a marble is molded and thrust on the point of a stick about three feet long, which is held by the opposite end, and by a sudden jerk the pellet is sent with considerable force and precision. They are experts in selecting cover, making feints, and taking advantage of any false move on the part of their opponents They are practicing a game which will train them for the real battles of the years to come.

October 9—A pleasant day. The restriction in regard to firing has been removed, and antelope steaks are again seen at our supper table. Next day we have more buffalo all around us; several are killed, and the Indians are in great glee. The squaws, who are hideously ugly, are all animation and activity when around a carcass.

October 11—A gala day among the buffalo. The Indians are in rapture over the prospect of replete stomachs.

October 12—A bright, clear morning. We pass over a hill which gives a fine view of the surrounding country. The Little Rockies loom up grandly. They will long remain pictured on my memory as one of the most delightful places that a hunter could visit. One man killed ten antelopes, and others were very successful.

The next day was chilly, cloudy, and windy. Buffalo are in sight, as they have been for many days. A huge fellow attempted to cross our trail. An old squaw with an emphatic gesture exclaimed in Chinook jargon, "Scucom muc-a-muc." (Heap meat.) I fired two shots from my rifle, and at the second fire an annoying accident occurred, which never happened to me before, although it does happen occasionally. The head of the shell was torn off by the ejector, leaving the balance in the chamber. I took the orderly's carbine, and at the third shot finished the magnificent monster, to the intense delight of the Indians. All three shots had taken effect. The tongue was handed over to me, while the rest was appropriated by the lighthearted followers of Joseph.

We arrived at the Missouri River in the afternoon, and the slow process of ferrying began. The majority of our wounded were sent down the river by steamer. An elk was killed at the mouth of Squaw Creek but a short distance from camp.

October 16—We start up Squaw Creek. A fine mountain sheep and three black-tailed deer were bagged during the day.

October 17—A small hunting party go out today. I saw two black-tailed deer and had a hasty shot at one. He came within eighty yards of me, but unfortunately two men were between the noble fellow and myself. As frequently happens, they were unconscious of his near proximity. An instant and he was gone. He was in sight again in 150 yards, but it was a farewell bound, and my shot did not stop him. He was such a splendid specimen that I had not the heart to grieve over his good luck.

Even mountain sheep were seen, and one enthusiastic young officer was determined to secure the head of the grand old ram, whose horns made one complete turn and half of the next circle. The experienced hunter of the party said they would weigh sixty pounds. A long chase, and they got a good shot, wounding the ram and a doe. The seven were seen to go into a cedar thicket, and only five left it. The blood marks were distinct, but the thicket was full of fallen timber. They could not ride through it. They were so far in rear of the column that they could not trust their horses on the outside of the thickets while they made a careful search on foot over a three-acre patch. They were liable to meet gentle savages who had left their pipes of peace at home, and so they reluctantly retraced their steps and left the sheep to the wolves.

We had an illustration of the amount of lead an antelope can sometimes carry. One was struck seven times, twice with explosive bullets, before he stopped running. Two men who went to the right of that trail killed two fine black-tailed deer.

An officer who left us yesterday morning to examine the valley of the Musselshell River returned this afternoon. He had a detachment of ten men. They saw plenty of elk, black-tailed deer, antelope, and two bears. The Musselshell is represented to be a splendid game region. It is the borderland between the Sioux and Crows. A party who ventures there must be prepared to fight. Until recently no white man could go five miles up the valley without the risk of leaving his remains, minus his scalp, for the wolves.

October 18—We reach a branch of the Big Dry Fork of the Missouri River. Fewer buffalo and more antelope are seen on the march.

October 19—We still have plenty of antelope about us. I saw a flock of sage hens.

October 20—A pleasant morning. I killed a fine doe antelope at long range. After reaching camp, a herd of buffalo passed near, and a few of us gave chase. Two are killed, a fine cow and calf. I wounded one but failed to bring her down, and after an exciting chase of four miles over a rough country, I gave it up, much to the disgust of my orderly, who would have gone until his horse dropped in his tracks. It requires a decided effort to give up a chase which is thrilling to the rider but death to the horse. It is a great abuse of horse-flesh to run buffalo after a forced march of seven hundred miles. The animals used for buffalo hunting should be led until the chase begins, and then a dash made regardless of the ground. Any attempt to favor a horse at the beginning of a run only leads to a long and frequently fruitless effort. It is easy enough to catch the bulls; the cows and calves require good horses and bold riding to overtake them.

We could see two immense herds a mile away as we reluctantly turned our horses' heads toward camp, but the sinking sun warned us to lose no time.

We got into the Badlands and meandered over a very rough, broken country, deep ravines, abrupt hills, fantastic mounds, yawning chasms—a very hell with the fires put out—but finally reached the open country and were not long in making camp. The next day we made the head of the main branch of Sunday Creek. A great many buffalo and antelope were killed.

After a march of over eight hundred miles, the command arrived at the cantonment on Tuesday, October 28. A lovely day. The scene was interesting and picturesque. The approach to the post on the north side of the Yellowstone is over a high plateau, from which a road winds down a ravine to the riverbank. First came the commanding officer and his staff, accompanied by Joseph and a few of his followers; then the advance guard, followed by Indians in picturesque groups; then the pack train and more troops; the wagon train and flanking columns; the pony herd and rear guard. As the command filed down the ravine, flags were unfurled, the band struck up "Hail to the Chief," while cannon thundered forth a salute of welcome to the troops who had so successfully ended the campaign against the Nez Perces.

The Capture of Chief Joseph and the Nez Perce Indians

HENRY ROMEYN[1]

Contributions to the Historical Society of Montana 2 (1896): 283–91

The campaign of 1876 in the vicinity of the Yellowstone had been nearly a fruitless one. The overwhelming disaster of the 7th U.S. Cavalry and the massacre of the greater part of its officers and enlisted men had been followed by an abortive attempt of the commanders of the departments of the Platte and Dakota to force the Indians to a fight, as it had been preceded by a drawn battle on the headwaters of the Rosebud. It fell to the lot of the 5th U.S. Infantry under its indefatigable leader to strike about the only blow of the year which had any lasting effect, when in late October that command met the Sioux north of the Yellowstone, not far below the mouth of Powder River, and forced them into a flight, and most of them finally into a surrender and return to the agencies on the Missouri River, Sitting Bull with most of his band, including several of the more prominent warriors, escaping across the Canadian line. This had been followed by the winter campaign against Crazy Horse and his band up the valley of the Tongue River, in which they were driven from their camps, which were destroyed, and this action by the surrender of most of the Northern Cheyenne at Tongue River cantonment.

Then in May, the band of Lame Deer had been struck in its camp on a tributary of the Rosebud and scattered over the country, with the loss of some its best warriors, all of its best horses, and its camp.

A month later a column consisting of portions of the 2nd and 7th Cavalry and 1st, 5th, and 22nd Infantry was sent into the field, the 5th being mounted on Indian horses captured as above stated. But no fight took place, though remnants of Lame Deer's camps were trailed over four hundred miles through eastern Montana, western Dakota, and northern Wyoming, to the end that the Indians finally abandoned the field and sought shelter at the agencies in the Department of the Platte.

Late in the autumn of 1876, the troops located at the mouth of Tongue River had constructed shelters made of logs placed on end in a trench dug in the soil and capped with a plate or log, on which rested a roof of poles and earth; not uncomfortable, as far as warmth was concerned, in the winter, but terribly damp and leaky in the heavy rains of spring. But material and labor for constructing a new post was on the way, and as soon as possible after the ice was out, the steamboats began to arrive.

A large portion of the army was represented at the new camp during the summer. The 1st, 5th, 6th, 7th, 11th, 17th, and 22nd regiments of infantry had each one or more companies there, with what was known as the "Montana Battalion" of the 2nd, and most of what remained of the 7th Cavalry. Scouting was kept up in all directions from the new camp, but with little result.

Meanwhile, far away to the westward, so far that the troops on the Yellowstone had no expectations of sharing in it, another war was in progress. Abandoning their reservations and homes, the Nez Perce Indians were on the warpath; their leader, leaving the country they had always held, had with his people started on that long march which, if made by a white chieftain, would have justly ranked with some of the most famous of ancient times. Beating off some of the forces which sought to impede his movement and skillfully avoiding others, he at length emerged from the mountains into the valley of the Yellowstone and, crossing to the left (northern) bank of that stream, turned his course toward the Canadian border. Six days after, on the afternoon of September 17, the news of his crossing reached the camp at the mouth of Tongue River. It did not take long for the commanding officer there to decide upon his course of action.

The courier reached the camp about 3:00 P.M.[2] By 4:00 P.M. orders were issued for a movement across the river, and everyone was busy. Twenty days' rations were to be taken, and the command was to move the next morning. It consisted of Companies B (Bennett),[3] F (Snyder),[4] G (Romeyn), I (Lt. M. Carter),[5] and K (Brotherton)[6] of the 5th Infantry; A (Moylan),[7] D (Godfrey),[8] and K[9] (Hale) of the 7th Cavalry; and F, G, and H of the 2nd Cavalry,[10] commanded by Tyler[11] and Lieutenants McClernand[12] and Jerome. Two companies of the battalion had previously been ordered to Fort Benton[13] to act as escort for the department commander from that point to the British line, where he was to meet the officer in command of the Canadian mounted police for a consultation on Indian affairs, but were halted two days' march from the river until the main body could overtake them. There was also a body of scouts, consisting of a detail from the different companies of the 5th Infantry, some thirty Cheyenne, and a few citizens employed as scouts and guides. A twelve-pounder brass gun and a Hotchkiss single-shot breechloader, caliber 1.67 inches, composed the artillery. A small wagon train and two good pack trains furnished transportation. Four of the infantry companies were mounted on horses captured from Lame Deer's band the previous spring. The entire command numbered about 350 men.[14]

It was thought that the Indians could be intercepted south of the Missouri, and the mouth of the Musselshell was the first objective point. Starting on September 18, the command reached the Missouri on the afternoon of the twenty-second, not at the designated point, however, owing to want of accurate knowledge of the country, but at the mouth of Squaw Creek, about eight miles below it and separated from it by country impassable for wagons.

Here his usual good fortune awaited the commander of the expedition. Camp had been made a few miles from the river, and at first some doubt was expressed as to the identity of the stream. The officer in command of the scouts was ordered to make a reconnaissance at once and, if satisfied that it was the Missouri, to encamp there and stop any boat which might happen to pass. On reaching the bank, he rode through some timber, out onto a bar and there, not one thousand yards above, coming down the stream was a steamer.[15] Fifteen minutes later she would have passed out of sight, going as she was with the current, and pursuit would have availed nothing. A hail brought her to, when upon inquiry it was learned that her captain had neither seen nor heard of any body of Indians crossing to the north bank, and it was supposed that the column had accomplished the first part of its design and was ahead of them.

Moving the camp down to the river, ten days' rations were taken from the wagons, when they were parked and left under the charge of Brotherton and his company, which was not mounted. The rations and the artillery were placed on the boat, and in the night it was taken up to the mouth of the Musselshell and landed on its left bank, while the mounted portion of the command led their horses across the badlands to the same point. Scouts thrown well out from the left flank of the column while on the march had reported signs of small parties of Indians, supposed to be "flankers" detached by the Nez Perce chief to guard his flank from surprise.

Everything was arranged for the march up the Musselshell, and the men were eating their breakfasts,[16] when a second strike of good fortune changed the whole plan. After the steamer had put off her load and dropped down the river about a mile to take on wood, a small "Mackinaw" boat containing two men came floating around a bend of the river above the camp. They informed us that the Indians had crossed the river at Cow Island two days before and gone north, carrying with them all the available stores landed by the boat we had been using, among which were supplies of clothing, groceries, hardware, and ammunition for merchants at Fort Benton and Helena. A gun was fired to attract the attention of the boats, and signals were made for her return. The crossing of the command was at once begun, and as soon as that of the mounted forces was completed, the boat dropped down to the camp of the wagon train, which it ferried over.

On first reaching the river, a citizen scout named Johnson offered to swim his horse across and view the country on the left bank. The man was drowned by his horse striking an obstruction and falling backward on its rider, who, loaded down with ammunition, did not rise to the surface.[17] No other accident happened to anyone or anything, but it was not until late the next morning, September 27, that the troops were ready to move out. The wagons were at first kept with the column, but this was found too slow, and in the afternoon the command was halted, ten days' rations were packed on the pack mules, [and]

the twelve-pounder was left with the wagon train, under command of Brotherton and Borden[18] with forty men, to follow the trail of the force as rapidly as
possible, and the march was resumed at a rapid gait.

It was late in the night when a halt was made at some pools of dirty water,
thick with mud, which had to be boiled and strained before it could be used.
Before daybreak on the twenty-eighth, the march was resumed in a northwesterly direction and continued the latter part of the day along the eastern side of
the Little Rockies, a broken, precipitous chain paralleling the desired course.

Large herds of buffalo started in amazement at sight of the column, but no
hunting was allowed. The night of the twenty-eighth, camp was made in a
deep ravine at the northern end of this chain. After carefully covering its fires at
daybreak, the column turned westward toward the Bear's Paw Mountains, distant about twenty-five miles. From the summits of the Little Rockies, scouts
had descried smoke far off to the southwest, and it was again thought that we
were ahead of the Indians.

Our camp on September 29 was made in a deep valley at a point northeast
of the main Bear's Paw,[19] and in a soaking rainstorm which had changed
to snow.

The Bear's Paw Mountains are not a continuous chain, nor from where we
saw them did they seem to be much more than high, steep hills partially
clothed in timber.[20] The camp was broken early, and the direction taken a little
south of west. An hour later two or three Indians were descried south of the
line of march and were supposed to be advance scouts or hunters of the Nez
Perces. The course was then changed more to the left (south), when a yell from
the Cheyenne scouts who were in advance of the troops announced that they
had discovered the trail, and a few moments afterwards the head of the column
reached the point and found it—broad, distinct, and fresh—leading due
north.[21] Like hounds on the fresh trace of game, the Cheyennes started on it,
while the command halted for a few minutes, then wheeled about "by fours"
and followed at a rapid pace.

Upon starting in the morning, the order of march for the day had been 5th
Infantry, 2nd Cavalry, 7th Cavalry, and the pack train in rear with a guard of
two men from each company. When the column was reversed, it of course
brought the 7th Cavalry in the van and the mounted infantry to the rear. A mile
along on the trail, a deep coulee had to be crossed by a path running diagonally
down its steep sides, a path that would not allow two men to pass at a time.
The first battalion had crossed and was forming upon level ground on the farther side when a Cheyenne warrior came flying back over the rising ground in
front, shouting his battle cry, announcing that the camp was only a short distance away and that the fight was on.

In the change of direction, the pack train had gotten into the column
instead of waiting to take its proper place at the rear, and now the packers were
crowding their mules down the narrow trail with all possible haste to make
way for the two battalions behind them, as well as to avoid being left in the

rear and exposed to the danger of attack from any rear guard of the enemy which might possibly be behind us. In the press, one of the smaller mules was crowded from the path and, with his pack, rolled over to the bottom of the ravine, only to scramble to his feet and resume his place without even a readjustment of his load.

By the time the packs were out of the way of the center and rear battalions, the 7th Cavalry had disappeared from view beyond the rise of ground. Mounting as rapidly as possible, these two battalions pushed on at a gallop. But the "short distance" stretched into miles, and not until three or four miles had been galloped over did we hear the first dropping shots, which, as we drew nearer, increased into a heavy fire, punctuated by both Indian yells and soldiers' cheers. There was an answering cheer from the mounted infantry battalion, and the pace, till now a gallop, became a ride "with loosened rein in horses' flanks."

The camp was located on a small stream called Snake Creek, as it proved an excellent position for defense, in a kidney shaped depression covering about six acres of ground, along the western side of which the stream ran in a tortuous course, while through it, from the steep bluffs forming its eastern and southern sides, ran coulees from two to six feet in depth and fringed with enough sagebrush to hide the heads of their occupants. Here the Nez Perce chieftain had pitched his camp, and here he now made his last stand for battle.

From the point whence the camp could first be seen, it appeared open to attack from all but its eastern side, and even that was overlooked by bluffs too steep to be readily ascended, and from twenty to thirty feet high. But at the south end of the valley or campground, there was an almost perpendicular bluff that afforded excellent cover for a line firing toward the point from which the attacking force was advancing, and this was instantly occupied by the Nez Perces who, withholding their fire until the 7th was within 200 yards, then delivered it with murderous effect. Hale and Biddle were killed at the first fire, and Captains Moylan and Godfrey wounded immediately thereafter, thereby leaving but one officer with the three troops.[22] All the first sergeants were also killed. Wherever the Indians heard a voice raised in command, there they at once directed their fire with the evident design of picking off the officers. Biddle had only joined in May, and it was his first battle.

Changing direction to the right and again to the left, the 7th was formed in line on the elevation east of the camp. On nearing the ground, the 2nd Cavalry had been sent off to the left and took up a position on the northwest of it, cutting off the herd and securing it. When the camp was first descried, a portion of the lodges had been struck and about one hundred ponies packed for the day's march. These, guided by women and children and accompanied by fifty or sixty warriors, were at once rushed out and started northward. An attempt was made to cut off their retreat, McClernand in command of G Troop, 2nd Cavalry, being sent in pursuit. The Indians halted for fight after going about five miles from the main body and, finding a large portion of their pursuers

The fight for the Nez Perce pony herd.
NELSON A. MILES. *PERSONAL RECOLLECTIONS AND OBSERVATIONS.*

encumbered by the care of the ponies they had secured, boldly assumed the offensive and forced the soldiers back toward the main body, although they failed in their attempts to retake the stock. Most of them succeeded in getting back through the investing lines and joining their companions in the defense.

So well had these succeeded in covering themselves that scarcely one could be seen; but from their concealment, they sent shots with unerring aim at every head exposed by the troops. Lt. G. W. Baird, adjutant of the 5th Infantry, acting assistant adjutant general of the command, had his left arm shattered and an ear shot away while carrying orders. When the cavalry occupied the bluffs east of the camp, they forced the abandonment of the steep bluff from which the Indians had first fired upon them, and as the 5th Infantry came up, it executed "left front into line" and was halted at this crest. Here it was greeted by a hot fire from the coulees immediately in front, in the low ground, some of them not more than fifty yards away, and men and horses began to drop before they could be dismounted.

The Hotchkiss gun was brought up and an attempt made to shell the Indians from their cover, but it could not be depressed enough to be effective and was soon driven from the position with severe loss to its gunners. The men behaved splendidly, and the coolness of some was wonderful. To get a position from which their fire could be made more effective, it was desired to deploy Company G of the 5th as skirmishers by the right flank, and the bugler was ordered to sound the deployment. "I can't blow, sir; I'm shot," said the brave fellow,[23] and a glance toward him showed him on the ground with a broken spine. A sergeant in his rear, creeping crabwise toward his new position, was directed to have him move along. "He can't do it, sir; he's dead" was the reply.

A small piece of ground directly in the rear of the steep bluff alluded to was sheltered from the enemy's fire, and here the wounded who could walk or crawl were gathered for the attention of the surgeons. Moylan, wounded in the thigh, came back to the line after having his wound attended to, but the effort was too much and had to be given up. Between fifty and sixty lodges were still standing. In them, and at any other place where they could be protected from fire, the Indian women began to sink pits for shelter. Many of the warriors worked their way up to the edges of the bluffs, through the coulees which seamed their faces, and digging into the banks, threw the soil thus obtained up over the top, soon having very formidable rifle pits in use. From these they picked off every man who rose to his feet on the level ground east of their defenses. As the distance was almost nil, every shot could be made to tell. An officer had one shot through his belt, another carried away his field glass, while a third took off his hunting knife and cut the skin from an ear.[24] Creeping carefully up to the edge of the bluff to look over, a bullet instantly lifted the hat and a lock of hair from a sergeant, and another went through the head of a comrade at his side.

By 3:00 P.M. it was evident that the attack must become a siege, and an attempt was made to get possession of the course of the creek to cut the Indians off from water. In order to effect this, Troops A and D of the 7th Cavalry, which had no officers with them, were placed under the command of the writer and, with his own company (G) of the 5th Infantry, were to be pushed by him up to the edge of the bluffs east of the valley in an attempt to dislodge the Indians there, and to direct a fire on those warriors who could be seen in the coulees in the bottom. Meanwhile, Company I, 5th Infantry, under command of 1st Lt. Mason Carter, was to charge down the slope on the southwestern side and get into the bed of the stream. The writer was to give the signal for the movement by swinging a hat when the three companies on the high ground were ready.

Crawling back to his command, the order was passed along the line. Then, rising to his feet, he swung the hat. The troops started with a cheer, some reaching the rifle pits, only to fall dead on their edge, while a shot through the lungs put their commanding officer out of the fight. Company I succeeded in getting across some of the smaller ravines, and certain of its numbers even among the tepees, but the Indians rallied and drove them out, with a loss of over a third of their number. The wounded who fell into the hands of the hostiles were not molested, otherwise than to be stripped of arms and ammunition, except one sergeant of the cavalry who, remembering the Little Bighorn, fired on an approaching Indian with his revolver and was killed because he refused to surrender. They even gave some of the wounded water after nightfall when it could be done with safety.

As soon as darkness closed in, the troops were posted around the valley to prevent, as far as possible, the escape of its defenders. The line was necessarily a thin one, and despite all precautions, a few, among them White Bird and some of his band who had been responsible for outrages leading to the first outbreak, succeeded in escaping and joining those already in Canadian territory. Aside from the Nez Perces, there was another possible, if not probable, element of danger and strife to be guarded against.

Sitting Bull, with a band reinforced by renegades from the agencies, was not far away, and should he and they decide to take part in the fray, there would be work cut out for every man. Hearing of the battle, and that "Bear Coat" was in command of the troops, they not only did not come, but struck camp and did not halt in their northward flight until more than a day's march had been placed between them and the line.[25]

If, to the men on duty, that night was one of watchfulness, to the wounded it was one of ceaseless agony. There was no fuel at hand, and none of the troops could be spared to obtain any from a distance. The night was bitterly cold, the train with the tents had not arrived, and the morning of October 1 dawned on a sad sight. Some had died during the night, while others supposed to be dead now revived to a sense of misery and suffering. Officers and enlisted men, white and Indian allies, to the number of fifty or more, lay in that little hollow place together. To add to the discomfort, a snowstorm set in, and by night four or five inches had fallen upon the combatants and disabled alike. Up to that time the Indians had the advantage of the troops in this respect, for their shelters had not been destroyed, and the wounded in the pits beneath them were, of course, protected to a great extent from the storm. During the night of September 30, however, the troops threw up such entrenchments as could be made with the few tools at hand, and from that time the losses were very few. With the Indians still in possession of the water, well supplied with provisions captured on the Missouri, able to utilize the meat of animals killed by our fire with considerable ammunition, the siege promised to extend indefinitely.

On the evening of October 1, the train under command of Brotherton arrived. Tents were at once put up to shelter the wounded, but in the darkness were so placed that they could be reached by the rifles of the Indians and, upon being lighted up, drew the fire of the enemy, whereby at least one man was wounded. The twelve-pounder was also with the train, and scarcely had day dawned on the second before its boom told the Indians that a new element had entered for their destruction. Still, it was almost impossible, owing to the shape of the ground, to bring it to bear on the pits now occupied by the hostiles, who, as soon as the shells fell into their camp, abandoned it and took refuge in the banks of the crooked coulees, where no direct fire could be made to reach and where the shells, if burst over them, were likewise liable to injure our men on the higher ground beyond. A dropping or mortar fire was, however, obtained by sinking the trail of the gun in a pit dug for it and using a high elevation with a small charge of powder. This made the fire effective, and late in the afternoon of the second, Joseph raised a white flag.[26] Cheers greeted its first appearance,

Carrying off the wounded from the Battle of Bear's Paw Mountain.
NELSON A. MILES. *PERSONAL RECOLLECTIONS AND OBSERVATIONS.*

and soon under it the Nez Perce chief, his clothing pierced with over a dozen bullets, although he was still unharmed, stood face to face with his opponent.

While he was willing to treat, he did not admit that his case was desperate, and his first proposition was to be allowed to march out armed and mounted, abandoning only the position to his foe. He was willing to fight still, but wished to save his women and children. So did the opposing commander, though refusing to entertain this proposition, and the Nez Perce went back to renew the battle.

The storm still continued. The troops in the trenches, unable to erect any shelters, were exposed to its inclemency, for all that the arrival of the wagon train with its guard had permitted [was] the gathering of fuel from some timber several miles away.[27]

Two days were spent at the battleground after the surrender, giving necessary attention to the wounded, burying the dead, and arranging for transportation of those unable to travel on horseback to the river. The only ambulance with the command was given up to two enlisted men, one of whom had a broken thigh, the other a shot through the hips. They lived to reach the river, but the latter[28] died as he was carried on board the steamer. Wagons, the beds of which were filled with small brush covered with grass, were utilized for the conveyance of such others as could not bear transportation on horseback. Much of the country was rough and broken in character, and though all possible care was exercised, the suffering of many of the injured was intense. The brush and grass soon became unevenly packed down, and every jolt of the wagon seemed to open fresh wounds.

The steamers had been ordered to the point where the column was to reach the river, and on them the crossing to the south bank was made, those of the whites too badly wounded to bear further land transportation being sent down the river—the infantry to Fort Buford, the cavalry to Fort Lincoln.

The campaign made by the troops from the Tongue River cantonment had been of the most brilliant character—short, sharp, and decisive. The element of chance had entered largely into it but did not detract in the least from the clearness of conception, while the manner in which the unforeseen changes were taken advantage of won the admiration of all who saw them.

Capture of Nez Perces

YOUNG TWO MOON[1]

Folder 59, Walter M. Camp Collection, Little Bighorn Battlefield
National Monument

When Chief Joseph and the Nez Perces were captured at the Bear's Paw
Mountains in 1877, there were about twenty enlisted Cheyenne and
Sioux scouts present. Among these were Young Two Moon, Little Old Man,
Ridge Bear, Brave Wolf, Magpie Eagle, and some Sioux—Hump, Roman
Nose Sioux, Iron Shirt, and No Scalp Lock. Besides these, there were a num-
ber of Cheyennes who went along as volunteers, not being enlisted as scouts
but induced to go by the hope of plunder, for they believed that a great many
horses would be taken from the Nez Perces. Such men were War Bonnet, Old
Wolf, Crazy Mule, High Wolf, Starving Elk, Tall White Antelope, White Wolf,
Little Sun, Spotted Black Bird, Little Yellow Man, Stands Different, Timber,
Sa-hut, Yellow Weasel, Medicine Flying, White Bear, Big Head, Bear Rope,
Elk Shows His Horns, and Hail. White Bear and White Bird got lost from the
command and did not see the fight.

After they had crossed the Missouri, and while they were traveling on the
north side of the river, they did not know where the Nez Perces were, but at
length someone happened on one of their old camps, but still they knew nothing of the actual whereabouts of the enemy. Some time later,[2] through the field
glasses a smoke was seen, and two scouts were sent ahead to try to find the
camp. These men were Starving Elk and Hump. An officer on a hill was able
to keep these scouts in sight. He had arranged with the scouts that if they saw
anything, they should separate and then ride across one another.

After a time they were seen to make this signal, and the troops started to
go to them. Some of the Indian scouts galloped on ahead and rode up to where
Starving Elk and Hump were waiting, and were told by them that the camp
was just over the next hill. Young Two Moon peeped over the hill and did not
see the camp but could see horses.

The scouts who had been sent on ahead had been ordered by a note given
to Johnny Bruguier, the interpreter, not to make any charge until Colonel Miles
got there. Bruguier read this note to the scouts, and they did not like the order at
all. They talked about it among themselves, and finally Crazy Mule told the

interpreter to write a letter and send it back to Colonel Miles, telling him that people never waited for each other, that he (Miles) would overtake them, and that he (Crazy Mule) wished to make a charge. Bruguier explained further that Colonel Miles's order had said that when they made their charge, they must go in on the right side of the command.

At Crazy Mule's request, the interpreter wrote the desired letter and sent it back to the commanding officer, but the scouts did not wait for a reply but charged on the Nez Perce camp, Young Two Moon leading. When they charged toward the camp, all began to shoot.[3] The Nez Perces all rode out and looked. Then they began to shoot, and the scouts began to charge back and forth in front of the camp. After they had charged on the camp, the Nez Perces retreated a little and began to dismount. Young Two Moon, Tall White Elk, War Bonnet, and No Scalp Lock stood there, and the Nez Perces charged on them, then turned and went back, and charged on them again and went back.

The scouts did not retreat, and the Nez Perces [went] back to their camp. Just as the Nez Perces reached their camp, the Cheyennes shot one of them off his horse.[4] When the four looked around, they saw behind them the other scouts dismounted and strung out in a line. After the Nez Perces had gone back to their camp, Young Two Moon mounted and rode along the line of the dismounted scouts and said, "Let us cross this creek and make another charge and try to drive them out of their camp."

All mounted and crossed the creek[5] and began to charge, but only three of them went. The others stayed behind. Those who charged were Young Two Moon, Starving Elk, and Little Sioux. They rode up almost to the breastworks of the camp, then turned and went back a little way, and turned again, and as they charged the second time, they could see the Nez Perces stringing out of the camp. They had driven them out of camp.[6]

After they had left the camp, the scouts rode along by the Nez Perces in the direction they were going, but did not get in front of them. After the Nez Perces had been traveling a little while, they began to split up. Some went in one direction and some in another. They had gone about two miles when the soldiers appeared and made a charge on the Nez Perces. Those Nez Perces who had split off had turned around and gone back to their camp.

While all this was going on, the scouts were driving off the horses. The Nez Perces who had returned to the camp were nearly all on foot. Those they kept after were mostly mounted. At length, one troop of cavalry[7] overtook the leading scouts. This was a black-horse company.[8] The Nez Perces in the lead still had a good many loose horses with them, but when the soldiers overtook them, they had to drop their horses and go on only with those they were riding.

After they had dropped the horses, they soon stopped to fight. The women were all following behind the men, and the troops and scouts tried to charge in between the Nez Perce men and women and capture the latter, but the Nez Perces charged back toward their women. Some of the scouts had already got between the women and the Nez Perces, but the women would not stop, and the Nez Perces crowded the scouts so closely that they had to get out on the other side of the Nez Perces. The soldiers did not reach the Nez Perce men. They stopped and dismounted and fought on foot. The Nez Perces were very brave and crowded on the soldiers, who after a little while mounted and rode off. Looking back, the officer in command[9] of the troops saw that he had left a man who could not mount his horse, and he wheeled his troops and charged back to save this man.

Here the soldiers and the Nez Perces got pretty close together. When this troop of cavalry got down into a gulch, the Nez Perces formed a line on both sides, and so surrounded the troops and the three scouts who were with them. There was hot fighting here down in this gulch for two and a half miles. Then the Nez Perces left them. Colonel Miles was still fighting at the camp.

When the Nez Perces left the troops, the troops rode toward the camp, on the way picking up all the loose horses that they could. The three Cheyenne scouts now left the black-horse troop and soon after met Colonel Miles. Young Two Moon, who had already taken a gun, asked Colonel Miles what they should do with the guns they captured. Colonel Miles said, "Right over there are some Nez Perces in breastworks. Try to drive them out."

It was here that White Wolf got shot in the head. They rode to the top of a little ridge and looked over, and then Big Head and White Wolf made a charge on the breastworks. White Wolf was shot, and they thought killed, close to the breastworks. He was shot in the top of the head and was senseless until the fight was over.

Now Hump and Young Two Moon began to consult as to how they could get this man's body away from the breastworks. Just then Starving Elk came up, and Hump said, "I will stay here and fight, and they will shoot at me and I at them, and you rush down and drag this man away."

It was done as he proposed. Hump stood out and the Nez Perces shot at him. Young Two Moon and Starving Elk made a charge and drew White Wolf away. Hump was shot in the breast while in sight and firing. When White Wolf was taken away, the firing ceased.

The troops were all around the Nez Perces except for a little opening. It was now drawing toward evening, and all around the Nez Perce camp, the soldiers were building their fires and cooking and eating. The sun went down, and during the night there was no shooting.

The next morning all were wondering—officers, soldiers, and scouts— what they could do today with the Nez Perces; whether they would surrender or keep on fighting. Colonel Miles did not know what the Indian scouts were going to do, but they had already planned to do something. The scouts had said to one another, "Let us try to take pity on the women and children here and see if today we cannot make peace with them." So far this day they had not done any shooting.

After breakfast three scouts—Young Two Moon, High Wolf, and Starving Elk—mounted and rode up near the breastworks, but out of sight. Then they rode up on top of the hill near the breastworks, two of them mounted but Starving Elk on foot. They had determined to ride down into the breastworks from this point.

When they reached the top of the hill, they heard someone shout out, "Colonel Miles does not wish you to go over the breastworks, for you will be killed." They paid no attention to this word.

When they rode down toward the breastworks in plain sight of the troops, the troops rode up in sight and stood in line looking at the three Cheyennes going toward the breastworks. As they drew near the breastworks, a man stood up in front of them, and a little later another two Nez Perces [stood] up. As they said they were not firing on them, the two men jumped out of the breastworks and came toward the Cheyennes, and then a third person came out; but the last was a young Nez Perce girl, so three people were going out to meet three other people.

They met and shook hands. One Nez Perce had his right arm broken and tied up. The girl met Starving Elk. She had a nice necklace of beads and took it from her neck and threw it over Starving Elk's head and shook hands.

The camp was a sad looking place. All about were lying the Nez Perces. Just outside of the breastworks were a few dead soldiers, but in the camp the bodies of the Nez Perces were everywhere.

The Nez Perces made signs asking which of the Cheyennes was the chief. Young Two Moon said, "No one of us is a chief." The Nez Perces asked, "What is the name of the white man who is in command?" "We call him 'Bear Coat,'" replied Young Two Moon. Then he made signs, "We three men rode in here today to try to take pity on the children and the women. If you will listen to us today, we will save all your lives."

The Nez Perces signed, "We are not chiefs. The chief is still in the breastworks. We will go back and tell him what you say." The Nez Perces asked in signs, saying, "When you tell this white man Bear Coat anything, will he take your words; will he listen to you?" Young Two Moon said, "Yes, whatever we tell that chief he will believe and he will do what we ask him." The Nez Perces said, "Let us separate now. We will go back to our breastworks and tell our chief, and you go back and tell yours." They separated.

The Cheyennes rode to the top of the hill and then on to Colonel Miles. Colonel Miles said to Young Two Moon, "When you met those three persons, what did you say?" Young Two Moon told him all that had passed. Colonel Miles said, "Go right back and tell these people to surrender to me. If they will do so, I will not hurt nor harm them. I will take good care of them. Choose any scout you wish to have to go with you, and take him down there."

Now Young Two Moon called on a chief, Magpie Eagle, asking him to go, but Magpie Eagle said, "Do not call me." Before he could speak again, Old Wolf said, "Do not ask me." Then he spoke to Brave Wolf, and Brave Wolf said, "I will go."

Young Two Moon called on Bear Robe, his cousin, to go, and Brave Wolf called on Tall White Elk, his relation. They set out for the Nez Perce camp. Before they reached the place where they had met the Nez Perces before, Brave Wolf and Bear Robe stopped and said, "We will wait here." The others went on. Out from the breastworks came five Nez Perces, four of them on foot in front, and behind them a chief[10] riding a fine sorrel horse. It was a wonder how a horse could be kept alive in these breastworks where there had been so much shooting. They did not see where the Nez Perces kept their horses, yet they must have had a number.

When these people came up, Young Two Moon was on foot and Tall White Elk on horseback. All the men were armed, and all held their guns pointed at the other party. It was a dangerous situation; almost anything might happen. The two parties stopped about twenty feet apart.

Young Two Moon made signs saying, "Today we have come to your camp because we have taken pity on your women and children. The great chief wants to see you and talk to you."

The Nez Perce chief made signs saying, "Which one of you is chief?" Young Two Moon replied, "Neither one of us is a chief. There is one chief," pointing to Brave Wolf. Then the Nez Perce [chief] made signs saying, "I think today that chief of yours is not a chief; that he is afraid of me. I am the chief of this camp you see here; the chief of these people. They are my people."

Young Two Moon replied, "If you are the chief of this camp, dismount from your horse. Today we want you to surrender to us."

The chief dismounted. When he got off his horse, he stepped out in front of the four men, and Young Two Moon heard the click of the locks as the four Nez Perces uncocked their guns. The two shook hands. One of the four Nez Perces jumped on the horse and rode back to the breastworks. The two parties shook hands, and the chief of the Nez Perces and the other three Nez Perces went on with the Cheyennes toward the soldier camp. When they reached Brave Wolf and Bear Robe, there were four Nez Perces and four Cheyennes. As they went up on the hill, the soldiers stood in line on either side in a "V," with Colonel Miles at a distance at the angle of the "V." When they reached Colonel Miles the soldiers closed in behind them. A little later a Nez Perce[11] rode up on a cavalry horse, which he must have captured. He came through the soldiers to where Colonel Miles was. He could speak English and interpreted for Colonel Miles.

Young Two Moon does not know what was said, but after a time the interpreter rode back to the camp. Colonel Miles let the four Nez Perces go but kept the chief. He told Young Two Moon to come with him and the Nez Perce chief and to talk with him by signs, and they went off to headquarters, Colonel Miles's tent. The guns carried by the Nez Perces were taken from them, but a pistol owned by the interpreter was not taken from him. With Colonel Miles and the two Indians went four soldiers for a guard for the chief. He was a fine-looking Nez Perce. Young Two Moon and the chief talked in signs, and Young

Two Moon advised the chief what he thought he ought to do for himself. This took place after they had fought four days and four nights. It was not until then that they gave up and surrendered.[12]

After they had eaten in the middle of the day [October 1], Starving Elk walked up to headquarters and said to Young Two Moon, "Let us go down to the breastworks again and talk to the whole tribe." Colonel Miles said to Starving Elk, "Go back and get the interpreter and bring him here." He told Young Two Moon to go down to the Nez Perce camp and try to persuade all the Nez Perces to surrender.

Young Two Moon mounted a horse and, with Starving Elk, went down to the camp. As they were going down there, about ten scouts and one officer,[13] who wore a buckskin shirt, joined them and went down with them.

The Nez Perces had left their breastworks and were in the camp, and the Cheyennes entered it. They talked there for quite a while, until nearly sundown. The twelve Cheyennes were scattered about, each one talking to a group of Nez Perces. All the group that Young Two Moon was talking to seemed to understand and speak English.

While they were talking to the Nez Perces, they heard a great shouting, and a Cheyenne scout mounted and rode away out of the camp to the top of the hill to see what was the matter. This scout called down to the others, "Try to get out of the camp and leave the Nez Perces to themselves." The scouts began to move out, and after they had got out of the camp, the shooting began, and the scouts started on a lope. Young Two Moon happened to look back and saw the three men holding the lieutenant's horse. Two men, holding each of his arms, led him back to the breastworks. He did not resist. They kept him that night, saying that the whites had their chief and that they now had a chief of the whites; that for one night they exchanged chiefs with the whites.

The soldiers were shouting because the government wagons had come in sight.[14] That night the government wagons were corralled, and the Nez Perces must have approached these wagons and fired at them. They could hear the balls strike the wagons. Seven mules were killed and one white man, but the soldiers did not reply to the fire.

Next morning nothing was done; no shots were fired. Colonel Miles said, "We must get that officer back from the Nez Perces. We will give up their chief if they will give up the officer." The chief Nez Perce called out to his people, and presently they led out the officer and his horse behind him. Colonel Miles told the scouts to take back the Nez Perce chief and meet the Nez Perces halfway and exchange the chief for the officer. They did so.

When the officer reached the command, he talked a great deal, but Young Two Moon did not understand what he said. Meantime, the soldiers were going over [to] the opposite field and were carrying away the dead and wounded soldiers.

After dinner[15] Young Two Moon heard a bugle call and saw that the soldiers had formed a line all about the Nez Perce camp. Three big guns were pointed at the breastworks, and they had a Gatling gun and many small cannon that went on wheels. Colonel Miles told the Nez Perces that unless they surrendered this afternoon, the soldiers would fire at them. The sign would be by bugle calls. After a time the troops did fire on the Nez Perces, and the firing did not cease until sundown. All the time the Nez Perces were firing. They were good shots.

That night after the firing had ceased, five Nez Perces, who must have been off on the war trail and have known nothing of what was going on, came right into the soldiers' camp and were captured there. Next morning, when they looked at the five Nez Perces, they saw that one of them wore citizen's clothing and had his hair cut. He talked good English. They talked a long time with these Nez Perces and finally sent the leader of the party, an oldish man, and one who could talk good English, he was about forty-five years, down to the Nez Perce camp.[16] They gave them a white flag made of a piece of canvas. For some time these two went back and forth carrying messages, but at length Colonel Miles said to the scouts, "They are going to surrender; you can all go." Then the scouts started back home to Fort Keogh.

Before long, Young Two Moon was ordered to go on and overtake the scouts and stop them, telling them to wait for the command. After the Nez Perces surrendered, Bruguier and Hump left the camp to overtake the scouts and go in with them. Colonel Miles told Bruguier to go right on in with the scouts; that he would bring in the Nez Perces. The scouts had many horses that they had captured.

Young Two Moon does not know how many soldiers were killed, but he guesses about fifty.[17] The Nez Perces were hard looking people; almost all were wounded, and many were being hauled along to die soon. They had suffered greatly, but they were brave and strong hearted.

Capture of Nez Perces

LUTHER S. KELLY[1]

Folder 69, Walter M. Camp Collection, Little Bighorn Battlefield
National Monument

Young Two Moon's narrative of the last engagement with the Nez Perce Indians in the Bear's Paw Mountains, Montana, in October 1877 is interesting but in some respects confusing, as he mixes up events occurring on different dates. This goes to show that no one man can give a concise history of a battle in which many participated.

The retreat of the Nez Perces would have been remarkable, even if they had not been encumbered with the women, children, and camp equipment. By skillful maneuvering, they kept in advance of General Howard's command and successfully eluded the 7th Cavalry, which blocked the only outlet from the mountains near Clark Fork, and were well under way to the crossing of the Yellowstone when overtaken.

It was then, September 17, [1877,] that Colonel Miles, learning of the situation, organized a force at the cantonment, Tongue River, and started to head off the Nez Perces. Although the destination and route of the Indians were largely a matter of conjecture, it later proved [that] the course pursued by Colonel Miles was exactly the proper one.

A couple of days before this, I had been detailed to accompany Lt. Hobart K. Bailey and a detachment to Carroll, on the Missouri River, to look after some military stores that had been left there.[2] Arriving at Carroll, I was surprised one evening to see one of our scouts riding in with orders for me to report at the mouth of the Musselshell River, distant about thirty miles down the river, at which point Colonel Miles and command were then encamped.

I reached the slumbering camp about midnight, September 24, and after securing forages for my horse, proceeded to the steamer Far West, where I found Colonel Miles and Lt. Frank D. Baldwin, his aide,[3] still awake and busy with unloading of supplies.

To show what a small thing makes or mars an enterprise, I will say that at that very moment, the Nez Perces were encamped some thirty miles north of us at the foot of the Bear's Paw Mountains and within a day's journey of the boundary line of Canadian territory. Secure of the line of pursuit (as they knew it), they had stopped one day to rest their broken-down stock and to hunt buffalo. Some of them had never seen a wild buffalo.

In the morning of September 25, the steamer <u>Far West</u> had cast off its mooring and was making down the river, when a small boat from the upper river came in with news that the Nez Perces had crossed the river the day before at Cow Island, sixty miles or more above.

Fortunately the steamer was not beyond recall, and I crossed at once with the white scouts, four in all, and pushed ahead to the Little Rockies, from which point a good view could be obtained of the country beyond. Colonel Miles crossed his command and pushed on to the northeast end of the Rockies, where he went into camp. He had with him quite a force of Indians, Sioux and Cheyennes, who were familiar with the country and rendered good service.

I reported to the colonel after he had established camp, and he directed me to join Lieutenant Maus, who had gone ahead with a few mounted infantrymen.

After joining Lieutenant Maus, we proceeded on until dark, when I suggested that we camp, as there was probability of our crossing the Nez Perces' trail in the darkness, it being a cloudy night with prospect of rain.[4] I felt certain that the trail, if we were not ahead of them, would cross Peoples Creek between the Little Rockies and the Bear's Paw Mountains.

In the morning we pushed on toward the base of the Bear's Paw, and as we neared the foothills, we saw two Indians driving some ponies. Our course was nearly at right angles to the route of the Nez Perces, and they were not looking for troops in our direction.

When we arrived at the point where we expected to intercept these people, we saw them in a valley at the foot of the mountain. They immediately abandoned their ponies and took to the rocks of the mountain, where it was not practicable to follow them. Personally, I was satisfied to let them go, as they were not close enough to perceive the military character of our party, and our object was to find the trail or camp of the Nez Perces.

Descending to the little valley, we came upon the broad trail and recently abandoned camp of the Nez Perces, as evidenced by the fresh ashes of campfires and remains of buffalo bones. Milan Tripp, one of the scouts,[5] having the fastest mount, volunteered to go back to the command, and Lieutenant Maus sent a dispatch to the colonel.

As the trail led up a pass through the mountains, I thought it best to await the arrival of the command, and so advised Lieutenant Maus, though he was eager to push on. The day was misty with rain, ideal conditions to effect a surprise. Instead of striking for the point where we had picked up the trail, Colonel Miles led his command to the right of the Bear's Paw Mountains and struck the Nez Perce camp in a gulch of Snake Creek that debouched from the mountains on the north side, and the fighting had commenced before we reached the scene.

A Hotchkiss gun was in operation shelling the camp, or such part of it as could be seen, for the Nez Perces, grown wise after the surprise at Big Hole, fortified nearly every camp they made. The main body of the Indians was concealed in a gulch, but around this gulch they had constructed a series of rock rifle pits that proved very effective when the attack was made by the troops.

The Sioux and Cheyennes were so eager for horses that they precipitated the fight before Colonel Miles was ready, otherwise it is probable the Nez Perces would have surrendered before so much blood had been shed on both sides, for it must be understood that the mist concealed the approach of the soldiers, so much so that they passed us without our knowledge.

The event [that Young Two Moon] relates of Hump standing out and drawing the fire of the Nez Perces in order to rescue White Wolf I can now understand, for with a companion,[6] I was trying to locate the exact spot in a rifle pit from which a Nez Perce was shooting at us, when I saw one of our Indian scouts dancing about on a little flat, while the bullets made little dust spots all about him, and I wondered why he acted so foolishly. It was but a moment later that my companion was shot through the head and instantly killed alongside of me. In the evening the troops, who had been heavily engaged during the day, were disposed around the camp in a manner to prevent the escape of the Indians.

The night was cloudy and very dark. I was sent by Colonel Miles to meet and bring in the wagon train but passed it in the darkness.

The next day, October 1, the investment was complete and there was little fighting, but communication was established with the Nez Perces, and Chief Joseph stayed in the military camp while Lieutenant Jerome remained as a hostage in the Nez Perce camp.

On October 4 General Howard arrived with an escort of two or three officers, and I remember well the council held in a circle of grass, in full view of the camp.

The Nez Perces surrendered to Colonel Miles on this day.[7]

The Sioux and Cheyenne Indians rendered good service in capturing the stock of the Nez Perces and thereby preventing them from escaping in the start, and were equally brave as the Nez Perces.

Chief Joseph's Fight and Surrender

NELSON A. MILES[1]

Cosmopolitan 51, no. 2 (July 1911): 249–52[2]

The period of tranquility following the avenging of Custer's death was not long to continue. Another Indian war was to occur; more strictly speaking, another cruel injustice was to be enacted. It would require a volume to record the history of the Nez Perce Indians, their loyalty to the government, their hospitality and kindness to the Lewis and Clark Expedition in 1804, and their truthful boast that no white man had ever been killed by a Nez Perce.

Long before 1877, the government had, for certain considerations, granted them a reservation. They prized this little section of their native land more than all other earthly possessions. The solemn dying injunction of Chief Joseph's father to him was to never give up the valley where his ashes were to rest. Yet the greed of the white race was too strong to permit the Nez Perces to retain the Wallowa Valley, their most cherished home.

A number of sharp engagements occurred between the troops under General Howard and the Indians under Looking Glass, who at the time was the principal chief. The Indians retreated up Clark's Fork of the Columbia, thence through the Big Hole Basin, where they were attacked by troops under command of Colonel Gibbon. After a sharp engagement, the attack was repulsed, and in turn the troops were surrounded and held until the approach of General Howard's command, following the trail. The Indians then retreated over the Rocky Mountains, through the Yellowstone Park, and down the Clark Fork of the Yellowstone, thence north toward Canada.

While these events were occurring, I received many reports of the approach of the Indians toward my district, and I sent two strong detachments of troops under Colonel Sturgis and Lieutenant Doane to intercept them as they came out of the Yellowstone Park. For weeks I anxiously waited for information. During the afternoon of September 17, I observed a dark object appear over the high bluff in the western horizon and wind its way down the trail to the bank of the Yellowstone. I soon recognized the object to be a cavalry soldier. He was ferried across the river and, riding up, dismounted and saluted. Colonel Sturgis reported that by a ruse, the Indians had evaded his command

Col. Nelson A. Miles. W. FLETCHER JOHNSON. *LIFE OF SITTING BULL.*

and turned his flank, leaving his troops hopelessly behind. General Howard reported the same. He had, with his command, joined that of Colonel Sturgis and assumed command of both. Later they followed the trail until it was scattered and lost in the Judith Basin.

This information had been five days in transmission, but when I finally received it, no time was lost in giving orders for the immediate equipment of six troops of cavalry, six companies of mounted infantry, two pieces of artillery, and a small body of Indian scouts. These were as rapidly as possible ferried over the Yellowstone River and started on a forced march of nearly two hundred miles to the northwest to intercept the hostile Nez Perces. Couriers were dispatched to Forts Peck and Buford on the Missouri, to send a steamer-load of supplies up the Missouri for my command and for those of General Howard and [Colonel] Sturgis.

On the evening of September 23, we reached a point six miles from the Missouri, after a forced march of fifty-two miles in twenty-four hours. Being desirous of taking every chance of success, I called upon Captain Hale, commanding one of the battalions, to send me a young officer who would ride forward and stop any steamer passing on the river before our arrival. Lieutenant Biddle quickly responded and in a few minutes was galloping down the valley. He reached the bank of the Missouri just in time to hail the last regular steamer going down the river that year. With it I transferred one battalion of troops to the north side of the Missouri to prevent the Indians from crossing. From all information obtainable from the steamer and other sources, I believed the hostile Indians to be about fifty miles south of the Missouri. As I could not well detain the steamer, she resumed her voyage down the river, and we started to move to the west with the remainder of the command. A half hour later, three

Capt. Owen Hale. NELSON A. MILES. *PERSONAL RECOLLECTIONS AND OBSERVATIONS.*

men came down the river in a rowboat, reporting that the Nez Perces had crossed the Missouri at a point forty miles to the west. I remembered that Lt. Frank D. Baldwin was invalided from hard service and was on board the steamer going down the river. I knew that if he was within sound of cannon shot, he would return, and that this was the only means of recalling the steamer. Quickly one of the guns was wheeled into position and commenced discharging shells down the valley of the Missouri. The sound of the gun and bursting shells, reechoing between the high bluffs, could be heard many miles. Soon we saw the black smoke rising above the steamer as she rounded the bend of the river far below and forced her way up against the strong current. The loyal instincts of the soldier had brought back the best means for our crossing the turbulent waters of the great Missouri. With the least possible delay, the troops were transferred to the north side, and then commenced anew the march to intercept and encounter the Indians.

On the evening of September 29, I received word from General Howard that the trail he was following had scattered; that he had given up the pursuit, turned back his cavalry, and was going to return his infantry to Idaho, leaving Colonel Sturgis's troops, as before, a part of my command. On the morning of September 30, we were early on the march, and soon one of our Indians came dashing back, reporting the discovery of the Indian camp. Without a halt, our troops formed in line of battle and galloped forward. A more resolute body of men I have never seen go into battle. As we galloped over the rolling prairies, the men were joking and laughing, and one even singing, "What shall the harvest be?" Captain Hale on his white steed was the picture of a dashing cavalier as he led his cavalry into action. Soon the slumbering camp of Indians was discovered, their large herd of horses, mules, and ponies grazing along the valley.

Captain Tyler's battalion of cavalry was ordered to sweep down the valley, stampede the herd, and "set the Indians afoot." But Captain Hale and Captain Tyler's battalions charged the enemy and, after desperate fighting, drove the Indians into a narrow ravine.

In the charge, the cavalry led, and at first were checked by the sharp fire of the Indians. The infantry, mounted on captured Indian ponies, galloped up close to the camp, threw themselves on the ground, and opened a short fire. The battalion of Captain Tyler soon after returned with eight hundred captured animals,[3] and Captain Brotherton came up with the reserve of two companies of infantry and a piece of artillery. These commands took position and strengthened the cordon of troops surrounding the Indians.

The siege lasted five days. At one time Chief Joseph came up to surrender, but Lieutenant Jerome, who had been directed to ascertain the condition of the camp, was seized by the Indians, and Chief Joseph had to be exchanged for him.

But on the morning of October 5, Chief Joseph agreed to surrender, and with much dignity and solemnity, he raised his hand and eyes toward heaven and said, "From where the sun now stands, I will fight no more against the white man."

With him surrendered four hundred of his people.[4] Our success was not without serious loss. Captain Hale and Lieutenant Biddle, with twenty soldiers, were killed.[5] Captains Moylan and Godfrey, Lieutenant Romeyn, and Assistant Adjutant General Baird, with twenty-eight soldiers, were wounded.[6] In the charge, Captain Carter had thirty-five percent of his company placed hors de combat. The Indians lost their veteran chief, Looking Glass, and four other chiefs, with twenty-six warriors killed and forty-six wounded.

Our band of thirty Indian allies, Sioux and Cheyennes, had fought bravely. Hump dashed into the Nez Perce lines and killed two with his own hands, but was severely wounded himself. After the surrender, each was allowed to select five captured ponies and return to the cantonment. They made the journey of two hundred miles, swimming the Missouri and the Yellowstone Rivers with their wounded. We made travois for our wounded, buried the dead, and started on our difficult march back. Our wounded suffered greatly, owing to the rough country passed over, and some died en route.

On reaching the Missouri, I found two steamers that had come up with supplies in response to my dispatch of September 17, and upon them I placed the severely wounded soldiers and Indians, and sent them to the nearest hospital. With the remainder, I moved across the country to the Yellowstone. Our Indian allies reached the cantonment days in advance of the command and several hours before the interpreters. They created consternation by shouting their victory, chanting their war songs, and exhibiting their captured trophies, and made signs that in the engagement two officers (shoulder straps) had been killed and

Chief Joseph surrenders to Colonel Miles.
CYRUS T. BRADY. *NORTHWESTERN FIGHTS AND FIGHTERS.*

several wounded. This greatly alarmed the officers' families. They, however, made it known that the big chief, Bear Coat, as they called me, was all right.

Four days later the command appeared, winding its way down the trail from the high mesa to the Yellowstone. The garrison, with military band, was gathered on the right bank to give us a cordial welcome. As we were ferried over, the band played, "Hail to the Chief," when suddenly they stopped and played a bar of the then popular air, "Not for Joe, oh no, no, not for Joseph."

All were placed in comfortable camps, and my desire was to send them back to Idaho, but orders were received sending them to the Indian Territory, where fifty percent of them died of low malarial fever. Although I constantly urged it, I was unable to have those that remained sent back to their native country until 1884.

Chief Joseph was the highest type of the Indian I have ever known—handsome, generous, and brave, quite an orator, and the idol of his tribe.

The Capture of Chief Joseph and the Nez Perces

GEORGE W. BAIRD[1]

The International Review 7 (August 1879): 209–15

The motive-causes which led to that modern "Anabasis" of the Nez Perce Joseph and his followers, wherein they marched from the Pacific slope across mountains and rivers, past the sources of the Missouri, through the world-famous [Yellowstone] National Park, and then onward to their last camping ground near the international boundary line, nearly a thousand miles from their starting point, involve the whole subject of the treatment of Indians by the United States, and are far too extensive to be treated in this article. It must suffice for present purposes to say that a system, and not an individual, is chiefly at fault.

Those interested in this unique and in every way remarkable march—a march not of warriors merely, but a hegira of the old and infirm, of women and babes—have had opportunity to learn, from participants or witnesses, concerning its initiation and earlier progress. I shall speak of some things connected with its later stages and its close. The command of Col. Nelson A. Miles had its headquarters at the mouth of Tongue River on the Yellowstone, and its field of operations included the valley of the Yellowstone and Little Missouri and their [tributaries] southward to Wyoming and the Black Hills; also, as the event proved, the region north of the Missouri to the dominion line.

The approach of the Nez Perces had been anticipated by Colonel Miles, and dispositions made to receive them even before the battle of Big Hole Pass. A strong detachment of troops, with a force of Crow Indian allies, was sent well up the Yellowstone in the early part of August (1877) with the purpose of intercepting and capturing the Nez Perces as they should emerge from the national park. The Indians, however, slipped by this detachment and, after a running rearguard fight with it, went on without further molestation, either from it or from any other force that had before pursued them. Their whole body thus reached a point a few miles north of the mouth of Clark Fork, near which they had crossed the Yellowstone, and thence had before them an unobstructed course through the valleys of the southern effluents of the Missouri to that river, to the buffalo range north of it, and to Dominion Territory.

Information of this state of facts reached Colonel Miles at the mouth of Tongue River—some two hundred miles from the point where the Nez Perces crossed the Yellowstone—on the evening of September 17, or about a week after they had accomplished the crossing. During that night, couriers were dispatched to secure the forwarding of supplies up the Missouri River, which, with troops, trains, and horses, were ferried across the Yellowstone in time for an early march on the eighteenth. Thence they proceeded over prairie, mesa, and badlands, across the Missouri at the mouth of the Musselshell; thence, curving northwestward, they held onward through the beautifully watered and grassy foothills, along the eastern and northern bases of the Little Rocky Mountains, a very Eden trailed over by the serpent of an unrighteous, because needless, war. Continuing on across the gap to Bear's Paw Mountains, and through that range, the command passed over two hundred and seventy miles in ten marching days and found themselves at the foot of the Bear's Paw Mountains, in the vicinity of the Indian village and undiscovered by its inhabitants.

There has not been lacking a disposition to represent the successful issue of this campaign as a result of good fortune merely. Its good fortune, however, consisted only in a slight chance which was availed of with great skill and astonishing energy. Supplies were accumulated from remote points, not by chance but by design, and the missile-like velocity of the march of the command along its appropriately parabolic trail was such as to make the cheerful but weary foot soldiers sigh audibly for "an old commanding officer who would not wish to get outside of a stockade."

While the courier was carrying to the mouth of Tongue River the news of the escape of the Indians near Clark Fork, and the command from the first-named point was pressing forward to overtake them, they had advanced to the Missouri River at Cow Island—the head of navigation during the period of low water—had overpowered the gallant little detachment of troops encountered at that point, had destroyed a vast amount of supplies awaiting transportation, had crossed the river, and had moved out northward between the Little Rocky and Bear's Paw Mountains. Near the river, they were attacked by a small force made up chiefly of civilians from Fort Benton; the loss on either side was inconsiderable, and the march or route of the Indians was not materially affected. It chanced that the Indians reached Cow Island on the same day that Colonel Miles's command arrived at the mouth of the Musselshell, some fifty miles below. Their arrival, depredations, and departure northward were communicated by a party who escaped in a small boat to a detachment of Colonel Miles's command which had been dispatched to Carroll—a small trading station a few miles below Cow Island—and thence the tidings were forwarded with speed to the main command. A boat which on the previous day had been employed to ferry over a portion of the command had been loosed from her moorings, and was round a curve and just passing out of sight as the news arrived on the morning of September 25. Instantly a small Hotchkiss gun was put in position and fired several times in rapid succession. This was recognized as a signal by those on board; the boat was brought back, and the remainder of the command, with train and supplies, was transported. Then, on the north bank of the Missouri, the force was put in order for what appeared to most of the participants to be a hard, hopeless march. Three companies each of the 2nd and 7th Cavalry; four companies of the 5th Infantry, mounted on ponies captured from the Sioux in the early spring of 1877; a gun detachment, with a Hotchkiss gun; and a small force of white and Indian scouts—an aggregate of 375, all told—struck out from their wagons, presenting a most picturesque spectacle. The possible proximity of the Indians made it necessary to interdict all shooting, and the antelope, deer, and buffaloes, seen in large bands and herds on either hand, seemed in doubt whether to be more astonished or frightened at so strange a spectacle. But they gazed unmolested, while the patient pack mules tottered along in the rear under their burdens, confidingly following the tinkling of the bell on the bell horse.

A glance at the map will show that the line of march of the Indians, after their escape from the force north of the mouth of Clark Fork, and of the command from the mouth of Tongue River, were almost exactly the perpendicular and hypotenuse of a right-angled triangle. Two hundred miles apart at the Yellowstone, and fifty miles apart at the Missouri, they intersected each other only a few miles from the scene of the battle, which was on a small southern affluent of Milk River.

At 7:00 A.M. on September 30—the command having been on the march since daylight—the village was reported to be three miles away. The command started at a trot; the three miles proved to be seven, and the trot became a swinging gallop, as horse and rider caught the spirit of the occasion, and comradeship and emulation urged them on. The camp was placed in a strong position for a defensive fight, under a high and crescent-shaped "cut bank," the bank itself being cut at intervals of a few rods by deep ravines heading in the open country from which the attack was made.

The column deployed to attack, charged promptly to close quarters, and dismounted. Then the fight raged with obstinacy, a spirit of "give-and-take," at short range, without yielding ground in spite of numerous casualties, such as fully warrant the name "battle," despite the paucity of numbers engaged. The village was surrounded; its herd, to the number of 730, was captured. The Indians, as the force under cover, would have had great advantage without the assistance received from the dry ravines before mentioned, but following the sinuous courses of these ravines, they could approach the troops without detection, and the deadly accuracy of their aim and their apparent singling out of officers are recorded in the list of casualties.

How shall the Indians be dislodged was now the question, and it was decided that an attempt be made to storm the ravines. At the bugle sound, a detachment of the 5th Infantry, led by Captain Carter, charged over the crest, down the steep declivity, and across the smooth bottomland. They reached the village and inflicted a severe loss upon the Indians; but thirty percent of the

An artist's conception of the Battle of Bear's Paw Mountain. HARPER'S WEEKLY, 1877.

charging party were killed or wounded, under the *feu d'enfer* from the Indians' magazine guns, in less time than is requisite to write or read the record of their brave action. It was evident that carrying the place by storm would be too costly, and already one-fifth of the command were killed or wounded. It remained to hold the Indians in a state of siege, to be in readiness to meet effectively the force which they expected would come to their rescue from over the border whither Sitting Bull had been driven, and to provide such shelter against the oncoming snowstorm as an utterly treeless region could furnish to the wounded of a command which had stripped for a rapid march and brought upon pack mules only such impedimenta as would enable it to eat sparingly and fight liberally.

While the fight was yet raging, Colonel Miles had ridden along the line and called to the Indians that they could surrender without further fighting if they should choose to do so. There were among them some who spoke a kind of English, and who during the first day replied stubbornly and with defiance. But on the morning of the second day, they were disposed to parley, and Joseph, with some of his chiefs, came out under a flag of truce. They were willing to surrender, provided they could be permitted to retain their arms. Meantime, taking advantage of the cessation of hostilities, they dug pits in the beds of the ravines and on adjacent knolls where they had taken refuge from the exposed valley of the creek. Occupying these, they were protected from direct fire, and seemed to be determined either to await their looked-for succor from the north, or to surrender only on their own conditions.

In the evening of October 1, the wagon train arrived, and with it a twelve-pounder Napoleon gun. The necessities of transportation had cut the artillery ammunition down to twenty-four shells, and probably never have sixteen shells—the number fired from the twelve-pounder—had equal moral or greater physical effect. The Indians admitted the loss of twenty-four killed and wounded by the fragments of the shells, which were the only missiles that could reach them in their deep, cellar-like pits constructed in the bottom of the sheltering ravines.

The unconditional surrender of the Indians was now only a question of time, unless the siege should be raised by their expected northern allies. To be prepared for any such attempt, the force which had last come in contact with the Nez Perces near the Yellowstone opposite the mouth of Clark Fork, and had moved thence northward to the Missouri about one hundred miles south of the battleground, was ordered forward and would have augmented the besieging force sufficiently for all contingencies. But after a short advance north of the Missouri, it was ordered back, inasmuch as the surrender of the Nez Perces, after a siege of four days, rendered its services unnecessary.

By this surrender, upwards of four hundred and twenty prisoners were obtained. The number who escaped northward with White Bird has been variously stated. I met White Bird at Fort Walsh in Dominion Territory in the summer of 1878 and held repeated conversations with him and others of his band.[2] They all agreed in saying that the number of lodges was twenty-five, but that they could give no exact statement as to the number of people. From other sources I have learned that it was one hundred five. Yellow Bull, one of the captured Nez Perce chiefs, was one of my companions in the summer of 1878 (our route lay in sight of the peaks which overlook the battlefield), and from him I learned that their loss in killed in that battle was thirty, which slightly exceeded that of the troops.

Without doubt it was the understanding, at the time of the surrender, that the Indians would be taken back to their old home. They have, however, been placed in the Indian Territory. The reason assigned for this departure from the terms of surrender is that the hostility to Joseph and his followers is so intense and inveterate among those who would be their neighbors in their former home that they would be insecure there. It is barely conceivable that there may be room for difference of opinion as to the sufficiency of this reason, but there can be no doubt whatever that the hostility, if it exists, illustrates the proverb "Whom one has injured, he hates."

The march of the Nez Perces—bold to rashness in conception, consummately skilful in execution—was marred by very few acts of savage violence; indeed, by none which came within my personal knowledge. In the fight herein described, the lines were so close that a charge from either side necessarily left the killed and wounded of the attacking party at the mercy of the attacked; but though the Indians took arms and ammunition from wounded soldiers, they did not otherwise molest them, nor did they mutilate the dead.

The results of the different encounters of this band with troops are forcible illustrations of the entire revolution in Indian warfare occasioned by their acquiring not only arms of precision, but skill in the use of them. They inflicted severe loss on every command with which they came fairly and fully in contact; they placed one command upon the defensive, and they showed themselves throughout to be skillful and courageous enemies. The time when it was possible safely to despise the prowess of a savage enemy is past. The time to fight them, when fighting is necessary, in accordance with the recognized principles of warfare has long since come; although some who are accounted high authorities in such matters have not recognized, and do not yet recognize, this truth. It is foreign to the purpose of this article to discuss the "Indian Question." It may not, however, be out of place to say that the policy which shapes the intercourse of whites with Indians resembles that of the gods, in that whom it would destroy it first makes mad—so mad from accumulated wrongs that they have nothing left them but to rush, destroying, upon their own destruction. The army, as the fundamental force element of society, by a sort of law of transmitted tension receives with augmented force every blow which bad judgment, incapacity, dishonesty, or injustice aims at the Indian. The needless, thankless, unrewarded task imposed by this condition of things has been met with rare self-sacrifice and courage, "though the soldier knew someone had blundered." On a bleak knoll in northern Montana, the snow-clad mountains rising coldly by, I saw more than a score of witnesses to the verity of all herein that seems like strong assertion; and none who looked upon their calm, upturned faces could ever discredit their testimony. On the field where they fought shoulder to shoulder, they lie side by side in the ceaseless comradeship of a soldier's grave.

Brave Jerome: A Dashing Lieutenant's Experience in Chief Joseph's Trenches

[ANONYMOUS]

New York *Herald*, October 30, 1877

CAMP OF THE SITTING BULL COMMISSION,
NORTHERN MONTANA, October 12–Midnight

The command, having encamped this afternoon in a desolate spot on the plains, discovered its escort of three companies of the 2nd Cavalry, which arrived and joined it this evening. These companies, commanded by Captain Tyler, were engaged under Colonel Miles in the recent battle with and victory over Chief Joseph and his Nez Perces. Among the commanders of companies is Lt. Lovell H. Jerome,[1] son of Lawrence Jerome of New York City, who distinguished himself in the action in a manner which has been partially described to you. His distinguishing feat during the battle was the saving of the 7th Cavalry from absolute annihilation. While the Indians, after Captain Hale's death, were pouring a deadly hurricane of lead upon the 7th's battalion, Lieutenant Jerome, coming up on the opposite side of the cut, bank, or ravine, assailed the savages with a deadly fusillade which continued for two or three minutes, drove them into their pits, and allowed the remnants of the 7th Cavalry to withdraw.

Lieutenant Jerome, like his brother officers, presents a highly unmilitary but very war-worn appearance. He is the most dashing and handsome of them all. His costume nearly resembles that of a prairie scout and would astonish the denizens of his father's household and the Union Club. He wears a velveteen coat, buckskin pantaloons, and heavy cavalry boots. On his head is a battered, drab, slouched hat with a black ribbon. He gave this evening, in the presence of one or two of his brother officers, an account of the battle and his share of it, which in essential respects had been anticipated by the stories of the scouts. But neither the scouts nor anyone else with whom I have conversed gave the twang, the peculiar flavor to the narrative which the young lieutenant himself gave it, and which he must have derived the knack of giving to any story from his inimitable sire.

It was this young man, as you will recollect, who after Joseph came into Miles's camp and made his first proposition to surrender, was ordered, or rather

590

permitted, by the colonel to go into the stronghold of the Nez Perces and reconnoiter. Indeed, Lieutenant Jerome suggested Joseph's presence and the temporary truce which then occurred as a good opportunity to recover the bodies of
Captain Hale and Lieutenant Biddle, both of whom were killed during the
charge of the 7th Cavalry at the opening of the fight. Says Lieutenant Jerome:

> The story about Hale's saying, "My God! Am I going to be killed so
> early in the morning?" is probably a fiction. What did occur was this.
> When the command halted just after the news that the Nez Perce vil-
> lage was in sight was received from the scout, and while the scout
> was riding back to the rear during the halt to inform Colonel Miles,
> Hale, who was spoiling for a fight, but who was evidently nervous
> and troubled, took out a charm given to him by a lady, which he wore
> around his neck, and said, "Jerome, if I should get killed this morning
> I want you to see that this gets back"—mentioning the lady's name. I
> bantered him a moment about it. Then he took it in his hand and
> threw it with a gesture against his heart, laughed his peculiar manner,
> and exclaimed, "There, nothing is going to harm me now." That was
> one of the reasons why I wanted to go down and recover Hale's body.

I asked Lieutenant Jerome if he recovered the charm. He answered that he
did, and went on with his account.

He proceeded into Joseph's camp, confident that he would be well
received there, knowing personally, as he did, so many of the Nez Perce warriors. It was not until he had fairly entered it that he perceived he was a prisoner. Since Miles had determined to hold Joseph, the Indians determined to
hold Jerome. They did not, however, treat him in the least like an enemy. In the
most laughing way, they insisted on his staying with them. They allowed him
to wander through their camp and examine their strange fortifications and
places of concealment. "At last," said he, "they put me into a pit where there
were about fifteen of them. The weather was bitterly cold, and I was glad that I
was sheltered. I had a pair of blankets that night and slept a little."

Here I asked the gallant young lieutenant to go on with his story in his
own way. He said:

> Well, what I did while I was in the Indian camp was to look around
> for the best places for Miles to put in his shells, and to see how their
> rifle pits were arranged, and whether it would be possible for us to
> take them by assault. I had the whole thing in my mind by the next
> day, when I expected to leave. On that day I received a message from
> Miles early in the forenoon. Miles evidently wanted to keep Joseph
> but wanted me to escape. I believe now that if I had not gone into that
> camp under the colonel's order, he, being deprived of the information

which I gave him afterward, would have withdrawn—holding Joseph as his prisoner—with his force to the cover of the distant woods, and there entrenched himself. The fact is, he was very anxious, as all of us were, lest Sitting Bull should come to the Nez Perces' assistance. I can testify that the Nez Perces really expected that Sitting Bull would aid them, though of course, I don't know how well their hope was grounded. While I was in their camp several warriors spoke of this matter.

For a long time after I reached their camp, the white flag floated over both encampments. But suddenly, while I was sitting in the pit I spoke of, a bullet came singing overhead. It was followed by others. These shots were from our own men, and I was alarmed and disgusted. In the first place, I didn't want to be killed by a friend; in the next instant, it struck me that the Indians suspected treachery. That they did suspect it, I found soon afterward. A couple of warriors, who had been especially friendly to me, took me out of that pit into another one, warning me that the other Indians were talking about my "forked tongue" and of the propriety of killing me then and there.

During the day Colonel Miles decided to surrender Joseph. So he was brought down under cover of a white flag to a space halfway between the Nez Perces' position and our own. The colonel himself was with Joseph and was accompanied by one of his staff officers.[2] There were three Indians along with me. I suppose that was an interesting position. With the suspicion of treachery on both sides, thirteen of our men lay in their trenches scarcely forty rods off, with the rifles held at a dead rest on Joseph and my three Indian guards. More than twenty Indians had an equally sure sight over their Winchesters and Henrys straight at Colonel Miles and me. I have since learned that Miles's staff officer held a cocked revolver in his bosom ready to fix Joseph if I should be harmed. The transfer passed without trouble, and I was restored to the command of my company.

While I was in their pits, the Indians behaved as I never saw Indians behave before. Some of their dead were brought in, but they paid no special attention to them and did not much grieve over them. One of the Indians would call out when a dead body arrived, "Hello! That fellow was shot yesterday," and that was about all. Neither did the Indians appear to care much whether they were fighting or not. It was the inconvenience of fighting or not fighting, as the case might be, that disturbed them. On the morning when I left, one approached me, saying in good English, which most of them spoke, "If it doesn't get warmer than this, we'll have to go to fighting again."

Lieutenant Jerome gives several vivacious incidents of the battle. From the first, Colonel Miles had ordered all the troops to push forward their entrenchments that night in order to get nearer and nearer to the enemy. When Lieutenant Jerome's line was within forty or fifty yards from that of the Nez Perces, it was so arranged between the soldiers and the Indians that either side being over fatigued from lying at full length on their bellies in the rifle pits might, by showing a white flag, arrest the firing and arise and stretch their limbs, and walk to and fro within full sight of each other at that deadly distance. Such a truce with white men on both sides has been frequent in American wars; never before had American soldiers such confidence in Indian magnanimity as they were justified in exhibiting on this occasion.

Said Lieutenant Jerome:

Why, these Indians are the bravest men on this continent. There, in the first night, when our men lay wounded after the charge when we lost so many, they wouldn't kill a wounded man. All they wanted was his gun and his cartridge belt. Several times the wounded would rise up in a sitting posture and stretch themselves. The Nez Perces never fired at them; yet if one of our men in the trenches showed his head, from five to ten bullets came whizzing at it on the instant.

Once when Colonel Miles was riding along the line, an Indian jumped up and raised his revolver at him and shouted, "We fight; we do, General, you bet!"

Throughout the action, there does not (according to the testimony of all the officers of Captain Tyler's command, including Captain Tyler himself, who were assembled in my tent tonight) appear to have been a single instance of mean or unheroic conduct on the part of these manly Nez Perces. They fought merrily—even as merrily as they lived—and died cheerily, with hardly a groan and never a complaint. So extraordinary a balance of the faculties, so complete an indifference to fate, such an apparent delight in mortal danger, have seldom been associated, at least in the annals of red men, with an absolute and knightly chivalry toward their foes.

The twenty or more Cheyenne scouts who headed Colonel Miles's advance did not emulate this chivalry but rivaled the bravery of the Nez Perces. The Cheyennes fought in sheer love of fighting; from the moment Joseph's village was discovered, they doffed their superfluous wear, donned their war paint, and rushed to the fray. Lieutenant Jerome describes their feats and marvels of hardihood and daring. Whenever during the four days of the engagement, the firing slackened, they fell to the rear and there took to comparative vagabondage, but when the fusillade of magazine rifles rolled around the line, they rushed to the front and recklessly exposed themselves.

Said Jerome:

They fought for the joy of it. At one time four of them formed a combination queerer than any Wall Street combination I ever heard of.

Three of them burrowed in a pit and put up a corner on Joseph's whole band. The fourth one—the man who did the most to win the corner—then used to jump and leap onto his horse and ride out to draw the Nez Perce fire. This bravado would, of course, oblige the Nez Perces who fired at him to expose their heads above the edges of their own trenches, whereupon the rider's three companions would lift up and give them hell.

The Surrender of Joseph

CHARLES E. S. WOOD[1]

Harper's Weekly, November 17, 1877

On September 30 Colonel Miles made a sudden attack on the enemy, whose camp was situated on a bench, or flat, in the creek bottom. The Indians occupied the crests of the surrounding hills and repulsed the charge made on the right by three companies of the 7th Cavalry. A line of dead horses marked the course of the charge; and the loss, either killed or wounded, of every commissioned officer but one, of every first sergeant and many noncommissioned officers, told how coolly it was received. [On] the skirmish line, the men dismounted, tied their lariats round the left arm, and led their horses. Whenever a soldier stopped for a moment, his horse would quietly graze—a strange sight on a battlefield! The Indians were finally forced to abandon their camp and to occupy the adjacent ravines, which were well protected from the fire and which they honeycombed with pits and bomb proofs. The Nez Perces occupied and held the crests on the north, immediately overlooking our own position. Things remained in this condition until the surrender.

The same bugler who sounded "To the charge!" on the thirtieth, trumpeting the death call of so many brave fellows, now blew the calming and welcome call of "Cease firing." The effect on the Indian camp was almost instantaneous. Where a moment before not a head was to be seen nor any sign of life, the ravines now swarmed with people, and little children capered in the sunshine and laughed in the face of death. They seemed to be the swarthy children of the earth, born in a moment, cast forth if by magic.

General Howard arrived on October 4, bringing with him his two herders, Captain John and George, friendly Nez Perces. Both these men had daughters in the hostile camp. Captain John is a friend of long standing to the whites. He fought by the side of Steptoe and helped him during his retreat. One parley with Joseph, held on October 2, had been unsuccessful; but after much discussion with the chief, old Captain John, with tears in his eyes, announced the surrender as concluded by Joseph's final reply.

Our artist was the only person present who committed the proceedings to writing and took the reply as it fell from the lips of the speaker. Joseph's little girl was lost in the hills during the first day's fight, his brother was killed, his relatives dead or fugitives; he upheld now only a lost cause. His answer was:

> Tell General Howard I know his heart. I am tired of fighting. Our chiefs are killed; Looking Glass is dead, Too-hool-hool-suit is dead. The old men are all dead. It is the young men who say yes or no. He who led the young men is dead. It is cold, and we have no blankets; the little children are freezing to death. My people, some of them, have run away to the hills and have no blankets, no food. No one knows where they are—perhaps freezing to death. I want to have time to look for my children and see how many of them I can find. Maybe I shall find them among the dead. Hear me, my chiefs! I am tired; my heart is sick and sad. From where the sun now stands, I will fight no more forever.

Attended by five warriors—he on horseback, they on foot—Joseph rode slowly up the hill, where General Howard and Colonel Miles stood to receive them. His hands were crossed on the pommel of his saddle, and his head was bowed upon his breast. After receiving him, General Howard and Colonel Miles mounted their horses and accompanied the chief to Miles's tent.

After the surrender, the Indian stronghold was filled with eager and curious visitors, who for days had invested the place, yet [had been] unable to get even a glimpse of its arrangement. The ravines were so crooked as to prevent enfilade fire, and so protected by hills as to be safe from our sharpshooters.

Joseph has a gentle face, somewhat feminine in its beauty, but intensely strong and full of character. A photograph could not do him justice. A bullet scratch has left a slight scar on his forehead. In each shirt sleeve and in the body of the shirt are bullet holes, and there was also a bullet hole in one of his leggings, a bullet scratch on his wrist, and one across the small of his back. Colonel Miles begged his shirt as a curiosity so full was it of visible evidence that Joseph had been where lead was flying.

George A. Huston, the guide, is a man of sterling integrity and indomitable pluck. He is the most famous and reliable "Yellowstone guide," the hero of many a thrilling bear or Indian fight, told so modestly that you do not suspect him of being [a] principal actor. He guided our column where no one else could take the lead, and brought us over the mountains two days nearer the Indians than we otherwise would have been.

Cavalry in the Nez Perce Campaign

OLIVER O. HOWARD

Army and Navy Journal 15, no. 40 (May 4, 1878): 629–30[1]

HEADQUARTERS DEPARTMENT OF THE COLUMBIA
PORTLAND, OREGON, January 19, 1878

Col. J. C. Kelton, Adjutant General, Military Division of the Pacific:

COLONEL: The following letter was received from your headquarters, December 11, 1877:

[Letter asking General Howard to furnish his own opinion and to "call for the views of the officers in command under you, not only of cavalry, but of infantry, artillery, and staff," as to the reason why the cavalry, as has been alleged, did not in the Nez Perce campaign fulfill the expectations of its friends, "the soldierly qualities of the officers and men" not being in question.]

In obedience to the instructions herein contained, I caused circular letters to be written to all the posts in my department calling for a full report from each of the officers. Some of them have been received. These I forward with this report.

I notice that several of the officers are sensitive and annoyed, probably disappointed that I should, in my interview with the division commander, let fall anything that could even seem to reflect upon the cavalry that had been so long under my command. On the contrary, there is an evident expectation of praise, and praise only.

Now let it be noticed that "the soldierly qualities of the officers and men are not in question." It is therefore not wise to assume that either the division or department commander had any intention of finding fault. On the contrary, neither in my report nor in my interview with the division commander, nor in private conversations, have I had occasion to complain of the officers and soldiers who labored hard, long, and successfully to make the late campaign complete and satisfactory to the government.

Still, if asked, did your cavalry at all times fulfill your expectations, I would say with regard to portions of the cavalry, no. It did not do so in its first engagement, June 17, though there were good reasons for this disappointment.

2nd. It did not do so in the skirmish with Looking Glass, July 1; though when I came to know better the difficulties of the situation, I imputed no official discredit to the officers in command.

3rd. I was disappointed somewhat after the battle of the Clearwater that we could not effect a prompter cavalry pursuit. Still, the reasons that caused the delay were in my judgment sufficient to exculpate the officer in charge from blame.

4th. I was somewhat disappointed at the Weippe. I believed that if I had sent my infantry and artillery, more would have been done. Here, too, good military reasons existed for the hasty return after a slight skirmish.

5th. I was also disappointed at Camas Meadows that the cavalry retired so rapidly and so far as to disconnect with Captain Norwood.

6th. I was often disappointed to find a feeling of depression exhibiting itself among some cavalry officers of undoubted bravery.

It showed itself at Dry Creek, Henry's Lake, Clark Fork, after Colonel Sturgis joined, and more or less at other times. I believed then that this feeling of depression arose partly because the cavalry officers felt that I expected too much of the commands, and partly, I thought, from want of confidence in their mount and arms as compared with the mount and arms of the enemy.

But notwithstanding these disappointing circumstances, on the whole march and campaign, the cavalry have and deserved high credit and are, I believe, equal to any other of our cavalry in the way of gallantry in action and long endurance of hardships.

Are There Improvements?
1. HORSES AND DRILL. Let us then ask ourselves what will improve our cavalry and make it more effective than now in the only kind of warfare that it is likely to engage in for many years, viz., Indian warfare.

Before our campaign began, many of the nontreaty Nez Perce Indians watched our cavalry as it appeared from time to time on drills and inspections at Lapwai and Walla Walla. These Indians stated, as I learned from the friendly Indians, that they "believed they could defeat this cavalry, for they could make our horses run."

The horses at White Bird Canyon became, as I understand, much excited; the holders were not able to manage them. On the retreat, those men who had their horses were much scattered and could not dismount to fire because their horses could not be controlled.

During our pursuit, I saw one company under a sudden fire from across the river at Kamiah. The horses became wild and unmanageable for the time, so that many men dismounted from them and let them go.

The remedy for this difficulty of managing horses in battle and in emergencies is, of course, more drill; better training of horses and men.

The American horse is intelligent and can be trained if taken young enough. He is not, in my judgment, taken young enough to make the essential training easy and certain. The Indians whom we opposed had the cayuses and half cayuse ponies. Their war ponies were carefully trained, probably beginning with the colts of two and three years. The Indian would throw his coil of the lariat upon the ground, one end being attached to the horse, [and] the horse would stand quietly waiting while the Indian delivered his fire, either in battle or in the chase. He could fire several times, and still his horse waited for him. This was the general rule. Early and persistent training of the horse is needed. Our cavalry soldiers have been obliged to work as laborers and have not, in consequence, been drilled enough, either with their horses or without their horses.

It should be remembered that the cavalry soldier has a double part to perform; namely, to care for and manage his horse, and besides, to acquire even more skill with his arms than the infantryman, more because he must learn to fire and fence on horseback as well as on foot.

I believe that the necessary skill will not be acquired except by the establishment of a cavalry school, through which the new men must pass before being sent to the field or post of active duty, and then have there, superadded, the most thorough and unremitting drills. If the horses and the men be trained sufficiently, the horse holders may be diminished in numbers, or some expedient resorted to like that suggested by Captain Babbitt[2] of automatic horse holding, or that of blinding mentioned by Lieutenant Egbert,[3] 2nd Infantry.

It is hard for a captain or a field officer to command several companies that have never acted together till the emergency of the battle or campaign calls them to this combined service. Large posts under the best field officers, instead of many small ones, are the economic remedies. The 7th Cavalry had this primary advantage over ours. They were often drilled and marched together over hundreds of miles in bodies of six and seven companies. Ours came together to fight at once and engage in rapid and unrelenting pursuit.

2. CONCERNING DRILL WITH ARMS. Our soldiers of all arms have had too little practice with their arms. The target practice and the firing with blank ammunition have been limited by a false idea of economy. It is now in better shape, but the necessity is the best limit in the expenditure of ammunition, for nobody but the post commander and those officers who are under him can tell beforehand how many times a man must fire to gain the requisite skill—some more and some less. The blank firing must be kept up to keep the horses in trim to stand the shock or become indifferent to it. Firing from the horse must be allowed, or no degree of accuracy can be attained by the man while mounted.

3. AS TO THE CHARACTER OF THE ARM, the same soldier gets altogether the best results with the Springfield rifle musket, now in the hands

of the infantry. The reasons, in my judgment, are first that there is a greater distance between the sights, and that the larger charge gives relatively greater velocity to the ball. The remedy is in lengthening somewhat the carbine, or in substituting for it the rifle musket. I noticed that quite a number of the 7th Cavalrymen carried the latter arm, and I think all felt increase of confidence from this fact.

Col. Miles's mounted infantry have the Springfield rifle-musket, and I know how self-possessed they appeared. Our own artillerymen and infantry were always satisfied with their arm whereas, on the other hand, I have heard of many cavalrymen expressing a distrust of theirs, as compared with those carried by the enemy's sharpshooters. Our scouts and the frontiersmen almost invariably prefer the Springfield rifle to the carbine, though it is heavy to carry. Some messengers preferred the carbine; yes, even the pistol to either carbine or rifle, because they had to ride so many miles that they would risk anything but a close assault to relieve them from the burden of a heavy arm.

4. THE KIND OF HORSE, TREATMENT, ETC. The character of the horse is a very important element in Indian warfare. How far the large, fine American breed of horses can be accustomed to the hardships of this warfare, if trained to it from colts and kept always without grain, I am not prepared to say. The cayuse ponies and half-breeds always have been grazed; never being grain fed, they want no grain. Those we had were generally much hardier than our cavalry horses. Still, it requires care and experience to graze horses properly, even Indian ponies.

We had two Indian herders who were quite successful in bringing horses nearly exhausted and quite thin into fair working condition while they kept up with us in the long daily marches. It was done by constantly watching their horses and seeing that they had the best grazing to be found, that they had short rests and grazing times frequently during the march, and also being very particular about the watering. My own judgment is that what I have called half-breed ponies would be the best for service in the field against Indians.

5. RAPIDITY OF MOVEMENT. Again, some remedy must be sought against the superiority of speed in movement which the Indians obtain. This is due to their driving along a herd of extra horses. The nontreaty Nez Perces had to begin with more than three ponies for each person, including men, women, and children. They replenished this herd at Bitterroot Valley. They added to it largely at Horse Prairie and Lemhi, and secured additional animals to replace those that had fallen out from exhaustion at the stampede of Camas Prairie and also by forays at other places a few miles off their route. We soon began to collect a small herd, and found it of great advantage from which to supply scouts, messengers, and officers called suddenly to long journeys.

Should ponies be allowed for this service, we could assign to each man two at least—one in the column and one in the herd—without much additional expense. For while the original cost of two of these animals would be more than one American horse, the difference would soon be compensated by the less cost of keeping.

6. FIGHTING MOUNTED. The opinion that seems to be gaining ground among cavalry officers and soldiers, that they are never to fight on horseback, I think is injurious to the morale of the men. A charge with sabers when the ground admits of it would be, I think, as effective against mounted Indians as it was against Confederate cavalry.

7. SKIRMISHING. The Indians frequently skirmished on horseback. Their quick flanking operation at the battle of the Clearwater, repeated two or three times, was while mounted. Their turning a flank of Major Sanford, which caused him to retire his force at Camas Meadows, was done without dismounting. Certainly it will require only equal arms, horses, and proper drill for us to excel the Indians in these military expedients.

8. SABERS AND THE CHARGE. The effect of a charge in a body was seen when our cavalry came down the steep hills upon the retreating Indians at Kamiah. Sabers would have added to the terror-inspiring movement. From this circumstance, it will be remembered the Indians' proposed battle for defending the crossing was given up. They sprang upon their skin rafts and fled, losing much property at the rapid and confident cavalry approach. The evident effect, however, was afterward lost by one company along the river, where several of the men abandoned their horses so as to take the fence for a cover. Had the men instantly returned the fire of the enemy without dismounting and maneuvered to cover, the shouts of triumph of the enemy would have been saved.

The saber might be used in drill, if not in campaign. The saber drill, when thoroughly conducted, increases a soldier's confidence in himself, for it makes him more agile in his motions, firmer in his seat, and skillful in the government of his horse.

9. PISTOL. As to the pistol, I would recommend that it be dispensed with for the cavalry soldier. The main reliance would then be upon the larger arm, with which firing can be frequent enough on the majority of occasions. I do not know that there is greater need of a pistol for the remarkably few cases of ultimate defense of life for the cavalry than for the infantrymen.

10. As fighting on foot, both in skirmishing and in regular action, will in most instances be absolutely necessary, it will add greatly to the soldier's confidence in himself to have with him an entrenching tool. Either the separate entrenching instrument or the trowel bayonet will do.

11. CROSSING RIVERS. There is one thing in which our cavalry appeared to me to be far less skilled than the Indians—that was in crossing rivers with their horses. Some whole companies of horses could not be made to take the water at Salmon River and had to be towed over by boats, two and four at a time.

Again I noticed the same difficulty in crossing the Clearwater at Kamiah. Few indeed, if any, of our soldiers could be made to swim their horses mounted at Craig's Ferry.

At each of these places, the Indians made a prompt crossing with a large number of ponies, certainly in half the time it took us to cross our cavalry. The only remedy is to be found in preliminary practice. It is quite an art to swim a horse well while on his back. Frequent repetition only will remove the horse's resistance to swimming by himself. The coaxing, driving, pounding, striking, shouting, chasing, plunging into the water, and emerging on the same side all along for half a mile, both at the Salmon River and the Clearwater, causing most vexatious delays, will not soon be forgotten by those of us who witnessed the exhibition. It is surely a matter of great importance to the cavalry officer to know beforehand whether his horses will take the water or not, and to have his men adept at making their horses swim, either with them on their backs or by themselves.

12. SADDLES AND EQUIPMENT. The objections to the saddle and other horse equipment are not material except to the cinch strap. The latigo, or cinch strap, ought to be made of thin, pliable leather instead of the thick, heavy tanned leather as now. The latter raises a swelling in the horse's side.

The bits ought to be averaged to accommodate the harder or more tender-mouthed horses; not being so uniform in size and shape, for of course a bit that will suit one horse would soon worry and fret another to death.

Again, there was during our march some complaint of the saddlebags chafing the legs of the men, as the corners project too far forward; either round the corners or shorten the rear strap.

I think the universal testimony of the officers is that the "side lines" for fettering the horse for purposes of grazing or preventing him from wandering away are the best.

13. REWARD FOR SERVICE. Now as I have intimated before, the cavalry soldier has much more to do in the way of preparation and subsequent work than the infantry soldier. We should then do all we can to have greater inducement for reenlistment. Give him a higher compensation and have some system of reward of merit most likely to increase his self-respect and awaken a pride in his profession.

My object will have been missed if there shall be a disposition to put on the coat of my criticism, and bring it home to lessen the good feeling that has existed and enabled us to accomplish so much as we have the past summer. But I shall be glad if any of the suggestions that I have made, or that other officers have made, may be of benefit, however slight to the cavalry of my command.

I append a summary of those reports received in time to be carefully considered. These reports themselves, as well as others received at later dates, are transmitted herewith. Respectfully submitted,

O. O. HOWARD, Brigadier General, commanding.

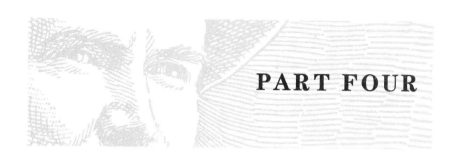

PART FOUR

The Bannock War, 1878

The Bannock War

OLIVER O. HOWARD

"Causes of the Paiute and Bannock War," *The Overland Monthly* 9 (May 1887): 492–98[1]

The Indian war of 1878, usually called the Paiute and Bannock War, originated with a small tribe of Indians in eastern Idaho. This tribe, the Bannocks,[2] have often been called the Snakes. They were once considerable in numbers and remarkable for their wars, particularly with other Indians.

During the summer of 1868, there was entered into between some agents of the government and the Bannocks at Fort Bridger, Wyoming, a sort of Indian treaty. This treaty stipulated that at any time, when the Bannocks should so elect, a reservation of public land should be given them. They were to have all the rights and privileges that had already been secured to their neighbors, the Shoshones, in Wyoming.

Subsequent to the treaty, a reservation some 100 miles north of Salt Lake, within the borders of the territory of Idaho, was set apart.[3] So far, there was good faith between those who made the promises and those who came after to execute them. But almost immediately the stipulations were modified and subsequently violated, for the Indian Department directed that all "roaming Indians" in southeastern Idaho should have a home on the same reserve.

As long as the Bannocks were more numerous than the roaming Indians not of their language or habits, they made no marked disturbance. In fact, the Bannocks had thousands of ponies and were nomadic, living principally by hunting the buffalo in the Yellowstone Valley. They came for the annuity goods and departed at will. But little by little, the Shoshones were allowed to come upon the reservation; goods, subsistence, and clothing intended for the Bannocks were issued to these roamers, and soon they outnumbered the lawful claimants nearly two to one.

The Bannocks, of course, grew dissatisfied, restless, and made bitter complaints that the Bridger treaty made with them was not kept.

People sitting in the office at Washington regarded such feelings as of little account. Were not all Indians Indians? What mattered it whether they were Shoshones or Bannocks? If there were room enough and supplies enough there, no Indian had a right to despise the hand that fed him. The Bannocks grew more and more restless, more and more quarrelsome, and not only hated, but robbed, the more industrious and more favored Shoshones.

At last, in August 1877, the work of revenge began. A Bannock near Fort Hall shot and killed two white teamsters. Matters were pretty quiet, even after this outrage, till the authorities, with a view of punishing the guilty, by their slow processes came at last to look into the matter. Mr. [W. P.] Danilson, the Indian agent, sent his interpreter to the Bannocks with a message that they should come to his office and bring with them Petope, who was believed to be the slayer of the two teamsters. The Indians seemed to obey. They came, and brought the suspected culprit. He was delivered to the marshal, who conveyed him to prison at Malad City to await his trial.[4]

There was thus far no opposition, but somehow Indians always deeply demur at the white man's methods of justice, and those who looked beyond the quiet demeanor could see signs of a gathering storm. Few Indians can understand why some white men should not suffer for other white men's offenses. They were merely squaring old scores when they, through Petope, slew the two teamsters.

So we are not surprised to hear that within an hour after the marshal had gone, the suppressed wrath began to show itself. Young Alexander Rhoden, who was attempting to issue cattle to the Indians, was killed by a weapon in the hands of Tambiago, and other mischief was threatened.[5]

Very properly, Fort Hall, several miles distant, was called upon for troops. The next morning my friend Captain Bainbridge,[6] who had the preceding summer, during the Nez Perce escapade, cooperated with me so heartily, was on the spot with a small detachment of his company.

The murderer was demanded at the hands of the Shoshones and the Bannocks. The Shoshones said that had he been a Shoshone, they would have arrested him and delivered him, but that his arrest should be made by the Bannocks. Those Bannocks who were listening feigned acquiescence and started off with apparent alacrity to make the arrest of the guilty Indian. But when night came, the pursuers returned without Tambiago. They declared that he had joined his father and brothers, and that all had escaped to the country that lies beyond the Snake River.

Again pursuers were dispatched, but always with like results. The Bannocks were now plainly hostile. They were armed, and many of them finely mounted. Their handsome ponies (some of them pure white) were fat and tough.

Soon more troops came, from Fort Douglass. Colonel John E. Smith[7] soon followed and held a council with the Bannocks: "Bring back that murderer, or you will be regarded as treaty breakers—yes, as hostiles."[8]

Still they did not comply. However, Tambiago did not get off. White men traced him up to a white settlement, and he was seized, tried, condemned, and executed.[9]

Soon after the [arrest] of the fierce Tambiago—about the middle of January 1878—an event occurred that has been named as the actual cause of the war. But the causes were really, like those of all wars, multifarious.

Colonel Smith had in hand on the ground three companies of infantry and three troops of cavalry. At dawn on January 16, he had so marched his small force as to completely surround and hem in two of the Bannock villages. Though the Indians were armed, yet they were taken so suddenly that both villages were captured, and upwards of fifty warriors and some 300 ponies were escorted to the agency. The father and two brothers of Tambiago were sent to Fort Hall for detention. The remainder, after Colonel Smith had counseled them well, were allowed their liberty. Their ponies, such as were captured, and rifles were kept from them.

For a time the Bannocks apparently acquiesced in this management, but they were angry at heart with the white man's administration of justice, and especially vexed at the loss of their rifles and ponies. They had many night talks among themselves and were for days hatching out plans for revenge.

As soon as the springtime gave them good weather and sufficient grass for the animals that they still had, the Bannocks left the reservation. Many of them had put in crops, but these were abandoned to the wary Shoshones, who reaped from their fields a goodly harvest.

Before following these warlike Indians into the actual campaign of 1878, let us notice them during the preceding year, in the troubles that the government had with their natural enemies, the Nez Perces. About a score of Bannocks were at that time employed by Maj. John Green as scouts. Accompanying the troops that had marched from Boise City to Kamiah, they joined me at the latter place, just after the battle of the Clearwater. Buffalo Horn, a handsome young Indian covered with plumage and dressed in skins, was at their head. These Bannock scouts had hardly come to my column, and been required to march with us across the mountains from Idaho into Montana, when they, hesitating to go, began to manifest a very insubordinate spirit. However, only three broke away from us at this time. Fortunately, Buffalo Horn then kept on my side of the controversy.

They were, after this, quite enterprising during the long march; yet it was exceedingly difficult to restrain them from acts of brutality. For example, they came at one time suddenly upon one of Joseph's abandoned camps. Finding in it an old woman who was too sick and infirm to keep on with the hostiles, the scouts instantly killed her and took her scalp as a trophy of victory. Again, there was another example of ferocity: The same scouts had come upon Colonel Gibbon's battlefield of Big Hole. The dead, including women and children, had been buried under the bank of a stream. The ferocious Bannocks quickly disinterred the bodies, robbed them of clothing, robes, and such various ornaments as had been buried with them; then they pierced and dishonored their naked bodies in a shocking way, and carried off their scalps. I noted at the time, "Our officers look sadly upon the scene, and then, as by a common impulse, deepen their beds (the places from which the bodies had been dug), and cover them with earth."

On the other hand, there was good behavior. Just before Chief Joseph's notable night attack on my camp at Camas Meadows, I recorded that one of Robbins's[10] scouts—a Bannock, the famous Buffalo Horn, who [has] since fought against us and been killed—at this time crept to the top of the mountain ridge, succeeded in getting upon a prominent point whence he could see Joseph's camp in the Camas Meadows below, and sent one of the Indians with a message, "Joseph with all his Indians are here."

After the night attack, and as we had resumed hot pursuit and were recovering the mules and horses which had been stolen, we had a pleasant surprise from the Bannock reserve. First a gay cavalcade, riding with the free and easy grace of Indians, appeared in the distance. It proved to be the advance guard of a company of scouts from Fort Hall, about 100 miles to the southwest. Their feathers and fur strips were flying in the breeze, and the bright colors and tasteful decorations of each man and horse added to the brilliant effect. They carried a white flag in the front rank and rode grandly into our camp. A thrill of joy ran through our weary and almost discouraged company at this accession. The leader of the scouts, in full buckskin dress, shaggy with strings, was a tall, pale man with fair proportions and slightly deaf. A stranger would see little that was remarkable in him; yet of all the scouts in our Indian campaign, none equaled this chief, Fisher.[11] Night and day, with guides and without, with force and without, Fisher fearlessly hung upon the skirts of the enemy. The accuracy, carefulness, and fullness of his reports to one attempting to chase Indians across a vast wilderness were a delight.

After this, I had occasion to distrust my Indian friends. for next there came to us here evidences of a Bannock treachery, which culminated a year later in the murder and outrages of the Bannock campaign. At the foot of the mountain near Mary Lake, where Spurgin made his zigzag road, forty horses belonging to civilian teams, which were doing the transporting work for us, were turned out to graze. During the night, these horses all mysteriously disappeared. The quartermaster's clerk, encountering some Bannock scouts who had suspiciously lingered in the rear, was treated to some very rough language by them.

Suspecting treachery, I sent at once a small detachment of mounted soldiers, who soon returned to the camp with ten of the Indian scouts as prisoners. Their leader—that is, the leader of this party—a half-breed by the name of Raine, was cross and mutinous in his language. I had them all disarmed and placed in the guard tent, and their handsome horses and rifles taken from them. I now also found on inquiry that all the Bannock scouts except one or two had deserted the brave Fisher, had come back from him to the troops, and were planning to return to Fort Hall.

An old chief of the tribe soon begged of me to let the prisoners go free, assuring me of their innocence. I said, "What you say may be true, but Indians are good to hunt horses. They follow blind trails better than white men. Send out some of your young men, and look up my lost horses. I will never set the prisoners free till the horses are brought back." The old man replied, "Yes, Indians good to hunt horses; I will send them."

In a few hours, twenty of the horses came galloping into camp, chased by his young Indians, who, with the old man, then came to me and declared that these twenty were all they could possibly find. I said, "All right. I shall never let the prisoners go till I see the other twenty horses."

The old Indian gave a grunt and shrug of the shoulders and left me. Soon after, I saw him mounted and then, with his party, leave the camp. That night the remaining twenty horses overtook us, and the prisoners were released, except Raine, who was dispatched under escort to Fort Ellis.

One night we had quite a scene, in which the brother of Raine figured. It occurred in a beautiful glade near the headwaters of the Snake River. The Bannocks, our scouts, had for their tepees a slight knoll near the beautiful and clear water, not far from my bivouac. Buffalo Horn came to me and asked that the Indians might have a dance. Consent was given. The echo of the wild singing, the weird shapes passing the fire during the dance, and the actual sense of danger, after Joseph's late-night attack, appeared to impress the whole command with a feeling of awe and apprehension; there was almost a panic. Add to this, I was intending to start the command at 2:00 A.M., and so there was an unusual stir of preparation kept up. The neighing of the horses and the braying of the mules, one occasionally giving a high and prolonged screech, sounded during the still night ten times louder than usual. It was a night to be remembered.

At midnight, after the war dance and its council had subsided, Buffalo Horn and Raine came to headquarters and asked for authority to kill our three Nez Perce herders—Captain John, Old George, and one other Indian of the tribe. Raine said that George and the two other Indians were traitors, that they had rejoiced openly at Joseph's success in the night battle in surprising our mule herd, and that Old George particularly ought to die.

We had George brought forward to face his accusers. He was so frank and evidently so honest that the story against him was not for a moment believed, and Buffalo Horn was denied that small favor of killing any of the three. He was very angry in consequence and never quite forgave me for this refusal. The third Indian may have been guilty. He, at any rate, so much feared these suspicous and exacting Bannocks that he escaped into the forest that night and went back to his people at Kamiah. But the jolly Captain John and the demure George, herding and bringing up the played-out horses from day to day in a wonderful manner, remained with the command to the close of the campaign.

All the Bannock scouts left me after the final battle with the Nez Perces and returned to their agency. And it is not doubted that some of them, particularly Buffalo Horn, puffed up with pride and self-confidence and hoping to do better than Joseph and his warriors, fomented the causes of dissatisfaction that I have herein related, and stimulated the Indians to revenge for real and fancied wrongs up to the time of their departure from their reservation in the spring of 1878.

Before proceeding with the direct accounts of the Bannock outbreak during the summer of 1878, it will be well to look into the Paiute country and see what causes induced that nation, or a part of them, to associate with the Bannocks during the dire conflict.

There is a strange story, a legend very old, told by Sarah Winnemucca concerning the early history of the Paiutes. It is to the effect that a barbarous people, who were cannibals of the worse sort, once dwelt in the long valley of the Humboldt River, while Sarah's forefathers occupied the country west of them, extending from what are now called the Muddy Lakes of Nevada northward to the Harney and Duck Lakes of Oregon and Idaho, inhabiting a broad landing sweeping off to the foothills of the Sierras.

The cannibals would set traps and lie in ambuscade for the more civilized Indians, catch them, kill them, and eat them as we do the cattle and sheep from the shambles.[12] The horrid creatures would, in extremities, even exhume and consume the bodies of those who had perished in war or died a natural death. Of course, they provoked wars with their neighbors, and in their wars, they were as regardless of life as the Bedouins of the desert, or as the reckless followers of the Mahdi. Sarah's ancient people at last undertook a war of extermination. They beat them in battle, they put large numbers to death and drove the remnant into the thick forest of bushes just north of Humboldt Lake. Fire set to the bushes drove them out of the forest. They fled to their bulrush boats. From these they were pierced with arrows as they approached the shore. At last the cannibals forced a landing on the eastern border of the lake and ran into a large cave situated near the mountains.

Here their relentless foes set a watch. They made some attempts to convert them to the use of the proper food of men and women, but the cannibals would not surrender their long-enjoyed rights and privileges, and so at last the mouth of the cave was filled with wood. As those within drew in the wood, it was replaced. When sufficiently filled, the cave was made into an oven by firing the wood, so that in smoke and heat, the last remnant of the ferocious tribe of cannibals were destroyed.

Hereafter, other Indians from the east and north called Sarah's people "Say-do-carah"—conquerors—because they had conquered and annihilated those terrible enemies. It is difficult to account for the name "Paiutes" that we gave the Say-do-carahs. It does not appear to be a word originating within the tribe itself. Fremont named their chief "Truckee," which signifies "All right."[13]

The cannibals had reddish hair. Sarah says that she has a dress trimmed with some of their hair. This dress is an heirloom in her royal family, and she calls it a "mourning dress."

Well, there always has been something remarkable about these Paiutes. They from the first desired greatly to have peace with the white men, who, following the paths of Fremont and others, began to cross over their country. But Anglo-Saxon greed is insatiable. Little by little their possessions were diminished. The lakes whence they took their fish in abundance were invaded by white settlers, and their hunting grounds were soon circumscribed.

The Paiutes have sometimes since 1860 been treated kindly by white settlers, as their later history shows; but though they had a reserve there given to them, yet the best part of it has since been taken away, and their best lake, where they obtained their largest trout (some weighing twenty pounds), was passed over from them to the new sovereigns of the soil.

Besides their love of peace, the Paiutes have generally exhibited good qualities. They, both men and women, have been ready to work and often have made headway by their industry in imitating the ways of their civilized neighbors. One example will explain their setbacks and discouragements:

Under advisement, they opened an acequia[14] near the railroad on the Pyramid Lake reservation and, with hard labor, extended it for a mile. This was for a flume and power to propel a saw and grist mill [that] had been promised them.

The saw and grist mill never came, except on paper. The lumber for Indian houses, which looks so well in the government reports, was never sent. The acequia is lost to them and used by Anglo-Saxons for purposes of irrigation.

I will venture to add a single instance to demonstrate the cruelty and wickedness that seemed to have pursued a people altogether predisposed, as we have seen, to peace and goodwill with all their "white brothers," as old Winnemucca's father named the first comers.

It was in 1865, just after our great war, that a cry arose among some of the white settlers around Harney Lake that the Indians had stolen some of their cattle. It might have been true, but the Paiutes were not engaged in theft. Winnemucca's tribe was then in Nevada. Many of the Paiutes were at Muddy Lake, engaged in fishing. A detachment of soldiers had came down from Harney, answering to the settlers' cry. Coming suddenly upon these peaceful Indians, they fired straight into the Indian camp and killed the old men, women, and children. Fortunately for the tribe, Winnemucca himself and his young men were then at another place on a hunting expedition.

After this terrible catastrophe, whoever was to be blamed, it is not at all strange that the Paiutes became filled with constant apprehension and suspicion. They were, of course, exceedingly ignorant and full of superstition, so that when some *tooat* (dreamer) arose and made predictions, many were ready to listen. A favorite idea was carried by the dreamers from tribe to tribe all through the northwest country; to wit: "There will soon be a resurrection of Indians—the whites will be killed by them, and our wrongs will speedily be avenged."

In process of time, after the close of another war, a band of Paiutes were gathered upon another section set apart from the public land, not far from Harney Lake; it was named the Malheur reservation. With my aide-de-camp, Captain Sladen, and my eldest daughter, I here paid the Indians a visit during the summer of 1874. I was looking for a better place for a post than Fort Harney, which, fifty miles distant, was on too elevated ground to enable the soldiers to raise vegetables or plant gardens of any sort. On a creek some ten miles distant from the Indian agency, I found a beautiful spot which would just suit, and which would put the garrison nearer the Indians, of whom the settlers, particularly the horse raisers, were ever making complaint. Thus the soldiers would get good gardens, the Indians be prevented from roaming, and the complaints be stifled.

This was my first personal acquaintance with the Paiutes. Here I found a full set of employees, an excellent agent, Mr. Sam Parish, and Sarah Winnemucca, acting as his interpreter. I had heard of her, and somewhat of her remarkable history. She spoke English perfectly, was very neat and tidy in her dress, and maintained an air of great self-respect.

Winnemucca was not then at Malheur, and Egan, the chief of that band, did not wish to decide the questions I put to him without consulting the old and respected head of his people. I was unwilling to force the soldiers upon the reserve, and so waited till the Indians should talk it over and decide. In spite of past troubles, they believed the soldiers at Fort Harney to be their friends, that [the soldiers] never had willingly injured them, and that they never would except when compelled to do so.

After I had stayed with them over one night and said all I could to encourage them in their evident industry and their school for the children, they in the morning, full of friendliness and with smiling faces, bid me adieu. Egan wanted me to visit them again and begged me to use my soldiers to keep bad white men off his reservation.

⊷ ⊱⬥⊰ ⊶

"Outbreak of the Paiute and Bannock War," *The Overland Monthly* 10 (June 1887): 587–92

During April and May 1878, there were a great many rumors of Indian troubles. They were found in the journals of the day and in the reports of army officers who were stationed in Washington Territory, eastern Oregon, and Idaho. I had heard something also of the state of things on the Fort Hall and Malheur reservations. The Indians all over the Northwest were much disturbed. Their wizard doctors insisted that the time had come when not only would the Indians of the different tribes unite, but there was to be an extensive resurrection of Indian heroes and fighting men, so that at last the double-tongued white men would be met with overwhelming force, and the land freed from their hateful presence and usurpations.

Looking closely to my correspondence, I discovered that Indian runners were passing from reservation to reservation; frequent visits on any ostensible plea were made, and secret meetings called and largely attended. As far as they dared, Indians who were really friendly to the whites gave unmistakable warning of danger at hand, and corroborating statements, more or less exaggerated, came in from the white men who were living in the vicinity of the plotting warriors.

Of course, I anticipated an outbreak somewhere and soon to come, but thought it would begin among what were called the Columbia Indians, or "Columbia renegades," who had escaped from their agencies and had expressed much dissatisfaction, and threatened white men because they had been required by the government to stop their wanderings and go back to their proper Indian reservation. These Indians seemed to be just waiting for us to use troops to carry out the orders which they had thus far disobeyed, and then they would begin their frightful massacres.

The various tribes up and down the Columbia were made the more restless and discontented at a governmental attempt to introduce a scheme known as "consolidation of agencies." Tribes of Indians who did not affiliate were to be taken from their existing homes or ranges, brought from afar, and placed—as we have seen with the Bannocks and Shoshones—in close association upon some common reserve. Many Indians would rather a thousand times die fighting than submit to what they considered such a wanton invasion of their rights.

Again, the stockmen who pastured their horses and cattle upon the public domain made unending complaints against the Indians, because the Indians' stallions were found amongst their herds, or because of the loss of horses or cattle, which the stockmen asserted (often wrongfully) had been stolen by the Indians. The Indians knew of these complaints and became secretive, restless, and at last, as they themselves said, "mad."

This condition of things, so unpleasant and troublesome, had made me feel sure, as I have intimated, that there would be during the summer an Indian war, and one, I feared, quite general in its scope. Accordingly, all practicable preparations for such an unwelcome event had been made prior to the first act of hostility. In the fullness of time the terrible war began, but not on the Columbia. The place of the outbreak, over 600 miles from me at Portland, Oregon, was between Boise City and Fort Hall.

As an instance of the exciting nature of the first alarm, I give an extract from a telegram sent me from Fort Boise, near Boise City, by its commanding officer:[15]

Bannock Indians have been making serious threats and ordering settlers off Big Camas Prairie. A man from there this evening reports
two settlers shot by Indians this morning, both wounded;[16] got to
Dixie Station, sixty miles distant, ninety miles to where Indians are
camped between Big Camas and Snake River, in lava beds. Bannocks
reported to have messengers out in the vicinity of Malheur agency.
Number of hostiles, two hundred, well armed and supplied with
ammunition.[17] Settlers counted sixty lodges, and twenty more lodges
with Buffalo Horn, who has just joined them.

The Bannocks had left Fort Hall, proceeded westward, and taken up their position among the ugly Lava Beds which are located amid that long stretch of camas prairie land over which the Short Line Railway now makes its daily journeys in passing from Pocatello in the Boise country and on to the Columbia. The Modocs had chosen the Lava Beds for the opening scenes of their awful tragedy, when General Canby fell, and Joseph had found them favorable to his bolder plans. So, doubtless, Buffalo Horn was following suit when, after the first bloodshed, he placed his lodges among the Lava Beds.

These beds are simply knolls of igneous rocks, over which debris and drift had gradually formed a soddy loam, and soon the surface became filled with briars and bushes. The knolls, generally a couple of rods across, were thrown together irregularly, alternating with spaces of prairie grassland. For miles the raised beds give so much sameness to the region that it is very difficult to find the way across it. They seem to be worse than forests in causing people to get lost. And they are well adapted to furnish cover to Indian braves in wartimes, for here all trails disappear—and the knolls are especially favorable to ambush, where the Indian may lie perfectly quiet till his enemy is within good range of his rifle.

The bloody affair on the Big Camas to which the telegram referred caused great excitement throughout the Northwest, and I confess that when the dispatches reaching me at Portland began to multiply and show me that another summer would have to be spent amid all the horrors of savage warfare, my heart for a moment shrank from the dire conflict and the responsibility. The last day of May I sat in my house, amid my family, with telegrams from official and unofficial sources from near the field of conflict in my hand, saying in substance: "The war is upon us; come, we entreat you, come to our help!" I said to my wife, "Is it possible that we must go through another such ordeal as that of last year?" I meant the Nez Perce War.

A soldier's conflict is not much prolonged. In a moment after my sorry remark, the proper spirit of decision came, and within an hour the troops of the department were holding themselves in readiness or preparing to go by water, by rail, or by marching toward Idaho and the scenes of strife.

General McDowell,[18] at San Francisco, was then my division commander. In answer to my dispatches, he promised at once to send troops, should their services be required, but he humanely ordered that "before troops should appear on the scene and a conflict begin," I "try to have it ascertained through reliable and discreet persons what has been the difficulty and who is to blame. If our people have done wrong, for which settlers have been shot," that I "endeavor if possible to do justice in the case by securing the offenders on both sides and delivering them to the civil authorities before resorting to so expensive a proceeding as war."

How thoroughly his instructions accorded with my own judgment! They were most earnestly complied with, though they were to meet with little real success. Governor [W. V.] Brayman, an elderly man, governor of the territory, was at his capital, Boise City. I telegraphed to him, among others, and received a reply June 2. Here are some of his words: "The right to Big Camas Prairie

[was] evidently the cause. Sheriff Hays informs me that 150 Indians are in Jordan Valley; King Hill Station, Overland stage road, raided, horses carried off." This Jordan Valley is a tributary of the Snake River. Very little time was given me to ascertain through discreet persons the cause of trouble, and none to negotiate a settlement, for the conflict was already begun.

Captain Bernard of the 1st Cavalry, who was the first, with his troop of horses,[19] to reach the Big Camas Prairie, found two men, herders, wounded. They were shot while in their tents by two Indians, and this was without apparent cause or provocation. After the wounded men had escaped, the Indians robbed the place of everything valuable and drove off thirty head of horses. From articles of wearing apparel discovered, Captain Bernard concluded that several bands had combined, mainly for plunder.

Mr. Rhinehart,[20] the Indian agent at Malheur agency, reporting on the causes of the war, believed stories brought to his Indians by visiting Bannocks as early as April that the Bannocks were angry because their horses had been taken from them, and because of the story spread among them that the Indian horses or ponies were to be taken away and given to the soldiers. Sarah Winnemucca speaks of this early visit of the Bannocks to the Paiutes and of their complaints:

It was Bannock Jack's band. They say that all their ponies have been taken from them, and all their guns too, for something two of their men had done. They [the Indians] got drunk, and went and shot two white men. One of the Indians (they allege) had a sister out digging some roots, and these white men went to the women who were digging, caught this girl, and used her shamefully. The other women ran away and left this girl to the mercy of those white men, and it was on her account that her brother went and shot them.

Sarah's account is evidently the Indian side of the Fort Hall story, which I have previously given.

When Bernard reached the Lava Beds [on] June 2, he found that the hostile bands which had been camped there in lodges, not daring to meet his approach, had abandoned their camps and fled. Indians' courage often weakens thus at the last moment. At once, as soon as he could discover their trail, he pursued it until he came upon other recent but deserted camps, which were evidently abandoned in great haste, for many important articles of food and clothing were left in them. The captain now pressed forward to the eastern portion of the Big Camas Prairie, where he struck an extensive lava country such as I have before described, one too rough and too dangerous in which to operate with his small cavalry troop.[21] He then turned off to the stage road. He found there the hamlet with [the] high-sounding name King Hill Station already deserted. The stage horses, ten in number, had been stolen by the Indians, who soon abandoned the Lava Beds, crossed over the Snake River at Glenn's Ferry, robbed the store and house there, turned the ferryboats loose, took everything they could carry off from some freight wagons, and gathered to themselves all the horses in stable or pasture that they could find.

Thus far there had been but little loss of life, for the settlements along the Snake River were scattered and isolated. Farmers, terrified by the first rumors, had quickly abandoned their homes and fled to the larger settlements and, as the people named the operation, "forted up." Our men found the dead body of a stranger, killed and thrown into the river, and several well-known persons had disappeared mysteriously.

Already it was evident from the reports that other Indians besides the Bannocks had joined these hostile raiding parties. A few Paiutes and Columbia River Indians were already present on the Big Camas Prairie before the first blow was struck. There were Indians there also from the Lemhi agency, and a few from elsewhere. They formed, after a consultation, a league, and agreed to move in such a way as to get the most plunder possible, and gradually passing from tribe to tribe in a circuit westward, to accumulate in time—like a huge snowball increases as it rolls—a force large enough to cope with all the troops I could bring to bear.

The Indians appear to have number at the outset between 300 and 400 warriors. Bernard, who was an old soldier, wrote, "This is the strongest outbreak I have ever known. They give no reasons of any kind for their actions, except the Bannocks, who had made some objections to white men coming on Big Camas Prairie with stock." The governor of Idaho in a letter to me mentioned the same complaint—that the cattle, horses, and hogs of white men were constantly pushing out upon the Big Camas Prairie. This was their ground, from which they had been accustomed to collect camas roots, and so they declared that white men were encroaching upon their most sacred rights.

However desirable it might be to so approach these savage raiders as to get from them the causes of their raiding, plunder, and murders, it could not be done with the small force which, at the outbreak, we had in that vicinity. There was, then, evidently, nothing left us to do but to pursue them rapidly, head them off where we could, and fight them fearlessly until they should be beaten. However often our officers have attempted to parley after hostilities have once been begun, the attempt has never been successful. The Indians laugh at such efforts and attribute them to a sense of weakness.

The Snake River between Boise City and Fort Hall on our maps resembles the trunk of a tree with many branches. In reality, the parallel streams are more abundant than those which are sketched on the maps. Several of the larger watercourses—tributaries of the Snake—have fertile valleys with a few settlements or detached ranches in each. The Indians sped on from one of these valleys to another, destroying as they went.

Captain Collins[22] of the 21st Infantry, setting out from Fort Boise with a small company of mounted infantry, had succeeded in joining Bernard near the Big Bend of the Snake River. June 5 he telegraphed from the nearest station:

"Scouts sent yesterday to the south of river, returned. They went to Bruneau Valley; found the people fortified, much property destroyed, [and] one man missing—supposed to be killed. Indians going south toward Juniper Mountains; they are believed to be Bannocks and Paiutes. All stock (cattle, horses, and mules) about Bruneau Valley taken by the Indians. They (this raiding party) are reported to be from 150 to 200 warriors."

That day Collins's command was transferred to Bernard, and Collins himself returned to Boise City to arrange for supplying Bernard's rapidly changing force. Bernard crossed the Snake River and put himself on the trail of the raiders. Though he was most energetic and persevering, it was difficult to gain upon his active enemy, who already had the best mounts the country could furnish, with two or three spare horses for each. Buffalo Horn was probably the field war chief at this time.

The next day, June 6, Bernard sent me a report from the upper Bruneau Valley. It informed me that the day before, he had, with his horses, swum the Snake River, reached the spot where the people had protected themselves by a unique fort, a sort of stockade. Resting at that place for a few hours, he sent some citizen scouts under a remarkable Boise City leader, Mr. [Orlando] Robbins; these were mounted upon fresh horses, with instructions to keep up the pursuit of the Indians, ascertain where they were at that time, and let him know as soon as possible.

The settlers declared that they, the Indians, had run into the Juniper or Battle Creek Valley—historic ground, upon which the Paiutes had more than once fought. The settlement in that valley is some thirty miles southeast of Silver City. Silver City itself, 100 miles south of Boise, was in 1878 a large mining town, having the usual combination of well-disposed, enterprising citizens, rough miners, and characteristic frontiersmen.

In the Bruneau Valley, Bernard found two more white men killed, one of them horridly mutilated. The next morning he escorted the settlers, who were unwilling to remain behind, away from their little fort to Duck Valley, from whence they thought they could get to Elko on the Central Pacific railway.

He pushed on his force next for Duck Flat, and then ran over into the Jordan Valley, where the Indians, according to his scouts, appeared to be making some delay. On June 8 everything had changed; for while Bernard's force was protecting citizens, his scouts, pressing up closer, had cautiously located the hostiles' bivouac, not far from Battle Creek.

Meanwhile, while Bernard's small mounted force, including his scouts, was thus watching and chasing, and chasing and watching, the raiders, Buffalo Horn was very wary and succeeded in avoiding battle with him. But this very day, in the afternoon, a small company of volunteers hurrying up from Silver City, led by Harper or Hill (for it is difficult to tell which of these men was really in command),[23] succeeded in heading off Buffalo Horn, with about sixty Bannocks. The place where they came together was seven miles from a small settlement called South Mountain. The Indians at once attacked the volunteers and drove them for several miles. They killed four white men and two friendly Paiutes, and wounded another man. One volunteer was reported missing—I think the schoolmaster of Silver City, the only white man that stood against the attack without retreating.[24]

"Paiute Joe," who went out with the volunteers, gave a different account of the fight. He said substantially that all the Bannocks were mad and on the warpath; that they were killing all the white people and such Indians as were friendly to them, but he and two other Paiutes had joined the volunteers as guides and taken them to South Mountain, where the volunteers proposed to annihilate the Bannocks; that the volunteers ran off at the first fire and left him and the poor old schoolmaster, who was badly wounded, close to the savages; that the schoolmaster was very angry and cursed his retreating friends while he was bleeding to death. Paiute Joe declared that it was he himself who fired the shot that killed Buffalo Horn. The fall of their leader checked the hostiles, so Paiute Joe, having a swift horse, succeeded in escaping. Joe also says that he and his companions, the other two Paiute guides, were all wounded, but that neither one of them were killed. I have not been able to verify the story about the volunteers, but it is certain that Buffalo Horn fell in that skirmish at South Mountain, and that shortly after this conflict, the hostiles pushed on as fast as they could to join the Malheur Paiutes at Juniper and Steen's Mountain.

It appears that Sarah Winnemucca, being much vexed because her friend and the Indians' good agent on the Malheur reservation, Samuel Parish, had been removed, had left the reserve and gone to live with a white family on the John Day River. A man by the name of Morton had hired Sarah to take him and his daughter in her wagon from John Day to Silver City. She was making the journey when, on June 11, she met Harper's volunteers and Paiute Joe at Fort Lyon, an old abandoned army post, then a station on the stage line. Next day Bernard (who was still in pursuit down the Boise and Kelton stage road), the volunteers, and Sarah came together at the next station further south, called the Sheep Ranch. On this day Bernard informed me by telegraph that the Indian raiders had descended the Owyhee River and gone toward Juniper Mountain, and were in a strong place in the Lava Canyon; that having captured a stage which was bringing military supplies from the railroad, they had seized two boxes of Winchester rifles and much ammunition; that they had, besides their mounts, some 400 horses; and that this band of hostiles had only about 60 warriors. Bernard thought that the other Bannocks—many of them, probably including their women and children—were not far from Battle Creek, a place south of Silver City, but were on the west side of the Owyhee. He adds to his report, "Sarah Winnemucca is in my camp offering her services for the good of her people; she wants to go to them with any message you or General McDowell might desire to send them—thinks if she can get to the Paiutes with a message from you or General McDowell, she could get all the well disposed of the people to come near the troops, where they could be safe and fed; says there is nothing at the Malheur agency to feed them with."

I answered: "Send Sarah with two or three friendly Indians, if you can get them, to go straight to her people and have them send a few of their principal men to you. I will see myself that all who behave well and come in are properly fed. Promise Sarah a reward if she succeeds."

Sarah Winnemucca, on horseback, with two friendly Paiutes, immediately set out on her journey of over 100 miles, through the roughest sort of country, to Juniper or Steen's Mountain, to communicate with her people who were already in the camp of the savage warriors and to accomplish, if possible, what she promised.

"The Bannock Campaign," *The Overland Monthly* 10 (July 1887): 95–101

Meanwhile, the entire Northwest was full of movement and excitement. The usual operations of mobilizing forces, which in Europe always creates consternation, occurs in any corner of this country the instant hostile Indians begin their work of murder, outrage, and robbery. Of course, here the numbers of men to be moved are small, but the posts are far apart, and great distances have to be spanned before any considerable force can get to a rendezvous.

A commander in Indian warfare is impatient and chafes at the exaggerated reports coming to him from every quarter. The experience, however, of the Nez Perce War and of the Custer massacre taught us never again, if it could possibly be avoided, to send an inadequate body of men against the Indians after they had had time to concentrate.

As a city fire-brigade promptly rushes at the first alarm to a burning building, so the troops of the Northwest sped on from every garrison toward the Camas Prairie and the Lava Beds, where the first bloodshed had occurred. They were hastening thither by water, by rail, and by marching—infantry and artillerymen from Fort Vancouver near Portland, from Forts Stevens and Canby near the mouth of the Columbia, and from Fort Townsend on Puget Sound. After reaching Umatilla, all these soldiers were to follow the Overland Stage road eastward for 100 miles, getting such lifts as they could in transportation wagons, riding and walking by turns. Fort Walla Walla furnished its contingent, two troops of cavalry—Whipple's and Perry's; Bendire's was already across the Blue Ridge, making for Walla Walla under previous instructions, but was quickly turned back, so that the beautiful route across the mountains was alive with marching men. Halfway between the Columbia and the California line was a frontier garrison at Camp Harney, which sent forward at once McGregor's[25] troop of cavalry and Downey's[26] company of infantry. They, with many misgivings, left behind them to protect their women and children but a small guard. At the same time, other detachments were approaching the scenes of disturbance by water, and by overland roads from California.

The morning of June 4, Col. Frank Wheaton, who was at Lapwai in Idaho, was fully warned of the Indian outbreak and of the perturbed condition of

The march out. RUFUS F. ZOGBAUM. *HORSE, FOOT, AND DRAGOON.*

affairs in the vicinity of Boise City. The following Saturday—June 9—was appointed for a consultation between him and me at Walla Walla. Col. Cuvier Grover, the commander at Walla Walla, was sent at the same time to the front under instructions to go to Boise City, "assume charge at that point, and remain there, opening communication with the department commander wherever he might be, and keeping him fully informed." The instructions to Grover indicated that I was to leave Portland Friday morning, go to Walla Walla, remain there one day, and go thence directly to Boise; he—Grover—was to furnish me with telegraphic reports at the various stations along the route.

There were still other preparations that I had to make before leaving my headquarters for the field.

There was a famous Indian not far from the Columbia (who is now living on a part of the Colville reservation in Washington Territory) by the name of Moses.[27] He is the acknowledged chief of several bands of Indians, and had then more or less influence over numerous restless tribes who were roaming over the upper region of the Columbia. I had great fears that certain wild white men, who preferred a state of riot and war to peace, might stir up trouble with this chief or among his followers. I knew, from my intercourse with him the previous year, that I had Moses's friendship, so I wrote him on the fourth substantially as follows: "I have already sent you word about the Bannocks; I send you word again. The Bannocks are giving me trouble, so that I cannot meet you as I promised at Spokane Falls. When I come back from the Bannocks, we will arrange for a meeting somewhere. I depend on you to keep the peace." Moses received this and several kindred communications. They had the effect that was desired, for he made no effort to combine with the Bannock hostiles or to give them aid in the war.

On the part of our eastern people, at times much objection has been raised, in letters and in the press, against the use of Indian scouts in dealing with Indians on the warpath. The fear is that by using Indians in trailing and skirmishing and other warlike operations, we keep them excited and diminish their interest in peaceful pursuits, so that they are more likely to shed blood among each other, and more inclined to retaliate their wrongs, or fancied wrongs, upon the settlers. Still, it is next to impossible for a commander successfully to follow Indian raiders or locate Indian camps without Indian scouts. We sought earnestly to obtain them in this war, first from the celebrated Capt. [John] Smith, the agent of the Warm Springs tribe. They were offered the privilege of furnishing their own horses, twenty-five of them, and they were to meet us en route at the Dalles, or afterward. No inducements, however, could procure them. Similar efforts were made to secure scouts from the Umatillas,[28] the Walla Wallas, the Nez Perces, and other Indians, but for quite a time without success. Those failures indicated beyond a doubt that there was a secret understanding among a score of tribes; in fact, among all those who range through Idaho, Oregon, and Washington Territory. No matter how advanced any of them were in knowledge and civilization, their "dreamers," or *tooats,* had over their minds a wonderful influence, and the hopeful predictions of ultimate success had for a time many ardent believers. However, the loyal Nez Perces, who during the previous war had remained our friends, did at last bring into the field fifteen of their number, and the wily Umatillas, under the persuasions of a half-breed interpreter, McBain, yielded us a few scouts—though not till after our battles in their vicinity had shown the futility of the enemy's attempts against us.

It was quite necessary in those Indian conflicts, where hostile bands changed their positions often and made rapid and long marches with their tough and numerous Indian ponies, to make on our part corresponding changes of position and plans. Certainly it is a difficult operation to ascertain and meet the shifting whims of an enemy more given to flight than to battle. These considerations determined me to be myself at the front, as near at hand as possible. With three staff officers, Maj. E. C. Mason and Lieutenants Wilkinson and Wood, I left Portland June 7 to go by way of the Columbia and the stage line across the Blue Ridge to Boise City. The previous engagement at Walla Walla for the ninth was met. Colonel Wheaton, who had arrived before me, took up his station there at Walla Walla to watch and guard the home district with small reserves, under his orders, stationed at several posts within his command, while the rest of us were endeavoring to arrest the depredators in Idaho and southern Oregon. We hoped speedily to beat them in battle or take them as captives.

On the afternoon of the twelfth, after a tedious journey, we reached Boise City, where we met Colonel Grover with several dispatches just received. A telegraph operator, a Mr. Calkins, kindly offered his office for temporary headquarters. It was situated in the city and every way convenient, for telegrams were constantly coming from all directions, so great was the alarm. It was at this point that I received the dispatch from Captain Bernard informing me of the position of the hostiles, their number, and of the bold proposition of Sarah Winnemucca to go, at the risk of her life, straight to their hostile camp.

There is a disposition on the part of men who have military knowledge, but who have only a limited military experience, severely to criticize all plans of operation. No commander can succeed in any warfare without formulated plans. Yet to make these good, it is necessary to have accurate knowledge of the country he occupies, and of the enemy. It does not do, however, to hesitate in Indian affairs. Use what information you can gather, and for the rest, conjecture what is most probable, plan quickly, and act at once.

With this theory in mind, there was no delay. As soon as Boise City was reached, my dispatch to General McDowell was as follows: "Arrived here this morning, sent force under Grover, including Sanford[29] [who was en route from Kelton, a Central Pacific Railroad station, towards Boise], to clear up scattering Indians eastward toward Fort Hall. Please ask commanding officer Fort Hall to work toward Grover; to detain the Bannock families reported going to Hall, particularly relatives of those on warpath. I am concentrating other troops against Bannocks and Malheurs at Sheep Ranch, six miles from Owyhee Ferry on Winnemucca stage road; taking charge of this column myself." This dispatch indicates the plan promptly taken at Boise City, founded upon the partial information which Colonel Grover brought.

At this time, the moving troops coming from Walla Walla and further west—cavalry, artillery, and infantry—were immersed in dust and pushing along the Baker wagon road, and yet considerably scattered. They were aiming for Sheep Ranch. The two companies from Camp Harney were supposed to be already near that station. They were to pass the Malheur agency and, if they had kept straight on, would not be more than three or four days' march from that point.

Just then, the Lemhi Indians and many friendly Bannocks appeared to have broken off from the hostile camp and were working back toward their homes. On the other hand, it was reported in dispatches that many Paiutes had already joined the hostile Bannocks in their raids. Buffalo Horn, it was asserted, but erroneously, was still alive and declared that the outbreak was begun by drunken Indians, and that as Captain Bainbridge, the Fort Hall commander, would hold the full tribe responsible, they might as well go to war at once, taking horses and other property. The bulk of the information represented that the main body of the Indians, with their women and children, were somewhere far in the rear of the active raiders, in the vicinity of Big Camas Prairie and the Lava Beds, and that the raiders had been comparatively few in number until they were reinforced about this time by all the Paiutes that belonged to the Malheur reservation.

The best approach to these conjoined enemies was from Sheep Ranch. I was quite sanguine that while my main force was marching to encounter this restless body, Colonel Grover, with the troops at his disposal pushing out eastward, would be able to sweep the others, with their families, towards Fort Hall and its troops and soon defeat and capture them. But a little later, as will appear, I discovered that the stories concerning the Indians on the prairie and

A moment's halt. RUFUS F. ZOGBAUM. *HORSE, FOOT, AND DRAGOON.*

among the Lava Beds were all incorrect. There were few Indians, if any, still in that region. Before, however, evolving a second plan, my staff and I hurried down the stage road to Sheep Ranch, arriving there June 14.

The next day, waiting for the scattered companies to come together, I was sitting with Captain Bernard at about 5:30 P.M. in a little room at the station, when it was reported that a mounted party was coming towards us from the west. It soon proved to be our messenger to the Paiutes, Sarah Winnemucca, with her companions. She came ahead of them, riding very rapidly. At first she could hardly speak for crying, she was so weary and excited. As soon as she was sufficiently quieted to speak intelligently, I received from her an account of her remarkable journey—over 200 miles long, rough, and evidently full of incident and excitement.

Though at the time, many of her statements appeared to the hearers to be considerably exaggerated, yet I put sufficient confidence in Sarah's story to change my whole plan of movement.

The following condensed account was crowded into a paragraph and recorded in the journal of the day:

> About 5:30 P.M., Sarah Winnemucca came in, riding fast; had been to hostile camp; brought out her father and brother; others followed and were pursued, overtaken, and taken back. She heard firing and fears her brother Lee was killed; says Natchez aided the white men to escape from the camp and went with them. She reports Oytez and Egan, with their bands, still detained in hostile camp; says arms and plunder were offered to tempt them to join hostiles; then threats and

coercion were tried; locates camp near Juniper Lake, Steen's Mountain; gives number at about 700; brought her sister-in-law into our camp and implores help for her father, whom she left behind with a few men and guns, guarding the fugitive women and children.

I may now add that Sarah's story, so far as subsequent information and evidence could affirm it, proved to be literally true. It is of sufficient historic interest to introduce here a few of those graphic incidents which she herself has since recorded:

"We (Sarah and the Indians George and John, Paiutes) followed the trail down the Owyhee River as much as fifteen miles, and then we came to where they had camp, and where they had been weeping and cutting their hair. So we knew that Buffalo Horn had been killed."

There were other indications of great grief besides the locks of hair on the ground; namely, pieces of manta and clothing, and numerous beads broken from the strings and strewn around. They found on the trail the whip of the stage driver who had been killed, and other articles from time to time, which made the blind trail when crossing the rocky beds easier to follow.

The first ranch the party came to had been owned by a frontier settler, Mr. G. B. Crawley. Everything combustible had been burned, but there were still considerable fire and fresh tracks about the premises. After delaying here to take a little food and rest, they determined to follow the fresher of two branching trails. This led them towards Steen's Mountain. That day they picked up a clock and a fiddle, and shot a mountain sheep, some strips from which added to their supplies. They were then near Juniper Lake. Five miles farther on they caught a glimpse of two people, dressed like Indians, on the slope of the mountain.

Sarah's account of this meeting is unique: "As we came nearer to them, I said to George, 'Call to them.' He did so. I saw them rise to their feet. I waved my handkerchief at them again, and one of them called out, 'Who are you?' I said, 'Your sister Sarah.' It was Lee Winnemucca, my brother, who had called out. Lee said, 'Oh, dear sister, you have come to save us, for we are all prisoners of the Bannocks.'"

Her brother represented that her father had been treated very badly; that his friends had been stripped of guns, horses, and blankets, and that there was great peril to her and her companions. "For," he said, "they will surely kill you, as they have said they will kill everyone who comes with messages from the white people, for Indians who come with messages are no friends of ours. They say so every night."

Immediately Sarah and her companions were transformed by the using of blankets and putting on of war paint into Indians proper; then altogether they went on to the grand encampment. "The mountain we had to go over was very rocky and steep, almost perpendicular. Sometimes it was very hard for us to climb up on our hands and knees, but we got up at last and looked down into the hostile encampment. Oh, such a sight my eyes met! It was beautiful; 327 lodges and about 450 warriors." Greater numbers were close at hand; they were down in Little Valley catching horses, and some were killing beef. This was part of the united camp of the Bannocks and Paiutes.

A little later, Sarah had worked her way into her father's lodge, containing several Paiute men and women. She says, "Everyone in the lodge whispered, 'Oh Sadie, you have come to save us!'" She and her brother succeeded in communicating with most of her father's friends. By concerted action, quite a number, estimated at seventy-five in all, left the camp in the night. When they were well on the way, they heard a horse running toward them. "We had to lie down close to the ground. It came close to us and stopped. Oh, how my heart beat. It stood a little while, and someone whistled. 'Yes,' the whistler said, 'where is father?'" It proved to be Lee Winnemucca's wife Mattie. After this, Mattie and Sarah rode together and tented together during the entire campaign.

Lee now turned back to endeavor to separate more Paiutes still from the hostiles and to act as a scout and guard to his father's little column. Old Winnemucca then said, "Ride two by two, keep close together. Men, march your children and your wives. Six men keep back, for fear we will be followed." Thus Winnemucca's family and friends, riding fast for six hours, hurried on for the remainder of the night, reaching Summit Springs at the break of day.

They had stopped for a little rest and food when, of a sudden, they saw one of their rear guard riding furiously toward them. He cried out as he approached, "We are followed by the Bannocks. I saw Lee running and them firing at him. I think he is killed." Of course, they mounted at once and rushed on again.

At this time, finding Winnemucca's column too slow to suit her impatient spirit, Sarah took her sister-in-law with her and two Indians, saying to her father, "Come father, give me your orders, as I am going back to the troops. What shall I tell General Howard, as I am going to where he is this very day?"

Winnemucca replied, "Tell him to send his soldiers to protect me and my people."

With this message, these brave women made the remainder of the distance to Sheep Ranch and reported to me as I have previously stated. Bernard's chief of scouts, Robbins, was immediately sent with his men to meet the old chief and his party, and bring them to the protection of the troops, to facilitate which, Sarah sent Paiute Joe as a guide.

I have been thus particular in recalling some of the incidents of this ride because of its extraordinary nature. It was a ride of over 200 miles, made between 10:00 A.M. of June 13 and 5:30 P.M. of June 15. Sarah says truly, "I went for the government when the officers could not get an Indian or a white man to go for love or money."

Information was now abundant. The reports from all sources showed that the Bannock raiders, those who had committed the most of the murders and robbery, had sent their women and children and bands of ponies in advance of them; so that those whom I had supposed still in the lava beds, as well as the raiders, had already formed junction with the Malheur Indians, and some others, probably Columbia River Indians and Klamaths, had made their way to them. They were all at Steen's Mountain. Their aggregate numbers varied in the account from 700 to 1,500 warriors. They had a strong position and expressed a determination to remain at Steen's Mountain and give battle.

The friendly Paiutes who had gone with Sarah Winnemucca and returned were so much alarmed at what they saw, and were so sure that the white men would eventually be defeated, that they could not be prevailed upon by any offer of reward to act as guides or interpreters, or even to continue with us. Furthermore, the sorrowful report reached us that the two companies from Camp Harney, affected by the extraordinary and unexpected danger, feared for their families left under an insufficient guard and had concluded, in spite of orders, to turn back to their post.

All communication was now, of course, interrupted. The experiment was afterward tried of getting a communication through to Camp Harney by using "Little Joe," a Paiute Indian. I had found Joe a prisoner at Silver City, suspected of being a spy, and after investigation, I had concluded to release him, principally in order that I might attach him to me and, if possible, send him with messages to his people in the enemy's camp. He was now trusted with a communication to Camp Harney. He gave strong promises but proved false, going straight to the hostiles.

With all these considerations in view, all the forces were now directed to make Steen's Mountains the objective point.

The field orders of June 16 sent toward the enemy what we called the right column under Maj. Joseph Stewart,[30] with two companies of the 4th Artillery and five of the 21st Infantry, changing his march from the Baker road southward; they sent Captain Bernard with his four troops of the 1st Cavalry, constituting a left column, straight from Sheep Ranch to the same point; while Colonel Grover's detachment of three troops of cavalry and one company of the 2nd Infantry was turned back from its eastward march toward Fort Hall and made a center column, to go directly from Boise City to Steen's Mountains. These little columns, moving rapidly toward the expected battlefield, were to be speedily followed by a reserve of five companies of the 12th Infantry under Major Egbert,[31] who had just come from the Department of California to join our force.

These columns were to move with the usual military precautions. They must carefully scout the country, pick up Indian men, women, and children, and avoid all ambuscades. None were to attack the enemy separately, except when there was a reasonable prospect of success, but if an attack was made, it must be delivered at once and be a quick, vigorous one. They were instructed to keep up constant intercommunication by scouts and couriers, so as to give one another the readiest information and the promptest support at whatever moment need might arise.

One paragraph of this field order indicates that several Indian tribes who were in Wheaton's district, then called the District of the Clearwater, were represented by warriors or sympathizers in the hostile camp. Colonel Wheaton was urged to watch with great care these tribes and guard against the return of the renegades, whether they were in small or in large parties.

Just as soon as these instructions were issued, my staff officers and I, taking with us Sarah Winnemucca and her sister Mattie as interpreters and guides, drove as rapidly as possible past Fort Lyons, where a short halt was made, back to the Baker road, and there joined the right column under Major Stewart, and pressed it as fast as men could march toward the position in which it now seemed probable the enemy would be found.

We began to realize something of the fear and demoralization of the citizens when we reached what was called Rhinehart's Corner. Here we found a large, brick house and outhouses filled to repletion with families that had come from the thinly settled valleys and cattle ranches more remote still from the hamlets. Lt. C. E. S. Wood, who had in charge the scouting parties, soon hired all the men from these crowded tenements and added them to his lists. They were sent out to ride with all their might upon their indefatigable half-breed cayuses till they should obtain sight of the hostiles or gather important news of camp, movements, or the present whereabouts of our changeable and rapid enemy.

The poor white women cried out, "What, send away our husbands! Who will care for us? Who will protect us?"

Lieutenant Wood replied, "There is your protection."

"Oh," they said in tears, "let the soldiers do that; let the soldiers do the fighting—it is their business!"

"Why yes," the humorous lieutenant remarked, "the soldiers will do the fighting—your friends only have to help them to find something to fight."

The new scouts accordingly soon sped off to comb down the woods and ravines, and trail up the canyons and mountains, to catch and bring back any lurking foes for the soldiers to fight.

<hr />

"Battle of Old Camp Curry," *The Overland Monthly* 10 (August 1887): 120–23

While the three columns were marching as fast as they could from different sides towards Steen's Mountains, which, at last accounts, had all told some two thousand Indians filling various camps, returning scouts and messengers met me every few hours. At last, on June 19, word came that the hostiles were no longer in those mountains, nor in that neighborhood; that they had on the approach of Bernard's troop lost courage and so made forced marches—or better, perhaps, a wild run—more than a hundred miles westward into a barren country, very hilly and heavily wooded, southwest of Camp Harney. In the evening of the same day, I heard from Captain Bernard that he had reached our point of concentration and, finding the Indians gone, had pressed on after them, following their plain trails and putting his troops to their utmost speed.

It is well now to pay a brief visit to the enemy's encampment, to inquire in the light of subsequent events what produced this sudden change of plan on his part and the strange abandonment of so strong a position as that in the Steen's Mountains.

No masses of men have ever accomplished much without organization and leadership. When the Indians set out from Fort Hall, the redoubtable Buffalo Horn, young brave, skillful, and energetic, was the Bannocks' chosen leader. When he was killed, there was no other Bannock chief whom the people would follow. Winnemucca, as before remarked, had no sympathy with the war and deserted the hostiles, coming to us. Egan, the next chief, the leader of all Paiutes at the Malheur agency, was at first very reluctant to fight. He, it was said, had even refused and had been made a prisoner by the others. An old tooat, or dreamer, Oytez by name, was for a time the actual chief. He was full of superstition, believing, or pretending to believe, that the time had come when the Indians were to rise in their might and regain all their old camping grounds and cherished haunts. While the Indians listened to his wizard performances and raving revelations, they looked upon him as civilized men do upon ministers—they wanted a regular military chief.

At last, after much pressure of threats and persuasion, Chief Egan, taking Oytez as counselor, resumed the chieftainship and became for the war the military head of all the Indians gathered. He had fought General Crook and other officers in former years. He had quite a reputation among both white men and Indians. His method was never to risk everything in a pitched battle. He heard that I was coming with three distinct bodies of fighting men, with plenty of guns and ammunition. He had no cannon and but a limited amount of cartridges and provisions. So he advised them to move rapidly westward to his old camping grounds, where the Indians would have the protection of extensive forests, where they could scatter and deceive, by numerous trails, the pursuing foe. He hoped, further, that some Klamaths and many Umatillas were watching to join him as soon as he got far enough west of Camp Harney. These allies would bring supplies.

Again, the hearts of the brave talkers, even the heart of old Oytez himself, began to weaken as their scouts rushed up the mountain crying that more than a thousand horsemen were moving to attack them. Then almost a panic ensued. Away they went, marching more than forty miles in a day, though they were encumbered with women, children, and baggage. No white community could stand such strain and fatigue.

As Major Stewart's command was threading its way toward Steen's Mountains by the route of Willow Creek and the Malheur agency, I left him for a while and passed on with my staff to a little mountain town called by the suggestive name of Malheur City. During Stewart's march, alarming reports and rumors of fresh Indian trails came from nearly every direction. One example will suffice to indicate their nature. A party of Indians—so said an excited citizen by the name of Harlan—had passed straight through the Burnt River country going northward, at least thirty miles off the main road. Lieutenant Shofner,[32] with a detachment using wagons so to make the quickest time, was sent by a night march to test the report. He found no Indians, and really no valid signs of them. The lieutenant returned to his command without delaying the column.

Such lateral marches, like reconnaissances, were frequently made. These, with the aid of our numerous citizen scouts, who had become spirited in their enterprising rides, soon put a stop to the small raiding parties of the hostiles and deceived them as to what we were really doing.

Meanwhile, I had sent Lieutenant Wilkinson, with two soldiers and the two Indian women, Sarah and Mattie, for guides, to take his way by the stars across the country to Camp Harney. I sent the party on this perilous journey, not only because of the rumored flight of the Indians and the vigorous pursuit by Bernard, but because of a report, which had a semblance of truth, that Captain McGregor's troop of cavalry had met Egan and had had a disastrous fight, ending in defeat and the loss of his horses. Could Wilkinson get through sixty or seventy miles to Camp Harney, he could quickly verify the report of Egan's presence in Harney Valley and satisfy me with regard to Bernard and McGregor's condition. For I firmly believed that by this time, McGregor's troop, which went from Camp Harney, must have joined Bernard, so that if McGregor had been badly handled, so had Bernard, and Camp Harney was in danger. In fact, the Indians' flight had changed the whole field of operations and necessitated new planning and new instructions.

Whilst everybody else was in motion, I held my staff at Malheur City for two days. All the workingmen who were employed on the immense mining ditch in that neighborhood were organized for scouting under a most enterprising citizen by the name of Packwood, a foreman on the work. They scouted and watched country, rough and wooded as it was, for the breadth of a hundred miles. From Mr. Packwood I obtained prompt and accurate information, and secured a few Indian prisoners who had strayed from Egan's flying column.

Major Stewart's command, never halting save for the necessary night camping, entered the famous Malheur agency grounds the morning of the twenty-third. Here the same morning, by a rapid crosscut with my staff and scouts, I overtook him.

The Indian agent, Rhinehart, who had fled from the agency at the first outbreak, now came back and joined us here. There was not at that time an Indian on any of the lands of the reservation. The buildings were standing but were in a deplorable condition. They appeared to have been robbed of every valuable. In the storehouses there was considerable flour and a little salt. Fortunately for our hungry soldiers, there was still unharvested a crop of potatoes and other vegetables in the garden. These they were not slow to find, harvest, and issue. Judging from Agent Rhinehart's account, a set of robbers, either white men or Indians, had, since he left seventeen days before made to the place a predatory excursion.

Making this a turning point in our ever-changing Indian campaign, I detached Major Stewart and Captain Cochran's[33] company of the 2nd Infantry to remain temporarily on the reservation. There were three objects in view: to take care of the property, what little there was left; to gather supplies and establish a sub-depot for the operating troops—one which would be temporarily much needed; and—a thing I had much at heart—to search out all the surrounding woods and ravines and bring in Indians who were reported as hiding in that neighborhood.

The moving column was placed under the command of Captain Rodney,[34] an active young officer of the 4th Artillery. All being assured that the Indians were already in Harney Valley, Rodney was allowed but the briefest halt. Turning westward, he pushed on with so much rapidity that he marched thirteen miles toward Camp Harney the very day of his arrival at the Malheur reservation, June 23.

I was with him at the head of the column. We had gone late into camp, but as we were unusually weary, an extraordinary silence reigned; when suddenly, at about 11:00 P.M., Lieutenant Wilkinson, with his Indian guides, startled the outposts by his sudden appearance, and then rode rapidly into camp. He and his attendants had come as fast as horses could bring them, forty-five miles from Camp Harney.

They brought good tidings. McGregor was united with Bernard. The day before, a battle had occurred, and instead of a defeat it was a complete victory. It was near Camp Curry on Curry Creek, forty-five miles beyond Camp Harney. The Indians had fled from the field but had rallied not far off. Bernard had managed to get four troops of cavalry into the engagement; but owing to their forced marches over rough ground and immense distances, his men were very weary, and he called strenuously for reinforcements.

The battle was not decisive enough to end the campaign. The rapid movements of the Indians had had the effect of stretching out my command: Bernard was at Camp Curry; Captain Miles with two companies at Camp Harney; Rodney's battalion with me; while Grover and Egbert, coming on, were still beyond Malheur agency, toward Boise. Sometimes a commander wishes that his men had wings and could fly together to a junction. To reinforce as speedily as possible, orders were sent at once to Miles to make forced marches to Bernard. Major Stewart, leaving only a small guard, was to hurry on with his company to take care of Camp Harney.

Before 11:00 A.M. the next morning, our advance entered Camp Harney. Taking a couple of hours for food and rest, that night Lieutenant Wood and myself rode out thirty miles farther and encamped with Captain Miles's infantry at a place called Sage Hen Springs. Early the following morning we were on the battlefield. Here leaving Lieutenant Wood, my aide, to make a sketch of the country, I rode on ten miles beyond to join the brave Bernard and his gallant men.

The Indians, after the battle, had made a halt and seemed at first to be waiting for another trial, but Egan was not confident enough to stand the onset. On our side, as is always the case after a victory, no matter how weary the men, they were highly elated. The officers, one after another, told me incidents of their bona fide cavalry engagement, where, as formerly, our horsemen, with sabers or pistols in hand, had charged an enemy well mounted, pretty well equipped, and as they confidently alleged, at least double their numbers.

From the few prisoners taken, the story was confirmed that some Klamaths and several Columbia River Indians had already joined the Bannocks and Paiutes, and that a body of Umatillas had come southward, perhaps fifty or sixty miles from their reservation, and gone into camp. They were evidently in sympathy with the hostiles.

After examining all sources of information, I concluded that our enemies under Egan, after their fight and brief subsequent halt, had turned northward, following up Silver Creek, and were making for the south fork of John Day River. They would certainly follow this fork as far as possible, and then go up Grand or Bridge Creek to join the Umatillas, or Cayuse Indians, as we named them, who had come southward to meet them. This was a new move, and like a snowball, the rolling mass was certainly increasing in size.

The mountains in the vicinity of the John Day River are remarkable for their roughness. They do not appear very high, but in passing from Camp Curry across the intervening range to what is usually called the John Day Valley, one finds every variety of country—jagged rocks, precipitous slopes, knife-edged divides, deep canyons with sides steep and difficult, sometimes four or five miles from the crest to the mountain stream that tumbles over the rocks in the hollow below. It is often the case that travelers crossing this well-known divide find hot weather on either side and severe cold—often hail, snow, and ice—at the summit. Even between old Camp Harney and Canyon City, the highest ground is always cold, suffering from frost every month of the year. It was on the north side of the John Day Divide that the Umatillas were waiting for the approach of Chief Egan.

While I determined to follow Egan's broad trail over the mountains, through extensive forests and almost impassable canyons, with my main force, the threatened outbreaks farther north, and particularly the dangers of the hostiles getting far enough to cross the Columbia River, now gave me unusual concern.

As we were just entering one of the trails of woodland, following up several different paths made by the Indians—for now they took no pains to conceal their northward push—through the firs and pines, many of which were completely peeled from the ground to the lower branches, we came suddenly upon a large log lying diagonally across our way. This log, like so many in veteran forests, was at one end simply a shell. Crowded close into the very center of the old log was found an old Indian woman. At first she was almost speechless; she was very decrepit and clad in tatters. She was hiding away without food and, as she afterwards declared, expecting to stay where she was till she died. We had her brought to our night encampment. She was fed and reclothed, being treated, of course, with great kindness by all. As soon as she came to herself, she cried bitterly and said her nephew Buffalo Horn was dead. She believed old Oytez was the chief in his place. Sarah and Mattie took charge of her, showed her much attention, and were rewarded by a very full and clear statement of all that had been done by the hostile Indians and of their plans and purposes in the future.

In Indian war, as in any other, the best possible policy is always to avoid harshness and unkindness toward prisoners—and of course, it is right and proper in any event so to do.

⊷⊶ ⊨✦⊨ ⊷⊶

"Birch Creek," *The Overland Monthly* 10 (October 1887): 347–52

We read of the wild tribes of Siberia, who, mounted on swift horses, were more terrible in their retreats from steppe to steppe than the cavalry of a Stuart in the advance; also of Arabs, Bedouins, of the desert, who could hide horses and luggage in some deep cut of the plain, spring up suddenly, fight furiously, and then disappear with the rapid motion of a wind cloud. Our Paiutes and their allies had some of these characteristics. Thus, some years before, by quick ambush and swift retreat, they set a high officer and all the cavalry with him afoot. Crestfallen, defeated, and half starved, he and his [men] found their way to a distant frontier post and were forced to begin their campaign over again. Some gray heads around me, recalling this incident, when it was known that Chief Egan was leading the hostiles and that some smart Umatillas had joined him, predicted similar results. "Ah, General, Indian Egan is great on hiding and running. He always takes to the wooded mountains. He is wary and swift!"

We had noticed Pilot Rock, a little hamlet north of the famous Blue Mountains—not far from the present charming town of Heppner—as the place where my pursuing column formed junction with Colonel Wheaton's men. Our scouts told me that I had passed the Indians; that is, all except those before named, who were farther north and trying to cross the Columbia.

There were two streams of water that had their rise in the Blue Mountains a few miles southeast of Pilot Rock and ran northeasterly, emptied into the Umatilla, and swelling that bigger stream, passed on into the grand Columbia near Umatilla Town. The mouths of these two streams or creeks (called Butter and Birch) are miles apart, but their headwaters are near together; so near, in fact, that the numerous little rivulets coursing around among the abrupt hills and tumbling down the mountain canyons hardly can determine which creek bed to take, till some chance knoll or rock has checked and turned their course to its proper destination. Oh, how rough that foothill country! High knolls round off between the creeks; deep ravines and high bluffs to the right and left; and behind all these, higher and higher steeps, with an open grazing space, the open ever diminishing in the distance till you attain the mountain crowned with its dense forest. It was delightful, then, to behold this lovely country, with its hundreds of hills rising rank above rank to the kingly crested summit. Chief

Egan, where two of my diligent scouts in the night had found and "placed" him, had chosen a broad and rugged height. It was favored with many large and dark-colored rocks. The Indians in motion on the top were multiplied in appearance by these natural shields. The slopes in front, after the large, detached hill was reached, were steep, stony, deceptive, and difficult. The chief had woods on his right a few hundred yards away, and hills as good as his and other woods behind him.

On paper and according to the maps, I had the hostiles pretty well hemmed in, for Bernard and Throckmorton's battalions were with me in front, Captain Miles's 21st Infantry battalion not far to his left and behind him, and Sanford with his column [were] coming up from Grande Ronde towards his right. Strategically, as a soldier would say, the sunrise of July 8 found everything most favorable for ending the campaign. True, Sarah Winnemucca said, "No, they will not stop long. The timber is near and the Paiutes will get away." I believed not; for when an enemy has chosen a good defensive position and put everything in order to deliver battle, he hopes to conquer and must stay and carry out his plan. I really thought that I had cut off Egan's retreat and that he had determined to make the most of his mountain fastness and give us a heavy blow.

On that beautiful morning, as the sun was coming up bright and clear, my columns were already in motion. Throckmorton, with a well-reputed guide, took the Butter Creek route. He had some artillery, infantry, and volunteers. Bernard, with seven troops of his cavalry, and Robbins, with civilian scouts and a Gatling gun, accompanied me. We went on up the foothills between the two creeks before named, passing rapidly from knoll to knoll, striking as directly as possible for the rocky height, which the scouts again said was held by the Indians.

There is always a feeling of dread in view of an approaching field of blood. It takes but a bullet to kill you. The thought of the fall of a comrade is not a happy one. Even the flowing blood of your country's foe has no attraction. The distinction, the glory, the reward—they are no compensation. What spirit, then, animates an officer in such a contest? Well, however men may cavil, it mainly is a sense of duty. It is the feeling of the policeman on his beat; the sentinel at the prison door; the juryman before his final verdict; the judge in delivering his charge; the father at a night robbery, guarding wife and child; or the executive pondering a long petition, whose last word sends a mortal man beyond the gates. The call of duty is imperative, unrelenting. The Indians, whoever is at fault at first, strike to destroy women and children and homes. We, the soldiers, at once take the field to stop the murders and cause the malcontents to submit to the authority which we represent.

Behold us, then, that lovely morning, under some exhilaration and excitement, which such action produces, pushing rapidly forward. After three miles of march, and seemingly about three miles still from the objective hill, as we rose upon a high crest, we could plainly see the Indians and discern their ponies among the rocks, with the mountain forest for their background. They

A cavalry charge. CENTURY MAGAZINE, 1889.

did not act as usual; they kept moving about; some jumped up and down as if in defiance. True, this was not like Apaches, hidden so that you do not catch the sight of a head or a hand till they have had the first fire. It was, however, like Joseph's Nez Perces at the Clearwater the year before, when, with blankets tossed high over their heads, they danced around far to our left, looking and acting like dervishes in their fetes and doubtless hoping to inspire terror in the breasts of their foes.

Just at this point of the picture, my own official report, taken straight from a war paper, has in it some vividness. "Bernard, taking the trot, moved quickly into position over these troublesome foothills, the last of which is fenced by a canyon, and over a mile in ascent. The cavalry sped from hill to hill, till it came into the vicinity of the enemy, strongly posted on a rocky crest."

On our advance men reaching the base of this occupied foothill, the Indians, with their sure rifles from between the rocks there high up, began to fire at Bernard's soldiers as well as men could down such a unpropitious grade. All the companies, six of them in number,[35] were deployed and used during the engagement. See the long, irregular, broken line of horsemen ascending the hill, with every man in place! They veer to the right and left, and they go up from different sides. It is a fine display—it would be formidable to any adversary. The fire of the Indians continues with briskness. Several men are hit, and several horses fall under the men, who, with difficulty, extricate themselves from their stirrups and save themselves from being crushed. Still the troops did not waver, but worked their way to the very summit. It was speedily done, wave after wave striking the Indians' position front and flank in quick succession.

But Egan and his warriors understood well their part. They were too quick for our breathless horses. They had already abandoned their stone-crowned hill, leaving here only a few old horses and played-out mules to fill the gaps between the dark rocks, while they appeared triumphant on the next height in the rear, and one as good as they could desire, prepared for them by a natural distribution of lava beds. Bernard was disappointed, for he had frayed away his game. Like a flock of birds, they had gathered on this pinnacle, and like a flock of birds, they had flown to the next. Sarah kindly says, "Dear reader, if you could only know the difficulties of this wilderness, you could then appreciate their [the soldiers'] loyal service. The fight commenced at 8:00 A.M. under a hot sun and with no water. The whole of it was watched by the general commanding. The bullets were whistling all around us, and the general said to me and Mattie, 'Get behind the rocks; you will be hit.'"

We heard the old Indian dreamer, Oytez, calling loudly. Sarah said, "Oytez says, 'Come on, you white dogs—what are you waiting for?'" She then begged to be allowed to get nearer so as to be sure of what he cried out. I let her go on, and she galloped to the place where our Gatling gun was in vain trying to throw its shower of bullets upon the lofty crest. Though the distance was favorable enough, the elevation was too great for effective firing. I joined the party at the Gatling, observed and listened, but the Indian dreamer did not call again; probably he was badly wounded at the time, for his arm was after this a long while in a sling.

As soon as our horses had rested and gathered a little strength, we struck for the next height in the same order as before, only endeavoring to fetch a compass and cut off their retreat, should the Indians fly again. But they were too wary. They would not hold the lava beds, but rushed for the thick pines farther eastward, where they now made a brief stand and fired weakly upon our men.

Again the cavalry came on, plunging their spurs into the sides of their tired horses, but again the Indians eluded the charge, and this time soon disappeared all together. My record says, "The rough country and the great exhaustion of the horses and men caused a cessation of the pursuit for today." On our side, wonderful to tell, we had not one man slain, because the Indians fired at us very far off. They killed for us, however, upwards of twenty horses and wounded five enlisted men. We captured from them at the first charge two hundred Indian ponies, mostly lame and worn, and considerable ammunition, food, and camp material. Their women, children, and best horses, in droves, were placed beyond danger before the battle began, and they left on the field and in the woods no dead or wounded men.

The Indians now ran through the thick pines toward the southeast and were reported to be aiming for Joseph's old haunts in the Wallowa country. Throckmorton's guide, a volunteer from Heppner, for some reason led his column farther and farther from us. I could not reach him with a dispatch. This disappointed me, but it served to keep Chief Egan from taking a turn in that direction and probably helped on the final consummation.

I felt, that night, tired and chagrined. To compare a great with a less, it was like a huntsman chasing antelope all the day, with several beautiful chances in his favor, but their quick ears and native fleetness had divined his approach and eluded his shots.

Another day dawned on my disappointment. It is said that Gen. Robert E. Lee said at Gettysburg, "We cannot always expect to win battles." In similar phrase, I said to myself, "We cannot always expect to catch Indians." But I bent myself again to the slippery task. The Paiutes, Bannocks, and a few Umatillas had divided into small parties and broken back along the headwaters of the Grande Ronde River, following its left bank, and thus keeping under cover of the forest that skirts the western slopes of the Blue Mountains, a wild, rough, dark trail, difficult to find and troublesome to follow. Should you join the points held by my nearest battalions, you would make a triangle, and the Indians were still within its sides; therefore, all hope of forcing a decisive battle had not yet been abandoned. Captain Miles must turn slightly eastward and run up the Grande Ronde, Bernard sending one troop, Bendire's, to get on the main trail, if there was one, and follow it till Miles and he came together. Sanford, coming from the opposite direction (Grande Ronde Valley east of the Blue Mountains), was to move straight on till these three forces came together; and if Chief Egan still escaped from them, Sanford, commanding the combined forces, was to push the pursuit wherever it led him. With Throckmorton's battalion and the remainder of Bernard's cavalry, I undertook to fill in the other, or northern, side of the triangle.

I hurried along the northern base of the Blue Mountains, watching against the Indians' possible turning toward the Columbia and hoping that Miles or Sanford, or both, might scare them towards me. It did seem that such a complete plan must win, but how many successes in war or peace hang more upon prompt and faithful execution than upon correct planning? Listen to the excuses: First, the couriers carrying dispatches for once failed me. They started up the old stage road toward the [A. B.] Meacham ranch. They saw some Indians, or imagined that they did, and so returned without delivering my orders. Again, some Indians whom we had deemed friendly went directly to Chief Egan and told him where I was and how to elude the nice traps that I had set for him. Next, Captain Miles's march was dreadfully delayed by a foolish guide, who led him for a long time along the wrong bank of the Grande Ronde, where a practicable route did not exist.

With Bernard, I set out to perform our part. Passing from Birch to McKay Creek, Bernard, with five companies, encamped at night and patrolled and scouted away up into the mountains, watching all tracks and trails, large and small, whence an enemy might break out of the forest. One of the troops (McGregor's) went with me still further, almost to the Umatilla Valley, to Cayuse Station, where the old stage road running eastward begins to ascend the Blue Mountains. Here I put Maj. E. C. Mason with headquarters, in my place, and set out with Lt. C. E. S. Wood, my aide, and Mr. Holland, the operator, to ascend the Umatilla some six miles farther into the mountain, to the point where the telegraph line crossed the river. Mr. Holland, a skillful man, believed he could attach his little instrument and thus communicate with the outer world. There was considerable risk in this journey, made after night, and it was not a success. We tried again and again but could get no reply. At last, in despair, I decided to gallop over to Weston.

Here again we found the wires down—but my trip was not in vain, for I was fortunate enough to meet there the two governors, [S. F.] Chadwick of Oregon and [Elisha P.] Ferry of Washington Territory. I laid before them the scheme that I have named, of clearing this part of the country of hostile Indians. One can hardly describe the feeling of the people in such small settlements as that of Weston. One can never hunt Indians or conduct battles to suit a frontier population, but I had the satisfaction of satisfying the governors and securing a cooperation with them in all matters.

It had become of the first importance for me to communicate back and forth with my headquarters at Vancouver, with General McDowell at San Francisco, and through these with Washington, so that, still trusting my admirable officer, Major Mason, to act for me in the field, I myself with my little party hurried on to Walla Walla, while all the battalions were as best they could carrying out such instructions as they had actually received. My information was so direct and so positive that the hostiles were making their way toward old Joseph's Wallowa country that I acted upon this as upon a fixed fact.

During Major Mason's stay at Cayuse Station, several Umatilla Indians professing great friendliness came into camp. They were kindly received and stayed with the soldiers overnight. They gathered much knowledge that they ought not to have had. Now, I have since learned, a few of these visitors went the next day into the mountains, found Egan, and told him the situation. These treacherous spirits were in some way connected with the Columbia bands that were fired into and stopped by the gunboats.[36] Balked in their proceedings and in their designs to help the hostiles, they determined to injure us as much as they could. Therefore, they hurried back to the Blue Mountains. Soon after, having conveyed all the information that they could gather, they hid among the trees on the side of the mountain and started out, as soon as it was safe for them, under the cover of night. They burned up the buildings and forage belonging to the Cayuse stage station; murdered a prominent citizen whom they caught driving along the road in that neighborhood; and finally, to the number of thirty-eight, united with the Paiutes and Bannocks to aid them in the next battle. All this took place between July 9–12.[37] Had I known of this treachery, or even suspected it, it would have constrained me to change my plans completely, for the hostile Indians whom we have represented as pushing on—men, women, children, and ponies—along the blind trails and through the rough forest of the north slope of the Blue Mountains, apparently making for the Wallowa country, then almost uninhabited, were suddenly arrested in their journey and turned back toward the Overland stage road. They were not far from the treacherous Columbias, whom I have just named; that is, not far from Cayuse Station the evening of July 11.

But I did not know these facts, for I was at Walla Walla that night. There Lieutenant Colonel Forsyth[38] of the 1st Cavalry, who had just come from the East, joined my command. He was at once directed to take charge of the several troops that the sturdy Bernard had been leading. To prevent the Indians from escaping through the Wallowa to the north, I organized another column, and as I was more familiar with the ground I wished it to pass through than any other officer, it was decided at this time to put Colonel Wheaton in charge of all the operations nearby in the Blue Mountains and to proceed myself as far as steamer could carry me to Lewiston. I reached Lewiston at 4:00 P.M. on the twelfth, and had not gone upon the little steamer *Northwest* many miles up the Snake River, for the current was strong, before an Indian courier riding furiously across the country overtook the steamer. His message was "Indians have turned back and have burned Cayuse Station!" The same report came from my aide-de-camp, who was with the governors, and from Colonel Wheaton, still at Walla Walla.

Wheaton had been directed to move Forsyth's cavalry toward the Wallowa very slowly, and to turn it back toward the Umatilla reservation in case the Indians changed their course and turned that way. So, regretting a personal absence but feeling sure that Wheaton had troops enough for a battle and would safely attend to everything the crisis demanded, I simply sent him words of encouragement, while I gathered two companies of the 8th Infantry under Captain Worth,[39] two of the 2nd under Captain Drum,[40] and a detachment of twenty more men to march at once westerly across the Wallowa to the Grande Ronde country. Those acquainted with the roughness, the mountains, the forests, and the extent of this region will have some idea of the energy and animation of the campaign.

These were the preliminaries to what had been called Captain Miles's engagement, a short, blind contest, but one quite effective in breaking up the unity of the Indians and bringing our trying campaign against the Paiutes and Bannocks to a speedy and decisive conclusion.

━━━ ⚔ ━━━

"Captain Miles' Engagement," *The Overland Monthly* 10 (November 1887): 533–39

In giving accounts of battles and campaigns, there is often confusion from several officers bearing the same name. During the War of the Rebellion, we had three of note by the name of Miles.

The first in order of time became famous while commanding General McDowell's reserve at Centreville during the battle of Bull Run, and then more so in his surrender of Harpers Ferry, where he lost his life. This was just before the battle of McClellan and Lee at Antietam. The second was the present

Brig. Gen. Nelson A. Miles, who rose from a lieutenant to a major general during the war, and whose name is closely identified with most of the hardest battles fought between the Armies of the Potomac and of Northern Virginia, and who has had as colonel and brigadier general in the Regular army, much prominent Indian campaigning to do since the war.

The third is Capt. Evan Miles, who became a lieutenant of the 12th Infantry in 1861 and was brevetted a captain for gallant services in Virginia, in operations near the Weldon Railroad. I found him a senior captain of the 21st Infantry. As such, he habitually commanded, as we have seen, the infantry battalion, consisting of from four to seven companies, according as the movements of troops permitted the smaller or larger number to be together. When I moved off to the extreme left to bring into the field of operations some troops via Wallowa, Captain Miles, with his infantry, was near Camas Meadows, some miles to the south of our battlefield of Birch Creek. It will be remembered that as he came forward in his northern march the second day after the battle, he was to push along the bank of the Grande Ronde, forming a junction with Captain Bendire's troop of cavalry, which I had sent from Birch Creek in the same direction. After considerable delay occasioned by the ignorance and clumsiness of his guides, he at last came upon the main trail of the fleeing Indians.

He says that he joined Bendire [on] July 10; that he also received instructions from me to push along the trail if, in his judgment, it "was sufficiently developed to warrant its continued pursuit," otherwise to go straight to Cayuse Station. So, falling upon a large and clear track, he took up pursuit as rapidly as he could. This course led him on the eleventh to McClellan's ranch on the Daley wagon road. Here Miles saw the results of fresh mischief—the premises having been rifled in Indian fashion and left in disorder. On the twelfth, wonderful to tell, most of the tracks that scattered out in the abundant timber led northward, instead of eastward, in the direction of Cayuse Station, or rather in the direction of the foothills of the Blue Mountains to the east of that little Cayuse hamlet, as if the hostiles were getting as near as they could to the Umatillas. They would naturally do this, even if they had no allies there and merely proposed to turn to the Wallowa along the north edge of the Long Mountain Range, but the signs seemed too clear and new to indicate great distance, and Miles said to himself, "They must be close at hand."

Next Captain Miles moved his troops to Weil's ranch, situated near the Pendleton stage road. He halted there a few hours for the purpose of replenishing his supplies, and then turned again eastward to get upon the Indian trails. At night he found himself upon those foothills of the Blue Mountains that overlook the Umatilla Indian Agency, having made with his infantry a remarkable march of thirty-five miles, and arriving for camp at the unseasonable hour of 2:00 A.M. on July 13.

What is more wearisome than those night marches? It is then that regular officers are apt to use the personal proverb "I have lost no Indians." It is then that soldiers get tired and cross and say things that their commanding officer ought never to hear. The morning light, after the short, refreshing sleep, puts a different aspect upon affairs.

"Here," says Captain Miles, "I was met by Mr. [N. A.] Cornoyer, the United States Indian agent for the Umatillas, who informed me of the immediate proximity of the enemy." Mr. Cornoyer was very active and helpful during this Paiute and Bannock war. He was a descendant of the voyageurs; a bright, tall, handsome man of French extraction. He wife was an Indian woman, and he had a fine family at the agency.

Of a nervous temperament and sanguine heart, it seemed at first impossible to him that any of his Indians—that is, any of those of different names congregated at the Umatilla agency—could be induced to favor the hostiles. He was up early that July morning, probably had been riding and working the whole night, and appeared at 2:00 A.M. at Miles's camp. At that time he declared with great disappointment that "the Indians of his agency had either knocked under to, or been murdered by, the Snakes." The Umatillas and Nez Perces always called the Bannocks the "Snakes."

And Mr. Cornoyer was right and was obliged to hang to the right horn of his dilemma. Only it was some, and not all, of the Indians of his agency, as we shall by and by see, who acted as spies; led the enemy to murder, arson, and depredation; next played neutrality, till it was evident that the savage Indians could not conquer; then turned squarely around and betrayed their late friends. As this miserable performance belongs to only a small minority, I love to acquit the remainder of the Umatillas proper—whether we call them Columbias, Walla Wallas, Cayuses, or only agency Indians—of having any hand in the evil work, except the fact that from sympathy with Indians, because they were Indians and not white men, they kept to themselves much knowledge of the Bannocks and their allies that they might have given Mr. Cornoyer or me.

In view of things as they appeared that morning on the round hills in sight of the agency, Captain Miles remarked that, "[Cornoyer] was unable to give the status of the Umatillas, as there had been more or less fraternization between them and the hostiles up to the time of his arrival."

Miles had, with a troop of cavalry, Bendire, who sometimes complained for, but never against, his men; who fed them so well as to produce contentment; and who marched and fought them as well as he fed them. Captain Rodney of the 4th Artillery brought up that morning two companies of his regiment.

The Umatillas who had been acting as scouts for Mr. Cornoyer and those who had joined them with arms in their hands formed a large group in plain sight of Miles and Rodney. They did not take any pains to conceal themselves, nor did they move towards our men. So Miles, as soon as it was light enough to see, caused Captain Rodney to put his two companies of the 4th Artillery into a single line, and covered their front and flanks by an open, fanlike formation of skirmishers, then set them in motion steadily toward the group of

Umatillas. As might have been expected, when the skirmishers came within rifle range, a party from the Indians bearing a white flag, the flag carried by one of the chiefs of the tribe, set out to meet them.

Some of our frontiersmen are very angry that our officers always respect a flag of truce. Indians may be treacherous. They may use the flag to decoy prominent leaders like Canby, and the others with him, to a terrible death, but we of the army never trifle with this sacred emblem of peace. Miles at once met the flag and had a parley that proved to him certainly the present friendliness on the eve of battle of that group of Umatilla Indians.

During all the trying operations of the day, these redoubtable "Indians remained neutral and passive spectators, safely sheltered by their flag of truce." The whole picture, with its varying positions, would remind one of old classic fields. For as the white men's lines were formed, and as the hostiles appeared here and there in the ravines, the Umatilla group remain like a royal arbiter, with escort and women spectators, watching the game of war. When the white men marched to the right, or left, or forward, the interested observers quickly moved to corresponding new positions, as if ready to crown the victors, whomever they might be. From one phase in Captain Miles's letter, it appears that this armed neutrality must have been a matter of prearrangement, for he says: "After this gratifying understanding with the Umatillas, I moved my command into the agency grounds for the preparation of coffee for the men, who were much worn by continued fatigue." The only wonder is that the hostiles had not divined something of this gratifying understanding, and fled and scattered after their old fashion. But fortunately it was not so.

The companies of infantry, one picket covering an overhanging ledge south and east of the agency, were a sufficiency, yes, probably a bait, that drew to them the searching eyes and cautious approach of the enemy. The fires for breakfast and coffee had hardly been lighted when the pickets descried the Paiutes and Bannocks coming toward them rapidly in considerable force. How often I have experienced just that state of things, where excitement has temporarily removed all appetite for food. Without waiting a moment, Miles deployed his forces, Rodney's companies on the left and facing southward, while six companies drew a semicircular line from Rodney's position westward. Putting Bendire's cavalry out on the extreme left, Miles held his remaining companies of the 21st Infantry in rear in reserve.

The reserve guarded the wagon train and the pack mules, which were parked and held in a ravine out of the track of immediate danger. Miles had two small howitzers which he brought into action a little to the left of his center, where two of his companies in the line could watch them and care for them in case of need. The Indians, as usual with them, stopped beyond the field of immediate danger. They ran into the crooked ravines and covered themselves as completely as they could, in fact, behaved naturally as our skirmishers are supposed to behave. The difference is that if you call out to our men, "There is the enemy," nearly every individual soldier will spring up or jump on a log, if there is one near, to see his opponent, while the Indians under like circumstances always remain motionless or hide more profoundly. From their hiding places, the Snakes fired irregularly, and though they occasionally ran to new places for better sight or range, still it was difficult for Miles's men to find anything to fire at except the occasional puffs of smoke. Still, this kind of fighting lasted a wonderfully long time, and much ammunition was expended, especially on our side, till about 2:00 P.M. Then Miles ordered Rodney to gain ground by his left to the east and, if possible, sweep out the ravine that his men were facing. At once, probably tired of bootless firing, his men sprang forward with enthusiasm and promptly set the enemy in motion, as Miles at the same time charged along his entire curvilinear front. This seems to have been unexpected by Chief Egan, for he was still commanding the Snakes in this, his last battle. So away his Indians ran, mounted on their swift ponies, over the foothills and the mountain, pursued by the excited white men, who seemed to have thought of neither breakfast nor dinner, till with the utmost rapidity, they had chased them at least three miles into the mountains.

When the exciting day began to wane, and Miles saw his men showing plain signs of exhaustion from want of rest and food, he halted and went into camp on the spot, expecting to take up the pursuit the next morning. But my friend Cornoyer, who had gone back to his home at the agency, for once was overexcited. Though the hostiles had fled and were running away into the mountains southward and eastward as fast as their hardy ponies could carry them, and had been pursued for several hours by Miles's eager men; though the troops, cavalry and infantry, were between the enemies and the peaceable Indians, and there was no likelihood of their return that night, particularly after their long and exhausting battle; still, Cornoyer sent a hurried dispatch to Miles, which he received about 8:00 P.M., just after the weary men had begun their much-needed sleep.

It was to the effect that he, Cornoyer, had received information, to which he gave credit, that the hostile Indians would return that very night and burn down all the buildings of the agency, and that they proposed to drive off the large herd of Indian horses or other stock which was pastured on the Umatilla reservation. Cornoyer begged for the immediate return of the troops. These astonishing reports, with the urgent request, were doubtless manufactured by the same cunning people who knew when to betray, when to be neutral, and when, in the interest of their beaten friends, according to their Indian notions, to lie. Someone asked me only yesterday if Indians were not habitually treacherous. I answered, "No, not generally."

After a long experience with them, and intercourse with perhaps a hundred tribes, I have found, on trial, that Indians have habitually kept their word with me. There have been, during war, a few notable exceptions to this rule. Still, as in war, every leader of an independent force, and everyone loyal to that leader's movements, undertakes to deceive and mislead an enemy in arms, so do the Indians. The Indians, all Indians in fact, own that when Indians are "mad," they go to war. When they go to war, they deceive, kill, scalp, rob, burn, destroy, and appropriate, beating all white men in atrocities and horrors.

Captain Miles exercised command *sans pitie*—either the long roll sounded or, more likely, captains, lieutenants, and noncommissioned officers crept quietly around and wakened every man. Silently but hurriedly, they marched back over their battlefield and were soon at the agency. The commander here put everything in the posture of defense. But there was no need; for as he with dignified simplicity remarks, "No attempt was made by the enemy in this direction, they being too demoralized by the result of the day to make any demonstration but the continuation of their precipitous retreat."

"But," says some military man—we know that many such are wise after the battle—"how came it that Captain Miles did not also have somebody follow up that demoralized foe?" Well, he did so. Some of those neutral Indians began to think of their future, and some others doubtless hated to be suspected of double-dealing. These came that night, through their headmen, in the language of Miles, "with offers to confirm their protestations of friendship by sending a number of warriors to cooperate with my command." This was fine; it was well timed. Miles at once closed in with the overtures—and Indian-like, without waiting for any positive directions, the savage allies set out on fresh horses to take up the pursuit. The reader will pardon me for giving the results of this pursuit and of the blind contest which took place somewhere in the dense forest of the Blue Mountains in the very words of Captain Miles himself: "The prompt and energetic action of this small band of allies was not, however, barren of good results, as on the fifteenth they returned to my camp, having attacked the fleeing hostiles successfully, as evidenced by their captured trophies, which consisted, among others, of seven warriors' scalps, one of which was subsequently proven to be that of the Paiute chief Egan."

The real leader of the allies had hitherto passed among the Paiutes as their special friend. The Indians called him "Umapine." He was about six feet in height, of large, closely knit frame, broad shouldered and thick chested, and when not on the warpath, he had a friendly eye of good size and a not unpleasant smile, yet the impression he gave you was of a predominant animal nature. When he ate, he consumed twice as much as the other strong men; yet doubtless when he fasted, he could go long without eating. When he undertook war, he displayed a profound treachery, and when he killed, he made it murder. Even his mates shuddered at his brutality, and his enemies hated him relentlessly. Yet after the wicked act, he strutted in pride and fine feather and boasted of his prowess.

It was this leader, Umapine, whom the Paiutes and Bannocks had leaned upon as a friend, who, now a secret foe, with his swiftest followers, overtook Egan and his beaten host. He brought back in the morning to Captain Miles and to Colonel Wheaton, who had just reached the agency, the signs of his terrible work. Truly such allies make one shudder anew at the horrors of Indian warfare. The old chief Winnemucca, Natchez, and Sarah were affected to tears by the loss of their old friends. They never could get over the shock that the stories of the murder of Egan and his companions produced upon them.

Many women prisoners, some of them young girls, were taken from the Paiutes at the time and kept in Indian fashion by Umapine and his Indians. Natchez's talk to the Umatillas in subsequent council is significant:

> If we had made war with you and you had taken us in battle, we would not say anything; but you helped the thing along, and for four years you have come on the Malheur reservation (Egan's place) and told Egan and Oytez to make war against the whites. You called them fools to stay on the reservation and starve; and another thing, you have helped the Bannocks to fight the soldiers. My friends, it must be a beautiful sensation to cut a man or woman to pieces and then skin their heads and fasten them on a pole, and dance around them as if you were indeed very happy.

It was believed by our officers that all the wounded and many of the dead were carried off the field by the Bannocks during the day's battle. Five bodies of the warriors, however, but no wounded, were found there after the conflict. Miles, strange to say, for the Indians are usually good marksmen, had none killed on his side and but few wounded.[41] At this time, the Indians attempted to shoot at too great a distance. He gives special credit to a small company of citizen volunteers who came out from the pretty village of Pendleton to help him in his assaults. He commended them particularly for their diligent conduct as skirmishers and flankers.

So much for what we have named "Miles's Engagement." It was, bating the position, much like Birch Creek—a brisk, animated combat, and then a chase. The Bannocks and Paiutes, by running, scattering, hiding, and then continuing their retreat in small, separate companies, succeeded in prolonging the tedious campaign and in spreading terror anew among the small villages and hamlets threatened with a wild visitation by the new routes which they chose.

Now we are prepared for the final work of this campaign. More than before I followed the example of my wily foe; that is, I divided my command and subdivided it, in order to visit every nook and hiding place and, like cranberry harvesters, "comb down" the entire field. This fatiguing work had two objects—first, to defeat or bring in the Indians as prisoners, and second, to allay if possible the wild fears of ranch people and inhabitants of small hamlets, who could never feel sure of protection till they saw the troops.

"The Back Tracks," *The Overland Monthly* 10 (December 1887): 653–59

It will be observed that the Paiutes and Bannocks had been arrested by the battle of Birch Creek on July 8, 1878, and by the work of the [three] steamers

The ride through the rain. RUFUS F. ZOGBAUM. *HORSE, FOOT, AND DRAGOON.*

converted into gunboats, which were running up and down the Columbia between Celilo and Wallula. The gunboats had hurled their shells into the camps of hostile allies and so terrified all Indians within hearing of the cannonade that the majority fled back from the Columbia toward the summit of the Blue Ridge and other mountain fastnesses.

Conceive now a new order of things existing after the second battle—namely, that of July 13 near the Umatilla agency, which I have just described and called Captain Miles's Engagement. Forsyth and Wheaton had hastened on, hearing the sound of battle, westward to the Umatilla agency or its vicinity. Throckmorton, with his companies, had come thither from the opposite direction. Sanford with his cavalry, moving north, had stopped and hurried back eastward to the Grande Ronde Valley, and I myself was coming with infantry and cavalry towards the same valley from the neighborhood of Lewiston, Idaho, and the Indians, broken into fragments, were following different paths, eastward and southward.

Captain Miles had sent the main body flying to Sanford's front. They were split by his column, part going almost south towards the rough mining regions west of Malheur City and Bakersfield, while a part escaped to the neighborhood of Joseph's old haunts in that immense Wallowa Valley.

The infantry and cavalry at first, under Miles and Throckmorton, were permitted to rest for a short time at the Umatilla agency, while Forsyth gathered together the troops of cavalry near at hand and proceeded at once to cross over the Blue Ridge Mountains and follow the main southward trail, hoping so to push his pursuit as to bring the band of Indians that ran in that direction to battle or, better, to a speedy surrender. He kept a scouting party consisting of a mixed body of white men and Umatilla Indians in his advance.

The whole command marched through the forests, the rocky ravines, over high mountains and across deep valleys, and broke through groves of small trees so straight, so thick and dry that they had impeded the progress of the Indians, left horses and mules broken and disabled, and were still a sufficient obstacle to render his own march one of extreme difficulty and danger.

A little farther to the left, setting out from La Grande in Grande Ronde Valley as a center, Sanford, with his cavalry, scouted the different approaches to that valley to the east and to the southeast, following up every road, trail, and footpath where there was the least recent sign of the presence of Indians. He had with him a small detachment of Nez Perce Indians, all of whom had been loyal to our people the year before and were now working hard under the command of Lieutenant Williams[42] of the 21st Infantry to clear the country of these parties of hostile Snakes, who, though flying in terror, were still slaying the stock of the settlers and terrifying anew men, women, and children, who could not help believing after nightfall that every stump and bush concealed a savage warrior.

Behold, then, the three columns in motion, substantially southward, directing their course, Forsyth on the right, Sanford in the center, and my own on the left. These officers were many miles apart, but every hour brought them nearer together. As soon as he could, Colonel Wheaton himself moved his headquarters, following up the movement of Forsyth over the Blue Mountains into the Grande Ronde, to the beautiful little town of La Grande.

I reached Colonel Wheaton here at La Grande July 19 in the night. All Indians running toward the Wallowa had been headed off. The old Lewiston and Wallowa Trail, which crossed the Grande Ronde about twelve miles above its confluence with the Snake River, was reached by my column so soon that the Indians could not have crossed in that direction without encountering immediate opposition sufficient to have defeated them and thrown them back upon the other troops. I had left the accompanying troop fifteen or sixteen miles to the east of La Grande, with a view of turning them southward, through Union, and facing toward Bakersfield. The visit to Wheaton was to ascertain just what had been done in the way of pursuit and to make plans at once for the following up of every trail until that whole vast region had been swept over and our troublesome enemy, now appearing and now disappearing, completely conquered and brought to bay.

I had consulted with Colonel Wheaton but a few minutes, when we saw plainly that either Wheaton or myself must at once take the field to keep the columns in rapid motion, to keep up a concert of action, to render sudden concentration of men practicable; in brief, to make our pursuit vigorous and effective. I determined again to take the laboring oar, and so, with a view to sending Wheaton further to the left and front, the following orders were at once issued: "Col. Frank Wheaton, 2nd Infantry, commanding the District of the Clearwater, will establish a headquarters temporarily at Baker City, organize a column (from all troops which I did not myself take to the front), and prepare it to take the field as soon as possible."

Captain Miles was to mount his infantry on Indian ponies and report to Wheaton. Drum, who had come with me across the Wallowa, commanding the infantry, and Egbert, who was marching towards us from the neighborhood of Boise City, Idaho, in command of a battalion of the 12th Infantry, were to do the same. Meanwhile, Major Mizner,[43] with his battalion, was to watch everything to the rear of us as far back as the Columbia River, to take care of the prisoners already in our hands, and give to Throckmorton the guardianship of the uneasy Umatilla agency.

Such was the new order of arrangement, and immediately upon the morning of July 20, it was rapidly and completely carried out from La Grande.

It was hardly dawn when I started out with a little company along the southeastern border of that magnificent Grande Ronde Valley. The eye from my pathway could encompass the entire prairie region, surrounded by superb mountains; covered with extensive farms filled with grain fields and half-grown orchards; and with the towns of Orodelle, La Grande, Union, and Summerville, with the spires of their churches and the towers of their new school buildings in plain sight.

The whole scene seemed then doubly beautiful and in wonderful contrast with the wilderness behind us and the sagebrush country in front, of which we caught glimpses as we neared the crest of the ridge over which we passed toward Sanford's command. I reached Major Sanford early in the day, in Ladd's Canyon, and then with him hastened on as rapidly as men could march, turning rightward and southward with the hope of forming a speedy junction with Forsyth, then reported to be at what was called Burnt River Meadows. To do this, it was necessary either to go around the eastern end of a short range called Burnt River Mountains, or to cross straight over it through a slight depression which exists between two of the central crags, or peaks. The distance around was thirty or forty miles or more, while if there were only a pathway, we ought to get to Forsyth in ten or twelve miles by crossing the divide. I sent for some frontier settlers who had a considerable interest in some country stores and hay ranches lying along the lengthy route. They declared with one voice that there was no trail, that there never had been even an Indian pathway across those rugged slopes.

Two feelings possessed me. One was a suspicion from the appearance of these men that they were not telling the truth, and the other a most earnest desire to go by the shortest route. I finally turned to the men and said, "If there is not a trail there, there ought to be one, and I am going to see for myself." I invited the sturdy pioneers to accompany me, which they did for a short distance, set my troops in motion, and putting myself at their head as a guide, went along to undertake what several of my officers felt to be simple foolhardiness. But fortunately, we soon found a house near the foot of the mountain where there lived a good guide, who took us over a fair, well-traveled Indian horse trail—steep, it is true, and wearisome to horses and men, but one which led, like the Pilgrim's straight road, to the desired haven. So without difficulty, July 22 found the troops of Forsyth and Sanford united under my command. The former (by some misapprehension or miscarriage of orders) had run short of rations and was glad enough to see us, for Sanford at once generously divided his supplies with him, running some risk of having his own command go hungry.

Next day, the twenty-third, we all took the Indian trails with renewed vigor, moved on rapidly for three days to the neighborhood of Ironsides Mountain. Here we were obliged to halt and bivouac at the crossing of Canyon City and Malheur City wagon roads, and wait a part of a day for the rations to come up. While here I sent out a scouting party to hunt through all the trails and hiding places, and go as far as the Malheur agency, to ascertain, if possible, if some of the escaping hostiles had not put in an appearance there. Furthermore, Colonel Forsyth now had time to give me a detailed account of his own eventful march which had been made since July 18. As his account is of intrinsic value and much condensed, I will insert a part of it in his own words:

> Our march was over the mountains and broken country bordering and bounding the headwaters of the Grande Ronde and John Day Rivers. The distance traveled in this interval of time from Meacham's to our camp, July 23, on the Burnt Meadows on Burnt River, was one hundred and twenty miles.
>
> The trail left by the retreating hostiles, over which we had to travel, was up and down steep canyons, over the highest ridges of the mountains, and through a perfect network of fallen timber. It was with great difficulty that the command labored through this jungle, till then unknown to the white man, encompassed as they were on either hand by rugged mountain peaks and deep canyons. The hostile Indians had, beyond a doubt, selected this route to move out of the country and back toward their agencies, so as to detain us as much as possible, and thereby gain time to push in advance of the troops their wounded and women and children.
>
> On the morning of July 20, I struck their rear guard in the canyon of the North Fork of the John Day River. This canyon is about twelve hundred feet deep, and as the walls are nearly perpendicular, my command literally slid down the trail that we were following into the stream which rushed down the bed of the canyon, and had to climb up the opposite side, leading our horses, the ascent being so steep that several of our pack animals fell over backward into the stream and were lost while trying to follow the puzzling zigzags of the trail. The Indians that constituted this rear guard numbered about forty. They had fortified themselves near the brow of the hill, on the trail, so as to command it for several hundred feet below their line of works. My scouts, numbering about eight, were a short distance ahead of my advance guard. The Indians who were in ambush permitted them to get almost up to their line of works, when the accidental discharge of a carbine of a man with the advance guard caused them to believe

they were discovered, and they at once opened fire upon the scouts, killing H. H. Froman, a courier, who was with the advance, and severely wounding a scout, John Campbell.

My advance guard was Company E, 1st Cavalry, under Capt. W. H. Winters.[44] At the sound of the firing, he deployed his company, dismounted, and took a strong position, which I reinforced by sending forward H Company, under Lieutenant Parnell, and I Company, under Lieutenant Shelton, and extended the line to the right by pushing G Company, under Captain Bernard and Lieutenant Pitcher,[45] up the side of the canyon to a projecting point which commanded and protected the trail and bench of land upon which we had corralled our stock. As soon as this formation was completed, which occupied us about an hour and a half and was made under the fire of the enemy, the line moved forward and the crest of the precipitous hill, or more properly speaking, bluff, was reached—not soon enough, however, to give us a chance at the foe, who had mounted and fled.

Major Sanford also had a story to tell, an interesting reference to which is recorded in his report. He says: "July 18 I received information from Lieutenant Williams, in command of Nez Perce scouts, that while in camp on the Daley road (a place not far from Ladd's Canyon), he had been fired into by a party of white men, and one of his Indians mortally wounded. The other Indians were very incensed at what they considered a wanton outrage and determined to return home." The parties who did this foul deed asserted that they saw these friendly Indians, and noticing their dress, their manner of going from place to place, and the subtleness of their motions, they came to the conclusion that they were Indians and belonged to the Snakes.

The Nez Perce scouts, however, declared that they moved as all Indians do when they are friendly, along the roads and the trail; that they were dressed in their scout's uniform; and that the least observation would have shown them to be friends and not enemies.

The scouts could never be made to believe but that these rough white men had intended to murder their companion, who lived but a short time after he was wounded. They at first insisted on returning to their agency but remained a while longer from a singular circumstance. These Nez Perce scouts were Christians; the wounded Indian sent for his enemy, that is, the man who shot him, and talked with him, took him by the hand, looked him in the face, and told him that he forgave him, and he besought the other scouts to forgive him also. After he was dead, the scouts themselves gave the deceased a marked but simple Christian burial. They had prayer, repeating of scripture, and solemn songs before they committed him to the earth. The whole bearing of the wounded scout and of his companions was a remarkable lesson to our white men who were engaged in the conflict and who, though nominally Christian and better educated than the Indians, yet were far more careless in Christian conduct and less thoughtful of Christian observance. Soon after this, Lieutenant Williams went back with his Indians, first to Union, the county seat, and thence he sent them later to the Lapwai reservation. The white men who were engaged in this sad affair appeared to be softened toward Indians. They were themselves arrested, held for a time by the local authorities, and then set at liberty without trial.

Let us return to our camp near the Ironsides Mountains. As we found some temporary supplies in the neighborhood, especially of cattle, our march was resumed early on Saturday morning. We went as straight as possible to the Malheur agency, a distance of about twenty-five miles, putting Lieutenant Cresson and others out on a scouting expedition. It was a fine, bright day, and as our troops were in good spirits, we made a brisk march and arrived at the agency before noon. We found the garden with unharvested vegetables comparatively undisturbed. There was great confusion inside of the buildings, articles being thrown hither and thither, especially in the storehouses, which had been generally robbed. There was, however, scattered around in broken bags a little flour and some grain, and from these supplies, the worn and half-famished troops were fed. The next day Capt. Marcus P. Miller, an officer whose name was frequently mentioned in the previous Nez Perce campaign, brought up plenty of rations, using his company of the 4th Artillery for a guard. He had taken the direct road from Baker City. The same day, important reports were brought in by numerous citizen scouts from the various officers and scouting parties who were scouring the country. With others, we had news from Maj. John Green, who had given up his leave of absence to do duty in this wearisome campaign.

I gathered from the reports that our Indians were no longer moving in any considerable detachments, but had broken up into very small, fragmentary parties, hurrying through the woods and across the lava rocks, which were here very extensive and barren of vegetation, and were endeavoring to cluster about Steen's Mountain, from whence Sarah Winnemucca, early in the conflict, had detached the old chief, her father, her brothers, and her friends from an immense hostile band. Some fresh trails led in precisely the opposite direction, toward the Weiser region, and others to a beaten route that led due east across the Owyhee. Comparing notes with others, I concluded that the Paiutes, what few there were left of them in that neighborhood, and the Weisers were endeavoring to hide in the vicinity of their old haunts, and that the Bannocks had separated themselves and were following the eastern trail back to Lemhi and Fort Hall. It was thought by some of our scouts that these had in mind a project of imitating Joseph's stampede of the year before, and purposed to lead a wild chase across the continent to the buffalo country and come under the fancied shelter of Sitting Bull, who was still reported to be beyond our boundaries in Canada. It may be interesting as part of these "Indian Papers" to introduce here a paper of instructions, to show how the different small columns, which had come together for supplies, were again spread out over the country to complete the campaign.

HEADQUARTERS DEPARTMENT OF THE COLUMBIA,
In the Field, Malheur Agency, Oregon, July 28, 1878
General Field Orders, No. 6.

General Field Orders, No. 5, July 26, current series, from these headquarters, is modified as follows.

I.—Maj. John Green, 1st Cavalry, being not too far to the left to execute his part of it, Lt. Col. James W. Forsyth, 1st Cavalry, will take his smaller battalion and one other, and execute what was assigned to Maj. John Green, 1st Cavalry. (Green had had orders to follow, in a constant pursuit, the hostile Indians by their principal trail.)

II.—The department commander will move to the vicinity of Camp Lyon, Oregon, with the other battalion, leaving one company of it to report to Capt. Marcus P. Miller, 4th Artillery, who will remain at this depot (the Malheur agency), under special instructions.

III.—Major John Green, 1st Cavalry, will, with his battalion, watch for a short time in his present neighborhood, and then move to form junction with department headquarters at or near Camp Lyon.

IV.—Col. Frank Wheaton, 2nd Infantry, will change his headquarters from Baker City, Oregon, to Boise City, I.T., commanding all troops along the stage road as now, holding himself in readiness to take the field should occasion demand it.

V.—Colonel Wheaton will move the subsistence depot at Baker City to Boise, as soon as it becomes certain that the hostiles have passed the Owyhee River.

By Command of Brigadier General Howard:
CHARLES E. S. WOOD, Aide-de-camp,
Acting Assistant Adjutant General. In the field.

For the right, Forsyth had planted Bernard's battalion. I took the central trail, using Sumner's troop of cavalry, and Major Green, having found some fresh trails, led the left column. We swept an extent of country as wide as that of Sherman's column in his march from Atlanta to the sea, running down every horse trail and footpath, clearing the mountains and valleys, and there are many of them, from the Snake River above Baker City southward as far as Steen's Mountain, all the time gaining ground toward the east. Meanwhile, Capt. M. P. Miller was anchored at the Malheur agency with his own company and a company of cavalry. He continuously probed the country in a circuit about the agency, caught up Indian stragglers, kept prisoners sent to him, and gathered those who blindly wandered hither and thither and so fell into his net. The old Indian woman who, it will be remembered, had been found in the mountains hiding in a log had been restored by the great care of Sarah Winnemucca and her sister-in-law, Mattie, to comparative health and strength. She was sent out by Miller to hunt up other frightened Indians and show them where they could come for food and shelter and permanent peace. Captain Miller's own words give an idea of his first success in this operation: "The pickets brought them in, and they had a talk with me, to the effect that their band desired to surrender; I told them that they could come in as prisoners of war. On August 5 they returned, and on the sixth this band came in, consisting of twenty-seven warriors, seventy-two women and children, fifty horses and ponies, and ten guns—worthless old muzzleloaders." These were the first prisoners taken; many others were to follow in a few days.

A singular accident occurred to me on my march across the sagebrush deserts, lying between the Malheur agency and the Owyhee River. I had a very tall, white mule which served me instead of a saddle horse. He was a very sensitive animal, and much to the discomfiture of the officers and men who followed, he took as an habitual walking gait a very rapid and lengthy stride. He had large ears and probably at some time a mane. But to beautify him in frontier style, the mane was roached (shorn) as closely as possible. As we were walking along rapidly, my staff officer near me, Major Mason, my inspector, was riding a few steps to my left and rear. Suddenly he cried out, as we were passing some dry, heavy knots of sagebrush lying in the trail, "Oh General, General, your cinch!" My large-eared mule had at that instant caught sign of that same cinch (girth), or rather, the shadow of it. The fastening had given way, and it was loose and pendent. Of course, there was nothing to hold my saddle, and there was no mane for my hands to seize. The mule bounded through the air like a frightened deer and sent me, saddle and all, headfirst to the ground. I landed upon some heavy sage knots, one of which struck my side, injured my ribs, and bruised me badly. At first, with the breath knocked out of my body, I could not move or speak, and I believed my ribs were broken. Very soon, however, by the kindly help of those around me, I was on my feet, and then, my mule being stopped in his wild flight and resaddled, I was lifted to his back and again continued the day's march. It was some time, however, before I recovered from that heavy fall. And since that time, no desire for extraordinary ornamentation ever leads me to believe in "roaching" a mule, for a reasonable mane would have saved me from the fall which nearly cost me my life.

⊷—⊨◈⊨—⊶

"Close of the Paiute and Bannock War," *The Overland Monthly* 11 (January 1888):101–6

At the time of my accident just related, there were four principal columns, of course none of them large, sweeping all the ground toward the east, toward that country from which the Bannocks had come. The Malheur River is a crooked one. I think some of the French voyageurs must have settled in this region, for, and I think very properly, everything had the word "Malheur" attached to it. There were the Malheur country, the Malheur reservation, the

Malheur River, and the Malheur City.[46] As, with my own immediate force, I passed down this river, I found the banks exceedingly rough and rocky, in places almost impassable for animals. We had to make diligent search for grass enough for their subsistence. The next day we broke away from the river, marching due east and passing over a waterless lava-rock plateau for seventy-eight miles. This day there was, as far as the eye could reach, a singular appearance of nature, owing to a partial eclipse of the sun. For a while everything appeared very much as when the heavens are obscured by the smoke of forest fires, only now the air was pure and the sky was clear. It seemed to the officers and men as if they had been suddenly ushered into another world. In a few hours, however, the realities of things were reestablished.

Owing to the ignorance or carelessness of a guide, we were at last led out of our direction and did not succeed in getting to the valley of the Owyhee as we had hoped, and what is always worrisome to tired men, we were forced to make a countermarch of three or four miles, where we had seen water pools at the bottom of a canyon between some ambitious cliffs. By 7:00 P.M. the troops, worn out and not a little cross, went into camp. I was annoyed to find that I had in some way lost the principal trail, for evidently only eight or ten Indians were ahead of us in the path that we were threading.

The next day was August 1. As I had frequently been obliged to do, I asserted my independence of guides, changed my direction to the left, and after a thirty-mile brisk march succeeded in gaining the Owyhee, but was again destined to disappointment, for there was not a spear of grass in the valley of this strange river. So, with a feeling of real grief, we encamped without a mouthful of food for our overworked and weary animals. The next morning, however, while ascending from the riverbed to the high tableland, we experienced the joy of the Psalmist when we came upon the water brooks, for we suddenly discovered a beautiful spring of clear water and an abundance of that bunchgrass which makes the horses glad and strong.

When fairly up the mountain, we came upon an extensive rolling country full of forage and running springs. The night of the second found us near old Camp Lyon. We bivouacked upon the level shore of a charming little lake. There are three such in that neighborhood. One of the officers, who had passed through that country years before and had been much troubled during the day for fear that we were lost, ascending a high bluff, suddenly saw these mirrorlike lakes. He cried out, "Now I know where we are; these are the lakes where General Crook, some years ago, had a battle with the Paiutes." The one nearest to us, instead of having a euphonic Indian or soft Spanish name, was called Cow Lake.

August 3 led us along through an extensive sagebrush prairie. The march of the day was a short one, for here we struck a telegraph line. Mr. Holland, our young operator, quickly hitched his instruments to the wire and made telegraphic connection with the outer world. So here, near Mr. Annawalt's, we encamped, and before morning had ascertained what the other actively moving troops had been doing.

Major Green, who, it will be remembered, was moving along a parallel trail several miles to my left, had been obliged for some reason to delay at McDowell's ranch. During the night of July 28, some Indians had crept up close to his camp, perhaps within a mile, driven away several horses, and then saucily set fire to a haystack. It was near dawn when Green discovered the fire, but [he] did not know that it was the haystack in flames until one of his pickets came in and so reported. Major Green immediately used the trail of these depredators, following it up rapidly in the hope of finding a larger one. This led him straight to the mouth of the Malheur River. He reached the place known as Rhinehart's Crossing the evening of the twenty-ninth. There scouting was continued. During the night of July 31, he received several reports, which showed him that somehow hostile Indians had managed to get beyond us and had already appeared in large numbers as far east on the Snake River as Mundy's Ferry,[47] where it was reported that the stage had been stopped and the driver, Mr. Hemingway, killed.

This is Major Green's dispatch: "August 1. I moved to McDowell's Ferry; sent two messengers with the news about the murder to the department commander, hoping they (the messengers) would reach him that day, as I believed if he received this dispatch my course would be changed, but unfortunately the messengers did not find him for several days."

How different officers are in interpreting and obeying commands! Sometimes it is necessary to deviate from literal instructions in order really to obey the plan or wish of a senior commander. During the Nez Perce campaign the year before the Bannock War, I received from my senior an order which detached from me a considerable portion of my troops. To obey the order was to imperil and probably defeat the expedition. There was no time to communicate. I did not hesitate. I deviated so far as to send an equivalent detachment, but not the one ordered. I can never forget when my general,[48] months afterwards, solemnly called me to an account for a direct infraction of discipline!

"You did not know what necessity lay behind that order, sir," he said, while looking sternly into my face.

"True," I replied, "but you were a thousand miles from me, and I did what I knew that you would have done had you been on the spot."

His face relaxed, and he said, "Well, I suppose it is necessary to give some discretion to an officer with large commands and situated as you were."

But Major Green would never risk so much; his designated route lay toward Camp Lyons, and thither he bent his way till, when six miles distant, he received instructions to turn to the left and go at once to Mundy's Ferry. Fortunately, while I was separated from the telegraph lines, my second in command, Colonel Wheaton, at Baker City, had heard of the stage-line outrage, and so took the responsibility of sending a message to Green not only to go to Mundy's Ferry, but beyond if necessary, following up our fourth column under Captain Egbert.

Egbert, on the north side of the Snake, had succeeded in finding the largest trail. He had put his men into wagons and rushed on like the hostiles themselves at forty and fifty miles a day. A part of the main hostiles, not more than a hundred, emerging from their hiding places in the Malheur country, had kept themselves south of the Snake, robbed the horse ranches along Sucker and Reynolds' creeks, and as we had before seen, struck the Boise stage near Mundy's Ferry and murdered the driver. There was a small detachment near the ferry from Captain Collins's 21st Infantry company, which skirmished with these raiders and drove them from the river. They then ran up the Snake River as far as Bruneau Valley. Here they crossed over the main river and hid themselves for quite a little time on a bushy island of a tributary of the Snake. Here, then, let us leave this rapid, energetic, fierce, depredating band, in fact the most important one which had succeeded in crossing the Malheur, Owyhee, and Snake Rivers.

Behold Captain Egbert and Major Green hastening their battalions through clouds of dust and under the intense heat of the August sun. While they are in eager pursuit, endeavoring to head the Indians off, beat them in battle, or capture them, let us turn for a few moments to bring up the other column moving over a country rougher than ours, miles away on the extreme right. I cannot do better than give Colonel Forsyth's own story of his march from Malheur agency to Steen's Mountain, and then beyond to that famous ground called Old Camp C. F. Smith. Here he arrived the same evening (August 3) that I reached Annawalt's, where young Holland had set in motion his telegraphic machine. Forsyth says:

From the time that we left the Malheur agency, up to our arrival at Old Camp C. F. Smith, no fresh signs of Indians were found in the country, and citizens living along the road reported that no Indians had been seen by them for ten or twelve days prior to our appearance. Distance traveled from the Malheur agency, 144 miles.

We were detained at Old Camp C. F. Smith from August 4–7 by signal fires in the mountains and reports made by citizens that there were Indians still hiding in them. To satisfy myself and clear the matter up, I sent out scouting parties, and they developed the fact that the signal fires were built by one Indian on foot, whom they brought in. No other signs of Indians, after a careful scout of the mountains, could be discovered.

Colonel Forsyth now swept that lower country by the way of Oregon Canyon to Antelope Springs. He kept on to the old Camp Three Forks, near the sources of the Owyhee, to the Flint River, to the Bruneau Valley, and thence up the Snake River itself to Payne's Ferry.

When his command had reached the mill on Sinker's Creek, it was divided. A part under Major Sanford went on to scout the Snake Valley further eastward, while the remainder under the famous Bernard turned southward and gathered up the scattering hostiles that were lurking in the neighborhood of Duck Valley, South Mountain, and the flat country stretching down as far as Fort McDermit.

When his command was divided, I brought Colonel Forsyth himself back to Boise City in order to give him general charge of all operations south and east of that city till the close of the campaign.

Meanwhile my own little column was itself bearing a part. August 5, taking Captain Sumner's battalion, I left our camp at Annawalt's by sunrise and made a rapid march of thirty miles toward Bruneau Valley, where excited citizens declared that hundreds of Indians were committing depredations. En route, I passed through that small mining town of Idaho named Silver City, going on to a rough camp in the mountains. I encountered at Silver City considerable hostile feeling from white men, particularly from the editor of a newspaper, who seemed extremely dissatisfied because the commanding officer could not be personally in more than one place at a time.

The place of encampment was at a queer little hamlet denominated Scotch Bob's, where the hills were so precipitous and the level spots so limited that it was next to impossible to find enough lodging ground for the night. Here my news was of such a character, and rumors from one quarter and another so conflicting, that I decided it best to break up my own little column, sending forward the troops to cross the river at Mundy's Ferry and report to Major Green, while I myself hastened northward to Boise City with a view to regulate all the operations from that center. The night of August 6, my aide-de-camp, Lieutenant Wood, and myself set out, rode all night and until noon of the next day. When we reached our destination at Boise City, I found about twenty Indian prisoners that Lt. Guy Howard[49] with a part of Captain Viven's[50] company, 12th Infantry, had succeeded in gathering up near Ladd's Canyon and had sent here to the fort for safekeeping.

A little later, August 9, a detachment of Egbert's battalion, which we left in hot pursuit of the Mundy's Ferry raiders under the immediate command of Captain Dove,[51] discovered unmistakable evidences of the presence of hostile Indians. They were about a hundred strong and hiding on the curious island before referred to, in the midst of Bennett Creek.[52] Captain Dove could only succeed in skirmishing, his combat lasting for some four hours. The island afforded the Indians a remarkably sheltered position. Egbert brought him reinforcements as soon as he could, and when the difficulties of the rapid stream and the concealing bushes had been overcome, a brisk charge was made, our men rushing through the fringes of trees; but the Indians were already on the alert and soon fled beyond danger. Then Captain Egbert followed up the hostiles without rest till they scattered out and lost their trail among the ledges and lava rocks of the mountains which lie between the Big Camas Prairie of Idaho and the Snake River.[53]

On the seventh I forwarded to General McDowell a dispatch, from which I make extract, which affords a significant picture of the condition of that section of the country at that time. In fact, it is typical of fevered disturbances occasioned by every Indian war:

Looking for Indian Sign. OUTING MAGAZINE, 1887.

The apprehensions of danger by the people are so great that I have located the troops so as to catch wandering parties, scout the country, and quiet this feeling, so that the farmers may return home and gather their crops. There is a great fear among the people that we shall be lenient toward the prisoners. It seems to me wise to keep the troops in this vicinity for a few weeks till all danger is over, all the prisoners gathered in, that proper punishment may be meted out to them.

As we have seen, Egbert, Green, Sumner, Sanford, and Bernard had kept their battalions, or detachments from them, in constant activity, following up every road and pathway, and ferreting out every possible hiding place. Colonel Wheaton, back at Baker City, had held Captain Worth in front of him near Old's Ferry and had sent Captain Drum with two infantry companies to push all the way northward to Mount Idaho, crossing the Snake at Brownlee's Ferry. The generous Captain Drum, finding the apprehensions of the people on his line of march very great, had halted near Salubria and made continuous efforts to capture Indians, which were confidently reported to be infesting that neighborhood. Meanwhile, the valley of the Boise River was scouted by a company of Miles's battalion of the 21st Infantry, which was serving under Captain Downey. They were mounted on Indian ponies and made a rapid run through the Boise Valley and along the Snake River, near its mouth, wherever the imagination of an overexcited people fancied there were hiding Indians. Captain Miles himself, with other mounted infantry, covered the country back to Baker City, while Major Mizner held his battalion upon the Blue Mountains on Meacham's ranch. All these active movements of battalions, detachments, and companies were necessitated by the singular conduct of our foes. They scattered, but not from fright. They ran hither and thither through this rough, wooded, and rocky region in ways that were puzzling to pursuers; persistency, however, brought its results. Dispatch from Boise City said, "I have now at different points some six hundred Indian prisoners (more or less), men, women, and children." After placing Lieutenant Colonel Forsyth in command of the Boise District, I turned back towards my permanent headquarters at Vancouver Barracks. The fighting was now over, and every dispatch showed the necessity of my immediate return to the Columbia.

On the fourteenth I met Colonel Wheaton at the Umatilla agency. Here, after consultation, with a view of settling their difficulties on a permanent basis, we had a council with the Umatilla and Columbia River Indians. It was plain that there was such a mingling of the loyal and the disloyal, and such a fever of accusation and apprehension among all the people there, both whites and Indians, that some measures must be speedily taken to relieve the troubles and preserve the peace. To this end we appointed a second council for Monday, August 26, and with a view to keep matters quiet and save the possibility of an outbreak, I ordered a small body of troops to bivouac at the agency and to remain there for a considerable length of time.

The results of this council and movement of troops were to take several prominent Indians and send them to safe forts to be kept as hostages for the good behavior of the remainder. These were harsh measures, war measures, where often innocent men were taken and made to suffer privation and hardship for the sake of securing the good behavior of a perturbed tribe. But owing to the manner in which Indians are influenced and governed, such measures appeared absolutely unavoidable.

By subsequent instructions and the gradual drawing back of the troops from the eastern portions of the Department of the Columbia, the prisoners themselves, made up principally of the Paiutes and Bannocks, were gathered together first at the Malheur agency, and then all transferred to Camp Harney, where there was a permanent garrison of troops some fifty miles from the Malheur agency. Then, with recommendations, the situation was reported to General McDowell, the division commander, and through him to Washington.

From the Umatilla councils, my aide-de-camp, Lieutenant Wood, and myself made our way to the Columbia and embarked on the first downriver steamer. The lieutenant was so worn by continued labors and loss of rest that he dropped down on a side seat of the steamer's cabin and went fast asleep. I was sitting near him and half dreaming, when a large man approached and roughly accosted me. He was tall and strongly built, had some pretensions to an education, but was coarse in his manner and language. He had evidently been drinking and, seeing me, had doubtless made his boast that he would show me how people such as he represented felt towards me and the authorities over me.

He said, "I hear that you have allowed those accursed Indians (perhaps using stronger terms) to surrender."

I answered, "Of course, I have. Whenever the Indians give up and put out the white flag, they are taken as prisoners of war."

He then said, "I wouldn't have done it. Every last one of them should have been killed."

"Then, sir," I replied, "you would have been a murderer. It would be more than my commission is worth to do such a dastardly thing as to kill prisoners."

He again, showing great anger, uttered more insulting language and imputed to my officers and myself the most unworthy conduct and motives. I felt great indignation, for a large crowd appeared, metaphorically, to be egging him on to keep up a quarrel with me. So I rose and said, probably with some decision of manner, "Sir, I do not know who you are, but I wish you to understand that I am a soldier, that I have never turned a corner to avoid a bullet; now, what do you want?"

He answered in a different tone, "Oh, nothing. Come take a drink."

I said, "No, I do not drink."

The crowd was now on my side, hurrahing for me, and I was left after that to join my aide-de-camp in his repose.

There is, however, little doubt but that many frontier people who have suffered extremely from Indian outrages entertain a feeling of soreness toward us army officers, who seem so much to sympathize with the Indians, and they decry overlenient policy and behavior. We should judge them to be wholly right, did we not know from long experience that primarily nine-tenths of our Indian outbreaks have been occasioned by the misconduct of wicked white men.

⊷ ⊫◊⊨ ⊶

"Results of the Paiute and Bannock War," *The Overland Monthly* 11 (February 1888): 192–97

All the Indians that had been connected with this war from the various tribes—Umatillas, Paiutes, Bannocks, Weisers, and Klamaths, were as far as possible gathered in as prisoners. The main portion of them, after considerable correspondence with General McDowell, were sent to Camp Harney. They came there particularly from Boise City and the Malheur reservation, and some fifty or more were brought up under escort from Fort Bidwell, California, to the same post.

It appears also that many of the friendly Paiutes, disturbed in all their usual operations and hindered by the war from gathering food, went to Fort McDermit entreating the garrison for supplies. One band of the latter, that of Leggins, made its way to Camp Harney and was counted, perhaps improperly, among the prisoners of war. I never knew why Leggins and his band were joined to the prisoners. From information that was brought me, however, I came at the time to the conclusion that he played both ways, and I believe that some of his people were among the hostiles. It is a fact, whether we like it or not, that many prominent Indians are very friendly after a war, and would have us believe that their sympathies had been with the whites all the while, when the reverse was actually the case.

Packing through the Bannock country. CENTURY MAGAZINE, 1889.

I think myself that if all the facts were known, at the beginning of the Paiute and Bannock conflict, nearly all the Paiute Indians, except old Winnemucca and his immediate family, sympathized with the Bannocks when they began the struggle.

After the war, as for a time it was under advisement to send the Indians back to the Malheur agency, Leggins said, "Rhinehart is there yet, we ought not to go there while he is there, for we shall die with hunger. We all know how we suffered while we were there." It is evident from this that he, Egan, and Oytez were in full sympathy as to the cause of the outbreak of the Paiutes, viz., the placing of Agent Rhinehart over them, and his manner of conducting the affairs of the agency.

Looking over a letter of the Department of the Interior of October 24, 1878, I notice that General McDowell recommended, first, that in conformity with the suggestion of the [commanding] general of the Army, from ten to fifteen of the leaders, those known to have been prominent in the recent hostilities, be sent to the Indian Territory; second, that the remainder of those who were on the Malheur reservation be sent to the Lemhi reservation; third, that provision be made for the small bands under Winnemucca, Ocheo, Natchez, and others who are off the Malheur reservation, by setting off small and separate reservations for them and breaking up the Malheur reservation and post of Camp Harney.

The first and third propositions were approved by the Hon. Carl Schurz, then secretary, but he said of the second proposition, "The information is not sufficient to enable at present to form a definite opinion as the capability and adaptability of the Lemhi reservation for the accommodation of the remainder of Indians on the Malheur reservation, and the future permanent location of these Indians will be hereafter determined."

The Indian prisoners, who were waiting with great anxiety to know what would be done with them, as I have said, had an intimation through Sarah Winnemucca, their interpreter, that they would go back to the Malheur for the winter. She says that she was told to go to Camp McDermit and bring all her people to Camp Harney; that she then made the journey in six days, and that was it due to this visit that Leggins and his band came to Harney.

How instructions to this effect could ever have been issued, I am unable to learn, but think that the officer temporarily commanding Camp Harney interpreted his orders, which were "to gather in all the prisoners," as meaning that he should bring together all the Paiutes that he could find. But fortunately for the peace of the camp, the subsequent recommendations of General McDowell, which were not adopted at Washington, that they should all go to the Lemhi reservation, did not reach them.

Correspondence with Washington created an unhappy delay. At last, on November 15, Mr. E. A. Hoyt, commissioner of Indian affairs, recommended "the necessary orders to be issued to General Howard to select from the prisoners in his charge the ringleaders engaged in the recent hostilities, and hold them until such time as the necessary arrangements can be made for their permanent disposition, and to deliver all others who are known to have been engaged in hostilities to the United States agent [James H.] Wilbur of the Yakima agency."

Mr. Schurz, the secretary, approved this paper November 21, and the [commanding] general of the army on November 27, 1878, started his instructions to General Howard to carry out the suggestion and recommendations of the Interior Department and conduct the prisoners intended for the Yakima agency under guard.

The next day, November 28, the substance of the orders was telegraphed to me at Vancouver Barracks. It was, as we have seen, to remove the Bannock and Paiute prisoners then under guard at Fort Harney, a distance of about three hundred and fifty miles, to the Yakima reservation, or what is more frequently called the Simcoe agency. I was further instructed to select a few of the worst and detain them at some post as prisoners in confinement.

In the region of Fort Harney, the severe winter had already set in, and in fact, the entire route was through a cold, bleak, and snowy country, and the prisoners would be obliged to cross the Columbia River and two ranges of mountains on the way. Before the receipt of the order, there had been an unaccountable stampede among them at Fort Harney, and several had escaped. Great effort was made by the troops to overtake them, and they were finally recaptured at places hundreds of miles away—a part of them near Fort Bidwell, California, and the remainder near the Klamath agency. Those retaken at Klamath were sent to me at Vancouver, and several besides, chosen at Fort Harney, were brought to the same place, and while waiting for their final disposition, I had them kept at Vancouver Barracks, and there constantly employed at some garrison work which they were capable of performing. Two or three of these so-called "hard cases" managed to escape after a time, but the remainder stayed with apparent willingness, behaved as well as men could, and labored diligently, doing whatever was required of them. I may say here that in process of time, they were finally sent, upon my recommendation, to their people at the Yakima agency. My report of the removal of the main body of the prisoners is brief and reads as follows:

The removal of some six hundred prisoners, men, women, and children, over the mountain roads in winter, from Harney to Simcoe, was a difficult and trying operation, and very costly. Capt. William H. Winters of the 1st Cavalry, who had charge of the work, exercised the greatest care. By short marches and the use of abundant transportation, he succeeded in taking them through, with an escort of two companies of cavalry, with but small loss of life—two adults who were already ill and three children perishing on the journey. He made the transfer to Agent Wilbur at Fort Simcoe February 10, 1879.

I notice that Mrs. Hopkins (Sarah Winnemucca) gives in her book[54] quite a detailed account of this removal, and regards it from beginning to end as a great outrage, indicating heartlessness and inhumanity on the part of all concerned in causing it. The pictures are graphic. When she first heard the news, she says, "It was just a little before Christmas. My people were given only one week to ready in. I said: 'What! In this cold winter, and in all this snow, and my people have so many little children? Why, they will all die. Oh, what can the president be thinking about? Oh! tell me, what is he? Is he man or beast? Yes, he must be beast; if he has no feeling for my people, surely he ought to have some for the soldiers. No human being would do such a thing as that, send people across [that] fearful mountain in midwinter.'"

She then gives an account of separating those who were regarded as the worst. They were Oytez, Bannock Joe, and nine others. Poor Sarah had been sent down to the Indian camp to select these men, and she did it by telling them that the commanding officer wanted to see them, and then started, with Oytez ahead, to lead them to his office.

"We had to go right by the guardhouse. Just as we got near it, the soldier on guard came out and headed us off, and took the men and put them in the guardhouse. After they were put in there, the soldiers told me to tell them they must not try to get away, or they would be shot."

After this, when the news came to the Indian camp, "Oh, how sad they were. Women cried and blamed their husbands for going with the Bannocks, but Leggins and his band were told they were not going with the prisoners of war.

"One afternoon Mattie and I were sent out to get five women who got away during the night; an officer was sent with us. We were riding very fast, and my sister Mattie's horse jumped to one side and threw her off and hurt her. The blood ran out of her mouth and I thought she would die right off, but poor dear, she went on, for an ambulance was at our command."

It will be remembered that Mattie, wife of Lee Winnemucca, had accompanied us, aiding Sarah as a scout and interpreter during the entire campaign. I never knew a better behaved or more worthy young person. This fall was the injury that finally caused her death. At last the Indians were in readiness for the severe trial. Citizens of the country who had wagons and teams were hired to use them in the transportation of the prisoners and all their belongings. As the escort and wagons, fifty in number, drew out, the column presented the appearance of one of our war trains, with the intervals greater or less according to the strength of the team; the train covered at no time less than a mile of wagon road.[55]

In three days careful Captain Winters had brought them safely as far as Canyon City, and then went into camp. Here he received a dispatch to send back for Leggins's band, which he had left behind at Fort Harney. Here, too, a brother of the old and much beloved agent, with his wife and children, came to see the Indians. I think some of the words of Sarah Winnemucca truthfully portray the feelings of the Indians, who certainly were hardly more than children themselves. For example:

> My people threw their arms around him and his wife, crying, "Oh, our father and mother, if you had stayed with us, we would not suffer this!"
>
> Poor Mrs. Parrish could not stop her tears at seeing the people who once loved her, the children whom she had taught—yes, the savage children who once called her their white lily mother, the children who used to bring her wildflowers with happy faces, now ragged, no clothes whatever.

She represents them as beseeching these good people, Mr. and Mrs. Parrish, thus: "Oh, good father and mother, talk for us! Don't let them take us away; take us back to our home!"

The wagons were made as comfortable as possible, and tents were there in plenty. Generally, they had wood enough for fires, but during the two days' delay, the cold was very severe, and it snowed most of the time. Leggins and his people had now come up. By some carelessness, an old Indian was left back in a wagon. Probably the wagon had met with some accident; in the morning it was found by the citizen owner, but the old Indian was frozen to death. The citizen put his body out of the wagon into the snow. Sarah thought this "the most fearful thing I ever saw in my life."

Chief Leggins was angry with her, holding her responsible for his detention. Her heart was nearly broken, because neither Leggins nor Lee Winnemucca would speak to her. Here is another picture of that journey: "We traveled all day. It snowed all day long. We camped, and that night a woman became a mother; and during the night the baby died and was put under the snow. The next morning the mother was put into the wagon; she was almost dead when we went into camp. That night she too was gone, and left on the roadside, her poor body not even covered with the snow."

During the five subsequent days, in spite of all the care that could be exercised, three more children perished with the cold. Sarah says mournfully, "All the time, my poor little Mattie was dying little by little."

I remember having gone up the Columbia and out on the Canyon City road for several miles to meet Captain Winters and his command. I came upon them just as they were going into camp, and I thought that no father could take more pains for the care and comfort of his children than did the noble captain. He had enough wagons and other conveniences, but he was not always able to procure good and sufficient wood for the fires, and the weather was bitterly cold. The soldiers were so well clad that they did not suffer much, but the Indians, particularly the women and children, after a summer of war, were in a state of destitution. The army had no clothing except blankets to issue them.

It was not long after passing the Columbia before this strange column reached the Yakima plain and went into camp, perhaps twenty miles from the home of the agent. While they were there, another Paiute died. Sarah says, "But thanks be to the good Father in the spirit land, he was buried as if he were a man."

At the end of about ten or twelve days, the Indians were transferred to the care of the venerable Indian agent, who has usually been called "Father Wilbur." Our friend Mrs. Hopkins had become so embittered by what she calls "the hardships of her people" that she retained and exhibited a good deal of this feeling towards the new friends that she met. For example, she says, "They did not come because they loved us, or because they were Christians; no, they were just like all civilized people; they came to take us up there (to the agency) because they were to be paid for it. You know what kind of a shed you make for your stock in wintertime. It [the shed for the people] was of that kind. Oh, how we did suffer with cold! There was no wood, and the snow was waist deep, and many died off just as cattle or horses do after traveling so long in the cold."

But I will not follow these Indians any farther. They remained, the most of them, through one season, working very hard to clear up some new land and to make themselves as comfortable as possible under the circumstances. They did not affiliate, however, with the so-called civilized Indians; they did not understand the taking of land in severalty; and they were always discontented because they were away from their own country. Where an ordinary white man would have built him a cabin, fenced in and cultivated a piece of land—for the land was rich and productive—the Indian made very little headway. When they worked together, there was considerable progress, but nowhere else. The interpreters quarreled with the agent, who doubtless did all he could, or all that he thought it his duty to do. There was, at that time, a constant pressure behind him from Washington to make all Indians self-supporting—to make them work for food, for clothing, and other supplies. So we may not wonder that these people cried out even about this agent, "Another Rhinehart! Don't you see, he is the same?"

And Sarah herself denounces not only the agent and other employees, but all the civilized Indians on the Yakima reservation. Soon after this trial near Fort Simcoe, Sarah came to me at Vancouver, and I gave her letters to Washington to allow her to plead the cause of her people in person.

Now, in closing this chapter, will not the friends of humanity say, "Are not the pictures you have given us sad enough, and do they not show how cruel the whites have been to the Indians?" Yes, if we take only their point of view, but those who have followed this campaign from the beginning to the close will find no army officers cruel toward the Indians. The Indians first believed one of their old tooats, who told them that there was to be a resurrection of Indians—that that time had now come. The Paiutes took advantage of a grievance; viz., the relief of a good agent and the putting in of one whom they claimed to be bad. They appealed to arms and believed for a time that they were strong enough, when all combined, to defeat the white troops and destroy all the white people in their region of country. The combination ran through various tribes, situated hundreds of miles apart.

The outbreak was met promptly by the troops. The Indians were defeated in battle, broken up into small parties, pursued relentlessly until captured or driven far beyond the field of operations. The prisoners were gathered together at Fort Harney and Vancouver Barracks, and the whole case at once submitted to the War Department for instructions. After careful consideration, it was determined to send these prisoners to the Yakima reservation, where civilization had already made great progress, and where there was abundance of the best soil for their cultivation.

They were ordered to be transported, clothed as well as the army could do it, and fed. It would have been simply to reward misconduct to have given back to them the reservation which they forfeited when they went to war.

Any hardships that occurred were merely incidental to the circumstances. Fort Harney, in the midst of the mountains, was not prepared to keep them through the winter, and it appeared necessary to the authorities to send them at once. Extraordinary expense was incurred for their protection and comfort. The extreme destitution of the women and children was due to the rigors of war—a war which every soldier would, if in his power, gladly have prevented. I believe that the Paiutes, had they heartily accepted the situation at Yakima, cultivated their fields, built houses and fences, and remained there as the Simcoe Indians have done, would have been prosperous and happy today. But perhaps in the nature of things, as it would first require a revolution in the arts of these people to bring it about, such desirable results could not be expected.

The Bannock Troubles

[ANONYMOUS]

Army and Navy Journal 15, no. 47 (June 29, 1878): 756

The bone of contention between the Bannock Indians and the white settlers is the Big Camas Prairie, a meadow-like valley affording excellent pasturage. It is some fifteen miles wide and extending in an easterly direction from a point seventy-five miles east of Boise City for a distance of thirty miles. The Indians claim this valley by virtue of prior occupancy, as well as from a clause in some old treaty. Between this prairie and the Snake River in Oregon lie the Lava Beds, extending easterly fifty miles or more, with a width of from six to eight miles, including every variety of sustenance, from grazing plains and gentle slopes to rugged, precipitous ridges of broken volcanic rock, which in many places completely surround large areas with high, jagged walls, behind which a well-armed band of Indians can defy the approach of many hundred troops. It is within these fastnesses that the Bannocks have made their headquarters and base of operations, raiding on the country and the lines of travel, and carrying consternation everywhere.

A correspondent of the Omaha, Nebraska, *Herald,* who has interviewed General Crook[1] with reference to this uprising, reports him as saying that the Indians engaged in it are the Bannocks, Paiutes, and some of the Shoshones, who complain of a want of supplies, which the agents say have not been furnished because the appropriations are exhausted, though General Crook believes it to be the fact that some of the supplies have been lying at some point out there all winter and had not been distributed.

These Indians have heretofore been friendly, and in answer to the suggestion of the reporter that "it is rather hard that men and officers should be sent out there to be killed by the Indians when all the trouble has been brought about by thieving agents," General Crook said, "That is not the hardest thing. A harder thing is to be forced to kill the Indians when they are clearly in the right." There is good ground, he continued, for apprehension:

> As long as the muzzle-loading arms were in use, we had the advantage of them, and twenty men could whip a hundred, but since the breechloaders came into use, it is entirely different; these they can

load on horseback, and now they are a match for any man. In regard to the Bannocks, I was up there last spring and found them in a desperate condition. I telegraphed, and the agent telegraphed, for supplies, but word came that no appropriation had been made. They have never been half supplied. The agent has sent them off for half a year to enable them to pick up something to live on, but there is nothing for them in that country. The buffalo is all gone, and an Indian can't catch enough jackrabbits to subsist himself and family, and then there aren't enough jackrabbits to catch. What are they to do? Starvation is staring them in the face, and if they wait much longer, they will not be able to fight. They understand the situation and fully appreciate what is before them. The encroachments upon the Camas Prairie was the cause of the trouble. Those prairies are their last source of subsistence. They are covered with water from April to June or July, and there is a sort of root, which grows in them under the water, which is very much like a sweet potato. A squaw can gather several bushels a day of them. Then they dig a hole and build a fire in it. After it is thoroughly heated, the roots are put in and baked, and when they are taken out, they are very sweet and nice. This root is their main source of food supply.

I do not wonder, and you will not either, that when these Indians see their wives and children starving and their last source of supplies cut off, they go to war. And then we are sent out there to kill them. It is an outrage. All the tribes tell the same story. They are surrounded on all sides, the game is destroyed or driven away, they are left to starve, and there remains but one thing for them to do—fight while they can. Some people think the Indians do not understand these things, but they do, and fully appreciate the circumstances in which they are placed. Our treatment of the Indian is an outrage.

The Hanging of Tambiago

ANONYMOUS

Idaho Weekly Statesman, June 29, 1878

Notwithstanding the heavy rain which poured down almost continuously yesterday, about 250 persons visited the territorial prison and witnessed the execution of Tambiago, the Bannock murderer of young Rhoden.

The war, which is now raging in all its fury, and the many recent murders and atrocities committed by the Indians, caused more interest than would otherwise have been felt in the case, and the almost total absence of sympathy which was manifested.

The prisoner was visited in his cell by Rev. Father Archambault, Judge Kelly of the *Statesman,* Mr. Joseph Perrault, and others. To Father Archambault, he expressed in his way a certain degree of sorrow for the sinfulness of his act and a desire to be prepared for his fate.

When asked as to the causes of the hostilities of the Bannocks, he said that it was owing to the discontent of the Indians with their agent at Fort Hall and with the *gray beard*—meaning the missionary—who had been sent there to teach them. When the father urged upon him, as a motive for telling all he knew, that his words would be written down and sent to Washington, from whence relief might come for his people, the prisoner laughed incredulously and sneeringly said, "Washington no good; no believe us at Washington; chief at Washington no do anything for Indians." Other causes of the war he said were his own arrest and conviction, and that of his brother, who occupies the cell adjoining his under sentence of long confinement, and also the arrest of four others of the tribe, of whose present whereabouts and fate the tribe is ignorant—many supposing them to have been killed.

The Camas Prairie, he said, belonged of right to the Indians, and that they needed it, but did not name this as one of the immediate causes of the outbreak. He persisted to the last in the presence of Father Archambault and several others in saying that Dempsey had been counseling the Bannocks to go to war for more than a year; that nine months ago Dempsey had bought guns and ammunition from the Mormons at Salt Lake, which he had traded to the Indians, giving ten guns to Buffalo Horn and sending fifteen guns to Tendoy[1] at

667

Lemhi; that Dempsey had written a letter to Tendoy. When told that Tendoy could not read, he said that Medicine John could read for Tendoy. He said that Dempsey traded some of the guns to Buffalo Horn for a woman.

When he saw that the people were assembling in and near the prison, he asked what it meant, and when told that it was near the hour for his execution, he said, "Me no die today; tomorrow die all right; one sleep more, then die with good heart." Questioned as to the reason why he wished the delay, he said that tomorrow his chief, Tagee, would come with the Indians to see him; that he knew they would come, and beseeched the father to intercede for him and obtain this respite.

When told that it was useless to hope for any delay, that the day had come, he seemed to be in terrible agony. He paced the floor of his cell, insisting that he would not walk to the scaffold; that they might shoot him where he was. In a former interview he had said that the Indians would come and rescue him, as he knew they were sorry for him, and seemed under the impression that they had made the mistake of a day, and that they would surely come on the morrow.

When the fatal moment arrived, however, he did not wait to be shot or dragged, but walked composedly to the scaffold, mounting the steps with a firm tread, and met his fate with the proverbial stoicism of his race. On the scaffold he took a calm glance at the crowd and surrounding objects, and indulged in a grim and somewhat ghastly smile at the scene. He resisted the placing of the black cap over his eyes, which he seemed to fear more than death itself.

Precisely at 1:00 P.M. the drop fell, and Tambiago went to join the good Bannocks in the happy hunting grounds.

As noted by Dr. Treadwell, who was in attendance, the pulse ceased to beat at the end of seven and a half minutes.

A Red Hot Fight with the Bannocks

ERNEST F. ALBRECHT

Winners of the West 1, no. 12 (November 1924): 6

I have just read Gen. Oliver O. Howard's *Life and Experiences among [Our] Hostile Indians.* In the main it is correct, as far as I know, but there are instances where he is misinformed, and does thereby a grievous wrong to two brave and gallant officers of our brave little army of Indian fighters. The instances alluded to are in the war with the Bannocks in 1878, and he says, for instance, "that Company K, 21st Infantry, and Troop A, 1st Cavalry, left Camp Harney after Indians and returned to their families." This is wrong. To correct that, I will give a short description of that war from memory, as I was a member of Troop A, 1st U.S. Cavalry at the time. About June 18 or 20, 1878, we were ordered to leave Camp Harney to hunt and fight Indians.[1] At that time, there were stationed at Camp Harney [Troops] A and G, 1st Cavalry, and Company K, 21st Infantry.

Troop A under Captain McGregor and Troop G under Captain Bernard at once left, leaving Captain Downey with Company K, 21st Infantry, to guard the post. We shortly struck an Indian trail as wide as a city street. After following it for a few days, the scouts reported the Indians a short distance ahead. We were halted and ordered to tighten our cinches and get ready, then mounted again, and we struck the Indians about five miles further on, as far as I can recollect, [on] June 23. When we first sighted them, they were in a small, round valley and twelve to fifteen hundred feet in diameter. From about the center of this valley to a gap in the surrounding hills, there were the headwaters of a stream,[2] covered with thick willow brush about ten or twelve feet high. Near the end of this brush, the chiefs of the different tribes were riding in a ring, waiting for us. As soon as we sighted the redskins, it was a trot, gallop, charge, while they fired at us. As soon as their revolvers were empty, they fled along the bushes towards the outlet of the stream.

Here they had a narrow trail leading out of the level valley to a palisade-like cliff that ran almost parallel with the bushes, about five hundred yards from them. We were ordered to dismount, firing at them and following them as fast

McGregor's advance at Silver Creek.
REUBEN F. BERNARD. *ONE HUNDRED THREE FIGHTS AND SCRIMMAGES.*

as we could. Now that was just what the Indians had expected, as the whole thing was a trap. The bushes to our left were full of Indians, planted there to massacre us from ambush, and the cliffs to our right were lined with Indians lying down, firing at us without giving us a chance at them. Not a man would have come out alive had it not been for two things. The first was that the Indians on the bluff, fearing to hit the bushes, fired a little too low, their bullets raising a cloud of dust about four or five yards to our right. The other was the fact that McGregor, being an old Indian fighter, saw the trap we were in and had the trumpeter sound cease firing and recall, besides sending Lt. Frank H. Edmunds[3] to bring us back.

We then went back to where the officers were and remained here with our mortally wounded, Cpl. Peter F. Grantsinger. We remained here in the hail of Indian bullets, to keep him from the torture, until he died, without disobeying orders, not firing at the Indians. We were then ordered to a small hill on the edge of the valley and dug in; that is, built a small breastwork, expecting the redskins to attack at daybreak next morning. We were, however, disappointed. We were left alone until night came. I was detailed for guard on the picket line that night and received the second relief from 11:00 P.M. to 1:00 A.M. Punctually at midnight, three shots were fired at us from the bushes, one striking the ground under the horses' feet, another making a couple of holes through Captain McGregor's tent, and the third went wild. The next morning a burial and firing party was detailed for poor Grantsinger.[4] As we rightly surmised, the redskins had gone. I asked some of the burial party afterwards how Grantsinger had looked, but even the most callous of them told me it was too revolting to relate.

During all this time, one of our scouts was missing,[5] and we believed he had taken French leave. Little did we dream what a terrible fate was his. He had been badly wounded in the first part of the battle, had fallen off his horse, and crawled into a nearby hole in the ground, thinking that he had not been seen. But the squaws had seen him, and as soon as we were out of the way, they pulled up sagebrush, piled it on top of the hole, and set fire to it. Anyone that ever burnt sagebrush knows what that means. It will flare up, but the thick stems will scale off and burn through anything they fall on, so they slowly burned him to death. We never found this out until afterwards, when everything was over, and the Indian prisoners boasted of it. Strange to say, the very Indians boasting were graduates of the government schools, and one of them a talented sculptor. After the burial, we broke camp and took up pursuit, and kept so hot after them that they had no time to go murdering through the country.

After the war was over, and we had to chain guard the prisoners at Camp Harney, it fell to our lot to learn a brand new method of making good Indians. The inventor of this new method was Lt. Thomas Drury,[6] a wise Irishman. He evidently knew Indians, because in a private conversation, he was heard to say that he would kill more Indians than the war, and he came near doing so. He was commissary officer, and he saw to it that the redskins got all they could eat, and the redskins promptly gorged themselves until they died like flies.

Vivid Tale of the Bannock War

HENRY E. HEPPNER[1]

Winners of the West 6, no. 6 (May 1929): 4

I was a resident of Canyon City, Oregon, during the Bannock Indian War of 1878, and during the month of June, reports began to come into Canyon to the effect that hostile Bannock and other Indians were likely to invade Grant County, Oregon, and that the people of said county were in serious danger from them. The situation became so serious that on or about June 23, 1878, a company of volunteers was organized at Canyon City and called the Grant County Home Guard for the purpose of defending the town and protecting it and the surrounding country and settlers from the depredations of hostile Indians. Of that company, F. C. Sells was elected captain; James N. Clark, first lieutenant; Henry G. Guild, second lieutenant, and a man, Jacoby, sergeant and drillmaster.

After the company had drilled from time to time, on June 28, 1878, in response to reports that arms were being sent from Vancouver, Washington, to Canyon City, a detachment of our company, consisting of about fifteen members, was sent out under orders from Captain Sells to act as an escort for the bringing of the said arms and ammunition into the valley. Included in this detachment were Henry E. Heppner, Henry G. Guild, Cal Berry, and about twelve others.

We went down the John Day River to the south fork, and then to Spanish Gulch, where we met the stage and learned that there were no arms or ammunition on the stage, but that a Mr. Gillenwater was on his way with ammunition from the Dalles. From there John Walsh, sheriff, and I went on as far as Bridge Creek, where we learned that Gillenwater had stopped at Antelope and turned back. We then returned to Canyon City, where the rest of the party had gone, and on their way warned some of the settlers and took some of the women and children from the valley into the city.

On June 29 a detachment was ordered out, and while scouting for hostile Indians we encountered the main body of Indians under Chief Egan about thirty miles south of Bayville, near the head of Murderer's Creek. There were quite a

Following the hostiles. NELSON A. MILES. *PERSONAL RECOLLECTIONS AND OBSERVATIONS.*

number of us in the detachment, including Frank and Oliver Aldrich, Joseph D. Combs, William Burnham, Henry Colby, J. W. Allen, Miles Andrews, J. W. Bates, John Clark, L. P. Davis, and Fred Williams.[2]

When the Indians came up, the detachment retreated to higher ground, the Indians following closely.[3] When they came within three hundred yards, they began shooting. Lieutenant Clark saw there were too many for his company, so decided to retreat. The ground was open but hilly and rocky, so in order to save our horses, the company would ride a mile or so and then stop, rest the horses, shoot at the Indians to hold them back, and then make another similar run, meanwhile maneuvering so that the Indians did not entirely surround us, but they did keep on both sides and behind the company and kept up their shooting. Miles Andrews[4] was shot in the leg.

At the next stand,[5] Oliver Aldrich was shot and killed. A little farther on, William Burnham was shot in the back, and at the next run, his horse was shot from under him. After we had been followed by the Indians ten or twelve miles, we came to a steep hill, where the Indians gained ground and the shooting was quite heavy. One of the men had the heel of his boot shot off, and Lieutenant Clark's horse was shot from under him and killed, and Clark shot in the arm.[6]

The next day we had another fight, in which two men were wounded and the [J.] Cummins house burned. Emil Shultz was one of those wounded at this place.[7] The Indians, who numbered several hundred at Murderer's Creek at the entrance of John Day Valley and the fight at Cummins ranch, caused the people at Canyon City to be very much wrought up. We did not know how many Indians were in the valley, but knew there were enough to overpower us if they attacked the town. We took the women and children and hid them in the mines and tunnels, and guarded the mouths of the tunnels, where we kept them for several days.

The members of our company continued on duty and continued to drill and go out on scouting parties all during the summer, ran down all reports of Indians in the valley, and watched for their expected return through the John Day Valley. Later in July 1878 they did return, and we dug rifle pits at Fort Defiance, from where we did various scouting and aided the settlers in defense against the Indians with the troops of Gen. Mark V. Brown.[8]

PART FIVE

The Sheepeater
Campaign,
1879

The Sheepeater Campaign

WILLIAM C. BROWN[1]

Winners of the West 5, nos. 9, 10, and 12 (August, September, and November 1928); 6, nos. 1, 3, and 5 (December 1928, February and April 1929)[2]

Indian hostilities which have received but little attention from historians are those known as the Sheepeater campaign in middle Idaho in 1879—a section at that time unexplored. Recently the War Department has officially recognized this as a campaign, and army regulations have been amended accordingly.

The writer, then a second lieutenant of the 1st U.S. Cavalry, was on duty with Lieutenant Farrow's[3] company of twenty Umatilla Indian Scouts, which, as will be seen below, was an important factor in bringing the campaign to a successful conclusion.

The Sheepeaters were a small band of renegade Bannocks, Shoshones, and Weisers, who derived their name from the fact that they subsisted largely on mountain sheep. They were strong, active, and capable of enduring great hardships, but they were not reservation Indians. Their existence had been known since the early sixties, at the time of the gold excitement at Florence, Warrens, and along the main Salmon River.

After the Bannock War of 1878, the Sheepeaters were joined by a few hostiles who, eluding the U.S. troops, sought refuge in that region of high timbered mountains. This section, on account of heavy snows, is particularly inaccessible for troops except from about the middle of July to the last of September.

Before proceeding to describe the military features of the campaign, the writer desires to invite attention and give credit to an entertaining description of it published in the July–August 1910 issue of the *Journal of the Military Service Institution* by a participant, Maj. Chas. B. Hardin, U.S.A., retired, from which extracts have been made. Since then, the writer has received considerable data from official War Department records, and diaries kept at the time, notably those of Captains R. F. Bernard and A. G. Forse, 1st Cavalry, and Mr. Edgar Hoffner, formerly a private in Company G, 1st U.S. Cavalry, who gave such graphic accounts of the hardships of that campaign, from hunger, snow, rain, crossing swollen streams, etc., that copies of them are to be filed with the Idaho Historical Records. What follows is taken from the above sources as

A Big Horn sheep. NELSON A. MILES. *PERSONAL RECOLLECTIONS AND OBSERVATIONS.*

well as from my personal diary. Memory of events which have taken place nearly half a century ago is so unreliable that recourse is had to it but seldom.

About May 1st, 1879, Brig. Gen. O. O. Howard, then commanding the Department of the Columbia, with headquarters at Vancouver Barracks, received the following telegram:

> San Francisco, May 1, 1879.
> COMMANDING OFFICER, Department Columbia,
> Vancouver, W.T.:
> Indian agent at Lemhi states that a murder of five Chinamen in February last in northern Idaho occurred at Oro Grande (now Casto) on Loon Creek, eighty miles northeast of Boise, and it is supposed was done by Indians, probably some of the hostiles of last summer who have been wintering with the Sheepeaters on the Middle Fork of the Salmon. The division commander directs that a detachment be sent out from Boise as soon as the trail can be traveled, and ascertain who the murderers were and, if Indians, to apprehend them and bring them into Boise.
> (Signed) KELTON, A.A.G.

Pursuant to the above instructions, Capt. Reuben F. Bernard and 2nd Lt. John Pitcher, with fifty-six men of Company G, 1st U.S. Cavalry, left Boise Barracks May 31, 1879. They were to proceed to Challis and, if information warranted it, were to operate from that point. At the instance of General Howard, there also left Camp Howard (near Grangeville) on June 4 a force of forty-eight mounted infantry under Lieutenants Henry Catley,[4] E. K. Webster and W. C. Muhlenberg, consisting of Company C and a detachment of Company K, 2nd U.S. Infantry, with directions to operate toward Challis and form junction with Bernard as soon as practicable. The original objective, Challis, was changed due to subsequent information of the killing (probably in May) of Hugh Johnson and Peter Dorsey at the former's ranch on the South Fork of the Salmon River, southeast of Warrens.

Bernard, being the senior and experienced in Indian campaigning, would command all forces in the field. Catley's first objective was Warrens, and thence northeast to Rains' ranch on the South Fork of the Salmon River. He, like Bernard, had a pack train of six packers, thirty-four packs, David R. Monroe and Josh Falkner as guides and scouts, and contract surgeon E. J. Pring as medical officer. Bernard had as guides and scouts Orlando "Rube" Robbins, Johnny Bose, and later John S. Ramey.

In connection with the above, General Howard was authorized to enlist twenty Umatilla scouts. These were enlisted June 9 at the Umatilla agency, Oregon, by 2nd Lt. E. S. Farrow, 21st Infantry, and 2nd Lt. William C. Brown, 1st Cavalry, and will be referred to herein as Farrow's scouts. Attached to the scout company were seven enlisted men mounted and a pack train of about twenty packs and four packers, with John Corliss as chief packer. The scouts were paid for use of but one horse and equipment each, but they brought with them a total of forty ponies. This command was organized and equipped in time to leave the agency July 7, and were instructed to form junction with the other troops as soon as possible. They marched via Brownlee's Ferry, crossing there July 14, and arrived at Upper Payette Lake July 19.

At this date, it may be remarked that Catley had, after repeated efforts on June 16, when he found a mile of snow five to eight feet deep and returned, and again June 26, when he was again turned back by deep snows, finally succeeded in getting through. He crossed the South Fork of the Salmon River, leaving Rains' ranch July 17, and July 19 was two marches east of there, about the head of Chamberlain Creek.

Bernard encountered almost insuperable difficulties in traveling through snow and in crossing swollen streams and rugged mountains. He lost many mules laden with rations and was at times thirty-six to seventy-two hours without food. He scouted the country northeast as far as Myers Cove on Camas Creek, along the Middle Fork of Salmon and the Loon Creek country, was now heading slightly west of north, and July 19 camped on Deer Creek, fifteen miles south of Warm Lake. All these commands were hunting for Indians, whose whereabouts, still undiscovered, were probably along Big Creek, between what is now known as Vinegar Hill and Soldier Bar. Neither command was in communication with either of the others.

At this point Farrow got reports of signs of hostiles in the Crooked River country north of Brownlee's Ferry and in the southern part of the Seven Devils Mountains. He then retraced his steps to Calvin R. White's ranch. White was the first settler in Little Salmon Meadows, now known as New Meadows; was the postmaster there and carried the mail on the route to Warrens. In addition to serving as guide for us in 1879, it is understood that he performed similar services for United States troops in 1877 and 1878. Sergeant Shaplish, with several scouts, was sent to return through Council Valley to Crooked River to investigate reports. Lieutenant Brown, with three scouts was sent down Payette (or Long) Valley as far as the falls (Cascade), Pearsall's Diggin's, and up Deep Creek on a similar mission.

Farrow on July 23 sent Bernard a dispatch stating that he had turned his command about and was now heading for Crooked River, in belief that the Indians were there. On July 27, from camp at Crooked River, he sent a dispatch to the assistant adjutant general at Vancouver Barracks, stating, "The hostile Indians, over 100 strong, are near the mouth of Crooked River. They have crossed most of their stock to the Oregon side of the river."

The reports of the Crooked River reconnaissance being such as to apparently justify our proceeding there, we went west to near Snake River and found there two men who reported having seen no Indians for a month. This unfortunate march over exceedingly rough country was very exhausting on both men and animals and, according to Howard's report, caused Bernard, who had heard of Farrow's move when at Warrens on July 31, to go some seventy miles out of his way. Farrow then marched southeast to Long Valley to investigate indications of hostiles reported there. During this time, several extensive side scouts were made. By July 31 we had arrived and camped on Gold Fork, where, in 1878, when commanding Company L, 1st Cavalry, the writer formed part of the command of Capt. W. F. Drum, 2nd Infantry, then operating against Bannocks. On August 3 Farrow camped at Warm Springs, at the falls of the North Fork of the Payette River. We learned that Bernard camped August 2 at the fishery north of Lower Payette Lake and was headed south. August 4 we received, through courier from Bernard, our first reliable information of Catley's defeat and the whereabouts of the hostiles.

Bernard took action promptly, sending word for the post surgeon at Boise Barracks to meet him on the South Fork of Salmon River and for supplies to be sent to the mouth of Loon Creek on the Middle Fork. August 6 Bernard and Farrow joined forces at Warm Springs, near the Falls of the North Fork of the Payette River, and under Bernard's command started northeast to the South Fork of Salmon River and down same to Johnson's ranch, arrived there August 10 after an exceedingly rough trip, having to cut their way through fallen timber with axes and losing in one day alone eight pack mules, killed by falling over precipices.

＋·　≡◆≡　·＋

We return now to Catley's operations. Leaving Rains' ranch July 17, he followed the trail shown on the map and camped at the caves on the night of July 28. We now quote from Bernard's report sent August 5 from Lake Creek in Long Valley:

A family group of Sheepeater Indians. SMITHSONIAN OFFICE OF ANTHROPOLOGY.

I have just received a dispatch from Catley, showing that the Indians attacked and defeated his command on the 29 ultimo, his loss being two wounded and all his provisions, greater portion of his baggage, and twenty-three pack mules. The force of Indians not large, though well posted at the mouth of Big Creek, a stream that flows from the west, emptying into the Middle Salmon thirty miles below the mouth of Loon Creek. I will get Farrow and go down South Salmon to a point where I ordered Catley to meet me, when we will cross over to the Indian position.

With a view of giving some idea of the skirmish which Captain Bernard denominates a defeat, I will insert a few extracts from Lieutenant Catley's report of August 2:

Having marched into the Big Creek country (Big Creek is a large tributary of the Middle Fork of the Salmon River), I found fresh Indian signs, which led me down Big Creek through a deep and rocky canyon, and the signs becoming fresher, I was obliged to follow their trail (which I believe to be the only way through that country) or give up the pursuit.

The result was that on July 29, my command struck an ambuscade, from which, after determining that it was impossible to do anything, the Indians being lodged in a point of rocks across the creek, where they had so fortified themselves that their exact location could not be discovered, I ordered a retreat. The first intimation I had of their presence was a few words spoken by one of their number, which was immediately followed by a volley. Two men, Privates Doyle, 2nd, and Holm, of Company C, 2nd Infantry, were seriously wounded but gotten out from under fire and carried about two miles back up the creek, to a point which I selected as one that could be held, where I met the pack train coming down the creek.

Here I camped, and the next morning, putting the wounded men upon hand litters, I moved up a ridge which I thought would lead me into the mountains somewhere near the route I had traveled to Big Creek.

In this I was mistaken. It proved to be an impracticable route, and being encumbered by the wounded men, I was unable to take and hold the points ahead of me, although the Indians were endeavoring to reach them first. They secured a high, rocky point ahead of me, and I fell back to a similar point, the wounded and the pack train arriving there at the same time. There were then Indians ahead and behind. I ordered the pack train unloaded and the men to take such cover as they could find in the rocks and behind the cargo, and hold the position if the Indians attempted to approach.

The Indians, seeing this determination, set the base of the mountain on fire. The wind was high, and the terrible roaring of smoke and flame seemed to approach us from every direction.

First Sergeant John A. Sullivan, Company C, 2nd Infantry, then took a party of men and worked bravely and hard to get a space burned off around us large enough to prevent the fire from reaching our position. This effort, and the fact that the wind seemed to shift just as we were in the greatest danger, alone saved the command.

That night, after the moon had got down, we moved down the side of the mountain, which was so precipitous that it was impossible to bring more than a very small portion of our baggage with us. Officers and men threw away the greater part of their effects, and I ordered most of the public property abandoned so that the train might be as lightly loaded as possible with what was absolutely necessary. Some of this was lost in descending the mountain by rolling and straying of the mules. At daylight we were ascending a ridge running parallel to the one we left, and which was found a fair route.

As I had not a sufficient command to establish and hold a camp to take care of my wounded men, and being crippled in every way by the loss of supplies, animals, equipage and clothing, I took up my march for Camp Howard, to which point it will be necessary to return and refit, if the command is to keep the field.

I shall order the purchase of sufficient rations at Warrens to last to Camp Howard, and continue my march in that direction as rapidly as the jaded animals and men can travel; at present both are exhausted from fatigue. No ammunition fell into the hands of the Indians. I think they got Private Doyle's rifle.

This rear movement of Lieutenant Catley was promptly arrested by an officer sent from Lapwai by Colonel Wheaton the instant the report of this defeat and run was made known to him. Very promptly also, Captain Forse, 1st Cavalry, with twenty-five men of his company, was dispatched to reinforce and turn him toward, and not from, this small body of Indians.

The following dispatch will indicate my action under the circumstances of these reports:

Vancouver Barracks, August 24, 1879.

CAPTAIN MCKEEVER,
Commanding Camp Howard (By mail from Lewiston) :
Department Commander directs you send the following to Bernard.
(Signed) SLADEN, Aide

CAPTAIN BERNARD,
In the Field:
Guard has been sent to Warrens. Indians have been encouraged by apparent misconduct of Catley. Possibly he may redeem himself under your eye, but his precipitate retreat before inferior numbers is astounding. Sorry for Farrow's unavoidable mistake. Think he will aid you materially. Must leave details to your discretion. Those Indians must be defeated, or trouble will extend.
(Signed) HOWARD, Commanding

In this engagement the hostiles fired about fifty shots at a range of less than 150 yards, wounding two men and killing a horse at the first fire. There were a few return shots fired. The strength of the enemy (by count) was given at from ten to twenty-seven.

The writer on August 18 visited and examined the hostile position on the south bank of Big Creek and at an elevation considerably above the trail, which was on the opposite (north) bank. The hostiles had built a wall of loose rock, where they were perfectly protected and could fire through loopholes in the wall. The narrow trail ran along a ledge 100 feet or more above the creek, which here runs through a canyon with walls perhaps 500 feet high and impracticable except along the trail; retreat could be made only by men turning about individually, which was done, and made in such haste that the two wounded men were left behind. Men were subsequently sent to bring them to the command, which had retreated (unpursued) about two miles up the creek to a flat, where it camped for the night.

July 30. In continuing the retreat (one and a half to two miles) to what was afterwards known as Vinegar Hill, there were about fifteen shots fired at the command, with no result save wounding a mule. Vinegar Hill was so called as, there being no water, the men slaked their thirst by sips of vinegar. July 31, 2:00 A.M., continuing the retreat; as the bell of the pack train was muffled, eleven mules were soon lost that night, mainly by straying. They marched that day to Cold Meadows, estimated at thirty miles. On August 1 they broke camp at 2:00 A.M. and camped within eight miles of the South Fork of the Salmon River at Tip Top. They arrived at Warm Springs (twelve miles west of Warrens) August 5.

If this little history is to be of value, it must be *complete*. This seems the appropriate place to record the fact that Lieutenant Catley was, for his conduct on this expedition tried by a general court-martial, found guilty of misbehavior in the presence of the enemy, and sentenced to be dismissed from the service. The sentence was, however, on the recommendation of the judge advocate general, set aside by the president.

Let us digress for a moment to refer to this little campaign from the viewpoint of the Sheepeater Indians, with whom history should deal fairly.

They had been in this unexplored and almost inaccessible region for generations, with apparently no hostility to the whites, and they might be there now but for the fact that in an evil day, they were joined by a few refugees from the Bannock War of 1878, and it seems probable that the murders of the Chinamen at Oro Grande (Casto) and Johnson and Dorsey on the South Fork of the Salmon in May were instigated by these new additions to the small tribe.

The real Sheepeaters, the old residents, resented Catley's invasion. He was trespassing on *their* country—theirs and their ancestors before them from time immemorial. They fought to repel their invader—and who would not! The attack on Rains was the legitimate sequel to Catley's defeat at Vinegar Hill. The Indians followed him up, found the isolated ranch unprotected and attacked it accordingly.

After the above mistakes and false movements, the several detachments formed junction and pushed toward the Indians, a few of whom had left their stronghold and, probably following up Catley, burned James Rains' ranch, killing the owner August 16 and wounding Albert Webber. James Edwards and Harry Serren (known as "Lemhi") escaped, carrying the news to Warrens.

Pursuant to instructions, Catley now marched to the mouth of Elk Creek, joining Bernard August 11.

⟶⟶ ⧏◊⧐ ⟵⟵

We now come to the *second stage*.

Bernard, Catley, and Farrow were at or near the mouth of Elk Creek, where Surgeon T. E. Wilcox and four men, after a hard trip from Boise Barracks, joined them on the thirteenth, picking up en route a pack mule loaded with 2,000 rounds of ammunition, which Bernard had lost on the tenth. August 13 the scouts started up Elk Creek, followed by the remainder of the command. On the fourteenth the latter camped on the head of Elk Creek, where Capt. A. G. Forse, 1st Cavalry, and Lt. Abner Haines,[5] 2nd Infantry, with 23 men of Company D, 1st Cavalry, from Camp Howard, joined him.

Through Catley's experience, it was now known that the enemy was located on Big Creek somewhere near Vinegar Hill. The command reached the headwaters of Big Creek (probably near the present site of Edwardsburg) August 15. Farrow's scouts proceeded about a march ahead of the main command as an advance guard. There was a dim Indian trail down this creek over which two horsemen had evidently passed about the previous February. The creek runs in a deep canyon its entire length. Frequently it was necessary to march for one or two hundred yards in the bed of the stream three feet or more in depth, covered with boulders, during which the hoofs of the scout ponies, which were unshod, became soft and soon wore down to the quick. This, more than anything else, used up our mounts, so that before the end of the campaign, we were obliged to abandon or shoot twenty of our forty ponies. About every five miles a little clear space with a few abandoned wickiups and a supply of winter fuel would be found, and occasional relatively fresh Indian signs, which became more plentiful as we proceeded down the canyon.

August 17. The scouts reached and camped two miles below the place where Catley's trail came down from the north to Big Creek. As we were apparently getting near the hostiles, Lieutenant Brown, with five scouts, started out at 4:20 P.M. down toward the site of Catley's engagement. They reached the caves about four miles after leaving camp and proceeded about three miles farther, finding salmon traps and plenty of fresh signs. By this time it was very dark, and they bivouacked on the trail.

This advance scouting party started at 2:45 A.M., August 18, and soon came to where Catley had been ambushed. A few hundred yards below here, halt was made in a clear space in the canyon, so narrow and with vertical cliffs towering above so precipitously that the sun set at 2:00 P.M. Here the main scout command came up, and Lieutenant Brown and a couple of scouts reconnoitered about a mile farther. A fresh sign was discovered below here, which caused ten of our scouts to start out August 19 at 2:30 A.M., proceeding only three miles when fired on from the rocks by ten or fifteen dismounted hostiles. On the fire being returned, the enemy ran up a side canyon pursued by our scouts. Meanwhile, Scout Spelia galloped back to camp, yelling: "Heap fight; heap Bannock!" Word was passed on back to Bernard, who, in view of the critical situation, had been closing up and was only two or three miles in the rear. The scouts saddled up and we hurried down the creek in single file as fast as the rough nature of the country permitted. We met our nine scouts where the action had commenced. They had sustained no casualties, except the loss of a horse. Half a mile farther, hostiles were seen on the hills ahead, so we kept on for several miles, and then climbed to a plateau, several acres in extent, with excellent grazing and a good spring. There were ten wickiups here which had been abandoned the day before. This place is now known as Soldier Bar. In the rocks above, the scouts found a number of caches with loot galore, including much which the Sheepeaters had taken at Vinegar Hill after Catley's retreat. The main command soon arrived, having crossed the stream about a dozen times en route, in places three or four feet deep. They camped at Soldier Bar, destroying the Indian village, while Farrow (minus his pack train) turned south up the mountain on the trail of the hostiles, finding more caches containing welcome food supplies. The hostiles were evidently lightening up to facilitate their escape. Subsequently, the whole hostile outit were seen hurrying away about a mile distant. Had our ponies been fresh, we might have captured them, but we were about all in and bivouacked that night near the summit above the snow line by a snowbank. Turning our ponies loose to graze, they naturally wandered off during the night.

August 20. Bernard, from Soldier Bar, ordered Catley back to Smead's ranch for supplies, while he and Forse followed Farrow, leaving all the trains to pack up and follow their respective commands; the latter were several miles from camp, and trains ready to follow them, when suddenly attacked by about fifteen hostiles who had crept down in the rocks above them. The train guards, though taken by surprise, soon repulsed the attack, though Pvt. Harry Eagan, Company G, 2nd Infantry, was shot through both thighs, necessitating amputation. He died under the operation and was buried on the spot. The War Department and his old regiment have (1925) erected a modest monument to mark his grave and the site of the engagement, at which a couple of animals were also killed and several wounded.

The little monument consists of a five-foot pile of boulders, set in cement and surmounted by a soldier's headstone, bearing the inscription, "Harry Eagan, private, Company C, 2nd Infantry. Killed in action here during an attack by Sheepeater Indians on rear guards and pack trains of Companies C, 2nd Infantry, and G and D, 1st Cavalry August 20, 1879." It is probably more remote from civilization, even today, than any similar monument in the United States. The headstone was transported from the nearest railroad station, McCall, on Payette Lake, some seventy miles by wagon and then nearly forty miles by pack mule, to its destination at Soldier Bar.

The firing brought all commands except Farrow back to Soldier Bar, where they remained until August 21, when they resumed the marches ordered for the 20th; Catley [arrived] at Smead's ranch on the twenty-fifth and remained there until the thirtieth. We now return to Farrow, whose scouts, in hunting for their ponies the next day (August 20), found twenty-nine horses and mules abandoned by the hostiles. Shaplish and a few scouts located the hostile camp at daybreak and fired a few shots at them as they fled. One of them threw away a bundle as he escaped, which proved to be the blouse with shoulder straps of one of Catley's lieutenants—Webster. Several caches were found with saddles and a much-needed 100 pounds of flour.

August 21. The scouts got their pack train this morning (civilian scouts, Robbins, and John S. Ramey), brought Farrow news of yesterday's attack on the pack trains. Bernard overtook Farrow, but his animals are fast giving out— lost seven today. A few hostiles seen by Bernard today, as yesterday, but they keep at a respectful distance.

August 22. Command marched only seven (or less) miles, scouts in the lead, toward Middle Fork of Salmon River. A few hostiles seen, but only one near enough to get a shot at him. Snow and rain today. Three more horses shot by Bernard to prevent their falling into hands of the enemy.

August 23. Marched eight miles (or less) over an old trail down a long bunchgrass slope to the Middle Fork, where we found an old winter camp of six lodges. This is just above what we then regarded as an impassable canyon. Bernard and Forse were now practically out of rations. Farrow had possibly enough for five days, except no bacon, which the scouts partly made up by fishing.

August 24. This is the last we are destined to hear of the hostiles for several weeks. Bernard, Forse, and Farrow's commands were all so short of supplies, and their animals so near the point of collapse, that it now becomes a question of getting to rations. Bernard and Forse leave this date for Loon Creek, where Lieutenant Patten had been ordered to meet them with rations from Boise but for some unknown reason was turned off to Warm Lake and did not reach Bernard until the thirty-first. By the night of the August 25, they arrived five miles north of the mouth of Loon Creek, losing six animals en route, only to learn that rations had not arrived; therefore, Forse, on August 26, marches back down the Middle Fork, arriving above Impassable Canyon just as the last of Farrow's men are taking the back trail.

Bernard, as will be seen later, reached his home station (Boise Barracks) September 8. Forse had a veritable starvation march back to Rains' ranch, following about a day behind Farrow, over to Soldier Bar and part of the way up Big Creek, where he fortunately shot a few salmon. A day or two later he met McKeever[6] and Catley with rations for him, and arrived at Rains' ranch September 3, returning to Camp Howard September 13–21.

On August 26 Captain McKeever, with fifteen mounted men of Company K, 2nd Infantry, left Camp Howard with rations, met Catley at Smead's ranch August 30, and assumed command; started up Elk and over onto and down Big Creek, meeting Farrow on the thirty-first and Forse a day or two later. He reached the caves September 4, Rains' ranch the tenth, and Camp Howard a week or more later.

Lieutenant Farrow, on his return march to Smead's ranch, lost twelve animals en route and, but for captured animals and picking up an occasional abandoned horse, would have had men dismounted. He was fortunate on August 27 to secure from hostile caches 100 pounds of flour, 30 pounds of bacon, and some dried salmon. On the thirtieth three scouts failed to get into camp. August 31 only seven or eight scouts arrived. They, however, joined the following day. September 1 Farrow arrived at Smead's.

Turning now to the official reports, General Howard states that Bernard reports from Loon Creek dated August 26:

Since my dispatch of the August 19 and 20, Lieutenant Farrow, with his scouts, has captured thirty-five head of stock from the hostiles and caused them to abandon all their baggage. They escaped down the Middle Salmon Canyon, abandoning everything. The command then turned south for a few miles, when they struck the Middle Salmon, just above what is called the Impassable Canyon. Here I left Lieutenant Farrow with his scouts to look after the Indians, while I, with my company and Captain Forse's twenty-four men, started to the mouth of Loon Creek, twenty miles distant, to meet the supply train.

I then ordered Captain Forse to return to Farrow's camp, when he would assume command of Catley's and Farrow's command and follow the Indians' trail, if possible, as long as his rations would allow him to do so.

Captain Forse's command consists of 103 persons (including Catley and Farrow), packers and all, and has now about eighteen days' provisions; that is, if the train from Camp Howard reaches them.

The hostiles do not exceed thirty warriors and, in my opinion, are short of that number. They are now destitute of everything and are believed by the scouts to be going toward Lemhi. The country they were in when we left the trail was so rough, animals could not be got through it at all. All our stock, except Captain Forse's horses and Farrow's captured stock, are exhausted. Many horses and mules have given out and been shot, and unless we have rest and forage, all will soon give out.

Five days later Bernard says,

The condition of my stock is such that few would be left at the close of the twenty-two days. It is my opinion that it will be both economy and for the interest of the service for this command to go to Boise and refit for the purpose of remaining in the Indian country as long as the Indians do.

A small force of troops should remain near Warrens' until a properly organized force can be sent against the Indians.

The stock of my command is much weaker than I thought they were when I last reported. Will remain in this vicinity until I get an answer.

I [General Howard] had already signified to Captain Bernard that he could best judge of the situation from the field, and also to distribute his command to their proper posts when the object of the expedition had been accomplished.

Fearing after his last dispatch, from the impassable nature of the country and on account of the weak condition of the animals, that I might endanger great loss and cause useless expenditure by an attempt to follow the few scattered Indians further, I sent the following telegram:

Vancouver Barracks, September 2, 1879.

CAPTAIN BERNARD,
      Care of Commanding Officer, Boise Barracks
      Dispatch of August 31 received. If, in your judgment, you have accomplished all you can, you will return with your company to Boise. Instruct Farrow to proceed to Lapwai and report. Send Forse, Catley, and McKeever to Camp Howard; Forse leaving a small guard of mounted men at Warrens. Pitcher can forward his field notes as soon as possible.
                  (Signed) HOWARD, Commanding Department

The expedition has not accomplished what was expected by myself or demanded by your instructions; still, it has revealed a country hitherto quite unknown and opened the way for more intelligent action in the future.

Lieutenant Catley appears to be much to blame for his timid action and hasty retreat for more than 10 miles. He will be given an opportunity to make full explanation.

After the foregoing was written, a missing dispatch from Captain Bernard has since come to hand via Fort Lapwai. From it, I [General Howard] make several extracts which show more effective work than previous reports gave me reason to anticipate.

Camp on Big Creek, ninety miles from Warrens, I.T.,
August 19, 1879

While the scouts were marching along the trail, the Indians fired upon them from the top of a rocky ridge; the scouts returned the fire, charged across the ridge, drove them from their position, and pushed them down the canyon to their camp, which they found deserted. They left much of their provisions, clothing, cooking utensils, skins, etc. They passed over a high, rocky mountain, going southeast, and have set fire to the country in our front and rear. Farrow and his scouts are now on their trail. They have done splendid service. The country is very rough, probably the roughest in the United States.

The Indians have but little stock; much of the property taken from Lieutenant Catley's command was found in the Indians' camp. Lieutenants Farrow and Brown deserve the greatest credit for the bravery and energy displayed since under my command. Their scouts also did splendidly. The entire command was kept close to the scouts during the chase.

Captain Forse's twenty-four men and Farrow's scouts will follow the Indians' trail as long as it continues toward Loon Creek, when we will go to the mouth of that stream and get supplies, then will again take up the trail, wherever it may go.

Farrow has just sent a report that the Indians are in full retreat, abandoning property all along the trail!

August 20, 1879. Just after the commands had moved out of camp this morning, and just as the pack train was moving out, the Indians fired on the rear guard and pack train from the rocks close by.

The Indians were soon dislodged and driven away after the commands returned. The Indians did not exceed ten or fifteen.

Acting on the above authority [from General Howard], Bernard returned to his home station, Boise Barracks, on September 8. He had been out since May 31, marched 1,168 miles, mostly over unexplored mountains, losing forty-five pack mules and eighteen horses, enduring hardships from snow and hunger seldom met with, even in those days. Surely no troop could have done more, and few as much.

Farrow now determined to make a final effort to strike the hostiles another blow, though the taking of an account of stock at this time would not appear encouraging. Half of our cayuse ponies were gone. We had, it is true, captured some stock and picked up a number of abandoned animals on our return from Middle Fork, but these, almost without exception, were played-out stock and not dependable for hard work. Lieutenant Farrow had an abundance of initiative, was very energetic, resourceful, and not deterred, though both the country and strength of the enemy were unknown. The scouts deserve more than passing notice. Sergeant Ya-tin-ow-itz was the war chief of the Cayuses and son-in-law of chief Howlish Wampo, who owned several thousand cayuse ponies. Ya-tin-ow-itz therefore started for the campaign with five selected ponies. Sergeant Shaplish (Whirlwind) spoke a little English, was of the Fenimore Cooper type, and as handsome a warrior as ever wore moccasins. Whenever there was a difficult piece of scouting to be done, Shaplish was usually selected to do it. Corporal Wah-tis-kow-kow's knowledge of Shoshone enabled him to assist materially at the surrender of Tamanmo, or War Jack, in which he took risks which should have won him a decoration. Lack of space prevents individual mention of others here. The Indian is more expert at hunting and fishing than the white man, an important consideration when the regular rations run short, which was frequently our misfortune.

Lieutenant Brown was sent September 2 to Camp Howard on a hurried mission, making a ride of about sixty-two miles in one day with dispatches, charged with securing supplies and, if possible, mounts to continue operations.

The best that could be done in that line was to charter Benson's pack train. Horses were promised from Fort Walla Walla, but they never came. On September 12 Farrow planned to go in for a week or more with ten of the best scouts and best horses, and a couple of packs. This plan, however, was wisely subsequently changed to leave two soldiers and three scouts at Smith's on the South Fork in charge of the weaker animals, so that we had really a strength of twenty-three men, including packers.

On September 17 we left Rains' ranch, following Catley's original trail until the afternoon of the twentieth, when we left it, striking out east and north for the section south of Salmon and west of the Middle Fork. Fortune smiled on us, for before noon the next day, we came on a party of two squaws, a papoose, and two boys about eight and seventeen years old. We took them in, except the older boy, who, though hotly pursued, made his escape.

Farrow made a short stop, while I took ten scouts and, going forward, soon struck fresh signs in shape of two recently occupied camps and the trail of a hunting party of about eight men (four of them mounted) heading north. Farrow, with the remainder of the command, overtook us at sundown, just as we arrived at the north edge of the general plateau overlooking the main Salmon, apparently about ten miles distant.

About dark, leaving here our packs and horses, and each taking a blanket or overcoat, we started on the trail afoot, losing it, as I had predicted, after going about two miles. We then made for a ridge about half a mile distant and, on reaching it, heard a dog bark about three-quarters of a mile distant. Scouts were sent out to more definitely locate the camp, while we waited, suffering considerably from the cold.

Starting again about 1:30 A.M., Farrow and I each took half our force and made our way stealthily to the camp, surrounding it at daylight. As we gradually closed in, we could see four horses and the place where the camp ought to be, but no fires—the Sheepeaters had escaped! The hostiles, realizing that the barking of the dog had revealed to us their whereabouts, had put out their fire, left four of their horses, stabbing one in the shoulder with a butcher knife, leaving the knife in, so the horse had to be shot. They had here about 600 pounds of meat, partly cured. Our pack train and prisoners, some four miles distant, were sent for. We spent the remainder of the day alternately sleeping and feasting on venison and elk meat. Shaplish was sent out with a white flag and with one of the squaws to induce the hostiles to come in for a parley. Poem and To-it-akas found the trail of several horse and foot tracks leading east. About two miles from camp, the dog whose barking had revealed to us their camp was found hanged directly over the trail, where we would be sure to see it. The dog had paid the supreme penalty for his watchfulness and for giving the alarm. It is possible, too, that the boy who had escaped may have reached the camp and warned them.

━•━ ≍✦≍ ━•━

On September 23 we started out on the trail, which took us in a complete circle to a fine meadow on our trail of the twenty-first. Here we made a base camp about eight miles west of Middle Fork, started civilian scout Bright and Private Smith to Warrens with dispatches and for flour and fifteen horses. After dark, leaving campfires burning brightly to indicate presence of the full command, Farrow and myself, with sixteen of the command, taking with us the squaw who had the papoose, started again on the trail.

The following day we camped in a gulch now marked on maps as Papoose Gulch, so called because the papoose of the squaw whom we sent out to bring in her people, retaining the papoose to ensure her return, kept the entire camp awake with its wailing. We discovered en route a lake to the north of us. Two camps, each several days old and each containing four to six lodges, were found. The squaw failed to get us in touch with her people, and we returned to our base camp on the twenty-fifth.

About two hours after we returned, we were startled by a loud yell in the timber half a mile from camp, and soon we discovered a hostile who evidently wanted to parley. Lieutenant Brown and Wah-tis-kow-kow left camp and approached him, but he moved, so that they, in following his movements, were soon out of sight of camp. When within 100 yards, it was discovered that he had a rifle, and he was warned that as we were unarmed he must drop it. He then asked who Lieutenant Brown was, and Wah-tis-kow-kow replied that he was the tenas tyee (little chief). Our scouts subsequently said that had the reply been "hyas tyee" (head chief), he would have shot us, as he might easily have done, and made his escape. However, he left his Henry rifle, approached, shook hands, and was brought into camp to Farrow. During the parley in camp, we discovered at his back a revolver which he had failed to leave with the rifle. There he said his name was Tamanmo (or War Jack), part Bannock and part Nez Perce, and successor to Chief Eagle Eye. He said that he was at the Malheur agency when the Bannock War broke out and, not being able to get back to Fort Hall, had participated in the outbreak and subsequently joined his friends here. He was tired of fighting and wanted to quit. He had crept down in the bushes last night close to our camp, and so learned that our Indians were Cayuses. He said that he and four others had planned to steal some of our horses tonight; therefore, we should guard them well. Farrow told him to go out and bring in his people, that it must be an unconditional surrender, [and] that no one not guilty of murder would be harmed. Tamanmo wanted a fresh horse, saying he had two played-out horses hid nearby in the timber. He was given one, and when his two jaded horses were driven in, either better than the one he got, we knew he would play fair.

Tamanmo said that part of the hostiles were at the mouth of Big Creek, and that he would either have them in or come himself tomorrow. Kept white flag out today and put on a strong guard at night.

September 26. Remained in camp. Tamanmo, with a Weiser named Buoyer, came in under white flag for a talk. Tamanmo, who has only been here about a year, is not well conversant with the country and had not succeeded in finding his people; says there are nine men with their families near here who belong here and know the country. The mother of the children whom we got on the twenty-first is Buoyer's squaw. Another party, consisting of twelve men, women, and children, are scattered through the country near here, and all are to be hunted up. Buoyer went out again, leaving his gun in camp. Courier David R. Monroe left for Warrens with dispatches for General Howard stating Indians were suing for peace, and if we failed to collect them all, we would start in again.

September 27. In camp. Considerable rain today. White flag still out. Command placed on half rations pending receipt of supplies from Warrens. September 28. Still in camp. Rain, sleet, and hard snowstorm. Night cold and hard on animals. September 29. Still in camp. Snow melting off slowly. Later learned that Captain Winters, 1st Cavalry, had left Camp Howard via Elk City for Mallard Bar on account of report of fifteen Indians seen near there.

September 30. Marched twenty miles (or less), camping where Lieutenant Brown left Farrow to go scouting in advance on the twenty-first. Buoyer came in.

October 1, marched five miles and camped where we halted on twenty-first ultimo, where the creek turns to the east. Snow last night and rain nearly all day today. Tamanmo, with another Indian (Weiser), came in this morning ahead of four lodges, consisting of eight men and twenty-four squaws and papooses (nearly all Sheepeaters), and doing justice to the occasion by liberal use of feathers and paint. A few still are out. Farrow is to wait a few days for Buoyer to bring them in. The muster roll reports thirty-nine surrendered up to this date. Later surrenders increased this to fifty-one, of whom fifteen may be classed as warriors. Their arms October 1 consisted of two Henry carbines; one Sharp's carbine; one Springfield carbine, caliber .45; one Springfield breech-loading rifle, caliber .50; two muzzle-loading rifles; and one double-barreled shotgun.

The aggressive part of the campaign being at an end, Farrow thought best to send Lieutenant Brown to Warrens in advance of the main party, carrying dispatches and arranging for rations and forage. The command was nearly out of rations; moreover, it was incumbent on us now to feed the prisoners. Captain Forse and Lieutenant Muhlenberg, with twenty-four men, had left camp Howard the previous day (September 30) with rations which reached Warrens about October 6 or 7. The matter of supply, etc., rendered it advisable that the prisoners be taken back via Camp Howard, Forts Lapwai [and] Walla Walla, and Umatilla agency. They arrived at the latter place in due time. Farrow and his scouts were justly given an enthusiastic reception by the Indians, as well as by the citizens of the nearby town of Pendleton. The scouts were furloughed from November 6 until December 9, their date of discharge, while the prisoners were taken by Lieutenant Farrow to Vancouver Barracks, and the following year they were sent to the Fort Hall, Idaho, reservation.

Meanwhile, Lieutenant Brown received orders from Farrow to return to the Umatilla agency via Indian and Council Valleys, proceeding to the Crooked River country en route, and to make a careful observation of the country thereabouts, reporting as to recent signs of Indians; also to permit citizens desirous of accompanying him to search for lost or stolen stock.

Lieutenant Brown left with three of the scouts and five of the detachment October 7 via Payette Lakes and Little Salmon Meadows, stopping at Grosclose ranch on Cottonwood Creek. There were no civilians who cared to go to Crooked River after horse thieves, but it was Lieutenant Brown's duty to go as far toward Crooked River as was physically possible in order to observe and report. This could be done with a single orderly as well as [if] escorted by the entire detachment, as the probabilities of finding anything were very remote. Taking, therefore, Private Ward, he left October 11, marched eighteen miles up Hornet Creek the twelfth, and the next day made fifteen miles, when the depth of snow became so great that the trail could no longer be followed, so he turned back five miles and camped, returning on the thirteenth. It had started to rain, which soon turned to snow, shortly after their departure on the eleventh. They had no transportation and came near perishing. It was the hardest trip of the entire summer. Homeward march was then resumed, and Umatilla agency reached October 22, 1879.

The department commander's appreciation of the services of the scouts was shown in the following appendix to his annual report:

(TELEGRAM)
Vancouver Barracks, Wash., Oct. 9, 1879.
ADJUTANT GENERAL,
 Military Division Pacific,
  Presidio, San Francisco
My Annual Report indicated a failure in the main object of the expedition against the Sheepeaters and renegades located between the Little Salmon and Snake Rivers.

Now it is reversed, and the expedition has handsomely been completed by Lieutenant Farrow and his scouts, having defeated the Indians in two skirmishes, capturing their camp, with stores and stock. He has finally forced the entire band to surrender and will deliver them as prisoners of war at this post.

Lieutenants Farrow, 21st Infantry, and W. C. Brown, 1st Cavalry, with their seven enlisted men, citizen employees, and Indian scouts, deserve special mention for gallantry, energy, and perseverance, resulting in success. There is not a rougher or more difficult country for campaigning in America.

Please add this to my report.
     HOWARD, Commanding Department

Lieutenants Farrow and Brown were each subsequently awarded (February 27, 1890) the brevet of first lieutenant for this service.

Any narrative of mountain campaigning such as this would be incomplete without reference to the splendid services of the civilian guides, couriers, and packers, not only in this, but in the two previous campaigns of 1877 and 1878, whose work calls for physical qualities and endurance of the highest order. Guides and couriers are daily called upon to take their lives in their hands in the performance of their duties, and it is unfortunate that our pension laws make no provisions for any of the above three classes. When away from the command, their food and bedding must be carried on the saddle, and their movements are necessarily largely restricted to trails which hostiles can easily watch, and where with safety to themselves they [the hostiles] can lie in ambush. In operations on the plains, these men usually travel by night, something ordinarily impracticable in a little known mountainous section. The packer must habitually be up long before daylight, pack his mules with ropes stiff with frost, and it is worthy of note here that in Bernard's command, Hoffner's diary mentions no less than thirty-seven of the marching days in this (midsummer) campaign when they were obliged to contend with snow, occasionally freshly fallen, but usually old drifts twenty to thirty feet deep.

The pack train necessarily occupies so much space in the column that as a rule, it trusts to luck that it may not be attacked, for the few men who can be spared for a guard could offer but little resistance to a determined assault by hostiles eager to secure the rich plunder carried by every military train. In our little commands that summer, as well as in the Indian campaigns of 1877 and 1878, the work and risks were such that the writer feels that the state of Idaho should hold in grateful remembrance the services of such men as Orlando ("Rube") Robbins, John S. Ramey, Geo. Shearer, Bright, Josh Falkner, Calvin R. White, Levi A. White, David R. Monroe, Johnny Bose, the Parker brothers, J. W. Redington, Jake Barnes, John Corliss, Alexander Foster, Harry Serren (Lemhi), and Uncle Dave ("Cougar") Lewis, who still lives in Big Creek, only a mile or two above the scene of the fight of August 20, 1879, and others whose names we cannot now recall.

The Sheepeater Campaign

CHARLES B. HARDIN

Journal of the Military Service Institution of the United States 47 (1910): 25–40

The days of campaigning against hostile Indians are past. Nearly all of our Indian campaigns have been written up, either by those who have taken part in them, or by professional writers who, in many cases, have added the embellishments necessary to make their stories commercially valuable. Almost nothing is known of the Sheepeater campaign of 1878 in middle Idaho, and but few people have ever heard of it. It took place in a section of Idaho which was very properly marked on the Department of Interior maps of that day as unexplored.

Hoping that the story of this campaign may be of interest to the friends of the army, and particularly to the few survivors of the campaign, the writer, who participated in the campaign as a corporal in Troop G, 1st Cavalry, has, with the aid of such data as he has been able to collect, and from personal recollections, attempted the task.

The band of Indians known as Sheepeaters was originally formed by outcasts from the Bannock and Shoshone tribes. Many years ago it was the custom of the Bannocks and Shoshones to meet each year in the neighborhood of the present site of Fort Hall, Idaho, to trade and gamble. These tribes were very friendly with each other, but this friendship was not strong enough to interfere with tribal pride, which would not countenance marriage between the tribes. But Cupid, who delights in interference with all laws and customs, was busy at these meetings, and the result was that in spite of the rulings of the elders, an occasional young buck of one tribe would find himself unable to resist the charms of a maiden of the other tribe and would steal and run off with his sweetheart. All who thus offended were repudiated by both tribes and became outcasts. Banding together, they took up their abode in the rough country about the South and Middle Forks of the Salmon River, where they were from time to time reinforced by who had in like manner offended their tribes. These Indians were known to placer miners as early as 1862. So far as I can learn, they led a lazy, peaceful life until after the close of the Bannock War of 1878, when they were joined by some bad Bannocks who had taken part in that war, and their troubles began.

Early in the spring of 1879, the Indian agent at Lemhi, Idaho, reported to the commanding general, Division of the Pacific, that five Chinamen had been murdered in February of that year at Oro Grande, a deserted mining camp on Loon Creek, about eighty miles northeast of Boise, Idaho, and that he supposed this murder had been done by some of the hostiles of the Bannock War who had been wintering with the Sheepeaters. This report was communicated to the commanding general, Department of the Columbia (General Howard), with orders for him to send a detachment of troops from Boise Barracks, Idaho, to ascertain who the murderers were and, if Indians, to apprehend and bring them to Boise. At the suggestion of General Howard, he was later authorized to send another detachment from Camp Howard, Idaho, as soon as the condition of the trails would permit. Accordingly, on May 7, 1879, General Howard sent orders to the commanding officer, Boise Barracks, directing him to send out Troop G, 1st Calvary—Capt. R. E. Bernard commanding—starting it on about June 1, the troop to proceed to Challis and operate from that point upon any information obtainable. At the same time, the commanding officer, District of the Clearwater, was directed to send about the same force (about fifty men) from Camp Howard toward Challis, to form a junction with Bernard as soon as possible. In his orders General Howard stated that it was his intention that when the two commands came together, Bernard being the ranking officer, the command should devolve upon him.

In compliance with these orders, Troop G, 1st Cavalry, about fifty men under Captain Bernard, and 2nd Lt. John Pitcher left Boise Barracks about the last of May; and a detachment of the 2nd Infantry, mounted and numbering about fifty men, under 1st Lt. Henry Catley, with Lieutenants E. K. Webster and W. C. Muhlenberg, 2nd Infantry, were ordered out from Camp Howard.

Bernard soon found that he had started too early. For when he reached Cape Horn Valley, he found that he was forty-eight hours ahead of his pack train, which was stuck in the snow. Here, at Camp Starvation, as it was called, the men who had not been sent back to assist in pulling the pack train out of the snow spent their time at tightening their belts and vainly hunting for game.

Having passed this point, Bernard moved on to Oro Grande, encountering more deep, soft snow en route but getting through with less difficulty. Finding no fresh signs of Indians at Oro Grande, he attempted to follow an old trail which led down Loon Creek; but heavy rains and melting snow had made a mighty river of this usually small stream, and as the trail down the canyon crossed and recrossed the creek many times in the distance to be covered in a day's march, and it was impossible to follow these crossings with the pack train, he was compelled to leave the creek and climb over the mountains. Thus he escaped danger from water, but only to encounter other difficulties almost as great. For, of course, there were no trails; the mountains were very rough and, in many places, covered with fallen timber on the slopes and deep snow on the summits. The wear on the pack mules was tremendous. After floundering about through the mountains for several days, finding no fresh Indian signs, Bernard returned to Cape Horn Valley, from which point he sent his pack train to Boise for rations.

From Cape Horn, Bernard reported to General Howard as follows:

> The country is, no doubt, as rough as any in the United States, and to get the Indians will be a work of great difficulty. Should they discover us before we do them, they can hide in the timbered, rocky mountains for a long time, and go from point to point much faster than we can, even if we knew where to go. We have traveled over much country that no white man ever saw before, old guides and miners declaring that we could not get through at all.

Indeed, Bernard had found some rough country; but it was nothing as compared with what he was to encounter later on in that unexplored region. Upon receipt of Bernard's description of the country, General Howard ordered Lt. E. S. Farrow, 21st Infantry, with his scouts, recently enlisted at the Umatilla agency, to take the field, crossing the Snake River at Brownlee's Ferry, with instructions to form a junction with the other troops as soon as possible.

An incident is related by one of the officers, which occurred as the scouts were leaving their reservation, which shows on the part of the red men an affection for their families, which those not acquainted with the Indian character would hardly suspect. Young Chief, one of the principal braves of the tribe, asked, as most of the scouts were enlisted from this camp, that the command stop there in passing to allow good-byes to be said, and his request was approved. As the column halted, the scouts of their own motion formed line, and Young Chief made them a farewell address and took occasion to hope that the officers would see that their men had enough to eat and wear at all times during the coming campaign, something, it is to be regretted, they found impossible to do. Then the chief, followed by his braves, shook hands all along the line, commencing with the officer. Then came the squaws with their papooses on their backs, taking care that each papoose placed its tiny, brown hand in that of the officer. As their families passed along the line, these stalwart braves, usually so stoical, could not conceal their emotions, and tears streamed down their cheeks as they realized the seriousness of the step they were taking, and that many moons must pass before they should see their squaws and papooses again.

Farrow had with him 2nd Lt. W. C. Brown, 1st Cavalry, seven enlisted men of the 21st Infantry, and twenty Umatilla Indians, all mounted. These two energetic young officers had used excellent judgment in selecting the soldiers and Indians to make up their organization, which, though small, was very efficient, as shall be seen later on.

These twenty Indian scouts were the pick of the Umatilla tribe, mounted on hardy little cayuse ponies selected from the countless herds then roaming over the Umatilla reservation—forty ponies for the twenty scouts. The head sergeant was Ya-tin-ow-itz, the war chief of the Umatillas. He was a grave, dignified Indian of the Fenimore Cooper type, whose word, on account of his tribal position, was law with other members of the band, and whose experience as a warrior was such that the young lieutenants commanding the detachment were glad to defer to his judgment in the trying situations in which they were placed at various times during the campaign.

Farrow's scouts left the Umatilla agency on July 1, crossed Snake River by swimming their herd near Brownlee's Ferry, and arrived at Upper Payette Lake July 19, where, learning that Indian sign had been seen near the headwaters of Crooked River in the Seven Devils Mountains, the detachment spent ten days of hard marching in that excessively rough country but found nothing.

On August 3 Farrow sent out another party to scout Long Valley and, on the same date, got in communication with Bernard, who was heading in that direction from Warrens, being lured by a report that Farrow was on the trail of a band of hostiles that had a large number of horses. Farrow had learned that this trail had not been made by Indians and had sent this information to Bernard, who, however, did not receive it until he had marched some seventy miles in what afterward proved to be the wrong direction.

About this time, Bernard received the first news of Lieutenant Catley, commanding the detachment sent out from Camp Howard. This officer had left Camp Howard on time as directed, proceeding as far as Warrens, where he was stopped by deep snow, and where he remained until the latter part of June. By July 11 he had succeeded in getting as far as the mouth of the South Fork of the Salmon, from which point he worked his way eastward over a very rough country to Big Creek, a tributary to the Middle Fork of the Salmon. Here, finding a fresh trail, he followed it down the creek, through a deep and rocky canyon, and on July 29 fell into an ambuscade, from which he felt obliged to retire with a loss of two men wounded. The Indians who attacked him probably numbered fifteen warriors. Falling back to his pack train, he started to climb out of the canyon, but the hostiles surrounded him on what was then named Vinegar Hill (prominently marked on recent maps of Idaho, though it is not a prominent peak), from which point, after being cut off from water for many hours, and after the Indians had made a fruitless effort to burn him out, he escaped in the night with the loss of the greater part of his baggage and rations and sixteen pack mules lost in the darkness. He then took up his march for Camp Howard, sending on ahead his report of the affair to Colonel Wheaton, commanding the District of the Clearwater, who, upon receipt of the report ordered Capt. A. G. Forse, with twenty-five men of his Troop D, 1st Cavalry, to reinforce Catley and stop the retreat.

Lieutenant Catley had been most unfortunate, but he had accomplished one very important piece of work. He had found the Indians.

A hot trail. RUFUS F. ZOGBAUM. HORSE, FOOT, AND DRAGOON.

Upon learning of Catley's defeat, Bernard sent orders directing that officer and Captain Forse to meet him at the mouth of Elk Creek, South Fork of
the Salmon; and having been joined by Farrow at Warm Springs, North Fork
of [the] Payette River, on August 6 he started for Elk Creek, trying a shortcut
across the mountains where there was no trail, and which proved to be disastrous to his saddle and pack animals, many of the latter being lost en route.

The mountains of Idaho are grand and beautiful but cannot be thoroughly
enjoyed by those who are compelled to cross them by forced marches and with
exhausted animals. The mounted troops usually made their day's march by

about noon—always before nightfall—but they usually had to wait in camp until late at night for the arrival of the pack train with provisions and bedding. Grass was scarce, and the poor animals had but little time in which to gather what there was of it. The result of this march was that Bernard's transportation was a wreck when he arrived at the mouth of Elk Creek.

Here he rested a day before pushing out into the terra incognita. Nearly two weeks before, he had sent in to Boise Barracks for a medical officer, and Assistant Surgeon Timothy E. Wilcox (now brigadier general, U.S.A., retired) was sent with a couple of guides and a few enlisted men to join the command. They expected to join Bernard in three days and were rationed accordingly. Bernard had changed his camp in the meanwhile, and guides sent to intercept Wilcox failed to find him, with the result that the latter's party marched some eight days before reaching the command on the twelfth.

They had eaten the last of their rations several days before and subsisted upon grizzly bear, salmon, and deer, which they were lucky enough to secure.

The various commands having assembled at Elk Creek, the expedition on August 13 started after the Sheepeaters. The entire march of the first day was made up the side of a mountain, so steep that it could be climbed only by making a zigzag trail. The distance marched was probably not more than eight miles, but it took the entire day in which to make it. On the second day the divide was crossed, and the command camped near the head of Big Creek. This stream was followed during the next five days along an old Indian trail, which crossed and recrossed the creek many times in the distance covered by a day's march. In many places, and for considerable distances, neither bank could be traversed, the command being obliged to march in the bed of the creek over rough boulders. Here in this deep canyon, we had sunset at 2:00 P.M. The Indians must have wondered at the nerve of white men who would attempt such a march with a pack train over such a trail. Evidently they were not looking for the accomplishment of such a feat, as there was no evidence that they were observing the invaders. During these days, Farrow and Brown, with the scouts, kept one day's march in advance of the main body of troops.

On the nineteenth the scouts drew the fire of the hostiles at a point a few miles below the scene of Catley's affair. This was what the scouts wanted, and they rushed the hostiles at once, charging their camp in fine style, and so quickly that they were glad to escape with their lives. Their camp was captured, and with it a number of caches, in which were found a quantity of rations and baggage which had been captured from Catley. In this rather brilliant affair, the scouts did not lose a man. In his report of this action, Captain Bernard said:

> While the scouts were marching along the trail, the Indians fired upon them from the top of a rocky ridge. The scouts returned the fire, charged across the ridge, drove them from their position, and pursued them down the canyon to their camp, which they found deserted. They left much of their provisions, clothing, cooking utensils, skins,

etc. They passed over a high, rocky mountain, going southeast, and have set fire to the country in our front and rear. Farrow and his scouts are now on their trail. They have done splendid service. The country is very rough, probably the roughest in the United States. The Indians have but little stock. Much of the property taken from Lieutenant Catley's command was found in the Indians' camp. Lieutenants Farrow and Brown deserve the greatest credit for bravery and energy displayed since under my command. Their scouts also did splendidly.

Bernard came up that evening and went into camp in the captured stronghold, which was located on a shelf of the mountain about 500 feet above the bed of the creek. This shelf contained about five or six acres of ground, covered with good grass. At one end were some trees and a fine spring of water. It was an ideal stronghold. On the morning of August 20, the command separated, Catley starting back toward Warrens to meet a train with rations now much needed by all, while Bernard and Forse moved out on the trail taken by Farrow's scouts in pursuit of the hostiles. Each separate command left camp before its pack train was ready to start, leaving a small rear guard to accompany the train. Bernard's rear guard consisted of a corporal and six privates, while Catley's rear guard consisted of a sergeant and six privates. The troops had been gone nearly an hour, and the trains were about ready to start, when the hostiles, perhaps twelve to fifteen in number, having doubled back to a bluff overlooking the camp, and about sixty feet above it, opened fire on the rear guards. One private of Catley's command was fatally shot, and the remainder of this detachment, headed by the sergeant, promptly stampeded. Bernard's men held together and, by a flanking movement up the side of the mountain, which movement was executed under fire from some of the soldiers who had stampeded, as well as from the hostiles, drove the latter off without further loss. In this affair the chief packer, Jake Barnes, showed up splendidly. Having moved his train to a sheltered position, under a heavy fire he recrossed the exposed ground, bringing ammunition to the troops engaged, and then, securing a rifle which had been thrown away by one of the stampeding men, he approached the corporal and, awkwardly executing the rifle salute, said with a laugh, "I want some of this myself. Pvt. Barnes reports for duty, sir." This had an excellent effect upon the men, who were naturally somewhat shaken by having seen half their number run away.

The firing in this little affair brought back Bernard and Catley; but when they arrived, the fight was over. This last statement is recorded because, probably through a typographical error, Bernard's report was made to read, "The Indians were soon dislodged and driven away after the commands returned."

The wounded man died that day, after having one leg amputated, and was buried near the camp.

The troops remained in this camp until the following morning, when they again separated, Catley to return to Warrens for rations, and Bernard and Forse making for the mouth of Loon Creek, where they expected to meet rations from Boise. Fourteen mules gave out and were shot on this day, during the hard climb out of Big Creek Canyon.

Bernard climbed the mountain and overtook the scouts that evening, August 21, and learned that during that day and the one previous, the scouts had picked up twenty-eight head of stock abandoned by the hostiles. During this and the following days, several hostiles were seen at a distance, but there was no fighting. It was evident that the enemy had scattered. The scouts remained with Bernard until the twenty-fourth, when the command separated near Impassable Canyon, Middle Fork of the Salmon, Bernard and Forse starting up the river for the mouth of Loon Creek, leaving Farrow and Brown to hunt the Indians.

Arriving at the mouth of Loon Creek and not finding the rations, Forse was sent back to meet Catley, who was to bring rations into the Big Creek country, while Bernard proceeded up Loon Creek in search of his missing train, his command being without food for three days before game of any kind could be found. Finally, one afternoon, some salmon were discovered and shot. The command went into camp at once, and the salmon were quickly devoured, without salt or bread. Some of the men were able to hold this load down, but many could not. Here the brave Jake Barnes again came to the front. Selecting two of his best pack mules, he made a wonderfully quick trip to Bonanza, a mining camp, where he secured provisions sufficient to keep down hunger for two days, by the expiration of which time the long-looked-for pack train from Boise was met. Bernard's animals being unfit for further field service, and his men in rags, he proceeded toward Boise as far as the Payette River, from which point he reported to General Howard, who, in a dispatch dated August 31, authorized his return to Boise Barracks.

The scouts under Farrow and Brown remained in camp near Impassable Canyon until August 26, sending out small parties to look for signs of hostiles and vainly endeavoring to open communication with them by means of a flag of truce. On the afternoon of the 26th, they started back on the old trail toward Warrens, and in quest of much-needed rations. Forse, returning from Bernard's command, entered the camp just as Farrow was leaving it. His command also was out of rations, and he was making for Warrens.

Farrow, returning via the old camp of the hostiles, was fortunate in finding, on the twenty-seventh, four more caches containing flour, bacon, soap, tobacco, dried salmon, blankets, and clothing, all of which (excepting the salmon) had been captured from Catley's command in July. He also found some stray cavalry horses but had to abandon several of his own animals. With great difficulty, owing to the condition of his animals, he continued his march with little to eat, abandoning and shooting exhausted animals, and picking up others which had been abandoned by other troops, until August 31, when he met Captain McKeever, 2nd Infantry, who had taken over the late command of Catley and was taking rations out to Forse, still somewhere in rear. Farrow secured three days' rations from McKeever and, on the same date, reached the head of Elk Creek. He arrived at Smead's ranch on the South Fork of the Salmon River on September 1, and on the following day Lieutenant Brown started for Camp Howard, bearing dispatches for the department commander. He arrived at Camp Howard on the fourth, received a reply to his dispatches on the seventh, and at once loaded a pack train with supplies and started back to Farrow's camp at Smead's ranch. He reported to Farrow on September 10 with orders from General Howard to complete the campaign. The pack train did not reach Farrow's camp until the afternoon of the fifteenth.

On September 16 Farrow again started out in search of the hostiles, marching via Rains' ranch and Chamberlain Creek, following the trail made by Lieutenant Catley when that officer first entered this section.

On the twenty-first instant two squaws, one small boy, and a papoose were captured and a trail discovered leading toward Salmon River, on which a small party was sent as a sort of advance on guard. They soon struck the trail of a small hunting party of the hostiles, which was followed, and at sunset they reached a ridge overlooking the canyon of Salmon River.

Evidently the hostile camp was not far distant. The remainder of the scouts having joined, a dry camp was made at which the prisoners and all impedimenta having been left under guard, the officers and about fifteen scouts started down on the trail, which led for some two miles over exceedingly rough country to a ridge. No sooner had they reached this ridge than the barking of a dog about three-fourths of a mile distant indicated the location of the camp. The party then halted, and two of the best scouts were sent to crawl up to the hostile camp, the fire of which could plainly be seen, and plans were made for an attack at daybreak.

It was a bitterly cold night, and no fires of course could be made; the party simply must shiver and await the return about midnight of the scouts, who had located the camp perfectly in a little, open valley, with their horses picketed about the campfire.

At 1:00 A.M. the party started, treading their way as softly as possible through the fallen timber and undergrowth. When near the camp they divided, each officer taking half the scouts and so disposing of them in extended order to make the escape of any hostile impossible. Orders were given to close in and open fire at daybreak. The campfire was no longer visible, but the horses could be seen, and at the first break of day, the lines closed in with every eye strained to catch a glimpse of the enemy. Nearer and nearer they closed in; the camp was there—but the hostiles had fled.

Some time between midnight and dawn, they had in some way been apprised of the coming of the scouts, and hastily extinguishing their fire by throwing water on it, and stabbing their ponies, they had hurriedly left. The last poor brute which had been stabbed had the six-inch butcher knife thrust to the hilt still sticking in his side. They had taken this means of disabling the animals rather than killing them, hoping that our people would leave them.

The hostiles had left five or six hundred pounds of partly cured elk meat and four horses. Having spent the previous night in reconnaissance, the command rested on the twenty-second, sending out one Umatilla scout and one of the captured squaws with a white flag to endeavor to communicate with the hostiles. Another scout found the trail of the hostiles leading eastward. He also found the carcass of the dog which had, by his barking, betrayed them. The dog had been hanged for his crime. On the twenty-third Farrow sent back two men for a doctor, more flour, and some horses, while he and Brown, with thirteen scouts, followed the hostiles. On September 24, with the assistance of a captured squaw, they found the trail, and on the same date found two small camps of from four to six lodges about three or four days old. A squaw was sent out to look for her people, she leaving her papoose with the scouts. She returned on the morning of the twenty-fifth, having found nothing, and was again sent out.

Matters seemed almost hopeless, but they say the darkest hour is just before dawn. Within two hours of their return on the twenty-fifth from a fruitless scout, the camp was startled by a shrill war whoop about half a mile distant in the open timber.

Careful search with field glasses finally revealed the Indian half concealed behind a tree. Taking Corporal Wah-tis-kow-kow, who could speak a little Shoshone, Brown advanced armed to meet the Indian, at the same time making peace signs. The Indian changed his location, and soon all were out of sight of camp, close to a large area of underbrush.

When within about 100 yards, Brown discovered that the Indian had a rifle and motioned him to leave it. After some parleying with Wah-tis-kow-kow as to who Brown was, and finding him only the second in command, the Indian complied, a fortunate thing for him, for the scouts said that had he been the chief officer, the Indian would doubtless have shot him.

When he squatted down to leave his rifle, he carefully adjusted his revolver at his back out of sight but within easy reach—he proposed to take no more chances than necessary. He was a Bannock who had taken part in the war of 1878. He said he was tired of fighting and wanted to quit. He had been near enough to Farrow's camp during the previous night to hear the scouts talking. This Indian was sent out to bring in his people, and he returned on the following morning, bringing in another Bannock and reporting that he had been unable to find the others. Farrow remained in one camp from September 26–30, flying a white flag over his camp. On the twenty-eighth a severe sleet and snowstorm came to remind the scouts that it was near the time to end the campaign.

It rained and snowed (mostly snow) for the next four days. Rations were getting so low that the command was placed on half rations. Their only tents were shelter halves, which by this time were worn full of holes.

Fortunately, the hostiles were not aware of the fact that snow and hunger must soon drive the scouts out of these mountains, on the trail for the nearest supplies. In fact, it was a question of soon getting out or of wintering in the

Reading the orders. OUTING MAGAZINE, 1887.

Salmon River Canyon, living on the game that abounded in this section and which, driven from the high mountains, came down along the streams to feed.

On October 1 a Bannock who had been sent out returned, bringing in nine bucks, twenty-four squaws and papooses, and eight guns. Four more bucks and enough squaws and papooses to swell the number of captives to fifty-one came in during the next day or two, and as these were all who could be located, Farrow started homeward.

On October 2, with a small detachment, Lieutenant Brown left Farrow, proceeding to Warrens, where he arrived on the third. Here he remained until the arrival of Farrow, pushing out horses and rations and attending to everything necessary the way of assisting Farrow. Upon the arrival of Farrow at Warrens, with his detachment Brown set out for the Crooked River country to hunt for horse thieves. He scouted the Crooked River country and Council Valley and other localities, finding no horse thieves or any evidence that horses had been recently stolen. This extra work had been thrust upon the scouts by reckless rumors. Not many white men had been encountered by the troops in the field, but the few who were seen seemed to be loaded with information concerning Indians and horse thieves, none of which information had any foundation in fact. Having finished his scouting, Brown proceeded to the Umatilla agency, arriving on October 22. Moving as rapidly as possible with his prisoners, Farrow came onto Umatilla agency, where he was given grand reception by the Umatillas and the citizens of Pendleton, Oregon, and later he delivered his prisoners at Vancouver Barracks. The campaign had been thoroughly completed.

This is the story of the Sheepeater campaign. Of course, the writer could have filled in with many stories of swimming of rivers; of the wonderful tumbles taken by pack mules without, in many cases, killing them; of encounters with bears and other large game; of the wonderful trout streams and the big catches made; of the fruits found; and of the many incidents—some very funny and some quite the reverse—connected with the everyday life of the soldier in the field. From lack of space, these side stories must be omitted. The campaign was one of hard work for all who were engaged in it; and the reader must not overlook the fact that those excellent officers, Bernard, Forse, Assistant Surgeon Wilcox, and Pitcher, and the men under them, contributed their full share of work and are entitled to credit for what they did. Farrow and Brown stand out prominently in this story because, having been in at the death, they seemed to have been entitled to receive the "brush."

Had the incidents which are herein recorded occurred since 1898, the names of Farrow and Brown would be familiar to every American citizen, but in the days of which I write, such deeds as theirs were too common to attract general notice.

Forgotten Tragedies of an Indian War

AARON F. PARKER[1]

William Carey Brown Collection, University of Colorado, Boulder

Indian hostilities in Central Idaho which have received no attention from historians are the Sheepeater campaigns of 1878 and 1879. Only recently the War Department has given these troubles official recognition as campaigns, and hereafter they will be so listed and army regulations amended accordingly. This recognition has proceeded so far that the cemetery division of the quartermaster general has sanctioned the erection over Pvt. Eagan's lonely grave of a five-foot conical monument of boulders laid in cement and surmounted by a marble headstone of the world war design, which will mark not only the grave, but also the site of the engagement of August 20, 1879, on Big Creek at Soldier Bar. So remote is this section, far up in the fastnesses of the Salmon River Canyon in the golden heart of Central Idaho, that the stone will have to be hauled about seventy miles by wagon and forty miles by pack mules to reach its destination.

In the absence of official data, the writer has related personal experiences, supplemented by verification from other active participants among the few survivors who still walk the earth.

The story of the Nez Perce War of 1877 is too familiar to need repetition here, and for the benefit of the new generations which have since entered the world, it may be said that it is the story of the epic flight of Chief Joseph and his tribesmen over 2,000 miles of the roughest country in North America; of a retreat conducted with such masterly skill as to win the highest praise for the Indian leader from the army officers who tried in vain to catch him. The war finally ended in the Bear's Paw Mountains of Montana when the late Col. Nelson A. Miles and the 5th Infantry finally intercepted him and held him at bay until the pursuing General Howard and his weary troopers came up, and the hostiles surrendered.

The Sheepeaters were a few mongrel Indians of unknown pedigree who inhabited the isolated, and at that period scantily settled, Council and Indian Valleys of the upper Weiser River. Except for their natural propensity for raiding ranches and running off stock, they were comparatively peaceful. Their name was derived from their subsistence on mountain sheep killed during their summer hunting trips into the rugged fastnesses of the mountain hinterland.

What is known as the Sheepeater country is to this day the wildest and most impenetrable region of indescribable ruggedness and grandeur. Lofty mountain summits alternate with abysmal canyons thousands of feet in depth, along whose depths the waters of mountain torrents dash along to free themselves from their rock-bound channels. The forests abound in game, the streams teem with fish, and these resources constituted the principal subsistence of the Sheepeaters. The bighorn or mountain sheep are still numerous despite the fact that the Indians were successful hunters of this elusive game and largely subsisted on their meat, from which they derived their name.

The Chief Joseph War of 1877 aroused general unrest among the tribal Indians of the entire Pacific Northwest, and this condition was further aggravated by the Bannock War of 1878, under the leadership of Buffalo Horn. Although the Bannock outbreak was neither so long nor so arduous as had been the Nez Perce War, it was filled with plenty of dangers and hardships. With the first defeat of Buffalo Horn in southeastern Idaho, many of his hostiles escaped to the Weiser country and joined forces with Eagle Eye, War Jack,[2] and Chuck, tribal chiefs of the Sheepeaters, thus strengthening and encouraging them to make trouble, with the probable view in their minds of inaugurating a distant flank attack, necessitating withdrawal of troops engaged in chasing Buffalo Horn and his myrmidons entirely out of Idaho.

This conjecture was justified when, on June 17, 1878, the Sheepeaters and their renegade Bannock recruits raided ranches in Indian Valley some hours before dawn and ran off with about sixty head of horses owned by William Monday, Tom Healy, and Jake Grosclose. Discovering their loss at daylight, these men, accompanied by "Three-Fingers" Smith, a veteran of the Modoc War of 1872–73, pursued the hostiles with intent to recover their stolen stock, following them over the divide between the Weiser and Payette watersheds to Long Valley, where, at a point on the old gold-seekers' trail between Lewiston, Idaho, and the Boise Basin, they were ambushed by the hostiles at the Payette Falls,[3] resulting in the killing of Monday, Healy, and Grosclose in the order named, and badly wounding Three Fingers and his mule after putting up a brave fight for their lives.

Smith, shot twice through the right groin and his left shoulder crippled by two more shots, and his mule practically out of commission, escaped to a grove of pine and willows, where he remained under cover until he observed the hostiles rounding up their stock, headed for the divide between the Payette and Salmon River waters. He then made the greatest effort of his life by climbing his crippled mule and headed for the Calvin R. White mail station on the Little Salmon Meadows, finally arriving at his destination after abandoning his mule and making the last lap of the journey on his hands and knees,[4] where he was given every care possible under the primitive conditions then existing.

The writer had been placer mining on Burnt River, Oregon, thirty-five miles west of Weiser that spring, and the water supply having given out early in June, he returned to Weiser, where in 1877 he had joined Company E, 1st Regiment Idaho Volunteers, Thomas C. Galloway commanding, for service during the Nez Perce War. Anticipating trouble from the Bannocks, who were raising all kinds of devilment in southern Idaho at that time, he returned for further service in his company. The day following his arrival at Weiser, Edgar Hall, mail carrier, arrived from the upper country with the first news of the massacre. Hall was on his way to Boise City to procure and accompany a doctor to the White station to doctor the wounds of Three Fingers.

That afternoon a company of four men comprising John Smith (a brother-in-law of Bill Monday), Steve Durbin, Ike McKinney, and the writer, all members of Company E, left Weiser for the mail station, intending to chase the hostiles, recapture the stolen stock for the benefit of the widows, and with the further hope in mind of capturing or otherwise disposing of the murderers.

Their equipment consisted of horse and saddle, a .50-caliber Springfield rifle, a very limited supply of cartridges, extra saddle blanket, one-half sack of "self-rising" flour, a few coffee berries and a pinch of tea to chew on and prevent headaches for those who were accustomed to the use of these beverages in peacetime.

In those primitive days all civilian volunteers furnished their own transportation, commissary and other equipment for light marching order at their own cost. Under such conditions most of the Indian wars of the Pacific Northwest have been fought, the volunteer companies being always in the field before troops arrived.

Thus equipped, the four men reached the mail station in the forenoon of the following day, making the ninety miles over a poor excuse for a wagon road in twenty-two hours. They camped at the mail station for rest and refreshment for man and beast until daylight next morning. Three Fingers was impatiently awaiting arrival of the Boise doctor but gave the pursuing party much valuable information concerning trails and distances, together with details of the massacre, which they subsequently verified.

Early dawn they headed for the scene of the tragedy, where they arrived at evening dusk, being unfamiliar with the country. Here they built a campfire, mixed a batch of "self-rising," toasted on willow twigs, and after a smoke and going through the motions of spreading their blankets, they silently stole away and back-trailed to another camp two miles up the trail they had followed in the hope of deceiving the Indians, if any were around in search of new victims. Here they camped for the night, each taking turns of vigilant watchful waiting until daylight, when they returned to the scene of the killings and reconnoitered the topography of the region and inspected the bodies, which lay in positions as outlined by Three Fingers.

The scene of the massacre and the details connected therewith will remain forever as a clear-cut picture never to be effaced from mind and memory.

Imagine for yourself a trail lying at the base of a timber-clad mountain with huge slabs of bare granite standing perpendicularly, from which twisted scrub pines and mountain mahogany had grown from the fissures. Beneath the

trail, the land sloped gently to the broad, open valley through which the river
sang, with no protection save a few wash boulders protruding a few inches
above the soil at frequent intervals. About one-half mile above this spot stood
the grove of pine and brush in which Three Fingers had sought shelter after the
death of his comrades.

Ambushed behind this natural and impregnable fortification, commanding
the trail and the open valley above and below, the hostiles picked them off one
by one as their victims, traveling in single file, approached, with no possibility
of escaping the deadly trap. From the version given them by Three Fingers,
Monday was in the advance and the first to be shot, his horse being killed
under him. He was not, however, instantly killed, and upon the fall of his
horse, he opened fire. His comrades rallied to the scene, dismounting as they
approached, except Three Fingers, whose experience had taught him never to
dismount under Indian fire.

As Healy walked, leading his horse, he became the next target, his horse
being first badly wounded and fractious, which engaged his attention so that he
became confused, and another shot from the ambush laid him low a short distance from Monday, who was still firing at the unseen enemy. No Indians were
visible throughout the melee. Grosclose was the next to fall, screaming as he
fell, "They have got me, Smith." Thus far, only single shots had been fired
from the ambush as the travelers approached, but as Smith drew nearer, the
hostiles fired in fusillades, and he and his mule were severely wounded. Smith
then exhausted his cartridges in aimless fire, and realizing that his comrades
were now dead, he escaped as above narrated.

A search of the soil revealed fourteen cartridge shells scattered around the
bodies of the victims; their cartridge belts were on the ground, all of them
empty. Examination of their rifles revealed only empty shells, showing that they
had fired as long as their scanty supply of ammunition held out. The bodies had
clearly been untouched, indicative that the Indians were either in a great hurry
to get away or were short of ammunition. The carcasses of the horses were far
apart in the valley. Realizing from these conditions that the Indians had
vamoosed directly after the murders, they scouted around and soon discovered
and followed the broad trail up the mountain in the soil of the hillside.

Anticipating that troops would soon be here and bury the dead, they maintained the pursuit for two days and nights, selecting well-protected spots for
camps and keeping vigilant lookouts for possible attacks. Approaching the
summit, the soil of the side hills gave way to bare granite; the tracks became
less recognizable, and a summer thunderstorm accompanied by hail and torrential rain wiped out the last vestige of the trail, eliminating all hope of again
picking up the hoofprints. The pursuers concluded to abandon the chase and
return from whence they came.

On the evening of the fifth day, they again reached the battlefield and found
that the bodies had been buried where they fell, and as a landmark to perpetuate
their memory, the troop had inscribed upon one of the slabs behind which the

enemy had lain concealed the names of the victims and the date of the event under crossed rifles. Here they camped for the night in peace, and after raking the still warm ashes of the troopers' campfires, they found bacon rinds which, after washing, [they] chewed to satisfy their hunger. Next morning they resumed the homeward march, intending to camp that night with the troops, who, they rightly surmised, would be near the outlet of the Big Payette Lake.

In the early forenoon, with the prospector's instinct, the writer left his companions to trace up some good-looking float quartz noted on the outward trip, following it well up the mountain side without finding "the other end of the rainbow." He was speeding for the valley when fresh bear tracks invited another chase, resulting in the sudden death of the animal. Realizing that his hungry comrades would consider a mess of fried bear steaks better than manna from heaven, he partially skinned the bear, carving out the two hams, and wrapping the hide around the carcass, dragged it down the mountainside with picket rope attached to the saddle and speedily rejoined his outfit, who were dismounted and chatting with two troopers wearing sergeants' chevrons, and by the insignia on their caps identified them as members of Company C, 2nd Infantry, in command of Capt. William F. Drum,[5] whose company had been detailed from Camp Howard, a cantonment which had been located near Grangeville[6] to protect the Camas Prairie settlers from possible Indian raids and further martyrdom such as they had undergone from the Chief Joseph hostiles in 1877.

The 2nd infantry had been sent out from Atlanta, Georgia, in 1877 under executive order issued by President Hayes withdrawing the troops from the Southern states during the Negro and carpetbag governments in the Reconstruction days. The two troopers whom we met were Sergeants Edward S. Beck and Nicholas Lamb. At the close of the Sheepeater troubles in 1879, they were again detailed to Camp Howard, where the writer became acquainted with both.

Sergeant Beck was postmaster at Grangeville for some years, and he and the writer organized there Company C, 1st Regiment, Idaho National Guard, of which Mr. Beck was elected captain and the writer quartermaster sergeant. This company later served in the Philippines during the Spanish War. Sergeant Lamb located a farm near Mount Idaho, where he lived and died some years later. Sergeant Beck also died at Grangeville and was given a military funeral by Company C.

They were out on scout duty, and being assured that the Payette watershed was clear of hostiles, they returned to the company camp near the outlet of Big Payette Lake as surmised. The civilians stayed behind to cook bear steaks and did not resume the march until the afternoon, reaching the military camp two hours after midnight. Camping for the rest of the night and eating breakfast with the boys in blue, and being unable to adjust their .45 cartridges to our .50 Springfields, they headed for the White mail station. They found Three Fingers still on his cot but recovering from his wounds. The doctor had left for Boise the day before, leaving the assurance that his patient "could not be killed with an axe."

Three Fingers was a prototype of the artist's picture delineating the pioneer, tall and stringy, and a typical mountain man accustomed to hardships. He was an early arrival in the Florence placer camp, where he discovered and developed Smith Gulch, from which he extracted $300 per day but was always broke at the end of the scanty water season. He later squatted on a garden spot at Elk Creek, on the South Fork of Salmon River, where the writer met him in 1883, when the events of the 1878 campaign were again gone over. He died there a few years later at a ripe old age. In due time the four men returned to Weiser, with entertainment at every house we stopped at en route.

During the month of August 1878, Dan Crooks and Boone Helm were killed in Round Valley, at that time totally uninhabited, presumably by Sheepeaters, no other Indians being in that country at that time. Their bodies were discovered and buried by a detachment of the 2nd Infantry from Camp Howard near Grangeville, where the parents of Crooks resided. The motive of these murders will never be known.[7]

Early in the spring of 1879, the Sheepeaters inaugurated another campaign of murder and depredations.[8] In the hostilities which ensued, they eluded three bodies of troops sent against them, defeating one, and resisted capture until late in the fall, when they surrendered with the honors of war—quite a record, considering the circumstances.

Along the South Fork of the Salmon River, there were four small farms or garden patches on narrow bars along the canyon, each isolated from the others, all having but one outlet by way of a rugged trail to Warrens, a prosperous placer mining camp. From James P. Rains' place, just above the mouth of the South Fork, to Hugh Johnson's place, on the main Salmon, the distance was forty miles, while between these two places were those of Sylvester S. Smith, known as Three Fingers, referred to frequently in these reminiscences. There were a few bars along the rivers where desultory placer mining was carried on, though most of these were deserted. All of the ranchers had families except Johnson.

In March or April of 1879 the hostiles made their first killings by the murders of Johnson and Peter Dorsey. This became known when Dorsey, living at the first ranch below, went to visit Johnson in the latter part of April and was greeted with death-dealing bullets from Indian rifles and his life blotted out. These men frequently visited Warrens for supplies and mail, and as they did not show up for some time, their friends in the camp decided in May to investigate the cause of their absence.

The party failed to find anyone at the Johnson house, and saw that the cabin had been plundered and the horses gone. Fearing the worst, they returned to Warrens, where they were reinforced by neighbors, and returned to the river for a more thorough search. In a nearby field they discovered the decomposed bodies of Johnson and Dorsey, bearing gunshot wounds. Indian signs were discovered, and the circumstances warranted the conclusion that the outrages had been committed by redskins.

A messenger was dispatched to Camp Howard requesting that a force be sent to protect the Warrens community and capture the Indians. Lt. Henry Catley set out with a detachment of sixty mounted men of the 2nd Infantry[9] early in July, accompanied by a large pack train with supplies for several weeks. Some civilians were recruited, making a total strength of seventy men.

The expedition reached Warrens by forced marches and proceeded into the Sheepeater country. They marched eastward for eleven days toward the Middle Fork of the Salmon River. No Indian signs appeared until July 28, when the civilian scouts discovered them eight miles below camp on Big Creek. This stream heads north of Thunder Mountain and runs northeasterly into the Middle Fork of the Salmon River. The creek runs through a box canyon, with infrequent bars along its course. Details of the happenings which followed—the discovery of the Indians, the attack on the troops, the retreat, the fight on Vinegar Hill, and the return to Warrens—was made public by an official report of Lieutenant Muhlenberg,[10] a member of the expedition, dated October 28, 1879, copies of which are still privately owned. From this source it appears that Catley placed no faith in the report of his scouts that Indians had been seen, although twice repeated to him by different persons cognizant of the facts, and ordered the troops to camp for the night over the protest of Lieutenant Webster,[11] who suggested sending out a scouting party.

Early next morning the troops broke camp and started down the Big Creek Canyon in single file, civilian scouts leading the way. The objective of the Indian camp was reached early in the forenoon and found deserted, evidently in a hurry, as large supplies of food and other equipment had been abandoned.

Destroying these supplies, the troops were ordered without customary precaution of an advance guard and flankers on the surrounding ridges. They were soon greeted by a volley from the opposite side of the creek. The troops quickly dismounted and sought protection from the enemy's fire. Two of their number, Privates James Doyle and A. R. Holmes of Company C, 2nd Infantry, were severely wounded. A detail of five men were ordered to bring them in. Catley then ordered a retreat to their last camp to await arrival of the pack train, which soon appeared, and the night was spent without alarm.

Early next morning Catley ordered the men to move up a long ridge to the summit of the high mountain on the north. They had hardly left the base of the ridge, when the pack train in the rear was attacked, but Muhlenberg and Webster brought them safely within the lines. However, the Indians also attacked the head of the column, thus placing the troops between a crossfire. Skirmishers were ordered out to drive back the redskins in front but were soon repulsed. The Indians fired the brush and grass to demoralize the troops and their mounts.

For fourteen hours the command was kept in this position, only five shots having been fired by the soldiers. Water was not accessible, owing to Indian command of the creek. So thirsty they became that, so the legend runs, they opened a keg of vinegar found in the pack train supplies and, with its contents, allayed their thirst. From this incident Vinegar Hill derived its name.

In the subsequent retreat, the greater part of the pack train was lost, furnishing the hostiles with needed provisions, equipment, and ammunition. They also secured the rifles and cartridge belts of the two wounded soldiers. In scaling the heights across the creek, Lieutenant Muhlenberg was thrown from his horse and one of his kneecaps dislocated. A short forced march the next morning brought the tired command to Warrens, where they rested, and when again on the march met up at the Burgdorf Hot Springs, with Capt. R. F. Bernard in command of a company of the 1st Cavalry, fresh from Boise Barracks.

Subsequently, Lieutenant Catley was subjected to a court-martial at Ft. Walla Walla in January 1880, on charges of "misbehavior, etc., in the presence of the enemy in connection with his retreats in Idaho in 1879." Among the dates mentioned in the charges are July 29, 30, 31 and August 1 and 2, 1879. The verdict of the court-martial was guilty as charged and recommended his dismissal from the service.

Many civilians familiar with military matters protested these charges were preferred because Catley had risen from the ranks, and that the court-martial was a matter of prejudices and clannishness on the part of West Point graduates. The verdict of the court-martial was set aside by President Hayes.

On Catley's arrival at the Burgdorf Springs, he was relieved of his command by Captain Bernard and ordered back to Camp Howard. With a portion of Catley's 2nd Infantry, Bernard moved into the Sheepeater country, leaving a guard of twelve cavalrymen to reinforce the stockaded civilian population of Warrens. In the absence of Bernard in the mountain fastness, the Indians inaugurated the second tragedy on the South Fork of the Salmon, a tragedy which fired the communities interested in a blaze of righteous indignation.

The scene is laid at the little farm of James P. Rains, who, with his family, had lived [there] for a number of years and had accumulated a valuable property by dint of hard work, supplying the Warrens population and surrounding mining camps with the products of his farm, raising and baling hay, which he packed into the camps and sold for $80 and $100 per ton. Mr. Rains had never quarreled with the Indians and was held in the highest respect by everybody in those mountains. He was never apprehensive of special danger to himself or family.

He was engaged in harvesting his hay crop when Catley's command traveled through his farm en route to Camp Howard and informed the family that they must get away to Warrens as speedily as possible, as the hostiles were in close pursuit. Mr. Rains promptly followed this advice, took his family safely to Warrens, and seeing nor hearing anything about Indians being anywhere in that region, he returned to his ranch, accompanied by James Edwards and Harry Serren, the latter being better known throughout Central Idaho as "Lemhi." Ten days had elapsed since Catley's return. Bernard was well on his way into the interior. Rains, Edwards, and Serren were gathering the hay crop. On Friday, August 15, Albert Webber, who lived near Grangeville and [was the] brother-in-law of Rains and now sole surviving witness of the tragedy, joined the party at the ranch and volunteered his services in the hay harvest. The August sun is almost tropical in those low-lying and enclosed canyons, and a long noon siesta is customary. They hoped to complete their work by Saturday and return to Warrens on the Sabbath.

From the first, they had carried rifles to their work as usual. At noon they returned to the house for lunch, resting until three o'clock. They discussed the advisability of carrying their weapons back to the hay press and decided to dispense with this precaution. They were putting the last bale through the press well towards evening; the twilight deepened, distant objects were becoming obscured, when a rifle shot from the direction of the house startled them. The others thought that Webber was shooting at a grouse. A volley of rifle fire followed, whizzing close to their ears. Edwards, who was on top of the press, yelled to his companions to drop behind the press and himself jumped from his exposed position. The Indians were at their bloody work, seeking the lives of the three unarmed men.

Between the men in the field and the house, a small creek flowed down from the steep mountain slope, cutting its course through the densely timbered channel forty feet in depth to the river. To this creek the three men stealthily made their way, consulting as to the best course to pursue. The longer they stayed, the more probable it was that they would be cut off from the house and their weapons, with absolute certainty of death. Notwithstanding the odds against them, they rushed for the house at all hazards, and cautiously climbing the bank of the creek, they started along the trail with Rains in the advance. The trail led over a small, exposed point. All were running rapidly when Edwards and Lemhi shouted to Rains, "Keep off the point!"

For some reason Rains kept to the trail, and as he reached the summit of the point, a gun flashed, and the brave pioneer staggered. A ball had pierced his right hip. Another shot rang out from the direction of the cabin, tearing a frightful wound in his body. Edwards and Lemhi saw him fall; they saw the flash of the gun from the direction of the cabin; they heard shooting in many directions, especially on the right, where it was afterwards learned that Webber had been firing at the Indians.

The two men decided that Webber had been taken, and that they had better retreat to the creek canyon, which they reached unharmed. No safety there, so they walked, crawled, and ran to the forks of the creek, a place they had never seen. From here they toiled over sharp rocks and through scattering pines, until they reached the summit, 2,500 feet above the creek canyon. Exhausted, they crawled into a thicket and slept for a short nap.

At daybreak they found an old trail, which they followed into Warrens, arriving about 7:00 A.M. A little later Webber arrived, much to the surprise of Edwards and Lemhi. His escape was as marvelous as that of his companions.

As soon as the Indians opened fire, Webber grasped the situation and prepared to defend the cabin. He had not done much shooting, because he was instantly expecting the men in the field to return for their rifles. Soon after dark, Rains reached the cabin and was admitted by Webber, who laid him on a couch and ministered to his wants as best as he could. Rains called for water and, after drinking a little, moaned in pain and peacefully passed away.

The Indians lighted several bonfires around the house for the purpose of watching his movements. Almost in despair, he noted that the fire in the rear of the cabin burned low. Now that Rains was beyond aid, Webber grasped the opportunity, and taking the best gun in the outfit, he crawled into an irrigating ditch with willows on both banks, which he followed to its source in the creek, and then began a terrible climb. He ascended the precipitous canyon and made the summit. From this point, he watched the Indians burn the buildings on the ranch and the few miners' cabins along the stream. He estimated the number of hostiles taking part in the attack as seven, although he thought there might be more.

At Warrens a volunteer company of eighteen well-armed men, under the leadership of Norman B. Willey, later a governor of the state of Idaho, took the field to pursue the Indians. A messenger was dispatched to Captain Bernard. The company proceeded to the Rains ranch and found the usual scene of desolation following an Indian attack. In the ruins of the cabin where the Rains family had made their home and where Webber made his brave stand, they found the charred bones of Rains' body, which were taken to Warrens and properly interred.

The damage to the property and contents of the building was estimated at $3,000, which the government was asked to pay to the widow and the two children. But her claim, like all of the depredation claims filed by the victims of Idaho County during the Nez Perce War, were thrown out by the claims commission, and the widows left absolutely destitute through the deviltry of the so-called "Wards of the Nation."

Such is the story of the Rains massacre, as personally narrated by Albert Webber on July 10, 1925. Mr. Webber was shot through the left shoulder, leaving a wound from the evil effects of which he still suffers in his advancing age. Rains at the time of his death was a young man, aged about thirty years. Edwards and Lemhi both resided in Grangeville for some years, finally passing on to a more peaceful land.

Captain Bernard remained in the mountains until early September but was unsuccessful in capturing the hostiles, though the presence of the troops kept the Indians from further outrages. Early in July, 2nd Lt. Edward S. Farrow was detailed with a force of forty men of the 21st Infantry and twenty Umatilla Indian scouts, with instructions to commence a fall campaign against the Sheepeaters. This force proceeded to Big Creek over the same route taken by Catley and Bernard. Farrow was energetic and profoundly impressed the hostiles with his determination to capture them. An official letter from the adjutant general of the War Department, Washington, D.C., dated June 18, 1925, in response to inquiries made by the writer, states:

Friendly Indians. RUFUS F. ZOGBAUM. *HORSE, FOOT, AND DRAGOON.*

Nothing has been found of record showing definitely the date of surrender of the last party of Sheepeater Indians to 2nd Lt. Edward S. Farrow, 21st Infantry, in 1879. However, the record indicates that Lieutenant Farrow and his force of Umatilla Indian scouts captured fourteen Sheepeaters at Big Salmon Meadows September 21; compelled the surrender of thirty-nine near the Middle Fork of Salmon River October 1; and compelled the surrender of twelve October 6, 1879, near Chamberlain Basin.

A report current at the time indicated that few Indians ever surrendered to United States troops under more favorable conditions. The Sheepeaters were allowed, according to this rumor, to retain their weapons and property [and] were exempted from prosecution by the civil authorities of Idaho County, in whose jurisdiction their atrocities were committed. The captives were brought out of the mountains by Lieutenant Farrow by way of Grangeville and, after being kept at Fort Vancouver for a time, were placed upon the Fort Hall reservation in the southeastern part of the state. About one-half of the prisoners were men. This total is supposed to represent their total strength, while others contend that not one-half of the Indians surrendered.

Speaking of their capture, the Warrens correspondent of the Lewiston *Teller,* October 8, 1879, says: "Too much praise cannot be accorded Lieutenant Farrow for his exertions in this affair. He has been thoroughly in earnest; has persevered when others weakened; has resolutely faced the inclemencies of the season; short supplies; poor and exhausted stock; and has achieved complete success. In these expressions of gratitude, I but echo the sentiment of every one of our citizens. The large scope of country thus cleared of Indians should recommend his promotion to a colonelcy."

The close of this Sheepeater War happily proved the conclusion of Indian disturbances in Idaho County.

NOTES

PART ONE: THE SNAKE-PAIUTE WAR AND AFTER, 1866–72

Albert G. Brackett: Fighting in the Sierras

1. Albert G. Brackett (1829–96) began his military career as a lieutenant in the 4th Indiana Volunteer Infantry during the Mexican War. Commissioned a captain in the 2nd U.S. Cavalry in March 1855, he saw service against the Lipan Apaches and Comanche in Texas. For three years during the Civil War, he commanded the 9th Illinois Volunteer Cavalry. Brackett emerged from the war a major in the 1st U.S. Cavalry. Besides duty in Nevada, Brackett saw postwar service in Arizona and Montana, and in the Ute War. He retired a colonel in February 1891.

2. A veteran of the Mexican War, Charles McDermit moved to California shortly thereafter. He superintended the building of Benicia Barracks in 1852 and served in the California state assembly.

3. McDermit was killed in the Quinn River Valley on August 8, 1865; the man who killed him was Captain John, a chief of the Warner Lake Shoshones.

4. Fort Churchill had been built in July 1860 to protect the main roads, mining camps, and outlying ranches of the area. It was abandoned in September 1869.

5. War Department records reproduced in *Chronological List of Actions, etc., with Indians from January 15, 1837, to January 1891* (Fort Collins, CO: Old Army Press, 1979), 23, and Hubert H. Bancroft, *History of Nevada, Colorado, and Wyoming, 1540–1888* (San Francisco: History Company, 1890), 220, give the date of the fight as January 12. Bancroft notes that eight civilians also accompanied the expedition. Captain John led the hostiles The fight occurred sixty-five miles west of Paradise Valley, Nevada.

6. The *Chronological List,* 23, gives army losses as five wounded, and hostile casualties as thirty-four killed; no mention is made of any Indians captured.

7. Bancroft, *Nevada, Colorado, and Wyoming,* 221, gives the same number of Indian losses; the *Chronological List,* 23, records hostile casualties as ninety-six killed, fifteen wounded, and nineteen captured.

8. Samuel P. Smith was commissioned a captain in the 8th U.S. Cavalry in July 1866 and was honorably discharged at his own request in October 1870. Henry B. Mellen was commissioned a second lieutenant in the 6th U.S. Cavalry in May 1866; he retired in October 1872.

9. Not recorded in the *Chronological List.*

10. The Washo spoke a language different from the Northern Paiutes, with whom they frequently were in contact. The Washo resided along the Truckee and Carson Rivers. The defeat to which Brackett refers occurred about 1860. By 1866 the Washo were estimated to have numbered five hundred. A. L. Kroeber, *Handbook of the Indians of California* (New York: Dover, 1976), 569–71.

11. Henry W. Halleck (1815–72) had been general-in-chief of the U.S. Army during much of the Civil War. He assumed command of the Military Division of the Pacific after the war.

12. Bancroft estimated the friendly Northern Paiutes from the Truckee and Walker River region to have numbered approximately one thousand; their reservation of 644,000 acres was confirmed in 1874. Bancroft, *Nevada, Colorado, and Wyoming,* 221.

13. The massacre occurred on May 19, 1866, at Battle Creek, Idaho. Travelers reported finding over one hundred bodies strewn along the road for nearly six miles. Some sources report that a Chinese boy escaped. The perpetrators were Snake Indians. Hubert H. Bancroft, *History of Oregon,* 2 vols. (San Francisco: History Company, 1886), 2:521–22.
14. Known as the Applegate Route.
15. This action is not found in the *Chronological List.*
16. The action occurred on October 26, 1867, near Camp Winfield Scott, Nevada. Three Indians were reported killed and four captured. *Chronological List,* 30.
17. Although Lafferty's action is not recorded in the *Chronological List,* there can be no doubt as to his courage. After Lafferty (1835–1899) had the lower part of his jaw shot away during a hard fight with Chiricahua Apaches on October 20, 1869, his commanding officer, Capt. Reuben F. Bernard, lamented that "the cavalry arm has lost for a time a good and brave officer." Dan L. Thrapp, *Encyclopedia of Frontier Biography,* 4 vols. (Spokane: Arthur H. Clark Company, 1988–94), 2:803–4.
18. Hayden De Lany (1845–90) later served with distinction in the Black Hills Expedition of 1874 and in General Crook's Yellowstone and Big Horn campaigns.
19. See Captain Munson's report of the action elsewhere in this volume.
20. Old Winnemucca (c. 1805–82) tolerated uncounted provocations from the whites during his many years as chief of the Paviotso, or Northern Paiutes, and remained a persistent advocate of peace.
21. Also known as Numaga, Young Winnemucca (d. 1871) of the Pyramid Lake, Nevada, band of Paiutes may have been the son of Old Winnemucca. Although he was active in the 1860 war and fought in the battle of Pyramid Lake, in which 105 territorial militia were killed or wounded, Young Winnemucca afterward became a fast friend of the whites. He died of tuberculosis on the Truckee River reservation.

William R. Parnell: Operations against Hostile Indians with General Crook, 1867–1868

1. William R. Parnell (1835–1910) of Dublin, Ireland, fought in the Crimean War and survived the Charge of the Light Brigade at Balaclava. He came to the United States in 1860, enlisted in the 4th New York Volunteer Cavalry at the outbreak of the Civil War, and rose to the volunteer rank of lieutenant colonel. Commissioned a lieutenant in the 1st U.S. Cavalry in February 1866, Parnell compiled a long and distinguished record in the Indian Wars, winning a Medal of Honor in action against the Nez Perce. Described as a "large, fleshy man" who "taxed the powers of his horse quite heavily," Parnell nonetheless was considered a superb officer. Thrapp, *Encyclopedia,* 3:1116–17. Parnell penned a poem entitled "The Infernal Caverns," which appeared in the October 26, 1872, *Army and Navy Journal.*
2. George Crook (1829–90) knew intimately the terrain over which he was to fight, having served as a company-grade officer in the Pacific Northwest before the Civil War. He saw action in the Rogue River War and was wounded in a skirmish with Pit River Indians in early 1857. Crook achieved corps command during the Civil War, earning the brevet rank of major general, and was appointed lieutenant colonel of the 23rd U.S. Infantry in July 1866.
3. Crook believed that in dry weather, the poison would retain its strength for a month. Martin F. Schmitt, ed., *General George Crook: His Autobiography* (Norman: University of Oklahoma Press, 1946), 41. Describing the same method of poisoning arrows that Parnell relates, Kroeber speculated that "the septic effect of such a preparation is likely to have been much greater than the toxic." Kroeber, *Handbook,* 417.

4. Old Camp Warner, established in August 1866 twenty miles east of Warner Lakes, near the Oregon Central Military Road.
5. Named for Maj. Enoch Steen of the Regular army, who drove a band of Snake Indians up its summit during an 1860 expedition, Steen's Mountain is the highest elevation in southeastern Oregon. Its east face is an escarpment rising five thousand feet above the Alvord Valley.
6. Named for Sgt. A. M. Beaty, who distinguished himself during an 1864 reconnaissance of the Owyhee by the 1st Oregon Volunteer Cavalry; elevation 7,916 feet.
7. Goose Lake was named in pioneer days, probably for the huge flocks of wild geese that frequented it.
8. David Perry (1841–1908) served during the Civil War a captain in the Regular army. He saw action in the Modoc War and was in command at the controversial fight at White Bird Canyon that opened the Nez Perce campaign, a battle in which he lost thirty-four men and was accused by some of dereliction of duty. Officially exonerated of any wrongdoing, he went on to serve in Arizona in the early 1880s. Perry retired as colonel of the 9th U.S. Cavalry in 1898 and was promoted to brigadier general on the retired list in 1904.
9. Archie McIntosh (1834–1902) was born in Canada to a Hudson's Bay Company employee and a Chippewa woman. He was well educated and studied two years in Edinburgh, Scotland. McIntosh served in the Oregon volunteer cavalry during the Civil War and afterward came to the attention of General Crook, who thought so highly of him that he took McIntosh with him as a scout upon his transfer to Arizona in 1871. McIntosh did good work in the unfamiliar surroundings, guiding troops at the battle of Salt River Cave in December 1872 and in the 1883 Sierra Madre campaign. McIntosh was dismissed from the government service in 1884 after it was found he had been diverting rations from the San Carlos Indian Reservation to his ranch for resale.
10. Isaac Wilson, also known as "Dad" Wilson, was a former stage driver who had been hired as a guide on May 15, 1867.
11. Richard I. Eskridge. For a biographical sketch, note 1 of the chapter entitled "The Battle of the Infernal Caverns," by Eskridge.
12. John Madigan (c. 1840–67) was born in Ireland and won a volunteer commission during the Civil War. He was commissioned a second lieutenant in the 1st U.S. Cavalry in February 1866, becoming a first lieutenant in April 1867.
13. The hostile force consisted of approximately seventy-five Northern Paiutes and thirty Pit River Indians, plus a handful of Modocs, all under Chief Si-e-ta.
14. Identified as Charles Brachet in Joseph Wasson's account and in regimental records. Conrad S. Babcock to the Quartermaster General, Washington D.C., February 19, 1929, William Carey Brown Collection, University of Colorado, Boulder.
15. The *Chronological List,* 30, places hostile losses at twenty killed, twelve wounded, and two captured.
15. The *Chronological List,* 30, gives total Federal losses as eight killed and eleven wounded.
17. New Camp Warner was thirty-five miles north of the California line.
18. The Blue Mountains form one of the largest ranges in Oregon, with elevations exceeding nine thousand feet. Their name apparently derived from their "azure-like appearance" when viewed from a distance. Lewis A. McArthur, *Oregon Geographical Names* (Portland: Oregon Historical Society, 1952), 58.
18. Named for Bvt. Capt. William H. Warner, killed by Indians in September 1849 just over the California border, Warner Lakes is a collective name referring to a north-south string of eleven lakes in Warner Valley.
20. Also known as the Donnor und Blitzen Valley, with a river of the same name passing through it. The valley and river were named after the German words for thunder

and lightning when a volunteer command under Col. George B. Currey crossed the stream in a thunderstorm during the Snake campaign of 1864.

21. The Northern Paiute chief We-ah-we-ah was elderly at the time of the Snake War and had been imprisoned briefly in 1859; his band roamed the region of the Malheur and Burnt Rivers and Harney Lake. His name has also been spelled as We-a-we-wah, Weawea, and Weyouwewah.
22. Camp Bidwell rested in the extreme northeast corner of California, having been established in July 1865.
23. John R. Eschenburg had served as an enlisted man in the California volunteers during the Civil War. He was appointed a second lieutenant in the 14th U.S. Infantry in February 1866, transferred as a first lieutenant to the 23rd Infantry in September 1866, and honorably mustered out in January 1871.
24. Azor H. Nickerson (1837–1910) was made a brevet major for gallantry at Antietam and at Gettysburg, where he sustained a severe chest wound. Nickerson served on Crook's staff for ten years, until his promotion to major on June 15, 1878. He retired four years later.
25. Duncan Sherman (d. 1879) was commissioned a second lieutenant in the 1st U.S. Cavalry in January 1867.
26. William Kelly (d. 1871) was an Irish immigrant and veteran of the Mexican War who had settled with his family in the Washington Territory in the 1850s. Kelly served as a captain in the 1st Oregon Volunteer Cavalry and was commissioned captain in the 8th U.S. Cavalry in 1866.
27. Crook reported losses of one officer and two enlisted men wounded; Indian casualties were placed at twelve killed and two captured. *Chronological List,* 32.
28. Donald McKay (1836–99) served as a military scout in most of the campaigns in Washington and eastern Oregon between 1852 and 1874 and commanded Indian irregulars in the Modoc War. Afterward, he joined a Wild West troupe, touring the Eastern states and Europe with a dozen Warm Springs Indians.
29. Ocheo, a chief of the Northern Paiute of central Oregon.
30. E. E. Gantt (also known as Egan), whom Bancroft characterized as a particularly malevolent subchief of We-ah-we-ah's band. Bancroft, *Oregon,* 2:548.
31. The action occurred on April 5. The *Chronological List,* 32, shows Indian losses as thirty-two killed and two captured; no troops were lost.
32. Total Indian losses during Crook's 1866–68 campaigns were reported as 329 killed, 20 wounded, and 225 captured. Robert M. Utley, *Frontier Regulars: The United States Army and the Indian, 1866–1890* (New York: MacMillan, 1973), 178.

Joseph P. Wasson: General Crook's Campaign

1. Twenty-six-year-old Joseph Wasson (1841–83) had been in the west seven years when he joined General Crook's expedition in the summer of 1867. Born in Wooster, Ohio, he studied the printer's trade before heading west after gold. In 1863 Wasson published the Boise *Idaho Union;* in August 1865 he and his brother John founded the Owyhee Avalanche Territory, a town that had sprung up two years earlier. Red-headed, muscular, and high-spirited, Wasson truly was first of the western war correspondents. Oliver Knight said, "He went into the field with troops to bring greater reliability to newspaper accounts of Indian fighting than could be obtained by correspondents in frontier towns." The distinguished newspaperman John W. Forney, editor of the Philadelphia *Press,* thought Wasson one of the best correspondents he had ever known. After Crook's campaign, Wasson traveled to New York and Europe on several occasions on newspaper assignments before striking it rich, apparently in California mines. Settling in California, he served in the state legislature until failing health took him to San Blas, Baja Cali-

fornia, Mexico, in 1883 as U.S. consul. There he died two months later. Oliver Knight, *Following the Indian Wars: The Story of the Newspaper Correspondents among the Indian Campaigners* (Norman: University of Oklahoma Press, 1960), 32, 325; biographical notes on Joseph Wasson in the Department of Special Collections, University of Oregon Library.

2. Wasson's dispatches from the field also appeared in the Portland *Morning Oregonian* and the San Francisco *Evening Bulletin.* Wasson sprinkled his dispatches with couplets from classical and popular poetry and with literary allusions having no direct bearing on the story, I have omitted these.

3. Wasson was in poor health when he took the field in the summer of 1867.

4. Camp C. F. Smith was established in June 1866 near the Pueblo mines. Named for Maj. Gen. Charles F. Smith, it was abandoned in November 1869.

5. An aparejo is a packsaddle for mules.

6. John Darragh (1830–post-1884) came to Oregon in 1851 from New York. He worked as a miller at the Warm Springs Indian Agency and as a packer for the Oregon volunteers during the Civil War. A frontier acquaintance described Darragh as "a morose, backward, unsocial man," who nonetheless was "esteemed highly by those who knew him best, but they were few, for he encouraged but few to come near enough to know him." After serving a term as superintendent of schools for Wasco County, Darragh moved to New York City to engage in construction work with his brother Robert L. Darragh, who had grown wealthy constructing Manhattan office buildings. Thrapp, *Encyclopedia,* 4:128–29.

7. Wasson corrects himself in a later article, noting that it was William C. McKay's scouts, and not Darragh's, who engaged in the fight in question.

8. In northern California.

9. John H. Walker (d. 1891) enlisted in the 13th New York State Militia at the start of the Civil War and ended the conflict a brevet major in the regular service.

10. John J. Coppinger was a Regular army captain who commanded the 15th New York Volunteer Cavalry during the Civil War. He was promoted to colonel in the regular service for his conduct during the Snake War. Coppinger saw service as a major general of volunteers in the Spanish-American War.

11. Camp Lyon, Idaho Territory, was founded in June 1865 on the north fork of Jordan Creek, the northernmost tributary of the Owyhee; it was abandoned in April 1869.

12. Col. Jefferson C. Davis (1828–79) did not assume district command, but instead was sent to Alaska.

13. Small, rounded huts made of tule rushes placed over a framework of poles, with the ground for a floor, a fire in the center in cold weather, and the top almost entirely open.

14. William H. Harris (d. 1895) of New York; brevetted lieutenant colonel for gallantry in the Civil War and honorably discharged in 1870.

15. William C. McKay (1824–93) was the son of a Chinook Indian mother and an Irish father prominent in the early Northwest fur trade. McKay completed his medical studies in Ohio at age nineteen. He has been described as "an energetic and outgoing individual with a keen eye for detail and memory . . . short and stocky with eyes, hair, and skin of the Indian." In 1861 President Abraham Lincoln appointed him physician at the Warm Springs Indian Agency. Thrapp, *Encyclopedia,* 4:327–28.

16. Crook was the lieutenant colonel of the 23rd U.S. Infantry at the time of the campaign. Wasson referred to him by brevet rank of major general. I have changed the text to reflect his regular rank in 1867.

17. Maj. Clinton Wagner, appointed an assistant surgeon in the Regular army on October 11, 1860, and brevetted lieutenant colonel in 1865 for meritorious service during the Civil War.

18. Richard I. Eskridge. For a biographical sketch, see note 1 of the chapter entitled "The Battle of the Infernal Caverns," by Eskridge.

19. Camp Number Two was located north of present-day Denio, Nevada.

20. Paulina, a leading hostile Northern Paiute chief whose band ranged from the upper Deschutes River to the upper John Day, had been killed on April 22, 1867.

21. George B. Curry, who as a captain of the 1st Oregon Volunteer Cavalry explored the barren region between the Snake River and Goose Creek Mountains and the Owyhee River during the Civil War.

22. An allusion to lice.

23. Lt. Col. C. S. Drew of the 1st Oregon Volunteer Cavalry conducted an extensive reconnaissance of the Owyhee country in 1864; his report was published the following year in the Jacksonville *Sentinel* and reprinted as a pamphlet. Although Bancroft was more positive than Wasson as to the results of what he termed Drew's "instructive and interesting" topographical reconnaissance, the two agreed that it was relatively economical. Bancroft, *Oregon,* 2: 503. Of Isaac's Springs, Drew had said, "[It] leaps directly out of the solid rock of the mountain's side, well up towards the summit, and [flows] through a grassy ravine wide enough for the passage of wagons to the desert below." Drew named the springs for his guide.

24. Spanish term for an Indian village.

25. Crook reported hostile losses for the day as forty-six killed and wounded. *Chronological List,* 29.

26. Frederick Steele (1819–68), a West Point graduate and major general of volunteers during the Civil War; he assumed command of the Department of the Columbia in February 1866.

27. Today known as Hart Mountain.

28. Bvt. Maj. Patrick Collins (d. 1879) of Company D, 23rd U.S. Infantry, was an Irish immigrant who rose from the ranks during the Civil War. Captain Hinton does not appear in Francis B. Heitman's two-volume, *Historical Register and Dictionary of the United States Army* (Washington, DC: Government Printing Office, 1903), the standard reference for nineteenth-century officers of the U.S. Army.

29. Joseph L. Jack was commissioned a second lieutenant in the 14th U.S. Infantry in February 1866, promoted to first lieutenant in July, and transferred to the 23rd Infantry in September 1866; he resigned in May 1868.

30. Known today as Crook Peak; elevation 7,834 feet.

31. Originally named for Gov. George I. Woods of Oregon, the post was renamed upon orders from department commander Maj. Gen. Henry W. Halleck, who told Crook on August 28, 1867, "As a general rule, I think military posts should not be named after civilians, but after military officers as a compliment for military services [and] think the new post should be called Camp Warner, or, if you prefer, New Camp Warner." Keith and Donna Clark, "William McKay's Journal, 1866–67: Indian Scouts, Part II," *Oregon Historical Quarterly* 79, no. 3 (Fall 1978): 284.

32. An obscure slang term for Northwestern Indians that may have been pejorative.

33. Located on the Silvies River and named for Brig. Gen. George Wright, Camp Wright was a temporary fortification erected in October 1865 and first garrisoned by Oregon volunteer cavalry.

34. Alexander H. Stanton (d. 1870) had entered the army from Ohio in 1861; his wife was a second cousin of Stephen A. Douglas.

35. McIntosh was mistaken; the river was named for Antoine Sylvaille, a trapper who found it unusually rich with beaver. Silvies is the anglicized form of the name.

36. Greenleaf A. Goodale began the Civil War as a volunteer private and ended the conflict as a brevet major. He received a commission as a first lieutenant in the 23rd U.S. Infantry in July 1866 and ended his career a brigadier general in 1903.

37. According to the *Chronological List,* 28, Capt. E. M. Baker and Troop I, 1st U.S. Cavalry, killed two Indians and captured fourteen during a July 8 engagement near the Malheur River; on July 19 they reportedly killed two more and captured another eight in a fight deeper in the Malheur country.
38. Established on August 16, 1867, Camp Steele was renamed Camp Harney on September 14, 1867.
39. In 1845 a party of immigrants passing through southeastern Oregon picked up yellow pebbles from a stream and hung them under a wagon in a blue wooden bucket. The bucket was lost or abandoned, after which the party realized that the pebbles may have been gold. They did not again find the stream, and the legend of Bluebucket Creek gave rise to numerous conjectures as to its location.
40. Wagontire Springs rested at the base of Wagontire Mountain (elevation 6,504 feet), so named because the tire of an immigrant wagon, said to have been burned by Indians, rested beside the road on the mountain's northern slope for many years.
41. Sixty square miles in size, Lake Abert was named for Col. J. J. Abert, chief topographical engineer of the U.S. Army, by Capt. John C. Frémont on December 20, 1843.
42. The fight occurred on Crane Mountain, then known as Lookout Mountain (elevation 8,454 feet).
43. A probable reference to the raid on Crook's horse herd on the night of March 20, 1868, described in Lieutenant Parnell's article, in which Crook's own mount was stolen and later butchered.
44. Not recorded in the *Chronological List.*
45. Also spelled Ocheo; a chief of the hostile Northern Paiutes who, with Paulina and We-ah-we-ah, had made war against settlers and miners in the interior of Oregon during the Civil War years.
46. The spelling of the surname is uncertain; district quartermaster records show one M. W. Holley as having been hired at Fort Harney in June 1867 for $150 a month as a quartermaster agent to furnish supplies and transportation for Crook's expedition. Clark, "McKay's Journal II," 292–93.
47. Unbeknownst to him, Wasson's brother John had sold the newspaper while Joseph was in the field; the new owners, W. J. Hill and H. W. Millard, kept Joseph Wasson on as a correspondent. The notice of the sale appeared in the August 17, 1867, *Avalanche.* Knight, *Following the Indian Wars,* 48.
48. Also known as Camas Meadows.
49. Also known as Plum Creek.
50. McKay and McIntosh had run into hostiles on the night of September 5 along Drew Creek.
51. Camp Creek.
52. Named for William C. McKay.
53. The water of Lake Abert was highly impregnated with sodium carbonates and other salts.
54. A reference to a map appearing in the Pacific Railroad Survey reports of the 1850s and drawn by Lt. R. S. Williamson during an 1849 expedition from Sacramento, California, to the upper reaches of Pit River.
55. Variously spelled as Brackett and Brachet in regimental records. The Acting Adjutant General to G. M. Saltsman, January 29, 1929, and Conrad S. Babcock to the Quartermaster General, Washington, D.C., February 19, 1929, both in William C. Brown Papers, University of Colorado, Boulder.
56. Last name shown as Braus in regimental records. Babcock to Quartermaster General, February 19, 1929, Brown Papers.

57. Regimental records show the last name as Embler. Austin A. Parker to William C. Brown, January 28, 1929, Brown Papers.

58. In his memoirs, Crook recorded that Wasson was one of the first to enter the fort. Schmitt, *Crook Autobiography*, 167.

59. Name shown as Shay in regimental returns. "Extract of Record of Events Taken from Regimental Return, 1st Cavalry for Month of September 1867, Pertaining to Company H," Brown Papers.

60. Name given as Bryan Carey in regimental records. Parker to Brown, January 28, 1929, Brown Papers.

61. In his annual report, Crook confessed that he could not ascertain the number of Indians killed. The *Chronological List*, 30, gives Indian losses as twenty killed, twelve wounded, and two captured.

62. Northern Paiutes who may have belonged to Winnemucca's band.

63. Patrick E. Connor (1820–70), an Irish immigrant who fought on the frontier from 1846, as a lieutenant in an independent company of Texas Volunteers, through the Civil War, as a brigadier general of volunteers. He won prestige for keeping open the Overland Stage route during the Civil War.

64. A pidgin language based on Chinook and other Native American languages, French, and English and formerly used as a lingua franca in the Pacific Northwest.

65. Richard Powell (d. 1872), an Irish immigrant who had entered the Civil War as assistant surgeon of the 88th New York Volunteer Infantry.

66. In his annual report, Crook said that Lt. John F. Small (d. 1869), with fifty-one men of Company A, 1st U.S. Cavalry, and ten Klamath Indian scouts, killed twenty-four warriors and captured ten women and children during an engagement in the Silver Lake country on September 2, 1867, at a cost of two men killed and one scout wounded. 40th Congress, 3rd Session, House Executive Document 1, *Annual Report of the Secretary of War,* 69. However, the *Chronological List,* 29, gives Indian losses as one killed and two captured. Small was promoted to captain for his conduct in the skirmish.

67. Thomas M. Fisher, an enlisted volunteer during the Civil War; commissioned second lieutenant in the 23rd U.S. Infantry in March 1867.

68. The order was revoked.

69. Frederick L. Dodge (d. 1891), a former private in the 44th Massachusetts Volunteer Infantry who was commissioned a second lieutenant in the 23rd U.S. Infantry in March 1867.

70. A gold-mining community in Baker County, Oregon.

71. McKay said they were to be gone ten to twelve days. Clark, "McKay's Journal," 2:268.

72. Abraham Bassford began the Civil War a private in the 8th New York State Militia and emerged colonel of the 14th New York Cavalry. He was commissioned a captain in the 8th U.S. Cavalry in 1866.

73. A probable reference to government contractors.

74. James Gilliss (d. 1898), chief quartermaster of the District of the Lakes.

75. Kelley and McKay's scout proved disappointing, as they encountered hostiles only briefly, on October 17, and took only one prisoner, who escaped the following day.

Richard I. Eskridge: The Battle of the Infernal Caverns

1. Richard I. Eskridge served in the Civil War as a company-grade officer in the Union's 14th Missouri Cavalry. Commissioned a second lieutenant in the 14th U.S. Infantry in February 1866, he was transferred to the 23rd Infantry in September 1866. Eskridge served as quartermaster for the District of the Owyhee during

the 1867 Snake-Paiute campaign and was brevetted captain for gallantry in the Infernal Caverns fight. He retired a colonel in 1901.

2. Eskridge's account was contained in a letter from Austin A. Parker, the colonel of the 23rd U.S. Infantry, to William C. Brown, a retired brigadier general who had served on the frontier and who researched the Indian Wars in his retirement. Writing from regimental headquarters at Fort Sam Houston, Parker told Brown that he had taken Eskridge's account from an unpublished history of the 23rd Infantry.

3. Eskridge erroneously gives the date as September 25 in his account.

4. Wasson gives the height as 300 feet; otherwise, his and Eskridge's descriptions of the terrain generally coincide.

5. A probable reference to Chief Si-e-ta.

Joseph W. Karge and Samuel Munson: Indian Affairs on the Pacific Coast

1. Pendleton Hunter was commissioned a second lieutenant in the 8th U.S. Cavalry in October 1867; he was honorably mustered out of the service in January 1871.

2. Joseph W. Karge (d. 1892) was a German immigrant who had attained the rank of brevet brigadier general of volunteers for gallant and meritorious service as a cavalry officer during the Civil War. He was commissioned a first lieutenant in the 8th U.S. Cavalry in June 1867 and honorably mustered out in January 1871.

3. In the Warner Valley, Oregon.

4. No Indian casualties are given in the *Chronological List*.

5. In his honor, the site of the fight was named Hoag's Bluff.

6. Samuel Munson (d. 1887) began the Civil War as a sergeant of Maine volunteers and ended the conflict a first lieutenant in the Regular army. He was promoted to captain in the 9th U.S. Infantry in September 1865.

Albert G. Forse: A Scout to Steen's Mountain

1. Albert G. Forse (1841–98) graduated with the West Point Class of 1865 and was commissioned a second lieutenant in Company E, 1st U.S. Cavalry. Except for two years of recruiting duty, Forse served in the West until the Spanish-American War. As a major of the 1st Cavalry, he was killed leading his squadron in the assault on San Juan Hill, Cuba.

2. Frederick W. Hodge estimated the Paiute population as between sixty-five hundred and seven thousand at the turn of the twentieth century. Hodge, *Handbook of American Indians North of Mexico,* 2 vols. (Washington, DC: Government Printing Office, 1905), 2:187.

3. The surrender that Crook negotiated with the Northern Paiutes in 1868 did not require them to go on reservations. "You are free as air so long as you keep the peace," Crook had told them. The Bureau of Indian Affairs gradually coaxed the majority onto reservations, but Winnemucca and his band generally held apart. In the autumn of 1873 a portion of his people were induced to go upon the Malheur River reservation, as Lieutenant Forse relates. Although Winnemucca withdrew to northernmost Nevada, being fed at Camp McDermit whenever he applied for rations, he did not cause significant trouble, and Forse's fears of an Indian war were not realized. Bancroft, *Nevada, Colorado, and Wyoming,* 222, and *Oregon,* 2:551–54.

PART TWO: THE MODOC WAR, 1872–73

James Jackson: The Modoc War—Its Origin, Incidents, and Peculiarities

1. James Jackson (b. 1833) enlisted in the 12th New Jersey Volunteer Infantry in 1861 and emerged from the Civil War a first lieutenant in the regular service. He was promoted to captain in 1868. Jackson was awarded the Medal of Honor for gallantry at Camas Meadows, Idaho, during the Nez Perce War. He retired a lieutenant colonel in 1903.

2. That portion of Jackson's article pertaining to the fight on November 29, 1872, at Captain Jack's camp was reprinted in Cyrus T. Brady's *Northwestern Fights and Fighters* (New York: Doubleday, Page, and Company, 1907). Jackson's article was derived from an address he presented before "The Canteen" on May 14, 1887. Excerpts from the talk, which differed but little from the article presented here, appeared in *The Public Service Review* 1, no. 5 (June 1887), 74–75, as "The Modoc War: A Personal Reminiscence."

3. Edward R. S. Canby (1819–73) graduated with the West Point Class of 1839 and served in the Seminole and Mexican Wars. During the Civil War, he held important commands in the Southwest until 1864, when, as a major general of volunteers, he was placed in command of the Military Division of Western Mississippi. He was promoted to brigadier general in the Regular army in July 1866 and served in the Reconstruction South until his assignment to the Department of the Columbia.

4. The Modocs and Klamaths drifted into the lakes region of southern Oregon and northern California in the fifteenth century and were closely associated for some two hundred years until, at about the time of the American Revolution, the Modocs separated from the Klamaths. When the first white men came into the Tule Lake basin, the Modocs numbered between four hundred and eight hundred, spread out over a territory of some five thousand square miles. They had at least twenty small, semipermanent villages, the farthest north being at present-day Klamath Falls, Oregon, and the easternmost along Sprague River. Keith A. Murray, *The Modocs and Their War* (Norman: University of Oklahoma Press, 1959), 8–9.

5. Jackson's reference to the Modocs as Digger Indians reflects a popular prejudice of the day. The term "digger" apparently was the English translation of the name of a small Paiute tribe of southwestern Utah that practiced agriculture. In time the term was applied to every northwestern tribe known to use roots extensively for food. As root eaters were supposed to be a low type of Indian, the term became a pejorative. The Modocs subsisted principally on meat, fish, and woka seeds taken from water lilies. Hodge, *Handbook,* 1:390; Kroeber, *Handbook,* 323–25.

6. Jackson is mistaken. The Modocs were most closely related to the Klamaths, a people of the Upper Klamath Lake and Williamson River region who lived at peace with the whites. The Modocs and Klamaths considered themselves branches of the same family and belonged to a group known to ethnologists as the Lutuamian. Although peaceably disposed toward the whites, the Klamath traditionally had joined their Modoc cousins in raids on other northern California Indian tribes. Kroeber, *Handbook,* 318–19.

7. Located on the northeastern side of Tule Lake, at a point where the Southern Emigrant road from Linkville to the Pitt River Valley passed between the lakeshore and a large lava outcropping, Bloody Point was the scene of several massacres of immigrants. The most notable occurred in the fall of 1852, when the Modocs struck several small caravans, killing an estimated thirty-six whites.

8. More commonly known as the Hot Creek Modocs. A small band, they lived on Hot Creek, which entered Lower Klamath Lake between the farms of John A. Fairchild

and P. A. Dorris. Although the Hot Creek were initially reluctant to fight, menacing whites caused most of the warriors joined Captain Jack in the stronghold.

9. In 1864 J. W. Perit Huntington, superintendent of Indian Affairs for Oregon, signed a treaty with the Klamaths, establishing the Klamath reservation. Before Huntington was able to secure the signatures of the Modoc leaders, Elijah Steele, a Yreka, California attorney, undertook to negotiate a private treaty with the Modocs allowing them to keep their lands north of Tule Lake along the lower Lost River. Bewildered and angry to learn their treaty with Steele had no authority, the Modocs moved to the Klamath reservation reluctantly. The tribe split: one portion followed Old Schonchin, who was willing to sign and comply with the Huntington treaty; a second band, under his brother, John Schonchin, and Captain Jack, returned to Lost River to reclaim their land.

10. The Klamaths and Modocs were not ancient foes, but Klamath attempts to exact tributes from the reservation Modocs and the friendly disposition of the Klamaths toward the whites, which included soldiering for them, strained relations between the two tribes intolerably.

11. Old Schonchin (c. 1797–1892) was not a hereditary leader but had attained chieftainship by ability; by 1846 he commanded several hundred warriors and took part in early hostilities against white settlers. During the 1860s he concluded that continued war meant only extermination for his people.

12. Captain Jack (c. 1839–73), whose Modoc name was Kientpoos or Kintpuash, was a subchief of the Lost River Modocs. As a young man he often visited Yreka and is said to have won his nickname there for his habit of wearing a brass-buttoned military jacket.

13. The ill child was Captain Jack's niece; the murdered man was a Klamath shaman who had been summoned because the Modoc shaman was absent.

14. White men married to Indian women, whose loyalties often were divided between their fellow settlers and the tribes into which they had wed.

15. Odeneal never visited the Modoc village nor spoke with Captain Jack, having been rebuffed in his attempts to meet with the Modoc leader in Linkville, Oregon, in late November 1872. "Say to the superintendent," Jack had told a messenger from Odeneal, "that we do not wish to see him or talk with him. We will not go upon the reservation. I am tired of talking and am done talking." Bancroft, *Oregon,* 2:572.

16. For a biographical sketch of Ivan D. Applegate, see note 1 of the chapter entitled "The Initial Shot of the Modoc War," by Applegate.

17. John Green (1825–1908), a German immigrant commissioned from the ranks as second lieutenant of the Second Dragoons in July 1855. Promoted to major of the 1st U.S. Cavalry in June 1868, Green served with distinction in Arizona before the Modoc War. He earned the Medal of Honor for gallantry during the January 17, 1873, attack on the Modoc stronghold and retired a lieutenant colonel in 1889.

18. Jackson started with between thirty and thirty-eight enlisted men at noon on November 28, 1872, for Captain Jack's camp of fifteen families, located along the south bank of Lost River near the northwestern shore of Tule Lake. A second Modoc camp of fourteen families under Hooker Jim lay a half mile downstream on the opposite side of the river.

19. The cabin of Dennis Crawley rested on the northeast side of Lost River, near Hooker Jim's camp.

20. Jackson's command arrived at Captain Jack's village on the morning of November 29.

21. The Modocs did not live in tepees, but rather in lodges of hewn or even-squared timber, covered with tule mats and earth, and dug three or four feet into the ground.

22. Jackson lost one man killed and seven wounded; the Modocs lost one warrior killed and one wounded. At least one Modoc woman and child were killed.

23. The Modocs from Captain Jack's village crossed Tule Lake by boat on the night of November 29 to reach their stronghold in the Lava Beds, thirteen miles distant. Warriors from the village of Hooker Jim reached the stronghold on horseback, killing at least fourteen settlers along the north and northeast shores of the lake en route. Reinforcements from the Hot Creek Modocs brought the number of warriors in the Stronghold to between fifty-five and seventy.

24. Frank Wheaton (1833–1903) left college in 1850 to accept a position with the United States and Mexican Boundary Commission; five years later he was appointed a first lieutenant in the 1st U.S. Cavalry. Wheaton rose steadily during the Civil War, ending the conflict a brevet major general of volunteers. He was appointed lieutenant colonel of infantry in the Regular army in 1866 and promoted to brigadier general while commanding the Department of Texas in 1892.

25. Capt. Reuben F. Bernard with Troop G, 1st U.S. Cavalry, arrived at Crawley's ranch on December 8, 1872, from Camp Bidwell. Major Green assumed command of the field forces on December 11; Capt. David Perry with Troop F and Lieutenant John G. Kyle with a detachment of Troop G, 1st Cavalry, arrived at Crawley's from Fort Klamath the same day. Colonel Wheaton assumed field command on December 21; that day, Maj. Edwin C. Mason arrived at Crawley's ranch with Companies B and C, 21st U.S. Infantry.

26. Thirty-six Klamath Indian volunteers arrived at Crawley's ranch on December 2. A company of Oregon volunteers joined the regular forces in December, as did a detachment of twenty-four California volunteers. By mid-January 1873 the regulars in the field numbered some 225 and the volunteers 175. Of this number, 175 regulars, 104 volunteers, and 20 Klamath scouts participated in the attack of January 17, 1873. Thompson, *Modoc War,* 43.

27. Reuben F. Bernard (1834–1903) enlisted in 1855, rose from the ranks to captain in July 1866, and made a reputation fighting the Apaches before, during, and after the Civil War. He was brevetted brigadier general in 1890 for his Indian war service and retired in 1896.

28. The directions of attack were, more precisely, from the south-southwest by Bernard's command and just north of east by Wheaton's. The assault was scheduled for the morning of January 17, 1873.

29. Bernard lost four men wounded in the encounter and fell back to a prominent outcropping known as Hospital Rock, approximately one mile northeast of the Stronghold.

30. Green had with him Troop F, 1st U.S. Cavalry, and the California volunteers.

31. Losses officially were reported as nine killed and twenty-eight wounded, of whom three later died. The Modocs may have suffered no casualties. Thompson, *Modoc War,* 43.

32. At Van Bremer's (also spelled Van Brimmer's) ranch, fifteen miles west of the Stronghold.

33. Jackson's recollection is faulty; not until January 30, 1873, did Secretary of War William Belknap issue orders that offensive operations be suspended and that the troops act only to protect settlers.

34. Alvan C. Gillem (1830–75) graduated with the West Point Class of 1851. He fought in the Seminole Wars and on the antebellum Texas frontier. Partly through the patronage of his friend Andrew Johnson, Gillem rose to the rank of brevet major general of volunteers in the Civil War.

35. Rev. Eleazar Thomas (1814–73) had been transferred to California as minister for the Powell Street Methodist Church in San Francisco in the late 1850s. From 1856 to 1865 he edited the *California Christian Advocate.*

36. As a young man, Alfred B. Meacham (1826–82) assisted in removing the Sauk and Fox Indians to a reservation assigned them after the Black Hawk War. He was

superintendent of Indian Affairs for Oregon from 1868 to 1872. In Washington, D.C., when the Modoc troubles erupted, Meacham secured appointment as nominal chairman of the peace commission.

37. Leroy S. Dyar (b. 1833) came to the Pacific Coast in 1858. After teaching at Willamette University and serving briefly as agent to the Grand Ronde reservation, he was appointed Indian agent to the Klamath agency.

38. Dyar and Thomas were not members of the commission as originally composed, but rather replaced Jesse Applegate and Samuel Case when they resigned (Applegate on February 26 and Case on March 2).

39. General Canby and the peace commission made their first effort at communicating with the Modocs on February 18, 1873.

40. This occurred when Canby believed he had a good-faith commitment on the part of the Modocs to surrender on March 10; probably because of dissension and uncertainty within their own ranks, no Modocs appeared.

41. Edwin C. Mason (1831–98) began the Civil War as a captain in the 2nd Ohio Volunteer Infantry and rose to the rank of brevet brigadier general of volunteers. He became major in the 21st U.S. Infantry in September 1871. For his service in the Modoc and Nez Perce Wars he was brevetted a brigadier general in the Regular army. Mason retired a colonel in 1895.

42. On March 24 Mason took up a position at Scorpion Point, slightly over five miles *east* of the Stronghold; on April 1 Canby and Gillem moved their headquarters, and Gillem's troops, to a spot known as Gillem's Camp, three miles *west* of the Stronghold.

43. Boston Charley was one of Captain Jack's most loyal followers. He was called Boston because of his light skin tone. His Indian name was Bostin Ah-gar.

44. Toby Riddle (1850–1920) was a cousin of Captain Jack; her Modoc name was Kaitchkana, or Nanooktowa. She was married at age twelve to Frank Riddle, a thirty-year-old settler who lived near Yreka. A devoted couple, their marriage endured until Frank's death in 1906. After Alfred B. Meacham recovered from his Modoc War wounds, he took the Riddles with him on lecture tours; Meacham gave Toby the name "Winema," for reasons never made clear. In 1890 Congress voted Toby a monthly pension of $25 for her interpretive services—and loyalty—during the Modoc War.

45. Jackson is mistaken as to the date; the fateful conference occurred on April 11.

46. William L. Sherwood of New York was commissioned a second lieutenant in the 21st U.S. Infantry in September 1867 and promoted to first lieutenant in July 1872.

47. William H. Boyle. For a biographical sketch, see note 1 of the chapter entitled "Personal Observations on the Conduct of the Modoc War," by Boyle.

48. The attack occurred on April 15–17, 1873.

49. Evan Thomas (1843–73), the son of Brig. Gen. Lorenzo Thomas, adjutant general of the army during the Civil War, was a veteran artillery officer who won brevets at Fredericksburg and Gettysburg.

50. Thomas led a sixty-six-man patrol from Gillem's Camp on the morning of April 26 to determine the feasibility of moving artillery into the Lava Beds. Twenty-four Modocs under Scarfaced Charley shadowed the patrol and ambushed it at Sand Butte. The command collapsed. Thomas and his officers were all killed or mortally wounded, and twenty-one enlisted men were killed and sixteen wounded.

51. A small body of water also known as Sorass Lake. The force attacked consisted of Battery B, 4th U.S. Artillery, Troops B and G, 1st Cavalry, and the Warm Springs scouts, all under the command of Capt. Henry C. Hasbrouck (b. 1839) of the 4th Artillery, later commandant of cadets at West Point.

52. Hasbrouck pursued the Modocs three to four miles before returning to Peninsula Camp, on the eastern edge of Tule Lake. Army losses were two enlisted men

killed and seven wounded. Hasbrouck claimed one Modoc killed and two wounded. *Chronological List,* 54.

53. These converging movements occurred on May 12–14, 1873.
54. The Hot Creek Modocs headed west, not south, toward the mountains beyond Van Bremer's ranch. After lingering a time at their Big Sand Butte stronghold, Captain Jack's band fled northeastward.
55. For a biographical sketch of Jefferson C. Davis, see note 1 of the chapter entitled "Observations on the Modoc War," by Davis.
56. Sixty-three Modocs, most of them of the Hot Creek band, surrendered at Fairchild's ranch on May 22.
57. Also known as Langell Valley.
58. Thirty-one Modocs surrendered on May 31, 1873.
59. Captain Jack was captured along Willow Creek, some six miles east of Clear Lake, on June 1, 1873.
60. A June 6, 1873, telegram to Davis related a War Department decision to defer any executions until the attorney general decided whether the Modocs were prisoners of war under military jurisdiction or murderers who should be turned over to civil authorities for prosecution. On June 9 the attorney general ruled that the Modocs' actions since November 29, 1872, had constituted war, subjecting them to military law.
61. October 3, 1873.

Ivan D. Applegate: The Initial Shot of the Modoc War

1. Ivan D. Applegate (1840–1918) was the brother of Oliver C. Applegate and the son of early Oregon settler Lindsey Applegate. At the age of ten, Ivan was with the party that found the bodies of emigrants the Modocs had massacred at Bloody Point on Tule Lake. Although the experience did not make Applegate a Modoc hater, he was ever after distrustful of them. Ivan and Oliver helped their father establish the Klamath Indian Agency. In 1869 Applegate made a lasting enemy of Captain Jack when he called for the recalcitrant chief's arrest. At the time of the Modoc War, Applegate was in charge of the government commissary at Yainax and agent for reservation Northern Paiute and Old Schonchin's Modoc band.

Maurice Fitzgerald: The Modoc War

1. Maurice Fitzgerald was a private in Troop K, 1st U.S. Cavalry during the campaign; he rose to the rank of sergeant in the regiment.
2. The complete title of the article as it originally appeared was "The Modoc War: Reminiscences of the Campaign against the Indian Uprising in the Lava Beds of Northern California and Southern Oregon in 1872–73. A First-Hand Account of the Murder of General Canby."
3. Jackson did not return to Fort Klamath, but remained at the Crawley ranch awaiting reinforcements.
4. Fitzgerald is incorrect. Hooker Jim's band killed only male settlers—at least fourteen, by most estimates.
5. For a biographical sketch of Oliver C. Applegate, see note 1 of the chapter entitled "The Modoc Peace Commission Massacre," by Applegate.
6. General Canby ordered Troop K to the front as soon as he learned of the failure of the January 17, 1873, attack on the Stronghold.
7. Perry was wounded only in the upper arm.

8. James Biddle (1832–1910) of the 1st U.S. Cavalry had been a brevet brigadier general of volunteers during the Civil War. He retired in 1896 as colonel of the 9th U.S. Cavalry.

9. Troop K arrived on February 14, 1873, seventy strong.

10. The ranch belonged to one Jesse Carr but had been surveyed for him by Jesse Applegate (1811–88), one of the Oregon Territory's most prominent early pioneers and the uncle of Ivan D. and Oliver C. Applegate. Jesse Applegate was living on Carr's place at the time of the Modoc War, and the army referred to the site of its camp as the Applegate ranch. Thompson, *Modoc War,* 51–54.

11. Troop K marched on March 11. Part of their route followed the Tickner road. In 1871 H. C. Tickner of Yreka had laid out a road south from Van Bremer's ranch, around the southern end of the Lava Beds, to join the existing road running from Linkville, down the east side of Tule Lake, and to the Pit River country. The route greatly shortened the distance between Yreka and the Pit River settlements. Thompson, *Modoc War,* 54–55.

12. A probable reference to Big Sand Butte.

13. Troop K arrived at Van Bremer's on the night of March 15. During its march across the Lava Beds, the troop captured thirty-four Modoc horses.

14. Fitzgerald's recollection is faulty; the reconnaissance occurred on March 23, 1873, eight days after Troop K arrived at Van Bremer's.

15. The party halted along the southwest corner of Tule Lake.

16. While Canby and Gillem conferred, Dr. Thomas Cabaniss and Edward Fox, a newspaper correspondent who had visited the Stronghold, wandered down the bluff to talk with the Indian. Learning that Captain Jack wanted to speak with Canby, they remained with the Indian as hostages of sorts while Captain Jack and Canby conferred. Thompson, *Modoc War,* 56–57.

17. Captain Jack.

18. The move to the base of the bluff occurred on April 1, 1873.

19. Mason moved from Scorpion Point to Hospital Rock.

20. Some sources place the number at six. Thompson, *Modoc War,* 60.

21. Most accounts have Dyar on horseback.

22. Dyar and Meacham said Toby had been knocked down at the first fire and had remained beside the wounded Meacham until the soldiers arrived.

23. Captain Jack also stabbed Canby in the throat after the general had been shot.

24. Thomas Cabaniss (c. 1826–87), a graduate of Maryland University Medical School, had come to California in 1849 in search of gold. Unsuccessful in mining, he returned to medicine. Cabaniss knew the Modocs well, having once set Captain Jack's arm. He offered his services as assistant army surgeon during the Modoc War.

25. Canby was fifty-five at the time of his murder.

26. Colonel Gillem was in charge of the operation. Major Green led the troops converging on the Stronghold from the west. The force was not, as Fitzgerald recalled, composed principally of cavalry. Green's command consisted of Troops F and K, 1st U.S. Cavalry; A, E, K, and M, 4th U.S. Artillery; and Companies E and G, 12th U.S. Infantry. The total strength was approximately 375 officers and men. Only the two cavalry troops moved out that night; the remainder of the command broke camp at 8:00 A.M., April 15.

27. Mason's command numbered approximately 300 and consisted of Troops B and G, 1st U.S. Cavalry; Companies B, C, and I, 21st U.S. Infantry; and the Warm Springs Indian scouts.

28. The peninsula Fitzgerald describes is known as Hovey Point and lay a mile west of the Stronghold. It was on Hovey Point that Troops F and K passed the early-morning hours of April 15.

29. The accidental discharge probably occurred as the artillery and infantry passed the cavalry on the morning of April 15. Murray, *Modocs,* 207–8, implies that the clumsy soldier was a member of Battery E, Fourth U.S. Artillery, which led the march column.
30. Green advanced Troops F and K at about 4:00 P.M. to occupy the extreme left of his line.
31. April 16, 1873.
32. Companies B, C, and I, 21st U.S. Infantry; Troops B and G, 1st U.S. Cavalry; Warm Springs Indian scouts; and howitzers, all under the command of Major Mason.
33. Bacon resigned his commission in June 1878.
34. Army losses were six killed and seventeen wounded; Modoc losses have been estimated at three warriors and eight women killed.
35. Eugene Hovey of Yreka, California, killed when Hooker Jim and a few cohorts, on their way to raid on Gillem's camp, came upon the unfortunate packer.
36. April 18, 1873.
37. April 26, 1873.
38. McKay had with him only twelve scouts. Gillem said the Warm Springs Indians tried to aid Thomas's patrol, but that the troops mistook them for Modocs and fired on them. More probably, McKay and his scouts realized that thirteen men could do little to help anyone but themselves.
39. May 30, 1873.
40. I have found no evidence that Scarfaced Charley was other than a Modoc.
41. Joel G. Trimble, a Regular army man who had begun his career in 1855 as a private.
42. In 1909 the government permitted any Modocs who wished to do so to return to the Klamath reservation.

Anonymous: The Modocs Laugh at the Soldiers

1. An abbreviated version of this article appeared in the *Army and Navy Journal* 10, no. 28 (February 22, 1873): 436.
2. Captain Jack met with Fairchild on the bluffs west of the Stronghold in early December to deny any responsibility for the Lost River battle and subsequent murder of Oregon settlers.

William H. Boyle: Personal Observations on the Conduct of the Modoc War

1. William H. Boyle (1837–1919) served in the 5th New York Artillery during the Civil War, rising to the volunteer rank of major. He was commissioned a second lieutenant in the 2nd U.S. Infantry in May 1866 and promoted to first lieutenant the following year. In December 1870 he joined the 21st U.S. Infantry. He saw service in the Nez Perce and Bannock campaigns. Boyle retired a lieutenant colonel in 1900.
2. Boyle penned his observations for Hubert H. Bancroft's use in the second volume of his history of Oregon. Boyle's grammar was faulty (I have corrected the most egregious errors), and he tended to write painfully long sentences strung together by an endless series of "ands" and "buts." I have broken up some of these to make for easier reading. Bancroft acknowledged that Boyle's Modoc War manuscript had been "of great service to me in enabling me to give a connected account of

that remarkable campaign." Bancroft, *History of Oregon, 1848–1888* (San Francisco: History Publishing Company, 1888), 2:582.
3. Col. Robert S. Granger (d. 1894) of the 21st U.S. Infantry.
4. Sixty-four officers and men.
5. 1st Lt. John Q. Adams, 1st U.S. Cavalry.
6. On December 21, 1872.
7. The escort consisted of six men.
8. Bernard himself did not go; rather, he sent 2nd Lt. John G. Kyle with ten men of Troop G, 1st Cavalry, to rescue the wagon party.
9. 2nd Lieutenant William H. Miller.
10. January 20, 1873.
11. A reference to President Lincoln's dismissal of Maj. Gen. George B. McClellan after the battle of Antietam in the autumn of 1862.
12. The ranch of Presley Dorris was located near the west bank of Little (Lower) Klamath Lake, approximately ten miles northwest of Van Bremer's place.
13. Boyle's recollection of the date is correct.
14. April 10, 1873.
15. Capt. Marcus Miller, 4th Artillery, whom Green had placed in charge of his main force.
16. Boyle's statement is misleading. No one from Gillem to the lowest private knew where the Modocs had gone; they certainly did not expose themselves to view that day.
17. Assistant Surgeon Henry McElderry, the chief medical officer of Gillem's command, recorded twenty-three casualties during the hostilities of April 15–17. Thompson, *Modoc War,* 75.
18. April 20, 1873.
19. Capt. John Mendenhall, commanding Battery G, 4th U.S. Artillery.
20. On April 21 the Modocs attacked a heavily escorted mule train between Scorpion Point and the Stronghold. Pvt. Morris Darcey, Battery M, 4th U.S. Artillery was killed, and Pvt. John Welsh, Co. G, 12th U.S. Infantry, wounded.
21. Eugene Hovey, a civilian packer. Hooker Jim and a small band of Modocs had made the raid.
22. The accounts of survivors do not suggest that any officers fell in the first fire, but rather were picked off slowly over the course of the fight. Boyle contradicts his own assertion in the next paragraph.
23. Official sources place the number of dead enlisted men at twenty.

Edward Fox: The Modoc Muddle
1. Edward Fox (d. 1895) was an Englishman of means who had served in the British Army. He was the yachting editor of the New York *Herald* at outbreak of the Modoc War. Learning from army sources that a competent interviewer might be able to reach Captain Jack, the *Herald*'s publisher, James G. Bennett, Jr., gave the assignment to Fox. He reached the front on February 5, 1873. Fox continued with the *Herald* for a time after the war, helping expose corruption in Indian affairs with stories of fraud and mismanagement at the Red Cloud agency. Fox eventually settled in Australia, where he copublished a newspaper called *The British Australian* and dabbled in mining ventures. He died in a yachting accident near Perth. Knight, *Following the Indian Wars,* 110, 320–21.
2. Fox's articles to the *Herald* were published as they were received from the front. I have placed them in chronological order, rather than in the sequence they appeared.
3. H. Wallace Atwell of the Sacramento *Record.*

4. Cattle rancher Presley "Press" Dorris, who enjoyed good relations with the Modocs.

5. The massacre occurred in November 1852. Among the few to escape was Schonchin Jim.

6. J. W. Petit Harrington.

7. Captain Jack did go to the reservation but quit it in the summer of 1867 after his split with Old Schonchin.

8. A possible reference to William J. Small of Linkville, Oregon.

9. I have omitted the remainder of Fox's first dispatch, which contained a sketch of the battle of January 17, 1873, because he treated the fight so fully in his dispatch of February 8, 1873.

10. Fox wrote the account that follows three days after arriving at Fairchild's ranch. Knight, *Following the Indian Wars,* 112, termed it "the outstanding story" of the battle of January 17, 1873. Fox interviewed participants scrupulously and presented the salient field orders and battle reports in his article, with but slight variance in details of phraseology, initials, and punctuation.

11. A reference to the Hot Creek band of Modocs.

12. George H. Burton (b. 1843) graduated with the West Point Class of 1865 and spent the next forty-one years of his life in the army, retiring as a lieutenant colonel in 1907. Burton was brevetted for distinguished service in the Lava Beds and also took part in the Nez Perce campaign.

13. Some accounts place the time of Perry's arrival at the chasm as 2:00 P.M.

14. Fox concluded the article with lengthy extracts from the reports of the officers involved, which I have omitted.

15. A probable reference to Toby Riddle.

16. Fox referred to himself as the "*Herald* commissioner," a term in vogue among *Herald* reporters.

17. Better known as the Siletz reservation, home to the Rogue River Indians.

18. February 13, 1873.

19. Henry R. Anderson, 4th U.S. Artillery.

20. Governor Grover was a Democrat; the commissioners were Republicans.

21. Robert Whittle's wife, Matilda.

22. February 17, 1873.

23. February 19, 1873.

24. Capt. O. C. Knapp was a veteran of the Civil War who had twice been brevetted for gallantry.

25. Brother-in-law of A. B. Meacham.

26. February 21, 1873.

27. A. M. Rosborough, county judge of Siskiyou County, California, and a business partner of Steele. During the three years Jack was off the reservation, he frequently came to Steele and Rosborough for advice and assistance.

28. Also known as Rock Dave.

29. Variously known as Hooker Jim, Hawker Jim, and Hooka Jim.

30. Also known as Miller's Charley.

31. O. C. Brown, better known as "One-Armed" Brown, a friend of Ivan D. Applegate.

32. The account that follows is the much fuller account of Fox's visit to the Lava Beds that he had promised readers of the *Herald.* As his shorter dispatch of February 25 had cost $500 or $600 to telegraph to the *Herald,* Fox was compelled to mail the longer story to New York. Knight, *Following the Indian Wars,* 126.

33. Fox's audacious visit to Captain Jack's camp the week before had paved the way for other journalists to interview the hostile Modocs. Accompanying Fox on March 1 were Alex McKay of the San Francisco *Evening Bulletin,* Robert D. Bogart of the San Francisco *Chronicle,* and H. Wallace Atwell of the Sacramento *Record.*

34. Historians of the Modoc War have discounted the belief, widely held at the time, that Snake Indians had reinforced the Modocs. However, no serious study of the Modoc War has made use of Fox's dispatches. In light of Jack's remarks to Fox, the matter may be open to re-examination.
35. J. H. Wilbur, agent of the Yakima agency, whom Meacham disliked for his paternalistic jurisdiction over all the Yakima, whether in the Yakima agency or in Meacham's Oregon superintendency.
36. Perhaps because of their dislike for Meacham, neither Odeneal nor Wilbur wanted to serve on the commission.
37. March 24 or 25, 1873.
38. March 21, 1873.
39. April 11, 1873.
40. The weight of testimony at the trial of the Modoc prisoners suggests that Canby remained frozen after the misfire and did not begin running, or lurching, toward the army camp until Jack had shot him in the face. Ellen's Man, rather than Shacknasty Jim, helped Jack dispatch Canby. Murray, *Modocs,* 189.
41. Boston Charley's first shot struck Thomas in the chest.
42. The Modocs in question were not Scarfaced Charley and Steamboat Frank, but rather Miller's Charley, Curly Headed Jack, and Comstock Dave.
43. Fox is incorrect; Battery E formed the initial skirmish line.
44. A spurious claim; only two Modocs were confirmed as killed during the fighting of April 15–17.
45. Captain Bernard was ill and did not participate in the second battle for the Stronghold.
46. Skinner and Stirling were civilian contract surgeons.
47. A rumor without foundation.
48. April 16, 1873.
49. Thompson, *Modoc War,* 168–70, places Modoc losses as two killed and none wounded. John Schonchin was not killed.
50. 1st Lt. Peter Leary, Jr., of Battery E, 4th U.S. Artillery.
51. A reference to Eugene Hovey, killed on April 17, 1873.
52. April 18, 1873.
53. William Simpson had been in San Francisco, during the course of a trip around the world, when he learned of Canby's murder.
54. May 2, 1873.
55. An obscure derivation of epizootic, which refers to any sort of disease affecting many animals of one kind simultaneously.
56. Edwin V. Sumner of the 1st Cavalry, aide-de-camp to Colonel Davis.
57. Garret J. Lydecker of the Engineer Corps accompanied Davis to prepare drawings of the Lava Beds and the Stronghold.
58. Confident that the fighting in the Lava Beds had drawn to a close, Fox left the field with William Simpson of the *Illustrated London News* on the morning of April 26, remaining just long enough to watch Thomas's doomed patrol set off. Fox reached Yreka on the twenty-eighth. There he penned an account of the slaughter of Thomas's patrol based on reports—and probably rumors—from the front; I have omitted it. Fox remained two weeks longer in Yreka before returning to New York.

P. W. Hamont: The Modoc Indian War, by One Who Was There

1. P. W. Hamont was the first sergeant of Battery A, 4th U.S. Artillery, during the Modoc War.
2. Hamont wrote his recollections of the Modoc War at his home in Hickory, North Carolina, in August 1910. They contained a good deal of preliminary material on

the antecedents of the war and of the fighting itself prior to the arrival of Battery A, 4th Artillery, on the field. I have omitted this portion.

3. The four units of the 4th Artillery, including Hamont's Battery A, arrived at Van Bremer's ranch on February 4, 1873.
4. Barncho and Slolux initially were to be hanged, but President Ulysses S. Grant commuted their sentence to life in prison. Ironically, it was the War Department that had requested the commutation, arguing that the two were unwitting participants in the massacre.
5. Boston Charley killed the Reverend Thomas.
6. A ricocheting bullet, and not a rifle butt, had caused Meacham's head wound.
7. In his confidential report of the affair, Colonel Gillem insisted that the commands of Green and Mason united north of the Stronghold on the afternoon of April 16. Both Maurice Fitzgerald, in his article appearing earlier in this section, and Hamont say otherwise.
8. Hamont meant that they should have made their junction south of the Stronghold, rather than north of it as they did.
9. Company G, 12th U.S. Infantry, did not participate in the patrol.
10. Lieutenant Wright, not Cranston, led the advance guard.
11. Other accounts say that Lieutenant Harris, rather than Howe, accompanied Thomas up the ridge.
12. Official casualty lists place the loss at forty. The casualties broke down as follows: Battery A, 4th Artillery, nine killed and four wounded; Battery K, 4th Artillery, five killed and five wounded; Company E, 12th Infantry, seven dead and seven wounded; from units not assigned to the patrol, one killed and one wounded; and one civilian packer killed. The Modocs apparently suffered no casualties. Murray, *Modocs and Their War*, 236.
13. On May 6 two friendly Indian women whom Colonel Davis had enlisted to search for Cranston's party found their bodies at the base of Sand Butte. Three days later a patrol buried them on the spot, the bodies having decomposed too far to be removed.
14. According to Charles B. Hardin, in his article elsewhere in this section, it was 1st Sgt. Thomas Kelly, or Kelley, Troop G, 1st Cavalry, who got the men started when he yelled, "Gosh dash it, let's charge!" Of course, more than one soldier may have uttered the same or similar words simultaneously.
15. The Warm Springs lost two killed.
16. Also known as Ellen's Man George.
17. The pursuit began on May 12, 1873.
18. Hooker's Jim band was not guilty of the murder of white women and children; during their ride through the settlements to join Captain Jack at the end of November 1872, these Modocs had killed only adult males.

Oliver C. Applegate: The Modoc Peace Commission Massacre

1. Oliver C. Applegate (1845–1938) was the son of prominent Northwest frontiersman Lindsey Applegate. A schoolteacher before the Civil War, he served three years as a captain in the territorial volunteers. In October 1865 he became assistant agent of the Klamath Indian Agency, his father being the agent. For some time before the Modoc War, Applegate was agent at the Yainax subagency. After the war, he held various political offices and in 1898 became agent of the Klamath reservation.

George W. Kingsbury: The Twelfth U.S. Infantry in the Lava Beds

1. George W. Kingsbury (d. 1897) rose from the ranks during the Civil War, ending the conflict a brevet captain of volunteers. Lieutenant Kingsbury was assigned to the 12th U.S. Infantry in January 1870 and retired in May 1886.
2. Wright failed to extend his company far enough to the left and right to cover the ridges on either side of the march column.
3. Other accounts assert that all but seven members of Company E deserted Wright and fled back they way they had come. Thompson, *Modoc War,* 86.
4. George M. Harris (c. 1846–73) of the West Point Class of 1868. He died of his wounds on May 12, 1873.

Charles B. Hardin: "Gosh Dash It, Let's Charge": A Story of the Modoc War

1. Charles B. Hardin entered the army as a private in Troop G, 1st U.S. Cavalry in August 1872. He rose to the rank of sergeant before being commissioned a second lieutenant in the 18th U.S. Infantry in March 1882. He retired a captain in April 1898.
2. Thomas had with him Batteries A and B, 4th U.S. Artillery, and Company E of the 12th U.S. Infantry.
3. Named for Lt. William H. Boyle; also known as the Peninsula Camp.
4. Learning that the Modocs were moving toward the southeast, Colonel Davis dispatched Hasbrouck to intercept them; that was the purpose of the patrol.
5. Battery B bivouacked at the northern base of Timber Mountain, just beyond the southern extreme of the Lava Beds.
6. Hasbrouck did in fact post guards, on a thirty-foot-high, rocky bluff 400 yards north of the cavalry camp.
7. The Modocs had crept past Hasbrouck's outposts and down onto a lower, east-west line of rock outcroppings.
8. Thompson, *Modoc War,* 98, speculates, probably correctly, that Kelley in fact shouted, "God damn it, let's charge!"
9. Thompson, *Modoc War,* 98, and Murray, *Modocs,* 248–49, record only one Modoc—Ellen's Man—as having been killed.
10. The *Chronological List,* 54, shows army casualties to have been two killed and seven wounded, with one Warm Springs Indian scout killed and two wounded.

Jefferson C. Davis: Observations on the Modoc War

1. Jefferson C. Davis (1828–79) served as an enlisted man during the Mexican War. Appointed a second lieutenant in the Regular army in 1848, Davis was at Fort Sumter when it was bombarded. Davis was appointed colonel of the 22nd Indiana Infantry in August 1861 and in December was promoted to brigadier general of volunteers. His further rise ended abruptly when he murdered a fellow general, William Nelson, in a Louisville hotel after a quarrel. Although he commanded a corps during the March to the Sea, Davis was denied a brigadier generalship in the Regular army. He was a colonel at time of the Modoc War.
2. Alex McKay, a thirty-five-year-old former surveyor from Rhode Island.
3. On June 7, 1873, four Modocs still at large surrendered themselves at Fairchild's ranch. James Fairchild was driving the Modocs to Davis's camp when two unknown white men accosted them, shooting the three Modoc men and one woman while holding Fairchild at gunpoint.

"Veritas": The Capture of Captain Jack

1. With Scarfaced Charley were twelve other warriors, ten women, and nine children.
2. Humpy Joe, a half-brother of Captain Jack.

H. Wallace Atwell: The Modoc Misery

1. H. Wallace Atwell (c. 1833–88) had been a California newspaperman for twenty-two years. He came to the Lava Beds to report for the Sacramento *Record,* but after Edward Fox returned to New York, Atwell took over as the *Herald*'s Modoc War correspondent. After the conflict, he continued in California journalism until his death.
2. Atwell is not referring to the famous Stronghold that the Modocs abandoned on April 17, but rather to Sand Butte, from which the Modocs had ambushed Thomas's patrol on April 26.
3. 1st Lt. Edward Field, acting commander of Battery A, led the remnants of Batteries A and K and of Company E, 12th U.S. Infantry, as well as Company G, 12th U.S. Infantry, in the search for the dead of Thomas's patrol.
4. Official reports place the number of wagons at four.
5. Captain Hasbrouck commanded the force, which consisted of Troops B and G of the 1st Cavalry, Battery B, 4th Artillery (mounted), and the Warm Springs scouts.
6. May 17, 1873.
7. Thompson, *Modoc War,* gives Modoc losses as two men and three women dead. Perhaps because Hasbrouck was loath to report that his men had killed women, the *Chronological List,* 54, gives Modoc losses as just two killed.
8. May 20, 1873.
9. Curly Headed Jack had been an advocate of war since at least mid-1870.
10. One of a number of names used to identify the Wasco, a Chinookan tribe that had been removed from their homeland near the Dalles, Oregon, in 1855 and resettled on the Warm Springs reservation.
11. Atwell left Perry's detachment on a $300 mule as soon as Jack was captured and tried to take a shortcut to Ashland, Oregon, to file his story ahead of the other correspondents. On the way, his mule fell and broke its neck. An injured Atwell stumbled into Boyle's camp. He later received medical treatment in Yreka.
12. Sgt. Michael McCarthy of the 1st Cavalry recorded in his diary that a detachment under his command, consisting of Captain Trimble, himself as sergeant, a corporal, fourteen privates, the civilian Charley Putnam, and two Warm Springs Indians, closed in on Captain Jack. According to McCarthy, Trimble wanted to rush the Modocs in a skirmish line, but the Warm Springs warned them to be patient. The troops, said McCarthy, "sat down out of sight of anybody in the canyon, but within a few yards of Jack's hiding place. . . . After some parley, Jack came up on our side and surrendered himself." Although McCarthy does not say so, it can be assumed that Jack had parleyed with the Warm Springs. Quoted in Thompson, *Modoc War,* 115.
13. The massacre occurred at Adams Point, seven miles from the Lost River ford, where Fairchild had come upon a company of recently recruited Oregon volunteers under Joseph W. Hyzer. The dead included Little John, Tee-He Jack, Pony, and Mooch; Little John's wife was wounded, perhaps accidentally. Hyzer was absolved of any responsibility for the act.
14. Mrs. William Boddy.
15. Accompanying Mrs. Boddy was her daughter, a Mrs. Schira.
16. That gentleman was none other than Atwell himself, who rushed into Davis's tent, yelling that the two women were about to kill the Modocs. Murray, *Modocs,* 274.
17. Davis took no action to find the murderers of the captive Modocs.

18. The deserters were sentenced to seven years at Alcatraz with ball and chain.
19. Hyzer's volunteers captured the Modocs on June 5, 1873.

PART THREE: THE NEZ PERCE CAMPAIGN, 1877

Heinmot Tooyalakekt (Chief Joseph): Chief Joseph's Own Story

1. Jacob B. Dunn, Jr. (1855–1924), a historical writer whose *Massacres of the Mountains: A History of the Indian Wars of the Far West,* published in 1886, is still regarded as one of the finest works on the subject, called "Chief Joseph's Own Story" the "most magnificent piece of Indian eloquence ever known." Dunn, *Massacres,* 672. While inaccurate in certain particulars, vague on dates, and subject to the vagaries of translation, the pathos and majesty of Joseph's words make their inclusion in this volume imperative. Rather than engage in a tiresome critique of Joseph's occasional lapses, for the most part I have limited my editorial remarks to biographical sketches of notable Nez Perces and Americans mentioned in the text. Joseph's narrative is best read in conjunction with Oliver O. Howard's prickly, but generally reliable, rejoinder, "The True Story of the Wallowa Campaign." It is the next article in this volume.

2. Heinmot Tooyalakekt (c. 1840–1904), known to history as Chief Joseph, was the son of Tuekakas, or Wellammootkin, whom the whites called Old Joseph. The great Nez Perce warrior Ollokot (Frog) was a brother of the young Joseph. Although he had had no war experience prior to the Nez Perce outbreak, and had only ventured onto the plains for one buffalo hunt, Joseph's courage and diplomatic skills made him a natural leader among the nontreaty Nez Perces. Standing over six feet tall, Joseph was handsome and an able orator.

3. Also known as the Wallowa band or Lower Nez Perces for their location within the tribal homelands.

4. European observers have assigned various Native American names to the tribe, often those by which other tribes referred to the Nez Perces. I have used Nee-Me-Poo, which Jerome A. Greene employs in his definitive *Nez Perce Summer, 1877* (Helena: Montana Historical Society, 2000).

5. Tuekakas (c. 1790–1871) embraced Christianity in the 1830s and baptized his son Joseph. He disavowed the faith in favor of the Smohalla (Dreamer) religion when whites began overrunning the Nez Perce homelands.

6. Henry H. Spalding (1803–74), a Presbyterian missionary who worked successfully among the Nez Perces at Lapwai from 1836 to 1847. Spalding befriended Old Joseph and converted a large portion of the Nez Perces to Christianity. He returned to the Nez Perces in 1871 as a member of the Presbyterian Board of Foreign Missions and was accorded an enthusiastic welcome.

7. Isaac I. Stevens, territorial governor of Washington, who later died in the Civil War. The conference occurred in June 1855.

8. Hallahotsoot, or Shadow of the Mountain (c. 1794–1876), was known to the whites as Lawyer because of his oratorical skills. A lifelong ally of the whites, Lawyer believed that only by assimilating their culture and giving up their nomadic way of life could the Nez Perces hope to survive.

9. For a biographical sketch of Brig. Gen. Oliver O. Howard, see note 1 of the chapter entitled "The True Story of the Wallowa Campaign," by Howard.

10. Toohoolhoolzote, or Sound (c. 1810–77), was the chosen spokesman of the nontreaty Nez Perces with whom Howard met. Toohoolhoolzote has been described as a tall, heavy man of uncommon strength.

11. Peopeo Kiskiok Hihih, or White Bird (c. 1807–82), was the eldest of the five non-treaty Nez Perce chiefs. Although an experienced warrior, White Bird was an advocate of peace.

12. Allalimya Takanin, or Looking Glass (c. 1823–77), was the son of a noted Nez Perce chief of the same name. Himself a prominent war chief, Looking Glass led the Alpowai band of nontreaty Nez Perces, which counted some forty warriors.

13. Arthur I. "Ad" Chapman (d. 1924) was among the first settlers of White Bird, Idaho. He operated a toll road in Idaho County and had several wives, among them an Umatilla woman. Other Nez Perce leaders were less forgiving of his conduct during the conflict than Joseph, considering him to be "a coward and a bad man who had given them nothing but trouble, and was not thought of as a friend, a reputation which has sometimes been given him." Thrapp, *Dictionary,* 1:252–53.

14. John Gibbon (1827–96), of the West Point Class of 1847, emerged from the Civil War a major general of volunteers and was appointed colonel of the 36th U.S. Infantry in July 1866, and of the 7th Infantry in March 1869.

15. Col. Samuel D. Sturgis (1833–89), the commander of the 7th U.S. Cavalry. A veteran of the Mexican War and of frontier service against the Apaches in the 1850s, Sturgis compiled a creditable record during the Civil War, earning the rank of brevet major general of volunteers.

16. Nelson A. Miles (1839–1925), an able but vain and insensitive officer who rose from the rank of lieutenant of volunteers during the Civil War to commander in chief of the U.S. Army in 1895.

17. For a biographical sketch of Yellow Bull, see note 1 of the chapter entitled "Yellow Bull's Story" by Chuslum Moxnox (Yellow Bull).

18. E. A. Hayt, the commissioner of Indian affairs, was sympathetic to the Nez Perce plight. He believed the conflict had been brought about "by the rascality of their agent and the encroachments of the whites," and also maintained that the Nez Perces had been treated with unwarranted harshness. Quoted in Merrill D. Beal, *"I Will Fight No More Forever," Chief Joseph and the Nez Perce War* (Seattle: University of Washington Press, 1963), 265.

19. John McNeill, the inspector general of the U.S. Army, visited Joseph in 1878 and made arrangements for him to meet with President Rutherford B. Hayes the following year.

20. Congressman Benjamin F. Butler of Massachusetts had been a major general of volunteers during the Civil War.

Oliver O. Howard: The True Story of the Wallowa Campaign

1. Oliver O. Howard (1830–1909) was a member of the West Point Class of 1854 who rose to the rank of major general of volunteers during the Civil War. A deeply religious man who championed the cause of freed slaves, Howard served as commissioner of the Bureau of Refugees, Freedmen, and Abandoned Lands from 1865 to 1872. He negotiated a fragile peace with the Apache chief Cochise in 1872 and also founded Howard University. Howard wrote widely of his Indian Wars service.

2. An abbreviated version of Howard's article appeared in Cyrus T. Brady, *Northwestern Fights and Fighters* (New York: Doubleday, Page and Company, 1907).

3. Palmer was the then superintendent of Indian affairs for Oregon.

4. In the spring of 1874 a white settler named Lawrence Ott murdered Tipyahlana Siskan, a nontreaty Nez Perce, in a dispute over land. Ott surrendered himself to authorities but went unpunished.

5. In June 1876 two white men named Findley and McNall entered a Nez Perce hunting camp and accused a Wallowa tribesman named Wilhautyah of having stolen their stock. When Wilhautyah tried to defend himself, Findley shot him.

6. "Dreamers" was the term whites gave to followers of Smohalla (c. 1818–1907), a Native American prophet who counted some two thousand adherents among the tribes of the Northwest. A hunchback and chief of the small Sokulk tribe, in his youth Smohalla had absorbed some Roman Catholic ritual and doctrine. Smohalla began preaching in 1850, and his fame aroused the wrath of Chief Moses of the neighboring Sinkiuse-Columbia. After having been left for dead in a battle against Moses, Smohalla left home secretly and roamed as far south as Mexico. Upon returning, he proclaimed that he had been to the spirit world and had returned to tell the Indians that they must reject the ways of the white man and return to their primitive way of life.
7. James Reuben, a Christian Nez Perce who also led a detachment of Nez Perce scouts for the army.
8. Nez Perce accounts tell the story differently. Yellow Wolf asserted that Toohool-hoolzote merely had demanded more time to move his people, saying, "You have brought a rifle to a peace council. If you mean but thirty suns for gathering our stock, yes. We will have to fight." Beal, *"I Will Fight No More,"* 41.

Melville C. Wilkinson: Origin of the Difficulties with the Nez Perces
1. Melville C. Wilkinson (1835–98) was aide to General Howard from April 1871 to August 1878. He won a brevet at the battle of Clearwater. Killed in a fight with the Chippewa at Leech Lake, Minnesota, on October 5, 1898, Wilkinson was the last soldier slain by hostile Indians on the continental United States.
2. Eugene A. Bancroft (1825–post-1903) earned a brevet at Clearwater and retired because of old age in 1889.
3. Charles A. Williams (1852–1926) earned a brevet for his service at the battle of Clearwater. He fought in the Spanish-American War and retired as colonel of the 21st U.S. Infantry in 1911.

Albert G. Forse: Chief Joseph as a Commander
1. Joseph also hoped to force the settlers to turn over to him the two white murderers of Wilhautyah.
2. Stephen G. Whipple (1840–95) of the 1st U.S. Cavalry.
3. Sevier M. Rains (1851–77) of the 1st U.S. Cavalry, a member of the West Point Class of 1876.
4. Government losses were eleven soldiers (including Rains) of Troops E and L, 1st U.S. Cavalry, and two civilians killed. There were no known Nez Perce casualties.
5. William H. Winters (1843–80) of the 1st U.S. Cavalry, a veteran of the Apache Wars.
6. Most sources agree that Howard's appearance had taken the Nez Perces by surprise.
7. Army reports place losses at twelve enlisted men killed, two officers and twenty-five men wounded, and one man missing, for a total of forty. Howard reported Nez Perce losses as twenty-three warriors killed and at least twice that number wounded. Based on a review of reliable Nez Perce sources, Greene, *Nez Perce Summer,* 95, concludes Nez Perce casualties to have been four killed and six wounded.
8. Charles C. Rawn (1837–87) of the 7th U.S. Infantry.
9. July 28, 1877.
10. Charles A. Coolidge (1844–1926) of the 7th U.S. Infantry, who also served from time to time as a surgeon. He became a brigadier general upon his retirement in 1903.

11. Gibbon had six companies with him—Companies A, D, F, G, I, and K of the 7th U.S. Infantry—plus the volunteers.
12. The unfortunate warrior was named Hahtalekin.
13. Contrary to Forse's understanding, it was White Bird and Looking Glass, rather than Joseph, who played the greater part in rallying the warriors and driving the soldiers from the village.
14. On August 20, 1877, Looking Glass orchestrated and led a raid on Howard's herd at Camas Meadows, Idaho. With him were Ollokot and Toohoolhoolzote. Whether Joseph even participated in the raid is uncertain. Greene, *Nez Perce Summer,* 154.
15. The battle of Canyon Creek, fought September 13, 1877, cost the army two dead and twelve wounded. Nez Perce losses were three wounded. Howard's cavalry had not reinforced Sturgis; the 7th Cavalry waged the fight alone.
16. Miles attacked from the *south* with his entire command except Troops F, G, and H of the 2nd Cavalry under Capt. George L. Tyler, which swung to the northwest a mile before Miles made contact in order to seize the Nez Perce pony herd.
17. Owen Hale (1843–77) of the 7th U.S. Cavalry.
18. The Nez Perces made it a practice throughout the campaign whenever possible to concentrate their fire on officers and noncommissioned officers.
19. Lovell H. Jerome (1849–1935) of the 2nd U.S. Cavalry. Jerome was twice arrested while serving on the postwar frontier and resigned in 1879. He returned to serve two years as an enlisted man before becoming general manager of a zinc mining operation in Tennessee.
20. Charles C. Gilbert (1822–1903), a member of the West Point Class of 1846 and a veteran of the Mexican and Civil Wars. He was lieutenant colonel of the 7th U.S. Infantry at the time of the Nez Perce campaign.
21. Joseph did not kill all armed males whom he took prisoner.

William R. Parnell: The Nez Perce War, 1877: The Battle of White Bird Canyon
1. Robert H. Fletcher received brevets for gallantry at the battles of Clearwater and Canyon Creek. He retired in 1886.
2. Henry Elfers was notorious in the area as an Indian hater.
3. Benjamin B. Norton, owner of Norton's ranch, also known as the Cottonwood House, had tried to remove his family from danger, only to fall into a Nez Perce ambush. Norton was mortally wounded; his wife, Jennie, and two ranch hands were wounded. Another settler, John Chamberlin, was killed, along with his infant daughter. His other daughter was wounded, and his wife shot with an arrow and raped.
4. The unfortunate woman was Mrs. Isabella Benedict.
5. Edward R. Theller (1831–77) served with the 2nd California Volunteer Infantry in the northwest during the Civil War and later fought creditably in the Modoc War. General Howard called him "a generous, brave man, with a warm heart." Thrapp, *Dictionary,* 3:1415.
6. The fire must have merely dismounted the Nez Perces, as no warriors were killed and only two wounded in the White Bird Canyon fight.

John P. Schorr: The White Bird Fight
1. Schorr was a member of Troop F, 1st U.S. Cavalry.
2. Trumpeter John Jones was killed at White Bird Canyon.
3. Some participants recalled the departure time as 10:00 P.M.

4. Other accounts place the arrival in Grangeville at sundown on June 16, and the departure at 9:00 or 10:00 P.M. Greene, *Nez Perce Summer,* 35; Beal, *"I Will Fight No More,"* 51.
5. Mrs. Isabella Benedict, whose four-year-old daughter had a broken arm.
6. Army casualties were thirty-four killed and two wounded.
7. Troops E and L.
8. There were no known Nez Perce casualties at Cottonwood.
9. Rumors of such fantastic accretions to the Nez Perce ranks suggest the deep fear the army had of the hostile warriors.

Luther P. Wilmot: Narratives of the Nez Perce War

1. Luther P. "Uncle Lew" Wilmot (1839–1922) was born in Freeport, Illinois, and moved west with his family in 1860. He was a successful miner and, after the Nez Perce War, served two terms in the territorial legislature. He died in Long Beach, California, while reading a book aloud to his wife.
2. Darius P. Randall (c. 1837–77), a Civil War veteran and respected Idaho settler whose volunteer company was attached to Capt. Stephen G. Whipple's squadron of the 1st Cavalry at the start of the Nez Perce campaign.
3. The Idaho volunteers were encamped at Mount Idaho.
4. Probably a relative of John M. Crooks, a Mount Idaho town father.
5. Charles Blewett and William Foster were scouting south of Cottonwood on July 3, looking for Nez Perce sign. Near Lawyer's Canyon, they spotted hostile warriors, and on returning to Captain Whipple's command, they were fired upon. Blewett was unhorsed and killed. Foster made it back to camp to report the Nez Perce presence, only to die with Rains's party later that day. Greene, *Nez Perce Summer,* 60–65.
6. July 5, 1877.
7. James C. Cearley was a volunteer lieutenant and local farmer.
8. In retreating from the White Bird Canyon fight, Captain Perry's frightened men passed by, and hid near, Henry C. Johnson's abandoned ranch south of Grangeville.
9. Peter H. Ready and Joseph Moore had sold their ranch at Cottonwood to Ben Norton before the Nez Perce outbreak. Greene, *Nez Perce Summer,* 59.
10. Perry renamed the entrenchments Camp Rains after he learned of the lieutenant's death.
11. Randall intended to charge through the Nez Perce lines to the creek, where he hoped to fashion a defense until Perry could assist him.
12. The low ridge upon which Wilmot and most of the others made their stand was one and a half miles southeast of Cottonwood.
13. Wilmot is mistaken in his recollection of the sequence of events. Captain Perry had directed Captains Whipple and Winters to go to the volunteers' relief with sixty men and a Gatling gun. Winters's detachment halted some 400 yards from the volunteers. Whipple and his men closed to within 200 yards, waited for the Nez Perce response—which was merely to watch the troops from afar—and then moved down to Wilmot's party. Winters followed them down. Greene, *Nez Perce Summer,* 70–71.
14. George Hunter, who commanded a volunteer outfit from Dayton, Washington Territory. With him were the Lewiston, Washington Territory, volunteers of Capt. Edward McConville.
15. The Washington and Idaho Territory volunteers reorganized into a single "regiment." Edward McConville was elected colonel; George Hunter, lieutenant colonel; George Shearer, major; and Benjamin F. Morris, adjutant.

16. In this story, Wilmot discusses events just prior to the Cottonwood fight.
17. Whipple also had orders from General Howard to scout aggressively for the Nez Perces.
18. July 3, 1877.
19. Based on an exhaustive review of relevant sources, Greene, *Nez Perce Summer,* 372–73, concluded that there were no Nez Perce casualties in the Rains fight.
20. I have omitted the remainder of this segment of Wilmot's narrative, as it consists of an inaccurate account of the origins of the Nez Perce outbreak and a confused telling of the White Bird Canyon fight, which Wilmot knew of only by hearsay.
21. Eugene T. Wilson, a volunteer lieutenant.
22. On the morning of July 8, 1877.
23. With the two men carrying the food was a small party from Mount Idaho under George Shearer.
24. Lawrence S. Babbitt, Howard's ordnance officer and acting aide.
25. July 11, 1877.
26. Wilmot erroneously recalled the day as a Sunday.
27. An intriguing but unsubstantiated allegation on the part of Wilmot, the more unlikely because Howard's attack came as a surprise to the Nez Perces. One treaty Nez Perce scout—Elaskolatat—did desert Howard's command during the Clearwater fight to join the hostiles, his father having been killed in the volunteers' fight at Cottonwood. Greene, *Nez Perce Summer,* 85. Perhaps Wilmot and others assumed he had been passing word to Joseph of the army's approach.
28. July 12, 1877.
29. Miller attacked with four companies of infantry, not eight.
30. Howard reported only one man wounded in the July 13, 1877, skirmish at Kamiah.
31. Wilmot's casualty count for the battle of Clearwater is far off the mark. Army casualties were thirteen killed and twenty-seven wounded (two mortally). Nez Perce losses were four killed and six wounded. Greene, *Nez Perce Summer,* 361–63, 373.
32. Better known as Dunwell's Ferry.

Thomas A. Sutherland: Howard's Campaign against the Nez Perce Indians, 1877

1. Thomas A. Sutherland (c. 1850–91) of the Portland *Standard* apparently was the only accredited newspaper correspondent with Howard's command. He also contributed reports to the New York *Herald* and the San Francisco *Chronicle.* At the time of the Nez Perce breakout, the Harvard-educated Californian had been an Oregon newspaperman for two years. Except for a two-year stint as clerk of the House Committee on Manufactures in Washington, D.C., Sutherland was a Portland journalist until his premature death.
2. Sutherland's *Standard* articles formed the basis of his 1878 pamphlet, *Howard's Campaign against the Nez Perce Indians, 1877.*
3. July 1, 1877.
4. Charles Bendire (d. 1897) enlisted in the 1st U.S. Dragoons in 1854 and rose to the volunteer rank of captain during the Civil War. He was commissioned captain in the 1st U.S. Cavalry in 1873.
5. James A. Haughey (d. 1890) was a volunteer captain during the Civil War who won a regular commission in July 1866.
6. There were slightly more than half that number of Nez Perce warriors.
7. A supposition on the part of Sutherland without foundation in Nez Perce testimony.

8. Seventeen warriors and twenty-eight women and children under a Nez Perce named Red Heart, recently returned from the buffalo country, surrendered, along with Three Feathers and a handful of his people.

9. Nez Perce sources concede no casualties at the Kamiah fight.

10. George S. Hoyle of the West Point Class of 1869. He retired a major in 1901.

11. Joseph A. Sladen of General Howard's staff.

12. Charles B. Throckmorton of the 4th U.S. Artillery.

13. Erwin C. Watkins, an inspector of the Bureau of Indian Affairs.

14. Henry Croasdaile, whose ranch was plundered and burned as the Nez Perces passed over the Camas Prairie.

15. Harry C. Cushing (d. 1902) enlisted as a corporal of Rhode Island volunteers in 1861 and ended the Civil War a major, with three brevets for gallantry. Edward Field was brevetted twice for gallantry in the Civil War. He retired a lieutenant colonel in 1900.

16. John L. Viven, an officer of the 100th New York Volunteers during the Civil War. He was commissioned a second lieutenant in the Regular army in 1866 and retired a lieutenant colonel in 1902.

17. Daniel T. Wells (d. 1899), twice brevetted during the Civil War for gallantry. He retired a major in 1897.

18. Maj. Charles T. Alexander entered the Regular army as a surgeon in 1856. He was promoted to colonel in 1890 for gallant service at the battle of Clearwater.

19. George B. Sanford (1842–1908) served widely on the military frontier. In addition to the Nez Perce campaign, Sanford saw action in Arizona and in the Bannock War. He retired as colonel of the 6th Cavalry in 1892. Sanford joined Howard with 140 cavalrymen and 24 Bannock scouts.

20. Edwin V. Sumner (1835–1912) was the son of Maj. Gen. Edwin V. Sumner, a prominent figure in the early months of the Civil War. The younger Sumner emerged from the Civil War a brevet brigadier general of volunteers. He spent fourteen years on the postwar frontier and retired a brigadier general in the Regular army in 1899.

21. Cuvier Grover (d. 1885), of the West Point Class of 1846, a brigadier general of volunteers during the Civil War.

22. Wahwookya Wasaw (Lean Elk), better known as Poker Joe, had been summering in the Bitterroot country. He brought with him six lodges, not eighteen. Greene, *Nez Perce Summer,* 122–23.

23. Ruby Creek was the name given the north fork of the Big Hole River.

24. Twenty cavalrymen and seventeen Bannock scouts.

25. August 9, 1877.

26. Other estimates place Nez Perce dead at forty-two. Greene, *Nez Perce Summer,* 374.

27. William Logan of Company A, 7th Infantry

28. James H. Bradley (1844–77) of Company B, 7th U.S. Infantry, was one of the most promising and intellectually gifted young officers in the army at the time of his death at the battle of the Big Hole. An excellent writer, Bradley penned dozens of narratives on diverse western topics—from Crow Indian history and culture to the early fur trade—before his tragic demise.

29. William L. English of Company I, 7th U.S. Infantry

30. Charles A. Woodruff of Company K, 7th U.S. Infantry. For a biographical sketch, see note 1 of the chapter entitled "The Battle of the Big Hole," by Woodruff.

31. There were six, not seventeen, civilians killed, and thirty-four soldiers wounded.

32. Charles F. Humphrey entered the Regular army as a private in 1863. Commissioned a second lieutenant three years later, he rose to the rank of brigadier general

and quartermaster general of the U.S. Army in 1903. He won the Medal of Honor for gallantry at the battle of the Clearwater.

33. Only some thirteen of the fifty-three Virginia City volunteers decamped; the remainder, with Captain Callaway, continued on with the troops.

34. George R. Bacon of the West Point Class of 1865.

35. Norwood's Company L, 2nd Cavalry, joined Howard on the morning of August 18.

36. Dry Creek Station.

37. Camas Creek and Spring Creek.

38. At about 3:30 A.M. on August 20, 1877.

39. Camillo C. C. Carr (1842–1914) edited the *Journal of the U.S. Cavalry Association* for four years and retired a brigadier general in 1906.

40. Trumpeter Bernard A. Brooks of Company H, 1st Cavalry, was killed, and seven enlisted men and Lieutenant Benson were wounded.

41. Stanton G. Fisher (1840–1915) journeyed from Wisconsin to San Francisco in 1860 and spent much of his adult life mining. Howard thought him the best scout to serve with the army during the Nez Perce campaign. In 1895 he was named agent for the Nez Perces.

42. Virginia City lay seventy-five miles from Howard's camp at Henry's Lake.

43. William F. Spurgin of the West Point Class of 1861, twice brevetted during the Civil War. He retired a brigadier general in 1902.

44. John Shively, a fifty-two-year-old prospector who had been traveling through the park from the Black Hills gold country.

45. September 11, 1877.

46. Harrison G. Otis of the West Point Class of 1870; he resigned in 1881.

47. Sturgis's soldiers at most killed one Nez Perce and wounded three; if there were six dead found, the remaining five might have been dispatched by the army's Crow allies.

48. September 14, 1877.

49. Greene, *Nez Perce Summer,* 232, estimates the number of Nez Perce ponies lost that day as closer to four hundred.

50. A private of the 7th U.S. Infantry was killed and two civilians wounded in the encounter at Cow Island on September 23, 1877; one Nez Perce warrior was slightly wounded.

51. Stephen P. Jocelyn enlisted in the 6th Vermont Infantry in 1863. Commissioned a lieutenant in the Regular army in 1866, he served forty-four years, retiring as a brigadier general. He was brevetted for gallantry at the battle of the Clearwater.

52. Sgt. John Workman, Battery A, 4th Artillery.

Harry L. Bailey: An Infantryman in the Nez Perce War of 1877

1. Harry L. Bailey (1854–1934) of the West Point Class of 1876 served off and on at northwestern posts until 1897. He won a Silver Star for heroism at the battle of Santiago in the Spanish-American War and retired a lieutenant colonel in 1910.

2. Bailey completed his reminiscences of the Nez Perce War, in the form of a letter to Nez Perce historian Lucullus V. McWhorter, on December 7, 1930, while living at Fort Davis in the old Panama Canal Zone. McWhorter made extensive use of them in his classic work, *Hear Me, My Chiefs! Nez Perce History and Legend* (Caldwell, ID: Caxton Printers, 1952).

3. Company F, 21st Infantry.

4. Oliver O. Howard, *Autobiography,* 2 vols. (New York: Baker and Taylor Company, 1907).

5. Stephen P. Jocelyn.

6. Howard contributed a series of articles called the "Nez Perce Campaign of 1877" in the January–October 1878 issues. These articles were incorporated in book form in Howard's *My Life and Experiences among Our Hostile Indians* (Hartford, CT, 1907).
7. Joseph W. Duncan won a brevet for gallantry at the battle of the Clearwater. In 1901 he was promoted to the lieutenant colonelcy of the 13th U.S. Infantry.
8. Norton's ranch at Cottonwood.
9. Bailey erred by a day; Howard's command crossed the river on July 1, 1877.
10. The principal guide was local resident James T. Silverwood. Ad Chapman led a contingent of scouts.
11. Howard had with him two mountain howitzers.
12. Pvt. Francis Winters received a flesh wound in the left thigh.
13. Battery (Company) A, 4th Artillery.
14. Robert Pollock (d. 1901) began his military career as a sergeant in the 1st Virginia Volunteer Infantry during the Mexican War. He closed the Civil War as colonel of the 2nd California Volunteer Infantry and retired as a captain in the Regular army in 1883.
15. Francis F. Eltonhead, 21st Infantry, won a brevet for gallantry at the battle of the Clearwater.
16. Williams received slight gunshot wounds to the right forearm and to the right thigh.
17. In reality, the Nez Perces had set up camp on the South Fork of the Clearwater River only seven or eight days earlier.
18. Summit Prairie, Montana Territory.

Charles A. Woodruff: The Battle of the Big Hole

1. 2nd Lt. Charles A. Woodruff (1845–1920) served as Col. John Gibbon's adjutant during the Nez Perce campaign. As an enlisted man with the 10th Vermont Infantry, Woodruff was thrice wounded at the battle of Cold Harbor in 1864. A fourth wound caused his discharge the following year, just after he had been commissioned a second lieutenant. Woodruff attended the U.S. Military Academy after the Civil War, graduating with the Class of 1871. After recovering from wounds sustained at the Battle of the Big Hole, Woodruff served principally in commissary assignments, retiring a brigadier general in 1903.
2. Pages 97–101 of Woodruff's address deal with miscellaneous topics, such as the Spanish-American War and the battle of the Little Bighorn, and consequently have been omitted here.
3. John Gibbon (1827–96) was among the more distinguished field grade officers to see action in the Indian Wars. A major general of volunteers with an outstanding record during the Civil War, Gibbon was named colonel of the 7th U.S. Infantry in 1869. From then until his retirement in 1891, Gibbon served on the frontier. He retired a brigadier general in 1891. A literate and careful observer, Gibbon wrote numerous magazine articles of lasting value. These have been collected as Alan and Maureen Gaff, eds., *Adventures on the Western Frontier* (Bloomington: Indiana University Press, 1994).
4. Richard Comba was one of several company-grade officers at the battle of the Big Hole eventually to rise to high rank. An Irish immigrant, Comba had enlisted in the 7th Infantry in 1855. Forty-three years later, he was named colonel of the 5th U.S. Infantry. He saw service as a brigadier general of volunteers during the Spanish-American War and retired in 1901.
5. From the Bitterroot Valley.
6. 1st Lt. Joshua W. Jacobs began the Civil War as a private in the 4th Kentucky Infantry (U.S.) and ended the conflict its major. He was the regimental quartermaster of the 7th U.S. Infantry from 1869 to 1882, and retired a lieutenant colonel in 1900.

7. Other participants place the number closer to sixty.

8. Placer Creek.

9. August 9, 1877.

10. James M. J. Sanno (1840–1907) graduated with the West Point Class of 1863 and was commissioned a second lieutenant in the 7th U.S. Infantry. He saw service in the Yellowstone and Bighorn expeditions of 1876 and retired a brigadier general in 1903.

11. George L. Browning (d. 1882) won a regular commission during the Civil War. He died a captain on active duty.

12. Constant Williams (1843–1922) entered the Civil War as an enlisted volunteer and was commissioned a second lieutenant in the 7th U.S. Infantry in 1863. He was brevetted for gallantry at the battle of the Big Hole and retired a brigadier general in 1907.

13. William Logan (1832–1877) was an Irish immigrant who enlisted in the army in 1850. He was killed at the Big Hole by the woman of a Nez Perce warrior whom he had just slain.

14. The unfortunate Nez Perce was the warrior Hahtalekin.

15. August 10, 1877.

16. Pvt. Charles Alberts, Company A, 7th Infantry.

17. August 11, 1877.

18. Howard reported that he had twenty soldiers with him, not twenty-seven.

19. Among the wounded was Lieutenant Woodruff, shot in the heel and both legs.

20. Nez Perce killed numbered between sixty and ninety, with twenty-two wounded (four mortally).

21. Surgeon Charles T. Alexander and Assistant Surgeon Jenkins A. Fitzgerald reached the Big Hole battlefield at 6:00 A.M. on August 12, 1877.

22. August 13, 1877.

23. The remainder of Woodruff's article consists largely of extracts from official reports and has been omitted here.

Charles N. Loynes: From Fort Fizzle to the Big Hole

1. Charles N. Loynes was a corporal in Company I, 7th U.S. Infantry, at the time of the battle of the Big Hole. George W. Webb, the editor of *Winners of the West*, called Loynes's reminiscences of the battle of the Big Hole "the best descriptive article we have ever read from the pen of any enlisted man of an engagement in which he actually participated." Loyne's article appeared as "The Battle of the Big Hole."

2. Captain Rawn established the post at Missoula on June 25, 1877; it was named Fort Missoula that November.

3. Rawn led a mixed command of four officers, thirty enlisted men, fifty volunteers, and twenty-one Flathead Indians up the Lolo Trail on July 25, 1877.

4. Nez Perce sources gave his name as Tom Hill.

5. July 28, 1877.

6. As many as forty volunteers may have accompanied Coolidge. Greene, *Nez Perce Summer,* 111.

7. The Nez Perce maneuver around Rawn's barricade became known as the "Fort Fizzle" affair.

8. August 6, 1877.

9. August 7, 1877.

10. Loynes's recollection is incorrect; Gibbon's main body reached Bradley's detachment one day after the lieutenant's departure.

11. William W. Watson of Company F, 7th Infantry.

12. Robert E. Sale of Company G, 7th Infantry.

13. Other accounts place the time as nearer 2:00 A.M., August 9, 1877.

14. Pvt. Patrick Fallon was wounded during the battle of the Big Hole.
15. Loynes is mistaken. Pvt. Charles B. Gould of the 2nd U.S. Cavalry was listed as wounded; no Private Scott appears among the killed or wounded. Greene, *Nez Perce Summer,* 364–65.
16. Pvt. Herman Broetz, Company I, 7th Infantry, apparently was finished off by the Nez Perces, as he is listed as killed in action at the Big Hole.
17. Frederick Stortz, Company K, 7th Infantry.
18. Robert L. Edgeworth of Company G, 7th Infantry.
19. Sergeants Michael Hogan, Company I, and William H. Martin, Company G, 7th Infantry; no enlisted man named Clark appears among the list of dead.
20. Corporals Daniel McCaffery, Company I; Dominick O'Connor, Company G; William H. Payne, Company D; and Jacob Eisenhut, also of Company D, 7th Infantry.
21. Unless the Nez Perce repeated their effort of August 9, Loynes's memory was faulty; the Nez Perces had attempted to burn out the soldiers on the first day of the battle.
22. Gibbon and the wounded reached Deer Lodge on August 15, 1877; the remainder of his command arrived the next day.
23. Gildo Ilges was then the post commander at Fort Benton.

John B. Catlin: The Battle of the Big Hole
1. August 7, 1877.
2. August 9, 1877.
3. Lt. Charles A. Woodruff.
4. Lt. William L. English of Company I, 7th Infantry, was shot through the back during the battle of the Big Hole; he died on August 19, 1877.
5. Like Woodruff, Catlin greatly exaggerated Nez Perce casualties.

Harry J. Davis: An Incident of the Nez Perce Campaign
1. Harry J. Davis was a sergeant in Troop (Company) L, 2nd U.S. Cavalry.
2. Randolph Norwood (1834–1901) had been a captain in the 1st Maryland (U.S.) Cavalry during the Civil War. He was commissioned a second lieutenant in the 2nd U.S. Cavalry in February 1866 and promoted to first lieutenant in August of that year. Promoted to captain in 1876, he received a brevet to major for his actions at the battle of the Rosebud and the Camas Meadows fight.
3. The arrival of Troop L of the 2nd Cavalry brought Howard's command to just over 260 men. Greene, *Nez Perce Summer,* 150.
4. A southward-flowing, intermittent tributary of Spring Creek, Idaho Territory.
5. Near the present town of Kilgore, Idaho.
6. Enough of the pickets, at least, were awake to challenge the Nez Perces. When the Indians failed to reply, the pickets opened fire, precipitating a general exchange. Greene, *Nez Perce Summer,* 151.
7. Maj. George B. Sanford (1842–1908) commanded the improvised squadron.
8. From every four enlisted men, one trooper—the "number four"—was the designated horse holder when the men dismounted.
9. Henry M. Benson was brevetted for gallantry at Camas Meadows. He retired a captain in 1885.
10. Benson's was a painful but simple flesh wound.
11. Captain Norwood said the distance was twelve hundred yards, which apparently was a more correct estimate. Greene, *Nez Perce Summer,* 427.
12. This spot was approximately seven miles northeast of Howard's camp.
13. Garland, Clark, and Jones were awarded the Medal of Honor for having stayed at their posts despite their wounds.
14. Nez Perce losses are uncertain but may have been six killed.

Duncan McDonald: The Nez Perce War of 1877—The Inside History from Indian Sources

1. Duncan McDonald was the agency trader for the Flathead tribe on the Jocko reservation in Montana. His father was Hudson Bay Fur Company manager Angus McDonald, and his Nez Perce mother was the sister-in-law of Eagle of the Light, chief of the band that White Bird later led. Fluent in both English and Nez Perce, McDonald was well regarded by the Nez Perce warriors. At the request of the editor of the *New North-West,* McDonald made a six-week trip to British America to obtain the particulars of the campaign from his relative, White Bird. Linwood Laughy, comp., *In Pursuit of the Nez Perces: The Nez Perce War of 1877* (Wrangell, AL: Mountain Meadow Press, 1993), iii, 213.
2. The first article carried the following introduction: "The writer, a relative of Looking Glass and White Bird, has entered into arrangements with the *New North-West* to prepare a series of papers giving the Nez Perce version of their troubles and their remarkable campaign. It is a condition of the publication that the views shall be related from their standpoint, and as full particulars as possible will be given of the tribe and their great expedition. The author has been for some time collecting data from the prominent actors in the great drama, and the time yet required to elicit incidents of the campaign will be occupied in preliminary narrative."
3. The elder Joseph.
4. A different man from the Nez Perce chief Eagle of the Light.
5. Also written as Sarpsisilpilp.
6. Also translated as Eagle from the Light.
7. Old Joseph and Looking Glass also signed the treaty.
8. Maj. Henry C. Wood, assistant adjutant general of the Department of the Columbia.
9. A reference to the June 14, 1877, attack on the Benjamin B. Norton party.
10. Other Nez Perce accounts place the number of warriors in White Bird's camp at closer to sixty.
11. According to Peopeo Tholekt (Bird Alighting), who left an account of Captain Whipple's July 1 attack, Looking Glass did not go forward, but rather sent Peopeo Tholekt to treat with the soldiers. Greene, *Nez Perce Summer,* 54–55.
12. A probable reference to the ambush of scouts William Foster and Charles Blewett on July 3, 1877.
13. Lt. Sevier M. Rains and his detachment.
14. July 5, 1877.
15. At the junction of Cottonwood Creek and the South Fork of the Clearwater River.
16. Six Nez Perce warriors—Mean Man, Wounded Breast, Five Wounds, Old Yellow Wolf, Yellow Wolf, and Animal Entering a Hole—were wounded in the two-day battle.
17. July 16, 1877.
18. July 26, 1877.
19. Wahlitits's wife was also killed.
20. August 15, 1877.
21. A reference to General Howard.

Chuslum Moxmox (Yellow Bull): Yellow Bull's Story

1. Chuslum Moxmox (Yellow Bull) was a Lamtama Nez Perce war leader. In the years after the Nez Perce surrender, he worked ably with Joseph to improve the lot of his people in the Indian Territory. Eventually he accepted a land allotment and removed his family to Lapwai.

2. Little is known of Pile of Clouds, apart from his unusual influence over the Nez Perce council of chiefs. It was Pile of Clouds who also had urged the return to the Salmon River country before the battle of the Big Hole.

3. September 30, 1877.

4. Both the date of White Bird's departure and the number of Nez Perces who accompanied him are open to question. Yellow Bull himself later said that White Bird had decamped on the night of October 2, 1877, with just fifty people. Weighing the varying testimony, Greene, *Nez Perce Summer,* 489, concludes that White Bird slipped away on the night of October 5.

5. Husis Kute (Bald Head), or Hush-hush-cute, was the leader of the Palouse band of nontreaty Nez Perces.

6. White Bird's murderer was Lamnisnim Husis (Shriveled Head), known to Canadian whites as Nez Perce Sam. Believing White Bird had threatened to use supernatural powers against his wife and son, Sam killed him with an axe on the evening of March 6, 1892.

Henry Buck: The Story of the Nez Perce Campaign during the Summer of 1877

1. Michigan native Henry Buck ran a general store with brothers Frank and Amos in Stevensville at the time of the Nez Perce campaign.

2. Buck completed his manuscript reminiscences in October 1922 at Stevensville, where he continued to reside. In a brief preface to his manuscript, which resides in the collections of the Montana Historical Society, Buck said, "This story of Joseph and Howard was written by me from memory, with the assistance of numerous authentic publications bearing on the subject, and then verified by trips subsequently taken by me in an automobile following Joseph's trail as closely as possible, all the way from Stevensville, Montana, through the Yellowstone Park, and on as far as Cook City."

3. The recalcitrant Nez Perce warriors from White Bird's actually had committed the first killings the day before, when they murdered four white men in the Salmon River settlements.

4. Capt. David L. Perry.

5. Lew Day of Mount Idaho.

6. Benjamin P. Norton, his family, and employees.

7. Buck underestimated Howard's strength; he had closer to 730 officers and men.

8. Howard had with him two Gatling guns, two howitzers, and a Coehorn mortar.

9. Considered as such only by the whites.

10. Aubrey L. Haines, *An Elusive Victory: The Battle of the Big Hole* (Helena, MT: Falcon Publishing, 1999), 17, speculates that Matte and Silverthorne may in fact have been en route to the Nez Perce reservation to steal horses when they stumbled upon the nontreaty Nez Perce. Matte was hanged for horse stealing later that year.

11. Also known as Woodman's Prairie.

12. Charlot, Charlos, or Charlo (1831–1910), was a hereditary Flathead chief, who clung tenaciously to his ancestral home in the Bitterroot Valley. In 1884 he achieved national fame for refusing government demands that he move onto a reservation. Charlot relented five years later and died on the Jock reservation, an embittered man.

13. In his account, Buck misidentified the chief as White Bird. Greene, *Nez Perce Summer,* 417n.

14. Possibly James Baker, killed near White Bird Creek on June 14, 1877, during the initial outburst of Nez Perce fury.

15. Wahwookya Wasaaw, or Poker Joe, had been summering in the Bitterroot country with six lodges of Nez Perces and had only joined the main body that day when they entered Stevensville; thus, his account of the Nez Perce travails in Idaho would have been secondhand. Greene, *Nez Perce Summer,* 122–23.

16. Nineteen miles by other accounts. Haines, *Elusive Victory,* 98.

17. For his account of the battle of the Big Hole, Henry Buck relied heavily on the recollections of his brother Amos, who fought in the encounter as a volunteer. Amos Buck's narrative was published as "Review of the Battle of the Big Hole," *Contributions to the Historical Society of Montana* 7 (1910): 117–30.

18. The Nez Perce, Hahtalekin, was not a medicine man.

19. By then, only a dozen or so warriors remained behind to keep the soldiers at bay, while the main party of Nez Perces broke contact to continue their march toward Canadian sanctuary.

20. Buck understated the amount and quality of water fetched. A detail of three volunteers from Company G, 7th Infantry, slipped down to the stream itself with four empty canteens apiece; all returned with full canteens.

21. Army casualties were three officers killed and four wounded, and twenty-two enlisted men killed and thirty wounded.

22. Nez Perce dead numbered closer to forty.

23. Perhaps to avenge the killing of their women and children during the battle of the Big Hole, on the evening of August 12 some Nez Perce warriors attacked the ranch belonging to W. L. Montague and Daniel Winters. They killed Montague and Thomas Flynn, the women and children having been evacuated, ransacked the ranch, then rode off and killed another white man five miles farther on. Greene, *Nez Perce Summer,* 143.

24. Howard detached the 7th Infantry on August 17 to return to its post at Missoula.

25. Francis E. Eltonhead of the West Point Class of 1871. As an officer in the 21st Infantry, he earned the Medal of Honor for distinguished service and gallantry at the battle of the Clearwater.

26. William F. Spurgin of the West Point Class of 1858 served with distinction during the Civil War, earning brevets for special gallantry in two battles and for meritorious service with the Freedmen's Bureau. In 1902 Spurgin was promoted to brigadier general in the Regular army.

27. The first shots were fired between 3:30 and 4:30 A.M.

28. Camas Meadows was dotted with large outcroppings of basalt lava, the residue of volcanic eruptions half a million years earlier.

29. Companies B and I, 1st U.S. Cavalry, joined by Company L, 2nd U.S. Cavalry.

30. One soldier was killed and eight wounded in the encounter, which occurred eight miles from Howard's camp. Six Nez Perces may have been killed, and at least one wounded.

31. Trumpeter Bernard A. Brooks, Company B, 1st Cavalry.

32. Joseph's participation in the Camas Meadows raid is uncertain; Yellow Wolf stated explicitly that Joseph was not with the raiding party. Greene, *Nez Perce Summer,* 154, 426n.

33. Shot-Gun Creek.

34. Frederick H. E. Ebstein, a Prussian immigrant who rose through the ranks. He earned brevets for his service at Cottonwood and Camas Meadows.

35. In Yellowstone National Park.

36. Albert Oldham of Helena, Montana.

37. The Radersburg party, as the group was also known, consisted of nine people: George F. Cowan and his wife, Emma; her brother, Frank D. Carpenter, and sister, Ida Carpenter; Charles Mann; teamster Henry Meyers; and three friends of Frank Carpenter's, Andrew J. Arnold, William Dingee, and Albert Oldham.

38. 2nd Lt. Charles B. Schofield.
39. The Nez Perces started forest fires in Yellowstone Park to retard Howard's pursuit.
40. Probably Major Spurgin.
41. The remainder of Buck's manuscript treats of the wagon train's journey from Yellowstone Park to Fort Ellis. As it is not germane to the Nez Perce War, I have omitted all but the last paragraph, which sums up Buck's feelings about his service.

Charles King: Where is Chief Joseph?

1. Charles King (1844–1933) was the son of Rufus King, part owner of the Milwaukee *Sentinel* and a brigadier general of volunteers during the Civil War. Charles King graduated with the West Point Class of 1866 and saw service in Arizona and on the Northern Plains. He was retired for disability in 1880 from a wound sustained in Arizona six years earlier. King went on to become a prolific and popular author of novels on the Civil, Indian, and Spanish-American Wars.
2. The 5th Cavalry was not the first unit to reach Chicago. Two companies of the 22nd Infantry from the Department of Dakota arrived in the city the day before the 5th Cavalry.
3. Verling K. Hart (d. 1883) had been brevetted lieutenant colonel for gallant and meritorious service during the Civil War. He was promoted to major of the 5th Cavalry in 1875.
4. The abode of the dead in early Hebrew thought.
5. Joel S. Bishop graduated with the West Point Class of 1869. He was still on active duty in 1902 as major of the 5th Cavalry.

Theodore W. Goldin: A Pleasure Ride in Montana

1. Theodore W. Goldin (1858–post-1927) enlisted in the 7th U.S. Cavalry in April 1876 at the age of seventeen. The army discharged Goldin in November 1877 after his father produced evidence that Goldin had enlisted before his eighteenth birthday. Returning to his Wisconsin home, Goldin went on to become a prominent lawyer and the chairman of the Republican State Central Committee of Wisconsin.
2. September 14, 1877.
3. Although it is not clear from the text, Goldin apparently is referring to himself. Goldin had a habit of exaggerating—and sometimes fabricating—his role in the campaigns in which he participated. His recollections of the Little Bighorn are particularly suspect. In another account of the 7th Cavalry in the Nez Perce campaign, Goldin wrote that he had watched the arrival of a large party of Crow Indian allies on September 14. Assuming both stories are true, Goldin must have watched the Crows come in as he was going out. See Greene, *Nez Perce Summer,* 232. If his later civilian accomplishments are any indication, Goldin was no doubt a particularly capable—if young—enlisted man, so it is reasonable to suppose his having been chosen for the demanding duty of courier.
4. Goldin incorrectly recorded the direction as west.

Peter Allen: Military Expedition and Campaign and Battle of Bear's Paw Mountains, Montana Territory, September 30, 1877

1. Allen dated his reminiscences July 11, 1913.
2. The 7th U.S. Cavalry was ordered to the Yellowstone country to help prevent a supposed foray by Sitting Bull into the region from Canada.
3. Troops A and D also remained at Fort Keogh. Capt. Owen Hale commanded the squadron.

4. The September 13, 1877 engagement at Canyon Creek, Montana.
5. At this juncture, Hale's squadron was two miles south of the Nez Perce camp.
6. Hale ordered the men of Troop K to dismount and advance in a skirmish line.
7. Indian Wars student Walter M. Camp (1867–1925) traveled to Peter Allen's home in Morristown, Tennessee, on October 17, 1913 to interview him further on his recollections of the Bear's Paw Mountain fight. (Peter Allen interview, October 17, 1913. Packet FF 12, Walter M. Camp Papers.) Allen told Camp:

> Three companies (D, A, and K) charged up in line mounted, with pistols drawn. While several miles distant from Snake Creek, up on the hills on high ground to the south we could see the Indian lodges, but as we neared the creek, we could not see the lodges, they being in the creek bottom. However, we expected to find the Indians where we had seen the lodges, and we were charging ahead as though making for the bottom, when all of a sudden the Indians rose up from the grass and gave us a volley, and then ran back for their pits at the edge of the bank.
>
> We charged on horseback very close to them, firing with our pistols, when we were ordered to dismount and fight on foot. Our horses went back without leaders. Every man stayed and fought—there were no horse holders. After the battle (that evening), our horses were found grazing back in the rear.
>
> We must have fought dismounted as long as an hour. Lieutenant Biddle was killed about one rod to my left. He had a rifle and had just knelt to fire it when he was hit and killed. I was wounded in the left arm, and Captain Hale asked me and a man named Fleck (who was wounded in the head) why we were not firing, and I told him my arm had been shattered. He then told me to go to the hospital, which was over to the west. We did so, having to cross a washout, or dry creekbed, on the way.
>
> After I had been in the hospital (that is, where a number of wounded men had gathered round the surgeon) awhile, a wounded man came in and said that Captain Hale, captain of my company (K), had been killed. Hale was therefore killed after Biddle.
>
> We were eight days getting to the boat that took the wounded down the Missouri to Fort Lincoln.
>
> After I was wounded I lay between the firing of our men and that of the Indians for some time.

8. There was no trooper named Fleck listed on the rolls of 7th Cavalrymen wounded at Bear's Paw Mountains. Greene, *Nez Perce Summer,* 368–70.
9. For a biographical sketch of Tilton, see note 1 of "After the Nez Perces," by Tilton.
10. Pvt. Emil Taube, Troop K, 7th Cavalry. Taube's wound was not serious.
11. Pvt. Jeanne B. D. Gallenne, Troop M, 7th Cavalry.
12. A Hotchkiss 1.65-inch breech-loading mountain gun.
13. The truce occurred on October 1, 1877; the officer whom the Nez Perces held hostage was Lt. Lovell H. Jerome of the 2nd Cavalry—not the 5th Infantry, as Allen supposed.
14. More precisely, the fourth day (October 5) after the abortive conference.
15. Pvt. Lewis Gensler, Company I, 5th Infantry.
16. Pvt. John Curran, Troop D, 7th Cavalry, lost his left index finger, not his thumb.
17. Howard arrived with his aides and a small escort on the evening of October 4, 1877.
18. To the credit of Surgeon Tilton and Assistant Surgeon Edward F. Gardner, only three of the fifty officers and men wounded at Bear's Paw Mountains died of their wounds.
19. Allen wrote his reminiscences from his home in Morristown, Tennessee.

Henry R. Tilton: After the Nez Perces

1. Henry R. Tilton (1836–1906) graduated in medicine from the University of Pennsylvania in 1859 and became an assistant surgeon with the army in 1861. Tilton was post surgeon at Fort Lyon, Colorado, from 1866 to 1870 and took part in Stanley's Yellowstone expedition. Tilton won the Medal of Honor for "fearlessly exposing his life and displaying great gallantry in rescuing and protecting the wounded men" at the battle of Bear's Paw Mountains. He retired a lieutenant colonel in 1900.
2. A skirmish between Troops A and B of the 7th Cavalry and the Sioux on August 4, 1873 near the Tongue River, during Col. David S. Stanley's Yellowstone expedition.
3. Miles's column marched thirty-one miles that day (September 20, 1877).
4. September 22, 1877. Miles's command traveled thirty-six miles that day.
5. September 26, 1877.
6. The upper Dry Fork Creek.
7. September 29, 1877.
8. Eagle Butte (later renamed McCann Butte), rising 900 feet above the plain, and Gray Butte (Miles Butte), rising 1,500 feet.
9. Lt. George A. Baird, acting assistant adjutant general on Miles's staff.
10. Colonel Miles.
11. Lovell H. Jerome (d. 1935) graduated with the West Point Class of 1866. His career ended in 1879 when he resigned rather than face a court-martial that his alcoholism had brought on. He enlisted in the 8th Cavalry in 1880 but was discharged two years later as a hopeless drunk. Still retaining a deep affection for his alma mater, Jerome became the founder of Alumni Day at West Point. In later life he worked for the U.S. Customs Service and engaged in mining in Alaska.

Henry Romeyn: The Capture of Chief Joseph and the Nez Perce Indians

1. Henry Romeyn (1833–1913) entered the Civil War as an enlisted member of the 105th Illinois Volunteer Infantry in 1862 and was commissioned captain in the 14th U.S. Colored Infantry the following year. He joined the 5th Infantry in 1869 and saw service on the Southern Plains and in the 1876 Sioux campaign. Romeyn was awarded a Medal of Honor for "most distinguished gallantry" at Bear's Paw Mountains. He retired in 1897, being promoted to major on the retired list. Thrapp, *Encyclopedia,* 4:1237.
2. Miles recalled the time as having been 6:00 P.M. Nelson A. Miles, *Serving the Republic* (New York: Harper and Brothers, 1911), 172.
3. Capt. Andrew S. Bennett (1834–78) was a volunteer officer in the Civil War who won a regular commission in 1867. He was killed in action during the Bannock War.
4. Capt. Simon Snyder (1839–1912), who commanded the mounted battalion of the 5th Infantry, had been with the regiment since 1861. He was promoted to brigadier general in the Regular army in 1902.
5. 1st Lt. Mason Carter (1834–1909) had been a lieutenant with the 5th Infantry since 1864. He was awarded the Medal of Honor for distinguished gallantry at Bear's Paw Mountains and retired a brevet major in 1898.
6. Capt. David H. Brotherton (d. 1889) of the West Point Class of 1850 had been with the 5th U.S. Infantry since 1854. He retired a lieutenant colonel in 1884.
7. Capt. Miles Moylan (1838–1909) began the Civil War a sergeant in the 2nd U.S. Dragoons. He ended the conflict a brevet major of volunteers. Reenlisting in the 7th U.S. Cavalry in 1866, he again rose through the ranks to captain in 1872. He was yet another officer to earn the Medal of Honor for distinguished gallantry at Bear's Paw Mountains. Moylan retired a major in 1893.

8. Capt. Edward S. Godfrey (1843–1932) served as an enlisted man in the 21st Ohio Volunteer Infantry during the Civil War. Afterward, he attended West Point and carved out a distinguished career on the frontier and in Cuba and the Philippines. He retired a brigadier general in 1907.
9. Troop K of the 7th Cavalry joined Miles's column on the march.
10. The battalion composed of Troops F, G, and H of the 2nd Cavalry also joined Miles's column on the march.
11. George L. Tyler (1839–81) had been a volunteer officer during the Civil War.
12. 2nd Lt. Edward J. McClernand (1849–1926) was still another Medal of Honor recipient for gallantry at Bear's Paw Mountains. (Though Miles was quarrelsome with superiors who stood in his way, he took care of subordinates who made him look good.)
13. Fort Benton, Montana Territory, was located on the left bank of the Missouri River at the head of navigation, some forty miles below the Great Falls of the river.
14. From a careful study of regimental returns and other official documents, Greene, *Nez Perce Summer,* 250, 457n., concluded that Miles had with him some 520 officers, men, scouts, and civilian employees.
15. 2nd Lt. Marion P. Maus (1850–1930) commanded Miles's scouts, but it was 2nd Lt. Jonathan W. Biddle (1855–77) of the 7th Cavalry who flagged down the steamboat *Fontenelle.*
16. On the morning of September 25, 1877.
17. Scout George Johnson drowned on the evening of September 23.
18. 2nd Lt. George P. Borden had graduated with the West Point Class of 1866.
19. Camp was made among foothills along a fork of Peoples Creek, some fifteen miles from the Nez Perce village on Snake Creek.
20. The Bear's Paw chain runs approximately twenty miles north to south and some forty miles east to west. The highest elevation, then called Bearpole Peak, rises 6,916 feet above the surrounding prairie; most of the remaining peaks are less than 6,000 feet in altitude.
21. At this point, Miles's column was within six miles of the Nez Perce camp.
22. Romeyn has his sequence of events wrong. None of the four officers named were struck in the first fire. Biddle was killed shortly after Hale ordered their troop to dismount. Godfrey fell next, with a bullet in the side. Dismounting to confer with Hale, Moylan took a bullet in his upper right thigh. Hale was the last of the four to fall. Greene, *Nez Perce Summer,* 274–78.
23. Pvt. Richard M. Peshall.
24. Here Romeyn is speaking of himself.
25. The Sioux leaders decided against helping the Nez Perces not from fear of Nelson A. Miles, but rather because the superintendent of the Northwest Mounted Police told them they would forfeit their Canadian sanctuary if they crossed into Montana.
26. Romeyn has his dates confused; Joseph called for a truce on October 1.
27. I have omitted six paragraphs that follow in the article as originally published, because Romeyn badly confuses the events of October 3–5, 1877, and misstates the casualty count on both sides.
28. Sgt. Otto Durselen, Troop A, 7th Cavalry.

Young Two Moon: Capture of Nez Perces

1. Young Two Moon (1847–c. 1917), also known as John Two Moon and Two Moon, was a Northern Cheyenne chief . He gained prominence fighting the army during Reynolds's 1876 Powder River campaign, after recapturing a pony herd that the soldiers had seized. Young Two Moon also fought the whites at the battles of the Rosebud and the Little Bighorn. He surrendered his people to Col. Nelson A.

Miles at Fort Keogh in April 1877, after which Miles made him head chief of the Northern Cheyennes. He lived at peace with the whites for the rest of his life and in 1914 met President Woodrow Wilson in Washington, D. C.

2. Early on the morning of September 30, 1877.
3. The Cheyennes and Sioux charged the Nez Perce camp from the southwest.
4. Shot in the Head, a Nez Perce warrior, said the Cheyennes did not shoot a warrior, but rather a woman who wanted only to escape danger. Greene, *Nez Perce Summer,* 470–71n.
5. Snake Creek.
6. The Nez Perces left camp to confront the 7th Cavalry assault to the south and east, not from fear of three reckless scouts.
7. Troop G, 2nd Cavalry.
8. By the 1870s, the U.S. Cavalry had adopted the practice of grouping horses of the same color, or color pattern, into particular companies, for ease of unit identification and esprit de corps.
9. Lt. Edward J. McClernand.
10. Chief Joseph.
11. Tom Hill, a mixed-blood Nez Perce and Delaware.
12. Here Young Two Moon confuses dates badly. The events he described to this point relating to Chief Joseph's discussions with Colonel Miles, and those that follow in his narrative, occurred on October 1, the day after the battle.
13. Lt. Lovell H. Jerome.
14. At about 4:00 P.M. on October 1, after Jerome was seized, Quartermaster Francis M. Gibson arrived with the expedition's wagon train.
15. At 11:00 A.M. on October 4, 1877.
16. The two Nez Perces sent to treat with Joseph on the morning of October 5 were Meopkowit, also known as Old George, and Jokais, also known as Captain John. They had not been captured, as Young Two Moon supposed, but had attached themselves to General Howard and his escort in the hope of saving members of their families who were in the hostile camp. Greene, *Nez Perce Summer,* 307–308.
17. Twenty-one soldiers were killed during the engagement and siege at Bear's Paw Mountains and fifty wounded, two mortally.

Luther S. Kelly: Capture of Nez Perces

1. Luther S. Kelly (1849–1928) enlisted in the 10th New York Infantry in the waning days of the Civil War and served out his enlistment in the Dakota Territory. He remained in the region, trapping, hunting, and serving occasionally as a dispatch courier. He began his army scouting career in 1873 and was chief scout for Miles from 1876 to 1878. Afterward, he was a War Department clerk. In 1898 and 1899 he guided exploring expeditions in Alaska. As a captain of volunteers, he saw action in the Philippines, then served as agent of the San Carlos Apache Reservation before retiring to a fruit ranch in Paradise, California, where he died.
2. In his memoirs Kelly said that Miles had ordered the detachment to Carroll to protect the ammunition depot there from Nez Perce raiders. M. M. Quaife, ed., *"Yellowstone Kelly," The Memoirs of Luther S. Kelly* (New Haven, CT: Yale University Press, 1926), 185–86.
3. Frank D. Baldwin (1842–1923) was one of Miles's most trusted and able subordinates. He won the Medal of Honor during the Civil War and on the frontier during the Red River War. He served with distinction during the Philippine insurrection and retired a brigadier general.
4. September 29, 1877.
5. Milan Tripp was a cattle driver whom Miles recently had hired on as a scout.

6. John Haddo, a young corporal of the 5th Infantry whom Miles had taken on as a scout, and whom he came to regard as "a fine fellow as well as a good shot." Quaife, *"Yellowstone Kelly,"* 180.

7. Kelly compresses the final events; the Nez Perces surrendered on October 5, the day after Howard arrived.

Nelson A. Miles: Chief Joseph's Fight and Surrender

1. Nelson A. Miles (1839–1925) was a pugnacious, controversial, but highly successful Indian-fighting officer. Commissioned a lieutenant in the 22nd Massachusetts Volunteer Infantry in September 1861, he fought in most of the major campaigns of the eastern theater of the Civil War, was wounded four times, and ended the conflict a brigadier general of volunteers. After extensive service on the postwar frontier, he became general in chief of the army in 1895. Miles oversaw recruitment and training for the Spanish-American War, and he led the forces that took Puerto Rico. He retired a lieutenant general in 1903.

2. Miles's narrative of the Nez Perce campaign appeared as the first four pages of an article entitled "On the Trail of Geronimo."

3. Estimates of the number of Nez Perce ponies captured range from five hundred to Miles's claim of eight hundred.

4. Small parties of Nez Perces picked up after Joseph's surrender brought the total number of Nez Perce captives to 448. Greene, *Nez Perce Summer,* 313.

5. Nineteen enlisted men were killed, and one mortally wounded.

6. Forty-six enlisted men were wounded.

George W. Baird: The Capture of Chief Joseph and the Nez Perces

1. George W. Baird (1839–1906) was colonel of the 32nd U.S. Colored Infantry during the Civil War. From 1871 to 1879 he was adjutant of the 5th U.S. Infantry. Baird won the Medal of Honor for gallantry at the battle of Bear's Paw Mountains. He retired a brigadier general in 1903.

2. Baird had been sent with three Nez Perce captives to ascertain under what, if any, conditions White Bird and his band would return to the United States. White Bird refused to consider leaving Canada until Chief Joseph was allowed to return to the Idaho Territory.

Lovell H. Jerome: Brave Jerome: A Dashing Lieutenant's Experience in Chief Joseph's Trenches

1. Lovell H. Jerome (d. 1935) of the West Point Class of 1866 had his promising career derailed by alcoholism, and he resigned his commission in 1879 while awaiting sentence of a court-martial. Jerome enlisted in the 8th Cavalry a year later but resumed his bibulous ways. Discharged in January 1882 in lieu of a second court-martial, Jerome went to work for the U.S. Customs Service and later in life held mining interests in Alaska.

2. Lt. Marion P. Maus.

Charles E. S. Wood: The Surrender of Joseph

1. Charles Erskine Scott Wood (1852–1944) of the West Point Class of 1874 gained fame as a writer, attorney, and social radical. He resigned from th army in 1884 to practice law. A crusader for social justice, Wood became known as a "philosophical anarchist."

PART FOUR: THE BANNOCK WAR, 1878

Oliver O. Howard: The Bannock War

1. Severely condensed version of this and Howard's second and third articles on the Bannock War appeared in his *My Life and Experiences among Our Hostile Indians* (Hartford, CT: A. D. Worthington and Company, 1907).
2. The Bannocks were a Shoshonean tribe that claimed as its native land much of southeastern Idaho. Their name is derived from their own word "Bampnack," meaning "to throw backward," a reference to the manner in which the warriors wore their hair in a lock tossed back from the forehead.
3. The Fort Hall reservation on the Portneuf River.
4. The Bannock warrior was found guilty and sentenced to a term in the Idaho territorial penitentiary.
5. Rhoden was shot on November 23, 1877, while walking to the barn to get his horse. Tambiago was a brother of Petope.
6. Augustus H. Bainbridge rose from the ranks during the Civil War. He retired a lieutenant colonel in 1898.
7. John E. Smith (1816–97) served with distinction in the western theater of the Civil War, ending the conflict a brevet major general of volunteers. He served on the postwar frontier until his retirement in 1881.
8. Smith arrived at the Fort Hall reservation on December 20, 1877, with three companies of the 14th U.S. Infantry.
9. Tambiago was hanged on June 28, 1878, at the territorial penitentiary in Boise City.
10. Orlando "Rube" Robbins.
11. Fisher was a white man who had lived with the Bannocks since 1869.
12. An archaic reference to the slaughterhouse, or the meat market.
13. Howard is mistaken as to the derivation of the name. Captain Truckee (d. 1860), a firm friend of the white man and a guide for Frémont's third expedition, was named after a French-Canadian scout.
14. Spanish word for irrigation ditch.
15. Capt. Reuben F. Bernard.
16. Two Bannock warriors shot and wounded stockmen George Nesbit and Louis Kensler after breakfasting with them on the morning of May 28, 1879.
17. Buffalo Horn was the war chief of these hostile Bannocks.
18. Maj. Gen. Irvin McDowell (1818–85), remembered principally for his defeat at the first battle of Bull Run.
19. G Troop, 1st U.S. Cavalry.
20. W. V. Rhinehart replaced the competent Sam Parrish, whom the reservation Indians trusted, in 1876. The Paiutes in particular detested Rhinehart, and Chief Natchez Winnemucca submitted a petition for his removal. Sarah Winnemucca added her own sworn statement accusing Rhinehart of mistreating and "systematically starving" her people. Army visitors to the agency corroborated Sarah Winnemucca's accusations, but no action was taken against Rhinehart. George F. Brimlow, *The Bannock War of 1878* (Caldwell, ID: Caxton Printers, 1938), 57–58.
21. Bernard was not alone with his troop. Orlando Robbins, a colonel in the Idaho militia who had scouted for General Howard during the Nez Perce campaign, and his volunteer scouts fell in with Bernard's command at Boise City. Thirty-seven volunteers from Alturas, Idaho Territory, under Capt. George M. Parsons, also augmented Bernard's cavalry troop. Brimlow, *Bannock War,* 82–83.
22. Patrick Collins (d. 1879) was an Irish immigrant who enlisted in the army in 1855 and rose through the ranks.
23. Capt. J. B. Harper led the volunteer company of twenty-six men.

24. The missing volunteer's name was Hastings.
25. Captain Thomas McGregor, a Scottish immigrant and former enlisted man who rose to the colonelcy of the 9th U.S. Cavalry during the Spanish-American War.
26. George M. Downey, brevetted for gallantry at Gettysburg.
27. Moses (1829–99) was a Sinkiuse-Columbia tribal leader who ruled his people for forty years. He took no part in the Bannock War hostilities.
28. The Umatillas were a Shahaptian tribe living on the Umatilla River and the adjacent banks of the Columbia River prior to the coming of the white man. In 1855 they signed a treat and settled on the Umatilla reservation in eastern Oregon.
29. George B. Sanford (1842–1908) served widely on the frontier, retiring a colonel in 1892.
30. Joseph Stewart of the West Point Class of 1838. He retired a lieutenant colonel in 1879.
31. Henry C. Egbert was twice brevetted for gallantry during the Civil War. As a brigadier general of volunteers, he was killed in action in the Philippines in 1899.
32. James C. Shofner of the West Point Class of 1873. He resigned in 1881.
33. Melville A. Cochran, appointed colonel of the 6th U. S. Infantry in 1890.
34. George B. Rodney entered the Civil War as a volunteer private and emerged with brevets to major. He was promoted a colonel in the artillery corps in 1901.
35. The *Chronological List,* 67, shows seven troops of the 1st Cavalry (A, E, F, G, H, K, and L) to have been engaged at Birch Creek.
36. Three steamers armed with Gatling guns and howitzers—the *Welcome,* the *Northwest,* and the *Spokane*—patrolled the Columbia River to prevent Indians sympathetic to the hostiles from crossing to join them. On July 8, 1878, the *Spokane* fired upon a band on the Washington Territory side of the river, wounding one and driving off the remainder. Brimlow, *Bannock War,* 137–39.
37. George Coggan was killed on July 11, 1878, and his traveling companion wounded.
38. James W. Forsyth (1834–1906) emerged from the Civil War a brevet brigadier general of volunteers. He served with Maj. Gen. Phillip H. Sheridan from 1869 to 1878, first as aide and then as military secretary. Forsyth commanded the 7th U.S. Cavalry at Wounded Knee in 1890 and retired a major general in 1897.
39. William S. Worth, a brigadier general during the Spanish-American War.
40. William F. Drum rose from private in the 3rd Ohio Volunteer Infantry in 1861 to the colonelcy of the 5th New York at the end of the Civil War.
41. Miles lost two enlisted men, seriously wounded—Corporals William Roberts, Company I, 21st Infantry, and Charles Brown, Company K, 1st Cavalry. *Chronological List,* 67; Brimlow, *Bannock War,* 151.
42. Charles A. Williams, brevetted for gallantry the year before at the battle of the Clearwater.
43. Henry R. Mizner, thrice brevetted for gallantry during the Civil War.
44. William H. Winters (d. 1880), commissioned from the ranks during the Civil War.
45. John Pitcher of the West Point Class of 1872.
46. Peter Skene Ogden, a Hudson's Bay Company trader, first gave the name *malheur* to an Oregon site during an expedition into the Snake River country with French-Canadian hunters in 1826. In his journal, Ogden wrote on February 14, "We encamped on *River au Malheur* [Unfortunate River], so called on account of property and furs having been hid here formerly, discovered and stolen by the natives." McArthur, *Oregon Place Names,* 383.
47. Also known as Munday's Ferry.
48. General McDowell.
49. Guy Howard (1855–99) was the eldest child of General Howard and served as his aide during the Nez Perce campaign. As a lieutenant colonel of volunteers, he was killed in action in the Philippines.

50. John L. Viven (d. 1896) of New Mexico served in the Southwest during the Civil War.
51. William E. Dove (d. 1884), commissioned from the ranks during the Civil War.
52. A tributary of the Snake River.
53. One enlisted man was wounded in the skirmish at Bennett Creek; Indian losses, if any, are unknown.
54. Sarah Winnemucca Hopkins, *Life among the Paiutes: Their Wrongs and Claims* (Boston, 1883).
55. Approximately six hundred Paiutes made the journey to the Yakima reservation.

George Crook: The Bannock Troubles
1. Brig. Gen. George Crook was then commander of the Military Department of the Platte.

Anonymous: The Hanging of Tambiago
1. Tendoy was chief of a mixed band of Bannocks, Shoshones, and Sheepeaters.

Ernest F. Albrecht: A Red Hot Fight with the Bannocks
1. General Howard issued the orders setting the forces of the Military Department of the Columbia in motion on June 16, 1878.
2. Silver Creek, Oregon, forty-five miles west of Camp Harney.
3. Albrecht misidentifies the lieutenant as Edwards. Frank H. Edmunds (d. 1900) of the West Point Class of 1866 served through the Spanish-American War.
4. Joseph Schultz, a saddler with Troop F, was also killed in the skirmish at Silver Creek.
5. William Meyers of Atlanta, Idaho Territory.
6. Thomas Drury (d. 1881) had enlisted in the army as a private in 1842 and was commissioned during the Civil War.

Henry E. Heppner: Vivid Tale of the Bannock War
1. Henry E. Heppner (d. 1905) came to the Pacific Northwest in 1853. In 1873 he and Jackson L. Morrow opened the first merchandise store in a town and county named for them—Heppner, Morrow County, Oregon. McArthur, *Oregon Place Names,* 297. Heppner presented his account in the form of an affidavit seeking a pension for volunteer service as a member of the Grant County Home Guard during the Bannock War. Three other members of the unit corroborated Heppner's sworn statement, and he was awarded a pension of $12 per month in 1929.
2. Also among the party were Sam Foss, Bert Williams, and Robert Hall. Canyon City *Times,* July 6, 1878.
3. According to the Canyon City *Times,* July 6, 1878, the Grant County volunteers battled with Chief Eagan's advance guard, consisting of some fifty warriors.
4. Also recorded as Mike Andross. Brimlow, *Bannock War,* 128.
5. At the foot of a rise known locally as Jackass Hill.
6. The volunteers stumbled onto Murray's ranch that evening, some twenty miles from the site of the first attack. Canyon City *Times,* July 6, 1878.
7. A volunteer named Nick Thornton was the other.
8. Brig. Gen. Mark V. Brown commanded the 2nd Brigade of the Oregon State Militia.

PART FIVE: THE SHEEPEATER CAMPAIGN, 1879

William C. Brown: The Sheepeater Campaign

1. William C. Brown (1854–1939) of the 2nd U.S. Cavalry participated in the Sioux campaign of 1890–91, the Spanish-American War, and the Mexican punitive expedition of 1916. He served in France in World War I and retired a brigadier general in 1927. During his retirement, Brown wrote widely on the Indian Wars.
2. Brown's article appeared first in the *Tenth Biennial Report of the Idaho Historical Society* in 1926.
3. Edward S. Farrow of the West Point Class of 1872 resigned his commission in 1892.
4. Henry Catley had been an enlisted man in the 9th U.S. Infantry during the Civil War. He retired a captain in 1891.
5. Abner Haines (d. 1903) entered the Civil War a private and emerged a captain of volunteers. In 1866 he was appointed a second lieutenant in the Regular army.
6. Samuel McKeever (d. 1902) was brevetted lieutenant colonel of volunteers for gallantry during the Civil War. Appointed a second lieutenant in the Regular army in 1866, McKeever retired a captain in 1889.

Aaron F. Parker: Forgotten Tragedies of an Indian War

1. Aaron F. Parker (1856–1930) recorded his recollections of the Sheepeater hostilities in the early 1920s. Born in England, Parker became a merchant mariner at age sixteen. After four years at sea, he jumped ship at San Francisco and set out for the mines of central Idaho. He served as a volunteer during the Nez Perce, Bannock, and Sheepeater Wars. Afterward, Parker alternated between mining and newspaper publishing. Active in politics and civic affairs, Parker was a signer of the Idaho state constitution.
2. The name that whites had given Chief Tamanmo.
3. At a point some thirty miles south of the Great Payette Lake. The ambush occurred on August 20, 1878.
4. The wounded Smith had traveled thirty miles.
5. William F. Drum (d. 1892) of the West Point Class of 1850 ended the Civil War as colonel of the 5th New York Volunteer Infantry. He retired as lieutenant colonel of the 8th U.S. Infantry.
6. Grangeville was located some 200 miles due north of Boise.
7. The Sheepeaters conducted several small raids of this sort during the summer of 1878, normally to steal livestock or to rob unwary whites.
8. The Sheepeaters inaugurated hostilities with a raid on a Chinese mining camp in the Payette Forest country. They continued on with forays against other camps and isolated ranches.
9. Official sources give Catley's command as forty-eight soldiers.
10. William C. Muhlenburg (d. 1888) had been commissioned a second lieutenant in December 1876.
11. Edmund K. Webster of the West Point Class of 1870. He retired a major in 1902.

INDEX

Author's note: In preparing the index for *Eyewitness to the Indian Wars, 1865–1890: The Wars for the Pacific Northwest*, I have deviated a bit from the standard indexing practice. As indexed items (names, places, concepts, etc.) generally appear frequently in the same article—sometimes on every page—I have cited only their first appearance in the article.

James Lawyer. *See* Lawyer.
Jerome, Lt. Lovell H., 341, 399, 491, 590, 757n., 760n.
Jocelyn, Capt. Stephen P., 407, 748n.
John Schonchin (Modoc), 133, 181, 260, 270
Johnson, Henry C., 361
Joseph. *See* Chief Joseph.
Journal of the Military Service Institution of the United States, 447, 695

Karge, Lt. Joseph W., 87, 727n.
Kelley, Sgt. Thomas, 277
Kelly, Capt. Harrison, 144
Kelly, Luther S., 576, 759n.
Kelly, Capt. William, 26, 722n.
King, Capt. Charles, 539, 755n.
Kingsbury, Lt. George W., 274, 739n.
Kirkendall, Hugh, 444
Klamath Falls *Express*, 110
Klamath Indians, 101, 145, 165, 729n.
Knapp, Capt. O. C., 179
Kulkulsuithim (Nez Perce), 378

Lafferty, Lt. John, 7, 87
Lake Abert, Or., 54
Lamb, Sgt. Nicholas, 711
Lapwai council (1877), 306, 321, 345, 356, 463
Lapwai reservation, 303, 345
Lava Beds, Ca., described, 98, 119, 142, 162, 193, 200, 612
Lawyer (Nez Perce), 302, 318, 377, 451, 498, 741n.
Leary, Lt. Peter, Jr., 256
Logan, Capt. William, 427, 432, 750n.
Lolo Trail, 371, 377, 383, 418, 433
Looking Glass (Nez Perce), 324, 327, 346, 373, 376, 386, 468, 494, 742
Lost River, Or., engagement on, 102, 111, 115, 160, 190
Loynes, Cpl. Charles N., 432, 750n.

Madigan, Lt. John, 14, 84, 721n.
Malheur Lake, Or., 52
Malheur River, Or., 651
Malheur reservation, Or., 610
Malheur River, Or., engagement near, 7, 51
Mason, Maj. Edward C., 106, 125, 138, 259, 379, 620, 635, 731n.
Matte, Peter, 502
Maus, Lt. Marion P., 577, 758n.
McCarthy, Sgt. Michael, 740n.
McClernand, Lt. Edward J., 563, 758n.
McConville, Col. Edward, 366, 405
McDermit, Col. Charles, 2, 719n.
McDonald, Duncan, 451, 752n.
McDowell, Maj. Gen. Irwin, 613
McElderry, Assistant Surgeon Henry, 164, 246

McElroy, Capt. James N., 7
McIntosh, Archie, 13, 38, 721n.
McKay, Donald, 29, 131, 137, 154, 248, 262, 288, 722n.
McKay, Capt. William C., 35, 723n.
McKay Valley, Or., 64
McKeever, Capt. Samuel, 686, 702, 764n.
Meacham, A. B., 101, 106, 119, 147, 169, 260, 730n.
Mears, Maj. Frederick, 87
Medcalfe, Lt. William M., 419
Medicine, 483
Miles, Capt. Evan, 410, 635, 637
Miles Fight, 637
Miles, Col. Nelson A., 311, 340, 398, 491, 571, 576, 579, 584, 591, 595, 760n.
Miller, Maj. Gen. John F., 142
Miller, Capt. Marcus P., 244, 330, 370, 410, 649
Miller, Lt. William H., 143
Misery Hill, Id., affair at, 365
Modoc Indians: characteristics of, 98; 74, 269; pre-1872 tribal history, 159, 194, 728n.; Hot Springs (Creek) band, 100, 728n.; Lost River band, 100; atrocities committed by, 100, 110, 116, 153, 160, 172, 280, 730n.; murder of peace commissioners by, 107, 119, 123, 146, 234, 261, 270, 737n.; surrender of, 109, 133, 268, 284, 291, 732n., 739n.; abandon Lava Beds, 133, 256, 264, 268; abandon Captain Jack's Stronghold, 151; dissension among, 168, 178, 257, 268; wrongs endured, 169, 189, 295
Modoc Sally (Modoc), 177
Montana volunteers, 405, 425, 445, 486, 512
Monteith, John B., 321, 326, 380
Moore, Lt. H. De Witt, 138
Mose, 293, 619
Moylan, Capt. Miles, 563, 757n.
Muddy Lake, Id., affair at, 610
Muhlenberg, Lt. William C., 677, 696, 764n.
Munson, Capt. Samuel, 7, 87, 727n.
Murderer's Creek, Or., affair at, 672

Nevada, Indian troubles in, 2
New York *Herald*, 135, 157, 287, 353, 590
Nez Perce Indians: pre-1877 tribal history, 300, 423, 451; origins of outbreak, 326, 342, 454, 496; treatment of prisoners, 310, 468, 588, 591; surrender of, 312, 325, 555, 567, 574, 578, 582, 588, 596; post-surrender fate of, 313, 342, 583; "nontreaty," 318, 326; "treaty," 318; wrongs endured, 346, 540; as warriors, 347, 393, 414, 423, 428, 435, 588, 593; dissension among, 376, 483, 490, 494; at Stevensville, Mt., 508
Nickerson, Lt. Azor H., 26, 722n.